PRINCIPLES OF
MICROECONOMICS

Selected Material from

Economics
Principles, Problems, and Policies
Nineteenth Edition

Campbell R. McConnell
University of Nebraska

Stanley L. Brue
Pacific Lutheran University

Sean M. Flynn
Scripps College

Study Guide for use with
Economics
Principles, Problems, and Policies
Nineteenth Edition

Campbell R. McConnell

Stanley L. Brue

Sean M. Flynn

William B. Walstad
Professor of Economics
University of Nebraska-Lincoln

ECO 212 | Economics
Anne Arundel Community College

 **Learning Solutions**

Boston   Burr Ridge, IL   Dubuque, IA   New York   San Francisco
St. Louis   Bangkok   Bogotá   Caracas   Lisbon   London   Madrid
Mexico City   Milan   New Delhi   Seoul   Singapore   Sydney   Taipei   Toronto

The McGraw-Hill Companies

PRINCIPLES OF M1CROECONOMICS
ECO 212 | Economics
Anne Arundel Community College

This book is a McGraw-Hill Learning Solutions textbook and contains selected materials from the following sources:
Economics: Principles, Problems, and Policies, Nineteenth Edition by Campbell R. McConnell, Stanley L. Brue and Sean M. Flynn. Copyright © 2012, 2009, 2008, 2005, 2002, 1999, 1996, 1993, 1990, 1987, 1984, 1981, 1978, 1975, 1972, 1969, 1966, 1963, 1960 by The McGraw-Hill Companies, Inc. Reprinted with permission of the publisher.
Study Guide for use with Economics: Principles, Problems, and Policies, Nineteenth Edition by Campbell R. McConnell, Stanley L. Brue, Sean M. Flynn and William B. Walstad. Copyright © 2012 by The McGraw-Hill Companies, Inc. Reprinted with permission of the publisher. Many custom published texts are modified versions or adaptations of our best-selling textbooks. Some adaptations are printed in black and white to keep prices at a minimum, while others are in color.

1 2 3 4 5 6 7 8 9 0 QDB QDB 14 13 12

ISBN-13: 978-0-07-775728-1
ISBN-10: 0 07-775728-9

Learning Solutions Representative: Dave Fleming
Production Editor: Connie Kuhl
Printer/Binder: Quad/Graphics

The Six Versions of McConnell, Brue, Flynn

Chapter	Economics	Microeconomics	Microeconomics: Brief Edition	Macroeconomics	Macroeconomics: Brief Edition	Essentials of Economics
1. Limits, Alternatives, and Choices	x	x	x	x	x	x
2. The Market System and the Circular Flow	x	x	x	x	x	x
3. Demand, Supply, and Market Equilibrium	x	x	x	x	x	x
4. Elasticity	x	x	x	x		x
5. Market Failures: Public Goods and Externalities	x	x		x	x	x
6. Consumer Behavior	x	x				
7. Businesses and the Costs of Production	x	x	x			x
8. Pure Competition in the Short Run	x	x	x			x
9. Pure Competition in the Long Run	x	x	x			x
10. Pure Monopoly	x	x	x			x
11. Monopolistic Competition and Oligopoly	x	x	x			x
11W. Technology, R&D, and Efficiency (Web Chapter)	x	x				
12. The Demand for Resources	x	x				
13. Wage Determination	x	x	x			x
14. Rent, Interest, and Profit	x	x				
15. Natural Resource and Energy Economics	x	x				
16. Public Finance: Expenditures and Taxes	x	x	x			
17. Asymmetric Information, Voting, and Public Choice	x	x				
18. Antitrust Policy and Regulation	x	x				
19. Agriculture: Economics and Policy	x	x				
20. Income Inequality, Poverty, and Discrimination	x	x	x			x
21. Health Care	x	x				
22. Immigration	x	x				
23. An Introduction to Macroeconomics	x			x		
24. Measuring Domestic Output and National Income	x			x	x	x
25. Economic Growth	x			x	x	x
26. Business Cycles, Unemployment, and Inflation	x			x	x	x
27. Basic Macroeconomic Relationships	x			x		
28. The Aggregate Expenditures Model	x			x		
29. Aggregate Demand and Aggregate Supply	x			x	x	x
30. Fiscal Policy, Deficits, and Debt	x			x	x	
31. Money, Banking, and Financial Institutions	x			x	x	x
32. Money Creation	x			x		
33. Interest Rates and Monetary Policy	x			x	x	x
34. Financial Economics	x			x		
35. Extending the Analysis of Aggregate Supply	x			x	x	
36. Current Issues in Macro Theory and Policy	x			x		
37. International Trade	x	x	x	x	x	x
38. The Balance of Payments, Exchange Rates, and Trade Deficits	x	x	x	x	x	x
39W. The Economics of Developing Countries (Web Chapter)	x			x		

*Chapter numbers refer to *Economics: Principles, Problems, and Policies.*
*A Red "X" indicates chapters that combine or consolidate content from two or more *Economics* chapters.

To **Mem** and to **Terri** and **Craig**, and to **past instructors**

About the Authors

CAMPBELL R. MCCONNELL earned his Ph.D. from the University of Iowa after receiving degrees from Cornell College and the University of Illinois. He taught at the University of Nebraska–Lincoln from 1953 until his retirement in 1990. He is also coauthor of *Contemporary Labor Economics*, ninth edition; *Essentials of Economics*, second edition; *Macroeconomics: Brief Edition*; and *Microeconomics: Brief Edition* (all The McGraw-Hill Companies), and has edited readers for the principles and labor economics courses. He is a recipient of both the University of Nebraska Distinguished Teaching Award and the James A. Lake Academic Freedom Award and is past president of the Midwest Economics Association. Professor McConnell was awarded an honorary Doctor of Laws degree from Cornell College in 1973 and received its Distinguished Achievement Award in 1994. His primary areas of interest are labor economics and economic education. He has an extensive collection of jazz recordings and enjoys reading jazz history.

STANLEY L. BRUE did his undergraduate work at Augustana College (South Dakota) and received its Distinguished Achievement Award in 1991. He received his Ph.D. from the University of Nebraska–Lincoln. He is retired from a long career at Pacific Lutheran University, where he was honored as a recipient of the Burlington Northern Faculty Achievement Award. Professor Brue has also received the national Leavey Award for excellence in economic education. He has served as national president and chair of the Board of Trustees of Omicron Delta Epsilon International Economics Honorary. He is coauthor of *Economic Scenes*, fifth edition (Prentice-Hall); *Contemporary Labor Economics*, ninth edition; *Essentials of Economics*, second edition; *Macroeconomics: Brief Edition*; *Microeconomics: Brief Edition* (all The McGraw-Hill Companies); and *The Evolution of Economic Thought*, seventh edition (South-Western). For relaxation, he enjoys international travel, attending sporting events, and skiing with family and friends.

SEAN M. FLYNN did his undergraduate work at the University of Southern California before completing his Ph.D. at U.C. Berkeley, where he served as the Head Graduate Student Instructor for the Department of Economics after receiving the Outstanding Graduate Student Instructor Award. He teaches at Scripps College (of the Claremont Colleges) and is the author of *Economics for Dummies* (Wiley) and coauthor of *Essentials of Economics*, second edition; *Macroeconomics: Brief Edition*; and *Microeconomics: Brief Edition* (all The McGraw-Hill Companies). His research interests include finance and behavioral economics. An accomplished martial artist, he has represented the United States in international aikido tournaments and is the author of *Understanding Shodokan Aikido* (Shodokan Press). Other hobbies include running, traveling, and enjoying ethnic food.

List of Key Graphs

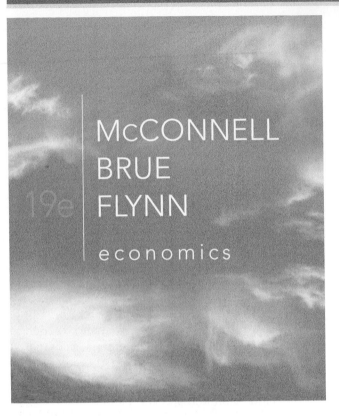

McCONNELL
BRUE
19e | FLYNN

economics

Welcome to the 19th edition of *Economics*, the best-selling economics textbook in the world. An estimated 14 million students have used *Economics* or its companion editions, *Macroeconomics* and *Microeconomics*. *Economics* has been adapted into Australian and Canadian editions and translated into Italian, Russian, Chinese, French, Spanish, Portuguese, and other languages. We are pleased that *Economics* continues to meet the market test: nearly one out of four U.S. students in principles courses used the 18th edition.

Fundamental Objectives

We have three main goals for *Economics*:

* Help the beginning student master the principles essential for understanding the economizing problem, specific economic issues, and policy alternatives.
* Help the student understand and apply the economic perspective and reason accurately and objectively about economic matters.
* Promote a lasting student interest in economics and the economy.

What's New and Improved?

One of the benefits of writing a successful text is the opportunity to revise—to delete the outdated and install the new, to rewrite misleading or ambiguous statements, to introduce more relevant illustrations, to improve the organizational structure, and to enhance the learning aids.

We trust that you will agree that we have used this opportunity wisely and fully. Some of the more significant changes include the following.

Restructured Introductory Chapters

We have divided the five-chapter grouping of introductory chapters common to *Economics, Microeconomics,* and *Macroeconomics* into two parts. Part 1 contains Chapter 1 (Limits, Alternatives, and Choices) and Chapter 2 (The Market System and the Circular Flow). The content in Part 2 has changed and now consists of three chapters: Chapter 3 (Demand, Supply, and Market Equilibrium), Chapter 4 (Elasticity), and Chapter 5 (Market Failures: Public Goods and Externalities).

The chapters in Part 2 are much more concept-oriented and analytical and much less general and descriptive than in the previous edition. Our new approach responds to suggestions by reviewers made over the years to:

* Locate the elasticity chapter immediately after the supply and demand chapter.
* Put the elasticity chapter into *Macroeconomics* for those who cover elasticity in their macro course.
* Eliminate the mainly descriptive Chapter 4 on the private and public sectors and move the relevant content to where it fits more closely with related micro and macro materials.
* Provide a single chapter on international trade, rather than two separate chapters that have overlapping coverage (Chapters 5 and 37 in the 18th edition).
* Boost the analysis of market failures (public goods and externalities) in the introductory sections to complement and balance the strong but highly stylized introduction to the market system discussed in Chapter 2.

Our new approach embraces these suggestions. For micro instructors, the new ordering provides a clear supply-and-demand path to the subsequent chapters on consumer and producer behavior. For macro instructors, the new ordering provides the option of assigning elasticity or market failures or both. And because this content is both optional and modular, macro instructors can also skip it and move directly to the macroeconomic analysis.

The content on the United States in the global economy that appeared in Chapter 5 of the 18th edition is now integrated into Chapter 37 (International Trade). Because Chapter 37 draws only on production possibilities analysis and supply and demand analysis, it can be assigned at any point after Chapter 3 (Demand, Supply, and Market Equilibrium). Therefore, instructors who want to introduce international economics early in their courses can assign Chapter 37 within the introductory chapters found in Parts 1 and 2.

For instructors who prefer Chapter 5 of the prior edition to Chapter 37 of the new edition, we have fully updated the previous Chapter 5 content and made it freely available for viewing and printing at both the instructor and student portions of our Web site, **www.mcconnell19e. com**. Look for it under the new category called Content Options for Instructors (COI). This substitute for Chapter 37 is fully supported by both the instructor supplement package and the student supplement package.

New "Consider This" and "Last Word" Pieces

Our "Consider This" boxes are used to provide analogies, examples, or stories that help drive home central economic

CONSIDER THIS . . .

The Fable of the Bees

Economist Ronald Coase received the Nobel Prize for his so-called **Coase theorem**, which pointed out that under the right conditions, private individuals could often negotiate their own mutually agreeable solutions to externality problems through *private bargaining* without the need for government interventions like pollution taxes.

This is a very important insight because it means that we shouldn't automatically call for government intervention every time we see a potential externality problem. Consider the positive externalities that bees provide by pollinating farmers' crops. Should we assume that beekeeping will be underprovided unless the government intervenes with, for instance, subsidies to encourage more hives and hence more pollination?

As it turns out, no. Research has shown that farmers and beekeepers long ago used private bargaining to develop customs and payment systems that avoid free riding by farmers and encourage beekeepers to keep the optimal number of hives. Free riding is avoided by the custom that all farmers in an area simultaneously hire beekeepers to provide bees to pollinate their crops. And farmers always pay the beekeepers for their pollination services because if they didn't, then no beekeeper would ever work with them in the future—a situation that would lead to massively reduced crop yields due to a lack of pollination.

The "Fable of the Bees" is a good reminder that it is a fallacy to assume that the market must always get involved to remedy externalities. In many cases, the private sector can solve both positive and negative externality problems on its own.

ideas in a student-oriented, real-world manner. For instance, a "Consider This" box titled "McHits and McMisses" illustrates consumer sovereignty through a listing of successful and unsuccessful products. How businesses exploit price discrimination is driven home in a "Consider This" box that explains why ballparks charge different admission prices for adults and children but only one set of prices at their concession stands. These brief vignettes, each accompanied by a photo, illustrate key points in a lively, colorful, and easy-to-remember way. We have added 16 new "Consider This" boxes in this edition.

Our "Last Word" pieces are lengthier applications or case studies that are placed near the end of each chapter. For example, the "Last Word" section for Chapter 1 (Limits, Alternatives, and Choices) examines pitfalls to sound economic reasoning, while the "Last Word" section for

LAST Word Carbon Dioxide Emissions, Cap and Trade, and Carbon Taxes

Cap-and-trade systems and carbon taxes are two approaches to reducing carbon dioxide (CO_2) emissions.

Externality problems are property rights problems. Consider a landfill. Because the owner of the landfill has full rights to his land, people wishing to dump their trash into the landfill have to pay him. This payment implies that there is no externality: He happily accepts their trash in exchange for a dumping fee. By contrast, because nobody owns the atmosphere, all air pollution is an externality, since there is no way for those doing the polluting to work out a payment to compensate those affected by the pollution or for those threatened with pollution to simply refuse to be polluted on.

Conventional property rights therefore cannot fix the externalities associated with air pollution. But that does not mean property rights can't help fight pollution. The trick to making them work is to assign property rights not to the atmosphere itself, but to *polluting* the atmosphere. This is done in "cap-and-trade" systems, under which the government sets an annual limit, or cap, to the number of tons of a pollutant that firms can emit into the atmosphere.

Consider carbon dioxide, or CO_2. It is a colorless, odorless

climate change, specifically global warming. To reduce CO_2 emissions, the U.S. government might set a cap of 5 billion tons of CO_2 emissions per year in the United States (which would be about 10 percent below 2009 emissions levels for that molecule). The government then prints out emissions permits that sum to the limit set in the cap and distributes them to polluting firms. Once they are distributed, the only way a firm can legally emit a ton of CO_2 is if it owns a permit to do so.

Under this policy, the government can obviously adjust the total amount of air pollution by adjusting the cap. This by itself improves efficiency, because the cap imposes scarcity. Because each firm has only a limited number of permits, each firm has a strong incentive to maximize the net benefit that it produces from every ton of pollution that it emits. But the *cap-and-trade* scheme leads to even greater improvements in efficiency, because firms are free to trade (sell) them to each other in what are referred to as *markets for externality rights*.

For instance, suppose Smokestack Toys owns permits for 100 tons of CO_2 emissions and that it could use them to produce toy cars that would generate profits of $100,000. There is a power plant, however, that could make up to $1 million of profits by using those 100 tons of emissions permits to generate electricity. Because firms can [...] their permits, Smok [...]

Chapter 5 (Market Failures: Public Goods and Externalities) examines cap-and-trade versus carbon taxes as policy responses to excessive carbon dioxide emissions. There are 10 new "Last Word" sections in this edition.

If you are unfamiliar with *Economics*, we encourage you to thumb through the chapters to take a quick look at these highly visible features.

New Content on Behavioral Economics

We have added new material covering the consumer-choice aspects of behavioral economics to the end of our chapter on Consumer Behavior (Chapter 6 of *Economics* and *Microeconomics*). The new material on behavioral economics covers prospect theory, framing effects, loss aversion, anchoring effects, mental accounting, and the endowment effect. The behavioral economics theory and examples are tightly focused on consumer-choice applications so as to flow smoothly from, and build upon, the standard utility-maximization theory and applications developed earlier in the chapter. The new material is intentionally at the end of the chapter, not only to show that behavioral economics extends standard theory (rather than replacing or refuting it) but also so that the new material is modular and thus can be skipped by instructors without loss of continuity. A new "Consider This" box on the "hedonic treadmill" and a new "Last Word" section on "nudges" bolster our overall coverage of behavioral economics.

Divided Pure Competition Chapter

We have divided the very long pure competition chapter (Chapter 9 of the 18th edition) into two logically distinct chapters, one on pure competition in the short run (Chapter 8) and the other on pure competition in the long run (Chapter 9). These more "bite-sized" chapters should improve student retention of the material. Students will first master the logic behind the MC = MR rule for setting output as well as the short-run shutdown condition. Students will then be able to pause to test their understanding of this content through end-of-chapter questions and problems and other supporting materials before moving on to the next chapter's coverage of pure competition in the long run.

We have also combined several table/figure pairs to improve pedagogy in the short-run chapter. In previous editions, the material for this chapter featured three figures that corresponded with the data in three separate tables. We have now combined all three such table/figure pairs, placing each data table directly above its accompanying figure to increase student comprehension. We have also used background highlights on equilibrium numbers in the tables to enable students to more easily move back and forth from references in the body to equilibrium numbers in the tables.

New Public Finance Chapter

By moving the discussion of market failure from Chapter 16 of the 18th edition to Chapter 5 of the 19th edition, we have made room for a new Chapter 16 (Public Finance: Taxation and Expenditures). This traditional public finance chapter adds considerable new content to existing material that previously appeared in Chapter 4 (The U.S. Economy: Private and Public Sectors) and Chapter 17 (Public Choice Theory and the Economics of Taxation). The material adopted from Chapter 4 of the 18th edition includes a circular flow diagram with government; an overview of Federal, state, and local tax revenues and expenditures; and explanations of marginal and average tax rates. The material adopted from Chapter 17 of the 18th edition includes discussions of the benefits-received and ability-to-pay principles of taxation; an explanation of progressive, regressive, and proportional taxes; tax incidence and efficiency losses due to taxation; and the redistributive incidence of the overall tax-spending system in the United States.

This chapter's new material includes a short section on government employment that is built around two pie charts. The first gives a breakdown of what fractions of state and local government employees are dedicated to certain tasks. The second gives a similar accounting for Federal government employees.

Also new to this chapter are "Consider This" boxes on state lotteries and value-added taxes and a "Last Word" section reviewing recent research on the redistributive effects of the *combined* taxation and spending system in the United States.

The new public finance chapter is followed by a restructured chapter covering asymmetric information, voting, and public choice. Reviewers agreed with us that this new two-chapter set covering the microeconomics of government is a major improvement over the prior edition.

New Discussions of the Financial Crisis and the Recession

Our modernization of the macroeconomics in the previous edition has met with great success, measured by reviews, instructor feedback, and market response. We recast the entire macro analysis in terms of the modern, dominant paradigm of macroeconomics, using economic growth as the central backdrop and viewing business fluctuations as significant and costly variations in the rate of growth. In this paradigm, business cycles result from demand shocks (or, less often, supply shocks) in conjunction with inflexible short-run product prices and wages. The degree of price and wage stickiness decreases with time. In our models, the *immediate short run* is a period in which both the price level and wages are not only sticky, but stuck; the *short run* is a period in which product prices are flexible but wages are not; and the *long run* is a period in which both product prices and wages are fully flexible. Each of these three periods—and thus each of the models based on them—is relevant to understanding the actual macro economy and its occasional difficulties.

In this edition, we have mainly focused on incorporating into our new macroeconomic schema an analysis of the financial crisis, the recession, and the hesitant recovery. We first introduce the recession in Chapter 23 (An Introduction to Macroeconomics) via a new "Consider This" box that ties to the chapter's discussion of Buzzer Auto, demand shocks, and short-run sticky prices. In Chapter 24 (Measuring Domestic Output and National Income) we point out that the main flows in the National Income and Product Accounts usually expand over time, but not always, as demonstrated by the recession. In Chapter 25 (Economic Growth) we discuss how the recession relates to the growth/production possibilities dynamics of Figure 25.2. In Chapter 26 (Business Cycles, Unemployment, and Inflation) we provide a telling comparison of unemployment rates for various demographic groups for the prerecession year 2007 and the recession year 2009.

In Chapter 27 (Basic Macroeconomic Relationships) we have added two "Consider This" boxes, one on how the paradox of thrift applied to consumer behavior during the recession and the other on the riddle of plunging investment spending at the same time the interest rate dropped to near zero during the recession. In Chapter 28 (The Aggregate Expenditures Model) we use the recession as a timely application of how a decline in aggregate expenditures can produce a recessionary expenditure gap and a highly negative GDP gap. In Chapter 29 (Aggregate Demand and Aggregate Supply) we use the recession as a good application of how negative demand shocks can produce large declines in real output with no or very little deflation. Chapter 30

(Fiscal Policy, Deficits, and Debt) provided a terrific opportunity to bring each of these timely and relevant subjects up-to-date, and we took full advantage of that opportunity.

In Chapter 31 (Money, Banking, and Financial Institutions) we added a major new section on the financial crisis, with emphasis on the mortgage debt crisis, mortgage-backed securities, failures and near-failures of financial firms, the Treasury's TARP rescue, the Fed's extraordinary use of lender-of-last-resort facilities, and the Wall Street Reform and Consumer Protection Act of 2010. In Chapter 32 (Money Creation), we stress that the Fed now pays interest on required reserves, and we also use the "Last Word" on the bank panics of 1930–1933 to explain how the Fed handled things very differently during the recent financial crisis.

Chapter 33 (Interest Rates and Monetary Policy) features several new discussions relating to Fed policies during the recession, including a new discussion on the liquidity trap. Along with giving the Fed high marks for dealing with the crisis, we also say that some economists think the Fed contributed to the financial crisis by keeping interest rates too low for too long during the recovery from the 2001 recession. We also replaced a dated "Consider This" piece with a new one on the ballooning Fed balance sheet and the problems it could pose for monetary policy during the eventual postrecession expansion. Chapter 34 (Financial Economics) presented a new opportunity for us to demonstrate how a sharp decline of the "appetite for risk" alters the slope of the Securities Market Line (SML) and changes investment patterns between stocks and bonds.

Other mentions of the recession are spread throughout the remainder of the macro chapters, including in the discussions of macro debates, trade protectionism, and trade deficits.

Although we found these various ways to work the recession into our macro chapters, we are confident that our basic macroeconomic models will serve equally well in explaining economic recovery and expansion back to the economy's historical growth path. The new inclusions relating to the recession simply help students see the relevance of the models to what they are seeing in the news and perhaps experiencing in their own lives. The overall tone of the book, including the macro, continues to be optimistic with respect to the long-term growth prospects of market economies.

Reworked End-of-Chapter Questions and Problems

We have extensively reworked the end-of-chapter Study Questions, splitting them into questions and problems and adding many new problems. The questions are analytic and often ask for free responses, whereas the problems are mainly quantitative. We have aligned the questions and problems with the learning objectives presented at the beginning of the chapters. All of the questions and problems are assignable through McGraw-Hill's *Connect Economics;* all of the problems also contain additional algorithmic variations and can be automatically graded within the system. The new lists of questions and problems were well-received by reviewers, many of them long-time users of the book.

Current Discussions and Examples

The 19th edition of *Economics* refers to and discusses many current topics. Examples include the cost of the war in Iraq; surpluses and shortages of tickets at the Olympics; the myriad impacts of ethanol subsidies; creative destruction; aspects of behavioral economics; applications of game theory; the most rapidly expanding and disappearing U.S. jobs; oil and gasoline prices; cap-and-trade systems and carbon taxes; the value-added tax; state lotteries; the Food, Conservation, and Energy Act of 2008; consumption versus income inequality; the Patient Protection and Affordable Care Act (PPACA) of 2010; immigration issues; core inflation; China's continued rapid growth; the severe recession of 2007–2009; the paradox of thrift; the stimulus package of 2008; ballooning Federal budget deficits and public debt; the long-run funding shortfalls in Social Security and Medicare; securitization and the mortgage debt crisis; the Wall Street Reform and Consumer Protection Act of 2010; recent Fed monetary policy; the liquidity trap; the Fed's new term auction facility; the Fed's payment of interest on required reserves; the Taylor rule in relation to Fed policy; the jump in the size of the Fed's balance sheet; U.S. trade deficits; offshoring of American jobs; trade adjustment assistance; the European Union and the Euro Zone; changes in exchange rates; and many other current topics.

Chapter-by-Chapter Changes

Each chapter of *Economics*, 19th edition, contains updated data reflecting the current economy, streamlined Learning Objectives, and reorganized end-of-chapter content.

Chapter-specific updates include:

Chapter 1: Limits, Alternatives, and Choices features a new Learning Objective on consumption possibilities and a revised definition of "entrepreneur" that clarifies why risk taking is socially beneficial and, thus, why entrepreneurial ability is a valuable economic resource.

Chapter 2: The Market System and the Circular Flow includes a revised explanation of property rights, a clarified discussion of firms' motives for choosing the lowest-cost production methods, an updated "McHits and McMisses"

"Consider This" box, and a revised discussion of the circular flow model.

Chapter 3: Demand, Supply, and Market Equilibrium contains wording improvements that clarify the main concepts.

Chapter 4: Elasticity is a new chapter that focuses solely on elasticity. This content has been moved forward from Chapter 6 of the 18th edition, allowing this topic to be covered directly after supply and demand. This content will be available in both the Macro and Micro splits. The material on consumer and producer surplus has been moved to Chapter 5.

Chapter 5: Market Failures: Public Goods and Externalities is a new chapter that first examines consumer surplus, producer surplus, efficiency, and efficiency losses (all from Chapter 6, 18th edition). It then devotes the remainder of the chapter to market failures, specifically public goods and externalities (both from Chapter 16, 18th edition). The chapter also features a new "Last Word" section that discusses the pros and cons of cap-and-trade emissions-control policies and a new "Consider This" box that concisely discusses the Coase Theorem.

Chapter 6: Consumer Behavior features additional coverage and discussion of the consumer-choice aspects of behavioral economics, including prospect theory, framing effects, loss aversion, anchoring effects, mental accounting, and the endowment effect. A new "Consider This" box discusses the hedonic treadmill and a new "Last Word" section explains how governments and firms may use the insights of behavioral economics to encourage desired outcomes.

Chapter 7: Businesses and the Costs of Production features a revised section on economic costs, explicit costs, implicit costs, accounting profit, normal profit, and economic profit; a new section on the rising price of gasoline that replaces the previous section on the doubling of the price of corn; and a rewritten example on daily newspapers.

Chapter 8: Pure Competition in the Short Run is a new chapter that contains information on pure competition in the short run from Chapter 9 of the 18th edition. This chapter features improved pedagogy and a new "Last Word" on the short-run shutdown condition.

Chapter 9: Pure Competition in the Long Run is a new chapter that contains information on pure competition in the long run from Chapter 9 of the 18th edition. This chapter features a new overview introductory section, a new figure clarifying decreasing-cost industries, and a revised discussion of why long-run equilibrium in pure competition yields allocative efficiency. This chapter also introduces creative destruction as a long-run competitive force.

Chapter 10: Pure Monopoly features a revised discussion of rate regulation for a natural monopoly and a precise identification of the income transfers of monopoly.

Chapter 11: Monopolistic Competition and Oligopoly features a revised Figure 11.2 with labels at key points, and an updated discussion of OPEC emphasizing the difficulty that it has had with its members complying with its established oil quotas.

Chapter 11 Web: Technology, R&D, and Efficiency contains a revised discussion of creative destruction.

Chapter 12: The Demand for Resources features improved discussions to clarify the main concepts.

Chapter 13: Wage Determination provides an improved introduction to monopsony.

Chapter 14: Rent, Interest, and Profit features a new section on the interest rate on money loans; an expanded explanation of the differences between insurable and noninsurable risks; an additional source of noninsurable risk (new products or production methods pioneered by rivals); and a new "Consider This" piece on Steve Jobs as an entrepreneur.

Chapter 15: Natural Resource and Energy Economics features a new "Consider This" piece that deals with the high risk associated with commercializing alternative fuel sources.

Chapter 16: Public Finance: Expenditures and Taxes is a new chapter on public finance that combines new material with topics from 18th edition Chapters 4, 16, and 17. This chapter features new pie charts on state and local government expenditures and tax revenues, two new "Consider This" boxes on state lotteries and value-added taxes, and a new "Last Word" on recent research that compares the redistributive effects of the tax system by itself with the redistributive effects of the *overall* tax-spending system.

Chapter 17: Asymmetric Information, Voting, and Public Choice adds new material to topics that were located in several other chapters in the 18th edition, including: asymmetric information from Chapter 16, government failures and voting inefficiencies and paradoxes from Chapter 17, and the principal-agent problem from Chapter 4. This chapter has a new "Consider This" box on the collective-action problem, a new discussion of political corruption, and a new "Global Perspective" piece comparing bribery rates in various countries.

Chapter 18: Antitrust Policy and Regulation now emphasizes that monopoly pricing raises significant concerns about income transfers (from consumers to producers) as well as efficiency losses.

Chapter 19: Agriculture: Economics and Policy contains a new update of the historical trends of real agricultural prices and clarifications of some of the main concepts.

Chapter 20: Income Inequality, Poverty, and Discrimination extensively updates the data on the distribution of income, poverty, and family wealth.

Chapter 21: Health Care features a detailed explanation and extensive coverage of the Patient Protection and Affordable Care Act of 2010, a new section that explains the history behind why the United States is uniquely dependent on employer-provided health insurance, an improved discussion of why insurance increases prices by increasing demand, and a new "Last Word" on how the health care system of Singapore uses high out-of-pocket costs to keep medical spending down.

Chapter 22: Immigration provides the latest available data on legal and illegal immigration.

Chapter 23: An Introduction to Macroeconomics includes two new "Consider This" boxes. The first contrasts economic investment with financial investment and the second discusses the recession of 2007–2009 in the context of the introductory analysis.

Chapter 24: Measuring Domestic Output and National Income adds new definitions and data for the terms *durable goods*, *nondurable goods*, and *services* in the discussion of personal consumption.

Chapter 25: Economic Growth has substantially revised Learning Objectives that provide a better preview of the chapter; tightened discussions in the "Consider This" boxes on patents in India and on women, the labor force, and economic growth; a new discussion relating the recession to the growth and production possibilities analysis in Figure 25.2; and updates on growth accounting from the *Economic Report of the President*.

Chapter 26: Business Cycles, Unemployment, and Inflation includes a revised discussion on business cycles, new data on unemployment rates during the recent recession, and a new discussion of core inflation.

Chapter 27: Basic Macroeconomic Relationships features new "Consider This" boxes discussing the Great Recession, the paradox of thrift, and the investment riddle, and an improved discussion of investment instability.

Chapter 28: The Aggregate Expenditures Model provides a revised introduction that links to the prior chapters, improved discussions in the "Assumptions and Simplifications" and "International Linkages" sections, and a new application that relates the Great Recession to the AE model.

Chapter 29: Aggregate Demand and Aggregate Supply has a new introduction that provides a current and relevant example for students, and a reorganized and updated "Last Word" on oil prices.

Chapter 30: Fiscal Policy, Deficits, and Debt provides explicit definitions of expansionary and contractionary fiscal policy and political business cycles, an updated discussion of current fiscal policy, detailed coverage of the 2008 and 2009 stimulus packages, and a new "Last Word" on Social Security and Medicare funding shortfalls.

Chapter 31: Money, Banking, and Financial Institutions features a new section on the financial crisis of 2007–2008, with emphasis on the mortgage default crisis, mortgage-backed securitization, failures and near failures of financial firms, the Treasury's TARP rescue, the Fed's extraordinary new lender-of-last resort facilities, and the Wall Street Reform and Consumer Protection Act of 2010. Also new is a "Last Word" on electronic banking.

Chapter 32: Money Creation contains a clarified discussion of a bank's balance sheet and an updated "Last Word" that contrasts the lack of action by the Fed during the early 1930s compared to the Fed's forceful actions during the financial crisis of 2007–2008.

Chapter 33: Interest Rates and Monetary Policy features a fully updated discussion of recent U.S. monetary policy, a new "Consider This" box on the ballooning balance sheet of the Fed during the recession of 2007–2009, and the conversion of the AD-AS summary figure from the previous edition to a new "Last Word" section.

Chapter 34: Financial Economics provides a revised introduction to the discussion of present value, a new section on applications of the security market line, and a new "Consider This" piece that discusses Ponzi schemes and Bernie Madoff.

Chapter 35: Extending the Analysis of Aggregate Supply features a crisper discussion of economic growth with ongoing inflation, along with a modified Figure 35.7, and an updated discussion of the Phillips Curve.

Chapter 36: Current Issues in Macro Theory and Policy has a new "Consider This" box on the Fed's actions prior to the financial crisis and an updated discussion of the Taylor Rule in the "Last Word."

Chapter 37: International Trade contains relevant content from Chapter 5 of the 18th edition. This chapter features additional explanation that clarifies how comparative advantage differs from absolute advantage, a new "Consider This" box on misunderstanding the gains from trade, and a streamlined discussion of multilateral trade agreements and free-trade zones.

Chapter 38: The Balance of Payments, Exchange Rates, and Trade Deficits features a streamlined explanation of why the balance-of-payments statement always balances, a revised discussion of official reserves and balance-of-payments deficits and surpluses, and updated discussions of exchange rates.

Chapter 39 Web: The Economics of Developing Countries includes a revised discussion of large populations and the standard of living and updated coverage of the role of government in improving the growth prospects of developing countries.

Distinguishing Features

Comprehensive Explanations at an Appropriate Level
Economics is comprehensive, analytical, and challenging yet fully accessible to a wide range of students. The thoroughness and accessibility enable instructors to select topics for special classroom emphasis with confidence that students can read and comprehend other independently assigned material in the book. Where needed, an extra sentence of explanation is provided. Brevity at the expense of clarity is false economy.

Fundamentals of the Market System
Many economies throughout the world are still making difficult transitions from planning to markets while a handful of other countries such as Venezuela seem to be trying to reestablish government-controlled, centrally planned economies. Our detailed description of the institutions and operation of the market system in Chapter 2 (The Market System and the Circular Flow) is therefore even more relevant than before. We pay particular attention to property rights, entrepreneurship, freedom of enterprise and choice, competition, and the role of profits because these concepts are often misunderstood by beginning students worldwide.

Extensive Treatment of International Economics
We give the principles and institutions of the global economy extensive treatment. The appendix to Chapter 3 (Demand, Supply, and Market Equilibrium) has an application on exchange rates. Chapter 37 (International Trade) examines key facts of international trade, specialization and comparative advantage, arguments for protectionism, impacts of tariffs and subsidies, and various trade agreements. Chapter 38 (Balance of Payments, Exchange Rates, and Trade Deficits) discusses the balance of payments, fixed and floating exchange rates, and U.S. trade deficits. Web Chapter 39 (The Economics of Developing Countries) takes a look at the special problems faced by developing countries and how the advanced industrial countries try to help them.

As noted previously in this preface, Chapter 37 (International Trade) is constructed such that instructors who want to cover international trade early in the course can assign it immediately after Chapter 3. Chapter 37 requires only a good understanding of production possibilities analysis and supply and demand analysis to comprehend. International competition, trade flows, and financial flows are integrated throughout the micro and macro sections. "Global Perspective" boxes add to the international flavor of the book.

Early and Extensive Treatment of Government
The public sector is an integral component of modern capitalism. This book introduces the role of government early. Chapter 5 (Market Failures: Public Goods and Externalities) systematically discusses public goods and government policies toward externalities. Chapter 16 (Public Finance: Expenditures and Taxes) examines taxation and government expenditures in detail, and Chapter 17 (Asymmetric Information, Voting, and Public Choice) looks at salient facets of asymmetric information, voting, and public choice theory as they relate to market failure and government failure. Both the micro and the macro sections of the text include issue- and policy-oriented chapters.

Stress on the Theory of the Firm
We have given much attention to microeconomics in general and to the theory of the firm in particular, for two reasons. First, the concepts of microeconomics are difficult for most beginning students; abbreviated expositions usually compound these difficulties by raising more questions than they answer. Second, we wanted to couple analysis of the various market structures with a discussion of the impact of each market arrangement on price, output levels, resource allocation, and the rate of technological advance.

Step-by-Step, Two-Path Macro
As in the previous edition, our macro continues to be distinguished by a systematic step-by-step approach to developing ideas and building models. Explicit assumptions about price and wage stickiness are posited and then systematically peeled away, yielding new models and extensions, all in the broader context of growth, expectations, shocks, and degrees of price and wage stickiness over time.

In crafting this step-by-step macro approach, we took care to preserve the "two-path macro" that many instructors appreciated. Instructors who want to bypass the immediate short-run model (Chapter 28: The Aggregate Expenditures Model) can proceed without loss of continuity directly to the short-run AD-AS model (Chapter 29: Aggregate Demand and Aggregate Supply), fiscal policy, money and banking, monetary policy, and the long-run AD-AS analysis.

Emphasis on Technological Change and Economic Growth This edition continues to emphasize economic growth. Chapter 1 (Limits, Alternatives, and Choices) uses the production possibilities curve to show the basic ingredients of growth. Chapter 25 (Economic Growth) explains how growth is measured and presents the facts of growth. It also discusses the causes of growth, looks at productivity growth, and addresses some controversies surrounding economic growth. Chapter 25's "Last Word" examines the rapid economic growth in China. Web Chapter 39 focuses on developing countries and the growth obstacles they confront. Web Chapter 11 (Technology, R&D, and Efficiency) provides an explicit and cohesive discussion of the microeconomics of technological advance, including topics such as invention, innovation, and diffusion; start-up firms; R&D decision making; market structure and R&D effort; and creative destruction.

Focus on Economic Policy and Issues For many students, the micro chapters on antitrust, agriculture, income inequality, health care, and immigration, along with the macro chapters on fiscal policy and monetary policy, are where the action is centered. We guide that action along logical lines through the application of appropriate analytical tools. In the micro, we favor inclusiveness; instructors can effectively choose two or three chapters from Part 6.

Integrated Text and Web Site *Economics* and its Web site are highly integrated through in-text Web buttons, Web-based end-of-chapter questions, bonus Web chapters, multiple-choice self-tests at the Web site, math notes, and other features. Our Web site is part and parcel of our student learning package, customized to the book.

The in-text Web buttons (or indicators) merit special mention. Three differing colors of rectangular indicators appear throughout the book, informing readers that complementary content on a subject can be found at our Web site, **www.mcconnell19e.com**. The indicator types are:

Worked Problems Written by Norris Peterson of Pacific Lutheran University (WA), these pieces consist of side-by-side computational questions and computational procedures used to derive the answers. In essence, they extend the textbook's explanations of various computations—for example, of real GDP, real GDP per capita, the unemployment rate, the inflation rate, per-unit production costs, economic profit, and more. From a student's perspective, they provide "cookbook" help for solving numerical problems.

WORKED PROBLEMS
W 1.1
Budget lines

Interactive Graphs These pieces (developed under the supervision of Norris Peterson) depict 30 major graphs and instruct students to shift the curves, observe the outcomes, and derive relevant generalizations. This hands-on graph work will greatly reinforce the graphs and their meaning.

INTERACTIVE GRAPHS
G 1.1
Production possibilities curve

Origin of the Ideas These pieces, written by Randy Grant of Linfield College (OR), are brief histories of 70 major ideas identified in the book. They identify the particular economists who developed ideas such as opportunity cost, equilibrium price, the multiplier, comparative advantage, and elasticity.

ORIGIN OF THE IDEA
O 1.1
Origin of the term "economics"

Organizational Alternatives

Although instructors generally agree on the content of principles of economics courses, they sometimes differ on how to arrange the material. *Economics* includes 11 parts, and thus provides considerable organizational flexibility. We place microeconomics before macroeconomics because this ordering is consistent with how contemporary economists view the direction of linkage between the two components. The introductory material of Parts 1 and 2, however, can be followed immediately by the macroanalysis of Parts 7 and 8. Similarly, the two-path macro enables covering the full aggregate expenditures model or advancing directly from the basic macro relationships chapter to the AD-AS model.

Some instructors will prefer to intersperse the microeconomics of Parts 3 and 4 with the problems chapters of Part 6. Chapter 19 on agriculture may follow Chapters 8 and 9 on pure competition; Chapter 18 on antitrust and regulation may follow Chapters 10, 11, and 11Web on imperfect competition models and technological advance. Chapter 22 on immigration may follow Chapter 13 on wages; and Chapter 20 on income inequality may follow Chapters 13 and 14 on distributive shares of national income.

Instructors who teach the typical two-semester course and feel comfortable with the book's organization will find that, by putting Parts 1 to 6 in the first semester and Parts 7 to 11 in the second, the material is divided logically between the two semesters.

Finally, as noted before, Chapter 37 on international trade can easily be moved up to immediately after Chapter 3 on supply and demand for instructors who want an early discussion of international trade.

Pedagogical Aids

Economics is highly student-oriented. The "To the Student" statement at the beginning of Part 1 details the book's many pedagogical aids. The 19th edition is also accompanied by a variety of high-quality supplements that help students master the subject and help instructors implement customized courses.

Supplements for Students and Instructors

Study Guide One of the world's leading experts on economic education, William Walstad of the University of Nebraska–Lincoln, prepared the *Study Guide*. Many students find either the printed or digital version indispensable. Each chapter contains an introductory statement, a checklist of behavioral objectives, an outline, a list of important terms, fill-in questions, problems and projects, objective questions, and discussion questions.

The *Guide* comprises a superb "portable tutor" for the principles student. Separate *Study Guides* are available for the macro and micro paperback editions of the text.

Instructor's Manual Laura Maghoney of Solano Community College revised and updated the *Instructor's Manual*, and Shawn Knabb of Western Washington University checked and brought the end-of-chapter questions, problems, and solutions to the *Manual*. The revised *Instructor's Manual* includes:

- Chapter summaries.
- Listings of "what's new" in each chapter.
- Teaching tips and suggestions.
- Learning objectives.
- Chapter outlines.
- Extra questions and problems.
- Answers to the end-of-chapter questions and problems, plus correlation guides mapping content to the learning objectives.

The *Instructor's Manual* is available on the instructor's side of the Online Learning Center.

Three Test Banks Test Bank I contains about 6500 multiple-choice and true-false questions, most of which were written by the text authors. Randy Grant revised Test Bank I for the 19th edition. Test Bank II contains around 6000 multiple-choice and true-false questions, updated by Felix Kwan of Maryville University. All Test Bank I and II questions are organized by learning objective, topic, AACSB Assurance of Learning, and Bloom's Taxonomy guidelines. Test Bank III, written by William Walstad, contains more than 600 pages of short-answer questions and problems created in the style of the book's end-of-chapter questions. Test Bank III can be used to construct student assignments or design essay and problem exams. Suggested answers to the essay and problem questions are included. In all, more than 14,000 questions give instructors maximum testing flexibility while ensuring the fullest possible text correlation.

Test Banks I and II are available in *Connect Economics*, through EZ Test Online, and in MS Word. EZ Test allows professors to create customized tests that contain both questions that they select from the test banks as well as questions that they craft themselves. Test Bank III is available in MS Word on the password-protected instructor's side of the Online Learning Center, and on the Instructor Resource CD.

PowerPoint Presentations With the assistance of Laura Maghoney, the PowerPoint Presentations for the 19th edition were updated by a dedicated team of instructors: Jill Beccaris-Pescatore of Montgomery County Community College, Stephanie Campbell of Mineral Area College, Amy Chataginer of Mississippi Gulf Coast Community College and Dorothy Siden of Salem State College. Each chapter is accompanied by a concise yet thorough tour of the key concepts. Instructors can use these Web-site presentations in the classroom, and students can use them on their computers.

Digital Image Library Every graph and table in the text is available on the instructor's side of the Web site and on the Instructor's Resource CD-ROM.

McGraw-Hill Connect Economics McGraw-Hill *Connect Economics* is an online assignment and assessment solution that connects students with  the tools and resources they'll need to achieve success. McGraw-Hill *Connect Economics* helps prepare students for their future by enabling faster learning, more efficient studying, and higher retention of knowledge.

All of the end-of-chapter questions and problems, the thousands of questions from Test Banks I and II, and additional resources are available in *Connect Economics*. For more information on *Connect Economics* and other technology, please see pages xii–xix.

Online Learning Center (www.mcconnell19e.com) The Web site accompanying this book is a central resource for students and instructors alike. The optional Web Chapters (Chapter 11W: Technology, R&D, and Efficiency and Chapter 39W: The Economics of Developing Countries) plus the two new Content Options for Instructors (The United States in the Global Economy and Previous International Exchange-Rate Systems), are posted as full-color PDF files. The in-text Web buttons alert the students to points in the book where they can springboard to the Web site to get more information. Students can also review PowerPoint presentations and test their knowledge of a chapter's concepts with a self-graded multiple-choice quiz. The password-protected Instructor Center houses the Instructor's Manual, all three Test Banks, and links to EZ Test Online, PowerPoint presentations, and the Digital Image Library.

Computerized Test Bank Online A comprehensive bank of test questions is provided within McGraw-Hill's flexible electronic testing program EZ Test Online (**www. eztestonline.com**). EZ Test Online allows instructors to simply and quickly create tests or quizzes for their students. Instructors can select questions from multiple McGraw-Hill test banks or author their own, and then either print the finalized test or quiz for paper distribution or publish it online for access via the Internet.

This user-friendly program allows instructors to sort questions by format; select questions by learning objectives or Bloom's taxonomy tags; edit existing questions or add new ones; and scramble questions for multiple versions of the same test. Instructors can export their tests for use in WebCT, Blackboard, and PageOut, making it easy to share assessment materials with colleagues, adjuncts, and TAs. Instant scoring and feedback is provided, and EZ Test Online's record book is designed to easily export to instructor gradebooks.

Assurance-of-Learning Ready Many educational institutions are focused on the notion of assurance of learning, an important element of some accreditation standards. *Economics* is designed to support your assurance-of-learning initiatives with a simple yet powerful solution. Each chapter in the book begins with a list of numbered learning objectives to which each end-of-chapter question and problem is then mapped. In this way, student responses to those questions and problems can be used to assess how well students are mastering each particular learning objective. Each test bank question for *Economics* also maps to a specific learning objective.

You can use our test bank software, EZ Test Online, or *Connect Economics* to easily query for learning outcomes and objectives that directly relate to the learning objectives for your course. You can then use the reporting features to aggregate student results in a similar fashion, making the collection and presentation of assurance-of-learning data simple and easy.

AACSB Statement The McGraw-Hill Companies is a proud corporate member of AACSB International. Understanding the importance and value of AACSB accreditation, *Economics*, 19th edition, has sought to recognize the curricula guidelines detailed in the AACSB standards for business accreditation by connecting end-of-chapter questions in *Economics*, 19th edition, and the accompanying test banks to the general knowledge and skill guidelines found in the AACSB standards.

This AACSB Statement for *Economics*, 19th edition, is provided only as a guide for the users of this text. The AACSB leaves content coverage and assessment within the purview of individual schools, their respective missions, and their respective faculty. While *Economics*, 19th edition, and the teaching package make no claim of any specific AACSB qualification or evaluation, we have, within *Economics*, 19th edition, labeled selected questions according to the six general knowledge and skills areas.

Acknowledgments

We give special thanks to Norris Peterson and Randy Grant, who created the "button" content on our Web site. We again thank James Reese of the University of South Carolina at Spartanburg, who wrote the original Internet exercises. Although many of those questions were replaced or modified in the typical course of revision, several remain virtually unchanged. We also thank Laura Maghoney and the team of instructors who updated the PowerPoint slides for the 19th edition. Shawn Knabb deserves great thanks for accuracy-checking the end-of-chapter questions and problems and their solutions, as well as for creating the variations of all of the problems. Thanks to the dedicated instructors who created and revised our additional study tools, including Steve Price, Shannon Aucoin, Brian Motii, Amy Scott, Emilio Gomez, Amy Stapp, Richard Kramer, and Mark Wilson. Finally, we thank William Walstad and Tom Barbiero (the coauthor of our Canadian edition) for their helpful ideas and insights.

We are greatly indebted to an all-star group of professionals at McGraw-Hill—in particular Douglas Reiner, Noelle Fox Bathurst, Harvey Yep, Lori Koetters, Jen Saxton, Melissa Larmon, and Brent Gordon—for their publishing and marketing expertise.

We thank Keri Johnson for her selection of the "Consider This" and "Last Word" photos and Mary Kazak Sander and Maureen McCutcheon for the design.

The 19th edition has benefited from a number of perceptive formal reviews. The reviewers, listed at the end of the preface, were a rich source of suggestions for this revision. To each of you, and others we may have inadvertently overlooked, thank you for your considerable help in improving *Economics*.

Stanley L. Brue
Sean M. Flynn
Campbell R. McConnell

Reviewers

Virden Harrison, *Modesto Junior College*
Richard Hawkins, *University of West Florida*
Kim Hawtrey, *Hope College*
Glenn Haynes, *Western Illinois University*
Michael Heslop, *NOVA Community College Annandale*
Jesse Hill, *Tarrant County College SE*
Calvin Hoy, *County College of Morris*
James Hubert, *Seattle Central Community College*
Greg Hunter, *California State Polytechnic University, Pomona*
Christos Ioannou, *University of Minnesota–Minneapolis*
Faridul Islam, *Utah Valley University*
Mahshid Jalilvand, *University of Wisconsin–Stout*
Ricot Jean, *Valencia Community College–Osceola*
Jonatan Jelen, *City College of New York*
Brad Kamp, *University of South Florida–Sarasota*
Kevin Kelley, *Northwest Vista College*
Chris Klein, *Middle Tennessee State University*
Barry Kotlove, *Edmonds Community College*
Richard Kramer, *New England College*
Felix Kwan, *Maryville University*
Ted Labay, *Bishop State Community College*
Tina Lance, *Germanna Community College–Fredericksburg*
Yu-Feng Lee, *New Mexico State University–Las Cruces*
Adam Lei, *Midwestern State University*
Phillip Letting, *Harrisburg Area Community College*
Brian Lynch, *Lake Land College*
Zagros Madjd-Sadjadi, *Winston-Salem State University*
Laura Maghoney, *Solano Community College*
Vincent Mangum, *Grambling State University*
Benjamin Matta, *New Mexico State University–Las Cruces*
Pete Mavrokordatos, *Tarrant County College NE*
Michael McIntyre, *Copiah Lincoln Community College*
Bob McKizzie, *Tarrant County College SE*
Kevin McWoodson, *Moraine Valley Community College*
Edwin Mensah, *University of North Carolina at Pembroke*
Randy Methenitis, *Richland College*
Ida Mirzaie, *Ohio State University*
David Mitch, *University of Maryland–Baltimore City*
Ramesh Mohan, *Bryant University*
Daniel Morvey, *Piedmont Technical College*
Shahriar Mostashari, *Campbell University*
Richard Mount, *Monmouth University*
Ted Muzio, *St. John's University*

Cliff Nowell, *Weber State University*
Albert Okunade, *University of Memphis*
Mary Ellen Overbay, *Seton Hall University*
Tammy Parker, *University of Louisiana at Monroe*
David Peterson, *American River College*
Alberto Perez, *Harford Community College*
Mary Anne Pettit, *Southern Illinois University*
Jeff Phillips, *Morrisville State College*
William Piper, *Piedmont College*
Robert Poulton, *Graceland University*
Dezzie Prewitt, *Rio Hondo College*
Joe Prinzinger, *Lynchburg College*
Jaishankar Raman, *Valparaiso University*
Natalie Reaves, *Rowan University*
Virginia Reilly, *Ocean County College*
Tim Reynolds, *Alvin Community College*
John Romps, *Saint Anselm College*
Tom Scheiding, *Elizabethtown College*
Amy Schmidt, *Saint Anselm College*
Ron Schuelke, *Santa Rosa Junior College*
Alexandra Shiu, *Temple College*
Dorothy Siden, *Salem State College*
Timothy Simpson, *Central New Mexico Community College*
Jonathan Sleeper, *Indian River State College Central*
Camille Soltau-Nelson, *Texas A&M University*
Robert Sonora, *Fort Lewis College*
Nick Spangenberg, *Ozarks Tech Community College*
Dennis Spector, *Naugatuck Valley Community College*
Thomas Stevens, *University of Massachusetts, Amherst*
Tamika Steward, *Tarrant Count College SE*
Robin Sturik, *Cuyahoga Community College Western–Parma*
Travis Taylor, *Christopher Newport University*
Ross Thomas, *Central New Mexico Community College*
Mark Thompson, *Augusta State University*
Deborah Thorsen, *Palm Beach Community College–Lake Worth*
Mike Toma, *Armstrong Atlantic State University*
Dosse Toulaboe, *Fort Hays State University*
Jeff Vance, *Sinclair Community College*
Cheryl Wachenheim, *North Dakota State University–Fargo*
Christine Wathen, *Middlesex County College*
Scott Williams, *County College of Morris*
Wendy Wysocki, *Monroe County Community College*
Edward Zajicek, *Winston-Salem State University*

Brief Contents

*From McConnel, Study Guide for Economics, 19e, ISBN: 978-0-07-733792-6

Contents

xxx | Contents

PART SIX
Microeconomic Issues and Policies   *373*

PART THREE
Microeconomics of Product Markets   *115*

PART FOUR
Microeconomics of Resource Markets   *247*

INTRODUCTION TO ECONOMICS AND THE ECONOMY

This book and its ancillaries contain several features designed to help you learn economics:

- *Web buttons (indicators)* A glance through the book reveals many pages with rectangular icons set into the text. These "buttons" alert you to helpful learning aids available with the book. The green button denotes "Interactive Graphs" found at the text's Web site, **www.mcconnell19e.com.** Brief exercises have you interact with the graphs, for example, by clicking on a specific curve and dragging it to a new location. These exercises will enhance your understanding of the underlying concepts. The blue button symbolizes "Worked Problems." Numeric problems are presented and then solved, side-by-side, step-by-step. Seeing how the problems are worked will help you solve similar problems on quizzes and exams. The purple button stands for "Origin of the Idea." Each of these pieces traces a particular idea to the person or persons who first developed it.

INTERACTIVE GRAPHS

G 3.1

Supply and demand

WORKED PROBLEMS

W 2.1

Least-cost production

ORIGIN OF THE IDEA

O 1.4

Ceteris paribus

After reading a chapter, thumb back through it to note the Web buttons and their associated numbers. On the home page of our Internet site select Student Edition and use the pull-down list under "Choose one" to find the Web button content for each chapter.

- *Other Internet aids* Our Web site contains many other aids. In the Student Edition you will find self-testing multiple-choice quizzes, PowerPoint presentations, and much more. For those of you with a very strong mathematics background, be sure to note the "See the Math" section on the Web site. There you will find nearly 50 notes that develop the algebra and, in a few cases, the calculus that underlie the economic concepts.

- *Appendix on graphs* Be assured, however, that you will need only basic math skills to do well in the principles course. In particular, you will need to be comfortable with basic graphical analysis and a few quantitative concepts. The appendix at the end of

Chapter 1 reviews graphs and slopes of curves. You may want to read it before starting Chapter 1.

- *Reviews* Each chapter contains two to four Quick Reviews and an end-of-chapter summary. These reviews will help you focus on essential ideas and study for exams.

- *Key terms and Key Graphs* Key terms are set in boldface type within the chapters, listed at the end of each chapter, and again defined in the glossary at the end of the book. Graphs with special importance are labeled Key Graphs, and each includes a multiple-choice Quick Quiz. Your instructor may or may not emphasize all of these figures, but you should pay special attention to those that are discussed in class; you can be certain there will be exam questions on them.

- *Consider This and Last Word boxes* Many chapters include a "Consider This" box. These brief pieces provide commonplace analogies, examples, and stories that help you understand and remember central economic ideas. Each chapter concludes with a "Last Word" box. Some of them are revealing applications of economic ideas; others are short case studies. While it is tempting to ignore in-text boxes, don't. Most are fun to read, and all will improve your grasp of economics.

- *Questions and Problems* The end of each chapter features separate sections of Questions and Problems. The Questions are analytic and often ask for free-responses, while the Problems are more computational. Each is keyed to a particular learning objective (LO) in the list of LOs at the beginning of the chapter. At the Web site is a multiple-choice quiz for each chapter.

- *Study Guide* We enthusiastically recommend the *Study Guide* accompanying this text. This "portable tutor" contains not only a broad sampling of various kinds of questions but a host of useful learning aids. Software-driven tutorials, including the Self Quiz and Study in *Connect Economics*, are also available with the text.

Our two main goals are to help you understand and apply economics and help you improve your analytical skills. An understanding of economics will enable you to comprehend a whole range of economic, social, and political problems that otherwise would seem puzzling and perplexing. Also, your study will enhance reasoning skills that are highly prized in the workplace.

Good luck with your study. We think it will be well worth your time and effort.

AFTER READING THIS CHAPTER, YOU SHOULD BE ABLE TO:

1 Define economics and the features of the economic perspective.

2 Describe the role of economic theory in economics.

3 Distinguish microeconomics from macroeconomics and positive economics from normative economics.

4 List the categories of scarce resources and delineate the nature of the economizing problem.

5 Apply production possibilities analysis, increasing opportunity costs, and economic growth.

6 Explain how economic growth and international trade increase consumption possibilities.

7 (Appendix) Understand graphs, curves, and slopes as they relate to economics.

Limits, Alternatives, and Choices

(An appendix on understanding graphs follows this chapter. If you need a quick review of this mathematical tool, you might benefit by reading the appendix first.) People's wants are numerous and varied. Biologically, people need only air, water, food, clothing, and shelter. But in modern societies people also desire goods and services that provide a more comfortable or affluent standard of living. We want bottled water, soft drinks, and fruit juices, not just water from the creek. We want salads, burgers, and pizzas, not just berries and nuts. We want jeans, suits, and coats, not just woven reeds. We want apartments, condominiums, or houses, not just mud huts. And, as the saying goes, "That is not the half of it." We also want flat-panel TVs, Internet service, education, homeland security, cell phones, health care, and much more.

Fortunately, society possesses productive resources, such as labor and managerial talent, tools and machinery, and land and mineral deposits. These resources, employed in the economic system (or simply the economy), help us produce goods and services that satisfy many of our economic wants. But the blunt reality is that our economic wants far exceed the productive capacity of our scarce (limited) resources. We are forced to make choices. This unyielding truth underlies the definition of **economics,** which is the social science concerned with how individuals, institutions, and society make optimal (best) choices under conditions of scarcity.

The Economic Perspective

Economists view things from a unique perspective. This **economic perspective,** or economic way of thinking, has several critical and closely interrelated features.

Scarcity and Choice

Scarce economic resources mean limited goods and services. Scarcity restricts options and demands choices. Because we "can't have it all," we must decide what we will have and what we must forgo.

At the core of economics is the idea that "there is no free lunch." You may be treated to lunch, making it "free" from your perspective, but someone bears a cost. Because all resources are either privately or collectively owned by members of society, ultimately society bears the cost. Scarce inputs of land, equipment, farm labor, the labor of cooks and waiters, and managerial talent are required. Because society could have used these resources to produce something else, it sacrifices those other goods and services in making the lunch available. Economists call such sacrifices **opportunity costs:** To obtain more of one thing, society forgoes the opportunity of getting the next best thing. That sacrifice is the opportunity cost of the choice.

Purposeful Behavior

Economics assumes that human behavior reflects "rational self-interest." Individuals look for and pursue opportunities to increase their **utility**—the pleasure, happiness, or satisfaction obtained from consuming a good or service. They allocate their time, energy, and money to maximize their satisfaction. Because they weigh costs and benefits, their economic decisions are "purposeful" or "rational," not "random" or "chaotic."

Consumers are purposeful in deciding what goods and services to buy. Business firms are purposeful in deciding what products to produce and how to produce them. Government entities are purposeful in deciding what public services to provide and how to finance them.

"Purposeful behavior" does not assume that people and institutions are immune from faulty logic and therefore are perfect decision makers. They sometimes make mistakes. Nor does it mean that people's decisions are unaffected by emotion or the decisions of those around them. Indeed, economists acknowledge that people are sometimes impulsive or emulative. "Purposeful behavior" simply means that people make decisions with some desired outcome in mind.

Rational self-interest is not the same as selfishness. In the economy, increasing one's own wage, rent, interest, or

4

profit normally requires identifying and satisfying *somebody else's* wants! Also, people make personal sacrifices for others. They contribute time and money to charities because they derive pleasure from doing so. Parents help pay for their children's education for the same reason. These self-interested, but unselfish, acts help maximize the givers'

CONSIDER THIS . . .

Fast-Food Lines

The economic perspective is useful in analyzing all sorts of behaviors. Consider an everyday example: the behavior of fast-food customers. When customers enter the restaurant, they go to the shortest line, believing that line will minimize their time cost of obtaining food. They are acting purposefully; time is limited, and people prefer using it in some way other than standing in line.

If one fast-food line is temporarily shorter than other lines, some people will move to that line. These movers apparently view the time saving from the shorter line (marginal benefit) as exceeding the cost of moving from their present line (marginal cost). The line switching tends to equalize line lengths. No further movement of customers between lines occurs once all lines are about equal.

Fast-food customers face another cost-benefit decision when a clerk opens a new station at the counter. Should they move to the new station or stay put? Those who shift to the new line decide that the time saving from the move exceeds the extra cost of physically moving. In so deciding, customers must also consider just how quickly they can get to the new station compared with others who may be contemplating the same move. (Those who hesitate in this situation are lost!)

Customers at the fast-food establishment do not have perfect information when they select lines. Thus, not all decisions turn out as expected. For example, you might enter a short line and find someone in front of you is ordering hamburgers and fries for 40 people in the Greyhound bus parked out back (and the employee is a trainee)! Nevertheless, at the time you made your decision, you thought it was optimal.

Finally, customers must decide what food to order when they arrive at the counter. In making their choices, they again compare marginal costs and marginal benefits in attempting to obtain the greatest personal satisfaction for their expenditure.

Economists believe that what is true for the behavior of customers at fast-food restaurants is true for economic behavior in general. Faced with an array of choices, consumers, workers, and businesses rationally compare marginal costs and marginal benefits in making decisions.

satisfaction as much as any personal purchase of goods or services. Self-interested behavior is simply behavior designed to increase personal satisfaction, however it may be derived.

Marginal Analysis: Comparing Benefits and Costs

The economic perspective focuses largely on **marginal analysis**—comparisons of marginal benefits and marginal costs, usually for decision making. To economists, "marginal" means "extra," "additional," or "a change in." Most choices or decisions involve changes in the status quo, meaning the existing state of affairs.

Should you attend school for another year? Should you study an extra hour for an exam? Should you supersize your fries? Similarly, should a business expand or reduce its output? Should government increase or decrease its funding for a missile defense system?

Each option involves marginal benefits and, because of scarce resources, marginal costs. In making choices rationally, the decision maker must compare those two amounts. Example: You and your fiancée are shopping for an engagement ring. Should you buy a $\frac{1}{2}$-carat diamond, a $\frac{3}{4}$-carat diamond, a 1-carat diamond, or something even larger? The marginal cost of a larger-size diamond is the added expense beyond the cost of the smaller-size diamond. The marginal benefit is the perceived lifetime pleasure (utility) from the larger-size stone. If the marginal benefit of the larger diamond exceeds its marginal cost (and you can afford it), buy the larger stone. But if the marginal cost is more than the marginal benefit, you should buy the smaller diamond instead—even if you can afford the larger stone!

ORIGIN OF THE IDEA
O 1.3
Marginal analysis

In a world of scarcity, the decision to obtain the marginal benefit associated with some specific option always includes the marginal cost of forgoing something else. The money spent on the larger-size diamond means forgoing some other product. An opportunity cost—the value of the next best thing forgone—is always present whenever a choice is made.

Theories, Principles, and Models

Like the physical and life sciences, as well as other social sciences, economics relies on the **scientific method**. That procedure consists of several elements:
- Observing real-world behavior and outcomes.
- Based on those observations, formulating a possible explanation of cause and effect (hypothesis).

- Testing this explanation by comparing the outcomes of specific events to the outcome predicted by the hypothesis.
- Accepting, rejecting, and modifying the hypothesis, based on these comparisons.
- Continuing to test the hypothesis against the facts. If favorable results accumulate, the hypothesis evolves into a theory. A very well-tested and widely accepted theory is referred to as an economic law or an **economic principle**—a statement about economic behavior or the economy that enables prediction of the probable effects of certain actions. Combinations of such laws or principles are incorporated into models, which are simplified representations of how something works, such as a market or segment of the economy.

Economists develop theories of the behavior of individuals (consumers, workers) and institutions (businesses, governments) engaged in the production, exchange, and consumption of goods and services. Theories, principles, and models are "purposeful simplifications." The full scope of economic reality itself is too complex and bewildering to be understood as a whole. In developing theories, principles, and models economists remove the clutter and simplify.

Economic principles and models are highly useful in analyzing economic behavior and understanding how the economy operates. They are the tools for ascertaining cause and effect (or action and outcome) within the economic system. Good theories do a good job of explaining and predicting. They are supported by facts concerning how individuals and institutions actually behave in producing, exchanging, and consuming goods and services.

There are some other things you should know about economic principles.

- *Generalizations* Economic principles are generalizations relating to economic behavior or to the economy itself. Economic principles are expressed as the tendencies of typical or average consumers, workers, or business firms. For example, economists say that consumers buy more of a particular product when its price falls. Economists recognize that some consumers may increase their purchases by a large amount, others by a small amount, and a few not at all. This "price-quantity" principle, however, holds for the typical consumer and for consumers as a group.
- *Other-things-equal assumption* In constructing their theories, economists use the *ceteris paribus* or

other-things-equal assumption—the assumption that factors other than those being considered do not change. They assume that all variables except those under immediate consideration are held constant for a particular analysis. For example, consider the relationship between the price of Pepsi and the amount of it purchased. Assume that of all the factors that might influence the amount of Pepsi purchased (for example, the price of Pepsi, the price of Coca-Cola,

> **ORIGIN OF THE IDEA**
> **O 1.4**
> Ceteris paribus

and consumer incomes and preferences), only the price of Pepsi varies. This is helpful because the economist can then focus on the relationship between the price of Pepsi and purchases of Pepsi in isolation without being confused by changes in other variables.

- *Graphical expression* Many economic models are expressed graphically. Be sure to read the special appendix at the end of this chapter as a review of graphs.

Microeconomics and Macroeconomics

Economists develop economic principles and models at two levels.

Microeconomics

Microeconomics is the part of economics concerned with decision making by individual customers, workers, households, and business firms. At this level of analysis, we observe the details of their behavior under a figurative microscope. We measure the price of a specific product, the number of workers employed by a single firm, the revenue or income of a particular firm or household, or the expenditures of a specific firm, government entity, or family. In microeconomics, we examine the sand, rocks, and shells, not the beach.

Macroeconomics

Macroeconomics examines either the economy as a whole or its basic subdivisions or aggregates, such as the government, household, and business sectors. An **aggregate** is a collection of specific economic units treated as if they were one unit. Therefore, we might lump together the millions of consumers in the U.S. economy and treat them as if they were one huge unit called "consumers."

In using aggregates, macroeconomics seeks to obtain an overview, or general outline, of the structure of the economy and the relationships of its major aggregates. Macroeconomics speaks of such economic measures as total output, total employment, total income, aggregate expenditures, and the general level of prices in analyzing various economic problems. Very little attention is given to the specific units making up the various aggregates.

Figuratively, macroeconomics looks at the beach, not the pieces of sand, the rocks, and the shells.

The micro–macro distinction does not mean that economics is so highly compartmentalized that every topic can be readily labeled as either micro or macro; many topics and subdivisions of economics are rooted in both. Example: While the problem of unemployment is usually treated as a macroeconomic topic (because unemployment relates to aggregate production), economists recognize that the decisions made by *individual* workers on how long to search for jobs and the way *specific* labor markets encourage or impede hiring are also critical in determining the unemployment rate.

Positive and Normative Economics

Both microeconomics and macroeconomics contain elements of positive economics and normative economics. **Positive economics** focuses on facts and cause-and-effect relationships. It includes description, theory development, and theory testing. Positive economics avoids value judgments. It tries to establish scientific statements about economic behavior and deals with what the economy is actually like. Such scientific-based analysis is critical to good policy analysis.

Economic policy, on the other hand, involves **normative economics,** which incorporates value judgments about what the economy should be like or what particular policy actions should be recommended to achieve a desirable goal. Normative economics looks at the desirability of certain aspects of the economy. It underlies expressions of support for particular economic policies.

Positive economics concerns *what is,* whereas normative economics embodies subjective feelings about *what ought to be.* Examples: Positive statement: "The unemployment rate in France is higher than that in the United States." Normative statement: "France ought to undertake policies to make its labor market more flexible to reduce unemployment rates." Whenever words such as "ought" or "should" appear in a sentence, you are very likely encountering a normative statement.

Most of the disagreement among economists involves normative, value-based policy questions. Of course, economists sometime disagree about which theories or models best represent the economy and its parts, but they agree on a full range of economic principles. Most economic controversy thus reflects differing opinions or value judgments about what society should be like.

QUICK REVIEW 1.1

- Economics examines how individuals, institutions, and society make choices under conditions of scarcity.
- The economic perspective stresses (a) resource scarcity and the necessity of making choices, (b) the assumption of purposeful (or rational) behavior, and (c) comparisons of marginal benefit and marginal cost.
- In choosing the best option, people incur an opportunity cost—the value of the next-best option.
- Economists use the scientific method to establish economic theories—cause-effect generalizations about the economic behavior of individuals and institutions.
- Microeconomics focuses on specific decision-making units of the economy, macroeconomics examines the economy as a whole.
- Positive economics deals with factual statements ("what is"); normative economics involves value judgments ("what ought to be").

Individual's Economizing Problem

A close examination of the **economizing problem**—the need to make choices because economic wants exceed economic means—will enhance your understanding of economic models and the difference between microeconomic and macroeconomic analysis. Let's first build a microeconomic model of the economizing problem faced by an individual.

Limited Income

We all have a finite amount of income, even the wealthiest among us. Even Donald Trump must decide how to spend his money! And the majority of us have much more limited means. Our income comes to us in the form of wages, interest, rent, and profit, although we may also receive money from government programs or family members. As Global Perspective 1.1 shows, the average income of Americans in 2008 was $47,580. In the poorest nations, it was less than $500.

GLOBAL PERSPECTIVE 1.1

Average Income, Selected Nations

Average income (total income/population) and therefore typical individual budget constraints vary greatly among nations.

Country	Per Capita Income, 2008 (U.S. dollars, based on exchange rates)
Switzerland	$65,330
United States	47,580
France	42,250
Japan	38,210
South Korea	21,530
Mexico	9980
Brazil	7350
China	2770
Nigeria	1160
India	1070
Rwanda	410
Liberia	170

Source: World Bank, **www.worldbank.org**.

Unlimited Wants

For better or worse, most people have virtually unlimited wants. We desire various goods and services that provide utility. Our wants extend over a wide range of products, from *necessities* (for example, food, shelter, and clothing) to *luxuries* (for example, perfumes, yachts, and sports cars). Some wants such as basic food, clothing, and shelter have biological roots. Other wants, for example, specific kinds of food, clothing, and shelter, arise from the conventions and customs of society.

Over time, as new and improved products are introduced, economic wants tend to change and multiply. Only recently have people wanted iPods, Internet service, or camera phones because those products did not exist a few decades ago. Also, the satisfaction of certain wants may trigger others: the acquisition of a Ford Focus or a Honda Civic has been known to whet the appetite for a Lexus or a Mercedes.

Services, as well as goods, satisfy our wants. Car repair work, the removal of an inflamed appendix, legal and accounting advice, and haircuts all satisfy human wants.

Actually, we buy many goods, such as automobiles and washing machines, for the services they render. The differences between goods and services are often smaller than they appear to be.

For most people, the desires for goods and services cannot be fully satisfied. Bill Gates may have all that he wants for himself, but his massive charitable giving suggests that he keenly wants better health care for the world's poor. Our desires for a particular good or service can be satisfied; over a short period of time we can surely get enough toothpaste or pasta. And one appendectomy is plenty. But our broader desire for more goods and services and higher-quality goods and services seems to be another story.

Because we have only limited income (usually through our work) but seemingly insatiable wants, it is in our self-interest to economize: to pick and choose goods and services that maximize our satisfaction given the limitations we face.

A Budget Line

We can clarify the economizing problem facing consumers by visualizing a **budget line** (or, more technically, a *budget constraint*). It is a schedule or curve that shows various combinations of two products a consumer can purchase with a specific money income. Although we assume two products, the analysis generalizes to the full range of products available to consumers.

To understand the idea of a budget line, suppose that you received a Barnes & Noble (or Borders) gift card as a birthday present. The $120 card is soon to expire. You take the card to the store and confine your purchase decisions to two alternatives: DVDs and paperback books. DVDs are $20 each and paperback books are $10 each. Your purchase options are shown in the table in Figure 1.1.

At one extreme, you might spend all of your $120 "income" on 6 DVDs at $20 each and have nothing left to spend on books. Or, by giving up 2 DVDs and thereby gaining $40, you can have 4 DVDs at $20 each and 4 books at $10 each. And so on to the other extreme, at which you could buy 12 books at $10 each, spending your entire gift card on books with nothing left to spend on DVDs.

The graph in Figure 1.1 shows the budget line. Note that the graph is not restricted to whole units of DVDs and books as is the table. Every point on the graph represents a possible combination of DVDs and books, including fractional quantities. The slope of the graphed budget line measures the ratio of the price of books (P_b) to the price of DVDs (P_{dvd}); more precisely, the slope is $P_b/P_{dvd} = \$-10/\$+20 = -\frac{1}{2}$. So you must forgo 1 DVD

FIGURE 1.1 A consumer's budget line. The budget line (or budget constraint) shows all the combinations of any two products that can be purchased, given the prices of the products and the consumer's money income.

The Budget Line: Whole-Unit Combinations of DVDs and Paperback Books Attainable with an Income of $120		
Units of DVDs (Price = $20)	Units of Books (Price = $10)	Total Expenditure
6	0	$120 (= $120 + $0)
5	2	$120 (= $100 + $20)
4	4	$120 (= $80 + $40)
3	6	$120 (= $60 + $60)
2	8	$120 (= $40 + $80)
1	10	$120 (= $20 + $100)
0	12	$120 (= $0 + $120)

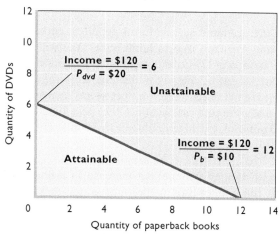

$\frac{\text{Income} = \$120}{P_{dvd} = \$20} = 6$

Unattainable

$\frac{\text{Income} = \$120}{P_b = \$10} = 12$

Attainable

Quantity of DVDs (vertical axis) / Quantity of paperback books (horizontal axis)

(measured on the vertical axis) to buy 2 books (measured on the horizontal axis). This yields a slope of $-\frac{1}{2}$ or $-.5$.

The budget line illustrates several ideas.

Attainable and Unattainable Combinations All the combinations of DVDs and books on or inside the budget line are *attainable* from the $120 of money income. You can afford to buy, for example, 3 DVDs at $20 each and 6 books at $10 each. You also can obviously afford to buy 2 DVDs and 5 books, thereby using up only $90 of the $120 available on your gift card. But to achieve maximum utility you will want to spend the full $120. The budget line shows all combinations that cost exactly the full $120.

In contrast, all combinations beyond the budget line are *unattainable*. The $120 limit simply does not allow you to purchase, for example, 5 DVDs at $20 each and 5 books at $10 each. That $150 expenditure would clearly exceed the $120 limit. In Figure 1.1 the attainable combinations are on and within the budget line; the unattainable combinations are beyond the budget line.

Trade-Offs and Opportunity Costs The budget line in Figure 1.1 illustrates the idea of trade-offs arising from limited income. To obtain more DVDs, you have to give up some books. For example, to obtain the first DVD, you trade off 2 books. So the opportunity cost of the first DVD

ORIGIN OF THE IDEA

O 1.5

Opportunity costs

is 2 books. To obtain the second DVD the opportunity cost is also 2 books. The straight-line budget constraint, with its constant slope, indicates constant opportunity cost. That is, the opportunity cost of 1 extra DVD remains the same (= 2 books) as more DVDs are purchased. And, in

CONSIDER THIS . . .

Did Gates, Winfrey, and Rodriguez Make Bad Choices?

Opportunity costs come into play in decisions well beyond simple buying decisions. Consider the different choices people make with respect to college. College graduates usually earn about 50 percent more during their lifetimes than persons with just high school diplomas. For most capable students, "Go to college, stay in college, and earn a degree" is very sound advice.

Yet Microsoft cofounder Bill Gates and talk show host Oprah Winfrey* both dropped out of college, and baseball star Alex Rodriguez ("A-Rod") never even bothered to start classes. What were they thinking? Unlike most students, Gates faced enormous opportunity costs for staying in college. He had a vision for his company, and his starting work young helped ensure Microsoft's success. Similarly, Winfrey landed a spot in local television news when she was a teenager, eventually producing and starring in the Oprah Winfrey Show when she was 32 years old. Getting a degree in her twenties might have interrupted the string of successes that made her famous talk show possible. And Rodriguez knew that professional athletes have short careers. Therefore, going to college directly after high school would have taken away four years of his peak earning potential.

So Gates, Winfrey, and Rodriguez understood opportunity costs and made their choices accordingly. The size of opportunity costs greatly matters in making individual decisions.

*Winfrey eventually went back to school and earned a degree from Tennessee State University when she was in her thirties.

reverse, the opportunity cost of 1 extra book does not change ($= \frac{1}{2}$ DVD) as more books are bought.

Choice Limited income forces people to choose what to buy and what to forgo to fulfill wants. You will select the combination of DVDs and paperback books that you think is "best." That is, you will evaluate your marginal benefits and marginal costs (here, product price) to make choices that maximize your satisfaction. Other people, with the same $120 gift card, would undoubtedly make different choices.

Income Changes The location of the budget line varies with money income. An increase in money income shifts the budget line to the right; a decrease in money income shifts it to the left. To verify this, recalculate the table in Figure 1.1, assuming the card value (income) is (a) $240 and (b) $60, and plot the new budget lines in the graph. No wonder people like to have more income: That shifts their budget lines outward and enables them to buy more goods and services. But even with more income, people will still face spending trade-offs, choices, and opportunity costs.

> **WORKED PROBLEMS**
>
> **W 1.1**
> Budget lines

> **QUICK REVIEW 1.2**
>
> - Because wants exceed incomes, individuals face an economizing problem; they must decide what to buy and what to forgo.
> - A budget line (budget constraint) shows the various combinations of two goods that a consumer can purchase with a specific money income.
> - Straight-line budget constraints imply constant opportunity costs for both goods.

Society's Economizing Problem

Society must also make choices under conditions of scarcity. It, too, faces an economizing problem. Should it devote more of its limited resources to the criminal justice system (police, courts, and prisons) or to education (teachers, books, and schools)? If it decides to devote more resources to both, what other goods and services does it forgo? Health care? Energy development?

Scarce Resources

Society has limited or scarce **economic resources,** meaning all natural, human, and manufactured resources that go into the production of goods and services. This includes the entire set of factory and farm buildings and all the equipment, tools, and machinery used to produce manufactured goods and agricultural products; all transportation and communication facilities; all types of labor; and land and mineral resources.

Resource Categories

Economists classify economic resources into four general categories.

Land Land means much more to the economist than it does to most people. To the economist **land** includes all natural resources ("gifts of nature") used in the production process. These include forests, mineral and oil deposits, water resources, wind power, sunlight, and arable land.

Labor The resource **labor** consists of the physical actions and mental activities that people contribute to the production of goods and services. The work-related activities of a logger, retail clerk, machinist, teacher, professional football player, and nuclear physicist all fall under the general heading "labor."

Capital For economists, **capital** (or capital goods) includes all manufactured aids used in producing consumer goods and services. Included are all factory, storage, transportation, and distribution facilities, as well as tools and machinery. Economists use the term **investment** to describe spending that pays for the production and accumulation of capital goods.

Capital goods differ from consumer goods because consumer goods satisfy wants directly, whereas capital goods do so indirectly by aiding the production of consumer goods. For example, large commercial baking ovens (capital goods) help make loaves of bread (consumer goods). Note that the term "capital" as used by economists refers not to money but to tools, machinery, and other productive equipment. Because money produces nothing, economists do not include it as an economic resource. Money (or money capital or financial capital) is simply a means for purchasing goods and services, including capital goods.

Entrepreneurial Ability Finally, there is the special human resource, distinct from labor, called **entrepreneurial ability.** The entrepreneur performs several socially useful functions:

- The entrepreneur takes the initiative in combining the resources of land, labor, and capital to produce a good or a service. Both a sparkplug and a catalyst, the entrepreneur is the driving force behind production and the agent who combines the other resources in what is hoped will be a successful business venture.

Principles of Economics II
Dr. Raymond F. Turner
Quiz 5 A B   Name_____
                            Please print. Thank you!

Answer all questions. Place answer in space provided. Show answer using BLOCK capital letters such as A,B,C,D,E,T,F. This quiz will be scored on the number right out of 10 which means that a score of 110% is possible. Failure to follow directions will result in a one question penalty.

Use the following to answer questions 1-3:

Output	Total cost
0	$10
1	20
2	28
3	38
4	53
5	73
6	98

A   1.   Refer to the above table. The average fixed cost for producing 3 units of output is:
          A) $3.33.   B) $10.   C) $12.67.   D) $38.

C   2.   Refer to the above table. The marginal cost of producing the sixth unit of output is:
          A) $10.   B) $16.33.   C) $25.   D) $98.

A   3.   Refer to the above table. The average variable cost of producing the first unit of output is:
          A) $10.   B) $20.   C) $30.   D) Unable to be determined from the information given.

B   4.   When the total product curve is falling, the:
          A) marginal product of labor is zero.   C) average product of labor is increasing.
          B) marginal product of labor is negative.   D) average product of labor must be negative.

C   5.   The reason the marginal cost curve eventually increases as output increases for the typical firm is because:
          A) of diseconomies of scale.   C) of the law of diminishing returns.
          B) of minimum efficient scale.   D) normal profit exceeds economic profit.

D   6.   A firm has total fixed costs of $8,000 a year. The average variable cost is $5.00 for 2,000 units of output. At this level of output, its average total costs are:
          A) $4.   B) $5.   C) $7.   D) $9.

ATC = AFC + AVC   AFC = $\frac{TFC}{Q}$
9.00   4.00   5.00

$\frac{8000}{2000} = 4$

B   7.   The term diseconomies of scale is reflected in:
          A) decreasing short-run average costs.   C) increasing short-run marginal costs.
          B) increasing long-run average costs.   D) decreasing long-run prices.

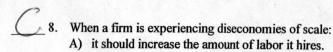 8. When a firm is experiencing diseconomies of scale:
   A) it should increase the amount of labor it hires.
   B) it should lower its price to the competitive level.
   C) its average total costs will decline if it reduces its scale of operations.
   D) it should increase the size of its plant to decrease its average total costs.

9. On the axis provided, *sketch* the AFC, AVC, ATC, and MC curves for a typical firm. Make sure the distances of separation the points of intersection correctly represent the relationships involving these functions. (4 points)

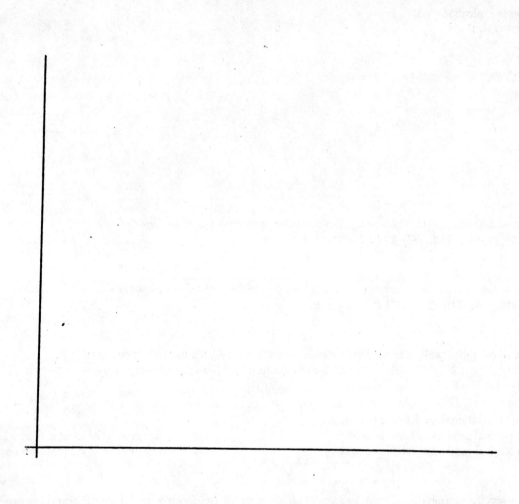

- The entrepreneur makes the strategic business decisions that set the course of an enterprise.
- The entrepreneur innovates. He or she commercializes new products, new production techniques, or even new forms of business organization.
- The entrepreneur bears risk. Innovation is risky, as nearly all new products and ideas are subject to the possibility of failure as well as success. Progress would cease without entrepreneurs who are willing to take on risk by devoting their time, effort, and ability—as well as their own money and the money of others—to commercializing new products and ideas that may enhance society's standard of living.

Because land, labor, capital, and entrepreneurial ability are combined to produce goods and services, they are called the **factors of production,** or simply "inputs."

Production Possibilities Model

Society uses its scarce resources to produce goods and services. The alternatives and choices it faces can best be understood through a macroeconomic model of production possibilities. To keep things simple, let's initially assume:

- *Full employment* The economy is employing all of its available resources.
- *Fixed resources* The quantity and quality of the factors of production are fixed.
- *Fixed technology* The state of technology (the methods used to produce output) is constant.
- *Two goods* The economy is producing only two goods: pizzas and industrial robots. Pizzas symbolize **consumer goods,** products that satisfy our wants directly; industrial robots (for example, the kind used to weld automobile frames) symbolize **capital goods,** products that satisfy our wants indirectly by making possible more efficient production of consumer goods.

Production Possibilities Table

A production possibilities table lists the different combinations of two products that can be produced with a specific set of resources, assuming full employment. Table 1.1 presents a simple, hypothetical economy that is producing pizzas and

industrial robots; the data are, of course, hypothetical. At alternative A, this economy would be devoting all its available resources to the production of industrial robots (capital goods); at alternative E, all resources would go to pizza production (consumer goods). Those alternatives are unrealistic extremes; an economy typically produces both capital goods and consumer goods, as in B, C, and D. As we move from alternative A to E, we increase the production of pizzas at the expense of the production of industrial robots.

Because consumer goods satisfy our wants directly, any movement toward E looks tempting. In producing more pizzas, society increases the satisfaction of its current wants. But there is a cost: More pizzas mean fewer industrial robots. This shift of resources to consumer goods catches up with society over time because the stock of capital goods expands more slowly, thereby reducing potential future production. By moving toward alternative E, society chooses "more now" at the expense of "much more later."

By moving toward A, society chooses to forgo current consumption, thereby freeing up resources that can be used to increase the production of capital goods. By building up its stock of capital this way, society will have greater future production and, therefore, greater future consumption. By moving toward A, society is choosing "more later" at the cost of "less now."

Generalization: At any point in time, a fully employed economy must sacrifice some of one good to obtain more of another good. Scarce resources prohibit such an economy from having more of both goods. Society must choose among alternatives. There is no such thing as a free pizza, or a free industrial robot. Having more of one thing means having less of something else.

Production Possibilities Curve

The data presented in a production possibilities table are shown graphically as a **production possibilities curve.** Such a curve displays the different combinations of goods and services that society can produce in a fully employed economy, assuming a fixed availability of supplies of resources and fixed technology. We arbitrarily represent the economy's output of capital goods (here, industrial robots) on the vertical axis and the output of consumer goods (here, pizzas) on the horizontal axis, as shown in **Figure 1.2 (Key Graph).**

Each point on the production possibilities curve represents some maximum output of the two products. The

INTERACTIVE GRAPHS

G 1.1

Production possibilities curve

TABLE 1.1 **Production Possibilities of Pizzas and Industrial Robots**

Type of Product	Production Alternatives				
	A	**B**	**C**	**D**	**E**
Pizzas (in hundred thousands)	0	1	2	3	4
Robots (in thousands)	10	9	7	4	0

key graph

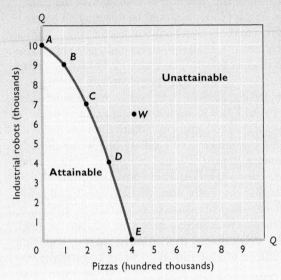

QUICK QUIZ FOR FIGURE 1.2

1. Production possibilities curve *ABCDE* is bowed out from the origin because:
   a. the marginal benefit of pizzas declines as more pizzas are consumed.
   b. the curve gets steeper as we move from *E* to *A*.
   c. it reflects the law of increasing opportunity costs.
   d. resources are scarce.

2. The marginal opportunity cost of the second unit of pizza is:
   a. 2 units of robots.
   b. 3 units of robots.
   c. 7 units of robots.
   d. 9 units of robots.

3. The total opportunity cost of 7 units of robots is:
   a. 1 unit of pizza.
   b. 2 units of pizza.
   c. 3 units of pizza.
   d. 4 units of pizza.

4. All points on this production possibilities curve necessarily represent:
   a. society's optimal choice.
   b. less than full use of resources.
   c. unattainable levels of output.
   d. full employment.

Answers: 1. c; 2. a; 3. b; 4. d

curve is a "constraint" because it shows the limit of attainable outputs. Points on the curve are attainable as long as the economy uses all its available resources. Points lying inside the curve are also attainable, but they reflect less total output and therefore are not as desirable as points on the curve. Points inside the curve imply that the economy could have more of both industrial robots and pizzas if it achieved full employment of its resources. Points lying beyond the production possibilities curve, like *W*, would represent a greater output than the output at any point on the curve. Such points, however, are unattainable with the current availability of resources and technology.

Law of Increasing Opportunity Costs

Figure 1.2 clearly shows that more pizzas means fewer industrial robots. The number of units of industrial robots that must be given up to obtain another unit of pizzas, of course, is the opportunity cost of that unit of pizzas.

In moving from alternative A to alternative B in Table 1.1, the cost of 1 additional unit of pizzas is 1 fewer unit of industrial robots. But when additional units are considered—B to C, C to D, and D to E—an important economic principle is revealed: For society, the opportunity cost of each additional unit of pizzas is greater than

12

the opportunity cost of the preceding one. When we move from A to B, just 1 unit of industrial robots is sacrificed for 1 more unit of pizzas; but in going from B to C we sacrifice 2 additional units of industrial robots for 1 more unit of pizzas; then 3 more of industrial robots for 1 more of pizzas; and finally 4 for 1. Conversely, confirm that as we move from E to A, the cost of an additional unit of industrial robots (on average) is $\frac{1}{4}, \frac{1}{3}, \frac{1}{2}$, and 1 unit of pizzas, respectively, for the four successive moves.

Our example illustrates the **law of increasing opportunity costs.** As the production of a particular good increases, the opportunity cost of producing an additional unit rises.

Shape of the Curve The law of increasing opportunity costs is reflected in the shape of the production possibilities curve: The curve is bowed out from the origin of the graph. Figure 1.2 shows that when the economy moves from *A* to *E*, it must give up successively larger amounts of industrial robots (1, 2, 3, and 4) to acquire equal increments of pizzas (1, 1, 1, and 1). This is shown in the slope of the production possibilities curve, which becomes steeper as we move from *A* to *E*.

Economic Rationale The law of increasing opportunity costs is driven by the fact that economic resources are not completely adaptable to alternative uses. Many resources are better at producing one type of good than at producing others. Consider land. Some land is highly suited to growing the ingredients necessary for pizza production. But as pizza production expands, society has to start using land that is less bountiful for farming. Other land is rich in mineral deposits and therefore well-suited to producing the materials needed to make industrial robots. That land will be the first land devoted to the production of industrial robots. But as society steps up the production of robots, it must use land that is less and less suited to making their components.

If we start at *A* and move to *B* in Figure 1.2, we can shift resources whose productivity is relatively high in pizza production and low in industrial robots. But as we move from *B* to *C*, *C* to *D*, and so on, resources highly productive in pizzas become increasingly scarce. To get more pizzas, resources whose productivity in industrial robots is relatively great will be needed. Increasingly more of such resources, and hence greater sacrifices of industrial robots, will be needed to achieve each 1-unit increase in pizzas. This lack of perfect flexibility, or interchangeability,

> **WORKED PROBLEMS**
> **W 1.2**
> Production possibilities

on the part of resources is the cause of increasing opportunity costs for society.

Optimal Allocation

Of all the attainable combinations of pizzas and industrial robots on the curve in Figure 1.2, which is optimal (best)? That is, what specific quantities of resources should be allocated to pizzas and what specific quantities should be allocated to industrial robots in order to maximize satisfaction?

Recall that economic decisions center on comparisons of marginal benefit (MB) and marginal cost (MC). Any economic activity should be expanded as long as marginal benefit exceeds marginal cost and should be reduced if marginal cost exceeds marginal benefit. The optimal amount of the activity occurs where MB = MC. Society needs to make a similar assessment about its production decision.

Consider pizzas. We already know from the law of increasing opportunity costs that the marginal cost of additional units of pizza will rise as more units are produced. At the same time, we need to recognize that the extra or marginal benefits that come from producing and consuming pizza decline with each successive unit of pizza. Consequently, each successive unit of pizza brings with it both increasing marginal costs and decreasing marginal benefits.

The optimal quantity of pizza production is indicated by point *e* at the intersection of the MB and MC curves: 200,000 units in Figure 1.3. Why is this amount the optimal quantity? If only 100,000 units of pizzas were

FIGURE 1.3 Optimal output: MB = MC. Achieving the optimal output requires the expansion of a good's output until its marginal benefit (MB) and marginal cost (MC) are equal. No resources beyond that point should be allocated to the product. Here, optimal output occurs at point e, where 200,000 units of pizzas are produced.

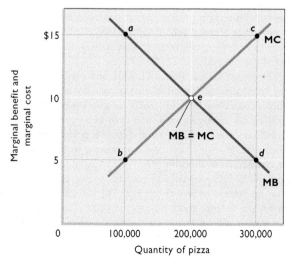

produced, the marginal benefit of an extra unit of pizza (point *a*) would exceed its marginal cost (point *b*). In money terms, MB is $15, while MC is only $5. When society gains something worth $15 at a marginal cost of only $5, it is better off. In Figure 1.3, net gains can continue to be realized until pizza-product production has been increased to 200,000.

CONSIDER THIS . . .

The Economics of War

Production possibilities analysis is helpful in assessing the costs and benefits of waging the broad war on terrorism, including the wars in Afghanistan and Iraq. At the end of 2010, the estimated cost of these efforts exceeded $1.05 trillion.

If we categorize all U.S. production as either "defense goods" or "civilian goods," we can measure them on the axes of a production possibilities diagram such as that shown in Figure 1.2. The opportunity cost of using more resources for defense goods is the civilian goods sacrificed. In a fully employed economy, more defense goods are achieved at the opportunity cost of fewer civilian goods—health care, education, pollution control, personal computers, houses, and so on. The cost of war and defense is the other goods forgone. The benefits of these activities are numerous and diverse but clearly include the gains from protecting against future loss of American lives, assets, income, and well-being.

Society must assess the marginal benefit (MB) and marginal cost (MC) of additional defense goods to determine their optimal amounts—where to locate on the defense goods–civilian goods production possibilities curve. Although estimating marginal benefits and marginal costs is an imprecise art, the MB-MC framework is a useful way of approaching choices. An optimal allocation of resources requires that society expand production of defense goods until MB = MC.

The events of September 11, 2001, and the future threats they foreshadowed increased the marginal benefits of defense goods, as perceived by Americans. If we label the horizontal axis in Figure 1.3 "defense goods" and draw in a rightward shift of the MB curve, you will see that the optimal quantity of defense goods rises. In view of the concerns relating to September 11, the United States allocated more of its resources to defense. But the MB-MC analysis also reminds us we can spend too much on defense, as well as too little. The United States should not expand defense goods beyond the point where MB = MC. If it does, it will be sacrificing civilian goods of greater value than the defense goods obtained.

In contrast, the production of 300,000 units of pizzas is excessive. There the MC of an added unit is $15 (point *c*) and its MB is only $5 (point *d*). This means that 1 unit of pizza is worth only $5 to society but costs it $15 to obtain. This is a losing proposition for society!

So resources are being efficiently allocated to any product when the marginal benefit and marginal cost of its output are equal (MB = MC). Suppose that by applying the same analysis to industrial robots, we find that the optimal (MB = MC) quantity of robots is 7000. This would mean that alternative *C* (200,000 units of pizzas and 7000 units of industrial robots) on the production possibilities curve in Figure 1.2 would be optimal for this economy.

QUICK REVIEW 1.3

- Economists categorize economic resources as land, labor, capital, and entrepreneurial ability.

- The production possibilities curve illustrates several ideas: (a) scarcity of resources is implied by the area of unattainable combinations of output lying outside the production possibilities curve; (b) choice among outputs is reflected in the variety of attainable combinations of goods lying along the curve; (c) opportunity cost is illustrated by the downward slope of the curve; (d) the law of increasing opportunity costs is reflected in the bowed-outward shape of the curve.

- A comparison of marginal benefits and marginal costs is needed to determine the best or optimal output mix on a production possibilities curve.

Unemployment, Growth, and the Future

In the depths of the Great Depression of the 1930s, one-quarter of U.S. workers were unemployed and one-third of U.S. production capacity was idle. Subsequent downturns have been much less severe. During the deep 2007–2009 recession, for instance, production fell by a comparably smaller 3.7 percent and 1-in-10 workers was without a job.

Almost all nations have experienced widespread unemployment and unused production capacity from business downturns at one time or another. Since 2000, for example, several nations—including Argentina, Japan, Mexico, Germany, and South Korea—have had economic downturns and unemployment.

How do these realities relate to the production possibilities model? Our analysis and conclusions change if we relax the assumption that all available resources are fully employed. The five alternatives in Table 1.1 represent

FIGURE 1.4 **Unemployment and the production possibilities curve.** Any point inside the production possibilities curve, such as *U*, represents unemployment or a failure to achieve full employment. The arrows indicate that by realizing full employment, the economy could operate on the curve. This means it could produce more of one or both products than it is producing at point *U*.

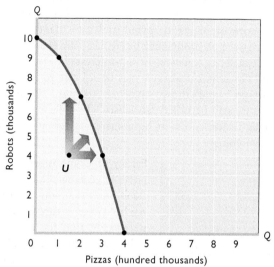

Pizzas (hundred thousands)

though unsteady, rate. And although some of our energy and mineral resources are being depleted, new sources are also being discovered. The development of irrigation systems, for example, adds to the supply of arable land.

The net result of these increased supplies of the factors of production is the ability to produce more of both consumer goods and capital goods. Thus, 20 years from now, the production possibilities may supersede those shown in Table 1.1. The new production possibilities might look like those in the table in Figure 1.5. The greater abundance of resources will result in a greater potential output of one or both products at each alternative. The economy will have achieved economic growth in the form of expanded potential output. Thus, when an increase in the quantity or quality of resources occurs, the production possibilities curve shifts outward and to the right, as illustrated by the move from the inner curve to curve *A'B'C'D'E'* in Figure 1.5. This sort of shift represents growth of economic capacity, which, when used, means **economic growth:** a larger total output.

maximum outputs; they illustrate the combinations of pizzas and industrial robots that can be produced when the economy is operating at full employment. With unemployment, this economy would produce less than each alternative shown in the table.

Graphically, we represent situations of unemployment by points inside the original production possibilities curve (reproduced here in Figure 1.4). Point *U* is one such point. Here the economy is falling short of the various maximum combinations of pizzas and industrial robots represented by the points on the production possibilities curve. The arrows in Figure 1.4 indicate three possible paths back to full employment. A move toward full employment would yield a greater output of one or both products.

A Growing Economy

When we drop the assumptions that the quantity and quality of resources and technology are fixed, the production possibilities curve shifts positions and the potential maximum output of the economy changes.

Increases in Resource Supplies Although resource supplies are fixed at any specific moment, they change over time. For example, a nation's growing population brings about increases in the supplies of labor and entrepreneurial ability. Also, labor quality usually improves over time via more education and training. Historically, the economy's stock of capital has increased at a significant,

FIGURE 1.5 **Economic growth and the production possibilities curve.** The increase in supplies of resources, improvements in resource quality, and technological advances that occur in a dynamic economy move the production possibilities curve outward and to the right, allowing the economy to have larger quantities of both types of goods.

Type of Product	Production Alternatives				
	A'	B'	C'	D'	E'
Pizzas (in hundred thousands)	0	2	4	6	8
Robots (in thousands)	14	12	9	5	0

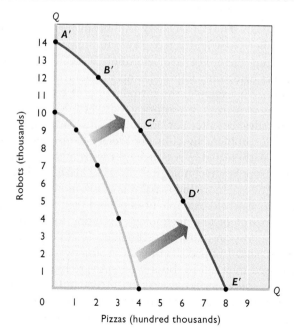

Pizzas (hundred thousands)

LAST Word Pitfalls to Sound Economic Reasoning

Because They Affect Us So Personally, We Often Have Difficulty Thinking Accurately and Objectively About Economic Issues.

Here are some common pitfalls to avoid in successfully applying the economic perspective.

Biases Most people bring a bundle of biases and preconceptions to the field of economics. For example, some might think that corporate profits are excessive or that lending money is always superior to borrowing money. Others might believe that government is necessarily less efficient than businesses or that more government regulation is always better than less. Biases cloud thinking and interfere with objective analysis. All of us must be willing to shed biases and preconceptions that are not supported by facts.

Loaded Terminology The economic terminology used in

newspapers and broadcast media is sometimes emotionally biased, or loaded. The writer or spokesperson may have a cause to promote or an ax to grind and may slant comments accordingly. High profits may be labeled "obscene," low wages may be called "exploitative" or self-interested behavior may be "greed." Government workers may be referred to as "mindless bureaucrats" and those favoring stronger government regulations may be called "socialists." To objectively analyze economic issues, you must be prepared to reject or discount such terminology.

Fallacy of Composition Another pitfall in economic thinking is the assumption that what is true for one individual or part of a whole is necessarily true for a group of individuals or the whole. This is a logical fallacy called the *fallacy of composition*; the assumption is not correct. A statement that is valid for an individual or part is not necessarily valid for the larger group or whole. You may see the action better if you leap to your feet to see an outstanding play at a

Advances in Technology An advancing technology brings both new and better goods and improved ways of producing them. For now, let's think of technological advance as being only improvements in the methods of production, for example, the introduction of computerized systems to manage inventories and schedule production. These advances alter our previous discussion of the economizing problem by allowing society to produce more goods with available resources. As with increases in resource supplies, technological advances make possible the production of more industrial robots *and* more pizzas.

A real-world example of improved technology is the recent surge of new technologies relating to computers, communications, and biotechnology. Technological advances have dropped the prices of computers and greatly increased their speed. Improved software has greatly increased the everyday usefulness of computers. Cellular phones and the Internet have increased communications capacity, enhancing production and improving the

efficiency of markets. Advances in biotechnology have resulted in important agricultural and medical discoveries. These and other new and improved technologies have contributed to U.S. economic growth (outward shifts of the nation's production possibilities curve).

Conclusion: Economic growth is the result of (1) increases in supplies of resources, (2) improvements in resource quality, and (3) technological advances. The consequence of growth is that a full-employment economy can enjoy a greater output of both consumption goods and capital goods. Whereas static, no-growth economies must sacrifice some of one good to obtain more of another, dynamic, growing economies can have larger quantities of both goods.

Present Choices and Future Possibilities

An economy's current choice of positions on its production possibilities curve helps determine the future location

16

football game. But if all the spectators leap to their feet at the same time, nobody—including you—will have a better view than when all remained seated.

Here are two economic examples: An individual stockholder can sell shares of, say, Google stock without affecting the price of the stock. The individual's sale will not noticeably reduce the share price because the sale is a negligible fraction of the total shares of Google being bought and sold. But if all the Google shareholders decide to sell their shares the same day, the market will be flooded with shares and the stock price will fall precipitously. Similarly, a single cattle ranch can increase its revenue by expanding the size of its livestock herd. The extra cattle will not affect the price of cattle when they are brought to market. But if all ranchers as a group expand their herds, the total output of cattle will increase so much that the price of cattle will decline when the cattle are sold. If the price reduction is relatively large, ranchers as a group might find that their income has fallen despite their having sold a greater number of cattle because the fall in price overwhelms the increase in quantity.

Post Hoc Fallacy You must think very carefully before concluding that because event A precedes event B, A is the cause of B. This kind of faulty reasoning is known as the *post hoc, ergo propter hoc*, or "after this, therefore because of this," fallacy. Noneconomic example: A professional football team hires a new coach and the team's record improves. Is the new coach the cause? Maybe. Perhaps the presence of more experienced and talented players or an easier schedule is the true cause. The rooster crows before dawn but does not cause the sunrise.

Economic example: Many people blamed the Great Depression of the 1930s on the stock market crash of 1929. But the crash did not cause the Great Depression. The same severe weaknesses in the economy that caused the crash caused the Great Depression. The depression would have occurred even without the preceding stock market crash.

Correlation but Not Causation Do not confuse correlation, or connection, with causation. Correlation between two events or two sets of data indicates only that they are associated in some systematic and dependable way. For example, we may find that when variable X increases, Y also increases. But this correlation does not necessarily mean that there is causation—that increases in X cause increases in Y. The relationship could be purely coincidental or dependent on some other factor, Z, not included in the analysis.

Here is an example: Economists have found a positive correlation between education and income. In general, people with more education earn higher incomes than those with less education. Common sense suggests education is the cause and higher incomes are the effect; more education implies a more knowledgeable and productive worker, and such workers receive larger salaries.

But might the relationship be explainable in other ways? Are education and income correlated because the characteristics required for succeeding in education—ability and motivation—are the same ones required to be a productive and highly paid worker? If so, then people with those traits will probably both obtain more education and earn higher incomes. But greater education will not be the sole cause of the higher income.

of that curve. Let's designate the two axes of the production possibilities curve as "goods for the future" and "goods for the present," as in Figure 1.6. Goods for the future are such things as capital goods, research and education, and preventive medicine. They increase the quantity and quality of property resources, enlarge the stock of technological information, and improve the quality of human resources. As we have already seen, goods for the future such as capital goods are the ingredients of economic growth. Goods for the present are consumer goods such as food, clothing, and entertainment.

Now suppose there are two hypothetical economies, Presentville and Futureville, that are initially identical in every respect except one: Presentville's current choice of

INTERACTIVE GRAPHS

G 1.2

Present choices and future possibilities

positions on its production possibilities curve strongly favors present goods over future goods. Point P in Figure 1.6a

indicates that choice. It is located quite far down the curve to the right, indicating a high priority for goods for the present, at the expense of less goods for the future. Futureville, in contrast, makes a current choice that stresses larger amounts of future goods and smaller amounts of present goods, as shown by point F in Figure 1.6b.

Now, other things equal, we can expect Futureville's future production possibilities curve to be farther to the right than Presentville's future production possibilities curve. By currently choosing an output more favorable to technological advances and to increases in the quantity and quality of resources, Futureville will achieve greater economic growth than Presentville. In terms of capital goods, Futureville is choosing to make larger current additions to its "national factory" by devoting more of its current output to capital than Presentville. The payoff from this choice for Futureville is greater future production capacity and economic growth. The opportunity cost is fewer consumer goods in the present for Futureville to enjoy.

FIGURE 1.6 **Present choices and future locations of production possibilities curves.** A nation's current choice favoring "present goods," as made by Presentville in (a), will cause a modest outward shift of the production possibilities curve in the future. A nation's current choice favoring "future goods," as made by Futureville in (b), will result in a greater outward shift of the curve in the future.

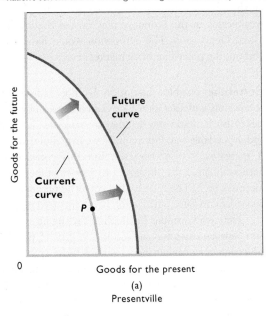

(a)
Presentville

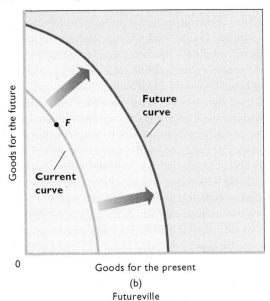

(b)
Futureville

Is Futureville's choice thus necessarily "better" than Presentville's? That, we cannot say. The different outcomes simply reflect different preferences and priorities in the two countries. But each country will have to live with the economic consequences of its choice.

A Qualification: International Trade

Production possibilities analysis implies that an individual nation is limited to the combinations of output indicated by its production possibilities curve. But we must modify this principle when international specialization and trade exist.

You will see in later chapters that an economy can circumvent, through international specialization and trade, the output limits imposed by its domestic production possibilities curve. Under international specialization and trade, each nation first specializes in the production of those items for which it has the lowest opportunity costs (due to an abundance of the necessary resources). Countries then engage in international trade, with each country exchanging the items that it can produce at the lowest opportunity costs for the items that other countries can produce at the lowest opportunity costs.

International specialization and trade allow a nation to get more of a desired good at less sacrifice of some other good. Rather than sacrifice three units of domestically-

produced robots to get a third unit of domestically-produced pizza, as in Table 1.1, a nation that engages in international specialization and trade might be able to do much better. If it specializes in robots while another country specializes in pizza, then it may be able to obtain the third unit of pizza by trading only two units of domestically-produced robots for one unit of foreign-produced pizza. Specialization and trade have the same effect as having more and better resources or discovering improved production techniques; both increase the quantities of capital and consumer goods available to society. Expansion of domestic production possibilities and international trade are two separate routes for obtaining greater output.

QUICK REVIEW 1.4

- Unemployment causes an economy to operate at a point inside its production possibilities curve.
- Increases in resource supplies, improvements in resource quality, and technological advance cause economic growth, which is depicted as an outward shift of the production possibilities curve.
- An economy's present choice of capital and consumer goods helps determine the future location of its production possibilities curve.
- International specialization and trade enable a nation to obtain more goods than its production possibilities curve indicates.

Summary

1. Economics is the social science that examines how individuals, institutions, and society make optimal choices under conditions of scarcity. Central to economics is the idea of opportunity cost: the value of the next-best good or service forgone to obtain something.

2. The economic perspective includes three elements: scarcity and choice, purposeful behavior, and marginal analysis. It sees individuals and institutions making rational decisions based on comparisons of marginal costs and marginal benefits.

3. Economists employ the scientific method, in which they form and test hypotheses of cause-and-effect relationships to generate theories, laws, and principles. Economists often combine theories into representations called models.

4. Microeconomics examines the decision making of specific economic units or institutions. Macroeconomics looks at the economy as a whole or its major aggregates.

5. Positive economic analysis deals with facts; normative economics reflects value judgments.

6. Individuals face an economizing problem. Because their wants exceed their incomes, they must decide what to purchase and what to forgo. Society also faces an economizing problem. Societal wants exceed the available resources necessary to fulfill them. Society therefore must decide what to produce and what to forgo.

7. Graphically, a budget line (or budget constraint) illustrates the economizing problem for individuals. The line shows the various combinations of two products that a consumer can purchase with a specific money income, given the prices of the two products.

8. Economic resources are inputs into the production process and can be classified as land, labor, capital, or entrepreneurial ability. Economic resources are also known as factors of production or inputs.

9. Economists illustrate society's economizing problem through production possibilities analysis. Production possibilities tables and curves show the different combinations of goods and services that can be produced in a fully employed economy, assuming that resource quantity, resource quality, and technology are fixed.

10. An economy that is fully employed and thus operating on its production possibilities curve must sacrifice the output of some types of goods and services to increase the production of others. The gain of one type of good or service is always accompanied by an opportunity cost in the form of the loss of some of the other type.

11. Because resources are not equally productive in all possible uses, shifting resources from one use to another creates increasing opportunity costs. The production of additional units of one product requires the sacrifice of increasing amounts of the other product.

12. The optimal (best) point on the production possibilities curve represents the most desirable mix of goods and is determined by expanding the production of each good until its marginal benefit (MB) equals its marginal cost (MC).

13. Over time, technological advances and increases in the quantity and quality of resources enable the economy to produce more of all goods and services, that is, to experience economic growth. Society's choice as to the mix of consumer goods and capital goods in current output is a major determinant of the future location of the production possibilities curve and thus of the extent of economic growth.

14. International trade enables a nation to obtain more goods from its limited resources than its production possibilities curve indicates.

Terms and Concepts

economics	macroeconomics	capital
economic perspective	aggregate	investment
opportunity cost	positive economics	entrepreneurial ability
utility	normative economics	factors of production
marginal analysis	economizing problem	consumer goods
scientific method	budget line	capital goods
economic principle	economic resources	production possibilities curve
other-things-equal assumption	land	law of increasing opportunity costs
microeconomics	labor	economic growth

Questions

1. What is an opportunity cost? How does the idea relate to the definition of economics? Which of the following decisions would entail the greater opportunity cost: Allocating a square block in the heart of New York City for a surface parking lot or allocating a square block at the edge of a typical suburb for such a lot? Explain. LO1

2. Cite three examples of recent decisions that you made in which you, at least implicitly, weighed marginal cost and marginal benefit. LO1

3. What is meant by the term "utility" and how does the idea relate to purposeful behavior? LO1

4. What are the key elements of the scientific method and how does this method relate to economic principles and laws? LO2

5. Indicate whether each of the following statements applies to microeconomics or macroeconomics: LO3
   a. The unemployment rate in the United States was 9.7 percent in March 2010.
   b. A U.S. software firm discharged 15 workers last month and transferred the work to India.
   c. An unexpected freeze in central Florida reduced the citrus crop and caused the price of oranges to rise.
   d. U.S. output, adjusted for inflation, decreased by 2.4 percent in 2009.
   e. Last week Wells Fargo Bank lowered its interest rate on business loans by one-half of 1 percentage point.
   f. The consumer price index rose by 2.7 percent from December 2008 to December 2009.

6. State (a) a positive economic statement of your choice, and then (b) a normative economic statement relating to your first statement. LO3

7. What are economic resources? What categories do economists use to classify them? Why are resources also called factors of production? Why are they called inputs? LO4

8. Why is money not considered to be a capital resource in economics? Why is entrepreneurial ability considered a category of economic resource, distinct from labor? What are the major functions of the entrepreneur? LO4

9. Specify and explain the typical shapes of marginal-benefit and marginal-cost curves. How are these curves used to determine the optimal allocation of resources to a particular product? If current output is such that marginal cost exceeds marginal benefit, should more or fewer resources be allocated to this product? Explain. LO5

10. Explain how (if at all) each of the following events affects the location of a country's production possibilities curve: LO5
    a. The quality of education increases.
    b. The number of unemployed workers increases.
    c. A new technique improves the efficiency of extracting copper from ore.
    d. A devastating earthquake destroys numerous production facilities.

11. Suppose that, on the basis of a nation's production possibilities curve, an economy must sacrifice 10,000 pizzas domestically to get the 1 additional industrial robot it desires but that it can get the robot from another country in exchange for 9000 pizzas. Relate this information to the following statement: "Through international specialization and trade, a nation can reduce its opportunity cost of obtaining goods and thus 'move outside its production possibilities curve.'" LO6

12. **LAST WORD** Studies indicate that married men on average earn more income than unmarried men of the same age and education level. Why must we be cautious in concluding that marriage is the cause and higher income is the effect?

Problems

1. Potatoes cost Janice $1 per pound, and she has $5.00 that she could possibly spend on potatoes or other items. If she feels that the first pound of potatoes is worth $1.50, the second pound is worth $1.14, the third pound is worth $1.05, and all subsequent pounds are worth $0.30, how many pounds of potatoes will she purchase? What if she only had $2 to spend? LO1

2. Pham can work as many or as few hours as she wants at the college bookstore for $9 per hour. But due to her hectic schedule, she has just 15 hours per week that she can spend working at either the bookstore or at other potential jobs. One potential job, at a café, will pay her $12 per hour for up to 6 hours per week. She has another job offer at a garage that will pay her $10 an hour for up to 5 hours per week. And she has a potential job at a daycare center that will pay her $8.50 per hour for as many hours as she can work. If her goal is to maximize the amount of money she can make each week, how many hours will she work at the bookstore? LO1

3. Suppose you won $15 on a lotto ticket at the local 7-Eleven and decided to spend all the winnings on candy bars and bags of peanuts. The price of candy bars is $0.75 and the price of peanuts is $1.50. LO4
   a. Construct a table showing the alternative combinations of the two products that are available.
   b. Plot the data in your table as a budget line in a graph. What is the slope of the budget line? What is the opportunity cost of one more candy bar? Of one more bag of peanuts? Do these opportunity costs rise, fall, or remain constant as each additional unit of the product is purchased?

c. Does the budget line tell you which of the available combinations of candy bars and bags of peanuts to buy?

d. Suppose that you had won $30 on your ticket, not $15. Show the $30 budget line in your diagram. Has the number of available combinations increased or decreased?

4. Suppose that you are on a desert island and possess exactly 20 coconuts. Your neighbor, Friday, is a fisherman, and he is willing to trade 2 fish for every 1 coconut that you are willing to give him. Another neighbor, Kwame, is also a fisherman, and he is willing to trade 3 fish for every 1 coconut. LO4

a. On a single figure, draw budget lines for trading with Friday and for trading with Kwame. (Put coconuts on the vertical axis.)

b. What is the slope of the budget line from trading with Friday?

c. What is the slope of the budget line from trading with Kwame?

d. Which budget line features a larger set of attainable combinations of coconuts and fish?

e. If you are going to trade coconuts for fish, would you rather trade with Friday or Kwame?

5. To the right is a production possibilities table for consumer goods (automobiles) and capital goods (forklifts): LO5

a. Show these data graphically. Upon what specific assumptions is this production possibilities curve based?

b. If the economy is at point C, what is the cost of one more automobile? Of one more forklift? Which characteristic of the production possibilities curve reflects the law of increasing opportunity costs: its shape or its length?

c. If the economy characterized by this production possibilities table and curve were producing 3 automobiles and 20 forklifts, what could you conclude about its use of its available resources?

d. Is production at a point outside the production possibilities curve currently possible? Could a future advance in technology allow production beyond the current production possibilities curve? Could international trade allow a country to consume beyond its current production possibilities curve?

Type of Production	Production Alternatives				
	A	B	C	D	E
Automobiles	0	2	4	6	8
Forklifts	30	27	21	12	0

6. Look at Figure 1.3. Suppose that the cost of cheese falls, so that the marginal cost of producing pizza decreases. Will the MC curve shift up or down? Will the optimal amount of pizza increase or decrease? LO5

7. Referring to the table in problem 5, suppose improvement occurs in the technology of producing forklifts but not in the technology of producing automobiles. Draw the new production possibilities curve. Now assume that a technological advance occurs in producing automobiles but not in producing forklifts. Draw the new production possibilities curve. Now draw a production possibilities curve that reflects technological improvement in the production of both goods. LO6

8. On average, households in China save 40 percent of their annual income each year, whereas households in the United States save less than 5 percent. Production possibilities are growing at roughly 9 percent annually in China and 3.5 percent in the United States. Use graphical analysis of "present goods" versus "future goods" to explain the differences in growth rates. LO6

FURTHER TEST YOUR KNOWLEDGE AT
www.mcconnell19e.com

At the text's Online Learning Center (OLC), **www.mcconnell19e.com**, you will find one or more Web-based questions that require information from the Internet to answer. We urge you to check them out; they will familiarize you with Web sites that may be helpful in other courses and perhaps even in your career. The OLC also features multiple-choice questions that give instant feedback and provides other helpful ways to further test your knowledge of the chapter.

Graphs and Their Meaning

If you glance quickly through this text, you will find many graphs. Some seem simple, while others seem more formidable. All are included to help you visualize and understand economic relationships. Physicists and chemists sometimes illustrate their theories by building arrangements of multicolored wooden balls, representing protons, neutrons, and electrons, that are held in proper relation to one another by wires or sticks. Economists most often use graphs to illustrate their models. By understanding these "pictures," you can more readily comprehend economic relationships. Most of our principles or models explain relationships between just two sets of economic facts, which can be conveniently represented with two-dimensional graphs.

Construction of a Graph

A *graph* is a visual representation of the relationship between two variables. The table in Figure 1 is a hypothetical illustration showing the relationship between income and consumption for the economy as a whole. Without even studying economics, we would logically expect that people would buy more goods and services when their incomes go up. Thus, it is not surprising to find in the table that total consumption in the economy increases as total income increases.

The information in the table is expressed graphically in Figure 1. Here is how it is done: We want to show visually how consumption changes as income changes. We therefore represent income on the **horizontal axis** of the graph and consumption on the **vertical axis.**

Now we arrange the vertical and horizontal scales of the graph to reflect the ranges of values of consumption and income and mark the scales in convenient increments. As you can see, the values marked on the scales cover all the values in the table. The increments on both scales are $100.

Because the graph has two dimensions, each point within it represents an income value and its associated consumption value. To find a point that represents one of the five income-consumption combinations in the table in Figure 1, we draw straight lines from the appropriate values on the vertical and horizontal axes. For example, to plot point *c* (the $200 income–$150 consumption point), we draw straight lines up from the horizontal (income) axis at $200 and across from the vertical (consumption) axis at $150. These lines intersect at point *c*, which represents this particular income-consumption combination. You should verify that the other income-consumption combinations shown in the table are properly located in the graph in Figure 1. Finally, by assuming that the same general relationship between income and consumption prevails for all other incomes, we draw a line or smooth curve to connect these points. That line or curve represents the income-consumption relationship.

If the curve is a straight line, as in Figure 1, we say the relationship is *linear*. (It is permissible, and even customary, to call straight lines in graphs "curves.")

FIGURE 1 **Graphing the direct relationship between consumption and income.** Two sets of data that are positively or directly related, such as consumption and income, graph as an upsloping line.

Income per Week	Consumption per Week	Point
$ 0	$ 50	a
100	100	b
200	150	c
300	200	d
400	250	e

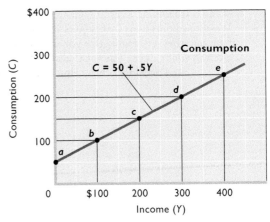

Direct and Inverse Relationships

The line in Figure 1 slopes upward to the right, so it depicts a direct relationship between income and consumption. By a **direct relationship** (or positive relationship) we mean that two variables—in this case, consumption and income—change in the *same* direction. An increase in consumption is associated with an increase in income; a decrease in consumption accompanies a decrease in income. When two sets of data are positively or directly related, they always graph as an *upsloping* line, as in Figure 1.

In contrast, two sets of data may be inversely related. Consider the table in Figure 2, which shows the relationship between the price of basketball tickets and game attendance at Gigantic State University (GSU). Here we have an **inverse relationship** (or negative relationship) because the two variables change in *opposite* directions. When ticket prices decrease, attendance increases. When ticket prices increase, attendance decreases. The six data points in the table in Figure 2 are plotted in the graph. Observe that an inverse relationship always graphs as a *downsloping* line.

Dependent and Independent Variables

Although it is not always easy, economists seek to determine which variable is the "cause" and which is the "effect." Or, more formally, they seek the independent variable and the dependent variable. The **independent variable** is the cause or source; it is the variable that changes first. The **dependent variable** is the effect or outcome; it is the variable that changes because of the change in the independent variable. As in our income-consumption example, income generally is the independent variable and consumption the dependent variable. Income causes consumption to be what it is rather than the other way around. Similarly, ticket prices (set in advance of the season and printed on the ticket) determine attendance at GSU basketball games; attendance at games does not determine the printed ticket prices for those games. Ticket price is the independent variable and the quantity of tickets purchased is the dependent variable.

You may recall from your high school courses that mathematicians put the independent variable (cause) on the horizontal axis and the dependent variable (effect) on the vertical axis. Economists are less tidy; their graphing of independent and dependent variables is more arbitrary. Their conventional graphing of the income-consumption relationship is consistent with mathematical convention, but economists put price and cost data on the vertical axis. Hence, economists' graphing of GSU's ticket price–attendance data differs from normal mathematical procedure. This does not present a problem, but we want you to be aware of this fact to avoid any possible confusion.

Other Things Equal

Our simple two-variable graphs purposely ignore many other factors that might affect the amount of consumption

---

FIGURE 2 **Graphing the inverse relationship between ticket prices and game attendance.** Two sets of data that are negatively or inversely related, such as ticket price and the attendance at basketball games, graph as a downsloping line.

Ticket Price	Attendance, Thousands	Point
$50	0	a
40	4	b
30	8	c
20	12	d
10	16	e
0	20	f

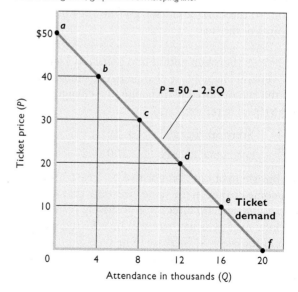

occurring at each income level or the number of people who attend GSU basketball games at each possible ticket price. When economists plot the relationship between any two variables, they employ the *ceteris paribus* (other-things-equal) assumption. Thus, in Figure 1 all factors other than income that might affect the amount of consumption are presumed to be constant or unchanged. Similarly, in Figure 2 all factors other than ticket price that might influence attendance at GSU basketball games are assumed constant. In reality, "other things" are not equal; they often change, and when they do, the relationship represented in our two tables and graphs will change. Specifically, the lines we have plotted would *shift* to new locations.

Consider a stock market "crash." The dramatic drop in the value of stocks might cause people to feel less wealthy and therefore less willing to consume at each level of income. The result might be a downward shift of the consumption line. To see this, you should plot a new consumption line in Figure 1, assuming that consumption is, say, $20 less at each income level. Note that the relationship remains direct; the line merely shifts downward to reflect less consumption spending at each income level.

Similarly, factors other than ticket prices might affect GSU game attendance. If GSU loses most of its games, attendance at GSU games might be less at each ticket price. To see this, redraw Figure 2 assuming that 2000 fewer fans attend GSU games at each ticket price.

Slope of a Line

Lines can be described in terms of their slopes. The **slope of a straight line** is the ratio of the vertical change (the rise or drop) to the horizontal change (the run) between any two points of the line.

Positive Slope Between point *b* and point *c* in Figure 1, the rise or vertical change (the change in consumption) is +$50 and the run or horizontal change (the change in income) is +$100. Therefore:

$$\text{Slope} = \frac{\text{vertical change}}{\text{horizontal change}} = \frac{+50}{+100} = \frac{1}{2} = .5$$

Note that our slope of $\frac{1}{2}$ or .5 is positive because consumption and income change in the same direction; that is, consumption and income are directly or positively related.

The slope of .5 tells us there will be a $1 increase in consumption for every $2 increase in income. Similarly, it indicates that for every $2 decrease in income there will be a $1 decrease in consumption.

Negative Slope Between any two of the identified points in Figure 2, say, point *c* and point *d*, the vertical change is −10 (the drop) and the horizontal change is +4 (the run). Therefore:

$$\text{Slope} = \frac{\text{vertical change}}{\text{horizontal change}} = \frac{-10}{+4}$$

$$= -2\frac{1}{2} = -2.5$$

This slope is negative because ticket price and attendance have an inverse relationship.

Note that on the horizontal axis attendance is stated in thousands of people. So the slope of −10/+4 or −2.5 means that lowering the price by $10 will increase attendance by 4000 people. This is the same as saying that a $2.50 price reduction will increase attendance by 1000 persons.

Slopes and Measurement Units The slope of a line will be affected by the choice of units for either variable. If, in our ticket price illustration, we had chosen to measure attendance in individual people, our horizontal change would have been 4000 and the slope would have been

$$\text{Slope} = \frac{-10}{+4000} = \frac{-1}{+400} = -.0025$$

The slope depends on the way the relevant variables are measured.

Slopes and Marginal Analysis Recall that economics is largely concerned with changes from the status quo. The concept of slope is important in economics because it reflects marginal changes—those involving 1 more (or 1 fewer) unit. For example, in Figure 1 the .5 slope shows that $.50 of extra or marginal consumption is associated with each $1 change in income. In this example, people collectively will consume $.50 of any $1 increase in their incomes and reduce their consumption by $.50 for each $1 decline in income.

Infinite and Zero Slopes Many variables are unrelated or independent of one another. For example, the quantity of wristwatches purchased is not related to the price of bananas. In Figure 3a we represent the price of bananas on the vertical axis and the quantity of watches demanded on the horizontal axis. The graph of their relationship is the line parallel to the vertical axis,

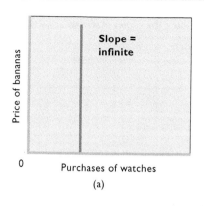
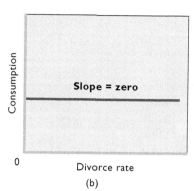

FIGURE 3 **Infinite and zero slopes.** (a) A line parallel to the vertical axis has an infinite slope. Here, purchases of watches remain the same no matter what happens to the price of bananas. (b) A line parallel to the horizontal axis has a slope of zero. In this case, consumption remains the same no matter what happens to the divorce rate. In both (a) and (b), the two variables are totally unrelated to one another.

indicating that the same quantity of watches is purchased no matter what the price of bananas. The slope of such a line is *infinite*.

Similarly, aggregate consumption is completely unrelated to the nation's divorce rate. In Figure 3b we put consumption on the vertical axis and the divorce rate on the horizontal axis. The line parallel to the horizontal axis represents this lack of relatedness. This line has a slope of *zero*.

Vertical Intercept

A line can be located on a graph (without plotting points) if we know just two things: its slope and its vertical intercept. We have already discussed slope. The **vertical intercept** of a line is the point where the line meets the vertical axis. In Figure 1 the intercept is $50. This intercept means that if current income were zero, consumers would still spend $50. They might do this through borrowing or by selling some of their assets. Similarly, the $50 vertical intercept in Figure 2 shows that at a $50 ticket price, GSU's basketball team would be playing in an empty arena.

Equation of a Linear Relationship

If we know the vertical intercept and slope, we can describe a line succinctly in equation form. In its general form, the equation of a straight line is

$$y = a + bx$$

where y = dependent variable
a = vertical intercept
b = slope of line
x = independent variable

For our income-consumption example, if C represents consumption (the dependent variable) and Y represents income (the independent variable), we can write $C = a + bY$.

By substituting the known values of the intercept and the slope, we get

$$C = 50 + .5Y$$

This equation also allows us to determine the amount of consumption C at any specific level of income. You should use it to confirm that at the $250 income level, consumption is $175.

When economists reverse mathematical convention by putting the independent variable on the vertical axis and the dependent variable on the horizontal axis, then y stands for the independent variable, rather than the dependent variable in the general form. We noted previously that this case is relevant for our GSU ticket price—attendance data. If P represents the ticket price (independent variable) and Q represents attendance (dependent variable), their relationship is given by

$$P = 50 - 2.5Q$$

where the vertical intercept is 50 and the negative slope is $-2\frac{1}{2}$, or -2.5. Knowing the value of P lets us solve for Q, our dependent variable. You should use this equation to predict GSU ticket sales when the ticket price is $15.

Slope of a Nonlinear Curve

We now move from the simple world of linear relationships (straight lines) to the more complex world of nonlinear relationships. The slope of a straight line is the same at all its points. The slope of a line representing a nonlinear relationship changes from one point to another. Such lines are always referred to as *curves*.

Consider the downsloping curve in Figure 4. Its slope is negative throughout, but the curve flattens as we move down along it. Thus, its slope constantly changes; the curve has a different slope at each point.

To measure the slope at a specific point, we draw a straight line tangent to the curve at that point. A straight line is *tangent* at a point if it touches, but does not intersect, the curve at that point. Thus line *aa* is tangent to the curve in Figure 4 at point *A*. The slope of the curve at that point is equal to the slope of the tangent line. Specifically, the total vertical change (drop) in the tangent line *aa* is -20 and the total horizontal change (run) is $+5$. Because the slope of the tangent line *aa* is $-20/+5$, or -4, the slope of the curve at point *A* is also -4.

> **INTERACTIVE GRAPHS**
> **G 1.3**
> Curves and slopes

Line *bb* in Figure 4 is tangent to the curve at point *B*. Following the same procedure, we find the slope at *B* to be $-5/+15$, or $-\frac{1}{3}$. Thus, in this flatter part of the curve, the slope is less negative.

FIGURE 4 Determining the slopes of curves.
The slope of a nonlinear curve changes from point to point on the curve. The slope at any point (say, *B*) can be determined by drawing a straight line that is tangent to that point (line *bb*) and calculating the slope of that line.

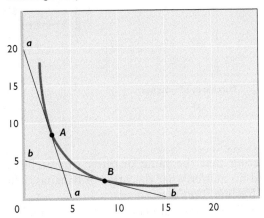

Appendix Summary

1. Graphs are a convenient and revealing way to represent economic relationships.
2. Two variables are positively or directly related when their values change in the same direction. The line (curve) representing two directly related variables slopes upward.
3. Two variables are negatively or inversely related when their values change in opposite directions. The line (curve) representing two inversely related variables slopes downward.
4. The value of the dependent variable (the "effect") is determined by the value of the independent variable (the "cause").
5. When the "other factors" that might affect a two-variable relationship are allowed to change, the graph of the relationship will likely shift to a new location.
6. The slope of a straight line is the ratio of the vertical change to the horizontal change between any two points. The slope of an upsloping line is positive; the slope of a downsloping line is negative.
7. The slope of a line or curve depends on the units used in measuring the variables. The slope is especially relevant for economics because it measures marginal changes.
8. The slope of a horizontal line is zero; the slope of a vertical line is infinite.
9. Together, the vertical intercept and slope of a line determine its location; they are used in expressing the line—and the relationship between the two variables—as an equation.
10. The slope of a curve at any point is determined by calculating the slope of a straight line tangent to the curve at that point.

Appendix Terms and Concepts

horizontal axis

vertical axis

direct relationship

inverse relationship

independent variable

dependent variable

slope of a straight line

vertical intercept

Appendix Questions

1. Briefly explain the use of graphs as a way to represent economic relationships. What is an inverse relationship? How does it graph? What is a direct relationship? How does it graph? LO7

2. Describe the graphical relationship between ticket prices and the number of people choosing to visit amusement parks. Is that relationship consistent with the fact that, historically, park attendance and ticket prices have both risen? Explain. LO7

3. Look back at Figure 2, which shows the inverse relationship between ticket prices and game attendance at Gigantic State University. (a) Interpret the meaning of both the slope and the intercept. (b) If the slope of the line were steeper, what would that say about the amount by which ticket sales respond to increases in ticket prices? (c) If the slope of the line stayed the same but the intercept increased, what can you say about the amount by which ticket sales respond to increases in ticket prices? LO7

Appendix Problems

1. Graph and label as either direct or indirect the relationships you would expect to find between (a) the number of inches of rainfall per month and the sale of umbrellas, (b) the amount of tuition and the level of enrollment at a university, and (c) the popularity of an entertainer and the price of her concert tickets. LO7

2. Indicate how each of the following might affect the data shown in the table and graph in Figure 2 of this appendix: LO7
   a. GSU's athletic director schedules higher-quality opponents.
   b. An NBA team locates in the city where GSU plays.
   c. GSU contracts to have all its home games televised.

3. The following table contains data on the relationship between saving and income. Rearrange these data into a meaningful order and graph them on the accompanying grid. What is the slope of the line? The vertical intercept? Write the equation that represents this line. What would you predict saving to be at the $12,500 level of income? LO7

Income per Year	Saving per Year
$15,000	$1,000
0	−500
10,000	500
5,000	0
20,000	1,500

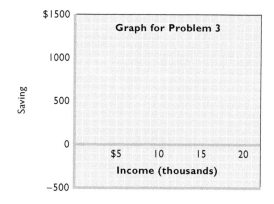

4. Construct a table from the data shown on the graph below. Which is the dependent variable and which the independent variable? Summarize the data in equation form. LO7

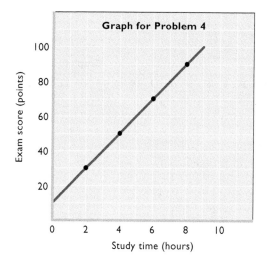

5. Suppose that when the interest rate on loans is 16 percent, businesses find it unprofitable to invest in machinery and equipment. However, when the interest rate is 14 percent, $5 billion worth of investment is profitable. At 12 percent interest, a total of $10 billion of investment is profitable. Similarly, total investment increases by $5 billion for each successive 2-percentage-point decline in the interest rate. Describe the relevant relationship between the interest rate and investment in a table, on a graph, and as an equation. Put the interest rate on the vertical axis and investment on the horizontal axis. In your equation use the form $i = a + bI$, where i is the interest rate, a is the vertical intercept, b is the slope of the line (which is negative), and I is the level of investment. LO7

6. Suppose that $C = a + bY$, where C = consumption, a = consumption at zero income, b = slope, and Y = income. LO7
   a. Are C and Y positively related or are they negatively related?

b. If graphed, would the curve for this equation slope upward or slope downward?

c. Are the variables C and Y inversely related or directly related?

d. What is the value of C if $a = 10$, $b = .50$, and $Y = 200$?

e. What is the value of Y if $C = 100$, $a = 10$, and $b = .25$?

7. The accompanying graph shows curve XX' and tangents at points A, B, and C. Calculate the slope of the curve at these three points. LO7

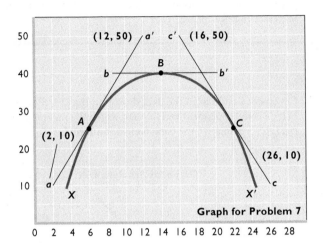

Graph for Problem 7

8. In the accompanying graph, is the slope of curve AA' positive or negative? Does the slope increase or decrease as we move along the curve from A to A'? Answer the same two questions for curve BB'. LO7

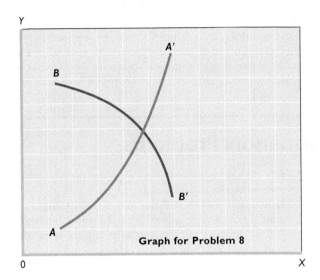

Graph for Problem 8

The Market System and the Circular Flow

You are at the mall. Suppose you were assigned to compile a list of all the individual goods and services there, including the different brands and variations of each type of product. That task would be daunting and the list would be long! And even though a single shopping mall contains a remarkable quantity and variety of goods, it is only a tiny part of the national economy.

Who decided that the particular goods and services available at the mall and in the broader economy should be produced? How did the producers determine which technology and types of resources to use in producing these particular goods? Who will obtain these products? What accounts for the new and improved products among these goods? This chapter will answer these and related questions.

Economic Systems

Every society needs to develop an **economic system**—a particular set of institutional arrangements and a coordinating mechanism—to respond to the economizing problem. The economic system has to determine what goods are produced, how they are produced, who gets them, how to accommodate change, and how to promote technological progress.

Economic systems differ as to (1) who owns the factors of production and (2) the method used to motivate, coordinate, and direct economic activity. Economic systems have two polar extremes: the command system and the market system.

The Command System

The **command system** is also known as *socialism* or *communism*. In a command system, government owns most property resources and economic decision making occurs through a central economic plan. A central planning board appointed by the government makes nearly all the major decisions concerning the use of resources, the composition and distribution of output, and the organization of production. The government owns most of the business firms, which produce according to government directives. The central planning board determines production goals for each enterprise and specifies the amount of resources to be allocated to each enterprise so that it can reach its production goals. The division of output between capital and consumer goods is centrally decided, and capital goods are allocated among industries on the basis of the central planning board's long-term priorities.

A pure command economy would rely exclusively on a central plan to allocate the government-owned property resources. But, in reality, even the preeminent command economy—the Soviet Union—tolerated some private ownership and incorporated some markets before its collapse in 1992. Recent reforms in Russia and most of the eastern European nations have to one degree or another transformed their command economies to capitalistic, market-oriented systems. China's reforms have not gone as far, but they have greatly reduced the reliance on central planning. Although government ownership of resources and capital in China is still extensive, the nation has increasingly relied on free markets to organize and coordinate its economy. North Korea and Cuba are the last prominent remaining examples of largely centrally planned economies. Other countries using mainly the command system include Turkmenistan, Laos, Belarus, Libya, Myanmar, and Iran. Later in this chapter, we will explore the main reasons for the general demise of the command systems.

The Market System

The polar alternative to the command system is the **market system,** or *capitalism*. The system is characterized by the private ownership of resources and the use of markets and prices to coordinate and direct economic activity. Participants act in their own self-interest. Individuals and businesses seek to achieve their economic goals through their own decisions regarding work, consumption, or production. The system allows for the private ownership of capital, communicates through prices, and coordinates economic activity through *markets*—places where buyers and sellers come together to buy and sell goods, services, and resources. Goods and services are produced and resources are supplied by whoever is willing and able to do so. The result is competition among independently acting buyers and sellers of each product and resource. Thus, economic decision making is widely dispersed. Also, the high potential monetary rewards create powerful incentives for existing firms to innovate and entrepreneurs to pioneer new products and processes.

In *pure* capitalism—or *laissez-faire* capitalism—government's role would be limited to protecting private property and establishing an environment appropriate

> **ORIGIN OF THE IDEA**
>
> O 2.1
>
> Laissez-faire

to the operation of the market system. The term "laissez-faire" means "let it be," that is, keep government from interfering with the economy. The idea is that such interference will disturb the efficient working of the market system.

But in the capitalism practiced in the United States and most other countries, government plays a substantial role in the economy. It not only provides the rules for economic activity but also promotes economic stability and growth, provides certain goods and services that would otherwise be underproduced or not produced at all, and modifies the distribution of income. The government, however, is not the dominant economic force in deciding what to produce, how to produce it, and who will get it. That force is the market.

Characteristics of the Market System

An examination of some of the key features of the market system in detail will be very instructive.

Private Property

In a market system, private individuals and firms, not the government, own most of the property resources (land

and capital). It is this extensive private ownership of capital that gives capitalism its name. This right of **private property,** coupled with the freedom to negotiate binding legal contracts, enables individuals and businesses to obtain, use, and dispose of property resources as they see fit. The right of property owners to designate who will receive their property when they die helps sustain the institution of private property.

The most important consequence of property rights is that they encourage people to cooperate by helping to ensure that only *mutually agreeable* economic transactions take place. To consider why this is true, imagine a world without legally enforceable property rights. In such a world, the strong could simply take whatever they wanted from the weak without giving them any compensation. But in a world of legally enforceable property rights, any person wanting something from you has to get you to agree to give it to them. And you can say no. The result is that if they really want what you have, they must offer you something that you value more highly in return. That is, they must offer you a mutually agreeable economic transaction—one that benefits you as well as them.

Property rights also encourage investment, innovation, exchange, maintenance of property, and economic growth. Nobody would stock a store, build a factory, or clear land for farming if someone else, or the government itself, could take that property for his or her own benefit.

Property rights also extend to intellectual property through patents, copyrights, and trademarks. Such long-term protection encourages people to write books, music, and computer programs and to invent new products and production processes without fear that others will steal them and the rewards they may bring.

Moreover, property rights facilitate exchange. The title to an automobile or the deed to a cattle ranch assures the buyer that the seller is the legitimate owner. Also, property rights encourage owners to maintain or improve their property so as to preserve or increase its value. Finally, property rights enable people to use their time and resources to produce more goods and services, rather than using them to protect and retain the property they have already produced or acquired.

Freedom of Enterprise and Choice

Closely related to private ownership of property is freedom of enterprise and choice. The market system requires that various economic units make certain choices, which are expressed and implemented in the economy's markets:

- **Freedom of enterprise** ensures that entrepreneurs and private businesses are free to obtain and use economic resources to produce their choice of goods and services and to sell them in their chosen markets.
- **Freedom of choice** enables owners to employ or dispose of their property and money as they see fit. It also allows workers to try to enter any line of work for which they are qualified. Finally, it ensures that consumers are free to buy the goods and services that best satisfy their wants and that their budgets allow.

These choices are free only within broad legal limitations, of course. Illegal choices such as selling human organs or buying illicit drugs are punished through fines and imprisonment. (Global Perspective 2.1 reveals that the degree of economic freedom varies greatly from economy to economy.)

Self-Interest

In the market system, **self-interest** is the motivating force of the various economic units as they express their free choices. Self-interest simply means that each economic unit tries to achieve its own particular goal, which usually requires delivering something of value to others. Entrepreneurs try to maximize

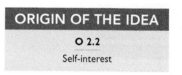

ORIGIN OF THE IDEA
O 2.2
Self-interest

profit or minimize loss. Property owners try to get the highest price for the sale or rent of their resources. Workers try to maximize their utility (satisfaction) by finding jobs that offer the best combination of wages, hours, fringe benefits, and working conditions. Consumers try to obtain the products they want at the lowest possible price and apportion their expenditures to maximize their utility. The motive of self-interest gives direction and consistency to what might otherwise be a chaotic economy.

Competition

The market system depends on **competition** among economic units. The basis of this competition is freedom of choice exercised in pursuit of a monetary return. Very broadly defined, competition requires

- Two or more buyers and two or more sellers acting independently in a particular product or resource market. (Usually there are many more than two buyers or sellers.)
- Freedom of sellers and buyers to enter or leave markets, on the basis of their economic self-interest.

Competition among buyers and sellers diffuses economic power within the businesses and households that make up the economy. When there are many buyers and sellers acting independently in a market, no single buyer

GLOBAL PERSPECTIVE 2.1

Index of Economic Freedom, Selected Economies

The Index of Economic Freedom measures economic freedom using 10 broad categories such as trade policy, property rights, and government intervention, with each category containing more than 50 specific criteria. The index then ranks 179 economies according to their degree of economic freedom. A few selected rankings for 2010 are listed below.

FREE

1 Hong Kong

3 Australia

6 Switzerland

MOSTLY FREE

8 United States

19 Japan

28 Botswana

MOSTLY UNFREE

113 Brazil

140 China

143 Russia

REPRESSED

168 Iran

174 Venezuela

179 North Korea

Source: Used by permission of The Heritage Foundation, **www.heritage.org**.

or seller can dictate the price of the product or resource because others can undercut that price.

Competition also implies that producers can enter or leave an industry; no insurmountable barriers prevent an industry's expanding or contracting. This freedom of an industry to expand or contract provides the economy with the flexibility needed to remain efficient over time. Freedom of entry and exit enables the economy to adjust to changes in consumer tastes, technology, and resource availability.

The diffusion of economic power inherent in competition limits the potential abuse of that power. A producer that charges more than the competitive market price will lose sales to other producers. An employer who pays less than the competitive market wage rate will lose workers to other employers. A firm that fails to exploit new technology will lose profits to firms that do. A firm that produces shoddy products will be punished as customers switch to higher-quality items made by rival firms. Competition is the basic regulatory force in the market system.

Markets and Prices

We may wonder why an economy based on self-interest does not collapse in chaos. If consumers want breakfast cereal but businesses choose to produce running shoes and resource suppliers decide to make computer software, production would seem to be deadlocked by the apparent inconsistencies of free choices.

In reality, the millions of decisions made by households and businesses are highly coordinated with one another by markets and prices, which are key components of the market system. They give the system its ability to coordinate millions of daily economic decisions. A **market** is an institution or mechanism that brings buyers ("demanders") and sellers ("suppliers") into contact. A market system conveys the decisions made by buyers and sellers of products and resources. The decisions made on each side of the market determine a set of product and resource prices that guide resource owners, entrepreneurs, and consumers as they make and revise their choices and pursue their self-interest.

Just as competition is the regulatory mechanism of the market system, the market system itself is the organizing and coordinating mechanism. It is an elaborate communication network through which innumerable individual free choices are recorded, summarized, and balanced. Those who respond to market signals and heed market dictates are rewarded with greater profit and income; those who do not respond to those signals and choose to ignore market dictates are penalized. Through this mechanism society decides what the economy should produce, how production can be organized efficiently, and how the fruits of production are to be distributed among the various units that make up the economy.

QUICK REVIEW 2.1

- The market system rests on the private ownership of property and on freedom of enterprise and freedom of choice.
- Property rights encourage people to cooperate and make mutually agreeable economic transactions.
- The market system permits consumers, resource suppliers, and businesses to pursue and further their self-interest.
- Competition diffuses economic power and limits the actions of any single seller or buyer.
- The coordinating mechanism of capitalism is a system of markets and prices.

Technology and Capital Goods

In the market system, competition, freedom of choice, self-interest, and personal reward provide the opportunity and motivation for technological advance. The monetary rewards for new products or production techniques accrue directly to the innovator. The market system therefore encourages extensive use and rapid development of complex capital goods: tools, machinery, large-scale factories, and facilities for storage, communication, transportation, and marketing.

Advanced technology and capital goods are important because the most direct methods of production are often the least efficient. The only way to avoid that inefficiency is to rely on capital goods. It would be ridiculous for a farmer to go at production with bare hands. There are huge benefits to be derived from creating and using such capital equipment as plows, tractors, and storage bins. The more efficient production means much more abundant output.

Specialization

The extent to which market economies rely on **specialization** is extraordinary. Specialization means using the resources of an individual, firm, region, or nation to produce one or a few goods or services rather than the entire range of goods and services. Those goods and services are then exchanged for a full range of desired products. The majority of consumers produce virtually none of the goods and services they consume, and they consume little or nothing of the items they produce. The person working nine to five installing windows in commercial aircraft may rarely fly. Many farmers sell their milk to the local dairy and then buy margarine at the local grocery store. Society learned long ago that self-sufficiency breeds inefficiency. The jack-of-all-trades may be a very colorful individual but is certainly not an efficient producer.

Division of Labor

Human specialization—called the **division of labor**—contributes to a society's output in several ways:

- *Specialization makes use of differences in ability.* Specialization enables individuals to take advantage of existing differences in their abilities and skills. If Peyton is strong, athletic, and good at throwing a football and Beyoncé is beautiful, agile, and can sing, their distribution of talents can be most efficiently used if Peyton plays professional football and Beyoncé records songs and gives concerts.

ORIGIN OF THE IDEA

O 2.3

Specialization: division of labor

- *Specialization fosters learning by doing.* Even if the abilities of two people are identical, specialization may still be advantageous. By devoting time to a single task, a person is more likely to develop the skills required and to improve techniques than by working at a number of different tasks. You learn to be a good lawyer by studying and practicing law.
- *Specialization saves time.* By devoting time to a single task, a person avoids the loss of time incurred in shifting from one job to another. Also, time is saved by not "fumbling around" with tasks that one is not trained to do.

For all these reasons, specialization increases the total output society derives from limited resources.

Geographic Specialization

Specialization also works on a regional and international basis. It is conceivable that oranges could be grown in Nebraska, but because of the unsuitability of the land, rainfall, and temperature, the costs would be very high. And it is conceivable that wheat could be grown in Florida, but such production would be costly for similar geographical reasons. So Nebraskans produce products—wheat in particular—for which their resources are best suited, and Floridians do the same, producing oranges and other citrus fruits. By specializing, both economies produce more than is needed locally. Then, very sensibly, Nebraskans and Floridians swap some of their surpluses—wheat for oranges, oranges for wheat.

Similarly, on an international scale, the United States specializes in producing such items as commercial aircraft and software, which it sells abroad in exchange for video cameras from Japan, bananas from Honduras, and woven baskets from Thailand. Both human specialization and geographic specialization are needed to achieve efficiency in the use of limited resources.

Use of Money

A rather obvious characteristic of any economic system is the extensive use of money. Money performs several functions, but first and foremost it is a **medium of exchange.** It makes trade easier.

Specialization requires exchange. Exchange can, and sometimes does, occur through **barter**—swapping goods for goods, say, wheat for oranges. But barter poses serious problems because it requires a *coincidence of wants* between the buyer and the seller. In our example, we assumed that Nebraskans had excess wheat to trade and wanted oranges. And we assumed that Floridians had excess oranges to trade and wanted wheat. So an exchange occurred. But if such a coincidence of wants is missing, trade is stymied.

FIGURE 2.1 **Money facilitates trade when wants do not coincide.** The use of money as a medium of exchange permits trade to be accomplished despite a noncoincidence of wants. (1) Nebraska trades the wheat that Florida wants for money from Floridians; (2) Nebraska trades the money it receives from Florida for the potatoes it wants from Idaho; (3) Idaho trades the money it receives from Nebraska for the oranges it wants from Florida.

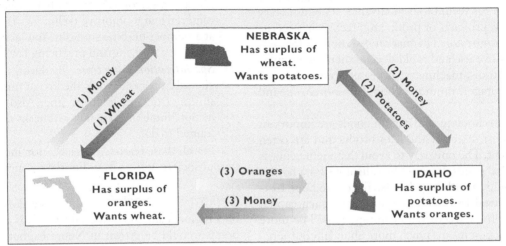

Suppose that Nebraska has no interest in Florida's oranges but wants potatoes from Idaho. And suppose that Idaho wants Florida's oranges but not Nebraska's wheat. And, to complicate matters, suppose that Florida wants some of Nebraska's wheat but none of Idaho's potatoes. We summarize the situation in Figure 2.1.

In none of the cases shown in the figure is there a coincidence of wants. Trade by barter clearly would be difficult. Instead, people in each state use **money,** which is simply a convenient social invention to facilitate exchanges of goods and services. Historically, people have used cattle, cigarettes, shells, stones, pieces of metal, and many other commodities, with varying degrees of success, as money. To serve as money, an item needs to pass only one test: It must be generally acceptable to sellers in exchange for their goods and services. Money is socially defined; whatever society accepts as a medium of exchange *is* money.

Today, most economies use pieces of paper as money. The use of paper dollars (currency) as a medium of exchange is what enables Nebraska, Florida, and Idaho to overcome their trade stalemate, as demonstrated in Figure 2.1.

On a global basis, specialization and exchange are complicated by the fact that different nations have different currencies. But markets in which currencies are bought and sold make it possible for people living in different countries to exchange goods and services without resorting to barter.

Active, but Limited, Government

An active, but limited, government is the final characteristic of market systems in modern advanced industrial economies. Although a market system promotes a high degree of efficiency in the use of its resources, it has certain inherent shortcomings, called "market failures." We will discover in subsequent chapters that government can increase the overall effectiveness of a market system in several ways.

QUICK REVIEW 2.2

- The market systems of modern industrial economies are characterized by extensive use of technologically advanced capital goods. Such goods help these economies achieve greater efficiency in production.
- Specialization is extensive in market systems; it enhances efficiency and output by enabling individuals, regions, and nations to produce the goods and services for which their resources are best suited.
- The use of money in market systems facilitates the exchange of goods and services that specialization requires.

Five Fundamental Questions

The key features of the market system help explain how market economies respond to five fundamental questions:

- What goods and services will be produced?
- How will the goods and services be produced?
- Who will get the goods and services?
- How will the system accommodate change?
- How will the system promote progress?

These five questions highlight the economic choices underlying the production possibilities curve discussed in

Chapter 1. They reflect the reality of scarce resources in a world of unlimited wants. All economies, whether market or command, must address these five questions.

What Will Be Produced?

How will a market system decide on the specific types and quantities of goods to be produced? The simple answer is this: The goods and services that can be produced at a continuing profit will be produced, while those whose production generates a continuing loss will be discontinued. Profits and losses are the difference between the total revenue (TR) a firm receives from the sale of its products and the total cost (TC) of producing those products. (For economists, total costs include not only wage and salary payments to labor, and interest and rental payments for capital and land, but also payments to the entrepreneur for organizing and combining the other resources to produce a product.)

Continuing economic profit (TR > TC) in an industry results in expanded production and the movement of resources toward that industry. Existing firms grow and new firms enter. The industry expands. Continuing losses (TC > TR) in an industry leads to reduced production and the exit of resources from that industry. Some existing firms shrink in size; others go out of business. The industry contracts. In the market system, consumers are sovereign (in command). **Consumer sovereignty** is crucial in determining the types and quantities of goods produced. Consumers spend their income on the goods they are most willing and able to buy. Through these **"dollar votes"** they register their wants in the market. If the dollar votes for a certain product are great enough to create a profit, businesses will produce that product and offer it for sale. In contrast, if the dollar votes do not create sufficient revenues to cover costs, businesses will not produce the product. So the consumers are sovereign. They collectively direct resources to industries that are meeting consumer wants and away from industries that are not meeting consumer wants.

The dollar votes of consumers determine not only which industries will continue to exist but also which products will survive or fail. Only profitable industries, firms, and products survive. So firms are not as free to produce whatever products they wish as one might otherwise think. Consumers' buying decisions make the production of some products profitable and the production of other products unprofitable, thus restricting the choice of businesses in deciding what to produce. Businesses must match their production choices with consumer choices or else face losses and eventual bankruptcy.

The same holds true for resource suppliers. The employment of resources derives from the sale of the goods

CONSIDER THIS ...

McHits and McMisses

McDonald's has introduced several new menu items over the decades. Some have been profitable "hits," while others have been "misses." Ultimately, consumers decide whether a menu item is profitable and therefore whether it stays on the McDonald's menu.

- Hulaburger (1962)—McMiss
- Filet-O-Fish (1963)—McHit
- Strawberry shortcake (1966)—McMiss
- Big Mac (1968)—McHit
- Hot apple pie (1968)—McHit
- Egg McMuffin (1975)—McHit
- Drive-thru (1975)—McHit
- Chicken McNuggets (1983)—McHit
- Extra Value Meal (1991)—McHit
- McLean Deluxe (1991)—McMiss
- Arch Deluxe (1996)—McMiss
- 55-cent special (1997)—McMiss
- Big Xtra (1999)—McHit
- McSalad Shaker (2000)—McMiss
- McGriddle (2003)—McHit
- Snack Wrap (2006)—McHit

Source: "Polishing the Golden Arches," *Forbes,* June 15, 1998, pp. 42–43, updated. Reprinted by permission of Forbes Media LLC © 2010.

and services that the resources help produce. Autoworkers are employed because automobiles are sold. There are few remaining professors of early Latin because there are few people desiring to learn the Latin language. Resource suppliers, desiring to earn income, are not truly free to allocate their resources to the production of goods that consumers do not value highly. Consumers register their preferences in the market; producers and resource suppliers, prompted by their own self-interest, respond appropriately.

How Will the Goods and Services Be Produced?

What combinations of resources and technologies will be used to produce goods and services? How will the production be organized? The answer: In combinations and ways that minimize the cost per unit of output. This is true

TABLE 2.1 **Three Techniques for Producing $15 Worth of Bar Soap**

Resource	Price per Unit of Resource	Units of Resource					
		Technique 1		Technique 2		Technique 3	
		Units	Cost	Units	Cost	Units	Cost
Labor	$2	4	$ 8	2	$ 4	1	$ 2
Land	1	1	1	3	3	4	4
Capital	3	1	3	1	3	2	6
Entrepreneurial ability	3	1	3	1	3	1	3
Total cost of $15 worth of bar soap			$15		$13		$15

because inefficiency drives up costs and lowers profits. As a result, any firm wishing to maximize its profits will make great efforts to minimize production costs. These efforts will include using the right mix of labor and capital, given the prices and productivity of those resources. They also mean locating production facilities optimally to hold down production and transportation expenses.

Those efforts will be intensified if the firm faces competition, as consumers strongly prefer low prices and will shift their purchases over to the firms that can produce a quality product at the lowest possible price. Any firm foolish enough to use higher-cost production methods will go bankrupt as it is undersold by its more efficient competitors who can still make a profit when selling at a lower price. Simply stated: Competition eliminates high-cost producers.

Least-cost production means that firms must employ the most economically efficient technique of production in producing their output. The most efficient production technique depends on

- The available technology, that is, the available body of knowledge and techniques that can be used to combine economic resources to produce the desired results.
- The prices of the needed resources.

A technique that requires just a few inputs of resources to produce a specific output may be highly inefficient economically if those resources are valued very highly in the market. Economic efficiency requires obtaining a particular output of product with the least input of scarce resources, when both output and resource inputs are measured in dollars and cents. The combination of resources that will produce, say, $15 worth of bathroom soap at the lowest possible cost is the most efficient.

Suppose there are three possible techniques for producing the desired $15 worth of bars of soap. Suppose also that the quantity of each resource required by each production technique and the prices of the required resources are as shown in Table 2.1. By multiplying the required

quantities of each resource by its price in each of the three techniques, we can determine the total cost of producing $15 worth of soap by means of each technique.

Technique 2 is economically the most efficient, because it is the least costly. It enables society to obtain $15 worth of output by using a smaller amount of resources—

WORKED PROBLEMS

W 2.1

Least-cost production

$13 worth—than the $15 worth required by the two other techniques. Competition will dictate that producers use technique 2. Thus, the question of how goods will be produced is answered. They will be produced in a least-cost way.

A change in either technology or resource prices, however, may cause a firm to shift from the technology it is using. If the price of labor falls to $.50, technique 1 becomes more desirable than technique 2. Firms will find they can lower their costs by shifting to a technology that uses more of the resource whose price has fallen. Exercise: Would a new technique involving 1 unit of labor, 4 of land, 1 of capital, and 1 of entrepreneurial ability be preferable to the techniques listed in Table 2.1, assuming the resource prices shown there?

Who Will Get the Output?

The market system enters the picture in two ways when determining the distribution of total output. Generally, any product will be distributed to consumers on the basis of their ability and willingness to pay its existing market price. If the price of some product, say, a small sailboat, is $3000, then buyers who are willing and able to pay that price will "sail, sail away." Consumers who are unwilling or unable to pay the price will be "sitting on the dock of the bay."

The ability to pay the prices for sailboats and other products depends on the amount of income that consumers have, along with the prices of, and preferences for, various goods. If consumers have sufficient income and want to spend their money on a particular good, they can have it.

The amount of income they have depends on (1) the quantities of the property and human resources they supply and (2) the prices those resources command in the resource market. Resource prices (wages, interest, rent, profit) are crucial in determining the size of each person's income and therefore each person's ability to buy part of the economy's output. If a lawyer earning $200 an hour and a janitor earning $10 an hour both work the same number of hours each year, then each year the lawyer will be able to purchase 20 times more of society's output than the janitor.

How Will the System Accommodate Change?

Market systems are dynamic: Consumer preferences, technology, and supplies of resources all change. This means that the particular allocation of resources that is now the most efficient for a specific pattern of consumer tastes, range of technological alternatives, and amount of available resources will become obsolete and inefficient as consumer preferences change, new techniques of production are discovered, and resource supplies change over time. Can the market economy adjust to such changes?

Suppose consumer tastes change. For instance, assume that consumers decide they want more fruit juice and less milk than the economy currently provides. Those changes in consumer tastes will be communicated to producers through an increase in spending on fruit and a decline in spending on milk. Other things equal, prices and profits in the fruit juice industry will rise and those in the milk industry will fall. Self-interest will induce existing competitors to expand output and entice new competitors to enter the prosperous fruit industry and will in time force firms to scale down—or even exit—the depressed milk industry.

The higher prices and greater economic profit in the fruit-juice industry will not only induce that industry to expand but will also give it the revenue needed to obtain the resources essential to its growth. Higher prices and profits will permit fruit producers to attract more resources from less urgent alternative uses. The reverse occurs in the milk industry, where fewer workers and other resources are employed. These adjustments in the economy are appropriate responses to the changes in consumer tastes. This is consumer sovereignty at work.

The market system is a gigantic communications system. Through changes in prices and profits, it communicates changes in such basic matters as consumer tastes and elicits appropriate responses from businesses and resource suppliers. By affecting price and profits, changes in consumer tastes direct the expansion of some industries and the contraction of others. Those adjustments are conveyed to the resource market. As expanding industries employ more resources and contracting industries employ fewer, the resulting changes in resource prices (wages and salaries, for example) and income flows guide resources from the contracting industries to the expanding industries.

This directing or guiding function of prices and profits is a core element of the market system. Without such a system, a government planning board or some other administrative agency would have to direct businesses and resources into the appropriate industries. A similar analysis shows that the system can and does adjust to other fundamental changes—for example, to changes in technology and in the prices of various resources.

How Will the System Promote Progress?

Society desires economic growth (greater output) and higher standards of living (greater output *per person*). How does the market system promote technological improvements and capital accumulation, both of which contribute to a higher standard of living for society?

Technological Advance The market system provides a strong incentive for technological advance and enables better products and processes to supplant inferior ones. An entrepreneur or firm that introduces a popular new product will gain revenue and economic profit at the expense of rivals. Firms that are highly profitable one year may find they are in financial trouble just a few years later. Technological advance also includes new and improved methods that reduce production or distribution costs. By passing part of its cost reduction on to the consumer through a lower product price, a firm can increase sales and obtain economic profit at the expense of rival firms.

Moreover, the market system promotes the *rapid spread* of technological advance throughout an industry. Rival firms must follow the lead of the most innovative firm or else suffer immediate losses and eventual failure. In some cases, the result is **creative destruction:** The creation of new products and production methods completely destroys the market positions of firms that are wedded to existing products and older ways of doing business. Example: The advent of compact discs largely demolished long-play vinyl records, and iPods and other digital technologies are now supplanting CDs.

Capital Accumulation Most technological advances require additional capital goods. The market system provides the resources necessary to produce additional capital goods through increased dollar votes for those goods. That is, the market system acknowledges dollar voting for capital goods as well as for consumer goods.

But who counts the dollar votes for capital goods? Answer: Entrepreneurs and business owners. As receivers of profit income, they often use part of that income to purchase capital goods. Doing so yields even greater profit income in the future if the technological innovation that required the additional capital goods is successful. Also, by paying interest or selling ownership shares, the entrepreneur and firm can attract some of the income of households as saving to increase their dollar votes for the production of more capital goods.

QUICK REVIEW 2.3

- The output mix of the market system is determined by profits, which in turn depend heavily on consumer preferences. Economic profits cause industries to expand; losses cause industries to contract.
- Competition forces industries to use the least costly production methods.
- Competitive markets reallocate resources in response to changes in consumer tastes, technological advances, and changes in availability of resources.
- In a market economy, consumer income and product prices determine how output will be distributed.
- Competitive markets create incentives for technological advance and capital accumulation, both of which contribute to increases in standards of living.

The "Invisible Hand"

In his 1776 book *The Wealth of Nations*, Adam Smith first noted that the operation of a market system creates a curious unity between private interests and social interests. Firms and resource suppliers, seeking to further their own self-interest and operating within the framework of a highly competitive market system, will simultaneously, as though guided by an **"invisible hand,"** promote the public or social interest. For example, we have seen that in a competitive environment, businesses seek to build new and improved products to increase profits. Those enhanced products increase society's well-being. Businesses also use the least costly combination of resources to produce a specific output because doing so is in their self-interest. To act otherwise would be to forgo profit or even to risk business failure. But, at the same time, to use scarce resources in the least costly way is clearly in the social interest as well. It "frees up" resources to produce something else that society desires.

Self-interest, awakened and guided by the competitive market system, is what induces responses appropriate to the changes in society's wants. Businesses seeking to make higher profits and to avoid losses, and resource suppliers pursuing greater monetary rewards, negotiate changes in the allocation of resources and end up with the output that society wants. Competition controls or guides self-interest such that self-interest automatically and quite unintentionally furthers the best interest of society. The invisible hand ensures that when firms maximize their profits and resource suppliers maximize their incomes, these groups also help maximize society's output and income.

Of the various virtues of the market system, three merit reemphasis:

- *Efficiency* The market system promotes the efficient use of resources by guiding them into the production of the goods and services most wanted by society. It forces the use of the most efficient techniques in organizing resources for production, and it encourages the development and adoption of new and more efficient production techniques.

- *Incentives* The market system encourages skill acquisition, hard work, and innovation. Greater work skills and effort mean greater production and higher incomes, which usually translate into a higher standard of living. Similarly, the assuming of risks by entrepreneurs can result in substantial profit incomes. Successful innovations generate economic rewards.

- *Freedom* The major noneconomic argument for the market system is its emphasis on personal freedom. In contrast to central planning, the market system coordinates economic activity without coercion. The market system permits—indeed, it thrives on—freedom of enterprise and choice. Entrepreneurs and workers are free to further their own self-interest, subject to the rewards and penalties imposed by the market system itself.

Of course, no economic system, including the market system, is flawless. In Chapter 5 we will explain two well-known shortcomings of the market system and examine the government policies that try to remedy them.

The Demise of the Command Systems

Our discussion of how a market system answers the five fundamental questions provides insights on why the command systems of the Soviet Union, eastern Europe, and China (prior to its market reforms) failed. Those systems encountered two insurmountable problems.

The Coordination Problem

The first difficulty was the coordination problem. The central planners had to coordinate the millions of individual decisions by consumers, resource suppliers, and businesses. Consider the setting up of a factory to produce tractors. The central planners had to establish a realistic annual production target, for example, 1000 tractors. They then had to make available all the necessary inputs—labor, machinery, electric power, steel, tires, glass, paint, transportation—for the production and delivery of those 1000 tractors.

Because the outputs of many industries serve as inputs to other industries, the failure of any single industry to achieve its output target caused a chain reaction of repercussions. For example, if iron mines, for want of machinery or labor or transportation, did not supply the steel industry with the required inputs of iron ore, the steel mills were unable to fulfill the input needs of the many industries that depended on steel. Those steel-using industries (such as tractor, automobile, and transportation) were unable to fulfill their planned production goals. Eventually the chain reaction spread to all firms that used steel as an input and from there to other input buyers or final consumers.

The coordination problem became more difficult as the economies expanded. Products and production processes grew more sophisticated and the number of industries requiring planning increased. Planning techniques that worked for the simpler economy proved highly inadequate and inefficient for the larger economy. Bottlenecks and production stoppages became the norm, not the exception. In trying to cope, planners further suppressed product variety, focusing on one or two products in each product category.

A lack of a reliable success indicator added to the coordination problem in the Soviet Union and China prior to its market reforms. We have seen that market economies rely on profit as a success indicator. Profit depends on consumer demand, production efficiency, and product quality. In contrast, the major success indicator for the command economies usually was a quantitative production target that the central planners assigned. Production costs, product quality, and product mix were secondary considerations. Managers and workers often sacrificed product quality and variety because they were being awarded bonuses for meeting quantitative, not qualitative, targets. If meeting production goals meant sloppy assembly work and little product variety, so be it.

It was difficult at best for planners to assign quantitative production targets without unintentionally producing distortions in output. If the plan specified a production target for producing nails in terms of *weight* (tons of nails), the enterprise made only large nails. But if it specified the target as a *quantity* (thousands of nails), the firm made all small nails, and lots of them! That is precisely what happened in the centrally planned economies.

The Incentive Problem

The command economies also faced an incentive problem. Central planners determined the output mix. When they misjudged how many automobiles, shoes, shirts, and chickens were wanted at the government-determined prices, persistent shortages and surpluses of those products arose. But as long as the managers who oversaw the production of those goods were rewarded for meeting their assigned production goals, they had no incentive to adjust production in response to the shortages and surpluses. And there were no fluctuations in prices and profitability to signal that more or less of certain products was desired. Thus, many products were unavailable or in short supply, while other products were overproduced and sat for months or years in warehouses.

The command systems of the former Soviet Union and China before its market reforms also lacked entrepreneurship. Central planning did not trigger the profit motive, nor did it reward innovation and enterprise.

CONSIDER THIS . . .

The Two Koreas

North Korea is one of the few command economies still standing. After the Second World War, the Korean peninsula was divided into North Korea and South Korea. North Korea, under the influence of the Soviet Union, established a command economy that emphasized government ownership and central government planning. South Korea, protected by the United States, established a market economy based upon private ownership and the profit motive. Today, the differences in the economic outcomes of the two systems are striking:

	North Korea	South Korea
GDP	$40 billion*	$1.3 trillion*
GDP per capita	$1800*	$27,700*
Exports	$2.0 billion	$355 billion
Imports	$3.5 billion	$313 billion
Agrculture as % of GDP	23 percent	3 percent

*Based on purchasing power equivalencies to the U.S. dollar.
Source: CIA World Fact Book, 2010, **www.cia.gov.**

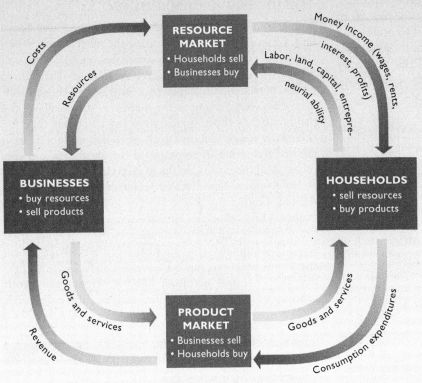

FIGURE 2.2 The circular flow diagram.
Resources flow from households to businesses through the resource market, and products flow from businesses to households through the product market. Opposite these real flows are monetary flows. Households receive income from businesses (their costs) through the resource market, and businesses receive revenue from households (their expenditures) through the product market.

QUICK QUIZ FOR FIGURE 2.2

1. The resource market is the place where:
   a. households sell products and businesses buy products.
   b. businesses sell resources and households sell products.
   c. households sell resources and businesses buy resources (or the services of resources).
   d. businesses sell resources and households buy resources (or the services of resources).

2. Which of the following would be determined in the product market?
   a. a manager's salary.
   b. the price of equipment used in a bottling plant.
   c. the price of 80 acres of farmland.
   d. the price of a new pair of athletic shoes.

3. In this circular flow diagram:
   a. money flows counterclockwise.
   b. resources flow counterclockwise.
   c. goods and services flow clockwise.
   d. households are on the selling side of the product market.

4. In this circular flow diagram:
   a. households spend income in the product market.
   b. firms sell resources to households.
   c. households receive income through the product market.
   d. households produce goods.

Answers: 1.c; 2. d; 3. b; 4. a

The route for getting ahead was through participation in the political hierarchy of the Communist Party. Moving up the hierarchy meant better housing, better access to health care, and the right to shop in special stores. Meeting production targets and maneuvering through the minefields of party politics were measures of success in "business." But a definition of business success based solely on political savvy was not conducive to technological advance, which is often disruptive to existing products, production methods, and organizational structures.

The Circular Flow Model

The dynamic market economy creates continuous, repetitive flows of goods and services, resources, and money. The **circular flow diagram**, shown in **Figure 2.2 (Key Graph)**, illustrates those flows for a simplified economy in which there is no government. Observe that in the diagram we group this economy's decision makers into *businesses*

ORIGIN OF THE IDEA

O 2.4

Circular flow diagram

and *households.* Additionally, we divide this economy's markets into the *resource market* and the *product market.*

Households

The blue rectangle on the right side of the circular flow diagram in Figure 2.2 represents **households,** which are defined as one or more persons occupying a housing unit. There are currently about 116 million households in the U.S. economy. Households buy the goods and services that businesses make available in the product market. Households obtain the income needed to buy those products by selling resources in the resource market.

All the resources in our no-government economy are ultimately owned or provided by households. For instance, the members of one household or another directly provide all of the labor and entrepreneurial ability in the economy. Households also own all of the land and all of the capital in the economy either directly, as personal property, or indirectly, as a consequence of owning all of the businesses in the economy (and thereby controlling all of the land and capital owned by businesses). Thus, all of the income in the economy—all wages, rents, interest, and profits—flows to households because they provide the economy's labor, land, capital, and entrepreneurial ability.

Businesses

The blue rectangle on the left side of the circular flow diagram represents **businesses,** which are commercial establishments that attempt to earn profits for their owners by offering goods and services for sale. Businesses fall into three main categories.

- A **sole proprietorship** is a business owned and managed by a single person. The proprietor (the owner) may work alone or have employees. Examples include a woman who runs her own tree-cutting business and an independent accountant who, with two assistants, helps his clients with their taxes.
- The **partnership** form of business organization is a natural outgrowth of the sole proprietorship. In a partnership, two or more individuals (the partners) agree to own and operate a business together. They pool their financial resources and business skills to operate the business, and they share any profits or losses that the business may generate. Many law firms and dental practices are organized as partnerships, as are a wide variety of firms in many other industries.
- A **corporation** is an independent legal entity that can—on its own behalf—acquire resources, own assets, produce and sell products, incur debts, extend

credit, sue and be sued, and otherwise engage in any legal business activity.

The fact that a corporation is an independent legal entity means that its owners bear no personal financial responsibility for the fulfillment of the corporation's debts and obligations. For instance, if a corporation has failed to repay a loan to a bank, the bank can sue the corporation but not its owners. Professional managers run most corporations. They are hired and supervised by a board of directors that is elected annually by the corporation's owners. Google, Ford, and American Airlines are examples of large corporations, but corporations come in all sizes and operate in every type of industry.

There currently are about 30 million businesses in the United States, ranging from enormous corporations like Walmart, with 2009 sales of $406 billion and 2.1 million employees, to single-person sole proprietorships with sales of less than $100 per day.

Businesses sell goods and services in the product market in order to obtain revenue, and they incur costs in the resource market when they purchase the labor, land, capital, and entrepreneurial ability that they need to produce their respective goods and services.

Product Market

The red rectangle at bottom of the diagram represents the **product market,** the place where the goods and services produced by businesses are bought and sold. Households use the income they receive from the sale of resources to buy goods and services. The money that they spend on goods and services flows to businesses as revenue.

Resource Market

Finally, the red rectangle at the top of the circular flow diagram represents the **resource market** in which households sell resources to businesses. The households sell resources to generate income, and the businesses buy resources to produce goods and services. Productive resources flow from households to businesses, while money flows from businesses to households in the form of wages, rents, interest, and profits.

To summarize, the circular flow model depicts a complex web of economic activity in which businesses and households are both buyers and sellers. Businesses buy resources and sell products. Households buy products and sell resources. The counterclockwise flow of economic resources and finished products that is illustrated by the red arrows in Figure 2.2 is paid for by the clockwise flow of money income and consumption expenditures illustrated by the blue arrows.

LAST Word Shuffling the Deck

Economist Donald Boudreaux Marvels at the Way the Market System Systematically and Purposefully Arranges the World's Tens of Billions of Individual Resources.

In *The Future and Its Enemies*, Virginia Postrel notes the astonishing fact that if you thoroughly shuffle an ordinary deck of 52 playing cards, chances are practically 100 percent that the resulting arrangement of cards has never before existed. *Never.* Every time you shuffle a deck, you produce an arrangement of cards that exists for the first time in history.

The arithmetic works out that way. For a very small number of items, the number of possible arrangements is small. Three items, for example, can be arranged only six different ways. But the number of possible arrangements grows very large very quickly. The number of different ways to arrange five items is 120 . . . for ten items it's 3,628,800 . . . for fifteen items it's 1,307,674,368,000.

The number of different ways to arrange 52 items is 8.066×10^{67}. This is a *big* number. No human can comprehend its enormousness. By way of comparison, the number of possible ways to arrange a mere 20 items is 2,432,902,008,176,640,000—a number larger than the total number of seconds that have elapsed since the beginning of time ten billion years ago—and this number is Lilliputian compared to 8.066×10^{67}.

What's the significance of these facts about numbers? Consider the number of different resources available in the world—my labor, your labor, your land, oil, tungsten, cedar, coffee beans, chickens, rivers, the Empire State Building, [Microsoft] Windows, the wharves at Houston, the classrooms at Oxford, the airport at Miami, and on and on and on. No one can possibly count all of the different productive resources available for our use. But we can be sure that this number is at least in the tens of billions.

When you reflect on how incomprehensibly large is the number of ways to arrange a deck containing a mere 52 cards, the mind boggles at the number of different ways to arrange all the world's resources.

If our world were random—if resources combined together haphazardly, as if a giant took them all into his hands and tossed them down like so many [cards]—it's a virtual certainty that the resulting combination of resources would be useless. Unless this chance arrangement were quickly rearranged according to some productive logic, nothing worthwhile would be produced. We would all starve to death. Because only a tiny fraction of possible arrangements serves human ends, any arrangement will be useless if it is chosen randomly or with inadequate knowledge of how each and every resource might be productively combined with each other.

And yet, we witness all around us an arrangement of resources that's productive and serves human goals. Today's arrangement of resources might not be perfect, but it is vastly superior to most of the trillions upon trillions of other possible arrangements.

How have we managed to get one of the minuscule number of arrangements that works? The answer is private property—a social institution that encourages mutual accommodation.

Private property eliminates the possibility that resource arrangements will be random, for each resource owner chooses a course of action only if it promises rewards to the owner that exceed the rewards promised by all other available courses.

[The result] is a breathtakingly complex and productive arrangement of countless resources. This arrangement emerged over time (and is still emerging) as the result of billions upon billions of individual, daily, small decisions made by people seeking to better employ their resources and labor in ways that other people find helpful.

Source: Abridged from Donald J. Boudreaux, "Mutual Accommodation," *Ideas on Liberty,* May 2000, pp. 4–5. Used by permission of *The Freeman.*

42

Summary

1. The market system and the command system are the two broad types of economic systems used to address the economizing problem. In the market system (or capitalism), private individuals own most resources, and markets coordinate most economic activity. In the command system (or socialism or communism), government owns most resources and central planners coordinate most economic activity.

2. The market system is characterized by the private ownership of resources, including capital, and the freedom of individuals to engage in economic activities of their choice to advance their material well-being. Self-interest is the driving force of such an economy and competition functions as a regulatory or control mechanism.

3. In the market system, markets, prices, and profits organize and make effective the many millions of individual economic decisions that occur daily.

4. Specialization, use of advanced technology, and the extensive use of capital goods are common features of market systems. Functioning as a medium of exchange, money eliminates the problems of bartering and permits easy trade and greater specialization, both domestically and internationally.

5. Every economy faces five fundamental questions: (a) What goods and services will be produced? (b) How will the goods and services be produced? (c) Who will get the goods and services? (d) How will the system accommodate change? (e) How will the system promote progress?

6. The market system produces products whose production and sale yield total revenue sufficient to cover total cost. It does not produce products for which total revenue continuously falls short of total cost. Competition forces firms to use the lowest-cost production techniques.

7. Economic profit (total revenue minus total cost) indicates that an industry is prosperous and promotes its expansion. Losses signify that an industry is not prosperous and hasten its contraction.

8. Consumer sovereignty means that both businesses and resource suppliers are subject to the wants of consumers. Through their dollar votes, consumers decide on the composition of output.

9. The prices that a household receives for the resources it supplies to the economy determine that household's income. This income determines the household's claim on the economy's output. Those who have income to spend get the products produced in the market system.

10. By communicating changes in consumer tastes to entrepreneurs and resource suppliers, the market system prompts appropriate adjustments in the allocation of the economy's resources. The market system also encourages technological advance and capital accumulation, both of which raise a nation's standard of living.

11. Competition, the primary mechanism of control in the market economy, promotes a unity of self-interest and social interests. As if directed by an invisible hand, competition harnesses the self-interest motives of businesses and resource suppliers to further the social interest.

12. The command systems of the Soviet Union and pre-reform China met their demise because of coordination difficulties caused by central planning and the lack of a profit incentive. The coordination problem resulted in bottlenecks, inefficiencies, and a focus on a limited number of products. The incentive problem discouraged product improvement, new product development, and entrepreneurship.

13. The circular flow model illustrates the flows of resources and products from households to businesses and from businesses to households, along with the corresponding monetary flows. Businesses are on the buying side of the resource market and the selling side of the product market. Households are on the selling side of the resource market and the buying side of the product market.

Terms and Concepts

economic system
command system
market system
private property
freedom of enterprise
freedom of choice
self-interest
competition
market

specialization
division of labor
medium of exchange
barter
money
consumer sovereignty
dollar votes
creative destruction
"invisible hand"

circular flow diagram
households
businesses
sole proprietorship
partnership
corporation
product market
resource market

Questions

1. Contrast how a market system and a command economy try to cope with economic scarcity. LO1
2. How does self-interest help achieve society's economic goals? Why is there such a wide variety of desired goods and services in a market system? In what way are entrepreneurs and businesses at the helm of the economy but commanded by consumers? LO2
3. Why is private property, and the protection of property rights, so critical to the success of the market system? How do property rights encourage cooperation? LO2
4. What are the advantages of using capital in the production process? What is meant by the term "division of labor"? What are the advantages of specialization in the use of human and material resources? Explain why exchange is the necessary consequence of specialization. LO2
5. What problem does barter entail? Indicate the economic significance of money as a medium of exchange. What is meant by the statement "We want money only to part with it"? LO2
6. Evaluate and explain the following statements: LO2
   a. The market system is a profit-and-loss system.
   b. Competition is the disciplinarian of the market economy.
7. Assume that a business firm finds that its profit is greatest when it produces $40 worth of product A. Suppose also that each of the three techniques shown in the table to the right will produce the desired output. LO3
   a. With the resource prices shown, which technique will the firm choose? Why? Will production using that technique entail profit or loss? What will be the amount of that profit or loss? Will the industry expand or contract? When will that expansion or contraction end?
   b. Assume now that a new technique, technique 4, is developed. It combines 2 units of labor, 2 of land, 6 of capital, and 3 of entrepreneurial ability. In view of the resource prices in the table, will the firm adopt the new technique? Explain your answer.
   c. Suppose that an increase in the labor supply causes the price of labor to fall to $1.50 per unit, all other resource prices remaining unchanged. Which technique will the producer now choose? Explain.
   d. "The market system causes the economy to conserve most in the use of resources that are particularly scarce

in supply. Resources that are scarcest relative to the demand for them have the highest prices. As a result, producers use these resources as sparingly as is possible." Evaluate this statement. Does your answer to part c, above, bear out this contention? Explain.

| | Price per Unit of Resource | Resource Units Required | | |
Resource		Technique 1	Technique 2	Technique 3
Labor	$3	5	2	3
Land	4	2	4	2
Capital	2	2	4	5
Entrepreneurial ability	2	4	2	4

8. Some large hardware stores, such as Home Depot, boast of carrying as many as 20,000 different products in each store. What motivated the producers of those individual products to make them and offer them for sale? How did the producers decide on the best combinations of resources to use? Who made those resources available, and why? Who decides whether these particular hardware products should continue to be produced and offered for sale? LO3
9. What is meant by the term "creative destruction"? How does the emergence of MP3 (or iPod) technology relate to this idea? LO3
10. In a sentence, describe the meaning of the phrase "invisible hand." LO4
11. In market economies, firms rarely worry about the availability of inputs to produce their products, whereas in command economies input availability is a constant concern. Why the difference? LO4
12. Distinguish between the resource market and the product market in the circular flow model. In what way are businesses and households both sellers and buyers in this model? What are the flows in the circular flow model? LO5
13. **LAST WORD** What explains why millions of economic resources tend to get arranged logically and productively rather than haphazardly and unproductively?

Problems

1. Table 2.1 contains information on three techniques for producing $15 worth of bar soap. Assume that we said "$15 worth of bar soap" because soap cost $3 per bar and all three techniques produce 5 bars of soap ($15 = $3 per bar × 5 bars). So you know each technique produces 5 bars of soap. LO3
   a. What technique will you want to use if the price of a bar of soap falls to $2.75? What if the price of a bar of soap rises to $4? To $5?
   b. How many bars of soap will you want to produce if the price of a bar of soap falls to $2.00?
   c. Suppose that the price of soap is again $3 per bar but that the prices of all four resources are now $1 per unit. Which is now the least-profitable technique?
   d. If the resource prices return to their original levels (the ones shown in the table) but a new technique is invented that can produce 3 bars of soap (yes, 3 bars, not 5 bars!)

using 1 unit of each of the four resources, will firms prefer the new technique?

2. Suppose Natasha currently makes $50,000 per year working as a manager at a cable TV company. She then develops two possible entrepreneurial business opportunities. In one, she will quit her job to start an organic soap company. In the other, she will try to develop an Internet-based competitor to the local cable company. For the soap-making opportunity, she anticipates annual revenue of $465,000 and costs for the necessary land, labor, and capital of $395,000 per year. For the Internet opportunity, she anticipates costs for land, labor, and capital of $3,250,000 per year as compared to revenues of $3,275,000 per year. (a) Should she quit her current job to become an entrepreneur? (b) If she does quit her current job, which opportunity would she pursue? LO3

3. With current technology, suppose a firm is producing 400 loaves of banana bread daily. Also assume that the least-cost combination of resources in producing those loaves is 5 units of labor, 7 units of land, 2 units of capital, and 1 unit of entrepreneurial ability, selling at prices of $40, $60, $60, and $20, respectively. If the firm can sell these 400 loaves at $2 per unit, what is its total revenue? Its total cost? Its profit or loss? Will it continue to produce banana bread? If this firm's situation is typical for the other makers of banana bread, will resources flow toward or away from this bakery good? LO3

4. Let's put dollar amounts on the flows in the circular flow diagram of Figure 2.2. LO5

   a. Suppose that businesses buy a total of $100 billion of the four resources (labor, land, capital, and entrepreneurial ability) from households. If households receive $60 billion in wages, $10 billion in rent, and $20 billion in interest, how much are households paid for providing entrepreneurial ability?

   b. If households spend $55 billion on goods and $45 billion on services, how much in revenues do businesses receive in the product market?

FURTHER TEST YOUR KNOWLEDGE AT
www.mcconnell19e.com

At the text's Online Learning Center (OLC), **www.mcconnell19e.com**, you will find one or more Web-based questions that require information from the Internet to answer. We urge you to check them out; they will familiarize you with Web sites that may be helpful in other courses and perhaps even in your career. The OLC also features multiple-choice questions that give instant feedback and provides other helpful ways to further test your knowledge of the chapter.

PRICE, QUANTITY, AND EFFICIENCY

AFTER READING THIS CHAPTER, YOU SHOULD BE ABLE TO:

1 Describe *demand* and explain how it can change.

2 Describe *supply* and explain how it can change.

3 Relate how supply and demand interact to determine market equilibrium.

4 Explain how changes in supply and demand affect equilibrium prices and quantities.

5 Identify what government-set prices are and how they can cause product surpluses and shortages.

6 (Appendix) Illustrate how supply and demand analysis can provide insights on actual-economy situations.

Demand, Supply, and Market Equilibrium

ORIGIN OF THE IDEA

O 3.1

Demand and supply

The model of supply and demand is the economics profession's greatest contribution to human understanding because it explains the operation of the markets on which we depend for nearly everything that we eat, drink, or consume. The model is so powerful and so widely used that to many people it *is* economics.

This chapter explains how the model works and how it can explain both the *quantities* that are bought and sold in markets as well as the *prices* at which they trade.

Markets

Markets bring together buyers ("demanders") and sellers ("suppliers"). The corner gas station, an e-commerce site, the local music store, a farmer's roadside stand—all are familiar markets. The New York Stock Exchange and the Chicago Board of Trade are markets in which buyers and sellers from all over the world communicate with one another to buy and sell bonds, stocks, and commodities. Auctioneers bring together potential buyers and sellers of art, livestock, used farm equipment, and, sometimes, real estate. In labor markets, new college graduates "sell" and employers "buy" specific labor services.

Some markets are local; others are national or international. Some are highly personal, involving face-to-face contact between demander and supplier; others are faceless, with buyer and seller never seeing or knowing each other.

To keep things simple, we will focus in this chapter on markets in which large numbers of independently acting buyers and sellers come together to buy and sell standardized products. Markets with these characteristics are the economy's most highly competitive. They include the wheat market, the stock market, and the market for foreign currencies. All such markets involve demand, supply, price, and quantity. As you will soon see, the price is "discovered" through the interacting decisions of buyers and sellers.

Demand

Demand is a schedule or a curve that shows the various amounts of a product that consumers are willing and able to purchase at each of a series of possible prices during a specified period of time.[1] Demand shows the quantities of a product that will be purchased at various possible prices, *other things equal*. Demand can easily be shown in table form. The table in Figure 3.1 is a hypothetical **demand schedule** for a *single consumer* purchasing bushels of corn.

The table reveals the relationship between the various prices of corn and the quantity of corn a particular consumer would be willing and able to purchase at each of these prices. We say "willing and able" because willingness alone is not effective in the market. You may be willing to buy a plasma television set, but if that willingness is not backed by the necessary dollars, it will not be effective and, therefore, will not be reflected in the market. In the table in Figure 3.1, if the price of corn were $5 per bushel, our consumer would be willing and able to buy 10 bushels per week; if it were $4, the consumer would be willing and able to buy 20 bushels per week; and so forth.

The table does not tell us which of the five possible prices will actually exist in the corn market. That depends

---

[1] This definition obviously is worded to apply to product markets. To adjust it to apply to resource markets, substitute the word "resource" for "product" and the word "businesses" for "consumers."

FIGURE 3.1 An individual buyer's demand for corn. Because price and quantity demanded are inversely related, an individual's demand schedule graphs as a downsloping curve such as *D*. Other things equal, consumers will buy more of a product as its price declines and less of the product as its price rises. (Here and in later figures, *P* stands for price and *Q* stands for quantity demanded or supplied.)

Demand for Corn	
Price per Bushel	Quantity Demanded per Week
$5	10
4	20
3	35
2	55
1	80

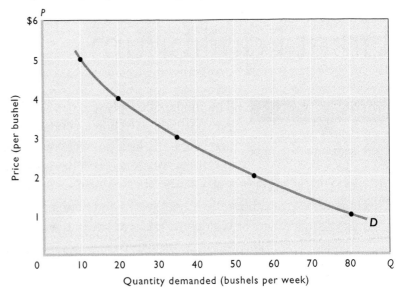

on the interaction between demand and supply. Demand is simply a statement of a buyer's plans, or intentions, with respect to the purchase of a product.

To be meaningful, the quantities demanded at each price must relate to a specific period—a day, a week, a month. Saying "A consumer will buy 10 bushels of corn at $5 per bushel" is meaningless. Saying "A consumer will buy 10 bushels of corn *per week* at $5 per bushel" is meaningful. Unless a specific time period is stated, we do not know whether the demand for a product is large or small.

Law of Demand

A fundamental characteristic of demand is this: Other things equal, as price falls, the quantity demanded rises, and as price rises, the quantity demanded falls. In short, there is a negative or *inverse* relationship between price and quantity demanded. Economists call this inverse relationship the **law of demand.**

ORIGIN OF THE IDEA
O 3.2
Law of demand

The other-things-equal assumption is critical here. Many factors other than the price of the product being considered affect the amount purchased. For example, the quantity of Nikes purchased will depend not only on the price of Nikes but also on the prices of such substitutes as Reeboks, Adidas, and New Balances. The law of demand in this case says that fewer Nikes will be purchased if the price of Nikes rises and if the prices of Reeboks, Adidas, and New Balances all remain constant. In short, if the *relative price* of Nikes rises, fewer Nikes will be bought. However, if the price of Nikes and the prices of all other competing shoes increase by some amount— say, $5—consumers might buy more, fewer, or the same number of Nikes.

Why the inverse relationship between price and quantity demanded? Let's look at three explanations, beginning with the simplest one:

- The law of demand is consistent with common sense. People ordinarily *do* buy more of a product at a low price than at a high price. Price is an obstacle that deters consumers from buying. The higher that obstacle, the less of a product they will buy; the lower the price obstacle, the more they will buy. The fact that businesses have "sales" to clear out unsold items is evidence of their belief in the law of demand.
- In any specific time period, each buyer of a product will derive less satisfaction (or benefit, or utility) from each successive unit of the product consumed. The second Big Mac will yield less satisfaction to the

ORIGIN OF THE IDEA
O 3.3
Diminishing marginal utility

consumer than the first, and the third still less than the second. That is, consumption is subject to **diminishing marginal utility.** And because successive units of a particular product yield less and less marginal utility, consumers will buy additional units only if the price of those units is progressively reduced.

- We can also explain the law of demand in terms of income and substitution effects. The **income effect** indicates that a lower price increases the purchasing power of a buyer's money income, enabling the buyer to purchase more of the product than before. A higher price has the opposite effect. The **substitution effect** suggests that at a lower price buyers have the incentive to substitute what is now a less expensive product for other products that are now *relatively* more expensive. The product whose price has fallen is now "a better deal" relative to the other products.

For example, a decline in the price of chicken will increase the purchasing power of consumer incomes, enabling people to buy more chicken (the income effect). At a lower price, chicken is relatively more attractive and consumers tend to substitute it for pork, lamb, beef, and fish (the substitution effect). The income and substitution effects combine to make consumers able and willing to buy more of a product at a low price than at a high price.

ORIGIN OF THE IDEA
O 3.4
Income and substitution effects

The Demand Curve

The inverse relationship between price and quantity demanded for any product can be represented on a simple graph, in which, by convention, we measure *quantity demanded* on the horizontal axis and *price* on the vertical axis. In the graph in Figure 3.1 we have plotted the five price-quantity data points listed in the accompanying table and connected the points with a smooth curve, labeled *D*. Such a curve is called a **demand curve.** Its downward slope reflects the law of demand—people buy more of a product, service, or resource as its price falls. The relationship between price and quantity demanded is inverse (or negative).

The table and graph in Figure 3.1 contain exactly the same data and reflect the same relationship between price and quantity demanded. But the graph shows that relationship much more simply and clearly than a table or a description in words.

Market Demand

So far, we have concentrated on just one consumer. But competition requires that more than one buyer be present in each market. By adding the quantities demanded by all consumers at each of the various possible prices, we can get from *individual* demand to *market* demand. If there are just three buyers in the market, as represented in the table in Figure 3.2, it is relatively easy to determine the total quantity demanded at each price. Figure 3.2 shows the graphical summing procedure: At each price we sum horizontally the quantities demanded by Joe, Jen, and Jay to obtain the total quantity demanded at that price; we then plot the price and the total quantity demanded as one point on the market demand curve.

Competition, of course, ordinarily entails many more than three buyers of a product. To avoid hundreds or thousands or millions of additions, we suppose that all the buyers in a market are willing and able to buy the same amounts at each of the possible prices. Then we just multiply those amounts by the number of buyers to obtain the market demand. That is how we arrived at the demand schedule and demand curve D_1 in Figure 3.3 for a market of 200 corn buyers, each with a demand as shown in the table in Figure 3.1.

In constructing a demand curve such as D_1 in Figure 3.3, economists assume that price is the most important influence on the amount of any product purchased. But economists know that other factors can and do affect purchases. These factors, called **determinants of demand,** are assumed to be constant when a demand curve like D_1 is drawn. They are the "other things equal" in the relationship between price and quantity demanded. When any of these determinants changes, the demand curve will shift to the right or left. For this reason, determinants of demand are sometimes referred to as *demand shifters.*

The basic determinants of demand are (1) consumers' tastes (preferences), (2) the number of buyers in the market, (3) consumers' incomes, (4) the prices of related goods, and (5) consumer expectations.

Changes in Demand

A change in one or more of the determinants of demand will change the demand data (the demand schedule) in the table accompanying Figure 3.3 and therefore the location of the demand curve there. A change in the demand schedule or, graphically, a shift in the demand curve is called a *change in demand.*

If consumers desire to buy more corn at each possible price than is reflected in column 2 in the table in Figure 3.3, that *increase in demand* is shown as a shift of the demand curve to the right, say, from D_1 to D_2. Conversely, a *decrease in demand* occurs when consumers buy less corn

FIGURE 3.2 Market demand for corn, three buyers. The market demand curve D is the horizontal summation of the individual demand curves (D_1, D_2, and D_3) of all the consumers in the market. At the price of $3, for example, the three individual curves yield a total quantity demanded of 100 bushels (= 35 + 39 + 26).

Market Demand for Corn, Three Buyers							
Price per Bushel	Quantity Demanded						Total Quantity Demanded per Week
	Joe		Jen		Jay		
$5	10	+	12	+	8	=	30
4	20	+	23	+	17	=	60
3	35	+	39	+	26	=	100
2	55	+	60	+	39	=	154
1	80	+	87	+	54	=	221

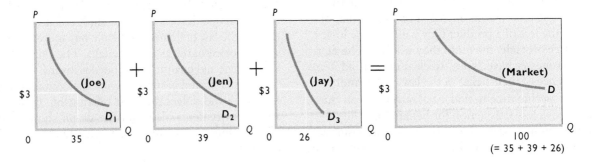

FIGURE 3.3 Changes in the demand for corn. A change in one or more of the determinants of demand causes a change in demand. An increase in demand is shown as a shift of the demand curve to the right, as from D_1 to D_2. A decrease in demand is shown as a shift of the demand curve to the left, as from D_1 to D_3. These changes in demand are to be distinguished from a change in quantity demanded, which is caused by a change in the price of the product, as shown by a movement from, say, point *a* to point *b* on fixed demand curve D_1.

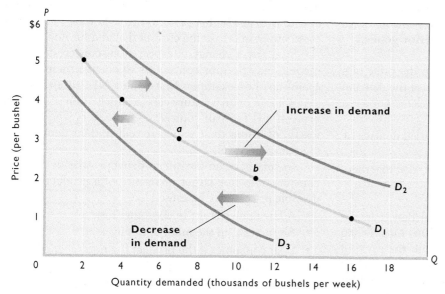

Market Demand for Corn, 200 Buyers, (D_1)	
(1) Price per Bushel	(2) Total Quantity Demanded per Week
$5	2000
4	4000
3	7000
2	11,000
1	16,000

at each possible price than is indicated in column 2. The leftward shift of the demand curve from D_1 to D_3 in Figure 3.3 shows that situation.

Now let's see how changes in each determinant affect demand.

Tastes A favorable change in consumer tastes (preferences) for a product—a change that makes the product more desirable—means that more of it will be demanded at each price. Demand will increase; the demand curve will shift rightward. An unfavorable change in consumer preferences will decrease demand, shifting the demand curve to the left.

New products may affect consumer tastes; for example, the introduction of digital cameras greatly decreased the demand for film cameras. Consumers' concern over the health hazards of cholesterol and obesity have increased the demand for broccoli, low-calorie beverages, and fresh fruit while decreasing the demand for beef, veal, eggs, and whole milk. Over the past several years, the demand for coffee drinks and table wine has greatly increased, driven by a change in tastes. So, too, has the demand for touch-screen mobile phones and fuel-efficient hybrid vehicles.

Number of Buyers An increase in the number of buyers in a market is likely to increase demand; a decrease in the number of buyers will probably decrease demand. For example, the rising number of older persons in the United

States in recent years has increased the demand for motor homes, medical care, and retirement communities. Large-scale immigration from Mexico has greatly increased the demand for a range of goods and services in the Southwest, including Mexican food products in local grocery stores. Improvements in communications have given financial markets international range and have thus increased the demand for stocks and bonds. International trade agreements have reduced foreign trade barriers to American farm commodities, increasing the number of buyers and therefore the demand for those products.

In contrast, emigration (out-migration) from many small rural communities has reduced the population and thus the demand for housing, home appliances, and auto repair in those towns.

Income How changes in income affect demand is a more complex matter. For most products, a rise in income causes an increase in demand. Consumers typically buy more steaks, furniture, and electronic equipment as their incomes increase. Conversely, the demand for such products declines as their incomes fall. Products whose demand varies *directly* with money income are called *superior goods*, or **normal goods.**

Although most products are normal goods, there are some exceptions. As incomes increase beyond some point, the demand for used clothing, retread tires, and third-hand automobiles may decrease, because the higher incomes enable consumers to buy new versions of those products. Rising incomes may also decrease the demand for soy-enhanced hamburger. Similarly, rising incomes may cause the demand for charcoal grills to decline as wealthier consumers switch to gas grills. Goods whose demand varies *inversely* with money income are called **inferior goods.**

Prices of Related Goods A change in the price of a related good may either increase or decrease the demand for a product, depending on whether the related good is a substitute or a complement:

- A **substitute good** is one that can be used in place of another good.
- A **complementary good** is one that is used together with another good.

Substitutes Häagen-Dazs ice cream and Ben & Jerry's ice cream are substitute goods or, simply, *substitutes*. When two products are substitutes, an increase in the price of one will increase the demand for the other. Conversely, a decrease in the price of one will decrease the demand for the other. For example, when the price of Häagen-Dazs ice cream rises, consumers will buy less of it and increase their demand for Ben & Jerry's ice cream. When the price of Colgate toothpaste declines, the demand for Crest decreases. So it is with other product pairs such as Nikes and Reeboks, Budweiser and Miller beer, or Chevrolets and Fords. They are *substitutes in consumption*.

Complements Because complementary goods (or, simply, *complements*) are used together, they are typically demanded jointly. Examples include computers and software, cell phones and cellular service, and snowboards and lift tickets. If the price of a complement (for example, lettuce) goes up, the demand for the related good (salad dressing) will decline. Conversely, if the price of a complement (for example, tuition) falls, the demand for a related good (textbooks) will increase.

Unrelated Goods The vast majority of goods are not related to one another and are called *independent goods*. Examples are butter and golf balls, potatoes and automobiles, and bananas and wristwatches. A change in the price of one has little or no effect on the demand for the other.

Consumer Expectations Changes in consumer expectations may shift demand. A newly formed expectation of higher future prices may cause consumers to buy now in order to "beat" the anticipated price rises, thus increasing current demand. That is often what happens in so-called hot real estate markets. Buyers rush in because

they think the price of new homes will continue to escalate rapidly. Some buyers fear being "priced out of the market" and therefore not obtaining the home they desire. Other buyers—speculators—believe they will be able to sell the houses later at a higher price. Whichever their motivation, these buyers increase the current demand for houses.

Similarly, a change in expectations concerning future income may prompt consumers to change their current spending. For example, first-round NFL draft choices may splurge on new luxury cars in anticipation of lucrative professional football contracts. Or workers who become fearful of losing their jobs may reduce their demand for, say, vacation travel.

In summary, an *increase* in demand—the decision by consumers to buy larger quantities of a product at each possible price—may be caused by:

- A favorable change in consumer tastes.
- An increase in the number of buyers.
- Rising incomes if the product is a normal good.
- Falling incomes if the product is an inferior good.
- An increase in the price of a substitute good.
- A decrease in the price of a complementary good.
- A new consumer expectation that either prices or income will be higher in the future.

You should "reverse" these generalizations to explain a *decrease* in demand. Table 3.1 provides additional illustrations of the determinants of demand.

TABLE 3.1 Determinants of Demand: Factors That Shift the Demand Curve

Determinant	Examples
Change in buyer tastes	Physical fitness rises in popularity, increasing the demand for jogging shoes and bicycles; cell phone popularity rises, reducing the demand for landline phones.
Change in number of buyers	A decline in the birthrate reduces the demand for children's toys.
Change in income	A rise in incomes increases the demand for normal goods such as restaurant meals, sports tickets, and necklaces while reducing the demand for inferior goods such as cabbage, turnips, and inexpensive wine.
Change in the prices of related goods	A reduction in airfares reduces the demand for bus transportation (substitute goods); a decline in the price of DVD players increases the demand for DVD movies (complementary goods).
Change in consumer expectations	Inclement weather in South America creates an expectation of higher future coffee bean prices, thereby increasing today's demand for coffee beans.

Changes in Quantity Demanded

A *change in demand* must not be confused with a *change in quantity demanded*. A **change in demand** is a shift of the demand curve to the right (an increase in demand) or to the left (a decrease in demand). It occurs because the consumer's state of mind about purchasing the product has been altered in response to a change in one or more of the determinants of demand. Recall that "demand" is a schedule or a curve; therefore, a "change in demand" means a change in the schedule and a shift of the curve.

In contrast, a **change in quantity demanded** is a movement from one point to another point—from one price-quantity combination to another—on a fixed demand curve. The cause of such a change is an increase or decrease in the price of the product under consideration. In the table in Figure 3.3, for example, a decline in the price of corn from $5 to $4 will increase the quantity demanded of corn from 2000 to 4000 bushels.

In Figure 3.3 the shift of the demand curve D_1 to either D_2 or D_3 is a change in demand. But the movement from point *a* to point *b* on curve D_1 represents a change in quantity demanded: Demand has not changed; it is the entire curve, and it remains fixed in place.

QUICK REVIEW 3.1

- Demand is a schedule or a curve showing the amount of a product that buyers are willing and able to purchase, in a particular time period, at each possible price in a series of prices.
- The law of demand states that, other things equal, the quantity of a good purchased varies inversely with its price.
- The demand curve shifts because of changes in (a) consumer tastes, (b) the number of buyers in the market, (c) consumer income, (d) the prices of substitute or complementary goods, and (e) consumer expectations.
- A change in demand is a shift of the demand curve; a change in quantity demanded is a movement from one point to another on a fixed demand curve.

Supply

Supply is a schedule or curve showing the various amounts of a product that producers are willing and able to make available for sale at each of a series of possible prices during a specific period.[2] The table in Figure 3.4 is a hypothetical

---

[2]This definition is worded to apply to product markets. To adjust it to apply to resource markets, substitute "resource" for "product" and "owners" for "producers."

---

supply schedule for a single producer of corn. It shows the quantities of corn that will be supplied at various prices, other things equal.

Law of Supply

The table in Figure 3.4 shows that a positive or direct relationship prevails between price and quantity supplied. As price rises, the quantity supplied rises; as price falls, the quantity supplied falls. This relationship is called the **law of supply.** A supply schedule tells us that, other things equal, firms will produce and offer for sale more of their product at a high price than at a low price. This, again, is basically common sense.

Price is an obstacle from the standpoint of the consumer, who is on the paying end. The higher the price, the less the consumer will buy. But the supplier is on the receiving end of the product's price. To a supplier, price represents *revenue*, which serves as an incentive to produce and sell a product. The higher the price, the greater this incentive and the greater the quantity supplied.

Consider a farmer who is deciding on how much corn to plant. As corn prices rise, as shown in the table in Figure 3.4, the farmer finds it profitable to plant more corn. And the higher corn prices enable the farmer to cover the increased costs associated with more intensive cultivation and the use of more seed, fertilizer, and pesticides. The overall result is more corn.

Now consider a manufacturer. Beyond some quantity of production, manufacturers usually encounter increases in *marginal cost*—the added cost of producing one more unit of output. Certain productive resources—in particular, the firm's plant and machinery—cannot be expanded quickly, so the firm uses more of other resources such as labor to produce more output. But as labor becomes more abundant relative to the fixed plant and equipment, the additional workers have relatively less space and access to equipment. For example, the added workers may have to wait to gain access to machines. As a result, each added worker produces less added output, and the marginal cost of successive units of output rises accordingly. The firm will not produce the more costly units unless it receives a higher price for them. Again, price and quantity supplied are directly related.

The Supply Curve

As with demand, it is convenient to represent individual supply graphically. In Figure 3.4, curve S is the **supply curve** that corresponds with the price–quantity supplied data in the accompanying table. The upward slope of the curve reflects the law of supply—producers offer more of

FIGURE 3.4 An individual producer's supply of corn. Because price and quantity supplied are directly related, the supply curve for an individual producer graphs as an upsloping curve. Other things equal, producers will offer more of a product for sale as its price rises and less of the product for sale as its price falls.

Supply of Corn	
Price per Bushel	Quantity Supplied per Week
$5	60
4	50
3	35
2	20
1	5

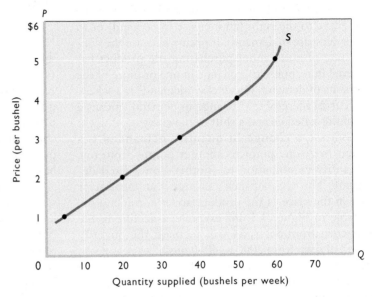

Quantity supplied (bushels per week)

a good, service, or resource for sale as its price rises. The relationship between price and quantity supplied is positive, or direct.

Market Supply

Market supply is derived from individual supply in exactly the same way that market demand is derived from individual demand. We sum the quantities supplied by each producer at each price. That is, we obtain the market supply curve by "horizontally adding" the supply curves of the individual producers. The price–quantity supplied data in the table accompanying Figure 3.5 are for an assumed 200 identical producers in the market, each willing to supply corn according to the supply schedule shown in Figure 3.4. Curve S_1 in Figure 3.5 is a graph of the market supply data. Note that the values of the axes in Figure 3.5 are the same as those used in our graph of market demand (Figure 3.3). The only difference is that we change the label on the horizontal axis from "quantity demanded" to "quantity supplied."

Determinants of Supply

In constructing a supply curve, we assume that price is the most significant influence on the quantity supplied of any product. But other factors (the "other things equal") can and do affect supply. The supply curve is drawn on the assumption that these other things are fixed and do not change. If one of them does change, a *change in supply* will occur, meaning that the entire supply curve will shift.

The basic **determinants of supply** are (1) resource prices, (2) technology, (3) taxes and subsidies, (4) prices of other goods, (5) producer expectations, and (6) the number of sellers in the market. A change in any one or more of these determinants of supply, or *supply shifters*, will move the supply curve for a product either right or left. A shift to the *right*, as from S_1 to S_2 in Figure 3.5, signifies an *increase* in supply: Producers supply larger quantities of the product at each possible price. A shift to the *left*, as from S_1 to S_3, indicates a *decrease* in supply: Producers offer less output at each price.

Changes in Supply

Let's consider how changes in each of the determinants affect supply. The key idea is that costs are a major factor underlying supply curves; anything that affects costs (other than changes in output itself) usually shifts the supply curve.

Resource Prices The prices of the resources used in the production process help determine the costs of production incurred by firms. Higher *resource* prices raise production costs and, assuming a particular *product* price, squeeze profits. That reduction in profits reduces the incentive for firms to supply output at each product price. For example, an increase in the price of sand, crushed rock, or Portland cement will increase the cost of producing concrete and reduce its supply.

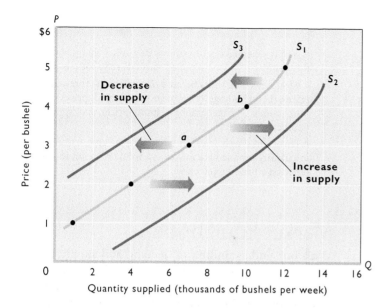

FIGURE 3.5 **Changes in the supply of corn.** A change in one or more of the determinants of supply causes a change in supply. An increase in supply is shown as a rightward shift of the supply curve, as from S_1 to S_2. A decrease in supply is depicted as a leftward shift of the curve, as from S_1 to S_3. In contrast, a change in the *quantity supplied* is caused by a change in the product's price and is shown by a movement from one point to another, as from b to a on fixed supply curve S_1.

Market Supply of Corn, 200 Producers, (S_1)	
(1) Price per Bushel	(2) Total Quantity Supplied per Week
$5	12,000
4	10,000
3	7000
2	4000
1	1000

In contrast, lower *resource* prices reduce production costs and increase profits. So when resource prices fall, firms supply greater output at each product price. For example, a decrease in the price of iron ore will decrease the price of steel.

Technology Improvements in technology (techniques of production) enable firms to produce units of output with fewer resources. Because resources are costly, using fewer of them lowers production costs and increases supply. Example: Technological advances in producing flat-panel computer monitors have greatly reduced their cost. Thus, manufacturers will now offer more such monitors than previously at the various prices; the supply of flat-panel monitors has increased.

Taxes and Subsidies Businesses treat most taxes as costs. An increase in sales or property taxes will increase production costs and reduce supply. In contrast, subsidies are "taxes in reverse." If the government subsidizes the production of a good, it in effect lowers the producers' costs and increases supply.

Prices of Other Goods Firms that produce a particular product, say, soccer balls, can sometimes use their plant and equipment to produce alternative goods, say, basketballs and volleyballs. The higher prices of these "other goods" may entice soccer ball producers to switch production to those other goods in order to increase profits. This *substitution in production* results in a decline in the supply of soccer balls. Alternatively, when the prices of basketballs and volleyballs decline relative to the price of soccer balls, producers of those goods may decide to produce more soccer balls instead, increasing their supply.

Producer Expectations Changes in expectations about the future price of a product may affect the producer's current willingness to supply that product. It is difficult, however, to generalize about how a new expectation of higher prices affects the present supply of a product. Farmers anticipating a higher wheat price in the future might withhold some of their current wheat harvest from the market, thereby causing a decrease in the current supply of wheat. In contrast, in many types of manufacturing industries, newly formed expectations that price will increase may induce firms to add another shift of workers or to expand their production facilities, causing current supply to increase.

Number of Sellers Other things equal, the larger the number of suppliers, the greater the market supply. As more firms enter an industry, the supply curve shifts to the right. Conversely, the smaller the number of firms in the industry, the less the market supply. This means that as firms leave an industry, the supply curve shifts to the left. Example: The United States and Canada have imposed restrictions on haddock fishing to replenish dwindling stocks. As part of that policy, the Federal government has bought the boats of some of the haddock fishers as a way of putting

TABLE 3.2 Determinants of Supply: Factors That Shift the Supply Curve

Determinant	Examples
Change in resource prices	A decrease in the price of microchips increases the supply of computers; an increase in the price of crude oil reduces the supply of gasoline.
Change in technology	The development of more effective wireless technology increases the supply of cell phones.
Changes in taxes and subsidies	An increase in the excise tax on cigarettes reduces the supply of cigarettes; a decline in subsidies to state universities reduces the supply of higher education.
Change in prices of other goods	An increase in the price of cucumbers decreases the supply of watermelons.
Change in producer expectations	An expectation of a substantial rise in future log prices decreases the supply of logs today.
Change in number of suppliers	An increase in the number of tattoo parlors increases the supply of tattoos; the formation of women's professional basketball leagues increases the supply of women's professional basketball games.

them out of business and decreasing the catch. The result has been a decline in the market supply of haddock.

Table 3.2 is a checklist of the determinants of supply, along with further illustrations.

Changes in Quantity Supplied

The distinction between a *change in supply* and a *change in quantity supplied* parallels the distinction between a change in demand and a change in quantity demanded. Because supply is a schedule or curve, a **change in supply** means a change in the schedule and a shift of the curve. An increase in supply shifts the curve to the right; a decrease in supply shifts it to the left. The cause of a change in supply is a change in one or more of the determinants of supply.

In contrast, a **change in quantity supplied** is a movement from one point to another on a fixed supply curve. The cause of such a movement is a change in the price of the specific product being considered.

Consider supply curve S_1 in Figure 3.5. A decline in the price of corn from $4 to $3 decreases the quantity of corn supplied per week from 10,000 to 7000 bushels. This movement from point *b* to point *a* along S_1 is a change in quantity supplied, not a change in supply. Supply is the full schedule of prices and quantities shown, and this schedule does not change when the price of corn changes.

Market Equilibrium

With our understanding of demand and supply, we can now show how the decisions of buyers of corn and sellers of corn interact to determine the equilibrium price and quantity of corn. In the table in Figure 3.6, columns 1 and 2 repeat the market supply of corn (from the table in Figure 3.5), and columns 2 and 3 repeat the market demand for corn (from the table in Figure 3.3). We assume this is a competitive market so that neither buyers nor sellers can set the price.

Equilibrium Price and Quantity

We are looking for the equilibrium price and equilibrium quantity. The **equilibrium price** (or *market-clearing price*) is the price where the intentions of buyers and sellers match. It is the price where quantity demanded equals quantity supplied. The table in Figure 3.6 reveals that at $3, *and only at that price*, the number of bushels of corn that sellers wish to sell (7000) is identical to the number consumers want to buy (also 7000). At $3 and 7000 bushels of corn, there is neither a shortage nor a surplus of corn. So 7000 bushels of corn is the **equilibrium quantity**: the quantity at which the intentions of buyers and sellers match, so that the quantity demanded and the quantity supplied are equal.

INTERACTIVE GRAPHS

G 3.1

Supply and demand

Graphically, the equilibrium price is indicated by the intersection of the supply curve and the demand curve in **Figure 3.6 (Key Graph).** (The horizontal axis now measures both quantity demanded and quantity supplied.) With neither a shortage nor a surplus at $3, the market is *in equilibrium*, meaning "in balance" or "at rest."

Competition among buyers and among sellers drives the price to the equilibrium price; once there, it will remain there unless it is subsequently disturbed by changes in

FIGURE 3.6 Equilibrium price and quantity. The intersection of the downsloping demand curve *D* and the upsloping supply curve *S* indicates the equilibrium price and quantity, here $3 and 7000 bushels of corn. The shortages of corn at below-equilibrium prices (for example, 7000 bushels at $2) drive up price. The higher prices increase the quantity supplied and reduce the quantity demanded until equilibrium is achieved. The surpluses caused by above-equilibrium prices (for example, 6000 bushels at $4) push price down. As price drops, the quantity demanded rises and the quantity supplied falls until equilibrium is established. At the equilibrium price and quantity, there are neither shortages nor surpluses of corn.

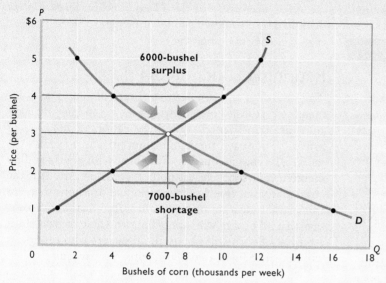

Market Supply of and Demand for Corn			
(1) Total Quantity Supplied per Week	(2) Price per Bushel	(3) Total Quantity Demanded per Week	(4) Surplus (+) or Shortage (−)*
12,000	$5	2000	+10,000 ↓
10,000	4	4000	+6000 ↓
7000	3	7000	0
4000	2	11,000	−7000 ↑
1000	1	16,000	−15,000 ↑

*Arrows indicate the effect on price.

QUICK QUIZ FOR FIGURE 3.6

1. Demand curve *D* is downsloping because:
   a. producers offer less of a product for sale as the price of the product falls.
   b. lower prices of a product create income and substitution effects that lead consumers to purchase more of it.
   c. the larger the number of buyers in a market, the lower the product price.
   d. price and quantity demanded are directly (positively) related.

2. Supply curve *S*:
   a. reflects an inverse (negative) relationship between price and quantity supplied.
   b. reflects a direct (positive) relationship between price and quantity supplied.
   c. depicts the collective behavior of buyers in this market.

   d. shows that producers will offer more of a product for sale at a low product price than at a high product price.

3. At the $3 price:
   a. quantity supplied exceeds quantity demanded.
   b. quantity demanded exceeds quantity supplied.
   c. the product is abundant and a surplus exists.
   d. there is no pressure on price to rise or fall.

4. At price $5 in this market:
   a. there will be a shortage of 10,000 units.
   b. there will be a surplus of 10,000 units.
   c. quantity demanded will be 12,000 units.
   d. quantity demanded will equal quantity supplied.

Answers: 1. b; 2. b; 3. d; 4. b

demand or supply (shifts of the curves). To better understand the uniqueness of the equilibrium price, let's consider other prices. At any above-equilibrium price, quantity supplied exceeds quantity demanded. For example, at the $4 price, sellers will offer 10,000 bushels of corn, but buyers will purchase only 4000. The $4 price encourages sellers to offer lots of corn but discourages many consumers from buying it. The result is a **surplus** (or *excess supply*) of 6000 bushels. If corn sellers produced them all, they would find themselves with 6000 unsold bushels of corn.

Surpluses drive prices down. Even if the $4 price existed temporarily, it could not persist. The large surplus would prompt competing sellers to lower the price to encourage buyers to take the surplus off their hands. As the price fell, the incentive to produce corn would decline and the incentive for consumers to buy corn would increase. As shown in Figure 3.6, the market would move to its equilibrium at $3.

Any price below the $3 equilibrium price would create a shortage; quantity demanded would exceed quantity

57

supplied. Consider a $2 price, for example. We see both from column 2 of the table and from the demand curve in Figure 3.6 that quantity demanded exceeds quantity supplied at that price. The result is a **shortage** (or *excess demand*) of 7000 bushels of corn. The $2 price discourages sellers from devoting resources to corn and encourages

CONSIDER THIS . . .

Ticket Scalping: A Bum Rap!

Ticket prices for athletic events and musical concerts are usually set far in advance of the events. Sometimes the original ticket price is too low to be the equilibrium price. Lines form at the ticket window and a severe shortage of tickets occurs at the printed price. What happens next? Buyers who are willing to pay more than the original price bid up the ticket price in resale ticket markets.

Tickets sometimes get resold for much greater amounts than the original price—market transactions known as "scalping." For example, an original buyer may resell a $75 ticket to a concert for $200. Reporters sometimes denounce scalpers for "ripping off" buyers by charging "exorbitant" prices.

But is scalping really a rip-off? We must first recognize that such ticket resales are voluntary transactions. If both buyer and seller did not expect to gain from the exchange, it would not occur! The seller must value the $200 more than seeing the event, and the buyer must value seeing the event at $200 or more. So there are no losers or victims here: Both buyer and seller benefit from the transaction. The scalping market simply redistributes assets (game or concert tickets) from those who would rather have the money (and the other things that the money can buy) to those who would rather have the tickets.

Does scalping impose losses or injury on the sponsors of the event? If the sponsors are injured, it is because they initially priced tickets below the equilibrium level. Perhaps they did this to create a long waiting line and the attendant news media publicity. Alternatively, they may have had a genuine desire to keep tickets affordable for lower-income, ardent fans. In either case, the event sponsors suffer an opportunity cost in the form of less ticket revenue than they might have otherwise received. But such losses are self-inflicted and separate and distinct from the fact that some tickets are later resold at a higher price.

So is ticket scalping undesirable? Not on economic grounds! It is an entirely voluntary activity that benefits both sellers and buyers.

consumers to desire more bushels than are available. The $2 price cannot persist as the equilibrium price. Many consumers who want to buy corn at this price will not obtain it. They will express a willingness to pay more than $2 to get corn. Competition among these buyers will drive up the price, eventually to the $3 equilibrium level. Unless disrupted by changes of supply or demand, this $3 price of corn will continue to prevail.

Rationing Function of Prices

The ability of the competitive forces of supply and demand to establish a price at which selling and buying decisions are consistent is called the rationing function of prices. In our case, the equilibrium price of $3 clears the market, leaving no burdensome surplus for sellers and no inconvenient shortage for potential buyers. And it is the combination of freely made individual decisions that sets this market-clearing price. In effect, the market outcome says that all buyers who are willing and able to pay $3 for a bushel of corn will obtain it; all buyers who cannot or will not pay $3 will go without corn. Similarly, all producers who are willing and able to offer corn for sale at $3 a bushel will sell it; all producers who cannot or will not sell for $3 per bushel will not sell their product.

Efficient Allocation

A competitive market such as that we have described not only rations goods to consumers but also allocates society's resources efficiently to the particular product. Competition among corn producers forces them to use the best technology and right mix of productive resources. If they didn't, their costs would be too high relative to the market price, and they would be unprofitable. The result is **productive efficiency:** the production of any particular good in the least costly way. When society produces corn at the lowest achievable per-unit cost, it is expending the least-valued combination of resources to produce that product and therefore is making available more-valued resources to produce other desired goods. Suppose society has only $100 worth of resources available. If it can produce a bushel of corn using $3 of those resources, then it will have available $97 of resources remaining to produce other goods. This is clearly better than producing the corn for $5 and having only $95 of resources available for the alternative uses.

Competitive markets also produce **allocative efficiency:** the *particular mix* of goods and services most highly valued by society (minimum-cost production assumed). For example, society wants land suitable for growing corn used for that purpose, not to grow dandelions. It wants diamonds to be used for jewelry, not crushed up and used as an additive to give concrete more sparkle. It wants iPods and MP4 players, not cassette players and tapes. Moreover, society does not want to devote all its resources to corn, diamonds, and portable digital media players. It wants to assign some resources to wheat, gasoline, and cell phones. Competitive markets make those allocatively efficient assignments.

The equilibrium price and quantity in competitive markets usually produce an assignment of resources that is "right" from an economic perspective. Demand essentially reflects the marginal benefit (MB) of the good, based on the utility received. Supply reflects the marginal cost (MC) of producing the good. The market ensures that firms produce all units of goods for which MB exceeds MC and no units for which MC exceeds MB. At the intersection of the demand and supply curves, MB equals MC and allocative efficiency results. As economists say, there is neither an "underallocaton of resources" nor an "overallocation of resources" to the product.

Changes in Supply, Demand, and Equilibrium

We know that demand might change because of fluctuations in consumer tastes or incomes, changes in consumer expectations, or variations in the prices of related goods. Supply might change in response to changes in resource prices, technology, or taxes. What effects will such changes in supply and demand have on equilibrium price and quantity?

Changes in Demand Suppose that the supply of some good (for example, health care) is constant and demand increases, as shown in Figure 3.7a. As a result, the new intersection of the supply and demand curves is at higher values on both the price and the quantity axes. Clearly, an increase in demand raises both equilibrium price and equilibrium quantity. Conversely, a decrease in demand such as that shown in Figure 3.7b reduces both equilibrium price and equilibrium quantity. (The value of graphical analysis is now apparent: We need not fumble with columns of figures to determine the outcomes; we need only compare the new and the old points of intersection on the graph.)

Changes in Supply What happens if the demand for some good (for example, flash drives) is constant but supply increases, as in Figure 3.7c? The new intersection of supply and demand is located at a lower equilibrium price but at a higher equilibrium quantity. An increase in supply

reduces equilibrium price but increases equilibrium quantity. In contrast, if supply decreases, as in Figure 3.7d, equilibrium price rises while equilibrium quantity declines.

Complex Cases When both supply and demand change, the effect is a combination of the individual effects.

Supply Increase; Demand Decrease What effect will a supply increase and a demand decrease for some good (for example, apples) have on equilibrium price? Both changes decrease price, so the net result is a price drop greater than that resulting from either change alone.

What about equilibrium quantity? Here the effects of the changes in supply and demand are opposed: the increase in supply increases equilibrium quantity, but the decrease in demand reduces it. The direction of the change in equilibrium quantity depends on the relative sizes of the changes in supply and demand. If the increase in supply is larger than the decrease in demand, the equilibrium quantity will increase. But if the decrease in demand is greater than the increase in supply, the equilibrium quantity will decrease.

Supply Decrease; Demand Increase A decrease in supply and an increase in demand for some good (for example, gasoline) both increase price. Their combined effect is an increase in equilibrium price greater than that caused by either change separately. But their effect on the equilibrium quantity is again indeterminate, depending on the relative sizes of the changes in supply and demand. If the decrease in supply is larger than the increase in demand, the equilibrium quantity will decrease. In contrast, if the increase in demand is greater than the decrease in supply, the equilibrium quantity will increase.

Supply Increase; Demand Increase What if supply and demand both increase for some good (for example, cell phones)? A supply increase drops equilibrium price, while a demand increase boosts it. If the increase in supply is greater than the increase in demand, the equilibrium price will fall. If the opposite holds, the equilibrium price will rise.

The effect on equilibrium quantity is certain: The increases in supply and demand both raise the equilibrium quantity. Therefore, the equilibrium quantity will increase by an amount greater than that caused by either change alone.

Supply Decrease; Demand Decrease What about decreases in both supply and demand for some good (for example, new homes)? If the decrease in supply is greater

FIGURE 3.7 **Changes in demand and supply and the effects on price and quantity.** The increase in demand from D_1 to D_2 in (a) increases both equilibrium price and equilibrium quantity. The decrease in demand from D_3 to D_4 in (b) decreases both equilibrium price and equilibrium quantity. The increase in supply from S_1 to S_2 in (c) decreases equilibrium price and increases equilibrium quantity. The decline in supply from S_3 to S_4 in (d) increases equilibrium price and decreases equilibrium quantity. The boxes in the top right corners summarize the respective changes and outcomes. The upward arrows in the boxes signify increases in equilibrium price (P) and equilibrium quantity (Q); the downward arrows signify decreases in these items.

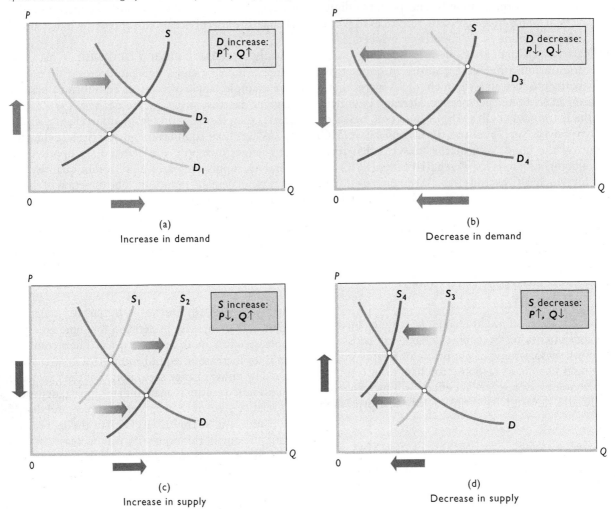

(a) Increase in demand

(b) Decrease in demand

(c) Increase in supply

(d) Decrease in supply

than the decrease in demand, equilibrium price will rise. If the reverse is true, equilibrium price will fall. Because the decreases in supply and demand each reduce equilibrium quantity, we can be sure that equilibrium quantity will fall.

Table 3.3 summarizes these four cases. To understand them fully, you should draw supply and demand diagrams for each case to confirm the effects listed in this table.

Special cases arise when a decrease in demand and a decrease in supply, or an increase in demand and an increase in supply, exactly cancel out. In both cases, the net effect on equilibrium price will be zero; price will not change.

The optional appendix accompanying this chapter provides additional examples of situations in which both supply and demand change at the same time.

TABLE 3.3 **Effects of Changes in Both Supply and Demand**

Change in Supply	Change in Demand	Effect on Equilibrium Price	Effect on Equilibrium Quantity
1. Increase	Decrease	Decrease	Indeterminate
2. Decrease	Increase	Increase	Indeterminate
3. Increase	Increase	Indeterminate	Increase
4. Decrease	Decrease	Indeterminate	Decrease

CONSIDER THIS . . .

Salsa and Coffee Beans

If you forget the other-things-equal assumption, you can encounter situations that *seem* to be in conflict with the laws of demand and supply. For example, suppose salsa manufacturers sell 1 million bottles of salsa at $4 a bottle in one year; 2 million bottles at $5 in the next year; and 3 million at $6 in the year thereafter. Price and quantity purchased vary directly, and these data seem to be at odds with the law of demand.

But there is no conflict here; the data do not refute the law of demand. The catch is that the law of demand's other-things-equal assumption has been violated over the three years in the example. Specifically, because of changing tastes and rising incomes, the demand for salsa has increased sharply, as in Figure 3.7a. The result is higher prices *and* larger quantities purchased.

Another example: The price of coffee beans occasionally shoots upward at the same time that the quantity of coffee beans harvested declines. These events seemingly contradict the direct relationship between price and quantity denoted by supply. The catch again is that the other-things-equal assumption underlying the upsloping supply curve is violated. Poor coffee harvests decrease supply, as in Figure 3.7d, increasing the equilibrium price of coffee and reducing the equilibrium quantity.

The laws of demand and supply are not refuted by observations of price and quantity made over periods of time in which either demand or supply curves shift.

Application: Government-Set Prices

Prices in most markets are free to rise or fall to their equilibrium levels, no matter how high or low those levels might be. However, government sometimes concludes that supply and demand will produce prices that are unfairly high for buyers or unfairly low for sellers. So government may place legal limits on how high or low a price or prices may go. Is that a good idea?

Price Ceilings on Gasoline

A **price ceiling** sets the maximum legal price a seller may charge for a product or service. A price at or below the ceiling is legal; a price above it is not. The rationale for establishing price ceilings (or ceiling prices) on specific products is that they purportedly enable consumers to obtain some "essential" good or service that they could not afford at the equilibrium price. Examples are rent controls and usury laws, which specify maximum "prices" in the forms of rent and interest that can be charged to borrowers.

Graphical Analysis We can easily show the effects of price ceilings graphically. Suppose that rapidly rising world income boosts the purchase of automobiles and shifts the demand for gasoline to the right so that the market equilibrium price reaches $3.50 per gallon, shown as P_0 in Figure 3.8. The rapidly rising price of gasoline greatly burdens low- and moderate-income households, which pressure government to "do something." To keep gasoline prices down, the government imposes a ceiling price P_c of $3 per gallon. To impact the market, a price ceiling must be below the equilibrium price. A ceiling price of $4, for example, would have had no effect on the price of gasoline in the current situation.

What are the effects of this $3 ceiling price? The rationing ability of the free market is rendered ineffective. Because the ceiling price P_c is below the market-clearing price P_0, there is a lasting shortage of gasoline. The quantity of gasoline demanded at P_c is Q_d and the quantity supplied is only Q_s; a persistent excess demand or shortage of amount $Q_d - Q_s$ occurs.

The price ceiling P_c prevents the usual market adjustment in which competition among buyers bids up price, inducing more production and rationing some buyers out of the market. That process would normally continue until the shortage disappeared at the equilibrium price and quantity, P_0 and Q_0.

By preventing these market adjustments from occurring, the price ceiling poses two related problems.

FIGURE 3.8 A price ceiling. A price ceiling is a maximum legal price such as P_c. When the ceiling price is below the equilibrium price, a persistent product shortage results. Here that shortage is shown by the horizontal distance between Q_d and Q_s.

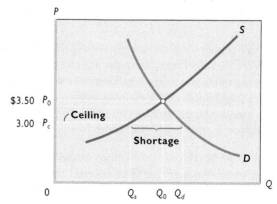

LAST Word A Legal Market for Human Organs?

A Legal Market Might Eliminate the Present Shortage of Human Organs for Transplant. But There Are Many Serious Objections to "Turning Human Body Parts into Commodities" for Purchase and Sale.

It has become increasingly commonplace in medicine to transplant kidneys, lungs, livers, corneas, pancreases, and hearts from deceased individuals to those whose organs have failed or are failing. But surgeons and many of their patients face a growing problem: There are shortages of donated organs available for transplant. Not everyone who needs a transplant can get one. In 2010, there were 105,000 Americans on the waiting list for transplants. Indeed, an inadequate supply of donated organs causes an estimated 6900 deaths in the United States each year.

Why Shortages? Seldom do we hear of shortages of desired goods in market economies. What is different about organs for transplant? One difference is that no legal market exists for human organs. To understand this situation,

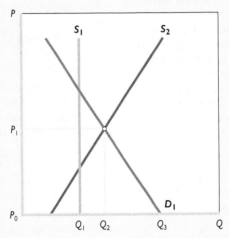

observe the demand curve D_1 and supply curve S_1 in the accompanying figure. The downward slope of the demand curve tells us that if there were a market for human organs, the quantity of organs demanded would be greater at lower prices than at higher prices. Vertical supply curve S_1 represents the fixed quantity of human organs now donated via consent before death. Because the price of these donated organs is in effect zero, quantity demanded Q_3 exceeds quantity supplied Q_1. The shortage of $Q_3 - Q_1$ is rationed through a waiting list of those in medical need of transplants. Many people die while still on the waiting list.

Use of a Market A market for human organs would increase the incentive to donate organs. Such a market might work like this: An individual might specify in a legal document that he or she is willing to sell one or more usable human organs upon death or near-death. The person could specify where the money from the sale would go, for example, to family, a church, an educational institution, or a charity. Firms would then emerge to purchase organs and resell them where needed for profit. Under such a

Rationing Problem How will the available supply Q_s be apportioned among buyers who want the greater amount Q_d? Should gasoline be distributed on a first-come, first-served basis, that is, to those willing and able to get in line the soonest or stay in line the longest? Or should gas stations distribute it on the basis of favoritism? Since an unregulated shortage does not lead to an equitable distribution of gasoline, the government must establish some formal system for rationing it to consumers. One option is to issue ration coupons, which authorize bearers to purchase a fixed amount of gasoline per month. The rationing system might entail first the printing of coupons for Q_s gallons of gasoline and then the equal distribution of the coupons among consumers so that the wealthy family of four and the poor family of four both receive the same number of coupons.

Black Markets But ration coupons would not prevent a second problem from arising. The demand curve in Figure 3.8 reveals that many buyers are willing to pay more than

the ceiling price P_c. And, of course, it is more profitable for gasoline stations to sell at prices above the ceiling. Thus, despite a sizable enforcement bureaucracy that would have to accompany the price controls, *black markets* in which gasoline is illegally bought and sold at prices above the legal limits will flourish. Counterfeiting of ration coupons will also be a problem. And since the price of gasoline is now "set by government," government might face political pressure to set the price even lower.

Rent Controls

About 200 cities in the United States, including New York City, Boston, and San Francisco, have at one time or another enacted rent controls: maximum rents established by law (or, more recently, maximum rent increases for existing tenants). Such laws are well intended. Their goals are to protect low-income families from escalating rents caused by perceived housing shortages and to make housing more affordable to the poor.

system, the supply curve of usable organs would take on the normal upward slope of typical supply curves. The higher the expected price of an organ, the greater the number of people who would be willing to have their organs sold at death. Suppose that the supply curve is S_2 in the figure. At the equilibrium price P_1, the number of organs made available for transplant (Q_2) would equal the number purchased for transplant (also Q_2). In this generalized case, the shortage of organs would be eliminated and, of particular importance, the number of organs available for transplanting would rise from Q_1 to Q_2. This means more lives would be saved and enhanced than under the present donor system.

Objections In view of this positive outcome, why is there no such market for human organs? Critics of market-based solutions have two main objections. The first is a moral objection: Critics feel that turning human organs into commodities commercializes human beings and diminishes the special nature of human life. They say there is something unseemly about selling and buying body organs as if they were bushels of wheat or ounces of gold. (There is, however, a market for blood!) Moreover, critics note that the market would

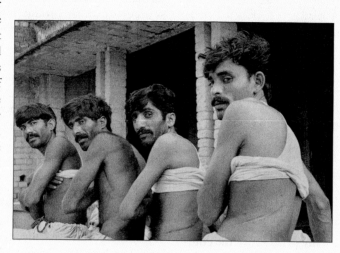

ration the available organs (as represented by Q_2 in the figure) to people who either can afford them (at P_1) or have health insurance for transplants. The poor and uninsured would be left out.

Second, a health-cost objection suggests that a market for body organs would greatly increase the cost of health care. Rather than obtaining freely donated (although "too few") body organs, patients or their insurance companies would have to pay market prices for them, further increasing the cost of medical care.

Rebuttal Supporters of market-based solutions to organ shortages point out that the laws against selling organs are simply driving the market underground. Worldwide, an estimated $1 billion-per-year illegal market in human organs has emerged. As in other illegal markets, the unscrupulous tend to thrive. This fact is dramatized by the accompanying photo, in which four Pakistani villagers show off their scars after they each sold a kidney to pay off debts. Supporters say that legalization of the market for human organs would increase organ supply from legal sources, drive down the price of organs, and reduce the abuses such as those now taking place in illegal markets.

What have been the actual economic effects? On the demand side, the below-equilibrium rents attract a larger number of renters. Some are locals seeking to move into their own places after sharing housing with friends or family. Others are outsiders attracted into the area by the artificially lower rents. But a large problem occurs on the supply side. Price controls make it less attractive for landlords to offer housing on the rental market. In the short run, owners may sell their rental units or convert them to condominiums. In the long run, low rents make it unprofitable for owners to repair or renovate their rental units. (Rent controls are one cause of the many abandoned apartment buildings found in larger cities.) Also, insurance companies, pension funds, and other potential new investors in housing will find it more profitable to invest in office buildings, shopping malls, or motels, where rents are not controlled.

In brief, rent controls distort market signals and thus resources are misallocated: Too few resources are allocated to rental housing and too many to alternative uses.

Ironically, although rent controls are often legislated to lessen the effects of perceived housing shortages, controls in fact are a primary cause of such shortages. For that reason, most American cities either have abandoned or are in the process of dismantling rent controls.

Price Floors on Wheat

A **price floor** is a minimum price fixed by the government. A price at or above the price floor is legal; a price below it is not. Price floors above equilibrium prices are usually invoked when society feels that the free functioning of the market system has not provided a sufficient income for certain groups of resource suppliers or producers. Supported prices for agricultural products and current minimum wages are two examples of price (or wage) floors. Let's look at the former.

Suppose that many farmers have extremely low incomes when the price of wheat is at its equilibrium value of $2 per bushel. The government decides to help out by establishing a legal price floor or price support of $3 per bushel.

FIGURE 3.9 A price floor. A price floor is a minimum legal price such as P_f. When the price floor is above the equilibrium price, a persistent product surplus results. Here that surplus is shown by the horizontal distance between Q_s and Q_d.

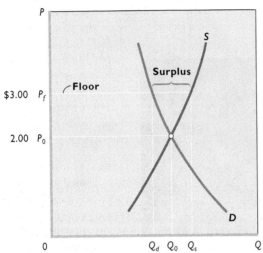

What will be the effects? At any price above the equilibrium price, quantity supplied will exceed quantity demanded—that is, there will be a persistent excess supply or surplus of the product. Farmers will be willing to produce and offer for sale more than private buyers are willing to purchase at the price floor. As we saw with a price ceiling, an imposed legal price disrupts the rationing ability of the free market.

Graphical Analysis Figure 3.9 illustrates the effect of a price floor graphically. Suppose that S and D are the supply and demand curves for wheat. Equilibrium price and quantity are P_0 and Q_0, respectively. If the government imposes a price floor of P_f, farmers will produce Q_s but private buyers will purchase only Q_d. The surplus is the excess of Q_s over Q_d.

The government may cope with the surplus resulting from a price floor in two ways:

- It can restrict supply (for example, by instituting acreage allotments by which farmers agree to take a certain amount of land out of production) or increase demand (for example, by researching new uses for the product involved). These actions may reduce the difference between the equilibrium price and the price floor and that way reduce the size of the resulting surplus.

- If these efforts are not wholly successful, then the government must purchase the surplus output at the $3 price (thereby subsidizing farmers) and store or otherwise dispose of it.

Additional Consequences Price floors such as P_f in Figure 3.9 not only disrupt the rationing ability of prices

but distort resource allocation. Without the price floor, the $2 equilibrium price of wheat would cause financial losses and force high-cost wheat producers to plant other crops or abandon farming altogether. But the $3 price floor allows them to continue to grow wheat and remain farmers. So society devotes too many of its scarce resources to wheat production and too few to producing other, more valuable, goods and services. It fails to achieve allocative efficiency.

That's not all. Consumers of wheat-based products pay higher prices because of the price floor. Taxpayers pay higher taxes to finance the government's purchase of the surplus. Also, the price floor causes potential environmental damage by encouraging wheat farmers to bring hilly, erosion-prone "marginal land" into production. The higher price also prompts imports of wheat. But, since such imports would increase the quantity of wheat supplied and thus undermine the price floor, the government needs to erect tariffs (taxes on imports) to keep the foreign wheat out. Such tariffs usually prompt other countries to retaliate with their own tariffs against U.S. agricultural or manufacturing exports.

So it is easy to see why economists "sound the alarm" when politicians advocate imposing price ceilings or price floors such as price controls, rent controls, interest-rate lids, or agricultural price supports. In all these cases, good intentions lead to bad economic outcomes. Government-controlled prices cause shortages or surpluses, distort resource allocation, and produce negative side effects.

INTERACTIVE GRAPHS

G 3.2

Price floors and ceilings

QUICK REVIEW 3.3

- In competitive markets, prices adjust to the equilibrium level at which quantity demanded equals quantity supplied.

- The equilibrium price and quantity are those indicated by the intersection of the supply and demand curves for any product or resource.

- An increase in demand increases equilibrium price and quantity; a decrease in demand decreases equilibrium price and quantity.

- An increase in supply reduces equilibrium price but increases equilibrium quantity; a decrease in supply increases equilibrium price but reduces equilibrium quantity.

- Over time, equilibrium price and quantity may change in directions that seem at odds with the laws of demand and supply because the other-things-equal assumption is violated.

- Government-controlled prices in the form of ceilings and floors stifle the rationing function of prices, distort resource allocations, and cause negative side effects.

Summary

1. Demand is a schedule or curve representing the willingness of buyers in a specific period to purchase a particular product at each of various prices. The law of demand implies that consumers will buy more of a product at a low price than at a high price. So, other things equal, the relationship between price and quantity demanded is negative or inverse and is graphed as a downsloping curve.

2. Market demand curves are found by adding horizontally the demand curves of the many individual consumers in the market.

3. Changes in one or more of the determinants of demand (consumer tastes, the number of buyers in the market, the money incomes of consumers, the prices of related goods, and consumer expectations) shift the market demand curve. A shift to the right is an increase in demand; a shift to the left is a decrease in demand. A change in demand is different from a change in the quantity demanded, the latter being a movement from one point to another point on a fixed demand curve because of a change in the product's price.

4. Supply is a schedule or curve showing the amounts of a product that producers are willing to offer in the market at each possible price during a specific period. The law of supply states that, other things equal, producers will offer more of a product at a high price than at a low price. Thus, the relationship between price and quantity supplied is positive or direct, and supply is graphed as an upsloping curve.

5. The market supply curve is the horizontal summation of the supply curves of the individual producers of the product.

6. Changes in one or more of the determinants of supply (resource prices, production techniques, taxes or subsidies, the prices of other goods, producer expectations, or the number of sellers in the market) shift the supply curve of a product. A shift to the right is an increase in supply; a shift to the left is a decrease in supply. In contrast, a change in the price of the product being considered causes a change in the quantity supplied, which is shown as a movement from one point to another point on a fixed supply curve.

7. The equilibrium price and quantity are established at the intersection of the supply and demand curves. The interaction of market demand and market supply adjusts the price to the point at which the quantities demanded and supplied are equal. This is the equilibrium price. The corresponding quantity is the equilibrium quantity.

8. The ability of market forces to synchronize selling and buying decisions to eliminate potential surpluses and shortages is known as the rationing function of prices. The equilibrium quantity in competitive markets reflects both productive efficiency (least-cost production) and allocative efficiency (producing the right amount of the product relative to other products).

9. A change in either demand or supply changes the equilibrium price and quantity. Increases in demand raise both equilibrium price and equilibrium quantity; decreases in demand lower both equilibrium price and equilibrium quantity. Increases in supply lower equilibrium price and raise equilibrium quantity; decreases in supply raise equilibrium price and lower equilibrium quantity.

10. Simultaneous changes in demand and supply affect equilibrium price and quantity in various ways, depending on their direction and relative magnitudes (see Table 3.3).

11. A price ceiling is a maximum price set by government and is designed to help consumers. Effective price ceilings produce persistent product shortages, and if an equitable distribution of the product is sought, government must ration the product to consumers.

12. A price floor is a minimum price set by government and is designed to aid producers. Effective price floors lead to persistent product surpluses; the government must either purchase the product or eliminate the surplus by imposing restrictions on production or increasing private demand.

13. Legally fixed prices stifle the rationing function of prices and distort the allocation of resources.

Terms and Concepts

demand	substitute good	change in quantity supplied
demand schedule	complementary good	equilibrium price
law of demand	change in demand	equilibrium quantity
diminishing marginal utility	change in quantity demanded	surplus
income effect	supply	shortage
substitution effect	supply schedule	productive efficiency
demand curve	law of supply	allocative efficiency
determinants of demand	supply curve	price ceiling
normal goods	determinants of supply	price floor
inferior goods	change in supply	

Questions

1. Explain the law of demand. Why does a demand curve slope downward? How is a market demand curve derived from individual demand curves? LO1

2. What are the determinants of demand? What happens to the demand curve when any of these determinants change? Distinguish between a change in demand and a movement along a fixed demand curve, noting the cause(s) of each. LO1

3. What effect will each of the following have on the demand for small automobiles such as the Mini-Cooper and Smart car? LO1
   a. Small automobiles become more fashionable.
   b. The price of large automobiles rises (with the price of small autos remaining the same).
   c. Income declines and small autos are an inferior good.
   d. Consumers anticipate that the price of small autos will greatly come down in the near future.
   e. The price of gasoline substantially drops.

4. Explain the law of supply. Why does the supply curve slope upward? How is the market supply curve derived from the supply curves of individual producers? LO2

5. What are the determinants of supply? What happens to the supply curve when any of these determinants changes? Distinguish between a change in supply and a change in the quantity supplied, noting the cause(s) of each. LO2

6. What effect will each of the following have on the supply of *auto* tires? LO2
   a. A technological advance in the methods of producing tires.
   b. A decline in the number of firms in the tire industry.
   c. An increase in the prices of rubber used in the production of tires.
   d. The expectation that the equilibrium price of auto tires will be lower in the future than currently.
   e. A decline in the price of the large tires used for semi trucks and earth-hauling rigs (with no change in the price of auto tires).
   f. The levying of a per-unit tax on each auto tire sold.
   g. The granting of a 50-cent-per-unit subsidy for each auto tire produced.

7. "In the corn market, demand often exceeds supply and supply sometimes exceeds demand." "The price of corn rises and falls in response to changes in supply and demand." In which of these two statements are the terms "supply" and "demand" used correctly? Explain. LO2

8. In 2001 an outbreak of hoof-and-mouth disease in Europe led to the burning of millions of cattle carcasses. What impact do you think this had on the supply of cattle hides, hide prices, the supply of leather goods, and the price of leather goods? LO4

9. Critically evaluate: "In comparing the two equilibrium positions in Figure 3.7b, I note that a smaller amount is actually demanded at a lower price. This refutes the law of demand." LO4

10. For each stock in the stock market, the number of shares sold daily equals the number of shares purchased. That is, the quantity of each firm's shares demanded equals the quantity supplied. So, if this equality always occurs, why do the prices of stock shares ever change? LO4

11. Suppose the total demand for wheat and the total supply of wheat per month in the Kansas City grain market are as shown in the table below. Suppose that the government establishes a price ceiling of $3.70 for wheat. What might prompt the government to establish this price ceiling? Explain carefully the main effects. Demonstrate your answer graphically. Next, suppose that the government establishes a price floor of $4.60 for wheat. What will be the main effects of this price floor? Demonstrate your answer graphically. LO5

Thousands of Bushels Demanded	Price per Bushel	Thousands of Bushels Supplied
85	$3.40	72
80	3.70	73
75	4.00	75
70	4.30	77
65	4.60	79
60	4.90	81

12. What do economists mean when they say "price floors and ceilings stifle the rationing function of prices and distort resource allocation"? LO5

13. **LAST WORD** In some countries, such as France, every corpse is available for doctors to "harvest" for organs unless the deceased, while still alive, signed a form forbidding the organs to be harvested. In the USA, it is the opposite: No harvesting is allowed unless the deceased had signed, while still alive, an organ donor form authorizing doctors to harvest any needed organs. Use supply and demand figures to show in which country organ shortages are likely to be less severe.

Problems

1. Suppose there are three buyers of candy in a market: Tex, Dex, and Rex. The market demand and the individual demands of Tex, Dex, and Rex are shown on the next page. LO1
   a. Fill in the table for the missing values.

   b. Which buyer demands the least at a price of $5? The most at a price of $7?
   c. Which buyer's quantity demanded increases the most when the price is lowered from $7 to $6?

d. Which direction would the market demand curve shift if Tex withdrew from the market? What if Dex doubled his purchases at each possible price?

e. Suppose that at a price of $6, the total quantity demanded increases from 19 to 38. Is this a "change in the quantity demanded" or a "change in demand"?

Price per Candy	Individual Quantities Demanded						Total Quantity Demanded
	Tex		Dex		Rex		
$8	3	+	1	+	0	=	___
7	8	+	2	+	___	=	12
6	___	+	3	+	4	=	19
5	17	+	___	+	6	=	27
4	23	+	5	+	8	=	___

2. The figure below shows the supply curve for tennis balls, S_1, for Drop Volley Tennis, a producer of tennis equipment. Use the figure and the table below to give your answers to the following questions. LO2

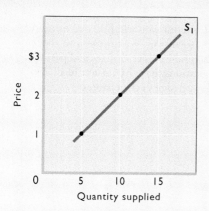

a. Use the figure to fill in the quantity supplied on supply curve S_1 for each price in the table below.

Price	S_1 Quantity Supplied	S_2 Quantity Supplied	Change in Quantity Supplied
$3	___	4	___
2	___	2	___
1	___	0	___

b. If production costs were to increase, the quantities supplied at each price would be as shown by the third column of the table ("S_2 Quantity Supplied"). Use that data to draw supply curve S_2 on the same graph as supply curve S_1.

c. In the fourth column of the table, enter the amount by which the quantity supplied at each price changes due to the increase in product costs. (Use positive numbers for increases and negative numbers for decreases.)

d. Did the increase in production costs cause a "decrease in supply" or a "decrease in quantity supplied"?

3. Refer to the expanded table below from question 11. LO3

a. What is the equilibrium price? At what price is there neither a shortage nor a surplus? Fill in the surplus-shortage column and use it to confirm your answers.

b. Graph the demand for wheat and the supply of wheat. Be sure to label the axes of your graph correctly. Label equilibrium price P and equilibrium quantity Q.

c. How big is the surplus or shortage at $3.40? At $4.90? How big a surplus or shortage results if the price is 60 cents higher than the equilibrium price? 30 cents lower than the equilibrium price?

Thousands of Bushels Demanded	Price per Bushel	Thousands of Bushels Supplied	Surplus (+) or Shortage (−)
85	$3.40	72	___
80	3.70	73	___
75	4.00	75	___
70	4.30	77	___
65	4.60	79	___
60	4.90	81	___

4. How will each of the following changes in demand and/or supply affect equilibrium price and equilibrium quantity in a competitive market; that is, do price and quantity rise, fall, or remain unchanged, or are the answers indeterminate because they depend on the magnitudes of the shifts? Use supply and demand to verify your answers. LO4

a. Supply decreases and demand is constant.

b. Demand decreases and supply is constant.

c. Supply increases and demand is constant.

d. Demand increases and supply increases.

e. Demand increases and supply is constant.

f. Supply increases and demand decreases.

g. Demand increases and supply decreases.

h. Demand decreases and supply decreases.

5. Use two market diagrams to explain how an increase in state subsidies to public colleges might affect tuition and enrollments in both public and private colleges. LO4

6. **ADVANCED ANALYSIS** Assume that demand for a commodity is represented by the equation $P = 10 - .2Q_d$ and supply by the equation $P = 2 + .2Q_s$, where Q_d and Q_s are quantity demanded and quantity supplied, respectively, and P is price. Using the equilibrium condition $Q_s = Q_d$, solve the equations to determine equilibrium price. Now determine equilibrium quantity. LO4

7. Suppose that the demand and supply schedules for rental apartments in the city of Gotham are as given in the table below. LO5

Monthly Rent	Apartments Demanded	Apartments Supplied
$2500	10,000	15,000
2000	12,500	12,500
1500	15,000	10,000
1000	17,500	7500
500	20,000	5000

a. What is the market equilibrium rental price per month and the market equilibrium number of apartments demanded and supplied?

b. If the local government can enforce a rent-control law that sets the maximum monthly rent at $1500, will there be a surplus or a shortage? Of how many units? And how many units will actually be rented each month?

c. Suppose that a new government is elected that wants to keep out the poor. It declares that the minimum rent that can be charged is $2500 per month. If the government can enforce that price floor, will there be a surplus or a shortage? Of how many units? And how many units will actually be rented each month?

d. Suppose that the government wishes to decrease the market equilibrium monthly rent by increasing the supply of housing. Assuming that demand remains unchanged, by how many units of housing would the government have to increase the supply of housing in order to get the market equilibrium rental price to fall to $1500 per month? To $1000 per month? To $500 per month?

FURTHER TEST YOUR KNOWLEDGE AT
www.mcconnell19e.com

At the text's Online Learning Center (OLC), **www.mcconnell19e.com**, you will find one or more Web-based questions that require information from the Internet to answer. We urge you to check them out; they will familiarize you with Web sites that may be helpful in other courses and perhaps even in your career. The OLC also features multiple-choice questions that give instant feedback and provides other helpful ways to further test your knowledge of the chapter.

Additional Examples of Supply and Demand

Our discussion has clearly demonstrated that supply and demand analysis is a powerful tool for understanding equilibrium prices and quantities. The information provided in the main body of this chapter is fully sufficient for moving forward in the book, but you may find that additional examples of supply and demand are helpful. This optional appendix provides several concrete illustrations of changes in supply and demand.

Your instructor may assign all, some, or none of this appendix, depending on time availability and personal preference.

Changes in Supply and Demand

As Figure 3.7 of this chapter demonstrates, changes in supply and demand cause changes in price, quantity, or both. The following applications illustrate this fact in several real-world markets. The simplest situations are those in which either supply changes while demand remains constant or demand changes while supply remains constant. Let's consider two such simple cases first, before looking at more complex applications.

Lettuce

Every now and then we hear on the news that extreme weather has severely reduced the size of some crop. Suppose, for example, that a severe freeze destroys a sizable portion of the lettuce crop. This unfortunate situation implies a significant decline in supply, which we represent as a leftward shift of the supply curve from S_1 to S_2 in Figure 1. At each price, consumers desire as much lettuce as before, so the freeze does not affect the demand for lettuce. That is, demand curve D_1 does not shift.

What are the consequences of the reduced supply of lettuce for equilibrium price and quantity? As shown in Figure 1, the leftward shift of the supply curve disrupts the previous equilibrium in the market for lettuce and drives the equilibrium price upward upward from P_1 to P_2. Consumers respond to that price hike by reducing the quantity of lettuce demanded from Q_1 to Q_2. Equilibrium is restored at P_2 and Q_2.

Consumers who are willing and able to pay price P_2 obtain lettuce; consumers unwilling or unable to pay that

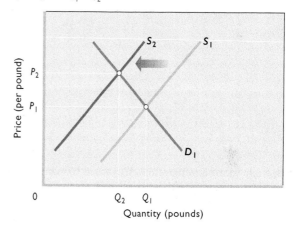

FIGURE 1 **The market for lettuce.** The decrease in the supply of lettuce, shown here by the shift from S_1 to S_2, increases the equilibrium price of lettuce from P_1 to P_2 and reduces the equilibrium quantity from Q_1 to Q_2.

price do not. Some consumers continue to buy as much lettuce as before, even at the higher price. Others buy some lettuce but not as much as before, and still others opt out of the market completely. The latter two groups use the money they would have spent on lettuce to obtain other products, say, carrots. (Because of our other-things-equal assumption, the prices of other products have not changed.)

Exchange Rates

Exchange rates are the prices at which one currency can be traded (exchanged) for another. Exchange rates are normally determined in foreign exchange markets. One of the largest foreign exchange markets is the euro-dollar market in which the currency used in most of Europe, the *euro*, is exchanged for U.S. dollars. In the United States, this market is set up so that euros are priced in dollars—that is, the "product" being traded is euros and the "price" to buy that product is quoted in dollars. Thus, the market equilibrium price one day might be $1.25 to buy 1 euro, while on another day it might be $1.50 to buy 1 euro.

Foreign exchange markets are used by individuals and companies that need to make purchases or payments in a different currency. U.S. companies exporting goods to Germany, for instance, wish to be paid in U.S. dollars.

FIGURE 2 The market for euros. The increase in the demand for euros, shown here by the shift from D_1 to D_2, increases the equilibrium price of one euro from \$1.25 to \$1.50 and increases the equilibrium quantity of euros that are exchanged from Q_1 to Q_2. The dollar has depreciated.

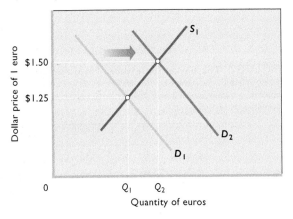

FIGURE 3 The market for pink salmon. In the last several decades, the supply of pink salmon has increased and the demand for pink salmon has decreased. As a result, the price of pink salmon has declined, as from P_1 to P_2. Because supply has increased by more than demand has decreased, the equilibrium quantity of pink salmon has increased, as from Q_1 to Q_2.

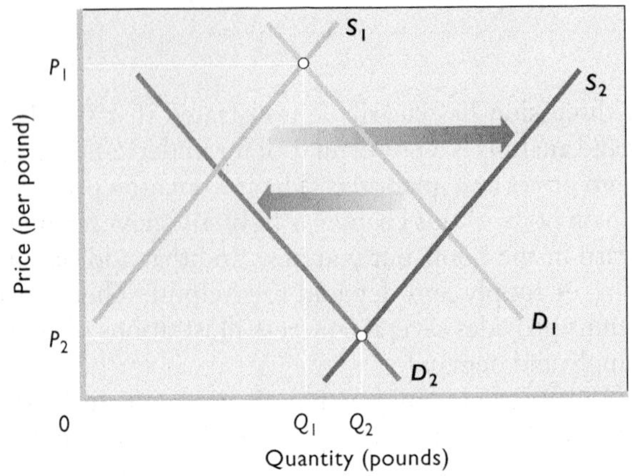

Thus, their German customers will need to convert euros into dollars. The euros that they bring to the euro-dollar market will become part of the overall market supply of euros. Conversely, an American mutual fund may wish to purchase some French real estate outside of Paris. But to purchase that real estate, it will need to pay in euros because the current French owners will only accept payment in euros. Thus, the American mutual fund has a demand to purchase euros that will form part of the overall market demand for euros. The fund will bring dollars to the euro-dollar foreign exchange market in order to purchase the euros it desires.

Sometimes, the demand for euros increases. This might be because a European product surges in popularity in foreign countries. For example, if a new German-made automobile is a big hit in the United States, American car dealers will demand more euros with which to pay for more units of that new model. This will shift the demand curve for euros to the right, as from D_1 to D_2 in Figure 2. Given the fixed euro supply curve S_1, the increase in demand raises the equilibrium exchange rate (the equilibrium number of dollars needed to purchase 1 euro) from \$1.25 to \$1.50. The equilibrium quantity of euros purchased increases from Q_1 to Q_2. Because a higher dollar amount is now needed to purchase one euro, economists say that the dollar has *depreciated*—gone down in value—relative to the euro. Alternatively, the euro has *appreciated*—gone up in value—relative to the dollar, because one euro now buys \$1.50 rather than \$1.25.

Pink Salmon

Now let's see what happens when both supply and demand change at the same time. Several decades ago, people who caught salmon earned as much as \$1 for each pound of pink salmon—the type of salmon most commonly used for canning. In Figure 3 that price is represented as P_1, at the intersection of supply curve S_1 and demand curve D_1. The corresponding quantity of pink salmon is shown as Q_1 pounds.

As time passed, supply and demand changed in the market for pink salmon. On the supply side, improved technology in the form of larger, more efficient fishing boats greatly increased the catch and lowered the cost of obtaining it. Also, high profits at price P_1 encouraged many new fishers to enter the industry. As a result of these changes, the supply of pink salmon greatly increased and the supply curve shifted to the right, as from S_1 to S_2 in Figure 3.

Over the same years, the demand for pink salmon declined, as represented by the leftward shift from D_1 to D_2 in Figure 3. That decrease was caused by increases in consumer income and reductions of the price of substitute products. As buyers' incomes rose, consumers shifted demand away from canned fish and toward higher-quality fresh or frozen fish, including more-valued Atlantic, chinook, sockeye, and coho salmon. Moreover, the emergence of fish farming, in which salmon are raised in ocean net pens, lowered the prices of these substitute species. That, too, reduced the demand for pink salmon.

The altered supply and demand reduced the price of pink salmon to as low as $.10 per pound, as represented by the drop in price from P_1 to P_2 in Figure 3. Both the supply increase and the demand decrease helped reduce the equilibrium price. However, in this particular case the equilibrium quantity of pink salmon increased, as represented by the move from Q_1 to Q_2. Both shifts reduced the equilibrium price, but equilibrium quantity increased because the increase in supply exceeded the decrease in demand.

Gasoline

The price of gasoline in the United States has increased rapidly several times during the past several years. For example, the average price of a gallon of gasoline rose from around $2.25 in January 2007 to about $4.10 in July 2008. What caused this 80 percent rise in the price of gasoline? How would we diagram this increase?

We begin in Figure 4 with the price of a gallon of gasoline at P_1, representing the $2.25 price. Simultaneous supply and demand factors disturbed this equilibrium. Supply uncertainties relating to Middle East politics and warfare and expanded demand for oil by fast-growing countries such as China pushed up the price of a barrel of oil from $50 per barrel in January 2007 to $145 per barrel in July 2008. Oil is the main input for producing gasoline, so any sustained rise in its price boosts the per-unit cost of producing gasoline. Such cost rises decrease the supply of gasoline, as represented by the leftward shift of the supply curve from S_1 to S_2 in Figure 4. At times refinery breakdowns in the United States also contributed to this reduced supply.

While the supply of gasoline declined between January 2007 and July 2008, the demand for gasoline increased, as depicted by the rightward shift of the demand curve from D_1 to D_2. Incomes in general were rising over this period because the U.S. economy was rapidly expanding. Rising incomes raise demand for all normal goods, including gasoline. An increased number of low-gas-mileage SUVs and light trucks on the road also contributed to growing gas demand.

The combined decline in gasoline supply and increase in gasoline demand boosted the price of gasoline from $2.25 to $4.10, as represented by the rise from P_1 to P_2 in Figure 4. Because the demand increase outweighed the supply decrease, the equilibrium quantity expanded, here from Q_1 to Q_2.

In other periods the price of gasoline has *declined* as the demand for gasoline has increased. Test your understanding of the analysis by explaining how such a price decrease could occur.

Sushi

Sushi bars are springing up like Starbucks in American cities (well, maybe not that fast!). Consumption of sushi, the raw-fish delicacy from Japan, has soared in the United States in recent years. Nevertheless, the price of sushi has remained relatively constant.

Supply and demand analysis helps explain this circumstance of increased quantity and constant price. A change in tastes has increased the U.S. demand for sushi. Many consumers of sushi find it highly tasty when they try it. And, as implied by the growing number of sushi bars in the United States, the supply of sushi has also expanded.

We represent these supply and demand changes in Figure 5 as the rightward shift of the demand curve from D_1 to D_2 and the rightward shift of the supply curve from S_1 to S_2. Observe that the equilibrium quantity of sushi increases from Q_1 to Q_2 and equilibrium price remains constant at P_1. The increase in supply, which taken alone would reduce price, has perfectly offset the increase in demand, which taken alone would raise price. The price of sushi does not change, but the equilibrium quantity greatly increases because both the increase in demand and the increase in supply expand purchases and sales.

Simultaneous increases in demand and supply can cause price to either rise, fall, or remain constant, depending on the relative magnitudes of the supply and demand increases. In this case, price remained constant.

FIGURE 4 The market for gasoline. An increase in the demand for gasoline, as shown by the shift from D_1 to D_2, coupled with a decrease in supply, as shown by the shift from S_1 to S_2, boosts equilibrium price (here from P_1 to P_2). In this case, equilibrium quantity increases from Q_1 to Q_2 because the increase in demand outweighs the decrease in supply.

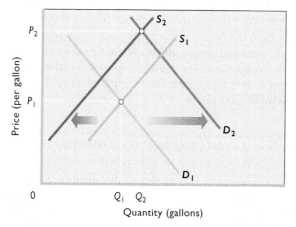

FIGURE 5 **The market for sushi.** Equal increases in the demand for sushi, as from D_1 to D_2, and in the supply of sushi, as from S_1 to S_2, expand the equilibrium quantity of sushi (here from Q_1 to Q_2) while leaving the price of sushi unchanged at P_1.

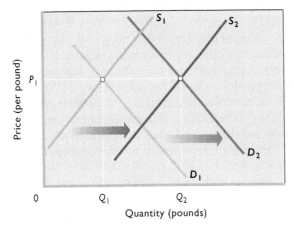

FIGURE 6 **The market for tickets to the Olympic women's figure skating finals.** The demand curve D and supply curve S for the Olympic women's figure skating finals produce an equilibrium price that is above the P_1 price printed on the ticket. At price P_1 the quantity of tickets demanded, Q_2, greatly exceeds the quantity of tickets available (Q_1). The resulting shortage of ab ($= Q_2Q_1$) gives rise to a legal or illegal secondary market.

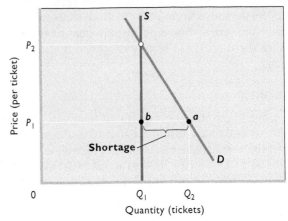

Preset Prices

In the body of this chapter, we saw that an effective government-imposed price ceiling (legal maximum price) causes quantity demanded to exceed quantity supplied—a shortage. An effective government-imposed price floor (legal minimum price) causes quantity supplied to exceed quantity demanded—a surplus. Put simply: Shortages result when prices are set below, and surpluses result when prices are set above, equilibrium prices.

We now want to establish that shortages and surpluses can occur in markets other than those in which government imposes price floors and ceilings. Such market imbalances happen when the seller or sellers set prices in advance of sales and the prices selected turn out to be below or above equilibrium prices. Consider the following two examples.

Olympic Figure Skating Finals

Tickets for the women's figure skating championship at the Olympics are among the world's "hottest tickets." The popularity of this event and the high incomes of buyers translate into tremendous ticket demand. The Olympic officials set the price for the tickets in advance. Invariably, the price, although high, is considerably below the equilibrium price that would equate quantity demanded and quantity supplied. A severe shortage of tickets therefore occurs in this *primary market*—the market involving the official ticket office.

The shortage, in turn, creates a *secondary market* in which buyers bid for tickets held by initial purchasers rather than the original seller. Scalping tickets—selling them above the original ticket price—may be legal or illegal, depending on local laws.

Figure 6 shows how the shortage in the primary ticket market looks in terms of supply and demand analysis. Demand curve D represents the strong demand for tickets and supply curve S represents the supply of tickets. The supply curve is vertical because a fixed number of tickets are printed to match the capacity of the arena. At the printed ticket price of P_1, the quantity of tickets demanded, Q_2, exceeds the quantity supplied, Q_1. The result is a shortage of ab—the horizontal distance between Q_2 and Q_1 in the primary market.

If the printed ticket price had been the higher equilibrium price P_2, no shortage of tickets would have occurred. But at the lower price P_1, a shortage and secondary ticket market will emerge among those buyers willing to pay more than the printed ticket price and those sellers willing to sell their purchased tickets for more than the original price. Wherever there are shortages and secondary markets, it is safe to assume the original price was set below the equilibrium price.

Olympic Curling Preliminaries

Contrast the shortage of tickets for the women's figure skating finals at the Olympics to the surplus of tickets for one of the preliminary curling matches. For the uninitiated, curling is a sport in which participants slide a heavy round object called a "stone" down the ice toward a target while teammates called "sweepers" use brooms to alter the course of the stone when desired.

Curling is a popular spectator sport in a few nations such as Canada, but it does not draw many fans in most countries. So the demand for tickets to most of the preliminary curling events is not very strong. We demonstrate this weak demand as D in Figure 7. As in our previous example, the supply of tickets is fixed by the size of the arena and is shown as vertical line S.

We represent the printed ticket price as P_1 in Figure 7. In this case the printed price is much higher than the equilibrium price of P_2. At the printed ticket price, quantity supplied is Q_1 and quantity demanded is Q_2. So a surplus of tickets of ba $(= Q_1 - Q_2)$ occurs. No ticket scalping occurs and there are numerous empty seats. Only if the Olympic officials had priced the tickets at the lower price P_2 would the event have been a sellout. (Actually, the Olympic officials try to adjust to demand realities for curling contests by holding them in smaller arenas and by charging less for tickets. Nevertheless, the stands are rarely full for the preliminary contests, which compete against final events in other winter Olympic sports.)

Appendix Summary

1. A decrease in the supply of a product increases its equilibrium price and reduces its equilibrium quantity. In contrast, an increase in the demand for a product boosts both its equilibrium price and its equilibrium quantity.

2. Simultaneous changes in supply and demand affect equilibrium price and quantity in various ways, depending on the relative magnitudes of the changes in supply and demand. Equal increases in supply and demand, for example, leave equilibrium price unchanged.

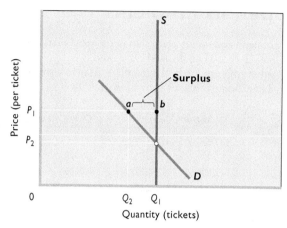

FIGURE 7 The market for tickets to the Olympic curling preliminaries. The demand curve D and supply curve S for the Olympic curling preliminaries produce an equilibrium price below the P_1 price printed on the ticket. At price P_1 the quantity of tickets demanded is less than the quantity of tickets available. The resulting surplus of ba $(= Q_1 - Q_2)$ means the event is not sold out.

3. Sellers set prices of some items such as tickets in advance of the event. These items are sold in the primary market that involves the original seller and buyers. If preset prices turn out to be below the equilibrium prices, shortages occur and scalping in legal or illegal secondary markets arises. The prices in the secondary market then rise above the preset prices. In contrast, surpluses occur when the preset prices happen to exceed the equilibrium prices.

Appendix Questions

1. Why are shortages or surpluses more likely with preset prices, such as those on tickets, than flexible prices, such as those on gasoline? LO6

2. Most scalping laws make it illegal to sell—but not to buy—tickets at prices above those printed on the tickets. Assuming that is the case, use supply and demand analysis to explain why the equilibrium ticket price in an illegal secondary market tends to be higher than in a legal secondary market. LO6

3. Go to the Web site of the Energy Information Administration, **www.eia.doe.gov**, and follow the links to find the current retail price of gasoline. How does the current price of regular gasoline compare with the price a year ago? What must have happened to either supply, demand, or both to explain the observed price change? LO6

4. Suppose the supply of apples sharply increases because of perfect weather conditions throughout the growing season. Assuming no change in demand, explain the effect on the equilibrium price and quantity of apples. Explain why quantity demanded increases even though demand does not change. LO6

5. Assume the demand for lumber suddenly rises because of a rapid growth of demand for new housing. Assume no change in supply. Why does the equilibrium price of lumber rise? What would happen if the price did not rise under the demand and supply circumstances described? LO6

6. Suppose both the demand for olives and the supply of olives decline by equal amounts over some time period. Use graphical analysis to show the effect on equilibrium price and quantity. LO6

7. Assume that both the supply of bottled water and the demand for bottled water rise during the summer but that supply increases more rapidly than demand. What can you conclude about the directions of the impacts on equilibrium price and equilibrium quantity? LO6

Appendix Problems

1. Demand and supply often shift in the retail market for gasoline. Here are two demand curves and two supply curves for gallons of gasoline in the month of May in a small town in Maine. Some of the data are missing. LO6

	Quantities Demanded		Quantities Supplied	
Price	D_1	D_2	S_1	S_2
$4.00	5000	7500	9000	9500
___	6000	8000	8000	9000
2.00	___	8500	___	8500
___	___	9000	5000	___

a. Use the following facts to fill in the missing data in the table. If demand is D_1 and supply is S_1, the equilibrium quantity is 7000 gallons per month. When demand is D_2 and supply is S_1, the equilibrium price is $3.00 per gallon. When demand is D_2 and supply is S_1, there is an excess demand of 4000 gallons per month at a price of $1.00 per gallon. If demand is D_1 and supply is S_2, the equilibrium quantity is 8000 gallons per month.
b. Compare two equilibriums. In the first, demand is D_1 and supply is S_1. In the second, demand is D_1 and supply is S_2. By how much does the equilibrium quantity change? By how much does the equilibrium price change?
c. If supply falls from S_2 to S_1 while demand declines from D_2 to D_1, does the equilibrium price rise, fall, or stay the same? What if only supply falls? What if only demand falls?
d. Suppose that supply is fixed at S_1 and that demand starts at D_1. By how many gallons per month would demand have to increase at each price level such that the equilibrium price per gallon would be $3.00? $4.00?

2. The table below shows two demand schedules for a given style of men's shoe—that is, how many pairs per month will be demanded at various prices at a men's clothing store in Seattle called Stromnord.

Price	D_1 Quantity Demanded	D_2 Quantity Demanded
$75	53	13
70	60	15
65	68	18
60	77	22
55	87	27

Suppose that Stromnord has exactly 65 pairs of this style of shoe in inventory at the start of the month of July and will not receive any more pairs of this style until at least August 1. LO6

a. If demand is D_1, what is the lowest price that Stromnord can charge so that it will not run out of this model of shoe in the month of July? What if demand is D_2?
b. If the price of shoes is set at $75 for both July and August and demand will be D_2 in July and D_1 in August, how many pairs of shoes should Stromnord order if it wants to end the month of August with exactly zero pairs of shoes in its inventory? What if the price is set at $55 for both months?

3. Use the table below to answer the questions that follow: LO6
a. If this table reflects the supply of and demand for tickets to a particular World Cup soccer game, what is the stadium capacity?
b. If the preset ticket price is $45, would we expect to see a secondary market for tickets? Would the price of a ticket in the secondary market be higher than, the same as, or lower than the price in the primary (original) market?
c. Suppose for some other World Cup game the quantity of tickets demanded is 20,000 lower at each ticket price than shown in the table. If the ticket price remains $45, would the event be a sellout?

Quantity Demanded, Thousands	Price	Quantity Supplied, Thousands
80	$25	60
75	35	60
70	45	60
65	55	60
60	65	60
55	75	60
50	85	60

Elasticity

In this chapter we extend Chapter 3's discussion of demand and supply by explaining *elasticity*, an extremely important concept that helps us answer such questions as: Why do buyers of some products (for example, ocean cruises) respond to price increases by substantially reducing their purchases while buyers of other products (say, gasoline) respond by only slightly cutting back their purchases? Why do higher market prices for some products (for example, chicken) cause producers to greatly increase their output while price rises for other products (say, gold) cause only limited increases in output? Why does the demand for some products (for example, books) rise a great deal when household income increases while the demand for other products (say, milk) rises just a little?

Elasticity extends our understanding of markets by letting us know the degree to which changes in prices and incomes affect supply and demand. Sometimes the responses are substantial, other times minimal or even nonexistent. But by knowing what to expect, businesses and the government can do a better job in deciding what to produce, how much to charge, and, surprisingly, what items to tax.

Price Elasticity of Demand

The law of demand tells us that, other things equal, consumers will buy more of a product when its price declines and less when its price increases. But how much more or less will they buy? The amount varies from product to product and over different price ranges for the same product. It also may vary over time. And such variations matter. For example, a firm contemplating a price hike will want to know how consumers will respond. If they remain highly loyal and continue to buy, the firm's revenue will rise. But if consumers defect en masse to other sellers or other products, the firm's revenue will tumble.

The responsiveness (or sensitivity) of consumers to a price change is measured by a product's **price elasticity of demand.** For some products—for example, restaurant meals—consumers are highly responsive to price changes. Modest price changes cause very large changes in the quantity purchased. Economists say that the demand for such products is *relatively elastic* or simply *elastic*.

ORIGIN OF THE IDEA

O 4.1

Price elasticity of demand

For other products—for example, toothpaste—consumers pay much less attention to price changes. Substantial price changes cause only small changes in the amount purchased. The demand for such products is *relatively inelastic* or simply *inelastic*.

The Price-Elasticity Coefficient and Formula

Economists measure the degree to which demand is price elastic or inelastic with the coefficient E_d, defined as

$$E_d = \frac{\text{percentage change in quantity demanded of product X}}{\text{percentage change in price of product X}}$$

The percentage changes in the equation are calculated by dividing the *change* in quantity demanded by the original quantity demanded and by dividing the *change* in price by the original price. So we can restate the formula as

$$E_d = \frac{\text{change in quantity demanded of X}}{\text{original quantity demanded of X}} \div \frac{\text{change in price of X}}{\text{original price of X}}$$

Using Averages Unfortunately, an annoying problem arises in computing the price-elasticity coefficient. A price change from, say, $4 to $5 along a demand curve is a 25 percent (= $1/$4) increase, but the opposite price change from $5 to $4 along the same curve is a 20 percent (= $1/$5) decrease. Which percentage change in price should we use in the denominator to compute the price-elasticity coefficient? And when quantity changes, for example, from 10 to 20, it is a 100 percent (=10/10) increase. But when quantity falls from 20 to 10 along the identical demand curve, it is a 50 percent (=10/20) decrease. Should we use 100 percent or 50 percent in the numerator of the elasticity formula? Elasticity should be the same whether price rises or falls!

The simplest solution to the problem is to use the **midpoint formula** for calculating elasticity. This formula simply averages the two prices and the two quantities as the reference points for computing the percentages. That is,

$$E_d = \frac{\text{change in quantity}}{\text{sum of quantities}/2} \div \frac{\text{change in price}}{\text{sum of prices}/2}$$

For the same $5–$4 price range, the price reference is $4.50 [= ($5 + $4)/2], and for the same 10–20 quantity range, the quantity reference is 15 units [= (10 + 20)/2]. The percentage change in price is now $1/$4.50, or about 22 percent, and the percentage change in quantity is $\frac{10}{15}$,

WORKED PROBLEMS

W 4.1

Elasticity of demand

or about 67 percent. So E_d is about 3. This solution eliminates the "up versus down" problem. All the price-elasticity coefficients that follow are calculated using this midpoint formula.

Using Percentages Why use percentages rather than absolute amounts in measuring consumer responsiveness? There are two reasons.

First, if we use absolute changes, the choice of units will arbitrarily affect our impression of buyer responsiveness. To illustrate: If the price of a bag of popcorn at the local softball game is reduced from $3 to $2 and consumers increase their purchases from 60 to 100 bags, it will seem that consumers are quite sensitive to price changes and therefore that demand is elastic. After all, a price change of 1 unit has caused a change in the amount demanded of 40 units. But by changing the monetary unit from dollars to pennies (why not?), we find that a price change of 100 units (pennies) causes a quantity change of 40 units. This may falsely lead us to believe that demand is inelastic. We avoid this problem by using percentage changes. This particular price decline is the same whether we measure it in dollars or pennies.

Second, by using percentages, we can correctly compare consumer responsiveness to changes in the prices of different products. It makes little sense to compare the effects on quantity demanded of (1) a \$1 increase in the price of a \$10,000 used car with (2) a \$1 increase in the price of a \$1 soft drink. Here the price of the used car has increased by .01 percent while the price of the soft drink is up by 100 percent. We can more sensibly compare the consumer responsiveness to price increases by using some common percentage increase in price for both.

Elimination of Minus Sign We know from the downsloping demand curve that price and quantity demanded are inversely related. Thus, the price-elasticity coefficient of demand E_d will always be a negative number. As an example, if price declines, then quantity demanded will increase. This means that the numerator in our formula will be positive and the denominator negative, yielding a negative E_d. For an increase in price, the numerator will be negative but the denominator positive, again yielding a negative E_d.

Economists usually ignore the minus sign and simply present the absolute value of the elasticity coefficient to avoid an ambiguity that might otherwise arise. It can be confusing to say that an E_d of −4 is greater than one of −2. This possible confusion is avoided when we say an E_d of 4 reveals greater elasticity than one of 2. So, in what follows, we ignore the minus sign in the coefficient of price elasticity of demand and show only the absolute value. Incidentally, the ambiguity does not arise with supply because price and quantity supplied are positively related. All elasticity of supply coefficients therefore are positive numbers.

Interpretations of E_d

We can interpret the coefficient of price elasticity of demand as follows.

Elastic Demand Demand is **elastic** if a specific percentage change in price results in a larger percentage change in quantity demanded. In such cases, E_d will be greater than 1. Example: Suppose that a 2 percent decline in the price of cut flowers results in a 4 percent increase in quantity demanded. Then demand for cut flowers is elastic and

$$E_d = \frac{.04}{.02} = 2$$

Inelastic Demand If a specific percentage change in price produces a smaller percentage change in quantity demanded, demand is **inelastic**. In such cases, E_d will be less than 1. Example: Suppose that a 2 percent decline in

the price of coffee leads to only a 1 percent increase in quantity demanded. Then demand is inelastic and

$$E_d = \frac{.01}{.02} = .5$$

Unit Elasticity The case separating elastic and inelastic demands occurs where a percentage change in price and the resulting percentage change in quantity demanded are the same. Example: Suppose that a 2 percent drop in the price of chocolate causes a 2 percent increase in quantity demanded. This special case is termed **unit elasticity** because E_d is exactly 1, or unity. In this example,

$$E_d = \frac{.02}{.02} = 1$$

Extreme Cases When we say demand is "inelastic," we do not mean that consumers are completely unresponsive to a price change. In that extreme situation, where a price change results in no change whatsoever in the quantity demanded, economists say that demand is **perfectly inelastic**. The price-elasticity coefficient is zero because there is no response to a change in price. Approximate examples include an acute diabetic's demand for insulin or an addict's demand for heroin. A line parallel to the vertical axis, such as D_1 in Figure 4.1a, shows perfectly inelastic demand graphically.

Conversely, when we say demand is "elastic," we do not mean that consumers are completely responsive to a price change. In that extreme situation, where a small price reduction causes buyers to increase their purchases from zero to all they can obtain, the elasticity coefficient is infinite ($= \infty$) and economists say demand is **perfectly elastic**. A line parallel to the horizontal axis, such as D_2 in Figure 4.1b, shows perfectly elastic demand. You will see in Chapter 8 that such a demand applies to a firm—say, a mining firm—that is selling its output in a purely competitive market.

The Total-Revenue Test

The importance of elasticity for firms relates to the effect of price changes on total revenue and thus on profits (= total revenue minus total costs).

Total revenue (TR) is the total amount the seller receives from the sale of a product in a particular time period; it is calculated by multiplying the product price (P) by the quantity sold (Q). In equation form:

$$TR = P \times Q$$

Graphically, total revenue is represented by the $P \times Q$ rectangle lying below a point on a demand curve. At point

FIGURE 4.1 Perfectly inelastic and elastic demands.

Demand curve D_1 in (a) represents perfectly inelastic demand ($E_d = 0$). A price increase will result in no change in quantity demanded. Demand curve D_2 in (b) represents perfectly elastic demand. A price increase will cause quantity demanded to decline from an infinite amount to zero ($E_d = \infty$).

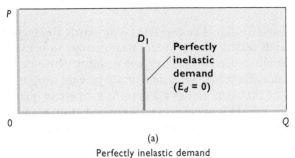

(a)
Perfectly inelastic demand

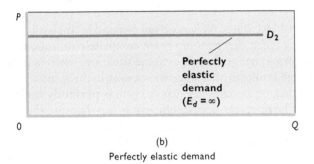

(b)
Perfectly elastic demand

CONSIDER THIS . . .

A Bit of a Stretch

The following analogy might help you remember the distinction between "elastic" and "inelastic." Imagine two objects—one an Ace elastic bandage used to wrap injured joints and the other a relatively firm rubber tie-down (rubber strap) used for securing items for transport. The Ace bandage stretches a great deal when pulled with a particular force; the rubber tie-down stretches some, but not a lot.

Similar differences occur for the quantity demanded of various products when their prices change. For some products, a price change causes a substantial "stretch" of quantity demanded. When this stretch in percentage terms exceeds the percentage change in price, demand is elastic. For other products, quantity demanded stretches very little in response to the price change. When this stretch in percentage terms is less than the percentage change in price, demand is inelastic.

In summary:
- Elastic demand displays considerable "quantity stretch" (as with the Ace bandage).
- Inelastic demand displays relatively little "quantity stretch" (as with the rubber tie-down).

And through extension:
- Perfectly elastic demand has infinite quantity stretch.
- Perfectly inelastic demand has zero quantity stretch.

a in Figure 4.2a, for example, price is $2 and quantity demanded is 10 units. So total revenue is $20 (= $2 × 10), shown by the rectangle composed of the yellow and green areas under the demand curve. We know from basic geometry that the area of a rectangle is found by multiplying one side by the other. Here, one side is "price" ($2) and the other is "quantity demanded" (10 units).

Total revenue and the price elasticity of demand are related. In fact, the easiest way to infer whether demand is elastic or inelastic is to employ the **total-revenue test.** Here is the test: Note what happens to total revenue when price changes. If total revenue changes in the opposite direction from price, demand is elastic. If total revenue changes in the same direction as price, demand is inelastic. If total revenue does not change when price changes, demand is unit-elastic.

Elastic Demand If demand is elastic, a decrease in price will increase total revenue. Even though a lesser price is received per unit, enough additional units are sold to more than make up for the lower price. For an example, look at demand curve D_1 in Figure 4.2a. We have already established that at point *a*, total revenue is $20 (= $2 × 10), shown as the yellow plus green area. If the price

declines from $2 to $1 (point *b*), the quantity demanded becomes 40 units and total revenue is $40 (= $1 × 40). As a result of the price decline, total revenue has increased from $20 to $40. Total revenue has increased in this case because the $1 decline in price applies to 10 units, with a consequent revenue loss of $10 (the yellow area). But 30 more units are sold at $1 each, resulting in a revenue gain of $30 (the blue area). Visually, the gain of the blue area clearly exceeds the loss of the yellow area. As indicated, the overall result is a net increase in total revenue of $20 (= $30 − $10).

The analysis is reversible: If demand is elastic, a price increase will reduce total revenue. The revenue gained on the higher-priced units will be more than offset by the

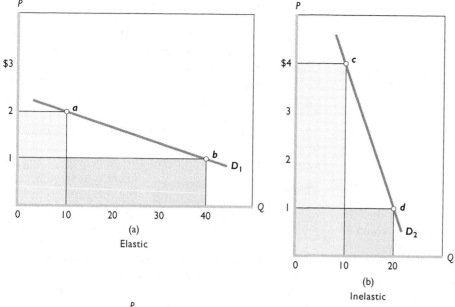

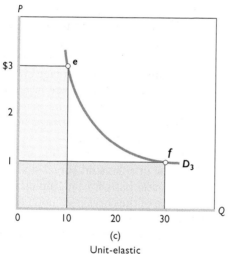

FIGURE 4.2 **The total-revenue test for price elasticity.** (a) Price declines from $2 to $1, and total revenue increases from $20 to $40. So demand is elastic. The gain in revenue (blue area) exceeds the loss of revenue (yellow area). (b) Price declines from $4 to $1, and total revenue falls from $40 to $20. So, demand is inelastic. The gain in revenue (blue area) is less than the loss of revenue (yellow area). (c) Price declines from $3 to $1, and total revenue does not change. Demand is unit-elastic. The gain in revenue (blue area) equals the loss of revenue (yellow area).

revenue lost from the lower quantity sold. Bottom line: Other things equal, when price and total revenue move in opposite directions, demand is elastic. E_d is greater than 1, meaning the percentage change in quantity demanded is greater than the percentage change in price.

Inelastic Demand If demand is inelastic, a price decrease will reduce total revenue. The increase in sales will not fully offset the decline in revenue per unit, and total revenue will decline. To see this, look at demand curve D_2 in Figure 4.2b. At point *c* on the curve, price is $4 and quantity demanded is 10. Thus total revenue is $40, shown by the combined yellow and green rectangle. If the price drops to $1 (point *d*), total revenue declines to $20, which

obviously is less than $40. Total revenue has declined because the loss of revenue (the yellow area) from the lower unit price is larger than the gain in revenue (the blue area) from the accompanying increase in sales. Price has fallen, and total revenue has also declined.

Our analysis is again reversible: If demand is inelastic, a price increase will increase total revenue. So, other things equal, when price and total revenue move in the same direction, demand is inelastic. E_d is less than 1, meaning the percentage change in quantity demanded is less than the percentage change in price.

WORKED PROBLEMS

W 4.2

Total-revenue test

Unit Elasticity In the special case of unit elasticity, an increase or a decrease in price leaves total revenue unchanged. The loss in revenue from a lower unit price is exactly offset by the gain in revenue from the accompanying increase in sales. Conversely, the gain in revenue from a higher unit price is exactly offset by the revenue loss associated with the accompanying decline in the amount demanded.

In Figure 4.2c (demand curve D_3) we find that at the price of $3, 10 units will be sold, yielding total revenue of $30. At the lower $1 price, a total of 30 units will be sold, again resulting in $30 of total revenue. The $2 price reduction causes the loss of revenue shown by the yellow area, but this is exactly offset by the revenue gain shown by the blue area. Total revenue does not change. In fact, that would be true for all price changes along this particular curve.

Other things equal, when price changes and total revenue remains constant, demand is unit-elastic (or unitary). E_d is 1, meaning the percentage change in quantity equals the percentage change in price.

Price Elasticity along a Linear Demand Curve

Now a major confession! Although the demand curves depicted in Figure 4.2 nicely illustrate the total-revenue test for elasticity, two of the graphs involve specific movements along linear (straight-line) demand curves. That presents no problem for explaining the total-revenue test. However, you need to know that elasticity typically varies over different price ranges of the same demand curve. (The exception is the curve in Figure 4.2c. Elasticity is 1 along the entire curve.)

Table 4.1 and Figure 4.3 demonstrate that elasticity typically varies over different price ranges of the same demand schedule or curve. Plotting the hypothetical data for movie tickets shown in columns 1 and 2 of Table 4.1 yields

demand curve *D* in Figure 4.3. Observe that the demand curve is linear. But we see from column 3 of the table that the price elasticity coefficient for this demand curve declines as we move from higher to lower prices. For all downsloping straight-line and most other demand curves, demand is more price-elastic toward the upper left (here, the $5–$8 price range of *D*) than toward the lower right (here, the $4–$1 price range of *D*).

This is the consequence of the arithmetic properties of the elasticity measure. Specifically, in the upper-left segment of the demand curve, the percentage change in

INTERACTIVE GRAPHS

G 4.1

Elasticity and revenue

quantity is large because the original reference quantity is small. Similarly, the percentage change in price is small in that segment because the original reference price is large. The relatively large percentage change in quantity divided by the relatively small change in price yields a large E_d—an elastic demand.

The reverse holds true for the lower-right segment of the demand curve. Here the percentage change in quantity is small because the original reference quantity is large; similarly, the percentage change in price is large because the original reference price is small. The relatively small percentage change in quantity divided by the relatively large percentage change in price results in a small E_d—an inelastic demand.

The demand curve in Figure 4.3a also illustrates that the slope of a demand curve—its flatness or steepness—is not a sound basis for judging elasticity. The catch is that the slope of the curve is computed from *absolute* changes in price and quantity, while elasticity involves *relative* or *percentage* changes in price and quantity. The demand curve

TABLE 4.1 Price Elasticity of Demand for Movie Tickets as Measured by the Elasticity Coefficient and the Total-Revenue Test

(1) Total Quantity of Tickets Demanded per Week, Thousands	(2) Price per Ticket	(3) Elasticity Coefficient (E_d)	(4) Total Revenue, (1) × (2)	(5) Total-Revenue Test
1	$8		$ 8000	
2	7	5.00	14,000	Elastic
3	6	2.60	18,000	Elastic
4	5	1.57	20,000	Elastic
5	4	1.00	20,000	Unit-elastic
6	3	0.64	18,000	Inelastic
7	2	0.38	14,000	Inelastic
8	1	0.20	8000	Inelastic

FIGURE 4.3 **The relation between price elasticity of demand for movie tickets and total revenue.** Demand curve D in (a) is based on Table 4.1 and is marked to show that the hypothetical weekly demand for movie tickets is elastic at higher price ranges and inelastic at lower price ranges. The total-revenue curve TR in (b) is derived from demand curve D. When price falls and TR increases, demand is elastic; when price falls and TR is unchanged, demand is unit-elastic; and when price falls and TR declines, demand is inelastic.

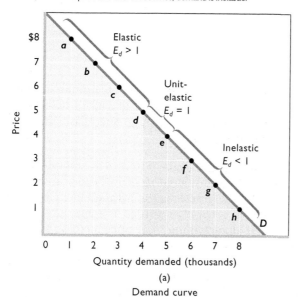

(a)
Demand curve

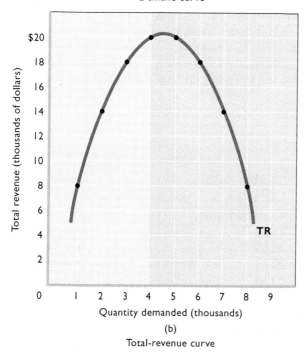

(b)
Total-revenue curve

Price Elasticity and the Total-Revenue Curve

In Figure 4.3b we plot the total revenue per week to the theater owner that corresponds to each price-quantity combination indicated along demand curve D in Figure 4.3a. The price–quantity-demanded combination represented by point a on the demand curve yields total revenue of $8000 (= $8×1000 tickets). In Figure 4.3b, we plot this $8000 amount vertically at 1 unit (1000 tickets) demanded. Similarly, the price–quantity-demanded combination represented by point b in the upper panel yields total revenue of $14,000 (= $7×2000 tickets). This amount is graphed vertically at 2 units (2000 tickets) demanded in the lower panel. The ultimate result of such graphing is total-revenue curve TR, which first slopes upward, then reaches a maximum, and finally turns downward.

Comparison of curves D and TR sharply focuses the relationship between elasticity and total revenue. Lowering the ticket price in the elastic range of demand—for example, from $8 to $5—increases total revenue. Conversely, increasing the ticket price in that range reduces total revenue. In both cases, price and total revenue change in opposite directions, confirming that demand is elastic.

The $5–$4 price range of demand curve D reflects unit elasticity. When price either decreases from $5 to $4 or increases from $4 to $5, total revenue remains $20,000. In both cases, price has changed and total revenue has remained constant, confirming that demand is unit-elastic when we consider these particular price changes.

In the inelastic range of demand curve D, lowering the price—for example, from $4 to $1—decreases total revenue, as shown in Figure 4.3b. Raising the price boosts total revenue. In both cases, price and total revenue move in the same direction, confirming that demand is inelastic.

Table 4.2 summarizes the characteristics of price elasticity of demand. You should review it carefully.

Determinants of Price Elasticity of Demand

We cannot say just what will determine the price elasticity of demand in each individual situation. However, the following generalizations are often helpful.

Substitutability Generally, the larger the number of substitute goods that are available, the greater the price elasticity of demand. Various brands of candy bars are generally substitutable for one another, making the demand for one brand of candy bar, say Snickers, highly elastic. Toward the other extreme, the demand for tooth repair (or

in Figure 4.3a is linear, which by definition means that the slope is constant throughout. But we have demonstrated that such a curve is elastic in its high-price ($8–$5) range and inelastic in its low-price ($4–$1) range.

TABLE 4.2 **Price Elasticity of Demand: A Summary**

Absolute Value of Elasticity Coefficient	Demand Is:	Description	Impact on Total Revenue of a:	
			Price Increase	Price Decrease
Greater than 1 ($E_d > 1$)	Elastic or relatively elastic	Quantity demanded changes by a larger percentage than does price	Total revenue decreases	Total revenue increases
Equal to 1 ($E_d = 1$)	Unit- or unitary elastic	Quantity demanded changes by the same percentage as does price	Total revenue is unchanged	Total revenue is unchanged
Less than 1 ($E_d < 1$)	Inelastic or relatively inelastic	Quantity demanded changes by a smaller percentage than does price	Total revenue increases	Total revenue decreases

tooth pulling) is quite inelastic because there simply are no close substitutes when those procedures are required.

The elasticity of demand for a product depends on how narrowly the product is defined. Demand for Reebok sneakers is more elastic than is the overall demand for shoes. Many other brands are readily substitutable for Reebok sneakers, but there are few, if any, good substitutes for shoes.

Proportion of Income Other things equal, the higher the price of a good relative to consumers' incomes, the greater the price elasticity of demand. A 10 percent increase in the price of low-priced pencils or chewing gum amounts to a few more pennies relative to a consumer's income, and quantity demanded will probably decline only slightly. Thus, price elasticity for such low-priced items tends to be low. But a 10 percent increase in the price of relatively high-priced automobiles or housing means additional expenditures of perhaps $3000 or $20,000, respectively. These price

increases are significant fractions of the annual incomes and budgets of most families, and quantities demanded will likely diminish significantly. The price elasticities for such items tend to be high.

Luxuries versus Necessities In general, the more that a good is considered to be a "luxury" rather than a "necessity," the greater is the price elasticity of demand. Electricity is generally regarded as a necessity; it is difficult to get along without it. A price increase will not significantly reduce the amount of lighting and power used in a household. (Note the very low price-elasticity coefficient of this good in Table 4.3.) An extreme case: A person does not decline an operation for acute appendicitis because the physician's fee has just gone up.

On the other hand, vacation travel and jewelry are luxuries, which, by definition, can easily be forgone. If the prices of vacation travel and jewelry rise, a consumer need not buy them and will suffer no great hardship without them.

TABLE 4.3 **Selected Price Elasticities of Demand**

Product or Service	Coefficient of Price Elasticity of Demand (E_d)	Product or Service	Coefficient of Price Elasticity of Demand (E_d)
Newspapers	.10	Milk	.63
Electricity (household)	.13	Household appliances	.63
Bread	.15	Liquor	.70
Major League Baseball tickets	.23	Movies	.87
Telephone service	.26	Beer	.90
Cigarettes	.25	Shoes	.91
Sugar	.30	Motor vehicles	1.14
Medical care	.31	Beef	1.27
Eggs	.32	China, glassware, tableware	1.54
Legal services	.37	Residential land	1.60
Automobile repair	.40	Restaurant meals	2.27
Clothing	.49	Lamb and mutton	2.65
Gasoline	.60	Fresh peas	2.83

Source: Compiled from numerous studies and sources reporting price elasticity of demand.

What about the demand for a common product like salt? It is highly inelastic on three counts: Few good substitutes are available; salt is a negligible item in the family budget; and it is a "necessity" rather than a luxury.

Time Generally, product demand is more elastic the longer the time period under consideration. Consumers often need time to adjust to changes in prices. For example, when the price of a product rises, time is needed to find and experiment with other products to see if they are acceptable. Consumers may not immediately reduce their purchases very much when the price of beef rises by 10 percent, but in time they may shift to chicken, pork, or fish.

Another consideration is product durability. Studies show that "short-run" demand for gasoline is more inelastic ($E_d = .2$) than is "long-run" demand ($E_d = .7$). In the short run, people are "stuck" with their present cars and trucks, but with rising gasoline prices they eventually replace them with smaller, more fuel-efficient vehicles. They also switch to mass transit where it is available.

Table 4.3 shows estimated price-elasticity coefficients for a number of products. Each reflects some combination of the elasticity determinants just discussed.

Applications of Price Elasticity of Demand

The concept of price elasticity of demand has great practical significance, as the following examples suggest.

Large Crop Yields The demand for most farm products is highly inelastic; E_d is perhaps .20 or .25. As a result, increases in the supply of farm products arising from a good growing season or from increased productivity tend to depress both the prices of farm products and the total revenues (incomes) of farmers. For farmers as a group, the inelastic demand for their products means that large crop yields may be undesirable. For policymakers it means that achieving the goal of higher total farm income requires that farm output be restricted.

Excise Taxes The government pays attention to elasticity of demand when it selects goods and services on which to levy excise taxes. If a $1 tax is levied on a product and 10,000 units are sold, tax revenue will be $10,000 (= $1 × 10,000 units sold). If the government raises the tax to $1.50 but the higher price that results reduces sales to 4000 because of elastic demand, tax revenue will decline to $6000 (= $1.50 × 4000 units sold). Because a higher tax on a product with elastic demand will bring in less tax revenue, legislatures tend to seek out products that have inelastic demand—such as liquor, gasoline, and cigarettes—when

levying excises. In fact, the Federal government, in its effort to reduce the budget deficit, increased taxes on those very categories of goods in 1991.

Decriminalization of Illegal Drugs In recent years proposals to legalize drugs have been widely debated. Proponents contend that drugs should be treated like alcohol; they should be made legal for adults and regulated for purity and potency. The current war on drugs, it is argued, has been unsuccessful, and the associated costs—including enlarged police forces, the construction of more prisons, an overburdened court system, and untold human costs—have increased markedly. Legalization would allegedly reduce drug trafficking significantly by taking the profit out of it. Crack cocaine and heroin, for example, are cheap to produce and could be sold at low prices in legal markets. Because the demand of addicts is highly inelastic, the amounts consumed at the lower prices would increase only modestly. Addicts' total expenditures for cocaine and heroin would decline, and so would the street crime that finances those expenditures.

Opponents of legalization say that the overall demand for cocaine and heroin is far more elastic than proponents think. In addition to the inelastic demand of addicts, there is another market segment whose demand is relatively elastic. This segment consists of the occasional users or "dabblers," who use hard drugs when their prices are low but who abstain or substitute, say, alcohol when their prices are high. Thus, the lower prices associated with the legalization of hard drugs would increase consumption by dabblers. Also, removal of the legal prohibitions against using drugs might make drug use more socially acceptable, increasing the demand for cocaine and heroin.

Many economists predict that the legalization of cocaine and heroin would reduce street prices by up to 60 percent, depending on if and how much they were taxed. According to an important study, price declines of that size would increase the number of occasional users of heroin by 54 percent and the number of occasional users of cocaine by 33 percent. The total quantity of heroin demanded would rise by an estimated 100 percent, and the quantity of cocaine demanded would rise by 50 percent.[1] Moreover, many existing and first-time dabblers might in time become addicts. The overall result, say the opponents of legalization, would be higher social costs, possibly including an increase in street crime.

---

[1]Henry Saffer and Frank Chaloupka, "The Demand for Illegal Drugs," *Economic Inquiry*, July 1999, pp. 401–411.

Price Elasticity of Supply

ORIGIN OF THE IDEA

O 4.2

Price elasticity of supply

The concept of price elasticity also applies to supply. If the quantity supplied by producers is relatively responsive to price changes, supply is elastic. If it is relatively insensitive to price changes, supply is inelastic.

We measure the degree of price elasticity or inelasticity of supply with the coefficient E_s, defined almost like E_d except that we substitute "percentage change in quantity supplied" for "percentage change in quantity demanded":

$$E_s = \frac{\text{percentage change in quantity supplied of product X}}{\text{percentage change in price of product X}}$$

For reasons explained earlier, the averages, or midpoints, of the before and after quantities supplied and the before and after prices are used as reference points for the percentage changes. Suppose an increase in the price of a good from \$4 to \$6 increases the quantity supplied from 10 units to 14 units. The percentage change in price would be $\frac{2}{5}$, or 40 percent, and the percentage change in quantity would be $\frac{4}{12}$, or 33 percent. Consequently,

$$E_s = \frac{.33}{.40} = .83$$

In this case, supply is inelastic because the price-elasticity coefficient is less than 1. If E_s is greater than 1, supply is elastic. If it is equal to 1, supply is unit-elastic. Also, E_s is never negative, since price and quantity supplied are directly related. Thus, there are no minus signs to drop, as was necessary with elasticity of demand.

The degree of **price elasticity of supply** depends on how easily—and therefore quickly—producers can shift resources between alternative uses. The easier and more rapidly producers can shift resources between alternative uses, the greater the price elasticity of supply. Take the case of Christmas trees. A firm's response to, say, an increase in the price of trees depends on its ability to shift resources from the production of other products (whose prices we assume remain constant) to the production of trees. And shifting resource takes time: The longer the time, the greater the "shiftability." So we can expect a greater response, and therefore greater elasticity of supply, the longer a firm has to adjust to a price change.

In analyzing the impact of time on elasticity, economists distinguish among the immediate market period, the short run, and the long run.

Price Elasticity of Supply: The Market Period

The **market period** is the period that occurs when the time immediately after a change in market price is too short for producers to respond with a change in quantity supplied. Suppose the owner of a small farm brings to market one truckload of tomatoes that is the entire season's output. The supply curve for the tomatoes is perfectly inelastic (vertical); the farmer will sell the truckload whether the price is high or low. Why? Because the farmer can offer only one truckload of tomatoes even if the price of tomatoes is much higher than anticipated. The farmer might like to offer more tomatoes, but tomatoes cannot be produced overnight. Another full growing season is needed to respond to a higher-than-expected price by producing more than one truckload. Similarly, because the product is perishable, the farmer cannot withhold it from the market. If the price is lower than anticipated, the farmer will still sell the entire truckload.

The farmer's costs of production, incidentally, will not enter into this decision to sell. Though the price of tomatoes may fall far short of production costs, the farmer will nevertheless sell everything he brought to market to avoid a total loss through spoilage. In the market period, both the supply of tomatoes and the quantity of tomatoes supplied are fixed. The farmer offers only one truckload no matter how high or low the price.

FIGURE 4.4 **Time and the elasticity of supply.** The greater the amount of time producers have to adjust to a change in demand, here from D_1 to D_2, the greater will be their output response. In the immediate market period (a) there is insufficient time to change output, and so supply is perfectly inelastic. In the short run (b) plant capacity is fixed, but changing the intensity of its use can alter output; supply is therefore more elastic. In the long run (c) all desired adjustments, including changes in plant capacity, can be made, and supply becomes still more elastic.

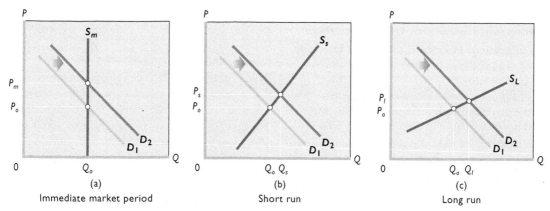

(a)
Immediate market period

(b)
Short run

(c)
Long run

Figure 4.4a shows the farmer's vertical supply curve during the market period. Supply is perfectly inelastic because the farmer does not have time to respond to a change in demand, say, from D_1 to D_2. The resulting price increase from P_0 to P_m simply determines which buyers get the fixed quantity supplied; it elicits no increase in output.

However, not all supply curves are perfectly inelastic immediately after a price change. If the product is not perishable and the price rises, producers may choose to increase quantity supplied by drawing down their inventories of unsold, stored goods. This will cause the market supply curve to attain some positive slope. For our tomato farmer, the market period may be a full growing season; for producers of goods that can be inexpensively stored, there may be no market period at all.

Price Elasticity of Supply: The Short Run

The **short run** in microeconomics is a period of time too short to change plant capacity but long enough to use the fixed-sized plant more or less intensively. In the short run, our farmer's plant (land and farm machinery) is fixed. But he does have time in the short run to cultivate tomatoes more intensively by applying more labor and more fertilizer and pesticides to the crop. The result is a somewhat greater output in response to a presumed increase in demand; this greater output is reflected in a more elastic supply of tomatoes, as shown by S_s in Figure 4.4b. Note now that the increase in demand from D_1 to D_2 is met by an increase in quantity (from Q_0 to Q_s), so there is a smaller price adjustment (from P_0 to P_s) than would be the case in the market period. The equilibrium price is therefore lower in the short run than in the market period.

Price Elasticity of Supply: The Long Run

The **long run** in microeconomics is a time period long enough for firms to adjust their plant sizes and for new firms to enter (or existing firms to leave) the industry. In the "tomato industry," for example, our farmer has time to acquire additional land and buy more machinery and equipment. Furthermore, other farmers may, over time, be attracted to tomato farming by the increased demand and higher price. Such adjustments create a larger supply response, as represented by the more elastic supply curve S_L in Figure 4.4c. The outcome is a smaller price rise (P_0 to P_l) and a larger output increase (Q_0 to Q_l) in response to the increase in demand from D_1 to D_2.

There is no total-revenue test for elasticity of supply. Supply shows a positive or direct relationship between price and amount supplied; the supply curve is upsloping. Regardless of the degree of elasticity or inelasticity, price and total revenue always move together.

Applications of Price Elasticity of Supply

The idea of price elasticity of supply has widespread applicability, as suggested by the following examples.

Antiques and Reproductions *Antiques Roadshow* is a popular PBS television program in which people bring antiques to a central location for appraisal by experts. Some people are pleased to learn that their old piece of furniture or funky folk art is worth a large amount, say, $30,000 or more.

The high price of an antique results from strong demand and limited, highly inelastic supply. Because a genuine antique can no longer be reproduced, its quantity

Word Elasticity and Pricing Power: Why Different Consumers Pay Different Prices

Firms and Nonprofit Institutions Often Recognize and Exploit Differences in Price Elasticity of Demand.

All the buyers of a product traded in a highly competitive market pay the same market price for the product, regardless of their individual price elasticities of demand. If the price rises, Jones may have an elastic demand and greatly reduce her purchases. Green may have a unit-elastic demand and reduce his purchases less than Jones. Lopez may have an inelastic demand and hardly curtail his purchases at all. But all three consumers will pay the single higher price regardless of their respective demand elasticities.

In later chapters we will find that not all sellers must passively accept a "one-for-all" price. Some firms have "market power" or "pricing power" that allows them to set their product prices in their best interests. For some goods and services, firms may find it advantageous to determine differences in price elasticity of demand and then charge different prices to different buyers.

It is extremely difficult to tailor prices for each customer on the basis of price elasticity of demand, but it is relatively easy to observe differences in group elasticities. Consider airline tickets. Business travelers generally have inelastic demand for air travel. Because their time is highly valuable, they do not see slower modes of transportation as realistic substitutes. Also, their employers pay for their tickets as part of their business expenses. In contrast, leisure travelers tend to have elastic demand. They have the option to drive rather than fly or to simply not travel at all. They also pay for their tickets out of their own pockets and thus are more sensitive to price.

Airlines recognize the difference between the groups in terms of price elasticity of demand and charge business travelers more than leisure travelers. To accomplish that, they have to dissuade business travelers from buying the less expensive round-trip tickets aimed at leisure travelers. One way to do this is by placing restrictions on the lower-priced tickets. For instance, airlines have at times made such tickets nonrefundable, required at least a 2-week advance purchase, and required Saturday-night stays. These restrictions chase off most business travelers who engage in last-minute travel and want to be home for the weekend. As a result, a business traveler often pays hundreds of dollars more for a ticket than a leisure traveler on the same plane.

supplied either does not rise or rises only slightly as price goes up. The higher price might prompt the discovery of a few more of the remaining originals and thus add to the quantity available for sale, but this quantity response is usually quite small. So the supply of antiques and other collectibles tends to be inelastic. For one-of-a-kind antiques, the supply is perfectly inelastic.

Factors such as increased population, higher income, and greater enthusiasm for collecting antiques have increased the demand for antiques over time. Because the supply of antiques is limited and inelastic, those increases in demand have greatly boosted the prices of antiques.

Contrast the inelastic supply of original antiques with the elastic supply of modern "made-to-look-old" reproductions. Such faux antiques are quite popular and widely available at furniture stores and knickknack shops. When the demand for reproductions increases, the firms making them simply boost production. Because the supply of reproductions is highly elastic, increased demand raises their prices only slightly.

Volatile Gold Prices The price of gold is quite volatile, sometimes shooting upward one period and plummeting downward the next. The main sources of these fluctuations are shifts in demand interacting with highly inelastic supply. Gold production is a costly and time-consuming process of exploration, mining, and refining. Moreover, the physical availability of gold is highly limited. For both reasons, increases in gold prices do not elicit substantial increases in quantity supplied. Conversely, gold mining is costly to shut down and existing gold bars are expensive to store. Price decreases therefore do not produce large drops in the quantity of gold supplied. In short, the supply of gold is inelastic.

The demand for gold is partly derived from the demand for its uses, such as for jewelry, dental fillings, and coins. But people also demand gold as a speculative financial investment. They increase their demand for gold when they fear general inflation or domestic or international turmoil that might undermine the value of currency and more traditional investments. They reduce

86

Discounts for children are another example of pricing based on group differences in price elasticity of demand. For many products, children have more elastic demands than adults because children have low budgets, often financed by their parents. Sellers recognize the elasticity difference and price accordingly. The barber spends as much time cutting a child's hair as an adult's but charges the child much less. A child takes up a full seat at the baseball game but pays a lower price than an adult. A child snowboarder occupies the same space on a chairlift as an adult snowboarder but qualifies for a discounted lift ticket.

Finally, consider pricing by colleges and universities. Price elasticity of demand for higher education is greater for prospective students from low-income families than similar students from high-income families. This makes sense because tuition is a much larger proportion of household income for a low-income student or family than for his or her high-income counterpart. Desiring a diverse student body, colleges charge different *net* prices (= tuition *minus* financial aid) to

the two groups on the basis of price elasticity of demand. High-income students pay full tuition, unless they receive merit-based scholarships. Low-income students receive considerable financial aid in addition to merit-based scholarships and, in effect, pay a lower *net* price.

It is common for colleges to announce a large tuition increase and immediately cushion the news by emphasizing that they also are increasing financial aid. In effect, the college is increasing the tuition for students who have inelastic demand by the full amount and raising the *net* tuition of those with elastic demand by some lesser amount or not at all. Through this strategy, colleges boost revenue to cover rising costs while maintaining affordability for a wide range of students.

There are a number of other examples of dual or multiple pricing. All relate directly to price elasticity of demand. We will revisit this topic again in Chapter 10 when we analyze *price discrimination*—charging different prices to different customers for the same product.

their demand when events settle down. Because of the inelastic supply of gold, even relatively small changes in demand produce relatively large changes in price. (This chapter's Web-based question 1 that is posted online provides an Internet source for finding current and past prices of gold.)

Cross Elasticity and Income Elasticity of Demand

Price elasticities measure the responsiveness of the quantity of a product demanded or supplied when its price changes. The consumption of a good also is affected by a change in the price of a related product or by a change in income.

Cross Elasticity of Demand

The **cross elasticity of demand** measures how sensitive consumer purchases of one product (say, X) are to a change in the price of some other product (say, Y). We calculate

the coefficient of cross elasticity of demand E_{xy} just as we do the coefficient of simple price elasticity, except that we relate the percentage change in the consumption of X to the percentage change in the price of Y:

$$E_{xy} = \frac{\text{percentage change in quantity demanded of product X}}{\text{percentage change in price of product Y}}$$

This cross-elasticity (or cross-price-elasticity) concept allows us to quantify and more fully understand substitute and complementary goods, introduced in Chapter 3. Unlike price elasticity, we allow the coefficient of cross elasticity of demand to be either positive or negative.

Substitute Goods If cross elasticity of demand is positive, meaning that sales of X move in the same direction as a change in the price of Y, then X and Y are substitute goods. An example is Evian water (X) and Dasani water (Y). An increase in the price of Evian causes consumers to buy more Dasani, resulting in a positive cross elasticity. The larger the positive cross-elasticity coefficient, the greater is the substitutability between the two products.

Complementary Goods When cross elasticity is negative, we know that X and Y "go together"; an increase in the price of one decreases the demand for the other. So the two are complementary goods. For example, a decrease in the price of digital cameras will increase the number of memory sticks purchased. The larger the negative cross-elasticity coefficient, the greater is the complementarity between the two goods.

Independent Goods A zero or near-zero cross elasticity suggests that the two products being considered are unrelated or independent goods. An example is walnuts and plums: We would not expect a change in the price of walnuts to have any effect on purchases of plums, and vice versa.

Application The degree of substitutability of products, measured by the cross-elasticity coefficient, is important to businesses and government. For example, suppose that Coca-Cola is considering whether or not to lower the price of its Sprite brand. Not only will it want to know something about the price elasticity of demand for Sprite (will the price cut increase or decrease total revenue?), but it will also be interested in knowing if the increased sales of Sprite will come at the expense of its Coke brand. How sensitive are the sales of one of its products (Coke) to a change in the price of another of its products (Sprite)? By how much will the increased sales of Sprite "cannibalize" the sales of Coke? A low cross elasticity would indicate that Coke and Sprite are weak substitutes for each other and that a lower price for Sprite would have little effect on Coke sales.

Government also implicitly uses the idea of cross elasticity of demand in assessing whether a proposed merger between two large firms will substantially reduce competition and therefore violate the antitrust laws. For

example, the cross elasticity between Coke and Pepsi is high, making them strong substitutes for each other. In addition, Coke and Pepsi together sell about 75 percent of all carbonated cola drinks consumed in the United States. Taken together, the high cross elasticities and the large market shares suggest that the government would likely block a merger between Coke and Pepsi because the merger would substantially lessen competition. In contrast, the cross elasticity between cola and gasoline is low or zero. A merger between Coke and Shell oil company would have a minimal effect on competition. So government would let that merger happen.

Income Elasticity of Demand

Income elasticity of demand measures the degree to which consumers respond to a change in their incomes by buying more or less of a particular good. The coefficient of income elasticity of demand E_i is determined with the formula

$$E_i = \frac{\text{percentage change in quantity demanded}}{\text{percentage change in income}}$$

Normal Goods For most goods, the income-elasticity coefficient E_i is positive, meaning that more of them are demanded as incomes rise. Such goods are called normal or superior goods (and were first described in Chapter 3). But the value of E_i varies greatly among normal goods. For example, income elasticity of demand for automobiles is about +3, while income elasticity for most farm products is only about +.20.

Inferior Goods A negative income-elasticity coefficient designates an inferior good. Retread tires, cabbage, long-distance bus tickets, used clothing, and muscatel wine are likely candidates. Consumers decrease their purchases of inferior goods as incomes rise.

Insights Coefficients of income elasticity of demand provide insights into the economy. For example, when

TABLE 4.4 Cross and Income Elasticities of Demand

Value of Coefficient	Description	Type of Good(s)
Cross elasticity: Positive ($E_{wz} > 0$)	Quantity demanded of W changes in same direction as change in price of Z	Substitutes
Negative ($E_{xy} < 0$)	Quantity demanded of X changes in opposite direction from change in price of Y	Complements
Income elasticity: Positive ($E_i > 0$)	Quantity demanded of the product changes in same direction as change in income	Normal or superior
Negative ($E_i < 0$)	Quantity demanded of the product changes in opposite direction from change in income	Inferior

recessions (business downturns) occur and incomes fall, income elasticity of demand helps predict which products will decline in demand more rapidly than others.

Products with relatively high income elasticity coefficients, such as automobiles ($E_i = +3$), housing ($E_i = +1.5$), and restaurant meals ($E_i = +1.4$), are generally hit hardest by recessions. Those with low or negative income elasticity coefficients are much less affected. For example, food products prepared at home ($E_i = +.20$) respond relatively little to income fluctuations. When incomes drop, purchases of food (and toothpaste and toilet paper) drop little compared to purchases of movie tickets, luxury vacations, and plasma screen TVs. Products we view as essential tend to have lower income elasticity coefficients than products we view as luxuries. When our incomes fall, we cannot easily eliminate or postpone the purchase of essential products.

In Table 4.4 we provide a convenient synopsis of the cross-elasticity and income-elasticity concepts.

Summary

1. Price elasticity of demand measures consumer response to price changes. If consumers are relatively sensitive to price changes, demand is elastic. If they are relatively unresponsive to price changes, demand is inelastic.

2. The price-elasticity coefficient E_d measures the degree of elasticity or inelasticity of demand. The coefficient is found by the formula

$$E_d = \frac{\text{percentage change in quantity demanded of X}}{\text{percentage change in price of X}}$$

Economists use the averages of prices and quantities under consideration as reference points in determining percentage changes in price and quantity. If E_d is greater than 1, demand is elastic. If E_d is less than 1, demand is inelastic. Unit elasticity is the special case in which E_d equals 1.

3. Perfectly inelastic demand is graphed as a line parallel to the vertical axis; perfectly elastic demand is shown by a line above and parallel to the horizontal axis.

4. Elasticity varies at different price ranges on a demand curve, tending to be elastic in the upper-left segment and inelastic in the lower-right segment. Elasticity cannot be judged by the steepness or flatness of a demand curve.

5. If total revenue changes in the opposite direction from prices, demand is elastic. If price and total revenue change in the same direction, demand is inelastic. Where demand is of unit elasticity, a change in price leaves total revenue unchanged.

6. The number of available substitutes, the size of an item's price relative to one's budget, whether the product is a luxury or a necessity, and length of time to adjust are all determinants of elasticity of demand.

7. The elasticity concept also applies to supply. The coefficient of price elasticity of supply is found by the formula

$$E_s = \frac{\text{percentage change in quantity supplied of X}}{\text{percentage change in price of X}}$$

The averages of the prices and quantities under consideration are used as reference points for computing percentage changes. Elasticity of supply depends on the ease of shifting resources between alternative uses, which varies directly with the time producers have to adjust to a price change.

8. Cross elasticity of demand indicates how sensitive the purchase of one product is to changes in the price of another product. The coefficient of cross elasticity of demand is found by the formula

$$E_{xy} = \frac{\text{percentage change in quantity demanded of X}}{\text{percentage change in price of Y}}$$

Positive cross elasticity of demand identifies substitute goods; negative cross elasticity identifies complementary goods.

9. Income elasticity of demand indicates the responsiveness of consumer purchases to a change in income. The coefficient of income elasticity of demand is found by the formula

$$E_i = \frac{\text{percentage change in quantity demanded of X}}{\text{percentage change in income}}$$

The coefficient is positive for normal goods and negative for inferior goods.

10. Industries that sell products which have high income elasticity of demand coefficients are particularly hard hit by recessions. Those with products that have low or negative income elasticity of demand coefficients fare much better.

Terms and Concepts

price elasticity of demand

midpoint formula

elastic demand

inelastic demand

unit elasticity

perfectly inelastic demand

perfectly elastic demand

total revenue (TR)

total-revenue test

price elasticity of supply

market period

short run

long run

cross elasticity of demand

income elasticity of demand

Questions

1. Explain why the choice between 1, 2, 3, 4, 5, 6, 7, and 8 "units," or 1000, 2000, 3000, 4000, 5000, 6000, 7000, and 8000 movie tickets, makes no difference in determining elasticity in Table 4.1. LO1

2. Graph the accompanying demand data, and then use the midpoint formula for E_d to determine price elasticity of demand for each of the four possible $1 price changes. What can you conclude about the relationship between the slope of a curve and its elasticity? Explain in a nontechnical way why demand is elastic in the northwest segment of the demand curve and inelastic in the southeast segment. LO1

Product Price	Quantity Demanded
$5	1
4	2
3	3
2	4
1	5

3. What are the major determinants of price elasticity of demand? Use those determinants and your own reasoning in judging whether demand for each of the following products is probably elastic or inelastic: (a) bottled water; (b) toothpaste, (c) Crest toothpaste, (d) ketchup, (e) diamond bracelets, (f) Microsoft's Windows operating system. LO1

4. What effect would a rule stating that university students must live in university dormitories have on the price elasticity of demand for dormitory space? What impact might this in turn have on room rates? LO1

5. Calculate total-revenue data from the demand schedule in question 2. Graph total revenue below your demand curve. Generalize about the relationship between price elasticity and total revenue. LO2

6. How would the following changes in price affect total revenue? That is, would total revenue increase, decrease, or remain unchanged? LO2
   a. Price falls and demand is inelastic.
   b. Price rises and demand is elastic.
   c. Price rises and supply is elastic.
   d. Price rises and supply is inelastic.
   e. Price rises and demand is inelastic.
   f. Price falls and demand is elastic.
   g. Price falls and demand is of unit elasticity.

7. In 2006, Willem de Kooning's abstract painting *Woman III* sold for $137.5 million. Portray this sale in a demand and supply diagram and comment on the elasticity of supply. Comedian George Carlin once mused, "If a painting can be forged well enough to fool some experts, why is the original so valuable?" Provide an answer. LO3

8. Suppose the cross elasticity of demand for products A and B is +3.6 and for products C and D is −5.4. What can you conclude about how products A and B are related? Products C and D? LO4

9. The income elasticities of demand for movies, dental services, and clothing have been estimated to be +3.4, +1, and +.5, respectively. Interpret these coefficients. What does it mean if an income elasticity coefficient is negative? LO4

10. Research has found that an increase in the price of beer would reduce the amount of marijuana consumed. Is cross elasticity of demand between the two products positive or negative? Are these products substitutes or complements? What might be the logic behind this relationship? LO4

11. **LAST WORD** What is the purpose of charging different groups of customers different prices? Supplement the three broad examples in the Last Word with two additional examples of your own. Hint: Think of price discounts based on group characteristics or time of purchase.

Problems

1. Look at the demand curve in Figure 4.2a. Use the midpoint formula and points *a* and *b* to calculate the elasticity of demand for that range of the demand curve. Do the same for the demand curves in Figures 4.2b and 4.2c using, respectively, points *c* and *d* for Figure 4.2b and points *e* and *f* for Figure 4.2c. LO1

2. Investigate how demand elasticities are affected by increases in demand. Shift each of the demand curves in Figures 4.2a, 4.2b, and 4.2c to the right by 10 units. For example, point *a* in Figure 4.2a would shift rightward from location (10 units, $2) to (20 units, $2), while point *b* would shift rightward from location (40 units, $1) to (50 units, $1). After making these shifts, apply the midpoint formula to calculate the demand elasticities for the shifted points. Are they larger or smaller than the elasticities you calculated in Problem 1 for the original points? In terms of the midpoint formula, what explains the change in elasticities? LO1

3. Suppose that the total revenue received by a company selling basketballs is $600 when the price is set at $30 per basketball and $600 when the price is set at $20 per basketball. Without using the midpoint formula, can you tell whether demand is elastic, inelastic, or unit-elastic over this price range? LO2

4. Danny "Dimes" Donahue is a neighborhood's 9-year old entrepreneur. His most recent venture is selling homemade brownies that he bakes himself. At a price of $1.50 each, he sells 100. At a price of $1.00 each, he sells 300. Is demand elastic or inelastic over this price range? *If* demand had the same elasticity for a price decline from $1.00 to $0.50 as it does for the decline from $1.50 to $1.00, would cutting the price from $1.00 to $0.50 increase or decrease Danny's total revenue? LO2

5. What is the formula for measuring the price elasticity of supply? Suppose the price of apples goes up from $20 to $22 a box. In direct response, Goldsboro Farms supplies 1200 boxes of apples instead of 1000 boxes. Compute the coefficient of price elasticity (midpoints approach) for Goldsboro's supply. Is its supply elastic, or is it inelastic? LO3

6. **ADVANCED ANALYSIS** Currently, at a price of $1 each, 100 popsicles are sold per day in the perpetually hot town of Rostin. Consider the elasticity of supply. In the short run, a price increase from $1 to $2 is unit-elastic ($E_s = 1.0$). So how many popsicles will be sold each day in the short run if the price rises to $2 each? In the long run, a price increase from $1 to $2 has an elasticity of supply of 1.50. So how many popsicles will be sold per day in the long run if the price rises to $2 each? (Hint: Apply the midpoints approach to the elasticity of supply.) LO3

7. Lorena likes to play golf. The number of times per year that she plays depends on both the price of playing a round of golf as well as Lorena's income and the cost of other types of entertainment—in particular, how much it costs to go see a movie instead of playing golf. The three demand schedules in the table below show how many rounds of golf per year Lorena will demand at each price under three different scenarios. In scenario D_1, Lorena's income is $50,000 per year and movies cost $9 each. In scenario D_2, Lorena's income is also $50,000 per year, but the price of seeing a movie rises to $11. And in scenario D_3, Lorena's income goes up to $70,000 per year, while movies cost $11. LO4

	Quantity Demanded		
Price	D_1	D_2	D_3
$50	15	10	15
35	25	15	30
20	40	20	50

a. Using the data under D_1 and D_2, calculate the cross elasticity of Lorena's demand for golf at all three prices. (To do this, apply the midpoints approach to the cross elasticity of demand.) Is the cross elasticity the same at all three prices? Are movies and golf substitute goods, complementary goods, or independent goods?

b. Using the data under D_2 and D_3, calculate the income elasticity of Lorena's demand for golf at all three prices. (To do this, apply the midpoints approach to the income elasticity of demand.) Is the income elasticity the same at all three prices? Is golf an inferior good?

FURTHER TEST YOUR KNOWLEDGE AT
www.mcconnell19e.com

At the text's Online Learning Center (OLC), **www.mcconnell19e.com**, you will find one or more Web-based questions that require information from the Internet to answer. We urge you to check them out; they will familiarize you with Web sites that may be helpful in other courses and perhaps even in your career. The OLC also features multiple-choice questions that give instant feedback and provides other helpful ways to further test your knowledge of the chapter.

Elasticity

Chapter 4 is basically a continuation of Chapter 3. The previous chapter provided a basic understanding of supply and demand. Now the economic principles, problems, and policies to be studied require a more detailed discussion of **elasticity** and how it relates to supply and demand.

The concept of **price elasticity of demand** is of great importance for studying the material found in the remainder of the text. You must understand (1) what price elasticity measures; (2) how the price-elasticity formula is applied to measure the price elasticity of demand; (3) the difference between price elastic, price inelastic, and unit elastic; (4) how total revenue varies by the type of price elasticity of demand; (5) the meaning of perfect price elasticity and of perfect price inelasticity of demand; (6) the four major determinants of price elasticity of demand; and (7) the practical application of the concept to many economic issues.

When you have become thoroughly acquainted with the concept of price elasticity of demand, you will find that you have very little trouble understanding the **price elasticity of supply.** The transition requires no more than the substitution of the words "quantity supplied" for the words "quantity demanded." You should concentrate your attention on the meaning of price elasticity of supply and how it is affected by time. Several examples are provided to show how it affects the prices of many products.

The chapter also introduces you to two other elasticity concepts. The **cross elasticity of demand** measures the sensitivity of a change in the quantity demanded for one product due to a change in the price of another product. This concept is especially important in identifying whether two goods are substitutes to each other, complements to each other, or independent of each other. The **income elasticity of demand** assesses the change in the quantity demanded of a product resulting from a change in consumer incomes. It is useful for categorizing goods as normal or inferior. For normal goods, as income increases, the demand for them increases, whereas for inferior goods as income increases, the demand for them decreases.

So elasticity as presented in this chapter is all about the responsiveness of changes in quantity to a change in price or income. Understanding this concept will be useful for answering many questions about demand and supply.

■ CHECKLIST

When you have studied this chapter you should be able to

☐ Describe the concept of the price elasticity of demand.

☐ Compute the coefficient for the price when given the demand data.

☐ State the midpoint formula for price elasticity of demand and explain how it refines the original formula for price elasticity.

☐ State two reasons why the formula for price elasticity of demand uses percentages rather than absolute amounts in measuring consumer responsiveness.

☐ Explain the meaning of elastic, inelastic, and unit elastic as they relate to demand.

☐ Describe the concepts of perfectly elastic demand and perfectly inelastic demand and illustrate them with graphs.

☐ Apply the total-revenue test to determine whether demand is elastic, inelastic, or unit-elastic.

☐ Describe the relationship between price elasticity of demand and the price range for most demand curves.

☐ Explain why the slope of the demand curve is not a sound basis for judging price elasticity.

☐ Illustrate graphically the relationship between price elasticity of demand and total revenue.

☐ List the four major determinants of the price elasticity of demand, and explain how each determinant affects price elasticity.

☐ Describe several applications of the concept of price elasticity of demand.

☐ Describe the concept of the price elasticity of supply.

☐ Compute the coefficient for the price elasticity of supply when given the relevant data.

☐ Explain the effect of three time periods (market period, short run, and long run) on price elasticity of supply.

☐ Describe several applications of price elasticity of supply.

☐ Describe the concept of the cross elasticity of demand.

☐ Compute the coefficient for the cross elasticity of demand when given relevant data.

☐ Use the cross elasticity of demand to categorize substitute goods, complementary goods, and independent goods.

☐ Give applications of cross elasticity of demand.

☐ Describe the concepts of the income elasticity of demand.

☐ Compute the coefficient for the income elasticity of demand when given relevant data.

☐ Use the income elasticity of demand to categorize goods as normal or inferior.

☐ Provide some insights using the concept of income elasticity.

☐ Use the concept of elasticity of demand to explain why different consumers pay different prices (*Last Word*).

■ **CHAPTER OUTLINE**

1. *Price elasticity of demand* is a measure of the responsiveness or sensitivity of quantity demanded to changes in the price of a product. When quantity demanded is relatively responsive to a price change, demand is said to be *elastic*. When quantity demanded is relatively unresponsive to a price change, demand is said to be *inelastic*.

   a. The degree of elasticity can be measured by using a formula to compute the elasticity coefficient. E_d = percentage change in quantity demanded of product X *divided by* the percentage change in the price of product X.

   (1) A *midpoint formula* calculates price elasticity across a price and quantity range to overcome the problem of selecting the reference points for the price range and the quantity range. In this formula, the *average* of the two quantities and the *average* of the two prices are used as reference points. This formula can be done in three steps: (a) calculate the change in quantity divided by the average of the two quantities; (b) calculate the change in price divided by the average of the two prices; (c) divide the quantity result from (a) by the price result from (b). For example, if the price falls from $5 to $4 while the quantity demanded rises from 10 units to 20 units, then using the midpoint formula, the price elasticity of demand is: (a) [10 − 20] divided by [(10 + 20)/2] = .67; (b) [(5 − 4) divided by [(5 + 4)/2] = .22; (c) thus .67 divided by .22 means that E_d is approximately equal to 3.

   (2) Economists use percentages rather than absolute amounts in measuring responsiveness because with absolute amounts the choice of units or scale can arbitrarily affect the perception of responsiveness.

   (3) The price elasticity of demand coefficient is a negative number (has a minus sign) because price and quantity demanded are inversely related. Economists ignore the minus sign in front of the coefficient and focus their attention on its absolute value.

   b. The coefficient of price elasticity has several interpretations.

   (1) *Elastic demand* occurs when the percentage change in quantity demanded is greater than the percentage change in price. The elasticity coefficient is greater than 1.

   (2) *Inelastic demand* occurs when the percentage change in quantity demanded is less than the percentage change in price. The elasticity coefficient is less than 1.

   (3) *Unit elasticity* occurs when the percentage change in quantity demanded is equal to the percentage change in price. The elasticity coefficient is equal to 1.

   (4) *Perfectly inelastic demand* means that a change in price results in no change in quantity demanded of a product, whereas *perfectly elastic demand* means that a small change in price causes buyers to purchase all they desire of a product.

   c. *Total revenue (TR)* changes when price changes. The *total-revenue test* shows that when demand is

   (1) *elastic,* a decrease in price will increase total revenue and an increase in price will decrease total revenue.

   (2) *inelastic,* a decrease in price will decrease total revenue and an increase in price will increase total revenue.

   (3) *unit-elastic,* an increase or decrease in price will not affect total revenue.

   d. Note several points about the graph of a linear demand curve and price elasticity of demand.

   (1) It is not the same at all prices. Demand is typically elastic at higher prices and inelastic at lower prices.

   (2) It cannot be judged from the slope of the demand curve.

   e. The relationship between price elasticity of demand and total revenue can be shown by graphing the demand curve and the total-revenue curve, one above the other. In this case, the horizontal axis for each graph uses the same quantity scale. The vertical axis for demand represents price. The vertical axis for the total-revenue graph measures total revenue.

   (1) When demand is price elastic, as price declines and quantity increases along the demand curve, total revenue increases in the total-revenue graph.

   (2) Conversely, when demand is price inelastic, as price declines and quantity increases along the demand curve, total revenue decreases.

   (3) When demand is unit-elastic, as price and quantity change along the demand curve, total revenue remains the same.

   f. The price elasticity of demand for a product depends on four determinants.

   (1) The number of good substitutes for the product. The more substitute products that are available for a product, the greater the price elasticity of demand for the product.

   (2) Its relative importance in the consumer's budget. The higher the price of product relative to consumers' incomes, the greater the price elasticity of demand.

   (3) Whether it is a necessity or a luxury. Luxuries typically have a greater price elasticity of demand than necessities.

   (4) The period of time under consideration. The longer the time period, the greater the elasticity of demand for a product.

   g. Price elasticity of demand has practical applications to public policy and business decisions. The concept is relevant to bumper crops in agriculture, excise taxes, and the decriminalization of illegal drugs.

2. *Price elasticity of supply* is a measure of the sensitivity of quantity supplied to changes in the price of a product. Both the general formula and the midpoint formula for price elasticity of supply are similar to those for the price elasticity of demand, but "quantity supplied" replaces "quantity demanded." This means that the price elasticity of supply is the percentage change in quantity supplied of a product divided by its percentage change in the price of the product. There is a midpoint formula that is an average of quantities and prices and is used for calculating the elasticity of supply across quantity or price ranges. The price elasticity of supply depends primarily on the

amount of time sellers have to adjust to a price change. The easier and faster suppliers can respond to changes in price, the greater the price elasticity of supply.

a. In the **market period,** there is too little time for producers to change output in response to a change in price. As a consequence supply is perfectly inelastic. Graphically, this means that the supply curve is vertical at that market level of output.

b. In the **short run,** producers have less flexibility to change output in response to a change in price because they have fixed inputs that they cannot change. They have only a limited control over the range in which they can vary their output. As a consequence, supply is *price inelastic* in the short run.

c. In the **long run,** producers can make adjustments to all inputs to vary production. As a consequence, supply is *price elastic* in the long run. There is no total-revenue test for price elasticity of supply because price and total revenue move in the same direction regardless of the degree of price elasticity of supply.

d. Price elasticity of supply has many practical applications for explaining price volatility. The concept is relevant to the pricing of antiques and gold, for which the supply is perfectly inelastic.

3. Two other elasticity concepts are important.

a. The **cross elasticity of demand** measures the degree to which the quantity demanded of one product is affected by a change in the price of another product. Cross elasticities of demand are

(1) positive for products that are substitutes;

(2) negative for products that are complements; and

(3) zero or near zero for products that are unrelated or independent.

b. The **income elasticity of demand** measures the effect of a change in income on the quantity demanded of a product. Income elasticities of demand are

(1) positive for normal or superior products, which means that more of them are demanded as income rises; and

(2) negative for inferior products, which means that less of them are demanded as income rises.

4. (*Last Word*). There are many examples of dual or multiple pricing of products. The main reason for the differences is differences in the price elasticity of demand among groups. Business travelers have a more inelastic demand for travel than leisure travelers and thus can be charged more for an airline ticket. Prices for children are often lower than prices for adults for the same service (for example, movie tickets or restaurant meals) because children have more elastic demand for the service. Low-income groups have a more elastic demand for higher education than high-income groups, so high-income groups are charged the full tuition price and lower-income groups get more financial aid to offset the tuition price.

■ **HINTS AND TIPS**

1. This chapter is an extension of the material presented in Chapter 3. Be sure you thoroughly read and study Chapter 3 again before you read and do the self-test exercises for this chapter.

2. You should **not judge** the price elasticity of demand based on the slope of the demand curve unless it is horizontal (*perfectly elastic*) or vertical (*perfectly inelastic*). Remember that elasticity varies from elastic to inelastic along a down-sloping, linear demand curve. The price elasticity equals 1 at the midpoint of a down-sloping linear demand curve.

3. Master the **total-revenue test** for assessing the price elasticity of demand (review Table 4.2). For many problems, the total-revenue test is easier to use than the midpoint formula for identifying the type of elasticity (elastic, inelastic, unit), and the test has many practical applications.

4. Do not just memorize the elasticity formulas in this chapter. Instead, work on understanding what they mean and how they are used for economic decisions. The elasticity formulas simply measure the *responsiveness* of a percentage change in *quantity* to a percentage change in some other characteristic (price or income). The elasticity formulas each have a similar structure: A percentage change in some type of *quantity* (demanded, supplied) is divided by a percentage change in the other variable. The price elasticity of demand measures the responsiveness of a percentage change in *quantity demanded* for a product to a percentage change in its *price*. The cross elasticity of demand measures the percentage change in the *quantity demanded of product X* to a percentage change in the *price of product Y*. The income elasticity of demand is the percentage change in *quantity demanded* for a product to a percentage change in *income*. The price elasticity of supply is the percentage change in the *quantity supplied* of a product to a percentage change in its price.

■ **IMPORTANT TERMS**

price elasticity of demand	total-revenue test
midpoint formula	price elasticity of supply
elastic demand	market period
inelastic demand	short run
unit elasticity	long run
perfectly inelastic demand	cross elasticity of demand
perfectly elastic demand	income elasticity of demand
total revenue	

SELF-TEST

■ **FILL-IN QUESTIONS**

1. If a relatively large change in price results in a relatively small change in quantity demanded, demand is (elastic, inelastic) _____. If a relatively small change in price results in a relatively large change in quantity demanded, demand is (elastic, inelastic) _____.

2. The midpoint formula for the price elasticity of demand uses the (total, average) _____ of the two quantities as a reference point in calculating the percentage change in quantity and the (total, average) _____ of the two prices as a reference point in calculating the percentage change in price.

3. The price elasticity formula is based on (absolute amounts, percentages) _____ because it avoids the problems caused by the arbitrary choice of units and permits meaningful comparisons of consumer (responsiveness, incomes) _____ to changes in the prices of different products.

4. If a change in price causes no change in quantity demanded, demand is perfectly (elastic, inelastic) _____ and the demand curve is (horizontal, vertical) _____. If an extremely small change in price causes an extremely large change in quantity demanded, demand is perfectly (elastic, inelastic) _____ and the demand curve is (horizontal, vertical) _____.

5. Two characteristics of the price elasticity of a linear demand curve are that elasticity (is constant, varies) _____ over the different price ranges, and that the slope is (a sound, an unsound) _____ basis for judging its elasticity.

6. Assume that the price of a product declines in cases a, b, and c.

　a. When demand is inelastic, the loss of revenue due to the lower price is (less, greater) _____ than the gain in revenue due to the greater quantity demanded.

　b. When demand is elastic, the loss of revenue due to the lower price is (less, greater) _____ than the gain in revenue due to the greater quantity demanded.

　c. When demand is unit-elastic, the loss of revenue due to the lower price (exceeds, is equal to) _____ the gain in revenue due to the greater quantity demanded.

7. Complete the following summary table.

If demand is	The elasticity coefficient is	If price rises, total revenue will	If price falls, total revenue will
Elastic	____	____	____
Inelastic	____	____	____
Unit-elastic	____	____	____

8. What are the four most important determinants of the price elasticity of demand?

　a. _____

　b. _____

　c. _____

　d. _____

9. The price elasticity of demand will tend to be greater when the number of substitute goods that are available for the product is (larger, smaller) _____.

10. The price elasticity of demand will tend to be greater when the price of the product relative to consumers' income is (lower, higher) _____.

11. The price elasticity of demand will tend to be greater when a product is considered to be a (necessity, luxury) _____.

12. The price elasticity of demand will tend to be greater when the time period under consideration for a change in quantity is (shorter, longer) _____.

13. The demand for most farm products is highly (elastic, inelastic) _____, which means that large crop yields will most likely (increase, decrease) _____ the total revenue of farmers. Governments often tax products such as liquor, gasoline, and cigarettes because the price elasticity of the demand is (elastic, inelastic) _____. A higher tax on such products will (increase, decrease) _____ tax revenue.

14. The price elasticity of supply measures the percentage change in (price, quantity supplied) _____ divided by the percentage change in _____. The most important factor affecting the price elasticity of supply is (revenue, time) _____. It is easier to shift resources to alternative uses when there is (more, less) _____ time.

15. In the market period, the price elasticity of supply will be perfectly (elastic, inelastic) _____ and the supply curve will be (horizontal, vertical) _____. Typically, in the short run the price elasticity of supply is (more, less) _____ elastic but in the long run the price elasticity of supply is _____ elastic.

16. There is a total-revenue test for the elasticity of (demand, supply) _____. There is no total-revenue test for the elasticity of (demand, supply) _____ because regardless of the degree of elasticity, price and total revenue are (directly, indirectly) _____ related.

17. The measure of the sensitivity of the consumption of one product given a change in the price of another product is the (cross, income) _____ elasticity of demand, while the measure of the responsiveness of consumer purchases to changes in income is the _____ elasticity of demand.

18. When the cross elasticity of demand is positive, two products are (complements, substitutes) _____, but when the cross elasticity of demand is negative, they are _____.

19. When a percentage change in the price of one product has no effect on another product, then the cross elasticity of demand will be (zero, one) _____ and the two products would be classified as being (dependent, independent) _____.

20. If consumers increase purchases of a product as consumer incomes increase, then a good is classified as (inferior, normal) _____, but if consumers decrease purchases of a product as consumer incomes increase, then a good is classified as _____.

■ **TRUE–FALSE QUESTIONS**

Circle T if the statement is true, F if it is false.

1. If the percentage change in price is greater than the percentage change in quantity demanded, the price elasticity coefficient is greater than 1. **T F**

2. If the quantity demanded for a product increases from 100 to 150 units when the price decreases from $14 to $10, using the midpoint formula, the price elasticity of demand for this product in this price range is 1.2. **T F**

3. A product with a price elasticity of demand equal to 1.5 is described as price inelastic. **T F**

4. If the price of a product increases from $5 to $6 and the quantity demanded decreases from 45 to 25, then according to the total-revenue test, the product is price inelastic in this price range. **T F**

5. Total revenue will not change when price changes if the price elasticity of demand is unitary. **T F**

6. When the absolute value of the price elasticity coefficient is greater than 1 and the price of the product decreases, then the total revenue will increase. **T F**

7. The flatness or steepness of a demand curve is based on absolute changes in price and quantity, while elasticity is based on relative or percentage changes in price and quantity. **T F**

8. Demand tends to be inelastic at higher prices and elastic at lower prices along a down-sloping linear demand curve. **T F**

9. Price elasticity of demand and the slope of the demand curve are two different things. **T F**

10. In general, the larger the number of substitute goods that are available, the less the price elasticity of demand. **T F**

11. Other things equal, the higher the price of a good relative to consumers' incomes, the greater the price elasticity of demand. **T F**

12. Other things equal, the higher the price of a good relative to the longer the time period the purchase is considered, the greater the price elasticity of demand. **T F**

13. The more that a good is considered to be a "luxury" rather than a "necessity," the less is the price elasticity of demand. **T F**

14. The demand for most agricultural products is price inelastic. Consequently, an increase in supply will reduce the total income of producers of agricultural products. **T F**

15. A state government seeking to increase its excise-tax revenues is more likely to increase the tax rate on restaurant meals than on gasoline. **T F**

16. The degree of price elasticity of supply depends on how easily and quickly producers can shift resources between alternative uses. **T F**

17. If an increase in product price results in no change in the quantity supplied, supply is perfectly elastic. **T F**

18. The market period is a time so short that producers cannot respond to a change in demand and price. **T F**

19. The price elasticity of supply will tend to be more elastic in the long run. **T F**

20. There is a total revenue test for the elasticity of supply. **T F**

21. Cross elasticity of demand is measured by the percentage change in quantity demanded over the percentage change in income. **T F**

22. For a substitute product, the coefficient of the cross elasticity of demand is positive. **T F**

23. Two products are considered to be independent or unrelated when the cross elasticity of demand is zero. **T F**

24. The degree to which consumers respond to a change in their incomes by buying more or less of a particular product is measured by the income elasticity of demand. **T F**

25. Inferior goods have a positive income elasticity of demand. **T F**

■ **MULTIPLE-CHOICE QUESTIONS**

Circle the letter that corresponds to the best answer.

1. If, when the price of a product rises from $1.50 to $2, the quantity demanded of the product decreases from 1000 to 900, the price elasticity of demand coefficient, using the midpoint formula, is.
   (a) 3.00
   (b) 2.71
   (c) 0.37
   (d) 0.33

2. If a 1% fall in the price of a product causes the quantity demanded of the product to increase by 2%, demand is
    (a) inelastic
    (b) elastic
    (c) unit-elastic
    (d) perfectly elastic

3. In the following diagram, D_1 is a

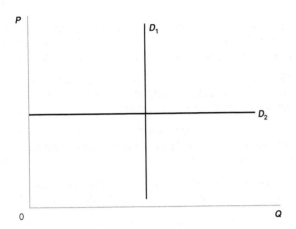

    (a) perfectly elastic demand curve
    (b) perfectly inelastic demand curve
    (c) unit-elastic demand curve
    (d) a long-run demand curve

4. Compared to the lower-right portion, the upper-left portion of most demand curves tends to be
    (a) more inelastic
    (b) more elastic
    (c) unit-elastic
    (d) perfectly inelastic

5. In which range of the demand schedule is demand price inelastic?

Price	Quantity demanded
$11	50
9	100
7	200
5	300
3	400

    (a) $11 − $9
    (b) $9 − $7
    (c) $7 − $5
    (d) $5 − $3

6. If a business increased the price of its product from $7 to $8 when the price elasticity of demand was inelastic, then
    (a) total revenues decreased
    (b) total revenues increased

    (c) total revenues remained unchanged
    (d) total revenues were perfectly inelastic

7. You are the sales manager for a pizza company and have been informed that the price elasticity of demand for your most popular pizza is greater than 1. To increase total revenues, you should.
    (a) increase the price of the pizza
    (b) decrease the price of the pizza
    (c) hold pizza prices constant
    (d) decrease demand for your pizza

8. Assume Amanda Herman finds that her total spending on compact discs remains the same after the price of compact discs falls, other things equal. Which of the following is true about Amanda's demand for compact discs with this price change?.
    (a) It is unit price elastic.
    (b) It is perfectly price elastic.
    (c) It is perfectly price inelastic.
    (d) It increased in response to the price change.

Questions 9, 10, and 11 are based on the following graph.

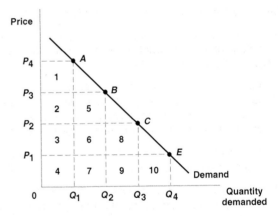

9. If price is P_3, then total revenue is measured by the area
    (a) $0P_3CQ_3$
    (b) $0P_3BQ_2$
    (c) $0P_3BQ_3$
    (d) $0P_3CQ_2$

10. If price falls from P_2 to P_1, then in this price range demand is
    (a) relatively inelastic because the loss in total revenue (areas 3 + 6 + 8) is greater than the gain in total revenue (area 10)
    (b) relatively elastic because the loss in total revenue (areas 3 + 6 + 8) is greater than the gain in total revenue (area 10)
    (c) relatively inelastic because the loss in total revenue (area 10) is less than the gain in total revenue (areas 3 + 6 + 8)
    (d) relatively inelastic because the loss in total revenue (areas 4 + 7 + 9 + 10) is greater than the gain in total revenue (areas 3 + 6 + 8)

11. As price falls from P_4 to P_3, you know that demand is
(a) elastic because total revenue decreased from $0P_4AQ_1$ to $0P_3BQ_2$
(b) inelastic because total revenue decreased from $0P_3BQ_2$ to $0P_4AQ_1$
(c) elastic because total revenue increased from $0P_4AQ_1$ to $0P_3BQ_2$
(d) inelastic because total revenue decreased from $0P_4AQ_1$ to $0P_3BQ_2$

12. Which is characteristic of a product whose demand is elastic?
(a) The price elasticity coefficient is less than 1.
(b) Total revenue decreases if price decreases.
(c) Buyers are relatively insensitive to price changes.
(d) The percentage change in quantity is greater than the percentage change in price.

13. The demand for Nike basketball shoes is more price elastic than the demand for basketball shoes as a whole. This is best explained by the fact that
(a) Nike basketball shoes are a luxury good, not a necessity
(b) Nike basketball shoes are the best made and widely advertised
(c) there are more complements for Nike basketball shoes than for basketball shoes as a whole
(d) there are more substitutes for Nike basketball shoes than for basketball shoes as a whole

14. Which is characteristic of a good whose demand is inelastic?
(a) There are a large number of good substitutes for the good for consumers.
(b) The buyer spends a small percentage of total income on the good.
(c) The good is regarded by consumers as a luxury.
(d) The period of time for which demand is given is relatively long.

15. From a time perspective, the demand for most products is
(a) less elastic in the short run and unit-elastic in the long run
(b) less elastic in the long run and unit-elastic in the short run
(c) more elastic in the short run than in the long run
(d) more elastic in the long run than in the short run

16. If a 5% fall in the price of a commodity causes quantity supplied to decrease by 8%, supply is
(a) inelastic
(b) unit-elastic
(c) elastic
(d) perfectly inelastic

17. In the following diagram, what is the price elasticity of supply between points **A** and **C** (using the midpoint formula)?.

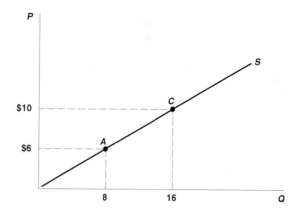

(a) 1.33
(b) 1.67
(c) 1.85
(d) 2.46

18. If supply is inelastic and demand decreases, the total revenue of sellers will
(a) increase
(b) decrease
(c) decrease only if demand is elastic
(d) increase only if demand is inelastic

19. The chief determinant of the price elasticity of supply of a product is
(a) the number of good substitutes the product has
(b) the length of time sellers have to adjust to a change in price
(c) whether the product is a luxury or a necessity
(d) whether the product is a durable or a nondurable good

20. A study shows that the coefficient of the cross elasticity of Coke and Sprite is negative. This information indicates that Coke and Sprite are
(a) normal goods
(b) complementary goods
(c) substitute goods
(d) independent goods

21. If a 5% increase in the price of one good results in a decrease of 2% in the quantity demanded of another good, then it can be concluded that the two goods are
(a) complements
(b) substitutes
(c) independent
(d) normal

22. Most goods can be classified as *normal* goods rather than inferior goods. The definition of a normal good means that
(a) the percentage change in consumer income is greater than the percentage change in price of the normal good
(b) the percentage change in quantity demanded of the normal good is greater than the percentage change in consumer income
(c) as consumer income increases, consumer purchases of a normal good increase
(d) the income elasticity of demand is negative

23. Based on the information in the table, which product would be an inferior good?

Product	% change in income	% change in quantity demanded
A	−10	+10
B	+10	+10
C	+5	+5
D	−5	−5

(a) Product A
(b) Product B
(c) Product C
(d) Product D

24. For which product is the income elasticity of demand most likely to be negative?
(a) automobiles
(b) bus tickets
(c) computers
(d) tennis rackets

25. During a recession, the quantity demanded for which product is likely to be most affected by the decline in consumer incomes?
(a) the buying of ketchup
(b) purchases of toothpaste
(c) the sales of toilet paper
(d) meals bought at restaurants

■ PROBLEMS

1. Complete the following table, using the demand data given, by computing total revenue at each of the seven prices and the six price elasticity coefficients between each of the seven prices, and indicate whether demand is elastic, inelastic, or unit-elastic between each of the seven prices.

Price	Quantity demanded	Total revenue	Elasticity coefficient	Character of demand
$1.00	300	____		
.90	400	____	____	____
.80	500	____	____	____
.70	600	____	____	____
.60	700	____	____	____
.50	800	____	____	____
.40	900	____	____	____

2. Use the data from the table for this problem. On the *first* of the two following graphs, plot the demand curve (price and quantity demanded) and indicate the elastic, inelastic, and unit-elastic portions of the demand curve. On the *second* graph, plot the total revenue on the vertical axis and the quantity demanded on the horizontal axis. (*Note:* The scale for quantity demanded that you

plot on the horizontal axis of each graph should be the same.)

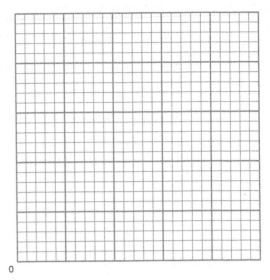

0

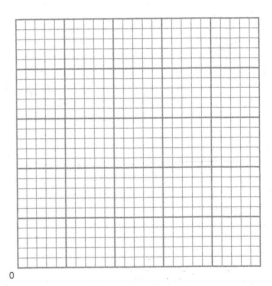

0

a. As price decreases from $1.00 to $0.70, demand is (elastic, inelastic, unit-elastic) _____ and total revenue (increases, decreases, remains the same) _____.

b. As price decreases from $0.70 to $0.60, demand is (elastic, inelastic, unit-elastic) _____ and total revenue (increases, decreases, remains the same) _____.

c. As price decreases from $0.60 to $0.40, demand is (elastic, inelastic, unit-elastic) _____ and total revenue (increases, decreases, remains the same) _____.

3. Using the supply data in the following schedule, complete the table by computing the six price elasticity of supply coefficients between each of the seven prices, and indicate whether supply is elastic, inelastic, or unit-elastic.

Price	Quantity demanded	Elasticity coefficient	Character of supply
$1.00	800		
.90	700	____	____
.80	600	____	____
.70	500	____	____
.60	400	____	____
.50	300	____	____
.40	200	____	____

4. The following graph shows three different supply curves (S_1, S_2, and S_3) for a product bought and sold in a competitive market.

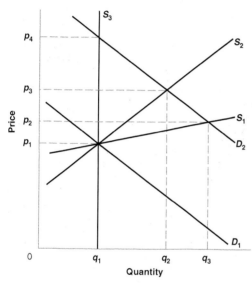

a. The supply curve for the

(1) market period is the one labeled _____.

(2) short run is the one labeled _____.

(3) long run is the one labeled _____.

b. No matter what the period of time under consideration, if the demand for the product were D_1, the equilibrium price of the product would be _____

and the equilibrium quantity would be _____.

(1) If demand were to increase to D_2 in the market period the equilibrium price would increase to

_____ and the equilibrium quantity would be

_____.

(2) In the short run the price of the product would

increase to _____ and the quantity would in-

crease to _____.

(3) In the long run the price of the product would be

_____ and the quantity would be _____.

c. The longer the period of time allowed to sellers to adjust their outputs the (more, less) _____ elastic is the supply of the product.

d. The more elastic the supply of a product, the

(greater, less) _____ the effect on equilibrium

price and the _____ the effect on equilibrium quantity of an increase in demand.

5. For the following three cases, use a midpoint formula to calculate the coefficient for the cross elasticity of demand and identify the relationship between the two goods (complement, substitute, or independent).

a. The quantity demanded for good A increases from 300 to 400 as the price of good B increases from $1 to $2.

Coefficient: _____ Relationship: _____

b. The quantity demanded for good J decreases from 2000 to 1500 as the price of good K increases from $10 to $15.

Coefficient: _____ Relationship: _____

c. The quantity demanded for good X increases from 100 to 101 units as the price of good Y increases from $8 to $15.

Coefficient: _____ Relationship: _____

6. Use the information in the following table to identify the income characteristic of each product A–E using the following labels: **N** = normal (or superior), **I** = inferior.

Product	% change in income	% change in quantity demanded	Income type (N or I)
A	10	10	____
B	1	15	____
C	5	-12	____
D	5	-2	____
E	10	1	____

■ **SHORT ANSWER AND ESSAY QUESTIONS**

1. Define and explain the price elasticity of demand in terms of the relationship between the relative (percentage) change in quantity demanded and the relative (percentage) change in price. Use the elasticity coefficient in your explanation.

2. What is meant by perfectly elastic demand? By perfectly inelastic demand? What does the demand curve look like when demand is perfectly elastic and when it is perfectly inelastic?.

3. Demand seldom has the same elasticity at all prices. What is the relationship between the price of most products and the price elasticity of demand for them?

4. What is the relationship—if there is one—between the price elasticity of demand and the slope of the demand curve?

5. When the price of a product declines, the quantity demanded of it increases. When demand is elastic, total revenue is greater at the lower price, but when demand is inelastic, total revenue is smaller. Explain why total revenue will sometimes increase and why it will sometimes decrease.

6. Explain the effect of the number of substitutes on the price elasticity of demand.

7. Why does the price elasticity of demand differ based on the price of a good as a proportion of household income? Give examples.

8. Is the quantity demanded for necessities more or less responsive to a change in price? Explain using examples.

9. What role does time play in affecting the elasticity of demand?

10. How do opponents of the decriminalization of illegal drugs use elasticity to make their arguments?

11. Explain what determines the price elasticity of supply of an economic good or service.

12. Why is there no total-revenue test for the elasticity of supply?

13. Discuss the supply and demand conditions for antiques. Why are antique prices so high?

14. Use the concepts of the elasticity of supply to explain the volatility of gold prices.

15. How can goods be classified as complementary, substitute, or independent? On what basis is this judgment made?

16. Explain why knowledge of the cross elasticity of demand is important to business.

17. Give an example showing how the government implicitly uses the idea of cross elasticity of demand in its policy-making.

18. Discuss the relationship between the quantity demand for a product and how that quantity responds to a change in income.

19. Supply definitions of a normal good and an inferior good. Illustrate each definition with an example.

20. What is an example of insights that income elasticity of demand coefficients provide about recessions?

ANSWERS

Chapter 4 Elasticity

FILL-IN QUESTIONS

1. inelastic, elastic
2. average, average
3. percentages, responsiveness
4. inelastic, vertical, elastic, horizontal
5. varies, an unsound
6. a. greater; b. less; c. is equal to
7. Elastic: greater than 1, decrease, increase; Inelastic: less than 1, increase, decrease; Unit-elastic: equal to 1, remain constant, remain constant

8. a. The number of good substitute products; b. The relative importance of the product in the total budget of the buyer; c. Whether the good is a necessity or a luxury; d. The period of time in which demand is being considered (any order a–d)
9. larger
10. higher
11. luxury
12. longer
13. inelastic, decrease, inelastic, increase
14. quantity supplied, price, time, more
15. inelastic, vertical, less, more
16. demand, supply, directly
17. cross, income
18. substitutes, complements
19. zero, independent
20. normal, inferior

TRUE-FALSE QUESTIONS

1. F, p. 76
2. T, p. 76
3. F, p. 77
4. F, pp. 77–78
5. T, p. 80
6. T, pp. 81–82
7. T, p. 80
8. F, pp. 80–81
9. T, pp. 80–81
10. F, pp. 81–82
11. T, p. 82
12. T, p. 83
13. F, p. 82
14. T, p. 83
15. F, p. 83
16. T, p. 84
17. F, p. 84
18. T, p. 84
19. T, p. 85
20. F, p. 85
21. F, p. 87
22. T, pp. 87–88
23. T, p. 88
24. T, p. 88
25. F, p. 88

MULTIPLE-CHOICE QUESTIONS

1. c, p. 76
2. b, p. 76
3. b, p. 77
4. b, pp. 80–81
5. d, p. 79
6. b, pp. 78–82
7. b, pp. 78–82
8. a, pp. 80–82
9. b, p. 77
10. a, pp. 80–82
11. c, pp. 80–82
12. d, pp. 81–82
13. d, p. 82
14. b, p. 82
15. d, p. 83
16. c, p. 84
17. a, p. 84
18. b, p. 84
19. b, pp. 84–85
20. b, p. 87–88
21. a, p. 87–88
22. c, p. 88
23. a, p. 88
24. b, p. 88
25. d, p. 89

PROBLEMS

1. Total revenue: $300, 360, 400, 420, 420, 400, 360; Elasticity coefficient: 2.71, 1.89, 1.36, 1, 0.73, 0.53; Character of demand: elastic, elastic, elastic, unit-elastic, inelastic, inelastic.
2. a. elastic, increases; b. unit-elastic, remains the same; c. inelastic, decreases.
3. Elasticity coefficient: 1.27, 1.31, 1.36, 1.44, 1.57, 1.8; Character of supply: elastic, elastic, elastic, elastic, elastic, elastic
4. a. (1) S_3; (2) S_2; (3) S_1; b. p_1, q_1, (1) p_4, q_1; (2) p_3, q_2; (3) p_2, q_3; c. more; d. less, greater
5. a. .43, substitute; b. −.71, complement; c. .02, independent
6. N, N, I, I, N

SHORT ANSWER AND ESSAY QUESTIONS

1. p. 76
2. pp. 77–78
3. pp. 77–78
4. pp. 78–82
5. pp. 78–82
6. pp. 81–82
7. p. 82
8. p. 82
9. p. 83
10. p. 83
11. p. 84
12. p. 85
13. pp. 85–86
14. pp. 86–87
15. pp. 87–88
16. p. 88
17. p. 88
18. p. 88
19. p. 88
20. p. 89

AFTER READING THIS CHAPTER, YOU SHOULD BE ABLE TO:

1 **Differentiate between demand-side market failures and supply-side market failures.**

2 **Explain the origin of both consumer surplus and producer surplus, and explain how properly functioning markets maximize their sum, total surplus, while optimally allocating resources.**

3 **Describe free riding and public goods, and illustrate why private firms cannot normally produce public goods.**

4 **Explain how positive and negative externalities cause under- and overallocations of resources.**

5 **Show why we normally won't want to pay what it would cost to eliminate every last bit of a negative externality such as air pollution.**

Market Failures: Public Goods and Externalities

Competitive markets usually do a remarkably effective job of allocating society's scarce resources to their most highly valued uses. Thus, we begin this chapter by demonstrating how properly functioning markets efficiently allocate resources. We then explore what happens when markets don't function properly. In some circumstances, economically desirable goods are not produced at all. In other situations, they are either overproduced or underproduced. This chapter focuses on these situations, which economists refer to as **market failures.**

In such situations, an economic role for government may arise. We will examine that role as it relates to public goods and so-called externalities—situations where market failures lead to suboptimal outcomes that the government may be able to improve upon by using its powers to tax, spend, and regulate. The government may, for instance, pay for the production of goods that the private sector fails to produce. It may also act to reduce the production of those goods and services that the private sector overproduces. Implementing such policies can, however, be both costly and complicated. Thus, we conclude the chapter by noting the government inefficiencies that can hinder government's efforts to improve economic outcomes.

Market Failures in Competitive Markets[1]

In Chapter 3 we asserted that "competitive markets usually produce an assignment of resources that is 'right' from an economic perspective." We now want to focus on the word "usually" and discuss exceptions. We must do this because it is unfortunately the case that the presence of robust competition involving many buyers and many sellers may not, by itself, be enough to guarantee that a market will allocate resources correctly. Market failures sometimes happen in competitive markets. The focus of this chapter is to explain how and why such market failures can arise.

Fortunately, the broad picture is simple. Market failures in competitive markets fall into just two categories:

- **Demand-side market failures** happen when demand curves do not reflect consumers' full willingness to pay for a good or service.
- **Supply-side market failures** occur when supply curves do not reflect the full cost of producing a good or service.

Demand-Side Market Failures

Demand-side market failures arise because it is impossible in certain cases to charge consumers what they are willing to pay for a product. Consider outdoor fireworks displays. People enjoy fireworks and would therefore be *willing* to pay to see a fireworks display if the only way to see it was to have to pay for the right to do so. But because such displays are outdoors and in public, people don't actually *have* to pay to see the display because there is no way to exclude those who haven't paid from also enjoying the show. Private firms will therefore be unwilling to produce outdoor fireworks displays, as it will be nearly impossible for them to raise enough revenue to cover production costs.

---

[1]Other market failures arise when there are not enough buyers or sellers to ensure competition. In those situations, the lack of competition allows either buyers or sellers to restrict purchases or sales below optimal levels for their own benefit. As an example, a monopoly—a firm that is the only producer in its industry—can restrict the amount of output that it supplies in order to drive up the market price and thereby increase its own profit.

Supply-Side Market Failures

Supply-side market failures arise in situations in which a firm does not have to pay the full cost of producing its output. Consider a coal-burning power plant. The firm running the plant will have to pay for all of the land, labor, capital, and entrepreneurship that it uses to generate electricity by burning coal. But if the firm is not charged for the smoke that it releases into the atmosphere, it will fail to pay another set of costs—the costs that its pollution imposes on other people. These include future harm from global warming, toxins that affect wildlife, and possible damage to agricultural crops downwind.

A market failure arises because it is not possible for the market to correctly weigh costs and benefits in a situation in which some of the costs are completely unaccounted for. The coal-burning power plant produces more electricity and generates more pollution than it would if it had to pay for each ton of smoke that it released into the atmosphere. The extra units that are produced are units of output for which the costs are *greater than* the benefits. Obviously, these units should not be produced.

Efficiently Functioning Markets

The best way to understand market failure is to first understand how properly functioning competitive markets achieve economic efficiency. We touched on this subject in Chapter 3, but we now want to expand and deepen that analysis, both for its own sake and to set up our discussion of public goods and externalities. Two conditions must hold if a competitive market is to produce efficient outcomes: The demand curve in the market must reflect consumers' full willingness to pay, and the supply curve in the market must reflect all the costs of production. If these conditions hold, then the market will produce only units for which benefits are at least equal to costs. It will also maximize the amount of "benefits surpluses" that are shared between consumers and producers.

Consumer Surplus

The benefit surplus received by a consumer or consumers in a market is called **consumer surplus.** It is defined as the difference between the maximum price a consumer is (or consumers are) willing to pay for a product and the actual price that they do pay.

93

The maximum price that a person is willing to pay for a unit of a product depends on the opportunity cost of that person's consumption alternatives. Suppose that Ted is offered the chance to purchase an apple. He would of course like to have it for free, but the maximum amount he would be willing to pay depends on the alternative uses to which he can put his money. If his maximum willingness to pay for that particular apple is $1.25, then we know that he is willing to forgo up to—but not more than—$1.25 of other goods and services. Paying even once cent more would entail having to give up too much of other goods and services.

It also means that if Ted is charged any market price less than $1.25, he will receive a consumer surplus equal to the difference between the $1.25 maximum price that he would have been willing to pay and the lower market price. For instance, if the market price is $.50 per apple, Ted will receive a consumer surplus of $.75 per apple (= $1.25 − $.50). In nearly all markets, consumers individually and collectively gain greater total utility or satisfaction in dollar terms from their purchases than the amount of their expenditures (= product price × quantity). This utility surplus arises because each consumer who buys the product only has to pay the equilibrium price even though many of them would have been willing to pay more than the equilibrium price to obtain the product.

The concept of maximum willingness to pay also gives us another way to understand demand curves. Consider Table 5.1, where the first two columns show the maximum amounts that six consumers would each be willing to pay for a bag of oranges. Bob, for instance, would be willing to pay a maximum of $13 for a bag of oranges. Betty, by contrast, would only be willing to pay a maximum of $8 for a bag of oranges.

Notice that the maximum prices that these individuals are willing to pay represent points on a demand curve because the lower the market price, the more bags of oranges will be demanded. At a price of $12.50, for instance, Bob will be the only person listed in the table who will purchase a

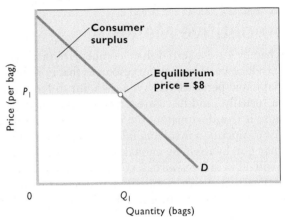

FIGURE 5.1 **Consumer surplus.** Consumer surplus— shown as the green triangle—is differences between the maximum prices consumers are willing to pay for a product and the lower equilibrium price, here assumed to be $8. For quantity Q_1, consumers are willing to pay the sum of the amounts represented by the green triangle and the yellow rectangle. Because they need to pay only the amount shown as the yellow rectangle, the green triangle shows consumer surplus.

bag. But at a price of $11.50, both Bob and Barb will want to purchase a bag. And at a price of $10.50, Bob, Barb, and Bill will each want to purchase a bag. The lower the price, the greater the total quantity demanded as the market price falls below the maximum prices of more and more consumers.

Lower prices also imply larger consumer surpluses. When the price is $12.50, Bob only gets $.50 in consumer surplus because his maximum willingness to pay of $13 is only $.50 higher than the market price of $12.50. But if the market price were to fall to $8, then his consumer surplus would be $5 (= $13 − $8). The third and fourth columns of Table 5.1 show how much consumer surplus each of our six consumers will receive if the market price of a bag of oranges is $8. Only Betty receives no consumer surplus, because her maximum willingness to pay exactly matches the $8 equilibrium price.

It is easy to show on a graph both the individual consumer surplus received by each particular buyer in a market as well as the collective consumer surplus received by all buyers. Consider Figure 5.1, which shows the market equilibrium price P_1 = $8 as well as the downsloping demand curve D for bags of oranges. Demand curve D includes not only the six consumers named in Table 5.1 but also every other consumer of oranges in the market. The individual consumer surplus of each particular person who is willing to buy at the $8 market price is simply the vertical distance from the horizontal line that marks the $8 market price up to that particular buyer's maximum willingness to pay. The collective consumer surplus obtained by all of our named and unnamed buyers is found

TABLE 5.1 Consumer Surplus

(1) Person	(2) Maximum Price Willing to Pay	(3) Actual Price (Equilibrium Price)	(4) Consumer Surplus
Bob	$13	$8	$5 (= $13 − $8)
Barb	12	8	4 (= $12 − $8)
Bill	11	8	3 (= $11 − $8)
Bart	10	8	2 (= $10 − $8)
Brent	9	8	1 (= $9 − $8)
Betty	8	8	0 (= $8 − $8)

by adding together each of their individual consumer surpluses. To obtain the Q_1 bags of oranges represented, consumers collectively are willing to pay the total amount shown by the sum of the green triangle and yellow rectangle under the demand curve and to the left of Q_1. But consumers need pay only the amount represented by the yellow rectangle ($= P_1 \times Q_1$). So the green triangle is the consumer surplus in this market. It is the sum of the vertical distances between the demand curve and the $8 equilibrium price at each quantity up to Q_1. Alternatively, it is the sum of the gaps between maximum willingness to pay and actual price, such as those we calculated in Table 5.1. Thus, consumer surplus can also be defined as the area that lies below the demand curve and above the price line that extends horizontally from P_1.

Consumer surplus and price are inversely (negatively) related. Given the demand curve, higher prices reduce consumer surplus; lower prices increase it. To test this generalization, draw in an equilibrium price above $8 in Figure 5.1 and observe the reduced size of the triangle representing consumer surplus. When price goes up, the gap narrows between the maximum willingness to pay and the actual price. Next, draw in an equilibrium price below $8 and see that consumer surplus increases. When price declines, the gap widens between maximum willingness to pay and actual price.

ORIGIN OF THE IDEA

O 5.1

Consumer surplus

Producer Surplus

Like consumers, producers also receive a benefit surplus in markets. This **producer surplus** is the difference between the actual price a producer receives (or producers receive) and the minimum acceptable price that a consumer would have to pay the producer to make a particular unit of output available.

A producer's minimum acceptable price for a particular unit will equal the producer's marginal cost of producing that particular unit. That marginal cost will be the sum of the rent, wages, interest, and profit that the producer will need to pay in order to obtain the land, labor, capital, and entrepreneurship required to produce that particular unit. In this section, we are assuming that the marginal cost of producing a unit will include *all* of the costs of production. Unlike the coal-burning power plant mentioned previously, the producer must pay for all of its costs, including the cost of pollution. In later sections, we will explore the market failures that arise in situations where firms do not have to pay all their costs.

In addition to equaling marginal cost, a producer's minimum acceptable price can also be interpreted as the opportunity cost of bidding resources away from the production of other products. To see why this is true, suppose that Leah is an apple grower. The resources necessary for her to produce one apple could be used to produce other things. To get them directed toward producing an apple, it is necessary to pay Leah what it will cost her to bid the necessary resources away from other entrepreneurs who would like to use them to produce other products. Leah would, naturally, like to get paid as much as possible to produce the apple for you. But her minimum acceptable price is the lowest price you could pay her such that she can just break even after bidding away from other uses the land, labor, capital, and entrepreneurship necessary to produce the apple.

The size of the producer surplus earned on any particular unit will be the difference between the market price that the producer actually receives and the producer's minimum acceptable price. Consider Table 5.2, which shows the minimum acceptable prices of six different orange growers. With a market price of $8, Carlos, for instance, has a producer surplus of $5, which is equal to the market price of $8 minus his minimum acceptable price of $3. Chad, by contrast, receives no producer surplus, because his minimum acceptable price of $8 just equals the market equilibrium price of $8.

Carlos's minimum acceptable price is lower than Chad's minimum acceptable price because Carlos is a more efficient producer than Chad, by which we mean that Carlos produces oranges using a less-costly combination of resources than Chad uses. The differences in efficiency between Carlos and Chad are likely due to differences in the type and quality of resources available to them. Carlos, for instance, may own land perfectly suited to growing oranges, while Chad has land in the desert that requires costly irrigation if it is to be used to grow oranges. Thus, Chad has a higher marginal cost of producing oranges.

TABLE 5.2 Producer Surplus

(1) Person	(2) Minimum Acceptable Price	(3) Actual Price (Equilibrium Price)	(4) Producer Surplus
Carlos	$3	$8	$5 (= $8 − $3)
Courtney	4	8	4 (= $8 − $4)
Chuck	5	8	3 (= $8 − $5)
Cindy	6	8	2 (= $8 − $6)
Craig	7	8	1 (= $8 − $7)
Chad	8	8	0 (= $8 − $8)

FIGURE 5.2 Producer surplus. Producer surplus—shown as the blue triangle—is the differences between the actual price producers receive for a product (here $8) and the lower minimum payments they are willing to accept. For quantity Q_1, producers receive the sum of the amounts represented by the blue triangle plus the yellow area. Because they need receive only the amount shown by the yellow area to produce Q_1, the blue triangle represents producer surplus.

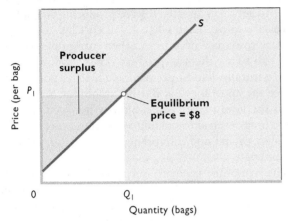

The minimum acceptable prices that producers are willing to accept form points on a supply curve, because the higher the price, the more bags of oranges will be supplied. At a price of $3.50, for instance, only Carlos would be willing to supply a bag of oranges. But at a price of $5.50, Carlos, Courtney, and Chuck would all be willing to supply a bag of oranges. The higher the market price, the more oranges will be supplied, as the market price surpasses the marginal costs and minimum acceptable prices of more and more producers. Thus, supply curves shown in this competitive market are both marginal-cost curves and minimum-acceptable-price curves.

The supply curve in Figure 5.2 includes not only the six producers named in Table 5.2 but also every other producer of oranges in the market. At the market price of $8 per bag, Q_1 bags are produced, because only those producers whose minimum acceptable prices are less than $8 per bag will choose to produce oranges with their resources. Those lower acceptable prices for each of the units up to Q_1 are shown by the portion of the supply curve lying to the left of and below the assumed $8 market price.

The individual producer surplus of each of these sellers is thus the vertical distance from each seller's respective minimum acceptable price on the supply curve up to the $8 market price. Their collective producer surplus is shown by the blue triangle in Figure 5.2. In that figure, producers collect revenues of $P_1 \times Q_1$, which is the sum of the blue triangle and the yellow area. As shown by the supply curve, however, revenues of only those illustrated by the yellow area would be required to entice producers to

offer Q_1 bags of oranges for sale. The sellers therefore receive a producer surplus shown by the blue triangle. That surplus is the sum of the vertical distances between the supply curve and the $8 equilibrium price at each of the quantities to the left of Q_1.

There is a direct (positive) relationship between equilibrium price and the amount of producer surplus. Given the supply curve, lower prices reduce producer surplus; higher prices increase it. If you pencil in a lower equilibrium price than $8, you will see that the producer surplus triangle gets smaller. The gaps between the minimum acceptable payments and the actual prices narrow when the price falls. If you pencil in an equilibrium price above $8, the size of the producer surplus triangle increases. The gaps between minimum acceptable payments and actual prices widen when the price increases.

WORKED PROBLEMS

W 5.1

Consumer and producer surplus

Efficiency Revisited

In Figure 5.3 we bring together the demand and supply curves of Figures 5.1 and 5.2 to show the equilibrium price and quantity and the previously described regions of consumer and producer surplus. All markets that have downsloping demand curves and upsloping supply curves yield consumer and producer surplus.

Because we are assuming in Figure 5.3 that the demand curve reflects buyers' full willingness to pay and the supply curve reflects all of the costs facing sellers, the

FIGURE 5.3 Efficiency: maximum combined consumer and producer surplus. At quantity Q_1 the combined amount of consumer surplus, shown as the green triangle, and producer surplus, shown as the blue triangle, is maximized. Efficiency occurs because, at Q_1, maximum willingness to pay, indicated by the points on the demand curve, equals minimum acceptable price, shown by the points on the supply curve.

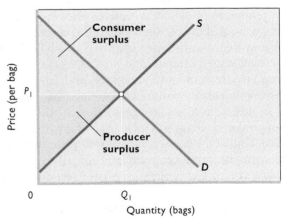

equilibrium quantity in Figure 5.3 reflects economic efficiency, which consists of productive efficiency and allocative efficiency.

- **Productive efficiency** is achieved because competition forces orange growers to use the best technologies and combinations of resources available. Doing so minimizes the per-unit cost of the output produced.
- **Allocative efficiency** is achieved because the correct quantity of oranges—Q_1—is produced relative to other goods and services.

There are two ways to understand why Q_1 is the correct quantity of oranges. Both involve realizing that any resources directed toward the production of oranges are resources that could have been used to produce other products. Thus, the only way to justify taking any amount of any resource (land, labor, capital, entrepreneurship) away from the production of other products is if it brings more utility or satisfaction when devoted to the production of oranges than it would if it were used to produce other products.

The first way to see why Q_1 is the allocatively efficient quantity of oranges is to note that demand and supply curves can be interpreted as measuring marginal benefit (MB) and marginal cost (MC). Recall from the discussion relating to Figure 1.3 that optimal allocation is achieved at the output level where MB = MC. We have already seen that supply curves are marginal cost curves. As it turns out, demand curves are marginal benefit curves. This is true because the maximum price that a consumer would be willing to pay for any particular unit is equal to the benefit that she would get if she were to consume that unit. Thus, each point on a demand curve represents both some consumer's maximum willingness to pay as well as the marginal benefit that he or she would get from consuming the particular unit in question.

Combining the fact that supply curves are MC curves with the fact that demand curves are MB curves, we see that points on the demand curve in Figure 5.3 measure the marginal benefit of oranges at each level of output, while points on the supply curve measure the marginal cost of oranges at each level of output. As a result, MB = MC where the demand and supply curves intersect—which means that the equilibrium quantity Q_1 must be allocatively efficient.

To gain a deeper understanding of why Q_1 is allocatively efficient, notice that for every unit up to Q_1 marginal benefit exceeds marginal cost (MB > MC). And because marginal cost includes the opportunity cost of not making other things with the resources needed to make these units, we know that people are made better off when the resources necessary to make these units are allocated to producing oranges rather than to producing anything else.

The second way to see why Q_1 is the correct quantity of oranges is based on our analysis of consumer and producer surplus and the fact that we can interpret demand and supply curves in terms of maximum willingness to pay and minimum acceptable price. In Figure 5.3, the maximum willingness to pay on the demand curve for each bag of oranges up to Q_1 exceeds the corresponding minimum acceptable price on the supply curve. Thus, each of these bags adds a positive amount (= maximum willingness to pay *minus* minimum acceptable price) to the *total* of consumer and producer surplus.

The fact that maximum willingness to pay exceeds minimum acceptable price for every unit up to Q_1 means that people gain more utility from producing and consuming those units than they would if they produced and consumed anything else that could be made with the resources that went into making those units. This is true because both the maximum willingness to pay and the minimum acceptable price take opportunity costs into account. As long as the maximum willingness to pay exceeds the minimum acceptable price, people are willing to pay more to consume a unit of the good in question (here, bags of oranges) than they would pay to consume anything else that could be made with the same resources. Only at the equilibrium quantity Q_1—where the maximum willingness to pay exactly equals the minimum acceptable price—does society exhaust all opportunities to produce units for which benefits exceed costs (including opportunity costs). Producing Q_1 units therefore achieves allocative efficiency because the market is producing and distributing only those units that make people happier with bags of oranges than they would be with anything else that could be produced with the same resources.

Geometrically, producing Q_1 units maximizes the combined area of consumer and producer surplus in Figure 5.3. In this context, the combined area is referred to as *total surplus*. Thus, when Q_1 units are produced, total surplus is equal to the large triangle formed by the green consumer-surplus triangle and the blue producer-surplus triangle.

When demand curves reflect buyers' full willingness to pay and when supply curves reflect all the costs facing sellers, competitive markets produce equilibrium quantities that maximize the sum of consumer and producer surplus. Allocative efficiency occurs at the market equilibrium quantity where three conditions exist simultaneously:

- MB = MC (Figure 1.3).
- Maximum willingness to pay = minimum acceptable price.
- Total surplus (= sum of consumer and producer surplus) is at a maximum.

Economists are enamored of markets because properly functioning markets automatically achieve allocative efficiency. Other methods of allocating resources—such as government central planning—do exist. But because other methods cannot do any better than properly functioning markets—and may in many cases do much worse—economists usually prefer that resources be allocated through markets whenever properly functioning markets are available.

Efficiency Losses (or Deadweight Losses)

Figures 5.4a and 5.4b demonstrate that **efficiency losses**—reductions of combined consumer and producer surplus—result from both underproduction and overproduction. First, consider Figure 5.4a, which analyzes the case of underproduction by considering what happens if output

falls from the efficient level Q_1 to the smaller amount Q_2. When that happens, the sum of consumer and producer surplus, previously *abc*, falls to *adec*. So the combined consumer and producer surplus declines by the amount of the gray triangle to the left of Q_1. That triangle represents an efficiency loss to buyers and sellers. And because buyers and sellers are members of society, it represents an efficiency loss (or a so-called **deadweight loss**) to society.

For output levels from Q_2 to Q_1, consumers' maximum willingness to pay (as reflected by points on the demand curve) exceeds producers' minimum acceptable price (as reflected by points on the supply curve). By failing to produce units of this product for which a consumer is willing to pay more than a producer is willing to accept, society suffers a loss of net benefits. As a concrete example, consider a particular unit for which a consumer is willing to pay $10 and a producer is willing to accept $6. The $4 difference between those values is a net benefit that will not be realized if this unit is not produced. In addition, the resources that should have gone to producing this unit will go instead to producing other products that will not generate as much utility as if those resources had been used here to produce this unit of this product. The triangle *dbe* in Figure 5.4a shows the total loss of net benefits that results from failing to produce the units from Q_2 to Q_1.

In contrast, consider the case of overproduction shown in Figure 5.4b, in which the number of oranges produced is Q_3 rather than the efficient level Q_1. In Figure 5.4b the combined consumer and producer surplus therefore declines by *bfg*—the gray triangle to the right of Q_1. This triangle subtracts from the total consumer and producer surplus of *abc* that would occur if the quantity had been Q_1. That is, for all units from 0 to Q_1, benefits exceed costs, so that those units generate the economic surplus shown by triangle *abc*. But the units from Q_1 to Q_3 are such that costs exceed benefits. Thus, they generate an economic loss shown by triangle *bfg*. The total economic surplus for all units from 0 to Q_3 is therefore the economic surplus given by *abc* for the units from 0 to Q_1 *minus* the economic loss given by *bfg* for the units from Q_1 to Q_3.

Producing any unit beyond Q_1 generates an economic loss, because the willingness to pay for such units on the part of consumers is less than the minimum acceptable price to produce such units on the part of producers. As a concrete example, note that producing an item for which the maximum willingness to pay is, say, $7 and the minimum acceptable price is, say, $10 subtracts $3 from society's net benefits. Such production is uneconomical and creates an efficiency loss (or deadweight loss) for society. Because the net benefit of each bag of oranges from Q_1 to Q_3 is negative, we know that the benefits from these units

FIGURE 5.4 Efficiency losses (or deadweight losses). Quantity levels either less than or greater than the efficient quantity Q_1 create efficiency losses. In (a), triangle *dbe* shows the efficiency loss associated with underproduction at output Q_2. Triangle *bfg* in (b) illustrates the efficiency loss associated with overproduction at output level Q_3.

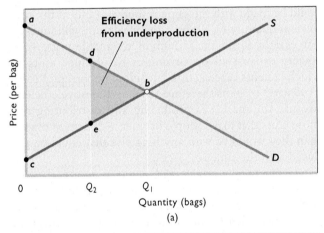

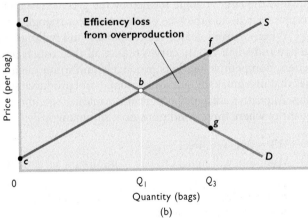

are smaller than the opportunity costs of the other products that could have been produced with the resources that were used to produce these bags of oranges. The resources used to produce the bags from Q_1 to Q_3 could have generated net benefits instead of net losses if they had been directed toward producing other products. The gray triangle *bfg* to the right of Q_1 in Figure 5.4b shows the total efficiency loss from overproduction at Q_3.

The magic of markets is that when demand reflects consumers' full willingness to pay and when supply reflects all costs, the market equilibrium quantity will automatically equal the allocatively efficient output level. Under these conditions, the market equilibrium quantity will ensure that there are neither efficiency losses from underproduction nor efficiency losses from overproduction. As we are about to see, however, such losses do happen when either demand does not reflect consumers' full willingness to pay or supply does not reflect all costs.

QUICK REVIEW 5.1

- Market failures in competitive markets have two possible causes: demand curves that do not reflect consumers' full willingness to pay, and supply curves that do not reflect producers' full cost of production.
- Consumer surplus is the difference between the maximum price that a consumer is willing to pay for a product and the lower price actually paid.
- Producer surplus is the difference between the minimum price that a producer is willing to accept for a product and the higher price actually received.
- At the equilibrium price and quantity in competitive markets, marginal benefit equals marginal cost, maximum willingness to pay equals minimum acceptable price, and the total of consumer surplus and producer surplus is maximized. Each of these conditions defines allocative efficiency.
- Quantities less than or greater than the allocatively efficient level of output create efficiency losses, often called deadweight losses.

Public Goods

Demand-side market failures arise in competitive markets when demand curves fail to reflect consumers' full willingness to pay for a good or service. In such situations, markets fail to produce all of the units for which there are net benefits, because demand curves underreport how much consumers are willing and able to pay. This underreporting problem reaches its most extreme form in the case of a public good: Markets may fail to produce *any* of the public good, because its demand curve may reflect *none* of its consumers' willingness to pay.

To understand public goods, we first need to understand the characteristics that define private goods.

Private Goods Characteristics

We have seen that the market system produces a wide range of **private goods.** These are the goods offered for sale in stores, in shops, and on the Internet. Examples include automobiles, clothing, personal computers, household appliances, and sporting goods. Private goods are distinguished by rivalry and excludability.

- **Rivalry** (in consumption) means that when one person buys and consumes a product, it is not available for another person to buy and consume. When Adams purchases and drinks a bottle of mineral water, it is not available for Benson to purchase and consume.
- **Excludability** means that sellers can keep people who do not pay for a product from obtaining its benefits. Only people who are willing and able to pay the market price for bottles of water can obtain these drinks and the benefits they confer.

Consumers fully express their personal demands for private goods in the market. If Adams likes bottled mineral water, that fact will be known by her desire to purchase the product. Other things equal, the higher the price of bottled water, the fewer bottles she will buy. So Adams's demand for bottled water will reflect an inverse relationship between the price of bottled water and the quantity of it demanded. This is simply *individual* demand, as described in Chapter 3.

The *market* demand for a private good is the horizontal summation of the individual demand schedules (review Figure 3.2). Suppose just two consumers comprise the market for bottled water and the price is $1 per bottle. If Adams will purchase 3 bottles and Benson will buy 2, the market demand will reflect consumers' demand for 5 bottles at the $1 price. Similar summations of quantities demanded at other prices will generate the market demand schedule and curve.

Suppose the equilibrium price of bottled water is $1. Adams and Benson will buy a total of 5 bottles, and the sellers will obtain total revenue of $5 (= $1 × 5). If the sellers' cost per bottle is $.80, their total cost will be $4 (= $.80 × 5). So sellers charging $1 per bottle will obtain $5 of total revenue, incur $4 of total cost, and earn $1 of profit on the 5 bottles sold.

Because firms can profitably "tap market demand" for private goods, they will produce and offer them for sale. Consumers demand private goods, and profit-seeking suppliers produce goods that satisfy the demand. Consumers willing to pay the market price obtain the goods; nonpayers go without. A competitive market not only makes private goods available to consumers but also allocates society's resources efficiently to the particular product. There is neither underproduction nor overproduction of the product.

Public Goods Characteristics

Public goods have the opposite characteristics of private goods. Public goods are distinguished by nonrivalry and nonexcludability.

- **Nonrivalry** (in consumption) means that one person's consumption of a good does not preclude consumption of the good by others. Everyone can simultaneously obtain the benefit from a public good such as national defense, street lighting, a global positioning system, or environmental protection.

- **Nonexcludability** means there is no effective way of excluding individuals from the benefit of the good once it comes into existence. Once in place, you cannot exclude someone from benefiting from national defense, street lighting, a global positioning system, or environmental protection.

These two characteristics create a **free-rider problem.** Once a producer has provided a public good, everyone, including nonpayers, can obtain the benefit.

Because most people do not voluntarily pay for something that they can obtain for free, most people become free riders. These free riders like the public good and would be willing to pay for it if producers could somehow force them to pay—but nonexcludability means that there is no way for producers to withhold the good from the free riders without also denying it to the few who do pay. As a result, free riding means that the willingness to pay of the free riders is not expressed in the market. From the viewpoint of producers, free riding reduces demand. The more free riding, the less demand. And if all consumers free ride, demand will collapse all the way to zero.

The low or even zero demand caused by free riding makes it virtually impossible for private firms to profitably provide public goods. With little or no demand, firms cannot effectively "tap market demand" for revenues and profits. As a result, they will not produce public goods. Society will therefore suffer efficiency losses because goods for which marginal benefits exceed marginal costs are not produced. Thus, if society wants a public good to be produced, it will have to direct government to provide it. Because the public good will still feature nonexcludability, the government won't have any better luck preventing free riding or charging people for it. But because the government can finance the provision of the public good through the taxation of other things, the government does not have to worry about profitability. It can therefore provide the public good even when private firms can't.

Street Entertainers

Street entertainers are often found in tourist areas of major cities. These entertainers illuminate the concepts of free riders and public goods.

Most street entertainers have a hard time earning a living from their activities (unless event organizers pay them) because they have no way of excluding nonpayers from the benefits of their entertainment. They essentially are providing public, not private, goods and must rely on voluntary payments.

The result is a significant free-rider problem. Only a few in the audience put money in the container or instrument case, and many who do so contribute only token amounts. The rest are free riders who obtain the benefits of the street entertainment and retain their money for purchases that they initiate.

Street entertainers are acutely aware of the free-rider problem, and some have found creative ways to lessen it. For example, some entertainers involve the audience directly in the act. This usually creates a greater sense of audience willingness (or obligation) to contribute money at the end of the performance.

"Pay for performance" is another creative approach to lessening the free-rider problem. A good example is the street entertainer painted up to look like a statue. When people drop coins into the container, the "statue" makes a slight movement. The greater the contributions, the greater the movement. But these human "statues" still face a free-rider problem: Nonpayers also get to enjoy the acts.

Examples of public goods include national defense, outdoor fireworks displays, the light beams thrown out by lighthouses, public art displays, public music concerts, MP3 music files posted to file-sharing Web sites, and ideas and inventions that are not protected by patents or copyrights. Each of these goods or services shows both nonrivalry and nonexcludability.

In a few special cases, private firms can provide public goods because the production costs of these public goods can be covered by the profits generated by closely related private goods. For instance, private companies can make a profit providing broadcast TV—which is a nonrival, nonexcludable public good—because they control who gets to air TV commercials, which are rival and excludable private goods. The money that broadcasters make from selling air time for ads allows them to turn a profit despite having to give their main product, broadcast TV, away for free.

Unfortunately, only a few public goods can be subsidized in this way by closely related private goods. For the large majority of public goods, private provision is unprofitable. As a result, there are only two remaining ways for a public good to be provided: private philanthropy or government provision. For many less expensive or less important public goods like fireworks displays or public art, society may feel comfortable relying on private philanthropy. But when it comes to public goods like national defense, people normally look to the government.

This leads to an important question: Once a government decides to produce a particular public good, how can it determine the optimal amount that it should produce? How can it avoid either underallocating or overallocating society's scarce resources to the production of the public good?

Optimal Quantity of a Public Good

If consumers need not reveal their true demand for a public good in the marketplace, how can society determine the optimal amount of that good? The answer is that the government has to try to estimate the demand for a public good through surveys or public votes. It can then compare the marginal benefit (MB) of an added unit of the good against the government's marginal cost (MC) of providing it. Adhering to the MB = MC rule, government can provide the "right," meaning "efficient," amount of the public good.

Demand for Public Goods

The demand for a public good is somewhat unusual. Suppose Adams and Benson are the only two people in the society, and their marginal willingness to pay for a public good, national defense, is as shown in columns 1 and 2 and columns 1 and 3 in Table 5.3. Economists might have discovered these schedules through a survey asking hypothetical questions about how much each citizen was willing to pay for various types and amounts of public goods rather than go without them.

Notice that the schedules in Table 5.3 are price-quantity schedules, implying that they are demand schedules. Rather than depicting demand in the usual way—the quantity of a product someone is willing to buy at each possible price—these schedules show the price someone is willing to pay for the extra unit of each possible quantity. That is, Adams is willing to pay $4 for the first unit of the public good, $3 for the second, $2 for the third, and so on.

Suppose the government produces 1 unit of this public good. Because of nonrivalry, Adams's consumption of the good does not preclude Benson from also consuming it, and vice versa. So both consume the good, and neither volunteers to pay for it. But from Table 5.3 we can find the

CONSIDER THIS . . .

Art for Art's Sake

Suppose an enterprising sculptor creates a piece of art costing $600 and, with permission, places it in the town square. Also suppose that Jack gets $300 of enjoyment from the art and Diane gets $400. Sensing this enjoyment and hoping to make a profit, the sculptor approaches Jack for a donation equal to his satisfaction. Jack falsely says that, unfortunately, he does not particularly like the piece. The sculptor then tries Diane, hoping to get $400 or so. Same deal: Diane professes not to like the piece either. Jack and Diane have become free riders. Although feeling a bit guilty, both reason that it makes no sense to pay for something when anyone can receive the benefits without paying for them. The artist is a quick learner; he vows never to try anything like that again.

amount these two people would be willing to pay, together, rather than do without this 1 unit of the good. Columns 1 and 2 show that Adams would be willing to pay $4 for the first unit of the public good; columns 1 and 3 show that Benson would be willing to pay $5 for it. So the two people are jointly willing to pay $9 (= $4 + $5) for this first unit.

For the second unit of the public good, the collective price they are willing to pay is $7 (= $3 from Adams + $4 from Benson); for the third unit they would pay $5 (= $2 + $3); and so on. By finding the collective willingness to pay for each additional unit (column 4), we can construct a collective demand schedule (a willingness-to-pay schedule) for the public good. Here we are *not* adding the quantities demanded at each possible price, as we do when we determine the market demand for a private good. Instead, we are

TABLE 5.3 Demand for a Public Good, Two Individuals

(1) Quantity of Public Good	(2) Adams's Willingness to Pay (Price)		(3) Benson's Willingness to Pay (Price)		(4) Collective Willingness to Pay (Price)
1	$4	+	$5	=	$9
2	3	+	4	=	7
3	2	+	3	=	5
4	1	+	2	=	3
5	0	+	1	=	1

FIGURE 5.5 The optimal amount of a public good.
The collective demand curve for a public good, as shown by D_c in (c), is found by summing vertically the individual willingness-to-pay curves D_1 in (a) and D_2 in (b) of Adams and Benson, the only two people in the economy. The supply curve of the public good represented in (c) slopes upward and to the right, reflecting rising marginal costs. The optimal amount of the public good is 3 units, determined by the intersection of D_c and S. At that output, marginal benefit (reflected in the collective demand curve D_c) equals marginal cost (reflected in the supply curve S).

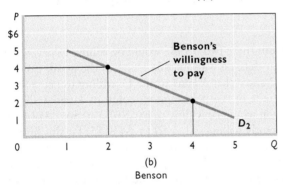

(c)
Collective demand and supply

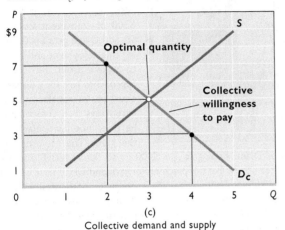

(b)
Benson

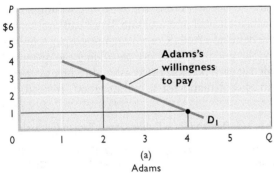

(a)
Adams

adding the prices that people are willing to pay for the last unit of the public good at each possible quantity demanded.

Figure 5.5 shows the same adding procedure graphically, using the data from Table 5.3. Note that we sum Adams's and Benson's willingness-to-pay curves *vertically* to derive the collective willingness-to-pay curve (demand curve). The summing procedure is upward from the lower graph to the middle graph to the top (total) graph. For example, the height of the collective demand curve D_c at 2 units of output in the top graph is $7, the sum of the amounts that Adams and Benson are each willing to pay for the second unit (= $3 + $4). Likewise, the height of the collective demand curve at 4 units of the public good is $3 (= $1 + $2).

What does it mean in Figure 5.5a that, for example, Adams is willing to pay $3 for the second unit of the public good? It means that Adams expects to receive $3 of extra benefit or utility from that unit. And we know from our discussion of diminishing marginal utility in Chapter 3 that successive units of any good yield less and less added benefit. This is also true for public goods, explaining the downward slope of the willingness-to-pay curves of Adams, Benson, and society. These curves, in essence, are marginal-benefit (MB) curves.

Comparing MB and MC

We can now determine the optimal quantity of the public good. The collective demand curve D_c in Figure 5.5c mea-

> **WORKED PROBLEMS**
>
> **W 5.2**
>
> Optimal amount of a public good

sures society's marginal benefit of each unit of this particular good. The supply curve S in that figure measures society's marginal cost of each unit. The optimal quantity of this public good occurs where marginal benefit equals marginal cost, or where the two curves intersect. In Figure 5.5c that point is 3 units of the public good, where the collective willingness to pay for the last (third) unit—the marginal benefit—just matches that unit's marginal cost ($5 = $5). As we saw in Chapter 1, equating marginal benefit and marginal cost efficiently allocates society's scarce resources.

Cost-Benefit Analysis

The above example suggests a practical means, called **cost-benefit analysis**, for deciding whether to provide a particular public good and how much of it to provide. Like our example, cost-benefit analysis (or marginal-benefit–marginal-cost analysis) involves a comparison of marginal costs and marginal benefits.

Concept Suppose the Federal government is contemplating a highway construction plan. Because the economy's resources are limited, any decision to use more resources in the public sector will mean fewer resources for the private sector. There will be an opportunity cost, as

TABLE 5.4 Cost-Benefit Analysis for a National Highway Construction Project (in Billions)

(1) Plan	(2) Total Cost of Project	(3) Marginal Cost	(4) Total Benefit	(5) Marginal Benefit	(6) Net Benefit (4) − (2)
No new construction	$ 0		$ 0		$ 0
		$ 4		$ 5	
A: Widen existing highways	4		5		1
		6		8	
B: New 2-lane highways	10		13		3
		8		10	
C: New 4-lane highways	18		23		5
		10		3	
D: New 6-lane highways	28		26		−2

well as a benefit. The cost is the loss of satisfaction resulting from the accompanying decline in the production of private goods; the benefit is the extra satisfaction resulting from the output of more public goods. Should the needed resources be shifted from the private to the public sector? The answer is yes if the benefit from the extra public goods exceeds the cost that results from having fewer private goods. The answer is no if the cost of the forgone private goods is greater than the benefit associated with the extra public goods.

Cost-benefit analysis, however, can indicate more than whether a public program is worth doing. It can also help the government decide on the *extent* to which a project should be pursued. Real economic questions cannot usually be answered simply by "yes" or "no" but, rather, involve questions such as "how much" or "how little."

Illustration Roads and highways can be run privately, as excludability is possible with toll gates. However, the Federal highway system is almost entirely nonexclusive, because anyone with a car can get on and off most Federal highways without restriction anytime they want. Federal highways therefore satisfy one characteristic of a public good, nonexcludability. The other characteristic, nonrivalry, is also satisfied by the fact that unless a highway is already extremely crowded, one person's driving on the highway does not preclude another person's driving on the highway. Thus, the Federal highway system is effectively a public good. This leads us to ask: Should the Federal government expand the Federal highway system? If so, what is the proper size or scope for the overall project?

Table 5.4 lists a series of increasingly ambitious and increasingly costly highway projects: widening existing two-lane highways; building new two-lane highways; building new four-lane highways; building new six-lane highways. The extent to which government should undertake highway construction depends on the costs and benefits. The costs are largely the costs of constructing and maintaining the highways; the benefits are improved flows of people and goods throughout the country.[2]

The table shows that total annual benefit (column 4) exceeds total annual cost (column 2) for plans A, B, and C, indicating that some highway construction is economically justifiable. We see this directly in column 6, where total costs (column 2) are subtracted from total annual benefits (column 4). Net benefits are positive for plans A, B, and C. Plan D is not economically justifiable because net benefits are negative.

But the question of optimal size or scope for this project remains. Comparing the marginal cost (the change in total cost) and the marginal benefit (the change in total benefit) relating to each plan determines the answer. The guideline is well known to you from previous discussions: Increase an activity, project, or output as long as the marginal benefit (column 5) exceeds the marginal cost (column 3). Stop the activity at, or as close as possible to, the point at which the marginal benefit equals the marginal cost. Do not undertake a project for which marginal cost exceeds marginal benefit.

In this case plan C (building new four-lane highways) is the best plan. Plans A and B are too modest; the marginal benefits exceed the marginal costs, and there is a better option. Plan D's marginal cost ($10 billion) exceeds the marginal benefit ($3 billion) and therefore cannot be justified; it overallocates resources to the project. Plan C is closest to the theoretical optimum because its marginal benefit ($10 billion) still exceeds marginal cost ($8 billion) but approaches the MB = MC (or MC = MB) ideal.

---

[2]Because the costs of public goods typically are immediate while the benefits often accrue over longer time periods, economists convert both costs and benefits to present values for comparison. Doing so properly accounts for the time-value of money, discussed in Chapters 14 and 15.

This **marginal-cost–marginal-benefit rule** actually tells us which plan provides the maximum excess of total benefits over total costs or, in other words, the plan that provides society with the maximum net benefit. You can confirm directly in column 6 that the maximum net benefit (= $5 billion) is associated with plan C.

Cost-benefit analysis shatters the myth that "economy in government" and "reduced government spending" are synonymous. "Economy" is concerned with using scarce resources efficiently. If the marginal cost of a proposed government program exceeds its marginal benefit, then the proposed public program should not be undertaken. But if the marginal benefit exceeds the marginal cost, then it would be uneconomical or "wasteful" not to spend on that government program. Economy in government does not mean minimization of public spending. It means allocating resources between the private and public sectors and among public goods to achieve maximum net benefit.

Quasi-Public Goods

Government provides many goods that fit the economist's definition of a public good. However, it also provides other goods and services that could be produced and delivered in such a way that exclusion would be possible. Such goods, called **quasi-public goods,** include education, streets and highways, police and fire protection, libraries and museums, preventive medicine, and sewage disposal. They could all be priced and provided by private firms through the market system. But, because the benefits of these goods flow well beyond the benefit to individual buyers, these goods would be underproduced by the market system. Therefore, government often provides them to avoid the underallocation of resources that would otherwise occur.

The Reallocation Process

How are resources reallocated from the production of private goods to the production of public and quasi-public goods? If the resources of the economy are fully employed, government must free up resources from the production of private goods and make them available for producing public and quasi-public goods. It does so by reducing private demand for them. And it does that by levying taxes on households and businesses, taking some of their income out of the circular flow. With lower incomes and hence less purchasing power, households and businesses must curtail their consumption and investment spending. As a result, the private demand for goods and services declines, as does the private demand for resources. So by diverting purchasing power from private spenders to government, taxes remove resources from private use.

Government then spends the tax proceeds to provide public and quasi-public goods and services. Taxation releases resources from the production of private consumer goods (food, clothing, television sets) and private investment goods (printing presses, boxcars, warehouses). Government shifts those resources to the production of public and quasi-public goods (post offices, submarines, parks), changing the composition of the economy's total output.

QUICK REVIEW 5.2

- Public goods are characterized by nonrivalry and nonexcludability.
- The demand (marginal-benefit) curve for a public good is found by vertically adding the prices that all the members of society are willing to pay for the last unit of output at various output levels.
- The socially optimal amount of a public good is the amount at which the marginal cost and marginal benefit of the good are equal.
- Cost-benefit analysis is the method of evaluating alternative projects or sizes of projects by comparing the marginal cost and marginal benefit and applying the MC = MB rule.
- The government uses taxes to reallocate resources from the production of private goods to the production of public and quasi-public goods.

Externalities

In addition to providing public goods, governments can also improve the allocation of resources in the economy by correcting for market failures caused by externalities. An **externality** occurs when some of the costs or the benefits of a good or service are passed onto or "spill over to" someone other than the immediate buyer or seller. Such spillovers are called externalities because they are benefits or costs that accrue to some third party that is external to the market transaction.

There are both positive and negative externalities. An example of a negative externality is the cost of breathing polluted air; an example of a positive externality is the benefit of having everyone else inoculated against some disease. When there are negative externalities, an overproduction of the related product occurs and there is an overallocation of resources to this product. Conversely, underproduction and underallocation of resources result when positive externalities are present.

Negative Externalities

Negative externalities cause supply-side market failures. These failures happen because producers do not take into account the costs that their negative externalities impose on others. This failure to account for all production costs causes firms' supply curves to shift to the right of (or below) where they would be if firms properly accounted for all costs. Consider the costs of breathing polluted air that are imposed on third parties living downwind of smoke-spewing factories. Because polluting firms do not take account of such costs, they oversupply the products they make, producing units for which total costs (including those that fall on third parties) exceed total benefits. The same is true when airlines fail to account for the costs that noisy jet engines impose on people living near airports and when biodiesel factories that convert dead animal parts into fuel release foul smelling gases that disgust those living nearby.

Figure 5.6a illustrates how negative externalities affect the allocation of resources. When producers shift some of their costs onto the community as external costs, producers' marginal costs are lower than they would be if they had to pay for those costs. So their supply curves do not include or "capture" all the costs legitimately associated with the production of their goods. A polluting producer's

> **INTERACTIVE GRAPHS**
> **G 5.1**
> Externalities

supply curve such as S in Figure 5.6a therefore understates the total cost of production. The firm's supply curve lies to the right of (or below) the total-cost supply curve S_t, which would include the spillover cost. Through polluting and thus transferring costs to society, the firm enjoys lower production costs and has the supply curve S.

The outcome is shown in Figure 5.6a, where equilibrium output Q_e is larger than the optimal output Q_o. This means that resources are overallocated to the production of this commodity; too many units of it are produced. In fact, there is a net loss to society for every unit from Q_o to Q_e because, for those units, the supply curve that accounts for all costs, S_t, lies above the demand curve. Therefore, MC exceeds MB for those units. The resources that went into producing those units should have been used elsewhere in the economy to produce other things.

In terms of our previous analysis, the negative externality results in an efficiency loss represented by triangle *abc*.

Positive Externalities

Positive externalities cause demand-side market failures. These failures happen because market demand curves in such cases fail to include the willingness to pay of the third parties who receive the external benefits caused by the positive externality. This failure to account for all benefits shifts market demand curves to the left of (or below) where they would be if they included all benefits and the willingness to pay of both the third parties as well as the primary beneficiaries. Because demand curves fail to take into account all benefits when there are positive externalities, markets in such cases fail to produce all units for which benefits (including those that are received by third parties) exceed costs. As a result, products featuring positive externalities are underproduced.

Vaccinations are a good example of how positive externalities reduce demand and shift demand curves down and to the left. When John gets vaccinated against a disease, he benefits not only himself (because he can no longer contract the disease) but also everyone else around him (because they know that in the future he will never be able to infect them). These other people would presumably be willing to pay some positive amount of money for the benefits they receive when John is vaccinated. But because his vaccination is a public good, there is no way to make them pay.

To see why his vaccination is a public good, note that the vaccination benefits that John provides to others feature nonrivalry and nonexcludability. There is nonrivalry

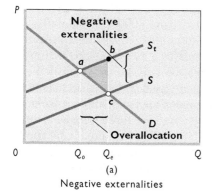

(a)
Negative externalities

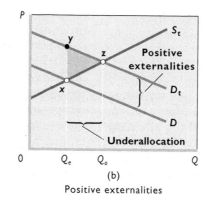

(b)
Positive externalities

FIGURE 5.6 **Negative externalities and positive externalities.** (a) With negative externalities borne by society, the producers' supply curve S is to the right of (below) the total-cost supply curve S_t. Consequently, the equilibrium output Q_e is greater than the optimal output Q_o, and the efficiency loss is *abc*. (b) When positive externalities accrue to society, the market demand curve D is to the left of (below) the total-benefit demand curve D_t. As a result, the equilibrium output Q_e is less than the optimal output Q_o, and the efficiency loss is *xyz*.

ORIGIN OF THE IDEA

O 5.2

Externalities

because the protection his vaccination provides to one person does not lessen the protection that it provides to other people. There is nonexcludability because once he is vaccinated, there is no way to exclude anyone in particular from benefiting from his vaccination. Thus, the market demand for vaccinations will only include John's personal willingness to pay for the benefits that he personally receives from the vaccination. The market demand will fail to include the benefits that others receive. As a result, demand will be too low and vaccinations will be underproduced.

Figure 5.6b shows the impact of positive externalities on resource allocation. When external benefits occur, the market demand curve D lies to the left of (or below) the total-benefits demand curve, D_t. That is, D does not include the external benefits of the product, whereas D_t does.

The outcome is that the equilibrium output Q_e is less than the optimal output Q_o. The market fails to produce enough vaccinations, and resources are underallocated to this product. The underproduction implies that society is missing out on a significant amount of potential net benefits. For every unit from Q_e to Q_o, the demand curve that accounts for all benefits, D_t, lies above the supply curve that accounts for all costs—including the opportunity cost of producing other items with the resources that would be needed to produce these units. Therefore, MB exceeds MC for each of these units, and we know that society should redeploy some of its resources away from the production of other things in order to produce these units that generate net benefits.

In terms of our previous analysis, the positive externality results in an efficiency loss represented by triangle xyz.

Government Intervention

Government intervention may be called upon to achieve economic efficiency when externalities affect large numbers of people or when community interests are at stake. Government can use direct controls and taxes to counter negative externalities; it may provide subsidies or public goods to deal with positive externalities.

Direct Controls The direct way to reduce negative externalities from a certain activity is to pass legislation limiting that activity. Such direct controls force the offending firms to incur the actual costs of the offending activity. Historically, direct controls in the form of uniform emission standards—limits on allowable pollution—have dominated American air pollution policy. For example, the Clean Air Act of 1990 (1) forced factories and businesses to install "maximum achievable control

CONSIDER THIS . . .

The Fable of the Bees

Economist Ronald Coase received the Nobel Prize for his so-called **Coase theorem,** which pointed out that under the right conditions, private individuals could often negotiate their own mutually agreeable solutions to externality problems through *private bargaining* without the need for government interventions like pollution taxes.

This is a very important insight because it means that we shouldn't automatically call for government intervention every time we see a potential externality problem. Consider the positive externalities that bees provide by pollinating farmers' crops. Should we assume that beekeeping will be underprovided unless the government intervenes with, for instance, subsidies to encourage more hives and hence more pollination?

As it turns out, no. Research has shown that farmers and beekeepers long ago used private bargaining to develop customs and payment systems that avoid free riding by farmers and encourage beekeepers to keep the optimal number of hives. Free riding is avoided by the custom that all farmers in an area simultaneously hire beekeepers to provide bees to pollinate their crops. And

ORIGIN OF THE IDEA

O 5.3

Coase theorem

farmers always pay the beekeepers for their pollination services because if they didn't, then no beekeeper would ever work with them in the future—a situation that would lead to massively reduced crop yields due to a lack of pollination.

The "Fable of the Bees" is a good reminder that it is a fallacy to assume that the government must always get involved to remedy externalities. In many cases, the private sector can solve both positive and negative externality problems on its own.

technology" to reduce emissions of 189 toxic chemicals by 90 percent between 1990 and 2000; (2) required a 30 to 60 percent reduction in tailpipe emissions from automobiles by 2000; (3) mandated a 50 percent reduction in the use of chlorofluorocarbons (CFCs), which deplete the ozone layer (CFCs were used widely as a coolant in refrigeration, a blowing agent for foam, and a solvent in the electronics industry); and (4) forced coal-burning utilities to cut their emissions of sulfur dioxide by about 50 percent to reduce the acid-rain destruction of lakes and forests. Clean-water legislation limits the amount of heavy metals, detergents, and other pollutants firms can discharge into rivers and bays. Toxic-waste laws dictate special

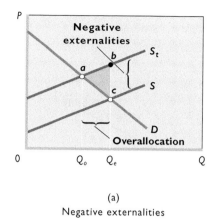

(a)
Negative externalities

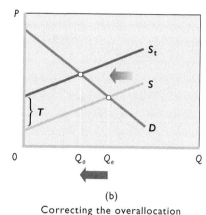

(b)
Correcting the overallocation
of resources via direct controls
or via a tax

FIGURE 5.7 Correcting for negative externalities. (a) Negative externalities result in an overallocation of resources. (b) Government can correct this overallocation in two ways: (1) using direct controls, which would shift the supply curve from S to S_t and reduce output from Q_e to Q_o, or (2) imposing a specific tax T, which would also shift the supply curve from S to S_t, eliminating the overallocation of resources and thus the efficiency loss.

procedures and dump sites for disposing of contaminated soil and solvents. Violating these laws means fines and, in some cases, imprisonment.

Direct controls raise the marginal cost of production because the firms must operate and maintain pollution-control equipment. The supply curve S in Figure 5.7b, which does not reflect the external costs, shifts leftward to the total-cost supply curve, S_t. Product price increases, equilibrium output falls from Q_e to Q_o, and the initial overallocation of resources shown in Figure 5.7a is corrected. Observe that the efficiency loss shown by triangle abc in 5.7a disappears after the overallocation is corrected in Figure 5.7b.

Specific Taxes

A second policy approach to negative externalities is for government to levy taxes or charges specifically on the related good. For example, the government has placed a manufacturing excise tax on CFCs, which deplete the stratospheric ozone layer protecting the earth from excessive solar ultraviolet radiation. Facing such an excise tax, manufacturers must decide whether to pay the tax or expend additional funds to purchase or develop substitute products. In either case, the tax raises the marginal cost of producing CFCs, shifting the private supply curve for this product leftward (or upward).

In Figure 5.7b, a tax equal to T per unit increases the firm's marginal cost, shifting the supply curve from S to S_t. The equilibrium price rises, and the equilibrium output declines from Q_e to the economically efficient level Q_o. The tax thus eliminates the initial overallocation of resources and therefore the efficiency loss.

Subsidies and Government Provision

Where spillover benefits are large and diffuse, as in our earlier example of inoculations, government has three options for correcting the underallocation of resources:

- *Subsidies to buyers* Figure 5.8a again shows the supply–demand situation for positive externalities. Government could correct the underallocation of resources, for example, to inoculations, by subsidizing consumers of the product. It could give each new mother in the United States a discount coupon to be used to obtain a series of inoculations for her child. The coupon would reduce the "price" to the mother by, say, 50 percent. As shown in Figure 5.8b, this program would shift the demand curve for inoculations from too-low D to the appropriate D_t. The number of inoculations would rise from Q_e to the economically optimal Q_o, eliminating the underallocation of resources and efficiency loss shown in Figure 5.8a.

- *Subsidies to producers* A subsidy to producers is a tax in reverse. Taxes are payments *to* the government that increase producers' costs. Subsidies are payments *from* the government that decrease producers' costs. As shown in Figure 5.8c, a subsidy of U per inoculation to physicians and medical clinics would reduce their marginal costs and shift their supply curve rightward from S_t to S_t'. The output of inoculations would increase from Q_e to the optimal level Q_o, correcting the underallocation of resources and efficiency loss shown in Figure 5.8a.

- *Government provision* Finally, where positive externalities are extremely large, the government may decide to provide the product for free to everyone. The U.S. government largely eradicated the crippling disease polio by administering free vaccines to all children. India ended smallpox by paying people in rural areas to come to public clinics to have their children vaccinated.

FIGURE 5.8 Correcting for positive externalities. (a) Positive externalities result in an underallocation of resources. (b) This underallocation can be corrected through a subsidy to consumers, which shifts market demand from D to D_t and increases output from Q_e to Q_o. (c) Alternatively, the underallocation can be eliminated by providing producers with a subsidy of U, which shifts their supply curve from S_t to $S_{t'}$, increasing output from Q_e to Q_o and eliminating the underallocation, and thus the efficiency loss, shown in graph a.

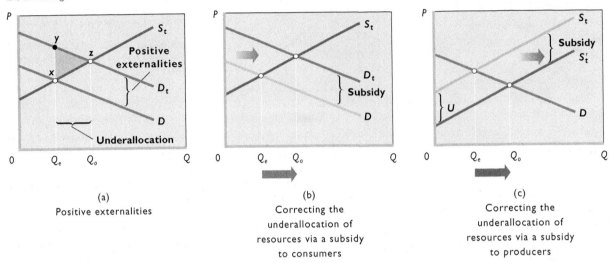

(a)
Positive externalities

(b)
Correcting the
underallocation of
resources via a subsidy
to consumers

(c)
Correcting the
underallocation of
resources via a subsidy
to producers

Table 5.5 lists several methods for correcting externalities, including those we have discussed thus far.

Society's Optimal Amount of Externality Reduction

Negative externalities such as pollution reduce the utility of those affected, rather than increase it. These spillovers are not economic goods but economic "bads." If something is bad, shouldn't society eliminate it? Why should society allow firms or municipalities to discharge *any* impure waste into public waterways or to emit *any* pollution into the air?

Economists answer these questions by pointing out that reducing pollution and negative externalities is not free.

There are costs as well as benefits to reducing pollution. As a result, the correct question to ask when it comes to cleaning up negative externalities is not, "Do we pollute a lot or pollute zero?" That is an all-or-nothing question that ignores marginal costs and marginal benefits. Instead, the correct question is, "What is the optimal amount to clean up—the amount that equalizes the marginal cost of cleaning up with the marginal benefit of a cleaner environment?"

If we ask that question, we see that reducing a negative externality has a "price." Society must decide how much of a reduction it wants to "buy." High costs may mean that totally eliminating pollution might not be desirable, even if it is technologically feasible. Because of the law of diminishing returns, cleaning up the second 10 percent of pollutants

TABLE 5.5 Methods for Dealing with Externalities

Problem	Resource Allocation Outcome	Ways to Correct
Negative externalities (spillover costs)	Overproduction of output and therefore overallocation of resources	1. Private bargaining 2. Liability rules and lawsuits 3. Tax on producers 4. Direct controls 5. Market for externality rights
Positive externalities (spillover benefits)	Underproduction of output and therefore underallocation of resources	1. Private bargaining 2. Subsidy to consumers 3. Subsidy to producers 4. Government provision

from an industrial smokestack normally is more costly than cleaning up the first 10 percent. Eliminating the third 10 percent is more costly than cleaning up the second 10 percent, and so on. Therefore, cleaning up the last 10 percent of pollutants is the most costly reduction of all.

The marginal cost (MC) to the firm and hence to society—the opportunity cost of the extra resources used—rises as pollution is reduced more and more. At some point MC may rise so high that it exceeds society's marginal benefit (MB) of further pollution abatement (reduction). Additional actions to reduce pollution will therefore lower society's well-being; total cost will rise more than total benefit.

MC, MB, and Equilibrium Quantity Figure 5.9 shows both the rising marginal-cost curve, MC, for pollution reduction and the downsloping marginal-benefit curve, MB, for pollution reduction. MB slopes downward because of the law of diminishing marginal utility: The more pollution reduction society accomplishes, the lower the utility (and benefit) of the next unit of pollution reduction.

The **optimal reduction of an externality** occurs when society's marginal cost and marginal benefit of reducing that externality are equal (MC = MB). In Figure 5.9 this optimal amount of pollution abatement is Q_1 units. When MB exceeds MC, additional abatement moves society toward economic efficiency; the added benefit of

cleaner air or water exceeds the benefit of any alternative use of the required resources. When MC exceeds MB, additional abatement reduces economic efficiency; there would be greater benefits from using resources in some other way than to further reduce pollution.

In reality, it is difficult to measure the marginal costs and benefits of pollution control. Nevertheless, Figure 5.9 demonstrates that some pollution may be economically efficient. This is so not because pollution is desirable but because beyond some level of control, further abatement may reduce society's net well-being. As an example, it would cost the government billions of dollars to clean up every last piece of litter in America. Thus, it would be better to tolerate some trash blowing around if the money saved by picking up less trash would yield larger net benefits when spent on other things.

Shifts in Locations of the Curves The locations of the marginal-cost and marginal-benefit curves in Figure 5.9 are not forever fixed. They can, and probably do, shift over time. For example, suppose that the technology of pollution-control equipment improved noticeably. We would expect the cost of pollution abatement to fall, society's MC curve to shift rightward, and the optimal level of abatement to rise. Or suppose that society were to decide that it wanted cleaner air and water because of new information about the adverse health effects of pollution. The MB curve in Figure 5.9 would shift rightward, and the optimal level of pollution control would increase beyond Q_1. Test your understanding of these statements by drawing the new MC and MB curves in Figure 5.9.

Government's Role in the Economy

Market failures can be used to justify government interventions in the economy. The inability of private-sector firms to break even when attempting to provide public goods and the over- and underproduction problems caused by positive and negative externalities mean that government can have an important role to play if society's resources are to be efficiently allocated to the goods and services that people most highly desire.

Correcting for market failures is not, however, an easy task. To begin with, government officials must correctly identify the existence and the cause of any given market failure. That by itself may be difficult, time consuming, and costly. But even if a market failure is correctly identified and diagnosed, government may still fail to take appropriate corrective action due to the fact that government undertakes its economic role in the context of politics.

FIGURE 5.9 Society's optimal amount of pollution abatement. The optimal amount of externality reduction—in this case, pollution abatement—occurs at Q_1, where society's marginal cost MC and marginal benefit MB of reducing the spillover are equal.

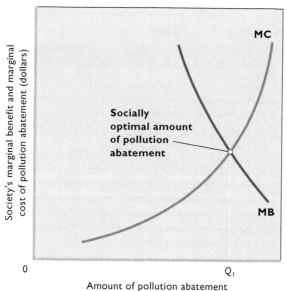

Word Carbon Dioxide Emissions, Cap and Trade, and Carbon Taxes

Cap-and-trade systems and carbon taxes are two approaches to reducing carbon dioxide (CO_2) emissions.

Externality problems are property rights problems. Consider a landfill. Because the owner of the landfill has full rights to his land, people wishing to dump their trash into the landfill have to pay him. This payment implies that there is no externality: He happily accepts their trash in exchange for a dumping fee. By contrast, because nobody owns the atmosphere, all air pollution is an externality, since there is no way for those doing the polluting to work out a payment to compensate those affected by the pollution or for those threatened with pollution to simply refuse to be polluted on.

Conventional property rights therefore cannot fix the externalities associated with air pollution. But that does not mean property rights can't help fight pollution. The trick to making them work is to assign property rights not to the atmosphere itself, but to *polluting* the atmosphere. This is done in "cap-and-trade" systems, under which the government sets an annual limit, or cap, to the number of tons of a pollutant that firms can emit into the atmosphere.

Consider carbon dioxide, or CO_2. It is a colorless, odorless gas that many scientists consider to be a contributing cause of climate change, specifically global warming. To reduce CO_2 emissions, the U.S. government might set a cap of 5 billion tons of CO_2 emissions per year in the United States (which would be about 10 percent below 2009 emissions levels for that molecule). The government then prints out emissions permits that sum to the limit set in the cap and distributes them to polluting firms. Once they are distributed, the only way a firm can legally emit a ton of CO_2 is if it owns a permit to do so.

Under this policy, the government can obviously adjust the total amount of air pollution by adjusting the cap. This by itself improves efficiency, because the cap imposes scarcity. Because each firm has only a limited number of permits, each firm has a strong incentive to maximize the net benefit that it produces from every ton of pollution that it emits. But the *cap-and-trade* scheme leads to even greater improvements in efficiency, because firms are free to trade (sell) them to each other in what are referred to as *markets for externality rights*.

For instance, suppose Smokestack Toys owns permits for 100 tons of CO_2 emissions and that it could use them to produce toy cars that would generate profits of $100,000. There is a power plant, however, that could make up to $1 million of profits by using those 100 tons of emissions permits to generate electricity. Because firms can trade their permits, Smokestack Toys will sell its permits to the power plant for more than the

---

To serve the public, politicians need to get elected. To stay elected, officials (presidents, senators, representatives, mayors, council members, school board members) need to satisfy their particular constituencies. At best, the political realities complicate government's role in the economy; at worst, they produce undesirable economic outcomes.

In the political context, overregulation can occur in some cases; underregulation, in others. Some public goods and quasi-public goods can be produced not because their benefits exceed their costs but because their benefits accrue to firms located in states served by powerful elected officials. Inefficiency can easily creep into government activities because of the lack of a profit incentive to hold down costs. Policies to correct negative externalities can be politically blocked by the very parties that are producing the spillovers. In short, the economic role of government, although critical to a well-functioning economy, is not always perfectly carried out.

Economists use the term "government failure" to describe economically inefficient outcomes caused by shortcomings in the public sector.

- Policies for coping with the overallocation of resources, and therefore efficiency losses, caused by negative externalities are (a) private bargaining, (b) liability rules and lawsuits, (c) direct controls, (d) specific taxes, and (e) markets for externality rights (Last Word).
- Policies for correcting the underallocation of resources, and therefore efficiency losses, associated with positive externalities are (a) private bargaining, (b) subsidies to producers, (c) subsidies to consumers, and (d) government provision.
- The optimal amount of negative-externality reduction occurs where society's marginal cost and marginal benefit of reducing the externality are equal.
- Political pressures often lead government to respond inefficiently when attempting to correct for market failures.

$100,000 in profits that it could make if it kept them and produced toy cars. And the power plant will gladly pay more than $100,00 for those permits, because it can turn around and use them to make up to $1 million of profits by using them to generate electricity.

Society will benefit hugely from this transaction, because while 100 tons of CO_2 will be emitted no matter which firm uses the permits, society will receive much greater net benefits when they are used by the power plant, as indicated by the fact that the power plant can produce much larger profits than the toy company when using the same amount of this scarce resource.

Several words of caution, however! Cap-and-trade systems have proven very difficult to implement in cases where it is difficult for regulators to effectively check whether firms are obeying the system. This has been a major problem with the European Union's cap-and-trade system for CO_2 emissions. Because nearly every type of industrial activity releases CO_2 into the atmosphere, enforcement involves monitoring many thousands of factories of all sizes. That is very difficult and cheating has resulted. In addition, politically connected industries got politicians to give them exemptions or free permits.

By contrast, a cap-and-trade system on sulfur dioxide emissions from coal-burning public utilities has worked well in the United States since the 1980s. But in that case, there were only a few hundred polluting utilities, and they were already being monitored for emissions. So there was little ability to cheat. In addition, all of the firms were treated equally, with no firms allowed exemptions or free permits.

Due to the mixed results, many economists have concluded that a cap-and-trade system would not be the best way to curb CO_2 emissions in the United States. They believe that there are simply too many sources of pollution to make monitoring either possible or cost-effective. And it seems likely that politically connected industries will be granted exemptions. So, instead, many economists favor a carbon tax, which would involve taxing each ton of coal, each gallon of gasoline, and each barrel of oil on the basis of how much carbon it contains (and thus how much CO_2 will eventually be released into the atmosphere when it is used). By raising the cost of polluting, the tax would reduce consumption and lessen the externalities associated with CO_2 emissions. It would also be nearly impossible to evade, so that we would not have to worry about cheating.

Summary

1. A market failure happens in a particular market when the market produces an equilibrium level of output that either overallocates or underallocates resources to the product being traded in the market. In competitive markets that feature many buyers and many sellers, market failures can be divided into two types: Demand-side market failures occur when demand curves do not reflect consumers' full willingness to pay; supply-side market failures occur when supply curves do not reflect all production costs, including those that may be borne by third parties.

2. Consumer surplus is the difference between the maximum price that a consumer is willing to pay for a product and the lower price actually paid; producer surplus is the difference between the minimum price that a producer is willing to accept for a product and the higher price actually received. Collectively, consumer surplus is represented by the triangle under the demand curve and above the actual price, whereas producer surplus is shown by the triangle above the supply curve and below the actual price.

3. Graphically, the combined amount of producer and consumer surplus is represented by the triangle to the left of the intersection of the supply and demand curves that is below the demand curve and above the supply curve. At the equilibrium price and quantity in competitive markets, marginal benefit equals marginal cost, maximum willingness to pay equals minimum acceptable price, and the combined amount of consumer surplus and producer surplus is maximized.

4. Output levels that are either less than or greater than the equilibrium output create efficiency losses, also called deadweight losses. These losses are reductions in the combined amount of consumer surplus and producer surplus.

111

Underproduction creates efficiency losses because output is not being produced for which maximum willingness to pay exceeds minimum acceptable price. Overproduction creates efficiency losses because output is being produced for which minimum acceptable price exceeds maximum willingness to pay.

5. Public goods are distinguished from private goods. Private goods are characterized by rivalry (in consumption) and excludability. One person's purchase and consumption of a private good precludes others from also buying and consuming it. Producers can exclude nonpayers (free riders) from receiving the benefits. In contrast, public goods are characterized by nonrivalry (in consumption) and nonexcludability. Public goods are not profitable to private firms because nonpayers (free riders) can obtain and consume those goods without paying. Government can, however, provide desirable public goods, financing them through taxation.

6. The collective demand schedule for a particular public good is found by summing the prices that each individual is willing to pay for an additional unit. Graphically, that demand curve is therefore found by summing vertically the individual demand curves for that good. The resulting total demand curve indicates the collective willingness to pay for (or marginal benefit of) any given amount of the public good.

7. The optimal quantity of a public good occurs where the society's willingness to pay for the last unit—the marginal benefit of the good—equals the marginal cost of the good.

8. Externalities, or spillovers, are costs or benefits that accrue to someone other than the immediate buyer or seller. Such costs or benefits are not captured in market demand or supply curves and therefore cause the output of certain goods to vary from society's optimal output. Negative externalities (or spillover costs or external costs) result in an overallocation of resources to a particular product. Positive externalities (or spillover benefits or external benefits) are accompanied by an underallocaton of resources to a particular product.

9. Direct controls and specific taxes can improve resource allocation in situations where negative externalities affect many people and community resources. Both direct controls (for example, smokestack emission standards) and specific taxes (for example, taxes on firms producing toxic chemicals) increase production costs and hence product price. As product price rises, the externality, overallocation of resources, and efficiency loss are reduced since less of the output is produced.

10. Government can correct the underallocation of resources and therefore the efficiency losses that result from positive externalities in a particular market either by subsidizing consumers (which increases market demand) or by subsidizing producers (which increases market supply). Such subsidies increase the equilibrium output, reducing or eliminating the positive externality and consequent underallocation of resources and efficiency loss.

11. The Coase theorem suggests that under the right circumstances private bargaining can solve externality problems. Thus, government intervention is not always needed to deal with externality problems.

12. The socially optimal amount of externality abatement occurs where society's marginal cost and marginal benefit of reducing the externality are equal. With pollution, for example, this optimal amount of pollution abatement is likely to be less than a 100 percent reduction. Changes in technology or changes in society's attitudes toward pollution can affect the optimal amount of pollution abatement.

13. Market failures present government with opportunities to improve the allocation of society's resources and thereby enhance society's total well-being. But even when government correctly identifies the existence and cause of a market failure, political pressures may make it difficult or impossible for government officials to implement a proper solution.

Terms and Concepts

market failures	private goods	free-rider problem
demand-side market failures	rivalry	cost-benefit analysis
supply-side market failures	excludability	quasi-public goods
consumer surplus	public goods	externality
producer surplus	nonrivalry	Coase theorem
efficiency losses (or deadweight losses)	nonexcludability	optimal reduction of an externality

Questions

1. Explain the two causes of market failures. Given their definitions, could a market be affected by both types of market failures simultaneously? LO1

2. Draw a supply and demand graph and identify the areas of consumer surplus and producer surplus. Given the demand curve, what impact will an increase in supply have on the amount of consumer surplus shown in your diagram? Explain why. LO2

3. Use the ideas of consumer surplus and producer surplus to explain why economists say competitive markets are

efficient. Why are below- or above-equilibrium levels of output inefficient, according to these two sets of ideas? LO2

4. What are the two characteristics of public goods? Explain the significance of each for public provision as opposed to private provision. What is the free-rider problem as it relates to public goods? Is U.S. border patrol a public good or a private good? Why? How about satellite TV? Explain. LO3

5. Draw a production possibilities curve with public goods on the vertical axis and private goods on the horizontal axis. Assuming the economy is initially operating on the curve, indicate how the production of public goods might be increased. How might the output of public goods be increased if the economy is initially operating at a point inside the curve? LO3

6. Use the distinction between the characteristics of private and public goods to determine whether the following should be produced through the market system or provided by government: (a) French fries, (b) airport screening, (c) court systems, (d) mail delivery, and (e) medical care. State why you answered as you did in each case. LO3

7. What divergences arise between equilibrium output and efficient output when (a) negative externalities and (b) positive externalities are present? How might government correct these divergences? Cite an example (other than the text examples) of an external cost and an external benefit. LO4

8. Why are spillover costs and spillover benefits also called negative and positive externalities? Show graphically how a tax can correct for a negative externality and how a subsidy to producers can correct for a positive externality. How does a subsidy to consumers differ from a subsidy to producers in correcting for a positive externality? LO4

9. An apple grower's orchard provides nectar to a neighbor's bees, while the beekeeper's bees help the apple grower by pollinating his apple blossoms. Use Figure 5.6b to explain why this situation of dual positive externalities might lead to an underallocation of resources to both apple growing and beekeeping. How might this underallocation get resolved via the means suggested by the Coase theorem? LO4

10. The LoJack car recovery system allows the police to track stolen cars. As a result, they not only recover 90 percent of LoJack-equipped cars that are stolen but also arrest many auto thieves and shut down many "chop shops" that take apart stolen vehicles to get at their used parts. Thus, LoJack provides both private benefits and positive externalities. Should the government consider subsidizing LoJack purchases? LO4

11. Explain the following statement, using the MB curve in Figure 5.9 to illustrate: "The optimal amount of pollution abatement for some substances, say, dirty water from storm drains, is very low; the optimal amount of abatement for other substances, say, cyanide poison, is close to 100 percent." LO5

12. Explain why zoning laws, which allow certain land uses only in specific locations, might be justified in dealing with a problem of negative externalities. Explain why in areas where buildings sit close together tax breaks to property owners for installing extra fire prevention equipment might be justified in view of positive externalities. Explain why excise taxes on beer might be justified in dealing with a problem of external costs. LO5

13. **LAST WORD** Distinguish between a carbon-tax and a cap-and-trade strategy for reducing carbon dioxide and other so-called greenhouse gases (that are believed by many scientists to be causing global warming). Which of the two strategies do you think would have the most political support in an election in your home state? Explain your thinking.

Problems

1. Refer to Table 5.1. If the six people listed in the table are the only consumers in the market and the equilibrium price is $11 (not the $8 shown), how much consumer surplus will the market generate? LO2

2. Refer to Table 5.2. If the six people listed in the table are the only producers in the market and the equilibrium price is $6 (not the $8 shown), how much producer surplus will the market generate? LO2

3. Look at Tables 5.1 and 5.2 together. What is the total surplus if Bob buys a unit from Carlos? If Barb buys a unit from Courtney? If Bob buys a unit from Chad? If you match up pairs of buyers and sellers so as to maximize the total surplus of all transactions, what is the largest total surplus that can be achieved? LO2

4. **ADVANCED ANALYSIS** Assume the following values for Figures 5.4a and 5.4b. $Q_1 = 20$ bags. $Q_2 = 15$ bags. $Q_3 = 27$ bags. The market equilibrium price is $45 per bag. The

price at a is $85 per bag. The price at c is $5 per bag. The price at f is $59 per bag. The price at g is $31 per bag. Apply the formula for the area of a triangle (Area = ½ × Base × Height) to answer the following questions. LO2

a. What is the dollar value of the total surplus (producer surplus plus consumer surplus) when the allocatively efficient output level is being produced? How large is the dollar value of the consumer surplus at that output level?

b. What is the dollar value of the deadweight loss when output level Q_2 is being produced? What is the total surplus when output level Q_2 is being produced?

c. What is the dollar value of the deadweight loss when output level Q_3 is produced? What is the dollar value of the total surplus when output level Q_3 is produced?

5. On the basis of the three individual demand schedules at the top of the next page, and assuming these three people are

the only ones in the society, determine (a) the market demand schedule on the assumption that the good is a private good and (b) the collective demand schedule on the assumption that the good is a public good. LO3

P	$Q_d(D_1)$	$Q_d(D_2)$	$Q_d(D_3)$
$8	0	1	0
7	0	2	0
6	0	3	1
5	1	4	2
4	2	5	3
3	3	6	4
2	4	7	5
1	5	8	6

6. Use your demand schedule for a public good, determined in problem 5, and the following supply schedule to ascertain the optimal quantity of this public good. LO3

P	Q_s
$19	10
16	8
13	6
10	4
7	2
4	1

7. Look at Tables 5.1 and 5.2, which show, respectively, the willingness to pay and willingness to accept of buyers and sellers of bags of oranges. For the following questions, assume that the equilibrium price and quantity will depend on the indicated changes in supply and demand. Assume that the only market participants are those listed by name in the two tables. LO4

a. What is the equilibrium price and quantity for the data displayed in the two tables?

b. What if, instead of bags of oranges, the data in the two tables dealt with a public good like fireworks displays? If all the buyers free ride, what will be the quantity supplied by private sellers?

c. Assume that we are back to talking about bags of oranges (a private good), but that the government has decided that tossed orange peels impose a negative externality on the public that must be rectified by imposing a $2-per-bag tax on sellers. What is the new equilibrium price and quantity? If the new equilibrium quantity is the optimal quantity, by how many bags were oranges being overproduced before?

FURTHER TEST YOUR KNOWLEDGE AT
www.mcconnell19e.com

At the text's Online Learning Center (OLC), **www.mcconnell19e.com**, you will find one or more Web-based questions that require information from the Internet to answer. We urge you to check them out; they will familiarize you with Web sites that may be helpful in other courses and perhaps even in your career. The OLC also features multiple-choice questions that give instant feedback and provides other helpful ways to further test your knowledge of the chapter.

MICROECONOMICS OF GOVERNMENT

16

AFTER READING THIS CHAPTER, YOU SHOULD BE ABLE TO:

1 Identify the main categories of government spending and the main sources of government revenue.

2 Summarize the different philosophies regarding the distribution of a nation's tax burden.

3 Explain the principles relating to tax shifting, tax incidence, and the efficiency losses caused by taxes.

4 Demonstrate how the distribution of income between rich and poor is affected by government taxes, transfers, and spending.

Public Finance: Expenditures and Taxes

As discussed in Chapter 2, the U.S. economy relies heavily on the private sector (households and businesses) and the market system to decide what gets produced, how it gets produced, and who gets the output. But the private sector is not the only entity in the decision process. The public sector (Federal, state, and local government) also affects these economic decisions.

Government influences what gets produced and how it gets produced through laws that regulate the activities of private firms and also by directly producing certain goods and services, such as national defense and education. As discussed in Chapter 5, many of these government-produced goods and services are *public goods* that the private sector has trouble producing because of free-rider problems. Also, government influences who receives society's output of goods and services through various taxes and through welfare and income-transfer payments that redistribute income from the rich to the poor.

336

Government-provided goods, services, and transfer payments are funded by taxes, borrowing, and *proprietary income*—the income that governments receive from running government-owned enterprises such as hospitals, utilities, toll roads, and lotteries.

Public finance is the subdiscipline of economics that studies the various ways in which governments raise and expend money. In this chapter we view the economy through the lens of public finance. Our main goal is to understand how taxes and income transfers not only pay for government-produced goods and services but also affect the distribution of income between rich and poor.

Government and the Circular Flow

In Figure 16.1 we integrate government into the circular flow model first shown in Figure 2.2. Here flows (1) through (4) are the same as the corresponding flows in that figure. Flows (1) and (2) show business expenditures for the resources provided by households. These expenditures are costs to businesses but represent wage, rent, interest, and profit income to households. Flows (3) and (4) show household expenditures for the goods and services produced by businesses.

Now consider what happens when we add government. Flows (5) through (8) illustrate that government makes purchases in both product and resource markets. Flows (5) and (6) represent government purchases of such products as paper, computers, and military hardware from private businesses. Flows (7) and (8) represent government purchases of resources. The Federal government employs and pays salaries to members of Congress, the armed forces, Justice Department lawyers, meat inspectors, and so on. State and local governments hire and pay teachers, bus drivers, police, and firefighters. The Federal government might also lease or purchase land to expand a

FIGURE 16.1 Government within the circular flow diagram. Government buys products from the product market and employs resources from the resource market to provide goods and services to households and businesses. Government finances its expenditures through the net taxes (taxes minus transfer payments) it receives from households and businesses.

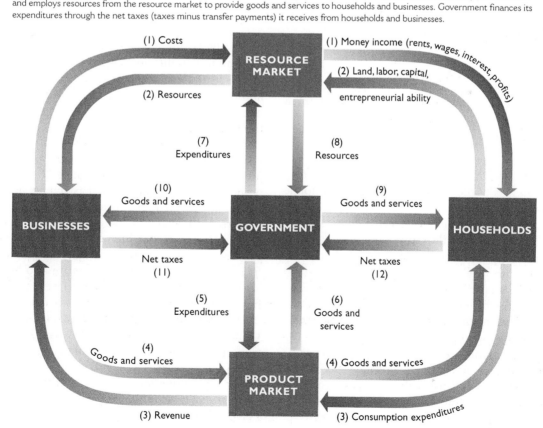

337

military base and a city might buy land on which to build a new elementary school.

Government then provides goods and services to both households and businesses, as shown by flows (9) and (10). Governments rely on three revenue sources to finance those goods and services: taxes, borrowing, and the proprietary income generated by government-run or government-sponsored businesses like public utilities and state lotteries. These revenues flowing from households and businesses to government are included in flows (11) and (12), which are labeled as "net taxes" for two reasons. First, the vast majority of the money raised by these three revenue sources comes from taxes; thus, it is sensible to have these labels refer to taxes. Second, the labels refer to *net* taxes to indicate that they also include "taxes in reverse" in the form of transfer payments to households and subsidies to businesses. Thus, flow (11) entails various subsidies to farmers, shipbuilders, and airlines as well as income, sales, and excise taxes paid by businesses to government. Most subsidies to business are "concealed" in the form of low-interest loans, loan guarantees, tax concessions, or public facilities provided at prices below their cost. Similarly, flow (12) includes not only taxes (personal income taxes, payroll taxes) collected by government from households but also transfer payments made by government to households. These include welfare payments and Social Security benefits.

Government Finance

How large is the U.S. public sector? What are the main expenditure categories of Federal, state, and local governments? How are these expenditures financed?

Government Purchases and Transfers

We can get an idea of the size of government's economic role by examining government purchases of goods and services and government transfer payments. There is a significant difference between these two kinds of outlays:

- **Government purchases** are *exhaustive;* the products purchased directly absorb (require the use of) resources and are part of the domestic output. For example, the purchase of a missile absorbs the labor of physicists and engineers along with steel, explosives, and a host of other inputs.

- **Transfer payments** are *nonexhaustive;* they do not directly absorb resources or create output. Social Security benefits, welfare payments, veterans' benefits, and unemployment compensation are examples of transfer payments. Their key characteristic is that

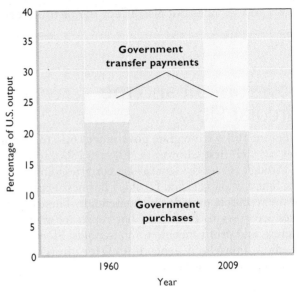

FIGURE 16.2 Government purchases, transfers, and total spending as percentages of U.S. output, 1960 and 2009. Government purchases have declined as a percentage of U.S. output since 1960. Transfer payments, however, have increased by more than this drop, raising total government spending (purchases plus transfers) from 27 percent of U.S. GDP in 1960 to about 35 percent today.

Source: Compiled from Bureau of Economic Analysis data, **www.bea.gov.**

recipients make no current contribution to domestic output in return for them.

Federal, state, and local governments spent $4989 billion (roughly $5 trillion) in 2009. Of that total, government purchases were $2855 billion and government transfers were $2134 billion. Figure 16.2 shows these amounts as percentages of U.S. domestic output for 2009 and compares them to percentages for 1960. Government purchases have declined from about 22 to 20 percent of output since 1960. But transfer payments have tripled as a percentage of output—from 5 percent in 1960 to about 15 percent in 2009. Relative to U.S. output, total government spending is thus higher today than it was 49 years earlier. This means that the tax revenues required to finance government expenditures are also higher. Today, government spending and the tax revenues needed to finance it are about 35 percent of U.S. output.

In 2010 the so-called Tax Freedom Day in the United States was April 9. On that day the average worker had earned enough (from the start of the year) to pay his or her share of the taxes required to finance government spending for the year. Tax Freedom Day arrives even later in several other countries, as implied in Global Perspective 16.1.

GLOBAL PERSPECTIVE 16.1

Total Tax Revenue as a Percentage of Total Output, Selected Nations, 2008*

A nation's "tax burden" is its tax revenue from all levels of government as a percentage of its total output (GDP). Among the world's industrialized nations, the United States has a very moderate tax burden.

Total Tax Revenue as Percentage of GDP, 2008

*Includes government nontax revenue from fees, charges, fines and sales of government property.

Source: OECD database, Revenue Statistics 1965–2008, 2009, OECD, accessed May 10, 2010.

government borrows when the economy is doing well, many economists worry that the opportunity cost may be high. In particular, the government's borrowing may "crowd out" private-sector investment. As an example, a billion dollars borrowed and spent by the Federal government on roads is a billion dollars that was not lent to private companies to fund the expansion of factories or the development of new technologies.

Government spending that is financed by borrowing is often referred to as *deficit spending*, because a government's budget is said to be "in deficit" if the government's spending in a given time period exceeds the money that it collects from taxes and proprietary income during that period.

QUICK REVIEW 16.1

- A circular flow diagram can be used to illustrate how the government affects the allocation of resources in the economy through its revenue and expenditure decisions.
- As percentages of GDP, government purchases are 20 percent; government transfers, 15 percent; and the two combined are 35 percent.
- The funds used to pay for government purchases and transfers come from taxes, proprietary income, and borrowing.
- The ability to borrow allows a government to maintain a high level of spending during an economic downturn even if taxes and proprietary income are falling.

Government Revenues

The funds used to pay for government purchases and transfers come from three sources: taxes, proprietary income, and funds that are borrowed by selling bonds to the public.

Government Borrowing and Deficit Spending

The ability to borrow allows a government to spend more in a given time period than it collects in tax revenues and proprietary income during that period. This flexibility is useful during an economic downturn because a government can use borrowed funds to maintain high levels of spending on goods, services, and transfer payments even if tax revenues and proprietary income are falling due to the slowing economy.

Any money borrowed by a government, however, is money that cannot be put to other uses. During an economic downturn, this opportunity cost is likely to be small because any funds that the government does not borrow are likely to sit idle and unused by other parties due to the lack of economic activity during the downturn. But if the

Federal Finance

Now let's look separately at each of the Federal, state, and local units of government in the United States and compare their expenditures and taxes. Figure 16.3 tells the story for the Federal government.

Federal Expenditures

Four areas of Federal spending stand out: (1) pensions and income security, (2) national defense, (3) health, and (4) interest on the public debt. The *pensions and income security* category includes the many income-maintenance programs for the aged, persons with disabilities or handicaps, the unemployed, the retired, and families with no breadwinner. This category—dominated by the $683 billion pension portion of the Social Security program—accounts for 35 percent of total Federal expenditures. *National defense* accounts for about 19 percent of the Federal budget, underscoring the high cost of military preparedness. *Health* reflects the cost of government health programs for the retired (Medicare) and poor

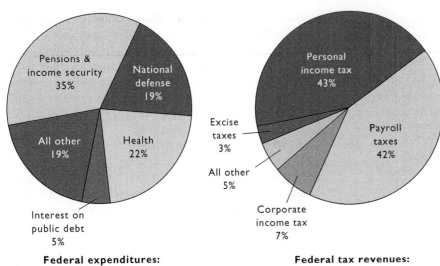

Federal expenditures:
$3522 billion

Federal tax revenues:
$2105 billion

Source: U.S. Treasury, *Combined Statement of Receipts, Outlays, and Balances, 2009*, **fms.treas.gov**.

FIGURE 16.3 **Federal expenditures and tax revenues, 2009.** Federal expenditures are dominated by spending for pensions and income security, health, and national defense. A full 85 percent of Federal tax revenue is derived from just two sources: the personal income tax and payroll taxes. The $1417 billion difference between expenditures and revenues reflects a budget deficit.

(Medicaid). *Interest on the public debt* accounts for 5 percent of Federal spending.

Federal Tax Revenues

The revenue side of Figure 16.3 shows that the personal income tax, payroll taxes, and the corporate income tax are the largest revenue sources, accounting respectively for 43, 42, and 7 cents of each dollar collected.

Personal Income Tax The **personal income tax** is the kingpin of the Federal tax system and merits special comment. This tax is levied on *taxable income*, that is, on the incomes of households and unincorporated businesses after certain exemptions ($3650 for each household member) and deductions (business expenses, charitable contributions, home mortgage interest payments, certain state and local taxes) are taken into account.

The Federal personal income tax is a *progressive tax*, meaning that people with higher incomes pay a larger percentage of their incomes as taxes than do people with lower incomes. The progressivity is achieved by applying higher tax rates to successive layers or brackets of income.

Columns 1 and 2 in Table 16.1 show the mechanics of the income tax for a married couple filing a joint return in 2010. Note that a 10 percent tax rate applies to all taxable income up to $16,750 and a 15 percent rate applies to additional income up to $68,000. The rates on additional layers of income then go up to 25, 28, 33, and 35 percent.

The tax rates shown in column 2 in Table 16.1 are marginal tax rates. A **marginal tax rate** is the rate at which the

TABLE 16.1 **Federal Personal Income Tax Rates, 2010***

(1) Total Taxable Income	(2) Marginal Tax Rate, %	(3) Total Tax on Highest Income In Bracket	(4) Average Tax Rate on Highest Income in Bracket, % (3) ÷ (1)
$1–$16,750	10	$ 1675	10
$16,751–$68,000	15	9363	14
$68,001–$137,300	25	26,688	19
$137,301–$209,250	28	46,834	22
$209,251–$373,650	33	101,086	27
Over $373,650	35		

*For a married couple filing a joint return.

tax is paid on each *additional* unit of taxable income. Thus, if a couple's taxable income is $80,000, they will pay the marginal rate of 10 percent on each dollar from $1 to $16,750, 15 percent on each dollar from $16,751 to $68,000, and 25 percent on each dollar from $68,001 to $80,000. You should confirm that their total income tax is $12,362.

The marginal tax rates in column 2 overstate the personal income tax bite because the rising rates in that column apply only to the income within each successive tax bracket. To get a better idea of the tax burden, we must consider average tax rates. The **average tax rate** is the total

WORKED PROBLEMS

W 16.1

Taxes and progressivity

tax paid divided by total taxable income. The couple in our previous example is in the 25 percent tax bracket because they pay a top marginal tax rate of 25 percent on the highest dollar of their income. But their *average* tax rate is 15 percent (= $12,362/$80,000).

As we will discuss in more detail shortly, a tax whose average rate rises as income increases is said to be a *progressive tax* because it claims both a progressively larger absolute amount of income as well as a progressively larger proportion of income as income rises. Thus we can say that the Federal personal income tax is progressive.

Payroll Taxes Social Security contributions are **payroll taxes**—taxes based on wages and salaries—used to finance two compulsory Federal programs for retired workers: Social Security (an income-enhancement program) and Medicare (which pays for medical services). Employers and employees pay these taxes equally. In 2010, employees and employers each paid 7.65 percent on the first $106,800 of an employee's annual earnings and 1.45 percent on all additional earnings.

Corporate Income Tax The Federal government also taxes corporate income. The **corporate income tax** is levied on a corporation's profit—the difference between its total revenue and its total expenses. For almost all corporations, the tax rate is 35 percent.

Excise Taxes Taxes on commodities or on purchases take the form of **sales and excise taxes.** The two differ primarily in terms of coverage. Sales taxes fall on a wide range of products, whereas excises are levied individually on a small, select list of commodities. An additional difference is that sales taxes are calculated as a percentage of the price paid for a product, whereas excise taxes are levied on a per-unit basis—for example, $2 per pack of cigarettes or $.50 per gallon of gasoline.

As Figure 16.3 suggests, the Federal government collects excise taxes of various rates (on the sale of such commodities as alcoholic beverages, tobacco, and gasoline) but does not levy a general sales tax; sales taxes are, however, the primary revenue source of most state governments.

State and Local Finance

State and local governments have different mixes of revenues and expenditures than the Federal government has.

State Finances

Figure 16.4 shows that the primary source of tax revenue for state governments is sales and excise taxes, which account for about 47 percent of all their tax revenue. State personal income taxes, which have much lower rates than the Federal income tax, are the second most important source of state tax revenue. They bring in about 35 percent of total state tax revenue. Corporate income taxes and license fees account for most of the remainder of state tax revenue.

Education expenditures account for about 36 percent of all state spending. State expenditures on public welfare are next in relative weight, at about 28 percent of the total. States also spend heavily on health and hospitals (7 percent), highway maintenance and construction (7 percent),

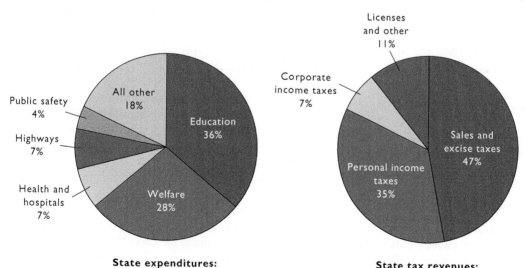

FIGURE 16.4 State expenditures and tax revenues, 2007. State governments spend largely on education and welfare. Their primary source of tax revenue is sales and excise taxes. The deficit between state expenditures and state tax revenues is filled by proprietary income and intergovernmental grants from the Federal government. The state expenditures numbers here include state grants to local governments.

State expenditures: $2000 billion

State tax revenues: $757 billion

Source: U.S. Census Bureau, *2007 Census of Government Finance,* **www.census.gov**.

CONSIDER THIS . . .

State Lotteries: A Good Bet?

State lotteries generated about $77.3 billion in revenue in 2008. Of that amount, $56.7 billion went to prizes and $2.4 billion went to administrative costs. That left $18.2 billion that could be spent by the states as they saw fit.

Though nowadays common, state lotteries are still controversial. Critics argue that (1) it is morally wrong for states to sponsor gambling; (2) lotteries generate compulsive gamblers who impoverish themselves and their families; (3) low-income families spend a larger portion of their incomes on lotteries than do high-income families; (4) as a cash business, lotteries attract criminals and other undesirables; and (5) lotteries send the message that luck and fate—rather than education, hard work, and saving—are the route to wealth.

Defenders contend that (1) lotteries are preferable to taxes, because they are voluntary rather than compulsory; (2) they are a relatively painless way to finance government services such as education, medical care, and welfare; and (3) lotteries compete with illegal gambling and are thus socially beneficial in curtailing organized crime.

As a further point for debate, also note that state lotteries are monopolies, with states banning competing private lotteries. The resulting lack of competition allows many states to restrict prizes to only about half the money wagered. These payout rates are substantially lower than the 80–95 percent payout rates typically found in private betting operations such as casinos.

Thus, while lotteries are indeed voluntary, they are overpriced and underprovided relative to what would happen if there were a free market in lotteries. But, then again, a free market in lotteries would eliminate monopoly profits for state lotteries and possibly add government costs for regulation and oversight. Consequently, the alternative of allowing a free market in lottery tickets and then taxing the firms selling lottery tickets would probably net very little additional revenue to support state spending programs.

and public safety (4 percent). That leaves about 18 percent of all state spending for a variety of other purposes.

These tax and expenditure percentages combine data from all the states, so they reveal little about the finances of individual states. States vary significantly in the taxes levied. Thus, although personal income taxes are a major source of revenue for all state governments combined, seven states do not levy a personal income tax. Also, there are great variations in the sizes of tax revenues and disbursements among the states, both in the aggregate and as percentages of personal income.

Forty-three states augment their tax revenues with state-run lotteries to help close the gap between their tax receipts and expenditures. Individual states also receive large intergovernmental grants from the Federal government. In fact, about 22 percent of their total revenue is in that form. States also take in revenue from miscellaneous sources such as state-owned utilities and liquor stores.

Local Finances

The local levels of government include counties, municipalities, townships, and school districts as well as cities and towns. Figure 16.5 shows that local governments obtain about 71 percent of their tax revenue from **property taxes.** Sales and excise taxes contribute about 17 percent of all local government tax revenue.

About 44 percent of local government expenditures go to education. Welfare, health, and hospitals (12 percent); public safety (11 percent); housing, parks, and sewerage (11 percent); and streets and highways (6 percent) are also major spending categories.

The tax revenues of local government cover less than one-half of their expenditures. The bulk of the remaining revenue comes from intergovernmental grants from the Federal and state governments. Also, local governments receive considerable amounts of proprietary income, for example, revenue from government-owned utilities providing water, electricity, natural gas, and transportation.

Local, State, and Federal Employment

In 2008, U.S. governments (local, state, and Federal) employed about 19.4 million workers, or about 13 percent of the U.S. labor force. Figure 16.6 shows the percentages of these government employees assigned to different tasks at both the Federal level and the state and local level.

As Figure 16.6 makes clear, the types of jobs done by government workers depend on the level of government. Over half of state and local government employment is focused on education. The next largest sector is hospitals and health care, which accounts for about 9 percent of state and local government employment. Police and corrections make up another 10 percent. Smaller categories like highways,

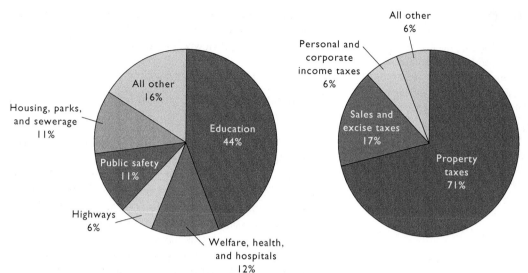

Source: U.S. Census Bureau, *2007 Census of Government Finance,* **www.census.gov**.

FIGURE 16.5 **Local expenditures and tax revenues, 2007.** The expenditures of local governments go largely to education, while a large majority of local tax collections are obtained via property taxes. The large deficit between local expenditures and local tax revenues is filled by proprietary income and Federal and state intergovernmental grants.

public welfare, and judicial together combine for less than 10 percent of state and local employment. The "other" category includes workers in areas such as parks and recreation, fire fighting, transit, and libraries.

Just over half of Federal government jobs are in national defense or the postal service. A further 12 percent of government jobs are in hospitals or health care. The natural resources, police, and financial administration categories each account for between 4 and 7 percent of Federal employment. The "other" category at the Federal level is composed of workers in areas such as justice and law, corrections, air transportation, and social insurance administration.

FIGURE 16.6 **Job functions of state and local employees and Federal employees, 2008.** A majority of state and local workers are employed in education. Federal employment is dominated by the postal service and national defense, which together employ just over half of Federal employees.

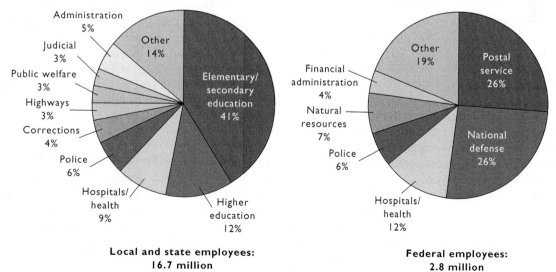

Source: U.S. Census Bureau, *State and Local Government Employment and Payroll Data, by State and Function,* and *Federal Government Employment by Function,* **www.census.gov**.

Apportioning the Tax Burden

Taxes are the major source of funding for the goods and services provided by government and the wages and salaries paid to government workers. Without taxes, there would be no public schools, no national defense, no public highways, no courts, no police, and no other government-provided public and quasi-public goods. As stated by Supreme Court Justice Oliver Wendell Holmes, "Taxes are the price we pay for civilization."

But taxes are controversial. To begin with, many people would prefer to obtain government goods and services without paying for them. Many others argue that certain taxes cause more harm than good, either by discouraging beneficial economic activity or by unfairly reducing the income flowing to workers and investors. And millions more chafe at the huge variety of taxes that governments levy, including income taxes, Social Security taxes, Medicare taxes, property taxes, sales taxes, liquor taxes, cigarette taxes, cell phone taxes, hotel taxes, gasoline taxes, profit taxes, and estate taxes. As the Beatles put it in their song "Taxman": "If you drive a car, I'll tax the street. If you try to sit, I'll tax your seat."

For these and other reasons, people are intently focused on the overall level of taxes, the amount they must personally pay, and the idea of tax fairness (which is often defined in terms of their own circumstances).

The public's attention to taxes has spurred public finance economists to undertake considerable research into the size, distribution, and impact of the total costs that taxes impose on society—the so-called tax burden. Their investigations reveal with reasonable clarity both the size of the tax burden as well as how it is apportioned across the income distribution.

Whether you consider their findings to be good news or bad news, however, depends significantly on your opinion about the fairest way to allocate taxes and the tax burden. So before turning to their findings, let's first discuss some of the major philosophical viewpoints regarding taxation.

Benefits Received versus Ability to Pay

Two basic philosophies coexist on how the economy's tax burden should be apportioned.

Benefits-Received Principle The **benefits-received principle** of taxation asserts that households should purchase the goods and services of government in the same way they buy other commodities. Those who benefit most from government-supplied goods or services should pay the taxes necessary to finance them. A few public goods are now financed on this basis. For example, money collected as gasoline taxes is typically used to finance highway construction and repairs. Thus people who benefit from good roads pay the cost of those roads. Difficulties immediately arise, however, when we consider widespread application of the benefits-received principle:

- How will the government determine the benefits that individual households and businesses receive from national defense, education, the court system, and police and fire protection? Recall from Chapter 5 that public goods are characterized by nonrivalry and nonexcludability. So benefits from public goods are especially widespread and diffuse. Even in the seemingly straightforward case of highway financing it is difficult to measure benefits. Good roads benefit owners of cars in different degrees. But others also benefit. For example, businesses benefit because good roads bring them workers and customers.
- The benefits-received principle cannot logically be applied to income redistribution programs. It would be absurd and self-defeating to ask poor families to pay the taxes needed to finance their welfare payments. It would also be self-defeating to tax only unemployed workers to finance the unemployment benefits they receive.

Ability-to-Pay Principle The **ability-to-pay principle** of taxation asserts that the tax burden should be apportioned according to taxpayers' income and wealth. In practice, this means that individuals and businesses with larger incomes should pay more taxes in both absolute and relative terms than those with smaller incomes.

In justifying the ability-to-pay principle, proponents contend that each additional dollar of income received by a household yields a smaller amount of satisfaction or marginal utility when it is spent. Because consumers act rationally, the first dollars of income received in any time period will be spent on high-urgency goods that yield the greatest marginal utility. Successive dollars of income will go for less urgently needed goods and finally for trivial goods and services. This means that a dollar taken through taxes from a poor person who has few dollars represents a greater utility sacrifice than a dollar taken through taxes from a rich person who has many dollars. To balance the sacrifices that taxes impose on income receivers, taxes should be apportioned according to the amount of income a taxpayer receives.

This argument is appealing, but application problems arise here too. Although we might agree that the household earning $100,000 per year has a greater ability to pay taxes than a household receiving $10,000, we don't know exactly how much more ability to pay the first family has. Should the wealthier family pay the *same* percentage of its larger income, and hence a larger absolute amount, as taxes? Or should it be made to pay a *larger* percentage of its income as taxes? And how much larger should that percentage be? Who is to decide?

There is no scientific way of making utility comparisons among individuals and thus of measuring someone's relative ability to pay taxes. That is the main problem. In practice, the solution hinges on guesswork, the tax views of the political party in power, expediency, and how urgently the government needs revenue.

Progressive, Proportional, and Regressive Taxes

Any discussion of taxation leads ultimately to the question of tax rates. Taxes are classified as progressive, proportional, or regressive, depending on the relationship between average tax rates and taxpayer incomes. We focus on incomes because all taxes—whether on income, a product, a building, or a parcel of land—are ultimately paid out of someone's income.

- A tax is **progressive** if its average rate increases as income increases. Such a tax claims not only a larger absolute (dollar) amount but also a larger percentage of income as income increases.
- A tax is **regressive** if its average rate declines as income increases. Such a tax takes a smaller proportion of income as income increases. A regressive tax may or may not take a larger absolute amount of income as income increases. (You may want to derive an example to substantiate this fact.)
- A tax is **proportional** if its average rate *remains the same* regardless of the size of income. Proportional income taxes are often referred to as *flat taxes* or *flat-rate taxes* because their average rates do not vary with (are flat with respect to) income levels.

We can illustrate these ideas with the personal income tax. Suppose tax rates are such that a household pays 10 percent of its income in taxes regardless of the size of its income. This is a *proportional* income tax. Now suppose the rate structure is such that a household with an annual taxable income of less than $10,000 pays 5 percent in income taxes; a household with an income of $10,000 to $20,000 pays 10 percent; one with a $20,000 to $30,000 income pays 15 percent; and so forth. This is a *progressive* income tax. Finally, suppose the rate declines as taxable income rises: You pay 15 percent if you earn less than $10,000; 10 percent if you earn $10,000 to $20,000; 5 percent if you earn $20,000 to $30,000; and so forth. This is a *regressive* income tax.

In general, progressive taxes are those that fall relatively more heavily on people with high incomes; regressive taxes are those that fall relatively more heavily on the poor.

Applications Let's examine the progressivity, or regressivity, of several taxes.

Personal Income Tax As noted earlier, the Federal personal income tax is progressive, with marginal tax rates (those assessed on additional income) ranging from 10 to 35 percent in 2010. Rules that allow individuals to deduct from income interest on home mortgages and property taxes and that exempt interest on state and local bonds from taxation tend to make the tax less progressive than these marginal rates suggest. Nevertheless, average tax rates rise with income.

Sales Taxes At first thought, a general sales tax with, for example, a 5 percent rate would seem to be proportional. But in fact it is regressive with respect to income. A larger portion of a low-income person's income is exposed to the tax than is the case for a high-income person; the rich pay no tax on the part of income that is saved, whereas the poor are unable to save. Example: "Low-income" Smith has an income of $15,000 and spends it all. "High-income" Jones has an income of $300,000 but spends only $200,000 and saves the rest. Assuming a 5 percent sales tax applies to all expenditures of each individual, we find that Smith pays $750 (5 percent of $15,000) in sales taxes and Jones pays $10,000 (5 percent of $200,000). But Smith pays $750/$15,000, or 5 percent of income as sales taxes while Jones pays $10,000/$300,000, or 3.3 percent of income. The general sales tax therefore is regressive.

Corporate Income Tax The Federal corporate income tax is essentially a proportional tax with a flat 35 percent tax rate. In the short run, the corporate owners (shareholders) bear the tax through lower dividends and share values. In the long run, workers may bear some of the tax since it reduces the return on investment and therefore slows capital accumulation. It also causes corporations to relocate to other countries that have lower tax rates. With less capital per worker, U.S. labor productivity may decline and wages may fall. To the extent this happens, the corporate income tax may be somewhat regressive.

Payroll Taxes Payroll taxes are taxes levied upon wages and salaries by certain states as well as by the Federal government. The Federal payroll tax is known as the FICA tax after the Federal Insurance Contributions Act, which mandated one payroll tax to fund the Social Security program and another to fund the Medicare program.

Both taxes are split equally between employer and employee. Thus, the 12.4 percent Social Security tax is split in half, with 6.2 percent paid by employees and an additional 6.2 percent paid by employers. In the same way, the 2.9 percent Medicare tax is also split in half, with 1.45 percent paid by employees and 1.45 percent paid by employers.

Crucially, however, only the Medicare tax applies to all wage and salary income without limit. The Social Security tax, by contrast, is "capped," meaning that it applies only up to a certain limit, or cap. In 2010, the cap was $106,800.

The fact that the Social Security tax applies only on income below the cap implies that the FICA tax is regressive. To see this, consider a person with $106,800 in wage income. He would pay $8170.20, or 7.65 percent (= 6.2 percent + 1.45 percent) of his wages in FICA taxes. By contrast, someone with twice that income, or $213,600, would pay $9718.80 (= $8170.20 on the first $106,800 + $1548.60 on the second $106,800), which is only 4.6 percent of his wage income. Thus the average FICA tax falls as income rises, thereby confirming that the FICA tax is regressive.

But payroll taxes are even more regressive than suggested by this example because they only apply to wage and salary income. People earning high incomes tend to derive a higher percentage of their total incomes from nonwage sources like rents and dividends than do people who have incomes below the $106,800 cap on which Social Security taxes are paid. Thus, if our individual with the $213,600 of wage income also received $213,600 of nonwage income, his $9718.80 of FICA tax would be only 2.2 percent of his total income of $427,200.

Property Taxes Most economists conclude that property taxes on buildings are regressive for the same reasons as are sales taxes. First, property owners add the tax to the

CONSIDER THIS . . .

The VAT: A Very Alluring Tax?

A value-added tax (VAT) is like a retail sales tax except that it applies only to the *difference* between the value of a firm's sales and the value of its purchases from other firms. For instance, Intel would pay the VAT—say, 7 percent—only on the difference between the value of the microchips it sells and the value of the materials used to make them. Dell, Lenovo, and other firms which buy chips and other components to make computers would subtract the value of their materials from the value of their sales of personal computers. They would pay the 7 percent tax on that difference—on the value that *they* added.

Economists reason that because the VAT would apply to all firms, sellers could shift their VATs to buyers in the form of higher prices without having to worry that their higher prices might cause them to lose sales to competitors. Final consumers, who cannot shift the tax, would be the ones who ultimately end up paying the full VAT as 7 percent higher prices. So the VAT would amount to a national sales tax on consumer goods.

Most other nations besides the United States have a VAT in addition to other taxes. Why the attraction? Proponents argue that it encourages savings and investment because it penalizes consumption. Unlike income taxes and profits taxes, which reduce the returns to working and investing, the VAT only taxes consumption. Thus, people might be expected to save and invest more if the government switched from taxing income and profits to taxing consumption via a VAT.

Opponents counter, however, that the VAT discourages savings and investment just as much as do income and profit taxes because the whole point of working hard, saving, and investing is the ability to reward yourself in the future with increased consumption. By making consumption more expensive, the VAT reduces this future reward. Also, because VATs are regressive, opponents argue that VATs lead to higher and more progressive income taxes as governments try to use the progressivity of income taxes to counter the regressivity of the VAT. Finally, critics note that the VAT is deeply buried within product prices and therefore is a *hidden tax*. Such taxes are usually easier to increase than other taxes and therefore can result in excessively large government.

rents that tenants are charged. Second, property taxes, as a percentage of income, are higher for low-income families than for high-income families because the poor must spend a larger proportion of their incomes for housing.

Tax Incidence and Efficiency Loss

Determining whether a particular tax is progressive, proportional, or regressive is complicated because those on whom taxes are levied do not always pay the taxes. This is true because some or all of the value of the tax may be passed on to others. We therefore need an understanding of **tax incidence,** the degree to which a tax falls on a particular person or group. The tools of elasticity of supply and demand will help. Let's focus on a hypothetical excise tax levied on wine producers. Do the producers really pay this tax, or is some fraction of the tax shifted to wine consumers?

Elasticity and Tax Incidence

In Figure 16.7, S and D represent the pretax market for a certain domestic wine; the no-tax equilibrium price and quantity are $8 per bottle and 15 million bottles. Suppose that government levies an excise tax of $2 per bottle at the winery. Who will actually pay this tax?

Division of Burden Since the government imposes the tax on the sellers (suppliers), we can view the tax as an

addition to the marginal cost of the product. Now sellers must get $2 more for each bottle to receive the same per-unit profit they were getting before the tax. While sellers are willing to offer, for example, 5 million bottles of untaxed wine at $4 per bottle, they must now receive $6 per bottle (= $4 + $2 tax) to offer the same 5 million bottles. The tax shifts the supply curve upward (leftward) as shown in Figure 16.7, where S_t is the "after-tax" supply curve.

The after-tax equilibrium price is $9 per bottle, whereas the before-tax equilibrium price was $8. So, in this case, consumers pay half the $2 tax as a higher price; producers pay the other half in the form of a lower after-tax per-unit revenue. That is, after remitting the $2 tax per unit to government, producers receive $7 per bottle, or $1 less than the $8 before-tax price. So, in this case, consumers and producers share the burden of the tax equally: Half of the $2 per bottle tax is shifted to consumers in the form of a higher price and half is paid by producers.

> **INTERACTIVE GRAPHS**
>
> **G 16.1**
>
> Tax incidence

Note also that the equilibrium quantity declines because of the tax levy and the higher price that it imposes on consumers. In Figure 16.7 that decline in quantity is from 15 million bottles to 12.5 million bottles per month.

Elasticities If the elasticities of demand and supply were different from those shown in Figure 16.7, the incidence of tax would also be different. Two generalizations are relevant.

With a specific supply, the more inelastic the demand for the product, the larger is the portion of the tax shifted to consumers. To verify this, sketch graphically the extreme cases in which demand is perfectly elastic and perfectly inelastic. In the first case, the incidence of the tax is entirely on sellers; in the second, the tax is shifted entirely to consumers.

Figure 16.8 contrasts the more usual cases where demand is either relatively elastic or relatively inelastic in the relevant price range. With elastic demand (Figure 16.8a), a small portion of the tax $(P_2 - P_1)$ is shifted to consumers and most of the tax $(P_1 - P_3)$ is borne by the producers. With inelastic demand (Figure 16.8b), most of the tax $(P_5 - P_4)$ is shifted to consumers and only a small amount $(P_4 - P_6)$ is paid by producers. In both graphs the per-unit tax is represented by the vertical distance between S_t and S.

Note also that the decline in equilibrium quantity (from Q_1 to Q_2 in Figure 16.8a and from Q_4 to Q_5 in Figure 16.8b) is smaller when demand is more inelastic. This is the basis of our previous applications of the elasticity concept to taxation in earlier chapters: Revenue-seeking

FIGURE 16.7 The incidence of an excise tax. An excise tax of a specified amount (here, $2 per unit) shifts the supply curve upward by the amount of the tax per unit: the vertical distance between S and S_t. This results in a higher price (here, $9) to consumers and a lower after-tax price (here, $7) to producers. Thus consumers and producers share the burden of the tax in some proportion (here, equally at $1 per unit).

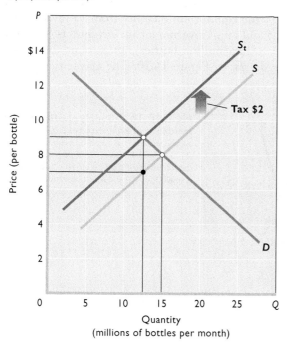

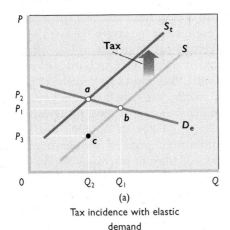

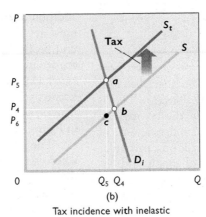

FIGURE 16.8 Demand elasticity and the incidence of an excise tax. (a) If demand is elastic in the relevant price range, price rises modestly (P_1 to P_2) when an excise tax is levied. Hence, the producers bear most of the tax burden. (b) If demand is inelastic, the price increases substantially (P_4 to P_5) and most of the tax is borne by consumers.

(a)
Tax incidence with elastic demand

(b)
Tax incidence with inelastic demand

legislatures place heavy excise taxes on liquor, cigarettes, automobile tires, telephone service, and other products whose demand is thought to be inelastic. Since demand for these products is relatively inelastic, the tax does not reduce sales by much, so the tax revenue stays high.

The second generalization is that, with a specific demand, the more inelastic the supply, the larger is the portion of the tax borne by producers. When supply is elastic (Figure 16.9a), consumers bear most of the tax ($P_2 - P_1$) while producers bear only a small portion ($P_1 - P_3$) themselves. But where supply is inelastic (Figure 16.9b), the reverse is true: The major portion of the tax ($P_4 - P_6$) falls on sellers, and a relatively small amount ($P_5 - P_4$) is shifted to buyers. The equilibrium quantity also declines less with an inelastic supply than it does with an elastic supply.

Gold is an example of a product with an inelastic supply and therefore one where the burden of an excise tax (such as an extraction tax) would mainly fall on producers.

On the other hand, because the supply of baseballs is relatively elastic, producers would pass on to consumers much of an excise tax on baseballs.

Efficiency Loss of a Tax

We just observed that producers and consumers typically each bear part of an excise tax levied on producers. Let's now look more closely at the overall economic effect of the excise tax. Consider Figure 16.10, which is identical to Figure 16.7 but contains the additional detail we need for our discussion.

Tax Revenues In our example, a $2 excise tax on wine increases its market price from $8 to $9 per bottle and reduces the equilibrium quantity from 15 million bottles to 12.5 million. Government tax revenue is $25 million (= $2 × 12.5 million bottles), an amount shown as the rectangle *efac* in Figure 16.10. The elasticities of supply

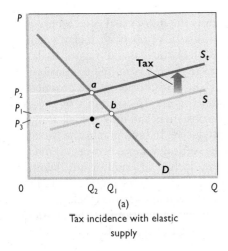

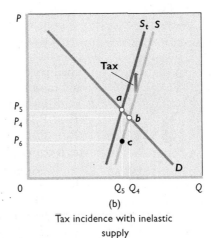

FIGURE 16.9 Supply elasticity and the incidence of an excise tax. (a) With elastic supply, an excise tax results in a large price increase (P_1 to P_2) and the tax is therefore paid mainly by consumers. (b) If supply is inelastic, the price rise is small (P_4 to P_5) and sellers bear most of the tax.

(a)
Tax incidence with elastic supply

(b)
Tax incidence with inelastic supply

FIGURE 16.10 Efficiency loss (or deadweight loss) of a tax.

The levy of a $2 tax per bottle of wine increases the price per bottle from $8 to $9 and reduces the equilibrium quantity from 15 million to 12.5 million. Tax revenue to the government is $25 million (area *efac*). The efficiency loss of the tax arises from the 2.5 million decline in output; the amount of that loss is shown as triangle *abc*.

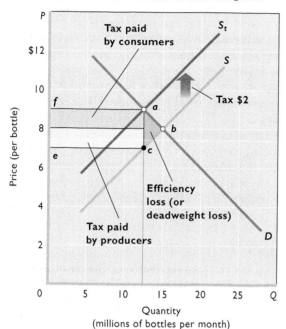

Quantity
(millions of bottles per month)

these 2.5 million bottles of wine reduces well-being by an amount represented by the triangle *abc*. The area of this triangle identifies the **efficiency loss of the tax** (also called the *deadweight loss of the tax*). This loss is society's sacrifice of net benefit, because the tax reduces production and consumption of the product below their levels of economic efficiency, where marginal benefit and marginal cost are equal.

Role of Elasticities Most taxes create some degree of efficiency loss, but just how much depends on the supply and demand elasticities. Glancing back at Figure 16.8, we see that the efficiency loss area *abc* is greater in Figure 16.8a, where demand is relatively elastic, than in Figure 16.8b, where demand is relatively inelastic. Similarly, area *abc* is greater in Figure 16.9a than in Figure 16.9b, indicating a larger efficiency loss where supply is more elastic. Other things equal, the greater the elasticities of supply and demand, the greater the efficiency loss of a particular tax.

Two taxes yielding equal revenues do not necessarily impose equal costs on society. The government must keep this fact in mind in designing a tax system to finance beneficial public goods and services. In general, it should minimize the efficiency loss of the tax system in raising any specific dollar amount of tax revenue.

Qualifications We must acknowledge, however, that other tax goals may be as important as, or even more important than, minimizing efficiency losses from taxes. Here are two examples:

- **Redistributive goals** Government may wish to impose progressive taxes as a way to redistribute income. The 10 percent excise tax the Federal government placed on selected luxuries in 1990 was an example. Because the demand for luxuries is elastic, substantial efficiency losses from this tax were to be expected. However, Congress apparently concluded that the benefits from the redistribution effects of the tax would exceed the efficiency losses.

  Ironically, in 1993 Congress repealed the luxury taxes on personal airplanes and yachts, mainly because the taxes had reduced quantity demanded so much that widespread layoffs of workers were occurring in those industries. But the 10 percent tax on luxury automobiles remained in place until it expired in 2003.

- **Reducing negative externalities** Our analysis of the efficiency loss of a tax assumes no negative externalities arising from either the production or consumption of the product in question. Where such spillover costs occur, an excise tax on producers might

and demand in this case are such that consumers and producers each pay half this total amount, or $12.5 million apiece (= $1 × 12.5 million bottles). The government uses this $25 million of tax revenue to provide public goods and services. So this transfer of dollars from consumers and producers to government involves no loss of well-being to society.

Efficiency Loss The $2 tax on wine does more than require consumers and producers to pay $25 million of taxes; it also reduces the equilibrium amount of wine produced and consumed by 2.5 million bottles. The fact that consumers and producers demanded and supplied 2.5 million more bottles of wine before the tax means that those 2.5 million bottles provided benefits in excess of their production costs. This is clear from the following analysis.

Segment *ab* of demand curve *D* in Figure 16.10 indicates the willingness to pay—the marginal benefit—associated with each of the 2.5 million bottles consumed before (but not after) the tax. Segment *cb* of supply curve *S* reflects the marginal cost of each of the bottles of wine. For all but the very last one of these 2.5 million bottles, the marginal benefit (shown by a point on *ab*) exceeds the marginal cost (shown by a point on *cb*). Not producing actually improve allocative efficiency by reducing output and thus lessening the negative externality. For example, the $2 excise tax on wine in our example might be part of a broader set of excise taxes on alcoholic beverages. The government may have concluded that the consumption of these beverages produces certain negative externalities. Therefore, it might have purposely levied this $2 tax to shift the market supply curve in Figure 16.10 to increase the price of wine, decrease alcohol consumption, and reduce the amount of resources devoted to wine.

Excise taxes that are intended to reduce the production and consumption of products with negative externalities are sometimes referred to as *sin taxes*. This name captures the idea that governments are motivated to impose these taxes to discourage activities that are perceived to be harmful or sinful. Excise taxes on cigarettes and alcohol in particular are commonly referred to as sin taxes.

QUICK REVIEW 16.3

- The benefits-received principle of taxation asserts that those who benefit from government services should pay the taxes needed to finance them; by contrast, the ability-to-pay principle asserts that taxes should be apportioned by income and wealth.
- A tax is (*a*) progressive if the average amount taxed away increases with income, (*b*) regressive if the average amount taxed away decreases with income, and (*c*) proportional if the average amount taxed away remains constant as income increases.
- Given fixed demand, more elastic supply shifts tax burdens to consumers; given fixed supply, more elastic demand shifts tax burdens to producers.
- Taxes imposed in markets raise the market equilibrium price, reduce the market equilibrium output, and normally generate efficiency losses.

Probable Incidence of U.S. Taxes

Let's look now at the probable incidence of each of the major sources of tax revenue in the United States.

Personal Income Tax

The incidence of the personal income tax generally is on the individual because there is little chance for shifting it. For every dollar paid to the tax, individuals have one less dollar in their pocketbooks. The same ordinarily holds true for inheritance taxes.

Payroll Taxes

As discussed earlier, employees and employers in 2010 *each* paid 7.65 percent in FICA taxes on a worker's annual earnings up to the 2010 Social Security cap of $106,800 and then 1.45 percent on any additional earnings.

Workers bear the full burden of their half of the Social Security and Medicare payroll taxes. As is true for the income tax, they cannot shift the payroll taxes that they pay to anyone else.

But what about the other half of the FICA tax that is levied on employers? Who pays that? The consensus view is that part of the employers' half of the FICA tax gets shifted to workers in the form of lower before-tax wages. By making it more costly to hire workers, the payroll tax reduces the demand for labor relative to supply. That reduces the market wages that employers pay workers. In a sense, employers "collect" some of the payroll tax they owe from their workers.

Corporate Income Tax

In the short run, the incidence of the corporate income tax falls on the company's stockholders (owners), who bear the burden of the tax through lower dividends or smaller amounts of retained corporate earnings. Here is why. A firm currently charging the profit-maximizing price and producing the profit-maximizing output will have no reason to change product price, output, or wages when a tax on corporate income (profit) is imposed. The price and output combination yielding the greatest profit before the tax will still yield the greatest profit after a fixed percentage of the firm's profit is removed by a corporate income tax. So, the company's stockholders will not be able to shift the tax to consumers or workers.

As previously indicated, the situation may be different in the long run. Workers, in general, may bear a significant part of the corporate income tax in the form of lower wage growth. Because it reduces the return on investment, the corporate income tax may slow the accumulation of capital (plant and equipment). It also may prompt some U.S. firms to relocate abroad in countries that have lower corporate tax rates. In either case, the tax may slow the growth of U.S. labor productivity, which depends on American workers having access to more and better equipment. We know from Figure 13.1 that the growth of labor productivity is the main reason labor demand grows over time. If the corporate income tax reduces the growth of labor productivity, then labor demand and wages my rise less rapidly. In this indirect way—and over long periods of time—workers may bear part of the corporate income tax.

Sales and Excise Taxes

A *sales tax* is a general excise tax levied on a full range of consumer goods and services, whereas a *specific excise tax* is one levied only on a particular product. Sales taxes are usually transparent to the buyer, whereas excise taxes are often "hidden" in the price of the product. But whether they are hidden or clearly visible, both are often partly or largely shifted to consumers through higher equilibrium product prices (as in Figures 16.7 through 16.9). Sales taxes and excise taxes may get shifted to different extents, however. Because a sales tax covers a much wider range of products than an excise tax, there is little chance for consumers to avoid the price boosts that sales taxes entail. They cannot reallocate their expenditures to untaxed, lower-priced products. Therefore, sales taxes tend to be shifted in their entirety from producers to consumers.

Excise taxes, however, fall on a select list of goods. Therefore, the possibility of consumers turning to substitute goods and services is greater. An excise tax on theater tickets that does not apply to other types of entertainment might be difficult to pass on to consumers via price increases. Why? The answer is provided in Figure 16.8a, where demand is elastic. A price boost to cover the excise tax on theater tickets might cause consumers to substitute alternative types of entertainment. The higher price would reduce sales so much that a seller would be better off to bear all, or a large portion of, the excise tax.

With other products, modest price increases to cover taxes may have smaller effects on sales. The excise taxes on gasoline, cigarettes, and alcoholic beverages provide examples. Here consumers have few good substitute products to which they can turn as prices rise. For these goods, the seller is better able to shift nearly all the excise tax to consumers. Example: Prices of cigarettes have gone up nearly in lockstep with the recent, substantial increases in excise taxes on cigarettes.

As indicated in Global Perspective 16.2, the United States depends less on sales and excise taxes for tax revenue than do several other nations.

Property Taxes

Many property taxes are borne by the property owner because there is no other party to whom they can be shifted. This is typically true for taxes on land, personal property,

GLOBAL PERSPECTIVE 16.2

Taxes on General Consumption as a Percentage of GDP, Selected Nations

A number of advanced industrial nations rely much more heavily on consumption taxes—sales taxes, specific excise taxes, and value-added taxes—than does the United States. A value-added tax, which the United States does not have, applies only to the difference between the value of a firm's sales and the value of its purchases from other firms. As a percentage of GDP, the highest tax rates on consumption are in countries that have value-added taxes.

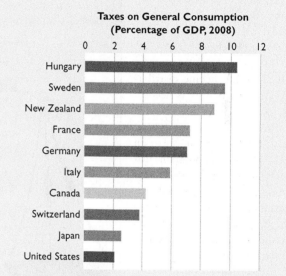

Taxes on General Consumption (Percentage of GDP, 2008)

Source: Organization for Economic Cooperation and Development, *OECD Stat Extracts*, **stats.oecd.org**.

and owner-occupied residences. Even when land is sold, the property tax is not likely to be shifted. The buyer will understand that future taxes will have to be paid on it, and this expected taxation would be reflected in the price the buyer is willing to offer for the land.

Taxes on rented and business property are a different story. Taxes on rented property can be, and usually are, shifted wholly or in part from the owner to the tenant by the process of boosting the rent. Business property taxes are treated as a business cost and are taken into account in establishing product price; hence such taxes are ordinarily shifted to the firm's customers.

Table 16.2 (on the following page) summarizes this discussion of the shifting and incidence of taxes.

Word Taxation and Spending: Redistribution versus Recycling

Many Think of Taxes as the Best Way to Level the Income Distribution, but the Real Action Is in Expenditures.

Modern governments face substantial political pressure to ensure a fair distribution of society's economic benefits. In most people's minds, this boils down to taxing the rich more than the poor, which is why there is such a focus on whether particular taxes are progressive or regressive.

But taxing the rich cannot by itself alter the income distribution. One other thing is needed: The taxes taken from the rich have to flow to the poor. In particular, they have to be spent on goods, services, and programs that are used mostly by the poor rather than on goods, services, and programs that are used mostly by the rich. If government doesn't do this, the tax revenues of the rich will simply be recycled back to the rich rather than being redistributed to the poor.

Until recently, however, economists had only patchy evidence about whether our system of taxation and spending actually redistributes income from the rich to the poor. The problem was that the U.S. government only publishes statistics on whether the

rich are being taxed more than the poor. It does not publish statistics on who receives most of its spending.

Fortunately, two economists from the nonpartisan Tax Foundation took it upon themselves to calculate those statistics. By combining data on government spending with household questionnaire responses in which people report what goods and services they consume, economists Andrew Chamberlain and Gerald Prante obtained the first reliable estimates of whether the government transfers significant amounts of income from the rich to the poor.*

As it turns out, the government *does* transfer an enormous amount of income from those with high incomes to those with low incomes. Not only do people with high incomes pay a much larger fraction of their incomes in taxes, it is also the case that the majority of that money gets transferred to the poor because government spending

*Andrew Chamberlain and Gerald Prante, "Who Pays Taxes and Who Receives Government Spending? An Analysis of Federal, State and Local Tax and Spending Distributions, 1991–2004," Tax Foundation Working Paper No. 1, 2007.

TABLE 16.2 The Probable Incidence of Taxes

Type of Tax	Probable Incidence
Personal income tax	The household or individual on which it is levied.
Payroll taxes	Workers pay the full tax levied on their earnings and part of the tax levied on their employers.
Corporate income tax	In the short run, the full tax falls on owners of the businesses. In the long run, some of the tax may be borne by workers through lower wages.
Sales tax	Consumers who buy the taxed products.
Specific excise taxes	Consumers, producers, or both, depending on elasticities of demand and supply.
Property taxes	Owners in the case of land and owner-occupied residences; tenants in the case of rented property; consumers in the case of business property.

352

is indeed concentrated on programs that are used more by the poor than by the rich. These include welfare, subsidized health care, public education, and jobs programs. The poor also benefit from government-provided public goods that are available to everyone on an equal basis—things like public roads, clean drinking water, national defense, and so on.

The size and impact of the income transfers from rich to poor are most clearly understood by looking at the nearby figure, which groups the 133 million households living in the United States in 2004 into one of five equally sized groups (or quintiles) on the basis of household income. The quintiles are labeled Bottom 20 Percent, Second 20 Percent, Third 20 Percent, Fourth 20 Percent, and Top 20 Percent. The yellow and blue bars above each quintile show, respectively, how much in taxes its members paid on average and how much in government spending they received on average during 2004.

The first thing to notice is how much more money the poor received in government spending than they paid in taxes that year. A comparison of the yellow and blue bars for the bottom quintile reveals that the poorest households received $31,185 (= $35,510 in government spending − $4,325 in taxes) more in government spending than they paid in taxes in 2004. By contrast, households in the top 20 percent of the income distribution paid

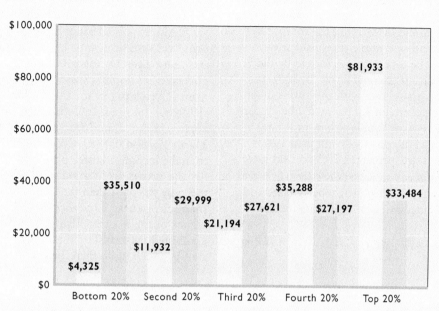

$48,449 more in taxes than they received in government spending that year.

This $48,449 per-household excess paid by households in the top quintile plus the $8091 per-household excess paid by the households in the second-highest quintile provided the money that allowed the members of the lower three quintiles to receive more in government spending than they paid in taxes. In total, the transfers from the top two quintiles to the bottom three quintiles amounted to more than $1 trillion in 2004, or about 10 percent of all income earned by households that year.

The authors also found that the average tax rates paid by the five quintiles were, respectively, 13 percent for the bottom quintile, 23.2 percent for the second quintile, 28.2 percent for the third quintile, 31.3 percent for the fourth quintile, and 34.5 percent for the top quintile. Thus, the overall tax system is highly progressive (due to the Federal income tax) despite many individual taxes being quite regressive.

But, more significantly, the spending made possible by taxing the rich more than the poor disproportionately flows back to the poor rather than being recycled to the rich. In fact, households in the top quintile receive back only 41 cents in government spending for each dollar they pay in taxes—which means that the remaining 59 cents are channeled to poorer households.

The U.S. Tax Structure

Is the overall U.S. tax structure—Federal, state, and local taxes combined—progressive, proportional, or regressive? The question is difficult to answer. Estimates of the distribution of the total tax burden depend on the extent to which the various taxes are shifted to others, and who bears the burden is subject to dispute. But the majority view of economists who study taxes is as follows:

- **_The Federal tax system is progressive._** Overall, higher-income groups pay larger percentages of

their income as Federal taxes than do lower-income groups. Although Federal payroll taxes and excise taxes are regressive, the Federal income tax is sufficiently progressive to make the overall Federal tax system progressive. About one-third of Federal income tax filers owe no tax at all. In fact, because of fully refundable tax credits designed to reduce poverty and promote work, millions of households receive tax rebates even though their income tax bill is zero. Most of the Federal income tax is paid by higher-income taxpayers. In 2007 (the latest year for which data have been compiled), the top 1 percent of income-tax filers paid 39.5 percent of the Federal income tax; the top 5 percent paid 61.0 percent of the tax.

The overall progressivity of the Federal tax system is confirmed by comparing effective (average) tax rates, which are found by dividing the total of Federal income, payroll, and excise taxes paid at various income levels by the total incomes earned by the people at those various income levels. In 2007, the 20 percent of the households with the lowest income paid an effective tax rate of 4.0 percent. The 20 percent of households with the highest income paid a 25.1 percent rate. The top 10 percent paid a 26.7 percent rate; the top 1 percent, a 29.5 percent rate.[2]

• *The state and local tax structures are largely regressive.* As a percentage of income, property taxes and sales taxes fall as income rises. Also, state income

---

[2]*Average Federal Tax Rates in 2007*, Congressional Budget Office, June 2010.

taxes are generally less progressive than the Federal income tax.

• *The overall U.S. tax system is progressive.* Higher-income people carry a substantially larger tax burden, as a percentage of their income, than do lower-income people, as discussed in this chapter's Last Word.

This chapter's Last Word also points out that the income tax system cannot be relied upon by itself to substantially alter the distribution of income, because the government might choose to spend the taxes collected from the rich to pay for things that are used more by the rich than the poor. In actual fact, however, this does not happen in the United States, because the government uses a large portion of the tax revenues collected from the rich to make income transfer payments to the poor and to pay for the provision of goods and services that are utilized more by the poor than the rich. The transfer payments by themselves are so large that they almost quadruple the incomes of the poorest fifth of U.S. households. Thus, the combined tax-transfer system levels the income distribution by much more than the tax system does on its own.

Summary

1. The funds used to pay for government purchases and transfers come from taxes, proprietary income, and borrowing. The ability to borrow allows governments to maintain high spending during economic downturns, but government borrowing when the economy is doing well may "crowd out" private-sector investment.

2. Government purchases exhaust (use up or absorb) resources; transfer payments do not. Government purchases have declined from about 22 percent of domestic output in 1960 to 20 percent today. Transfer payments, however, have grown rapidly. As a percentage of GDP, total government spending (purchases plus transfers) now stands at about 35 percent, up from 27 percent in 1960.

3. The main categories of Federal spending are pensions and income security, national defense, health, and interest on the public debt; Federal revenues come primarily from personal income taxes, payroll taxes, and corporate income taxes.

4. States derive their revenue primarily from sales and excise taxes and personal income taxes; major state expenditures go to education, public welfare, health and hospitals, and highways. Local communities derive most of their revenue from property taxes; education is their most important expenditure. State and local tax revenues are supplemented by sizable revenue grants from the Federal government.

5. Slightly over half of state and local government employees work in education. Just over half of Federal government

employees work for either the postal service or in national defense.

6. The benefits-received principle of taxation states that those who receive the benefits of goods and services provided by government should pay the taxes required to finance them. The ability-to-pay principle states that those who have greater income should be taxed more, absolutely and relatively, than those who have less income.

7. The Federal personal income tax is progressive. The corporate income tax is roughly proportional. General sales, excise, payroll, and property taxes are regressive.

8. Excise taxes affect supply and therefore equilibrium price and quantity. The more inelastic the demand for a product, the greater is the portion of an excise tax that is borne by consumers. The greater the inelasticity of supply, the larger is the portion of the tax that is borne by the seller.

9. Taxation involves the loss of some output whose marginal benefit exceeds its marginal cost. The more elastic the supply and demand curves, the greater is the efficiency loss (or deadweight loss) resulting from a particular tax.

10. Some taxes are borne by those taxed; other taxes are shifted to someone else. The income tax, the payroll tax levied on workers, and the corporate income tax (in the short run) are borne by those taxed. In contrast, sales taxes are shifted to consumers, part of the payroll tax levied on employers is shifted to workers, and, in the long run, part of the

corporate income tax is shifted to workers. Specific excise taxes may or may not be shifted to consumers, depending on the elasticities of demand and supply. Property taxes on owner-occupied property are borne by the owner; those on rental property are borne by tenants.

11. The Federal tax structure is progressive; the state and local tax structure is regressive; and the overall tax structure is progressive.

12. As discussed in the Last Word, the overall tax-spending system in the United States redistributes significant amounts of income from high-income individuals to low-income individuals. Because of the highly progressive Federal income tax, the overall tax system is progressive. In addition, spending flows disproportionately to those with lower incomes, so that the tax collections from the rich are redistributed to the poor rather than being recycled back to the rich.

Terms and Concepts

government purchases	corporate income tax	regressive tax
transfer payments	sales and excise taxes	proportional tax
personal income tax	property taxes	tax incidence
marginal tax rate	benefits-received principle	efficiency loss of a tax
average tax rate	ability-to-pay principle	
payroll taxes	progressive tax	

Questions

1. Use a circular flow diagram to show how the allocation of resources and the distribution of income are affected by each of the following government actions. LO1
   a. The construction of a new high school.
   b. A 2-percentage-point reduction of the corporate income tax.
   c. An expansion of preschool programs for disadvantaged children.
   d. The levying of an excise tax on polluters.

2. What do economists mean when they say government purchases are "exhaustive" expenditures whereas government transfer payments are "nonexhaustive" expenditures? Cite an example of a government purchase and a government transfer payment. LO1

3. What is the most important source of revenue and the major type of expenditure at the Federal level? At the state level? At the local level? LO1

4. Distinguish between the benefits-received and the ability-to-pay principles of taxation. Which philosophy is more evident in our present tax structure? Justify your answer. To which principle of taxation do you subscribe? Why? LO2

5. What is meant by a progressive tax? A regressive tax? A proportional tax? Comment on the progressivity or regressivity of each of the following taxes, indicating in each case where you think the tax incidence lies: (*a*) the Federal personal income tax, (*b*) a 4 percent state general sales tax, (*c*) a Federal excise tax on automobile tires, (*d*) a municipal property tax on real estate, (*e*) the Federal corporate income tax, (*f*) the portion of the payroll tax levied on employers. LO3

6. What is the tax incidence of an excise tax when demand is highly inelastic? Highly elastic? What effect does the elasticity of supply have on the incidence of an excise tax? What is the efficiency loss of a tax, and how does it relate to elasticity of demand and supply? LO3

7. Given the inelasticity of cigarette demand, discuss an excise tax on cigarettes in terms of efficiency loss and tax incidence. LO3

8. **ADVANCED ANALYSIS** Suppose the equation for the demand curve for some product X is $P = 8 - .6Q$ and the supply curve is $P = 2 + .4Q$. What are the equilibrium price and quantity? Now suppose an excise tax is imposed on X such that the new supply equation is $P = 4 + .4Q$. How much tax revenue will this excise tax yield the government? Graph the curves, and label the area of the graph that represents the tax collection "TC" and the area that represents the efficiency loss of the tax "EL." Briefly explain why area EL is the efficiency loss of the tax but TC is not. LO3

9. Is it possible for a country with a regressive tax system to have a tax-spending system that transfers resources from the rich to the poor? LO4

10. **LAST WORD** Does a progressive tax system by itself guarantee that resources will be redistributed from the rich to the poor? Explain. Is the *tax* system in the United States progressive, regressive, or proportional? Does the *tax-spending* system in the United States redistribute resources from higher-income earners to lower-income earners?

Problems

1. Suppose a tax is such that an individual with an income of $10,000 pays $2000 of tax, a person with an income of $20,000 pays $3000 of tax, a person with an income of $30,000 pays $4000 of tax, and so forth. What is each person's average tax rate? Is this tax regressive, proportional, or progressive? LO3

2. Suppose in Fiscalville there is no tax on the first $10,000 of income, but a 20 percent tax on earnings between $10,000 and $20,000 and a 30 percent tax on income between $20,000 and $30,000. Any income above $30,000 is taxed at 40 percent. If your income is $50,000, how much will you pay in taxes? Determine your marginal and average tax rates. Is this a progressive tax? LO3

3. For tax purposes, "gross income" is all the money a person receives in a given year from any source. But income taxes are levied on "taxable income" rather than gross income. The difference between the two is the result of many exemptions and deductions. To see how they work, suppose you made $50,000 last year in wages, $10,000 from investments, and were given $5000 as a gift by your grandmother. Also assume that you are a single parent with one small child living with you. LO3

   a. What is your gross income?

   b. Gifts of up to $13,000 per year from any person are not counted as taxable income. Also, the "personal exemption" allows you to reduce your taxable income by $3650 for each member of your household. Given these exemptions, what is your taxable income?

   c. Next, assume you paid $700 in interest on your student loans last year, put $2000 into a health savings account (HSA), and deposited $4000 into an individual retirement account (IRA). These expenditures are all *tax exempt*, meaning that any money spent on them reduces taxable income dollar-for-dollar. Knowing that fact, what is now your taxable income?

   d. Next, you can either take the so-called standard deduction or apply for itemized deductions (which involve a lot of tedious paperwork). You opt for the standard deduction that allows you as head of your household to exempt another $8500 from your taxable income. Taking that into account, what is your taxable income?

   e. Apply the tax rates shown in Table 16.1 to your taxable income. How much Federal tax will you owe? What is the marginal tax rate that applies to your last dollar of taxable income?

   f. As the parent of a dependent child, you qualify for the government's $1000 per-child "tax credit." Like all tax credits, this $1000 credit "pays" for $1000 of whatever amount of tax you owe. Given this credit, how much money will you actually have to pay in taxes? Using that actual amount, what is your average tax rate relative to your taxable income? What about your average tax rate relative to your gross income?

FURTHER TEST YOUR KNOWLEDGE AT
www.mcconnell19e.com

At the text's Online Learning Center (OLC), **www.mcconnell19e.com**, you will find one or more Web-based questions that require information from the Internet to answer. We urge you to check them out; they will familiarize you with Web sites that may be helpful in other courses and perhaps even in your career. The OLC also features multiple-choice questions that give instant feedback and provides other helpful ways to further test your knowledge of the chapter.

6

AFTER READING THIS CHAPTER, YOU SHOULD BE ABLE TO:

1 **Define** and explain the relationship between total utility, marginal utility, and the law of diminishing marginal utility.

2 **Describe** how rational consumers maximize utility by comparing the marginal utility-to-price ratios of all the products they could possibly purchase.

3 **Explain** how a demand curve can be derived by observing the outcomes of price changes in the utility-maximization model.

4 **Discuss** how the utility-maximization model helps highlight the income and substitution effects of a price change.

5 **Relate** how behavioral economics and prospect theory shed light on many consumer behaviors.

6 **(Appendix) Relate** how the indifference curve model of consumer behavior derives demand curves from budget lines, indifference curves, and utility maximization.

Consumer Behavior

If you were to compare the shopping carts of almost any two consumers, you would observe striking differences. Why does Paula have potatoes, peaches, and Pepsi in her cart, while Sam has sugar, saltines, and 7-Up in his? Why didn't Paula also buy pasta and plums? Why didn't Sam have soup and spaghetti on his grocery list?

In this chapter, you will see how individual consumers allocate their incomes among the various goods and services available to them. Given a certain budget, how does a consumer decide which goods and services to buy? This chapter will develop a model to answer this question.

This chapter will also survey some of the recent insights about consumer behavior provided by the field of behavioral economics. These insights explain many of the less-rational and oftentimes quirky behaviors exhibited by consumers. Better yet, they also suggest concrete policies that individuals, companies, and governments can use to make consumers better off by working with—rather than against—people's behavioral quirks.

116

Law of Diminishing Marginal Utility

The simplest theory of consumer behavior rests squarely on the **law of diminishing marginal utility.** This principle, first discussed in Chapter 3, is that added satisfaction declines as a consumer acquires additional units of a given product. Although consumer wants in general may be insatiable, wants for particular items can be satisfied. In a specific span of time over which consumers' tastes remain unchanged, consumers can obtain as much of a particular good or service as they can afford. But the more of that product they obtain, the less they want still more of it.

Consider durable goods, for example. A consumer's desire for an automobile, when he or she has none, may be very strong. But the desire for a second car is less intense; and for a third or fourth, weaker and weaker. Unless they are collectors, even the wealthiest families rarely have more than a half-dozen cars, although their incomes would allow them to purchase a whole fleet of vehicles.

Terminology

Evidence indicates that consumers can fulfill specific wants with succeeding units of a product but that each added unit provides less utility than the last unit purchased. Recall that a consumer derives utility from a product if it can satisfy a want: **Utility** is want-satisfying power. The utility of a good or service is the satisfaction or pleasure one gets from consuming it. Keep in mind three characteristics of this concept:

- "Utility" and "usefulness" are not synonymous. Paintings by Picasso may offer great utility to art connoisseurs but are useless functionally (other than for hiding a crack on a wall).
- Utility is subjective. The utility of a specific product may vary widely from person to person. A lifted pickup truck may have great utility to someone who drives off-road but little utility to someone unable or unwilling to climb into the rig. Eyeglasses have tremendous utility to someone who has poor eyesight but no utility to a person with 20-20 vision.
- Utility is difficult to quantify. But for purposes of illustration we assume that people can measure satisfaction with units called *utils* (units of utility). For example, a particular consumer may get 100 utils of satisfaction from a smoothie, 10 utils of satisfaction from a candy bar, and 1 util of satisfaction from a stick of gum. These imaginary units of satisfaction are convenient for quantifying consumer behavior for explanatory purposes.

Total Utility and Marginal Utility

Total utility and marginal utility are related, but different, ideas. **Total utility** is the total amount of satisfaction or pleasure a person derives from consuming some specific quantity—for example, 10 units—of a good or service. **Marginal utility** is the *extra* satisfaction a consumer realizes from an additional unit of that product—for example, from the eleventh unit. Alternatively, marginal utility is the change in total utility that results from the consumption of 1 more unit of a product.

Figure 6.1 (Key Graph) and the accompanying table demonstrate the relation between total utility and marginal

CONSIDER THIS . . .

Vending Machines and Marginal Utility

Newspaper dispensing devices and soft-drink vending machines are similar in their basic operations. Both enable consumers to buy a product by inserting coins. But there is an important difference in the two devices. The newspaper dispenser opens to the full stack of papers and seemingly "trusts" the customer to take only a single copy, whereas the vending machine displays no such "trust," requiring the consumer to buy one can at a time. Why the difference?

The idea of diminishing marginal utility is key to solving this puzzle. Most consumers take only single copies from the newspaper box because the marginal utility of a second newspaper is nearly zero. They could grab a few extra papers and try to sell them on the street, but the revenue obtained would be small relative to their time and effort. So, in selling their product, newspaper publishers rely on "zero marginal utility of the second unit," not on "consumer honesty." Also, newspapers have little "shelf life"; they are obsolete the next day. In contrast, soft-drink sellers do not allow buyers to make a single payment and then take as many cans as they want. If they did, consumers would clean out the machine because the marginal utility of successive cans of soda diminishes slowly and buyers could take extra sodas and consume them later. Soft-drink firms thus vend their products on a pay-per-can basis.

In summary, newspaper publishers and soft-drink firms use alternative vending techniques because of the highly different rates of decline in marginal utility for their products. The newspaper seller uses inexpensive dispensers that open to the full stack of papers. The soft-drink seller uses expensive vending machines that limit the consumer to a single can at a time. Each vending technique is optimal under the particular economic circumstance.

key graph

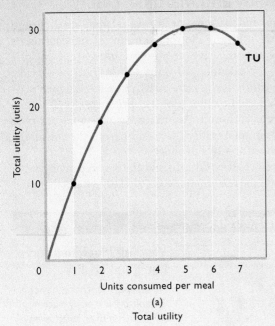

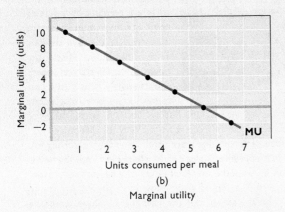

(a)
Total utility

(b)
Marginal utility

FIGURE 6.1 **Total and marginal utility.** Curves TU and MU are graphed from the data in the table. (a) As more of a product is consumed, total utility increases at a diminishing rate, reaches a maximum, and then declines. (b) Marginal utility, by definition, reflects the changes in total utility. Thus marginal utility diminishes with increased consumption, becomes zero when total utility is at a maximum, and is negative when total utility declines. As shown by the shaded rectangles in (a) and (b), marginal utility is the change in total utility associated with each additional taco. Or, alternatively, each new level of total utility is found by adding marginal utility to the preceding level of total utility.

(1) Tacos Consumed per Meal	(2) Total Utility, Utils	(3) Marginal Utility, Utils
0	0	
		10
1	10	
		8
2	18	
		6
3	24	
		4
4	28	
		2
5	30	
		0
6	30	
		−2
7	28	

QUICK QUIZ FOR FIGURE 6.1

1. Marginal utility:
   a. is the extra output a firm obtains when it adds another unit of labor.
   b. explains why product supply curves slope upward.
   c. typically rises as successive units of a good are consumed.
   d. is the extra satisfaction from the consumption of 1 more unit of some good or service.

2. Marginal utility in Figure 6.1b is positive, but declining, when total utility in Figure 6.1a is positive and:
   a. rising at an increasing rate.
   b. falling at an increasing rate.
   c. rising at a decreasing rate.
   d. falling at a decreasing rate.

3. When marginal utility is zero in graph (b), total utility in graph (a) is:
   a. also zero.
   b. neither rising nor falling.
   c. negative.
   d. rising, but at a declining rate.

4. Suppose the person represented by these graphs experienced a diminished taste for tacos. As a result the:
   a. TU curve would get steeper.
   b. MU curve would get flatter.
   c. TU and MU curves would shift downward.
   d. MU curve, but not the TU curve, would collapse to the horizontal axis.

118

utility. The curves reflect the data in the table. Column 2 shows the total utility associated with each level of consumption of tacos. Column 3 shows the marginal utility—the change in total utility—that results from the consumption of each successive taco. Starting at the origin

in Figure 6.1a, observe that each of the first five units increases total utility (TU), but by a diminishing amount. Total utility reaches a maximum with the addition of the sixth unit and then declines.

So in Figure 6.1b marginal utility (MU) remains positive but diminishes through the first five units (because total utility increases at a declining rate). Marginal utility

is zero for the sixth unit (because that unit doesn't change total utility). Marginal utility then becomes negative with the

seventh unit and beyond (because total utility is falling). Figure 6.1b and table column 3 reveal that each successive taco yields less extra utility, meaning fewer utils, than the preceding taco.[1] That is, the table and graph illustrate the law of diminishing marginal utility.

Marginal Utility and Demand

The law of diminishing marginal utility explains why the demand curve for a given product slopes downward. If successive units of a good yield smaller and smaller amounts of marginal, or extra, utility, then the consumer will buy additional units of a product only if its price falls. The consumer for whom Figure 6.1 is relevant may buy two tacos at a price of $1 each. But because he or she obtains less marginal utility from additional tacos, the consumer will choose not to buy more at that price. The consumer would rather spend additional dollars on products that provide more utility, not less utility. Therefore, additional tacos with less utility are not worth buying unless the price declines. (When marginal utility becomes negative, Taco Bell would have to pay you to consume another taco!) Thus, diminishing marginal utility supports the idea that price must decrease in order for quantity demanded to increase. In other words, consumers behave in ways that make demand curves downsloping.

---

[1]Technical footnote: In Figure 6.1b we graphed marginal utility at half-units. For example, we graphed the marginal utility of 4 utils at $3\frac{1}{2}$ units because "4 utils" refers neither to the third nor the fourth unit per se but to the *addition* or *subtraction* of the fourth unit.

- Utility is the benefit or satisfaction a person receives from consuming a good or a service.
- The law of diminishing marginal utility indicates that gains in satisfaction become smaller as successive units of a specific product are consumed.
- Diminishing marginal utility provides a simple rationale for the law of demand.

Theory of Consumer Behavior

In addition to explaining the law of demand, the idea of diminishing marginal utility explains how consumers allocate their money incomes among the many goods and services available for purchase.

Consumer Choice and the Budget Constraint

For simplicity, we will assume that the situation for the typical consumer has the following dimensions.

- *Rational behavior* The consumer is a rational person, who tries to use his or her money income to derive the greatest amount of satisfaction, or utility, from it. Consumers want to get "the most for their money" or, technically, to maximize their total utility. They engage in **rational behavior.**
- *Preferences* Each consumer has clear-cut preferences for certain of the goods and services that are available in the market. Buyers also have a good idea of how much marginal utility they will get from successive units of the various products they might purchase.
- *Budget constraint* At any point in time the consumer has a fixed, limited amount of money income. Since each consumer supplies a finite amount of human and property resources to society, he or she earns only limited income. Thus, as noted in Chapter 1, every consumer faces a **budget constraint,** even consumers who earn millions of dollars a year. Of course, this budget limitation is more severe for a consumer with an average income than for a consumer with an extraordinarily high income.
- *Prices* Goods are scarce relative to the demand for them, so every good carries a price tag. We assume that the price of each good is unaffected by the amount of it that is bought by any particular person. After all, each person's purchase is a tiny part of total demand. Also, because the consumer has a limited number of dollars, he or she cannot buy everything wanted. This point drives home the reality of scarcity to each consumer.

So the consumer must compromise; he or she must choose the most personally satisfying mix of goods and services. Different individuals will choose different mixes.

Utility-Maximizing Rule

Of all the different combinations of goods and services a consumer can obtain within his or her budget, which specific combination will yield the maximum utility or satisfaction? *To maximize satisfaction, the consumer should allocate his or her money income so that the last dollar spent on each product yields the same amount of extra (marginal) utility.* We call this the **utility-maximizing rule.** When the consumer has "balanced his margins" using this rule, he has achieved **consumer equilibrium** and has no incentive to alter his expenditure pattern. In fact, any person who has achieved consumer equilibrium would be worse off—total utility would decline—if there were any alteration in the bundle of goods purchased, providing there is no change in taste, income, products, or prices.

Numerical Example

An illustration will help explain the utility-maximizing rule. For simplicity we limit our example to two products, but the analysis also applies if there are more. Suppose consumer Holly is analyzing which combination of two products she should purchase with her fixed daily income of $10. Let's suppose these products are apples and oranges.

Holly's preferences for apples and oranges and their prices are the basic data determining the combination that will maximize her satisfaction. Table 6.1 summarizes those data, with column 2a showing the amounts of marginal utility she will derive from each successive unit of A (apples) and with column 3a showing the same thing for product B (oranges). Both columns reflect the law of diminishing marginal utility, which, in this example, is assumed to begin with the second unit of each product purchased.

Marginal Utility per Dollar To see how the utility-maximizing rule works, we must put the marginal-utility information in columns 2a and 3a on a per-dollar-spent basis. A consumer's choices are influenced not only by the extra utility that successive apples will yield but also by how many dollars (and therefore how many oranges) she must give up to obtain additional apples.

The rational consumer must compare the extra utility from each product with its added cost (that is, its price). Switching examples for a moment, suppose that you prefer a pizza whose marginal utility is, say, 36 utils to a movie whose marginal utility is 24 utils. But if the pizza's price is $12 and the movie costs only $6, you would choose the

TABLE 6.1 The Utility-Maximizing Combination of Apples and Oranges Obtainable with an Income of $10*

(1) Unit of Product	(2) Apple (Product A): Price = $1		(3) Orange (Product B): Price = $2	
	(a) Marginal Utility, Utils	(b) Marginal Utility per Dollar (MU/Price)	(a) Marginal Utility, Utils	(b) Marginal Utility per Dollar (MU/Price)
First	10	10	24	12
Second	8	8	20	10
Third	7	7	18	9
Fourth	6	6	16	8
Fifth	5	5	12	6
Sixth	4	4	6	3
Seventh	3	3	4	2

*It is assumed in this table that the amount of marginal utility received from additional units of each of the two products is independent of the quantity of the other product. For example, the marginal-utility schedule for apples is independent of the number of oranges obtained by the consumer.

movie rather than the pizza! Why? Because the marginal utility per dollar spent would be 4 utils for the movie (= 24 utils/$6) compared to only 3 utils for the pizza (= 36 utils/$12). You could see two movies for $12 and, assuming that the marginal utility of the second movie is, say, 16 utils, your total utility would be 40 utils. Clearly, 40 units of satisfaction (= 24 utils + 16 utils) from two movies are superior to 36 utils from the same $12 expenditure on one pizza.

To make the amounts of extra utility derived from differently priced goods comparable, marginal utilities must be put on a per-dollar-spent basis. We do this in columns 2b and 3b by dividing the marginal-utility data of columns 2a and 3a by the prices of apples and oranges—$1 and $2, respectively.

Decision-Making Process Table 6.1 shows Holly's preferences on a unit basis and a per-dollar basis as well as the price tags of apples and oranges. With $10 to spend, in what order should Holly allocate her dollars on units of apples and oranges to achieve the highest amount of utility within the $10 limit imposed by her income? And what specific combination of the two products will she have obtained at the time she uses up her $10?

Concentrating on columns 2b and 3b in Table 6.1, we find that Holly should first spend $2 on the first orange because its marginal utility per dollar of 12 utils is higher than the first apple's 10 utils. But now Holly finds herself indifferent about whether to buy a second orange or the first apple because the marginal utility per dollar of both is

10 utils per dollar. So she buys both of them. Holly now has 1 apple and 2 oranges. Also, the last dollar she spent on each good yielded the same marginal utility per dollar (10). But this combination of apples and oranges does not represent the maximum amount of utility that Holly can obtain. It cost her only $5 [= (1 × $1) + (2 × $2)], so she has $5 remaining, which she can spend to achieve a still higher level of total utility.

Examining columns 2b and 3b again, we find that Holly should spend the next $2 on a third orange because marginal utility per dollar for the third orange is 9 compared with 8 for the second apple. But now, with 1 apple and 3 oranges, she is again indifferent between a second apple and a fourth orange because both provide 8 utils per dollar. So Holly purchases 1 more of each. Now the last dollar spent on each product provides the same marginal utility per dollar (8), and Holly's money income of $10 is exhausted.

The utility-maximizing combination of goods attainable by Holly is 2 apples and 4 oranges. By summing marginal-utility information from columns 2a and 3a, we find that Holly is obtaining 18 (= 10 + 8) utils of satisfaction from the 2 apples and 78 (= 24 + 20 + 18 + 16) utils of satisfaction from the 4 oranges. Her $10, optimally spent, yields 96 (= 18 + 78) utils of satisfaction.

Table 6.2 summarizes our step-by-step process for maximizing Holly's utility. Note that we have implicitly assumed that Holly spends her entire income. She neither borrows nor saves. However, saving can be regarded as a "commodity" that yields utility and can be incorporated into our analysis. In fact, we treat it that way in problem 4 at the end of this chapter.

Inferior Options Holly can obtain other combinations of apples and oranges with $10, but none will yield as great a total utility as do 2 apples and 4 oranges. As an example, she can obtain 4 apples and 3 oranges for $10. But this combination yields only 93 utils, clearly inferior to the 96 utils

---

WORKED PROBLEMS

W 6.1

Consumer choice

---

provided by 2 apples and 4 oranges. True, there are other combinations apples and oranges (such as 4 apples and 5 oranges or 1 apple and 2 oranges) in which the marginal utility of the last dollar spent is the same for both goods. But all such combinations either are unobtainable with Holly's limited money income (as 4 apples and 5 oranges) or do not exhaust her money income (as 1 apple and 2 oranges) and therefore do not yield the maximum utility attainable.

Algebraic Generalization

Economists generalize the utility-maximizing rule by saying that a consumer will maximize her satisfaction when she allocates her money income so that the last dollar spent on product A, the last on product B, and so forth, yield equal amounts of additional, or marginal, utility. The marginal utility per dollar spent on A is indicated by the MU of product A divided by the price of A (column 2b in Table 6.1), and the marginal utility per dollar spent on B by the MU of product B divided by the price of B (column 3b in Table 6.1). Our utility-maximizing rule merely requires that these ratios be equal for the last dollar spent on A and the last dollar spent on B. Algebraically,

$$\frac{\text{MU of product A}}{\text{Price of A}} = \frac{\text{MU of product B}}{\text{Price of B}}$$

And, of course, the consumer must exhaust her available income. Table 6.1 shows us that the combination of 2 units of A (apples) and 4 of B (oranges) fulfills these conditions in that

$$\frac{8 \text{ utils}}{\$1} = \frac{16 \text{ utils}}{\$2}$$

and the consumer's $10 income is all spent.

TABLE 6.2 Sequence of Purchases to Achieve Consumer Equilibrium, Given the Data in Table 6.1

Choice Number	Potential Choices	Marginal Utility per Dollar	Purchase Decision	Income Remaining
1	First apple	10	First orange for $2	$8 = $10 − $2
	First orange	12		
2	First apple	10	First apple for $1	$5 = $8 − $3
	Second orange	10	and second orange for $2	
3	Second apple	8	Third orange for $2	$3 = $5 − $2
	Third orange	9		
4	Second apple	8	Second apple for $1	$0 = $3 − $3
	Fourth orange	8	and fourth orange for $2	

If the equation is not fulfilled, then some reallocation of the consumer's expenditures between A and B (from the low to the high marginal-utility-per-dollar product) will increase the consumer's total utility. For example, if the consumer spent $10 on 4 of A (apples) and 3 of B (oranges), we would find that

$$\frac{\text{MU of A of 6 utils}}{\text{Price of A of \$1}} < \frac{\text{MU of B of 18 utils}}{\text{Price of B of \$2}}$$

Here the last dollar spent on A provides only 6 utils of satisfaction, while the last dollar spent on B provides 9 (= 18/$2). So the consumer can increase total satisfaction by purchasing more of B and less of A. As dollars are reallocated from A to B, the marginal utility per dollar of A will increase while the marginal utility per dollar of B will decrease. At some new combination of A and B the two will be equal and consumer equilibrium will be achieved. Here that combination is 2 of A (apples) and 4 of B (oranges).

Utility Maximization and the Demand Curve

Once you understand the utility-maximizing rule, you can easily see why product price and quantity demanded are inversely related. Recall that the basic determinants of an individual's demand for a specific product are (1) preferences or tastes, (2) money income, and (3) the prices of other goods. The utility data in Table 6.1 reflect our consumer's preferences. We continue to suppose that her money income is $10. And, concentrating on the construction of an individual demand curve for oranges, we assume that the price of apples, now representing all "other goods," is still $1.

Deriving the Demand Schedule and Curve

We can derive a single consumer's demand schedule for oranges by considering alternative prices at which oranges might be sold and then determining the quantity the consumer will purchase. We already know one such price-quantity combination in the utility-maximizing example: Given tastes, income, and the prices of other goods, Holly will purchase 4 oranges at $2.

Now let's assume the price of oranges falls to $1. The marginal-utility-per-dollar data of column 3b in Table 6.1 will double because the price of oranges has been halved; the new data for column 3b are (by coincidence) identical to the data in column 3a. The doubling of the MU per dollar for each successive orange means that the purchase of 2

FIGURE 6.2 Deriving an individual demand curve. The consumer represented by the data in the table maximizes utility by purchasing 4 oranges at a price of $2. The decline in the price of oranges to $1 disrupts the consumer's initial utility-maximizing equilibrium. The consumer restores equilibrium by purchasing 6 rather than 4 oranges. Thus, a simple price-quantity schedule emerges, which locates two points on a downsloping demand curve.

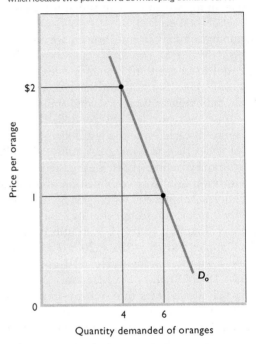

Price per Orange	Quantity Demanded
$2	4
1	6

apples and 4 oranges is no longer an equilibrium combination. By applying the same reasoning we used previously, we now find that Holly's utility-maximizing combination is 4 apples and 6 oranges. As summarized in the table in Figure 6.2, Holly will purchase 6 oranges when the price of oranges is $1. Using the data in this table, we can sketch the downward-sloping demand curve for oranges, D_o, shown in Figure 6.2. This exercise, then, clearly links the utility-maximizing behavior of a consumer and that person's downsloping demand curve for a particular product.

Income and Substitution Effects

Recall from Chapter 3 that the **income effect** is the impact that a change in the price of a product has on a consumer's real income and consequently on the quantity demanded of that good. In contrast, the **substitution effect** is the impact that a change in a product's price has on its relative expensiveness and consequently on the quantity demanded. Both effects help explain why a demand curve such as that in Figure 6.2 is downsloping.

Let's first look at the substitution effect. Recall that before the price of oranges declined, Holly was in equilibrium when purchasing 2 apples and 4 oranges because

$$\frac{\text{MU of apples of } 8}{\text{Price of apples of } \$1} = \frac{\text{MU of oranges of } 16}{\text{Price of oranges of } \$2}$$

But after the price of oranges declines from \$2 to \$1,

$$\frac{\text{MU of apples of } 8}{\text{Price of apples of } \$1} < \frac{\text{MU of oranges of } 16}{\text{Price of oranges of } \$1}$$

Clearly, the last dollar spent on oranges now yields greater utility (16 utils) than does the last dollar spent on apples (8 utils). This will lead Holly to switch, or substitute, purchases away from apples and towards oranges so as to restore consumer equilibrium. This substitution effect contributes to the inverse relationship between price and quantity that is found along her demand curve for oranges: When the price of oranges declines, the substitution effect causes Holly to buy more oranges.

What about the income effect? The decline in the price of oranges from \$2 to \$1 increases Holly's real income. Before the price decline, she maximized her utility and achieved consumer equilibrium by selecting 2 apples and 4 oranges. But at the lower \$1 price for oranges, Holly would have to spend only \$6 rather than \$10 to buy that particular combination of goods. That means that the lower price of oranges has freed up \$4 that can be spent on buying more apples, more oranges, or more of both. How many more of each fruit she ends up buying will be determined by applying the utility-maximizing rule to the new situation. But it is quite likely that the increase in real income caused by the reduction in the price of oranges will cause Holly to end up buying more oranges than before the price reduction. Any such increase in orange purchases is referred to as the income effect of the reduction in the price of oranges and it, too, helps to explain why demand curves are downward sloping: When the price of oranges falls, the income effect causes Holly to buy more oranges.

ORIGIN OF THE IDEA

O 6.2

Income and substitution effects

QUICK REVIEW 6.2

- The theory of consumer behavior assumes that, with limited income and a set of product prices, consumers make rational choices on the basis of well-defined preferences.

- A consumer maximizes utility by allocating income so that the marginal utility per dollar spent is the same for every good purchased.

- A downsloping demand curve can be derived by changing the price of one product in the consumer-behavior model and noting the change in the utility-maximizing quantity of that product demanded.

- By providing insights on the income effect and substitution effects of a price decline, the utility-maximization model helps explain why demand curves are downsloping.

Applications and Extensions

Many real-world phenomena can be explained by applying the theory of consumer behavior.

iPods

Every so often a new product totally captures consumers' imaginations. One such product is Apple's iPod, which debuted in November 2001. Less than six years later, Apple sold its 100 millionth unit. Furthermore, those units enabled Apple to sell more than 2.5 billion songs through its online iTunes Store.

The swift ascendancy of the iPod resulted mainly from a leapfrog in technology. Not only is the iPod much more compact than the portable digital CD player that it replaced, it can store and play back several thousand songs—whereas a single CD only has a 74-minute recording capacity. The improved portability and storage—and enhanced consumer satisfaction—caused a major shift in consumer demand away from the portable CD player and toward the iPod.

In the language of our analysis, Apple's introduction of the iPod severely disrupted consumer equilibrium. Consumers en masse concluded that iPods had a higher marginal-utility-to-price ratio (= MU/P) than the ratios for alternative products. They therefore shifted spending away from those other products and toward iPods as a way to increase total utility. Of course, for most people the marginal utility of a second or third iPod relative to price is quite low, so most consumers purchased only a single iPod. But Apple continued to enhance the iPod, enticing some of the buyers of older models to buy new models.

This example demonstrates a simple but important point: New products succeed by enhancing consumers' total utility. This "delivery of value" generates a revenue stream. If revenues exceed production costs, substantial profits can result—as they have for Apple.

The Diamond-Water Paradox

Early economists such as Adam Smith were puzzled by the fact that some "essential" goods had much lower prices than some "unimportant" goods. Why would water, essential to life, be priced below diamonds, which have much less usefulness? The paradox is resolved when we acknowledge that water is in great supply relative to demand and thus has a very low price per gallon. Diamonds, in contrast, are rare. Their supply is small relative to demand and, as a result, they have a very high price per carat.

Moreover, the marginal utility of the last unit of water consumed is very low. The reason follows from our utility-maximizing rule. Consumers (and producers) respond to the very low price of water by using a great deal of it—for generating electricity, irrigating crops, heating buildings, watering lawns, quenching thirst, and so on. Consumption is expanded until marginal utility, which declines as more water is consumed, equals its low price. On the other hand, relatively few diamonds are purchased because of their prohibitively high price, meaning that their marginal utility remains high. In equilibrium:

$$\frac{\text{MU of water (low)}}{\text{Price of water (low)}} = \frac{\text{MU of diamonds (high)}}{\text{Price of diamonds (high)}}$$

Although the marginal utility of the last unit of water consumed is low and the marginal utility of the last diamond purchased is high, the total utility of water is very high and the total utility of diamonds quite low. The total utility derived from the consumption of water is large because of the enormous amounts of water consumed. Total utility is the sum of the marginal utilities of all the gallons of water consumed, including the trillions of gallons that have far higher marginal utilities than the last unit consumed. In contrast, the total utility derived from diamonds is low since their high price means that relatively few of them are bought. Thus the water-diamond "paradox" is solved: Water has much more total utility (roughly, usefulness) than diamonds even though the price of diamonds greatly exceeds the price of water. These relative prices relate to marginal utility, not total utility.

ORIGIN OF THE IDEA

O 6.3

Diamond-water paradox

Opportunity Cost and the Value of Time

The theory of consumer behavior has been generalized to account for the economic value of *time*. Both consumption and production take time. Time is a valuable economic commodity; by using an hour in productive work a person can earn $6, $10, $50, or more, depending on her or his education and skills. By using that hour for leisure or in consumption activities, the individual incurs the opportunity cost of forgone income; she or he sacrifices the $6, $10, or $50 that could have been earned by working.

Imagine a self-employed consumer named Linden who is considering buying a round of golf, on the one hand, and a concert, on the other. The market price of the golf game is $30 and that of the concert is $40. But the golf game takes more time than the concert. Suppose Linden spends 4 hours on the golf course but only 2 hours at the concert. If her time is worth $10 per hour, as evidenced by the $10 wage she can obtain by working, then the "full price" of the golf game is $70 (the $30 market price plus $40 worth of time). Similarly, the full price of the concert is $60 (the $40 market price plus $20 worth of time). We find that, contrary to what market prices alone indicate, the full price of the concert is really less than the full price of the golf game.

If we now assume that the marginal utilities derived from successive golf games and concerts are identical, traditional theory would indicate that Linden should consume more golf games than concerts because the market price of the former ($30) is lower than that of the latter ($40). But when time is taken into account, the situation is reversed and golf games ($70) are more expensive than concerts ($60). So it is rational for Linden to consume more concerts than golf games.

By accounting for the opportunity cost of a consumer's time, we can explain certain phenomena that are otherwise quite puzzling. It may be rational for the unskilled worker or retiree whose time has little market value to ride a bus from Chicago to Pittsburgh. But the corporate executive, whose time is very valuable, will find it cheaper to fly, even though bus fare is only a fraction of plane fare. It is sensible for the retiree, living on a modest company pension and a Social Security check, to spend many hours shopping for bargains at the mall or taking long trips in a motor home. It is equally intelligent for the highly paid physician, working 55 hours per week, to buy a new personal computer over the Internet and take short vacations at expensive resorts.

People in other nations often feel affluent Americans are "wasteful" of food and other material goods but "overly economical" in their use of time. Americans who visit developing countries find that time is used casually or "squandered," while material goods are very highly prized and carefully used. These differences are not a paradox or a case of radically different temperaments. The differences are primarily a rational reflection of the fact that the high productivity of labor in an industrially advanced society gives time a high market value, whereas the opposite is true in a low-income, developing country.

Medical Care Purchases

The method of payment for certain goods and services affects their prices at the time we buy them and significantly changes the amount purchased. Let's go back to Table 6.1. Suppose the $1 price for apples is its "true" value or opportunity cost. But now, for some reason, its price is only, say, $.20. A rational consumer clearly would buy more apples at the $.20 price than at the $1 price.

That is what happens with medical care. People in the United States who have health insurance pay a fixed premium once a month that covers, say, 80 percent of all incurred health care costs. This means that when they actually need health care, its price to them will be only 20 percent of the actual market price. How would you act in such a situation? When you are ill, you would likely purchase a great deal more medical care than you would if you were confronted with the full price. As a result, financing health care through insurance is an important factor in explaining today's high expenditures on health care and the historical growth of such spending as a percentage of domestic output.

Similar reasoning applies to purchases of buffet meals. If you buy a meal at an all-you-can-eat buffet, you will tend to eat more than if you purchased it item by item. Why not eat that second dessert? Its marginal utility is positive and its "price" is zero!

Cash and Noncash Gifts

Marginal-utility analysis also helps us understand why people generally prefer cash gifts to noncash gifts costing the same amount. The reason is simply that the noncash gifts may not match the recipient's preferences and thus may not add as much as cash to total utility. Thought of differently, consumers know their own preferences better than the gift giver does, and the $100 cash gift provides more choices.

Look back at Table 6.1. Suppose Holly has zero earned income but is given the choice of a $2 cash gift or a noncash gift of 2 apples. Because 2 apples can be bought with $2, these two gifts are of equal monetary value. But by spending the $2 cash gift on the first orange, Holly could obtain 24 utils. The noncash gift of the first 2 apples would yield only 18 (= 10 + 8) units of utility. Conclusion: The noncash gift yields less utility to the beneficiary than does the cash gift.

Since giving noncash gifts is common, a considerable value of those gifts is potentially lost because they do not match their recipients' tastes. For example, Uncle Fred may have paid $15 for the Frank Sinatra CD he gave you for the holidays, but you would pay only $7.50 for it. Thus, a $7.50, or 50 percent, value loss is involved. Multiplied by billions of gifts a year, the total potential loss of value is huge.

But some of that loss is avoided by the creative ways individuals handle the problem. For example, newlyweds set up gift registries for their weddings to help match up their wants to the noncash gifts received. Also, people obtain cash refunds or exchanges for gifts so they can buy goods that provide more utility. And people have even been known to "recycle gifts" by giving them to someone else at a later time. All three actions support the proposition that individuals take actions to maximize their total utility.

Prospect Theory

Up to this point, we have restricted ourselves to dealing with consumer-choice situations in which people only have to deal with "goods" as opposed to "bads." When deciding on how to spend a budget, people only consider items that can bring them positive marginal utility—that is "good" things. They then use the utility-maximizing rule to select how much of each of those good things they should consume to get as much utility as possible from their limited budgets.

Unfortunately, life often forces us to deal with bad things, too. Our houses may burn down. A potential investment may go bad. The money we lend out may not be repaid.

How people deal with these negative possibilities is a central focus of **behavioral economics**—the branch of economics that combines insights from economics, psychology, and neuroscience to better understand those situations in which actual choice behavior deviates from the predictions made by earlier theories, which incorrectly concluded that people were *always* rational, deliberate, and unswayed by emotions. By studying how people actually deal with the prospect of bad things as well as good things, behavioral economists discovered three very interesting facts about how people react to goods and bads:

- People judge good things and bad things in relative terms, as gains and losses relative to their current situation, or **status quo.**
- People experience both diminishing marginal utility for gains (as you have already seen) as well as diminishing marginal disutility for losses (meaning that each successive unit of loss hurts, but less painfully than the previous unit).

- People are **loss averse,** meaning that for losses and gains near the status quo, losses are felt *much* more intensely than gains—in fact, about 2.5 times more intensely. Thus, for instance, the pain experienced by an investor who loses one dollar from his current status quo level of wealth will be about 2.5 times more intense than the pleasure he would have felt if he had gained one dollar relative to his current level of wealth.

These three facts about how people deal with goods and bads form the basis of **prospect theory,** which sheds important light on how consumers plan for and deal with

CONSIDER THIS . . .

Rising Consumption and the Hedonic Treadmill

For many sensations, people's brains are wired to notice changes rather than states. For example, your brain can sense acceleration—your change in speed—but not speed itself. As a result, standing still feels the same as moving at a constant 50 miles per hour. And if you accelerate from one constant speed to another—say, from 50 miles per hour to 70 miles per hour—you will feel the acceleration only while it's happening. Once you settle down at the new higher speed, it will feel like you are standing still again.

Consumption appears to work in much the same way. If you are used to a given level of consumption—say, $50,000 per year—then you will get a lot of enjoyment for a while if your consumption accelerates to $100,000 per year. But, as time passes, you will get used to that higher level of consumption, so that $100,000 per year seems ordinary and doesn't bring you any more pleasure than $50,000 per year used to bring you when it was your status quo.

Economist Richard Easterlin coined the term *hedonic treadmill* (pleasure treadmill) to describe this phenomenon. Just as a person walking on a real treadmill gets nowhere, people trying to make themselves permanently happier by consuming more also get nowhere, because they end up getting used to any higher level of consumption. Indeed, except for the extremely poor, people across the income spectrum report similar levels of happiness and satisfaction with their lives. This has led several economists, including Robert Frank, to argue that we should all stop trying to consume more, because doing so doesn't make us any happier in the long run. What do you think? Should we all step off of the hedonic treadmill?

ORIGIN OF THE IDEA

O 6.4

Prospect theory

life's ups and downs as well as why they often appear narrow-minded and fail to "see the big picture." To give you an idea of how powerful prospect theory is—and why its pioneer, Daniel Kahneman, was awarded the Nobel Prize in Economics—let's go through some examples of consumer behavior that would be hard to explain without the insights provided by prospect theory.

Losses and Shrinking Packages

Because people see the world in terms of gains and losses relative to the status quo situations that they are used to, businesses have to be very careful about increasing the prices they charge for their products. This is because once consumers become used to a given price, they will view any increase in the price as a loss relative to the status quo price they were used to.

The fact that consumers may view a price increase as a loss explains the otherwise curious fact that many food producers react to rising input costs by shrinking the sizes of their products. The company most famous for doing this was Hershey's chocolates, which during its first decades of operation about 100 years ago would always charge exactly 5 cents for one of its Hershey's chocolate bars. But the size of the bars would increase or decrease depending on the cost of the company's inputs. When the cost of raw materials rose, the company would keep the price fixed at 5 cents but decrease the size of the bar. When the cost of raw materials fell, it would again keep the price fixed at 5 cents but increase the size of the bar.

This seems rather bizarre when you consider that consumers were not in any way *actually* being shielded from the changes in input prices. That is because what should rationally matter to consumers is the price per ounce that they are paying for Hershey's Bars. And that *does* go up and down when the price remains fixed but the size of the bars changes.

But people aren't being fully rational here. They mentally fixate on the product's price because that is the characteristic that they are used to focusing on when making their purchasing decisions. And because the 5-cent price had become the status quo that they were used to, Hershey's understood that any price increase would be mentally categorized as a loss. Thus, Hershey's wisely chose to keep the price of its product fixed at 5 cents even when input prices were rising.

Other companies employ the same strategy today. In 2008, the prices of many raw materials, including sugar, wheat, and corn, rose substantially. Many major manufacturers reacted by reducing product sizes while keeping prices fixed. Kellogg's reduced the size of its Frosted Flakes and Rice Krispies cereal boxes from 19 to 18 ounces. Frito-Lay reduced Doritos bags from 12 to 10 ounces. Dial Soap bars shrank from 4.5 to 4 ounces. And Procter and Gamble reduced the size of Bounty paper towel rolls from 60 to 52 sheets.

Framing Effects and Advertising

Because people evaluate situations in terms of gains and losses, their decision-making can be very sensitive to the *mental frame* that they use to evaluate whether a possible outcome should be viewed as a gain or a loss. Here are a couple of examples in which differences in the context or "frame" change the perception of whether a situation should be treated as a gain or loss. See how you react to them.

- Would you be happy with a salary of $100,000 per year? You might say yes. But what if your salary last year had been $140,000? Are you still going to say yes? Now that you know you are taking a $40,000 pay cut, does that $100,000 salary seem as good as it did before?
- Similarly, suppose you have a part-time job. One day, your boss Joe walks in and says that he is going to give you a 10 percent raise. Would that please you? Now, what if he also mentioned that *everyone else* at your firm would be getting a 15 percent raise. Are you still going to be just as pleased? Or does your raise now seem like a loss compared to what everyone else will be getting?

Changes in people's preferences that are caused by new information that alters the frame used to define whether situations are gains or losses are referred to as **framing effects.** These are important to recognize because they can be manipulated by advertisers, lawyers, and politicians to try to alter people's decisions. For instance, would an advertising company be better off marketing a particular brand of hamburger as "20% fat" or as "80% lean"? Both phrases describe the same meat, but one frames the situation as a loss (20 percent fat) while the other frames it as a gain (80 percent lean).

And would you be more willing to take a particular medicine if you were told that 99.9 percent of the people who take it live or if you were told that 0.1 percent of the people who take it die? Continuing to live is a gain, whereas dying is clearly a loss. Which frame sounds better to you?

Finally, note that framing effects have important consequences for the utility-maximizing rule that we studied earlier in this chapter. If a frame alters people's valuations of marginal utility, it *will* affect their consumption decisions!

Anchoring and Credit Card Bills

Before people can calculate their gains and losses, they must first define the status quo from which to measure those changes. But it turns out that irrelevant information can unconsciously influence people's feelings about the status quo. Here's a striking example. Find a group of people and ask each person to write down the last two digits of his or her Social Security number. Then ask each person to write down his or her best estimate of the value of some object that you display to them—say, a nice cordless keyboard. What you will find is that the people whose Social Security numbers end in higher numbers—say, 67 or 89—will give higher estimates for the value of the keyboard than people whose Social Security numbers end in smaller numbers like 18 or 37. The effect can be huge. Among students in one MBA class at MIT, those with Social Security numbers ending between 80 and 99 gave average estimates of $56 for a cordless keyboard, while their classmates whose Social Security numbers ended in numbers from 00 to 20 gave average estimates of just $16.

Psychologists and behavioral economists refer to this phenomenon as **anchoring** because people's estimates about the value of the keyboard are influenced, or "anchored," by the recently considered information about the last two digits of their Social Security numbers. Why irrelevant information can anchor subsequent valuations is not fully understood. But the anchoring effect is real and can lead people to unconsciously alter how they evaluate different options.

Unfortunately, credit card companies have figured this out. They use anchoring to increase their profits by showing very small minimum-payment amounts on borrowers' monthly credit card statements. The companies could require larger minimum payments, but the minimum-payment numbers that they present are only typically about 2% of what a customer owes. Why such a small amount? Because it acts as an anchor that causes people to unconsciously make smaller payments each month. This can make a huge difference in how long it takes to pay off their bill and how much in total interest they will end up paying. For a customer who owes $1000 on a credit card that charges the typical interest rate of 19 percent per year, it will take 22 years and $3398.12 in total payments (including accumulated interest) to pay off the debt if he only makes 2 percent monthly payments. By showing such small minimum-payment amounts, credit card companies anchor many customers into the expensive habit of paying off their debts slowly rather than quickly.

LAST
Word Nudging People Toward Better Decisions

Behavioral Economists Have Recently Found Success in Using People's Behavioral Quirks to "Nudge" Them Toward Making Better Decisions.*

Behavioral economics began as a descriptive science, meaning that its first goal was to develop theories that accurately described human economic behavior. In particular, it sought to explain a number of behaviors that at first glance seemed irrational. Now that behavioral economics has made significant headway in explaining many of those behaviors, some economists are suggesting that its insights be used to nudge people toward choices that are better for themselves and others.

A key feature of "nudges" is that they are subtle. This subtlety means that nudges can cause large changes in behavior without making people feel bullied or coerced—and also without imposing stringent new rules or having to offer people big monetary incentives or disincentives to get them to do what you want.

Take retirement savings. As you may know, people tend to consume too much in the present and therefore undersave for

---

*The term "nudge" was popularized by Richard Thaler and Cass Sunstein in their book *Nudge: Improving Decisions about Health, Wealth, and Happiness*, Yale University Press, 2008.

retirement. But as it turns out, this unfortunate behavioral tendency can be easily offset by another behavioral tendency: the tendency people have to stick with default options. In terms of retirement savings, this comes down to designing corporate retirement programs in which each worker is "defaulted into" her company's retirement savings program.

Under those savings programs, money is automatically deducted each month from a worker's paycheck and deposited in her retirement savings account. It used to be the case that the default for such programs was for workers to start out *not* enrolled in them. To get enrolled, they would have to request to join the program. That is, they would have to choose to go against the default option of not being enrolled.

And because people have the behavioral tendency of sticking with whatever option is presented to them as the default, relatively few workers would make the change and enroll in their company's savings program. That was disappointing. But instead of being deterred, behavioral economists saw an opportunity. Why not change the default? Why not make automatic enrollment the default option? By making that change, people's tendency to stick with default options would work in their own favor—they would stay enrolled and save money for retirement.

When this strategy of switching the default was actually implemented, the number of workers participating in retirement

Mental Accounting and Overpriced Warranties

The utility-maximizing rule assumes that people will look at all of their potential consumption options simultaneously when trying to maximize the total utility that they can get from spending their limited incomes. But economist Richard Thaler famously noted that people sometimes look at consumption options in isolation, thereby irrationally failing to look at all their options simultaneously. Thaler coined the term **mental accounting** to describe this behavior, because it was as if people arbitrarily put certain options into totally separate "mental accounts" that they dealt with without any thought to options outside of those accounts.

An example of where this suboptimal tendency leads is the warranties that patrons of big electronic stores are offered when they purchase an expensive product, such as a plasma TV that costs $1000. These

warranties are very much overpriced given that the products they insure hardly ever break down. Personal financial experts universally tell people not to buy them. Yet many people do buy them because they engage in mental accounting.

They do this by mentally labeling their purchase of the TV as an isolated, individual transaction, sticking it into a separate mental account in their brain that might have a title like, "Purchase of New TV." Viewing the purchase in isolation exaggerates the size of the potential loss that would come from a broken TV. Customers who view the transaction in isolation see the possibility of a $1000 loss on their $1000 purchase as a potential total loss—"Holy cow! I could lose $1000 on a $1000 TV!" By contrast, people who see the big picture compare the potential loss with their entire future income stream—thereby seeing it correctly as a relatively minor loss. Because of this difference, mental accounting inclines people to pay for overpriced warranties.

savings programs skyrocketed—jumping from 60 percent to 98 percent. Those workers can now look forward to much more pleasant retirements thanks to this simple change that works *with* people's preference to stick with default options.

People's tendency to look around them for social cues as to what constitutes good behavior can also be exploited to modify their consumption behavior. But you have to be careful about how you do it, as was discovered by a California power company that wanted to encourage its customers to conserve electricity. Its first attempt to use social cues involved sending each customer a bill that showed not only his or her own usage of electricity in kilowatt-hours, but also the average usage of nearby houses. The company hoped that by showing the average usage of neighbors, customers would receive a subtle hint about their own usage. In particular, it was hoped that customers who used more than their neighbors would feel that they were being wasteful and would thus cut back on their usage.

And that did indeed happen. *But*, their reduction in electricity usage ended up being completely swamped by an increase in electricity usage on the part of the customers who had previously been below-average users. Those customers interpreted the new information that they were below-average electricity users to mean that they should feel free to consume more. After all, why should they use so little when their neighbors were using so much more?

The power company finally hit upon a solution that worked. Smilies. Yes, symbols like ☺ and ☹. In addition to printing people's own usage and the average usage of their neighbors, the company also started printing a ☺ on a customer's bill if his usage was below average and a ☹ on his bill if his usage was above average. The unhappy smilies embarrassed the heavy users into reducing their consumption even more, while the happy smilies gave a pat on the back to the light users—a pat on the back that kept their usage low.

Bear in mind that both the electricity customers and the workers saving for retirement were being *manipulated* by the people who designed the nudges. This fact is perhaps even more disturbing when you consider that the changes in behavior that were caused by the nudges were most likely *unconscious* on the part of those being manipulated. Keep this in mind as you consider for yourself when and if it is morally or ethically acceptable to use nudges to guide people's behavior.

The Endowment Effect and Market Transactions

Prospect theory also offers an explanation for the **endowment effect,** which is the tendency that people have to put a higher valuation on anything that they currently possess (are endowed with) than on identical items that they do not own but might purchase. For instance, if we show a person a new coffee mug and ask him what the maximum amount is that he would pay to buy it, he might say $10. But if we then give the mug to him so that he now owns it, and we then ask how much we would have to pay him to buy it back, he will very likely report a much higher value—say, $15.

The interesting thing is that he is not just bluffing or driving a hard bargain. Human brains appear wired to do this, to put a higher value on things we own than on things we don't. Economist John List has shown that this tendency can moderate if people are used to buying things for resale—that is, buying them with the intention of getting rid of them—but without such experience the endowment effect can be quite strong. If it is, it can make market transactions between buyers and sellers harder because sellers will be demanding higher prices for the items they are selling ("Hey, *my* mug is worth $15 to me!") than the values put on those items by potential buyers ("Dude, *your* mug is only worth $10 to me").

Several researchers have pointed to the fact that human beings are loss averse as providing an explanation for the endowment effect. Once a person possesses something, the thought of parting with it seems like a potential loss. And because potential losses are felt so intensely (2.5 times more intensely than potential gains), the owners of items end up demanding a lot of money as compensation when asked to sell their property. The potential purchasers, on the other hand, do not own the property and thus do not feel any potential sense of loss. So they put lower valuations on the items in question than do the sellers.

129

Summary

1. The law of diminishing marginal utility states that beyond a certain quantity, additional units of a specific good will yield declining amounts of extra satisfaction to a consumer.

2. The utility-maximization model assumes that the typical consumer is rational and acts on the basis of well-defined preferences. Because income is limited and goods have prices, the consumer cannot purchase all the goods and services he or she might want. The consumer therefore selects the attainable combination of goods that maximizes his or her utility or satisfaction.

3. A consumer's utility is maximized when income is allocated so that the last dollar spent on each product purchased yields the same amount of extra satisfaction. Algebraically, the utility-maximizing rule is fulfilled when

$$\frac{\text{MU of product A}}{\text{Price of A}} = \frac{\text{MU of product B}}{\text{Price of B}}$$

and the consumer's total income is spent.

4. The utility-maximizing rule and the demand curve are logically consistent. Because marginal utility declines, a lower price is needed to induce the consumer to buy more of a particular product.

5. The utility-maximization model illuminates the income and substitution effects of a price change. The income effect implies that a decline in the price of a product increases the consumer's real income and enables the consumer to buy more of that product with a fixed money income. The substitution effect implies that a lower price makes a product relatively more attractive and therefore increases the consumer's willingness to substitute it for other products.

6. Behavioral economics explains many consumption behaviors, including why irrelevant information can anchor valuations, how people value possibilities in terms of gains and losses relative to a status quo, and how framing effects can change people's decisions by affecting whether particular consumption possibilities seem like gains or losses.

Terms and Concepts

law of diminishing marginal utility

utility

total utility

marginal utility

rational behavior

budget constraint

utility-maximizing rule

consumer equilibrium

income effect

substitution effect

behavioral economics

status quo

loss averse

prospect theory

framing effects

anchoring

mental accounting

endowment effect

Questions

1. Complete the following table and answer the questions below: LO1

Units Consumed	Total Utility	Marginal Utility
0	0	
1	10	10
2	—	8
3	25	—
4	30	—
5	—	3
6	34	—

   a. At which rate is total utility increasing: a constant rate, a decreasing rate, or an increasing rate? How do you know?

   b. "A rational consumer will purchase only 1 unit of the product represented by these data, since that amount maximizes marginal utility." Do you agree? Explain why or why not.

   c. "It is possible that a rational consumer will not purchase any units of the product represented by these data." Do you agree? Explain why or why not.

2. Mrs. Simpson buys loaves of bread and quarts of milk each week at prices of $1 and 80 cents, respectively. At present she is buying these products in amounts such that the marginal utilities from the last units purchased of the two products are 80 and 70 utils, respectively. Is she buying the utility-maximizing combination of bread and milk? If not, how should she reallocate her expenditures between the two goods? LO2

3. How can time be incorporated into the theory of consumer behavior? Explain the following comment: "Want to make

millions of dollars? Devise a product that saves Americans lots of time." LO2

4. Explain: LO2
   a. Before economic growth, there were too few goods; after growth, there is too little time.
   b. It is irrational for an individual to take the time to be completely rational in economic decision making.
   c. Telling your spouse where you would like to go out to eat for your birthday makes sense in terms of utility maximization.

5. In the last decade or so, there has been a dramatic expansion of small retail convenience stores (such as 7-Eleven, Kwik Shop, and Circle K), although their prices are generally much higher than prices in large supermarkets. What explains the success of the convenience stores? LO2

6. Many apartment-complex owners are installing water meters for each apartment and billing the occupants according to the amount of water they use. This is in contrast to the former procedure of having a central meter for the entire complex and dividing up the collective water expense as part of the rent. Where individual meters have been installed, water usage has declined 10 to 40 percent. Explain that drop, referring to price and marginal utility. LO3

7. Using the utility-maximization rule as your point of reference, explain the income and substitution effects of an increase in the price of product B, with no change in the price of product A. LO4

8. **ADVANCED ANALYSIS** A "mathematically fair bet" is one in which the amount won will on average equal the amount bet,

for example, when a gambler bets, say, $100 for a 10 percent chance to win $1000 ($100 = .10 × $1000). Assuming diminishing marginal utility of dollars, explain why this is *not* a fair bet in terms of utility. Why is it even a less fair bet when the "house" takes a cut of each dollar bet? So is gambling irrational? LO4

9. Suppose that Ike is loss averse. In the morning, Ike's stockbroker calls to tell him that he has gained $1000 on his stock portfolio. In the evening, his accountant calls to tell him that he owes an extra $1000 in taxes. At the end of the day, does Ike feel emotionally neutral since the dollar value of the gain in his stock portfolio exactly offsets the amount of extra taxes he has to pay? Explain. LO5

10. You just accepted a campus job helping to raise money for your school's athletic program. You are told to draft a fundraising letter. The bottom of the letter asks recipients to write down a donation amount. If you want to raise as much money as possible, would it be better if the text of that section mentioned that your school is #3 in the nation in sports or that you are better than 99% of other schools at sports? Explain. LO5

11. **LAST WORD** What do you think of the ethics of using unconscious nudges to alter people's behavior? Before you answer, consider the following argument made by economists Richard Thaler and Cass Sunstein, who favor the use of nudges. They argue that in most situations, we couldn't avoid nudging even if we wanted to, because whatever policy we choose will contain some set of unconscious nudges and incentives that will influence people. Thus, they say, we might as well choose the wisest set of nudges.

Problems

1. Mylie's total utility from singing the same song over and over is 50 utils after one repetition, 90 utils after two repetitions, 70 utils after three repetitions, 20 utils after four repetitions, −50 utils after five repetitions, and −200 utils after six repetitions. Write down her marginal utility for each repetition. Once Mylie's total utility begins to decrease, does each additional singing of the song hurt more than the previous one or less than the previous one? LO1

2. John likes Coca-Cola. After consuming one Coke, John has a total utility of 10 utils. After two Cokes, he has a total utility of 25 utils. After three Cokes, he has a total utility of 50 utils. Does John show diminishing marginal utility for Coke, or does he show increasing marginal utility for Coke? Suppose that John has $3 in his pocket. If Cokes cost $1 each and John is willing to spend one of his dollars on purchasing a first can of Coke, would he spend his second dollar on a Coke, too? What about the third dollar? If John's marginal utility for Coke keeps on increasing no matter

how many Cokes he drinks, would it be fair to say that he is addicted to Coke? LO1

3. Suppose that Omar's marginal utility for cups of coffee is constant at 1.5 utils per cup no matter how many cups he drinks. On the other hand, his marginal utility per doughnut is 10 for the first doughnut he eats, 9 for the second he eats, 8 for the third he eats, and so on (that is, declining by 1 util per additional doughnut). In addition, suppose that coffee costs $1 per cup, doughnuts cost $1 each, and Omar has a budget that he can spend only on doughnuts, coffee, or both. How big would that budget have to be before he would spend a dollar buying a first cup of coffee? LO2

4. Columns 1 through 4 in the table at the top of the next page show the marginal utility, measured in utils, that Ricardo would get by purchasing various amounts of products A, B, C, and D. Column 5 shows the marginal utility Ricardo gets from saving. Assume that the prices of A, B, C, and D are, respectively, $18, $6, $4, and $24 and that Ricardo has an income of $106. LO2

Column 1		Column 2		Column 3		Column 4		Column 5	
Units of A	MU	Units of B	MU	Units of C	MU	Units of D	MU	Number of Dollars Saved	MU
1	72	1	24	1	15	1	36	1	5
2	54	2	15	2	12	2	30	2	4
3	45	3	12	3	8	3	24	3	3
4	36	4	9	4	7	4	18	4	2
5	27	5	7	5	5	5	13	5	1
6	18	6	5	6	4	6	7	6	$\frac{1}{2}$
7	15	7	2	7	$3\frac{1}{2}$	7	4	7	$\frac{1}{4}$
8	12	8	1	8	3	8	2	8	$\frac{1}{8}$

a. What quantities of A, B, C, and D will Ricardo purchase in maximizing his utility?

b. How many dollars will Ricardo choose to save?

c. Check your answers by substituting them into the algebraic statement of the utility-maximizing rule.

5. You are choosing between two goods, X and Y, and your marginal utility from each is as shown in the table below. If your income is $9 and the prices of X and Y are $2 and $1, respectively, what quantities of each will you purchase to maximize utility? What total utility will you realize? Assume that, other things remaining unchanged, the price of X falls to $1. What quantities of X and Y will you now purchase? Using the two prices and quantities for X, derive a demand schedule (a table showing prices and quantities demanded) for X. LO3

Units of X	MU_x	Units of Y	MU_y
1	10	1	8
2	8	2	7
3	6	3	6
4	4	4	5
5	3	5	4
6	2	6	3

6. **ADVANCED ANALYSIS** Let $MU_A = z = 10 - x$ and $MU_B = z = 21 - 2y$, where z is marginal utility per dollar measured in utils, x is the amount spent on product A, and y is the amount spent on product B. Assume that the consumer has $10 to spend on A and B—that is, $x + y = 10$. How is the $10 best allocated between A and B? How much utility will the marginal dollar yield? LO3

7. Suppose that with a budget of $100, Deborah spends $60 on sushi and $40 on bagels when sushi costs $2 per piece and bagels cost $2 per bagel. But then, after the price of bagels falls to $1 per bagel, she spends $50 on sushi and $50 on bagels. How many pieces of sushi and how many bagels did Deborah consume before the price change? At the new prices, how much money would it have cost Deborah to buy those same quantities (the ones that she consumed before the price change)? Given that it used to take Deborah's entire $100 to buy those quantities, how big is the income effect caused by the reduction in the price of bagels? LO4

FURTHER TEST YOUR KNOWLEDGE AT
www.mcconnell19e.com

At the text's Online Learning Center (OLC), **www.mcconnell19e.com**, you will find one or more Web-based questions that require information from the Internet to answer. We urge you to check them out; they will familiarize you with Web sites that may be helpful in other courses and perhaps even in your career. The OLC also features multiple-choice questions that give instant feedback and provides other helpful ways to further test your knowledge of the chapter.

Indifference Curve Analysis

The utility-maximization rule previously discussed requires individuals to measure and compare utility, much as a business would measure and compare costs or revenues. Such *cardinal utility* is measured in units such as 1, 2, 3, and 4 and can be added, subtracted, multiplied, and divided, just like the cardinal numbers in mathematics. More importantly, cardinal utility allows precise quantification of the marginal utilities upon which the utility-maximizing rule depends. In fact, the marginal-utility theory of consumer demand that we explained in the body of this chapter rests squarely on the assumption that economists be able to measure cardinal utility. The reality, however, is that measuring cardinal utility is highly difficult, at best. (Can you, for instance, state exactly how many utils you are getting from reading this book right now or how many utils you would get from watching a sunset?)

To avoid this measurement problem, economists have developed an alternative explanation of consumer behavior and equilibrium in which cardinal measurement is not required. In this more-advanced analysis, the consumer must simply *rank* various combinations of goods in terms of preference. For instance, Sally can simply report that she *prefers* 4 units of A to 6 units of B without having to put number values on how much she likes either option. The model of consumer behavior that is based upon such *ordinal utility* rankings is called indifference curve analysis. It has two main elements: budget lines and indifference curves.

The Budget Line: What Is Attainable

We know from Chapter 1 that a **budget line** (or, more technically, a *budget constraint*) is a schedule or curve showing various combinations of two products a consumer can purchase with a specific money income. If the price of product A is $1.50 and the price of product B is $1, a consumer could purchase all the combinations of A and B shown in the table in Figure 1 with $12 of money income. At one extreme, the consumer might spend all of his or her income on 8 units of A and have nothing left to spend on B. Or, by giving up 2 units of A and thereby "freeing" $3, the consumer could have 6 units of A and 3 of B. And so on to the other extreme, at which the consumer could buy 12 units of B at $1 each, spending his or her entire money income on B with nothing left to spend on A.

Figure 1 also shows the budget line graphically. Note that the graph is not restricted to whole units of A and B as is the table. Every point on the graph represents a possible combination of A and B, including fractional quantities. The slope of the graphed budget line measures the ratio of the price of B to the price of A; more precisely, the absolute value of the slope is $P_B/P_A = \$1.00/\$1.50 = \frac{2}{3}$. This is the mathematical way of saying that the consumer must forgo 2 units of A (measured on the vertical axis) to buy

FIGURE 1 A consumer's budget line. The budget line shows all the combinations of any two products that someone can purchase, given the prices of the products and the person's money income.

Units of A (Price = $1.50)	Units of B (Price = $1)	Total Expenditure
8	0	$12 (= $12 + $0)
6	3	$12 (= $9 + $3)
4	6	$12 (= $6 + $6)
2	9	$12 (= $3 + $9)
0	12	$12 (= $0 + $12)

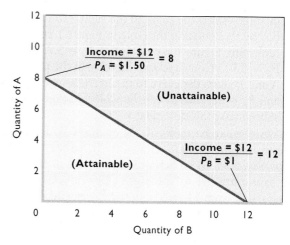

FIGURE 2 A consumer's indifference curve. Every point on indifference curve *I* represents some combination of products A and B, and all those combinations are equally satisfactory to the consumer. That is, each combination of A and B on the curve yields the same total utility.

Combination	Units of A	Units of B
j	12	2
k	6	4
l	4	6
m	3	8

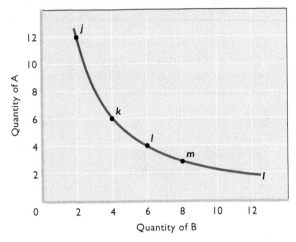

3 units of B (measured on the horizontal axis). In moving down the budget or price line, 2 units of A (at $1.50 each) must be given up to obtain 3 more units of B (at $1 each). This yields a slope of $\frac{2}{3}$.

The budget line has two other significant characteristics:

- **Income changes** The location of the budget line varies with money income. An increase in money income shifts the budget line to the right; a decrease in money income shifts it to the left. To verify this, recalculate the table in Figure 1, assuming that money income is (a) $24 and (b) $6, and plot the new budget lines in Figure 1.

- **Price changes** A change in product prices also shifts the budget line. A decline in the prices of both products—the equivalent of an increase in real income—shifts the curve to the right. (You can verify this by recalculating the table in Figure 1 and replotting Figure 1 assuming that P_A = $.75 and P_B = $.50.) Conversely, an increase in the prices of A and B shifts the curve to the left. (Assume P_A = $3 and P_B = $2, and rework the table and Figure 1 to substantiate this statement.)

Note what happens if P_B changes while P_A and money income remain constant. In particular, if P_B drops, say, from $1 to $.50, the lower end of the budget line fans outward to the right. Conversely, if P_B increases, say, from $1 to $1.50, the lower end of the line fans inward to the left. In both instances the line remains "anchored" at 8 units on the vertical axis because P_A has not changed.

Indifference Curves: What Is Preferred

Budget lines reflect "objective" market data, specifically income and prices. They reveal combinations of products A and B that can be purchased, given current money income and prices.

Indifference curves, on the other hand, reflect "subjective" information about consumer preferences for A and B. An **indifference curve** shows all the combinations of two products A and B that will yield the same total satisfaction or total utility to a consumer. The table and graph in Figure 2 present a hypothetical indifference curve for products A and B. The consumer's subjective preferences are such that he or she will realize the same total utility from each combination of A and B shown in the table or on the curve. So the consumer will be indifferent (will not care) as to which combination is actually obtained.

Indifference curves have several important characteristics.

ORIGIN OF THE IDEA

O 6.5

Indifference curves

Indifference Curves Are Downsloping

An indifference curve slopes downward because more of one product means less of the other if total utility is to remain unchanged. Suppose the consumer moves from one combination of A and B to another, say, from *j* to *k* in Figure 2. In so doing, the consumer obtains more of product B, increasing his or her total utility. But because total utility is the same everywhere on the curve, the consumer must give up some of the other product, A, to reduce total utility by a precisely offsetting amount. Thus "more of B" necessitates "less of A," and the quantities of A and B are inversely related. A curve that reflects inversely related variables is downsloping.

Indifference Curves Are Convex to the Origin

Recall from the appendix to Chapter 1 that the slope of a curve at a particular point is measured by drawing a straight line that is tangent to that point and then measuring the "rise over run" of the straight line. If you drew such straight lines for several points on the curve in Figure 2, you would find that their slopes decline (in absolute terms) as you move down the curve. An indifference curve is therefore convex (bowed inward) to the origin of the graph. Its slope diminishes or becomes flatter as we move down the curve from j to k to l, and so on. Technically, the slope of an indifference curve at each point measures the **marginal rate of substitution (MRS)** of the combination of two goods represented by that point. The slope or MRS shows the rate at which the consumer who possesses the combination must substitute one good for the other (say, B for A) to remain equally satisfied. The diminishing slope of the indifference curve means that the willingness to substitute B for A diminishes as more of B is obtained.

The rationale for this convexity—that is, for a diminishing MRS—is that a consumer's subjective willingness to substitute B for A (or A for B) will depend on the amounts of B and A he or she has to begin with. Consider the table and graph in Figure 2 again, beginning at point j. Here, in relative terms, the consumer has a substantial amount of A and very little of B. Within this combination, a unit of B is very valuable (that is, its marginal utility is high), while a unit of A is less valuable (its marginal utility is low). The consumer will then be willing to give up a substantial amount of A to get, say, 2 more units of B. In this case, the consumer is willing to forgo 6 units of A to get 2 more units of B; the MRS is $\frac{6}{2}$, or 3, for the jk segment of the curve.

But at point k the consumer has less A and more B. Here A is somewhat more valuable, and B less valuable, "at the margin." In a move from point k to point l, the consumer is willing to give up only 2 units of A to get 2 more units of B, so the MRS is only $\frac{2}{2}$, or 1. Having still less of A and more of B at point l, the consumer is willing to give up only 1 unit of A in return for 2 more units of B and the MRS falls to $\frac{1}{2}$ between l and m.[1]

---

[1] MRS declines continuously between j and k, k and l, and l and m. Our numerical values for MRS relate to the curve segments between points and are not the actual values of the MRS at each point. For example, the MRS *at* point l is $\frac{2}{3}$.

In general, as the amount of B *increases*, the marginal utility of additional units of B *decreases*. Similarly, as the quantity of A *decreases*, its marginal utility *increases*. In Figure 2 we see that in moving down the curve, the consumer will be willing to give up smaller and smaller amounts of A to offset acquiring each additional unit of B. The result is a curve with a diminishing slope, a curve that is convex to the origin. The MRS declines as one moves southeast along the indifference curve.

The Indifference Map

The single indifference curve of Figure 2 reflects some constant (but unspecified) level of total utility or satisfaction. It is possible and useful to sketch a whole series of indifference curves or an **indifference map,** as shown in Figure 3. Each curve reflects a different level of total utility and therefore never crosses another indifference curve. Specifically, each curve to the right of our original curve (labeled I_3 in Figure 3) reflects combinations of A and B that yield more utility than I_3. Each curve to the left of I_3 reflects less total utility than I_3. As we move out from the origin, each successive indifference curve represents a higher level of utility. To demonstrate this fact, draw a line in a northeasterly direction from the origin; note that its points of intersection with successive curves entail larger

FIGURE 3 An indifference map. An indifference map is a set of indifference curves. Curves farther from the origin indicate higher levels of total utility. Thus any combination of products A and B represented by a point on I_4 has greater total utility than any combination of A and B represented by a point on I_3, I_2, or I_1.

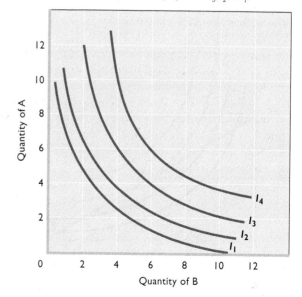

amounts of both A and B and therefore higher levels of total utility.

Equilibrium at Tangency

Since the axes in Figures 1 and 3 are identical, we can superimpose a budget line on the consumer's indifference map, as shown in Figure 4. By definition, the budget line indicates all the combinations of A and B that the consumer can attain with his or her money income, given the prices of A and B. Of these attainable combinations, the consumer will prefer the combination that yields the greatest satisfaction or utility. Specifically, the utility-maximizing combination will be the combination lying on the highest attainable indifference curve. It is called the consumer's **equilibrium position.**

In Figure 4 the consumer's equilibrium position is at point X, where the budget line is *tangent* to I_3. Why not point Y? Because Y is on a lower indifference curve, I_2. By moving "down" the budget line—by shifting dollars from purchases of A to purchases of B—the consumer can attain an indifference curve farther from the origin and thereby increase the total utility derived from the same income. Why not point Z? For the same reason: Point Z is on a lower indifference curve, I_1. By moving "up" the budget line—by reallocating dollars from B to A—the consumer can get on higher indifference curve I_3 and increase total utility.

How about point W on indifference curve I_4? While it is true that W would yield a greater total utility than X, point W is beyond (outside) the budget line and hence is *not* attainable by the consumer. Point X represents the optimal *attainable* combination of products A and B. Note that at the equilibrium position, X, the definition of tangency implies that the slope of the highest attainable indifference curve equals the slope of the budget line. Because the slope of the indifference curve reflects the MRS (marginal rate of substitution) and the slope of the budget line is P_B/P_A, the consumer's optimal or equilibrium position is the point where

$$\text{MRS} = \frac{P_B}{P_A}$$

(You may benefit by trying Appendix Question 3 at this time.)

Equivalency at Equilibrium

As indicated at the beginning of this appendix, an important difference exists between the marginal-utility theory of consumer demand and the indifference curve theory. The marginal-utility theory assumes that utility is *numerically* measurable, that is, that the consumer can say how much extra utility he or she derives from each extra unit of A or B. The consumer needs that information to determine the utility-maximizing (equilibrium) position, which is defined by

$$\frac{\text{Marginal utility of A}}{\text{Price of A}} = \frac{\text{Marginal utility of B}}{\text{Price of B}}$$

The indifference curve approach imposes a less stringent requirement on the consumer. He or she need only specify whether a particular combination of A and B will yield more than, less than, or the same amount of utility as some other combination of A and B will yield. The consumer need only say, for example, that 6 of A and 7 of B will yield more (or less) satisfaction than will 4 of A and 9 of B. Indifference curve theory does not require that the consumer specify *how much* more (or less) satisfaction will be realized.

That being said, it is a remarkable mathematical fact that both models of consumer behavior will, in any given situation, point to exactly the same consumer equilibrium and, consequently, exactly the same demand behavior. This fact allows us to combine the separate pieces of information that each theory gives us about equilibrium in order to deduce an interesting property about marginal utilities that must also hold true in equilibrium. To see this, note that when we compare the equilibrium situations in the two theories, we find that in the indifference curve analysis the MRS equals P_B/P_A at equilibrium; however, in the marginal-utility approach the ratio of marginal

FIGURE 4 The consumer's equilibrium position. The consumer's equilibrium position is represented by point X, where the black budget line is tangent to indifference curve I_3. The consumer buys 4 units of A at $1.50 per unit and 6 of B at $1 per unit with a $12 money income. Points Z and Y represent attainable combinations of A and B but yield less total utility, as is evidenced by the fact that they are on lower indifference curves. Point W would entail more utility than X, but it requires a greater income than the $12 represented by the budget line.

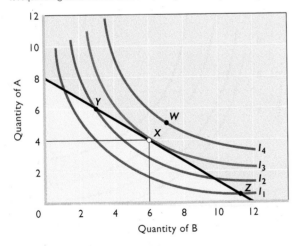

CONSIDER THIS . . .

Indifference Maps and Topographical Maps

The familiar topographical map may help you understand the idea of indifference curves and indifference maps. Each line on a topographical map represents a particular elevation above sea level, say, 500 feet. Similarly, an indifference curve represents a particular level of total utility. When you move from one point on a specific elevation line to another, the elevation remains the same. So it is with an indifference curve. A move from one position to another on the curve leaves total utility unchanged. Neither elevation lines nor indifference curves can intersect. If they did, the meaning of each line or curve would be violated. An elevation line is "an equal-elevation line"; an indifference curve is "an equal-total-utility curve."

Like the topographical map, an indifference map contains not just one line but a series of lines. That is, the topographical map may have elevation lines representing successively higher elevations of 100, 200, 300, 400, and 500 feet. Similarly, the indifference curves on the indifference map represent successively higher levels of total utility. The climber whose goal is to maximize elevation wants to get to the highest attainable elevation line; the consumer desiring to maximize total utility wants to get to the highest attainable indifference curve.

Finally, both topographical maps and indifference maps show only a few of the many such lines that could be drawn. The topographical map, for example, leaves out the elevation lines for 501 feet, 502, 503, and so on. The indifference map leaves out all the indifference curves that could be drawn between those that are displayed.

utilities equals P_B/P_A. We therefore deduce that at equilibrium the MRS is equivalent in the marginal-utility approach to the ratio of the marginal utilities of the last purchased units of the two products.[2]

---

[2]Technical footnote: If we begin with the utility-maximizing rule, $MU_A/P_A = MU_B/P_B$, and then multiply through by P_B and divide through by MU_A, we obtain $P_B/P_A = MU_B/MU_A$. In indifference curve analysis we know that at the equilibrium position MRS = P_B/P_A. Hence, at equilibrium, MRS also equals MU_B/MU_A.

The Derivation of the Demand Curve

We noted earlier that with a fixed price for A, an increase in the price of B will cause the bottom of the budget line to fan inward to the left. We can use that fact to derive a demand curve for product B. In Figure 5a we reproduce the part of Figure 4 that shows our initial consumer equilibrium at point X. The budget line determining this

FIGURE 5 Deriving the demand curve. (a) When the price of product B is increased from $1 to $1.50, the equilibrium position moves from X to X', decreasing the quantity demanded of product B from 6 to 3 units. (b) The demand curve for product B is determined by plotting the $1–6-unit and the $1.50–3-unit price-quantity combinations for product B.

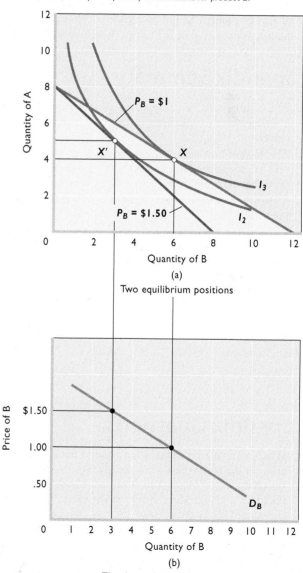

equilibrium position assumes that money income is $12 and that P_A = $1.50 and P_B = $1. Let's see what happens to the equilibrium position when we increase P_B to $1.50 and hold both money income and the price of A constant. The result is shown in Figure 5a. The budget line fans to the left, yielding a new equilibrium point X' where it is tangent to lower indifference curve I_2. At X' the consumer buys 3 units of B and 5 of A, compared with 4 of A and 6 of B at X. Our interest is in B, and we now have sufficient information to locate two points on the demand curve for product B. We know that at equilibrium point X the price of B is $1 and 6 units are purchased; at equilibrium point X' the price of B is $1.50 and 3 units are purchased.

These data are shown graphically in Figure 5b as points on the consumer's demand curve for B. Note that the horizontal axes of Figures 5a and 5b are identical; both measure the quantity demanded of B. We can therefore drop vertical reference lines from Figure 5a down to the horizontal axis of Figure 5b. On the vertical axis of Figure 5b we locate the two chosen prices of B. Knowing that these prices yield the relevant quantities demanded, we locate two points on the demand curve for B. By simple manipulation of the price of B in an indifference curve–budget line context, we have obtained a downward-sloping demand curve for B. We have thus again derived the law of demand assuming "other things equal," since only the price of B was changed (the price of A and the consumer's money income and tastes remained constant). But, in this case, we have derived the demand curve without resorting to the questionable assumption that consumers can measure utility in units called "utils." In this indifference curve approach, consumers simply compare combinations of products A and B and determine which combination they prefer, given their incomes and the prices of the two products.

Appendix Summary

1. The indifference curve approach to consumer behavior is based on the consumer's budget line and indifference curves.

2. The budget line shows all combinations of two products that the consumer can purchase, given product prices and his or her money income.

3. A change in either product prices or money income moves the budget line.

4. An indifference curve shows all combinations of two products that will yield the same total utility to a consumer. Indifference curves are downsloping and convex to the origin.

5. An indifference map consists of a number of indifference curves; the farther from the origin, the higher the total utility associated with a curve.

6. The consumer is in equilibrium (utility is maximized) at the point on the budget line that lies on the highest attainable indifference curve. At that point the budget line and indifference curve are tangent.

7. Changing the price of one product shifts the budget line and determines a new equilibrium point. A downsloping demand curve can be determined by plotting the price-quantity combinations associated with two or more equilibrium points.

Appendix Terms and Concepts

budget line

indifference curve

marginal rate of substitution (MRS)

indifference map

equilibrium position

Appendix Questions

1. What information is embodied in a budget line? What shifts occur in the budget line when money income (*a*) increases and (*b*) decreases? What shifts occur in the budget line when the price of the product shown on the vertical axis (*c*) increases and (*d*) decreases? LO6

2. What information is contained in an indifference curve? Why are such curves (*a*) downsloping and (*b*) convex to the origin? Why does total utility increase as the con-

sumer moves to indifference curves farther from the origin? Why can't indifference curves intersect? LO6

3. Using Figure 4, explain why the point of tangency of the budget line with an indifference curve is the consumer's equilibrium position. Explain why any point where the budget line intersects an indifference curve is not equilibrium. Explain: "The consumer is in equilibrium where MRS = P_B/P_A." LO6

Appendix Problems

1. Assume that the data in the accompanying table give an indifference curve for Mr. Chen. Graph this curve, putting A on the vertical axis and B on the horizontal axis. Assuming that the prices of A and B are $1.50 and $1, respectively, and that Mr. Chen has $24 to spend, add his budget line to your graph. What combination of A and B will Mr. Chen purchase? Does your answer meet the MRS = P_B/P_A rule for equilibrium? LO6

Units of A	Units of B
16	6
12	8
8	12
4	24

2. Explain graphically how indifference analysis can be used to derive a demand curve. LO6

3. **ADVANCED ANALYSIS** First, graphically illustrate a doubling of income without price changes in the indifference curve model. Next, on the same graph, show a situation in which the person whose indifference curves you are drawing buys considerably more of good B than good A after the income increase. What can you conclude about the relative coefficients of the income elasticity of demand for goods A and B (Chapter 4)? LO6

CHAPTER 6

Consumer Behavior

Previous chapters explained that consumers typically buy more of a product as its price decreases and less of a product as its price increases. Chapter 6 looks behind this law of demand to explain why consumers behave this way. It also explains factors that influence consumer decisions when they act in less rational ways and are confronted with good or bad decisions.

The chapter first explains the **law of diminishing marginal utility** and uses it to explain why the demand curve slopes downward. This explanation is based on the concept of marginal utility. In this view, the additional satisfaction (or marginal utility) that a consumer obtains from the consumption of each additional unit of a product will tend to decline; therefore a consumer will have an incentive to purchase additional units of a product only if its price falls. (Another explanation of the law of demand that is more complete, but more complex, is based on indifference curves and is presented in the appendix to this chapter.)

Most of this chapter presents the **marginal-utility** view of consumer behavior. This explanation requires that you first understand the concepts and assumptions on which this theory of consumer behavior rests, and second, do some rigorous reasoning using these concepts and assumptions. It is an exercise in logic, but be sure that you follow the reasoning. To help you, the text provides several numerical examples for you to follow.

No one believes that consumers actually perform these mental gymnastics before they spend their incomes or make purchases. But we study the marginal-utility approach to consumer behavior because the consumers behave as if they made their purchases on the basis of very fine calculations. Thus, this approach explains what we do in fact observe and makes it possible for us to predict with a good deal of precision how consumers will react to changes in their incomes and the prices of products.

The final section of the chapter describes how the theory of consumer behavior can be used to explain many economic events in the real world. The five applications discussed are the takeover by iPods of the market for recorded music, the water–diamond paradox, the value of time in consumption, the reasons for increased consumer purchases of medical care, and the economic effects of cash and noncash gifts. Be sure you understand how consumer theory is used to explain these five phenomena.

The chapter also offers insights about consumer behavior from the field of **behavioral economics.** Here you will learn about **prospect theory** and how it can be used to explain situations in which consumers are presented with good or bad choices and may be less rational in their decision making than has been assumed in previous theory. This interesting section of the chapter presents the concepts of loss aversion, framing effects, anchoring, mental accounting, and the endowment effect. Each concept is illustrated with a practical example showing how it changes the evaluations of gains and losses by consumers.

■ CHECKLIST

When you have studied this chapter you should be able to

☐ Describe the law of diminishing marginal utility.

☐ Define utility, marginal utility, and total utility.

☐ Explain the relationship of the law of diminishing marginal utility to demand.

☐ List four dimensions of the typical consumer's situation.

☐ State the utility-maximizing rule.

☐ Use the utility-maximizing rule to determine how consumers would spend their fixed incomes when given the utility and price data.

☐ Explain how a consumer decides between an optimal solution and an inferior solution to a utility-maximization problem.

☐ Give an algebraic restatement of the utility-maximizing rule based on an example using two products, A and B.

☐ Derive a consumer's demand schedule for a product from utility, income, and price data.

☐ Explain how the income and substitution effects affect utility maximization and the deriving of the product demand curve.

☐ Use consumer theory to explain the popularity of iPods.

☐ Describe the diamond–water paradox in terms of the theory of consumer behavior.

☐ Generalize the theory of consumer behavior to account for the economic value of time.

☐ Discuss how the method of payments affects consumer purchases of medical care.

☐ Describe the economic trade-offs between cash and noncash gifts.

☐ State three facts about how people deal with good and bad situations that form the basis for prospect theory.

☐ Explain why a manufacturer will keep the price constant for a product while shrinking its size when input costs rise.

☐ Describe how framing effects influence consumers' perceptions of product purchases.

☐ Discuss the role of anchoring in affecting later consumer decisions or purchases.

☐ Give an example of how mental accounting influences the buying of a warranty.

☐ Use the endowment effect to explain why people put different valuations on what they own or would like to own.

☐ Describe two "nudges" based on behavioral economics that were used to influence consumer decisions (*Last Word*).

■ CHAPTER OUTLINE

1. The *law of diminishing marginal utility* can be used to explain why the demand curve slopes downward.

 a. *Utility* is subjective and difficult to quantify. For the purposes of this chapter it will be assumed that utility is the satisfaction or pleasure a person gets from consuming a product. It will be measured in hypothetical units called *utils*.

 b. *Total utility* is the total amount of satisfaction that a consumer obtains from consuming a product. *Marginal utility* is the extra satisfaction that a consumer obtains from consuming an additional or extra unit of a product. The principle that the marginal utility of a product falls as a consumer uses (consumes) additional units of a product is the law of diminishing marginal utility. There is a relationship between total and marginal utility. As shown in text Figure 6.1, total utility increases, but at a decreasing rate until it reaches a maximum and then declines. Marginal utility decreases as total utility increases. When total utility reaches a maximum, marginal utility is zero. When total utility declines, marginal utility is negative.

 c. The law of diminishing marginal utility explains why the demand curve for a product slopes downward. As more and more of a product is consumed, each additional unit consumed provides less satisfaction. The consumer will only buy more of a product if the price falls.

2. The law of diminishing marginal utility is also the basis of the **theory of consumer behavior** that explains how consumers will spend their incomes for particular goods and services.

 a. In the simple case, it is assumed that the typical consumer engages in **rational behavior,** knows marginal-utility schedules for the various goods available (has preferences), has a limited money income to spend (a **budget constraint**), and must pay a price to acquire each of the goods that yield utility.

 b. Given these assumptions, the consumer maximizes the total utility obtained when the marginal utility of the last dollar spent on each product is the same for all products (the **utility-maximizing rule**). When the consumer follows this rule, he or she has achieved **consumer equilibrium** and has no incentive to change expenditures.

 c. A numerical example is used to illustrate the rule using two products, A and B, and assuming that all money income is spent on one of the two products. In

making the decision, the rational consumer must compare the extra or marginal utility from each product with its added cost (as measured by its price). Thus, marginal utility is compared on a per dollar basis.

 d. The allocation rule states that consumers will maximize their satisfaction when they allocate their money income so that the last dollar spent on each product yields the same marginal utility. In the two-product case, this can be stated algebraically as

$$\frac{\text{Marginal utility of A}}{\text{Price of A}} = \frac{\text{Marginal utility of B}}{\text{Price of B}}$$

Total utility is a maximum when the marginal utility of the last unit of a product purchased divided by its price is the same for all products.

3. The utility-maximizing rule can be applied to determine the amount of the product the consumer will purchase at different prices with income, tastes, and the prices of other products remaining constant.

 a. The numerical example that is used is based on one price for a product. If the price of the product falls, it is possible to use the utility-maximizing rule to determine how much more of the product the consumer will purchase. Based on this exercise it is possible to show the inverse relationship between price and quantity demanded as shown by a demand curve.

 b. Utility maximization also can be understood in terms of the **income effect** and the **substitution effect** to explain the law of demand. As the price of a product drops, a consumer increases the amounts purchased to restore equilibrium following the utility-maximizing rule. The change can be viewed as the consumer substituting more of the now less expensive product for another product and having more real income to spend.

4. Five of the many **applications** and **extensions** of consumer theory for the real world are discussed in this chapter.

 a. iPods have gained popularity among consumers relative to portable CD players because many consumers have concluded that iPods have a higher ratio of marginal utility to price than the ratio for portable CD players.

 b. Diamonds are high in price, but of limited usefulness, while water is low in price, but essential for life. This diamond–water paradox is explained by distinguishing between marginal and total utility. Water is low in price because it is generally in plentiful supply and thus has low marginal utility. Diamonds are high in price because they are relatively scarce and thus have high marginal utility. Water, however, is considered more useful than diamonds because it has much greater total utility.

 c. The facts that consumption takes time and time is a scarce resource can be included in the marginal-utility theory. The full price of any consumer good or service is equal to its market price plus the value of time taken to consume it (i.e., the income the consumer could have earned had he or she used that time for work).

 d. Expenditures on medical care have increased because of its financing through insurance. The consumer does not pay the full price of medical care services and thus has an incentive to consume more than if the consumer paid the full price.

e. Cash gifts tend to be more efficient for consumers because they are more likely to match consumer preferences and increase the total utility compared to non-cash gifts that restrict consumer choice.

5. *Behavioral economics* combines insights from economics, psychology, and neuroscience to understand decision making when people are not always rational, deliberate, or unemotional. *Prospect theory* is a part of behavioral economics that takes into account decision making when outcomes are bad or good. It is based on three facts or insights: people judge good and bad things relative to their current situation or the *status quo;* people experience both diminishing marginal utility for gains and diminishing marginal disutility for losses; and people are *loss adverse,* which means that losses are experienced more intensely than gains.

a. Consumers often fixate on a price increase rather than other product characteristics when assessing a loss. For example, if the costs of inputs increase for a product, businesses can respond by raising its price or by reducing its size. Businesses may not increase price but shrink size because they know consumers view price increases more adversely than a size reduction.

b. *Framing effects* can affect perceptions of gains or losses. New information changes the mental frame people use for evaluating whether outcomes are good or bad. For example, getting a 10-percent wage increase would typically be considered good, but not if the person found out that everyone else working in a business received a 15-percent wage increase.

c. *Anchoring* produces situations where irrelevant information affects people's perceptions of the status quo and decisions. For example, students who recently received a high grade on a test might be more likely to purchase a product such as candy bars because their assessment of the product is influenced by the positive feedback from the test.

d. Consumers may not look at their consumption options simultaneously, but rather use *mental accounting* to separate items and consider them in isolation. For example, people would be less likely to purchase a warranty for a TV if they did not separate the TV purchase from the warranty purchase, thus recognizing that a TV is not likely to break and future income will cover a loss.

e. The *endowment effect* refers to situations where people place greater value on items they possess or own than identical items they might want to purchase. For example, people who value coffee mugs at $10 each might sell them for a higher price (say $15 each) if they were given possession of the mugs and wanted to sell them.

6. (*Last Word*). Studies in behavioral economics offer suggestions to "nudge" people to make better economic and financial decisions. For example, enrollments in retirement plans are higher when people are enrolled and then given the option to opt out than if they are not enrolled and given the option to opt in. Also, people are more likely to reduce their electricity usage when given positive or negative feedback about how their behavior compares with other similar users.

■ HINTS AND TIPS

1. Utility is simply an abstraction useful for explaining consumer behavior. Do not become overly concerned with the precise measurement of utility or satisfaction. What you should focus on is the relative comparison of the additional satisfaction (marginal utility) from a dollar spent on one good to the additional satisfaction obtained from a dollar spent on another good. The choice of producing more additional utility satisfaction from one good than the other will maximize consumer satisfaction. Thus, you just need to know which good won the contest, not the final score (how much additional utility was added).

2. Master the difference between marginal utility and total utility. Once you think you understand the difference, use the concepts to explain to someone the diamond–water paradox at the end of the chapter.

3. The utility-maximization model provides insights about the income and substitution effects that occur with a change in price. For most products, a price decrease gives consumers more income to spend on that product and other products, so the quantity demanded for that product increases. The three steps in the logic for a typical product A are (1) $P_A\downarrow$, (2) income$\uparrow$, and (3) $Q_{dA}\uparrow$. A price decrease also makes product A more attractive to buy relative to its substitutes, so the demand for these substitutes decreases and the quantity demanded for product A increases. Again, there are three steps in the logic: (1) $P_A\downarrow$, (2) demand for substitutes$\downarrow$, and (3) $Q_{dA}\uparrow$. In both cases, the end result is the same: $Q_{dA}\uparrow$. Practice your understanding by showing the logic for an increase in the price of product A.

4. Prospect theory offers interesting explanations for some economic decisions and outcomes. To gain mastery of the different terms used throughout this section, think of one aspect of the theory (loss aversion, framing effects, anchoring, mental accounting, and the endowment effect) and a related example to explain it.

■ IMPORTANT TERMS

law of diminishing marginal utility	substitution effect
utility	behavioral economics
total utility	prospect theory
marginal utility	status quo
rational behavior	loss averse
budget constraint	framing effects
utility-maximizing rule	anchoring
consumer equilibrium	mental accounting
income effect	endowment effect

SELF-TEST

■ FILL-IN QUESTIONS

1. Utility is (an objective, a subjective) _____ concept and is not the same thing as usefulness. The overall satisfaction a consumer gets from consuming a good or service is (marginal, total) _____ utility, but the extra or additional satisfaction that a consumer gets from a good or service is (marginal, total) _____ utility.

2. A graph of total utility and marginal utility shows that when total utility is increasing, marginal utility is (positive, negative) _____, and when total utility is at a maximum, marginal utility is at (a maximum, zero, a minimum) _____.

3. The law of diminishing marginal utility states that marginal utility will (increase, decrease) _____ as a consumer increases the quantity consumed of a product. This law explains why the (demand, supply) _____ curve slopes downward.

4. The marginal-utility theory of consumer behavior assumes that the consumer is (wealthy, rational) _____ and has certain (preferences, discounts) _____ for various goods. A consumer cannot buy every good and service desired because income is (subsidized, limited) _____ and goods and services are scarce in relation to the demand for them; thus they have (prices, quantities) _____ attached to them.

5. When the consumer is maximizing the utility the consumer's income will obtain, the ratio of the marginal utility of the (first, last) _____ unit purchased of a product to its price is (the same, greater than) _____ for all the products bought.

6. If the marginal utility of the last dollar spent on one product is greater than the marginal utility of the last dollar spent on another product, the consumer should (increase, decrease) _____ purchases of the first and _____ purchases of the second product.

7. Assume there are only two products, X and Y, that a consumer can purchase with a fixed income. The consumer is maximizing utility algebraically when:

a. _____   b. _____

c. _____ = d. _____

8. In deriving a consumer's demand for a particular product, the two factors (other than the preferences or tastes of the consumer) that are held constant are

a. _____

b. _____

9. The utility-maximizing rule and the demand curve are logically (consistent, inconsistent) _____. Because marginal utility declines, a lower price is needed to get the consumer to buy (less, more) _____ of a particular product.

10. A fall in the price of a product tends to (increase, decrease) _____ a consumer's real income, and a rise in its price tends to _____ real income. This is called the (substitution, income) _____ effect.

11. When the price of a product increases, the product becomes relatively (more, less) _____ expensive than it was and the prices of other products become relatively (higher, lower) _____ than they were; the consumer will therefore buy (less, more) _____ of the product in question and _____ of the other products. This is called the (substitution, income) _____ effect.

12. When consumer preferences changed from portable CD players to iPods, and the prices of iPods (increased, decreased) _____ significantly, this led to (increased, decreased) _____ purchases of iPods.

13. Water is low in price because its (total, marginal) _____ utility is low, while diamonds are high in price because their _____ utility is high. Water, however, is more useful than diamonds because the (total, marginal) _____ utility of water is much greater than the _____ utility of diamonds.

14. The theory of consumer behavior has been generalized to account for (supply, time) _____. This is a valuable economic resource because it is (limited, unlimited) _____. Its value is (greater than, equal to) _____ the income that can be earned with it. The full price to the consumer of any product is, therefore, the market (time, price) _____ plus the value of the consumption _____.

15. With health insurance coverage, the price consumers pay for health care services is less than the "true" value or opportunity (benefit, cost) _____. The lower price to consumers encourages them to consume (more, less) _____ health care services.

16. Comparing food consumption at an all-you-can-eat buffet with a pay-per-item cafeteria would show that people eat (less, more) _____ at the buffet because the marginal utility of an extra food is (positive, zero) _____ while its price is _____.

17. Noncash gifts are (less, more) _____ preferred than cash gifts because they yield (less, more) _____ total utility to consumers.

18. Prospect theory suggests that people judge good and bad things relative to the (status quo, future) _____. People experience diminishing marginal utility for (losses, gains) _____ and diminishing marginal disutility for _____. People are loss adverse and experience losses (less, more) _____intensely than they do gains.

19. Changes in people's preferences that are caused by new information that changes their perspectives on whether there are gains or losses are referred to as (framing, endowment) _____ effects whereas the tendency that people have to put a higher valuation on anything they currently possess than identical items they do not own is a(n) _____ effect.

20. When consumers consider purchasing a warranty for a large consumer product such as a TV in isolation without thinking about the other options or aspects of the purchase, they are using mental (accounting, economics) _____ that often can lead to (overpayment, underpayment) _____ for the warranty protection.

■ TRUE–FALSE QUESTIONS

Circle T if the statement is true, F if it is false.

1. Utility is the benefit or satisfaction a person receives from consuming a good or service.   T F

2. Utility and usefulness are not synonymous.   T F

3. Marginal utility is the change in total utility from consuming one more unit of a product.   T F

4. Because utility cannot actually be measured, the marginal-utility theory cannot really explain how consumers will behave.   T F

5. The law of diminishing marginal utility indicates that gains in satisfaction become smaller as successive units of a specific product are consumed.   T F

6. A consumer's demand curve for a product is downsloping because total utility decreases as more of the product is consumed.   T F

7. If total utility is increasing, then marginal utility is positive and may be either increasing or decreasing.   T F

8. The theory of consumer behavior assumes that consumers act rationally to get the most from their money.   T F

9. All consumers are subject to budget constraints. T F

10. To find a consumer's demand for a product, the price of the product is varied while tastes, income, and the prices of other products remain unchanged.   T F

11. The theory of consumer behavior assumes that consumers attempt to maximize marginal utility.   T F

12. If the marginal utility per dollar spent on product A is greater than the marginal utility per dollar spent on product B, then to maximize utility, the consumer should purchase less of A and more of B.   T F

13. When consumers are maximizing total utility, the marginal utilities of the last unit of every product they buy are identical.   T F

14. The marginal utility of product X is 15 and its price is $5, while the marginal utility of product Y is 10 and its price is $2. The utility-maximizing rule suggests that there should be less consumption of product Y.   T F

15. In most cases, a change in incomes will cause a change in the portfolio of goods and services purchased by consumers.   T F

16. An increase in the real income of a consumer will result from an increase in the price of a product the consumer is buying.   T F

17. The income and substitution effects will induce the consumer to buy less of normal good Z when the price of Z increases.   T F

18. A fall in the price of iPods will decrease the demand for iTunes.   T F

19. The diamond–water paradox is explained by the fact that the total utility derived from water is low while the total utility derived from diamonds is high.   T F

20. If a consumer can earn $10 an hour and it takes 2 hours to consume a product, the value of the time required for the consumption of the product is $5.   T F

21. One reason for the increased use of health care services is that consumers pay only part of the full price of the services.   T F

22. People tend to eat more at an "all-you-can-eat buffet" because the "price" of additional items is zero but the marginal utility for these items is likely to be positive.   T F

23. Noncash gifts add more to total utility than cash gifts.   T F

24. If the price of a consumer product rather than its size is the status quo for assessing losses, then when input costs rise, a business is more likely to increase the price of the product rather than reduce its size to help pay for these additional costs.   T F

25. When people's decisions are influenced by irrelevant information that they recently considered, this phenomenon is referred to in behavior economics as anchoring.   T F

■ MULTIPLE-CHOICE QUESTIONS

Circle the letter that corresponds to the best answer.

1. Utility as defined in this chapter refers to the
   (a) usefulness of a purchased product
   (b) value of the money a consumer spends on a good
   (c) satisfaction or pleasure from consuming a good
   (d) extra income a consumer gets from buying a good at a lower price

2. Which best expresses the law of diminishing marginal utility?
   (a) The more a person consumes of a product, the smaller becomes the utility that he receives from its consumption.
   (b) The more a person consumes of a product, the smaller becomes the additional utility that she receives as a result of consuming an additional unit of the product.
   (c) The less a person consumes of a product, the smaller becomes the utility that she receives from its consumption.
   (d) The less a person consumes of a product, the smaller becomes the additional utility that he receives as a result of consuming an additional unit of the product.

3. Summing the marginal utilities of each unit consumed will determine total
   (a) cost
   (b) revenue
   (c) utility
   (d) consumption

The following table shows a hypothetical total utility schedule for a consumer of chocolate candy bars. Use the table to answer Questions 4, 5, and 6.

Number consumed	Total utility
0	0
1	9
2	19
3	27
4	35
5	42
6	42
7	40

4. This consumer begins to experience diminishing marginal utility when he consumes the
   (a) first candy bar
   (b) second candy bar
   (c) third candy bar
   (d) fourth candy bar

5. Marginal utility becomes negative with the consumption of the
   (a) fourth candy bar
   (b) fifth candy bar
   (c) sixth candy bar
   (d) seventh candy bar

6. Based on the data, you can conclude that the
   (a) marginal utility of the fourth unit is 6
   (b) marginal utility of the second unit is 27
   (c) total utility of 5 units is 42
   (d) total utility of 3 units is 55

7. After eating eight chocolate chip cookies, you are offered a ninth cookie. You turn down the cookie. Your refusal indicates that the
   (a) marginal utility for chocolate chip cookies is negative
   (b) total utility for chocolate chip cookies is negative
   (c) marginal utility is positive for the eighth and negative for the ninth cookie
   (d) total utility was zero because you ate one cookie and refused the other

8. Which is a dimension or assumption of the marginal-utility theory of consumer behavior?
   (a) The consumer has a small income.
   (b) The consumer is rational.
   (c) Goods and services are free.
   (d) Goods and services yield continually increasing amounts of marginal utility as the consumer buys more of them.

9. A consumer is making purchases of products A and B such that the marginal utility of product A is 20 and the marginal utility of product B is 30. The price of product A is $10 and the price of product B is $20. The utility-maximizing rule suggests that this consumer should
   (a) increase consumption of product B and decrease consumption of product A
   (b) increase consumption of product B and increase consumption of product A
   (c) increase consumption of product A and decrease consumption of product B
   (d) make no change in consumption of A or B

10. Suppose that the prices of A and B are $3 and $2, respectively, that the consumer is spending her entire income and buying 4 units of A and 6 units of B, and that the marginal utility of both the fourth unit of A and the sixth unit of B is 6. It can be concluded that the consumer should buy
    (a) more of both A and B
    (b) more of A and less of B
    (c) less of A and more of B
    (d) less of both A and B

11. Robert Woods is maximizing his satisfaction consuming two goods, X and Y. If the marginal utility of X is half that of Y, what is the price of X if the price of Y is $1.00?
    (a) $0.50
    (b) $1.00
    (c) $1.50
    (d) $2.00

Answer Questions 12, 13, and 14 based on the following table showing the marginal-utility schedules for goods X and Y for a hypothetical consumer. The price of good X is $1 and the price of good Y is $2. The income of the consumer is $9.

Good *X*		Good *Y*	
Quantity	MU	Quantity	MU
1	8	1	10
2	7	2	8
3	6	3	6
4	5	4	4
5	4	5	3
6	3	6	2
7	2	7	1

12. To maximize utility, the consumer will buy
(a) 7*X* and 1*Y*
(b) 5*X* and 2*Y*
(c) 3*X* and 3*Y*
(d) 1*X* and 4*Y*

13. When the consumer purchases the utility-maximizing combination of goods *X* and *Y*, total utility will be
(a) 36
(b) 45
(c) 48
(d) 52

14. Suppose that the consumer's income increased from $9 to $12. What would be the utility-maximizing combination of goods *X* and *Y*?
(a) 5*X* and 2*Y*
(b) 6*X* and 3*Y*
(c) 2*X* and 5*Y*
(d) 4*X* and 4*Y*

15. A decrease in the price of product Z will
(a) increase the marginal utility per dollar spent on Z
(b) decrease the marginal utility per dollar spent on Z
(c) decrease the total utility per dollar spent on Z
(d) cause no change in the marginal utility per dollar spent on Z

Answer Questions 16, 17, 18, and 19 on the basis of the following total utility data for products A and B. Assume that the prices of A and B are $6 and $8, respectively, and that consumer income is $36.

Units of A	Total utility	Units of B	Total utility
1	18	1	32
2	30	2	56
3	38	3	72
4	42	4	80
5	44	5	84

16. What is the level of total utility for the consumer in equilibrium?
(a) 86
(b) 102
(c) 108
(d) 120

17. How many units of the two products will the consumer buy?
(a) 1 of A and 4 of B
(b) 2 of A and 2 of B
(c) 2 of A and 3 of B
(d) 3 of A and 4 of B

18. If the price of A decreases to $4, then the utility-maximizing combination of the two products is
(a) 2 of A and 2 of B
(b) 2 of A and 3 of B
(c) 3 of A and 3 of B
(d) 4 of A and 4 of B

19. Which of the following represents the demand curve for A?

(a)		(b)		(c)		(d)	
P	*Q$_d$*	*P*	*Q$_d$*	*P*	*Q$_d$*	*P*	*Q$_d$*
$6	1	$6	2	$6	2	$6	2
4	4	4	5	4	3	4	4

20. Kristin Hansen buys only two goods, food and clothing. Both are normal goods for Kristin. Suppose the price of food decreases. Kristin's consumption of clothing will
(a) decrease due to the income effect
(b) increase due to the income effect
(c) increase due to the substitution effect
(d) not change due to the substitution effect

21. The reason the substitution effect works to encourage a consumer to buy more of a product when its price decreases is because
(a) the real income of the consumer has been increased
(b) the real income of the consumer has been decreased
(c) the product is now relatively less expensive than it was
(d) other products are now relatively less expensive than they were

22. The price of water is substantially less than the price of diamonds because
(a) the marginal utility of a diamond is significantly less than the marginal utility of a gallon of water
(b) the marginal utility of a diamond is significantly greater than the marginal utility of a gallon of water
(c) the total utility of diamonds is greater than the total utility of water
(d) diamonds have a low marginal utility

23. A consumer has two basic choices: rent a movie for $4.00 and spend 2 hours of time watching it or spend $15 for dinner at a restaurant that takes 1 hour of time. If the marginal utilities of the movie and the dinner are the same, and the consumer values time at $15 an hour, the rational consumer will most likely
(a) rent more movies and buy fewer restaurant dinners
(b) buy more restaurant dinners and rent fewer movies
(c) buy fewer restaurant dinners and rent fewer movies
(d) make no change in the consumption of both

24. Compared to cash gifts, noncash gifts are preferred
(a) more because they decrease total utility
(b) more because they increase total utility
(c) less because they increase total utility
(d) less because they decrease total utility

25. According to prospect theory, for gains or losses near the status quo
(a) gains and losses are experienced more intensely
(b) gains and losses are experienced less intensely
(c) losses are experienced more intensely while gains are experienced less intensely
(d) losses are experienced less intensely while gains are experienced more intensely

■ PROBLEMS

1. Assume that Harriet Palmer finds only three goods, A, B, and C, for sale and that the amounts of utility that their consumption will yield her are as shown in the table below. Compute the marginal utilities for successive units of A, B, and C and enter them in the appropriate columns.

	Good A			Good B			Good C	
Quantity	Total utility	Marginal utility	Quantity	Total utility	Marginal utility	Quantity	Total utility	Marginal utility
1	21	___	1	7	___	1	23	___
2	41	___	2	13	___	2	40	___
3	59	___	3	18	___	3	52	___
4	74	___	4	22	___	4	60	___
5	85	___	5	25	___	5	65	___
6	91	___	6	27	___	6	68	___
7	91	___	7	28.2	___	7	70	___

2. Using the marginal-utility data for goods A, B, and C that you obtained in problem 1, assume that the prices of A, B, and C are $5, $1, and $4, respectively, and that Palmer has an income of $37 to spend.

   a. Complete the table below by computing the *marginal utility per dollar* for successive units of A, B, and C.

	Good A		Good B		Good C
Quantity	Marginal utility per dollar	Quantity	Marginal utility per dollar	Quantity	Marginal utility per dollar
1	___	1	___	1	___
2	___	2	___	2	___
3	___	3	___	3	___
4	___	4	___	4	___
5	___	5	___	5	___
6	___	6	___	6	___
7	___	7	___	7	___

   b. Palmer would *not* buy 4 units of A, 1 unit of B, and 4 units of C because _____.

   c. Palmer would *not* buy 6 units of A, 7 units of B, and 4 units of C because _____.

   d. When Palmer is maximizing her utility, she will buy _____ units of A, _____ units of B, _____ units of C; her total utility will be _____, and the marginal utility of the last dollar spent on each good will be

   _____.

   e. If Palmer's income increased by $1, she would spend it on good _____, assuming she can buy fractions of a unit of a good, because _____.

3. Sam Thompson has an income of $36 to spend each week. The only two goods he is interested in purchasing are H and J. The marginal-utility schedules for these two goods are shown in the table below.

   The price of J does not change from week to week and is $4. The marginal utility per dollar from J is also shown in the table. But the price of H varies from one week to the next. The marginal utilities per dollar from H when the prices of H are $6, $4, $3, $2, and $1.50 are shown in the table.

	Good H						Good J	
Quantity	MU	MU/$6	MU/$4	MU/$3	MU/$2	MU/$1.50	MU	MU/$4
1	45	7.5	11.25	15	22.5	30	40	10
2	30	5	7.5	20	15	20	36	9
3	20	3.33	5	6.67	10	13.33	32	8
4	15	2.5	3.75	5	7.5	10	28	7
5	12	2	3	4	6	8	24	6
6	10	1.67	2.5	3.33	5	6.67	20	5
7	9	1.5	2.25	3	4.5	6	16	4
8	7.5	1.25	1.88	2.5	3.75	5	12	3

a. Complete the table below to show how much of H Thompson will buy each week at each of the five possible prices of H.

Price of H	Quantity of H demanded
$6.00	_____
4.00	_____
3.00	_____
2.00	_____
1.50	_____

b. What is the table you completed in part **a** called?

_____

4. Assume that a consumer can purchase only two goods: R (recreation) and M (material goods). The market price of R is $2 and the market price of M is $1. The consumer spends all her income in such a way that the marginal utility of the last unit of R she buys is 12 and the marginal utility of the last unit of M she buys is 6.

a. If we ignore the time it takes to consume R and M, is the consumer maximizing the total utility she obtains from the two goods? _____

b. Suppose it takes 4 hours to consume each unit of R, 1 hour to consume each unit of M, and the consumer can earn $2 an hour when she works.

(1) The full price of a unit of R is $_____.

(2) The full price of a unit of M is $_____.

c. If we take into account the full price of each of the commodities, is the consumer maximizing her total utility? _____ How do you know this? _____

d. If the consumer is not maximizing her utility, should she increase her consumption of R or of M? _____

Why should she do this? _____

e. Will she use more or less of her time for consuming R? _____

5. Match one of the terms from behavioral economics to an example using the appropriate number.

1. status quo	4. loss aversion
2. endowment effect	5. framing effects
3. mental accounting	6. anchoring

a. You always buy a warranty for every major consumer product you purchase regardless of whether a product is highly reliable or whether you can afford to take the loss if something should happen. _____

b. You like the number 99. Whenever you see a product sold for $0.99 you will often buy it even if you have no practical or valid use for the product. _____

c. You buy some stock in a drug company, but then the price drops sharply because one of the major drugs it sells is found to have bad side effects. You think you should sell the stock but don't want to lose money on what you purchased. _____

d. You tend to judge your gains or losses relative to your current situation. _____

e. You go to the store and purchase a gas grill and get 5 percent off, and think you got a good deal. You then talk with your neighbor who purchased the same gas grill and received 15 percent off and think you did not get a good deal. _____

f. You buy a new GPS device for $50 and start using it. Then you happen to meet a friend who sees your device and wants to buy it from you on the spot. You think about it and say fine, but state an asking price of $75. _____

■ **SHORT ANSWER AND ESSAY QUESTIONS**

1. Define the law of diminishing marginal utility and give an example of it in practice.

2. How does the subjective nature of utility limit the practical usefulness of the marginal-utility theory of consumer behavior?

3. Define total utility and marginal utility. What is the relationship between total utility and marginal utility?

4. What is the law of diminishing marginal utility?

5. What essential assumptions are made about consumers and the nature of goods and services in developing the marginal-utility theory of consumer behavior?

6. When is the consumer in equilibrium and maximizing total utility? Explain why any deviation from this equilibrium will decrease the consumer's total utility.

7. Why must the amounts of extra utility derived from differently priced goods mean that marginal utility must be put on a per-dollar-spent basis? Give an example.

8. How can saving be incorporated into the utility-maximizing analysis?

9. Give and explain an algebraic restatement of the utility-maximizing rule.

10. Using the marginal-utility theory of consumer behavior, explain how an individual's demand schedule for a particular consumer good can be obtained.

11. Why does the demand schedule that is based on the marginal-utility theory almost invariably result in an inverse or negative relationship between price and quantity demanded?

12. What insights does the utility-maximization model provide about the income and substitution effects from a price decline?

13. What aspects of the theory of consumer behavior explain why consumers started buying iPods in larger numbers instead of portable CD players in the past decade?

14. Why does water have a lower price than diamonds despite the fact that water is more useful than diamonds?

15. Explain how a consumer might determine the value of his or her time. How does the value of time affect the full price the consumer pays for a good or service?

16. What does taking time into account explain that the traditional approach to consumer behavior does not explain?

17. How does the way that we pay for goods and services affect the quantity purchased? Explain using medical care as an example.

18. Why are noncash gifts less preferred than cash gifts?

19. Explain what three "facts" about how people deal with goods and bads form the basis for prospect theory.

20. Discuss how anchoring can be used to explain the amount set for minimum payments on credit card bills.

ANSWERS

Chapter 6 Consumer Behavior

FILL-IN QUESTIONS

1. subjective, total, marginal
2. positive, zero
3. decrease, demand
4. rational, preferences, limited, prices
5. last, the same
6. increase, decrease
7. *a.* MU of product *X*; *b.* MU of product *Y*; *c.* price of *X*; *d.* price of *Y*
8. *a.* the income of the consumer; *b.* the prices of other products
9. consistent, more
10. increase, decrease, income
11. more, lower, less, more, substitution
12. decreased, increased
13. marginal, marginal, total, total
14. time, limited, equal to, price, time
15. cost, more
16. more, positive, zero
17. less, less
18. status quo, gains, losses, more
19. framing, endowment
20. accounting, overpayment

TRUE–FALSE QUESTIONS

1. T, p. 117
2. T, p. 117
3. T, pp. 117–119
4. F, pp. 117–119
5. T, p. 117
6. F, p. 119
7. T, pp. 117–119
8. T, pp. 119–120
9. T, pp. 119–120
10. T, pp. 119–120
11. F, pp. 119–120
12. F, p. 120
13. F, pp. 120–121
14. F, pp. 120–121
15. T, pp. 122–123
16. F, pp. 122–123
17. T, pp. 122–123
18. F, pp. 122–123
19. F, p. 124
20. F, pp. 124–125
21. T, p. 125
22. T, p. 125
23. F, p. 125
24. F, pp. 126–127
25. T, p. 127

MULTIPLE-CHOICE QUESTIONS

1. c, p. 117
2. b, p. 117
3. c, pp. 117–119
4. c, pp. 117–119
5. d, pp. 117–119
6. c, pp. 117–119
7. c, pp. 117–119
8. b, pp. 119–120
9. c, pp. 120–121
10. c, pp. 120–121
11. a, pp. 120–121
12. b, pp. 121–122
13. c, pp. 121–122
14. b, pp. 121–122
15. a, pp. 121–122
16. b, pp. 117–119
17. c, pp. 118–119
18. c, pp. 117–119
19. c, p. 122
20. b, pp. 122–123
21. c, pp. 122–123
22. b, p. 124
23. b, pp. 124–125
24. d, p. 125
25. c, pp. 125–126

PROBLEMS

1. marginal utility of good A: 21, 20, 18, 15, 11, 6, 0; marginal utility of good B: 7, 6, 5, 4, 3, 2, 1.2; marginal utility of good C: 23, 17, 12, 8, 5, 3, 2
2. *a.* marginal utility per dollar of good A: 4.2, 4, 3.6, 3, 2.2, 1.2, 0; marginal utility per dollar of good B: 7, 6, 5, 4, 3, 2, 1.2; marginal utility of good C: 5.75, 4.25, 3, 2, 1.25, .75, .5; *b.* the marginal utility per dollar spent on good B (7) is greater than the marginal utility per dollar spent on good A (3), and the latter is greater than the marginal utility per dollar spent on good C (2); *c.* she would be spending more than her $37 income; *d.* 4, 5, 3, 151, 3; *e.* A, she would obtain the greatest marginal utility for her dollar (2.2)
3. *a.* 2, 3, 4, 6, 8; *b.* the demand schedule (for good H)
4. *a.* yes; *b.* (1) 10, (2) 3; *c.* no, the marginal utility to price ratios are not the same for the two goods; *d.* of M, because its MU/P ratio is greater; *e.* less
5. *a.* 3; *b.* 6; *c.* 4; *d.* 1; *e.* 5; *f.* 2

SHORT ANSWER AND ESSAY QUESTIONS

1. p. 119
2. p. 119
3. p. 119
4. pp. 119–121
5. p. 119
6. pp. 119–120
7. p. 119
8. pp. 120–121
9. p. 120
10. pp. 120–121
11. pp. 121–122
12. p. 122
13. p. 122
14. pp. 122–123
15. pp. 123–124
16. p. 124
17. p. 125
18. p. 125
19. pp. 125–126
20. p. 127

Indifference Curve Analysis

This brief appendix contains another explanation of or approach to the theory of consumer behavior. It is based on *ordinal utility* (the rank-ordering of consumer preferences) rather than *cardinal utility* (the precise measurement of utility). For this explanation you are introduced first to the **budget line** and then to the **indifference curve.** These two geometrical concepts are then combined to explain when a consumer is purchasing the combination of two products that maximizes the satisfaction obtainable with his or her income. The last step is to vary the price of one of the products to find the consumer's demand (schedule or curve) for the product.

■ APPENDIX CHECKLIST

When you have studied this appendix you should be able to

☐ Distinguish between cardinal utility and ordinal utility.
☐ Describe the concept of a budget line and its characteristics.
☐ Explain how to measure the slope of a budget line and determine the location of the budget line.
☐ Describe the concept of an indifference curve.
☐ State two characteristics of indifference curves.
☐ Explain the meaning of an indifference map.
☐ Given an indifference map, determine which indifference curves bring more or less total utility to consumers.
☐ Use indifference curves to identify which combination of two products maximizes the total utility of consumers.
☐ Derive a consumer's demand for a product using indifference curve analysis.
☐ Compare and contrast the marginal-utility and the indifference curve analyses of consumer behavior.

■ APPENDIX OUTLINE

1. Indifference curve analysis is based on ordinal utility in which consumer preferences are rank-ordered, but not measured. By contrast, the utility-maximization analysis and rule presented in Chapter 6 is based on cardinal utility, or the precise measurement of utility or satisfaction.

2. A **budget line** shows graphically the different combinations of two products a consumer can purchase with a particular money income. A budget line has a negative slope.

    a. An increase in the money income of the consumer will shift the budget line to the right without affecting its slope. A decrease in money income will shift the budget line to the left.

    b. An increase in the prices of both products shifts the budget line to the left. A decrease in the prices of both products shifts the budget line to the right. An increase (decrease) in the price of the product, the quantity of which is measured horizontally (the price of the other product remaining constant), pivots the budget line around a fixed point on the vertical axis in a clockwise (counterclockwise) direction.

3. An **indifference curve** shows graphically the different combinations of two products that bring a consumer the same total utility.

    a. An indifference curve is down-sloping. If the utility is to remain the same when the quantity of one product increases, the quantity of the other product must decrease.

    b. An indifference curve is also convex to the origin. The more a consumer has of one product, the smaller the quantity of a second product he or she is willing to give up to obtain an additional unit of the first product. The slope of an indifference curve is the **marginal rate of substitution** (MRS), the rate at which the consumer will substitute one product for another to remain equally satisfied.

4. The consumer has an indifference curve for every level of total utility or satisfaction. The nearer a curve is to the origin in this **indifference map**, the smaller is the utility of the combinations on that curve. The further a curve is from the origin, the larger is the utility of the combinations on that curve.

5. The consumer is in an **equilibrium position** and purchasing the combination of two products that brings the maximum utility to her or him when the budget line is tangent to the highest attainable indifference curve.

6. In the marginal-utility approach to consumer behavior, it is assumed that utility is cardinal and it is measurable. In the indifference-curve approach, utility is ordinal and rank-ordered. It need only be assumed that a consumer can say whether a combination of products has more utility than, less utility than, or the same amount of utility as another combination.

7. The demand (schedule or curve) for one of the products is derived by varying the price of that product and shifting the budget line, holding the price of the other product and the consumer's income constant, and finding the quantity of the product the consumer will purchase at each price when in equilibrium.

■ HINTS AND TIPS

1. This appendix simplifies the analysis by limiting consumer choice to just two goods. The **budget line** shows the consumer what it is possible to purchase in the two-good world, given an income. Make sure that you understand what a budget line is. To test your understanding, practice with different income levels and prices. For example, assume you had an income of $100 to spend for two goods (A and B). Good A costs $10 and Good B costs $5. Draw a budget line to show the possible combinations of A and B that you could purchase.

2. **Indifference curves** and the marginal rate of substitution are perhaps the most difficult concepts to understand in this appendix. Remember that the points on the curve show the possible combinations of two goods for which the consumer is *indifferent,* and thus does not care what combination is chosen. The **marginal rate of substitution** is the rate at which the consumer gives up units of one good for units of another along the indifference curve. This rate will change (diminish) as the consumer moves down an indifference curve because the consumer is less willing to *substitute* one good for the other.

■ IMPORTANT TERMS

budget line

indifference curve

marginal rate of
 substitution (MRS)

indifference map

equilibrium position

SELF-TEST

■ FILL-IN QUESTIONS

1. A schedule or curve that shows the various combinations of two products a consumer can buy with a specific (income, feature) _____ is called (a budget, an indifference) _____ line.

2. Given two products, X and Y, and a graph with the quantities of X measured horizontally and the quantities of Y measured vertically, the budget line has a slope equal to the ratio of the _____ to the _____.

3. When a consumer's income increases, the budget line shifts to the (left, right) _____, while a decrease in income shifts the budget line to the _____.

4. Given two products, A and B, and a budget line graph with the quantities of A measured horizontally and the quantities of B measured vertically, an increase in the price of A will fan the budget line (outward, inward) _____, and a decrease in the price of A will fan the budget line _____ around a fixed point on the (A, B) _____ axis.

5. (A demand, An indifference) _____ curve shows the various combinations of two products that give a consumer the same total satisfaction or total (cost, utility) _____.

6. An indifference curve slopes (upward, downward) _____ and is (concave, convex) _____ to the origin.

7. The slope of the indifference curve at each point measures the (marginal, total) _____ rate of substitution of the combination represented by that point.

8. The more a consumer has of the first product than the second product, the (greater, smaller) _____ is the quantity of the first product the consumer will give up to obtain an additional unit of the second product. As a result, the marginal rate of substitution (MRS) of the first for the second product (increases, decreases) _____ as a consumer moves from left to right (downward) along an indifference curve.

9. A set of indifference curves reflects different levels of (marginal, total) _____ utility and is called an indifference (plan, map) _____.

10. The farther from the origin an indifference curve lies, the (greater, smaller) _____ the total utility obtained from the combinations of products on that curve.

11. A consumer obtains the greatest attainable total utility or satisfaction when he or she purchases that combination of two products at which his or her budget line is (tangent to, greater than) _____ an indifference curve. At this point the consumer's marginal rate of substitution is equal to the (slope, axis) _____ of the budget line.

12. Were a consumer to purchase a combination of two products that lie on her budget line and at which her budget line is steeper than the indifference curve intersecting that point, she could increase her satisfaction by trading (down, up) _____ her budget line.

13. The marginal-utility approach to consumer behavior requires that we assume utility is (cardinal, ordinal) _____, or numerically measurable; the indifference-curve approach assumes the utility is _____, and that preferences are ranked.

14. When quantities of product X are measured along the horizontal axis, a decrease in the price of X

 a. fans the budget line (inward, outward) _____ and to the (right, left) _____,

 b. puts the consumer, when in equilibrium, on a (higher, lower) _____ indifference curve; and

 c. normally induces the consumer to purchase (more, less) _____ of product X.

15. Using indifference curves and different budget lines to determine how much of a particular product an individual consumer will purchase at different prices makes it possible to derive that consumer's (supply, demand)

_____ curve or schedule for that product.

■ TRUE–FALSE QUESTIONS

Circle T if the statement is true, F if it is false.

1. The budget line shows all combinations of two products that the consumer can purchase, given money income and the prices of the products.　　**T　F**

2. The slope of the budget line when quantities of Alpha are measured horizontally and quantities of Beta are measured vertically is equal to the price of Beta divided by the price of Alpha.　　**T　F**

3. A consumer is unable to purchase any of the combinations of two products which lie below (or to the left) of the consumer's budget line.　　**T　F**

4. An increase in the money income of a consumer shifts the budget line to the right.　　**T　F**

5. If a consumer moves from one combination (or point) on an indifference curve to another combination (or point) on the same curve, the total utility obtained by the consumer does not change.　　**T　F**

6. An indifference curve is concave to the origin.　**T　F**

7. The marginal rate of substitution shows the rate, at the margin, at which the consumer is prepared to substitute one good for the other so as to remain equally satisfied.　　**T　F**

8. The closer to the origin an indifference curve lies, the smaller the total utility a consumer obtains from the combinations of products on that indifference curve.　　**T　F**

9. On an indifference map, the further from the origin, the lower the level of utility associated with each indifference curve.　　**T　F**

10. There can be an intersection of consumer indifference curves.　　**T　F**

11. A consumer maximizes total utility when she or he purchases the combination of the two products at which her or his budget line crosses an indifference curve.　　**T　F**

12. On an indifference map, the consumer's equilibrium position will be where the slope of the highest attainable indifference curve equals the slope of the budget line.　　**T　F**

13. It is assumed in the marginal-utility approach to consumer behavior that utility is cardinal, or numerically measurable.　　**T　F**

14. In both the marginal-utility and indifference curve approaches to consumer behavior, it is assumed that a consumer is able to say whether the total utility obtained from combination A is greater than, equal to, or less than the total utility obtained from combination B.　　**T　F**

15. A decrease in the price of a product normally enables a consumer to reach a higher indifference curve.　　**T　F**

■ MULTIPLE-CHOICE QUESTIONS

Circle the letter that corresponds to the best answer.

1. Suppose a consumer has an income of $8, the price of **R** is $1, and the price of **S** is $0.50. Which of the following combinations is on the consumer's budget line?
 (a) 8**R** and 1**S**
 (b) 7**R** and 1**S**
 (c) 6**R** and 6**S**
 (d) 5**R** and 6**S**

2. If a consumer has an income of $100, the price of **U** is $10, and the price of **V** is $20, the maximum quantity of **U** the consumer is able to purchase is
 (a) 5
 (b) 10
 (c) 20
 (d) 30

3. When the income of a consumer is $20, the price of **T** is $5, the price of **Z** is $2, and the quantity of **T** is measured horizontally, the slope of the budget line is
 (a) 0.4
 (b) 2.5
 (c) 4
 (d) 10

4. Assume that everything else remains the same, but there is a decrease in a consumer's money income. The most likely effect is
 (a) an inward shift in the indifference curves because the consumer can now satisfy fewer wants
 (b) an inward shift in the budget line because the consumer can now purchase less of both products
 (c) an increase in the marginal rate of substitution
 (d) no change in the equilibrium of the consumer

5. An indifference curve is a curve that shows the different combinations of two products that
 (a) give a consumer equal marginal utilities
 (b) give a consumer equal total utilities
 (c) cost a consumer equal amounts
 (d) have the same prices

6. In the following schedule for an indifference curve, how much of **G** is the consumer willing to give up to obtain the third unit of **H**?
 (a) 3
 (b) 4
 (c) 5
 (d) 6

Quantity of G	Quantity of H
18	1
12	2
7	3
3	4
0	5

7. The slope of the indifference curve measures the
  (a) slope of the budget line
  (b) total utility of a good
  (c) space on an indifference map
  (d) marginal rate of substitution

8. The marginal rate of substitution
  (a) may rise or fall, depending on the slope of the budget line
  (b) rises as you move downward along an indifference curve
  (c) falls as you move downward along an indifference curve
  (d) remains the same along a budget line

9. Which of the following is characteristic of indifference curves?
  (a) They are concave to the origin.
  (b) They are convex to the origin.
  (c) Curves closer to the origin have the highest level of total utility.
  (d) Curves closer to the origin have the highest level of marginal utility.

10. To derive the demand curve of a product, the price of the product is varied. For the indifference curve analysis, the
  (a) budget line is held constant
  (b) money income of the consumer changes
  (c) tastes and preferences of the consumer are held constant
  (d) prices of other products the consumer might purchase change

Questions 11, 12, 13, and 14 are based on the diagram below.

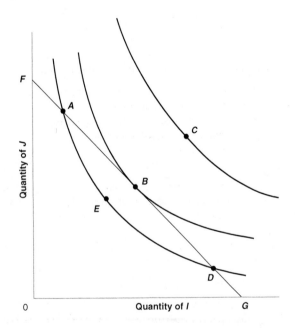

11. The budget line is best represented by line
  (a) *AB*
  (b) *AD*
  (c) *FG*
  (d) *DG*

12. Which combination of goods *I* and *J* will the consumer purchase?
  (a) *A*
  (b) *B*
  (c) *C*
  (d) *E*

13. Suppose the price of good *I* increases. The budget line will shift
  (a) inward around a point on the *J* axis
  (b) outward around a point on the *J* axis
  (c) inward around a point on the *I* axis
  (d) outward around a point on the *I* axis

14. If the consumer chooses the combination of goods *I* and *J* represented by point *E*, then the consumer could
  (a) obtain more goods with the available money income
  (b) not obtain more goods with the available money income
  (c) shift the budget line outward so that it is tangent with point *C*
  (d) shift the budget line inward so that it is tangent with point *E*

15. In indifference curve analysis, the consumer will be in equilibrium at the point where the
  (a) indifference curve is concave to the origin
  (b) budget line crosses the vertical axis
  (c) two indifference curves intersect and are tangent to the budget line
  (d) budget line is tangent to an indifference curve

16. If a consumer is initially in equilibrium, a decrease in money income will
  (a) move the consumer to a new equilibrium on a lower indifference curve
  (b) move the consumer to a new equilibrium on a higher indifference curve
  (c) make the slope of the consumer's indifference curves steeper
  (d) have no effect on the equilibrium position

Questions 17, 18, 19, and 20 are based on the following graph.

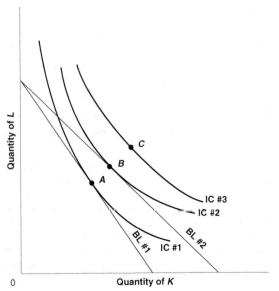

17. If the budget line shifts from **BL #1** to **BL #2**, it is because the price of
(a) *K* increased
(b) *K* decreased
(c) *L* increased
(d) *L* decreased

18. If the budget line shifts from **BL #2** to **BL #1**, it is because the price of
(a) *K* increased
(b) *K* decreased
(c) *L* increased
(d) *L* decreased

19. When the budget line shifts from **BL #2** to **BL #1**, the consumer will buy
(a) more of *K* and *L*
(b) less of *K* and *L*
(c) more of *K* and less of *L*
(d) less of *K* and more of *L*

20. Point *C* on indifference curve **IC #3** can be an attainable combination of products *K* and *L* if
(a) the price of *K* increases
(b) the price of *L* increases
(c) money income increases
(d) money income decreases

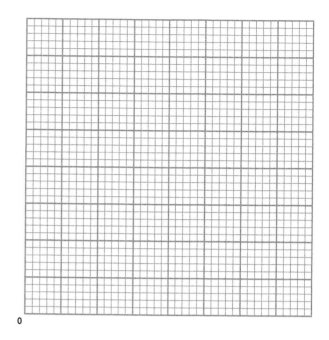

0

■ **PROBLEMS**

1. Following are the schedules for three indifference curves.

Indifference schedule 1		Indifference schedule 2		Indifference schedule 3	
A	B	A	B	A	B
1	28	0	36	0	45
2	21	1	28	1	36
3	15	2	21	2	28
4	10	3	15	3	21
5	6	4	11	4	15
6	3	5	7	5	10
7	1	6	4	6	6
	0	7	1	7	3
			0	8	1
				9	0

a. On the following graph measure quantities of *A* along the horizontal axis (from 0 to 9) and quantities of *B* along the vertical axis (from 0 to 45).
(1) Plot the 8 combinations of *A* and *B* from indifference schedule 1 and draw through the 8 points a curve which is in no place a straight line. Label this curve **IC #1**.
(2) Do the same for the 9 points in indifference schedule 2 and label it **IC #2.**
(3) Repeat the process for the 10 points in indifference schedule 3 and label the curve **IC #3.**
b. Assume the price of *A* is $12, the price of *B* is $2.40, and a consumer has an income of $72.

(1) Complete the following table to show the quantities of *A* and *B* this consumer is able to purchase.

A	B
0	_____
1	_____
2	_____
3	_____
4	_____
5	_____
6	_____

(2) Plot this budget line on the graph you completed in part **a.**

(3) This budget line has a slope equal to _____.
c. To obtain the greatest satisfaction or utility from his income of $72 this consumer will

(1) purchase _____ units of *A* and _____ of *B*;

(2) and spend _____ $ on *A* and $ _____ on *B*.

2. Following is a graph with three indifference curves and three budget lines. This consumer has an income of $100, and the price of *Y* remains constant at $5.
a. When the price of *X* is $10, the consumer's budget line is **BL #1** and the consumer

(1) purchases _____ *X* and _____ *Y*;

(2) and spends $ _____ on *X* and $ _____on *Y*.
b. If the price of X is $6.67, 2/3 the budget line is **BL #2** and the consumer

(1) purchases _____ *X* and _____ *Y*;

(2) 2 and spends $ _____ for *X* and $ for _____ *Y*.

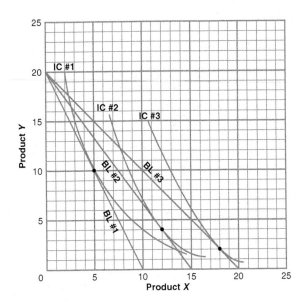

c. And when the price of **X** is $5, the consumer has budget line **BL #3** and

(1) buys _____ **X** and _____ **Y**; and

(2) spends $_____ on **X** and $ _____ on **Y**.

d. On the following graph, plot the quantities of **X** demanded at the three prices.

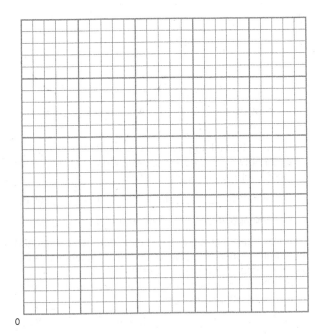

a. Between $10 and $5 this consumer's demand for

X is (elastic, inelastic) _____, and for him products **X** and **Y** are (substitutes, complements) _____.

■ SHORT ANSWER AND ESSAY QUESTIONS

1. Why is the slope of the budget line negative?

2. How will each of the following events affect the budget line?
   a. a decrease in the money income of the consumer
   b. an increase in the prices of both products
   c. a decrease in the price of one of the products

3. Explain why the budget line can be called "objective" and an indifference curve "subjective."

4. What is the relationship between an indifference curve and total utility? Between an indifference map and total utility?

5. Why is the slope of an indifference curve negative and convex to the origin?

6. You are given two products, alpha and beta. Why will the utility-maximizing combination of the two products be the one lying on the highest attainable indifference curve?

7. Suppose a consumer purchases a combination of two products that is on her budget line but the budget line is not tangent to an indifference curve at that point. Of which product should the consumer buy more, and of which should she buy less? Why?

8. What is the important difference between the marginal-utility theory and the indifference-curve theory of consumer demand in terms of how utility is considered or measured?

9. Explain how the indifference map of a consumer and the budget line are utilized to derive the consumer's demand for one of the products. In deriving demand, what is varied and what is held constant?

10. How does a change in the price of one product shift the budget line and determine a new equilibrium point? Explain and illustrate with a graph.

ANSWERS

Appendix to Chapter 6 Indifference Curve Analysis

FILL-IN QUESTIONS

1. income, a budget
2. price of X, price of Y
3. right, left
4. inward, outward, B
5. An indifference, utility
6. downward, convex
7. marginal
8. greater, decreases
9. total, map
10. greater
11. tangent, slope
12. up
13. cardinal, ordinal
14. *a.* outward, right; *b.* higher; *c.* more
15. demand

TRUE–FALSE QUESTIONS

1. T, pp. 133–134   **6.** F, pp. 134–135   **11.** F, p. 136
2. F, pp. 133–134   **7.** T, p. 135   **12.** T, p. 136
3. F, pp. 133–134   **8.** T, pp. 135–136   **13.** T, p. 136
4. T, p. 134   **9.** F, pp. 135–136   **14.** T, p. 136
5. T, p. 134   **10.** F, p. 135   **15.** T, pp. 136–137

MULTIPLE-CHOICE QUESTIONS

1. d, pp. 133–134   **8.** c, pp. 134–135   **15.** d, p. 136
2. b, pp. 133–134   **9.** b, p. 135   **16.** a, pp. 134, 136
3. b, pp. 133–134   **10.** c, pp. 134–135   **17.** b, pp. 137–138
4. b, p. 134   **11.** c, pp. 135–136   **18.** a, pp. 137–138
5. b, p. 134   **12.** b, pp. 135–136   **19.** b, pp. 137–138
6. c, p. 134   **13.** a, p. 136   **20.** c, pp. 134, 136
7. d, pp. 134–135   **14.** a, pp. 135–136

PROBLEMS

1. *a.* graph; *b.* (1) 30, 25, 20, 15, 10, 5, 0, (2) graph, (3) −5; *c.* (1) 3, 15, (2) 36, 36
2. *a.* (1) 5, 10, (2) 50, 50; *b.* (1) 12, 4, (2) 80, 20; *c.* (1) 18, 2, (2) 90, 10; *d.* graph; *e.* elastic, substitutes

SHORT ANSWER AND ESSAY QUESTIONS

1. pp. 133–134   **5.** pp. 134–135   **9.** pp. 137–138
2. p. 134   **6.** p. 136   **10.** pp. 137–138
3. pp. 133–134   **7.** p. 136
4. pp. 134–135   **8.** pp. 136–137

AFTER READING THIS CHAPTER, YOU SHOULD BE ABLE TO:

1 Explain why economic costs include both explicit (revealed and expressed) costs and implicit (present but not obvious) costs.

2 Relate the law of diminishing returns to a firm's short-run production costs.

3 Describe the distinctions between fixed and variable costs and among total, average, and marginal costs.

4 Use economies of scale to link a firm's size and its average costs in the long run.

Businesses and the Costs of Production

Our attention now turns from the behavior of consumers to the behavior of producers. In market economies, a wide variety of businesses produce an even wider variety of goods and services. Each of those businesses requires economic resources in order to produce its products. In obtaining and using resources, a firm makes monetary payments to resource owners (for example, workers) and incurs opportunity costs when using resources it already owns (for example, entrepreneurial talent). Those payments and opportunity costs together make up the firm's *costs of production*, which we discuss in this chapter.

Then, in the next several chapters, we bring product demand, product prices, and revenue back into the analysis and explain how firms compare revenues and costs in determining how much to produce. Our ultimate purpose is to show how those comparisons relate to economic efficiency.

Economic Costs

Firms face costs because the resources they need to produce their products are scarce and have alternative uses. Because of scarcity, firms wanting a particular resource have to bid it away from other firms. That process is costly for firms because it requires a payment to the resource owner. This reality causes economists to define **economic cost** as the payment that must be made to obtain and retain the services of a resource. It is the income the firm must provide to resource suppliers to attract resources away from alternative uses.

This section explains how firms incorporate opportunity costs to calculate economic costs. If you need a refresher on opportunity costs, a brief review of the section on opportunity costs in Chapter 1 might be useful before continuing on with the rest of this section.

Explicit and Implicit Costs

To properly calculate a firm's economic costs, you must remember that *all* of the resources used by the firm have an opportunity cost. This is true both for the resources that a firm purchases from outsiders as well as for the resources that it already owns.

As an example, consider a table-making firm that starts this month with $5000 in cash as well as ownership of a small oak forest from which it gets the oak that it turns into tables.

Suppose that during the month the firm uses the entire $5000 of cash to pay its workers. Clearly, the $5000 it spends purchasing their labor comes at the opportunity cost of forgoing the best alternatives that could have been bought with that money.

Less obvious, however, is the opportunity cost of the oak that the firm grows itself and which it uses to make tables. Suppose that the oak has a market value of $1500, meaning that our table-making firm could sell it to outsiders for $1500. This implies that using the oak to make tables has an opportunity cost of $1500. Choosing to convert the oak into tables means giving up the best alternatives that the firm could have purchased with the $1500.

As a result, keep in mind that *all* of the resources that a firm uses—whether purchased from outside or already owned—have opportunity costs and thus economic costs. Economists refer to these two types of economic costs as *explicit costs* and *implicit costs*:

- A firm's **explicit costs** are the monetary payments it makes to those from whom it must purchase resources that it does not own. Because these costs involve an obvious cash transaction, they are referred to as explicit costs. Be sure to remember that explicit costs are opportunity costs because every monetary payment used to purchase outside resources necessarily involves forgoing the best alternatives that could have been purchased with the money.

- A firm's **implicit costs** are the opportunity costs of using the resources that it already owns to make the firm's own product rather than selling those resources to outsiders for cash. Because these costs are present but not obvious, they are referred to as implicit costs.

A firm's economic costs are the sum of its explicit costs and its implicit costs:

$$\underset{\text{costs}}{\text{Economic}} = \underset{\text{costs}}{\text{explicit}} + \underset{\text{costs}}{\text{implicit}}$$

The following example makes clear how both explicit costs and implicit costs affect firm profits and firm behavior.

Accounting Profit and Normal Profit

Suppose that after many years working as a sales representative for a large T-shirt manufacturer, you decided to strike out on your own. After considering many potential business ventures, you decide to open a retail T-shirt shop. As we explain in Chapter 2, you will be providing two different economic resources to your new enterprise: labor and entrepreneurial ability. The part of your job that involves providing labor includes any of the routine tasks that are needed to help run the business—things like answering customer e-mails, taking inventory, and sweeping the floor. The part of your job that involves providing entrepreneurial ability includes any of the nonroutine tasks involved with organizing the business and directing its strategy—things like deciding on whether to use Internet ads or in-person events to promote your business, whether to include children's clothing in your product mix, and how to decorate your store to maximize its appeal to potential customers.

You begin providing entrepreneurial ability to your new firm by making some initial organizational decisions. You decide to work full time at your new business, so you quit your old job that paid you $22,000 per year. You invest $20,000 of savings that has been earning $1000 per year. You decide that your new firm will occupy a small retail space that you own and had been previously renting out for $5000 per year. Finally, you decide to hire one clerk to help you in the store. She agrees to work for you for $18,000 per year.

After a year in business, you total up your accounts and find the following:

Total sales revenue		$120,000
Cost of T-shirts	$40,000	
Clerk's salary	18,000	
Utilities	5000	
Total (explicit) costs		63,000
Accounting profit		57,000

These numbers look very good. In particular, you are happy with your $57,000 **accounting profit,** the profit number that accountants calculate by subtracting total explicit costs from total sales revenue. This is the profit (or net income) that would appear on your accounting statement and that you would report to the government for tax purposes.

But don't celebrate yet! Your $57,000 accounting profit overstates the economic success of your business because it ignores your implicit costs. Success is not defined as "having a total sales revenue that exceeds total explicit costs." Rather, the true measure of success is doing as well as you possibly can—that is, making more money in your new venture selling T-shirts than you could pursuing any other business venture.

To figure out whether you are achieving that goal, you must take into account all of your opportunity costs—both your implicit costs as well as your explicit costs. Doing so will indicate whether your new business venture is earning more money than what you could have earned in any other business venture.

To see how these calculations are made, let's continue with our example.

By providing your own financial capital, retail space, and labor, you incurred three different implicit costs during the year: $1000 of forgone interest, $5000 of forgone rent, and $22,000 of forgone wages. But don't forget that there is another implicit cost that you must also take account of—how much income you chose to forgo by applying your entrepreneurial abilities to your current retail T-shirt venture rather than applying them to other potential business ventures.

But what dollar value should we place on the size of the profits that you might have made if you had provided your entrepreneurial ability to one of those other ventures?

The answer is given by estimating a **normal profit,** the typical (or "normal") amount of accounting profit that you would most likely have earned in one of these other ventures. For the sake of argument, let us assume that with your particular set of skills and talents your entrepreneurial abilities would have on average yielded a normal profit of

$5000 in one of the other potential ventures. Knowing that value, we can take all of your implicit costs properly into account by subtracting them from your accounting profit:

Accounting profit		$57,000
Forgone interest	$ 1000	
Forgone rent	5000	
Forgone wages	22,000	
Forgone entrepreneurial income	5000	
Total implicit costs		33,000
Economic profit		24,000

Economic Profit

After subtracting your $33,000 of implicit costs from your accounting profit of $57,000, we are left with an *economic profit* of $24,000.

Please distinguish clearly between accounting profit and economic profit. Accounting profit is the result of subtracting only explicit costs from revenue: *Accounting Profit = Revenue − Explicit Costs.* By contrast, **economic profit** is the result of subtracting all of your economic costs—both explicit costs and implicit costs—from revenue: *Economic Profit = Revenue − Explicit Costs − Implicit Costs.*

WORKED PROBLEMS

W 7.1

Economic profit

By subtracting all of your economic costs from your revenue, you determine how your current business venture compares with your best alternative business venture. In our example, the fact that you are generating an economic profit of $24,000 means that you are making $24,000 more than you could expect to make in your best alternative business venture.

By contrast, suppose that you had instead done poorly in business, so that this year your firm generated an economic loss (a negative economic profit) of $8000. This would mean that you were doing worse in your current venture than you could have done in your best alternative venture. You would, as a result, wish to switch to that alternative.

Generalizing this point, we see that there is an important behavioral threshold at $0 of economic profit. If a firm is breaking even (that is, earning exactly $0 of economic profit), then its entrepreneurs know that they are doing exactly as well as they could expect to do in their best alternative business venture. They are earning enough to cover all their explicit and implicit costs, including the normal profit that they could expect to earn in other business ventures. Thus, they have no incentive to change. By

FIGURE 7.1 **Economic profit versus accounting
profit.** Economic profit is equal to total revenue less economic costs.
Economic costs are the sum of explicit and implicit costs and include a
normal profit to the entrepreneur. Accounting profit is equal to total
revenue less accounting (explicit) costs.

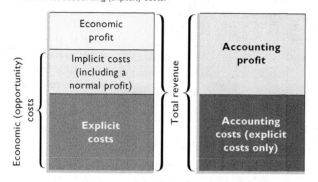

contrast, anyone running a positive economic profit knows they are doing better than they could in alternative ventures and will want to continue doing what they are doing or maybe even expand their business. And anyone running an economic loss (a negative economic profit) knows that they could do better by switching to something else.

It is for this reason that economists focus on economic profits rather than accounting profits. Simply put, economic profits direct how resources are allocated in the economy. Entrepreneurs running economic losses close their current businesses, thereby freeing up the land, labor, capital, and entrepreneurial ability that they had been using. These resources are freed up to be used by firms that are generating positive economic profits or which are at least breaking even. Resources thus flow from producing goods and services with lower net benefits toward producing goods and services with higher net benefits. Allocative efficiency increases as firms are led by their profit signals to produce more of what consumers want the most.

Figure 7.1 shows the relationship among the various cost and profit concepts that we have just discussed. To test yourself, you might want to enter cost data from our example in the appropriate blocks.

Short Run and Long Run

When the demand for a firm's product changes, the firm's profitability may depend on how quickly it can adjust the amounts of the various resources it employs. It can easily and quickly adjust the quantities employed of many resources such as hourly labor, raw materials, fuel, and power. It needs much more time, however, to adjust its *plant capacity*—the size of the factory building, the amount of machinery and equipment, and other capital resources. In some heavy industries such as aircraft manufacturing, a firm may need several years to alter plant capacity. Because

of these differences in adjustment time, economists find it useful to distinguish between two conceptual periods: the short run and the long run. We will discover that costs differ in these two time periods.

Short Run: Fixed Plant In microeconomics, the **short run** is a period too brief for a firm to alter its plant capacity, yet long enough to permit a change in the degree to which the plant's current capacity is used. The firm's plant capacity is fixed in the short run. However, the firm can vary its output by applying larger or smaller amounts of labor, materials, and other resources to that plant. It can use its existing plant capacity more or less intensively in the short run.

Long Run: Variable Plant In microeconomics, the **long run** is a period long enough for it to adjust the quantities of all the resources that it employs, including plant capacity. From the industry's viewpoint, the long run also includes enough time for existing firms to dissolve and leave the industry or for new firms to be created and enter the industry. While the short run is a "fixed-plant" period, the long run is a "variable-plant" period.

Illustrations If Boeing hires 100 extra workers for one of its commercial airline plants or adds an entire shift of workers, we are speaking of the short run. If it adds a new production facility and installs more equipment, we are referring to the long run. The first situation is a *short-run adjustment*; the second is a *long-run adjustment*.

The short run and the long run are conceptual periods rather than calendar time periods. In light-manufacturing industries, changes in plant capacity may be accomplished almost overnight. A small T-shirt manufacturer can increase its plant capacity in a matter of days by ordering and installing two or three new cutting tables and several extra sewing machines. But for heavy industry the long run is a different matter. Shell Oil may require several years to construct a new gasoline refinery.

QUICK REVIEW 7.1

- Explicit costs are money payments a firm makes to outside suppliers of resources; implicit costs are the opportunity costs associated with a firm's use of resources it owns.
- Normal profit is the implicit cost of entrepreneurship. Economic profit is total revenue less all explicit and implicit costs, including normal profit.
- In the short run, a firm's plant capacity is fixed; in the long run, a firm can vary its plant size and firms can enter or leave the industry.

Short-Run Production Relationships

A firm's costs of producing a specific output depend on the prices of the needed resources and the quantities of resources (inputs) needed to produce that output. Resource supply and demand determine resource prices. The technological aspects of production, specifically the relationships between inputs and output, determine the quantities of resources needed. Our focus will be on the *labor*-output relationship, given a fixed plant capacity. But before examining that relationship, we need to define three terms:

- **Total product (TP)** is the total quantity, or total output, of a particular good or service produced.
- **Marginal product (MP)** is the extra output or added product associated with adding a unit of a variable resource, in this case labor, to the production process. Thus,

$$\text{Marginal product} = \frac{\text{change in total product}}{\text{change in labor input}}$$

- **Average product (AP),** also called labor productivity, is output per unit of labor input:

$$\text{Average product} = \frac{\text{total product}}{\text{units of labor}}$$

In the short run, a firm can for a time increase its output by adding units of labor to its fixed plant. But by how much will output rise when it adds more labor? Why do we say "for a time"?

Law of Diminishing Returns

The answers are provided in general terms by the **law of diminishing returns.** This law assumes that technology is

ORIGIN OF THE IDEA

O 7.1

Law of diminishing returns

fixed and thus the techniques of production do not change. It states that as successive units of a variable resource (say, labor) are added to a fixed resource (say, capital or land), beyond some point the extra, or marginal, product that can be attributed to each additional unit of the variable resource will decline. For example, if additional workers are hired to work with a constant amount of capital equipment, output will eventually rise by smaller and smaller amounts as more workers are hired.

Rationale Suppose a farmer has a fixed resource—80 acres of land—planted in corn. If the farmer does not cultivate the cornfields (clear the weeds) at all, the yield will be

CONSIDER THIS . . .

Diminishing Returns from Study

Here is a noneconomic example of a relationship between "inputs" and "output" that may help you better understand the idea of diminishing returns. Suppose for an individual that

Total course learning = f (intelligence, quality of course materials, instructor effectiveness, class time, and study time)

where f means "function of" or "depends on." So this relationship supposes that total course learning depends on intelligence (however defined), quality of course materials such as the textbook, the effectiveness of the instructor, the amount of class time, and the amount of personal study time outside the class.

For analytical purposes, let's assume that one's intelligence, the quality of course materials, the effectiveness of the instructor, and the amount of class time are *fixed*—meaning they do not change over the length of the course. Now let's add units of study time per day over the length of the course to "produce" greater course learning. The first hour of study time per day increases total course learning. Will the second hour enhance course learning by as much as the first? By how much will the third, fourth, fifth, . . . fifteenth hour of study per day contribute to total course learning relative to the *immediate previous hour*?

We think you will agree that eventually diminishing returns to course learning will set in as successive hours of study are added each day. At some point the marginal product of an extra hour of study time will decline and, at some further point, become zero.

This is also true of production relationships within firms. As successive units of a variable input (say, labor) are added to a fixed input (say, capital), the marginal product of the variable input eventually declines. In short, diminishing returns will occur sooner or later. Total product eventually will rise at a diminishing rate, reach a maximum, and then decline.

40 bushels per acre. If he cultivates the land once, output may rise to 50 bushels per acre. A second cultivation may increase output to 57 bushels per acre, a third to 61, and a fourth to 63. Succeeding cultivations will add less and less to the land's yield. If this were not so, the world's needs for corn could be fulfilled by extremely intense cultivation of this single 80-acre plot of land. Indeed, if diminishing returns did not occur, the world could be fed out of a flowerpot. Why not? Just keep adding more seed, fertilizer, and harvesters!

TABLE 7.1 Total, Marginal, and Average Product: The Law of Diminishing Returns

(1) Units of the Variable Resource (Labor)	(2) Total Product (TP)	(3) Marginal Product (MP), Change in (2)/ Change in (1)		(4) Average Product (AP), (2)/(1)
0	0			—
1	10	10	Increasing marginal returns	10.00
2	25	15		12.50
3	45	20		15.00
4	60	15	Diminishing marginal returns	15.00
5	70	10		14.00
6	75	5		12.50
7	75	0	Negative marginal returns	10.71
8	70	−5		8.75

The law of diminishing returns also holds true in non-agricultural industries. Assume a wood shop is manufacturing furniture frames. It has a specific amount of equipment such as lathes, planes, saws, and sanders. If this shop hired just one or two workers, total output and productivity (output per worker) would be very low. The workers would have to perform many different jobs, and the advantages of specialization would not be realized. Time would be lost in switching from one job to another, and machines would stand idle much of the time. In short, the plant would be understaffed, and production would be inefficient because there would be too much capital relative to the amount of labor.

The shop could eliminate those difficulties by hiring more workers. Then the equipment would be more fully used, and workers could specialize on doing a single job. Time would no longer be lost switching from job to job. As more workers were added, production would become more efficient and the marginal product of each succeeding worker would rise.

But the rise could not go on indefinitely. Beyond a certain point, adding more workers would cause overcrowding. Since workers would then have to wait in line to use the machinery, they would be underused. Total output would increase at a diminishing rate because, given the fixed size of the plant, each worker would have less capital equipment to work with as more and more labor was hired. The marginal product of additional workers would decline because there would be more labor in proportion to the fixed amount of capital. Eventually, adding still more workers would cause so much congestion that marginal product would become negative and total product would decline. At the extreme, the addition of more and more labor would exhaust all the standing room, and total product would fall to zero.

Note that the law of diminishing returns assumes that all units of labor are of equal quality. Each successive worker is presumed to have the same innate ability, motor coordination, education, training, and work experience. Marginal product ultimately diminishes, but not because successive workers are less skilled or less energetic. It declines because the firm is using more workers relative to the amount of plant and equipment available.

Tabular Example Table 7.1 is a numerical illustration of the law of diminishing returns. Column 2 shows the total product, or total output, resulting from combining each level of a variable input (labor) in column 1 with a fixed amount of capital.

Column 3 shows the marginal product (MP), the change in total product associated with each additional unit of labor. Note that with no labor input, total product is zero; a plant with no workers will produce no output. The first three units of labor reflect increasing marginal returns, with marginal products of 10, 15, and 20 units, respectively. But beginning with the fourth unit of labor, marginal product diminishes continuously, becoming zero with the seventh unit of labor and negative with the eighth.

WORKED PROBLEMS

W 7.2

Total, marginal, and average product

Average product, or output per labor unit, is shown in column 4. It is calculated by dividing total product (column 2) by the number of labor units needed to produce it (column 1). At 5 units of labor, for example, AP is 14 (= 70/5).

Graphical Portrayal **Figure 7.2 (Key Graph)** shows the diminishing-returns data in Table 7.1 graphically and further clarifies the relationships between total, marginal,

key graph

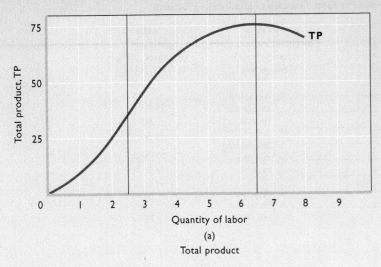

(a)
Total product

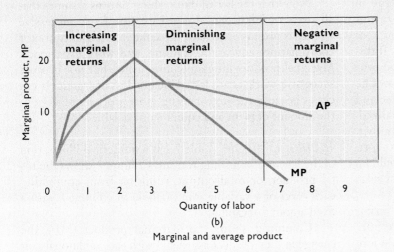

(b)
Marginal and average product

FIGURE 7.2 The law of diminishing returns. (a) As a variable resource (labor) is added to fixed amounts of other resources (land or capital), the total product that results will eventually increase by diminishing amounts, reach a maximum, and then decline.
(b) Marginal product is the change in total product associated with each new unit of labor. Average product is simply output per labor unit. Note that marginal product intersects average product at the maximum average product.

QUICK QUIZ FOR FIGURE 7.2

1. Which of the following is an assumption underlying these figures?
   a. Firms first hire "better" workers and then hire "poorer" workers.
   b. Capital and labor are both variable, but labor increases more rapidly than capital.
   c. Consumers will buy all the output (total product) produced.
   d. Workers are of equal quality.

2. Marginal product is:
   a. the change in total product divided by the change in the quantity of labor.
   b. total product divided by the quantity of labor.
   c. always positive.
   d. unrelated to total product.

3. Marginal product in graph (b) is zero when:
   a. average product in graph (b) stops rising.
   b. the slope of the marginal-product curve in graph (b) is zero.
   c. total product in graph (a) begins to rise at a diminishing rate.
   d. the slope of the total-product curve in graph (a) is zero.

4. Average product in graph (b):
   a. rises when it is less than marginal product.
   b. is the change in total product divided by the change in the quantity of labor.
   c. can never exceed marginal product.
   d. falls whenever total product in graph (a) rises at a diminishing rate.

Answers: 1. d; 2. a; 3. d; 4. a

146

and average products. (Marginal product in Figure 7.2b is plotted halfway between the units of labor since it applies to the addition of each labor unit.)

Note first in Figure 7.2a that total product, TP, goes through three phases: It rises initially at an increasing rate; then it increases, but at a diminishing rate; finally, after reaching a maximum, it declines.

Geometrically, marginal product—shown by the MP curve in Figure 7.2b—is the slope of the total-product curve. Marginal product measures the change in total product associated with each succeeding unit of labor. Thus, the three phases of total product are also reflected in marginal product. Where total product is increasing at an increasing rate, marginal product is rising. Here, extra units of labor are adding larger and larger amounts to total product. Similarly, where total product is increasing but at a decreasing rate, marginal product is positive but falling. Each additional unit of labor adds less to total product than did the previous unit. When total product is at a maximum, marginal product is zero. When total product declines, marginal product becomes negative.

Average product, AP (Figure 7.2b), displays the same tendencies as marginal product. It increases, reaches a maximum, and then decreases as more and more units of labor are added to the fixed plant. But note the relationship between marginal product and average product: Where marginal product exceeds average product, average product rises. And where marginal product is less than average product, average product declines. It follows that marginal product intersects average product where average product is at a maximum.

This relationship is a mathematical necessity. If you add a larger number to a total than the current average of that total, the average must rise. And if you add a smaller number to a total than the current average of that total, the average must fall. You raise your average examination grade only when your score on an additional (marginal) examination is greater than the average of all your past scores. You lower your average when your grade on an additional exam is below your current average. In our production example, when the amount an extra worker adds to total product exceeds the average product of all workers currently employed, average product will rise. Conversely, when the amount an extra worker adds to total product is less than the current average product, average product will decrease.

ORIGIN OF THE IDEA

O 7.2

Production relationship

The law of diminishing returns is embodied in the shapes of all three curves. But, as our definition of the law

of diminishing returns indicates, economists are most concerned with its effects on marginal product. The regions of increasing, diminishing, and negative marginal product (returns) are shown in Figure 7.2b.

Short-Run Production Costs

Production information such as that provided in Table 7.1 and Figures 7.2a and 7.2b must be coupled with resource prices to determine the total and per-unit costs of producing various levels of output. We know that in the short run, resources associated with the firm's plant are fixed. Other resources, however, are variable in the short run. As a result, short-run costs can be either fixed or variable.

Fixed, Variable, and Total Costs

Let's see what distinguishes fixed costs, variable costs, and total costs from one another.

Fixed Costs **Fixed costs** are those costs that do not vary with changes in output. Fixed costs are associated with the very existence of a firm's plant and therefore must be paid even if its output is zero. Such costs as rental payments, interest on a firm's debts, a portion of depreciation on equipment and buildings, and insurance premiums are generally fixed costs; they are fixed and do not change even if a firm produces more. In column 2 of Table 7.2 we assume that the firm's total fixed cost is $100. By definition, this fixed cost is incurred at all levels of output, including zero. The firm cannot avoid paying fixed costs in the short run.

Variable Costs **Variable costs** are those costs that change with the level of output. They include payments for materials, fuel, power, transportation services, most labor, and similar variable resources. In column 3 of Table 7.2 we find that the total of variable costs changes directly with output. But note that the increases in variable cost associated with succeeding one-unit increases in output are not equal. As production begins, variable cost will for a time increase by a decreasing amount; this is true through the fourth unit of output in Table 7.2. Beyond the fourth unit, however, variable cost rises by increasing amounts for succeeding units of output.

The reason lies in the shape of the marginal-product curve. At first, as in Figure 7.2b, marginal product is increasing, so smaller and smaller increases in the amounts of variable resources are needed to produce successive units of output. Hence the variable cost of successive units of output decreases. But when, as diminishing returns are encountered, marginal product begins to decline, larger and larger additional amounts of variable resources are

TABLE 7.2 **Total-, Average-, and Marginal-Cost Schedules for an Individual Firm in the Short Run**

	Total-Cost Data			Average-Cost Data			Marginal Cost
(1) Total Product (Q)	**(2)** Total Fixed Cost (TFC)	**(3)** Total Variable Cost (TVC)	**(4)** Total Cost (TC) TC = TFC + TVC	**(5)** Average Fixed Cost (AFC) $AFC = \dfrac{TFC}{Q}$	**(6)** Average Variable Cost (AVC) $AVC = \dfrac{TVC}{Q}$	**(7)** Average Total Cost (ATC) $ATC = \dfrac{TC}{Q}$	**(8)** Marginal Cost (MC) $MC = \dfrac{\text{change in TC}}{\text{change in Q}}$
0	$100	$ 0	$ 100				
							$ 90
1	100	90	190	$100.00	$90.00	$190.00	
							80
2	100	170	270	50.00	85.00	135.00	
							70
3	100	240	340	33.33	80.00	113.33	
							60
4	100	300	400	25.00	75.00	100.00	
							70
5	100	370	470	20.00	74.00	94.00	
							80
6	100	450	550	16.67	75.00	91.67	
							90
7	100	540	640	14.29	77.14	91.43	
							110
8	100	650	750	12.50	81.25	93.75	
							130
9	100	780	880	11.11	86.67	97.78	
							150
10	100	930	1030	10.00	93.00	103.00	

needed to produce successive units of output. Total variable cost therefore increases by increasing amounts.

Total Cost

Total cost is the sum of fixed cost and variable cost at each level of output:

$$TC = TFC + TVC$$

TC is shown in column 4 of Table 7.2. At zero units of output, total cost is equal to the firm's fixed cost. Then for each unit of the 10 units of production, total cost increases by the same amount as variable cost.

Figure 7.3 shows graphically the fixed-, variable-, and total-cost data given in Table 7.2. Observe that total variable cost, TVC, is measured vertically from the horizontal axis at each level of output. The amount of fixed cost, shown as TFC, is added vertically to the total-variable-cost curve to obtain the points on the total-cost curve TC.

The distinction between fixed and variable costs is significant to the business manager. Variable costs can be controlled or altered in the short run by changing production levels. Fixed costs are beyond the business manager's current control; they are incurred in the short run and must be paid regardless of output level.

Per-Unit, or Average, Costs

Producers are certainly interested in their total costs, but they are equally concerned with per-unit, or average, costs. In particular, average-cost data are more meaningful for making comparisons with product price, which is always stated on a per-unit basis. Average fixed cost, average variable

cost, and average total cost are shown in columns 5 to 7, Table 7.2.

AFC

Average fixed cost (AFC) for any output level is found by dividing total fixed cost (TFC) by that amount of output (Q). That is,

$$AFC = \frac{TFC}{Q}$$

FIGURE 7.3 Total cost is the sum of fixed cost and variable cost. Total variable cost (TVC) changes with output. Total fixed cost (TFC) is independent of the level of output. The total cost (TC) at any output is the vertical sum of the fixed cost and variable cost at that output.

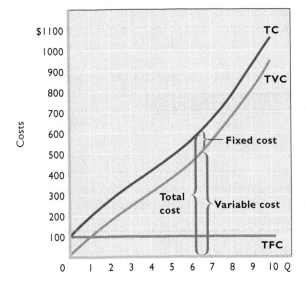

FIGURE 7.4 The average-cost curves. AFC falls as a given amount of fixed costs is apportioned over a larger and larger output. AVC initially falls because of increasing marginal returns but then rises because of diminishing marginal returns. Average total cost (ATC) is the vertical sum of average variable cost (AVC) and average fixed cost (AFC).

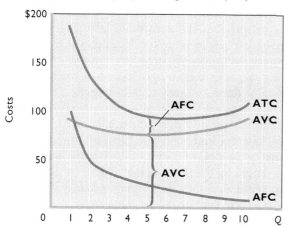

Rephrased, production is relatively inefficient—and therefore costly—at low levels of output. Because the firm's fixed plant is understaffed, average variable cost is relatively high. As output expands, however, greater specialization and better use of the firm's capital equipment yield more efficiency, and variable cost per unit of output declines. As still more variable resources are added, a point is reached where crowding causes diminishing returns to set in. Once diminishing returns start, each additional unit of input does not increase output by as much as preceding units did. This means that AVC eventually increases.

You can verify the U or saucer shape of the AVC curve by returning to Table 7.1. Assume the price of labor is $10 per unit. Labor cost per unit of output is then $10 (the price per labor unit in this example) divided by average product (output per labor unit). Because we have assumed labor to be the only variable input, the labor cost per unit of output is the variable cost per unit of output, or AVC. When average product is initially low, AVC is high. As workers are added, average product rises and AVC falls. When average product is at its maximum, AVC is at its minimum. Then, as still more workers are added and average product declines, AVC rises. The "hump" of the average-product curve is reflected in the saucer or U shape of the AVC curve. As you will soon see, the two are mirror images of each other.

ATC **Average total cost (ATC)** for any output level is found by dividing total cost (TC) by that output (*Q*) or by adding AFC and AVC at that output:

$$ATC = \frac{TC}{Q} = \frac{TFC}{Q} + \frac{TVC}{Q} = AFC + AVC$$

Graphically, ATC can be found by adding vertically the AFC and AVC curves, as in Figure 7.4. Thus the vertical distance between the ATC and AVC curves measures AFC at any level of output.

Marginal Cost

One final and very crucial cost concept remains: **Marginal cost (MC)** is the extra, or additional, cost of producing one more unit of output. MC can be determined for each added unit of output by noting the change in total cost that unit's production entails:

$$MC = \frac{\text{change in TC}}{\text{change in } Q}$$

Calculations In column 4, Table 7.2, production of the first unit of output increases total cost from $100 to $190. Therefore, the additional, or marginal, cost of that first

Because the total fixed cost is, by definition, the same regardless of output, AFC must decline as output increases. As output rises, the total fixed cost is spread over a larger and larger output. When output is just 1 unit in Table 7.2, TFC and AFC are the same at $100. But at 2 units of output, the total fixed cost of $100 becomes $50 of AFC or fixed cost per unit; then it becomes $33.33 per unit as $100 is spread over 3 units, and $25 per unit when spread over 4 units. This process is sometimes referred to as "spreading the overhead." Figure 7.4 shows that AFC graphs as a continuously declining curve as total output is increased.

AVC **Average variable cost (AVC)** for any output level is calculated by dividing total variable cost (TVC) by that amount of output (*Q*):

$$AVC = \frac{TVC}{Q}$$

Due to increasing and then diminishing returns, AVC declines initially, reaches a minimum, and then increases again. A graph of AVC is a U-shaped or saucer-shaped curve, as shown in Figure 7.4.

Because total variable cost reflects the law of diminishing returns, so must AVC, which is derived from total variable cost. Because marginal returns increase initially, fewer and fewer additional variable resources are needed to produce each of the first four units of output. As a result, variable cost per unit declines. AVC hits a minimum with the fifth unit of output, and beyond that point AVC rises as diminishing returns require more and more variable resources to produce each additional unit of output.

unit is $90 (column 8). The marginal cost of the second unit is $80 (= $270 − $190); the MC of the third is $70 (= $340 − $270); and so forth. The MC for each of the 10 units of output is shown in column 8.

MC can also be calculated from the total-variable-cost column because the only difference between total cost and total variable cost is the constant amount of fixed costs ($100). Thus, the change in total cost and the change in total variable cost associated with each additional unit of output are always the same.

Marginal Decisions Marginal costs are costs the firm can control directly and immediately. Specifically, MC

> **WORKED PROBLEMS**
>
> **W 7.3**
>
> Per-unit cost

designates all the cost incurred in producing the last unit of output. Thus, it also designates the cost that can be "saved" by not producing that last unit. Average-cost figures do not provide this information. For example, suppose the firm is undecided whether to produce 3 or 4 units of output. At 4 units Table 7.2 indicates that ATC is $100. But the firm does not increase its total costs by $100 by producing the fourth unit, nor does it save $100 by not producing that unit. Rather, the change in costs involved here is only $60, as the MC column in Table 7.2 reveals.

A firm's decisions as to what output level to produce are typically marginal decisions, that is, decisions to produce a few more or a few less units. Marginal cost is the change in costs when one more or one less unit of output is produced. When coupled with marginal revenue (which, as you will see in Chapter 8, indicates the change in revenue from one more or one less unit of output), marginal cost allows a firm to determine if it is profitable to expand or contract its production. The analysis in the next four chapters focuses on those marginal calculations.

Graphical Portrayal Marginal cost is shown graphically in **Figure 7.5 (Key Graph)**. Marginal cost at first

> **INTERACTIVE GRAPHS**
>
> **G 7.1**
>
> Production and costs

declines sharply, reaches a minimum, and then rises rather abruptly. This reflects the fact that variable cost, and therefore total cost, increase at first by decreasing amounts and then by increasing amounts (see columns 3 and 4, Table 7.2).

MC and Marginal Product The marginal-cost curve's shape is a consequence of the law of diminishing returns. Looking back at Table 7.1, we can see the relationship between marginal product and marginal cost. If

all units of a variable resource (here labor) are hired at the same price, the marginal cost of each extra unit of output will fall as long as the marginal product of each additional worker is rising. This is true because marginal cost is the (constant) cost of an extra worker divided by his or her marginal product. Therefore, in Table 7.1, suppose that each worker can be hired for $10. Because the first worker's marginal product is 10 units of output, and hiring this worker increases the firm's costs by $10, the marginal cost of each of these 10 extra units of output is $1 (= $10/10 units). The second worker also increases costs by $10, but the marginal product is 15, so the marginal cost of each of these 15 extra units of output is $.67 (= $10/15 units). Similarly, the MC of each of the 20 extra units of output contributed by the third worker is $.50 (= $10/20 units). To generalize, as long as marginal product is rising, marginal cost will fall.

But with the fourth worker diminishing returns set in and marginal cost begins to rise. For the fourth worker, marginal cost is $.67 (= $10/15 units); for the fifth worker, MC is $1 ($10/10 units); for the sixth, MC is $2 (= $10/5 units); and so on. If the price (cost) of the variable resource remains constant, increasing marginal returns will be reflected in a declining marginal cost, and diminishing marginal returns in a rising marginal cost. The MC curve is a mirror reflection of the marginal-product curve. As you can see in Figure 7.6, when marginal product is rising, marginal cost is necessarily falling. When marginal product is at its maximum, marginal cost is at its minimum. And when marginal product is falling, marginal cost is rising.

Relation of MC to AVC and ATC Figure 7.5 shows that the marginal-cost curve MC intersects both the AVC and the ATC curves at their respective minimum points. As noted earlier, this marginal-average relationship is a mathematical necessity, which a simple illustration will reveal. Suppose an NBA basketball player has scored an average of 20 points a game over the first three games of the season. Now, whether his average rises or falls as a result of playing a fourth (marginal) game will depend on whether the additional points he scores in that game are fewer or more than his current 20-point average. If in the fourth game he scores fewer than 20 points, his average will fall. For example, if he scores 16 points in the fourth game, his total points will rise from 60 to 76 and his average will fall from 20 to 19 (= 76/4). Conversely, if in the fourth (marginal) game he scores more than 20 points, say, 24, his total will increase from 60 to 84 and his average will rise from 20 to 21 (= 84/4).

So it is with costs. When the amount (the marginal cost) added to total cost is less than the current average

key graph

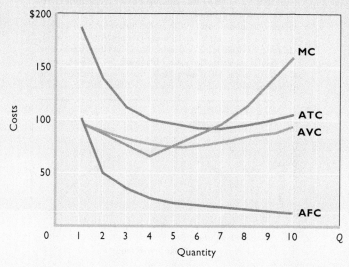

FIGURE 7.5 The relationship of the marginal-cost curve to the average-total-cost and average-variable-cost curves. The marginal-cost (MC) curve cuts through the average-total-cost (ATC) curve and the average-variable-cost (AVC) curve at their minimum points. When MC is below average total cost, ATC falls; when MC is above average total cost, ATC rises. Similarly, when MC is below average variable cost, AVC falls; when MC is above average variable cost, AVC rises.

QUICK QUIZ FOR FIGURE 7.5

1. The marginal-cost curve first declines and then increases because of:
   a. increasing, then diminishing, marginal utility.
   b. the decline in the gap between ATC and AVC as output expands.
   c. increasing, then diminishing, marginal returns.
   d. constant marginal revenue.

2. The vertical distance between ATC and AVC measures:
   a. marginal cost.
   b. total fixed cost.
   c. average fixed cost.
   d. economic profit per unit.

3. ATC is:
   a. AVC − AFC.
   b. MC + AVC.
   c. AFC + AVC.
   d. (AFC + AVC) × Q.

4. When the marginal-cost curve lies:
   a. above the ATC curve, ATC rises.
   b. above the AVC curve, ATC rises.
   c. below the AVC curve, total fixed cost increases.
   d. below the ATC curve, total fixed cost falls.

total cost, ATC will fall. Conversely, when the marginal cost exceeds ATC, ATC will rise. This means in Figure 7.5 that as long as MC lies below ATC, ATC will fall, and whenever MC lies above ATC, ATC will rise. Therefore, at the point of intersection where MC equals ATC, ATC has just ceased to fall but has not yet begun to rise. This, by definition, is the minimum point on the ATC curve. The marginal-cost curve intersects the average-total-cost curve at the ATC curve's minimum point.

Marginal cost can be defined as the addition either to total cost or to total variable cost resulting from one more unit of output; thus this same rationale explains why the MC curve also crosses the AVC curve at the AVC curve's minimum point. No such relationship exists between the MC curve and the average-fixed-cost curve because the two are not related; marginal cost includes only those costs that change with output, and fixed costs by definition are those that are independent of output.

Shifts of the Cost Curves

Changes in either resource prices or technology will cause costs to change and cost curves to shift. If fixed costs double from $100 to $200, the AFC curve in Figure 7.5 would be shifted upward. At each level of output, fixed costs are higher. The ATC curve would also move upward because AFC is a component of ATC. But the positions of the AVC and MC curves would be unaltered because their locations are based on the prices of variable rather than fixed resources. However, if the price (wage) of labor or some

151

other variable input rose, AVC, ATC, and MC would rise and those cost curves would all shift upward. The AFC curve would remain in place because fixed costs have not changed. And, of course, reductions in the prices of fixed or variable resources would reduce costs and produce shifts of the cost curves exactly opposite to those just described.

The discovery of a more efficient technology would increase the productivity of all inputs. The cost figures in Table 7.2 would all be lower. To illustrate, if labor is the only variable input, if wages are $10 per hour, and if average product is 10 units, then AVC would be $1. But if a technological improvement increases the average product of labor to 20 units, then AVC will decline to $.50. More generally, an upward shift in the productivity curves shown in Figure 7.6a means a downward shift in the cost curves portrayed in Figure 7.6b.

QUICK REVIEW 7.2

- The law of diminishing returns indicates that, beyond some point, output will increase by diminishing amounts as more units of a variable resource (labor) are added to a fixed resource (capital).
- In the short run, the total cost of any level of output is the sum of fixed and variable costs (TC = TFC + TVC).
- Average fixed, average variable, and average total costs are fixed, variable, and total costs per unit of output; marginal cost is the extra cost of producing one more unit of output.
- Average fixed cost declines continuously as output increases; the average-variable-cost and average-total-cost curves are U-shaped, reflecting increasing and then diminishing returns; the marginal-cost curve falls but then rises, intersecting both the average-variable-cost curve and the average-total-cost curve at their minimum points.

FIGURE 7.6 The relationship between productivity curves and cost curves. The marginal-cost (MC) curve and the average-variable-cost (AVC) curve in (b) are mirror images of the marginal-product (MP) and average-product (AP) curves in (a). Assuming that labor is the only variable input and that its price (the wage rate) is constant, then when MP is rising, MC is falling, and when MP is falling, MC is rising. Under the same assumptions, when AP is rising, AVC is falling, and when AP is falling, AVC is rising.

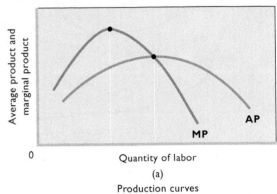

(a)
Production curves

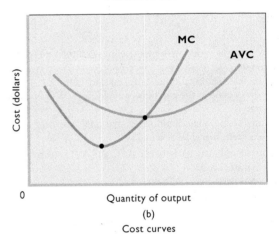

(b)
Cost curves

Long-Run Production Costs

In the long run an industry and its individual firms can undertake all desired resource adjustments. That is, they can change the amount of all inputs used. The firm can alter its plant capacity; it can build a larger plant or revert to a smaller plant than that assumed in Table 7.2. The industry also can change its overall capacity; the long run allows sufficient time for new firms to enter or for existing firms to leave an industry. We will discuss the impact of the entry and exit of firms to and from an industry in the next chapter; here we are concerned only with changes in plant capacity made by a single firm. Let's couch our analysis in terms of average total cost (ATC), making no distinction between fixed and variable costs because all resources, and therefore all costs, are variable in the long run.

Firm Size and Costs

Suppose a manufacturer with a single plant begins on a small scale and, as the result of successful operations, expands to successively larger plant sizes with larger output capacities. What happens to average total cost as this occurs? For a time, successively larger plants will reduce average total cost. However, eventually the building of a still larger plant will cause ATC to rise.

Figure 7.7 illustrates this situation for five possible plant sizes. ATC-1 is the short-run average-total-cost curve for the smallest of the five plants, and ATC-5, the curve for the largest. Constructing larger plants will lower the minimum average total costs through plant size 3. But then larger plants will mean higher minimum average total costs.

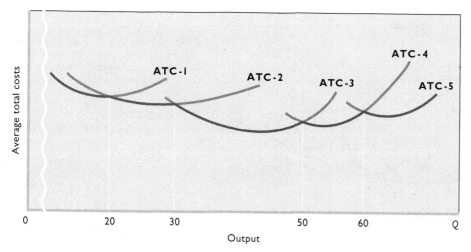

FIGURE 7.7 The long-run average-total-cost curve: five possible plant sizes. The long-run average-total-cost curve is made up of segments of the short-run cost curves (ATC-1, ATC-2, etc.) of the various-size plants from which the firm might choose. Each point on the bumpy planning curve shows the lowest unit cost attainable for any output when the firm has had time to make all desired changes in its plant size.

The Long-Run Cost Curve

The vertical lines perpendicular to the output axis in Figure 7.7 indicate the outputs at which the firm should change plant size to realize the lowest attainable average total costs of production. These are the outputs at which the per-unit costs for a larger plant drop below those for the current, smaller plant. For all outputs up to 20 units, the lowest average total costs are attainable with plant size 1. However, if the firm's volume of sales expands beyond 20 units but less than 30, it can achieve lower per-unit costs by constructing a larger plant, size 2. Although total cost will be higher at the expanded levels of production, the cost per unit of output will be less. For any output between 30 and 50 units, plant size 3 will yield the lowest average total costs. From 50 to 60 units of output, the firm must build the size-4 plant to achieve the lowest unit costs. Lowest average total costs for any output over 60 units require construction of the still larger plant, size 5.

Tracing these adjustments, we find that the long-run ATC curve for the enterprise is made up of segments of the short-run ATC curves for the various plant sizes that can be constructed. The long-run ATC curve shows the lowest average total cost at which *any output level* can be produced after the firm has had time to make all appropriate adjustments in its plant size. In Figure 7.7 the blue, bumpy curve is the firm's long-run ATC curve or, as it is often called, the firm's *planning curve.*

In most lines of production the choice of plant size is much wider than in our illustration. In many industries the number of possible plant sizes is virtually unlimited, and in time quite small changes in the volume of output will lead to changes in plant size. Graphically, this implies an unlimited number of short-run ATC curves, one for each output level, as suggested by **Figure 7.8 (Key Graph).** Then, rather than being made up of segments of short-run ATC curves as in Figure 7.7, the long-run ATC curve is made up of all the points of tangency of the unlimited number of short-run ATC curves from which the long-run ATC curve is derived. Therefore, the planning curve is smooth rather than bumpy. Each point on it tells us the minimum ATC of producing the corresponding level of output.

Economies and Diseconomies of Scale

We have assumed that, for a time, larger and larger plant sizes will lead to lower unit costs but that, beyond some point, successively larger plants will mean higher average total costs. That is, we have assumed the long-run ATC curve is U-shaped. But why should this be? It turns out that the U shape is caused by economies and diseconomies of large-scale production, as we explain in a moment. But before we do, please understand that the U shape of the long-run average-total-cost curve *cannot* be the result of rising resource prices or the law of diminishing returns. First, our discussion assumes that resource prices are constant. Second, the law of diminishing returns does not apply to production in the long run. This is true because the law of diminishing returns only deals with situations in which a productive resource or input is held constant. Under our definition of "long run," all resources and inputs are variable.

Economies of Scale **Economies of scale,** or economies of mass production, explain the downsloping part of

key graph

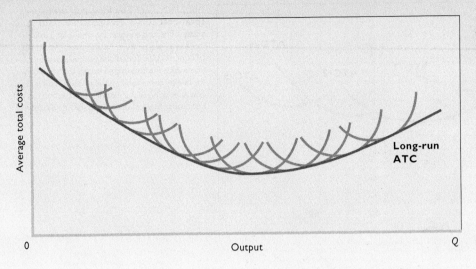

FIGURE 7.8 The long-run average-total-cost curve: unlimited number of plant sizes. If the number of possible plant sizes is very large, the long-run average-total-cost curve approximates a smooth curve. Economies of scale, followed by diseconomies of scale, cause the curve to be U-shaped.

QUICK QUIZ FOR FIGURE 7.8

1. The unlabeled red curves in this figure illustrate the:
   a. long-run average-total-cost curves of various firms constituting the industry.
   b. short-run average-total-cost curves of various firms constituting the industry.
   c. short-run average-total-cost curves of various plant sizes available to a particular firm.
   d. short-run marginal-cost curves of various plant sizes available to a particular firm.

2. The unlabeled red curves in this figure derive their shapes from:
   a. decreasing, then increasing, short-run returns.
   b. increasing, then decreasing, short-run returns.
   c. economies, then diseconomies, of scale.
   d. diseconomies, then economies, of scale.

3. The long-run ATC curve in this figure derives its shape from:
   a. decreasing, then increasing, short-run returns.
   b. increasing, then decreasing, short-run returns.
   c. economies, then diseconomies, of scale.
   d. diseconomies, then economies, of scale.

4. The long-run ATC curve is often called the firm's:
   a. planning curve.
   b. capital-expansion path.
   c. total-product curve.
   d. production possibilities curve.

Answers: 1. c; 2. b; 3. c; 4. a

the long-run ATC curve, as indicated in Figure 7.9, graphs (a), (b), and (c). As plant size increases, a number of factors will for a time lead to lower average costs of production.

Labor Specialization Increased specialization in the use of labor becomes more achievable as a plant increases in size. Hiring more workers means jobs can be divided and subdivided. Each worker may now have just one task to perform instead of five or six. Workers can work full-time on the tasks for which they have special skills. By contrast, skilled machinists in a small plant may spend half their time performing unskilled tasks, leading to higher production costs.

Further, by working at fewer tasks, workers become even more proficient at those tasks. The jack-of-all-trades doing five or six jobs is not likely to be efficient in any of them. Concentrating on one task, the same worker may become highly efficient.

Finally, greater labor specialization eliminates the loss of time that occurs whenever a worker shifts from one task to another.

Managerial Specialization Large-scale production also means better use of, and greater specialization in, management. A supervisor who can handle 20 workers is underused in a small plant that employs only 10 people. The production staff could be doubled with no increase in supervisory costs.

Small firms cannot use management specialists to best advantage. For example, a marketing specialist working in

154

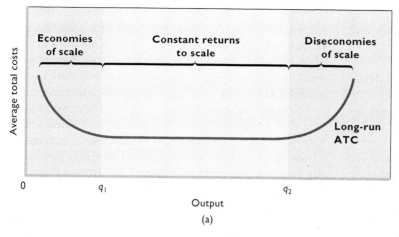

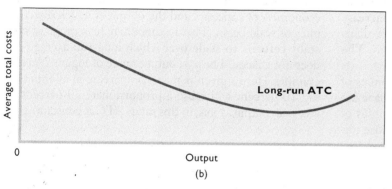

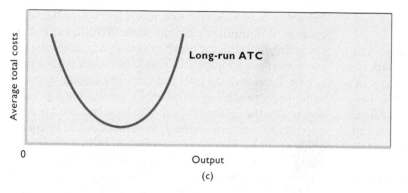

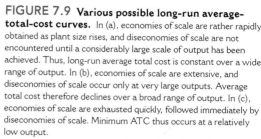

FIGURE 7.9 **Various possible long-run average-total-cost curves.** In (a), economies of scale are rather rapidly obtained as plant size rises, and diseconomies of scale are not encountered until a considerably large scale of output has been achieved. Thus, long-run average total cost is constant over a wide range of output. In (b), economies of scale are extensive, and diseconomies of scale occur only at very large outputs. Average total cost therefore declines over a broad range of output. In (c), economies of scale are exhausted quickly, followed immediately by diseconomies of scale. Minimum ATC thus occurs at a relatively low output.

a small plant may have to spend some of her time on functions outside of her area of expertise—for example, accounting, personnel, and finance. A larger scale of operations would allow her to supervise marketing full-time, while other specialists perform other managerial functions. Greater productivity and efficiency, along with lower unit costs, would be the net result.

Efficient Capital Small firms often cannot afford the most efficient equipment. In many lines of production such machinery is available only in very large and extremely expensive units. Furthermore, effective use of

the equipment demands a high volume of production, and that again requires large-scale producers.

In the automobile industry the most efficient fabrication method employs robotics and elaborate assembly-line equipment. Effective use of this equipment demands an annual output of several hundred thousand automobiles. Only very large-scale producers can afford to purchase and use this equipment efficiently. The small-scale producer is faced with a dilemma. To fabricate automobiles using other equipment is inefficient and therefore more costly per unit. But so, too, is buying and underutilizing the equipment used by the large manufacturers. Because it cannot spread the high equipment cost over very many units of output, the small-scale producer will be stuck with high costs per unit of output.

Other Factors Many products entail design and development costs, as well as other "start-up" costs, which must be incurred regardless of projected sales. These costs decline per unit as output is increased. Similarly, advertising costs decline per auto, per computer, per stereo system, and per box of detergent as more units are produced and sold. Also, the firm's production and marketing expertise usually rises as it produces and sells more output. This *learning by doing* is a further source of economies of scale.

All these factors contribute to lower average total costs for the firm that is able to expand its scale of operations. Where economies of scale are possible, an increase in all resources of, say, 10 percent will cause a more-than-proportionate increase in output of, say, 20 percent. The result will be a decline in ATC.

In many U.S. manufacturing industries, economies of scale have been of great significance. Firms that have expanded their scale of operations to obtain economies of mass production have survived and flourished. Those unable to expand have become relatively high-cost producers, doomed to struggle to survive.

Diseconomies of Scale In time the expansion of a firm may lead to diseconomies and therefore higher average total costs.

The main factor causing **diseconomies of scale** is the difficulty of efficiently controlling and coordinating a firm's operations as it becomes a large-scale producer. In a small plant a single key executive may make all the basic decisions for the plant's operation. Because of the firm's small size, the executive is close to the production line, understands the firm's operations, and can make efficient decisions because the small plant size requires only a relatively small amount of information to be examined and understood in optimizing production.

This neat picture changes as a firm grows. One person cannot assemble, digest, and understand all the information essential to decision making on a large scale. Authority must be delegated to many vice presidents, second vice presidents, and so forth. This expansion of the management hierarchy leads to problems of communication and cooperation, bureaucratic red tape, and the possibility that decisions will not be coordinated. At the same time, each new manager must be paid a salary. Thus, declining efficiency in making and executing decisions goes hand-in-hand with rising average total costs as bureaucracy expands beyond a certain point.

Also, in massive production facilities workers may feel alienated from their employers and care little about working efficiently. Opportunities to shirk, by avoiding work in favor of on-the-job leisure, may be greater in large plants than in small ones. Countering worker alienation and shirking may require additional worker supervision, which increases costs.

Where diseconomies of scale are operative, an increase in all inputs of, say, 10 percent will cause a less-than-proportionate increase in output of, say, 5 percent. As a consequence, ATC will increase. The rising portion of the long-run cost curves in Figure 7.9 illustrates diseconomies of scale.

Constant Returns to Scale In some industries a rather wide range of output may exist between the output at which economies of scale end and the output at which diseconomies of scale begin. That is, there may be a range of **constant returns to scale** over which long-run average cost does not change. The q_1q_2 output range of Figure 7.9a is an example. Here a given percentage increase in all inputs of, say, 10 percent will cause a proportionate 10 percent increase in output. Thus, in this range ATC is constant.

Minimum Efficient Scale and Industry Structure

Economies and diseconomies of scale are an important determinant of an industry's structure. Here we introduce the concept of **minimum efficient scale (MES)**, which is the lowest level of output at which a firm can minimize long-run average costs. In Figure 7.9a that level occurs at q_1 units of output. Because of the extended range of constant returns to scale, firms producing substantially greater outputs could also realize the minimum attainable long-run average costs. Specifically, firms within the q_1 to q_2 range would be equally efficient. So we would not be surprised to find an industry with such cost conditions to be populated by firms of quite different sizes. The apparel, food processing, furniture, wood products, snowboard, banking, and small-appliance industries are examples. With an extended range of constant returns to scale, relatively large and relatively small firms can coexist in an industry and be equally successful.

Compare this with Figure 7.9b, where economies of scale continue over a wide range of outputs and diseconomies of scale appear only at very high levels of output. This pattern of declining long-run average total cost occurs in the automobile, aluminum, steel, and other heavy industries. The same pattern holds in several of the new industries related to information technology, for example, computer microchips, operating system software, and Internet service provision.

Given consumer demand, efficient production will be achieved with a few large-scale producers. Small firms cannot realize the minimum efficient scale and will not be able to compete. In the extreme, economies of scale might extend beyond the market's size, resulting in what is termed **natural monopoly,** a relatively rare market situation in which average total cost is minimized when only one firm produces the particular good or service.

Where economies of scale are few and diseconomies come into play quickly, the minimum efficient size occurs at a low level of output, as shown in Figure 7.9c. In such industries a particular level of consumer demand will support a large number of relatively small producers. Many retail trades and some types of farming fall into this category. So do certain kinds of light manufacturing such as the baking, clothing, and shoe industries. Fairly small firms are more efficient than larger-scale producers in such industries.

Our point here is that the shape of the long-run average-total-cost curve is determined by technology and

> **ORIGIN OF THE IDEA**
>
> **O 7.3**
>
> Minimum efficient scale and natural monopoly

the economies and diseconomies of scale that result. The shape of the long-run ATC curve, in turn, can be significant in determining whether an industry is populated by a relatively large number of small firms or is dominated by a few large producers, or lies somewhere in between.

But we must be cautious in our assessment because industry structure does not depend on cost conditions alone. Government policies, the geographic size of markets, managerial strategy and skill, and other factors must be considered in explaining the structure of a particular industry.

> **QUICK REVIEW 7.3**
>
> - Most firms have U-shaped long-run average-total-cost curves, reflecting economies and then diseconomies of scale.
> - Economies of scale are the consequence of greater specialization of labor and management, more efficient capital equipment, and the spreading of start-up costs over more units of output.
> - Diseconomies of scale are caused by the problems of coordination and communication that arise in large firms.
> - Minimum efficient scale (MES) is the lowest level of output at which a firm's long-run average total cost is at a minimum.

Applications and Illustrations

The business world offers many examples relating to short-run costs, economies of scale, and minimum efficient scale (MES). Here are just a few.

Rising Gasoline Prices

As we discuss in the appendix to Chapter 3, changes in supply and demand often lead to rapid increases in the price of gasoline. Because gasoline is used to power nearly all motor vehicles, including those used by businesses, increases in the price of gasoline lead to increases in firms' short-run variable costs, marginal costs, and average total costs. In terms of our analysis, their AVC, MC, and ATC curves all shift upward when an increase in the price of gasoline increases their production costs.

The extent of these upward shifts depends upon the relative importance of gasoline as a variable input in the various firms' individual production processes. Package-delivery companies like FedEx that use a lot of gasoline-powered vehicles will see substantial upward shifts while software companies like Symantec (Norton) that mainly deliver their products through Internet downloads may see only small upward shifts.

Successful Start-Up Firms

The U.S. economy has greatly benefited over the past several decades from the explosive growth of scores of highly successful start-up firms. These firms typically reduce their costs by moving from higher to lower points on their short-run cost curves and by downward and to-the-right shifts of their short-run cost curves via economies of scale. That has certainly been the case for such former start-up firms as Intel (microchips), Starbucks (coffee), Microsoft (software), Dell (personal computers), Google (Internet searches), and Cisco Systems (Internet switching).

A major source of lower average total cost for rapidly growing firms is the ability to spread huge product development and advertising costs over a larger number of units of output. These firms also achieve economies of scale from learning by doing and through increased specialization of labor, management, and equipment. After starting up, such firms experience declining average total costs over the years or even decades it takes them to eventually reach their respective MESs.

The Verson Stamping Machine

In 1996 Verson (a U.S. firm located in Chicago) introduced a 49-foot-tall metal-stamping machine that is the size of a house and weighs as much as 12 locomotives.

LAST
Word Don't Cry over Sunk Costs

Sunk Costs Are Irrelevant in Decision Making.

There is an old saying: Don't cry over spilt milk. The message is that once you have spilled a glass of milk, there is nothing you can do to recover it, so you should forget about it and "move on from there." This saying has great relevance to what economists call sunk costs. Once these costs are incurred, they cannot be recovered.

Let's gain an understanding of this idea by applying it first to consumers and then to businesses. Suppose you buy an expensive ticket to an upcoming football game, but the morning of the game you wake up with a bad case of the flu. Feeling miserable, you step outside to find that the windchill is about −10 degrees. You absolutely do not want to go to the game, but you remind yourself that you paid a steep price for the ticket. You call several people to try to sell the ticket, but you soon discover that no one is interested in it, even at a discounted price. You conclude that everyone who wants a ticket has one.

Should you go to the game? Economic analysis says that you should not take actions for which marginal cost exceeds marginal benefit. In this case, if the marginal cost of going to the game is greater than the marginal benefit, the best decision is to go back to bed. In correctly applying this rule, however, it is crucial that you recognize that the price you paid for the ticket is *not* a marginal cost. Even if the ticket was hideously expensive, it was purchased previously. Thus, its cost is not a marginal, extra cost that depends on whether or not you go to the game. The cost has already been incurred and must therefore be dealt with even if you decide not to attend!

With the cost of the ticket out of the picture, your cost-benefit analysis is going to be settled by your opinion that "you absolutely do not want to go." With such a strongly negative opinion, the marginal cost obviously exceeds the marginal benefit, and you should not go.

Here is a second consumer example: Suppose a family is on vacation and stops at a roadside stand to buy some apples. The kids get back into the car and bite into their apples, immediately pronouncing them "totally mushy" and unworthy of another bite. Both parents agree that the apples are "terrible," but the father continues to eat his because, as he says, "We paid a premium price for them." One of the older children replies, "Dad, that is irrelevant."

This $30 million machine, which cuts and sculpts raw sheets of steel into automobile hoods and fenders, enables automakers to make new parts in just 5 minutes, compared with 8 hours for older stamping presses. A single machine is designed to make 5 million auto parts per year. So, to achieve the cost saving from the machine, an auto manufacturer must have sufficient auto production to use all these parts. By allowing the use of this cost-saving piece of equipment, large firm size achieves economies of scale.

The Daily Newspaper

Daily newspapers have been going bankrupt in rapid succession over the past several years as both advertising dollars and news readership have shifted to the Internet. The falling circulation numbers have caused average fixed costs to rise significantly as newspapers are forced to spread their substantial fixed costs over fewer and fewer papers. The spike in average fixed costs has, in turn, forced newspapers to sharply increase their prices. Between July 2007 and July 2009, for instance, the *New York Times* had to raise its cover price three times as advertising revenues plunged and fixed costs had to be spread over fewer and fewer papers. Starting at $1 per copy, the cover price had to be raised to $1.25, then $1.50, and then $2.00.

With readership continuing to fall, newspapers face an average-fixed-cost death spiral. The more they raise their prices, the less they will sell. But the less their sales, the higher their average fixed costs and thus the more they must raise their prices. As a result, printed newspapers could ultimately be a thing of the past, with both advertising and news delivery shifting mainly to the Internet.

Aircraft and Concrete Plants

Why are there only two plants in the United States (both operated by Boeing) that produce large commercial aircraft and thousands of plants (owned by hundreds of firms) that produce ready-mixed concrete? The simple answer is that MES is radically different in the two industries. Why is that? First, while economies of scale are extensive in assembling large commercial aircraft, they are only very modest in mixing concrete. Manufacturing airplanes is a complex process that requires huge facilities, thousands of workers, and very expensive, specialized machinery. Economies of scale extend to huge plant sizes.

158

Although not stated very diplomatically, the child is exactly right. In making a new decision, you should ignore all costs that are not affected by the decision. The prior bad decision (in retrospect) to buy the apples should not dictate a second decision for which marginal benefit is less than marginal cost.

Now let's apply the idea of sunk costs to firms. Some of a firm's costs are not only fixed (recurring, but unrelated to the level of output) but sunk (unrecoverable). For example, a nonrefundable annual lease payment for the use of a store cannot be recouped once it has been paid. A firm's decision about whether to move from the store to a more profitable location does not depend on the amount of time remaining on the lease. If moving means greater profit, it makes sense to move whether there are 300 days, 30 days, or 3 days left on the lease.

Or, as another example, suppose a firm spends $1 million on R&D to bring out a new product, only to discover that

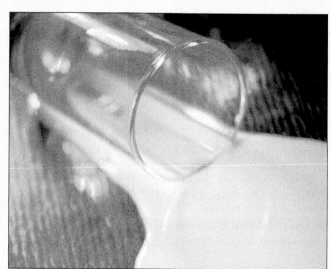

the product sells very poorly. Should the firm continue to produce the product at a loss even when there is no realistic hope for future success? Obviously, it should not. In making this decision, the firm realizes that the amount it has spent in developing the product is irrelevant; it should stop production of the product and cut its losses. In fact, many firms have dropped products after spending millions of dollars on their development.

A recent example is Pfizer's decision in 2007 to shelve its novel insulin inhaler because of poor sales and concerns about long-term side effects. The product withdrawal forced Pfizer to take a $2.8 billion pretax loss on this highly touted product.

In short, if a cost has been incurred and cannot be partly or fully recouped by some other choice, a rational consumer or firm should ignore it. Sunk costs are irrelevant. Don't cry over sunk costs.

But mixing portland cement, sand, gravel, and water to produce concrete requires only a handful of workers and relatively inexpensive equipment. Economies of scale are exhausted at relatively small size.

The differing MESs also derive from the vastly different sizes of the geographic markets. The market for commercial airplanes is global, and aircraft manufacturers

can deliver new airplanes anywhere in the world by flying them there. In contrast, the geographic market for a concrete plant is roughly the 50-mile radius within which the concrete can be delivered before it "sets up." So thousands of small concrete plants locate close to their customers in hundreds of small and large cities in the United States.

Summary

1. The economic cost of using a resource to produce a good or service is the value or worth that the resource would have had in its best alternative use. Economic costs include explicit costs, which flow to resources owned and supplied by others, and implicit costs, which are payments for the use of self-owned and self-employed resources. One implicit cost is a normal profit to the entrepreneur. Economic profit occurs when total revenue exceeds total cost (= explicit costs + implicit costs, including a normal profit).

2. In the short run a firm's plant capacity is fixed. The firm can use its plant more or less intensively by adding or subtracting units of variable resources, but it does not have sufficient time in the short run to alter plant size.

3. The law of diminishing returns describes what happens to output as a fixed plant is used more intensively. As successive units of a variable resource such as labor are added to a fixed plant, beyond some point the marginal product associated with each additional unit of a resource declines.

4. Because some resources are variable and others are fixed, costs can be classified as variable or fixed in the short run. Fixed costs are independent of the level of output; variable costs vary with output. The total cost of any output is the sum of fixed and variable costs at that output.

5. Average fixed, average variable, and average total costs are fixed, variable, and total costs per unit of output. Average fixed cost declines continuously as output increases because a fixed sum is being spread over a larger and larger number of units of production. A graph of average variable cost is U-shaped, reflecting increasing returns followed by diminishing returns. Average total cost is the sum of average fixed and average variable costs; its graph is also U-shaped.

6. Marginal cost is the extra, or additional, cost of producing one more unit of output. It is the amount by which total cost and total variable cost change when one more or one less unit of output is produced. Graphically, the marginal-cost curve intersects the ATC and AVC curves at their minimum points.

7. Lower resource prices shift cost curves downward, as does technological progress. Higher input prices shift cost curves upward.

8. The long run is a period of time sufficiently long for a firm to vary the amounts of all resources used, including plant size. In the long run all costs are variable. The long-run ATC, or planning, curve is composed of segments of the short-run ATC curves, and it represents the various plant sizes a firm can construct in the long run.

9. The long-run ATC curve is generally U-shaped. Economies of scale are first encountered as a small firm expands. Greater specialization in the use of labor and management, the ability to use the most efficient equipment, and the spreading of start-up costs among more units of output all contribute to economies of scale. As the firm continues to grow, it will encounter diseconomies of scale stemming from the managerial complexities that accompany large-scale production. The output ranges over which economies and diseconomies of scale occur in an industry are often an important determinant of the structure of that industry.

10. A firm's minimum efficient scale (MES) is the lowest level of output at which it can minimize its long-run average cost. In some industries, MES occurs at such low levels of output that numerous firms can populate the industry. In other industries, MES occurs at such high output levels that only a few firms can exist in the long run.

Terms and Concepts

economic cost

explicit costs

implicit costs

accounting profit

normal profit

economic profit

short run

long run

total product (TP)

marginal product (MP)

average product (AP)

law of diminishing returns

fixed costs

variable costs

total cost

average fixed cost (AFC)

average variable cost (AVC)

average total cost (ATC)

marginal cost (MC)

economies of scale

diseconomies of scale

constant returns to scale

minimum efficient scale (MES)

natural monopoly

Questions

1. Distinguish between explicit and implicit costs, giving examples of each. What are some explicit and implicit costs of attending college? LO1

2. Distinguish between accounting profit, economic profit, and normal profit. Does accounting profit or economic profit determine how entrepreneurs allocate resources between different business ventures? Explain. LO1

3. Which of the following are short-run and which are long-run adjustments? LO1
   a. Wendy's builds a new restaurant.
   b. Harley-Davidson Corporation hires 200 more production workers.
   c. A farmer increases the amount of fertilizer used on his corn crop.
   d. An Alcoa aluminum plant adds a third shift of workers.

4. Complete the table directly below by calculating marginal product and average product.

Inputs of Labor	Total Product	Marginal Product	Average Product
0	0		
1	15	_____	_____
2	34	_____	_____
3	51	_____	_____
4	65	_____	_____
5	74	_____	_____
6	80	_____	_____
7	83	_____	_____
8	82	_____	_____

Plot the total, marginal, and average products and explain in detail the relationship between each pair of curves. Explain why marginal product first rises, then declines, and ultimately becomes negative. What bearing does the law of diminishing returns have on short-run costs? Be specific. "When marginal product is rising, marginal cost is falling. And when marginal product is diminishing, marginal cost is rising." Illustrate and explain graphically. LO2

5. Why can the distinction between fixed costs and variable costs be made in the short run? Classify the following as fixed or variable costs: advertising expenditures, fuel, interest on company-issued bonds, shipping charges, payments for raw materials, real estate taxes, executive salaries, insurance premiums, wage payments, depreciation and obsolescence charges, sales taxes, and rental payments on leased office machinery. "There are no fixed costs in the long run; all costs are variable." Explain. LO3

6. List several fixed and variable costs associated with owning and operating an automobile. Suppose you are considering whether to drive your car or fly 1000 miles to Florida for spring break. Which costs—fixed, variable, or both—would you take into account in making your decision? Would any implicit costs be relevant? Explain. LO3

7. A firm has fixed costs of $60 and variable costs as indicated in the table at the bottom of this page. Complete the table and check your calculations by referring to question 4 at the end of Chapter 8. LO3

   a. Graph total fixed cost, total variable cost, and total cost. Explain how the law of diminishing returns influences the shapes of the variable-cost and total-cost curves.

   b. Graph AFC, AVC, ATC, and MC. Explain the derivation and shape of each of these four curves and their relationships to one another. Specifically, explain in nontechnical terms why the MC curve intersects both the AVC and the ATC curves at their minimum points.

   c. Explain how the location of each curve graphed in question 7b would be altered if (1) total fixed cost had been $100 rather than $60 and (2) total variable cost had been $10 less at each level of output.

8. Indicate how each of the following would shift the (1) marginal-cost curve, (2) average-variable-cost curve, (3) average-fixed-cost curve, and (4) average-total-cost curve of a manufacturing firm. In each case specify the direction of the shift. LO3

   a. A reduction in business property taxes.

   b. An increase in the nominal wages of production workers.

   c. A decrease in the price of electricity.

   d. An increase in insurance rates on plant and equipment.

   e. An increase in transportation costs.

9. Suppose a firm has only three possible plant-size options, represented by the ATC curves shown in the accompanying figure. What plant size will the firm choose in producing (a) 50, (b) 130, (c) 160, and (d) 250 units of output? Draw the firm's long-run average-cost curve on the diagram and describe this curve. LO4

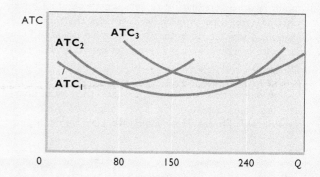

10. Use the concepts of economies and diseconomies of scale to explain the shape of a firm's long-run ATC curve. What is the concept of minimum efficient scale? What bearing can the shape of the long-run ATC curve have on the structure of an industry? LO4

11. **LAST WORD** What is a sunk cost? Provide an example of a sunk cost other than one from this book. Why are such costs irrelevant in making decisions about future actions?

Total Product	Total Fixed Cost	Total Variable Cost	Total Cost	Average Fixed Cost	Average Variable Cost	Average Total Cost	Marginal Cost
0	$_____	$ 0	$_____			$_____	
1	_____	45	_____	$_____	$_____	_____	$_____
2	_____	85	_____	_____	_____	_____	_____
3	_____	120	_____	_____	_____	_____	_____
4	_____	150	_____	_____	_____	_____	_____
5	_____	185	_____	_____	_____	_____	_____
6	_____	225	_____	_____	_____	_____	_____
7	_____	270	_____	_____	_____	_____	_____
8	_____	325	_____	_____	_____	_____	_____
9	_____	390	_____	_____	_____	_____	_____
10	_____	465	_____	_____	_____	_____	_____

Problems

1. Gomez runs a small pottery firm. He hires one helper at $12,000 per year, pays annual rent of $5000 for his shop, and spends $20,000 per year on materials. He has $40,000 of his own funds invested in equipment (pottery wheels, kilns, and so forth) that could earn him $4000 per year if alternatively invested. He has been offered $15,000 per year to work as a potter for a competitor. He estimates his entrepreneurial talents are worth $3000 per year. Total annual revenue from pottery sales is $72,000. Calculate the accounting profit and the economic profit for Gomez's pottery firm. LO1

2. Imagine you have some workers and some handheld computers that you can use to take inventory at a warehouse. There are diminishing returns to taking inventory. If one worker uses one computer, he can inventory 100 items per hour. Two workers sharing a computer can together inventory 150 items per hour. Three workers sharing a computer can together inventory 160 items per hour. And four or more workers sharing a computer can together inventory fewer than 160 items per hour. Computers cost $100 each and you must pay each worker $25 per hour. If you assign one worker per computer, what is the cost of inventorying a single item? What if you assign two workers per computer? Three? How many workers per computer should you assign if you wish to minimize the cost of inventorying a single item? LO2

3. You are a newspaper publisher. You are in the middle of a one-year rental contract for your factory that requires you to pay $500,000 per month, and you have contractual labor obligations of $1 million per month that you can't get out of. You also have a marginal printing cost of $.25 per paper as well as a marginal delivery cost of $.10 per paper. If sales fall by 20 percent from 1 million papers per month to 800,000 papers per month, what happens to the AFC per paper, the MC per paper, and the minimum amount that you must charge to break even on these costs? LO3

4. There are economies of scale in ranching, especially with regard to fencing land. Suppose that barbed-wire fencing costs $10,000 per mile to set up. How much would it cost to fence a single property whose area is one square mile if that property also happens to be perfectly square, with sides that are each one mile long? How much would it cost to fence exactly four such properties, which together would contain four square miles of area? Now, consider how much it would cost to fence in four square miles of ranch land if, instead, it comes as a single large square that is two miles long on each side. Which is more costly—fencing in the four, one-square-mile properties or the single four-square-mile property? LO4

FURTHER TEST YOUR KNOWLEDGE AT
www.mcconnell19e.com

At the text's Online Learning Center (OLC), **www.mcconnell19e.com**, you will find one or more Web-based questions that require information from the Internet to answer. We urge you to check them out; they will familiarize you with Web sites that may be helpful in other courses and perhaps even in your career. The OLC also features multiple-choice questions that give instant feedback and provides other helpful ways to further test your knowledge of the chapter.

Businesses and the Costs of Production

Previous chapters discussed consumer behavior and product demand. This chapter switches to producer behavior and business firms. It explains how a firm's **costs of production** change as the firm's output changes, in the short run and in the long run.

This chapter begins with a definition of cost and profit. You should be somewhat familiar with these terms because they were first introduced in Chapters 1 and 2. The explanation is now more detailed. Several definitions of cost and profit are given in the chapter, so you must know the distinctions if you are to understand the true meaning of **economic cost** and **economic profit.**

The second and third sections of the chapter focus on **short-run** variable relationships and production costs for the firm. You are first introduced to the important **law of diminishing returns,** which defines the relationship between the quantity of resources used by the firm and the output the firm produces in the short run. The chapter discussion then shifts to costs because resource prices are associated with the fixed and variable resources the typical firm uses to produce its output. The three basic types of short-run costs—total, average, and marginal—vary for the firm as the quantity of resources and output changes. The chapter describes the relationship among the various cost curves and how they are shaped by the law of diminishing returns.

The fourth section of the chapter looks at production costs in the **long run.** All resources, and also production costs, are variable in the long run. You will learn that the long-run cost curve for the typical firm is based on the short-run cost curves for firms of different sizes. In the long run, firms can experience **economies of scale** and **diseconomies of scale** that will shape the long-run cost curve for the firm. The chapter concludes with several practical applications of the concept of scale economies.

It is important that you master this material on the costs of production because it sets the foundation for understanding the price and output decisions of a firm operating under different market structures that you will be reading about in the next three chapters.

■ CHECKLIST

When you have studied this chapter you should be able to

☐ Define economic cost in terms of opportunity cost.
☐ Distinguish between an explicit cost and an implicit cost.
☐ Define accounting profit in terms of revenue and costs.

☐ Describe how normal profit is measured.
☐ Define economic profit in terms of revenue and costs.
☐ Distinguish between the short run and the long run in production.
☐ Define total product, marginal product, and average product.
☐ State the law of diminishing returns and explain its rationale.
☐ Compute marginal product and average product to illustrate the law of diminishing returns when you are given the necessary data.
☐ Describe the relationship between marginal product and average product.
☐ Define fixed costs, variable costs, and total cost.
☐ Define average fixed cost, average variable cost, and average total cost.
☐ Explain how average product is related to average variable cost.
☐ Define marginal cost.
☐ Explain how marginal product is related to marginal cost.
☐ Compute and graph average fixed cost, average variable cost, average total cost, and marginal cost when given total-cost data.
☐ Describe the relation of marginal cost to average variable cost and average total cost.
☐ Explain why short-run cost curves shift.
☐ Illustrate the difference between short-run average total cost curves for a firm at different outputs and its long-run average total cost curve.
☐ Describe various possible long-run average total cost curves.
☐ Define and list reasons for the economies and diseconomies of scale.
☐ Explain the concept of minimum efficient scale and its relation to industry structure.
☐ Give examples of short-run costs, economies of scale, and minimum efficient scale in the real world.
☐ Explain why sunk costs are irrelevant in decision making (*Last Word*).

■ CHAPTER OUTLINE

1. Resources are scarce and are used to produce many different products. The **economic cost** of using resources to produce a product is an opportunity cost: the value or worth of the resources in their best alternative use.

   a. Economic costs can be explicit or implicit. **Explicit costs** are the monetary payments that a firm makes

85

to obtain resources from nonowners of the firm. *Implicit costs* are the monetary payments that would have been paid for self-owned or self-employed resources if they had been used in their next best alternative outside the firm. Both types of costs are opportunity costs because the use of the resources for this use means that they are not available for use in the next best alternative use.

b. *Accounting profit* is the difference between a firm's total sales revenue and its total explicit costs. *Normal profit* is an implicit cost and is the typical or normal amount of accounting profit that an entrepreneur would have received for working at other firms of this type and supplying entrepreneurial resources.

c. *Economic profit* is the revenue a firm receives in excess of all its explicit and implicit economic costs. These economic costs are opportunity costs that measure the value of the forgone use of the resources. Included in the implicit costs is a normal profit which represents the entrepreneur's forgone income. The firm's accounting profit will be greater than its economic costs because accounting profit is the total of its sales revenue minus its explicit costs.

d. A distinction is made between the *short run* and the *long run.* The firm's economic costs vary as the firm's output changes. These costs depend on whether the firm is able to make short-run or long-run changes in its resource use. In the short run, the firm's plant is a fixed resource, but in the long run it is a variable resource. So, in the short run the firm cannot change the size of its plant and can vary its output only by changing the quantities of the variable resources it employs.

2. There are *short-run* relationships between inputs and outputs in the production process.

a. Several product terms need to be defined to show these relationships. *Total product (TP)* is the total quantity of output produced. *Marginal product (MP)* is the change made in total product from a change in a variable resource input. *Average product (AP),* or productivity, is the total product per unit of resource input.

b. The *law of diminishing returns* determines the manner in which the costs of the firm change as it changes its output in the short run. As more units of a variable resource are added to a fixed resource, beyond some point the marginal product from each additional unit of a variable resource will decline.

(1) There are three phases reflected in a graph of the total product and marginal product curves: increasing, decreasing, and negative marginal returns.

(2) When total product is increasing at an increasing rate, marginal product is rising; when total product is increasing at a decreasing rate, marginal product is falling; and when total product declines, marginal product is negative.

(3) When marginal product is greater than average product, average product rises, and when marginal product is less than average product, average product falls.

3. When input, output, and price information is available, it is possible to calculate **short-run production costs.**

a. The *total cost* is the sum of the firm's fixed costs and variable costs. As output increases,

(1) *fixed costs* do not change;

(2) at first, the *variable costs* increase at a decreasing rate, and then increase at an increasing rate;

(3) and at first total costs increase at a decreasing rate and then increase at an increasing rate.

b. **Average costs** consist of *average fixed costs (AFC), average variable costs (AVC),* and *average total costs (ATC).* They are equal, respectively, to the firm's fixed, variable, and total costs divided by its output. As output increases,

(1) average fixed cost decreases

(2) at first, average variable cost decreases and then increases

(3) and at first, average total cost also decreases and then increases

c. *Marginal cost (MC)* is the extra cost incurred in producing one additional unit of output.

(1) Because the marginal product of the variable resource increases and then decreases (as more of the variable resource is employed to increase output), marginal cost decreases and then increases as output increases.

(2) At the output at which average variable cost is a minimum, average variable cost and marginal cost are equal, and at the output at which average total cost is a minimum, average total cost and marginal cost are equal.

(3) On a graph, marginal cost will always intersect average variable cost at its minimum point and marginal cost will always intersect average total cost at its minimum point. These intersections will always have marginal cost approaching average variable cost and average total cost from below.

d. Changes in either resource prices or technology will cause the cost curves to shift.

4. In the long run, all the resources employed by the firm are variable resources. **Long-run production costs** are all variable costs.

a. As the firm expands its output by increasing the size of its plant, average total cost tends to fall at first because of the *economies of scale,* but as this expansion continues, sooner or later, average total cost begins to rise because of the *diseconomies of scale.*

b. The long-run average total cost curve shows the least average total cost at which any output can be produced after the firm has had time to make all changes in its plant size. Graphically, it is made up of all the points of tangency of the unlimited number of short-run average total cost curves.

c. The economies and diseconomies of scale encountered in the production of different goods are important factors influencing the structure and competitiveness of various industries.

(1) *Economies of scale* (a decline in long-run average total costs) arise because of labor specialization, managerial specialization, efficient capital, and other factors such as spreading the start-up, advertising, or development costs over an increasing level of output.

(2) *Diseconomies of scale* arise primarily from the problems of efficiently managing and coordinating the firm's operations as it becomes a large-scale producer.

(3) *Constant returns to scale* are the range of output where long-run average total cost does not change.

d. Economies and diseconomies of scale can determine the structure in an industry. *Minimum efficient scale (MES)* is the smallest level of output at which a firm can minimize long-run average costs. This concept explains why relatively large and small firms could co-exist in an industry and be viable when there is an extended range of constant returns to scale.

(1) In some industries the long-run average cost curve will decline over a range of output. Given consumer demand, efficient production will be achieved only with a small number of large firms.

(2) If economies of scale extend beyond the market size, the conditions for a *natural monopoly* are produced, which is a rare situation where unit costs are minimized by having a single firm produce a product.

(3) If there are few economies of scale, then there is minimum efficient size at a low level of output and there are many firms in an industry.

5. There are several applications and illustrations of short-run costs, economies of scale, and minimum efficient cost.

a. A rise in the price of gasoline raises short-run cost curves (AVC, MC, ATC) for businesses that use gasoline as an input for trucks and vehicles used to produce a product.

b. Economies of scale can be seen in successful start-up firms such as Intel, Microsoft, or Starbucks.

c. Economies of scale are also exhibited in the Verson stamping machine that makes millions of auto parts per year.

d. As the number of newspaper readers has fallen due to the shift of readership to the Internet, the average fixed cost of producing a newspaper has risen. In response, some newspapers have raised their prices, thus further reducing the number of readers. This situation creates a back (few readers) and forth (rising newspaper prices) problem that has the potential to bankrupt many newspapers.

e. Economies of scale are extensive in aircraft production, but modest in concrete mixing, which achieves minimum efficient scale at a low level of output. As a consequence, there are few aircraft factories and many concrete mixing companies.

6. (*Last Word*). Sunk costs are irrelevant to economic decision making because they are already incurred and cannot be recovered. Sunk costs are the result of making a past decision, not a current decision. A current decision is made on the basis of evaluating marginal costs and marginal benefits. If the marginal costs are less than the marginal benefits, the action will be taken.

■ **HINTS AND TIPS**

1. Many **cost** terms and **profit** terms are described in this chapter. Make yourself a glossary so that you can distinguish among them. You need to know what each one

means if you are to master the material in the chapter. If you try to learn them in the order in which you encounter them, you will have little difficulty because the later terms build on the earlier ones.

2. Make sure you know the difference between **marginal** and **average** relationships in this chapter. Marginal product (MP) shows the *change* in total output associated with each additional input. Average product (AP) is simply the output per unit of resource input. Marginal cost (MC) shows the change in total cost associated with producing another unit of output. Average cost shows the per-unit cost of producing a level of output.

3. Practice drawing the different sets of **cost curves** used in this chapter: (1) short-run total cost curves, (2) short-run average and marginal cost curves, and (3) long-run cost curves. Also, explain to yourself the relationship between the curves in each set that you draw.

4. In addition to learning *how* the costs of the firm vary as its output varies, be sure to understand *why* the costs vary the way they do. In this connection note that the behavior of short-run costs is the result of the law of diminishing returns and that the behavior of long-run costs is the consequence of economies and diseconomies of scale.

■ **IMPORTANT TERMS**

economic cost	fixed costs
explicit costs	variable costs
implicit costs	average fixed cost (AFC)
accounting profit	average variable cost (AVC)
normal profit	average total cost (ATC)
economic profit	marginal cost (MC)
short run	economies of scale
long run	diseconomies of scale
total product (TP)	constant returns to scale
marginal product (MP)	minimum efficient scale (MES)
average product (AP)	natural monopoly
law of diminishing returns	
total cost (TC)	

SELF-TEST

■ **FILL-IN QUESTIONS**

1. The value or worth of any resource in its best alternative use is called the (out-of-pocket, opportunity) _____ cost of that resource.

2. The economic cost of producing a product is the amount of money or income the firm must pay or provide to (government, resource suppliers) _____ to attract land, labor, and capital goods away from alternative uses in the economy. The monetary payments for resources used for production are (explicit, implicit) _____ costs, and the self-owned or self-employed resources used by the firm are _____ costs.

3. Accounting profit is equal to the firm's total revenue less its (explicit, implicit) _____ costs. Normal profit is an (explicit, implicit) _____ cost because it represents the forgone income that the entrepreneur could have earned working at another firm. Economic profit is equal to the firm's total (costs, revenues) _____ minus all its economic _____, both explicit and implicit.

4. In the short run the firm can change its output by changing the quantity of the (fixed, variable) _____ resources it employs, but it cannot change the quantity of the _____ resources. This means that the firm's plant capacity is fixed in the (short, long) _____ run and variable in the _____ run.

5. The law of diminishing returns is that as successive units of a (fixed, variable) _____ resource are added to a _____ resource, beyond some point the (total, marginal) _____ product of the former resource will decrease. The law assumes that all units of input are of (equal, unequal) _____ quality.

6. If the total product increases at an increasing rate, the marginal product is (rising, falling) _____. If it increases at a decreasing rate, the marginal product is (positive, negative, zero) _____, but (rising, falling) _____.

7. If total product is at a maximum, the marginal product is (positive, negative, zero) _____, but if it decreases, the marginal product is _____.

8. If the marginal product of any input exceeds its average product, the average product is (rising, falling) _____, but if it is less than its average product, the average product is _____. If the marginal product is equal to its average product, the average product is at a (minimum, maximum) _____.

9. Those costs that in total do not vary with changes in output are (fixed, variable) _____ costs, but those costs that in total change with the level of output are _____ costs. The sum of fixed and variable costs at each level of output is (marginal, total) _____ cost.

10. The law of diminishing returns explains why a firm's average variable, average total, and marginal cost may at first tend to (increase, decrease) _____ but ultimately _____ as the output of the firm increases.

11. Marginal cost is the increase in (average, total) _____ variable cost or _____ cost that occurs when the firm increases its output by one unit.

12. If marginal cost is less than average variable cost, average variable cost will be (rising, falling, constant) _____, but if average variable cost is less than marginal cost, average variable cost will be _____.

13. Assume that labor is the only variable input in the short run and that the wage rate paid to labor is constant.
    a. When the marginal product of labor is rising, the marginal cost of producing a product is (rising, falling) _____.
    b. When the average variable cost of producing a product is falling, the average product of labor is (rising, falling) _____.
    c. At the output at which marginal cost is at a minimum, the marginal product of labor is at a (minimum, maximum) _____.
    d. At the output at which the average product of labor is at a maximum, the average variable cost of producing the product is at a (minimum, maximum) _____.
    e. At the output at which the average variable cost is at a minimum, average variable cost and (marginal, total) _____ cost are equal and average product and _____ product are equal.

14. Changes in either resource prices or technology will cause cost curves to (shift, remain unchanged) _____. If average fixed costs increase, then the average fixed costs curve will (shift up, shift down, remain unchanged) _____ and the average total cost curve will _____, but the average variable cost curve will _____ and the marginal cost curve will (shift up, shift down, remain unchanged) _____.

15. If average variable costs increase, then the average variable cost curve will (shift up, shift down, remain unchanged) _____ and the average total cost curve will _____, and the marginal cost curve will (shift up, shift down, remain unchanged) _____, but the average fixed cost curve would _____.

16. The short-run costs of a firm are fixed and variable costs, but in the long run all costs are (fixed, variable) _____. The long-run average total cost of producing a product is equal to the lowest of the short-run costs of producing that product after the firm has had all the time it requires to make the appropriate adjustments in the size of its (workforce, plant) _____.

17. List the three important sources of economies of scale:

a. _____

b. _____

c. _____

18. When the firm experiences diseconomies of scale, it has (higher, lower) _____ average total costs as output increases. Where diseconomies of scale are operative, an increase in all inputs will cause a (greater, less) _____-than-proportionate increase in output. The factor that gives rise to large diseconomies of scale is managerial (specialization, difficulties) _____.

19. The smallest level of output at which a firm can minimize long-run average costs is (maximum, minimum) _____ efficient scale. Relatively large and small firms could coexist in an industry and be equally viable when there is an extended range of (increasing, decreasing, constant) _____ returns to scale.

20. In some industries, the long-run average cost curve will (increase, decrease) _____ over a long range of output and efficient production will be achieved with only a few (small, large) _____ firms. The conditions for a natural monopoly are created when (economies, diseconomies) _____ of scale extend beyond the market's size so that unit costs are minimized by having a single firm produce a product.

■ **TRUE–FALSE QUESTIONS**

Circle T if the statement is true, F if it is false.

1. The economic costs of a firm are the explicit or implicit costs for resources used for production by the firm. **T F**

2. Economic profit is an explicit cost, while normal profit is an implicit cost. **T F**

3. In the short run the size (or capacity) of a firm's plant is fixed. **T F**

4. The resources employed by a firm are all variable in the long run and all fixed in the short run. **T F**

5. The law of diminishing returns states that as successive amounts of a variable resource are added to a fixed resource, beyond some point total output will diminish. **T F**

6. An assumption of the law of diminishing returns is that all units of variable inputs are of equal quality. **T F**

7. When total product is increasing at a decreasing rate, marginal product is positive and increasing. **T F**

8. When average product is falling, marginal product is greater than average product. **T F**

9. When marginal product is negative, total production (or output) is decreasing. **T F**

10. The larger the output of a firm, the smaller the fixed cost of the firm. **T F**

11. The law of diminishing returns explains why increases in variable costs associated with each 1-unit increase in output become greater and greater after a certain point. **T F**

12. Fixed costs can be controlled or altered in the short run. **T F**

13. Total cost is the sum of fixed and variable costs at each level of output. **T F**

14. Marginal cost is the change in fixed cost divided by the change in output. **T F**

15. The marginal cost curve intersects the average total cost (ATC) curve at the ATC curve's minimum point. **T F**

16. If the fixed cost of a firm increases from one year to the next (because the premium it must pay for the insurance on the buildings it owns has been increased) while its variable cost schedule remains unchanged, its marginal cost schedule also will remain unchanged. **T F**

17. Marginal cost is equal to average variable cost at the output at which average variable cost is at a minimum. **T F**

18. When the marginal product of a variable resource increases, the marginal cost of producing the product will decrease, and when marginal product decreases, marginal cost will increase. **T F**

19. If the price of a variable input should increase, the average variable cost, average total cost, and marginal cost curves would all shift upward, but the position of the average fixed cost curve would remain unchanged. **T F**

20. One explanation why the long-run average total cost curve of a firm rises after some level of output has been reached is the law of diminishing returns. **T F**

21. If a firm increases all its inputs by 20% and its output increases by 30%, the firm is experiencing economies of scale. **T F**

22. The primary cause of diseconomies of scale is increased specialization of labor. **T F**

23. If a firm has constant returns to scale in the long run, the *total* cost of producing its product does not change when it expands or contracts its output. **T F**

24. Minimum efficient scale occurs at the largest level of output at which a firm can minimize long-run average costs. **T F**

25. One reason many daily newspapers are going bankrupt is that their average fixed costs are rising because more people are getting their news from the Internet and there are fewer subscribers to newspapers. **T F**

■ **MULTIPLE-CHOICE QUESTIONS**

Circle the letter that corresponds to the best answer.

1. Suppose that a firm produces 100,000 units a year and sells them all for $5 each. The explicit costs of production are $350,000 and the implicit costs of production are $100,000. The firm has an accounting profit of
(a) $200,000 and an economic profit of $25,000
(b) $150,000 and an economic profit of $50,000
(c) $125,000 and an economic profit of $75,000
(d) $100,000 and an economic profit of $50,000

2. Economic profit for a firm is defined as the total revenue of the firm minus its
(a) accounting profit
(b) normal profit
(c) implicit costs
(d) economic costs

3. Which would best describe the short run for a firm as defined by economists?
(a) The plant capacity for a firm is variable.
(b) The plant capacity for a firm is fixed.
(c) There are diseconomies of scale.
(d) There are economies of scale.

4. Which is most likely to be a long-run adjustment for a firm that manufactures golf carts on an assembly line basis?
(a) an increase in the amount of steel the firm buys
(b) a reduction in the number of shifts of workers from three to two
(c) a change in the production managers of the assembly line
(d) a change from the production of golf carts to motorcycles

5. The change in total product divided by the change in resource input defines
(a) total cost
(b) average cost
(c) average product
(d) marginal product

Use the following table to answer Questions 6 and 7. Assume that the only variable resource used to produce output is labor.

Amount of labor	Amount of output
1	3
2	8
3	12
4	15
5	17
6	18

6. The marginal product of the fourth unit of labor is
(a) 2 units of output
(b) 3 units of output
(c) 4 units of output
(d) 15 units of output

7. When the firm hires four units of labor the average product of labor is
(a) 3 units of output
(b) 3.75 units of output
(c) 4.25 units of output
(d) 15 units of output

8. Because the marginal product of a variable resource initially increases and later decreases as a firm increases its output,
(a) average variable cost decreases at first and then increases
(b) average fixed cost declines as the output of the firm expands
(c) variable cost at first increases by increasing amounts and then increases by decreasing amounts
(d) marginal cost at first increases and then decreases

9. Because the marginal product of a resource at first increases and then decreases as the output of the firm increases,
(a) average fixed cost declines as the output of the firm increases
(b) average variable cost at first increases and then decreases
(c) variable cost at first increases by increasing amounts and then increases by decreasing amounts
(d) total cost at first increases by decreasing amounts and then increases by increasing amounts

For Questions 10, 11, and 12, use the data given in the following table. The fixed cost of the firm is $500, and the firm's total variable cost is indicated in the table.

Output	Total variable cost
1	$ 200
2	360
3	500
4	700
5	1000
6	1800

10. The average variable cost of the firm when 4 units of output are produced is
(a) $175
(b) $200
(c) $300
(d) $700

11. The average total cost of the firm when 4 units of output are being produced is
(a) $175
(b) $200
(c) $300
(d) $700

12. The marginal cost of the sixth unit of output is
(a) $200
(b) $300
(c) $700
(d) $800

13. Marginal cost and average variable cost are equal at the output at which
   (a) marginal cost is a minimum
   (b) marginal product is a maximum
   (c) average product is a maximum
   (d) average variable cost is a maximum

14. Average variable cost may be either increasing or decreasing when
   (a) marginal cost is decreasing
   (b) marginal product is increasing
   (c) average fixed cost is decreasing
   (d) average total cost is increasing

15. Why does the short-run marginal cost curve eventually increase for the typical firm?
   (a) diseconomies of scale
   (b) minimum efficient scale
   (c) the law of diminishing returns
   (d) economic profit eventually decreases

16. If the price of labor or some other variable resource increased, the
   (a) AVC curve would shift downward
   (b) AFC curve would shift upward
   (c) AFC curve would shift downward
   (d) MC curve would shift upward

Questions 17, 18, 19, and 20 are based on the following figure.

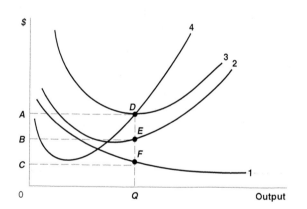

17. In the figure, curves **1, 3,** and **4,** respectively, represent
   (a) average variable cost, marginal cost, and average total cost
   (b) average total cost, average variable cost, and marginal cost
   (c) average fixed cost, average total cost, and marginal cost
   (d) marginal cost, average total cost, and average variable cost

18. At output level **Q,** the average fixed cost is measured by the vertical distance represented by
   (a) *DE*
   (b) *DF*
   (c) *DQ*
   (d) *EF*

19. As output increases beyond the level represented by **Q,**
   (a) marginal product is rising
   (b) marginal product is falling
   (c) total fixed costs are rising
   (d) total costs are falling

20. If the firm is producing at output level **Q,** then the total variable costs of production are represented by area
   (a) 0**QFC**
   (b) 0**QEB**
   (c) 0**QDC**
   (d) **CFEB**

21. At an output of 10,000 units per year, a firm's total variable costs are $50,000 and its average fixed costs are $2. The total costs per year for the firm are
   (a) $50,000
   (b) $60,000
   (c) $70,000
   (d) $80,000

22. A firm has total fixed costs of $4,000 a year. The average variable cost is $3.00 for 2000 units of output. At this level of output, its average total costs are
   (a) $2.50
   (b) $3.00
   (c) $4.50
   (d) $5.00

23. If you know that total fixed cost is $100, total variable cost is $300, and total product is 4 units, then
   (a) marginal cost is $50
   (b) average fixed cost is $45
   (c) average total cost is $125
   (d) average variable cost is $75

24. If the short-run average variable costs of production for a firm are falling, then this indicates that
   (a) average variable costs are above average fixed costs
   (b) marginal costs are below average variable costs
   (c) average fixed costs are constant
   (d) total costs are falling

Answer Questions 25 and 26 using the following table. Three short-run cost schedules are given for three plants of different sizes that a firm might build in the long run.

Plant 1		Plant 2		Plant 3	
Output	ATC	Output	ATC	Output	ATC
10	$10	10	$15	10	$20
20	9	20	10	20	15
30	8	30	7	30	10
40	9	40	10	40	8
50	10	50	14	50	9

25. What is the long-run average cost of producing 40 units of output?
   (a) $7
   (b) $8
   (c) $9
   (d) $10

26. At what output is long-run average cost at a minimum?
  (a) 20
  (b) 30
  (c) 40
  (d) 50

27. If the long-run average total cost curve for a firm is down-sloping, then it indicates that there
  (a) is a minimum efficient scale
  (b) are constant returns to scale
  (c) are diseconomies of scale
  (d) are economies of scale

28. Which factor contributes to economies of scale?
  (a) less efficient use of capital goods
  (b) less division of labor and specialization
  (c) greater specialization in management of a firm
  (d) greater difficulty controlling the operations of a firm

29. A firm is encountering constant returns to scale when it increases all of its inputs by 20% and its output increases by
  (a) 10%
  (b) 15%
  (c) 20%
  (d) 25%

30. If economies of scale are limited and diseconomies appear quickly in an industry, then minimum efficient scale occurs at a
  (a) high level of output, and there will be a few firms
  (b) high level of output, and there will be many firms
  (c) low level of output, and there will be few firms
  (d) low level of output, and there will be many firms

■ **PROBLEMS**

1. On the following graph, sketch the way in which the average product and the marginal product of a resource change as the firm increases its employment of that resource.

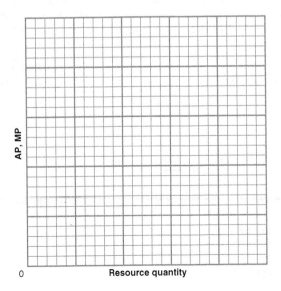

2. The table shows the total production of a firm as the quantity of labor employed increases. The quantities of all other resources employed remain constant.
  a. Compute the marginal products of the first through the eighth units of labor and enter them in the table.

Units of labor	Total production	Marginal product of labor	Average product of labor
0	0		0
1	80	____	____
2	200	____	____
3	330	____	____
4	400	____	____
5	450	____	____
6	480	____	____
7	490	____	____
8	480	____	____

  b. Now compute the average products of the various quantities of labor and enter them in the table.
  c. There are increasing returns to labor from the first through the _____ units of labor and decreasing returns from the _____ through the eighth units.
  d. When total production is increasing, marginal product is (positive, negative) _____ and when total production is decreasing, marginal product is _____.
  e. When marginal product is greater than average product, then average product will (rise, fall) _____, and when marginal product is less than average product, the average product will _____.

3. On the graph below sketch the manner in which fixed cost, variable cost, and total cost change as the output the firm produces in the short run changes.

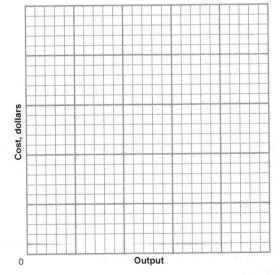

4. Assume that a firm has a plant of fixed size and that it can vary its output only by varying the amount of labor it employs. The table below shows the relationships among

Quantity of labor employed	Total ouput	Marginal product of labor	Average product of labor	Total cost	Marginal cost	Average variable cost
0	0	—	—	$_____	—	—
1	5	5	5	_____	$_____	$_____
2	11	6	5.50	_____	_____	_____
3	18	7	6	_____	_____	_____
4	24	6	6	_____	_____	_____
5	29	5	5.80	_____	_____	_____
6	33	4	5.50	_____	_____	_____
7	36	3	5.14	_____	_____	_____
8	38	2	4.75	_____	_____	_____
9	39	1	4.33	_____	_____	_____
10	39	0	3.90	_____	_____	_____

the amount of labor employed, the output of the firm, the marginal product of labor, and the average product of labor.

a. Assume each unit of labor costs the firm $10. Compute the total cost of labor for each quantity of labor the firm might employ, and enter these figures in the table.

b. Now determine the marginal cost of the firm's product as the firm increases its output. Divide the increase in total labor cost by the *increase* in total output to find the marginal cost. Enter these figures in the table.

c. When the marginal product of labor

(1) increases, the marginal cost of the firm's product

(increases, decreases) _____.

(2) decreases, the marginal cost of the firm's product

_____.

d. If labor is the only variable input, the total labor cost and total variable cost are equal. Find the average variable cost of the firm's product (by dividing the total labor cost by total output) and enter these figures in the table.

e. When the average product of labor

(1) increases, the average variable cost (increases,

decreases) _____.

(2) decreases, the average variable cost _____.

5. The law of diminishing returns causes a firm's average variable, average total, and marginal cost to decrease at first and then to increase as the output of the firm increases.

Sketch these three cost curves on the following graph in such a way that their proper relationship to each other is shown.

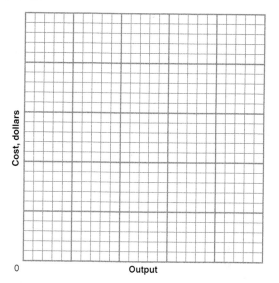

6. The table that follows is a schedule of a firm's fixed cost and variable cost.

a. Complete the table by computing total cost, average fixed cost, average total cost, and marginal cost.

b. On the graph at the top of the next page, plot and label fixed cost, variable cost, and total cost.

c. On the graph at the bottom of the next page, plot average fixed cost, average variable cost, average total cost, and marginal cost. Label the four curves.

Output	Total fixed cost	Total variable cost	Total cost	Average fixed cost	Average variable cost	Average total cost	Marginal cost
0	$200	$ 0	$_____				
1	200	50	_____	$_____	$50.00	$_____	$_____
2	200	90	_____	_____	45.00	_____	_____
3	200	120	_____	_____	40.00	_____	_____
4	200	160	_____	_____	40.00	_____	_____
5	200	220	_____	_____	44.00	_____	_____
6	200	300	_____	_____	50.00	_____	_____
7	200	400	_____	_____	57.14	_____	_____
8	200	520	_____	_____	65.00	_____	_____
9	200	670	_____	_____	74.44	_____	_____
10	200	900	_____	_____	90.00	_____	_____

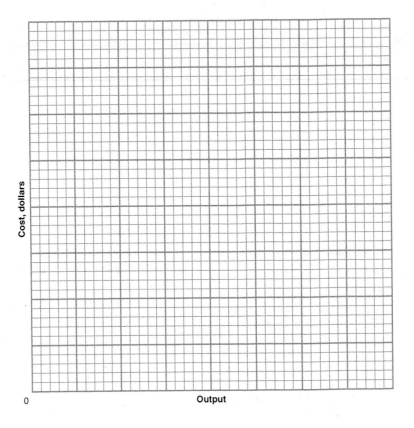

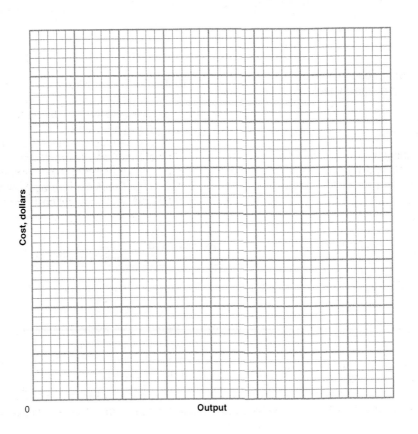

7. Following are the short-run average cost curves of producing a product with three different sizes of plants, Plant 1, Plant 2, and Plant 3. Draw the firm's long-run average cost on this graph.

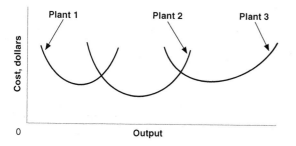

8. Following are the short-run average total cost schedules for three plants of different sizes that a firm might build to produce its product. Assume that these are the only possible sizes of plants that the firm might build.

Plant size A		Plant size B		Plant size C	
Output	ATC	Output	ATC	Output	ATC
10	$ 7	10	$17	10	$53
20	6	20	13	20	44
30	5	30	9	30	35
40	4	40	6	40	27
50	5	50	4	50	20
60	7	60	3	60	14
70	10	70	4	70	11
80	14	80	5	80	8
90	19	90	7	90	6
100	25	100	10	100	5
110	32	110	16	110	7
120	40	120	25	120	10

a. Complete the long-run average cost schedule for the firm in the following table.

Output	Average cost	Output	Average cost
10	$_____	70	$_____
20	_____	80	_____
30	_____	90	_____
40	_____	100	_____
50	_____	110	_____
60	_____	120	_____

b. For outputs between

(1) _____ and _____, the firm should build Plant A.

(2) _____ and _____, the firm should build Plant B.

(3) _____ and _____, the firm should build Plant C.

■ **SHORT ANSWER AND ESSAY QUESTIONS**

1. Explain the meaning of the opportunity cost of producing a product and the difference between an explicit cost and an implicit cost. How would you determine the implicit money cost of a resource?

2. What is the difference between normal profit and economic profit? Why is the former an economic cost? How do you define accounting profit?

3. What type of adjustments can a firm make in the long run that it cannot make in the short run? What adjustments can it make in the short run? How long is the short run?

4. Why is the distinction between the short run and the long run important?

5. State precisely the law of diminishing returns. Exactly what is it that diminishes, and why does it diminish?

6. Distinguish between a fixed cost and a variable cost.

7. Why are short-run total costs partly fixed and partly variable costs, and why are long-run costs entirely variable?

8. Why do short-run variable costs increase at first by decreasing amounts and later increase by increasing amounts?

9. How does the behavior of short-run variable costs influence the behavior of short-run total costs?

10. Describe the ways in which short-run average fixed cost, average variable cost, average total cost, and marginal cost vary as the output of the firm increases.

11. What are the connections between marginal product and marginal cost, and between average product and average variable cost? How will marginal cost behave as marginal product decreases and increases? How will average variable cost change as average product rises and falls?

12. What are the precise relationships between marginal cost and minimum average variable cost, and between marginal cost and minimum average total cost? Why are these relationships necessarily true?

13. What happens to the average total cost, average variable cost, average fixed cost, and marginal cost curves when the price of a variable input increases or decreases? Describe what other factor can cause short-run cost curves to shift.

14. What does the long-run average cost curve of a firm show? What relationship is there between long-run average cost and the short-run average total cost schedules of the different-sized plants which a firm might build?

15. Why is the long-run average cost curve of a firm U-shaped?

16. What is meant by economies of scale and by diseconomies of scale?

17. What are factors that contribute to economies of scale?

18. What causes diseconomies of scale?

19. What is minimum efficient scale? How can this concept, combined with economies and diseconomies of scale, be used to describe the number and size of firms in an industry?

20. Describe real examples of short-run costs, economies of scale, and minimum efficient scale.

ANSWERS

Chapter 7 Businesses and the Costs of Production

FILL-IN QUESTIONS

1. opportunity
2. resource suppliers, explicit, implicit
3. explicit, implicit, revenues, costs
4. variable, fixed, short, long
5. variable, fixed, marginal, equal
6. rising, positive, falling
7. zero, negative
8. rising, falling, maximum
9. fixed, variable, total
10. decrease, increase
11. total, total
12. falling, rising
13. *a.* falling; *b.* rising; *c.* maximum; *d.* minimum; *e.* marginal, marginal
14. shift, shift up, shift up, remain unchanged, remain unchanged
15. shift up, shift up, shift up, remain unchanged
16. variable, plant
17. *a.* labor specialization; *b.* managerial specialization; *c.* more efficient use
18. higher, less, difficulties
19. minimum, constant
20. decrease, large, economies

TRUE–FALSE QUESTIONS

1. T, p. 141	10. F, p. 147	19. T, pp. 151–152
2. F, pp.141–143	11. T, pp. 147–148	20. F, pp. 152–153
3. T, p. 143	12. F, pp. 147–149	21. T, pp. 153–154
4. F, p. 143	13. T, p. 148	22. F, p. 156
5. F, p. 144	14. F, pp. 149–150	23. F, p. 156
6. T, pp. 144–145	15. T, pp. 149–150	24. F, pp. 156–157
7. F, pp. 145–147	16. T, pp. 150–151	25. T, p. 158
8. F, pp. 145–147	17. T, pp. 150–151	
9. T, pp. 145–147	18. T, pp. 150–151	

MULTIPLE-CHOICE QUESTIONS

1. b, pp. 141–143	11. c, p. 149	21. c, pp. 148–149
2. d, pp. 142–143	12. d, pp. 149–150	22. d, pp. 148–149
3. b, p. 143	13. c, pp. 150–151	23. d, pp. 148–149
4. d, p. 143	14. c, pp. 150–151	24. b, pp. 149–152
5. d, p. 144	15. c, p. 150	25. b, pp. 152–153
6. b, p. 144	16. d, pp. 150–151	26. b, pp. 153–154
7. b, p. 144	17. c, p. 151	27. d, pp. 152–154
8. a, pp. 149–151	18. a, p. 151	28. c, pp. 154–156
9. d, pp. 149–151	19. b, pp. 150–152	29. c, p. 156
10. a, p. 149	20. b, pp. 148–149	30. d, p. 156

PROBLEMS

1. see Figure 7.2(b) of the text
2. *a.* 80, 120, 130, 70, 50, 30, 10, −10; *b.* 80, 100, 110, 100, 90, 80, 70, 60; *c.* third, fourth; *d.* positive, negative; *e.* rise, fall
3. see Figure 7.3 of the text
4. *a.* $0, 10, 20, 30, 40, 50, 60, 70, 80, 90, 100; *b.* $2.00, 1.67, 1.43, 1.67, 2.00, 2.50, 3.33, 5.00, 1.00, NA; *c.* (1) decreases, (2) increases; *d.* 2.00, 1.82, 1.67, 1.67, 1.72, 1.82, 1.94, 2.11, 2.31, 2.56; *e.* (1) decreases, (2) increases
5. see Figure 7.5 of the text
6. *a.* see table below; *b.* graph; *c.* graph

Total cost	Average fixed cost	Average total cost	Marginal cost
$ 200	—	—	—
250	$200.00	$250.00	$ 50
290	100.00	145.00	40
320	66.67	106.67	30
360	50.00	90.00	40
420	40.00	84.00	60
500	33.33	83.33	80
600	28.57	85.71	100
720	25.00	90.00	120
870	22.22	96.67	150
1100	20.00	110.00	230

7. see Figures 7.7 and 7.8 of the text
8. *a.* $7.00, 6.00, 5.00, 4.00, 4.00, 3.00, 4.00, 5.00, 6.00, 5.00, 7.00, 10.00; *b.* (1) 10, 40, (2) 50, 80, (3) 90, 120

SHORT ANSWER AND ESSAY QUESTIONS

1. p. 141	8. pp. 148–152	15. pp. 153–154
2. pp. 141–143	9. pp. 148–149	16. pp. 153–156
3. p. 143	10. pp. 148–152	17. pp. 153–156
4. p. 143	11. pp. 149–152	18. p. 156
5. pp. 144–146	12. pp. 149–152	19. pp. 156–157
6. pp. 147–148	13. pp. 152–153	20. pp. 157–159
7. pp. 147, 151	14. pp. 153–154	

AFTER READING THIS CHAPTER, YOU SHOULD BE ABLE TO:

1 Give the names and summarize the main characteristics of the four basic market models.

2 List the conditions required for purely competitive markets.

3 Convey how purely competitive firms maximize profits or minimize losses in the short run.

4 Explain why a competitive firm's marginal cost curve is the same as its supply curve.

Pure Competition in the Short Run

In Chapter 4 we examined the relationship between product demand and total revenue, and in Chapter 7 we discussed production costs. Now we want to connect revenues and costs to see how a business decides what price to charge and how much output to produce. A firm's decisions concerning price and production depend greatly on the character of the industry in which it is operating. There is no "average" or "typical" industry. At one extreme is an industry in which a single producer dominates the market; at the other extreme are industries in which thousands of firms each produce a tiny fraction of market supply. Between these extremes are many other types of industries.

Since we cannot examine each industry individually, we will focus on four basic *models* of market structure. Together, these models will help you understand how price and output are determined in the many product markets in the economy. They also will help you evaluate the efficiency or inefficiency of those markets. Finally, these four models will provide a crucial background for assessing public policies (such as antitrust policy) relating to certain firms and industries.

TABLE 8.1 **Characteristics of the Four Basic Market Models**

	Market Model			
Characteristic	**Pure Competition**	**Monopolistic Competition**	**Oligopoly**	**Pure Monopoly**
Number of firms	A very large number	Many	Few	One
Type of product	Standardized	Differentiated	Standardized or differentiated	Unique; no close substitutes
Control over price	None	Some, but within rather narrow limits	Limited by mutual interdependence; considerable with collusion	Considerable
Conditions of entry	Very easy, no obstacles	Relatively easy	Significant obstacles	Blocked
Nonprice competition	None	Considerable emphasis on advertising, brand names, trademarks	Typically a great deal, particularly with product differentiation	Mostly public relations advertising
Examples	Agriculture	Retail trade, dresses, shoes	Steel, automobiles, farm implements, many household appliances	Local utilities

Four Market Models

Economists group industries into four distinct market structures: pure competition, pure monopoly, monopolistic competition, and oligopoly. These four market models differ in several respects: the number of firms in the industry, whether those firms produce a standardized product or try to differentiate their products from those of other firms, and how easy or how difficult it is for firms to enter the industry.

Very briefly the four models are as follows:

- **Pure competition** involves a very large number of firms producing a standardized product (that is, a product like cotton, for which each producer's output is virtually identical to that of every other producer.) New firms can enter or exit the industry very easily.
- **Pure monopoly** is a market structure in which one firm is the sole seller of a product or service (for example, a local electric utility). Since the entry of additional firms is blocked, one firm constitutes the entire industry. The pure monopolist produces a single unique product, so product differentiation is not an issue.
- **Monopolistic competition** is characterized by a relatively large number of sellers producing differentiated products (clothing, furniture, books). Present in this model is widespread *nonprice competition*, a selling strategy in which a firm does not try to distinguish its product on the basis of price but instead on attributes like design and workmanship (an approach called *product differentiation*). Either entry to or exit from monopolistically competitive industries is quite easy.
- **Oligopoly** involves only a few sellers of a standardized or differentiated product, so each firm is affected by the

decisions of its rivals and must take those decisions into account in determining its own price and output.

Table 8.1 summarizes the characteristics of the four models for easy comparison and later reference. In discussing these market models, we will occasionally distinguish the characteristics of *pure competition* from those of the three other basic market structures, which together we will designate as **imperfect competition.**

Pure Competition: Characteristics and Occurrence

Although pure competition is relatively rare in the real world, this market model is highly relevant to several industries. In particular, we can learn much about markets for agricultural goods, fish products, foreign exchange, basic metals, and stock shares by studying the pure-competition model. Also, pure competition is a meaningful starting point for any discussion of price and output determination. Moreover, the operation of a purely competitive economy provides a standard, or norm, for evaluating the efficiency of the real-world economy.

Let's take a fuller look at pure competition, the focus of the remainder of this chapter:

- *Very large numbers* A basic feature of a purely competitive market is the presence of a large number of independently acting sellers, often offering their products in large national or international markets. Examples: markets for farm commodities, the stock market, and the foreign exchange market.
- *Standardized product* Purely competitive firms produce a standardized (identical or homogeneous) product. As long as the price is the same, consumers

will be indifferent about which seller to buy the product from. Buyers view the products of firms B, C, D, and E as perfect substitutes for the product of firm A. Because purely competitive firms sell standardized products, they make no attempt to differentiate their products and do not engage in other forms of nonprice competition.

- *"Price takers"* In a purely competitive market, individual firms do not exert control over product price. Each firm produces such a small fraction of total output that increasing or decreasing its output will not perceptibly influence total supply or, therefore, product price. In short, the competitive firm is a **price taker:** It cannot change market price; it can only adjust to it. That means that the individual competitive producer is at the mercy of the market. Asking a price higher than the market price would be futile. Consumers will not buy from firm A at $2.05 when its 9999 competitors are selling an identical product, and therefore a perfect substitute, at $2 per unit. Conversely, because firm A can sell as much as it chooses at $2 per unit, it has no reason to charge a lower price, say, $1.95. Doing that would shrink its profit.
- *Free entry and exit* New firms can freely enter and existing firms can freely leave purely competitive industries. No significant legal, technological, financial, or other obstacles prohibit new firms from selling their output in any competitive market.

Demand as Seen by a Purely Competitive Seller

We begin by examining demand from a purely competitive seller's viewpoint to see how it affects revenue. This seller might be a wheat farmer, a strawberry grower, a sheep rancher, a foreign-currency broker, or some other pure competitor. Because each purely competitive firm offers only a negligible fraction of total market supply, it must accept the price determined by the market; it is a price taker, not a price maker.

Perfectly Elastic Demand

The demand schedule faced by the *individual firm* in a purely competitive industry is perfectly elastic at the market price, as demonstrated in Figure 8.1. As shown in column 1 of the table in Figure 8.1, the market price is $131. The firm represented cannot obtain a higher price by restricting its output, nor does it need to lower its price to increase its sales volume. Columns 1 and 2 show that the firm can produce and sell as many or as few units as it likes at the market price of $131.

We are *not* saying that *market* demand is perfectly elastic in a competitive market. Rather, market demand graphs as a downsloping curve. An entire industry (all firms producing a particular product) can affect price by changing industry output. For example, all firms, acting independently but simultaneously, can increase price by reducing output. But the individual competitive firm cannot do that because its output represents such a small fraction of its industry's total output. For the individual competitive firm, the market price is therefore a fixed value at which it can sell as many or as few units as it cares to. Graphically, this implies that the individual competitive firm's demand curve will plot as a straight, horizontal line such as *D* in Figure 8.1

Average, Total, and Marginal Revenue

The firm's demand schedule is also its average-revenue schedule. Price per unit to the purchaser is also revenue per unit, or average revenue, to the seller. To say that all buyers must pay $131 per unit is to say that the revenue per unit, or **average revenue** received by the seller, is $131. Price and average revenue are the same thing.

The **total revenue** for each sales level is found by multiplying price by the corresponding quantity the firm can sell. (Column 1 multiplied by column 2 in the table in Figure 8.1 yields column 3.) In this case, total revenue increases by a constant amount, $131, for each additional unit of sales. Each unit sold adds exactly its constant price—no more or no less—to total revenue.

When a firm is pondering a change in its output, it will consider how its total revenue will change as a result. **Marginal revenue** is the change in total revenue (or the extra revenue) that results from selling one more unit of output. In column 3 of the table in Figure 8.1, total revenue is zero when zero units are sold. The first unit of output sold increases total revenue from zero to $131, so marginal revenue for that unit is $131. The second unit sold increases total revenue from $131 to $262, and marginal revenue is again $131. Note in column 4 that marginal revenue is a constant $131, as is price. *In pure competition, marginal revenue and price are equal.*

Figure 8.1 shows the purely competitive firm's total-revenue, demand, marginal-revenue, and average-revenue curves. Total revenue (TR) is a straight line that slopes upward to the right. Its slope is constant because each extra unit of sales increases TR by $131. The demand curve (*D*) is horizontal, indicating perfect price elasticity. The marginal-revenue (MR) curve coincides with the demand curve because the product price (and hence MR) is constant. The average revenue (AR) curve equals price and therefore also coincides with the demand curve.

FIGURE 8.1 **A purely competitive firm's demand and revenue curves.** The demand curve (*D*) of a purely competitive firm is a horizontal line (perfectly elastic) because the firm can sell as much output as it wants at the market price (here, $131). Because each additional unit sold increases total revenue by the amount of the price, the firm's total-revenue (TR) curve is a straight upsloping line and its marginal-revenue (MR) curve coincides with the firm's demand curve. The average-revenue (AR) curve also coincides with the demand curve.

Firm's Demand Schedule		Firm's Revenue Data	
(1) Product Price (P) (Average Revenue)	(2) Quantity Demanded (Q)	(3) Total Revenue (TR), (1) × (2)	(4) Marginal Revenue (MR)
$131	0	$ 0	
131	1	131	$131
131	2	262	131
131	3	393	131
131	4	524	131
131	5	655	131
131	6	786	131
131	7	917	131
131	8	1048	131
131	9	1179	131
131	10	1310	131

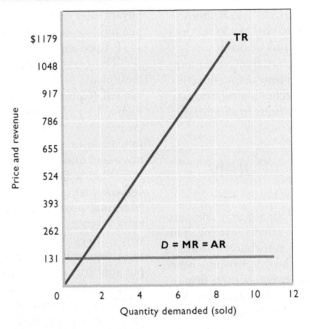

Profit Maximization in the Short Run: Total-Revenue–Total-Cost Approach

Because the purely competitive firm is a price taker, it cannot attempt to maximize its profit by raising or lowering the price it charges. With its price set by supply and demand in the overall market, the only variable that the firm can control is its output. As a result, the purely competitive firm attempts to maximize its economic profit (or minimize its economic loss) by adjusting its *output*. And, in the short run, the firm has a fixed plant. Thus it can adjust its output only through changes in the amount of variable resources (materials, labor) it uses. It adjusts its variable resources to achieve the output level that maximizes its profit.

There are two ways to determine the level of output at which a competitive firm will realize maximum profit or minimum loss. One method is to compare total revenue and total cost; the other is to compare marginal revenue and marginal cost. Both approaches apply to all firms, whether they are pure competitors, pure monopolists, monopolistic competitors, or oligopolists.[1]

We begin by examining profit maximization using the total-revenue–total-cost approach. Confronted with the market price of its product, the competitive producer will ask three questions: (1) Should we produce this product? (2) If so, in what amount? (3) What economic profit (or loss) will we realize?

Let's demonstrate how a pure competitor answers these questions, given a particular set of cost data and a

WORKED PROBLEMS

W 8.1

Profit maximization: TR–TC approach

specific market price. Our cost data are already familiar because they are the fixed-cost, variable-cost, and total-cost data in Table 7.2, repeated in columns 1 to 4 of the table in Figure 8.2. (Recall that these data reflect explicit and implicit costs, including a normal profit.) Assuming that the market price is $131, the total revenue for each output level is found by multiplying output (total product) by price. Total-revenue data are in column 5. Then in column 6 we find the profit or loss at each output level by subtracting total cost, TC (column 4), from total revenue, TR (column 5).

Should the firm produce? Definitely. It can obtain a profit by doing so. How much should it produce? Nine units. Column 6 tells us that this is the output at which total economic profit is at a maximum. What economic profit (or loss) will it realize? A $299 economic profit— the difference between total revenue ($1179) and total cost ($880).

Figure 8.2a compares total revenue and total cost graphically for this profit-maximizing case. Observe again that the total-revenue curve for a purely competitive firm

is a straight line (Figure 8.1). Total cost increases with output because more production requires more resources. But the *rate* of increase in total cost varies with the efficiency of the firm, which in turn varies with the amount of variable inputs that are being combined with the firm's current amount of capital (which is fixed in the short run). Stated slightly differently, the cost data reflect Chapter 7's law of diminishing returns. From zero to four units of output, total cost increases at a decreasing rate as the firm temporarily experiences increasing returns. At higher levels of output, however, efficiency falls as crowding causes diminishing returns to set in. Once that happens, the firm's total cost increases at an increasing rate because each additional unit of input yields less output than the previous unit.

Total revenue and total cost are equal where the two curves in Figure 8.2a intersect (at roughly 2 units of output). Total revenue covers all costs (including a normal profit, which is included in the cost curve), but there is no economic profit. For this reason economists call this output a **break-even point**: an output at which a firm makes a *normal profit* but not an economic profit. If we extended the data beyond 10 units of output, another break-even point would occur where total cost catches up with total revenue, somewhere between 13 and 14 units of output in Figure 8.2a. Any output within the two break-even points identified in the figure will yield an economic profit. The firm achieves maximum profit, however, where the vertical distance between the total-revenue and total-cost curves is greatest. For our particular data, this is at 9 units of output, where maximum profit is $299.

The profit-maximizing output is easier to see in Figure 8.2b, where total profit is graphed for each level of output. Where the total-revenue and total-cost curves intersect in Figure 8.2a, economic profit is zero, as shown by the total-profit line in Figure 8.2b. Where the vertical distance between TR and TC is greatest in the upper graph, economic profit is at its peak ($299), as shown in the lower graph. This firm will choose to produce 9 units since that output maximizes its profit.

Profit Maximization in the Short Run: Marginal-Revenue– Marginal-Cost Approach

In the second approach, the firm compares the amounts that each *additional* unit of output would add to total revenue and to total cost. In other words, the firm compares the *marginal revenue* (MR) and the *marginal cost* (MC) of each successive unit of output. Assuming that producing

---

[1]To make sure you understand these two approaches, we will apply both of them to output determination under pure competition. But since we want to emphasize the marginal approach, we will limit our graphical application of the total-revenue approach to a situation where the firm maximizes profits. We will then use the marginal approach to examine three cases: profit maximization, loss minimization, and shutdown.

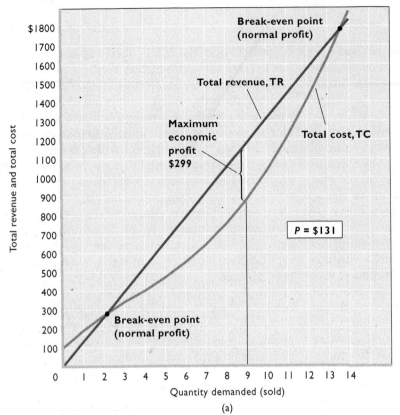

FIGURE 8.2 Total-revenue–total-cost approach to profit maximization for a purely competitive firm. (a) The firm's profit is maximized at that output (9 units) where total revenue, TR, exceeds total cost, TC, by the maximum amount. (b) The vertical distance between TR and TC in (a) is plotted as a total-economic-profit curve. Maximum economic profit is $299 at 9 units of output.

(a)
Profit-maximizing case

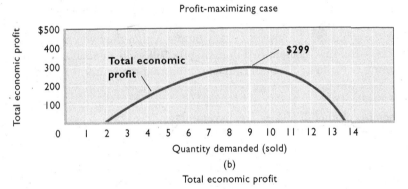

(b)
Total economic profit

				PRICE: $131	
(1) Total Product (Output) (Q)	(2) Total Fixed Cost (TFC)	(3) Total Variable Cost (TVC)	(4) Total Cost (TC)	(5) Total Revenue (TR)	(6) Profit (+) or Loss (−)
0	$100	$ 0	$ 100	$ 0	$−100
1	100	90	190	131	−59
2	100	170	270	262	−8
3	100	240	340	393	+53
4	100	300	400	524	+124
5	100	370	470	655	+185
6	100	450	550	786	+236
7	100	540	640	917	+277
8	100	650	750	1048	+298
9	100	780	800	1179	+299
10	100	930	1030	1310	+280

is preferable to shutting down, the firm should produce any unit of output whose marginal revenue exceeds its marginal cost because the firm would gain more in revenue from selling that unit than it would add to its costs by producing it. Conversely, if the marginal cost of a unit of output exceeds its marginal revenue, the firm should not produce that unit. Producing it would add more to costs than to revenue, and profit would decline or loss would increase.

In the initial stages of production, where output is relatively low, marginal revenue will usually (but not always) exceed marginal cost. So it is profitable to produce through this range of output. But at later stages of production, where output is relatively high, rising marginal costs will exceed marginal revenue. Obviously, a profit-maximizing firm will want to avoid output levels in that range. Separating these two production ranges is a unique point at which marginal revenue equals marginal cost. This point is the key to the output-determining rule: *In the short run, the firm will maximize profit or minimize loss by producing the output at which marginal revenue equals marginal cost (as long as producing is preferable to shutting down).* This profit-maximizing guide is known as the **MR = MC rule.**

Keep in mind these features of the MR = MC rule:

- For most sets of MR and MC data, MR and MC will be precisely equal at a fractional level of output. In such instances the firm should produce the last complete unit of output for which MR exceeds MC.
- As noted, the rule applies only if producing is preferable to shutting down. We will show shortly that if marginal revenue does not equal or exceed average variable cost, the firm will shut down rather than produce the amount of output at which MR = MC.
- The rule is an accurate guide to profit maximization for all firms whether they are purely competitive, monopolistic, monopolistically competitive, or oligopolistic.
- The rule can be restated as $P = MC$ when applied to a purely competitive firm. Because the demand schedule faced by a competitive seller is perfectly elastic at the going market price, product price and marginal revenue are equal. So under pure competition (and only under pure competition) we may substitute P for MR in the rule: When producing is preferable to shutting down, the competitive firm that wants to maximize its profit or minimize its loss should produce at that point where price equals marginal cost ($P = MC$).

Now let's apply the MR = MC rule or, because we are considering pure competition, the $P = MC$ rule, first using the same price as used in our total-revenue–total-cost approach to profit maximization. Then, by considering other prices, we will demonstrate two additional cases: loss minimization and shutdown. It is crucial that you understand the MR = MC analysis that follows since it reappears in Chapters 10, 11, and 12.

Profit-Maximizing Case

The first five columns of the table in **Figure 8.3 (Key Graph)** reproduce the AFC, AVC, ATC, and MC data derived for our product in Table 7.2. It is the marginal-cost data of column 5 that we will compare with price (equals marginal revenue) for each unit of output. Suppose first that the market price, and therefore marginal revenue, is $131, as shown in column 6.

What is the profit-maximizing output? Every unit of output up to and including the ninth unit represents greater marginal revenue than marginal cost of output. Each of the first 9 units therefore adds to the firm's profit and should be produced. The tenth unit, however, should not be produced. It would add more to cost ($150) than to revenue ($131). So 9 units is the profit-maximizing output.

The economic profit realized by producing 9 units can be calculated by subtracting total cost from total revenue. Multiplying price ($131) by output (9), we find that total revenue is $1179. From the average-total-cost data in column 4, we see that ATC is $97.78 at 9 units of output. Multiplying $97.78 by 9 gives us total cost of $880.[2] The difference of $299 (= $1179 − $880) is the economic profit. Clearly, this firm will prefer to operate rather than shut down.

Perhaps an easier way to calculate the economic profit is to use this simple equation, in which A is average total cost:

$$\text{Profit} = (P - A) \times Q$$

So by subtracting the average total cost ($97.78) from the product price ($131), we obtain a per-unit profit of $33.22.

WORKED PROBLEMS

W 8.2

Profit maximization: MR = MC approach

Multiplying that amount by 9 units of output, we determine that the profit is $299. Take some time now to verify the num-

---

[2]Most of the unit-cost data are rounded figures. Therefore, economic profits calculated from them will typically vary by a few cents from the profits determined in the total-revenue–total-cost approach. Here we simply ignore the few-cents differentials to make our answers consistent with the results of the total-revenue–total-cost approach.

FIGURE 8.3 Short-run profit maximization for a purely competitive firm. The MR = MC output enables the purely competitive firm to maximize profits or to minimize losses. In this case MR (= P in pure competition) and MC are equal at an output Q of 9 units. There, P exceeds the average total cost A = $97.78, so the firm realizes an economic profit of P − A per unit. The total economic profit is represented by the green rectangle and is 9 × (P − A).

(1) Total Product (Output)	(2) Average Fixed Cost (AFC)	(3) Average Variable Cost (AVC)	(4) Average Total Cost (ATC)	(5) Marginal Cost (MC)	(6) Price = Marginal Revenue (MR)	(7) Total Economic Profit (+) or Loss (−)
0						$−100
1	$100.00	$90.00	$190.00	$ 90	$131	−59
2	50.00	85.00	135.00	80	131	−8
3	33.33	80.00	113.33	70	131	+53
4	25.00	75.00	100.00	60	131	+124
5	20.00	74.00	94.00	70	131	+185
6	16.67	75.00	91.67	80	131	+236
7	14.29	77.14	91.43	90	131	+277
8	12.50	81.25	93.75	110	131	+298
9	11.11	86.67	97.78	130	131	+299
10	10.00	93.00	103.00	150	131	+280

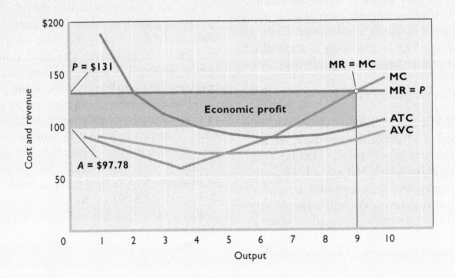

QUICK QUIZ FOR FIGURE 8.3

1. Curve MR is horizontal because:
   a. product price falls as output increases.
   b. the law of diminishing marginal utility is at work.
   c. the market demand for this product is perfectly elastic.
   d. the firm is a price taker.

2. At a price of $131 and 7 units of output:
   a. MR exceeds MC, and the firm should expand its output.
   b. total revenue is less than total cost.
   c. AVC exceeds ATC.
   d. the firm would earn only a normal profit.

3. In maximizing profits at 9 units of output, this firm is adhering to which of the following decision rules?

   a. Produce where MR exceeds MC by the greatest amount.
   b. Produce where P exceeds ATC by the greatest amount.
   c. Produce where total revenue exceeds total cost by the greatest amount.
   d. Produce where average fixed costs are zero.

4. Suppose price declined from $131 to $100. This firm's:
   a. marginal-cost curve would shift downward.
   b. economic profit would fall to zero.
   c. profit-maximizing output would decline.
   d. total cost would fall by more than its total revenue.

Answers: 1. d; 2. a; 3. c; 4. c

170

bers in column 7. You will find that any output other than that which adheres to the MR = MC rule will mean either profits below $299 or losses.

The graph in Figure 8.3 shows price (= MR) and marginal cost graphically. Price equals marginal cost at the profit-maximizing output of 9 units. There the per-unit economic profit is $P - A$, where P is the market price and A is the average total cost for an output of 9 units. The total economic profit is $9 \times (P - A)$, shown by the green rectangular area.

Note that the firm wants to maximize its total profit, not its per-unit profit. Per-unit profit is greatest at 7 units of output, where price exceeds average total cost by $39.57

INTERACTIVE GRAPHS

G 8.1

Short-run profit maximization

(= $131 - $91.43). But by producing only 7 units, the firm would be forgoing the production of 2 additional units of output that would clearly contribute to total profit. The firm is happy to accept lower per-unit profits for additional units of output because they nonetheless add to total profit.

Loss-Minimizing Case

Now let's assume that the market price is $81 rather than $131. Should the firm still produce? If so, how much? And what will be the resulting profit or loss? The answers, respectively, are "Yes," "Six units," and "A loss of $64."

The first five columns of the table in Figure 8.4 are the same as the first five columns of the table in Figure 8.3. But column 6 of the table in Figure 8.4 shows the new price (equal to MR), $81. Comparing columns 5 and 6, we find that the first unit of output adds $90 to total cost but only $81 to total revenue. One might conclude: "Don't produce—close down!" But that would be hasty. Remember that in the very early stages of production, marginal product is low, making marginal cost unusually high. The price–marginal cost relationship improves with increased production. For units 2 through 6, price exceeds marginal cost. Each of these 5 units adds more to revenue than to cost, and as shown in column 7, they decrease the total loss. Together they more than compensate for the "loss" taken on the first unit. Beyond 6 units, however, MC exceeds MR (= P). The firm should therefore produce 6 units. In general, the profit-seeking producer should always compare marginal revenue (or price under pure competition) with the rising portion of the marginal-cost schedule or curve.

Will production be profitable? No, because at 6 units of output the average total cost of $91.67 exceeds the price

of $81 by $10.67 per unit. If we multiply that by the 6 units of output, we find the firm's total loss is $64. Alternatively, comparing the total revenue of $486 (= 6 × $81) with the total cost of $550 (= 6 × $91.67), we see again that the firm's loss is $64.

Then why produce? Because this loss is less than the firm's $100 of fixed costs, which is the $100 loss the firm would incur in the short run by closing down. The firm receives enough revenue per unit ($81) to cover its average variable costs of $75 and also provide $6 per unit, or a total of $36, to apply against fixed costs. Therefore, the firm's loss is only $64 (= $100 − $36), not $100.

This loss-minimizing case is illustrated in the graph in Figure 8.4. Wherever price P exceeds average variable cost AVC but is less than ATC, the firm can pay part, but not all, of its fixed costs by producing. The loss is minimized by producing the output at which MC = MR (here, 6 units). At that output, each unit contributes $P - V$ to covering fixed cost, where V is the AVC at 6 units of output. The per-unit loss is $A - P = $10.67, and the total loss is $6 \times (A - P)$, or $64, as shown by the red area.

Shutdown Case

Suppose now that the market yields a price of only $71. Should the firm produce? No, because at every output level the firm's average variable cost is greater than the price (compare columns 3 and 8 of the table in Figure 8.4). The smallest loss it can incur by producing is greater than the $100 fixed cost it will lose by shutting down (as shown by column 9). The best action is to shut down.

You can see this shutdown situation in Figure 8.5. Price comes closest to covering average variable costs at the MR (= P) = MC output of 5 units. But even here, price or revenue per unit would fall short of average variable cost by $3 (= $74 − $71). By producing at the MR (= P) = MC output, the firm would lose its $100 worth of fixed cost plus $15 ($3 of variable cost on each of the 5 units), for a total loss of $115. This compares unfavorably with the $100 fixed-cost loss the firm would incur by shutting down and producing no output. So it will make sense for the firm to shut down rather than produce at a $71 price—or at any price less than the minimum average variable cost of $74.

The shutdown case reminds us of the qualifier to our MR (= P) = MC rule. A competitive firm will maximize profit or minimize loss in the short run by producing that output at which MR (= P) = MC, *provided that market price exceeds minimum average variable cost.*

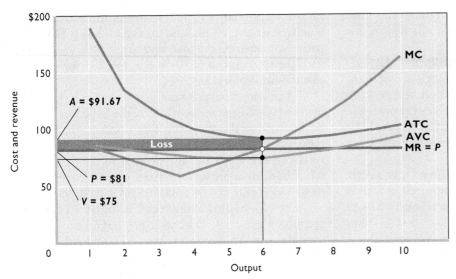

FIGURE 8.4 Short-run loss minimization for a purely competitive firm. If price P exceeds the minimum AVC (here, $74 at $Q = 5$) but is less than ATC, the MR = MC output (here, 6 units) will permit the firm to minimize its losses. In this instance the loss is $A - P$ per unit, where A is the average total cost at 6 units of output. The total loss is shown by the red area and is equal to $6 \times (A - P)$.

					Loss-Minimizing Case		Shutdown Case	
(1) Total Product (Output)	(2) Average Fixed Cost (AFC)	(3) Average Variable Cost (AVC)	(4) Average Total Cost (ATC)	(5) Marginal Cost (MC)	(6) $81 Price = Marginal Revenue (MR)	(7) Profit (+) or Loss (−), $81 Price	(8) $71 Price = Marginal Revenue (MR)	(9) Profit (+) or Loss (−), $71 Price
0						$−100		$−100
1	$100.00	$90.00	$190.00	$90	$81	−109	$71	−119
2	50.00	85.00	135.00	80	81	−108	71	−128
3	33.33	80.00	113.33	70	81	−97	71	−127
4	25.00	75.00	100.00	60	81	−76	71	−116
5	20.00	74.00	94.00	70	81	−65	71	−115
6	16.67	75.00	91.67	80	81	−64	71	−124
7	14.29	77.14	91.43	90	81	−73	71	−143
8	12.50	81.25	93.75	110	81	−102	71	−182
9	11.11	86.67	97.78	130	81	−151	71	−241
10	10.00	93.00	103.00	150	81	−220	71	−320

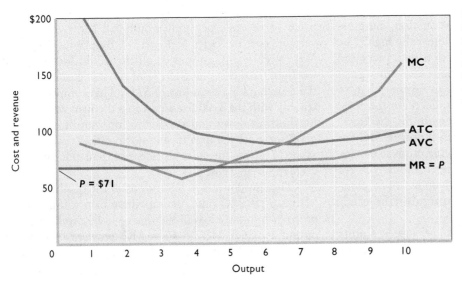

FIGURE 8.5 The short-run shutdown case for a purely competitive firm. If price P falls below the minimum AVC (here, $74 at $Q = 5$), the competitive firm will minimize its losses in the short run by shutting down. There is no level of output at which the firm can produce and incur a loss smaller than its total fixed cost.

- A firm will choose to produce if it can at least break even and generate a normal profit.
- Profit is maximized, or loss minimized, at the output at which marginal revenue (or price in pure competition) equals marginal cost, provided that price exceeds variable cost.
- If the market price is below the minimum average variable cost, the firm will minimize its losses by shutting down.

Marginal Cost and Short-Run Supply

In the preceding section we simply selected three different prices and asked what quantity the profit-seeking competitive firm, faced with certain costs, would choose to offer in the market at each price. This set of product prices and corresponding quantities supplied constitutes part of the supply schedule for the competitive firm.

Table 8.2 summarizes the supply schedule data for those three prices ($131, $81, and $71) and four others. This table confirms the direct relationship between product price and quantity supplied that we identified in Chapter 3. Note first that the firm will not produce at price $61 or $71 because both are less than the $74 minimum AVC. Then note that quantity supplied increases as price increases. Observe finally that economic profit is higher at higher prices.

Generalized Depiction

Figure 8.6 (Key Graph) generalizes the MR = MC rule and the relationship between short-run production costs and the firm's supply behavior. The ATC, AVC, and MC curves are shown, along with several marginal-revenue lines drawn at possible market prices. Let's observe quantity supplied at each of these prices:

- Price P_1 is below the firm's minimum average variable cost, so at this price the firm won't operate at all.

TABLE 8.2 **The Supply Schedule of a Competitive Firm Confronted with the Cost Data in the table in Figure 8.3**

Price	Quantity Supplied	Maximum Profit (+) or Minimum Loss (−)
$151	10	$+480
131	9	+299
111	8	+138
91	7	−3
81	6	−64
71	0	−100
61	0	−100

The Still There Motel

Have you ever driven by a poorly maintained business facility and wondered why the owner does not either fix up the property or go out of business? The somewhat surprising reason is that it may be unprofitable to improve the facility yet profitable to continue to operate the business as it deteriorates. Seeing why will aid your understanding of the "stay open or shut down" decision facing firms experiencing declining demand.

Consider the story of the Still There Motel on Old Highway North, Anytown, USA. The owner built the motel on the basis of traffic patterns and competition existing several decades ago. But as interstate highways were built, the motel found itself located on a relatively untraveled stretch of road. Also, it faced severe competition from "chain" motels located much closer to the interstate highway.

As demand and revenue fell, Still There moved from profitability to loss ($P <$ ATC). But at first its room rates and annual revenue were sufficient to cover its total variable costs and contribute some to the payment of fixed costs such as insurance and property taxes ($P >$ AVC). By staying open, Still There lost less than it would have if it shut down. But since its total revenue did not cover its total costs (or $P <$ ATC), the owner realized that something must be done in the long run. The owner decided to lower total costs by reducing annual maintenance. In effect, the owner opted to allow the motel to deteriorate as a way of regaining temporary profitability.

This renewed profitability of Still There cannot last because in time no further reduction of maintenance costs will be possible. The deterioration of the motel structure will produce even lower room rates, and therefore even less total revenue. The owner of Still There knows that sooner or later total revenue will again fall below total cost (or P will again fall below ATC), even with an annual maintenance expense of zero. When that occurs, the owner will close down the business, tear down the structure, and sell the vacant property. But, in the meantime, the motel is still there—open, deteriorating, and profitable.

Quantity supplied will be zero, as it will be at all other prices below P_2.

- Price P_2 is just equal to the minimum average variable cost. The firm will supply Q_2 units of output (where $MR_2 = MC$) and just cover its total variable cost. Its loss will equal its total fixed cost. (Actually, the firm would be indifferent as to shutting down

key graph

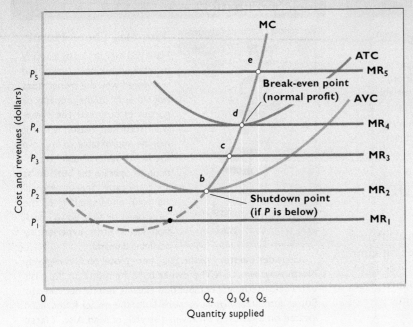

FIGURE 8.6 **The $P = $ MC rule and the competitive firm's short-run supply curve.** Application of the $P = $ MC rule, as modified by the shutdown case, reveals that the (solid) segment of the firm's MC curve that lies above AVC is the firm's short-run supply curve. More specifically, at price P_1, $P = $ MC at point a, but the firm will produce no output because P_1 is less than minimum AVC. At price P_2 the firm will operate at point b, where it produces Q_2 units and incurs a loss equal to its total fixed cost. At P_3 it operates at point c, where output is Q_3 and the loss is less than total fixed cost. With the price of P_4, the firm operates at point d; in this case the firm earns a normal profit because at output Q_4 price equals ATC. At price P_5 the firm operates at point e and maximizes its economic profit by producing Q_5 units.

QUICK QUIZ FOR FIGURE 8.6

1. Which of the following might increase product price from P_3 to P_5?
   a. An improvement in production technology.
   b. A decline in the price of a substitute good.
   c. An increase in the price of a complementary good.
   d. Rising incomes if the product is a normal good.

2. An increase in price from P_3 to P_5 would:
   a. shift this firm's MC curve to the right.
   b. mean that MR_5 exceeds MC at Q_3 units, inducing the firm to expand output to Q_5.
   c. decrease this firm's average variable costs.
   d. enable this firm to obtain a normal, but not an economic, profit.

3. At P_4:
   a. this firm has no economic profit.
   b. this firm will earn only a normal profit and thus will shut down.
   c. MR_4 will be less than MC at the profit-maximizing output.
   d. the profit-maximizing output will be Q_5.

4. Suppose P_4 is \$10, P_5 is \$15, Q_4 is 8 units, and Q_5 is 10 units. This firm's:
   a. supply curve is elastic over the Q_4–Q_5 range of output.
   b. supply curve is inelastic over the Q_4–Q_5 range of output.
   c. total revenue will decline if price rises from P_4 to P_5.
   d. marginal-cost curve will shift downward if price falls from P_5 to P_4.

Answers: 1. d; 2. b; 3. a; 4. b

or supplying Q_2 units of output, but we assume it produces.)

- At price P_3 the firm will supply Q_3 units of output to minimize its short-run losses. At any of the other prices between P_2 and P_4 the firm will also minimize its losses by producing and supplying the quantity at which MR (= P) = MC.

- The firm will just break even at price P_4. There it will supply Q_4 units of output (where MR_4 = MC), earning a normal profit but not an economic profit. Total revenue will just cover total cost, including a

normal profit, because the revenue per unit (MR_4 = P_4) and the total cost per unit (ATC) are the same.

- At price P_5 the firm will realize an economic profit by producing and supplying Q_5 units of output. In fact, at any price above P_4 the firm will obtain economic profit by producing to the point where MR (= P) = MC.

Note that each of the MR (= P) = MC intersection points labeled b, c, d and e in Figure 8.6 indicates a possible product price (on the vertical axis) and the corresponding quantity that the firm would supply at that price (on the

TABLE 8.3 **Output Determination in Pure Competition in the Short Run**

Question	Answer
Should this firm produce?	Yes, if price is equal to, or greater than, minimum average variable cost. This means that the firm is profitable or that its losses are less than its fixed cost.
What quantity should this firm produce?	Produce where MR (= P) = MC; there, profit is maximized (TR exceeds TC by a maximum amount) or loss is minimized.
Will production result in economic profit?	Yes, if price exceeds average total cost (so that TR exceeds TC). No, if average total cost exceeds price (so that TC exceeds TR).

horizontal axis). Thus, points such as these are on the upsloping supply curve of the competitive firm. Note, too, that quantity supplied would be zero at any price below the minimum average variable cost (AVC). *We can conclude that the portion of the firm's marginal-cost curve lying above its average-variable-cost curve is its short-run supply curve.* In Figure 8.6, the solid segment of the marginal-cost curve MC is this firm's **short-run supply curve.** It tells us the amount of output the firm will supply at each price in a series of prices.

Table 8.3 summarizes the MR = MC approach to determining the competitive firm's profit-maximizing output level. It also shows the equivalent analysis in terms of total revenue and total cost.

Diminishing Returns, Production Costs, and Product Supply

We have now identified the links between the law of diminishing returns (Chapter 7), production costs, and product supply in the short run. Because of the law of diminishing returns, marginal costs eventually rise as more units of output are produced. And because marginal costs rise with output, a purely competitive firm must get successively higher prices to motivate it to produce additional units of output.

Viewed alternatively, higher product prices and marginal revenue encourage a purely competitive firm to expand output. As its output increases, the firm's marginal costs rise as a result of the law of diminishing returns. At some now greater output, the higher MC equals the new product price and MR. Profit once again is maximized, but at a greater total amount. Quantity supplied has increased in direct response to an increase in product price and the desire to maximize profit.

Changes in Supply

In Chapter 7 we saw that changes in such factors as the prices of variable inputs or in technology will alter costs and shift the marginal-cost or short-run supply curve to a new location. All else equal, for example, a wage increase would increase marginal cost and shift the supply curve in Figure 8.6 upward as viewed from the horizontal axis (leftward as viewed from the vertical axis). That is, supply would decrease. Similarly, technological progress that increases the productivity of labor would reduce marginal cost and shift the marginal-cost or supply curve downward as viewed from the horizontal axis (rightward as viewed from the vertical axis). This represents an increase in supply.

Firm and Industry: Equilibrium Price

In the preceding section we established the competitive firm's short-run supply curve by applying the MR (= P) = MC rule. But which of the various possible prices will actually be the market equilibrium price?

From Chapter 3 we know that the market equilibrium price will be the price at which the total quantity supplied of the product equals the total quantity demanded. So to determine the equilibrium price, we first need to obtain a total supply schedule and a total demand schedule. We find the total supply schedule by assuming a particular number of firms in the industry and supposing that each firm has the same individual supply schedule as the firm represented in Figure 8.6. Then we sum the quantities supplied at each price level to obtain the total (or market) supply schedule. Columns 1 and 3 in Table 8.4 repeat the supply schedule for the individual competitive firm, as derived in Table 8.2.

TABLE 8.4 **Firm and Market Supply and Market Demand**

(1) Quantity Supplied, Single Firm	(2) Total Quantity Supplied, 1000 Firms	(3) Product Price	(4) Total Quantity Demanded
10	10,000	$151	4000
9	9000	131	6000
8	8000	111	8000
7	7000	91	9000
6	6000	81	11,000
0	0	71	13,000
0	0	61	16,000

Suppose 1000 firms compete in this industry, all having the same total and unit costs as the single firm we discussed. This lets us calculate the market supply schedule (columns 2 and 3) by multiplying the quantity-supplied figures of the single firm (column 1) by 1000.

Market Price and Profits

To determine the equilibrium price and output, these total-supply data must be compared with total-demand data. Let's assume that total demand is as shown in columns 3 and 4 in Table 8.4. By comparing the total quantity supplied and the total quantity demanded at the seven possible prices, we determine that the equilibrium price is $111 and the equilibrium quantity is 8000 units for the industry—8 units for each of the 1000 identical firms.

Will these conditions of market supply and demand make this a profitable or unprofitable industry? Multiplying product price ($111) by output (8 units), we find that the total revenue of each firm is $888. The total cost is $750, found by looking at column 4 of the table in Figure 8.2. The $138 difference is the economic profit of each firm. For the industry, total economic profit is $138,000. This, then, is a profitable industry.

Another way of calculating economic profit is to determine per-unit profit by subtracting average total cost ($93.75) from product price ($111) and multiplying the difference (per-unit profit of $17.25) by the firm's equilibrium level of output (8). Again we obtain an economic profit of $138 per firm and $138,000 for the industry.

Figure 8.7 shows this analysis graphically. The individual supply curves of each of the 1000 identical firms—one of which is shown as $s = MC$ in Figure 8.7a—are summed horizontally to get the total-supply curve $S =$ ΣMC of Figure 8.7b. With total-demand curve D, it yields the equilibrium price $111 and equilibrium quantity (for the industry) 8000 units. This equilibrium price is given and unalterable to the individual firm; that is, each firm's demand curve is perfectly elastic at the equilibrium price, as indicated by d in Figure 8.7a. Because the individual firm is a price taker, the marginal-revenue curve coincides with the firm's demand curve d. This $111 price exceeds the average total cost at the firm's equilibrium MR = MC output of 8 units, so the firm earns an economic profit represented by the green area in Figure 8.7a.

Assuming no changes in costs or market demand, these diagrams reveal a genuine equilibrium in the short run. No shortages or surpluses occur in the market to cause price or total quantity to change. Nor can any firm in the industry increase its profit by altering its output. Note, too, that higher unit and marginal costs, on the one hand, or weaker market demand, on the other, could change the situation so that Figure 8.7a resembles Figure 8.4 or Figure 8.5.

Firm versus Industry

Figure 8.7 underscores a point made earlier: Product price is a given fact to the *individual* competitive firm, but the supply plans of all competitive producers *as a group* are a basic determinant of product price. If

> **WORKED PROBLEMS**
> **W 8.3**
> Short-run competitive equilibrium

we recall the fallacy of composition (Last Word, Chapter 1), we find there is no inconsistency here. Although one firm, supplying a negligible fraction of total supply, cannot affect price, the sum of the supply curves of all the firms in the industry constitutes the industry supply curve, and that curve does have an important bearing on price.

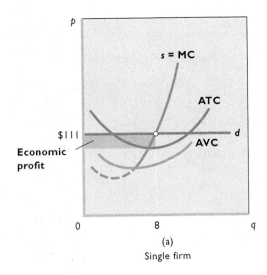

(a)
Single firm

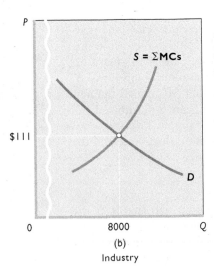

(b)
Industry

FIGURE 8.7 Short-run competitive equilibrium for (a) a firm and (b) the industry. The horizontal sum of the 1000 firms' individual supply curves (s) determines the industry supply curve (S). Given industry demand (D), the short-run equilibrium price and output for the industry are $111 and 8000 units. Taking the equilibrium price as given, the individual firm establishes its profit-maximizing output at 8 units and, in this case, realizes the economic profit represented by the green area.

Word Fixed Costs: Digging Yourself Out of a Hole

For Firms Facing Losses Due to Fixed Costs, Shutting Down in the Short Run Does Not Mean Shutting Down Forever.

A firm with fixed costs starts each month standing at the bottom of a deep financial hole. The depth of that "money pit" is equal to the dollar value of all the payments that the firm is legally obligated to make even if it is producing nothing. These fixed costs include contractually guaranteed salaries, interest payments on loans, and equipment rental fees that are locked-in by long-term contracts. As the firm stands at the bottom of this fixed-cost financial hole and stares upward looking for a way out, it has to ask itself the following question: Will producing output make the hole even deeper?

Naturally, the firm hopes that producing output will generate positive cash flows that will offset its fixed costs and start filling in the hole. If those positive flows are large enough, they may completely offset the firm's fixed costs and fill up the hole, thereby allowing the firm to break even. And if they are just a bit larger, they will not only fill up the hole but also accumulate a nice little pile of profits above ground.

But those are just the firm's hopes. The firm's reality may be quite unpleasant. In particular, the firm may be facing a situation in which producing output would make its financial situation worse rather than better. As explained in this chapter, if the price of the firm's output falls too low, then producing output will yield cash flows that are negative rather than positive because revenues will be less than variable costs. If that happens, producing output will lose money for the firm so that the firm would be better off shutting down production rather than producing output. By shutting down, it will lose only its fixed costs. By shutting down, its financial hole won't get even deeper.

A crucial thing to understand, however, is that the low prices that cause firms to shut down production are often temporary—so that shutdowns are also often temporary. Just because a firm shuts down at a given moment to prevent its financial hole from getting any deeper does not mean that the firm will go out of business forever. To the contrary, many industries are characterized by firms that regularly switch production on and off depending upon the market price they can get for their output and,

consequently, whether producing output will generate positive or negative cash flows.

Oil production is a good example. Different wells have different variable production costs. If the price of oil drops below a given well's variable costs, then it would be better to halt production on that well and just lose the value of its fixed costs rather than pumping oil whose variable costs exceed the revenue that it generates when sold.

Seasonal resorts are another good example of turning production on and off depending on the price. The demand for hotel rooms near ski resorts in New Hampshire, for instance, is much higher during the winter ski season than it is during the summer. As a result, the market price of hotel rooms falls so low during the summer that many inns and resorts close during the warmer months. They have all sorts of fixed costs, but it makes more sense for them to shut down rather than remain open, because operating in the summer would cost more in variable costs than it would generate in revenues. Better to lose only their fixed costs.

Numerous other examples of temporary shutdowns occur during recessions, the occasional economy-wide economic slowdowns during which demand declines for nearly all goods and services. The 2007–2009 recession in the United States, for instance, saw many manufacturing companies temporarily shut down and mothball their production facilities. The recession witnessed the mothballing of electric generating plants, factories that make fiber optic cable, automobile factories, chemical plants, textile mills, and even the plant in McIntosh, Alabama, that makes the artificial sweetener Splenda. Many other firms also shut down production to wait out the recession—so many, in fact, that there was a mini-boom for consulting firms that specialized in helping firms mothball their factories (the main problem being how to properly store idle machinery so that it will work again when it is eventually brought back into service).

Firms that mothball factories or equipment during a recession do so expecting to eventually turn them back on. But the lengths of recessions vary, as do the specific circumstances of individual firms. So while many firms shut down in the short run with the expectation of reopening as soon as their particular business conditions improve, sometimes their business conditions do not improve. Sometimes the only way to terminate fixed costs is to terminate the firm.

Summary

1. Economists group industries into four models based on their market structures: (a) pure competition, (b) pure monopoly, (c) monopolistic competition, and (d) oligopoly.

2. A purely competitive industry consists of a large number of independent firms producing a standardized product. Pure competition assumes that firms and resources are mobile among different industries.

3. In a competitive industry, no single firm can influence market price. This means that the firm's demand curve is perfectly elastic and price equals marginal revenue.

4. We can analyze short-run profit maximization by a competitive firm by comparing total revenue and total cost or by applying marginal analysis. A firm maximizes its short-run profit by producing the output at which total revenue exceeds total cost by the greatest amount.

5. Provided price exceeds minimum average variable cost, a competitive firm maximizes profit or minimizes loss in the short run by producing the output at which price or marginal revenue equals marginal cost.

6. If price is less than minimum average variable cost, a competitive firm minimizes its loss by shutting down. If price is greater than average variable cost but is less than average total cost, a competitive firm minimizes its loss by producing the $P = MC$ amount of output. If price also exceeds average total cost, the firm maximizes its economic profit at the $P = MC$ amount of output.

7. Applying the MR $(= P) = MC$ rule at various possible market prices leads to the conclusion that the segment of the firm's short-run marginal-cost curve that lies above the firm's average-variable-cost curve is its short-run supply curve.

8. A competitive firm shuts down production at least temporarily if price is less than minimum average variable cost, because in those situations, producing any amount of output will always result in variable costs exceeding revenues. Shutting down therefore results in a smaller loss, because the firm will lose only its fixed cost, whereas, if it operated, it would lose its fixed cost plus whatever money is lost due to variable costs exceeding revenues.

9. Competitive firms choose to operate rather than shut down whenever price is greater than average variable cost but less than average total cost, because in those situations, revenues will always exceed variable costs. The amount by which revenues exceed variable costs can be used to help pay down some of the firms fixed costs. Thus, the firm loses less money by operating (and paying down some of its fixed costs) than it would if it shut down (in which case it would suffer a loss equal to the full amount of its fixed costs).

Terms and Concepts

pure competition	imperfect competition	marginal revenue
pure monopoly	price taker	break-even point
monopolistic competition	average revenue	MR = MC rule
oligopoly	total revenue	short-run supply curve

Questions

1. Briefly state the basic characteristics of pure competition, pure monopoly, monopolistic competition, and oligopoly. Under which of these market classifications does each of the following most accurately fit? (a) a supermarket in your hometown; (b) the steel industry; (c) a Kansas wheat farm; (d) the commercial bank in which you or your family has an account; (e) the automobile industry. In each case, justify your classification. LO1

2. Strictly speaking, pure competition is relatively rare. Then why study it? LO2

3. Use the demand schedule to the right to determine total revenue and marginal revenue for each possible level of sales: LO2

   a. What can you conclude about the structure of the industry in which this firm is operating? Explain.

Product Price	Quantity Demanded	Total Revenue	Marginal Revenue
$2	0	$_____	$_____
2	1	_____	_____
2	2	_____	_____
2	3	_____	_____
2	4	_____	_____
2	5	_____	

   b. Graph the demand, total-revenue, and marginal-revenue curves for this firm.

   c. Why do the demand and marginal-revenue curves coincide?

d. "Marginal revenue is the change in total revenue associated with additional units of output." Explain verbally and graphically, using the data in the table.

4. "Even if a firm is losing money, it may be better to stay in business in the short run." Is this statement ever true? Under what condition(s)? LO3

5. Consider a firm that has no fixed costs and which is currently losing money. Are there any situations in which it would want to stay open for business in the short run? If a firm has no fixed costs, is it sensible to speak of the firm distinguishing between the short run and the long run? LO3

6. Why is the equality of marginal revenue and marginal cost essential for profit maximization in all market structures? Explain why price can be substituted for marginal revenue in the MR = MC rule when an industry is purely competitive. LO3

7. "That segment of a competitive firm's marginal-cost curve that lies above its average-variable-cost curve constitutes the short-run supply curve for the firm." Explain using a graph and words. LO4

8. **LAST WORD** If a firm's current revenues are less than its current variable costs, when should it shut down? If the firm decides to shut down, should we expect that decision to be final? Explain using an example that is not in the book.

Problems

1. A purely competitive firm finds that the market price for its product is $20. It has a fixed cost of $100 and a variable cost of $10 per unit for the first 50 units and then $25 per unit for all successive units. Does price exceed average variable cost for the first 50 units? What about for the first 100 units? What is the marginal cost per unit for the first 50 units? What about for units 51 and higher? For each of the first 50 units, does MR exceed MC? What about for units 51 and higher? What output level will yield the largest possible profit for this purely competitive firm? (Hint: Draw a graph similar to Figure 8.2 using data for this firm.) LO3

2. A purely competitive wheat farmer can sell any wheat he grows for $10 per bushel. His five acres of land show diminishing returns, because some are better suited for wheat production than others. The first acre can produce 1000 bushels of wheat, the second acre 900, the third 800, and so on. Draw a table with multiple columns to help you answer the following questions. How many bushels will each of the farmer's five acres produce? How much revenue will each acre generate? What are the TR and MR for each acre? If the marginal cost of planting and harvesting an acre is $7000 per acre for each of the five acres, how many acres should the farmer plant and harvest? LO3

3. Karen runs a print shop that makes posters for large companies. It is a very competitive business. The market price is currently $1 per poster. She has fixed costs of $250. Her variable costs are $1000 for the first thousand posters, $800 for the second thousand, and then $750 for each additional thousand posters. What is her AFC per poster (not per thousand!) if she prints 1000 posters? 2000? 10,000? What is her ATC per poster if she prints 1000? 2000? 10,000? If the market price fell to 70 cents per poster, would there be *any* output level at which Karen would *not* shut down production immediately? LO3

4. Assume that the cost data in the top table of the next column are for a purely competitive producer: LO3

Total Product	Average Fixed Cost	Average Variable Cost	Average Total Cost	Marginal Cost
0				
1	$60.00	$45.00	$105.00	$45
2	30.00	42.50	72.50	40
3	20.00	40.00	60.00	35
4	15.00	37.50	52.50	30
5	12.00	37.00	49.00	35
6	10.00	37.50	47.50	40
7	8.57	38.57	47.14	45
8	7.50	40.63	48.13	55
9	6.67	43.33	50.00	65
10	6.00	46.50	52.50	75

a. At a product price of $56, will this firm produce in the short run? If it is preferable to produce, what will be the profit-maximizing or loss-minimizing output? What economic profit or loss will the firm realize per unit of output?

b. Answer the questions of 4a assuming product price is $41.

c. Answer the questions of 4a assuming product price is $32.

d. In the table below, complete the short-run supply schedule for the firm (columns 1 and 2) and indicate the profit or loss incurred at each output (column 3).

(1) Price	(2) Quantity Supplied, Single Firm	(3) Profit (+) or Loss (−)	(4) Quantity Supplied 1500 Firms
$26	_____	$_____	_____
32	_____	_____	_____
38	_____	_____	_____
41	_____	_____	_____
46	_____	_____	_____
56	_____	_____	_____
66	_____	_____	_____

e. Now assume that there are 1500 identical firms in this competitive industry; that is, there are 1500 firms, each of which has the cost data shown in the table. Complete the industry supply schedule (column 4).

f. Suppose the market demand data for the product are as follows:

Price	Total Quantity Demanded
$26	17,000
32	15,000
38	13,500
41	12,000
46	10,500
56	9500
66	8000

What will be the equilibrium price? What will be the equilibrium output for the industry? For each firm? What will profit or loss be per unit? Per firm? Will this industry expand or contract in the long run?

FURTHER TEST YOUR KNOWLEDGE AT
www.mcconnell19e.com

At the text's Online Learning Center (OLC), **www.mcconnell19e.com**, you will find one or more Web-based questions that require information from the Internet to answer. We urge you to check them out; they will familiarize you with Web sites that may be helpful in other courses and perhaps even in your career. The OLC also features multiple-choice questions that give instant feedback and provides other helpful ways to further test your knowledge of the chapter.

Pure Competition in the Short Run

Chapter 8 is the first of four chapters that bring together the previous discussion of demand and production costs. These chapters examine demand and production costs in four different market structures: pure competition, monopoly, oligopoly, and monopolistic competition. This chapter focuses exclusively on the market structure for pure competition, which is characterized by (1) a large number of firms, (2) the selling of a standardized product, (3) firms that are price takers rather than price makers, and (4) ease of entry into and exit from the industry.

The main section of the chapter describes profit maximization for the purely competitive firm in the **short run.** In the short run the firm has a fixed plant and adjusts its output through changes in the amount of variable resources it uses. Although two approaches to profit maximization are presented, the one given the greatest emphasis is the **marginal revenue–marginal cost** approach. You will learn the rule that a firm maximizes profit or minimizes losses by producing the output level at which marginal revenue equals marginal cost. Finding this equality provides the answers to the three central questions each firm has to answer: (1) Should we produce? (2) If so, how much output? (3) What profit (or loss) will be realized?

Answers to these questions also give insights about the **short-run supply curve** for the individual firm. The firm will find it profitable to produce at any output level where marginal revenue is greater than marginal costs. The firm also will produce in the short run, but it will experience losses if marginal revenue is less than marginal costs and greater than the minimum of average total cost. You will be shown how to construct the short-run supply curve for the purely competitive firm, given price and output data. The market supply curve for the industry is the sum of all supply curves for individual firms.

This chapter limits the discussion of pure competition to the short run where there are fixed costs and the size of plants producing the output do not change. In the next chapter you will learn about pure competition in the long run, where all costs are variable and firms are free to change plant size. In the long run, there is also ease of entry and exit from the industry that can change the level of output and market prices.

You must understand the purely competitive model because it is the efficiency standard or norm for evaluating different market structures. You will be using it often for comparison with the pure monopoly model in Chapter 10 and with the models for monopolistic competition and oligopoly in Chapter 11. Understanding pure competition in the short run is a start to developing this evaluation perspective and sets the basis for comprehending pure competition in the long run as presented in the next chapter.

■ **CHECKLIST**

When you have studied this chapter you should be able to

☐ List the five characteristics of each of the four basic market models.
☐ Give examples of industries related to the four basic market models.
☐ Describe four major features of pure competition.
☐ Explain why a purely competitive firm is a price taker.
☐ Describe the elasticity of the demand curve for a purely competitive firm.
☐ Distinguish between average revenue, total revenue, and marginal revenue.
☐ Explain the relationship between average revenue, marginal revenue, and price in pure competition.
☐ Compute average, total, and marginal revenues when given a demand schedule faced by a purely competitive firm.
☐ Use the total-revenue and total-cost approaches to determine the output that a purely competitive firm will produce in the short run in the profit-maximizing case when given the necessary data.
☐ Draw a total revenue and total cost graph illustrating the break-even points and the level of output producing maximum economic profit.
☐ State characteristics of the MR = MC rule.
☐ Use the marginal-revenue and marginal-cost approach to determine the output that a purely competitive firm will produce in the short run in the three different cases: profit-maximizing, loss-minimizing, and shutdown.
☐ Draw a graph with average cost, marginal cost, marginal revenue, and price illustrating output and the area of profit in the profit-maximizing case and the area of loss in the loss-minimizing case.
☐ Discuss the reasons why a firm will shut down in the short run and not produce any output.
☐ Find the firm's short-run supply curve when you are given the firm's short-run cost schedules.
☐ Explain the links among the law of diminishing returns, production costs, and product supply in the short run.
☐ Graph a shift in the firm's short-run supply curve and cite factors that cause the curve to increase or decrease.
☐ Find the industry's short-run supply curve (or schedule) when you are given the typical firm's short-run cost schedules.

☐ Determine, under short-run conditions, the price at which the product will sell, the output of the industry, and the output of the individual firm.

☐ Discuss why shutting down a business in the short run makes economic sense and may be temporary (*Last Word*).

■ CHAPTER OUTLINE

1. The price a firm charges for the good or service it produces and its output of that product depend not only on the demand for and the cost of producing it, but on the characteristics of the market (industry) in which it sells the product. The *four market models* are *pure competition, pure monopoly, monopolistic competition,* and *oligopoly.* These models are defined by the number of firms, whether the product is standardized or differentiated, the firm's control over price, the conditions for entry into the industry, and degree of nonprice competition (see Table 8.1 in text). Compared with *pure competition,* the other three market models are considered different forms of *imperfect competition.*

2. This chapter examines *pure competition,* in which a very large number of independent firms, no one of which is able to influence market price by itself, sell a standardized product in a market where firms are free to enter and to leave in the long run. Although pure competition is rare in practice, it is the standard against which the *efficiency* of the economy and other market models can be compared.

3. *Demand* as seen by the purely competitive firm is unique because a firm selling its product cannot influence the price at which the product sells, and therefore is a *price taker.*

   a. The demand for its product is perfectly elastic.

   b. There are three types of revenue. *Average revenue* is the amount of revenue per unit of output. *Total revenue* is calculated as the price times the quantity a firm can produce. *Marginal revenue* is the change in total revenue from selling one more unit. Average revenue (or price) and marginal revenue are equal and constant at the fixed (equilibrium) market price ($AR = P = MR$). Total revenue increases at a constant rate as the firm increases its output.

   c. The demand (average revenue) and marginal revenue curves faced by the firm are horizontal and identical at the market price. The total revenue curve has a constant positive slope.

4. The purely competitive firm operating in the *short run* is a price taker that can maximize profits (or minimize losses) only by changing its level of output. Two approaches can be used to determine the optimal level of output for the firm.

   a. The *total revenue–total cost* approach to profit maximization sets the level of output at that quantity where the difference between total revenue and total cost is greatest. An output at which total revenue covers total costs (including a normal profit) is a *break-even point.*

   b. The *marginal revenue–marginal cost* approach to profit maximization basically sets the level of output at the quantity where marginal revenue (or price) equals marginal cost. There are three possible cases to consider when using this approach.

   (1) The firm uses the *MR = MC rule* to evaluate profit maximization. The firm will produce that level of output where the marginal revenue from each additional unit produced is equal to the marginal cost of each additional unit produced. The rule is an accurate guide to profit maximization for the four basic types of firms. For the purely competitive firm, however, the rule can be restated as $P = $ MC.

   (2) The firm will *maximize profits* when MR = MC at an output level where price is greater than average total cost.

   (3) The firm will *minimize losses* when MR = MC at an output level where price is greater than the minimum average variable cost (but less than average total cost).

   (4) The firm will *shut down* when MR = MC at an output level where price is less than average variable cost.

5. There is a close relationship between marginal cost and the *short-run supply curve* for the purely competitive firm and industry.

   a. The short-run supply curve for the purely competitive firm is the portion of the marginal cost curve that lies above average variable cost.

   b. There are links among the law of diminishing returns, production costs, and product supply. The law of diminishing returns suggests that marginal costs will increase as output expands. The firm must receive more revenue (get higher prices for its products) if it is to expand output.

   c. Changes in variable inputs will change the marginal cost or supply curve for the purely competitive firm. For example, an improvement in technology that increases productivity will decrease the marginal cost curve (shift it downward).

   d. The *short-run supply curve of the industry* (which is the sum of the supply curves of the individual firms) and the total demand for the product determine the short-run equilibrium price and equilibrium output of the industry. Firms in the industry may be either prosperous or unprosperous in the short run.

6. (*Last Word*). If a firm finds that the revenue it earns from the output it produces and sells does not even cover its fixed costs, then the firm will shut down. In many cases in the real world, the shutdown is temporary and part of business conditions firms may face. For example, oil wells are shut down if the price of oil does not cover the fixed costs of oil production. Seasonal resorts shut down over the off-season months because there are not enough paying customers to cover the fixed costs. During recessions, businesses shut down factories because product demand and revenue are insufficient to cover fixed costs. Shutdowns are more common than typically thought and are often temporary until economic conditions and revenues expand to cover the fixed costs.

■ **HINTS AND TIPS**

1. The purely competitive model is extremely important for you to master even if examples of it in the real world are rare. The model is the standard against which the other market models—pure monopoly, monopolistic competition, and oligopoly—will be compared for effects on economic efficiency. Spend extra time learning the material in this chapter so you can make model comparisons in later chapters.

2. Make sure that you understand why a purely competitive firm is a **price "taker"** and not a price "maker." The purely competitive firm has no influence over the price of its product and can only make decisions about the level of output.

3. Construct a table for explaining how the purely competitive firm maximizes profits or minimizes losses in the short run. Ask yourself the three questions in the table: (1) Should the firm produce? (2) What quantity should be produced to maximize profits? (3) Will production result in economic profit? Answer the questions using a marginal revenue–marginal cost approach. Check your answers against those presented in the text Table 8.3.

■ **IMPORTANT TERMS**

pure competition	average revenue
pure monopoly	total revenue
monopolistic competition	marginal revenue
oligopoly	break-even point
imperfect competition	MR = MC rule
price taker	short-run supply curve

SELF-TEST

■ **FILL-IN QUESTIONS**

1. The four market models examined in this and the next three chapters are

   a. _____

   b. _____

   c. _____

   d. _____

2. The four market models differ in terms of the (age, number) _____ of firms in the industry, whether the product is (a consumer good, standardized) _____ or (a producer good, differentiated) _____, and how easy or difficult it is for new firms to (enter, leave) _____ the industry.

3. What are the four specific conditions that characterize pure competition?

   a. _____

   b. _____

   c. _____

   d. _____

4. The individual firm in a purely competitive industry is a price (maker, taker) _____ and finds that the demand for its product is perfectly (elastic, inelastic) _____. The demand curve for the individual firm is graphed as a (vertical, horizontal) _____ line.

5. The price per unit to the seller is (marginal, total, average) _____ revenue; price multiplied by the quantity the firm can sell is _____ revenue; and the extra revenue that results from selling one more unit of output is _____ revenue.

6. In pure competition, as an individual firm increases output, the product price (rises, falls, is constant) _____. Marginal revenue is (less than, greater than, equal to) _____ product price and average revenue is _____ product price.

7. The purely competitive firm's demand schedule is a (cost, revenue) _____ schedule. Demand is equal to (marginal, total) _____ revenue and is equal to (average, total) _____ revenue.

8. There are two ways to determine the level of output at which the competitive firm will realize maximum (loss, profit) _____ or minimum _____. One method is to compare total revenue with (total, marginal) _____ cost and the other way is to compare marginal revenue with _____ cost.

9. Economic profit is total revenue (plus, minus) _____ total cost. If the firm is making only a normal profit, total revenue is (greater than, equal to) _____ total cost. This output level is called the (profit, break-even) _____ point by economists. A firm will produce a level of output where the difference between total revenue and total cost is at a (minimum, maximum) _____.

10. The rule for profit maximization is that marginal revenue (MR) is (less than, equal to, greater than) _____ marginal cost (MC), and in the case of pure competition this rule can be restated as price is _____ marginal cost; but this rule implies that price is _____ minimum average variable cost.

11. In a graph with marginal and average cost curves, the way to calculate economic profit is to take the difference between average total cost and (price, output) _____ and multiply it by _____.

12. If a purely competitive firm produces any output at all, it will produce that output at which its profit is at a (maximum, minimum) _____ or its loss is at a _____. Or, said another way, the firm will produce output at which marginal cost is (equal to, greater than) _____ marginal revenue.

13. In the short run, a firm will be willing to produce its output at an economic loss if the price which it receives is less than its average (fixed, variable, total) _____ cost but greater than its average _____ cost.

14. In the short run, a firm will choose to shut down and not produce output if the price which it receives is less than its average (fixed, variable, total) _____ cost.

15. In the short run, the individual firm's supply curve in pure competition is that portion of the firm's (total, marginal) _____ cost curve which lies (above, below) _____ the average variable cost curve. The break-even point for a firm is where price equals average (total, variable) _____ cost.

16. Because of the law of diminishing returns, marginal costs eventually (fall, rise) _____ as more units of output are produced, and to be motivated to produce more units of output at higher marginal costs, the price of the product must _____.

17. An increase in the price of variable inputs such as worker wages will shift the marginal-cost or short-run supply curve of the individual firm (upward, downward) _____ while a decrease in the price of variable input or an improvement in technology will shift this curve _____.

18. The short-run market supply curve is the (average, sum) _____ of the (short-run, long-run) _____ supply curves of all firms in the industry.

19. In the short run in a purely competitive industry, the equilibrium price is the price at which quantity demanded is (greater than, equal to, less than) _____ quantity supplied, and the equilibrium quantity is the quantity at which quantity demanded is _____ quantity supplied at the equilibrium price.

20. Product price is a given fact to the (firm, industry) _____ but the supply plans of the _____ as a group of firms are a basic determinant of product price.

■ **TRUE–FALSE QUESTIONS**

Circle T if the statement is true, F if it is false.

1. The structures of the markets in which business firms sell their products in the U.S. economy are very similar.　**T　F**

2. There are significant obstacles to entry in a purely competitive industry.　**T　F**

3. In a purely competitive industry individual firms do not have control over the price of their product.　**T　F**

4. Imperfectly competitive markets are defined as all markets except those that are purely competitive.　**T　F**

5. One reason for studying the pure competition model is that most industries are purely competitive.　**T　F**

6. The purely competitive firm views an average revenue schedule as identical to its marginal revenue schedule.　**T　F**

7. The demand curves for an individual firm in a purely competitive industry are perfectly inelastic.　**T　F**

8. Price and average revenue are the same in pure competition.　**T　F**

9. Total revenue for each sales level is found by multiplying price by the quantity the firm can sell at that price.　**T　F**

10. Marginal revenue is the change in average revenue that results from selling one more unit of output.　**T　F**

11. In pure competition, price is equal to marginal revenue and also equal to average revenue.　**T　F**

12. Under purely competitive conditions, the product price charged by the firm increases as output increases.　**T　F**

13. The purely competitive firm can maximize its economic profit (or minimize its loss) only by adjusting its output.　**T　F**

14. Economic profit is the difference between total revenue and average revenue.　**T　F**

15. The break-even point means that the firm is realizing normal profits, but not economic profits.　**T　F**

16. A purely competitive firm that wishes to produce and not close down will maximize profits or minimize losses at that output at which marginal costs and marginal revenue are equal.　**T　F**

17. Assuming that the purely competitive firm chooses to produce and not close down, to maximize profits or minimize losses it should produce at that point where price equals average cost.　**T　F**

18. If a purely competitive firm is producing output less than its profit-maximizing output, marginal revenue is greater than marginal cost.　**T　F**

19. If, at the profit-maximizing level of output for the purely competitive firm, price exceeds the minimum average variable cost but is less than average total cost, the firm will make a profit.　**T　F**

20. A purely competitive firm will produce in the short run the output at which marginal cost and marginal revenue are equal provided that the price of the product is greater than its average variable cost of production.　**T　F**

21. The short-run supply curve of the purely competitive firm is the segment of the firm's short-run marginal cost curve that lies above the firm's average variable cost curve.　**T　F**

22. The short-run supply curve of a purely competitive firm tends to slope upward from left to right because of the law of diminishing returns. **T F**

23. An increase in the price of a variable input will shift the marginal cost or short-run supply curve downward. **T F**

24. An improvement in technology that raises productivity will shift the marginal cost or short-run supply curve downward. **T F**

25. Product price is a given fact to the individual competitive firm, but the supply plans of all competitive firms as a group are a basic determinant of product price. **T F**

■ **MULTIPLE-CHOICE QUESTIONS**

Circle the letter that corresponds to the best answer.

1. For which market model are there a very large number of firms?
 (a) monopolistic competition
 (b) oligopoly
 (c) pure monopoly
 (d) pure competition

2. In which market model is the individual seller of a product a price taker?
 (a) pure competition
 (b) pure monopoly
 (c) monopolistic competition
 (d) oligopoly

3. Which industry comes *closest* to being purely competitive?
 (a) agriculture
 (b) retail trade
 (c) electricity
 (d) automobile

4. In a purely competitive industry,
 (a) each existing firm will engage in various forms of nonprice competition
 (b) new firms are free to enter and existing firms are able to leave the industry very easily
 (c) individual firms have a price policy
 (d) each firm produces a differentiated (nonstandardized) product

5. The demand schedule or curve confronted by the individual purely competitive firm is
 (a) perfectly inelastic
 (b) inelastic but not perfectly inelastic
 (c) perfectly elastic
 (d) elastic but not perfectly elastic

6. Total revenue for producing 10 units of output is $6. Total revenue for producing 11 units of output is $8. Given this information, the
 (a) average revenue for producing 11 units is $2.
 (b) average revenue for producing 11 units is $8.
 (c) marginal revenue for producing the 11th unit is $2.
 (d) marginal revenue for producing the 11th unit is $8.

7. In pure competition, product price is
 (a) greater than marginal revenue
 (b) equal to marginal revenue
 (c) equal to total revenue
 (d) greater than total revenue

8. Suppose that when 2000 units of output are produced, the marginal cost of the 2001st unit is $5. This amount is equal to the minimum of average total cost, and marginal cost is rising. If the optimal level of output in the short run is 2500 units, then at that level,
 (a) marginal cost is greater than $5 and marginal cost is less than average total cost
 (b) marginal cost is greater than $5 and marginal cost is greater than average total cost
 (c) marginal cost is less than $5 and marginal cost is greater than average total cost
 (d) marginal cost is equal to $5 and marginal cost is equal to average total cost

9. The Zebra, Inc., is selling in a purely competitive market. Its output is 250 units, which sell for $2 each. At this level of output, marginal cost is $2 and average variable cost is $2.25. The firm should
 (a) produce zero units of output
 (b) decrease output to 200 units
 (c) continue to produce 250 units
 (d) increase output to maximize profits

Questions 10, 11, 12, and 13 are based on the following graph.

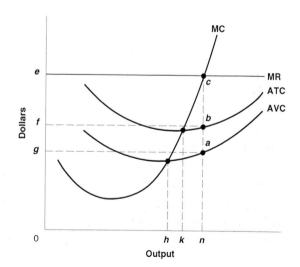

10. If the firm is producing at output level 0*n*, the rectangular area *fecb* is
 (a) total variable cost
 (b) total fixed costs
 (c) total revenue
 (d) total economic profit

11. At the profit-maximizing output, average fixed cost is
 (a) *ab*
 (b) *ac*
 (c) *na*
 (d) *nb*

12. At the profit-maximizing output, the total variable costs are equal to the area
(a) 0*fbn*
(b) 0*ecn*
(c) 0*gan*
(d) *gfba*

13. The demand curve for this firm is equal to
(a) **MR**, and the supply curve is the portion of the **MC** curve where output is greater than level *n*
(b) **MR**, and the supply curve is the portion of the **MC** curve where output is greater than level *k*
(c) **MR**, and the supply curve is the portion of the **MC** curve where output is greater than level *h*
(d) **MR**, and the supply curve is the portion of the **ATC** curve where output is greater than level *k*

Answer Questions 14 through 20 on the basis of the following cost data for a firm that is selling in a purely competitive market.

Output	AFC	AVC	ATC	MC
0				
1	$300	$100	$400	$100
2	150	75	225	50
3	100	70	170	60
4	75	73	148	80
5	60	80	140	110
6	50	90	140	140
7	43	103	146	180
8	38	119	156	230
9	33	138	171	290
10	30	160	190	360

14. If the market price for the firm's product is $140, the competitive firm will produce
(a) 5 units
(b) 6 units
(c) 7 units
(d) 8 units

15. If the market price for the firm's product is $140, the competitive firm will
(a) have an economic loss of $50
(b) have an economic profit of $50
(c) have an economic profit of $840
(d) break even

16. If the market price for the firm's product is $290, the competitive firm will produce
(a) 7 units
(b) 8 units
(c) 9 units
(d) 10 units

17. If the market price for the firm's product is $290, the competitive firm will produce an economic profit of
(a) $1071
(b) $1368
(c) $1539
(d) $2610

18. If the product price is $179, the *per-unit* economic profit at the profit-maximizing output is
(a) $15
(b) $23
(c) $33
(d) $39

19. If the market price for the firm's product is $60, the competitive firm will produce
(a) 0 units
(b) 1 units
(c) 2 units
(d) 3 units

20. For this firm, the total fixed costs are
(a) $100
(b) $200
(c) $300
(d) $400

Assume there are 100 identical firms in this industry and total or market demand is as shown.

Price	Quantity demanded
$360	600
290	700
230	800
180	900
140	1000
110	1100
80	1200

21. The equilibrium price will be
(a) $140
(b) $180
(c) $230
(d) $290

22. The individual firm's short-run supply curve is that part of its marginal cost curve lying above its
(a) average total cost curve
(b) average variable cost curve
(c) average fixed cost curve
(d) average revenue curve

23. Which statement is true of a purely competitive industry in short-run equilibrium?
(a) Price is equal to average total cost.
(b) Total quantity demanded is equal to total quantity supplied.
(c) Profits in the industry are equal to zero.
(d) Output is equal to the output at which average total cost is a minimum.

24. Because of the law of diminishing marginal returns, marginal costs eventually
(a) fall as fewer units of output are produced, thus higher prices are required to motivate producers to supply less
(b) fall as fewer units of output are produced, thus higher prices are required to motivate producers to supply more

(c) rise as more units of output are produced, thus lower prices are required to motivate producers to supply less

(d) rise as more units of output are produced, thus higher prices are required to motivate producers to supply more

25. If other factors are held constant, an increase in wages for a purely competitive firm would result in a shift

(a) downward in the marginal cost curve

(b) downward in the average fixed cost curve

(c) upward in the marginal cost curve

(d) upward in the average fixed cost curve

■ PROBLEMS

1. Using the following set of terms, complete the following table by inserting the appropriate letter or letters in the blanks.

a. one
b. few
c. many
d. a very large number
e. standardized
f. differentiated
g. some

h. considerable
i. very easy
j. blocked
k. fairly easy
l. fairly difficult
m. none
n. unique

Market characteristics	Market model			
	Pure competition	Monopolistic competition	Oligopoly	Pure monopoly
Number of firms	___	___	___	___
Type of product	___	___	___	___
Control over price	___	___	___	___
Conditions of entry	___	___	___	___
Nonprice competition	___	___	___	___

2. Following is the demand schedule facing the individual firm.

Price	Quantity demanded	Average revenue	Total revenue	Marginal revenue
$10	0	$___	$___	—
10	1	___	___	$___
10	2	___	___	___
10	3	___	___	___
10	4	___	___	___
10	5	___	___	___
10	6	___	___	___

a. Complete the table by computing average revenue, total revenue, and marginal revenue.

b. Is this firm operating in a market that is purely competitive?_____ How can you tell?_____

_____

c. The coefficient of the price elasticity of demand is the same between every pair of quantities demanded.

What is it? _____

d. What relationship exists between average revenue and marginal revenue? _____

_____

e. On the graph below, plot the demand schedule, average revenue, total revenue, and marginal revenue; label each curve.

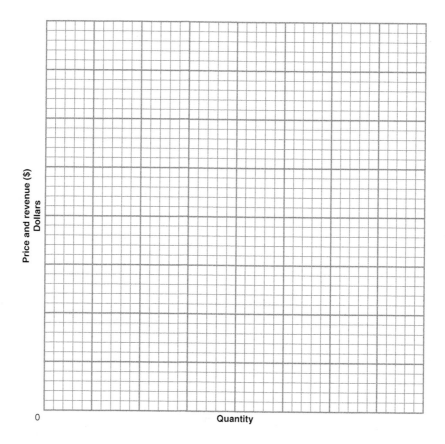

251

f. The demand, average revenue, and marginal revenue curves are all _____ lines at a price of $_____ across all quantities.

g. The total revenue curve is an up-sloping line with a _____ slope because marginal revenue is _____.

3. Assume that a purely competitive firm has the following schedule of costs.

Output	TFC	TVC	TC
0	$300	$ 0	$ 300
1	300	100	400
2	300	150	450
3	300	210	510
4	300	290	590
5	300	400	700
6	300	540	840
7	300	720	1020
8	300	950	1250
9	300	1240	1540
10	300	1600	1900

a. Complete the following table to show the total revenue and total profit of the firm at each level of output the firm might produce. Assume the market price is $200.

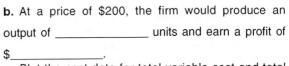

Output	Market price = $200	
	Revenue	Profit
0	$_____	$_____
1	_____	_____
2	_____	_____
3	_____	_____
4	_____	_____
5	_____	_____
6	_____	_____
7	_____	_____
8	_____	_____
9	_____	_____
10	_____	_____

b. At a price of $200, the firm would produce an output of _____ units and earn a profit of $_____.

c. Plot the cost data for total variable cost and total cost on the graph below. Then plot the total revenue when the price is $200. For this price, indicate the level of output and the economic profit or loss on the graph.

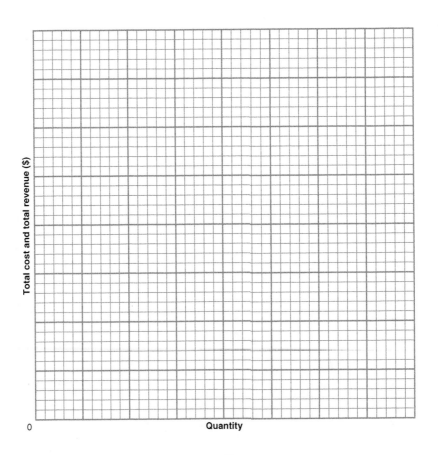

Total cost and total revenue ($)

0   Quantity

4. Now assume that the same purely competitive firm has the following schedule of average and marginal costs.

Output	AFC	AVC	ATC	MC
0				
1	$300	$100	$400	$100
2	150	75	225	50
3	100	70	170	60
4	75	73	148	80
5	60	80	140	110
6	50	90	140	140
7	43	103	146	180
8	38	119	156	230
9	33	138	171	290
10	30	160	190	360

a. At a price of $55, the firm would produce _____ units of output. At a price of $120, the firm would produce _____ units of output. At a price of $200, the firm would produce _____ units of output. At the $200 price compare your answers to those you gave in problem 3.

b. The *per-unit* economic profit (or loss) is calculated by subtracting _____ at a particular level of output from the product price. This *per-unit* economic profit is then multiplied by the number of units of _____ to determine the economic profit for the competitive firm.

(1) At the product price of $200, the average total costs are $_____, so *per-unit* economic profit is $_____. Multiplying this amount by the number of units of output results in an economic profit of $_____.

(2) At the product price of $120, the average total costs are $_____, so *per-unit* economic losses are $_____. Multiplying this amount by the number of units of output results in an economic loss of $_____.

c. Plot the data for average and marginal cost in the graph at bottom of the page. Then plot each marginal revenue when the price is $55, $120, and $200. For each price, indicate the level of output and the economic profit or loss on the graph.

5. Use the average and marginal cost data in problem 4 in your work on problem 5.

a. In the following table, complete the supply schedule for the competitive firm and state what the economic profit will be at each price.

Price	Quantity supplied	Profit
$360	_____	$_____
290	_____	_____
230	_____	_____
180	_____	_____
140	_____	_____
110	_____	_____
80	_____	_____
60	_____	_____

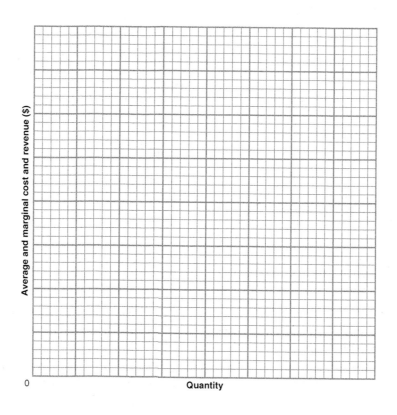

b. If there are 100 firms in the industry and all have the same cost schedule,

(1) Complete the market supply schedule in the following table.

Quantity demanded	Price	Quantity supplied
400	$360	_____
500	290	_____
600	230	_____
700	180	_____
800	140	_____
900	110	_____
1000	80	_____

(2) Using the demand schedule given in (1):
(a) What will the market price of the product be?

$_____

(b) What quantity will the individual firm produce?

_____

(c) How large will the firm's profit be? $_____

■ **SHORT ANSWER AND ESSAY QUESTIONS**

1. What are the four market models (or situations) that economists employ, and what are the major characteristics of each type of market?

2. Describe in detail four characteristics of pure competition.

3. If pure competition is so rare in practice, why are students of economics asked to study it?

4. Explain how the firm in a purely competitive industry sees the demand for the product it produces in terms of the price elasticity of demand.

5. Describe the differences between average revenue, total revenue, and marginal revenue.

6. What happens to total average, revenue, and marginal revenue as the output of the firm increases?

7. Why is price equal to marginal revenue and also equal to average revenue for the purely competitive firm?

8. Describe the total revenue–total cost approach to profit maximization.

9. In the total revenue–total cost approach to profit maximization, what is the break-even point and how is it related to normal profit?

10. Compare and contrast the total revenue–total cost approach with the marginal revenue–marginal cost approach to profit maximization. Are the two approaches consistent?

11. Explain the MR = MC rule and its characteristics.

12. Why do the MC = MR rule and MC = P rule mean the same thing under conditions of pure competition?

13. Why does the purely competitive firm want to maximize total profit but not its per-unit profit?

14. Use an equation to calculate the area of economic profit and draw marginal and average graphs to show the area.

15. Why is a firm willing to produce at a loss in the short run if the loss is no greater than the fixed costs of the firm?

16. In the MR = MC approach, under which conditions will the firm shut down production? Supply a graph of the shutdown case.

17. Use the price equals marginal cost rule to describe the firm's short-run supply curve.

18. Explain the links between the law of diminishing returns, production costs, and product supply in the short run.

19. Explain how the short-run supply of an individual firm and of the purely competitive industry is each determined.

20. What determines the equilibrium price and output of a purely competitive industry in the short run? Will economic profits in the industry be positive or negative?

ANSWERS

Chapter 8 Pure Competition in the Short Run

FILL-IN QUESTIONS

1. *a.* pure competition; *b.* pure monopoly; *c.* monopolistic competition; *d.* oligopoly (any order *a–d*)
2. number, standardized, differentiated, enter
3. *a.* a large number of sellers; *b.* a standardized product; *c.* firms are price takers; *d.* free entry and exit of firms
4. taker, elastic, horizontal
5. average, total, marginal
6. is constant, equal to, equal to
7. revenue, marginal, average
8. profit, loss, total, marginal
9. minus, equal to, break-even, maximum
10. equal to, equal to, greater than
11. price, output
12. maximum, minimum, equal to
13. total, variable
14. fixed
15. marginal, above, total
16. rise, rise
17. upward, downward
18. sum, short-run
19. equal to, equal to
20. firm, industry

TRUE–FALSE QUESTIONS

1. F, p. 164	**10.** F, p. 165	**19.** F, p. 171
2. F, pp. 164–165	**11.** T, pp. 165–166	**20.** T, pp. 171–172
3. T, p. 165	**12.** F, pp. 165–167	**21.** T, pp. 173–174
4. T, p. 164	**13.** I, pp. 166–167	**22.** T, p. 175
5. F, p. 164	**14.** F, p. 167	**23.** F, p. 175
6. T, p. 165	**15.** T, p. 167	**24.** T, p. 175
7. T, p. 165	**16.** T, p. 169	**25.** T, p. 176
8. T, p. 165	**17.** F, pp. 169–171	
9. T, p. 165	**18.** T, pp. 169–171	

MULTIPLE-CHOICE QUESTIONS

1. d, p. 164
2. a, p. 164
3. a, p. 164
4. b, p. 165
5. c, p. 165
6. c, p. 165
7. b, p. 165
8. b, pp. 169–171
9. a, pp. 169–171
10. d, pp. 169–171
11. a, pp. 169–171
12. c, pp. 169–171
13. c, pp. 173–174
14. b, pp. 169–171
15. d, pp. 169–171
16. c, pp. 169–171
17. a, pp. 169–171
18. d, pp. 169–171
19. a, pp. 171–171
20. c, pp. 169–171
21. c, pp. 175–176
22. b, pp. 175–176
23. b, p. 175
24. d, p. 175
25. c, p. 175

PROBLEMS

1. Number of firms: d, a, c, b; Type of product: e, n, f, e, or f; Control over price: m, h, g, g; Conditions of entry: i, j, k, l; Non-price competition: m, g, h, g, or h

2. *a.* Average revenue: all are $10.00; Total revenue: $0, 10.00, 20.00, 30.00, 40.00, 50.00, 60.00; Marginal revenue: all are $10.00; *b.* yes, because price (average revenue) is constant and equal to marginal revenue; *c.* infinity; *d.* they are equal; *e.* see Figure 8.1 of the text for an example; *f.* horizontal, $10; *g.* constant, constant

3. *a.* see following table; *b.* 7, 380; *c.* see Figure 8.2 of the text for an example

Output	Market price = $200	
	Revenue	Profit
0	$ 0	$ −300
1	200	−200
2	400	−50
3	600	90
4	800	210
5	1000	300
6	1200	360
7	1400	380
8	1600	350
9	1800	260
10	2000	100

4. *a.* 0, 5, 7 (last answer is the same as 3b); *b.* average total cost, output; (1) $146, ($200 − $146 = $54), ($54 × 7 = $378), (2) $140, ($120 − $140 = −$20), (−$20 × 5 = −$100); *c.* see Figure 8.3 of the text for an example

5. *a.* see following table; *b.* (1) Quantity supplied: 1000, 900, 800, 700, 600, 500, 400, (2) (*a*) 180, (*b*) 7, (*c*) 238

Price	Quantity supplied	Profit
$360	10	$1700
290	9	1071
230	8	592
180	7	238
140	6	0
110	5	−150
80	4	−272
60	0	−300

SHORT ANSWER AND ESSAY QUESTIONS

1. p. 164
2. pp. 164–165
3. p. 165
4. p. 165
5. pp. 165–166
6. pp. 165–167
7. p. 165
8. pp. 166–167
9. p. 167
10. pp. 166–171
11. p. 169
12. p. 169
13. pp. 169–171
14. pp. 169–171
15. pp.171–172
16. pp. 171–172
17. pp. 173–175
18. p. 175
19. p. 175
20. p.175–176

AFTER READING THIS CHAPTER, YOU SHOULD BE ABLE TO:

1 Explain how the long run differs from the short run in pure competition.

2 Describe why profits encourage entry into a purely competitive industry and losses result in firms exiting the industry.

3 Explain how the entry and exit of firms affects resource flows and long-run profits and losses.

4 Explain the differences between constant-cost, increasing-cost, and decreasing-cost industries.

5 Show how long-run equilibrium in pure competition produces an efficient allocation of resources.

6 Discuss creative destruction and the profit incentives for innovation.

Pure Competition in the Long Run

The previous chapter discussed how pure competition operates in the short run, the time period during which the individual firms in an industry are stuck with their current plant sizes and fixed-cost commitments. As you know, pure competitors shut down their operation if prices are too low or, if prices are high enough, produce where MR = MC to minimize their losses or maximize their profits. Whether they make a profit or a loss depends on how high the market price is relative to their costs.

That being said, profits and losses cannot be the end of the pure competition story because one of the key characteristics of pure competition is the freedom of firms to enter or exit the industry. We know from Chapter 2 that profits attract entry and losses prompt exit.

In this chapter, we are keenly interested in how entry and exit relate to allocative and productive efficiency. We are also interested in how continuing competition leads to new products and new business methods replacing older products and older business methods through a process aptly referred to as *creative destruction*.

The Long Run in Pure Competition

The entry and exit of firms in our market models can only take place in the long run. In the short run, the industry is composed of a specific number of firms, each with a plant size that is fixed and unalterable in the short run. Firms may shut down in the sense that they can produce zero units of output in the short run, but they do not have sufficient time to liquidate their assets and go out of business.

In the long run, by contrast, the firms already in an industry have sufficient time to either expand or contract their capacities. More important, the number of firms in the industry may either increase or decrease as new firms enter or existing firms leave.

The length of time constituting the long run varies substantially by industry, however, so that you should not fix in your mind any specific number of years, months, or days. Instead, focus your attention on the incentives provided by profits and losses for the entry and exit of firms into any purely competitive industry and, later in the chapter, on how those incentives lead to productive and allocative efficiency. The time horizons are far less important than the process by which profits and losses guide business managers toward the efficient use of society's resources.

Profit Maximization in the Long Run

The first part of the pure competition story (Chapter 8) was about profit, loss, and shutdown in the short run. The rest of the story (this chapter) is about entry and exit and their effects on industry size and allocative and productive efficiency in the long run.

To tell the rest of story well, we need to return to our graphical analysis and examine profit maximization by pure competitors in the long run. Several assumptions, none of which affect our conclusions, will keep things simple:

- *Entry and exit only* The only long-run adjustment in our graphical analysis is caused by the entry or exit of firms. Moreover, we ignore all short-run adjustments in order to concentrate on the effects of the long-run adjustments.
- *Identical costs* All firms in the industry have identical cost curves. This assumption lets us discuss an "average," or "representative," firm, knowing that all other firms in the industry are similarly affected by any long-run adjustments that occur.
- *Constant-cost industry* The industry is a constant-cost industry. This means that the entry and exit of firms does not affect resource prices or, consequently, the locations of the average-total-cost curves of individual firms.

Goal of Our Analysis

The basic conclusion we seek to explain is this: After all long-run adjustments are completed in a purely competitive industry, product price will be exactly equal to, and production will occur at, each firm's minimum average total cost.

This conclusion follows from two basic facts: (1) Firms seek profits and shun losses, and (2) under pure competition, firms are free to enter and leave an industry. If market price initially exceeds minimum average total costs, the resulting economic profits will attract new firms to the industry. But this industry expansion will increase supply until price is brought back down to equality with minimum average total cost. Conversely, if price is initially less than minimum average total cost, the resulting losses will cause firms to leave the industry. As they leave, total supply will decline, bringing the price back up to equality with minimum average total cost.

Long-Run Equilibrium

Consider the average firm in a purely competitive industry that is initially in long-run equilibrium. This firm is represented in Figure 9.1a, where MR = MC and price and minimum average total cost are equal at $50. Economic profit here is zero; the industry is in equilibrium or "at rest" because there is no tendency for firms to enter or to leave. The existing firms are earning normal profits, which means that their accounting profits are equal to those that the owners of these firms could expect to receive on average in other industries. It is because their current profits are the same as they could expect to earn elsewhere that there is no tendency for firms to enter or leave the industry. The $50 market price is determined in Figure 9.1b by market or industry demand D_1 and supply S_1. (S_1 is a short-run supply curve; we will develop the long-run industry supply curve in our discussion.) And remember that normal profits earned by these firms are considered an opportunity cost and, therefore, are included in the firms' cost curves.

As shown on the quantity axes of the two graphs, equilibrium output in the industry is 100,000 while equilibrium output for the single firm is 100. If all firms in the industry are identical, there must be 1000 firms (= 100,000/100).

Entry Eliminates Economic Profits Let's upset the long-run equilibrium in Figure 9.1 and see what happens. Suppose a change in consumer tastes increases product demand from D_1 to D_2. Price will rise to $60, as determined at the intersection of D_2 and S_1, and the firm's

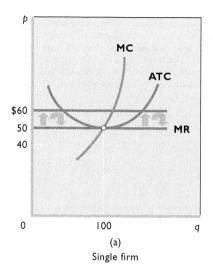

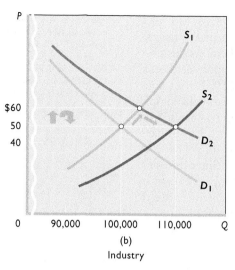

FIGURE 9.1 Temporary profits and the reestablishment of long-run equilibrium in (a) a representative firm and (b) the industry. A favorable shift in demand (D_1 to D_2) will upset the original industry equilibrium and produce economic profits. But those profits will entice new firms to enter the industry, increasing supply (S_1 to S_2) and lowering product price until economic profits are once again zero.

marginal-revenue curve will shift upward to $60. This $60 price exceeds the firm's average total cost of $50 at output 100, creating an economic profit of $10 per unit. This economic profit will lure new firms into the industry. Some entrants will be newly created firms; others will shift from less prosperous industries.

As firms enter, the market supply of the product increases, pushing the product price below $60. Economic profits persist, and entry continues until short-run supply increases to S_2. Market price falls to $50, as does marginal revenue for the firm. Price and minimum average total cost are again equal at $50. The economic profits caused by the boost in demand have been eliminated, and, as a result, the previous incentive for more firms to enter the industry has disappeared because the firms that remain are earning only a normal profit (zero economic

profit). Entry ceases and a new long-run equilibrium is reached.

Observe in Figure 9.1a and 9.1b that total quantity supplied is now 110,000 units and each firm is producing 100 units. Now 1100 firms rather than the original 1000 populate the industry. Economic profits have attracted 100 more firms.

Exit Eliminates Losses Now let's consider a shift in the opposite direction. We begin in Figure 9.2b with curves S_1 and D_1 setting the same initial long-run equilibrium situation as in our previous analysis, including the $50 price.

Suppose consumer demand declines from D_1 to D_3. This forces the market price and marginal revenue down to $40, making production unprofitable at the minimum ATC of $50. In time the resulting economic losses will

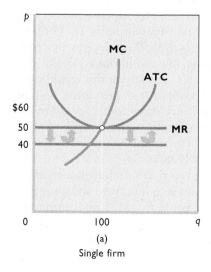

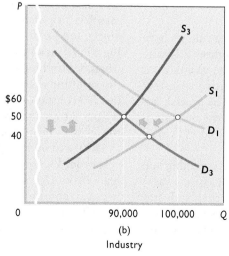

FIGURE 9.2 Temporary losses and the reestablishment of long-run equilibrium in (a) a representative firm and (b) the industry. An unfavorable shift in demand (D_1 to D_3) will upset the original industry equilibrium and produce losses. But those losses will cause firms to leave the industry, decreasing supply (S_1 to S_3) and increasing product price until all losses have disappeared.

induce firms to leave the industry. Their owners will seek a normal profit elsewhere rather than accept the below-normal profits (losses) now confronting them. As this exodus of firms proceeds, however, industry supply decreases, pushing the price up from $40 toward $50. Losses continue and more firms leave the industry until the supply curve shifts to S_3. Once this happens, price is again $50, just equal to the minimum average total cost. Losses have been eliminated so that the firms that remain are earning only a normal profit (zero economic profit). Since this is no better or worse than entrepreneurs could expect to earn in other business ventures, there is no longer any incentive to exit the industry. Long-run equilibrium is restored.

In Figure 9.2a and 9.2b, total quantity supplied is now 90,000 units and each firm is producing 100 units. Only 900 firms, not the original 1000, populate the industry. Losses have forced 100 firms out.

You may have noted that we have sidestepped the question of which firms will leave the industry when losses occur by assuming that all firms have identical cost curves. In the real world, of course, managerial talents differ. Even if resource prices and technology are the same for all firms, less skillfully managed firms tend to incur higher costs and therefore are the first to leave an industry when demand declines. Similarly, firms with less productive labor forces or higher transportation costs will be higher-cost producers and likely candidates to quit an industry when demand decreases.

We have now reached an intermediate goal: Our analysis verifies that competition, reflected in the entry and exit of firms, eliminates economic profits or losses by adjusting price to equal minimum long-run average total cost. In addition, this competition forces firms to select output levels at which average total cost is minimized.

Long-Run Supply for a Constant-Cost Industry

Although our analysis has dealt with the long run, we have noted that the market supply curves in Figures 9.1b and 9.2b are short-run curves. What then is the character of the **long-run supply curve** of a competitive industry? Our analysis points us toward an answer. The crucial factor here is the effect, if any, that changes in the number of firms in the industry will have on costs of the individual firms in the industry.

In our analysis of long-run competitive equilibrium we assumed that the industry under discussion was a **constant-cost industry.** This means that industry expansion or contraction will not affect resource prices and therefore production costs. Graphically, it means

FIGURE 9.3 The long-run supply curve for a constant-cost industry is horizontal. In a constant-cost industry, the entry and exit of firms does not affect resource prices, or, therefore, unit costs. So an increase in demand (D_1 to D_2) raises industry output (Q_1 to Q_2) but not price ($50). Similarly, a decrease in demand (D_1 to D_3) reduces output (Q_1 to Q_3) but not price. Thus the long-run industry supply curve (S) is horizontal through points Z_1, Z_2 and Z_3.

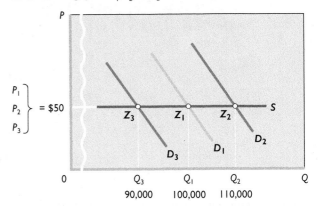

that the entry or exit of firms does not shift the long-run ATC curves of individual firms. This is the case when the industry's demand for resources is small in relation to the total demand for those resources. Then the industry can expand or contract without significantly affecting resource prices and costs.

What does the long-run supply curve of a constant-cost industry look like? The answer is contained in our previous analysis. There we saw that the entry and exit of firms changes industry output but always brings the product price back to its original level, where it is just equal to the constant minimum ATC. Specifically, we discovered that the industry would supply 90,000, 100,000, or 110,000 units of output, all at a price of $50 per unit. In other words, the long-run supply curve of a constant-cost industry is perfectly elastic.

This is demonstrated graphically in Figure 9.3, which uses data from Figures 9.1 and 9.2. Suppose industry demand is originally D_1, industry output is Q_1 (100,000 units), and product price is P_1 ($50). This situation, from Figure 9.1, is one of long-run equilibrium. We saw that when demand increases to D_2, upsetting this equilibrium, the resulting economic profits attract new firms. Because this is a constant-cost industry, entry continues and industry output expands until the price is driven back down to the level of the unchanged minimum ATC. This is at price P_2 ($50) and output Q_2 (110,000).

From Figure 9.2, we saw that a decline in market demand from D_1 to D_3 causes an exit of firms and ultimately restores equilibrium at price P_3 ($50) and output Q_3 (90,000 units). The points Z_1, Z_2, and Z_3 in Figure 9.3 represent these three price-quantity combinations. A line or curve connecting all such points shows the various price-quantity combinations that firms would produce if they had enough time to make all desired adjustments to changes in demand. This line or curve is the industry's long-run supply curve. In a constant-cost industry this curve (straight line) is horizontal, as in Figure 9.3, thus representing perfectly elastic supply.

Long-Run Supply for an Increasing-Cost Industry

Constant-cost industries are a special case. Most industries are **increasing-cost industries,** in which firms' ATC curves shift upward as the industry expands and downward as the industry contracts. Usually, the entry of new firms will increase resource prices, particularly in industries using specialized resources whose long-run supplies do not readily increase in response to increases in resource demand. Higher resource prices result in higher long-run average total costs for all firms in the industry. These higher costs cause upward shifts in each firm's long-run ATC curve.

Thus, when an increase in product demand results in economic profits and attracts new firms to an increasing-cost industry, a two-way squeeze works to eliminate those profits. As before, the entry of new firms increases market supply and lowers the market price. But now each firm's entire ATC curve also shifts upward. The overall result is a higher-than-original equilibrium price. The industry produces a larger output at a higher product price because the industry expansion has increased resource prices and the minimum average total cost.

Since greater output will be supplied at a higher price, the long-run industry supply curve is upsloping. Instead of supplying 90,000, 100,000, or 110,000 units at the same price of $50, an increasing-cost industry might supply 90,000 units at $45, 100,000 units at $50, and 110,000 units at $55. A higher price is required to induce more production, because costs per unit of output increase as production rises.

Figure 9.4 nicely illustrates the situation. Original market demand is D_1 and industry price and output are P_1 ($50) and Q_1 (100,000 units), respectively, at equilibrium point Y_1. An increase in demand to D_2 upsets this equilibrium and leads to economic profits. New firms enter the industry, increasing both market supply and the production costs of individual firms. A new price is established at point Y_2, where P_2 is $55 and Q_2 is 110,000 units.

Conversely, a decline in demand from D_1 to D_3 makes production unprofitable and causes firms to leave the industry. The resulting decline in resource prices reduces

FIGURE 9.4 The long-run supply curve for an increasing-cost industry is upsloping. In an increasing-cost industry, the entry of new firms in response to an increase in demand (D_3 to D_1 to D_2) will bid up resource prices and thereby increase unit costs. As a result, an increased industry output (Q_3 to Q_1 to Q_2) will be forthcoming only at higher prices ($55 > $50 > $45). The long-run industry supply curve (S) therefore slopes upward through points Y_3, Y_1, and Y_2.

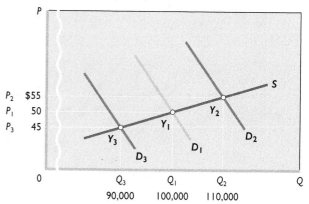

the minimum average total cost of production for firms that stay. A new equilibrium price is established at some level below the original price, say, at point Y_3, where P_3 is $45 and Q_3 is 90,000 units. Connecting these three equilibrium positions, we derive the upsloping long-run supply curve S in Figure 9.4.

Long-Run Supply for a Decreasing-Cost Industry

In **decreasing-cost industries,** firms experience lower costs as their industry expands. The personal computer industry is an example. As demand for personal computers increased, new manufacturers of computers entered the industry and greatly increased the resource demand for the components used to build them (for example, memory chips, hard drives, monitors, and operating software). The expanded production of the components enabled the producers of those items to achieve substantial economies of scale. The decreased production costs of the components reduced their prices, which greatly lowered the computer manufacturers' average costs of production. The supply of personal computers increased by more than demand, and the price of personal computers declined.

Unfortunately, however, the industries that show decreasing costs when output expands also show increasing costs if output contracts. A good example is the American shoe-manufacturing industry as it contracted due to

INTERACTIVE GRAPHS

G 9.1

Long-run competitive supply

FIGURE 9.5 **The long-run supply curve for a decreasing-cost industry is downsloping.** In a decreasing-cost industry, the entry of new firms in response to an increase in demand (D_3 to D_1 to D_2) will lead to decreased input prices and, consequently, decreased unit costs. As a result, an increase in industry output (Q_3 to Q_1 to Q_2) will be accompanied by lower prices ($55 > $50 > $45). The long-run industry supply curve (S) therefore slopes downward through points X_3, X_1, and X_2.

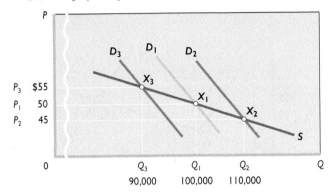

foreign competition. Back when the industry was doing well and there were many shoemaking firms, the cost of specialized technicians who repair shoemaking machinery could be spread across many firms. This was because the repairmen worked as independent contractors going from one firm's factory to another firm's factory on a daily basis as various pieces of equipment at different factories needed repairs. But as the demand for American footwear fell over time, there were fewer and fewer factories, so the cost of a repair technician had to be spread over fewer and fewer firms. Thus, costs per firm and per unit of output increased.

Figure 9.5 illustrates the situation. The original market demand is D_1 and industry price and output are P_1($50) and Q_1(100,000 units), respectively, at equilibrium point X_1. An increase in demand to D_2 upsets this equilibrium and leads to economic profits. New firms enter the industry, increasing market supply but decreasing the production costs of individual firms. A new price is established at point X_2, where P_2 is $45 and Q_2 is 110,000 units.

Conversely, a decline in demand from D_1 to D_3 makes production unprofitable and causes firms to leave the industry. The resulting increase in input prices increases the minimum average total cost of production for the firms that remain. A new equilibrium price is established at some level above the original price, say at point X_3, where P_3 is $55 and Q_3 is 90,000 units. Connecting these three equilibrium positions in Figure 9.5, we derive the downsloping long-run supply curve S for this decreasing-cost industry.

Pure Competition and Efficiency

Figure 9.6 (Key Graph) demonstrates the efficiency characteristics of the individual firms (Figure 9.6a) and the market (Figure 9.6b) after long-run adjustments in pure competition. Assuming a constant- or increasing-cost industry, the final long-run equilibrium positions of all firms have the same basic efficiency characteristics. As shown in Figure 9.6a, price (and marginal revenue) will settle where it is equal to minimum average total cost: P (and MR) = minimum ATC. Moreover, since the marginal-cost curve intersects the average-total-cost curve at its minimum point, marginal cost and average total cost are equal: MC = minimum ATC. So in long-run equilibrium a triple equality occurs: P (and MR) = MC = minimum ATC. Thus, in long-run equilibrium, each firm produces at the output level Q_f that is associated with this triple equality.[1]

The triple equality tells us two very important things about long-run equilibrium. First, it tells us that although a competitive firm may realize economic profit or loss in the short run, it will earn only a normal profit by producing in accordance with the MR (= P) = MC rule in the long run. Second, the triple equality tells us that in long-run equilibrium, the profit-maximizing decision rule that leads each firm to produce the quantity at which P = MR also implies that each firm will produce at the output level Q_f that is associated with the minimum point on each identical firm's ATC curve.

This is very important because it suggests that pure competition leads to the most efficient possible use of society's resources. Indeed, subject only to Chapter 5's

---

[1]This triple equality does not always hold for decreasing-cost industries in which individual firms produce a large fraction of the total market output. In such cases, MC may remain below ATC if average costs are decreasing. We will discuss this situation of "natural monopoly" in Chapter 10.

key graph

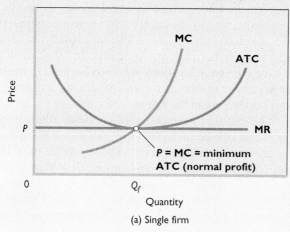

(a) Single firm

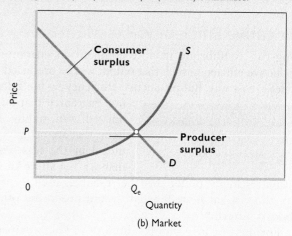

(b) Market

QUICK QUIZ FOR FIGURE 9.6

1. We know the firm is a price taker because:
   a. its MC curve slopes upward.
   b. its ATC curve is U-shaped.
   c. its MR curve is horizontal.
   d. MC and ATC are equal at the profit-maximizing output.

2. At this firm's profit-maximizing output:
   a. total revenue equals total cost.
   b. it is earning an economic profit.
   c. allocative, but not necessarily productive, efficiency is achieved.
   d. productive, but not necessarily allocative, efficiency is achieved.

3. The equality of *P*, MC, and minimum ATC:
   a. occurs only in constant-cost industries.
   b. encourages entry of new firms.
   c. means that the "right goods" are being produced in the "right ways."
   d. results in a zero accounting profit.

4. When *P* = MC = lowest ATC for individual firms, in the market:
   a. consumer surplus necessarily exceeds producer surplus.
   b. consumer surplus plus producer surplus is at a maximum.
   c. producer surplus necessarily exceeds consumer surplus.
   d. supply and demand are identical.

Answers: 1. c; 2. a; 3. c; 4. b

---

qualifications relating to public goods and externalities, an idealized purely competitive market economy composed of constant- or increasing-cost industries will generate both productive efficiency and allocative efficiency.

Productive Efficiency: P = Minimum ATC

Productive efficiency requires that goods be produced in the least costly way. In the long run, pure competition forces firms to produce at the minimum average total cost of production and to charge a price that is just consistent with that cost. This is true because firms that do not use the best available (least-cost) production methods and combinations of inputs will not survive.

To see why that is true, let's suppose that Figure 9.6 has to do with pure competition in the cucumber industry. In the final equilibrium position shown in Figure 9.6a, suppose each firm in the cucumber industry is producing 100 units (say, truckloads) of cucumbers by using $5000 (equal to average total cost of $50 × 100 units) worth of resources. If any firm produced that same amount of output at any higher total cost, say $7000, it would be wasting resources because all of the other firms in the industry are able to produce that same amount of output using only $5000 of resources. Society would be faced with a net loss of $2000 worth of alternative products. But this cannot happen in pure competition; this firm would incur a loss of $2000, requiring it either to reduce its costs or to go out of business.

187

Note, too, that consumers benefit from productive efficiency by paying the lowest product price possible under the prevailing technology and cost conditions. And the firm receives only a normal profit, which is part of its economic costs and thus incorporated in its ATC curve.

Allocative Efficiency: $P = MC$

Long-run equilibrium in pure competition guarantees productive efficiency, such that output will be produced in the least-cost way. But productive efficiency by itself does not guarantee that anyone will want to buy the items that are being produced in the least-cost manner. For all we know, consumers might prefer that the resources used to produce those items be redirected toward producing other products instead.

ORIGIN OF THE IDEA

O 9.1

Allocative efficiency

Fortunately, long-run equilibrium in pure competition also guarantees **allocative efficiency,** so we can be certain that society's scarce resources are directed toward producing the goods and services that people most want to consume. Stated formally, allocative efficiency occurs when it is impossible to produce any net gains for society by altering the combination of goods and services that are produced from society's limited supply of resources.

To understand how pure competition leads to allocative efficiency, recall the concept of opportunity cost while looking at Figure 9.6b, where Q_e total units are being produced in equilibrium by the firms in a purely competitive industry. For every unit up to Q_e, market demand curve D lies above market supply curve S. Recall from Chapter 5 what this means in terms of marginal benefits and marginal costs.

- For each unit of output on the horizontal axis, the point directly above it on demand curve D shows how many dollars' worth of other goods and services consumers are willing to give up to obtain that unit of output. Consequently, the demand curve shows the dollar value of the marginal benefit that consumers place on each unit.

- For each unit of output on the horizontal axis, the point directly above it on supply curve S shows how many dollars' worth of other products have to be sacrificed in order to direct the underlying resources toward producing each unit of this product. Consequently, the supply curve shows the dollar value of the marginal opportunity cost of each unit.

Keeping these definitions in mind, the fact that the demand curve lies above the supply curve for every unit up to Q_e means that marginal benefit exceeds marginal cost for every one of these units. Stated slightly differently,

producing and consuming these units brings net benefits, because consumers are willing to give up more of other goods to obtain these units than must actually be forgone to produce them. Furthermore, because the supply curve includes the opportunity cost of the other goods that must be given up when resources are directed to producing these units, we can be certain that consumers prefer to have the necessary resources directed toward producing these units rather than anything else. In other words, allocative efficiency has been achieved because redirecting the necessary resources toward producing anything else would make people less happy.

The fact that pure competition yields allocative efficiency can also be understood by looking at the situation facing each individual firm in long-run equilibrium. To see this, take the market equilibrium price P that is determined in Figure 9.6b and see how it affects the behavior of the individual firm shown in Figure 9.6a. This profit-maximizing firm takes P as fixed and produces Q_f units, the output level at which $P = MC$.

By comparing the horizontal line at P with the upsloping MC curve, it is clear that for every unit up to Q_f, the price at which each unit can be sold exceeds the marginal cost of producing it. That is equivalent to saying that these units are worth more to consumers than they cost to make. Why? Because consumers are willing to forgo P dollars' worth of other goods and services when they pay P dollars for these units, but at the same time the firm only has to use less than P dollars' worth of resources to produce them. Thus, if these units are produced and consumed, there are net benefits and society comes out ahead. And, as with our previous analysis, allocative efficiency also obtains because by spending their P dollars per unit on these units rather than anything else, consumers are indicating that they would rather have the necessary resources directed toward producing these units rather than anything else.

Maximum Consumer and Producer Surplus

We confirm the existence of allocative efficiency in Figure 9.6b, where we see that pure competition maximizes the sum of the "benefit surpluses" to consumers and producers. Recall from Chapter 5 that **consumer surplus** is the difference between the maximum prices that consumers are willing to pay for a product (as shown by the demand curve) and the market price of that product. In Figure 9.6b, consumer surplus is the green triangle, which is the sum of the vertical distances between the demand curve and equilibrium price. In contrast, **producer surplus** is the difference between the minimum prices that producers are willing to accept for a product (as shown by the supply curve) and the market price of the product. Producer surplus is the sum of the vertical distances between the equilibrium price and the supply curve. Here producer surplus is the blue area.

At the equilibrium quantity Q_e, the combined amount of consumer surplus and producer surplus is maximized. Allocative efficiency occurs because, at Q_e, marginal benefit, reflected by points on the demand curve, equals marginal cost, reflected by the points on the supply curve. Alternatively, the maximum willingness of consumers to pay for unit Q_e equals the minimum acceptable price of that unit to producers. At any output less than Q_e, the sum of consumer and producer surplus—the combined size of the green and blue area—would be less than that shown. At any output greater than Q_e, an efficiency loss (deadweight loss) would subtract from the combined consumer and producer surplus shown by the green and blue area.

After long-run adjustments, pure competition produces both productive and allocative efficiency. It yields a level of output at which $P =$ MC $=$ lowest ATC, marginal benefit $=$ marginal cost, maximum willingness to pay for the last unit $=$ minimum acceptable price for that unit, and combined consumer and producer surplus are maximized.

Dynamic Adjustments

A further attribute of purely competitive markets is their ability to restore the efficiency just described when disrupted by changes in the economy. A change in consumer tastes, resource supplies, or technology will automatically set in motion the appropriate realignments of resources. For example, suppose that cucumbers and pickles become dramatically more popular. First, the demand for cucumbers will increase in the market, increasing the price of cucumbers. So, at current output, the price of cucumbers will exceed their marginal cost. At this point efficiency will be lost, but the higher price will create economic profits in the cucumber industry and stimulate its expansion. The profitability of cucumbers will permit the industry to bid resources away from now less pressing uses, say, watermelons. Expansion of the industry will end only when the supply of cucumbers has expanded such that the price of cucumbers and their marginal cost are equal—that is, when allocative efficiency has been restored.

Similarly, a change in the supply of a particular resource—for example, the field laborers who pick cucumbers—or in a production technique will upset an existing price–marginal-cost equality by either raising or lowering marginal cost. The resulting inequality of MC and P will cause producers, in either pursuing profit or avoiding loss, to reallocate resources until product supply is such that price once again equals marginal cost. In so doing, they

will correct any inefficiency in the allocation of resources that the original change may have temporarily imposed on the economy.

"Invisible Hand" Revisited

The highly efficient allocation of resources that a purely competitive economy promotes comes about because businesses and resource suppliers seek to further their self-interest. For private goods with no externalities (Chapter 5), the "invisible hand" (Chapter 2) is at work. The competitive system not only maximizes profits for individual producers but also, at the same time, creates a pattern of resource allocation that maximizes consumer satisfaction. The invisible hand thus organizes the private interests of producers in a way that is fully in sync with society's interest in using scarce resources efficiently. Striving to obtain a profit produces highly desirable economic outcomes.

Technological Advance and Competition

In explaining the model of pure competition, we assumed for simplicity that all the firms in an industry had the same cost curves. Competition, as a result, only involved entrepreneurs entering and exiting industries in response to changes in profits caused by changes in the market price. This form of competition is important, but it is just a game of copycat, because firms entering an industry simply duplicate the production methods and cost curves of existing firms in order to duplicate their above-normal profits. In this type of competition, there is no dynamism and no innovation, just more of the same.

By contrast, the most dynamic and interesting parts of competition are the fights between firms over the creation of new production technologies and new products. As we explain in detail in Web Chapter 11, firms have a strong profit incentive to develop both improved ways of making existing products as well as totally new products. To put that incentive in context, recall what you just learned about long-run equilibrium in perfect competition. When each firm in a purely competitive industry has the same productive technology and therefore the same cost structure for producing output, entry and exit assure that in the long run every firm will make the exact same normal profit.

Entrepreneurs, of course, would like to earn more than a normal profit. As a result, they are constantly attempting two different strategies for increasing their profits. The first involves attempting to lower the production costs of existing products through better technology or improved business organization. Because pure competition implies that individual firms cannot affect the market price, anything that lowers an innovating firm's production costs will result in higher profits, since the innovating firm's revenues per unit (which are equal to the market price per unit) will stay the same while its costs per unit fall due to its improved production technology.

The second strategy for earning a rate of return greater than a normal profit is to try to develop a totally new product that is popular with consumers. If a firm is first-to-market with a popular new product, it will face no competition, as it is the only producer. As long as the product remains popular and the firm remains the only producer, it will be able to charge prices that are higher than production costs, thereby allowing it to earn above-normal profits. (We say much more about this in the next chapter, which covers pure monopoly).

Notably, however, any advantages that innovative firms gain either by lowering the production costs of existing products or by introducing entirely new products will not normally persist. An innovative entrepreneur may put some of her current rivals out of business, but there are always other entrepreneurs with new ideas so that soon it may be *her* firm that is going out of business due to innovations made by others. The Consider This box below shows just how rapid the destruction and creation of new firms is.

CONSIDER THIS . . .

Running a Company Is Hard Business

The life expectancy of a U.S. business is just 10.2 years. About 9.5 percent of U.S. firms go out of business each year. In addition, 22 percent of new start-up firms go bankrupt within 2 years, 53 percent within 5 years, and nearly 65 percent within 10 years.

These numbers testify to the ability of competition to quickly dispose of firms that have high production costs or unpopular products. In a competitive environment, such firms quickly prove unprofitable and are shut down by their owners.

Balancing out the bankrupt firms are start-ups that hope to use the resources freed up by the closed firms to deliver better products or lower costs. In a typical year, more than 650,000 new businesses are started in the United States. Most of these new firms will themselves eventually fall victim to creative destruction and the pressures of competition, but one of them may just be the next Google, Starbucks, or Walmart.

Creative Destruction

The innovations that firms achieve thanks to competition are considered by many economists to be the driving force behind economic growth and rising living standards. The

> **ORIGIN OF THE IDEA**
> **O 9.2**
> Creative destruction

transformative effects of competition are often referred to as **creative destruction** to capture the idea that the creation of new products and new production methods destroys the market positions of firms committed to existing products and old ways of doing business. In addition, just the *threat* that a rival may soon come out with a new technology or product can cause other firms to innovate and thereby replace or destroy their old ways of doing business. As argued decades ago by Harvard economist Joseph Schumpeter, the most important type of competition is

> competition from the new commodity, the new technology, the new source of supply, the new type of business organization—competition which commands a decisive cost or quality advantage and which strikes not at the margins of profits of the existing firms but at their foundation and their very lives. This kind of competition is . . . so . . . important that it becomes a matter of comparative indifference whether competition in the ordinary [short-run or long-run] sense functions more or less promptly. . . .
>
> . . . competition of the kind we now have in mind acts not only when in being but also when it is merely an ever-present threat. It disciplines before it attacks. The business-man feels himself to be in a competitive situation even if he is alone in his field.[2]

There are many examples of creative destruction. In the 1800s wagons, ships, and barges were the only means of transporting freight until the railroads broke up their monopoly; the dominant market position of the railroads was, in turn, undermined by trucks and, later, by airplanes. Movies brought new competition to live theater, at one time the "only show in town." But movies were later challenged by broadcast television, which was then challenged by cable TV. Both are now challenged by Hulu, YouTube, and other online video-on-demand services. Cassettes replaced records before compact discs undermined cassettes. Now iPods, MP3 players, and Internet music downloads will soon make the compact disc obsolete. Electronic communications—including faxes and e-mails—have greatly affected the United States Postal Service. And online retailers like Amazon.com have stolen substantial business away from brick-and-mortar retailers.

---

[2]Joseph A. Schumpeter, *Capitalism, Socialism, and Democracy*, 3d ed. (New York: Harper & Row, 1950), pp. 84–85.

Word Efficiency Gains from Entry: The Case of Generic Drugs

When a Generic Drug Becomes Available, the Price of the Drug Falls, Consumer Surplus Rises, and Society Experiences an Efficiency Gain.

The competitive model predicts that entry will lower price, expand output, and increase efficiency. A good actual-economy test of this prediction occurs where entry of new producers occurs in a formerly monopolized market. Such a situation occurs when prescription drugs lose their patent protection. A patent on a prescription drug gives the pharmaceutical company that developed it an exclusive right to produce and sell the medication for 20 years from the time of patent application. Because the FDA approval process averages 8 years, the exclusive right may last for as few as 12 years. The purpose of drug patents is to encourage research and development (R&D) leading to new medications and the increased well-being they enable. With patent protection, a firm can charge prices that exceed marginal cost and average total cost and thus earn economic profits on its popular brand-name medicines. Those economic profits provide a return on past development costs and help fund more R&D.

Although competitors can and often do develop similar drugs, they cannot copy and sell the patented medication. Such drugs as Lipitor (for high cholesterol), Singulair (for allergies), and Nexium (for gastrointestinal disorders) are examples of best-selling brand-name, patented drugs.

When a patent expires, any pharmaceutical company can produce and sell the drug under the generic name for the medication. An example of a generic is metoprolol (a substitute for the brand-name drug Lopressor), a beta-blocker used to treat high blood pressure. Because such generic drugs have the same chemical composition as the branded drug, they directly compete against it. The generic price is lower than the branded price, so the price of the drug (at least on average) drops as generics claim a share of the market. Studies indicate that price drop is typically 30–40 percent. Medical insurance plans either mandate that patients buy generics or provide financial incentives to encourage them do so when generics become available. Today, generics make up about 63 percent of all prescription drugs dispensed in the United States.

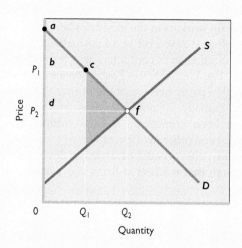

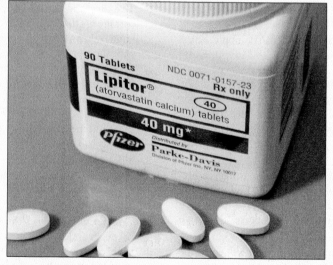

Seeing how patent expiration and the competition from generic drugs relate to consumer surplus and efficiency gains is useful. Consider the accompanying figure, which is similar to Figure 9.6b. The patent gives the firm monopoly power that allows it to charge a higher-than-competitive price. Suppose that the sole seller's profit-maximizing price is P_1. (In Chapter 10 we explain how a monopolist chooses this price.)

The expiration of the patent creates competition from generics, which reduces the price of the medication from P_1 to, say, P_2. If you compare the consumer surplus triangles above the price lines, you can see that consumer surplus rises from *bac* to *daf* when the price falls. As the price of the medication drops from P_1 to P_2, output increases from Q_1 to Q_2. In this case, the efficiency gain from competition is shown by the addition of the gray triangle. At price P_2 and quantity Q_2, the combined amounts of consumer surplus and producer surplus are at a maximum. (In reality, the price might not drop all the way to P_2 because of continued loyalty to the branded drug by prescribing physicians.)

Patents aid consumers and society by encouraging the development of new medicines that might otherwise not be available. Entry of the generics at the time of patent expiration further helps consumers by lowering prices, increasing consumer surplus, and enhancing efficiency—just like the competitive model predicts.

191

The "creative" part of "creative destruction" leads to new products and lower-cost production methods that are of great benefit to society because they allow for a more efficient use of society's scarce resources. Keep in mind, however, that the "destruction" part of "creative destruction" can be hard on workers in the industries being displaced by new technologies. A worker at a CD-making factory may see her job eliminated as consumers switch to online music downloads. The United States Postal Service cut thousands of jobs in 2010 partly because of the impact that e-mail has had on the demand for postal services. And many jobs in retail have been eliminated due to competition with Amazon.com and other online retailers.

Normally, the process of creative destruction goes slowly enough that workers at firms being downsized can transition smoothly to jobs in firms that are expanding. But sometimes the change is too swift for all of them to find new jobs easily. And in other instances, such as a town with only one major employer—like a rural coal-mining town or a small town with a large auto factory—the loss of that one major employer can be devastating because there are not enough other firms in the local area to employ the workers laid off by the major employer.

While the net effects of creative destruction are indisputably positive—including ongoing economic growth and rising living standards—creative destruction involves costs as well as benefits. And while the benefits are widespread, the costs tend to be borne almost entirely by the relatively few workers in declining industries who are not positioned to make easy transitions to new jobs.

Summary

1. In the short run, when plant and equipment are fixed, the firms in a purely competitive industry may earn profits or suffer losses. In the long run, when plant and equipment are adjustable, profits will attract new entrants, while losses will cause existing firms to leave the industry.

2. The entry or exit of firms will change industry supply. Entry or exit will continue until the market price determined by industry supply interacting with market demand generates a normal profit for firms in the industry. With firms earning a normal profit, there will be no incentive to either enter or exit the industry. This situation constitutes long-run equilibrium in a purely competitive industry.

3. Entry and exit help to improve resource allocation. Firms that exit an industry due to low profits release their resources to be used more profitably in other industries. Firms that enter an industry chasing higher profits bring with them resources that were less profitably used in other industries. Both processes increase allocative efficiency.

4. In the long run, the market price of a product will equal the minimum average total cost of production. At a higher price, economic profits would cause firms to enter the industry until those profits had been competed away. At a lower price, losses would force the exit of firms from the industry until the product price rose to equal average total cost.

5. The long-run supply curve is horizontal for a constant-cost industry, upsloping for an increasing-cost industry, and downsloping for a decreasing-cost industry.

6. The long-run equality of price and minimum average total cost means that competitive firms will use the most efficient known technology and charge the lowest price consistent with their production costs. That is, the purely competitive firms will achieve productive efficiency.

7. The long-run equality of price and marginal cost implies that resources will be allocated in accordance with consumer tastes. Allocative efficiency will occur. In the market, the combined amount of consumer surplus and producer surplus will be at a maximum.

8. The competitive price system will reallocate resources in response to a change in consumer tastes, in technology, or in resource supplies and will thereby maintain allocative efficiency over time.

9. Competition involves the never-ending attempts by entrepreneurs and managers to earn above-normal profits by either creating new products or developing lower-cost production methods for existing products. These efforts cause creative destruction, the financial undoing of the market positions of firms committed to existing products and old ways of doing business by new firms with new products and innovative ways of doing business.

Terms and Concepts

long run supply curve

constant-cost industry

increasing-cost industry

decreasing-cost industry

productive efficiency

allocative efficiency

consumer surplus

producer surplus

creative destruction

Questions

1. Explain how the long run differs from the short run in pure competition. **LO1**
2. Relate opportunity costs to why profits encourage entry into purely competitive industries and how losses encourage exit from purely competitive industries. **LO2**
3. How do the entry and exit of firms in a purely competitive industry affect resource flows and long-run profits and losses? **LO3**
4. Using diagrams for both the industry and a representative firm, illustrate competitive long-run equilibrium. Assuming constant costs, employ these diagrams to show how (a) an increase and (b) a decrease in market demand will upset that long-run equilibrium. Trace graphically and describe verbally the adjustment processes by which long-run equilibrium is restored. Now rework your analysis for increasing- and decreasing-cost industries and compare the three long-run supply curves. **LO4**
5. In long-run equilibrium, P = minimum ATC = MC. Of what significance for economic efficiency is the equality of P and minimum ATC? The equality of P and MC? Distinguish between productive efficiency and allocative efficiency in your answer. **LO5**
6. Suppose that purely competitive firms producing cashews discover that P exceeds MC. Will their combined output of cashews be too little, too much, or just right to achieve allocative efficiency? In the long run, what will happen to the supply of cashews and the price of cashews? Use a supply and demand diagram to show how that response will change the combined amount of consumer surplus and producer surplus in the market for cashews. **LO5**
7. The basic model of pure competition reviewed in this chapter finds that in the long run all firms in a purely competitive industry will earn normal profits. If all firms will only earn a normal profit in the long run, why would any firms bother to develop new products or lower-cost production methods? Explain. **LO6**
8. "Ninety percent of new products fail within two years—so you shouldn't be so eager to innovate." Do you agree? Explain why or why not. **LO6**
9. **LAST WORD** How does a generic drug differ from its brand-name, previously patented equivalent? Explain why the price of a brand-name drug typically declines when an equivalent generic drug becomes available. Explain how that drop in price affects allocative efficiency.

Problems

1. A firm in a purely competitive industry has a typical cost structure. The normal rate of profit in the economy is 5 percent. This firm is earning $5.50 on every $50 invested by its founders. What is its percentage rate of return? Is the firm earning an economic profit? If so, how large? Will this industry see entry or exit? What will be the rate of return earned by firms in this industry once the industry reaches long-run equilibrium? **LO3**
2. A firm in a purely competitive industry is currently producing 1000 units per day at a total cost of $450. If the firm produced 800 units per day, its total cost would be $300, and if it produced 500 units per day, its total cost would be $275. What are the firm's ATC per unit at these three levels of production? If every firm in this industry has the same cost structure, is the industry in long-run competitive equilibrium? From what you know about these firms' cost structures, what is the highest possible price per unit that could exist as the market price in long-run equilibrium? If that price ends up being the market price and if the normal rate of profit is 10 percent, then how big will each firm's accounting profit per unit be? **LO5**
3. There are 300 purely competitive farms in the local dairy market. Of the 300 dairy farms, 298 have a cost structure that generates profits of $24 for every $300 invested. What is their percentage rate of return? The other two dairies have a cost structure that generates profits of $22 for every $200 invested. What is their percentage rate of return? Assuming that the normal rate of profit in the economy is 10 percent, will there be entry or exit? Will the change in the number of firms affect the two that earn $22 for every $200 invested? What will be the rate of return earned by most firms in the industry in long-run equilibrium? If firms can copy each other's technology, what will be the rate of return eventually earned by all firms? **LO5**

FURTHER TEST YOUR KNOWLEDGE AT
www.mcconnell19e.com

At the text's Online Learning Center (OLC), **www.mcconnell19e.com**, you will find one or more Web-based questions that require information from the Internet to answer. We urge you to check them out; they will familiarize you with Web sites that may be helpful in other courses and perhaps even in your career. The OLC also features multiple-choice questions that give instant feedback and provides other helpful ways to further test your knowledge of the chapter.

CHAPTER 9

Pure Competition in the Long Run

This chapter discusses what happens to competitive firms in the long run as equilibrium conditions change. Over time, new firms will enter an industry that is making economic profits. As a result, product supply will increase and the price of the product will fall, thereby eroding economic profits until firms earns just a normal profit. Also, when an industry is realizing economic losses, then over time firms will exit the industry. As a consequence, product supply will decrease and the product price will increase to eliminate the economic losses and restore a normal profit for firms.

In this chapter too you will learn that the shape of the **long-run supply curve** is directly affected by the resource cost characteristics of the industry. Three possible shapes of the long-run supply curve are described and discussed: a constant-cost industry with a horizontal long-run supply curve, an increasing-cost industry with an up-sloping long-run supply curve, and a decreasing-cost industry with a down-sloping long-run supply curve.

In the long run, pure competition produces almost ideal conditions for **economic efficiency.** These ideal conditions and their qualifications are discussed in the chapter. Pure competition results in products produced in the least costly way, and thus it is *productively efficient.* Pure competition also allocates resources to firms so that they produce the products most wanted by society, and therefore it is *allocatively efficient.* You will find out that these two efficiency conditions can be expressed in the triple equality: price (and marginal revenue) = marginal cost = minimum of average total cost.

The last section of the chapter discusses competition in a broader context. It describes the role of entrepreneurs and how they can change industries and bring innovation and technological advance. Competition has transformative effects that are both creative (think new products) and at the same time destructive (think of bankrupt firms). Although this **creative destruction** has net positive benefits for society, it is not without costs.

■ CHECKLIST

When you have studied this chapter you should be able to

☐ Explain the role played by the entry and exit of firms in a purely competitive industry in achieving equilibrium in the long run.
☐ Specify three assumptions used in the chapter to reduce the complexity of the long-run analysis in pure competition.

☐ Describe the basic goal for long-run adjustments in pure competition.
☐ Explain using graphs what happens to price, profit, and output for the firm and the industry in pure competition when firms enter the industry because there are economic profits.
☐ Explain using graphs what happens to price, profit, and output for the firm and the industry in pure competition when firms exit the industry when there are economic losses.
☐ Describe the characteristics of the long-run supply curve in a constant-cost industry.
☐ State a rationale for the long-run supply curve in an increasing-cost industry.
☐ Illustrate the shape of the long-run supply curve in a decreasing-cost industry.
☐ Demonstrate with a graph the efficiency characteristics of firms and the market after long-run adjustments in pure competition.
☐ Describe the rationale and requirements for productive efficiency in pure competition.
☐ State the conditions for achieving allocative efficiency in pure competition.
☐ Explain the significance of MR (= P) = MC = minimum ATC.
☐ Describe how allocative efficiency maximizes the combined consumer and producer surplus.
☐ Discuss how pure competition makes dynamic adjustments.
☐ Describe how the "invisible hand" works in competitive markets.
☐ Explain the role of the entrepreneur and innovation in pure competition.
☐ Discuss and give examples of how creative destruction transforms industries.
☐ Explain how a fall in the price of drugs increases the consumer surplus and society experiences efficiency gains (*Last Word*).

■ CHAPTER OUTLINE

1. This chapter focuses on how the entry and exit of firms leads to long-run equilibrium in a purely competitive industry.
   a. Three assumptions are made in the chapter to simplify the analysis, but none of them affect the conclusions presented in the chapter: the only long-run adjustment is the entry and exit of firm; all firms in the

109

industry have identical costs; and the industry is a constant-cost industry.

b. The basic conclusion that is explained by the chapter is that when all long-run adjustments have been made, the price of a product will be equal to the minimum average total cost (**P = minimum ATC**) and output will occur at this level. The conclusion arises from the fact that firms want to earn profits and want to avoid losses and also the fact that firms are free to enter or exit an industry.

c. In long-run equilibrium, purely competitive firms in the industry will neither earn economic profits nor suffer economic losses.

(1) If economic profits are being received in the industry in the short run, firms will enter the industry in the long run (attracted by the profits), increase total supply, and thereby force price down to the minimum average total cost, leaving only a normal profit.

(2) If losses are being suffered in the industry in the short run, firms will leave the industry in the long run (seeking to avoid losses), reduce total supply, and thereby force price up to the minimum average total cost, leaving only a normal profit.

d. Each industry has a *long-run supply curve.* If an industry is a *constant-cost industry,* the entry of new firms will not affect the average-total-cost schedules or cost curves of firms in the industry. An increase in demand will result in no increase in the long-run equilibrium price, and the industry will be able to supply larger outputs at a constant price. Graphically, the long-run supply curve in a constant-cost industry is horizontal at the minimum of the average-total-cost curve, indicating that firms make only normal profits, but not economic profits.

e. If an industry is an *increasing-cost industry,* the entry of new firms will raise the average-total-cost schedules or curves of firms in the industry. An increase in demand will result in an increase in the long-run equilibrium price, and the industry will be able to supply larger outputs only at higher prices. Graphically, the long-run supply curve in an increasing-cost industry is up-sloping at the minimum of the average-total-cost curve, indicating that firms make only normal profits but not economic profits.

f. If an industry is a *decreasing-cost industry,* the entry of new firms will lower the average-total-cost schedules or curves of firms in the industry. An increase in demand will result in a decrease in the long-run equilibrium price, and the industry will be able to supply larger outputs only at lower prices. Graphically, the long-run supply curve in a decreasing-cost industry is down-sloping at the minimum of the average-total-cost curve, indicating that firms make only normal profits, but not economic profits.

2. In the long run, *competition* and *efficiency* compel the purely competitive firm to produce that output at a price at which marginal revenue, average cost, and marginal cost are equal and average total cost is a minimum. An economy in which all industries are purely competitive makes efficient use of its resources.

a. *Productive efficiency* requires that each good be produced in the least costly way. In the long run, competition forces firms to produce at the point of minimum average total cost and to charge a price which is just equal to those costs. Buyers benefit most from this efficiency when they are charged a price just equal to minimum average total cost (**P = minimum ATC**).

b. *Allocative efficiency* means that resources are distributed among firms such that a mix of products is produced that is most desired by society. The price of any product is society's measure of its perceived marginal benefit from consumption of the product. The marginal cost measures the relative value of the resources that were used to produce the product. Pure competition is allocatively efficient because P equals MC (**P = MC**), or society's perceived marginal benefit from the consumption of the product just equals the opportunity cost of the resources used to produce the product. When $P >$ MC, there is an *underallocation* of resources to the production of a product. When $P <$ MC, and price is less than marginal cost, there is an *overallocation* of resources to the production of a product.

c. Pure competition is allocatively efficient because it maximizes the combined consumer surplus and producer surplus. The **consumer surplus** is the difference between the maximum prices that consumers are willing to pay for a product and the market price of that product. The **producer surplus** is the difference between the minimum prices that producers are willing to accept for a product and the market price of the product. In long-run equilibrium, the maximum willingness to pay for the last unit of a product is equal to the minimum acceptable price for that unit.

d. Dynamic adjustments will occur automatically in pure competition from changes in demand, changes in resource supplies, or changes in technology. These adjustments will restore allocative efficiency. For example, if demand for a product increases, the price of the product will increase ($P >$ MC). This situation means there is an underallocation of resources to the production of the product. It will create temporary economic profits for firms in the industry. The economic profits will attract new firms to the industry to supply output. This increased supply will result in a decline in price until the equilibrium of $P =$ MC is restored.

e. The "invisible hand" is at work in a competitive market system by organizing the private interests of producers that will help achieve society's interest in the efficient allocation and use of scarce resources.

3. So far the assumption has been that firms in an industry have identical cost curves. This condition implies that the only change to a purely competitive industry comes from the entry or exit of firms and there is no technological change or innovation. From a broader perspective, however, industries are changed by competition. Entrepreneurs will try to earn more than the normal profit earned in pure competition either by lowering the cost of production with new production methods or by developing new products for which they are the unique producers. These actions, however, will eventually stimulate competition from other firms that adopt the new production methods or develop competing products, so that in the long run with competition the above normal profit will not persist.

a. Competition has transformative effects for firms and industries through a process described by economist Joseph Schumpeter as *creative destruction*. Firms are "creative" in the sense that they develop new production methods and new products. In the long run, these new products and methods cause "destruction" in the sense that firms go bankrupt and workers lose their jobs in dying industries. There are net benefits to society from this transformative process arising from competition, but there are costs imposed on particular industries and their workers. There are many examples of creative destruction throughout economic history (the railroads displacing barges and canals) and in more recent times (e-mail undermining the use of regular mail).

4. (*Last Word*). The competitive model predicts that when there are new entrants into a previously monopolized market, prices will fall, output will increase, and efficiency will improve. Such is the case in the drug market when a drug patent expires and the drug can be produced as a generic. Generic drugs are cheaper for consumers. The decline in price for these drugs compared with the patented versions boosts output and increases the consumer surplus.

■ HINTS AND TIPS

1. The average purely competitive firm in long-run equilibrium will not make economic profits. Find out why by following the graphical analysis in Figures 9.1 and 9.2.

2. The triple equality of MR (= P) = MC = minimum ATC is the most important equation in the chapter because it allows you to judge the allocative and productive efficiency of a purely competitive economy. Check your understanding of this triple equality by explaining what happens to productive efficiency when $P >$ minimum ATC, or to allocative efficiency when $P < $ MC or $P >$ MC.

■ IMPORTANT TERMS

long-run supply curve
constant-cost industry
increasing-cost industry
decreasing-cost industry
productive efficiency
allocative efficiency
consumer surplus
producer surplus

SELF-TEST

■ FILL-IN QUESTIONS

1. The entry and exit of firms in a purely competitive market can only occur in the (short run, long run) _____. In the short run, the industry is composed of a specific number of firms, each with a plant size

that is (fixed, variable) _____, but in the long run the number of firms is _____.

2. State three assumptions about profit maximization in the long run to keep the analysis simple in this chapter.

a. _____

b. _____

c. _____

3. After all long-run adjustments are made in a purely competitive industry, product price will be equal to, and production will occur at, each firm's minimum average (variable, total) _____ cost because firms (shut down production, seek profits) _____ and firms are free to (enter or exit, raise prices or lower prices) _____ in an industry.

4. An industry will be in long-run equilibrium when firms are earning (normal, economic) _____ profits, which means that the firms are earning what they could be earning elsewhere in the economy and there (is, is not) _____ an incentive for change.

5. When a purely competitive industry is in long-run equilibrium, the price that the individual firm is paid for its product is equal to (total, marginal) _____ revenue and its _____ cost. Also in this case the long-run average total cost for the firm is at a (maximum, minimum) _____.

6. New firms will enter an industry In the long run if the existing firms in the industry are earning (accounting, economic) _____ profits. As new firms enter, the market supply of the product will (decrease, increase) _____ and this change will _____ the market price until it is equal to minimum long-run average total cost.

7. Existing firms will leave an industry in the long run if they are realizing economic (profits, losses) _____. As firms leave the industry, the market supply of the product will (decrease, increase) _____ and this change will _____ the market price until it is equal to minimum long-run average total cost.

8. If the entry of new firms into an industry does not change the costs of all firms in the industry, the industry is said to be (a constant-, an increasing-, a decreasing-) _____ cost industry. Its long-run supply curve is (horizontal, down-sloping, up-sloping) _____.

9. If the entry of new firms into an industry raises costs of all firms in the industry, the industry is said to be (a constant-, an increasing-, a decreasing-) _____ cost industry. Its long-run supply curve is (horizontal, down-sloping, up-sloping) _____.

10. If the entry of new firms into an industry lowers costs of all firms in the industry, the industry is said to be (a constant-, an increasing-, a decreasing-) _____ cost industry. Its long-run supply curve is (horizontal, down-sloping, up-sloping) _____.

11. The purely competitive economy achieves productive efficiency in the long run because price and average (variable, total) _____ cost are equal and the latter is at a (maximum, minimum) _____.

12. In the long run the purely competitive economy is allocatively efficient because price and (total, marginal) _____ cost are equal and it implies that resources will be allocated according to the "tastes and preferences" of (producers, consumers) _____.

13. Another way to think about allocative efficiency is that it occurs because, at the equilibrium level of output, the marginal benefit to consumers, as reflected by points on the (supply, demand) _____ curve, equal marginal cost for producers, as reflected by the points on the _____ curve.

14. Consumer surplus is the difference between the (minimum, maximum) _____ prices that consumers are willing to pay for a product and the market price of that product whereas producer surplus is the difference between the _____ prices that producers are willing to accept for a product and the market price of a product. At the long-run equilibrium level of output, the (minimum, maximum) _____ willingness to pay for the last unit is just equal to the _____ acceptable price for that unit so that the combined consumer and producer surplus is at a _____.

15. One of the attributes of purely competitive markets is their ability to restore (surplus, efficiency) _____ when disrupted by changes in the economy. If the demand for a product increases, this change will (increase, decrease) _____ price so that it is greater than marginal cost. This situation in turn will (increase, decrease) _____ profits and give incentive to expand supply so that price will _____ and return to an equilibrium where price is equal to marginal cost.

16. The "invisible hand" also operates in a competitive market system because it (maximizes, minimizes) _____ the profits of individual producers and at the same time the system creates a pattern of resource allocation that _____ consumer satisfaction.

17. The model of pure competition used in this chapter assumed that all firms in the industry had the same cost curves and production technology, so as a result, firms entering an industry just duplicate the production methods

of other firms, so there (is, is no) _____ innovation and there _____ dynamism. Entries and exits of firms in pure competition will ensure that every firm will make the same (normal, economic) _____ profit in the long run.

18. An entrepreneur will improve production methods to earn more than a(n) (normal, economic) _____ profit typically earned by firms in pure competition. A successful new method of production will reduce the firm's cost, and if revenues stay the same, the firm will earn a(n) (normal, economic) _____ profit for a while; but if other firms copy those production methods and increase production eventually there will be return to a(n) _____ profit typically earned by firms.

19. A second strategy for an entrepreneur trying to earn more than a (normal, economic) _____ profit typically earned by firms in pure competition would be to develop a new product that is popular with consumers. If the product is successful, then the firm will be able to earn a(n) _____ profit for a while; but, when other firms develop similar products, then eventually there will be a return to a(n) _____ profit typically earned by firms.

20. The dynamism and change arising from competition and the search for economic profit is often referred to as creative (construction, destruction) _____, where the creative part leads to new products and lower-cost production methods and the _____ part leads to the loss of jobs and bankruptcy of businesses.

■ **TRUE–FALSE QUESTIONS**

Circle T if the statement is true, F if it is false.

1. In the long run in pure competition, economic profits will attract new firms to enter an industry, while economic losses will cause existing firms to leave an industry. **T F**

2. The long-run equilibrium for firms in pure competition is for marginal revenue to equal marginal cost (MR = MC) and for price to equal the minimum of average total cost. **T F**

3. When there is long-run equilibrium in pure competition, the normal profit is zero for the existing firms. **T F**

4. The existence of economic profits in an industry will attract new firms to enter an industry. **T F**

5. When new firms enter a purely competitive industry it will lead to an increase in market demand. **T F**

6. As new firms enter a purely competitive industry with economic profits, product price for the typical firm will decrease until eventually price equals marginal cost at the minimum of average total cost. **T F**

7. When there are economic losses in a purely competitive industry, some of the existing firms will exit the industry. **T F**

8. When firms in a purely competitive industry are earning profits that are less than normal, the supply of the product will eventually decrease. **T F**

9. As firms experiencing economic losses exit a purely competitive industry, product price for the typical firm will decrease until eventually price equals marginal cost and the minimum of average total cost. **T F**

10. In a constant-cost industry in pure competition, an expansion of the industry will increase resource prices. **T F**

11. The long-run supply curve for a constant-cost industry in pure competition is horizontal. **T F**

12. In an increasing-cost industry in pure competition, an expansion of the industry will increase resource prices. **T F**

13. The long-run supply curve for an increasing-cost industry in pure competition is downsloping. **T F**

14. In a decreasing-cost industry in pure competition, an expansion of the industry will decrease resource prices. **T F**

15. The long-run supply curve for a decreasing-cost industry in pure competition is vertical. **T F**

16. Assuming a constant- or increasing-cost industry, the final long-run equilibrium positions of all firms have the same basic efficiency characteristics: $P > \text{MC} > \text{ATC}$. **T F**

17. Under conditions of pure competition, firms achieve productive efficiency by producing in the least costly way. **T F**

18. In the long run, pure competition forces firm to produce at the minimum average total cost of production and to charge a price that is just consistent with the cost. **T F**

19. In a purely competitive market, product price measures the marginal benefit, or additional satisfaction, that society obtains from producing additional units of the product. **T F**

20. In pure competition, allocative efficiency is achieved when product price is greater than marginal cost. **T F**

21. Pure competition minimizes the combined consumer and producer surplus. **T F**

22. A major attribute of pure competition is the ability to restore productive and allocative efficiency when it is disrupted by changes in the economy. **T F**

23. The "invisible hand" of the competitive market system organizes the private interests of producers in a way that complements society's interest in the efficient use of scarce resources. **T F**

24. With pure competition any advantage that innovative firms gain by either lowering production costs or by introducing new products will not persist over time. **T F**

25. Creative destruction is the concept that the creation of new products and new production methods are beneficial for society, but that it also leads to the destruction of jobs, businesses, and even industries. **T F**

■ **MULTIPLE-CHOICE QUESTIONS**

Circle the letter that corresponds to the best answer.

1. Pure competition in the long run in an industry is most affected by
  (a) the fixed costs of firms
  (b) the normal profit of firms
  (c) the entry and exit of firms
  (d) the identical costs of firms

2. For a purely competitive firm in long-run equilibrium,
  (a) MR = MC = minimum ATC
  (b) MR = MC = maximum ATC
  (c) $P > \text{MR} > \text{ATC}$
  (d) MR > MC

3. Assume that the market for wheat is purely competitive. Currently, firms growing wheat are experiencing economic losses. In the long run, we can expect this market's
  (a) supply curve to increase
  (b) demand curve to increase
  (c) supply curve to decrease
  (d) demand curve to decrease

Use the two graphs below to answer questions 4, 5, 6, and 7. Graph A represents a typical firm in a purely competitive industry. Graph B represents the supply and demand conditions in that industry. Assume that the marginal cost curve is an up-sloping curve that intersects ATC at its minimum.

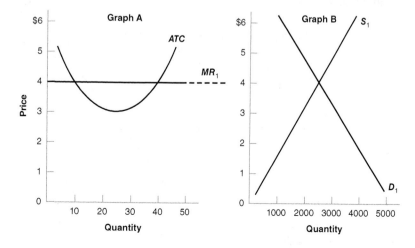

4. If the price of the product in this industry is $4, the typical firm in this industry is
  (a) earning a normal profit
  (b) earning an economic profit
  (c) realizing an economic loss
  (d) breaking even

5. Given the economic conditions shown in the graphs, what is most likely to occur in graph B?
  (a) Firms will exit the industry and the demand curve will shift to the left.
  (b) Firms will enter the industry and the supply curve will shift to the right.
  (c) Firms will exit the industry and the supply curve will shift to the right.
  (d) Firms will enter the industry and the demand curve will shift to the right.

6. As this industry moves toward long-run equilibrium, the market price will
  (a) increase and the marginal revenue for the firm will decrease
  (b) decrease and the marginal revenue for the firm will increase
  (c) decrease and the marginal revenue for the firm will decrease
  (d) increase and the marginal revenue for the firm will increase

7. Long-run equilibrium will be restored in this industry when
  (a) product price and marginal revenue fall to $3
  (b) product price and marginal revenue fall to $2
  (c) product price and marginal revenue rise to $5
  (d) product price and marginal revenue remain at $4

Use the two graphs below to answer questions 8, 9, 10, and 11. Graph A represents a typical firm in a purely competitive industry. Graph B represents the supply and demand conditions in that industry. Assume that the marginal cost curve is an up-sloping curve that intersects ATC at its minimum.

8. If the price of the product in this industry is $3, the typical firm in this industry is
  (a) earning a normal profit
  (b) earning an economic profit
  (c) realizing an economic loss
  (d) breaking even

9. Given the economic conditions shown in the graphs, what is most likely to occur?
  (a) Demand will increase as firms will exit the industry.
  (b) Supply will increase as firms enter the industry.
  (c) Supply will decrease as firms exit the industry.
  (d) Demand will decrease as firms exit the industry.

10. As this industry moves to long-run equilibrium, the market price will
  (a) increase and the marginal revenue for the firm will decrease
  (b) decrease and the marginal revenue for the firm will increase
  (c) decrease and the marginal revenue for the firm will decrease
  (d) increase and the marginal revenue for the firm will increase

11. Long-run equilibrium will be restored in this industry when
  (a) product price and marginal revenue fall to $2
  (b) product price and marginal revenue rise to $5
  (c) product price and marginal revenue rise to $4
  (d) product price and marginal revenue remain at $3

12. The long-run supply curve under pure competition will be
  (a) down-sloping in an increasing-cost industry and up-sloping in a decreasing-cost industry
  (b) horizontal in a constant-cost industry and up-sloping in a decreasing-cost industry
  (c) horizontal in a constant-cost industry and up-sloping in an increasing-cost industry
  (d) up-sloping in an increasing-cost industry and vertical in a constant-cost industry

13. The long-run supply curve in a constant-cost industry will be
  (a) perfectly elastic
  (b) perfectly inelastic
  (c) unit-elastic
  (d) income elastic

14. In a decreasing-cost industry, the long-run
  (a) demand curve would be perfectly inelastic
  (b) demand curve would be perfectly elastic
  (c) supply curve would be up-sloping
  (d) supply curve would be down-sloping

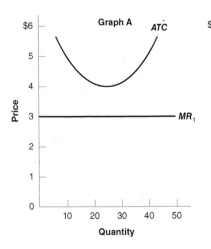

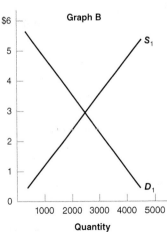

15. Increasing-cost industries find that their costs rise as a consequence of an increased demand for their product because of

(a) the diseconomies of scale
(b) diminishing returns
(c) higher resource prices
(d) a decreased supply of the product

16. When a purely competitive industry is in long-run equilibrium, which statement is true?

(a) Firms in the industry are earning normal profits.
(b) Price and long-run average total cost are not equal to each other.
(c) Marginal cost is at its minimum level.
(d) Marginal cost is equal to total revenue.

17. Which triple identity results in the most efficient use of resources?

(a) $P = MC =$ minimum ATC
(b) $P = AR = MR$
(c) $P = MR =$ minimum MC
(d) $TR = MC = MR$

18. An economy is producing the goods most wanted by society when, for each and every good, its

(a) price and average cost are equal
(b) price and marginal cost are equal
(c) marginal revenue and marginal cost are equal
(d) price and marginal revenue are equal

Answer questions 19, 20, 21, and 22 on the basis of the following supply and demand graph.

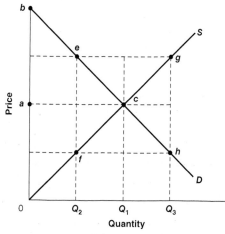

19. The area of consumer surplus would be shown by the area

(a) 0bc
(b) 0ac
(c) abc
(d) cef

20. The area of producer surplus would be shown by the area

(a) 0bc
(b) 0ac
(c) abc
(d) cgh

21. The area that maximizes the combined consumer surplus and producer surplus would be shown by the area

(a) 0bc
(b) 0ac

(c) abc
(d) efgh

22. Allocative efficiency occurs at Q_1 because marginal benefit, reflected in points on the

(a) demand curve equal price as reflected by the points on the supply curve
(b) supply curve equal marginal cost as reflected by the points on the demand curve
(c) demand curve equal marginal cost as reflected by the points on the supply curve
(d) supply curve equal minimum average cost as reflected by the points on the supply curve

23. If there is an increase in demand for a product in a purely competitive industry, it results in a dynamic adjustment in which there is an industry

(a) contraction that will end when the price of the product is greater than its marginal cost
(b) contraction that will end when the price of the product is equal to its marginal cost
(c) expansion that will end when the price of the product is greater than its marginal cost
(d) expansion that will end when the price of the product is equal to its marginal cost

24. The idea of the "invisible hand" operating in the competitive market system means that

(a) there is a unity of private and social interests that promotes efficiency
(b) the industries in this system are described as decreasing-cost industries
(c) there is an overallocation of resources to the production of goods and services
(d) productive efficiency is more important than allocative efficiency

25. The elimination of the market positions of firms and their products by new firms with new products and innovative ways of doing business would be most closely associated with the concept of

(a) consumer surplus
(b) producer surplus
(c) creative destruction
(d) an increasing-cost industry

■ **PROBLEMS**

1. If the average total costs assumed for the individual firm below were long-run average total costs and if the industry were a constant-cost industry,

Output	ATC	MC
1	$400	$100
2	225	50
3	170	60
4	148	80
5	140	110
6	140	140
7	146	180
8	156	230
9	171	290
10	190	360

a. what would be the market price of the product in the long run? $ _____

b. what output would each firm produce when the industry was in long-run equilibrium? _____

c. approximately how many firms would there be in the industry in the long run, given the present demand for the product as shown in the table below?

_____

Quantity demanded	Price	Quantity supplied
400	$360	1000
500	290	900
600	230	800
700	180	700
800	140	600
900	110	500
1000	80	400

d. if the following table were the market demand schedule for the product, how many firms would there be in the long run in the industry? _____

Price	Quantity demanded
$360	500
290	600
230	700
180	800
140	900
110	1000
80	1100

2. On the following graph, draw a long-run supply curve of
  a. a constant-cost industry
  b. an increasing-cost industry
  c. a decreasing-cost industry

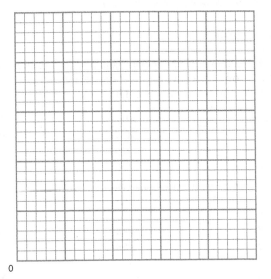

0

■ **SHORT ANSWER AND ESSAY QUESTIONS**

1. What are the important distinctions between the short run and the long run and between equilibrium in the short run and in the long run in a competitive industry?

2. When is the purely competitive industry in long-run equilibrium? What forces the purely competitive firm into this position?

3. Assume that a firm is in a purely competitive industry. Assume that the demand for the product increases and it increases the product price. Describe what happens over time to industry supply and product price. What happens to the firm's profit? What will the economic conditions be when long-run equilibrium is restored?

4. Assume that a firm is in a purely competitive industry. Assume that the demand for the product decreases and it decreases the product price. Describe what happens over time to industry supply and product price. What happens to the firm's profits? What will the economic conditions be when long-run equilibrium is restored?

5. What is a constant-cost industry? Explain what happens in this industry when demand increases or decreases.

6. What is an increasing-cost industry? Why will costs increase in this industry?

7. What is a decreasing-cost industry? Why will costs decrease in this industry?

8. What is the triple equality as it relates to economic efficiency and what two things does it tell us?

9. Explain the conditions for productive efficiency in an economy.

10. Describe the conditions for allocative efficiency. Why is it said that a purely competitive economy is an efficient economy?

11. What is the relationship between demand and supply curves and allocative efficiency?

12. Explain how pure competition maximizes consumer and producer surpluses.

13. How does a purely competitive economy eliminate an overallocation for resources for the production of a product and correct for an underallocation?

14. Explain how dynamic adjustments are made in pure competition as a result of changes in demand for a product or the supply of a resource.

15. In what way does an "invisible hand" work to ensure an efficient allocation of society's scare resources?

16. Describe how entrepreneurs affect profits by improving production methods. What happens in the long run to these changes in pure competition?

17. What role does innovation play in fostering competition? Explain what occurs in the long run to new products or innovations that create economic profit.

18. Why is running a company a hard business?

19. Describe the concept of creative destruction. How does it create and how does it destroy?

20. Give examples of creative destruction activity in the past and in recent years.

ANSWERS

Chapter 9 Pure Competition in the Long Run

FILL-IN QUESTIONS

1. long run, fixed, variable
2. *a.* only entry and exits affects long-run adjustments; *b.* firms in the industry have identical costs; *c.* the industry is a constant-cost industry
3. total, seek profit, enter or exit
4. normal, is not
5. economic, increase, decrease
6. marginal, marginal, minimum
7. losses, decrease, increase
8. a constant-, horizontal
9. an increasing-, up-sloping
10. a decreasing-, down-sloping
11. total, minimum
12. marginal, consumers
13. demand, supply
14. maximum, minimum, maximum, minimum, maximum
15. efficiency, increase, increase, decrease
16. maximizes, maximizes
17. is no, is no, normal
18. normal, economic, normal
19. normal, economic, normal
20. destruction, destruction

TRUE–FALSE QUESTIONS

1. T, p. 182
2. T, p. 182
3. F, p. 182
4. T, p. 182
5. F, pp. 182–183
6. T, pp. 182–183
7. T, pp. 183–184
8. T, p. 183
9. F, pp. 182–183
10. F, p. 184
11. T, p. 184
12. T, p. 185
13. F, p. 185
14. T, pp. 185–186
15. F, pp. 185–186
16. F, pp. 186–187
17. T, pp. 186–187
18. T, p. 187
19. T, p. 188
20. F, p. 188
21. F, pp. 188–189
22. T, p. 189
23. T, p. 189
24. T, p. 190
25. T, pp. 190–191

MULTIPLE-CHOICE QUESTIONS

1. c, p. 182
2. a, pp. 182, 186
3. c, pp. 183–184
4. b, p. 183
5. b, p. 183
6. c, p. 183
7. a, p. 183
8. c, pp. 183–184
9. c, pp. 183–184
10. d, pp. 183–184
11. c, p. 183
12. c, pp. 184–186
13. a, p. 184
14. d, pp. 185–186
15. c, p. 185
16. a, p. 182
17. a, p. 186
18. b, p. 188
19. c, pp. 188–189
20. b, pp. 188–189
21. a, pp. 188–189
22. c, p. 189
23. d, p. 189
24. a, p. 189
25. c, pp. 190, 192

PROBLEMS

1. *a.* 140; *b.* 6; *c.* 133 = 800 [the total quantity demanded at $140 divided by 6 (the output of each firm)]; *d.* 150 = 900 divided by 6
2. *a.* The curve is a horizontal line (see Figure 9.3 in the text); *b.* the curve slopes upward (see Figure 9.4 in the text); *c.* the curve slopes downward (see Figure 9.5 in the text)

SHORT ANSWER AND ESSAY QUESTIONS

1. pp. 181–182
2. p. 182
3. pp. 182–183
4. pp. 182–183
5. pp. 184–185
6. pp. 184–185
7. p. 185
8. p. 186
9. p. 187
10. p. 188
11. p. 188
12. pp. 188–189
13. pp. 188–189
14. p. 189
15. p. 189
16. pp. 189–190
17. p. 190
18. p. 190
19. pp. 190, 192
20. pp. 190, 192

10

AFTER READING THIS CHAPTER, YOU SHOULD BE ABLE TO:

1 List the characteristics of pure monopoly.

2 Explain how a pure monopoly sets its profit-maximizing output and price.

3 Discuss the economic effects of monopoly.

4 Describe why a monopolist might prefer to charge different prices in different markets.

5 Distinguish between the monopoly price, the socially optimal price, and the fair-return price of a government-regulated monopoly.

Pure Monopoly

We turn now from pure competition to pure monopoly, which is at the opposite end of the spectrum of industry structures listed in Table 8.1. You deal with monopolies more often than you might think. If you see the logo for Microsoft's Windows on your computer, you are dealing with a monopoly (or, at least, a near-monopoly). When you purchase certain prescription drugs, you are buying monopolized products. When you make a local telephone call, turn on your lights, or subscribe to cable TV, you may be patronizing a monopoly, depending on your location.

What precisely do we mean by pure monopoly, and what conditions enable it to arise and survive? How does a pure monopolist determine its profit-maximizing price and output? Does a pure monopolist achieve the efficiency associated with pure competition? If not, what, if anything, should the government do about it? A simplified model of pure monopoly will help us answer these questions. It will be the first of three models of imperfect competition.

An Introduction to Pure Monopoly

Pure monopoly exists when a single firm is the sole producer of a product for which there are no close substitutes. Here are the main characteristics of pure monopoly:

- *Single seller* A pure, or absolute, monopoly is an industry in which a single firm is the sole producer of a specific good or the sole supplier of a service; the firm and the industry are synonymous.
- *No close substitutes* A pure monopoly's product is unique in that there are no close substitutes. The consumer who chooses not to buy the monopolized product must do without it.
- *Price maker* The pure monopolist controls the total quantity supplied and thus has considerable control over price; it is a *price maker* (unlike a pure competitor, which has no such control and therefore is a *price taker*). The pure monopolist confronts the usual downsloping product demand curve. It can change its product price by changing the quantity of the product it produces. The monopolist will use this power whenever it is advantageous to do so.
- *Blocked entry* A pure monopolist has no immediate competitors because certain barriers keep potential competitors from entering the industry. Those barriers may be economic, technological, legal, or of some other type. But entry is totally blocked in pure monopoly.
- *Nonprice competition* The product produced by a pure monopolist may be either standardized (as with natural gas and electricity) or differentiated (as with Windows or Frisbees). Mo-

ORIGIN OF THE IDEA

O 10.1

Monopoly

nopolists that have standardized products engage mainly in public relations advertising, whereas those with differentiated products sometimes advertise their products' attributes.

Examples of Monopoly

Examples of *pure* monopoly are relatively rare, but there are many examples of less pure forms. In most cities, government-owned or government-regulated public utilities—natural gas and electric companies, the water company, the cable TV company, and the local telephone company—are all monopolies or virtually so.

There are also many "near-monopolies" in which a single firm has the bulk of sales in a specific market. Intel, for example, produces 80 percent of the central microprocessors used in personal computers. First Data Corporation, via its Western Union subsidiary, accounts for 80 percent of the market for money order transfers. Brannock Device Company has an 80 percent market share of the shoe sizing devices found in shoe stores. Wham-O, through its Frisbee brand, sells 90 percent of plastic throwing disks. The De Beers diamond syndicate effectively controls 55 percent of the world's supply of rough-cut diamonds (see this chapter's Last Word).

Professional sports teams are, in a sense, monopolies because they are the sole suppliers of specific services in large geographic areas. With a few exceptions, a single major-league team in each sport serves each large American city. If you want to see a live Major League Baseball game in St. Louis or Seattle, you must patronize the Cardinals or the Mariners, respectively. Other geographic monopolies exist. For example, a small town may be served by only one airline or railroad. In a small, isolated community, the local barber shop, dry cleaner, or grocery store may approximate a monopoly.

Of course, there is almost always some competition. Satellite television is a substitute for cable, and amateur softball is a substitute for professional baseball. The Linux operating system can substitute for Windows, and so on. But such substitutes are typically either more costly or in some way less appealing.

Dual Objectives of the Study of Monopoly

Monopoly is worth studying both for its own sake and because it provides insights about the more common market structures of monopolistic competition and oligopoly (Chapter 11). These two market structures combine, in differing degrees, characteristics of pure competition and pure monopoly.

Barriers to Entry

The factors that prohibit firms from entering an industry are called **barriers to entry.** In pure monopoly, strong barriers to entry effectively block all potential competition. Somewhat weaker barriers may permit oligopoly, a market structure dominated by a few firms. Still weaker barriers may permit the entry of a fairly large number of competing firms giving rise to monopolistic competition. And the absence of any effective entry barriers permits the entry of a very large number of firms, which provide the basis of pure competition. So barriers to entry are pertinent not only to the extreme case of pure monopoly but also to other market structures in which there are monopoly-like characteristics or monopoly-like behaviors.

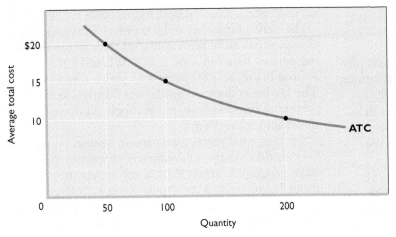

FIGURE 10.1 **Economies of scale: the natural monopoly case.** A declining long-run average-total-cost curve over a wide range of output quantities indicates extensive economies of scale. A single monopoly firm can produce, say, 200 units of output at lower cost ($10 each) than could two or more firms that had a combined output of 200 units.

We now discuss the four most prominent barriers to entry.

Economies of Scale

Modern technology in some industries is such that economies of scale—declining average total cost with added firm size—are extensive. In such cases, a firm's long-run average-cost schedule will decline over a wide range of output. Given market demand, only a few large firms or, in the extreme, only a single large firm can achieve low average total costs.

Figure 10.1 indicates economies of scale over a wide range of outputs. If total consumer demand is within that output range, then only a single producer can satisfy demand at least cost. Note, for example, that a monopolist can produce 200 units at a per-unit cost of $10 and a total cost of $2000. If the industry has two firms and each produces 100 units, the unit cost is $15 and total cost rises to $3000 (= 200 units × $15). A still more competitive situation with four firms each producing 50 units would boost unit and total cost to $20 and $4000, respectively. Conclusion: When long-run ATC is declining, only a single producer, a monopolist, can produce any particular output at minimum total cost.

If a pure monopoly exists in such an industry, economies of scale will serve as an entry barrier and will protect the monopolist from competition. New firms that try to enter the industry as small-scale producers cannot realize the cost economies of the monopolist. They therefore will be undercut and forced out of business by the monopolist, which can sell at a much lower price and still make a profit because of its lower per-unit cost associated with its economies of scale. A new firm might try to start out big, that is, to enter the industry as a large-scale producer so as to achieve the necessary economies of scale. But the massive plant facilities required would necessitate huge amounts of financing, which a new and untried enterprise would find difficult to secure. In most cases the financial obstacles and risks to "starting big" are prohibitive. This explains why efforts to enter such industries as computer operating software, commercial aircraft, and basic steel are so rare.

A monopoly firm is referred to as a *natural monopoly* if the market demand curve intersects the long-run ATC curve at any point where average total costs are declining. If a natural monopoly were to set its price where market demand intersects long-run ATC, its price would be lower than if the industry were more competitive. But it will probably set a higher price. As with any monopolist, a natural monopolist may, instead, set its price far above ATC and obtain substantial economic profit. In that event, the lowest-unit-cost advantage of a natural monopolist would accrue to the monopolist as profit and not as lower prices to consumers. That is why the government regulates some natural monopolies, specifying the price they may charge. We will say more about that later.

ORIGIN OF THE IDEA
O 10.2
Natural monopoly

Legal Barriers to Entry: Patents and Licenses

Government also creates legal barriers to entry by awarding patents and licenses.

Patents A *patent* is the exclusive right of an inventor to use, or to allow another to use, her or his invention. Patents and patent laws aim to protect the inventor from rivals who would use the invention without having shared in the effort and expense of developing it. At the same time, patents provide the inventor with a monopoly position for the life of the patent. The world's nations have agreed on a uniform patent length of 20 years from the time of application. Patents have figured prominently in the growth of modern-day giants such as IBM, Pfizer, Intel, Xerox, General Electric, and DuPont.

Research and development (R&D) is what leads to most patentable inventions and products. Firms that gain monopoly power through their own research or by purchasing the patents of others can use patents to strengthen their market position. The profit from one patent can finance the research required to develop new patentable products. In the pharmaceutical industry, patents on prescription drugs have produced large monopoly profits that have helped finance the discovery of new patentable medicines. So monopoly power achieved through patents may well be self-sustaining, even though patents eventually expire and generic drugs then compete with the original brand.

Licenses Government may also limit entry into an industry or occupation through *licensing*. At the national level, the Federal Communications Commission licenses only so many radio and television stations in each geographic area. In many large cities one of a limited number of municipal licenses is required to drive a taxicab. The consequent restriction of the supply of cabs creates economic profit for cab owners and drivers. New cabs cannot enter the industry to drive down prices and profits. In a few instances the government might "license" itself to provide some product and thereby create a public monopoly. For example, in some states only state-owned retail outlets can sell liquor. Similarly, many states have "licensed" themselves to run lotteries.

Ownership or Control of Essential Resources

A monopolist can use private property as an obstacle to potential rivals. For example, a firm that owns or controls a resource essential to the production process can prohibit the entry of rival firms. At one time the International Nickel Company of Canada (now called Inco) controlled 90 percent of the world's known nickel reserves. A local firm may own all the nearby deposits of sand and gravel. And it is very difficult for new sports leagues to be created because existing professional sports leagues have contracts with the best players and have long-term leases on the major stadiums and arenas.

Pricing and Other Strategic Barriers to Entry

Even if a firm is not protected from entry by, say, extensive economies of scale or ownership of essential resources, entry may effectively be blocked by the way the monopolist responds to attempts by rivals to enter the industry. Confronted with a new entrant, the monopolist may "create an entry barrier" by slashing its price, stepping up its advertising, or taking other strategic actions to make it difficult for the entrant to succeed.

Examples of entry deterrence: In 2005 Dentsply, the dominant American maker of false teeth (70 percent market share) was found to have unlawfully precluded independent distributors of false teeth from carrying competing brands. The lack of access to the distributors deterred potential foreign competitors from entering the U.S. market. As another example, in 2001 a U.S. court of appeals upheld a lower court's finding that Microsoft used a series of illegal actions to maintain its monopoly in Intel-compatible PC operating systems (95 percent market share). One such action was charging higher prices for its Windows operating system to computer manufacturers that featured Netscape's Navigator rather than Microsoft's Internet Explorer.

Monopoly Demand

Now that we have explained the sources of monopoly, we want to build a model of pure monopoly so that we can analyze its price and output decisions. Let's start by making three assumptions:

- Patents, economies of scale, or resource ownership secure the firm's monopoly.
- No unit of government regulates the firm.
- The firm is a single-price monopolist; it charges the same price for all units of output.

The crucial difference between a pure monopolist and a purely competitive seller lies on the demand side of the market. The purely competitive seller faces a perfectly elastic demand at the price determined by market supply and demand. It is a price taker that can sell as much or as little as it wants at the going market price. Each additional unit sold will add the amount of the constant product price to the firm's total revenue. That means that marginal revenue for the competitive seller is constant and equal to product price. (Refer to the table and graph in Figure 8.1 for price, marginal-revenue, and total-revenue relationships for the purely competitive firm.)

The demand curve for the monopolist (and for any imperfectly competitive seller) is quite different from that of the pure competitor. Because the pure monopolist *is* the industry, its demand curve *is* the market demand curve. And because market demand is not perfectly elastic, the monopolist's demand curve is downsloping. Columns 1 and 2 in Table 10.1 illustrate this concept. Note that quantity demanded increases as price decreases.

TABLE 10.1 Revenue and Cost Data of a Pure Monopolist

	Revenue Data				Cost Data		
(1) Quantity of Output	(2) Price (Average Revenue)	(3) Total Revenue, (1) × (2)	(4) Marginal Revenue	(5) Average Total Cost	(6) Total Cost, (1) × (5)	(7) Marginal Cost	(8) Profit [+] or Loss [−]
0	$172	$ 0			$ 100		$−100
1	162	162	$162	$190.00	190	$ 90	−28
2	152	304	142	135.00	270	80	+34
3	142	426	122	113.33	340	70	+86
4	132	528	102	100.00	400	60	+128
5	122	610	82	94.00	470	70	+140
6	112	672	62	91.67	550	80	+122
7	102	714	42	91.43	640	90	+74
8	92	736	22	93.75	750	110	−14
9	82	738	2	97.78	880	130	−142
10	72	720	−18	103.00	1030	150	−310

In Figure 8.7 we drew separate demand curves for the purely competitive industry and for a single firm in such an industry. But only a single demand curve is needed in pure monopoly because the firm and the industry are one and the same. We have graphed part of the demand data in Table 10.1 as demand curve *D* in Figure 10.2. This is the monopolist's demand curve *and* the market demand curve. The downsloping demand curve has three implications that are essential to understanding the monopoly model.

FIGURE 10.2 Price and marginal revenue in pure monopoly. A pure monopolist, or any other imperfect competitor with a downsloping demand curve such as *D*, must set a lower price in order to sell more output. Here, by charging $132 rather than $142, the monopolist sells an extra unit (the fourth unit) and gains $132 from that sale. But from this gain must be subtracted $30, which reflects the $10 less the monopolist charged for each of the first 3 units. Thus, the marginal revenue of the fourth unit is $102 (= $132 − $30), considerably less than its $132 price.

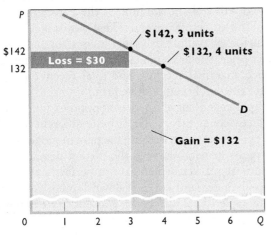

Marginal Revenue Is Less Than Price

With a fixed downsloping demand curve, the pure monopolist can increase sales only by charging a lower price. Consequently, marginal revenue—the change in total revenue associated with a one unit change in output—is less than price (average revenue) for every unit of output except the first. Why so? The reason is that the lower price of the extra unit of output also applies to all prior units of output. The monopolist could have sold these prior units at a higher price if it had not produced and sold the extra output. Each additional unit of output sold increases total revenue by an amount equal to its own price less the sum of the price cuts that apply to all prior units of output.

Figure 10.2 confirms this point. There, we have highlighted two price-quantity combinations from the monopolist's demand curve. The monopolist can sell 1 more unit at $132 than it can at $142 and that way obtain $132 (the blue area) of extra revenue. But to sell that fourth unit for $132, the monopolist must also sell the first 3 units at $132 rather than $142. The $10 reduction in revenue on 3 units results in a $30 revenue loss (the red area). Thus, the net difference in total revenue from selling a fourth unit is $102: the $132 gain from the fourth unit minus the $30 forgone on the first 3 units. This net gain (marginal revenue) of $102 from the fourth unit is clearly less than the $132 price of the fourth unit.

Column 4 in Table 10.1 shows that marginal revenue is always less than the corresponding product price in column 2, except for the first unit of output. Because marginal revenue is the change in total revenue associated with each additional unit of output, the declining amounts of marginal revenue in column 4 mean that total revenue increases at a diminishing rate (as shown in column 3).

We show the relationship between the monopolist's marginal-revenue curve and total-revenue curve in Figure 10.3. For this figure, we extended the demand and revenue data of columns 1 through 4 in Table 10.1, assuming that successive $10 price cuts each elicit 1 additional unit of sales. That is, the monopolist can sell 11 units at $62, 12 units at $52, and so on.

Note that the monopolist's MR curve lies below the demand curve, indicating that marginal revenue is less than price at every output quantity but the very first unit. Observe also the special relationship between total revenue (shown in the lower graph) and marginal revenue (shown in the top graph). Because marginal revenue is the change in total revenue, marginal revenue is positive while total revenue is increasing. When total revenue reaches its maximum, marginal revenue is zero. When total revenue is diminishing, marginal revenue is negative.

The Monopolist Is a Price Maker

All imperfect competitors, whether pure monopolists, oligopolists, or monopolistic competitors, face downsloping demand curves. As a result, any change in quantity produced causes a movement along their respective demand curves and a change in the price they can charge for their respective products. Economists summarize this fact by saying that firms with downsloping demand curves are *price makers*.

This is most evident in pure monopoly, where an industry consists of a single monopoly firm so that total industry output is exactly equal to whatever the single monopoly firm chooses to produce. As we just mentioned, the monopolist faces a downsloping demand curve in

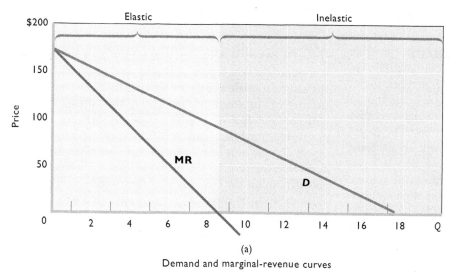

(a)
Demand and marginal-revenue curves

FIGURE 10.3 Demand, marginal revenue, and total revenue for a pure monopolist. (a) Because it must lower price on all units sold in order to increase its sales, an imperfectly competitive firm's marginal-revenue curve (MR) lies below its downsloping demand curve (D). The elastic and inelastic regions of demand are highlighted. (b) Total revenue (TR) increases at a decreasing rate, reaches a maximum, and then declines. Note that in the elastic region, TR is increasing and hence MR is positive. When TR reaches its maximum, MR is zero. In the inelastic region of demand, TR is declining, so MR is negative.

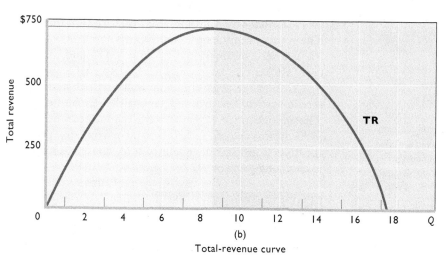

(b)
Total-revenue curve

which each amount of output is associated with some unique price. Thus, in deciding on the quantity of output to produce, the monopolist is also determining the price it will charge. Through control of output, it can "make the price." From columns 1 and 2 in Table 10.1 we find that the monopolist can charge a price of $72 if it produces and offers for sale 10 units, a price of $82 if it produces and offers for sale 9 units, and so forth.

The Monopolist Sets Prices in the Elastic Region of Demand

The total-revenue test for price elasticity of demand is the basis for our third implication. Recall from Chapter 4 that the total-revenue test reveals that when demand is elastic, a decline in price will increase total revenue. Similarly, when demand is inelastic, a decline in price will reduce total revenue. Beginning at the top of demand curve D in Figure 10.3a, observe that as the price declines from $172 to approximately $82, total revenue increases (and marginal revenue therefore is positive). This means that demand is elastic in this price range. Conversely, for price declines below $82, total revenue decreases (marginal revenue is negative), indicating that demand is inelastic there.

The implication is that a monopolist will never choose a price-quantity combination where price reductions cause total revenue to decrease (marginal revenue to be negative). The profit-maximizing monopolist will always want to avoid the inelastic segment of its demand curve in favor of some price-quantity combination in the elastic region. Here's why: To get into the inelastic region, the monopolist must lower price and increase output. In the inelastic region a lower price means less total revenue. And increased output always means increased total cost. Less total revenue and higher total cost yield lower profit.

QUICK REVIEW 10.1

- A pure monopolist is the sole supplier of a product or service for which there are no close substitutes.
- A monopoly survives because of entry barriers such as economies of scale, patents and licenses, the ownership of essential resources, and strategic actions to exclude rivals.
- The monopolist's demand curve is downsloping and its marginal-revenue curve lies below its demand curve.
- The downsloping demand curve means that the monopolist is a price maker.
- The monopolist will operate in the elastic region of demand since in the inelastic region it can increase total revenue and reduce total cost by reducing output.

Output and Price Determination

At what specific price-quantity combination will a profit-maximizing monopolist choose to operate? To answer this question, we must add production costs to our analysis.

Cost Data

On the cost side, we will assume that although the firm is a monopolist in the product market, it hires resources competitively and employs the same technology and, therefore, has the same cost structure as the purely competitive firm that we studied in Chapters 9 and 10. By using the same cost data that we developed in Chapter 7 and applied to the competitive firm in Chapters 9 and 10, we will be able to directly compare the price and output decisions of a pure monopoly with those of a pure competitor. This will help us demonstrate that the price and output differences between a pure monopolist and a pure competitor are not the result of two different sets of costs. Columns 5 through 7 in Table 10.1 restate the pertinent cost data from Table 7.2.

MR = MC Rule

A monopolist seeking to maximize total profit will employ the same rationale as a profit-seeking firm in a competitive industry. If producing is preferable to shutting down, it will produce up to the output at which marginal revenue equals marginal cost (MR = MC).

A comparison of columns 4 and 7 in Table 10.1 indicates that the profit-maximizing output is 5 units because the fifth unit is the last unit of output whose marginal revenue exceeds its marginal cost. What price will the monopolist charge? The demand schedule shown as columns 1 and 2 in Table 10.1 indicates there is only one price at which 5 units can be sold: $122.

This analysis is shown in **Figure 10.4 (Key Graph)**, where we have graphed the demand, marginal-revenue, average-total-cost, and marginal-cost data of Table 10.1. The profit-maximizing output occurs at 5 units of output (Q_m), where the marginal-revenue (MR) and marginal-cost (MC) curves intersect. There, MR = MC.

To find the price the monopolist will charge, we extend a vertical line from Q_m up to the demand curve D. The unique price P_m at which Q_m units can be sold is $122. In this case, $122 is the profit-maximizing price. So the monopolist sets the quantity at Q_m to charge its profit-maximizing price of $122.

INTERACTIVE GRAPHS

G 10.1

Monopoly

Columns 2 and 5 in Table 10.1 show that at 5 units of output, the product price ($122) exceeds the average total

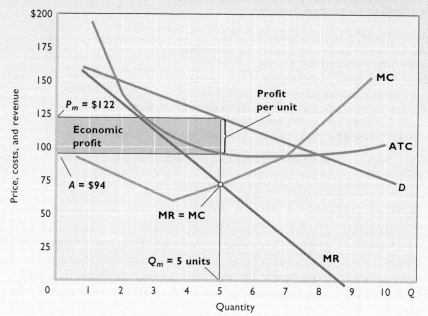

FIGURE 10.4 Profit maximization by a pure monopolist. The pure monopolist maximizes profit by producing at the MR = MC output, here Q_m = 5 units. Then, as seen from the demand curve, it will charge price P_m = $122. Average total cost will be A = $94, meaning that per-unit profit is $P_m - A$ and total profit is 5 × ($P_m - A$). Total economic profit is thus represented by the green rectangle.

QUICK QUIZ FOR FIGURE 10.4

1. The MR curve lies below the demand curve in this figure because the:
   a. demand curve is linear (a straight line).
   b. demand curve is highly inelastic throughout its full length.
   c. demand curve is highly elastic throughout its full length.
   d. gain in revenue from an extra unit of output is less than the price charged for that unit of output.

2. The area labeled "Economic profit" can be found by multiplying the difference between P and ATC by quantity. It also can be found by:
   a. dividing profit per unit by quantity.
   b. subtracting total cost from total revenue.
   c. multiplying the coefficient of demand elasticity by quantity.
   d. multiplying the difference between P and MC by quantity.

3. This pure monopolist:
   a. charges the highest price that it could achieve.
   b. earns only a normal profit in the long run.
   c. restricts output to create an insurmountable entry barrier.
   d. restricts output to increase its price and total economic profit.

4. At this monopolist's profit-maximizing output:
   a. price equals marginal revenue.
   b. price equals marginal cost.
   c. price exceeds marginal cost.
   d. profit per unit is maximized.

Answers: 1. d; 2. b; 3. d; 4. c

cost ($94). The monopolist thus obtains an economic profit of $28 per unit, and the total economic profit is $140 (= 5 units × $28). In Figure 10.4, per-unit profit is $P_m - A$, where A is the average total cost of producing Q_m units. Total economic profit—the green rectangle—is found by multiplying this per-unit profit by the profit-maximizing output Q_m.

Another way to determine the profit-maximizing output is by comparing total revenue and total cost at each possible level of production and choosing the output with the greatest positive difference. Use columns 3 and 6 in Table 10.1 to

WORKED PROBLEMS

W 10.1

Monopoly price and output

verify that 5 units is the profit-maximizing output. An accurate graphing of total revenue and total cost against output would also show the greatest difference (the maximum profit) at 5 units of output. Table 10.2 summarizes the process for determining the profit-maximizing output, profit-maximizing price, and economic profit in pure monopoly.

No Monopoly Supply Curve

Recall that MR equals P in pure competition and that the supply curve of a purely competitive firm is determined by applying the MR (= P) = MC profit-maximizing rule. At

201

TABLE 10.2 Steps for Graphically Determining the Profit-Maximizing Output, Profit-Maximizing Price, and Economic Profit (if Any) in Pure Monopoly

Step 1.	Determine the profit-maximizing output by finding where MR = MC.
Step 2.	Determine the profit-maximizing price by extending a vertical line upward from the output determined in step 1 to the pure monopolist's demand curve.
Step 3.	Determine the pure monopolist's economic profit using one of two methods:
	Method 1. Find profit per unit by subtracting the average total cost of the profit-maximizing output from the profit-maximizing price. Then multiply the difference by the profit-maximizing output to determine economic profit (if any).
	Method 2. Find total cost by multiplying the average total cost of the profit-maximizing output by that output. Find total revenue by multiplying the profit-maximizing output by the profit-maximizing price. Then subtract total cost from total revenue to determine economic profit (if any).

any specific market-determined price, the purely competitive seller will maximize profit by supplying the quantity at which MC is equal to that price. When the market price increases or decreases, the competitive firm produces more or less output. Each market price is thus associated with a specific output, and all such price-output pairs define the supply curve. This supply curve turns out to be the portion of the firm's MC curve that lies above the average-variable-cost curve (see Figure 8.6).

At first glance we would suspect that the pure monopolist's marginal-cost curve would also be its supply curve. But that is *not* the case. *The pure monopolist has no supply curve.* There is no unique relationship between price and quantity supplied for a monopolist. Like the competitive firm, the monopolist equates marginal revenue and marginal cost to determine output, but for the monopolist marginal revenue is less than price. Because the monopolist does not equate marginal cost to price, it is possible for different demand conditions to bring about different prices for the same output. To understand this point, refer to Figure 10.4 and pencil in a new, steeper marginal-revenue curve that intersects the marginal-cost curve at the same point as does the present marginal-revenue curve. Then draw in a new demand curve that is roughly consistent with your new marginal-revenue curve. With the new curves, the same MR = MC output of 5 units now means a higher profit-maximizing price. Conclusion: There is no single, unique price associated with each output level Q_m, and so there is no supply curve for the pure monopolist.

Misconceptions Concerning Monopoly Pricing

Our analysis exposes two fallacies concerning monopoly behavior.

Not Highest Price Because a monopolist can manipulate output and price, people often believe it "will charge the highest price possible." That is incorrect. There are many prices above P_m in Figure 10.4, but the monopolist shuns them because they yield a smaller-than-maximum total profit. The monopolist seeks maximum total profit, not maximum price. Some high prices that could be charged would reduce sales and total revenue too severely to offset any decrease in total cost.

Total, Not Unit, Profit The monopolist seeks maximum *total* profit, not maximum *unit* profit. In Figure 10.4 a careful comparison of the vertical distance between average total cost and price at various possible outputs indicates that per-unit profit is greater at a point slightly to the left of the profit-maximizing output Q_m. This is seen in Table 10.1, where the per-unit profit at 4 units of output is $32 (= $132 − $100) compared with $28 (= $122 − $94) at the profit-maximizing output of 5 units. Here the monopolist accepts a lower-than-maximum per-unit profit because additional sales more than compensate for the lower unit profit. A monopolist would rather sell 5 units at a profit of $28 per unit (for a total profit of $140) than 4 units at a profit of $32 per unit (for a total profit of only $128).

Possibility of Losses by Monopolist

The likelihood of economic profit is greater for a pure monopolist than for a pure competitor. In the long run the pure competitor is destined to have only a normal profit, whereas barriers to entry mean that any economic profit realized by the monopolist can persist. In pure monopoly there are no new entrants to increase supply, drive down price, and eliminate economic profit.

But pure monopoly does not guarantee profit. The monopolist is not immune from changes in tastes that reduce the demand for its product. Nor is it immune from upward-shifting cost curves caused by escalating resource prices. If the demand and cost situation faced by the monopolist is far less favorable than that in Figure 10.4, the

FIGURE 10.5 The loss-minimizing position of a pure monopolist. If demand D is weak and costs are high, the pure monopolist may be unable to make a profit. Because P_m exceeds V, the average variable cost at the MR = MC output Q_m, the monopolist will minimize losses in the short run by producing at that output. The loss per unit is $A - P_m$, and the total loss is indicated by the red rectangle.

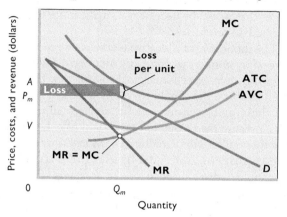

monopolist will incur losses in the short run. Despite its dominance in the market (as, say, a seller of home sewing machines), the monopoly enterprise in Figure 10.5 suffers a loss, as shown, because of weak demand and relatively high costs. Yet it continues to operate for the time being because its total loss is less than its fixed cost. More precisely, at output Q_m the monopolist's price P_m exceeds its average variable cost V. Its loss per unit is $A - P_m$, and the total loss is shown by the red rectangle.

Like the pure competitor, the monopolist will not persist in operating at a loss. Faced with continuing losses, in the long run the firm's owners will move their resources to alternative industries that offer better profit opportunities. A monopolist such as the one depicted in Figure 10.5 must obtain a minimum of a normal profit in the long run or it will go out of business.

Economic Effects of Monopoly

Let's now evaluate pure monopoly from the standpoint of society as a whole. Our reference for this evaluation will be the outcome of long-run efficiency in a purely competitive market, identified by the triple equality $P = MC =$ minimum ATC.

Price, Output, and Efficiency

Figure 10.6 graphically contrasts the price, output, and efficiency outcomes of pure monopoly and a purely competitive *industry*. The $S = MC$ curve in Figure 10.6a reminds us that the market supply curve S for a purely competitive industry is the horizontal sum of the marginal-cost curves of all the firms in the industry. Suppose there are 1000 such firms. Comparing their combined supply curves S with market demand D, we see that the purely competitive price and output are P_c and Q_c.

Recall that this price-output combination results in both productive efficiency and allocative efficiency.

FIGURE 10.6 Inefficiency of pure monopoly relative to a purely competitive industry. (a) In a purely competitive industry, entry and exit of firms ensure that price (P_c) equals marginal cost (MC) and that the minimum average-total-cost output (Q_c) is produced. Both productive efficiency (P = minimum ATC) and allocative efficiency (P = MC) are obtained. (b) In pure monopoly, the MR curve lies below the demand curve. The monopolist maximizes profit at output Q_m, where MR = MC, and charges price P_m. Thus, output is lower (Q_m rather than Q_c) and price is higher (P_m rather than P_c) than they would be in a purely competitive industry. Monopoly is inefficient, since output is less than that required for achieving minimum ATC (here, at Q_c) and because the monopolist's price exceeds MC. Monopoly creates an efficiency loss (here, of triangle *abc*). There is also a transfer of income from consumers to the monopoly (here, of rectangle P_cP_mbd).

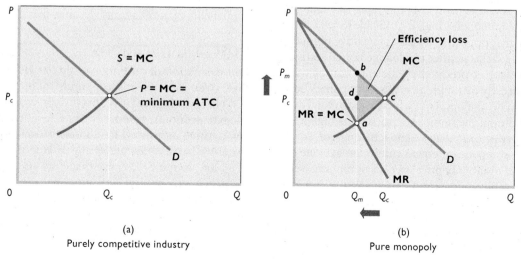

(a)
Purely competitive industry

(b)
Pure monopoly

Productive efficiency is achieved because free entry and exit force firms to operate where average total cost is at a minimum. The sum of the minimum-ATC outputs of the 1000 pure competitors is the industry output, here, Q_c. Product price is at the lowest level consistent with minimum average total cost. The *allocative efficiency* of pure competition results because production occurs up to that output at which price (the measure of a product's value or marginal benefit to society) equals marginal cost (the worth of the alternative products forgone by society in producing any given commodity). In short: $P = MC = $ minimum ATC.

Now let's suppose that this industry becomes a pure monopoly (Figure 10.6b) as a result of one firm acquiring all its competitors. We also assume that no changes in costs or market demand result from this dramatic change in the industry structure. What formerly were 1000 competing firms is now a single pure monopolist consisting of 1000 noncompeting branches.

The competitive market supply curve S has become the marginal-cost curve (MC) of the monopolist, the summation of the individual marginal-cost curves of its many branch plants. (Since the monopolist does not have a supply curve, as such, we have removed the S label.) The important change, however, is on the demand side. From the viewpoint of each of the 1000 individual competitive firms, demand was perfectly elastic, and marginal revenue was therefore equal to the market equilibrium price P_c. So each firm equated its marginal revenue of P_c dollars per unit with its individual marginal cost curve to maximize profits. But market demand and individual demand are the same to the pure monopolist. The firm *is* the industry, and thus the monopolist sees the downsloping demand curve D shown in Figure 10.6b.

This means that marginal revenue is less than price, that graphically the MR curve lies below demand curve D. In using the MR = MC rule, the monopolist selects output Q_m and price P_m. A comparison of both graphs in Figure 10.6 reveals that the monopolist finds it profitable to sell a smaller output at a higher price than do the competitive producers.

Monopoly yields neither productive nor allocative efficiency. The lack of productive efficiency can be understood most directly by noting that the monopolist's output Q_m is less than Q_c, the output at which average total cost is lowest. In addition, the monopoly price P_m is higher than the competitive price P_c that we know in long-run equilibrium in pure competition equals minimum average total cost. Thus, the monopoly price exceeds minimum average total cost, thereby demonstrating in another way that the monopoly will not be productively efficient.

The monopolist's underproduction also implies allocative inefficiency. One way to see this is to note that at the monopoly output level Q_m, the monopoly price P_m that consumers are willing to pay exceeds the marginal cost of production. This means that consumers value additional units of this product more highly than they do the alternative products that could be produced from the resources that would be necessary to make more units of the monopolist's product.

The monopolist's allocative inefficiency can also be understood by noting that for every unit between Q_m and Q_c, marginal benefit exceeds marginal cost because the demand curve lies above the supply curve. By choosing not to produce these units, the monopolist reduces allocative efficiency because the resources that should have been used to make these units will be redirected instead toward producing items that bring lower net benefits to society. The total dollar value of this efficiency loss (or *deadweight loss*) is equal to the area of the gray triangle labeled *abc* in Figure 10.6b.

Income Transfer

In general, a monopoly transfers income from consumers to the owners of the monopoly. The income is received by the owners as revenue. Because a monopoly has market power, it can charge a higher price than would a purely competitive firm with the same costs. So the monopoly in effect levies a "private tax" on consumers. This private tax can often generate substantial economic profits that can persist because entry to the industry is blocked.

The transfer from consumers to the monopolist is evident in Figure 10.6b. For the Q_m units of output demanded, consumers pay price P_m rather than the price P_c that they would pay to a pure competitor. The total amount of income transferred from consumers to the monopolist is $P_m - P_c$ multiplied by the number of units sold, Q_m. So the total transfer is the dollar amount of rectangle $P_c P_m bd$. What the consumer loses, the monopolist gains. In contrast, the efficiency loss *abc* is a *deadweight* loss—society totally loses the net benefits of the Q_c minus Q_m units that are not produced.

Cost Complications

Our evaluation of pure monopoly has led us to conclude that, given identical costs, a purely monopolistic industry will charge a higher price, produce a smaller output, and allocate economic resources less efficiently than a purely competitive industry. These inferior results are rooted in the entry barriers characterizing monopoly.

Now we must recognize that costs may not be the same for purely competitive and monopolistic producers. The unit cost incurred by a monopolist may be either larger or smaller than that incurred by a purely competitive firm. There are four reasons why costs may differ: (1) economies of scale, (2) a factor called "X-inefficiency," (3) the need for monopoly-preserving expenditures, and (4) the "very long run" perspective, which allows for technological advance.

Economies of Scale Once Again

Where economies of scale are extensive, market demand may not be sufficient to support a large number of competing firms, each producing at minimum efficient scale. In such cases, an industry of one or two firms would have a lower average total cost than would the same industry made up of numerous competitive firms. At the extreme, only a single firm—a natural monopoly—might be able to achieve the lowest long-run average total cost.

Some firms relating to new information technologies—for example, computer software, Internet service, and wireless communications—have displayed extensive economies of scale. As these firms have grown, their long-run average total costs have declined because of greater use of specialized inputs, the spreading of product development costs, and learning by doing. Also, *simultaneous consumption* and *network effects* have reduced costs.

A product's ability to satisfy a large number of consumers at the same time is called **simultaneous consumption** (or *nonrivalrous consumption*). Dell Computers needs to produce a personal computer for each customer, but Microsoft needs to produce its Windows program only once. Then, at very low marginal cost, Microsoft delivers its program by disk or Internet to millions of consumers. Similar low cost of delivering product to additional customers is true for Internet service providers, music producers, and wireless communication firms. Because marginal costs are so low, the average total cost of output declines as more customers are added.

Network effects are present if the value of a product to each user, including existing users, increases as the total number of users rises. Good examples are computer software, cell phones, and Web sites like Facebook where the content is provided by users. When other people have Internet service and devices to access it, a person can conveniently send e-mail messages to them. And when they have similar software, various documents, spreadsheets, and photos can be attached to the e-mail messages. The greater the number of persons connected to the system, the more the benefits of the product to each person are magnified.

Such network effects may drive a market toward monopoly because consumers tend to choose standard products that everyone else is using. The focused demand for these products permits their producers to grow rapidly and thus achieve economies of scale. Smaller firms, which either have higher-cost "right" products or "wrong" products, get acquired or go out of business.

Economists generally agree that some new information firms have not yet exhausted their economies of scale. But most economists question whether such firms are truly natural monopolies. Most firms eventually achieve their minimum efficient scale at less than the full size of the market. That means competition among firms is possible.

But even if natural monopoly develops, the monopolist is unlikely to pass cost reductions along to consumers as price reductions. So, with perhaps a handful of exceptions, economies of scale do not change the general conclusion that monopoly industries are inefficient relative to competitive industries.

X-Inefficiency

In constructing all the average-total-cost curves used in this book, we have assumed that the firm uses the most efficient existing technology. This assumption is only natural, because firms cannot maximize profits

> **ORIGIN OF THE IDEA**
> **O 10.3**
> X-inefficiency

unless they are minimizing costs. **X-inefficiency** occurs when a firm produces output at a higher cost than is necessary to produce it. In Figure 10.7 X-inefficiency is represented by operation at points X and X' above the lowest-cost ATC curve. At these points, per-unit costs are ATC_X (as opposed to ATC_1) for output Q_1 and $ATC_{X'}$ (as opposed to ATC_2) for output Q_2. Producing at any point above the average-total-cost curve in Figure 10.7 reflects inefficiency or "bad management" by the firm.

Why is X-inefficiency allowed to occur if it reduces profits? The answer is that managers may have goals, such as expanding power, an easier work life, avoiding business risk, or giving jobs to incompetent relatives, that conflict with cost minimization. Or X-inefficiency may arise because a firm's workers are poorly motivated or ineffectively supervised. Or a firm may simply become lethargic and inert, relying on rules of thumb in decision making as opposed to careful calculations of costs and revenues.

For our purposes the relevant question is whether monopolistic firms tend more toward X-inefficiency than competitive producers do. Presumably they do. Firms in competitive industries are continually under pressure from rivals, forcing them to be internally efficient to survive. But monopolists are sheltered from such competitive forces by entry barriers. That lack of pressure may lead to X-inefficiency.

Rent-Seeking Expenditures

Rent-seeking behavior is any activity designed to transfer income or wealth to a particular firm or resource supplier at someone else's, or

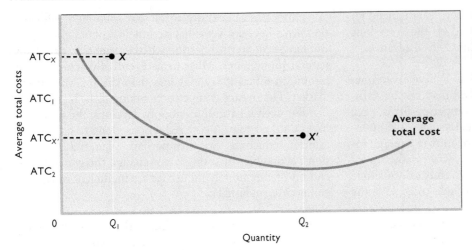

FIGURE 10.7 X-inefficiency. The average-total-cost curve (ATC) is assumed to reflect the minimum cost of producing each particular level of output. Any point above this "lowest-cost" ATC curve, such as X or X', implies X-inefficiency: operation at greater than lowest cost for a particular level of output.

even society's, expense. We have seen that a monopolist can obtain an economic profit even in the long run. Therefore, it is no surprise that a firm may go to great expense to acquire or maintain a monopoly granted by government through legislation or an exclusive license. Such rent-seeking expenditures add nothing to the firm's output, but they clearly increase its costs. Taken alone, rent-seeking implies that monopoly involves higher costs and less efficiency than suggested in Figure 10.6b.

Technological Advance In the very long run, firms can reduce their costs through the discovery and implementation of new technology. If monopolists are more likely than competitive producers to develop more efficient production techniques over time, then the inefficiency of monopoly might be overstated. Because research and development (R&D) is the topic of optional Web Chapter 11, we will provide only a brief assessment here.

The general view of economists is that a pure monopolist will not be technologically progressive. Although its economic profit provides ample means to finance research and development, it has little incentive to implement new techniques (or products). The absence of competitors means that there is no external pressure for technological advance in a monopolized market. Because of its sheltered market position, the pure monopolist can afford to be complacent and lethargic. There simply is no major penalty for not being innovative.

One caveat: Research and technological advance may be one of the monopolist's barriers to entry. Thus, the monopolist may continue to seek technological advance to avoid falling prey to new rivals. In this case technological advance is essential to the maintenance of monopoly. But then it is *potential* competition, not the monopoly market structure, that is driving the technological advance. By

assumption, no such competition exists in the pure monopoly model; entry is completely blocked.

Assessment and Policy Options

Monopoly is a legitimate concern. Monopolists can charge higher-than-competitive prices that result in an underallocation of resources to the monopolized product. They can stifle innovation, engage in rent-seeking behavior, and foster X-inefficiency. Even when their costs are low because of economies of scale, there is no guarantee that the price they charge will reflect those low costs. The cost savings may simply accrue to the monopoly as greater economic profit.

Fortunately, however, monopoly is not widespread in the United States. Barriers to entry are seldom completely successful. Although research and technological advance may strengthen the market position of a monopoly, technology may also undermine monopoly power. Over time, the creation of new technologies may work to destroy monopoly positions. For example, the development of courier delivery, fax machines, and e-mail has eroded the monopoly power of the U.S. Postal Service. Similarly, cable television monopolies are now challenged by satellite TV and by technologies that permit the transmission of audio and video over the Internet.

Patents eventually expire; and even before they do, the development of new and distinct substitutable products often circumvents existing patent advantages. New sources of monopolized resources sometimes are found and competition from foreign firms may emerge. (See Global Perspective 10.1.) Finally, if a monopoly is sufficiently fearful of future competition from new products, it may keep its prices relatively low so as to discourage rivals from developing such products. If so, consumers may pay nearly competitive prices even though competition is currently lacking.

So what should government do about monopoly when it arises in the real world? Economists agree that government needs to look carefully at monopoly on a case-by-case basis. Three general policy options are available:

- If the monopoly is achieved and sustained through anticompetitive actions, creates substantial economic inefficiency, and appears to be long-lasting, the government can file charges against the monopoly under the antitrust laws. If found guilty of monopoly abuse, the firm can either be expressly prohibited from engaging in certain business activities or be broken into two or more competing firms. An example of the breakup approach was the dissolution of Standard Oil into several competing firms in 1911. In contrast, in 2001 an appeals court overruled a lower-court decision to divide Microsoft into two firms. Instead, Microsoft was prohibited from engaging in a number of specific anticompetitive business activities. (We discuss the antitrust laws and the Microsoft case in Chapter 18.)
- If the monopoly is a natural monopoly, society can allow it to continue to expand. If no competition

emerges from new products, government may then decide to regulate its prices and operations. (We discuss this option later in this chapter and also in Chapter 18.)
- If the monopoly appears to be unsustainable because of emerging new technology, society can simply choose to ignore it. In such cases, society simply lets the process of creative destruction (discussed in Chapter 9) do its work. In Web Chapter 11, we discuss in detail the likelihood that real-world monopolies will collapse due to creative destruction and competition brought on by new technologies.

QUICK REVIEW 10.2

- The monopolist maximizes profit (or minimizes loss) at the output where MR = MC and charges the price that corresponds to that output on its demand curve.
- The monopolist has no supply curve, since any of several prices can be associated with a specific quantity of output supplied.
- Assuming identical costs, a monopolist will be less efficient than a purely competitive industry because it will fail to produce units of output for which marginal benefits exceed marginal costs.
- The inefficiencies of monopoly may be offset or lessened by economies of scale and, less likely, by technological progress, but they may be intensified by the presence of X-inefficiency and rent-seeking expenditures.

Price Discrimination

We have assumed in this chapter that the monopolist charges a single price to all buyers. But under certain conditions the monopolist can increase its profit by charging different prices to different buyers. In so doing, the monopolist is engaging in **price discrimination,** the practice of selling a specific product at more than one price when the price differences are not justified by cost differences. Price discrimination can take three forms:

ORIGIN OF THE IDEA
O 10.4
Price discrimination

- Charging each customer in a single market the maximum price she or he is willing to pay.
- Charging each customer one price for the first set of units purchased and a lower price for subsequent units purchased.
- Charging some customers one price and other customers another price.

Conditions

The opportunity to engage in price discrimination is not readily available to all sellers. Price discrimination is possible when the following conditions are met:

- *Monopoly power* The seller must be a monopolist or, at least, must possess some degree of monopoly power, that is, some ability to control output and price.
- *Market segregation* At relatively low cost to itself, the seller must be able to segregate buyers into distinct classes, each of which has a different willingness or ability to pay for the product. This separation of buyers is usually based on different price elasticities of demand, as the examples below will make clear.
- *No resale* The original purchaser cannot resell the product or service. If buyers in the low-price segment of the market could easily resell in the high-price segment, the monopolist's price-discrimination strategy would create competition in the high-price segment. This competition would reduce the price in the high-price segment and undermine the monopolist's price-discrimination policy. This condition suggests that service industries such as the transportation industry or legal and medical services, where resale is impossible, are good candidates for price discrimination.

Examples of Price Discrimination

Price discrimination is widely practiced in the U.S. economy. For example, we noted in Chapter 4's Last Word that airlines charge high fares to business travelers, whose demand for travel is inelastic, and offer lower, highly restricted, nonrefundable fares to attract vacationers and others whose demands are more elastic.

Electric utilities frequently segment their markets by end uses, such as lighting and heating. The absence of reasonable lighting substitutes means that the demand for electricity for illumination is inelastic and that the price per kilowatt-hour for such use is high. But the availability of natural gas and petroleum for heating makes the demand for electricity for this purpose less inelastic and the price lower.

Movie theaters and golf courses vary their charges on the basis of time (for example, higher evening and weekend rates) and age (for example, lower rates for children, senior discounts). Railroads vary the rate charged per ton-mile of freight according to the market value of the product being shipped. The shipper of 10 tons of television sets or refrigerators is charged more than the shipper of 10 tons of gravel or coal.

The issuance of discount coupons, redeemable at purchase, is a form of price discrimination. It enables firms to give price discounts to their most price-sensitive

Price Discrimination at the Ballpark

Take me out to the ball game . . .

Buy me some peanuts and Cracker Jack . . .

Professional baseball teams earn substantial revenues through ticket sales. To maximize profit, they offer significantly lower ticket prices for children (whose demand is elastic) than for adults (whose demand is inelastic). This discount may be as much as 50 percent.

If this type of price discrimination increases revenue and profit, why don't teams also price discriminate at the concession stands? Why don't they offer half-price hot dogs, soft drinks, peanuts, and Cracker Jack to children?

The answer involves the three requirements for successful price discrimination. All three requirements are met for game tickets: (1) The team has monopoly power; (2) it can segregate ticket buyers by age group, each group having a different elasticity of demand; and (3) children cannot resell their discounted tickets to adults.

It's a different situation at the concession stands. Specifically, the third condition is *not* met. If the team had dual prices, it could not prevent the exchange or "resale" of the concession goods from children to adults. Many adults would send children to buy food and soft drinks for them: "Here's some money, Billy. Go buy *six* hot dogs." In this case, price discrimination would reduce, not increase, team profit. Thus, children and adults are charged the same high prices at the concession stands. (These prices are high relative to those for the same goods at the local convenience store because the stadium sellers have a captive audience and thus considerable monopoly power.)

customers who have elastic demand. Less price-sensitive consumers who have less elastic demand are not as likely to take the time to clip and redeem coupons. The firm thus makes a larger profit than if it had used a single-price, no-coupon strategy.

Finally, price discrimination often occurs in international trade. A Russian aluminum producer, for example, might sell aluminum for less in the United States than in Russia. In the United States, this seller faces an elastic demand because several substitute suppliers are available. But in Russia, where the manufacturer dominates the market and trade barriers impede imports, consumers have fewer choices and thus demand is less elastic.

FIGURE 10.8 Price discrimination to different groups of buyers. The price-discriminating monopolist represented here maximizes its total profit by dividing the market into two segments based on differences in elasticity of demand. It then produces and sells the MR = MC output in each market segment. (For visual clarity, average total cost (ATC) is assumed to be constant. Therefore MC equals ATC at all output levels.) (a) The firm charges a higher price (here, P_b) to customers who have a less elastic demand curve and (b) a lower price (here, P_s) to customers with a more elastic demand. The price discriminator's total profit is larger than it would be with no discrimination and therefore a single price.

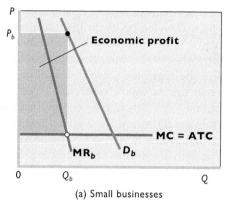

(a) Small businesses

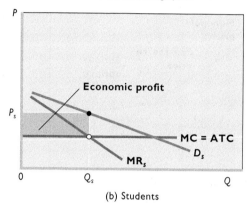

(b) Students

Graphical Analysis

Figure 10.8 demonstrates graphically the most frequently seen form or price discrimination—charging different prices to different classes of buyers. The two side-to-side graphs are for a single pure monopolist selling its product, say, software, in two segregated parts of the market. Figure 10.8a illustrates demand for software by small-business customers; Figure 10.8b, the demand for software by students. Student versions of the software are identical to the versions sold to businesses but are available (1 per person) only to customers with a student ID. Presumably, students have lower ability to pay for the software and are charged a discounted price.

The demand curve D_b in the graph to the left indicates a relatively inelastic demand for the product on the part of business customers. The demand curve D_s in the righthand graph reflects the more elastic demand of students. The marginal revenue curves (MR_b and MR_s) lie below their respective demand curves, reflecting the demand–marginal revenue relationship previously described.

For visual clarity we have assumed that average total cost (ATC) is constant. Therefore marginal cost (MC) equals average total cost (ATC) at all quantities of output. These costs are the same for both versions of the software and therefore appear as the identical straight lines labeled "MC = ATC."

What price will the pure monopolist charge to each set of customers? Using the MR = MC rule for profit

WORKED PROBLEMS

W 10.2

Price discrimination

maximization, the firm will offer Q_b units of the software for sale to small businesses. It can sell that profit-maximizing output by charging price P_b. Again using the MR = MC rule, the monopolist will offer Q_s units of software to students. To sell those Q_s units, the firm will charge students the lower price P_s.

Firms engage in price discrimination because it enhances their profit. The numbers (not shown) behind the curves in Figure 10.8 would clearly reveal that the sum of the two profit rectangles shown in green exceeds the single profit rectangle the firm would obtain from a single monopoly price. How do consumers fare? In this case, students clearly benefit by paying a lower price than they would if the firm charged a single monopoly price; in contrast, the price discrimination results in a higher price for business customers. Therefore, compared to the single-price situation, students buy more of the software and small businesses buy less.

Such price discrimination is widespread in the economy and is illegal only when it is part of a firm's strategy to lessen or eliminate competition. We will discuss illegal price discrimination in Chapter 18, which covers antitrust policy.

Regulated Monopoly

Natural monopolies traditionally have been subject to *rate regulation* (price regulation), although the recent trend has been to deregulate wherever competition seems possible. For example, long-distance telephone calls, natural gas distribution, wireless communications, cable television, and long-distance electricity transmission have been, to one degree or another, deregulated over the past several decades. And regulators in some states are beginning to allow new entrants to compete with existing local telephone and electricity providers. Nevertheless, state and local regulatory commissions still regulate the prices that most local natural

FIGURE 10.9 Regulated monopoly. The socially optimal price P_r, found where D and MC intersect, will result in an efficient allocation of resources but may entail losses to the monopoly. The fair-return price P_f will allow the monopolist to break even but will not fully correct the underallocation of resources.

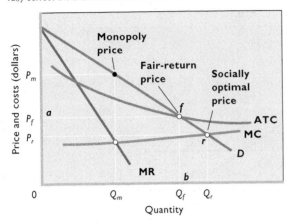

gas distributors, regional telephone companies, and local electricity suppliers can charge. These locally regulated monopolies are commonly called "public utilities."

Let's consider the regulation of a local natural monopoly. Our example will be a single firm that is the only seller of natural gas in the town of Springfield. Figure 10.9 shows the demand and the long-run cost curves facing our firm. Because of extensive economies of scale, the demand curve cuts the natural monopolist's long-run average-total-cost curve at a point where that curve is still falling. It would be inefficient to have several firms in this industry because each would produce a much smaller output, operating well to the left on the long-run average-total-cost curve. In short, each firm's lowest average total cost would be substantially higher than that of a single firm. So efficient, lowest-cost production requires a single seller.

We know by application of the MR = MC rule that Q_m and P_m are the profit-maximizing output and price that an unregulated monopolist would choose. Because price exceeds average total cost at output Q_m, the monopolist enjoys a substantial economic profit. Furthermore, price exceeds marginal cost, indicating an underallocation of resources to this product or service. Can government regulation bring about better results from society's point of view?

Socially Optimal Price: P = MC

One sensible goal for regulators would be to get the monopoly to produce the allocatively efficient output level. For our monopolist in Figure 10.9, this is output level Q_r, determined by where the demand curve D intersects the MC curve. Q_r is the allocatively efficient output level,

because for each unit of output up to Q_r, the demand curve lies above the MC curve, indicating that for all of these units marginal benefits exceed marginal costs.

But how can the regulatory commission actually motivate the monopoly to produce this output level? The trick is to set the regulated price P_r at a level such that the monopoly will be led by its profit-maximizing rule to voluntarily produce the allocatively efficiently level of output. To see how this works, note that because the monopoly will receive the regulated price P_r for all units that it sells, P_r becomes the monopoly's marginal revenue per unit. Thus, the monopoly's MR curve becomes the horizontal white line moving rightward from price P_r on the vertical axis.

The monopoly will at this point follow its usual rule for maximizing profits or minimizing losses: It will produce where marginal revenue equals marginal cost. As a result, the monopoly will produce where the horizontal white MR ($= P_r$) line intersects the MC curve at point r. That is, the monopoly will end up producing the socially optimal output Q_r not because it is socially minded but because Q_r happens to be the output that either maximizes profits or minimizes losses when the firm is forced by the regulators to sell all units at the regulated price P_r.

The regulated price P_r that achieves allocative efficiency is called the **socially optimal price**. Because it is determined by where the MC curve intersects the demand curve, this type of regulation is often summarized by the equation P = MC.

Fair-Return Price: P = ATC

The socially optimal price suffers from a potentially fatal problem. P_r may be so low that average total costs are not covered, as is the case in Figure 10.9. In such situations, forcing the socially optimal price on the regulated monopoly would result in short-run losses and long-run exit. In our example, Springfield would be left without a gas company and its citizens without gas.

What can be done to rectify this problem? One option is to provide a public subsidy to cover the loss that the socially optimal price would entail. Another possibility is to condone price discrimination, allow the monopoly to charge some customers prices above P_r, and hope that the additional revenue that the monopoly gains from price discrimination will be enough to permit it to break even.

In practice, regulatory commissions in the United States have often pursued a third option that abandons the goal of producing every unit for which marginal benefits exceed marginal costs but which guarantees that regulated monopolies will be able to break even and continue in operation. Under this third option, regulators set a regulated price that is high enough for monopolists to break even and continue in operation. This price has come to be referred to as a **fair-return price** because of a ruling in which the Supreme Court held that regulatory agencies must permit regulated utility owners to enjoy a "fair return" on their investments.

In practice, a fair return is equal to a normal profit. That is, a fair return is an accounting profit equal in size to what the owners of the monopoly would on average receive if they entered another type of business.

The regulator determines the fair-return price P_f by where the average total cost curve intersects the demand curve at point f. As we will explain, setting the regulated price at this level will cause the monopoly to produce Q_f units while guaranteeing that it will break even and not wish to exit the industry. To see why the monopoly will voluntarily produce Q_f units, note that because the monopoly will receive P_f dollars for each unit it sells, its marginal revenue per unit becomes P_f dollars so that the horizontal line moving rightward from P_f on the vertical axis becomes the regulated monopoly's MR curve. Because this horizontal MR curve is always higher than the monopoly's MC curve, it is obvious that marginal revenues will exceed marginal costs for every possible level of output shown in Figure 10.9. Thus, the monopoly should be willing to supply whatever quantity of output is demanded by consumers at the regulated price P_f. That quantity is, of course, given by the demand curve. At price P_f consumers will demand exactly Q_f units. Thus, by setting the regulated price at P_f, the regulator gets the monopoly to voluntarily supply exactly Q_f units.

Even better, the regulator also guarantees that the monopoly firm will earn exactly a normal profit. This can be seen in Figure 10.9 by noting that the rectangle $0afb$ is equal to both the monopoly's total cost and its total revenue. Its economic profit is therefore equal to zero, implying that it must be earning a normal accounting profit for its owners.

One final point about allocative efficiency: By choosing the fair-return price P_f, the regulator leads the monopoly to produce Q_f units. This is less than the socially optimal quantity Q_r, but still more than the Q_m units that the monopolist would produce if left unregulated. So while fair-return pricing does not lead to full allocative efficiency, it is still an improvement on what the monopoly would do if left to its own devices.

Dilemma of Regulation

Comparing results of the socially optimal price ($P = MC$) and the fair-return price ($P = ATC$) suggests a policy dilemma, sometimes termed the *dilemma of regulation*. When

its price is set to achieve the most efficient allocation of resources ($P = MC$), the regulated monopoly is likely to suffer losses. Survival of the firm would presumably depend on permanent public subsidies out of tax revenues. On the other hand, although a fair-return price ($P = ATC$) allows the monopolist to cover costs, it only partially resolves the underallocation of resources that the unregulated monopoly price would foster. Despite this dilemma, regulation can improve on the results of monopoly from the social point of view. Price regulation (even at the fair-return price) can simultaneously reduce price, increase output, and reduce the economic profits of monopolies.

That said, we need to provide an important caution: "Fair-price" regulation of monopoly looks rather simple in theory but is amazingly complex in practice. In the actual economy, rate regulation is accompanied by large, expensive rate-setting bureaucracies and maze-like sets of procedures. Also, rate decisions require extensive public input via letters and through public hearings. Rate decisions are subject to lengthy legal challenges. Further, because regulatory commissions must set prices sufficiently above costs to create fair returns, regulated monopolists have little incentive to minimize average total costs. When these costs creep up, the regulatory commissions must set higher prices.

Regulated firms therefore are noted for higher-than-competitive wages, more managers and staff than necessary, nicer-than-typical office buildings, and other forms of X-inefficiency. These inefficiencies help explain the trend of Federal, state, and local governments abandoning price regulation where the possibility of competition looks promising.

QUICK REVIEW 10.3

- Price discrimination occurs when a firm sells a product at different prices that are not based on cost differences.

- The conditions necessary for price discrimination are (a) monopoly power, (b) the ability to segregate buyers on the basis of demand elasticities, and (c) the inability of buyers to resell the product.

- Compared with single pricing by a monopolist, perfect price discrimination results in greater profit and greater output. Many consumers pay higher prices, but other buyers pay prices below the single price.

- Monopoly price can be reduced and output increased through government regulation.

- The socially optimal price ($P = MC$) achieves allocative efficiency but may result in losses; the fair-return price ($P = ATC$) yields a normal profit but fails to achieve allocative efficiency.

De Beers Was One of the World's Strongest and Most Enduring Monopolies. But in Mid-2000 It Announced That It Could No Longer Control the Supply of Diamonds and Thus Would Abandon Its 66-Year Policy of Monopolizing the Diamond Trade.

De Beers, a Swiss-based company controlled by a South African corporation, produces about 45 percent of the world's rough-cut diamonds and purchases for resale a sizable number of the rough-cut diamonds produced by other mines worldwide. As a result, De Beers markets about 55 percent of the world's diamonds to a select group of diamond cutters and dealers. But that percentage has declined from 80 percent in the mid-1980s. Therein lies the company's problem.

Classic Monopoly Behavior

De Beers's past monopoly behavior is a classic example of the unregulated monopoly model illustrated in Figure 10.4. No matter how many diamonds it mined or purchased, it sold only the quantity of diamonds that would yield an "appropriate" (monopoly) price. That price was well above production costs, and De Beers and its partners earned monopoly profits.

When demand fell, De Beers reduced its sales to maintain price. The excess of production over sales was then reflected in growing diamond stockpiles held by De Beers. It also attempted to bolster demand through advertising ("Diamonds are forever"). When demand was strong, it increased sales by reducing its diamond inventories.

De Beers used several methods to control the production of many mines it did not own. First, it convinced a number of independent producers that "single-channel" or monopoly marketing through De Beers would maximize their profit. Second, mines that circumvented De Beers often found their market suddenly flooded with similar diamonds from De Beers's vast stockpiles. The resulting price decline and loss of profit often would encourage a "rogue" mine into the De Beers fold. Finally, De Beers simply purchased and stockpiled diamonds produced by independent mines so that their added supplies would not "undercut" the market.

An End of an Era? Several factors have come together to unravel the De Beers monopoly. New diamond discoveries resulted in a growing leakage of diamonds into world markets outside De Beers's control. For example, significant prospecting and trading in Angola occurred. Recent diamond discoveries in Canada's Northwest Territories pose another threat. Although De Beers is a participant in that region, a large uncontrolled supply of diamonds is expected to emerge. Another challenge has been technological improvements that now allow chemical firms to manufacture flawless artificial diamonds. To prevent consumers from switching to synthetic diamonds, De Beers had to launch a costly campaign to promote "mined diamonds" over synthetics.

If that was not enough, Australian diamond producer Argyle opted to withdraw from the De Beers monopoly. Its annual production of mostly low-grade industrial diamonds accounts for about 6 percent of the global $8 billion diamond market. Moreover, the international media began to focus heavily on the role that diamonds play in financing bloody civil wars in Africa. Fearing a consumer boycott of diamonds, De Beers pledged not to buy these "conflict" diamonds or do business with any firm that did. These diamonds, however, continue to find their way into the marketplace, eluding De Beers's control.

In mid-2000 De Beers abandoned its attempt to control the supply of diamonds. It announced that it planned to transform itself from a diamond cartel to a modern firm selling "premium" diamonds and other luxury goods under the De Beers label. It therefore would gradually reduce its $4 billion stockpile of diamonds and turn its efforts to increasing the overall demand for diamonds through advertising. De Beers proclaimed that it was changing its strategy to being "the diamond supplier of choice."

Diamonds may be forever, but the DeBeers diamond monopoly was not. Nevertheless, with its high market share and ability to control its own production levels, De Beers will continue to wield considerable influence over the price of rough-cut diamonds.

212

Summary

1. A pure monopolist is the sole producer of a commodity for which there are no close substitutes.

2. The existence of pure monopoly and other imperfectly competitive market structures is explained by barriers to entry in the form of (a) economies of scale, (b) patent ownership and research, (c) ownership or control of essential resources, and (d) pricing and other strategic behavior.

3. The pure monopolist's market situation differs from that of a competitive firm in that the monopolist's demand curve is downsloping, causing the marginal-revenue curve to lie below the demand curve. Like the competitive seller, the pure monopolist will maximize profit by equating marginal revenue and marginal cost. Barriers to entry may permit a monopolist to acquire economic profit even in the long run. However, (a) the monopolist does not charge "the highest price possible"; (b) the price that yields maximum total profit to the monopolist rarely coincides with the price that yields maximum unit profit; (c) high costs and a weak demand may prevent the monopolist from realizing any profit at all; and (d) the monopolist avoids the inelastic region of its demand curve.

4. With the same costs, the pure monopolist will find it profitable to restrict output and charge a higher price than would sellers in a purely competitive industry. This restriction of output causes resources to be misallocated, as is evidenced by the fact that price exceeds marginal cost in monopolized markets. Monopoly creates an efficiency loss (or deadweight loss) for society.

5. Monopoly transfers income from consumers to monopolists because a monopolist can charge a higher price than would

a purely competitive firm with the same costs. So monopolists in effect levy a "private tax" on consumers and, if demand is strong enough, obtain substantial economic profits.

6. The costs monopolists and competitive producers face may not be the same. On the one hand, economies of scale may make lower unit costs available to monopolists but not to competitors. Also, pure monopoly may be more likely than pure competition to reduce costs via technological advance because of the monopolist's ability to realize economic profit, which can be used to finance research. On the other hand, X-inefficiency—the failure to produce with the least costly combination of inputs—is more common among monopolists than among competitive firms. Also, monopolists may make costly expenditures to maintain monopoly privileges that are conferred by government. Finally, the blocked entry of rival firms weakens the monopolist's incentive to be technologically progressive.

7. A monopolist can increase its profit by practicing price discrimination, provided (a) it can segregate buyers on the basis of elasticities of demand and (b) its product or service cannot be readily transferred between the segregated markets.

8. Price regulation can be invoked to eliminate wholly or partially the tendency of monopolists to underallocate resources and to earn economic profits. The socially optimal price is determined where the demand and marginal-cost curves intersect; the fair-return price is determined where the demand and average-total-cost curves intersect.

Terms and Concepts

pure monopoly

barriers to entry

simultaneous consumption

network effects

X-inefficiency

rent-seeking behavior

price discrimination

socially optimal price

fair-return price

Questions

1. "No firm is completely sheltered from rivals; all firms compete for consumer dollars. If that is so, then pure monopoly does not exist." Do you agree? Explain. How might you use Chapter 4's concept of cross elasticity of demand to judge whether monopoly exists? LO1

2. Discuss the major barriers to entry into an industry. Explain how each barrier can foster either monopoly or oligopoly. Which barriers, if any, do you feel give rise to monopoly that is socially justifiable? LO1

3. How does the demand curve faced by a purely monopolistic seller differ from that confronting a purely competitive firm? Why does it differ? Of what significance is the differ-

ence? Why is the pure monopolist's demand curve not perfectly inelastic? LO1

4. Use the demand schedule at the top of the next page to calculate total revenue and marginal revenue at each quantity. Plot the demand, total-revenue, and marginal-revenue curves, and explain the relationships between them. Explain why the marginal revenue of the fourth unit of output is $3.50, even though its price is $5. Use Chapter 4's total-revenue test for price elasticity to designate the elastic and inelastic segments of your graphed demand curve. What generalization can you make as to the relationship between marginal revenue and elasticity of demand? Suppose the

marginal cost of successive units of output was zero. What output would the profit-seeking firm produce? Finally, use your analysis to explain why a monopolist would never produce in the inelastic region of demand. LO1

Price (P)	Quantity Demanded (Q)	Price (P)	Quantity Demanded (Q)
$7.00	0	$4.50	5
6.50	1	4.00	6
6.00	2	3.50	7
5.50	3	3.00	8
5.00	4	2.50	9

5. Assume that a pure monopolist and a purely competitive firm have the same unit costs. Contrast the two with respect to (a) price, (b) output, (c) profits, (d) allocation of resources, and (e) impact on income transfers. Since both monopolists and competitive firms follow the MC = MR rule in maximizing profits, how do you account for the different results? Why might the costs of a purely competitive firm and those of a monopolist be different? What are the implications of such a cost difference? LO3

6. Critically evaluate and explain each statement: LO3
   a. Because they can control product price, monopolists are always assured of profitable production by simply charging the highest price consumers will pay.
   b. The pure monopolist seeks the output that will yield the greatest per-unit profit.
   c. An excess of price over marginal cost is the market's way of signaling the need for more production of a good.
   d. The more profitable a firm, the greater its monopoly power.

e. The monopolist has a pricing policy; the competitive producer does not.
f. With respect to resource allocation, the interests of the seller and of society coincide in a purely competitive market but conflict in a monopolized market.

7. Assume a monopolistic publisher has agreed to pay an author 10 percent of the total revenue from the sales of a text. Will the author and the publisher want to charge the same price for the text? Explain. LO3

8. U.S. pharmaceutical companies charge different prices for prescription drugs to buyers in different nations, depending on elasticity of demand and government-imposed price ceilings. Explain why these companies, for profit reasons, oppose laws allowing reimportation of drugs to the United States. LO4

9. Explain verbally and graphically how price (rate) regulation may improve the performance of monopolies. In your answer distinguish between (a) socially optimal (marginal-cost) pricing and (b) fair-return (average-total-cost) pricing. What is the "dilemma of regulation"? LO5

10. It has been proposed that natural monopolists should be allowed to determine their profit-maximizing outputs and prices and then government should tax their profits away and distribute them to consumers in proportion to their purchases from the monopoly. Is this proposal as socially desirable as requiring monopolists to equate price with marginal cost or average total cost? LO5

11. **LAST WORD** How was De Beers able to control the world price of diamonds even though it produced only 45 percent of the diamonds? What factors ended its monopoly? What is its new strategy for earning economic profit, rather than just normal profit?

Problems

1. Suppose a pure monopolist is faced with the demand schedule shown below and the same cost data as the competitive producer discussed in problem 4 at the end of Chapter 8. Calculate the missing total-revenue and marginal-revenue amounts, and determine the profit-maximizing price and profit-maximizing output for this monopolist. What is the monopolist's profit? Verify your answer graphically and by comparing total revenue and total cost. LO2

Price	Quantity Demanded	Total Revenue	Marginal Revenue
$115	0	$_____	
100	1	_____	$_____
83	2	_____	_____
71	3	_____	_____
63	4	_____	_____
55	5	_____	_____
48	6	_____	_____
42	7	_____	_____
37	8	_____	_____
33	9	_____	_____
29	10	_____	_____

2. Suppose that a price-discriminating monopolist has segregated its market into two groups of buyers. The first group is described by the demand and revenue data that you developed for problem 1. The demand and revenue data for the second group of buyers is shown in the table at the top-left corner of the next page. Assume that MC is $13 in both markets and MC = ATC at all output levels. What price will the firm charge in each market? Based solely on these two prices, which market has the higher price elasticity of demand? What will be this monopolist's total economic profit? LO4

Price	Quantity Demanded	Total Revenue	Marginal Revenue
$71	0	$ 0	
63	1	63	$63
55	2	110	47
48	3	144	34
42	4	168	24
37	5	185	17
33	6	198	13
29	7	203	5

Output	TC
25,000	$50,000
50,000	70,000
75,000	75,000
100,000	80,000

3. Assume that the most efficient production technology available for making vitamin pills has the cost structure given in the following table. Note that output is measured as the number of bottles of vitamins produced per day and that costs include a normal profit. LO4

Output	TC	MC
25,000	$100,000	$0.50
50,000	150,000	1.00
75,000	187,500	2.50
100,000	275,500	3.00

a. What is ATC per unit for each level of output listed in the table?
b. Is this a decreasing-cost industry? (Answer yes or no).
c. Suppose that the market price for a bottle of vitamins is $2.50 and that at that price the total market quantity demanded is 75,000,000 bottles. How many firms will there be in this industry?
d. Suppose that, instead, the market quantity demanded at a price of $2.50 is only 75,000. How many firms do you expect there to be in this industry?
e. Review your answers to parts b, c, and d. Does the level of demand determine this industry's market structure?

4. A new production technology for making vitamins is invented by a college professor who decides not to patent it. Thus, it is available for anybody to copy and put into use. The TC per bottle for production up to 100,000 bottles per day is given in the following table. LO4
a. What is ATC for each level of output listed in the table?
b. Suppose that for each 25,000-bottle-per-day increase in production above 100,000 bottles per day, TC increases

by $5000 (so that, for instance, 125,000 bottles per day would generate total costs of $85,000 and 150,000 bottles per day would generate total costs of $90,000). Is this a decreasing-cost industry?
c. Suppose that the price of a bottle of vitamins is $1.33 and that at that price the total quantity demanded by consumers is 75,000,000 bottles. How many firms will there be in this industry?
d. Suppose that, instead, the market quantity demanded at a price of $1.33 is only 75,000. How many firms do you expect there to be in this industry?
e. Review your answers to parts b, c, and d. Does the level of demand determine this industry's market structure?
f. Compare your answer to part d of this problem with your answer to part d of problem 3. Do both production technologies show constant returns to scale?

5. Suppose you have been tasked with regulating a single monopoly firm that sells 50-pound bags of concrete. The firm has fixed costs of $10 million per year and a variable cost of $1 per bag no matter how many bags are produced. LO5
a. If this firm kept on increasing its output level, would ATC per bag ever increase? Is this a decreasing-cost industry?
b. If you wished to regulate this monopoly by charging the socially optimal price, what price would you charge? At that price, what would be the size of the firm's profit or loss? Would the firm want to exit the industry?
c. You find out that if you set the price at $2 per bag, consumers will demand 10 million bags. How big will the firm's profit or loss be at that price?
d. If consumers instead demanded 20 million bags at a price of $2 per bag, how big would the firm's profit or loss be?
e. Suppose that demand is perfectly inelastic at 20 million bags, so that consumers demand 20 million bags no matter what the price is. What price should you charge if you want the firm to earn only a fair rate of return? Assume as always that TC includes a normal profit.

FURTHER TEST YOUR KNOWLEDGE AT
www.mcconnell19e.com

At the text's Online Learning Center (OLC), **www.mcconnell19e.com**, you will find one or more Web-based questions that require information from the Internet to answer. We urge you to check them out; they will familiarize you with Web sites that may be helpful in other courses and perhaps even in your career. The OLC also features multiple-choice questions that give instant feedback and provides other helpful ways to further test your knowledge of the chapter.

Pure Monopoly

This chapter looks at the other end of the spectrum and examines pure monopoly, a market structure in which there is a **single seller**. Like pure competition, pure monopoly is rarely found in the U.S. economy, but it is still important. Many government-owned or government-regulated public utilities (electricity, water, natural gas, or cable television) are close to being pure monopolies, and other business firms are near monopolies because they have a large share of a market. Monopolies play a key role in the allocation of resources and the production of goods and services in the economy.

It is possible for a single seller or pure monopolist to dominate an industry if firms are prevented in some way from entering the industry. Factors that restrict firms from entering an industry are referred to as **barriers to entry**. The second section of this chapter is devoted to a description of the more important types of these barriers, such as economies of scale, patents and licenses, control of essential resources, and strategies for product pricing.

The chapter answers certain questions about the pure monopolist, such as what output the firm will produce, what price it will charge, and the amount of profit for the firm. In answering these questions and in comparing pure competition and pure monopoly, note the following:

1. Both the competitive and monopoly firm try to maximize profits by producing the output at which marginal cost and marginal revenue are equal (**MR = MC**).

2. The individual firm in a perfectly competitive industry sees a perfectly price elastic demand for its product at the going market price because it is but one of many firms in the industry, but the monopolist sees a market demand schedule that is less than perfectly price elastic because the **monopolist is the industry**. The purely competitive firm has *only* an output policy and is a price taker, but the monopolist is able to determine the price at which it will sell its product and is a price maker.

3. When demand is perfectly price elastic, price is equal to marginal revenue and is constant, but when demand is less than perfectly price elastic, marginal revenue is less than price and both decrease as the output of the firm increases.

4. Because entry is blocked in the long run, firms cannot enter a monopolistic industry to compete away profits as they can under conditions of pure competition.

This chapter has three other goals that deserve your study time and careful attention. One goal is to evaluate **economic efficiency** under pure monopoly. Here the purely competitive industry that you read about in Chapters 8 and 9 serves as the standard for comparison. You will learn that unlike the purely competitive industry, pure monopoly does not result in allocative efficiency. Although the inefficiencies of monopoly are offset or reduced by economies of scale and technological progress, they are reinforced by the presence of X-inefficiency and rent-seeking behavior.

The second goal is to discuss the possible pricing strategies of the pure monopolist. The monopolist may be able to set multiple prices for the same product even when the price differences are not justified by cost differences, a situation called **price discrimination.** This type of pricing power works only under certain conditions, and when it is effective it results in higher profits for the monopolist and also greater output.

The pricing power and inefficiency of the pure monopoly have made it a target for **regulation.** Therefore, the last section of the chapter explains the economic choices a regulatory agency faces when it must determine the maximum price that a public utility will be allowed to charge for its product. Here you will learn about the **socially optimum price** and the **fair-return price** and their effects on efficiency and profits. You will also discover the difficult economic dilemma regulatory officials face as they decide what prices they should permit a monopolist to charge.

■ CHECKLIST

When you have studied this chapter you should be able to

☐ Define pure monopoly based on five characteristics.
☐ Give several examples of monopoly and explain its importance.
☐ List and explain four potential barriers that would prevent or deter the entry of new firms into an industry.
☐ Define a natural monopoly using an average total cost curve.
☐ Compare the demand curve for the pure monopolist with that of the purely competitive firm.
☐ Compute marginal revenue when you are given the demand for the monopolist's product.
☐ Explain the relationship between the price a monopolist charges and the marginal revenue from the sale of an additional unit of the product.
☐ Explain why the monopolist is a price maker.
☐ Use elasticity to explain the region of the demand curve where the monopolist produces.

119

☐ State the rule that explains what output the monopolist will produce and the price that will be charged.

☐ Determine the profit-maximizing output and price for the pure monopolist when you are given the demand and cost data.

☐ Explain why there is no supply curve for the pure monopolist.

☐ Counter two popular misconceptions about the price charged and the profit target in pure monopoly.

☐ Explain why monopolists can experience losses.

☐ Compare the economic effects of pure monopoly in terms of price, output, efficiency, and income distribution with a purely competitive industry producing the same product.

☐ Discuss the cost complications caused by economies of scale, X-inefficiency, rent-seeking behavior, and technological advance for pure monopoly and a purely competitive industry.

☐ Describe three general policy options for dealing with the economic inefficiency of monopoly.

☐ Define and give examples of price discrimination.

☐ List three conditions that are necessary for price discrimination.

☐ Explain the economic consequences of price discrimination.

☐ Use graphical analysis to identify the socially optimal price and the fair-return price for the regulated monopoly.

☐ Explain the dilemma of regulation based on a graphical analysis of a regulated monopoly.

☐ Discuss the market forces that made De Beers change its monopoly behavior and end its attempts to control the diamond market (*Last Word*).

■ **CHAPTER OUTLINE**

1. ***Pure monopoly*** is a market structure in which a single firm sells a product for which there are no close substitutes. These characteristics make the monopoly firm a **price maker** rather than a price taker, as was the case for the purely competitive firm. Entry into the industry is blocked, and there can be nonprice competition through advertising to influence the demand for the product.

    a. Examples of monopolies typically include regulated public utilities such as firms providing electricity, natural gas, local telephone service, and cable television, but they can also be unregulated, such as the De Beers diamond syndicate.

    b. The study of monopoly is useful for understanding the economic effects of other market structures—oligopoly and monopolistic competition—where there is some degree of monopoly power.

2. Pure monopoly can exist in the long run only if potential competitors find there are *barriers* that prevent their entry into the industry. There are four major **barriers to entry** that can prevent or severely restrict entry into an industry.

    a. ***Economies of scale*** can reduce production costs in the long run so that one producer can supply a range of output at a minimum total cost. If other producers try to enter the industry, extensive financing would be

required and they may not be able to produce output at a lower cost than the monopolist. The conditions for a ***natural monopoly*** arise in the extreme case in which the market demand curve cuts the long-run ATC curve where they are still declining. One firm can supply the market demand at a minimum cost.

    b. Government creates legal restrictions through issuing patents and licenses. ***Patents*** give the inventor the exclusive right to use or allow others to use the invention. ***Licenses*** give a firm the exclusive right to provide a good or service.

    c. The ownership or control of essential resources can effectively block entry into an industry.

    d. Pricing and other strategic practices, such as price cuts, advertising campaigns, and producing excess capacity, can deter entry into an industry by making entry very costly for a firm.

3. The ***demand curve*** of the pure monopolist is downsloping because the monopolist is the industry. By contrast, the purely competitive firm has a horizontal (perfectly price elastic) demand curve because it is only one of many small firms in an industry. There are several implications of the down-sloping shape of the monopolist's demand curve.

    a. The monopolist can increase sales only by lowering product price; thus price will exceed marginal revenue ($P > MR$) for every unit of output but the first.

    b. The monopolist will have a pricing policy, and is a *price maker;* the purely competitive firm has no price policy and is a price taker.

    c. The monopolist will avoid setting price in the inelastic segment of its demand curve because total revenue will be decreasing and marginal revenue will be negative; price will be set in the *elastic* portion of the demand curve.

4. The ***output*** and ***price determination*** of the profit-maximizing pure monopolist entails several considerations.

    a. Monopoly power in the sale of a product does not necessarily affect the prices that the monopolist pays for resources or the costs of production; an assumption is made in this chapter that the monopolist hires resources in a competitive market and uses the same technology as competitive firms.

    b. The monopolist produces that output at which marginal cost and marginal revenue are equal (**MR = MC**) and charges a price at which this profit-maximizing output can be sold.

    c. The monopolist has **no supply curve** because there is no unique relationship between price and quantity supplied; price and quantity supplied will change when demand and marginal revenue change. By contrast, a purely competitive firm has a supply curve that is the portion of the marginal cost curve above average variable cost, and there is a unique relationship between price and quantity supplied.

    d. Two popular misconceptions about monopolists are that they charge as high a price as possible and that they seek maximum profit per unit of output.

    e. The monopolist is **not guaranteed a profit** and can experience losses because of weak demand for a product or high costs of production.

5. Pure monopoly has significant *economic effects* on the economy when compared to outcomes that would be produced in a purely competitive market.

a. The pure monopolist charges a *higher price* and *produces less output* than would be produced by a purely competitive industry. Pure monopoly is **not productively efficient** because price is greater than the minimum of average cost. It is **not allocatively efficient** because price is greater than marginal cost.

b. Monopoly transfers income from consumers to the owners of the monopoly because these consumers pay a higher price for the product than they otherwise would have to pay if the product was produced by a purely competitive firm with a similar cost structure.

c. A pure monopolist in an industry may produce output at a lower or higher average cost than would be the case for a purely competitive industry producing the same product. The costs of production may differ between the two industries for four reasons.

(1) **Economies of scale** in the production of the product allow the pure monopolist to produce it at a lower long-run average cost than a large number of small pure competitors. In the extreme, a firm may be a **natural monopoly** that can supply the market demand at the lowest average cost. There can also be other factors such as **simultaneous consumption** (a product's ability to satisfy a large number of consumers at the same time) and **network effects** (increases in the value of the product for users as the number of users increase) that create extensive economies of scale for firms, especially those firms involved in information technology.

(2) If a pure monopolist is more susceptible to **X-inefficiency** (having an output level that is higher than the lowest possible cost of producing it) than firms in a purely competitive industry, then long-run average costs at every level of output for the monopolist are higher than those purely competitive firms.

(3) **Rent-seeking** expenditures in the form of legal fees, lobbying, and public-relations expenses to obtain or maintain a position as a monopoly add nothing to output, but do increase monopoly costs.

(4) Monopoly is not likely to contribute to technological advance because there is little incentive for the monopolist to produce a more advanced product. The threat of potential competition, however, may stimulate research and more technological advance, but the purpose of this effort is often to restrict or block entry into the industry.

d. Monopoly causes problems for an economy because of higher prices and restricted output. Monopoly, however, is relatively rare. Technological advance and the development of substitute products can also undermine a monopoly. The policy options for dealing with the economic inefficiency of monopoly include the use of antitrust laws and the breakup of firms, the regulation of price, output, and profits of the monopolist, and simply ignoring the monopoly because its position cannot be sustained.

6. To increase profits a pure monopolist may engage in **price discrimination** by charging different prices to different buyers of the same product (when the price differences do not represent differences in the costs of producing the product).

a. To discriminate, the seller must have some monopoly power, be capable of separating buyers into groups with different price elasticities of demand, and be able to prevent the resale of the product from one group to another group.

b. Price discrimination is common in the U.S. economy. Airlines charge different fares to different passengers for the same flight. Movie theaters vary prices for the same product based on time of day or age. Discount coupons allow firms to charge different prices to different customers for the purchase of the same product.

c. Graphical analysis can be used to show price discrimination to different groups of buyers. The monopolist maximizes its total profit by dividing the market in the segmented groups based on the differences in elasticity of demand. It then produces and sells that output in each market where **MR = MC**. It charges a higher price to customers with a less elastic demand and a lower price to customers with a more elastic demand.

7. Monopolies are often **regulated** by government to reduce the misallocation of resources and control prices.

a. One goal of regulation is to get the monopolist to be allocatively efficient. A regulated price determined by the intersection of the marginal cost and demand curve is the **socially optimal price,** or where $P = MC$. This price becomes the marginal revenue for the monopolist and gives the monopolist an incentive to increase output until marginal revenue equals marginal cost.

b. The socially optimal price, however, may force the firm to produce at a loss if the price is set below average total costs. The government regulator, therefore, may set the price at a level determined by the intersection of the average total cost and demand schedules to allow the monopolist a **fair-return price** or where $P = ATC$. In this case the monopolist covers its cost of production and earns a normal profit, but not an economic profit.

c. The dilemma of regulation is that the socially optimal price may cause losses for the monopolist, and a fair-return price may result in a less efficient allocation of resources. Also, fair-return price regulation can be complex to conduct in the real world.

8. (*Last Word*). The price and output decisions of the original De Beers firm fit the monopoly model. It controlled a large supply of diamonds and was able to sell a limited quantity to yield price that was in excess of production costs, and thus obtain monopoly profits. Several factors undercut the monopoly power of De Beers. New discoveries increased supply and previous agreements to sell diamonds exclusively to De Beers were terminated. The firm could no longer control price by manipulating supply and placed more emphasis on increasing demand to maintain price.

■ **HINTS AND TIPS**

1. Make sure you understand **how pure monopoly differs from pure competition.** Here are key distinctions: (a) The monopolist's demand curve is down-sloping, not horizontal as in pure competition; (b) the monopolist's marginal revenue is less than price (or average revenue) for each level of output except the first, whereas in pure competition marginal revenue equals price; (c) the monopoly firm is a price maker, not a price taker as in pure competition; (d) *the firm is the industry* in monopoly, but not in pure competition; (e) there is the potential for long-run economic profits in pure monopoly, but purely competitive firms will only break even in the long run; and (f) there is no supply curve for a pure monopoly, but there is one for the purely competitive firm.

2. A key similarity between a profit-maximizing pure monopolist and a purely competitive firm is that both types of firms will produce up to that output level at which marginal revenue equals marginal cost (**MR = MC**).

3. Figure 10.3 helps explain why the profit-maximizing monopolist will always want to select some price and quantity combination in the **elastic** and not in the **inelastic** portion of the demand curve. In the inelastic portion, total revenue declines and marginal revenue is negative.

4. Drawing the marginal revenue curve for a monopolist with a linear demand curve is easy if you remember that the marginal revenue curve will always be a straight line that intersects the quantity axis at half of the level of output as the demand curve. (See Figure 10.3.)

5. Spend extra time studying Figure 10.8 and reading the related discussion. It will help you see how **price discrimination** results in more profits, a greater output, and a higher price for some consumers and lower prices for other consumers.

■ **IMPORTANT TERMS**

pure monopoly	rent-seeking behavior
barriers to entry	price discrimination
simultaneous consumption	socially optimal price
network effects	fair-return price
X-inefficiency	

SELF-TEST

■ **FILL-IN QUESTIONS**

1. Pure monopoly is an industry in which a single firm is the sole producer of a product for which there are no close (substitutes, complements) _____ and into which entry in the long run is effectively (open, blocked) _____.

2. The closest example of pure monopoly would be government-regulated (nonprofit organizations, public utilities) _____ that provide water, electricity, or natural gas. There are also "near monopolies," such as private businesses that might account for (40, 80) _____% of a particular market, or businesses in a geographic region that are the (multiple, sole) _____ suppliers of a good or service.

3. If there are substantial economies of scale in the production of a product, a small-scale firm will find it difficult to enter into and survive in an industry because its average costs will be (greater, less) _____ than those of established firms, and a firm will find it (easy, difficult) _____ to start out on a large scale because it will be nearly impossible to acquire the needed financing.

4. Legal barriers to entry by government include granting an inventor the exclusive right to produce a product for 20 years, or a (license, patent) _____, and limiting entry into an industry or occupation through its issuing of a _____.

5. Other barriers to entry include the ownership of essential (markets, resources) _____ and strategic changes in product (price, regulation) _____.

6. The demand schedule confronting the pure monopolist is (perfectly elastic, down-sloping) _____. This means that marginal revenue is (greater, less) _____ than average revenue (or price) and that both marginal revenue and average revenue (increase, decrease) _____ as output increases.

7. When demand is price elastic, a decrease in price will (increase, decrease) _____ total revenue, but when demand is price inelastic, a decrease in price will _____ total revenue. The demand curve for the purely competitive firm is (horizontal, down-sloping) _____, but it is _____ for the monopolist. The profit-maximizing monopolist will want to set price in the price (elastic, inelastic) _____ portion of its demand curve.

8. The supply curve for a purely competitive firm is the portion of the (average variable cost, marginal cost) _____ curve that lies above the _____ curve. The supply curve for the monopolist (is the same, does not exist) _____.

9. When the economic profit of a monopolist is at a maximum, (marginal, average) _____ revenue equals _____ cost and price is (greater, less) _____ than marginal cost.

10. Two common misconceptions about pure monopoly are that it charges the (lowest, highest) _____ price possible and seeks the maximum (normal, per-unit) _____ profit.

11. The pure monopolist (is, is not) _____ guaranteed an economic profit; in fact, the pure monopolist can experience economic losses in the (short run, long run) _____ because of (strong, weak) _____ demand for the monopoly product.

12. The monopolist will typically charge a (lower, higher) _____ price and produce (less, more) _____ output and is (less, more) _____ efficient than if the product was produced in a purely competitive industry.

   a. The monopolist is inefficient *productively* because the average (variable, total) _____ cost of producing a product is not at a (maximum, minimum) _____.

   b. It is inefficient *allocatively* because (marginal revenue, price) _____ is not equal to (marginal, total) _____ cost.

   c. A monopoly will charge a (lower, higher) _____ price than would a purely competitive firm with same costs, and as a result consumers pay a _____ price and this income gets transferred as revenue to the owners of the monopoly.

13. Resources can be said to be more efficiently allocated by pure competition than by pure monopoly only if the purely competitive firms and the monopoly have the same (costs, revenues) _____, and they will not be the same if the monopolist

   a. by virtue of being a large firm enjoys (economies, diseconomies) _____ of scale not available to a pure competitor;

   b. is more susceptible to X-(efficiency, inefficiency) _____ than pure competitors;

   c. may need to make (liability, rent-seeking) _____ expenditures to obtain or maintain monopoly privileges granted by government; and

   d. reduces costs through adopting (higher prices, new technology) _____.

14. The incidence of pure monopoly is relatively (rare, common) _____ because eventually new developments in technology (strengthen, weaken) _____ monopoly power or (substitute, complementary) _____ products are developed.

15. Three general policy options to reduce the economic (losses, inefficiency) _____ of a monopoly are to file charges against it through (liability, antitrust) _____ laws, have government regulate it if it is a (conglomerate, natural monopoly) _____, or ignore it if it is unsustainable.

16. Price discrimination occurs whenever a product is sold at different (markets, prices) _____, and these differences are not equal to the differences in the (revenue from, cost of) _____ producing the product.

17. Price discrimination is possible when the following three conditions exist:

   a. _____

   b. _____

   c. _____

18. One economic consequence of a monopolist's use of price discrimination is (an increase, a decrease) _____ in profits.

19. If the monopolist were regulated and a socially optimal price for the product were sought, the price would be set equal to (marginal, average total) _____ cost. Such a legal price would achieve (productive, allocative) _____ efficiency but might result in losses for the monopolist.

20. If a regulated monopolist is allowed to earn a fair return, the price the government regulators let the monopolist charge for the price would be set equal to (marginal, average total) _____ cost. Such a regulated price falls short of (allocative, productive) _____ efficiency, but it is an improvement over the unregulated case in terms of price and output.

■ **TRUE–FALSE QUESTIONS**

Circle T if the statement is true, F if it is false.

1. The pure monopolist produces a product for which there are no close substitutes.   **T   F**

2. The weaker the barriers to entry into an industry, the more competition there will be in the industry, other things equal.   **T   F**

3. In pure monopoly, there are strong barriers to entry.   **T   F**

4. A monopolist may create an entry barrier by price cutting or substantially increasing the advertising of its product.   **T   F**

5. The monopolist can increase the sales of its product if it charges a lower price.   **T   F**

6. As a monopolist increases its output, it finds that its total revenue at first decreases, and that after some output level is reached, its total revenue begins to increase.   **T   F**

7. A purely competitive firm is a price taker but a monopolist is a price maker.   **T F**

8. A monopolist will avoid setting a price in the *inelastic* segment of the demand curve and prefer to set the price in the e*lastic* segment.   **T F**

9. The monopolist determines the profit-maximizing output by producing that output at which marginal cost and marginal revenue are equal and sets the product price equal to marginal cost and marginal revenue at that output.   **T F**

10. The supply curve for a monopolist is the up-sloping portion of the marginal cost curve that lies above the average variable cost.   **T F**

11. A monopolist will charge the highest price it can get.   **T F**

12. A monopolist seeks maximum total profits, not maximum unit profits.   **T F**

13. Pure monopoly guarantees economic profits.   **T F**

14. Resources are misallocated by monopoly because price is not equal to marginal cost.   **T F**

15. One of the economic effects of monopoly is the transfer of income from consumers to the owners of the monopoly.   **T F**

16. When there are substantial economies of scale in the production of a product, the monopolist may charge a price that is lower than the price that would prevail if the product were produced by a purely competitive industry.   **T F**

17. The purely competitive firm is more likely to be affected by X-inefficiency than a monopolist.   **T F**

18. Rent-seeking expenditures that monopolists make to obtain or maintain monopoly privilege have no effect on the firm's costs.   **T F**

19. The general view of economists is that a pure monopoly is efficient because it has strong incentives to be technologically progressive.   **T F**

20. One general policy option for a monopoly that creates substantial economic inefficiency and is long lasting is to directly regulate its prices and operation.   **T F**

21. Price discrimination occurs when a given product is sold at more than one price and these price differences are not justified by cost differences.   **T F**

22. A discriminating monopolist who can segment its market based on elasticity of demand will charge a higher price to the customers with a less elastic demand and a lower price to customers with a more elastic demand.   **T F**

23. The regulated utility is likely to make an economic profit when price is set to achieve the most efficient allocation of resources ($P = MC$).   **T F**

24. A fair-return price for a regulated utility would have price set to equal average total cost.   **T F**

25. The dilemma of monopoly regulation is that the production by a monopolist of an output that causes no misallocation of resources may force the monopolist to suffer an economic loss.   **T F**

■ **MULTIPLE-CHOICE QUESTIONS**

Circle the letter that corresponds to the best answer.

1. Which would be defining characteristics of pure monopoly?
   (a) The firm does no advertising and it sells a standardized product.
   (b) No close substitutes for the product exist and there is one seller.
   (c) The firm can easily enter into or exit from the industry and profits are guaranteed.
   (d) The firm holds a patent and is technologically progressive.

2. A barrier to entry that significantly contributes to the establishment of a monopoly would be
   (a) economies of scale
   (b) price-taking behavior
   (c) technological progress
   (d) X-inefficiency

3. The demand curve for the pure monopolist is
   (a) perfectly price elastic
   (b) perfectly price inelastic
   (c) down-sloping
   (d) up-sloping

4. Which is true with respect to the demand data confronting a monopolist?
   (a) Marginal revenue is greater than average revenue.
   (b) Marginal revenue decreases as average revenue decreases.
   (c) Demand is perfectly price elastic.
   (d) Average revenue (or price) increases as the output of the firm increases.

5. When the monopolist is maximizing total profits or minimizing losses,
   (a) total revenue is greater than total cost
   (b) average revenue is greater than average total cost
   (c) average revenue is greater than marginal cost
   (d) average total cost is less than marginal cost

6. At which combination of price and marginal revenue is the price elasticity of demand less than 1?
   (a) Price equals $102, marginal revenue equals $42.
   (b) Price equals $92, marginal revenue equals $22.
   (c) Price equals $82, marginal revenue equals $2.
   (d) Price equals $72, marginal revenue equals −$18.

7. The region of demand in which the monopolist will choose a price-output combination will be the
   (a) elastic one because total revenue will increase as price declines and output increases
   (b) inelastic one because total revenue will increase as price declines and output increases

(c) elastic one because total revenue will decrease as price declines and output increases
(d) inelastic one because total revenue will decrease as price declines and output increases

8. At present output a monopolist determines that its marginal cost is $18 and its marginal revenue is $21. The monopolist will maximize profits or minimize losses by
  (a) increasing price while keeping output constant
  (b) decreasing price and increasing output
  (c) decreasing both price and output
  (d) increasing both price and output

Answer Questions 9, 10, and 11 based on the demand and cost data for a pure monopolist given in the following table.

Quantity demanded	Price	Total cost
0	$700	$ 300
1	650	400
2	600	450
3	550	510
4	500	590
5	450	700
6	400	840
7	350	1020
8	300	1250
9	250	1540
10	200	1900

9. The profit-maximizing output and price for this monopolist would be
  (a) 5 units and $450
  (b) 6 units and $400
  (c) 7 units and $350
  (d) 8 units and $300

10. The profit-maximizing price for this monopolist would be
  (a) $300 price
  (b) $350 price
  (c) $400 price
  (d) $450 price

11. At the profit-maximizing price and output, the amount of profit for the monopolist would be
  (a) $1410
  (b) $1430
  (c) $1550
  (d) $1560

12. The supply curve for a pure monopolist
  (a) is the portion of the marginal cost curve that lies above the average variable cost curve
  (b) is perfectly price elastic at the market price
  (c) is up-sloping
  (d) does not exist

13. The analysis of monopoly indicates that the monopolist
  (a) will charge the highest price it can get
  (b) will seek to maximize total profits
  (c) is guaranteed an economic profit
  (d) is only interested in normal profit

14. When compared with the purely competitive industry with identical costs of production, a monopolist will charge a
  (a) higher price and produce more output
  (b) lower price and produce more output
  (c) lower price and produce less output
  (d) higher price and produce less output

15. At an equilibrium level of output, a monopolist is *not* productively efficient because
  (a) the average total cost of producing the product is not at a minimum
  (b) the marginal cost of producing the last unit is equal to its price
  (c) it is earning a profit
  (d) average revenue is less than the cost of producing an extra unit of output

16. A product's ability to satisfy a large number of consumers at the same time is called
  (a) network effects
  (b) X-inefficiciency
  (c) economies of scale
  (d) simultaneous consumption

17. Which will tend to increase the inefficiencies of the monopoly producer?
  (a) price-taking behavior
  (b) rent-seeking behavior
  (c) economies of scale
  (d) technological progress

18. Which is one of the conditions that must be met before a seller finds that price discrimination is workable?
  (a) The demand for the product is perfectly elastic.
  (b) The seller must be able to segment the market.
  (c) The buyer must be able to resell the product.
  (d) The product must be a service.

19. A monopolist can segment two groups of buyers of its product based on elasticity of demand. Assume that ATC remains constant. The monopolist will maximize profit by charging
  (a) the highest price to all customers
  (b) the lowest price to all customers
  (c) a higher price to customers with an elastic demand and a lower price to customers with an inelastic demand
  (d) a lower price to customers with an elastic demand and a higher price to customers with an inelastic demand

Answer Questions 20, 21, and 22 based on the demand and cost data for a pure monopolist given in the following table.

Output	Price	Total cost
0	$1000	$ 500
1	600	520
2	500	580
3	400	700
4	300	1000
5	200	1500

20. The profit-maximizing output and price for this monopolist would be
(a) 1 and $100
(b) 2 and $200
(c) 3 and $400
(d) 4 and $300

21. At the profit-maximizing price and output, the amount of profit for the monopolist would be
(a) $200
(b) $340
(c) $420
(d) $500

22. If the monopolist were forced to produce the socially optimal output by the imposition of a government-set price, the regulated price would have to be
(a) $200
(b) $300
(c) $400
(d) $500

23. A monopolist who is limited by the imposition of a government-set or regulated price to a fair return would sell the product at a price equal to
(a) average total cost
(b) average variable cost
(c) marginal cost
(d) average fixed cost

Questions 24 and 25 are based on the following graph.

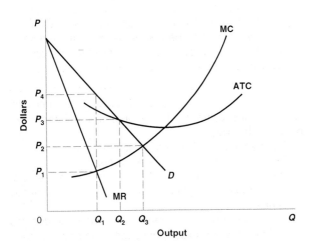

24. The price and output combination for the unregulated profit-maximizing monopoly compared with the socially optimal price and output combination for the regulated monopoly would be, respectively,
(a) P_4 and Q_1 versus P_3 and Q_2
(b) P_4 and Q_1 versus P_2 and Q_3
(c) P_3 and Q_2 versus P_4 and Q_1
(d) P_2 and Q_3 versus P_3 and Q_2

25. The dilemma of regulation that compares the fair-return price and output with the socially optimal price and output would be, respectively,

(a) P_4 and Q_1 versus P_3 and Q_2
(b) P_4 and Q_1 versus P_2 and Q_3
(c) P_3 and Q_2 versus P_4 and Q_1
(d) P_2 and Q_3 versus P_3 and Q_2

■ **PROBLEMS**

1. The demand schedule for the product produced by a monopolist is given in the following table.

Quantity demanded	Price	Total revenue	Marginal revenue	Price elasticity
0	$700	$_____		
1	650	_____	$_____	_____
2	600	_____	_____	_____
3	550	_____	_____	_____
4	500	_____	_____	_____
5	450	_____	_____	_____
6	400	_____	_____	_____
7	350	_____	_____	_____
8	300	_____	_____	_____
9	250	_____	_____	_____
10	200	_____	_____	_____
11	150	_____	_____	_____
12	100	_____	_____	_____
13	50	_____	_____	_____
14	0	_____	_____	_____

a. Complete the table by computing total revenue, marginal revenue, and the price elasticity of demand (use midpoints formula).
b. The relationships in the table indicate that
(1) total revenue rises from $0 to a maximum of

$_____ as price falls from $700 to $_____, and as price falls to $0, total revenue falls from its maximum to $_____;
(2) the relationship between price and total revenue suggests that demand is price (elastic, inelastic)

_____ when quantity demanded is between 0 and 7 units of output, but that demand is price (elastic,

inelastic) _____ when quantity demanded is between 8 units and 14 units;
(3) when demand is price elastic and total revenue rises from $0 to a maximum, marginal revenue is

(negative, positive) _____, but when demand is price inelastic and total revenue falls from its

maximum, marginal revenue is _____.
c. Use the data in the previous table and the following graph to plot and graph the demand curve and the marginal revenue curve for the monopolist. Indicate the portion of the demand curve that is price elastic and the portion that is price inelastic.

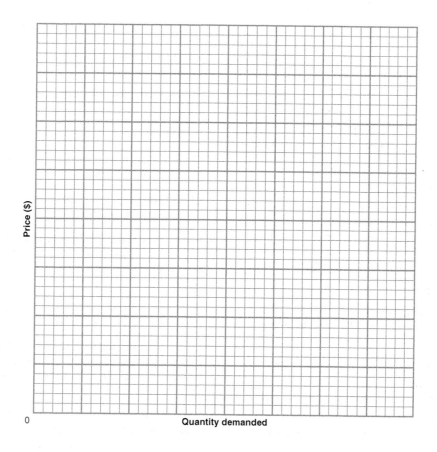

Price ($)

0 Quantity demanded

2. The following table shows demand and cost data for a pure monopolist.

Quantity demanded	Price	Total revenue	Marginal revenue	Total cost	Marginal cost
0	$17	$____		$10	
1	16	____	$____	18	$____
2	15	____	____	23	____
3	14	____	____	25	____
4	13	____	____	27	____
5	12	____	____	28	____
6	11	____	____	32	____
7	10	____	____	40	____
8	9	____	____	50	____
9	8	____	____	64	____
10	7	____	____	80	____

a. Complete the table by filling in the columns for total revenue, marginal revenue, and marginal cost.
b. Answer the next three questions using the data you calculated in the table.
(1) What output will the monopolist produce?

_____

(2) What price will the monopolist charge?

_____

(3) What total profit will the monopolist receive at the profit-maximizing level of output? _____

3. In the following table are cost and demand data for a pure monopolist.

Quantity demanded	Price	Marginal revenue	Average cost	Marginal cost
0	$17.50			
1	16.00	$16.00	$24.00	$24.00
2	14.50	13.00	15.00	6.00
3	13.00	10.00	11.67	5.00
4	11.50	7.00	10.50	7.00
5	10.00	4.00	10.00	8.00
6	8.50	1.00	9.75	8.50
7	7.00	−2.00	9.64	9.00
8	5.50	−5.00	9.34	9.25
9	4.00	−8.00	9.36	9.50

a. An unregulated monopolist would produce _____ units of this product, sell it at a price of $ _____, and receive a total profit of $_____.
b. If this monopolist were regulated and the maximum price it could charge were set equal to marginal cost, it would produce _____ units of a product, sell it at a price of $ _____, and receive a total profit of $_____. Such regulation would either _____ the firm or require that the regulating (bankrupt, subsidize) government _____ the firm.

c. If the monopolist were regulated and allowed to charge a fair-return price, it would produce _____ units of product, charge a price of $_____, and receive a profit of $_____.

d. From which situation—*a, b,* or *c*—does the most efficient allocation of resources result? _____ From which situation does the least efficient allocation result? _____ In practice, government would probably select situation _____.

4. Identify whether the following long-run conditions apply to a firm under pure monopoly (**M**), pure competition (**C**), or both. Put the appropriate letter(s) (**M** or **C**) next to the condition.

    a. There is the potential for long-run profits because price is greater than or equal to average total cost. _____

    b. The firm's demand curve is perfectly elastic. _____

    c. The firm maximizes profits at the output level where MC = MR. _____

    d. The firm exhibits productive efficiency because price is equal to the minimum average total cost. _____

    e. Price is greater than marginal revenue for each output level except the first. _____

    f. There is an optimal allocation of resources because price is equal to marginal cost. _____

■ SHORT ANSWER AND ESSAY QUESTIONS

1. What is pure monopoly? Define its characteristics.

2. Give examples of monopoly. How might a professional sports team be considered a monopoly when there are other such teams in the nation?

3. Why are the economies of scale a barrier to entry?

4. Why are most natural monopolies also public utilities? What does government hope to achieve by granting exclusive franchises to and regulating such natural monopolies?

5. How do patents and licenses create barriers to entry? Cite examples.

6. How can the monopolist use changes in price and other strategic actions to maintain a monopoly position?

7. Compare the pure monopolist and the individual pure competitor with respect to: (a) the demand schedule; (b) the marginal revenue schedule; (c) the relationship between marginal revenue and average revenue; (d) price policy, and (e) the ability to administer (or set) price.

8. Explain why marginal revenue is always less than average revenue (price) when demand is less than perfectly elastic.

9. Suppose a pure monopolist discovered it was producing and selling an output at which the demand for its product was inelastic. Explain why a decrease in its output would increase its economic profits.

10. How does the profit-maximizing monopolist determine what output to produce? What price will it charge?

11. Why is there no supply curve for a monopoly?

12. Why does the monopolist not charge the highest possible price for its product?

13. Why does the monopolist not set the price for its product in such a way that average profit is a maximum?

14. Why are some monopolies unprofitable? Explain what will happen to the firm in the short run and the long run in this situation.

15. In what sense are resource allocation and production more efficient under conditions of pure competition than under monopoly conditions?

16. How do monopolies allegedly affect the distribution of income in the economy and why do monopolies seemingly have this effect on income distribution in the U.S. economy?

17. What are some reasons why costs might differ between a monopoly and purely competitive firms operating in the same industry? Give at least four possible reasons.

18. Explain how economies of scale offset some of the economic inefficiencies of a monopoly. Evaluate the importance of this factor in reducing a monopolist's cost.

19. What is X-inefficiency? How does it affect the cost of production for the monopolist?

20. A monopolist will often engage in rent-seeking behavior. Explain what this means and how it changes a monopolist's cost.

21. Evaluate this statement from an economic perspective: "A pure monopoly has great incentive to discover and use new technology."

22. What is meant by price discrimination? Define it. What conditions must be met before it is workable?

23. Explain how a monopolist who can segment its market based on elasticity determines the price to charge for each unit of the product sold (or to charge each group of buyers).

24. How does price discrimination affect the profits and the output of the monopolist? How does it affect consumers?

25. Explain what public-utility regulatory agencies attempt to do to eliminate the misallocation of resources that results from monopoly. Describe the dilemma of regulation for these agencies and explain why a fair-return policy only reduces but does not eliminate misallocation.

ANSWERS

Chapter 10 Pure Monopoly

FILL-IN QUESTIONS

1. substitutes, blocked
2. public utilities, 80, sole
3. greater, difficult
4. patent, license
5. resources, price
6. down-sloping, less, decrease
7. increase, decrease, horizontal, down-sloping, elastic
8. marginal cost, average variable cost, does not exist
9. marginal, marginal, greater
10. highest, per-unit
11. is not, short run, weak
12. higher, less, less; *a.* total, minimum; *b.* price, marginal; *c.* higher, higher
13. costs; *a.* economies; *b.* inefficiency; *c.* rent-seeking; *d.* new technology
14. rare, weaken, substitute
15. inefficiency, antitrust, natural monopoly
16. prices, cost of
17. *a.* the seller has some monopoly power; *b.* the seller is able to separate buyers into groups that have different elasticities of demand for the product; *c.* the original buyers cannot resell the product
18. an increase
19. marginal, allocative
20. average total, allocative

TRUE–FALSE QUESTIONS

1. T, p.195
2. T, p. 195
3. T, p. 195
4. T, pp. 196–197
5. T, pp. 197–198
6. F, pp. 198–199
7. T, pp. 199–200
8. T, p. 200
9. F, pp. 200–201
10. F, pp. 201–202
11. F, p. 202
12. T, p. 202
13. F, pp. 202–203
14. T, pp. 203–204
15. T, p. 204
16. T, p. 205
17. F, p. 205
18. F, pp. 205–206
19. F, p. 206
20. T, pp. 206–207
21. T, pp. 207–208
22. T, pp. 207–208
23. F, pp. 209–210
24. T, pp. 210–211
25. T, p. 211

MULTIPLE-CHOICE QUESTIONS

1. b, p. 195
2. a, p. 196
3. c, pp. 197–198
4. b, pp. 198–199
5. c, pp. 198–199
6. d, pp. 198–199
7. a, p. 200
8. b, pp. 200–201
9. b, pp. 200–201
10. c, pp. 200–201
11. d, pp. 200–201
12. d, pp. 201–202
13. b, p. 202
14. d, pp. 203–204
15. a, pp. 203–204
16. d, p. 205
17. b, pp. 205–206
18. b, pp. 207–208
19. d, pp. 208–209
20. c, pp. 203–204
21. d, pp. 203–204
22. b, p. 210
23. a, pp. 210–211
24. b, pp. 202–203, 210
25. d, p. 211

PROBLEMS

1. *a.* Total revenue: $0, 650, 1200, 1650, 2000, 2250, 2400, 2450, 2400, 2250, 2000, 1650, 1200, 650, 0; Marginal revenue: $650, 550, 450, 350, 250, 150, 50, −50, −150, −250, −350, −450, −550, −650; Price elasticity: 27, 8.33, 4.60, 3.00, 2.11, 1.55, 1.15, .87, .65, .47, .33, .22, .12, .04; *b.* (1) $2450, $350, 0, (2) elastic, inelastic, (3) positive, negative; *c.* see Figure 10.3a in the text as an example
2. *a.* Total revenue: $0, 16, 30, 42, 52, 60, 66, 70, 72, 72, 70; Marginal revenue: $16, 14, 12, 10, 8, 6, 4, 2, 0, −2; Marginal cost: $8, 5, 2, 2, 1, 4, 8, 10, 14, 16; *b.* (1) 6, (2) $11, (3) $34 (TR of $66 minus TC of $32)
3. *a.* 4, 11.50, 4.00; *b.* 6, 8.50, −7.50, bankrupt, subsidize; *c.* 5, 10.00, zero; *d.* b, a, c
4. *a.* M; *b.* C; *c.* C, M; *d.* C; *e.* M; *f.* C

SHORT ANSWER AND ESSAY QUESTIONS

1. p. 195
2. p. 195
3. p. 196
4. p. 197
5. pp. 196–197
6. p. 197
7. pp. 197–200
8. pp. 198–199
9. p. 200
10. pp. 200–201
11. pp. 201–202
12. p. 202
13. p. 202
14. pp. 202–203
15. pp. 203–204
16. p. 204
17. pp. 204–206
18. p. 205
19. p. 205
20. pp. 205–206
21. p. 206
22. pp. 207–208
23. p. 207
24. pp. 208–209
25. pp. 209–211

18

AFTER READING THIS CHAPTER, YOU SHOULD BE ABLE TO:

1 List and explain the core elements of the major antitrust (antimonopoly) laws in the United States.

2 Describe some of the key issues relating to the interpretation and application of antitrust laws.

3 Identify and explain the economic principles and difficulties relating to the setting of prices (rates) charged by so-called natural monopolies.

4 Discuss the nature of "social regulation," its benefits and costs, and its optimal level.

Antitrust Policy and Regulation

We now can apply the economics of product markets (Part 3), resource markets (Part 4), and government (Part 5) to selected microeconomic issues and policies.

In this chapter we look at three sets of government policies toward business: antitrust policy, industrial regulation, and social regulation. **Antitrust policy** consists of laws and government actions designed to prevent monopoly and promote competition. **Industrial regulation** pertains to government regulation of firms' prices (or "rates") within selected industries. **Social regulation** is government regulation of the conditions under which goods are produced, the physical characteristics of goods, and the impact of the production and consumption of goods on society.

Then, in the remaining four chapters of Part 6, we discuss issues and policies relating to agriculture, income inequality, health care, and immigration.

The Antitrust Laws

The underlying purpose of antitrust policy (antimonopoly policy) is to prevent monopolization, promote competition, and achieve allocative efficiency. Although all economists would agree that these are meritorious goals, there is sharp conflict of opinion about the appropriateness and effectiveness of U.S. antitrust policy. As we will see, antitrust policy over the years has been neither clear-cut nor consistent.

Historical Background

Just after the U.S. Civil War (1861–1865), local markets widened into national markets because of improved transportation facilities, mechanized production methods, and sophisticated corporate structures. In the 1870s and 1880s, dominant firms formed in several industries, including petroleum, meatpacking, railroads, sugar, lead, coal, whiskey, and tobacco. Some of these oligopolists, near-monopolists, or monopolists were known as *trusts*—business combinations that assign control to a single decision group ("trustees"). Because these trusts "monopolized" industries, the word "trust" became synonymous with "monopoly" in common usage. The public, government, and historians began to define a business monopoly as a large-scale dominant seller, even though that seller was not always "a sole seller" as specified in the model of pure monopoly.

These dominant firms often used questionable tactics in consolidating their industries and then charged high prices to customers and extracted price concessions from resource suppliers. Farmers and owners of small businesses were particularly vulnerable to the power of large corporate monopolies and were among the first to oppose them. Consumers, labor unions, and economists were not far behind in their opposition.

The main economic case against monopoly is familiar to you from Chapter 10. Monopolists tend to produce less output and charge higher prices than would be the case if their industries were competitive. With pure competition, each competitive firm maximizes profit by producing the output level at which $P = MC$. That output level generates allocative efficiency because price P measures the marginal benefit to society of an extra unit of output while marginal cost MC reflects the cost of an extra unit. When $P = MC$, society cannot gain by producing 1 more or 1 less unit of the product. In contrast, a monopolist maximizes profit by producing the lower output level at which marginal revenue (rather than price) equals marginal cost. At this MR = MC point, price exceeds marginal cost, meaning that society would obtain more benefit than it would incur cost by producing extra units. An underallocation of resources to the monopolized product occurs, and the economy suffers

an efficiency loss. So society's economic well-being is less than it would be with greater competition.

But an efficiency loss isn't the only consequence of the monopolist's higher-than-competitive price. The higher price also transfers income from consumers to the monopolist. This transfer causes significant resentment because it results purely from the monopolist's ability to restrict output and cannot be justified on the basis of increased production costs. Consumers consequently express their ire to elected officials to "do something about the situation."

Responding to that pressure, government officials concluded in the late 1800s and early 1900s that monopolized industries lacked enough of the beneficial market forces that in competitive industries help to protect consumers, achieve fair competition, and achieve allocative efficiency. So the government instituted two alternative means of control as substitutes for, or supplements to, market forces:

- *Regulatory agencies* In the few markets where the nature of the product or technology creates a *natural monopoly*, the government established public regulatory agencies to control economic behavior.
- *Antitrust laws* In most other markets, social control took the form of antitrust (antimonopoly) legislation designed to inhibit or prevent the growth of monopoly.

Four particular pieces of Federal legislation, as refined and extended by various amendments, constitute the basic law relating to monopoly structure and conduct.

Sherman Act of 1890

The public resentment of trusts that emerged in the 1870s and 1880s culminated in the **Sherman Act** of 1890. This cornerstone of antitrust legislation is surprisingly brief and, at first glance, directly to the point. The core of the act resides in two provisions:

- *Section 1* "Every contract, combination in the form of a trust or otherwise, or conspiracy, in restraint of trade or commerce among the several States, or with foreign nations is declared to be illegal."
- *Section 2* "Every person who shall monopolize, or attempt to monopolize, or combine or conspire with any person or persons, to monopolize any part of the trade or commerce among the several states, or with foreign nations, shall be deemed guilty of a felony" (as later amended from "misdemeanor").

The Sherman Act thus outlawed *restraints of trade* (for example, collusive price-fixing and dividing up markets) as well as *monopolization*. Today, the U.S. Department of Justice, the Federal Trade Commission, injured private parties, or state attorney generals can file antitrust suits against alleged violators of the act. The courts can issue injunctions to prohibit anticompetitive practices or, if necessary, break up monopolists into competing firms. Courts can also fine and imprison violators. Further, parties injured by illegal combinations and conspiracies can sue the perpetrators for *treble damages*—awards of three times the amount of the monetary injury done to them.

The Sherman Act seemed to provide a sound foundation for positive government action against business monopolies. However, early court interpretations limited the scope of the act and created ambiguities of law. It became clear that a more explicit statement of the government's antitrust sentiments was needed. The business community itself sought a clearer statement of what was legal and what was illegal.

Clayton Act of 1914

The **Clayton Act** of 1914 contained the desired elaboration of the Sherman Act. Four sections of the act, in particular, were designed to strengthen and make explicit the intent of the Sherman Act:

- Section 2 outlaws *price discrimination* when such discrimination is not justified on the basis of cost differences and when it reduces competition.
- Section 3 prohibits **tying contracts,** in which a producer requires that a buyer purchase another (or others) of its products as a condition for obtaining a desired product.
- Section 7 prohibits the acquisition of stocks of competing corporations when the outcome would be less competition.
- Section 8 prohibits the formation of **interlocking directorates**—situations where a director of one firm is also a board member of a competing firm—in large corporations where the effect would be reduced competition.

The Clayton Act simply sharpened and clarified the general provisions of the Sherman Act. It also sought to outlaw the techniques that firms might use to develop monopoly power and, in that sense, was a preventive measure. Section 2 of the Sherman Act, by contrast, was aimed more at breaking up existing monopolies.

Federal Trade Commission Act of 1914

The **Federal Trade Commission Act** created the five-member Federal Trade Commission (FTC), which has joint Federal responsibility with the U.S. Justice Department for enforcing the antitrust laws. The act gave the FTC the power to investigate unfair competitive practices on its own initiative or at the request of injured firms. It can hold public hearings on such complaints and, if necessary, issue

cease-and-desist orders in cases where it discovers "unfair methods of competition in commerce."

The **Wheeler-Lea Act** of 1938 amended the Federal Trade Commission Act to give the FTC the additional responsibility of policing "deceptive acts or practices in commerce." In so doing, the FTC tries to protect the public against false or misleading advertising and the misrepresentation of products. So the Federal Trade Commission Act, as modified by the Wheeler-Lea Act, (1) established the FTC as an independent antitrust agency and (2) made unfair and deceptive sales practices illegal.

The FTC is highly active in enforcing the deceptive advertising statues. As one recent example, in 2007 the FTC fined four makers of over-the-counter diet pills a collective $25 million for claiming their products produced fast and permanent weight loss.

Celler-Kefauver Act of 1950

The **Celler-Kefauver Act** amended the Clayton Act, Section 7, which prohibits a firm from merging with a competing firm (and thereby lessening competition) by acquiring its stock. Firms could evade Section 7, however, by instead acquiring the physical assets (plant and equipment) of competing firms. The Celler-Kefauver Act closed that loophole by prohibiting one firm from obtaining the physical assets of another firm when the effect would be reduced competition. Section 7 of the Clayton Act now prohibits anticompetitive mergers no matter how they are undertaken.

Antitrust Policy:
Issues and Impacts

The effectiveness of any law depends on how the courts interpret it and on the vigor of government enforcement. The courts have been inconsistent in interpreting the antitrust laws. At times, they have applied them vigorously, adhering closely to their spirit and objectives. At other times, their interpretations have rendered certain laws nearly powerless. The Federal government itself has varied considerably in its aggressiveness in enforcing the antitrust laws. Some administrations have made tough antitrust enforcement a high priority. Other administrations have taken a more laissez-faire approach, initiating few antitrust actions or even scaling back the budgets of the enforcement agencies.

Issues of Interpretation

Differences in judicial interpretations have led to vastly different applications of the antitrust laws. Two questions, in particular, have arisen: (1) Should the focus of antitrust policy be on monopoly behavior or on monopoly structure? (2) How broadly should markets be defined in antitrust cases?

Monopoly Behavior versus Monopoly Structure

A comparison of three landmark Supreme Court decisions reveals two distinct interpretations of Section 2 of the Sherman Act as it relates to monopoly behavior and structure.

In the 1911 **Standard Oil case,** the Supreme Court found Standard Oil guilty of monopolizing the petroleum industry through a series of abusive and anticompetitive actions. The Court's remedy was to divide Standard Oil into several competing firms. But the Standard Oil case left open an important question: Is every monopoly in violation of Section 2 of the Sherman Act or just those created or maintained by anticompetitive actions?

In the 1920 **U.S. Steel case,** the courts established the so-called **rule of reason,** under which not every monopoly is illegal. Only monopolies that "unreasonably" restrain trade violate Section 2 of the Sherman Act and are subject to antitrust action. Size alone is not an offense. Under the rule of reason, U.S. Steel was innocent of "monopolizing" because it had not resorted to illegal acts against competitors in obtaining and then maintaining its monopoly power. Unlike Standard Oil, which was a so-called bad trust, U.S. Steel was a "good trust" and therefore not in violation of the law.

In the **Alcoa case** of 1945 the courts touched off a 20-year turnabout. The Supreme Court sent the case to the U.S. court of appeals in New York because four of the Supreme Court justices had been involved with litigation of the case before their appointments. Led by Judge Learned Hand, the court of appeals held that, even though a firm's behavior might be legal, the mere possession of monopoly power (Alcoa held 90 percent of the aluminum ingot market) violated the antitrust laws. So Alcoa was found guilty of violating the Sherman Act.

These two cases point to a controversy in antitrust policy. Should a firm be judged by its behavior (as in the U.S. Steel case) or by its structure or market share (as in the Alcoa case)?

- "Structuralists" assume that any firm with a very high market share will behave like a monopoly. As a result, they assert that any firm with a very high market share is a legitimate target for antitrust action. Structuralists argue that changes in the structure of an industry, say, by splitting the monopolist into several smaller firms, will improve behavior and performance.

- "Behavioralists" assert that the relationship among structure, behavior, and performance is tenuous and unclear. They feel a monopolized or highly concentrated industry may be technologically progressive and have a good record of providing products of increasing quality at reasonable prices. If a firm has served society well and has engaged in no anticompetitive practices, it should not be accused of antitrust violation just because it has an extraordinarily large market share. That share may be the product of superior technology, superior products, and economies of scale. "Why use antitrust laws to penalize efficient, technologically progressive, well-managed firms?" they ask.

Over the past 25 years, the courts have returned to the rule of reason first established in the 1920 U.S. Steel case, and most contemporary economists and antitrust enforcers reject strict structuralism. For instance, in 1982 the government dropped its 13-year-long monopolization case against IBM on the grounds that IBM had not unreasonably restrained trade, despite having possessed extremely high market share in the market for mainframe computers. More recently, the government has made no attempt to break up Intel's near monopoly in the sale of microprocessors for personal computers. And in prosecuting the Microsoft case (the subject of this chapter's Last Word), the Federal government made it clear that the behavior used by Microsoft to maintain and extend its monopoly, not the presence of its large market share, violated the Sherman Act. In essence, the government declared Microsoft to be "a bad monopoly" that could become a good monopoly if it stopped doing bad things.

The Relevant Market Courts often decide whether or not market power exists by considering the share of the market held by the dominant firm. They have roughly adhered to a "90-60-30 rule" in defining monopoly: If a firm has a 90 percent market share, it is definitely a monopolist; if it has a 60 percent market share, it probably is a monopolist; if it has a 30 percent market share, it clearly is not a monopolist. The market share will depend on how the market is defined. If the market is defined broadly to include a wide range of somewhat similar products, the firm's market share will appear small. If the market is defined narrowly to exclude such products, the market share will seem large. The Supreme Court has the final say on how broadly to define relevant markets, but the Supreme Court has not always been consistent.

In the Alcoa case, the Court used a narrow definition of the relevant market: the aluminum ingot market. But in the **DuPont cellophane case** of 1956 the Court defined the market very broadly. The government contended that DuPont, along with a licensee, controlled 100 percent of the cellophane market. But the Court accepted DuPont's contention that the relevant market included all "flexible packaging materials"—waxed paper, aluminum foil, and so forth, in addition to cellophane. Despite DuPont's monopoly in the "cellophane market," it controlled only 20 percent of the market for "flexible wrapping materials." The Court ruled that this did not constitute a monopoly.

Issues of Enforcement

Some U.S. presidential administrations have enforced the antitrust laws more strictly than others. The degree of Federal antitrust enforcement makes a difference in the overall degree of antitrust action in the economy. It is true that individual firms can sue other firms under the antitrust laws. For example, in 2005 AMD—a maker of microprocessors—filed an antitrust suit against Intel, claiming that Intel was a monopolist that used anticompetitive business practices to thwart the growth of AMD's market share. But major antitrust suits often last years and are highly expensive. Injured parties therefore often look to the Federal government to initiate and litigate such cases. Once the Federal government gains a conviction, the injured parties no longer need to prove guilt and can simply sue the violator to obtain treble damages. In many cases, lack of Federal antitrust action therefore means diminished legal action by firms.

Why might one administration enforce the antitrust laws more or less strictly than another? The main reason is differences in political philosophies about the market economy and the wisdom of intervention by government. There are two contrasting general perspectives on antitrust policy.

The *active antitrust perspective* is that competition is insufficient in some circumstances to achieve allocative efficiency and ensure fairness to consumers and competing firms. Firms occasionally use illegal tactics against competitors to dominate markets. In other instances, competitors collude to fix prices or merge to enhance their monopoly power. Active, strict enforcement of the antitrust laws is needed to stop illegal business practices, prevent anticompetitive mergers, and remedy monopoly. This type of government intervention maintains the viability and vibrancy of the market system and thus allows society to reap its full benefits. In this view, the antitrust authorities need to act much like the officials in a football game. They must observe the players, spot infractions, and enforce the rules.

In contrast, the *laissez-faire perspective* holds that antitrust intervention is largely unnecessary, particularly as it relates to monopoly. Economists holding this position view competition as a long-run dynamic process in which firms battle against each other for dominance of markets. In some markets, a firm successfully monopolizes the market, usually because of its superior innovativeness or business skill. But in exploiting its monopoly power to raise prices, these firms inadvertently create profit incentives and profit opportunities for other entrepreneurs and firms to develop alternative technologies and new products to better serve consumers. As discussed in Chapter 2 and expanded upon in Chapter 9, a process of *creative destruction* occurs in which today's monopolies are eroded and eventually destroyed by tomorrow's technologies and products. The government therefore should not try to break up a monopoly. It should stand aside and allow the long-run competitive process to work.

> **ORIGIN OF THE IDEA**
> **O 18.1**
> Creative destruction

The extent to which a particular administration adheres to—or leans toward—one of these contrasting antitrust perspectives usually gets reflected in the appointments to the agencies overseeing antitrust policy. Those appointees help determine how strictly the laws are enforced.

Effectiveness of Antitrust Laws

Have the antitrust laws been effective? Although this question is difficult to answer, we can at least observe how the laws have been applied to monopoly, mergers, price-fixing, price discrimination, and tying contracts.

Monopoly On the basis of the rule of reason, the government has generally been lenient in applying antitrust laws to monopolies that have developed naturally. Generally, a firm will be sued by the Federal government only if it has a very high market share and there is evidence of abusive conduct in achieving, maintaining, or extending its market dominance.

But even if the Federal government wins the antitrust lawsuit, there is still the matter of *remedy:* What actions should the court order to correct for the anticompetitive practices of the monopoly that lost the lawsuit?

The issue of remedy arose in two particularly noteworthy monopoly cases. The first was the AT&T (American Telephone and Telegraph) case in which the government charged AT&T with violating the Sherman Act by engaging in anticompetitive practices designed to maintain its domestic telephone monopoly. As part of an out-of-court settlement between the government and AT&T, in 1982 AT&T agreed to divest itself of its 22 regional telephone-operating companies.

A second significant monopoly case was the **Microsoft case.** In 2000 Microsoft was found guilty of violating the Sherman Act by taking several unlawful actions designed to maintain its monopoly of operating systems for

FIGURE 18.1 **Types of mergers.** Horizontal mergers (T + U) bring together firms selling the same product in the same geographic market; vertical mergers (F + Z) connect firms having a buyer-seller relationship; and conglomerate mergers (C + D) join firms in different industries or firms operating in different geographic areas.

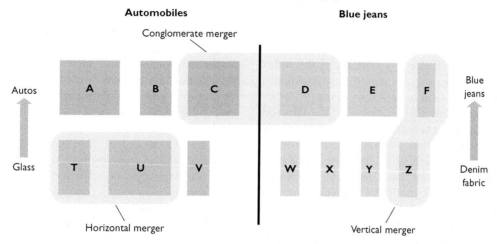

personal computers. A lower court ordered that Microsoft be split into two competing firms. A court of appeals upheld the lower-court finding of abusive monopoly but rescinded the breakup of Microsoft. Instead of the structural remedy, the eventual outcome was a behavioral remedy in which Microsoft was prohibited from engaging in a set of specific anticompetitive business practices.

The antitrust agency for the European Union (EU) has generally been more aggressive than the United States in prosecuting monopolists. For example, in 2004 the EU fined Microsoft $600 million for monopolization and required it to share its computer code with other firms that supplied Windows applications (such as media players). The purpose of the code-sharing requirement was to enable competitors to compete on an equal footing against Microsoft's own application software. Microsoft was fined a further $1.3 billion by the EU in 2008 for failing to quickly and fully comply with the 2004 remedy ordering Microsoft to share its computer code.

Mergers The treatment of mergers, or combinations of existing firms, varies with the type of merger and its effect on competition.

Merger Types

There are three basic types of mergers, as represented in Figure 18.1. This figure shows two stages of production (the input stage and the output, or final-product, stage) for two distinct final-goods industries (autos and blue jeans). Each rectangle (A, B, C, . . . X, Y, Z) represents a particular firm.

A **horizontal merger** is a merger between two competitors that sell similar products in the same geographic market. In Figure 18.1 this type of merger is shown as a combination of glass producers T and U. Actual examples of such mergers include Chase Manhattan's merger with Chemical Bank, Boeing's merger with McDonnell Douglas, and Exxon's merger with Mobil.

A **vertical merger** is a merger between firms at different stages of the production process. In Figure 18.1, the merger between firm Z, a producer of denim fabric, and firm F, a producer of blue jeans, is a vertical merger. Vertical mergers are mergers between firms that have buyer-seller relationships. Actual examples of such mergers are PepsiCo's mergers with Pizza Hut, Taco Bell, and Kentucky Fried Chicken. PepsiCo supplies soft drinks to each of these fast-food outlets. (In 1997, PepsiCo spun off these entities into a separate company now called Yum! Brands.)

A **conglomerate merger** is officially defined as any merger that is not horizontal or vertical; in general, it is the combination of firms in different industries or firms operating in different geographic areas. Conglomerate mergers can extend the line of products sold, extend the territory in which products are sold, or combine totally unrelated companies. In Figure 18.1, the merger between firm C, an auto manufacturer, and firm D, a blue jeans producer, is a conglomerate merger. Real-world examples of conglomerate mergers include the merger between Walt Disney Company (movies) and the American Broadcasting Company (radio and television) and the merger between America Online (Internet service provider) and Time Warner (communications).

Merger Guidelines: The Herfindahl Index

The Federal government has established very loose merger

guidelines based on the Herfindahl index. Recall from Chapter 11 that this measure of concentration is the sum of the squared percentage market shares of the firms within an industry. An industry of only four firms, each with a 25 percent market share, has a Herfindahl index of $2500 (= 25^2 + 25^2 + 25^2 + 25^2)$. In pure competition, where each firm's market share is minuscule, the index approaches $0 (= 0^2 + 0^2 + \ldots + 0^2)$. In pure monopoly, the index for that single firm is $10,000 (= 100^2)$.

The U.S. government uses Section 7 of the Clayton Act to block horizontal mergers that will substantially lessen competition. It is likely to challenge a horizontal merger if the postmerger Herfindahl index would be high (above 1800) and if the merger has substantially increased the index (added 100 or more points). However, other factors, such as economies of scale, the degree of foreign competition, and the ease of entry of new firms, are also considered. Furthermore, horizontal mergers are usually allowed if one of the merging firms is suffering major and continuing losses. (This is one reason Boeing was allowed to acquire McDonnell Douglas in 1996: MD was losing money in producing its commercial airplanes.)

During the past several decades, the Federal government has blocked several proposed horizontal mergers. For example, it blocked mergers between Staples and Office Depot, two major office-supply retailers; WorldCom and Sprint, two competing telecommunications firms; and Hughes (DirecTV) and Echostar (DISH Network), providers of direct-broadcast satellite television.

More recently, the Federal government successfully challenged mergers between Snyder's of Hanover and Utz Quality Foods, makers of pretzels; Polypore and Microporous, battery-parts makers; and Blue Cross Blue Shield of Michigan and Physician's Health Plan of Michigan, health insurance providers.

Most *vertical mergers* escape antitrust prosecution because they do not substantially lessen competition in either of the two markets. (In Figure 18.1 neither the Herfindahl index in the industry producing denim fabric nor the index in the blue jeans industry changes when firms Z and F merge vertically.) However, a vertical merger between large firms in highly concentrated industries may be challenged. For example, in 1999 the threat of FTC action spurred Barnes & Noble to abandon its merger with Ingram Book Company, the nation's largest book wholesaler. The merger would have enabled Barnes & Noble to set the wholesale price of books charged to its direct retail competitors such as Borders and Amazon.com.

Conglomerate mergers are generally permitted. If an auto manufacturer acquires a blue jeans producer, no antitrust action is likely since neither firm has increased its own market share as a result. That means the Herfindahl index remains unchanged in each industry.

Price-Fixing Price-fixing among competitors is treated strictly. Evidence of price-fixing, even by small firms, will bring antitrust action, as will other collusive activities such as scheming to rig bids on government contracts or dividing up sales in a market. In antitrust law, these activities are known as **per se violations;** they are "in and of themselves" illegal, and therefore are *not* subject to the rule of reason. To gain a conviction, the government or other party making the charge need show only that there was a conspiracy to fix prices, rig bids, or divide up markets, not that the conspiracy succeeded or caused serious damage to other parties.

Price-fixing investigations and court actions are common. (See the Consider This box to the right).

Price Discrimination Price discrimination is a common business practice that rarely reduces competition and therefore is rarely challenged by government. The exception occurs when a firm engages in price discrimination as part of a strategy to block entry or drive out competitors.

Tying Contracts The Federal government strictly enforces the prohibition of tying contracts, particularly when practiced by dominant firms. For example, it stopped movie distributors from forcing theaters to buy the projection rights to a full package of films as a condition of showing a blockbuster movie. Also, it prevented Kodak—the dominant maker of photographic film—from requiring that consumers process their film only through Kodak.

What then can we conclude about the overall effectiveness of antitrust laws? Antitrust policy has not been very effective in restricting the rise of or in breaking up monopolies or oligopolies resulting from legally undertaken internal expansions of firms. But most economists do not deem that to be a flaw. The antitrust laws have been used more effectively against predatory or abusive monopoly, but that effectiveness has been diminished by the slow legal process and consequently long time between the filing of charges and the implementation of remedies. In contrast, antitrust policy *has* been effective in blocking blatantly anticompetitive mergers and in identifying and prosecuting price-fixing and tying contracts.

Most economists conclude that, overall, U.S. antitrust policy has been moderately effective in achieving its goal of promoting competition and efficiency. Much of the success of antitrust policy arises from its deterrent effect on price-fixing and anticompetitive mergers. Some

CONSIDER THIS . . .

Of Catfish and Art (and Other Things in Common)

Examples of price-fixing are numerous. Here are just a few:

- In 1996 ConAgra and Hormel agreed to pay more than $21 million to settle their roles in a nationwide price-fixing case involving catfish.
- In 1996 Archer Daniels Midland (ADM) and other agribusinesses admitted fixing the prices of citric acid and an additive to livestock feed. In the early 2000s ADM, Cargill, and Corn Products admitted fixing the price of high-fructose syrup, a sweetener made from corn. In 2004 ADM paid $430 million to resolve the government's antitrust action.
- The U.S. Justice Department fined UCAR International $110 million in 1998 for scheming with competitors to fix prices and divide up the world market for graphite electrodes used in steel mills.
- In 2001 a court found the auction houses Sotheby's and Christie's guilty of conspiring over a 6-year period to set the same commission rates for sellers at auctions.
- In the early 2000s Samsung (South Korea), Hynix Semiconductor (South Korea), Infineon (Germany), and Micron (United States) were found to have fixed the price of dynamic random access memory chips (DRAMs), which are used in personal computers, printers, cell phones, and other electronic devices. In 2004 and 2005, the companies paid fines totaling $645 million.
- In 2007 British Airlines and Korean Air agreed to pay fines of $300 million each for conspiring to fix fuel surcharges on passenger tickets and cargo.
- Between 2008 and 2010, five manufacturers of liquid crystal displays—LG, Sharp, Hitachi, Chi Mei Optoelectronics, and Chunghwa Picture Tubes—were fined a total of over $860 million by the U.S. Justice Department for fixing the prices of the displays they sold to computer maker Dell Inc.
- In 2009, three international cargo airlines—Cargolux of Luxembourg, Nippon Cargo of Japan, and Asiana Airlines of South Korea—were fined $214 million by the U.S. Justice Department for conspiring to fix international airline cargo rates.

economists, however, think that enforcement of antitrust laws has been too weak. Others believe that parts of U.S. antitrust policy are anachronistic in an era of rapidly changing technology that continuously undermines existing monopoly power.

Industrial Regulation

Antitrust policy assumes that society will benefit if a monopoly is prevented from evolving or if it is dissolved where it already exists. We now return to a special situation in which there is an economic reason for an industry to be organized monopolistically.

Natural Monopoly

A **natural monopoly** exists when economies of scale are so extensive that a single firm can supply the entire market at a lower average total cost than could a number of competing firms. Clear-cut circumstances of natural monopoly are relatively rare, but such conditions exist for many *public utilities,* such as local electricity, water, and natural gas providers. As discussed in Chapter 10, large-scale operations in some cases are necessary to obtain low unit costs and a low product price. Where natural monopoly occurs, competition is uneconomical. If the market were divided among many producers, economies of scale would not be achieved and unit costs and prices would be higher than necessary.

There are two possible alternatives for promoting better economic outcomes where natural monopoly exists. One is public ownership, and the other is public regulation.

TABLE 18.1 The Main Regulatory Commissions Providing Industrial Regulation

Commission (Year Established)	Jurisdiction
Federal Energy Regulatory Commission (1930)*	Electricity, gas, gas pipelines, oil pipelines, water-power sites
Federal Communications Commission (1934)	Telephones, television, cable television, radio, telegraph, CB radios, ham operators
State public utility commissions (various years)	Electricity, gas, telephones

*Originally called the Federal Power Commission; renamed in 1977.

Public ownership or some approximation of it has been established in a few instances. Examples: the Postal Service, the Tennessee Valley Authority, and Amtrak at the national level and mass transit, water supply systems, and garbage collection at the local level.

But *public regulation*, or what economists call *industrial regulation*, has been the preferred option in the United States. In this type of regulation, government commissions regulate the prices (or "rates") charged by natural monopolists. Table 18.1 lists the two major Federal regulatory commissions and their jurisdictions. It also notes that all 50 states have commissions that regulate the intrastate activities and "utility rates" of local natural monopolies.

The economic objective of industrial regulation is embodied in the **public interest theory of regulation.** In that theory, industrial regulation is necessary to keep a natural monopoly from charging monopoly prices and thus harming consumers and society. The goal of such regulation is to garner for society at least part of the cost reductions associated with natural monopoly while avoiding the restrictions of output and high prices associated with unregulated monopoly. If competition is inappropriate or impractical, society should allow or even encourage a monopoly but regulate its prices. Regulation should then be structured so that ratepayers benefit from the economies of scale—the lower per-unit costs—that natural monopolists are able to achieve.

In practice, regulators seek to establish rates that will cover production costs and yield a "fair" return to the enterprise. The goal is to set price equal to average total cost so that the regulated firm receives a normal profit, as described in the "Regulated Monopoly" section of Chapter 10. In particular, you should carefully review Figure 10.9.

Problems with Industrial Regulation

There is considerable disagreement on the effectiveness of industrial regulation. Let's examine two criticisms.

Costs and Inefficiency An unregulated firm has a strong incentive to reduce its costs at each level of output because that will increase its profit. The regulatory commission, however, confines the regulated firm to a normal profit or a "fair return" on the value of its assets. If a regulated firm lowers its operating costs, the rising profit eventually will lead the regulatory commission to require that the firm lower its rates in order to return its profits to normal. The regulated firm therefore has little or no incentive to reduce its operating costs.

Worse yet, higher costs do not result in lower profit. Because the regulatory commission must allow the public utility a fair return, the regulated monopolist can simply pass through higher production costs to consumers by charging higher rates. A regulated firm may reason that it might as well have high salaries for its workers, opulent working conditions for management, and the like, since the "return" is the same in percentage terms whether costs are minimized or not. So, although a natural monopoly reduces costs through economies of scale, industrial regulation fosters considerable X-inefficiency (Figure 10.7). Due to the absence of competition, the potential cost savings from natural monopoly may never actually materialize.

Perpetuating Monopoly A second general problem with industrial regulation is that it sometimes perpetuates monopoly long after the conditions of natural monopoly have ended.

Technological change often creates the potential for competition in some or even all portions of the regulated industry. Examples: Trucks began competing with railroads; transmission of voice and data by microwave and satellites began competing with transmission over telephone wires; satellite television began competing with cable television; and cell phones began competing with landline phones.

But spurred by the firms they regulate, commissions often protect the regulated firms from new competition by either blocking entry or extending regulation to competitors. Industrial regulation therefore may perpetuate a monopoly that is no longer a natural monopoly and would otherwise erode. Ordinary monopoly, protected by government, may supplant natural monopoly. If so, the regulated prices may exceed those that would occur with competition. The beneficiaries of outdated regulation are the regulated firms and their employees. The losers are consumers and the potential entrants.

Example: Regulation of the railroads by the Interstate Commerce Commission (ICC) was justified in the late 1800s and early 1900s. But by the 1930s, with the emergence of a network of highways, the trucking industry had seriously undermined the monopoly power of the railroads.

That is, for the transport of many goods over many routes, railroad service was no longer a natural monopoly. At that time it would have been desirable to dismantle the ICC and let railroads and truckers, along with barges and airlines, compete with one another. Instead, in the 1930s the ICC extended regulation of rates to interstate truckers. The ICC remained in place until its elimination in 1996. It was eliminated because the deregulation of railroads and trucking in the late 1970s and early 1980s had made its work irrelevant.

Second example: Until recently, both long-distance telephone companies such as AT&T as well as cable-television providers such as Time Warner were prohibited from offering local telephone services in competition with regulated local and regional telephone companies. But the very fact that AT&T, Time Warner, and other firms wanted to compete with regulated monopolies calls into question whether those local providers are in fact natural monopolies or government-protected monopolies.

Legal Cartel Theory

The regulation of potentially competitive industries has produced the **legal cartel theory of regulation.** In place of having socially minded officials forcing regulation on natural monopolies to protect consumers, holders of this view see practical politicians "supplying" regulation to local, regional, and national firms that fear the impact of competition on their profits or even on their long-term survival. These firms desire regulation because it yields a legal monopoly that can virtually guarantee a profit. Specifically, the regulatory commission performs such functions as blocking entry (for example, in local telephone service). Or, where there are several firms, the commission divides up the market much like an illegal cartel (for example, prior to airline deregulation, the Civil Aeronautics Board assigned routes to specific airlines). The commission may also restrict potential competition by enlarging the "cartel" (for example, the ICC's addition of trucking to its regulatory domain).

While private cartels are illegal and unstable and often break down, the special attraction of a government-sponsored cartel under the guise of regulation is that it endures. The legal cartel theory of regulation suggests that regulation results from the rent-seeking activities of private firms and the desire of politicians to be responsive in order to win reelection (Chapter 17).

Proponents of the legal cartel theory of regulation note that the Interstate Commerce Commission was welcomed by the railroads and that the trucking and airline industries both supported the extension of ICC regulation to their industries, arguing that unregulated competition was severe and destructive.

Occupational licensing is a labor market application of the legal cartel theory. Certain occupational groups—barbers, dentists, hairstylists, interior designers, dietitians, lawyers—demand stringent licensing on the grounds that it protects the public from charlatans and quacks. But skeptics say the real reason may be to limit entry into the occupational group so that practitioners can receive monopoly incomes.

Deregulation

Beginning in the 1970s, evidence of inefficiency in regulated industries and the contention that the government was regulating potentially competitive industries contributed to a wave of deregulation. Since then, Congress and many state legislatures have passed legislation that has deregulated in varying degrees the airline, trucking, banking, railroad, natural gas, television, and electricity industries. Deregulation has also occurred in the telecommunications industry, where antitrust authorities dismantled the regulated monopoly known as the Bell System (AT&T). Deregulation in the 1970s and 1980s was one of the most extensive experiments in economic policy to take place during the last 50 years.

The overwhelming consensus among economists is that deregulation has produced large net benefits for consumers and society. Most of the gains from deregulation have occurred in three industries: airlines, railroads, and trucking. Airfares (adjusted for inflation) declined by about one-third, and airline safety has continued to improve. Trucking and railroad freight rates (again, adjusted for inflation) dropped by about one-half.

Significant efficiency gains were also realized in long-distance telecommunications, and there have been slight efficiency gains in cable television, stock brokerage services, and the natural gas industry. Moreover, deregulation has unleashed a wave of technological advances that have resulted in such new and improved products and services as fax machines, cellular phones, fiber-optic cable, microwave communication systems, and the Internet.

The most recent and perhaps controversial industry to be deregulated is electricity. Deregulation is relatively advanced at the wholesale level, where firms can buy and sell electricity at market prices. They are also free to build generating facilities and sell electricity to local electricity providers at unregulated prices. In addition, several states have deregulated retail prices and encouraged households and businesses to choose among available electricity suppliers. This competition has generally lowered electricity rates for consumers and enhanced allocative efficiency.

But deregulation suffered a severe setback in California, where wholesale electricity prices, but not retail rates, were deregulated. Wholesale electricity prices surged in 2001 when California experienced electricity shortages. Because they could not pass on wholesale price increases to consumers, California electric utilities suffered large financial losses. California then filed lawsuits against several energy-trading companies that allegedly manipulated electricity supplies to boost the wholesale price of electricity during the California energy crisis. One multibillion-dollar energy trader—Enron—collapsed in 2002 when Federal investigators uncovered a pattern of questionable and fraudulent business and accounting practices.

The California deregulation debacle and the Enron collapse have muddied the overall assessment of electricity deregulation in the United States. It is simply much too soon to declare that deregulation of electricity is either a success or a failure.

QUICK REVIEW 18.2

- Natural monopoly occurs where economies of scale are so extensive that only a single firm can produce the product at minimum average total cost.
- The public interest theory of regulation says that government must regulate natural monopolies to prevent abuses arising from monopoly power. Regulated firms, however, have less incentive than competitive firms to reduce costs. That is, regulated firms tend to be X-inefficient.
- The legal cartel theory of regulation suggests that some firms seek government regulation to reduce price competition and ensure stable profits.
- Deregulation initiated by government in the past several decades has yielded large annual efficiency gains for society.

Social Regulation

The industrial regulation discussed in the preceding section has focused on the regulation of prices (or rates) in natural monopolies. But in the early 1960s a new type of regulation began to emerge. This *social regulation* is concerned with the conditions under which goods and services are produced, the impact of production on society, and the physical qualities of the goods themselves.

The Federal government carries out most of the social regulation, although states also play a role. In Table 18.2 we list the main Federal regulatory commissions engaged in social regulation.

Distinguishing Features

Social regulation differs from industrial regulation in several ways.

First, social regulation applies to far more firms than does industrial regulation. Social regulation is often

TABLE 18.2 The Main Federal Regulatory Commissions Providing Social Regulation

Commission (Year Established)	Jurisdiction
Food and Drug Administration (1906)	Safety and effectiveness of food, drugs, and cosmetics
Equal Employment Opportunity Commission (1964)	Hiring, promotion, and discharge of workers
Occupational Safety and Health Administration (1971)	Industrial health and safety
Environmental Protection Agency (1972)	Air, water, and noise pollution
Consumer Product Safety Commission (1972)	Safety of consumer products

applied "across the board" to all industries and directly affects more producers than does industrial regulation. For instance, while the industrial regulation of the Federal Energy Regulatory Commission (FERC) applies to a relatively small number of firms, the rules and regulations issued by the Occupational Safety and Health Administration (OSHA) apply to firms in all industries.

Second, social regulation intrudes into the day-to-day production process to a greater extent than industrial regulation. While industrial regulation focuses on rates, costs, and profits, social regulation often dictates the design of products, the conditions of employment, and the nature of the production process. As examples, the Consumer Product Safety Commission (CPSC) regulates the design of potentially unsafe products, and the Environmental Protection Agency (EPA) regulates the amount of pollution allowed during production.

Finally, social regulation has expanded rapidly during the same period in which industrial regulation has waned. Between 1970 and 1980, the U.S. government created 20 new social regulatory agencies. More recently, Congress has established new social regulations to be enforced by existing regulatory agencies. For example, the Equal Employment Opportunity Commission, which is responsible for enforcing laws against workplace discrimination on the basis of race, gender, age, or religion, has been given the added duty of enforcing the Americans with Disabilities Act of 1990. Under this social regulation, firms must provide reasonable accommodations for qualified workers and job applicants with disabilities. Also, sellers must provide reasonable access for customers with disabilities.

The names of the regulatory agencies in Table 18.2 suggest the reasons for their creation and growth. As much of our society had achieved a fairly affluent standard of living by the 1960s, attention shifted to improvement in the nonmaterial quality of life. The new focus called for safer products, less pollution, improved working conditions, and greater equality of economic opportunity.

The Optimal Level of Social Regulation

While economists agree on the need for social regulation, they disagree on whether or not the current level of such regulation is optimal. Recall that an activity should be expanded as long as its marginal benefit (MB) exceeds its marginal cost (MC). If the MB of social regulation exceeds its MC, then there is too little social regulation. But if MC exceeds MB, there is too much (review Figure 5.9). Unfortunately, the marginal costs and benefits of social regulation are not always easy to measure. So ideology about the proper size and role of government often drives the debate over social regulation as much as, or perhaps more than, economic cost-benefit analysis.

In Support of Social Regulation Defenders of social regulation say that it has achieved notable successes and, overall, has greatly enhanced society's well-being. They point out that the problems that social regulation confronts are serious and substantial. According to the National Safety Council, about 5000 workers die annually in job-related accidents and 3.7 million workers suffer injuries that force them to miss a day or more of work. Air pollution continues to cloud major U.S. cities, imposing large costs in terms of reduced property values and increased health care expense. Numerous children and adults die each year because of poorly designed or manufactured products (for example, car tires) or tainted food (for example, *E. coli* in beef). Discrimination against some ethnic and racial minorities, persons with disabilities, and older workers reduces their earnings and imposes heavy costs on society.

Proponents of social regulation acknowledge that social regulation is costly. But they correctly point out that a high "price" for something does not necessarily mean that it should not be purchased. They say that the appropriate economic test should be not whether the costs of social regulation are high or low but, rather, whether the benefits of social regulation exceed the costs. After decades of neglect, they further assert, society cannot expect to cleanse the environment, enhance the safety of the workplace, and promote economic opportunity for all without incurring substantial costs. So statements about the huge costs of social regulation are irrelevant, say defenders, since the benefits are even greater. The public often underestimates those benefits since they are more difficult to measure than costs and often become apparent only after

some time has passed (for example, the benefits of reducing global warming).

Proponents of social regulation point to its many specific benefits. Here are just a few examples: It is estimated that highway fatalities would be 40 percent greater annually in the absence of auto safety features mandated through regulation. Compliance with child safety-seat and seat belt laws has significantly reduced the auto fatality rate for small children. The national air quality standards set by law have been reached in nearly all parts of the nation for sulfur dioxide, nitrogen dioxide, and lead. Moreover, recent studies clearly link cleaner air, other things equal, with increases in the values of homes. Affirmative action regulations have increased the labor demand for racial and ethnic minorities and females. The use of child-proof lids has resulted in a 90 percent decline in child deaths caused by accidental swallowing of poisonous substances.

Some defenders of social regulation say there are many remaining areas in which greater regulation would generate net benefits to society. For instance, some call for greater regulation of the meat, poultry, and seafood industries to improve food safety. Others favor greater regulation of health care organizations and insurance companies to ensure "patients' rights" for consumers of health care services. Still others say that more regulation is needed to ensure that violent movies, CDs, and video games are not marketed to children.

Advocates of social regulation say that the benefits of such regulation are well worth the considerable costs. The costs are simply the price we must pay to create a hospitable, sustainable, and just society.

Criticisms of Social Regulation Critics of social regulation contend that, in many instances, it has been expanded to the point where the marginal costs exceed the marginal benefits. In this view, society would achieve net benefits by cutting back on irritating social regulation. Critics say that many social regulation laws are poorly written, making regulatory objectives and standards difficult to understand. As a result, regulators pursue goals well beyond the original intent of the legislation. Businesses complain that regulators often press for additional increments of improvement, unmindful of costs.

Also, decisions must often be made and rules formed on the basis of inadequate information. Examples: Consumer Product Safety Commission (CPSC) officials may make decisions about certain ingredients in products on the basis of limited laboratory experiments that suggest that those ingredients might cause cancer. Or government agencies may establish costly pollution standards to attack

Word United States v. Microsoft

The Microsoft Antitrust Case Is the Most Significant Monopoly Case since the Breakup of AT&T in the Early 1980s.

The Charges In May 1998 the U.S. Justice Department (under President Clinton), 19 individual states, and the District of Columbia (hereafter, "the government") filed antitrust charges against Microsoft under the Sherman Antitrust Act. The government charged that Microsoft had violated Section 2 of the act through a series of unlawful actions designed to maintain its "Windows" monopoly. It also charged that some of that conduct violated Section 1 of the Sherman Act.

Microsoft denied the charges, arguing it had achieved its success through product innovation and lawful business practices. Microsoft contended it should not be penalized for its superior foresight, business acumen, and technological prowess. It also pointed out that its monopoly was highly transitory because of rapid technological advance.

The District Court Findings In June 2000 the district court ruled that the relevant market was software used to operate Intel-compatible personal computers (PCs). Microsoft's 95 percent share of that market clearly gave it monopoly power. The court pointed out, however, that being a monopoly is not illegal. The violation of

the Sherman Act occurred because Microsoft used anticompetitive means to maintain its monopoly power.

According to the court, Microsoft feared that the success of Netscape's Navigator, which allowed people to browse the Internet, might allow Netscape to expand its software to include a competitive PC operating system—software that would threaten the Windows monopoly. It also feared that Sun's Internet applications of its Java programming language might eventually threaten Microsoft's Windows monopoly.

To counter these and similar threats, Microsoft illegally signed contracts with PC makers that required them to feature Internet Explorer on the PC desktop and penalized companies that promoted software products that competed with Microsoft products. Moreover, it gave friendly companies coding that linked Windows to software applications and withheld such coding from companies featuring Netscape. Finally, under license from Sun, Microsoft developed Windows-related Java software that made Sun's own software incompatible with Windows.

The District Court Remedy The district court ordered Microsoft to split into two competing companies, one initially selling the Windows operating system and the other initially selling Microsoft applications (such as Word, Hotmail, MSN, PowerPoint, and Internet Explorer). Both companies would be free to develop new products that compete with each other, and both could derive

the global-warming problem without knowing for certain whether pollution is the main cause of the problem. These efforts, say critics, lead to excessive regulation of business.

Moreover, critics argue that social regulations produce many unintended and costly side effects. For instance, the Federal gas mileage standard for automobiles has been blamed for an estimated 2000 to 3900 traffic deaths a year because auto manufacturers have reduced the weight of vehicles to meet the higher miles-per-gallon standards. Other things equal, drivers of lighter cars have a higher fatality rate than drivers of heavier vehicles.

Finally, opponents of social regulation say that the regulatory agencies may attract overzealous workers who are hostile toward the market system and "believe" too fervently in regulation. For example, some staff members of government agencies may see large corporations as "bad guys" who regularly cause pollution, provide inadequate safety for workers, deceive their customers, and

generally abuse their power in the community. Such biases can lead to seemingly never-ending calls for still more regulation, rather than objective assessments of the costs and benefits of added regulation.

Two Reminders

The debate over the proper amount of social regulation will surely continue. By helping determine costs and benefits, economic analysis can lead to more informed discussions and to better decisions. In this regard, economic analysis provides pertinent reminders for both ardent supporters and ardent opponents of social regulation.

There Is No Free Lunch Fervent supporters of social regulation need to remember that "there is no free lunch." Social regulation can produce higher prices, stifle innovation, and reduce competition.

386

those products from the intellectual property embodied in the common products existing at the time of divestiture.

The Appeals Court Ruling In late 2000 Microsoft appealed the district court decision to a U.S. court of appeals. In 2001 the higher court affirmed that Microsoft illegally maintained its monopoly but tossed out the district court's decision to break up Microsoft. It agreed with Microsoft that the company was denied due process during the penalty phase of the trial and concluded that the district court judge had displayed an appearance of bias by holding extensive interviews with the press. The appeals court sent the remedial phase of the case to a new district court judge to determine appropriate remedies. The appeals court also raised issues relating to the wisdom of a structural remedy.

The Final Settlement At the urging of the new district court judge, the Federal government (then under President George W. Bush) and Microsoft negotiated a proposed settlement. With minor modification, the settlement became the final court order in 2002. The breakup was rescinded and replaced with a behavioral remedy. It (1) prevents Microsoft from retaliating against any firm that is developing, selling, or using software that competes with Microsoft Windows or Internet Explorer or is shipping a personal computer that includes both Windows and a non-Microsoft operating system; (2) requires Microsoft to establish uniform royalty and licensing terms for computer manufacturers wanting to include Windows on their PCs; (3) requires that manufacturers be allowed to remove Microsoft icons and replace them with other icons on the Windows desktop; and (4) calls for Microsoft to provide technical information to other companies so that they can develop programs that work as well with Windows as Microsoft's own products.

The Microsoft actions and conviction have indirectly resulted in billions of dollars of fines and payouts by Microsoft. Main examples: To AOL Time Warner (Netscape), $750 million; to the European Commission, $1.9 billion; to Sun Microsystems, $1.6 billion; to Novell, $536 million; to Burst.com, $60 million; to Gateway, $150 million; to InterTrust, $440 million; to RealNetworks, $761 million; and to IBM, $850 million.

Source: United States v. Microsoft (District Court Conclusions of Law), April 2000; *United States v. Microsoft* (Court of Appeals), June 2001; *U.S. v. Microsoft* (Final Judgment), November 2002; and Reuters and Associated Press News Services.

Social regulation raises product prices in two ways. It does so directly because compliance costs normally get passed on to consumers, and it does so indirectly by reducing labor productivity. Resources invested in making workplaces accessible to disabled workers, for example, are not available for investment in new machinery designed to increase output per worker. Where the wage rate is fixed, a drop in labor productivity increases the marginal and average total costs of production. In effect, the supply curve for the product shifts leftward, causing the price of the product to rise.

Social regulation may have a negative impact on the rate of innovation. Technological advance may be stifled by, say, the fear that a new plant will not meet EPA guidelines or that a new medicine will require years of testing before being approved by the Food and Drug Administration (FDA).

Social regulation may weaken competition since it usually places a relatively greater burden on small firms than on large ones. The costs of complying with social regulation are, in effect, fixed costs. Because smaller firms produce less output over which to distribute those costs, their compliance costs per unit of output put them at a competitive disadvantage with their larger rivals. Social regulation is more likely to force smaller firms out of business, thus contributing to the increased concentration of industry.

Finally, social regulation may prompt some U.S. firms to move their operations to countries in which the rules are not as burdensome and therefore production costs are lower.

Less Government Is Not Always Better Than More On the opposite side of the issue, opponents of social regulation need to remember that less government is not always better than more government. While the market system is a powerful engine for producing goods and services and generating income, it has certain flaws and can camouflage certain abuses. Through appropriate amounts of social regulation government can clearly increase economic efficiency and thus society's well-being. Ironically, by "taking the rough edges off of capitalism," social regulation may be a strong pro-capitalism force. Properly conceived and executed, social regulation helps maintain political support for the market system. Such support could quickly wane should there be a steady drumbeat of reports of unsafe workplaces, unsafe products, discriminatory hiring, choking pollution, deceived loan customers, and the like. Social regulation helps the market system deliver not only goods and services but also a "good society."

> **QUICK REVIEW 18.3**
>
> - Social regulation is concerned with the conditions under which goods and services are produced, the effects of production on society, and the physical characteristics of the goods themselves.
> - Defenders of social regulation point to the benefits arising from policies that keep dangerous products from the marketplace, reduce workplace injuries and deaths, contribute to clean air and water, and reduce employment discrimination.
> - Critics of social regulation say uneconomical policy goals, inadequate information, unintended side effects, and overzealous personnel create excessive regulation, for which regulatory costs exceed regulatory benefits.

Summary

1. The cornerstones of antitrust policy are the Sherman Act of 1890 and the Clayton Act of 1914. The Sherman Act specifies that "every contract, combination . . . or conspiracy in the restraint of interstate trade . . . is . . . illegal" and that any person who monopolizes or attempts to monopolize interstate trade is guilty of a felony.

2. If a company is found guilty of violating the antimonopoly provisions of the Sherman Act, the government can either break up the monopoly into competing firms (a structural remedy) or prohibit it from engaging in specific anticompetitive business practices (a behavioral remedy).

3. The Clayton Act was designed to bolster and make more explicit the provisions of the Sherman Act. It declares that price discrimination, tying contracts, intercorporate stock acquisitions, and interlocking directorates are illegal when their effect is to reduce competition.

4. The Federal Trade Commission Act of 1914 created the Federal Trade Commission to investigate antitrust violations and to prevent the use of "unfair methods of competition." The FTC Act was amended by the Wheeler-Lea Act of 1938 to outlaw false and deceptive representation of products to consumers. Empowered by cease-and-desist orders, the FTC serves as a watchdog agency over unfair, deceptive, or false claims made by firms about their own products or the products of their competitors.

5. The Celler-Kefauver Act of 1950 amended the Clayton Act of 1914 to prohibit one firm from acquiring the assets of another firm when doing so would substantially reduce competition.

6. Issues in applying antitrust laws include (a) determining whether an industry should be judged by its structure or by its behavior; (b) defining the scope and size of the dominant firm's market; and (c) deciding how strictly to enforce the antitrust laws.

7. The courts treat price-fixing among competitors as a *per se violation*, meaning that the conduct is illegal independently of whether the conspiracy causes harm. In contrast, a *rule of reason* is used to assess monopoly. Only monopolies that unreasonably (abusively) achieve or maintain their status violate the law. Antitrust officials are more likely to challenge price-fixing, tying contracts, and horizontal mergers than to try to break up existing monopolies. Nevertheless, antitrust suits by the Federal government led to the breakup of the AT&T monopoly in the early 1980s.

8. The objective of industrial regulation is to protect the public from the market power of natural monopolies by regulating prices and quality of service.

9. Critics of industrial regulation contend that it can lead to inefficiency and rising costs and that in many instances it constitutes a legal cartel for the regulated firms. Legislation passed in the late 1970s and the 1980s has brought about varying degrees of deregulation in the airline, trucking, banking, railroad, and television broadcasting industries.

10. Studies indicate that deregulation of airlines, railroads, trucking, and telecommunications is producing sizable annual gains to society through lower prices, lower costs, and increased output. Less certain is the effect of the more recent deregulation of the electricity industry.

11. Social regulation is concerned with product safety, working conditions, and the effects of production on society. Whereas industrial regulation is on the wane, social regulation continues to expand. The optimal amount of social regulation occurs where MB = MC.

12. People who support social regulation point to its numerous specific successes and assert that it has greatly enhanced society's well-being. Critics of social regulation contend that businesses are excessively regulated to the point where marginal costs exceed marginal benefits. They also say that social regulation often produces unintended and costly side effects.

Terms and Concepts

antitrust policy

industrial regulation

social regulation

Sherman Act

Clayton Act

tying contracts

interlocking directorates

Federal Trade Commission Act

cease-and-desist order

Wheeler-Lea Act

Celler-Kefauver Act

Standard Oil case

U.S. Steel case

rule of reason

Alcoa case

DuPont cellophane case

Microsoft case

horizontal merger

vertical merger

conglomerate merger

per se violations

natural monopoly

public interest theory of regulation

legal cartel theory of regulation

Questions

1. Both antitrust policy and industrial regulation deal with monopoly. What distinguishes the two approaches? How does government decide to use one form of remedy rather than the other? LO1, LO3

2. Describe the major provisions of the Sherman and Clayton acts. What government entities are responsible for enforcing those laws? Are firms permitted to initiate antitrust suits on their own against other firms? LO1

3. Contrast the outcomes of the Standard Oil and U.S. Steel cases. What was the main antitrust issue in the DuPont cellophane case? In what major way do the Microsoft and Standard Oil cases differ? LO2

4. Why might one administration interpret and enforce the antitrust laws more strictly than another? How might a change of administrations affect a major monopoly case in progress? LO2

5. How would you expect antitrust authorities to react to: LO2
   a. A proposed merger of Ford and General Motors.
   b. Evidence of secret meetings by contractors to rig bids for highway construction projects.
   c. A proposed merger of a large shoe manufacturer and a chain of retail shoe stores.
   d. A proposed merger of a small life-insurance company and a regional candy manufacturer.
   e. An automobile rental firm that charges higher rates for last-minute rentals than for rentals reserved weeks in advance.

6. Suppose a proposed merger of firms would simultaneously lessen competition and reduce unit costs through economies of scale. Do you think such a merger should be allowed? LO2

7. In the 1980s, PepsiCo Inc., which then had 28 percent of the soft-drink market, proposed to acquire the Seven-Up Company. Shortly thereafter, the Coca-Cola Company, with 39 percent of the market, indicated it wanted to acquire the Dr Pepper Company. Seven-Up and Dr Pepper each

controlled about 7 percent of the market. In your judgment, was the government's decision to block these mergers appropriate? LO2

8. Why might a firm charged with violating the Clayton Act, Section 7, try arguing that the products sold by the merged firms are in separate markets? Why might a firm charged with violating Section 2 of the Sherman Act try convincing the court that none of its behavior in achieving and maintaining its monopoly was illegal? LO2

9. "The social desirability of any particular firm should be judged not on the basis of its market share but on the basis of its conduct and performance." Make a counterargument, referring to the monopoly model in your statement. LO2

10. What types of industries, if any, should be subjected to industrial regulation? What specific problems does industrial regulation entail? LO3

11. In view of the problems involved in regulating natural monopolies, compare socially optimal (marginal-cost) pricing and fair-return pricing by referring again to Figure 10.9. Assuming that a government subsidy might be used to cover any loss resulting from marginal-cost pricing, which pricing policy would you favor? Why? What problems might such a subsidy entail? LO3

12. How does social regulation differ from industrial regulation? What types of benefits and costs are associated with social regulation? LO4

13. Use economic analysis to explain why the optimal amount of product safety may be less than the amount that would totally eliminate risks of accidents and deaths. Use automobiles as an example. LO4

14. **LAST WORD** Under what law and on what basis did the Federal district court find Microsoft guilty of violating the antitrust laws? What was the initial district court's remedy? How did Microsoft fare with its appeal to the court of appeals? Was the final remedy in the case a structural remedy or a behavioral remedy?

Problems

1. Suppose that there are only three types of fruit sold in the United States. Annual sales are 1 million tons of blueberries, 5 million tons of strawberries, and 10 million tons of bananas. Suppose that of those total amounts, the Sunny Valley Fruit Company sells 900,000 tons of blueberries, 900,000 tons of strawberries, and 7.9 million tons of bananas. LO2

    a. What is Sunny Valley's market share if the relevant market is blueberries? If a court applies the "90-60-30 rule" when considering just the blueberry market, would it rule that Sunny Valley is a monopoly?

    b. What is Sunny Valley's market share if the relevant market is all types of berries? Would the court rule Sunny Valley to be a monopolist in that market?

    c. What if the relevant market is all types of fruit? What is Sunny Valley's market share, and would the court consider Sunny Valley to be a monopolist?

2. Carrot Computers and its competitors purchase touch screens for their handheld computers from several suppliers. The six makers of touch screens have market shares of, respectively, 19 percent, 18 percent, 14 percent, 16 percent, 20 percent, and 13 percent. LO2

    a. What is the Herfindahl index for the touch screen manufacturing industry?

    b. By how much would a proposed merger between the two smallest touch screen makers increase the Herfindahl index? Would the government be likely to challenge that proposed merger?

    c. If Carrot Computers horizontally merges with its competitor Blueberry Handhelds, by how much would the Herfindahl index change for the touch screen industry?

FURTHER TEST YOUR KNOWLEDGE AT
www.mcconnell19e.com

At the text's Online Learning Center (OLC), **www.mcconnell19e.com**, you will find one or more Web-based questions that require information from the Internet to answer. We urge you to check them out; they will familiarize you with Web sites that may be helpful in other courses and perhaps even in your career. The OLC also features multiple-choice questions that give instant feedback and provides other helpful ways to further test your knowledge of the chapter.

11

Monopolistic Competition and Oligopoly

In the United States, most industries have a market structure that falls somewhere between the two poles of pure competition and pure monopoly. To begin with, most real-world industries have fewer than the large number of producers required for pure competition but more than the single producer that defines pure monopoly. In addition, most firms in most industries have both distinguishable rather than standardized products as well as some discretion over the prices they charge. As a result, competition often occurs on the basis of price, quality, location, service, and advertising. Finally, entry to most real-world industries ranges from easy to very difficult but is rarely completely blocked.

This chapter examines two models that more closely approximate these widespread industry structures. You will discover that *monopolistic competition* mixes a small amount of monopoly power with a large amount of competition. *Oligopoly,* in contrast, blends a large amount of monopoly power with both considerable rivalry among existing firms and the threat of increased future competition due to foreign firms and new technologies. (You should quickly review Table 8.1, page 164, at this point.)

Monopolistic Competition

Let's begin by examining **monopolistic competition,** which is characterized by (1) a relatively large number of

ORIGIN OF THE IDEA

O 11.1

Monopolistic competition

sellers, (2) differentiated products (often promoted by heavy advertising), and (3) easy entry to, and exit from, the industry. The first and third characteristics provide the "competitive" aspect of monopolistic competition; the second characteristic provides the "monopolistic" aspect. In general, however, monopolistically competitive industries are much more competitive than they are monopolistic.

Relatively Large Number of Sellers

Monopolistic competition is characterized by a fairly large number of firms, say, 25, 35, 60, or 70, not by the hundreds or thousands of firms in pure competition. Consequently, monopolistic competition involves:

- *Small market shares* Each firm has a comparatively small percentage of the total market and consequently has limited control over market price.
- *No collusion* The presence of a relatively large number of firms ensures that collusion by a group of firms to restrict output and set prices is unlikely.
- *Independent action* With numerous firms in an industry, there is no feeling of interdependence among them; each firm can determine its own pricing policy without considering the possible reactions of rival firms. A single firm may realize a modest increase in sales by cutting its price, but the effect of that action on competitors' sales will be nearly imperceptible and will probably trigger no response.

Differentiated Products

In contrast to pure competition, in which there is a standardized product, monopolistic competition is distinguished by **product differentiation.** Monopolistically competitive firms turn out variations of a particular product. They produce products with slightly different physical characteristics, offer varying degrees of customer service, provide varying amounts of locational convenience, or proclaim special qualities, real or imagined, for their products.

Let's examine these aspects of product differentiation in more detail.

Product Attributes Product differentiation may entail physical or qualitative differences in the products themselves. Real differences in functional features, materials, design, and workmanship are vital aspects of product differentiation. Personal computers, for example, differ in terms of storage capacity, speed, graphic displays, and included software. There are dozens of competing principles of economics textbooks that differ in content, organization, presentation and readability, pedagogical aids, and graphics and design. Most cities have a variety of retail stores selling men's and women's clothes that differ greatly in styling, materials, and quality of work. Similarly, one pizza place may feature thin-crust Neapolitan style pizza, while another may tout its thick-crust Chicago-style pizza.

Service Service and the conditions surrounding the sale of a product are forms of product differentiation too. One shoe store may stress the fashion knowledge and helpfulness of its clerks. A competitor may leave trying on shoes and carrying them to the register to its customers but feature lower prices. Customers may prefer one-day over three-day dry cleaning of equal quality. The prestige appeal of a store, the courteousness and helpfulness of clerks, the firm's reputation for servicing or exchanging its products, and the credit it makes available are all service aspects of product differentiation.

Location Products may also be differentiated through the location and accessibility of the stores that sell them. Small convenience stores manage to compete with large supermarkets, even though these minimarts have a more limited range of products and charge higher prices. They compete mainly on the basis of location—being close to customers and situated on busy streets. A motel's proximity to an interstate highway gives it a locational advantage that may enable it to charge a higher room rate than nearby motels in less convenient locations.

Brand Names and Packaging Product differentiation may also be created through the use of brand names and trademarks, packaging, and celebrity connections. Most aspirin tablets are very much alike, but many headache sufferers believe that one brand—for example, Bayer, Anacin, or Bufferin—is superior and worth a higher price than a generic substitute. A celebrity's name associated

217

with watches, perfume, or athletic shoes may enhance the appeal of those products for some buyers. Many customers prefer one style of ballpoint pen to another. Packaging that touts "natural spring" bottled water may attract additional customers.

Some Control over Price Despite the relatively large number of firms, monopolistic competitors do have some control over their product prices because of product differentiation. If consumers prefer the products of specific sellers, then within limits they will pay more to satisfy their preferences. Sellers and buyers are not linked randomly, as in a purely competitive market. But the monopolistic competitor's control over price is quite limited since there are numerous potential substitutes for its product.

Easy Entry and Exit

Entry into monopolistically competitive industries is relatively easy compared to oligopoly or pure monopoly. Because monopolistic competitors are typically small firms, both absolutely and relatively, economies of scale are few and capital requirements are low. On the other hand, compared with pure competition, financial barriers may result from the need to develop and advertise a product that differs from rivals' products. Some firms have trade secrets relating to their products or hold trademarks on their brand names, making it difficult and costly for other firms to imitate them.

Exit from monopolistically competitive industries is relatively easy. Nothing prevents an unprofitable monopolistic competitor from holding a going-out-of-business sale and shutting down.

Advertising

The expense and effort involved in product differentiation would be wasted if consumers were not made aware of product differences. Thus, monopolistic competitors advertise their products, often heavily. The goal of product differentiation and advertising—so-called **nonprice competition**—is to make price less of a factor in consumer purchases and make product differences a greater factor. If successful, the firm's demand curve will shift to the right and will become less elastic.

Monopolistically Competitive Industries

Table 11.1 lists several manufacturing industries that approximate monopolistic competition. Economists measure the degree of industry concentration—the extent to which the largest firms account for the bulk of the industry's output—to identify monopolistically competitive (versus oligopolistic) industries. Two such measures are the four-firm concentration ratio and the Herfindahl index. They are listed in columns 2 and 3 of the table.

A **four-firm concentration ratio**, expressed as a percentage, is the ratio of the output (sales) of the four largest firms in an industry relative to total industry sales.

$$\text{Four-firm concentration ratio} = \frac{\text{Output of four largest firms}}{\text{Total output in the industry}}$$

Four-firm concentration ratios are very low in purely competitive industries in which there are hundreds or even

TABLE 11.1 Percentage of Output Produced by Firms in Selected Low-Concentration U.S. Manufacturing Industries

(1) Industry	(2) Percentage of Industry Output* Produced by the Four Largest Firms	(3) Herfindahl Index for the Top 50 Firms	(1) Industry	(2) Percentage of Industry Output* Produced by the Four Largest Firms	(3) Herfindahl Index for the Top 50 Firms
Asphalt paving	25	207	Metal windows and doors	14	114
Plastic pipe	24	262	Women's dresses	13	84
Textile bags	24	263	Ready-mix concrete	11	63
Bolts, nuts, and rivets	24	205	Wood trusses	10	50
Plastic bags	23	240	Stone products	10	59
Quick printing	22	319	Metal stamping	8	31
Textile machinery	20	206	Wood pallets	7	24
Sawmills	18	117	Sheet metal work	6	25
Jewelry	16	117	Signs	5	19
Curtains and draperies	16	111	Retail bakeries	4	7

*As measured by value of shipments. Data are for 2002. See **www.census.gov/epcd/www/concentration.html**.

Source: Bureau of Census, *Census of Manufacturers, 2002.*

thousands of firms, each with a tiny market share. In contrast, four-firm ratios are high in oligopoly and pure monopoly. Industries in which the largest four firms account for 40 percent or more of the market are generally considered to be oligopolies. If the largest four firms account for less than 40 percent, they are likely to be monopolistically competitive. Observe that the four-firm concentration ratios in Table 11.1 range from 4 percent to 25 percent.

Published concentration ratios such as those in Table 11.1 are helpful in categorizing industries but must be used cautiously because the market shares (percentage of total sales) that they list are national in scope, whereas competition in many industries is often local in scope. As a result, some industries with low national concentration ratios are in fact substantially concentrated if one focuses on local markets.

As an example, the national four-firm concentration ratio for ready-mix concrete shown in Table 11.1 is only 11 percent. This suggests that ready-mix concrete is a monopolistically competitive industry. But the sheer bulk of ready-mix concrete and the fact that it "sets up" as it dries limits the relevant market to a specific town, city, or metropolitan area. In most of these local markets, only a few firms compete, not the numerous firms needed for monopolistic competition.

Column 3 of Table 11.1 lists a second measure of concentration: the **Herfindahl index.** This index is the sum of the squared percentage market shares of all firms in the industry. In equation form:

$$\text{Herfindahl index} = (\%S_1)^2 + (\%S_2)^2 + (\%S_3)^2 + \cdots + (\%S_n)^2$$

where $\%S_1$ is the percentage market share of firm 1, $\%S_2$ is the percentage market share of firm 2, and so on for each of the n total firms in the industry. By squaring the percentage market shares of all firms in the industry, the Herfindahl index purposely gives much greater weight to larger, and thus more powerful, firms than to smaller ones. For a purely competitive industry, the index would approach zero since each firm's market share—$\%S$ in the equation—is extremely small. In the case of a single-firm industry, the index would be at its maximum of 10,000 (= 100^2), indicating an industry with complete monopoly power.

We will discover later in this chapter that the Herfindahl index is important for assessing oligopolistic industries. But for now, the relevant generalization is that the lower the Herfindahl index, the greater is the likelihood that an industry is monopolistically competitive rather than oligopolistic. Column 3 of Table 11.1 lists the Herfindahl index (computed for the top 50 firms, not all the industry firms) for several industries. Note that the index

values are decidedly closer to the bottom limit of the Herfindahl index—0—than to its top limit—10,000.

The numbers in Table 11.1 are for manufacturing industries. In addition, many retail establishments in metropolitan areas are monopolistically competitive, including grocery stores, gasoline stations, hair salons, dry cleaners, clothing stores, and restaurants. Also, many providers of professional services such as medical care, legal assistance, real estate sales, and basic bookkeeping are monopolistic competitors.

Price and Output in Monopolistic Competition

How does a monopolistic competitor decide on its price and output? To explain, we initially assume that each firm in the industry is producing a specific differentiated product and engaging in a particular amount of advertising. Later we will see how changes in the product and in the amount of advertising modify our conclusions.

The Firm's Demand Curve

Our explanation is based on **Figure 11.1 (Key Graph),** which shows that the demand curve faced by a monopolistically competitive seller is highly, but not perfectly, elastic. It is precisely this feature that distinguishes monopolistic competition from both pure monopoly and pure competition. The monopolistic competitor's demand is more elastic than the demand faced by a pure monopolist because the monopolistically competitive seller has many competitors producing closely substitutable goods. The pure monopolist has no rivals at all. Yet, for two reasons, the monopolistic competitor's demand is not perfectly elastic like that of the pure competitor. First, the monopolistic competitor has fewer rivals; second, its products are differentiated, so they are not perfect substitutes.

The price elasticity of demand faced by the monopolistically competitive firm depends on the number of rivals and the degree of product differentiation. The larger the number of rivals and the weaker the product differentiation, the greater the price elasticity of each seller's demand, that is, the closer monopolistic competition will be to pure competition.

The Short Run: Profit or Loss

In the short run, monopolistically competitive firms maximize profit or minimize loss using exactly the same strategy as pure competitors and monopolists: They produce the level of output at which marginal revenue equals marginal cost (MR = MC). Thus, the monopolistically

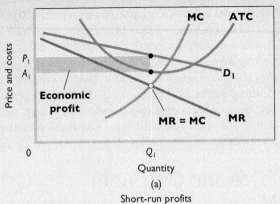

FIGURE 11.1 A monopolistically competitive firm: short run and long run. The monopolistic competitor maximizes profit or minimizes loss by producing the output at which MR = MC. The economic profit shown in (a) will induce new firms to enter, eventually eliminating economic profit. The loss shown in (b) will cause an exit of firms until normal profit is restored. After such entry and exit, the price will settle in (c) to where it just equals average total cost at the MR = MC output. At this price P_3 and output Q_3, the monopolistic competitor earns only a normal profit, and the industry is in long-run equilibrium.

(a)
Short-run profits

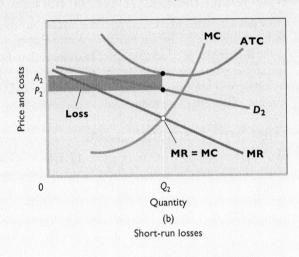

(b)
Short-run losses

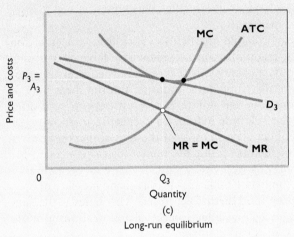

(c)
Long-run equilibrium

QUICK QUIZ FOR FIGURE 11.1

1. Price exceeds MC in:
   a. graph (a) only.
   b. graph (b) only.
   c. graphs (a) and (b) only.
   d. graphs (a), (b), and (c).

2. Price exceeds ATC in:
   a. graph (a) only.
   b. graph (b) only.
   c. graphs (a) and (b) only.
   d. graphs (a), (b), and (c).

3. The firm represented by Figure 11.1c is:
   a. making a normal profit.
   b. incurring a loss.

   c. producing at the same level of output as a purely competitive firm.
   d. producing a standardized product.

4. Which of the following pairs are both "competitionlike elements" in monopolistic competition?
   a. Price exceeds MR; standardized product.
   b. Entry is relatively easy; only a normal profit in the long run.
   c. Price equals MC at the profit-maximizing output; economic profits are likely in the long run.
   d. The firms' demand curve is downsloping; differentiated products.

Answers: 1. d; 2. a; 3. a; 4. b

competitive firm in Figure 11.1a produces output Q_1, where MR = MC. As shown by demand curve D_1, it then can charge price P_1. It realizes an economic profit, shown by the green area [$= (P_1 - A_1) \times Q_1$].

But with less favorable demand or costs, the firm may incur a loss in the short run. We show this possibility in Figure 11.1b, where the firm's best strategy is to minimize its loss. It does so by producing output Q_2 (where MR =

MC) and, as determined by demand curve D_2, by charging price P_2. Because price P_2 is less than average total cost A_2, the firm incurs a per-unit loss of $A_2 - P_2$ and a total loss represented as the red area $[= (A_2 - P_2) \times Q_2]$.

The Long Run: Only a Normal Profit

In the long run, firms will enter a profitable monopolistically competitive industry and leave an unprofitable one. So a monopolistic competitor will earn only a normal profit in the long run or, in other words, will only break even. (Remember that the cost curves include both explicit and implicit costs, including a normal profit.)

Profits: Firms Enter In the case of short-run profit (Figure 11.1a), economic profits attract new rivals because entry to the industry is relatively easy. As new firms enter, the demand curve faced by the typical firm shifts to the left (falls). Why? Because each firm has a smaller share of total demand and now faces a larger number of close-substitute products. This decline in the firm's demand reduces its economic profit. When entry of new firms has reduced demand to the extent that the demand curve is tangent to the average-total-cost curve at the profit-maximizing output, the firm is just making a normal profit. This situation is shown in Figure 11.1c, where demand is D_3 and the firm's long-run equilibrium output is Q_3. As Figure 11.1c indicates, any greater or lesser output will entail an average total cost that exceeds product price P_3, meaning a loss for the firm. At the tangency point between the demand curve and ATC, total revenue equals total costs. With the economic profit gone, there is no further incentive for additional firms to enter.

Losses: Firms Leave When the industry suffers short-run losses, as in Figure 11.1b, some firms will exit in the long run. Faced with fewer substitute products and blessed with an expanded share of total demand, the surviving firms will see their demand curves shift to the right (rise), as to D_3. Their losses will disappear and give way to normal profits (Figure 11.1c). (For simplicity we have assumed constant costs; shifts in the cost curves as firms enter or leave would complicate our discussion slightly but would not alter our conclusions.)

Complications The representative firm in the monopolistic competition model earns only a normal profit in the long run. That outcome may not always occur, however, in the real world of small firms as opposed to the theoretical model.

- Some firms may achieve sufficient product differentiation such that other firms cannot duplicate them,

even over time. One hotel in a major city may have the best location relative to business and tourist activities. Or a firm may have developed a well-known brand name that gives it a slight but very long-lasting advantage over imitators. Such firms may have sufficient monopoly power to realize modest economic profits even in the long run.

- Entry to some industries populated by small firms is not as free in reality as it is in theory. Because of product differentiation, financial barriers to entry are likely to be greater than they would be if the product were standardized. This suggests some monopoly power, with small economic profits continuing even in the long run.

INTERACTIVE GRAPHS
G 11.1
Monopolistic competition

With all things considered, however, the outcome that yields only a normal profit—the long-run equilibrium shown in Figure 11.1c—is a reasonable approximation of reality.

Monopolistic Competition and Efficiency

We know from Chapter 9 that economic efficiency requires each firm to produce the amount of output at which $P = MC = $ minimum ATC. The equality of price and minimum average total cost yields *productive efficiency*. The good is being produced in the least costly way, and the price is just sufficient to cover average total cost, including a normal profit. The equality of price and marginal cost yields *allocative efficiency*. The right amount of output is being produced, and thus the right amount of society's scarce resources is being devoted to this specific use.

How efficient is monopolistic competition, as measured against this triple equality? In particular, do monopolistically competitive firms produce the efficient output level associated with $P = MC = $ minimum ATC?

Neither Productive nor Allocative Efficiency

In monopolistic competition, neither productive nor allocative efficiency occurs in long-run equilibrium. Figure 11.2 includes an enlargement of part of Figure 11.1c and clearly shows this. First note that the profit-maximizing price P_3 slightly exceeds the lowest average total cost, A_4. In producing the profit-maximizing output Q_3, the firm's average total cost therefore is slightly higher than optimal from society's perspective—productive efficiency is not

FIGURE 11.2 The inefficiency of monopolistic competition. In long-run equilibrium a monopolistic competitor achieves neither productive nor allocative efficiency. Productive efficiency is not realized because production occurs where the average total cost A_3 exceeds the minimum average total cost A_4. Allocative efficiency is not achieved because the product price P_3 exceeds the marginal cost M_3. The results are an underallocation of resources as well as an efficiency loss and excess production capacity at every firm in the industry. This firm's efficiency loss is area acd and its excess production capacity is $Q_4 - Q_3$.

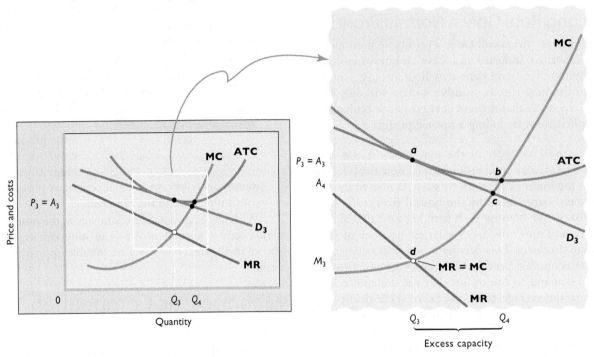

achieved. Also note that the profit-maximizing price P_3 exceeds marginal cost (here M_3), meaning that monopolistic competition causes an underallocation of resources. To measure the size of this inefficiency, note that the allocatively optimal amount of output is determined by point c, where demand curve D intersects the MC curve. So for all units between Q_3 and the level of output associated with point c, marginal benefits exceed marginal costs. Consequently, by producing only Q_3 units, this monopolistic competitor creates an efficiency loss (deadweight loss) equal in size to area acd. The total efficiency loss for the industry as a whole will be the sum of the individual efficiency losses generated by each of the firms in the industry.

Excess Capacity

In monopolistic competition, the gap between the minimum-ATC output and the profit-maximizing output identifies **excess capacity:** plant and equipment that are underused because firms are producing less than the minimum-ATC output. This gap is shown as the distance between Q_4 and Q_3 in Figure 11.2. Note in the figure that the minimum ATC is at point b. If each monopolistic competitor could profitably produce at this point on its ATC curve,

the lower average total cost would enable a lower price than P_3. More importantly, if each firm produced at b rather than at a, fewer firms would be needed to produce the industry output. But because monopolistically competitive firms produce at a in long-run equilibrium, monopolistically competitive industries are overpopulated with firms, each operating below its optimal capacity. This situation is typified by many kinds of retail establishments. For example, in most cities there is an abundance of small motels and restaurants that operate well below half capacity.

Product Variety

The situation portrayed in Figures 11.1c and 11.2 is not very satisfying to monopolistic competitors, since it foretells only a normal profit. But the profit-realizing firm of Figure 11.1a need not stand by and watch new competitors eliminate its profit by imitating its product, matching its customer service, and copying its advertising. Each firm has a product that is distinguishable in some way from those of the other producers. So the firm can attempt to stay ahead of competitors and sustain its profit through further product differentiation and better advertising. By developing or improving its product, it may be able to postpone, at least for a while, the outcome of Figure 11.1c.

Although product differentiation and advertising will add to the firm's costs, they can also increase the demand for its product. If demand increases by more than enough to compensate for the added costs, the firm will have improved its profit position. As Figure 11.2 suggests, the firm has little or no prospect of increasing profit by price cutting. So why not engage in nonprice competition?

Benefits of Product Variety

The product variety and product improvement that accompany the drive to maintain economic profit in monopolistic competition are a benefit for society—one that may offset the cost of the inefficiency associated with monopolistic competition. Consumers have a wide diversity of tastes: Some like regular fries, others like curly fries; some like contemporary furniture, others like traditional furniture. If a product is differentiated, then at any time the consumer will be offered a wide range of types, styles, brands, and quality gradations of that product. Compared with pure competition, this provides an advantage to the consumer. The range of choice is widened, and producers more fully meet the wide variation in consumer tastes.

The product improvement promoted by monopolistic competition further differentiates products and expands choices. And a successful product improvement by one firm obligates rivals to imitate or improve on that firm's temporary market advantage or else lose business. So society benefits from better products.

In fact, product differentiation creates a trade-off between consumer choice and productive efficiency. The stronger the product differentiation, the greater is the excess capacity and, therefore, the greater is the productive inefficiency. But the greater the product differentiation, the more likely it is that the firms will satisfy the great diversity of consumer tastes. The greater the excess-capacity problem, the wider the range of consumer choice.

Further Complexity

Finally, the ability to engage in nonprice competition makes the market situation of a monopolistic competitor more complex than Figure 11.1 indicates. That figure assumes a given (unchanging) product and a given level of advertising expenditures. But we know that, in practice, product attributes and advertising are not fixed. The monopolistically competitive firm juggles three factors—price, product, and advertising—in seeking maximum profit. It must determine what variety of product, selling at what price, and supplemented by what level of advertising will

result in the greatest profit. This complex situation is not easily expressed in a simple, meaningful economic model. At best, we can say that each possible combination of price, product, and advertising poses a different demand and cost (production cost plus advertising cost) situation for the firm and that one combination yields the maximum profit. In practice, this optimal combination cannot be readily forecast but must be found by trial and error.

QUICK REVIEW 11.1

- Monopolistic competition involves a relatively large number of firms operating in a noncollusive way and producing differentiated products with easy industry entry and exit.
- In the short run, a monopolistic competitor will maximize profit or minimize loss by producing that output at which marginal revenue equals marginal cost.
- In the long run, easy entry and exit of firms cause monopolistic competitors to earn only a normal profit.
- A monopolistic competitor's long-run equilibrium output is such that price exceeds the minimum average total cost (implying that consumers do not get the product at the lowest price attainable) and price exceeds marginal cost (indicating that resources are underallocated to the product).
- The efficiency loss (or deadweight loss) associated with monopolistic competition is greatly muted by the benefits consumers receive from product variety.

Oligopoly

In terms of competitiveness, the spectrum of market structures reaches from pure competition, to monopolistic competition, to oligopoly, to pure monopoly (review Table 8.1). We now direct our attention to **oligopoly**, a market dominated by a few large producers of a homogeneous or differentiated product. Because of their "fewness," oligopolists have considerable control over their prices, but each must consider the possible reaction of rivals to its own pricing, output, and advertising decisions.

A Few Large Producers

The phrase "a few large producers" is necessarily vague because the market model of oligopoly covers much ground, ranging between pure monopoly, on the one hand, and monopolistic competition, on the other. Oligopoly encompasses the U.S. aluminum industry, in which three huge firms dominate an entire national market, and the situation in which four or five much smaller auto-parts stores enjoy roughly equal shares of the market in a medium-size town. Generally, however, when you hear a term such as "Big

Three," "Big Four," or "Big Six," you can be sure it refers to an oligopolistic industry.

Homogeneous or Differentiated Products

An oligopoly may be either a **homogeneous oligopoly** or a **differentiated oligopoly**, depending on whether the firms in the oligopoly produce standardized (homogeneous) or differentiated products. Many industrial products (steel, zinc, copper, aluminum, lead, cement, industrial alcohol) are virtually standardized products that are produced in oligopolies. Alternatively, many consumer goods industries (automobiles, tires, household appliances, electronics equipment, breakfast cereals, cigarettes, and many sporting goods) are differentiated oligopolies. These differentiated oligopolies typically engage in considerable nonprice competition supported by heavy advertising.

Control over Price, but Mutual Interdependence

Because firms are few in oligopolistic industries, each firm is a "price maker"; like the monopolist, it can set its price and output levels to maximize its profit. But unlike the monopolist, which has no rivals, the oligopolist must consider how its rivals will react to any change in its price, output, product characteristics, or advertising. Oligopoly is thus characterized by *strategic behavior* and *mutual interdependence*. By **strategic behavior,** we simply mean self-interested behavior that takes into account the reactions of others. Firms develop and implement price, quality, location, service, and advertising strategies to "grow their business" and expand their profits. But because rivals are few, there is **mutual interdependence:** a situation in which each firm's profit depends not just on its own price and sales strategies but also on those of the other firms in its highly concentrated industry. So oligopolistic firms base their decisions on how they think their rivals will react. Example: In deciding whether to increase the price of its cosmetics, L'Oreal will try to predict the response of the other major producers, such as Clinique. Second example: In deciding on its advertising strategy, Burger King will take into consideration how McDonald's might react.

Entry Barriers

The same barriers to entry that create pure monopoly also contribute to the creation of oligopoly. Economies of scale are important entry barriers in a number of oligopolistic industries, such as the aircraft, rubber, and copper industries. In those industries, three or four firms might each

Creative Strategic Behavior

The following story, offered with tongue in cheek, illustrates a localized market that exhibits some characteristics of oligopoly, including strategic behavior.

Tracy Martinez's Native American Arts and Crafts store is located in the center of a small tourist town that borders on a national park. In its early days, Tracy had a minimonopoly. Business was brisk, and prices and profits were high.

To Tracy's annoyance, two "copycat" shops opened adjacent to her store, one on either side of her shop. Worse yet, the competitors named their shops to take advantage of Tracy's advertising. One was "Native Arts and Crafts"; the other, "Indian Arts and Crafts." These new sellers drew business away from Tracy's store, forcing her to lower her prices. The three side-by-side stores in the small, isolated town constituted a localized oligopoly for Native American arts and crafts.

Tracy began to think strategically about ways to boost profit. She decided to distinguish her shop from those on either side by offering a greater mix of high-quality, expensive products and a lesser mix of inexpensive souvenir items. The tactic worked for a while, but the other stores eventually imitated her product mix.

Then, one of the competitors next door escalated the rivalry by hanging up a large sign proclaiming: "We Sell for Less!" Shortly thereafter, the other shop put up a large sign stating: "We Won't Be Undersold!"

Not to be outdone, Tracy painted a colorful sign of her own and hung it above her door. It read: "Main Entrance."

have sufficient sales to achieve economies of scale, but new firms would have such a small market share that they could not do so. They would then be high-cost producers, and as such they could not survive. A closely related barrier is the large expenditure for capital—the cost of obtaining necessary plant and equipment—required for entering certain industries. The jet engine, automobile, commercial aircraft, and petroleum-refining industries, for example, are all characterized by very high capital requirements.

The ownership and control of raw materials help explain why oligopoly exists in many mining industries, including gold, silver, and copper. In the computer, chemicals, consumer electronics, and pharmaceutical industries, patents have served as entry barriers. Moreover, oligopolists can preclude the entry of new competitors through preemptive and retaliatory pricing and advertising strategies.

Mergers

Some oligopolies have emerged mainly through the growth of the dominant firms in a given industry (examples: breakfast cereals, chewing gum, candy bars). But for other industries the route to oligopoly has been through mergers (examples: steel, in its early history, and, more recently, airlines, banking, and entertainment). The merging, or combining, of two or more competing firms may substantially increase their market share, and this in turn may allow the new firm to achieve greater economies of scale.

Another motive underlying the "urge to merge" is the desire for monopoly power. The larger firm that results from a merger has greater control over market supply and thus the price of its product. Also, since it is a larger buyer of inputs, it may be able to demand and obtain lower prices (costs) on its production inputs.

Oligopolistic Industries

Previously, we listed the four-firm concentration ratio—the percentage of total industry sales accounted for by the four largest firms—for a number of monopolistically competitive industries (see Table 11.1). Column 2 of Table 11.2 shows the four-firm concentration ratios for 21 oligopolistic industries. For example, the four largest U.S. producers of breakfast cereals make 78 percent of all breakfast cereals produced in the United States.

When the largest four firms in an industry control 40 percent or more of the market (as in Table 11.2), that

industry is considered oligopolistic. Using this benchmark, about one-half of all U.S. manufacturing industries are oligopolies.

Although concentration ratios help identify oligopoly, they have four shortcomings.

Localized Markets We have already noted that concentration ratios apply to the nation as a whole, whereas the markets for some products are highly localized because of high transportation costs. Local oligopolies can exist even though national concentration ratios are low.

Interindustry Competition Concentration ratios are based on somewhat arbitrary definitions of industries. In some cases, they disguise significant **interindustry competition**—competition between two products associated with different industries. The high concentration ratio for the copper industry shown in Table 11.2 understates the competition in that industry because aluminum competes with copper in many applications (for example, in the market for long-distance power lines).

World Trade The data in Table 11.2 are only for products produced in the United States and may overstate concentration because they do not account for the **import competition** of foreign suppliers. The truck and auto tire industry is a good example. Although Table 11.2 shows that four U.S. firms produce 77 percent of the domestic output of tires, it ignores the fact that a very large portion

TABLE 11.2 Percentage of Output Produced by Firms in Selected High-Concentration U.S. Manufacturing Industries

(1) Industry	(2) Percentage of Industry Output* Produced by the Four Largest Firms	(3) Herfindahl Index for the Top 50 Firms	(1) Industry	(2) Percentage of Industry Output* Produced by the Four Largest Firms	(3) Herfindahl Index for the Top 50 Firms
Primary copper	99	ND†	Petrochemicals	85	2662
Cane sugar refining	99	ND	Small-arms ammunition	83	1901
Cigarettes	95	ND	Motor vehicles	81	2321
Household laundry equipment	93	ND	Men's slacks and jeans	80	2515
Beer	91	ND	Aircraft	81	ND
Electric light bulbs	89	2582	Breakfast cereals	78	2521
Glass containers	88	2582	Household vacuum cleaners	78	2096
Turbines and generators	88	ND	Phosphate fertilizers	78	1853
Household refrigerators and freezers	85	1986	Tires	77	1807
Primary aluminum	85	ND	Electronic computers	76	2662
			Alcohol distilleries	71	1609

*As measured by value of shipments. Data are for 2002. See **www.census.gov/epcd/www/concentration.html**.
†ND = not disclosed.
Source: Bureau of Census, *Census of Manufacturers, 2002.*

of the truck and auto tires bought in the United States are imports. Many of the world's largest corporations are foreign, and many of them do business in the United States.

Dominant Firms

The four-firm concentration ratio does not reveal the extent to which one or two firms dominate an industry. Suppose that in industry X one firm produces the entire industry output. In a second industry, Y, four firms compete, each with 25 percent of the market. The concentration ratio is 100 percent for both these industries. But industry X is a pure monopoly, while industry Y is an oligopoly that may be experiencing significant economic rivalry. Most economists would agree that monopoly power (or market power) is substantially greater in industry X than in industry Y, a fact disguised by their identical 100 percent concentration ratios.

The Herfindahl index addresses this problem. Recall that this index is the sum of the squared percentage market shares of all firms in the industry. In equation form:

$$\text{Herfindahl index} = (\%S_1)^2 + (\%S_2)^2 + (\%S_3)^2 + \cdots + (\%S_n)^2$$

where $\%S_1$ is the percentage market share of firm 1, $\%S_2$ is the percentage market share of firm 2, and so on for each firm in the industry. Also remember that by squaring the percentage market shares of all firms in the industry, the Herfindahl index gives much greater weight to larger, and thus more powerful, firms than to smaller ones. In the case of the single-firm industry X, the index would be at its maximum of 100^2, or 10,000, indicating an industry with complete monopoly power. For our supposed four-firm industry Y, the index would be $25^2 + 25^2 + 25^2 + 25^2$, or 2500, indicating much less market power.

WORKED PROBLEMS

W 11.1

Measures of industry competition

The larger the Herfindahl index, the greater the market power within an industry. Note in Table 11.2 that the four-firm concentration ratios for the electronic computer industry and the tire industry are similar: 76 and 77 percent. But the Herfindahl index of 2662 for the electronic computer industry suggests greater market power than the 1807 index for the tire industry. Also, contrast the much larger Herfindahl indexes in Table 11.2 with those for the low-concentration industries in Table 11.1.

Oligopoly Behavior: A Game-Theory Overview

Oligopoly pricing behavior has the characteristics of certain games of strategy such as poker, chess, and bridge. The best way to play such a game depends on the way

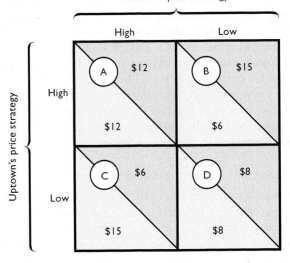

FIGURE 11.3 Profit payoff (in millions) for a two-firm oligopoly. Each firm has two possible pricing strategies. RareAir's strategies are shown in the top margin, and Uptown's in the left margin. Each lettered cell of this four-cell payoff matrix represents one combination of a RareAir strategy and an Uptown strategy and shows the profit that combination would earn for each. Assuming no collusion, the outcome of this game is Cell D, with both parties using low price strategies and earning $8 million of profits.

one's opponent plays. Players (and oligopolists) must pattern their actions according to the actions and expected reactions of rivals. The study of how people behave in strategic situations is called **game theory.** A classic example of game theory is called the prisoner's dilemma, in which each of two prisoners confess to a crime even though they might go free if neither confesses. The logic of this outcome is explained in the nearby Consider This box, which you should read now.

ORIGIN OF THE IDEA

O 11.2

Game theory

The "confess-confess" outcome of the prisoner's dilemma is conceptually identical to the "low price–low price" outcome in the game shown in Figure 11.3. In Figure 11.3 we assume that a duopoly, or two-firm oligopoly, is producing athletic shoes. Each of the two firms—let's call them RareAir and Uptown—has a choice of two pricing strategies: price high or price low. The profit each firm earns will depend on the strategy it chooses *and* the strategy its rival chooses.

There are four possible combinations of strategies for the two firms, and a lettered cell in Figure 11.3 represents each combination. For example, cell C represents a low-price strategy for Uptown along with a high price strategy for RareAir. Figure 11.3 is called a *payoff matrix* because each cell shows the payoff (profit) to each firm that would result

The Prisoner's Dilemma

One of the classic illustrations of game theory is the prisoner's dilemma game in which two people—let's call them Betty and Al—have committed a diamond heist and are being detained by the police as prime suspects. Unbeknownst to the two, the evidence against them is weak, so the best hope the police have for getting a conviction is if one or both of the thieves confess to the crime. The police place Betty and Al in separate holding cells and offer each the same deal: Confess to the crime and receive a lighter prison sentence.

Each detainee therefore faces a dilemma. If Betty remains silent and Al confesses, Betty will end up with a long prison sentence. If Betty confesses and Al says nothing, Al will receive a long prison sentence. What happens? Fearful that the other person will confess, both confess, even though they each would be better off saying nothing.

from each combination of strategies. Cell C shows that if Uptown adopts a low-price strategy and RareAir a high-price strategy, then Uptown will earn $15 million (yellow portion) and RareAir will earn $6 million (blue portion).

Mutual Interdependence Revisited

The data in Figure 11.3 are hypothetical, but their relationships are typical of real situations. Recall that oligopolistic firms can increase their profits, and influence their rivals' profits, by changing their pricing strategies. Each firm's profit depends on its own pricing strategy and that of its rivals. This mutual interdependence of oligopolists is the most obvious point demonstrated by Figure 11.3. If Uptown adopts a high-price strategy, its profit will be $12 million provided that RareAir also employs a high-price strategy (cell A). But if RareAir uses a low-price strategy against Uptown's high-price strategy (cell B), RareAir will increase its market share and boost its profit from $12 to $15 million. RareAir's higher profit will come at the expense of Uptown, whose profit will fall from $12 million to $6 million. Uptown's high-price strategy is a good strategy only if RareAir also employs a high-price strategy.

Collusion

Figure 11.3 also suggests that oligopolists often can benefit from **collusion**—that is, cooperation with rivals. To see the benefits of collusion, first suppose that both firms in

Figure 11.3 are acting independently and following high-price strategies. Each realizes a $12 million profit (cell A).

Note that either RareAir or Uptown could increase its profit by switching to a low-price strategy (cell B or C). The low-price firm would increase its profit to $15 million and the high-price firm's profit would fall to $6 million. The high-price firm would be better off if it, too, adopted a low-price policy. Doing so would increase its profit from $6 million to $8 million (cell D). The effect of all this independent strategy shifting would be the reduction of both firms' profits from $12 million (cell A) to $8 million (cell D).

In real situations, too, independent action by oligopolists may lead to mutually "competitive" low-price strategies: Independent oligopolists compete with respect to price, and this leads to lower prices and lower profits. This outcome is clearly beneficial to consumers but not to the oligopolists, whose profits decrease.

How could oligopolists avoid the low-profit outcome of cell D? The answer is that they could collude, rather than establish prices competitively or independently. In our example, the two firms could agree to establish and maintain a high-price policy. So each firm will increase its profit from $8 million (cell D) to $12 million (cell A).

Incentive to Cheat

The payoff matrix also explains why an oligopolist might be strongly tempted to cheat on a collusive agreement.

Suppose Uptown and RareAir agree to maintain high-price policies, with each earning $12 million in profit (cell A). Both are tempted to cheat on this collusive pricing agreement because either firm can increase its profit to $15 million by lowering its price. For instance, if Uptown secretly cheats and sells at the low price while RareAir keeps on charging the high price, the payoff would move from cell A to cell C so that Uptown's profit would rise to $15 million while RareAir's profit would fall to $6 million. On the other hand, if RareAir cheats and sets a low price while Uptown keeps the agreement and charges the high price, the payoff matrix would move from cell A to cell B so that RareAir would get $15 million while Uptown would get only $6 million. As you can see, cheating is both very lucrative to the cheater as well as very costly to the firm that gets cheated on. As a result, both firms will probably cheat so that the game will settle back to cell D, with each firm using its low-price strategy. (The Consider This box on the prisoner's dilemma is highly relevant and we urge you to read it now. Also, the appendix to this chapter provides several additional applications of game theory.)

- An oligopoly is made up of relatively few firms producing either homogeneous or differentiated products; these firms are mutually interdependent.

- Barriers to entry such as scale economies, control of patents or strategic resources, or the ability to engage in retaliatory pricing characterize oligopolies. Oligopolies may result from internal growth of firms, mergers, or both.

- The four-firm concentration ratio shows the percentage of an industry's sales accounted for by its four largest firms; the Herfindahl index measures the degree of market power in an industry by summing the squares of the percentage market shares held by the individual firms in the industry.

- Game theory reveals that (a) oligopolies are mutually interdependent in their pricing policies; (b) collusion enhances oligopoly profits; and (c) there is a temptation for oligopolists to cheat on a collusive agreement.

Three Oligopoly Models

To gain further insight into oligopolistic pricing and output behavior, we will examine three distinct pricing models: (1) the kinked-demand curve, (2) collusive pricing, and (3) price leadership.

Why not a single model, as in our discussions of the other market structures? There are two reasons:

- *Diversity of oligopolies* Oligopoly encompasses a greater range and diversity of market situations than do other market structures. It includes the *tight* oligopoly, in which two or three firms dominate an entire market, and the *loose* oligopoly, in which six or seven firms share, say, 70 or 80 percent of a market while a "competitive fringe" of firms shares the remainder. It includes both differentiated and standardized products. It includes cases in which firms act in collusion and those in which they act independently. It embodies situations in which barriers to entry are very strong and situations in which they are not quite so strong. In short, the diversity of oligopoly does not allow us to explain all oligopolistic behaviors with a single market model.

- *Complications of interdependence* The mutual interdependence of oligopolistic firms complicates matters significantly. Because firms cannot predict the reactions of their rivals with certainty, they cannot estimate their own demand and marginal-revenue data. Without such data, firms cannot determine their profit-maximizing price and output, even in theory, as we will see.

Despite these analytical difficulties, two interrelated characteristics of oligopolistic pricing have been observed. First, if the macroeconomy is generally stable, oligopolistic prices are typically inflexible (or "rigid" or "sticky"). Prices change less frequently under oligopoly than under pure competition, monopolistic competition, and, in some instances, pure monopoly. Second, when oligopolistic prices do change, firms are likely to change their prices together, suggesting that there is a tendency to act in concert, or collusively, in setting and changing prices (as we mentioned in the preceding section). The diversity of oligopolies and the presence of mutual interdependence are reflected in the models that follow.

Kinked-Demand Theory: Noncollusive Oligopoly

Imagine an oligopolistic industry made up of three hypothetical firms (Arch, King, and Dave's), each having about one-third of the total market for a differentiated product. Assume that the firms are "independent," meaning that they do not engage in collusive price practices. Assume, too, that the going price for Arch's product is P_0 and its current sales are Q_0, as shown in **Figure 11.4a (Key Graph)**.

Now the question is, "What does the firm's demand curve look like?" Mutual interdependence and the uncertainty about rivals' reactions make this question hard to answer. The location and shape of an oligopolist's demand curve depend on how the firm's rivals will react to a price change introduced by Arch. There are two plausible assumptions about the reactions of Arch's rivals:

- *Match price changes* One possibility is that King and Dave's will exactly match any price change initiated by Arch. In this case, Arch's demand and marginal-revenue curves will look like the straight lines labeled D_1 and MR_1 in Figure 11.4a. Why are they so steep? Reason: If Arch cuts its price, its sales will increase only modestly because its two rivals will also cut their prices to prevent Arch from gaining an advantage over them. The small increase in sales that Arch (and its two rivals) will realize is at the expense of other industries; Arch will gain no sales from King and Dave's. If Arch raises its price, its sales will fall only modestly because King and Dave's will match its price increase. The industry will lose sales to other industries, but Arch will lose no customers to King and Dave's.

- *Ignore price changes* The other possibility is that King and Dave's will ignore any price change by Arch. In this case, the demand and marginal-revenue curves faced by Arch will resemble the straight lines D_2 and MR_2 in Figure 11.4a. Demand in this case is considerably more

FIGURE 11.4 **The kinked-demand curve.** (a) The slope of a noncollusive oligopolist's demand and marginal-revenue curves depends on whether its rivals match (straight lines D_1 and MR_1) or ignore (straight lines D_2 and MR_2) any price changes that it may initiate from the current price P_0. (b) In all likelihood an oligopolist's rivals will ignore a price increase but follow a price cut. This causes the oligopolist's demand curve to be kinked (D_2eD_1) and the marginal-revenue curve to have a vertical break, or gap (fg). Because any shift in marginal costs between MC_1 and MC_2 will cut the vertical (dashed) segment of the marginal-revenue curve, no change in either price P_0 or output Q_0 will result from such a shift.

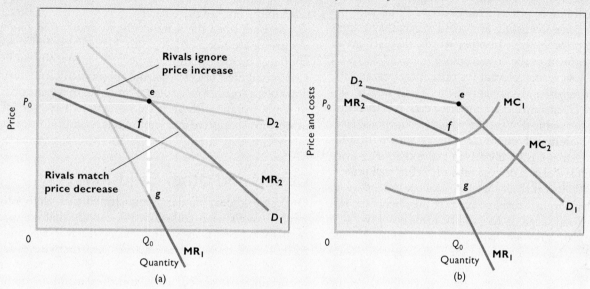

QUICK QUIZ FOR FIGURE 11.4

1. Suppose Q_0 in this figure represents annual sales of 5 million units for this firm. The other two firms in this three-firm industry sell 3 million and 2 million units, respectively. The Herfindahl index for this industry is:
   a. 100 percent.
   b. 400.
   c. 10.
   d. 3800.

2. The D_2e segment of the demand curve D_2eD_1 in graph (b) implies that:
   a. this firm's total revenue will fall if it increases its price above P_0.
   b. other firms will match a price increase above P_0.
   c. the firm's relevant marginal-revenue curve will be MR_1 for price increases above P_0.
   d. the product in this industry is necessarily standardized.

3. By matching a price cut, this firm's rivals can:
   a. increase their market shares.
   b. increase their marginal revenues.
   c. maintain their market shares.
   d. lower their total costs.

4. A shift of the marginal-cost curve from MC_2 to MC_1 in graph (b) would:
   a. increase the "going price" above P_0.
   b. leave price at P_0 but reduce this firm's total profit.
   c. leave price at P_0 but reduce this firm's total revenue.
   d. make this firm's demand curve more elastic.

Answers: 1. d; 2. a; 3. c; 4. b

elastic than it was under the previous assumption. The reasons are clear: If Arch lowers its price and its rivals do not, Arch will gain sales significantly at the expense of its two rivals because it will be underselling them. Conversely, if Arch raises its price and its rivals do not, Arch will lose many customers to King and Dave's, which will be underselling it. Because of product differentiation, however, Arch's sales will not fall to zero

when it raises its price; some of Arch's customers will pay the higher price because they have a strong preference for Arch's product. Nevertheless, Arch's demand curve will be much more elastic when its rivals ignore price changes than when they match them.

A Combined Strategy Now, which is the most logical assumption for Arch to make about how its rivals will react

229

to any price change it might initiate? The answer is, "It depends on the direction of the price change." Common sense and observation of oligopolistic industries suggest that a firm's rivals will match price declines below P_0 as they act to prevent the price cutter from taking their customers. But they will ignore price increases above P_0 because the rivals of the price-increasing firm stand to gain the business lost by the price booster. In other words, the dark-green left-hand segment of the "rivals ignore" demand curve D_2 in Figure 11.4a seems relevant for price increases, and the dark-green right-hand segment of the "rivals match" demand curve D_1 seems relevant for price cuts. It is therefore reasonable to assume that the noncollusive oligopolist faces the **kinked-demand curve** D_2eD_1, as shown in Figure 11.4b. Demand is highly elastic above the going price P_0 but much less elastic or even inelastic below that price.

Note also that if rivals match a price cut but ignore an increase, the marginal-revenue curve of the oligopolist will also have an odd shape. It, too, will be made up of two segments: the dark gray left-hand part of marginal-revenue curve MR_2 in Figure 11.4a and the dark gray right-hand part of marginal-revenue curve MR_1. Because of the sharp difference in elasticity of demand above and below the going price, there is a gap, or what we can simply treat as a vertical segment, in the marginal-revenue curve. We show this gap as the dashed segment in the combined marginal-revenue curve MR_2fgMR_1 in Figure 11.4b.

Price Inflexibility This analysis helps explain why prices are generally stable in noncollusive oligopolistic industries. There are both demand and cost reasons.

On the demand side, the kinked-demand curve gives each oligopolist reason to believe that any change in price will be for the worse. If it raises its price, many of its customers will desert it. If it lowers its price, its sales at best will increase very modestly since rivals will match the lower price. Even if a price cut increases the oligopolist's total revenue somewhat, its costs may increase by a greater amount, depending on demand elasticity. For instance, if its demand is inelastic to the right of Q_0, as it may well be, then the firm's profit will surely fall. A price decrease in the inelastic region lowers the firm's total revenue, and the production of a larger output increases its total costs.

On the cost side, the broken marginal-revenue curve suggests that even if an oligopolist's costs change substantially, the firm may have no reason to change its price. In particular, all positions of the marginal-cost curve between MC_1 and MC_2 in Figure 11.4b will result in the firm's deciding on exactly the same price and output. For all those positions, MR equals MC at output Q_0; at that output, it will charge price P_0.

Criticisms of the Model The kinked-demand analysis has two shortcomings. First, it does not explain how the going price gets to be at P_0 in Figure 11.4 in the first place. It only helps explain why oligopolists tend to stick with an existing price. The kinked-demand curve explains price inflexibility but not price itself.

Second, when the macroeconomy is unstable, oligopoly prices are not as rigid as the kinked-demand theory implies. During inflationary periods, many oligopolists have raised their prices often and substantially. And during downturns (recessions), some oligopolists have cut prices. In some instances these price reductions have set off a **price war:** successive and continuous rounds of price cuts by rivals as they attempt to maintain their market shares.

Cartels and Other Collusion

Our game-theory model demonstrated that oligopolists might benefit from collusion. We can say that collusion occurs whenever firms in an industry reach an agreement to fix prices, divide up the market, or otherwise restrict competition among themselves. The disadvantages and uncertainties of noncollusive, kinked-demand oligopolies are obvious. There is always the danger of a price war breaking out, especially during a general business recession. Then each firm finds that, because of unsold goods and excess capacity, it can reduce per-unit costs by increasing market share. Then, too, a new firm may surmount entry barriers and initiate aggressive price cutting to gain a foothold in the market. In addition, the kinked-demand curve's tendency toward rigid prices may adversely affect profits if general inflationary pressures increase costs. However, by controlling price through collusion, oligopolists may be able to reduce uncertainty, increase profits, ` and perhaps even prohibit the entry of new rivals.

Price and Output Assume once again that there are three hypothetical oligopolistic firms (Gypsum, Sheetrock, and GSR) producing, in this instance, gypsum drywall panels for finishing interior walls. All three firms produce a homogeneous product and have identical cost curves. Each firm's demand curve is indeterminate unless we know how its rivals will react to any price change. Therefore, we suppose each firm assumes that its two rivals will match either a price cut or a price increase. In other words, each firm has a demand curve like the straight line D_1 in Figure 11.4a. And since they have identical cost data, and the same demand and thus marginal-revenue data, we can say that Figure 11.5 represents the position of each of our three oligopolistic firms.

What price and output combination should, say, Gypsum select? If Gypsum were a pure monopolist, the answer

FIGURE 11.5 Collusion and the tendency toward joint-profit maximization. If oligopolistic firms face identical or highly similar demand and cost conditions, they may collude to limit their joint output and to set a single, common price. Thus each firm acts as if it were a pure monopolist, setting output at Q_0 and charging price P_0. This price and output combination maximizes each oligopolist's profit (green area) and thus the combined or joint profit of the colluding firms.

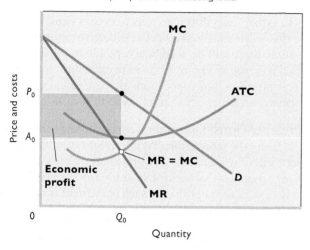

The 12 OPEC Nations, Daily Oil Production, October 2009

The OPEC nations produce about 41 percent of the world's oil and about 43 percent of the oil sold in world markets.

OPEC Country	Barrels of Oil
Saudi Arabia	8,092,000
Iran	3,743,000
Iraq	2,470,000
Venezuela	2,311,000
Kuwait	2,275,000
UAE	2,258,000
Angola	1,879,000
Nigeria	1,856,000
Libya	1,560,000
Algeria	1,281,000
Qatar	790,000
Ecuador	478,000

Source: OPEC, **www.opec.org**; *CIA World Factbook*, **www.cia.gov**.

would be clear: Establish output at Q_0, where marginal revenue equals marginal cost, charge the corresponding price P_0, and enjoy the maximum profit attainable. However, Gypsum does have two rivals selling identical products, and if Gypsum's assumption that its rivals will match its price of P_0 proves to be incorrect, the consequences could be disastrous for Gypsum. Specifically, if Sheetrock and GSR actually charge prices below P_0, then Gypsum's demand curve D will shift sharply to the left as its potential customers turn to its rivals, which are now selling the same product at a lower price. Of course, Gypsum can retaliate by cutting its price too, but this will move all three firms down their demand curves, lowering their profits. It may even drive them to a point where average total cost exceeds price and losses are incurred.

So the question becomes, "Will Sheetrock and GSR want to charge a price below P_0?" Under our assumptions, and recognizing that Gypsum has little choice except to match any price they may set below P_0, the answer is no. Faced with the same demand and cost circumstances, Sheetrock and GSR will find it in their interest to produce Q_0 and charge P_0. This is a curious situation; each firm finds it most profitable to charge the same price, P_0, but only if its rivals actually do so! How can the three firms ensure the price P_0 and quantity Q_0 solution in which each is keenly interested? How can they avoid the less profitable outcomes associated with either higher or lower prices?

The answer is evident: They can collude. They can get together, talk it over, and agree to charge the same price, P_0.

In addition to reducing the possibility of price wars, this will give each firm the maximum profit. (But it will also subject them to antitrust prosecution if they are caught!) For society, the result will be the same as would occur if the industry were a pure monopoly composed of three identical plants.

Overt Collusion: The OPEC Cartel Collusion may assume a variety of forms. The most comprehensive form of collusion is the **cartel**, a group of producers that typically creates a formal written agreement specifying how much each member will produce and charge. Output must be controlled—the market must be divided up—in order to maintain the agreed-upon price. The collusion is overt, or open to view.

Undoubtedly the most significant international cartel is the Organization of Petroleum Exporting Countries (OPEC), comprising 12 oil-producing nations (see Global Perspective 11.1). OPEC produces 41 percent of the world's oil and supplies 43 percent of all oil traded internationally.

OPEC has in some cases been able to drastically alter oil prices by increasing or decreasing supply. In 1973 for instance, it caused the price of oil to more than triple by getting its members to restrict output. And again, in the late 1990s it caused oil prices to rise from $11 per barrel to $34 per barrel over a 15-month period.

That being said, it should be kept in mind that most increases in the price of oil are not caused by OPEC. Between 2005 and 2008, for example, oil prices went from $40 per barrel to $140 per barrel due to rapidly rising demand from China and supply uncertainties related to armed conflict in the Middle East. But as the recession that began in December 2007 took hold, demand slumped and oil prices collapsed back down to about $40 per barrel. OPEC was largely a nonfactor in this rise and fall in the price of oil. But in those cases where OPEC can effectively enforce its production agreements, there is little doubt that it can hold the price of oil substantially above the marginal cost of production.

Covert Collusion: Examples

Cartels are illegal in the United States, and hence any collusion that exists is covert or secret. Yet there are numerous examples, as shown by evidence from antitrust (antimonopoly) cases. In 1993 the Borden, Pet, and Dean food companies, among others, either pleaded guilty to or were convicted of rigging bids on the prices of milk products sold to schools and military bases. By phone or at luncheons, company executives agreed in advance on which firm would submit the low bid for each school district or military base. In 1996 American agribusiness Archer Daniels Midland and three Japanese and South Korean firms were found to have conspired to fix the worldwide price and sales volume of a livestock feed additive. Executives for the firms secretly met in Hong Kong, Paris, Mexico City, Vancouver, and Zurich to discuss their plans.

In many other instances collusion is much subtler. Unwritten, informal understandings (historically called "gentlemen's agreements") are frequently made at cocktail parties, on golf courses, through phone calls, or at trade association meetings. In such agreements, executives reach verbal or even tacit (unspoken) understandings on product price, leaving market shares to be decided by nonprice competition. Although these agreements, too, violate antitrust laws—and can result in severe personal and corporate penalties—the elusive character of informal understandings makes them more difficult to detect.

Obstacles to Collusion

Normally, cartels and similar collusive arrangements are difficult to establish and maintain. Here are several barriers to collusion:

Demand and Cost Differences When oligopolists face different costs and demand curves, it is difficult for them to agree on a price. This is particularly the case in industries where products are differentiated and change frequently. Even with highly standardized products, firms usually have somewhat different market shares and operate with differing degrees of productive efficiency. Thus it is unlikely that even homogeneous oligopolists would have the same demand and cost curves.

In either case, differences in costs and demand mean that the profit-maximizing price will differ among firms; no single price will be readily acceptable to all, as we assumed was true in Figure 11.5. So price collusion depends on compromises and concessions that are not always easy to obtain and hence act as an obstacle to collusion.

Number of Firms Other things equal, the larger the number of firms, the more difficult it is to create a cartel or some other form of price collusion. Agreement on price by three or four producers that control an entire market may be relatively easy to accomplish. But such agreement is more difficult to achieve where there are, say, 10 firms, each with roughly 10 percent of the market, or where the Big Three have 70 percent of the market while a competitive fringe of 8 or 10 smaller firms battles for the remainder.

Cheating As the game-theory model makes clear, collusive oligopolists are tempted to engage in secret price cutting to increase sales and profit. The difficulty with such cheating is that buyers who are paying a high price for a product may become aware of the lower-priced sales and demand similar treatment. Or buyers receiving a price concession from one producer may use the concession as a wedge to get even larger price concessions from a rival producer. Buyers' attempts to play producers against one another may precipitate price wars among the producers. Although secret price concessions are potentially profitable, they threaten collusive oligopolies over time. Collusion is more likely to succeed when cheating is easy to detect and punish. Then the conspirators are less likely to cheat on the price agreement.

Recession Long-lasting recession usually serves as an enemy of collusion because slumping markets increase average total cost. In technical terms, as the oligopolists' demand and marginal-revenue curves shift to the left in Figure 11.5 in response to a recession, each firm moves leftward and upward to a higher operating point on its average-total-cost curve. Firms find they have substantial excess production capacity, sales are down, unit costs are up, and profits are being squeezed. Under such conditions, businesses may feel they can avoid serious profit reductions (or even losses) by cutting price and thus gaining sales at the expense of rivals.

Potential Entry The greater prices and profits that result from collusion may attract new entrants, including foreign firms. Since that would increase market supply and reduce prices and profits, successful collusion requires that colluding oligopolists block the entry of new producers.

Legal Obstacles: Antitrust Law

U.S. antitrust laws prohibit cartels and price-fixing collusion. So less obvious means of price control have evolved in this country.

Price Leadership Model

Price leadership entails a type of implicit understanding by which oligopolists can coordinate prices without engaging in outright collusion based on formal agreements and secret meetings. Rather, a practice evolves whereby the "dominant firm"—usually the largest or most efficient in the industry—initiates price changes and all other firms more or less automatically follow the leader. Many industries, including farm machinery, cement, copper, newsprint, glass containers, steel, beer, fertilizer, cigarettes, and tin, are practicing, or have in the recent past practiced, price leadership.

Leadership Tactics

An examination of price leadership in a variety of industries suggests that the price leader is likely to observe the following tactics.

Infrequent Price Changes

Because price changes always carry the risk that rivals will not follow the lead, price adjustments are made only infrequently. The price leader does not respond to minuscule day-to-day changes in costs and demand. Price is changed only when cost and demand conditions have been altered significantly and on an industrywide basis as the result of, for example, industrywide wage increases, an increase in excise taxes, or an increase in the price of some basic input such as energy. In the automobile industry, price adjustments traditionally have been made when new models are introduced each fall.

Communications

The price leader often communicates impending price adjustments to the industry through speeches by major executives, trade publication interviews, or press releases. By publicizing "the need to raise prices," the price leader seeks agreement among its competitors regarding the actual increase.

Limit Pricing

The price leader does not always choose the price that maximizes short-run profits for the industry because the industry may want to discourage new firms from entering. If the cost advantages (economies of scale) of existing firms are a major barrier to entry, new entrants could surmount that barrier if the price leader and the other firms set product price high enough. New firms that are relatively inefficient because of their small size might survive and grow if the industry sets price very high. So, in order to discourage new competitors and to maintain the current oligopolistic structure of the industry, the price leader may keep price below the short-run profit-maximizing level. The strategy of establishing a price that blocks the entry of new firms is called *limit pricing*.

Breakdowns in Price Leadership: Price Wars

Price leadership in oligopoly occasionally breaks down, at least temporarily, and sometimes results in a price war. An example of price leadership temporarily breaking down occurred in the breakfast cereal industry, in which Kellogg traditionally had been the price leader. General Mills countered Kellogg's leadership in 1995 by reducing the prices of its cereals by 11 percent. In 1996 Post responded with a 20 percent price cut, which Kellogg then followed. Not to be outdone, Post reduced its prices by another 11 percent.

As another example, in October 2009 with the Christmas shopping season just getting underway, Walmart cut its price on 10 highly anticipated new books to just $10 each. Within hours, Amazon.com matched the price cut. Walmart then retaliated by cutting its price for the books to just $9 each. Amazon.com matched that reduction—at which point Walmart went to $8.99! Then, out of nowhere, Target jumped in at $8.98, a price that Amazon.com and Walmart immediately matched. And that is where the price finally came to rest—at a level so low that each company was losing money on each book it sold.

Most price wars eventually run their course. After a period of low or negative profits, they again yield price leadership to one of the industry's leading firms. That firm then begins to raise prices, and the other firms willingly follow suit.

QUICK REVIEW 11.3

- In the kinked-demand theory of oligopoly, price is relatively inflexible because a firm contemplating a price change assumes that its rivals will follow a price cut and ignore a price increase.
- Cartels agree on production limits and set a common price to maximize the joint profit of their members as if each were a unit of a single pure monopoly.
- Collusion among oligopolists is difficult because of (a) demand and cost differences among sellers, (b) the complexity of output coordination among producers, (c) the potential for cheating, (d) a tendency for agreements to break down during recessions, (e) the potential entry of new firms, and (f) antitrust laws.
- Price leadership involves an informal understanding among oligopolists to match any price change initiated by a designated firm (often the industry's dominant firm).

Oligopoly and Advertising

We have noted that oligopolists would rather not compete on the basis of price and may become involved in price collusion. Nonetheless, each firm's share of the total market is typically determined through product development and advertising, for two reasons:

- Product development and advertising campaigns are less easily duplicated than price cuts. Price cuts can be quickly and easily matched by a firm's rivals to cancel any potential gain in sales derived from that strategy. Product improvements and successful advertising, however, can produce more permanent gains in market share because they cannot be duplicated as quickly and completely as price reductions.
- Oligopolists have sufficient financial resources to engage in product development and advertising. For most oligopolists, the economic profits earned in the past can help finance current advertising and product development.

Product development (or, more broadly, "research and development") is the subject of Web Chapter 11, so we will confine our present discussion to advertising. In 2008, firms spent an estimated $137 billion on advertising in the United States and $490 billion worldwide. Advertising is prevalent in both monopolistic competition and oligopoly. Table 11.3 lists the 10 leading U.S. advertisers in 2008.

Advertising may affect prices, competition, and efficiency both positively and negatively, depending on the circumstances. While our focus here is on advertising by oligopolists, the analysis is equally applicable to advertising by monopolistic competitors.

Positive Effects of Advertising

In order to make rational (efficient) decisions, consumers need information about product characteristics and prices. Media advertising may be a low-cost means for consumers to obtain that information. Suppose you are in the market for a high-quality camera that is not advertised or promoted in newspapers, in magazines, or on the Internet. To make a rational choice, you may have to spend several days visiting stores to determine the availability, prices, and features of various brands. This search entails both direct costs (gasoline, parking fees) and indirect costs (the value of your time). By providing information about the available options, advertising and Internet promotion reduce your search time and minimize these direct and indirect costs.

By providing information about the various competing goods that are available, advertising diminishes monopoly power. In fact, advertising is frequently associated with the introduction of new products designed to compete with existing brands. Could Toyota and Honda have so strongly

TABLE 11.3 **The Largest U.S. Advertisers, 2008**

Company	Advertising Spending Millions of $
Procter & Gamble	$4831
Verizon	3700
AT&T	3073
General Motors	2901
Johnson & Johnson	2529
Unilever	2423
Walt Disney	2218
Time Warner	2208
General Electric	2019
Sears	1865

Source: Advertising Age, **www.adage.com**. Copyright 2010, Crain Communications. 69284-36mpf.

challenged U.S. auto producers without advertising? Could FedEx have sliced market share away from UPS and the U.S. Postal Service without advertising?

Viewed this way, advertising is an efficiency-enhancing activity. It is a relatively inexpensive means of providing useful information to consumers and thus lowering their search costs. By enhancing competition, advertising results in greater economic efficiency. By facilitating the introduction of new products, advertising speeds up technological progress. By increasing sales and output, advertising can reduce long-run average total cost by enabling firms to obtain economies of scale.

Potential Negative Effects of Advertising

Not all the effects of advertising are positive, of course. Much advertising is designed simply to manipulate or persuade consumers—that is, to alter their preferences in favor of the advertiser's product. A television commercial that indicates that a popular personality drinks a particular brand of soft drink—and therefore that you should too—conveys little or no information to consumers about price or quality. In addition, advertising is sometimes based on misleading and extravagant claims that confuse consumers rather than enlighten them. Indeed, in some cases advertising may well persuade consumers to pay high prices for much-acclaimed but inferior products, forgoing better but unadvertised products selling at lower prices. Example: *Consumer Reports* has found that heavily advertised premium motor oils provide no better engine performance and longevity than do cheaper brands.

Firms often establish substantial brand-name loyalty and thus achieve monopoly power via their advertising (see Global Perspective 11.2). As a consequence, they are able to increase their sales, expand their market shares,

GLOBAL PERSPECTIVE 11.2

The World's Top 10 Brand Names, 2009

Here are the world's top 10 brands, based on four criteria: the brand's market share within its category, the brand's world appeal across age groups and nationalities, the loyalty of customers to the brand, and the ability of the brand to "stretch" to products beyond the original product.

World's Top 10 Brands

Coca-Cola

IBM

Microsoft

General Electric

Nokia

McDonald's

Google

Toyota

Intel

Disney

Source: 100 Best Global Brands, 2009. Used with permission of Interbrand, **www.interbrand.com.**

and enjoy greater profits. Larger profits permit still more advertising and further enlargement of the firm's market share and profit. In time, consumers may lose the advantages of competitive markets and face the disadvantages of monopolized markets. Moreover, new entrants to the industry need to incur large advertising costs in order to establish their products in the marketplace; thus, advertising costs may be a barrier to entry.

Advertising can also be self-canceling. The advertising campaign of one fast-food hamburger chain may be offset by equally costly campaigns waged by rivals, so each firm's demand actually remains unchanged. Few, if any, extra burgers will be purchased and each firm's market share will stay the same. But because of the advertising, all firms will experience higher costs and either their profits will fall or, through successful price leadership, their product prices will rise.

When advertising either leads to increased monopoly power or is self-canceling, economic inefficiency results.

Oligopoly and Efficiency

Is oligopoly, then, an efficient market structure from society's standpoint? How do the price and output decisions of the oligopolist measure up to the triple equality $P = MC =$ minimum ATC that occurs in pure competition?

Productive and Allocative Efficiency

Many economists believe that the outcome of some oligopolistic markets is approximately as shown in Figure 11.5. This view is bolstered by evidence that many oligopolists sustain sizable economic profits year after year. In that case, the oligopolist's production occurs where price exceeds marginal cost and average total cost. Moreover, production is below the output at which average total cost is minimized. In this view, neither productive efficiency (P = minimum ATC) nor allocative efficiency (P = MC) is likely to occur under oligopoly.

A few observers assert that oligopoly is actually less desirable than pure monopoly because government usually regulates pure monopoly in the United States to guard against abuses of monopoly power. Informal collusion among oligopolists may yield price and output results similar to those under pure monopoly yet give the outward appearance of competition involving independent firms.

Qualifications

We should note, however, three qualifications to this view:

- **Increased foreign competition** In recent decades foreign competition has increased rivalry in a number of oligopolistic industries—steel, automobiles, video games, electric shavers, outboard motors, and copy machines, for example. This has helped to break down such cozy arrangements as price leadership and to stimulate much more competitive pricing.

- **Limit pricing** Recall that some oligopolists may purposely keep prices below the short-run profit-maximizing level in order to bolster entry barriers. In essence, consumers and society may get some of the benefits of competition—prices closer to marginal cost and minimum average total cost—even without the competition that free entry would provide.

- **Technological advance** Over time, oligopolistic industries may foster more rapid product development and greater improvement of production techniques than would be possible if they were purely competitive. Oligopolists have large economic profits from which they can fund expensive research and development (R&D). Moreover, the existence of barriers to entry may give the oligopolist some assurance that it will reap the rewards of successful R&D. Thus, the short-run economic inefficiencies of oligopolists may be partly or wholly offset by the oligopolists' contributions to better products, lower prices, and lower costs over time. We say more about these dynamic aspects of rivalry in optional Web Chapter 11.

Word Oligopoly in the Beer Industry

The Beer Industry Was Once Populated by Hundreds of Firms and an Even Larger Number of Brands. But It Now Is an Oligopoly Dominated by a Handful of Producers.

Since the Second World War, profound changes have increased the level of concentration in the U.S. beer industry. In 1947 more than 400 independent brewing companies operated in the United States. By 1967, the number had declined to 124 and by 1980 it had dropped to just 33. In 1947 the largest five brewers sold only 19 percent of the nation's beer. In 2007, the Big Three brewers (Anheuser-Busch, SABMiller, and Molson Coors) sold 76 percent. In 2007, Anheuser-Busch (48 percent) and SABMiller (18 percent) alone combined for 66 percent of industry sales. And, in late 2007, SABMiller acquired the U.S. operations of Molson Coors, thus creating MillerCoors and turning the Big Three into the Big Two. In 2008, Belgian brewer InBev purchased Anheuser-Busch, thereby forming international brewing giant A-B. The U.S. beer industry clearly meets all the criteria of oligopoly.

Changes on the demand side of the market have contributed to the "shakeout" of small brewers from the industry. First, consumer tastes in the mass market have generally shifted from the stronger-flavored beers of the small brewers to the light products of the larger brewers. Second, there has been a shift from the consumption of beer in taverns to consumption of it in the home. The beer consumed in taverns was mainly "draft" or "tap" beer from kegs, supplied by local and regional brewers that could deliver the kegs in a timely fashion at relatively low transportation cost. But the large increase in the demand for beer consumed at home opened the door for large brewers that sold their beer in bottles and aluminum cans. The large brewers could ship their beer by truck or rail over long distances and compete directly with the local brewers.

Developments on the supply side of the market have been even more profound. Technological advances speeded up the bottling and canning lines. Today, large brewers can fill and close 2000 cans per line per minute. Large plants are also able to reduce labor costs through the automating of brewing and warehousing. Furthermore, plant construction costs per barrel of production capacity are about one-third less for a 4.5-million-barrel plant than for a 1.5-million-barrel plant. As a consequence of these and other factors, the minimum efficient scale in brewing is a plant size of about 4.5 million barrels. Additionally, studies indicate that further cost savings are available to brewing firms that have two or more separate large breweries in different regions of the country. Between the economies of scale from plant size and these cost savings from multiple plants, cost considerations deter entry to the mainline beer industry.

"Blindfold" taste tests confirm that most mass-produced American beers taste alike. Undaunted, brewers spend large amounts of money touting the supposed differences between their brands in order to build brand loyalty. And here Anheuser-Busch and MillerCoors, which sell national brands, enjoy major cost advantages over producers such as Pabst that have many regional brands (for example, Lone Star, Rainier, Schaefer, and Schmidt). The reason is that national television advertising is less costly per viewer than local TV advertising.

Up until the recent combination of Molson Coors and SABMiller, mergers had not been the dominant factor in explaining the industry consolidation. Rather, that was largely caused by failing smaller breweries (such as Heileman's) selling their assets and brands to competitors. Dominant firms have

Summary

1. The distinguishing features of monopolistic competition are (a) there are enough firms in the industry to ensure that each firm has only limited control over price, mutual interdependence is absent, and collusion is nearly impossible; (b) products are characterized by real or perceived differences so that economic rivalry entails both price and nonprice competition; and (c) entry to the industry is relatively easy. Many aspects of retailing, and some manufacturing industries in which economies of scale are few, approximate monopolistic competition.

2. The four-firm concentration ratio measures the percentage of total industry output accounted for by the largest four firms. The Herfindahl index sums the squares of the percent market shares of all firms in the industry.

expanded by heavily advertising their main brands and by creating new brands such as Lite, Bud Light, Genuine Draft, Keystone Light, and Icehouse rather than acquiring other brewers. This has sustained significant product differentiation, despite the declining number of major brewers.

The rise of the Miller Brewing Company from the seventh- to the second-largest producer in the 1970s was due in large measure to advertising and product differentiation. When the Philip Morris Company acquired Miller in 1970, the new management made two big changes. First, it "repositioned" Miller High Life beer into that segment of the market where potential sales were the greatest. Sold previously as the "champagne of beers," High Life had appealed heavily to upper-income consumers and to occasional women beer drinkers. Miller's new television ads featured young blue-collar workers, who were known to be larger consumers of beer. Second, Miller then developed its low-calorie Lite beer, which was extensively promoted with Philip Morris advertising dollars. Lite proved to be the most popular new product in the history of the beer industry. Miller later introduced its Genuine Draft beer, which found its place within the top 10 brands.

But the story of the last three decades has been Anheuser-Busch InBev, (A-B), which has greatly expanded its market share. A-B now makes the nation's top two brands: Bud Light and Budweiser account for nearly half the beer sold in the United States. Part of A-B's success owes to the demise of regional competitors. But part also is the result of A-B's competitive prowess. It has constructed state-of-the-art breweries, created effective advertising campaigns, and forged strong relationships with regional distributors. Meanwhile, Miller's market share has declined slightly in recent years. In 2002 Philip Morris sold Miller to London-based SAB. SABMiller, as the combined firm was called, significantly redesigned Miller's labeling and marketing to enhance its appeal both domestically and overseas. Perhaps of greater importance, SABMiller's acquisition of Coors to form MillerCoors immediately expanded its U.S. market share from 18 percent to 29 percent. MillerCoors thus became the number two brewer in the United States after A-B, which controls 49 percent of the market.

Imported beers such as Heineken, Corona, and Guinness constitute about 15 percent of the market, with individual brands seeming to wax and wane in popularity. Some local or regional microbreweries such as Samuel Adams and Pyramid, which brew "craft" or specialty beers and charge super-premium prices, have whittled into the sales of the major brewers. Craft and specialty beers account for only 6 percent of beer consumed in the United States, but they are the fastest-growing segment of the U.S. industry. A-B, Miller, and Coors have taken notice, responding with specialty brands of their own (for example, Red Wolf, Red Dog, Killarney's Red Lager, Icehouse, and Blue Moon) and by buying stakes in microbrewers Redhook Ale and Celis.

Sources: Based on Kenneth G. Elzinga, "Beer," in Walter Adams and James Brock (eds.), *The Structure of American Industry*, 10th ed. (Upper Saddle River, N.J.: Prentice Hall, 2001), pp. 85–113; and Douglas F. Greer, "Beer: Causes of Structural Change," in Larry Duetsch (ed.), *Industry Studies*, 2d ed. (New York: M. E. Sharpe, 1998), pp. 28–64. Updated data and information are mainly from *Beer Marketer's Insights*, **www.beerinsights.com**, and the Association of Brewers, **www.beertown.com**.

3. Monopolistically competitive firms may earn economic profits or incur losses in the short run. The easy entry and exit of firms results in only normal profits in the long run.

4. The long-run equilibrium position of the monopolistically competitive producer is less efficient than that of the pure competitor. Under monopolistic competition, price exceeds marginal cost, indicating an underallocation of resources to the product, and price exceeds minimum average total cost, indicating that consumers do not get the product at the lowest price that cost conditions might allow.

5. Nonprice competition provides a way that monopolistically competitive firms can offset the long-run tendency for economic profit to fall to zero. Through product differentiation, product development, and advertising, a firm may

237

strive to increase the demand for its product more than enough to cover the added cost of such nonprice competition. Consumers benefit from the wide diversity of product choice that monopolistic competition provides.

6. In practice, the monopolistic competitor seeks the specific combination of price, product, and advertising that will maximize profit.

7. Oligopolistic industries are characterized by the presence of few firms, each having a significant fraction of the market. Firms thus situated engage in strategic behavior and are mutually interdependent: The behavior of any one firm directly affects, and is affected by, the actions of rivals. Products may be either virtually uniform or significantly differentiated. Various barriers to entry, including economies of scale, underlie and maintain oligopoly.

8. High concentration ratios are an indication of oligopoly (monopoly) power. By giving more weight to larger firms, the Herfindahl index is designed to measure market dominance in an industry.

9. Game theory (a) shows the interdependence of oligopolists' pricing policies, (b) reveals the tendency of oligopolists to collude, and (c) explains the temptation of oligopolists to cheat on collusive arrangements.

10. Noncollusive oligopolists may face a kinked-demand curve. This curve and the accompanying marginal-revenue curve help explain the price rigidity that often characterizes oligopolies; they do not, however, explain how the actual prices of products were first established.

11. The uncertainties inherent in oligopoly promote collusion. Collusive oligopolists such as cartels maximize joint profits—that is, they behave like pure monopolists. Demand and cost differences, a "large" number of firms, cheating through secret price concessions, recessions, and the antitrust laws are all obstacles to collusive oligopoly.

12. Price leadership is an informal means of collusion whereby one firm, usually the largest or most efficient, initiates price changes and the other firms in the industry follow the leader.

13. Market shares in oligopolistic industries are usually determined on the basis of product development and advertising. Oligopolists emphasize nonprice competition because (a) advertising and product variations are less easy for rivals to match and (b) oligopolists frequently have ample resources to finance nonprice competition.

14. Advertising may affect prices, competition, and efficiency either positively or negatively. Positive: It can provide consumers with low-cost information about competing products, help introduce new competing products into concentrated industries, and generally reduce monopoly power and its attendant inefficiencies. Negative: It can promote monopoly power via persuasion and the creation of entry barriers. Moreover, it can be self-canceling when engaged in by rivals; then it boosts costs and creates inefficiency while accomplishing little else.

15. Neither productive nor allocative efficiency is realized in oligopolistic markets, but oligopoly may be superior to pure competition in promoting research and development and technological progress.

16. Table 8.1, page 164, provides a concise review of the characteristics of monopolistic competition and oligopoly as they compare to those of pure competition and pure monopoly.

Terms and Concepts

monopolistic competition	homogeneous oligopoly	collusion
product differentiation	differentiated oligopoly	kinked-demand curve
nonprice competition	strategic behavior	price war
four-firm concentration ratio	mutual interdependence	cartel
Herfindahl index	interindustry competition	price leadership
excess capacity	import competition	
oligopoly	game theory	

Questions

1. How does monopolistic competition differ from pure competition in its basic characteristics? From pure monopoly? Explain fully what product differentiation may involve. Explain how the entry of firms into its industry affects the demand curve facing a monopolistic competitor and how that, in turn, affects its economic profit. LO1

2. Compare the elasticity of a monopolistic competitor's demand with that of a pure competitor and a pure monopolist. Assuming identical long-run costs, compare graphically the prices and outputs that would result in the long run under pure competition and under monopolistic competition. Contrast the two market structures in terms of productive

and allocative efficiency. Explain: "Monopolistically competitive industries are populated by too many firms, each of which produces too little." LO2

3. "Monopolistic competition is monopolistic up to the point at which consumers become willing to buy close-substitute products and competitive beyond that point." Explain. LO2

4. "Competition in quality and service may be just as effective as price competition in giving buyers more for their money." Do you agree? Why? Explain why monopolistically competitive firms frequently prefer nonprice competition to price competition. LO2

5. Critically evaluate and explain: LO2
   a. In monopolistically competitive industries, economic profits are competed away in the long run; hence, there is no valid reason to criticize the performance and efficiency of such industries.
   b. In the long run, monopolistic competition leads to a monopolistic price but not to monopolistic profits.

6. Why do oligopolies exist? List five or six oligopolists whose products you own or regularly purchase. What distinguishes oligopoly from monopolistic competition? LO3

7. Answer the following questions, which relate to measures of concentration: LO3
   a. What is the meaning of a four-firm concentration ratio of 60 percent? 90 percent? What are the shortcomings of concentration ratios as measures of monopoly power?
   b. Suppose that the five firms in industry A have annual sales of 30, 30, 20, 10, and 10 percent of total industry sales. For the five firms in industry B, the figures are 60, 25, 5, 5, and 5 percent. Calculate the Herfindahl index for each industry and compare their likely competitiveness.

8. Explain the general meaning of the profit payoff matrix at the top of the next column for oligopolists X and Y. All profit figures are in thousands. LO4
   a. Use the payoff matrix to explain the mutual interdependence that characterizes oligopolistic industries.
   b. Assuming no collusion between X and Y, what is the likely pricing outcome?
   c. In view of your answer to 8b, explain why price collusion is mutually profitable. Why might there be a temptation to cheat on the collusive agreement?

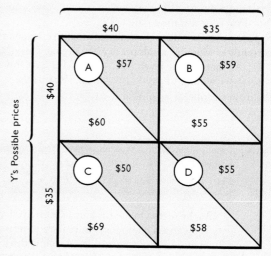

9. What assumptions about a rival's response to price changes underlie the kinked-demand curve for oligopolists? Why is there a gap in the oligopolists' marginal-revenue curve? How does the kinked-demand curve explain price rigidity in oligopoly? What are the shortcomings of the kinked-demand model? LO5

10. Why might price collusion occur in oligopolistic industries? Assess the economic desirability of collusive pricing. What are the main obstacles to collusion? Speculate as to why price leadership is legal in the United States, whereas price-fixing is not. LO6

11. Why is there so much advertising in monopolistic competition and oligopoly? How does such advertising help consumers and promote efficiency? Why might it be excessive at times? LO7

12. **ADVANCED ANALYSIS** Construct a game-theory matrix involving two firms and their decisions on high versus low advertising budgets and the effects of each on profits. Show a circumstance in which both firms select high advertising budgets even though both would be more profitable with low advertising budgets. Why won't they unilaterally cut their advertising budgets? LO7

13. **LAST WORD** What firm dominates the U.S. beer industry? What demand and supply factors have contributed to "fewness" in this industry?

Problems

1. Suppose that a small town has seven burger shops whose respective shares of the local hamburger market are (as percentages of all hamburgers sold): 23%, 22%, 18%, 12%, 11%, 8%, and 6%. What is the four-firm concentration ratio of the hamburger industry in this town? What is the Herfindahl index for the hamburger industry in this town?

If the top three sellers combined to form a single firm, what would happen to the four-firm concentration ratio and to the Herfindahl index? LO3

2. Suppose that the most popular car dealer in your area sells 10 percent of all vehicles. If all other car dealers sell either the same number of vehicles or fewer, what is the largest

value that the Herfindahl index could possibly take for car dealers in your area? In that same situation, what would the four-firm concentration ratio be? LO3

3. Suppose that an oligopolistically competitive restaurant is currently serving 230 meals per day (the output where MR = MC). At that output level, ATC per meal is $10 and consumers are willing to pay $12 per meal. What is the size of this firm's profit or loss? Will there be entry or exit? Will this restaurant's demand curve shift left or right? In long-run equilibrium, suppose that this restaurant charges $11 per meal for 180 meals and that the marginal cost of the 180th meal is $8. What is the size of the firm's profit? Suppose that the allocatively efficient output level in long-run equilibrium is 200 meals. Is the deadweight loss for this firm greater than or less than $60? LO3

FURTHER TEST YOUR KNOWLEDGE AT
www.mcconnell19e.com

At the text's Online Learning Center (OLC), **www.mcconnell19e.com**, you will find one or more Web-based questions that require information from the Internet to answer. We urge you to check them out; they will familiarize you with Web sites that may be helpful in other courses and perhaps even in your career. The OLC also features multiple-choice questions that give instant feedback and provides other helpful ways to further test your knowledge of the chapter.

Additional Game Theory Applications

We have seen that game theory is helpful in explaining mutual interdependence and strategic behavior by oligopolists. This appendix provides additional oligopoly-based applications of game theory.

A One-Time Game: Strategies and Equilibrium

Consider Figure 1, which lists strategies and outcomes for two fictitious producers of the computer memory chips referred to as DRAMs (Dynamic Random Access Memory circuits). Chipco is the single producer of these chips in the United States and Dramco is the only producer in China. Each firm has two alternative strategies: an international strategy, in which it competes directly against the other firm in both countries; and a national strategy, in which it sells only in its home country.

The game and payoff matrix shown in Figure 1 is a **one-time game** because the firms select their optimal strategies in a single time period without regard to possible interactions in subsequent time periods. The game is also a **simultaneous game** because the firms choose their strategies at the same time; and a **positive-sum game**, a game in which the sum of the two firms' outcomes (here, profits) is positive. In contrast, the net gain in a **zero-sum game** is zero because one firm's gain must equal the other firm's loss, and the net gain in a **negative-sum game** is negative. In some positive-sum games, both firms may have positive outcomes. That is the case in Figure 1.

To determine optimal strategies, Chipco looks across the two rows in the payoff matrix (yellow portion of cells in millions of dollars) and Dramco looks down the two columns (blue portion of cells). These payoffs indicate that both firms have a **dominant strategy**—an option that is better than any alternative option *regardless of what the other firm does*. To see this, notice that Chipco's international strategy will give it a higher profit than its national strategy—regardless of whether Dramco chooses to utilize an international or a national strategy. An international strategy will produce an $11 million profit for Chipco (yellow portion of cell A) if Dramco also uses an international strategy while a national strategy will result in a $20 million profit for Chipco (yellow portion of cell B) if Dramco uses a national strategy. Chipco's possible $11 million and $20 million outcomes are clearly better than the $5 million (cell C) and $17 million (cell D) outcomes it could receive if it chose to pursue a national strategy. Chipco's international strategy is, consequently, its dominant strategy. Using similar logic, Dramco also concludes that its international strategy is its dominant strategy.

In this particular case, the outcome (cell A) of the two dominant strategies is the game's **Nash equilibrium**—an outcome from which neither rival wants to deviate.[1] At the Nash equilibrium, both rivals see their current strategy as optimal *given the other firm's strategic choice*. The Nash equilibrium is the only outcome in the payoff matrix in Figure 1 that, once achieved, is stable and therefore will persist.[2]

Credible and Empty Threats

In looking for optimal strategies, Chipco and Dramco both note that they could increase their profit from $11 million to $17 million if they could agree to jointly pursue national strategies (cell D) instead of independently

FIGURE 1 A One-Time Game In this single-period, positive-sum game, Chipco's international strategy is its dominant strategy—the alternative that is superior to any other strategy regardless of whatever Dramco does. Similarly, Dramco's international strategy is also its dominant strategy. With both firms choosing international strategies, the outcome of the game is Cell A, where each firm receives an $11 million profit. Cell A is a Nash equilibrium because neither firm will independently want to move away from it given the other firm's strategy.

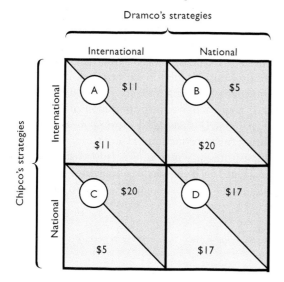

---

[1]The Nash equilibrium is named for its discoverer, John F. Nash. Nash's life and Nobel Prize are the subject of the motion picture *A Beautiful Mind*, directed by Ron Howard and starring Russell Crowe.

[2]Nash equilibriums can exist even in games that lack dominant strategies.

pursuing international strategies (cell A). Presumably the national strategies would leave the firms as pure monopolists in their domestic economies, with each able to set higher prices and obtain greater profits as a result. But if this territorial agreement were put in place, both firms would have an incentive to cheat on the agreement by secretly selling DRAMs in the other's country. That would temporarily move the game to either cell B or cell C. Once discovered, however, such cheating would undermine the territorial agreement and return the game to the Nash equilibrium (cell A).

Now let's add a new twist—a credible threat—to the game shown in Figure 1. A **credible threat** is a statement of coercion (a threat!) that is believable by the other firm. Suppose that Chipco is the lower-cost producer of DRAMs because of its superior technology. Also, suppose that Chipco approaches Dramco saying that Chipco intends to use its national strategy and expects Dramco to do the same. If Dramco decides against the national strategy or agrees to the strategy and then later cheats on the agreement, Chipco will immediately drop its price to an ultra-low level equal to its average total cost (ATC). Both firms know that Chipco's ATC price is below Dramco's ATC. Although Chipco will see its economic profit fall to zero, Dramco will suffer an economic loss and possibly go out of business.

If Chipco's threat is credible, the two firms represented in Figure 1 will abandon the Nash equilibrium (cell A) to deploy their national strategies and achieve highly profitable cell D. In game theory, credible threats such as this can help establish and maintain collusive agreements. A strong "enforcer" can help prevent cheating and maintain the group discipline needed for cartels, price-fixing conspiracies, and territorial understandings to successfully generate high profits.

But credible threats are difficult to achieve in the actual economy. For example, Dramco might rightly wonder why Chipco had not previously driven it out of business through an ultra-low price strategy. Is Chipco fearful of the U.S. antitrust authorities?

If Dramco does not wish to participate in the proposed scheme, it might counter Chipco's threat with its own: Forget that you ever talked to us and we will not take this illegal "offer" to the U.S. Justice Department. Dramco can make this threat because strict laws are in place against attempts to restrain trade through price-fixing and territorial agreements.

So Dramco may view Chipco's threat as simply an **empty threat**—a statement of coercion that is not believable by the threatened firm. If so, the Nash equilibrium will prevail, with both firms pursuing an international strategy.

Repeated Games and Reciprocity Strategies

The Chipco-Dramco game was a one-time game, but many strategic situations are repeated by the same oligopolists over and over again. For example, Coca Cola and Pepsi are mutually interdependent on pricing, advertising, and product development year after year, decade after decade. The same is true for Boeing and Airbus, Walmart and Target, Toyota and General Motors, Budweiser and Miller, Nike and Adidas, and numerous other dominant pairs.

In a **repeated game**—a game that recurs more than once—the optimal strategy may be to cooperate and restrain oneself from competing as hard as possible so long as the other firm reciprocates by also not competing as hard as possible.[3] To see how this works, consider two hypothetical producers of soft drinks: 2Cool and ThirstQ. If ThirstQ competes hard with 2Cool in today's situation in which 2Cool would like ThirstQ to take things easy, 2Cool will most likely retaliate against ThirstQ in any subsequent situation where the circumstances are reversed. In contrast, if ThirstQ cooperates with 2Cool in game 1, ThirstQ can expect 2Cool to reciprocate in game 2 of their repeated interaction. Both firms know full well the negative long-run consequences of ever refusing to cooperate. So the cooperation continues, not only in game 2, but in games 3, 4, 5, and beyond.

Figure 2 shows two side-by-side payoff matrixes for the two games. In Figure 2a, 2Cool and ThirstQ face a situation in which 2Cool is introducing a new cola called Cool Cola and has two advertising options: a high promotional budget to introduce the new product and a normal advertising budget. ThirstQ has the same two options: a high promotional budget to try to counter 2Cool's product introduction and a normal advertising budget.

The analysis is now familiar to you. The dominant strategies for both firms in game 1 (Figure 2a) are their large promotional advertising budgets and the Nash equilibrium is cell A. Both firms could do better at cell D if each agreed to use normal advertising budgets. But 2Cool could do better still. It could achieve the $16 million of profit in cell B, but only if ThirstQ holds its advertising budget to its normal level during the introduction of Cool Cola.

ThirstQ might voluntarily do just that! It knows that game 2 (Figure 2b) is forthcoming in which it will be introducing its new product, Quench It. By leaving its

---

[3]We are assuming either an infinitely repeated game or a game of unknown time-horizon. Games with a known ending date undermine reciprocity strategies.

FIGURE 2 A Repeated Game with Reciprocity (a) in the payoff matrix to the left, 2Cool introduces its new Cool Cola with a large promotional advertising budget, but its rival ThirstQ maintains its normal advertising budget even though it could counter 2Cool with a large advertising budget of its own and drive the outcome from Cell B to Cell A. ThirstQ forgoes this $2 million of extra profit because it knows that it will soon be introducing its own new product (Quench It). (b) In the payoff matrix to the right, ThirstQ introduces Quench It with a large promotional advertising budget. Cool2 reciprocates ThirstQ's earlier accommodation by not matching ThirstQ's promotional advertising budget and instead allowing the outcome of the repeated game to be Cell C. The profit of both 2Cool and ThirstQ therefore is larger over the two periods than if each firm had aggressively countered each other's single-period strategy.

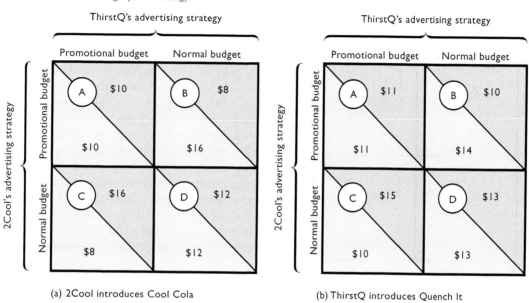

(a) 2Cool introduces Cool Cola   (b) ThirstQ introduces Quench It

advertising budget at its normal level during 2Cool's introduction of Cool Cola, and thereby sacrificing profit of $2 million (= $10 million in cell A − $8 million in cell B), ThirstQ can expect 2Cool to reciprocate in the subsequent game in which ThirstQ introduces Quench It. Without formally colluding—and risking antitrust penalties—game 1 ends at cell B and repeated game 2 ends at cell C. With reciprocity, 2Cool's total profit of $26 million (= $16 million in game 1 + $10 million in game 2) exceeds the $21 million (= $10 million + $11 million) it would have earned without the reciprocity. ThirstQ similarly benefits. To check your understanding, confirm this fact using the numbers in the two matrixes.

First-Mover Advantages and Preemption of Entry

The games we have highlighted thus far have been games in which the two firms simultaneously select their optimal strategies. But in some actual economic circumstances, firms apply strategies sequentially: One firm moves first and commits to a strategy to which a rival firm must subsequently respond. In such a **sequential game,** the final outcome may depend critically upon which firm

moves first since the first mover may have the opportunity to establish a Nash equilibrium that works in its favor.

Consider Figure 3, which identifies a game in which two large retailers—let's call them Big Box and Huge Box—are each considering building a large retail store in a small rural city. As indicated in the figure, each firm has two strategies: build or don't build. The payoff matrix reflects the fact that the city is not large enough to support two big box retailers profitably. If both retailers simultaneously build, the outcome will be cell A and each firm will lose $5 million. If neither firm builds, the outcome will be cell D with both firms securing zero profit. If only Big Box builds, the outcome will be cell C and Big Box will profit handsomely at $12 million. If Huge Box builds, but Big Box stays out, the outcome will be cell B and Huge Box will secure the $12 million profit. Either cell B or cell C is the possible Nash equilibrium. At either cell, both firms will have selected their best option in view of the strategy taken by the other firm.

The payoff matrix in Figure 3 clearly reveals that whoever builds first will preempt the other retailer from entering the market. An extremely large **first-mover advantage** exists in this particular game. Suppose that a well-thought-out strategy and adequate financing leave Big Box better prepared than Huge Box to move quickly to

FIGURE 3 A First-Mover Advantage and the Preemption of Entry In this game in which strategies are pursued sequentially, the firm that moves first can take advantage of the particular situation represented in which only a single firm can exist profitably in some geographical market. Here, we suppose that Big Box moves first with its "Build" strategy to achieve the $12 million profit outcome in Cell C. Huge Box then will find that it will lose money if it also builds because that will result in a $5 million loss, as shown in Cell A.

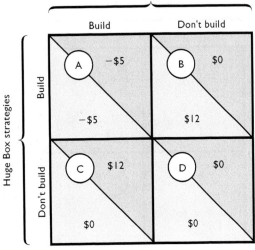

build a large retail store in this city. By exploiting its first-mover advantage, Big Box drives the outcome to Cell C and preempts Huge Box's entry into this market.

Many firms in the actual economy have used variations of this first-mover strategy to a greater or lesser extent to preempt major rivals, or at least greatly slow their entry. Examples are Walmart, Home Depot, Costco, Walgreens, Starbucks, and many more. The strategy, however, is highly risky because it requires the commitment of huge amounts of investment funds to saturate the market and preclude entry by other firms. Also, to be the first-mover in places that are being transformed from rural land into urban areas, firms may need to build their stores many months prior to the time when the area in question becomes developed enough to provide the store with significant business. That may mean losses until the market grows sufficiently for profitability. Some firms such as Walmart have become huge, profitable international enterprises by using a first-mover strategy. Other firms, such as Krispy Kreme Donuts, have lost millions of dollars because their extremely rapid expansion turned out to be unprofitable in many of their outlets because the expected customers never materialized.

Appendix Summary

1. Positive-sum games are games in which the payoffs to the firms sum to a positive number; zero-sum games are games in which the payoffs sum to zero; and negative-sum games are games in which the payoffs sum to less than zero. Positive-sum games allow for "win-win" opportunities, whereas zero-sum games always feature "I win-you lose" outcomes. Games can be either one-time games or repeated games. Decisions in games may be made either simultaneously or sequentially.

2. When two firms are playing a strategic game, a firm is said to have a dominant strategy if there is an option that leads to better outcomes than all other options regardless of what the other firm does. Not all games have dominant strategies. The Nash equilibrium is an outcome from which neither firm wants to deviate because both firms see their current strategy as optimal given the other firm's chosen strategy. The Nash equilibrium is stable and persistent. Attempts by the firms to rig games to achieve some other outcome are difficult to accomplish and maintain, although

credible threats can sometimes work. In contrast, empty threats accomplish nothing and leave the outcome at the Nash equilibrium.

3. Reciprocity can improve outcomes for firms participating in repeated games. In such games, one firm avoids taking advantage of the other firm because it knows that the other firm can take advantage of it in subsequent games. This reciprocity increases firm profits relative to what they would have been without reciprocity.

4. Two possible Nash equilibriums can exist in sequential games with first-mover advantages. Which one occurs depends on which firm moves first since that firm can preempt the other firm, making it unprofitable for the other firm to match the move. Several real-world firms, including Walmart, have successfully used first-mover advantages to saturate markets and preempt entry by rivals.

Appendix Terms and Concepts

one-time game	negative-sum game	empty threat
simultaneous game	dominant strategy	repeated game
positive-sum game	Nash equilibrium	sequential game
zero-sum game	credible threat	first-mover advantage

Appendix Questions

1. Is the game shown by Figure 11.3 in the chapter (not this appendix) a zero-sum game or is it a positive-sum game? How can you tell? Are there dominant strategies in this game? If so, what are they? What cell represents a Nash equilibrium and why? Explain why it is so difficult for Uptown and RareAir to achieve and maintain a more favorable cell than the Nash equilibrium in this single-period pricing game. LO8

2. Refer to the payoff matrix in question 8 at the end of this chapter. First, assume this is a one-time game. Explain how the $60/$57 outcome might be achieved through a credible threat. Next, assume this is a repeated game (rather than a one-time game) and that the interaction between the two firms occurs indefinitely. Why might collusion with a credible threat not be necessary to achieve the $60/$57 outcome? LO8

3. Refer to the payoff matrix below. LO8

Firm A

	Build aircraft	Don't build
Build aircraft	A −$10 / $10	B 0 / $25
Don't build	C $25 / 0	D 0 / 0

Firm B

Assuming this is a sequential game with no collusion, what is the outcome if Firm A moves first to build a new type of commercial aircraft? Explain why first-mover strategies in the real world are only as good as the profit projections on which they are based. How could a supposed "win" from moving first turn out to be a big loss, whereas the "loss" of being preempted turn out to be a blessing in disguise?

4. **ADVANCED** Suppose you are playing a game in which you and one other person each pick a number between 1 and 100, with the person closest to some randomly selected number between 1 and 100 winning the jackpot. (Ask your instructor to fund the jackpot.) Your opponent picks first. What number do you expect her to choose? Why? What number would you then pick? Why are the two numbers so close? How might this example relate to why Home Depot and Lowes, Walgreens and Rite-Aid, McDonald's and Burger King, Borders and Barnes & Noble, and other major pairs of rivals locate so close to each other in many well-defined geographical markets that are large enough for both firms to be profitable? LO8

Appendix Problems

1. Consider a "punishment" variation of the two-firm oligopoly situation shown in Figure 11.3 in the chapter (not in this appendix). Suppose that if one firm sets a low price while the other sets a high price, then the firm setting the high price can fine the firm setting the low price. Suppose that whenever a fine is imposed, X dollars is taken from the low-price firm and given to the high-price firm. What is the smallest amount that the fine X can be such that both firms will want to always set the high price? LO8

2. Consider whether the promises and threats made toward each other by duopolists and oligopolists are always credible (believable). Look back at Figure 11.3 in the chapter (not in this appendix). Imagine that the two firms will play this game twice in sequence and that each firm claims the following policy. Each says that if both it and the other firm choose the high price in the first game, then it will also choose the high price in the second game (as a reward to the other firm for cooperating in the first game). LO8

   a. As a first step toward thinking about whether this policy is credible, consider the situation facing both firms in the second game. If each firm bases its decision on what to do in the second game entirely on the payouts facing the firms in the second game, which strategy will each firm choose in the second game?

   b. Now move backward in time one step. Imagine that it is the start of the first game and each firm must decide what to do during the first game. Given your answer to 2a, is the publicly stated policy credible? (Hint: No matter what happens in the first game, what will both firms do in the second game?)

   c. Given your answers to 2a and 2b, what strategy will each firm choose in the first game?

CHAPTER 11

Monopolistic Competition and Oligopoly

This chapter examines two market structures, monopolistic competition and oligopoly, that fall between the extremes of pure competition and pure monopoly. Both structures are important because they offer descriptions of firms and industries typically found in the U.S. economy.

Monopolistically competitive firms are prevalent because most retail establishments, such as clothing stores and restaurants, fall into the monopolistically competitive category. In such industries, there are a relatively large number of firms, so no one has a large market share, they sell differentiated products, and each has limited pricing power.

Economists use **four-firm concentration ratios** and the **Herfindahl index** to measure the degree of firm dominance of an industry and to determine whether an industry is monopolistically competitive or oligopolistic.

The first part of the chapter focuses on the **demand curve** for the monopolistically competitive firm. This demand curve differs from those found in pure competition and pure monopoly. As the individual firm changes the character of its product, or changes product promotion, both the costs of the firm and the demand for its product will change.

The **price–output** analysis of the monopolistic competitor is relatively simple. In the short run, this analysis is identical with the analysis of the price–output decision of a pure monopolist. Only in the long run does the competitive element make itself apparent: The entry of firms forces the price a firm charges to fall. This price, however, is not equal either to minimum average cost or to marginal cost; consequently, monopolistic competition can be said to be less efficient than pure competition.

This chapter also discusses **product variety** under monopolistic competition. A part of the competitive effort of individual firms is devoted to product differentiation, product development, and advertising. Each firm has three things to manipulate—price, product, and advertising—in maximizing profits. Although monopolistic competition has been characterized as inefficient, some of the positive benefits of product variety may offset some of the inefficiencies of this market structure.

The concept of **oligopoly** is fairly easy to grasp: a few firms that are mutually interdependent dominate the market for a product. The underlying causes of oligopoly are economies of scales and barriers to entry. More difficult to grasp is oligopoly behavior. **Game theory** helps explain what is meant by mutual interdependence and why it exists in an oligopoly. It also explains why specific conclusions cannot be drawn about the price and output decisions of individual firms. Oligopolists are loath to engage in price competition because of **mutual interdependence,** and fre-

quently resort to **collusion** to set prices and sometimes use nonprice competition to determine market share. Collusion does not give firms complete protection from competition because there are incentives to cheat on agreements.

There is no standard model of oligopoly because of the diversity of markets and the uncertainty caused by mutual interdependence among firms. **Three oligopoly models,** however, cover the range of most market situations. The **kinked-demand curve** explains why, in the absence of collusion, oligopolists will not raise or lower their prices even when their costs change. This model does not explain what price oligopolists will set; it only explains why prices will be relatively inflexible.

The second model examines how oligopolists resort to **collusion** to set price. The collusion can be **overt,** as in a cartel agreement, or the collusion can be **covert,** as in a secret agreement. The OPEC oil cartel is a classic example of covert collusion. Obstacles, such as cheating on price, make collusive agreements difficult to establish and maintain.

The third model of oligopoly is **price leadership.** In some industries a dominant firm serves as the price leader for other firms. There is no overt collusion, only unwritten, informal (tacit) understandings about price and competition among firms. This model explains why there are infrequent price changes, why the lead firm makes price and output announcements for other firms to follow, and why low pricing is used to prevent new entry. Such covert collusion, however, can be undermined by price wars.

The next-to-last section of the chapter looks at **advertising** in oligopoly. Product development and advertising are often the means of competition in oligopoly. Drawing conclusions about the effects of advertising, however, is difficult. Reasonable arguments can be made that advertising is both beneficial and costly for consumers and about whether advertising helps or hurts economic efficiency.

Compared with pure competition, oligopoly does not result in allocative or productive efficiency. Nevertheless, the qualifications noted at the end of the chapter may offset some of oligopoly's shortcomings.

■ CHECKLIST

When you have studied this chapter you should be able to

☐ Describe monopolistic competition in terms of the number of sellers, type of product, entry and exit conditions, and advertising.
☐ Cite three consequences from having relatively large numbers of sellers in monopolistic competition.

131

☐ Describe five aspects of differentiated products in monopolistic competition.
☐ Describe the entry and exit conditions in monopolistic competition.
☐ State the role of advertising and nonprice competition in monopolistic competition.
☐ Define four-firm concentration ratio and use it to describe whether industries are monopolistically competitive or oligopolistic.
☐ Define the Herfindahl index and use it to assess influence of dominant firms in different types of industries.
☐ Compare the firm's demand curve under monopolistic competition with firms' demand curves in pure competition and pure monopoly.
☐ Determine the output of and the price charged by a monopolistic competitor in the short run when given cost and demand data.
☐ Explain why the price charged by a monopolistic competitor will in the long run tend to equal average cost and result in only a normal profit.
☐ Cite two real-world complications that may affect the outcome for monopolistically competitive firms in the long run.
☐ Show graphically how the typical firm in monopolistic competition achieves neither productive nor allocative efficiency and how excess capacity occurs.
☐ Discuss the effects of product variety in monopolistic competition.
☐ Explain why monopolistic competition is more complex in practice.
☐ Define oligopoly in terms of the number of producers, type of product, control over price, and interdependence.
☐ Explain how entry barriers and mergers contribute to the existence of oligopolies.
☐ Use game theory to explain three characteristics of oligopoly behavior.
☐ Cite two reasons why there is no standard model of oligopoly.
☐ Use the kinked-demand theory to explain the tendency for prices to be inflexible in a noncollusive model oligopoly.
☐ Describe the price and output conditions for a cartel or collusive pricing model of oligopoly.
☐ Give real examples of overt and covert collusion.
☐ State six obstacles to collusion.
☐ Describe the price leadership model of oligopoly and its outcomes.
☐ Explain why advertising is often heavily used in oligopoly.
☐ Cite the potential positive and negative effects of advertising.
☐ Compare economic efficiency in oligopoly to other market structures.
☐ Describe the major demand and supply factors over the years that turned the beer industry into an oligopoly (*Last Word*).

■ **CHAPTER OUTLINE**

   1. **Monopolistic competition** has several defining characteristics.
      a. The *relatively large number of sellers* means that each has a small market share, there is no collusion,
and firms take actions that are independent of each other.
      b. Monopolistic competition exhibits **product differentiation.** This differentiation occurs through differences in attributes or features of products; services to customers; location and accessibility; brand names and packaging; and some control over price.
      c. *Entry* into the industry or *exit* is relatively easy.
      d. There is **nonprice competition** in the form of product differentiation and advertising.
      e. Monopolistically competitive firms are common, and examples include asphalt paving, quick printing, saw mills, retail bakeries, clothing stores, restaurants, and grocery stores (see Table 11.1). (An explanation of how all industries are classified based on market type or market power is provided in section 5g of this chapter outline.)

   2. Given the products produced in a monopolistically competitive industry and the amounts of promotional activity, it is possible to analyze the **price and output decisions** of a firm.
      a. The **demand curve** confronting each firm will be highly but not perfectly price elastic because each firm has many competitors who produce close but not perfect substitutes for the product it produces.
      (1) Comparing the demand curve for the monopolistic competitor to other market structures suggests that it is not perfectly elastic, as is the case with the pure competitor, but it is also more elastic than the demand curve of the pure monopolist.
      (2) The degree of elasticity, however, for each monopolistic competitor will depend on the number of rivals and the extent of product differentiation.
      b. In the **short run** the individual firm will produce the output at which marginal cost and marginal revenue are equal and charge the price at which the output can be sold; either economic profits or losses may result in the short run.
      c. In the **long run** the entry and exodus of firms will tend to change the demand for the product of the individual firm in such a way that economic profits are eliminated and there are only normal profits. (Price and average costs are made equal to each other.)

   3. Monopolistic competition among firms producing a given product and engaged in a given amount of promotional activity results in **less economic efficiency and more excess capacity** than does pure competition.
      a. The average cost of each firm is equal in the long run to its price. The industry **does not achieve allocative efficiency** because output is smaller than the output at which marginal cost and price are equal. The industry **does not achieve productive efficiency** because the output is less than the output at which average cost is a minimum.
      b. **Excess capacity** results because firms produce less output than at the minimum of average total cost. In monopolistic competition, many firms operate below optimal capacity.

4. Each monopolistically competitive firm attempts to differentiate its product and advertise it to increase the firm's profit. These activities give rise to **nonprice competition** among firms.

  a. The benefit of product variety is that firms offer consumers a wide range of types, style, brands, and quality variants of a product. Products can also be improved. The expanded range of consumer choice from product differentiation and improvement may offset some of the economic inefficiency (excess capacity problem) of monopolistic competition.

  b. Monopolistic competition is more complex than the simple model presented in the chapter because the firm must constantly juggle three factors—price, product characteristics, and advertising—in seeking to maximize profits.

5. Oligopoly is frequently encountered in the U.S. economy.

  a. It is composed of a few firms that dominate an industry.

  b. It can be a **homogeneous oligopoly** that produces standardized industrial products such as steel, or a **differentiated oligopoly** that produces different types of consumer products such as automobiles.

  c. Firms have control over price, and thus are price makers. Oligopolistic firms engage in **strategic behavior,** which means they take into account the actions of other firms in making their decisions. **Mutual interdependence** exists because firms must consider the reaction of rivals to any change in price, output, product characteristic, or advertising.

  d. Barriers to entry, such as economies of scale or ownership, control over raw materials, patents, and pricing strategies, can explain the existence of oligopoly.

  e. Some industries have become oligopolistic not from internal growth but from external factors such as mergers.

  f. Most large industries are oligopolistic. They include ones such as primary copper, electric light bulbs, petrochemicals, motor vehicles, tires, and breakfast cereals (see Table 11.2).

  g. The degree of concentration or market power in an industry is measured in several ways. A **four-firm concentration ratio** gives the percentage of an industry's total sales provided by the four largest firms. If the ratio is very small, the industry is competitive. If the ratio is less than 40 percent, but not very small, the industry is considered monopolistically competitive. If the ratio is 40 percent or greater, the industry is classified as oligopolistic. There are, however, shortcomings with concentration ratios:

  (1) The ratio may understate concentration if markets are more local than national because the ratio is based on national data.

  (2) The ratio may overstate concentration because definitions of industries can be somewhat arbitrary and there may be substantial **interindustry competition.**

  (3) The ratio may overstate concentration if there is **import competition** because the ratio does not account for world trade.

  (4) The ratio may understate concentration if there is a dominant firm or firms among the firms in an industry. The **Herfindahl index** addresses the dominant firm problem because it accounts for the market share of each firm. It is the sum of the squared percentage market shares of all firms in the industry. This formula gives a greater weight in the index to larger firms in an industry.

6. Insight into the pricing behavior of oligopolists can be gained by thinking of the oligopoly as a game of strategy. This **game-theory model** leads to three conclusions.

  a. Firms in an oligopolistic industry are mutually interdependent and must consider the actions of rivals when they make price decisions.

  b. Oligopoly often leads to overt or covert collusion among the firms to fix prices or to coordinate pricing because competition among oligopolists results in low prices and profits; collusion helps maintain higher prices and profits.

  c. Collusion creates incentives to cheat among oligopolists by lowering prices or increasing production to obtain more profit.

7. Economic analysis of oligopoly is difficult because of the diversity among the firms and complications resulting from mutual interdependence. Nevertheless, two important characteristics of oligopoly are inflexible prices and simultaneous price changes by firms. An analysis of three oligopoly models helps explain the pricing practices of oligopolists.

  a. In the **kinked-demand model** there is no collusion. Each firm believes that if it lowers its price its rivals will lower their prices, but if it raises its price its rivals *will not* increase their prices. Therefore, the firm is reluctant to change its price for fear of reducing its profits. The model has two shortcomings: it does not explain how the going price gets set; prices are not as rigid as the model implies.

  b. Mutual interdependence indicates there is **collusion** among oligopoly firms to maintain or increase profits.

  (1) Firms that collude tend to set their prices and joint output at the same level a pure monopolist would set them.

  (2) Collusion may be overt, as in a **cartel** agreement. The OPEC cartel is an example of effective overt collusion.

  (3) Collusion may be covert whereby agreements or unwritten, informal (tacit) understandings between firms set price or market share. Examples of such collusion have included bid rigging on milk prices for schools or fixing worldwide prices for a livestock feed additive.

  (4) At least six obstacles make it difficult for firms to collude or maintain collusive arrangements: difference in demand and cost among firms, the number of firms in the arrangement, incentives to cheat, changing economic conditions, potential for entry by other firms, and legal restrictions and penalties.

  c. Price leadership is a form of covert collusion in which one firm initiates price changes and the other firms in the industry follow the lead. Three price leadership tactics have been observed.

(1) Price adjustments tend to be made infrequently, only when cost and demand conditions change to a significant degree.

(2) The price leader announces the price change in various ways, through speeches, announcements, or other such activities.

(3) The price set may not maximize short-run profits for the industry, especially if the industry wants to prevent entry by other firms.

(4) Price leadership can break down and result in a **price war.** Eventually the wars end, and a price leader re-emerges.

8. Oligopolistic firms often avoid price competition but engage in **product development and advertising** for two reasons: Price cuts are easily duplicated, but nonprice competition is more unique; and firms have more financial resources for advertising and product development.

a. The potential positive effects of advertising include providing low-cost information to consumers that reduces search time and monopoly power, thus enhancing economic efficiency.

b. The potential negative effects of advertising include manipulating consumers to pay higher prices, serving as a barrier to entry into an industry, and offsetting campaigns that raise product costs and prices.

9. The **efficiency of oligopoly** is difficult to evaluate.

a. Many economists think that oligopoly price and output characteristics are similar to those of monopoly. Oligopoly firms set output where price exceeds marginal cost and the minimum of average total cost. Oligopoly is allocatively inefficient ($P > \text{MC}$) and productively inefficient ($P > \text{minimum ATC}$).

b. This view must be qualified because of increased foreign competition to oligopolistic firms, the use of limit pricing that sets prices at less than the profit-maximizing price, and the technological advances arising from this market structure.

10. (*Last Word*). In 1947, there were over 400 independent brewers in the United States, but today the two major brewers account for 76 percent of the market. One reason for this change is that demand changed. Preferences shifted from stronger-flavored beers to lighter, dryer products. Consumption also shifted from taverns to homes, which results in different packaging. On the supply side, technology changed to produce significant economies of scale that now are barriers to entry. Mergers have occurred, but they are not the fundamental cause of increased concentration. Advertising and product differentiation have also been important in the growth of some firms.

■ HINTS AND TIPS

1. Review the four basic market models in Table 8.1 so that you see how monopolistic competition and oligopoly compare with the other market models on five characteristics.

2. The same **MC = MR** rule for maximizing profits or minimizing losses for the firm from previous chapters is now used to determine output and price in monopolistic competition and in certain oligopoly models. If you understood how the rule applied under pure competition and pure monopoly, you should have no trouble applying it here.

3. Make sure you know how to interpret Figure 11.1 because it is an important graph. It illustrates why a representative firm in monopolistic competition just breaks even in the long run and earns just a normal rather than an economic profit. It also shows how economic inefficiency in monopolistic competition produces excess capacity.

4. Where is the kink in the kinked-demand model? To find out, practice drawing the model. Then use Figure 11.4 to check your answer. Explain to yourself what each line means in the graph.

5. Price and output determinations under collusive oligopoly or a cartel are essentially the same as those for pure monopoly.

■ IMPORTANT TERMS

monopolistic competition	strategic behavior
product differentiation	mutual interdependence
nonprice competition	interindustry competition
four-firm concentration ratio	import competition
	game theory
Herfindahl index	collusion
excess capacity	kinked-demand curve
oligopoly	price war
homogeneous oligopoly	cartel
differentiated oligopoly	price leadership

SELF-TEST

■ FILL-IN QUESTIONS

1. In a monopolistically competitive market, there are a relatively (large, small) _____ number of producers who sell (standardized, differentiated) _____ products. Entry into such a market is relatively (difficult, easy) _____. The number of firms means that each one has a (large, small) _____ market share, the firms (do, do not) _____ collude, and they operate in (an independent, a dependent) _____ manner.

2. Identify the different aspects of production differentiation in monopolistic competition:

a. _____

b. _____

c. _____

d. _____

e. _____

3. In the *short run* for a monopolistically competitive firm,

   a. the demand curve will be (more, less) _____

   elastic than that facing a monopolist and _____
   elastic than that facing a pure competitor;

   b. the elasticity of this demand curve will depend on

   (1) _____ and

   (2) _____; and

   c. it will produce the output level where marginal cost

   is (less than, equal to, greater than) _____
   marginal revenue.

4. In the *long run* for a monopolistically competitive
industry,

   a. the *entry* of new firms will (increase, decrease)

   _____ the demand for the product produced by

   each firm in the industry and _____ the elasticity
   of that demand; and

   b. the price charged by the individual firm will tend

   to equal (average, marginal) _____ cost, its
   economic profits will tend to be (positive, zero)

   _____, and its average cost will be (greater,

   less) _____ than the minimum average cost of
   producing and promoting the product.

5. Although representative firms in monopolistic compe-

tition tend to earn (economic, normal) _____ profits
in the long run, there can be complications that may result

in firms earning _____ profits in the long run. Some
firms may achieve a degree of product differentiation that

(can, cannot) _____ be duplicated by other firms.

There may be (collusion, barriers to entry) _____
that prevent penetration of the market by other firms.

6. In monopolistic competition, price is (less than, equal

to, greater than) _____ marginal cost, and so the

market structure (does, does not) _____ yield allocative efficiency. Also, average total cost is (less than,

equal to, greater than) _____ the minimum of
average total cost, and so the market structure (does,

does not) _____ result in (allocative, productive)

_____ efficiency.

7. In the long run, the monopolistic competitor tries to
earn economic profits by using (price, nonprice)

_____ competition in the form of product differentiation and advertising. This results in a trade-off between
a choice of more consumer goods and services and

(more, less) _____ economic efficiency.

8. The more complex model of monopolistic competition
suggests that in seeking to maximize profits, each firm

juggles the factors of (losses, price) _____, changes

in (collusion, product) _____, and decisions about

(controls, advertising) _____ until the firm feels
no further change in the variables will result in greater
profit.

9. The percentage of the total industry sales accounted
for by the top four firms in an industry is known as a four-

firm (Herfindahl index, concentration ratio) _____,
whereas summing the squared percentage market shares
of each firm in the industry is the way to calculate the

_____.

10. In an oligopoly (many, a few) _____ large
firms produce either a differentiated or a (heterogeneous,

homogeneous) _____ product, and entry into such

an industry is (easy, difficult) _____. The oligopo-

listic firm is a price (maker, taker) _____ and there

is mutual (independence, interdependence) _____
among firms in an industry. The existence of oligopoly can

be explained by (exit, entry) _____ barriers and

by (markets, mergers) _____.

11. The basics of the pricing behavior of oligopolists can

be understood from a (game, advertising) _____
theory perspective. Oligopoly consists of a few firms that

are mutually (funded, interdependent) _____.
This means that when setting the price of its product,

each producer (does, does not) _____ consider
the reaction of its rivals. The monopolist (does, does

not) _____ face this problem because it has no
rivals, and the pure competitor, or monopolistic com-

petitor, _____ face the problem because it has
many rivals.

12. It is difficult to use formal economic analysis to explain
the prices and outputs of oligopolists because oligopoly

encompasses (diverse, similar) _____ market
situation(s), and when firms are mutually interdependent,

each firm is (certain, uncertain) _____ about how
its rivals will react when it changes the price of its product.
Despite the analytical problems, oligopoly prices tend to

be (flexible, inflexible) _____ and oligopolists tend to

change their prices (independently, together) _____.

13. The noncolluding oligopolist has a kinked-demand
curve that

   a. is highly (elastic, inelastic) _____ at prices
   above the current or going price and tends to be only

   slightly _____ or (elastic, inelastic) _____
   below that price.

   b. is drawn on the assumption that if the oligopolist

   raises its price its rivals (will, will not) _____
   raise their prices or if it lowers its price its rivals

   _____ lower their prices.

c. has an associated marginal (cost, revenue) _____ curve with a gap, such that small changes in the marginal _____ curve do not change the price the oligopolist will charge.

14. A situation in which firms in an industry reach an agreement to fix prices, divide up the market, or otherwise restrict competition among themselves is called (concentration, collusion) _____. In this case, the prices they set and their combined output tend to be the same as that found with pure (competition, monopoly) _____.

15. A formal written agreement among sellers in which the price and the total output of the product and each seller's share of the market are specified is a (cartel, duopoly) _____. It is a form of (covert, overt) _____ collusion, whereas tacit understandings among firms to divide up a market would be _____ collusion.

16. Six obstacles to collusion among oligopolists are

a. _____

b. _____

c. _____

d. _____

e. _____

f. _____

17. When one firm in an oligopoly is almost always the first to change its price and the other firms change their prices after the first firm has changed its price, the oligopoly model is called the (price war, price leadership) _____ model. The tactics of this model include (infrequent, frequent) _____ price changes, announcements of such price changes, and (limit, no limit) _____ pricing. One event that can undermine this practice is (price leadership, price wars) _____.

18. There tends to be very little (price, nonprice) _____ competition among oligopolists and a great deal of _____ competition such as product development and advertising used to determine each firm's share of the market.

   a. The positive view of advertising contends that it is (efficient, inefficient) _____ because it provides important information that (increases, reduces) _____ search costs, and information about competing goods _____ monopoly power.

   b. The negative view of advertising suggests that it is (inefficient, efficient) _____ because the advertising campaigns are (offsetting, reinforcing) _____, the creation of brand loyalty serves as a barrier to (entry, exit) _____, and consumers are persuaded to pay (lower, higher) _____ prices than they would have paid otherwise.

19. Although it is difficult to evaluate the economic efficiency of oligopoly, when comparisons are made to pure competition, the conclusion drawn is that oligopoly (is, is not) _____ allocatively efficient and (is, is not) _____ productively efficient. The price and output behavior of the oligopolist is more likely to be similar to that found under (competition, monopoly) _____.

20. The view that oligopoly is inefficient in the short run needs to be qualified because of the effects of (decreased, increased) _____ foreign competition that make pricing more competitive, policies to restrict entry into an industry that keep consumer prices (high, low) _____, and profits that are used to fund (more, less) _____ research and development that produces improved products.

■ **TRUE–FALSE QUESTIONS**

Circle T if the statement is true, F if it is false.

1. Monopolistic competitors have no control over the price of their products.　　　　　　　　　**T　F**

2. The firm's reputation for servicing or exchanging its product is a form of product differentiation under monopolistic competition.　　　　　　　　　**T　F**

3. Entry is relatively easy in pure competition, but there are significant barriers to entry in monopolistic competition.　　　　　　　　　**T　F**

4. The smaller the number of firms in an industry and the greater the extent of product differentiation, the greater will be the elasticity of the individual seller's demand curve.　　　　　　　　　**T　F**

5. The demand curve of the monopolistic competitor is likely to be less elastic than the demand curve of the pure monopolist.　　　　　　　　　**T　F**

6. In the short run, firms that are monopolistically competitive may earn economic profits or incur losses.　　　　　　　　　**T　F**

7. The long-run equilibrium position in monopolistic competition would be where price is equal to marginal cost.　　　　　　　　　**T　F**

8. Representative firms in a monopolistically competitive market earn economic profits in the long run.　　**T　F**

9. One reason why monopolistic competition is economically inefficient is that the average cost of producing the product is greater than the minimum average cost at which the product could be produced.　　　　　　　　　**T　F**

10. The more product variety offered to consumers by a monopolistically competitive industry, the less excess capacity there will be in that industry.　　　　**T　F**

11. Successful product improvement by one firm has little or no effect on other firms under monopolistic competition. **T F**

12. The products produced by the firms in an oligo‐polistic industry may be either homogeneous or differentiated. **T F**

13. Oligopolistic industries contain a few large firms that act independently of one another. **T F**

14. Concentration ratios include adjustments for inter‐industry competition in measuring concentration in an industry. **T F**

15. The Herfindahl index is the sum of the market shares of all firms in the industry. **T F**

16. Game theory analysis of oligopolist behavior suggests that oligopolists will not find any benefit in collusion. **T F**

17. One shortcoming of kinked-demand analysis is that it does not explain how the going oligopoly price was established in the first place. **T F**

18. Collusion occurs when firms in an industry reach an overt or covert agreement to fix prices, divide or share the market, and in some way restrict competition among the firms. **T F**

19. A cartel is usually a written agreement among firms which sets the price of the product and determines each firm's share of the market. **T F**

20. Secret price concessions and other forms of cheating will strengthen collusion. **T F**

21. The practice of price leadership is almost always based on a formal written or oral agreement. **T F**

22. Limit pricing is the leadership tactic of limiting price increases to a certain percentage of the basic price of a product. **T F**

23. Those contending that advertising contributes to mo‐nopoly power argue that the advertising by established firms creates barriers to the entry of new firms into an industry. **T F**

24. Oligopolies are allocatively and productively effi‐cient when compared with the standard set in pure competition. **T F**

25. Increased competition from foreign firms in oligopo‐listic industries has stimulated more competitive pricing in those industries. **T F**

■ **MULTIPLE-CHOICE QUESTIONS**

Circle the letter that corresponds to the best answer.

1. Which would be most characteristic of monopolistic competition?
  (a) collusion among firms
  (b) firms selling a homogeneous product
  (c) a relatively large number of firms
  (d) difficult entry into and exit from the industry

2. The concern that monopolistically competitive firms express about product attributes, services to customers, or brand names are aspects of
  (a) allocative efficiency in the industry
  (b) collusion in the industry
  (c) product differentiation
  (d) concentration ratios

3. The demand curve a monopolistically competitive firm faces is
  (a) perfectly elastic
  (b) perfectly inelastic
  (c) highly, but not perfectly inelastic
  (d) highly, but not perfectly elastic

4. In the short run, a typical monopolistically competitive firm will earn
  (a) only a normal profit
  (b) only an economic profit
  (c) only an economic or normal profit
  (d) an economic or normal profit or suffer an economic loss

5. A monopolistically competitive firm is producing at an output level in the short run where average total cost is $3.50, price is $3.00, marginal revenue is $1.50, and mar‐ginal cost is $1.50. This firm is operating
  (a) with an economic loss in the short run
  (b) with an economic profit in the short run
  (c) at the break-even level of output in the short run
  (d) at an inefficient level of output in the short run

6. If firms enter a monopolistically competitive in‐dustry, we would expect the typical firm's demand curve to
  (a) increase and the firm's price to increase
  (b) decrease and the firm's price to decrease
  (c) remain the same but the firm's price to increase
  (d) remain the same and the firm's price to remain the same

Answer Questions 7, 8, 9, and 10 on the basis of the following diagram for a monopolistically competitive firm in short-run equilibrium.

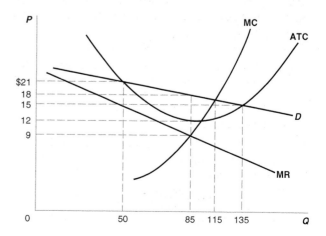

7. The firm's profit-maximizing price will be
   (a) $9
   (b) $12
   (c) $15
   (d) $18

8. The equilibrium output for this firm will be
   (a) 50
   (b) 85
   (c) 115
   (d) 135

9. This firm will earn an economic profit of
   (a) $510
   (b) $765
   (c) $1021
   (d) $1170

10. If firms enter this industry in the long run,
    (a) demand will decrease
    (b) demand will increase
    (c) the marginal revenue curve will shift upward
    (d) economic profits will increase

11. Given a representative firm in a typical monopolistically competitive industry, in the long run
    (a) the firm will produce that output at which marginal cost and price are equal
    (b) the elasticity of demand for the firm's product will be less than it was in the short run
    (c) the number of competitors the firm faces will be greater than it was in the short run
    (d) the economic profits being earned by the firm will tend to equal zero

12. *Productive* efficiency is not achieved in monopolistic competition because production occurs where
    (a) MR is greater than MC
    (b) MR is less than MC
    (c) ATC is greater than minimum ATC
    (d) ATC is less than MR and greater than MC

13. The *underallocation* of resources in monopolistic competition means that at the profit-maximizing level of output, price is
    (a) greater than MC
    (b) less than MC
    (c) less than MR
    (d) greater than minimum ATC

14. Excess capacity occurs in a monopolistically competitive industry because firms
    (a) advertise and promote their product
    (b) charge a price that is less than marginal cost
    (c) produce at an output level short of the least-cost output
    (d) have a perfectly elastic demand for the products that they produce

15. Were a monopolistically competitive industry in long-run equilibrium, a firm in that industry might be able to increase its economic profits by
    (a) increasing the price of its product
    (b) increasing the amounts it spends to advertise its product

(c) decreasing the price of its product
(d) decreasing the output of its product

16. Which would be most characteristic of oligopoly?
    (a) easy entry into the industry
    (b) a few large producers
    (c) product standardization
    (d) no control over price

17. Mutual interdependence means that
    (a) each firm produces a product similar but not identical to the products produced by its rivals
    (b) each firm produces a product identical to the products produced by its rivals
    (c) each firm must consider the reactions of its rivals when it determines its price policy
    (d) each firm faces a perfectly elastic demand for its product

18. One major problem with concentration ratios is that they fail to take into account
    (a) the national market for products
    (b) competition from imported products
    (c) excess capacity in production
    (d) mutual interdependence

19. Industry A is composed of four large firms that hold market shares of 40, 30, 20, and 10. The Herfindahl index for this industry is
    (a) 100
    (b) 1000
    (c) 3000
    (d) 4500

Questions 20, 21, and 22 are based on the following pay-off matrix for a duopoly in which the numbers indicate the profit in thousands of dollars for a high-price or a low-price strategy.

		Firm A Strategy	
		High-price	Low-price
Firm B Strategy	High-price	A = $425 B = $425	A = $525 B = $275
	Low-price	A = $275 B = $525	A = $300 B = $300

20. If both firms collude to maximize joint profits, the total profits for the two firms will be
    (a) $400,000
    (b) $800,000
    (c) $850,000
    (d) $950,000

21. Assume that Firm B adopts a low-price strategy while Firm A maintains a high-price strategy. Compared to the results from a high-price strategy for both firms, Firm B will now
    (a) lose $150,000 in profit and Firm A will gain $150,000 in profit

(b) gain $100,000 in profit and Firm A will lose $150,000 in profit

(c) gain $150,000 in profit and Firm A will lose $100,000 in profit

(d) gain $525,000 in profit and Firm A will lose $275,000 in profit

22. If both firms operate independently and do not collude, the most likely profit is
- **(a)** $300,000 for Firm A and $300,000 for Firm B
- **(b)** $525,000 for Firm A and $275,000 for Firm B
- **(c)** $275,000 for Firm A and $525,000 for Firm B
- **(d)** $425,000 for Firm A and $425,000 for Firm B

23. If an individual oligopolist's demand curve is kinked, it is necessarily
- **(a)** perfectly elastic at the going price
- **(b)** less elastic above the going price than below it
- **(c)** more elastic above the going price than below it
- **(d)** of unitary elasticity at the going price

Use the following diagram to answer Question 24.

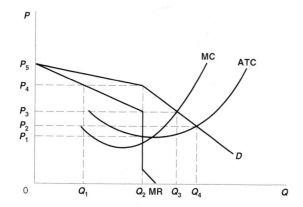

24. The profit-maximizing price and output for this oligopolistic firm is
- **(a)** P_5 and Q_2
- **(b)** P_4 and Q_2
- **(c)** P_3 and Q_3
- **(d)** P_2 and Q_4

25. What is the situation called whenever firms in an industry reach an agreement to fix prices, divide up the market, or otherwise restrict competition?
- **(a)** interindustry competition
- **(b)** incentive to cheat
- **(c)** price leadership
- **(d)** collusion

26. When oligopolists collude the results are generally
- **(a)** greater output and higher price
- **(b)** greater output and lower price
- **(c)** smaller output and lower price
- **(d)** smaller output and higher price

27. To be successful, collusion requires that oligopolists be able to
- **(a)** keep prices and profits as low as possible
- **(b)** block or restrict the entry of new producers

(c) reduce legal obstacles that protect market power

(d) keep the domestic economy from experiencing high inflation

28. Which is a typical tactic that has been used by the price leader in the price leadership model of oligopoly?
- **(a)** limit pricing
- **(b)** frequent price changes
- **(c)** starting a price war with competitors
- **(d)** giving no announcement of a price change

29. Market shares in oligopoly are typically determined on the basis of
- **(a)** product development and advertising
- **(b)** covert collusion and cartels
- **(c)** tacit understandings
- **(d)** joint profit maximization

30. Many economists think that relative to pure competition, oligopoly is
- **(a)** allocatively efficient, but not productively efficient
- **(b)** productively efficient, but not allocatively efficient
- **(c)** both allocatively and productively efficient
- **(d)** neither allocatively nor productively efficient

■ **PROBLEMS**

1. Assume that the short-run cost and demand data given in the following table confront a monopolistic competitor selling a given product and engaged in a given amount of product promotion.

Output	Total cost	Marginal cost	Quantity demanded	Price	Marginal revenue
0	$ 50		0	$120	
1	80	$_____	1	110	$_____
2	90	_____	2	100	_____
3	110	_____	3	90	_____
4	140	_____	4	80	_____
5	180	_____	5	70	_____
6	230	_____	6	60	_____
7	290	_____	7	50	_____
8	360	_____	8	40	_____
9	440	_____	9	30	_____
10	530	_____	10	20	_____

a. Compute the marginal cost and marginal revenue of each unit of output and enter these figures in the table.

b. In the short run the firm will (1) produce _____ units of output, (2) sell its output at a price of $_____, and (3) have a total economic profit of $_____.

c. In the long run, (1) the demand for the firm's product will _____, (2) until the price of the product equals _____, and (3) the total economic profits of the firm are _____.

2. Match the following descriptions to the six graphs below. Indicate on each graph the area of economic profit or loss or state if the firm is just making normal profits.

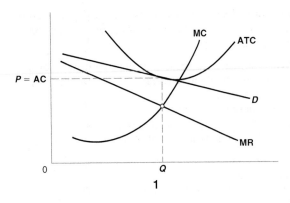

1

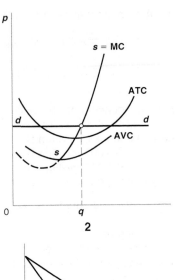

2

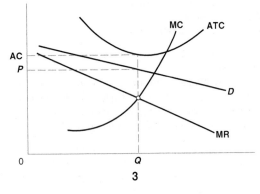

3

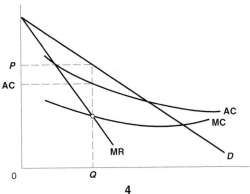

4

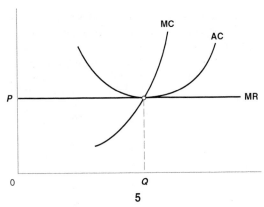

5

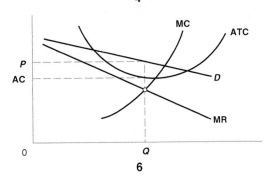

6

a. a purely competitive firm earning economic profits in the short run   Graph _____

b. a purely competitive firm in long-run equilibrium   Graph _____

c. a natural monopoly   Graph _____

d. a monopolistically competitive firm earning economic profits in the short run   Graph _____

e. a monopolistically competitive firm experiencing economic losses in the short run   Graph _____

f. a monopolistically competitive firm in long-run equilibrium   Graph _____

3. Consider the following payoff matrix in which the numbers indicate the profit in millions of dollars for a duopoly based on either a high-price or a low-price strategy.

| | | Firm X Strategy | |
		High-price	Low-price
Firm Y Strategy	**High-price**	X = $200 Y = $200	X = $250 Y = $ 50
	Low-price	X = $ 50 Y = $250	X = $ 50 Y = $ 50

a. *Situation 1:* Each firm chooses a high-price strategy. *Result:* Each firm will earn $_____ million in profit for a total of $_____ million for the two firms.

b. *Situation 2:* Firm X chooses a low-price strategy while Firm Y maintains a high-price strategy. *Result:* Firm X will earn $_____ million and Firm Y will earn $_____ million. Compared to Situation 1, Firm X has an incentive to cut prices because it will earn $_____ million more in profit and Firm Y will earn $_____ million less in profit. Together, the firms will earn $_____ million in profit, which is $_____ million less than in Situation 1.

c. *Situation 3:* Firm Y chooses a low-price strategy while Firm X maintains a high-price strategy. ***Result:*** Compared to Situation 1, Firm Y has an incentive to cut prices because it will earn $_____ million and Firm X will earn $_____. Compared to Situation 1, Firm Y will earn $_____ million more in profit and Firm X will earn $_____ million less in profit. Together, the firms will earn $_____ million in profit, which is $_____ less than in Situation 1.

d. *Situation 4:* Each firm chooses a low-price strategy. ***Result:*** Each firm will earn $_____ million in profit for a total of $_____ million for the two firms. This total is $_____ less than in Situation 1.

e. *Conclusions:*

(1) The two firms have a strong incentive to collude and adopt the high-price strategy because there is the potential for $_____ million more in profit for the two firms than with a low-price strategy (Situation 4), or the potential for $_____ million more for the two firms than with a mixed-price strategy (Situations 2 or 3).

(2) There is also a strong incentive for each firm to cheat on the agreement and adopt a low-price strategy when the other firm maintains a high-price strategy because this situation will produce $_____ million more in profit for the cheating firm compared to its honoring a collusive agreement for a high-price strategy.

4. The kinked-demand schedule which an oligopolist believes confronts the firm is presented in the following table.

Price	Quantity demanded	Total revenue	Marginal revenue per unit
$2.90	100	$_____	
2.80	200	_____	$_____
2.70	300	_____	_____
2.60	400	_____	_____
2.50	500	_____	_____
2.40	525	_____	_____
2.30	550	_____	_____
2.20	575	_____	_____
2.10	600	_____	_____

a. Compute the oligopolist's total revenue at each of the nine prices and enter these figures in the table.

b. Also compute marginal revenue *for each unit* between the nine prices and enter these figures in the table.

c. What is the current, or going, price for the oligopolist's product? $_____ How much is it selling? _____

d. On the graph below plot the oligopolist's demand curve and marginal revenue curve. Connect the demand points and the marginal revenue points with as straight a line as possible. (Be sure to plot the marginal revenue figures at the average of the two quantities involved, that is, at 150, 250, 350, 450, 512.5, 537.5, 562.5, and 587.5.)

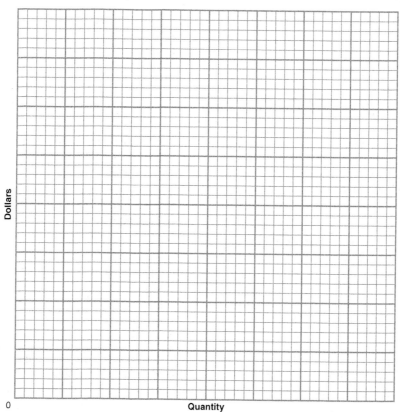

Dollars

0   Quantity

373

e. Assume that the marginal cost schedule of the oligopolist is given in columns 1 and 2 of the following table. Plot the marginal cost curve on the graph on which demand and marginal revenue were plotted.

(1) Output	(2) MC	(3) MC′	(4) MC″
150	$1.40	$1.90	$.40
250	1.30	1.80	.30
350	1.40	1.90	.40
450	1.50	2.00	.50
512.5	1.60	2.10	.60
537.5	1.70	2.20	.70
562.5	1.80	2.30	.80
587.5	1.90	2.40	.90

(1) Given demand and marginal cost, what price should the oligopolist charge to maximize profits? $_____ How many units of product will it sell at this price? _____

(2) If the marginal cost schedule changed from that shown in columns 1 and 2 to that shown in columns 1 and 3, what price should it charge? $_____ What level of output will it produce? _____ How have profits changed as a result of the change in costs? _____ Plot the new marginal cost curve on the graph.

(3) If the marginal-cost curve schedule changed from that shown in columns 1 and 2 to that shown in columns 1 and 4, what price should it charge? $_____ What level of output will it produce? _____ How have profits changed as a result of the change in costs? _____ Plot the new marginal cost curve on the graph.

5. An oligopoly producing a homogeneous product is composed of three firms. Assume that these three firms have identical cost schedules. Assume also that if any one of these firms sets a price for the product, the other two firms charge the same price. As long as the firms all charge the same price they will share the market equally, and the quantity demanded of each will be the same.

Following is the total cost schedule of one of these firms and the demand schedule that confronts it when the other firms charge the same price as this firm.

Output	Total cost	Marginal cost	Price	Quantity demanded	Marginal revenue
0	$ 0		$140	0	
1	30	$____	130	1	$____
2	50	____	120	2	____
3	80	____	110	3	____
4	120	____	100	4	____
5	170	____	90	5	____
6	230	____	80	6	____
7	300	____	70	7	____
8	380	____	60	8	____

a. Complete the marginal cost and marginal revenue schedules facing the firm.
b. What price would this firm set if it wished to maximize its profits? $_____
c. How much would

(1) it sell at this price? _____

(2) its profits be at this price? $_____
d. What would be the industry's

(1) total output at this price? _____

(2) joint profits at this price? $_____
e. Is there any other price this firm can set, assuming that the other two firms charge the same price, that would result in a greater joint profit for them? _____
f. If these three firms colluded in order to maximize their joint profit, what price would they charge? $_____

■ **SHORT ANSWER AND ESSAY QUESTIONS**

1. What are the three characteristics of monopolistic competition?

2. What is meant by product differentiation? By what methods can products be differentiated?

3. How does product differentiation affect the kind of competition and the degree of monopoly in monopolistic competition?

4. Describe the elasticity of the demand curve faced by a monopolistically competitive firm in the short run.

5. Assume that the firm is producing a given product and is engaged in a given amount of promotional activity. What two factors determine how elastic the demand curve will be for a monopolistic competitor?

6. At what level of output will the monopolistic competitor produce in the short run? What price will it charge for its product? Draw a graph to help explain your answer.

7. What determines whether a monopolistically competitive firm will earn economic profits or suffer economic losses in the short run?

8. What will be the level of economic profit that the monopolistic competitor will tend to receive in the long run? What forces economic profits toward this level? Why is this just a *tendency*?

9. What are two complications that would explain why the representative firm may not earn only a normal profit in the long run and may earn economic profits?

10. Use the concepts of allocative and productive efficiency to explain excess capacity and the level of prices under monopolistic competition.

11. Describe the methods, other than price cutting, that a monopolistic competitor can use to protect and increase its economic profits in the long run.

12. Explain how product variety and improvement may offset the economic inefficiency associated with monopolistic competition.

13. What are the essential characteristics of an oligopoly? How does oligopoly differ from pure competition, pure monopoly, and monopolistic competition?

14. Explain how the concentration ratio in a particular industry is computed. What is the relationship between this ratio and fewness? What are the shortcomings of the concentration ratio as a measure of the extent of competition in an industry?

15. What is the Herfindahl index? How can it be used to correct problems with concentration ratios?

16. How can game theory be used to explain strategic behavior under oligopoly? What do mutual interdependence and collusion mean with respect to oligopoly?

17. Why is it difficult to use one standard model to explain the prices charged by and the outputs of oligopolists?

18. How can the kinked-demand curve be used to explain why oligopoly prices are relatively inflexible?

19. Suppose a few firms produce a homogeneous product, have identical cost curves, and charge the same price (act as a cartel). Compare the results in terms of price, combined output, and joint profits with those from a pure monopoly producing the same market output.

20. Why do oligopolists find it advantageous to collude? What are the obstacles to collusion?

21. What is the price leadership model, and what leadership tactics do oligopolistic firms use?

22. Why do oligopolists engage in little price competition and in extensive product development and advertising?

23. How is it possible for consumers to get a lower price on a product with advertising than they would in its absence?

24. Explain how the advertising efforts of firms may be offsetting and lead to higher prices for consumers.

25. Evaluate the economic efficiency of the oligopoly market structure. What qualifications should be noted for the evaluation?

ANSWERS

Chapter 11 Monopolistic Competition and Oligopoly

FILL-IN QUESTIONS

1. large, differentiated, easy, small, do not, an independent
2. *a.* product attributes; *b.* services; *c.* location; *d.* brand names and packaging; *e.* some control over price
3. *a.* more, less; *b.* (1) number of rivals the firm has, (2) the degree of product differentiation; *c.* equal to
4. *a.* decrease, increase; *b.* average, zero, greater

5. normal, economic, cannot, barriers to entry
6. greater than, does not, greater than, does not, productive
7. nonprice, more
8. price, product, advertising
9. concentration ratio, Herfindahl index
10. a few, homogeneous, difficult, maker, interdependence, entry, mergers
11. game, interdependent, does, does not, does not
12. diverse, uncertain, inflexible, together
13. *a.* elastic, elastic, inelastic; *b.* will not, will; *c.* revenue, cost
14. collusion, monopoly
15. cartel, overt, covert
16. *a.* demand and cost differences; *b.* a large number of firms; *c.* cheating (secret price cutting); *d.* a recession; *e.* potential entry; *f.* legal obstacles (antitrust laws) (any order for *a–f*)
17. price leadership, infrequent, limit, price wars
18. price, nonprice; *a.* efficient, reduces, reduces; *b.* inefficient, offsetting, entry, higher
19. is not, is not, monopoly
20. increased, low, more

TRUE–FALSE QUESTIONS

1. F, pp. 217–218	**10.** F, pp. 222–223	**19.** T, pp. 230–232
2. T, p. 217	**11.** F, p. 223	**20.** F, p. 232
3. F, p. 218	**12.** T, p. 224	**21.** F, p. 233
4. F, pp. 219–220	**13.** F, p. 223	**22.** F, p. 233
5. F, pp. 219–220	**14.** F, p. 225	**23.** T, pp. 234–235
6. T, pp. 219–221	**15.** F, p. 226	**24.** F, p. 235
7. F, pp. 220–221	**16.** F, pp. 226–227	**25.** T, p. 235
8. F, p. 221	**17.** T, pp. 228–230	
9. T, pp. 221–222	**18.** T, pp. 230–232	

MULTIPLE-CHOICE QUESTIONS

1. c, p. 217	**11.** d, pp. 219–220	**21.** b, p. 226
2. c, pp. 217–218	**12.** c, pp. 221–222	**22.** a, pp. 226
3. d, pp. 219–220	**13.** a, pp. 221–222	**23.** c, pp. 228–230
4. d, pp. 219–220	**14.** c, p. 222	**24.** b, pp. 228–230
5. a, pp. 219–220	**15.** b, pp. 222–223	**25.** d, pp. 230–231
6. b, p. 221	**16.** b, p. 223	**26.** d, pp. 230–231
7. d, pp. 219–220	**17.** c, p. 224	**27.** b, p. 233
8. b, pp. 219–220	**18.** b, p. 225	**28.** a, p. 233
9. a, pp. 219–220	**19.** c, p. 226	**29.** a, pp. 234–235
10. a, pp. 220–221	**20.** c, p. 226	**30.** d, p. 235

PROBLEMS

1. *a.* Marginal cost: $30, 10, 20, 30, 40, 50, 60, 70, 80, 90, Marginal revenue: $110, 90, 70, 50, 30, 10, −10, −30, −50, −70; *b.* (1) 4, (2) $80, (3) $180; *c.* (1) decrease, (2) average cost, (3) equal to zero
2. *a.* 2; *b.* 5; *c.* 4; *d.* 6; *e.* 3; *f.* 1
3. *a.* 200, 400; *b.* 250, 50, 50, 150, 300, 100; *c.* 250, 50, 50, 150, 300, 100; *d.* 50, 100, 300; *e.* (1) 300, 100, (2) 50
4. *a.* Total revenue: 290, 560, 810, 1,040, 1,250, 1,260, 1,265, 1,265, 1,260; *b.* Marginal revenue: 2.70, 2.50, 2.30, 2.10, 0.40, 0.20, 0, −0.20; *c.* 2.50, 500; *d.* graph; *e.* (1) 2.50, 500, (2) 2.50, 500, they have decreased, (3) 2.50, 500, they have increased
5. *a.* Marginal cost: $30, 20, 30, 40, 50, 60, 70, 80; Marginal revenue: $130, 110, 90, 70, 50, 30, 10, −10; *b.* $90; *c.* (1) 5, (2) $280; *d.* (1) 15, (2) $840; *e.* no; *f.* $90

SHORT ANSWER AND ESSAY QUESTIONS

1. p. 217
2. pp. 217–218
3. pp. 217–218
4. p. 219
5. p. 219
6. pp. 219–220
7. pp. 219–220
8. p. 221
9. p. 221

10. pp. 221–222
11. pp. 222–223
12. pp. 222–223
13. pp. 223–224
14. pp. 225–226
15. p. 226
16. p. 226
17. p. 228
18. pp. 228–230

19. pp. 230–231
20. pp. 230–233
21. p. 233
22. p. 234
23. p. 234
24. pp. 234–235
25. p. 235

Additional Game Theory Applications

This appendix provides some additional applications of oligopoly based on game theory and behavior. The first section of the appendix discusses strategies and equilibrium for games that occur just one time between two rivals. Here you will learn about the **Nash equilibrium,** which is an outcome from which neither rival wants to deviate because each firm sees its strategy as optimal given the strategy of its rival. The second section introduces the ideas of a **credible threat** and an **empty threat** and evaluates how each will affect Nash equilibrium. The third section turns to **repeated games,** which are games played more than once, and explains how strategies are influenced by the thought that there will be reciprocity from a rival, or less direct or intense competition. The final section turns to the topic of **sequential games,** in which the outcome depends on **first-mover advantage** and the ability to preclude entry by rivals.

■ APPENDIX CHECKLIST

When you have studied this appendix you should be able to

☐ Describe a one-time game and simultaneous game.
☐ Define positive-sum game, zero-sum game, and negative-sum game.
☐ Give an example of a dominant strategy in a game.
☐ Define the Nash equilibrium for a one-time game.
☐ Explain how a credible threat affects the Nash equilibrium.
☐ Explain how an empty threat affects the Nash equilibrium.
☐ Describe a repeated game and the effect of a reciprocity strategy on game outcomes.
☐ Supply an example of a sequential game.
☐ Explain how first-mover advantages in a sequential game affect decisions by rivals and entry into markets.

■ APPENDIX OUTLINE

1. In a *one-time game,* two firms (rivals) select their optimal strategies in a single time period without considering subsequent time periods. If both firms make their strategies at the same time, it is also a *simultaneous game.*
   a. If the net outcome from such one-time and simultaneous games is positive, it is a *positive-sum game.* If the net outcome is negative, it a *negative-sum game.* If the net outcome is zero, it is a *zero-sum game.*

   b. If one option in a game is better for a firm than any alternative option in a game regardless of the choice made by another firm, the better option is a *dominant strategy.* Not all games have a dominant strategy, however.
   c. The dominant strategy for each firm determines the game's *Nash equilibrium.* It is the outcome from which neither firm wants to deviate because it is optimal given the strategic choice made by the other firm.

2. If there is a *credible threat* in a single-period and simultaneous game, then it can cause the firms to abandon the Nash equilibrium. The credible threat can occur if one firm is believed to have the power to dictate the decision of another firm and thus the firms collude. It is, however, difficult to enforce such a threat and if it is not credible, it is an *empty threat.* In this case, the Nash equilibrium will hold.

3. A *repeated game* is not a one-time event, but occurs more often or somewhat regularly. In this situation, the optimal strategy for a firm may be to limit competition with the other firm, if the other firm reciprocates by limiting its competition. Thus reciprocity strategies, and whether they will be used, are important for determining outcomes in repeated games.

4. A **sequential game** is one in which the final outcome may depend on which firm makes the first move because the first-mover may be able to establish the Nash equilibrium. A real-world example would be a large store such as Walmart that, by making a first-mover decision to enter a market, prevents other large firms from also entering the same market because it would not be profitable.

■ HINTS AND TIPS

1. This appendix extends your understanding of game theory and strategic behavior described in Chapter 11. Before you start the appendix, make sure you master how the profit-payoff matrix works for two-firm oligopolies as in the example shown in Figure 11.3. A similar matrix is used to illustrate each two-firm game discussed in this appendix.

2. There is nothing complicated about the content of this appendix, but it does introduce subtle distinctions in the definitions and conditions for games that you will need to learn as shown in the following list of important terms.

145

■ IMPORTANT TERMS

one-time game	Nash equilibrium
simultaneous games	credible threat
positive-sum games	empty threat
zero-sum games	repeated games
negative-sum games	sequential games
dominant strategy	first-mover advantage

SELF-TEST

■ FILL-IN QUESTIONS

1. If firms select their optimal strategies in a single time period, it is a (one-time, repeated) _____ game, but if firms select their optimal strategies based on a situation that is recurring, it is a _____ game.

2. Outcomes from games can be used to categorize games: if there is an "I win and you lose" outcome, it is a (positive, zero, negative) _____-sum game; if there is a "win-win" outcome, it is a _____-sum game; and, if there is a "lose-lose" outcome, it is a _____-sum game.

3. A strategic choice for a firm that is better than any other option is a (subordinate, dominant) _____ strategy.

4. In a two-firm game, the dominant strategy for each firm determines the (Crowe, Nash) _____ equilibrium.

5. At such an equilibrium, both firms consider their current strategy as optimal and (do, do not) _____ want to deviate from it; so such an equilibrium is (stable, unstable) _____.

6. If a firm is capable or likely to use coercion to force a desired decision on a rival firm, the threat is (credible, empty) _____, but if the firm cannot use coercion to force a desired decision, the threat is _____.

7. If a threat is credible, firms will (deviate, not deviate) _____ from the Nash equilibrium and seek greater profits, but if a threat is empty, threatening firms will _____ from the Nash equilibrium and be unable to seek greater profits.

8. In a repeated game, if one firm avoids taking advantage of another firm because the firm knows the other firm will take advantage of it in a subsequent game, then there is likely to be a (monopolistic, reciprocity) _____ strategy enacted by the firms that can (harm, improve) _____ the outcomes from such games.

9. If one firm moves first and commits to a strategy and the other firm must then respond, it is a (repeated, sequential) _____ game.

10. In a sequential game involving two large, but similar retailers, the first-mover retailer may have the opportunity to (establish, destroy) _____ a Nash equilibrium and it may make it (profitable, unprofitable) _____ for the other retailer to enter the market.

■ TRUE–FALSE QUESTIONS

Circle T if the statement is true, F if it is false.

1. Games can either be one-time games or repeated games.   **T   F**

2. Negative-sum games feature an "I win and you lose" outcome.   **T   F**

3. Decisions in games may be made simultaneously, but not sequentially.   **T   F**

4. When two firms are playing a strategic game, a firm has a dominant strategy if one option leads to a better result than all other options no matter what the other firm does.   **T   F**

5. The Nash equilibrium is an outcome from which neither firm wants to deviate because both firms see their current strategy as optimal given the selected strategy of the other firm.   **T   F**

6. A Nash equilibrium is unstable and changing.   **T   F**

7. An empty threat in a two-firm game will change outcomes and the Nash equilibrium.   **T   F**

8. Reciprocity means that one firm avoids taking advantage of the other firm because it knows that the other firm can take advantage of it in subsequent games.   **T   F**

9. Reciprocity makes outcomes worse for firms participating in repeated games.   **T   F**

10. If there is a first-mover advantage for two rival firms seeking to enter a market, it may be possible for the first-mover firm to preempt entry by the other firm.   **T   F**

■ MULTIPLE-CHOICE QUESTIONS

Circle the letter that corresponds to the best answer.

1. If one firm's gain equals another firm's loss it is a
   (a) negative-sum game
   (b) zero-sum game
   (c) repeated game
   (d) sequential game

*Questions 2, 3, and 4 are based on the following payoff matrix for a single-period, two-firm game for firms **Rig** and **Dig**. The numbers in the matrix indicate the profit in* millions of dollars for a national or regional strategy. The profit outcome cells are **A**, **B**, **C**, and **D**.

Rig Strategy

		National	Regional
Dig Strategy	**National**	Ⓐ Rig = $24 / Dig = $24	Ⓑ Rig = $12 / Dig = $42
	Regional	Ⓒ Rig = $42 / Dig = $12	Ⓓ Rig = $36 / Dig = $36

2. Which strategies are the dominant ones for Rig and Dig?
(a) national for Rig and regional for Dig
(b) regional for Rig and national for Dig
(c) national for Rig and national for Dig
(d) regional for Rig and regional for Dig

3. The Nash equilibrium will be represented by which cell showing the set of profit outcomes for the two firms?
(a) A
(b) B
(c) C
(d) D

4. If Dig can make a credible threat that determines the strategy for Rig, then which combinations of strategies will be selected?
(a) national for Rig and regional for Dig
(b) regional for Rig and national for Dig
(c) national for Rig and national for Dig
(d) regional for Rig and regional for Dig

5. If Dig makes a threat, but it is an empty threat that is not believable for Rig, then which cell shows the set of profit outcomes for the two firms?
(a) A
(b) B
(c) C
(d) D

6. In a repeated game among two firms, if the optimal strategy for one firm is to cooperate with the other firm and restrain competition in the expectation that the other firm will do the same, then the firm is using a
(a) dominant strategy
(b) reciprocity strategy
(c) credible threat strategy
(d) empty threat strategy

7. If one firm make the first move and then the other firm responds, it would be a
(a) zero-sum game
(b) negative-sum game
(c) simultaneous game
(d) sequential game

Questions 8, 9, and 10 are based on the following payoff matrix for a single-period, two-firm game for the two major aircraft makers, **Fly** *and* **Sky**. *The numbers in the matrix* indicate the profit in billions of dollars if a firm builds or does not build a new aircraft to compete with the other firm. The profit outcome cells are **A**, **B**, **C**, and **D**.

Fly Strategy

		Build	Don't build
Sky Strategy	**Build**	Ⓐ Fly = $12 / Sky = $12	Ⓑ Fly = $0 / Sky = $15
	Don't build	Ⓒ Fly = $15 / Sky = $0	Ⓓ Fly = $0 / Sky = $0

8. What will be the total amount of profit or losses for both firms if both firms decide simultaneously to build a new aircraft?
(a) $0
(b) $15 billion
(c) −$12 million
(d) −$24 million

9. Which pair of cells contains the possible Nash equilibrium?
(a) A and B
(b) B and C
(c) C and D
(d) A and D

10. If Sky makes the first move and builds an aircraft then
(a) Sky will earn $15 billion and Fly will earn $0
(b) Sky will lose $12 billion and Fly will lose $12 billion
(c) Sky will earn $15 billion and Fly will earn $15 billion
(d) Neither firm will make a profit, but neither firm will suffer a loss

■ PROBLEMS

For problems 1 to 4 use the following payoff matrix for two retail firms, **Top** *and* **Pop,** *in a single-period, one-time game. The numbers in each cell (**A**, **B**, **C**, or **D**) indicate the profit in millions of dollars based on whether they adopt a high-price or a low-price strategy.*

Top Strategy

		High-price	Low-price
Pop Strategy	**High-price**	Ⓐ Top = $30 / Pop = $30	Ⓑ Top = $15 / Pop = $60
	Low-price	Ⓒ Top = $60 / Pop = $15	Ⓓ Top = $45 / Pop = $45

1. Determine the dominant strategy for Pop.
a. If Top adopts a high-price strategy, then Pop will be better off if it chooses a high-price strategy because it

can earn $_____ million. By contrast, if Pop had used a low-price strategy in this case, it only

would earn $_____ million in profit.

b. If Top adopts a low-price strategy, then Pop will be better off if it chooses a high-price strategy because it can earn $_____ million. By contrast, if Pop used a low-price strategy in this case, it only would earn $_____ million in profit.

c. Regardless of whether Top adopts a high-price or low-price strategy, Pop will be better off it if adopts a high-price strategy because it can earn either $_____ million or $_____ million. A high-price strategy is the dominant strategy for Pop.

2. Determine the dominant strategy for Pop.
   a. If Pop adopts a high-price strategy, then Top will be better off if it chooses a high-price strategy because it can earn $_____ million. By contrast, if Top used a low-price strategy in this case, it only would earn $_____ million in profit.
   b. If Pop adopts a low-price strategy, then Top will still be better off if it chooses a high-price strategy because it can earn $_____ million. By contrast, if Top used a low-price strategy in this case, it only would earn $_____ million in profit.
   c. Regardless of whether Pop adopts a high-price or low-price strategy, Top will be better off it if adopts a high-price strategy because it can earn either $_____ million or $_____ million. A high-price strategy is the dominant strategy for Top.

3. Identify the Nash equilibrium.
   a. Each firm will adopt a _____-price strategy because such a strategy is dominant over all other choices for each firm. The Nash equilibrium will be in cell _____.
   b. At the Nash equilibrium each firm will earn $_____ million.

4. Identify the effects of credible and empty threats.
   a. If Pop chooses a low-price strategy and makes a credible threat to get Top to adopt a low-price strategy, then both firms will abandon the Nash equilibrium at cell _____ and move to cell _____ in the profit-payoff matrix. Pop will earn a profit of $_____ million.
   b. If Pop chooses a low-price strategy and makes a threat to get Top to adopt a low-price strategy, but Pop cannot enforce that threat or it is not believable, then the Nash equilibrium will be at cell _____. The profit for each firm will be $_____.

5. Determine outcomes from repeated games and reciprocity.

*Use the following payoff matrix for two shoe firms, **Skip** and **Jump**, which are involved in a two-period game. The numbers in each cell (**A**, **B**, **C**, or **D**) indicate the profit in millions of dollars based on whether they adopt more*

advertising or less advertising for the introduction of a new shoe. Assume that in period 1, Jump introduces a new shoe, Clog, and it adopts an advertising strategy of placing more ads to sell the new shoe.

Period 1: Jump introduces a new shoe, Clog

		Skip Strategy	
		More-ads	Fewer-ads
Jump Strategy	More-ads	(A) Skip = $20 / Jump = $20	(B) Skip = $16 / Jump = $32
	Fewer-ads	(C) Skip = $32 / Jump = $16	(D) Skip = $24 / Jump = $24

a. If, in response, Skip counters by placing more ads, the amount of profit for each firm will be $_____ million. The profit outcomes for both firms will be at cell _____.

b. But if, in response, Skip adopts a fewer-ads strategy in hopes that Jump will do the same when Skip launches its new shoe, then Skip will earn $_____ million in profit. The profit outcomes for both firms will be at cell _____.

Now assume that in period 2 Skip launches its new shoe, Fleet, and adopts a more-ads strategy.

Period 2: Skip introduces a new shoe, Fleet

		Skip Strategy	
		More-ads	Fewer-ads
Jump Strategy	More-ads	(A) Skip = $22 / Jump = $22	(B) Skip = $20 / Jump = $28
	Fewer-ads	(C) Skip = $30 / Jump = $20	(D) Skip = $26 / Jump = $26

c. If, in response, Jump counters by placing more ads, the amount of profit earned by each firm will be $_____ million. The profit outcomes for both firms will be at cell _____.

d. But if, in response, Jump cooperates and adopts a reciprocity strategy of fewer ads, Jump will earn $_____ million. The profit outcomes for both firms will be at cell _____.

e. By cooperating and showing reciprocity to each other, the firms will earn more total profit. In period 1, Jump will earn $_____ million and in period 2 Jump will earn $_____ million, for a total of $_____ million. In period 1, Skip will earn $_____ million and in period 2 Skip will earn $_____ million for a total of $_____ million.

f. Had there been no cooperation or reciprocity, each firm would have earned $_____ million in the first period and $_____ million in the second period, for a total of $_____ million.

■ **SHORT ANSWER AND ESSAY QUESTIONS**

1. What are the differences between positive-sum, negative-sum, and zero-sum games?

2. How can decisions in games be either simultaneous or sequential? Give examples of each type.

3. Explain what is meant by a dominant strategy in a one-period game involving two rival firms.

4. Define the Nash equilibrium. Is it stable or unstable?

5. How does the use of credible threats or empty threats from firms affect outcomes and the Nash equilibrium in one-period games?

6. Give examples of real-world companies for which repeated games apply.

7. What strategies might two dominant firms use in repeated games to increase profits over what might be achieved with competitive strategies?

8. Explain how the first mover might have an advantage in a sequential game. Does such an advantage always produce a positive outcome?

9. Why might there be two outcomes that could create the Nash equilibrium in sequential games with first-mover advantages?

10. Supply some real-world examples of firms that have used first-mover advantages to saturate markets or preempt entry by rivals.

ANSWERS

Appendix to Chapter 11: Additional Game Theory Applications

FILL-IN QUESTIONS

1. one-time, repeated
2. zero, positive, negative
3. dominant
4. Nash
5. do not, stable
6. credible, empty
7. deviate, not deviate
8. reciprocity, improve
9. sequential
10. establish, unprofitable

TRUE–FALSE QUESTIONS

1. T, pp. 241–242	5. T, p. 241	9. F, p. 243
2. F, p. 241	6. F, p. 241	10. T, pp. 243–244
3. F, pp. 241, 243	7. F, p. 242	
4. T, p. 241	8. T, p. 242	

MULTIPLE-CHOICE QUESTIONS

1. b, p. 241	5. a, p. 242	9. b, pp. 243–244
2. c, p. 241	6. b, p. 242	10. a, pp. 243–244
3. a, p. 241	7. d, p. 243	
4. d, pp. 241–242	8. d, pp. 243–244	

PROBLEMS

1. *a.* 30, 15; *b.* 60, 45; *c.* 30, 60
2. *a.* 30, 15; *b.* 60, 45; *c.* 30, 60
3. *a.* high, A; *b.* 30
4. *a.* A, D, 45; *b.* A, 30
5. *a.* 20, A; *b.* 16, B; *c.* 22, A; *d.* 20, C; *e.* 32, 20, 52, 16, 46, 46; *f.* 20, 22, 42

SHORT ANSWER AND ESSAY QUESTIONS

1. p. 242	5. pp. 242–243	9. p. 244
2. pp. 242, 244	6. p. 242	10. p. 244
3. p. 242	7. p. 243	
4. p. 242	8. pp. 243–244	

12

AFTER READING THIS CHAPTER, YOU SHOULD BE ABLE TO:

1 Explain the significance of resource pricing.

2 Convey how the marginal revenue productivity of a resource relates to a firm's demand for that resource.

3 List the factors that increase or decrease resource demand.

4 Discuss the determinants of elasticity of resource demand.

5 Determine how a competitive firm selects its optimal combination of resources.

The Demand for Resources

When you finish your education, you probably will be looking for a new job. But why would someone want to hire you? The answer, of course, is that you have a lot to offer. Employers have a demand for educated, productive workers like you.

We need to learn more about the demand for labor and other resources. So, we now turn from the pricing and production of *goods and services* to the pricing and employment of *resources*. Although firms come in various sizes and operate under highly different market conditions, each has a demand for productive resources. Firms obtain needed resources from households—the direct or indirect owners of land, labor, capital, and entrepreneurial resources. So, referring to the circular flow model (Figure 2.2, page 40), we shift our attention from the bottom loop of the diagram (where businesses supply products that households demand) to the top loop (where businesses demand resources that households supply).

This chapter looks at the *demand* for economic resources. Although the discussion is couched in terms of labor, the principles developed also apply to land, capital, and entrepreneurial ability. In

Chapter 13 we will combine resource (labor) demand with labor *supply* to analyze wage rates. In Chapter 14 we will use resource demand and resource supply to examine the prices of, and returns to, other productive resources. Issues relating to the use of natural resources are the subject of Chapter 15.

Significance of Resource Pricing

Studying resource pricing is important for several reasons:

- *Money-income determination* Resource prices are a major factor in determining the income of households. The expenditures that firms make in acquiring economic resources flow as wage, rent, interest, and profit incomes to the households that supply those resources.
- *Cost minimization* To the firm, resource prices are costs. And to obtain the greatest profit, the firm must produce the profit-maximizing output with the most efficient (least costly) combination of resources. Resource prices play the main role in determining the quantities of land, labor, capital, and entrepreneurial ability that will be combined in producing each good or service (see Table 2.1, p. 36).
- *Resource allocation .*Just as product prices allocate finished goods and services to consumers, resource prices allocate resources among industries and firms. In a dynamic economy, where technology and product demand often change, the efficient allocation of resources over time calls for the continuing shift of resources from one use to another. Resource pricing is a major factor in producing those shifts.
- *Policy issues* Many policy issues surround the resource market. Examples: To what extent should government redistribute income through taxes and transfers? Should government do anything to discourage "excess" pay to corporate executives? Should it increase the legal minimum wage? Is the provision of subsidies to farmers efficient? Should government encourage or restrict labor unions? The facts and debates relating to these policy questions are grounded on resource pricing.

Marginal Productivity Theory of Resource Demand

In discussing resource demand, we will first assume that a firm sells its output in a purely competitive product market and hires a certain resource in a purely competitive resource market. This assumption keeps things simple and is consistent with the model of a competitive labor market that we will develop in Chapter 13. In a competitive *product market*, the firm is a "price taker" and can dispose of as little or as much output as it chooses at the market price. The firm is

selling such a negligible fraction of total output that its output decisions exert no influence on product price. Similarly, the firm also is a "price taker" (or "wage taker") in the competitive *resource market*. It purchases such a negligible fraction of the total supply of the resource that its buying (or hiring) decisions do not influence the resource price.

Resource Demand as a Derived Demand

Resource demand is the starting point for any discussion of resource prices. Resource demand is a schedule or a curve showing the amounts of a resource that buyers are willing and able to purchase at various prices over some period of time. Crucially, resource demand is a **derived demand,** meaning that the demand for a resource is derived from the demand for the products that the resource helps to produce. This is true because resources usually do not directly satisfy customer wants but do so indirectly through their use in producing goods and services. Almost nobody wants to consume an acre of land, a John Deere tractor, or the labor services of a farmer, but millions of households do want to consume the food and fiber products that these resources help produce. Similarly, the demand for airplanes generates a demand for assemblers, and the demands for such services as income-tax preparation, haircuts, and child care create derived demands for accountants, barbers, and child care workers.

Marginal Revenue Product

Because resource demand is derived from product demand, the strength of the demand for any resource will depend on:

- The productivity of the resource in helping to create a good or service.
- The market value or price of the good or service it helps produce.

Other things equal, a resource that is highly productive in turning out a highly valued commodity will be in great demand. On the other hand, a relatively unproductive resource that is capable of producing only a minimally valued commodity will be in little demand. And no demand whatsoever will exist for a resource that is phenomenally efficient in producing something that no one wants to buy.

Productivity Table 12.1 shows the roles of resource productivity and product price in determining resource

TABLE 12.1 The Demand for Labor: Pure Competition in the Sale of the Product

(1) Units of Resource	(2) Total Product (Output)	(3) Marginal Product (MP)	(4) Product Price	(5) Total Revenue, (2) × (4)	(6) Marginal Revenue Product (MRP)
0	0		$2	$ 0	
1	7	7	2	14	$14
2	13	6	2	26	12
3	18	5	2	36	10
4	22	4	2	44	8
5	25	3	2	50	6
6	27	2	2	54	4
7	28	1	2	56	2

demand. Here we assume that a firm adds a single variable resource, labor, to its fixed plant. Columns 1 and 2 give the number of units of the resource applied to production and the resulting total product (output). Column 3 provides the **marginal product (MP)**, or additional output, resulting from using each additional unit of labor. Columns 1 through 3 remind us that the law of diminishing returns applies here, causing the marginal product of labor to fall beyond some point. For simplicity, we assume that these diminishing marginal returns—these declines in marginal product—begin with the first worker hired.

Product Price But the derived demand for a resource depends also on the price of the product it produces. Column 4 in Table 12.1 adds this price information. Product price is constant, in this case at $2, because the product market is competitive. The firm is a price taker and can sell units of output only at this market price.

Multiplying column 2 by column 4 provides the total-revenue data of column 5. These are the amounts of revenue the firm realizes from the various levels of resource usage. From these total-revenue data we can compute **marginal revenue product (MRP)**—the change in total revenue resulting from the use of each additional unit of a resource (labor, in this case). In equation form,

$$\text{Marginal revenue product} = \frac{\text{change in total revenue}}{\text{unit change in resource quantity}}$$

The MRPs are listed in column 6 in Table 12.1.

Rule for Employing Resources: MRP = MRC

The MRP schedule, shown as columns 1 and 6, is the firm's demand schedule for labor. To understand why, you must first know the rule that guides a profit-seeking firm in hiring

any resource: To maximize profit, a firm should hire additional units of a specific resource as long as each successive unit adds more to the firm's total revenue than it adds to the firm's total cost.

Economists use special terms to designate what each additional unit of labor or other variable resource adds to total cost and what it adds to total revenue. We have seen that MRP measures how much each successive unit of a resource adds to total revenue. The amount that each additional unit of a resource adds to the firm's total (resource) cost is called its **marginal resource cost (MRC).**

In equation form,

$$\text{Marginal resource cost} = \frac{\text{change in total (resource) cost}}{\text{unit change in resource quantity}}$$

So we can restate our rule for hiring resources as follows: It will be profitable for a firm to hire additional units of a resource up to the point at which that resource's MRP is equal to its MRC. For example, as the rule applies to labor, if the number of workers a firm is currently hiring is such that the MRP of the last worker exceeds his or her MRC, the firm can profit by hiring more workers. But if the number being hired is such that the MRC of the last worker exceeds his or her MRP, the firm is hiring workers who are not "paying their way" and it can increase its profit by discharging some workers. You may have recognized that this **MRP = MRC rule** is similar to the MR = MC profit-maximizing rule employed throughout our discussion of price and output determination. The rationale of the two rules is the same, but the point of reference is now *inputs* of a resource, not *outputs* of a product.

MRP as Resource Demand Schedule

Let's continue with our focus on labor, knowing that the analysis also applies to other resources. In a purely competitive labor market, market supply and market demand establish the wage rate. Because each firm hires such a small fraction of market supply, it cannot influence the market wage rate; it is a wage taker, not a wage maker. This means that for each additional unit of labor hired, each firm's total resource cost increases by exactly the amount of the constant market wage rate. More specifically, the MRC of labor exactly equals the market wage rate. Thus, resource "price" (the market wage rate) and resource "cost" (marginal resource cost) are equal for a firm that hires a resource in a competitive labor market. As a result, the MRP = MRC rule tells us that, in pure competition, the firm will hire workers up to the point at which the market *wage rate* (its MRC) is equal to its MRP.

In terms of the data in columns 1 and 6 of Table 12.1, if the market wage rate is, say, $13.95, the firm will hire only one worker. This is so because only the hiring of the first worker results in an increase in profits. To see this, note that for the first worker MRP (= $14) exceeds MRC (= $13.95). Thus, hiring the first worker is profitable. For each successive worker, however, MRC (= $13.95) exceeds MRP (= $12 or less), indicating that it will not be profitable to hire any of those workers. If the wage rate is $11.95, by the same reasoning we discover that it will pay the firm to hire both the first and second workers. Similarly, if the wage rate is $9.95, three workers will be hired. If it is $7.95, four. If it is $5.95, five. And so forth. So here is the key generalization: The MRP schedule constitutes the firm's demand for labor because each point on this schedule (or curve) indicates the number of workers the firm would hire at each possible wage rate.

In Figure 12.1, we show the D = MRP curve based on the data in Table 12.1.[1] The competitive firm's resource demand curve identifies an inverse relationship between the wage rate and the quantity of labor demanded, other things equal. The curve slopes downward because of diminishing marginal returns.

Resource Demand under Imperfect Product Market Competition

Resource demand (here, labor demand) is more complex when the firm is selling its product in an imperfectly competitive market, one in which the firm is a price maker. That is because imperfect competitors (pure monopolists,

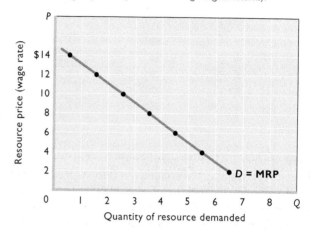

FIGURE 12.1 The purely competitive seller's demand for a resource. The MRP curve is the resource demand curve; each of its points relates a particular resource price (= MRP when profit is maximized) with a corresponding quantity of the resource demanded. Under pure competition, product price is constant; therefore, the downward slope of the D = MRP curve is due solely to the decline in the resource's marginal product (law of diminishing marginal returns).

oligopolists, and monopolistic competitors) face downsloping product demand curves. As a result, whenever an imperfect competitor's product demand curve is fixed in place, the only way to increase sales is by setting a lower price (and thereby moving down along the fixed demand curve).

The productivity data in Table 12.1 are retained in columns 1 to 3 in Table 12.2. But here in Table 12.2 we show in column 4 that product price must be lowered to sell the marginal product of each successive worker. The MRP of the purely competitive seller of Table 12.1 falls for only one reason: Marginal product diminishes. But the MRP of the imperfectly competitive seller of Table 12.2 falls for two reasons: Marginal product diminishes *and* product price falls as output increases.

We emphasize that the lower price accompanying each increase in output (total product) applies not only to the marginal product of each successive worker but also to all prior output units that otherwise could have been sold at a higher price. Observe that the marginal product of the second worker is 6 units of output. These 6 units can be sold for $2.40 each, or, as a group, for $14.40. But $14.40 is not the MRP of the second worker. To sell these 6 units, the firm must take a 20-cent price cut on the 7 units produced by the first worker—units that otherwise could have been sold for $2.60 each. Thus, the MRP of the second worker is only $13 [= $14.40 − (7 × 20 cents)], as shown.

Similarly, the third worker adds 5 units to total product, and these units are worth $2.20 each, or $11 total. But to sell these 5 units, the firm must take a 20-cent price cut on the 13 units produced by the first two workers. So the

---

[1]Note that we plot the points in Figure 12.1 halfway between succeeding numbers of resource units because MRP is associated with the addition of 1 more unit. Thus in Figure 12.1, for example, we plot the MRP of the second unit ($12) not at 1 or 2 but at 1½. This "smoothing" enables us to sketch a continuously downsloping curve rather than one that moves downward in discrete steps (like a staircase) as each new unit of labor is hired.

TABLE 12.2 The Demand for Labor: Imperfect Competition in the Sale of the Product

(1) Units of Resource	(2) Total Product (Output)	(3) Marginal Product (MP)	(4) Product Price	(5) Total Revenue, (2) × (4)	(6) Marginal Revenue Product (MRP)
0	0		$2.80	$ 0	
		7			$18.20
1	7		2.60	18.20	
		6			13.00
2	13		2.40	31.20	
		5			8.40
3	18		2.20	39.60	
		4			4.40
4	22		2.00	44.00	
		3			2.25
5	25		1.85	46.25	
		2			1.00
6	27		1.75	47.25	
		1			−1.05
7	28		1.65	46.20	

third worker's MRP is only $8.40 [= $11 − (13 × 20 cents)]. The numbers in column 6 reflect such calculations.

In Figure 12.2 we graph the MRP data from Table 12.2 and label it "*D* = MRP (imperfect competition)." The broken-line resource demand curve, in contrast, is that of the purely competitive seller represented in Figure 12.1. A comparison of the two curves demonstrates that, other things equal, the resource demand curve of an imperfectly competitive seller is less elastic than that of a purely competitive seller. Consider the effects of an identical percentage decline in the wage rate (resource price) from $11 to $6 in Figure 12.2. Comparison of the two

curves reveals that the imperfectly competitive seller (solid curve) does not expand the quantity of labor it employs by as large a percentage as does the purely competitive seller (broken curve).

It is not surprising that the imperfectly competitive producer is less responsive to resource price cuts than the purely competitive producer. When resource prices fall, MC per unit declines for both imperfectly competitive firms as well as purely competitive firms. Because both types of firms maximize profits by producing where MR = MC, the decline in MC will cause both types of firms to produce more. But the effect will be muted for imperfectly competitive firms because their downsloping demand curves cause them to also face downsloping MR curves—so that for each additional unit sold, MR declines. By contrast, MR is constant (and equal to the market equilibrium price *P*) for competitive firms, so that they do not have to worry about MR per unit falling as they produce more units. As a result, competitive firms increase production by a larger amount than imperfectly competitive firms whenever resource prices fall.

WORKED PROBLEMS

W 12.1

Resource demand

Market Demand for a Resource

The total, or market, demand curve for a specific resource shows the various total amounts of the resource that firms will purchase or hire at various resource prices, other things equal. Recall that the total, or market, demand curve for a *product* is found by summing horizontally the demand curves of all individual buyers in the market. The market demand curve for a particular *resource* is derived in essentially the same way—by summing horizontally the individual demand or MRP curves for all firms hiring that resource.

FIGURE 12.2 The imperfectly competitive seller's demand curve for a resource. An imperfectly competitive seller's resource demand curve *D* (solid) slopes downward because both marginal product and product price fall as resource employment and output rise. This downward slope is greater than that for a purely competitive seller (dashed resource demand curve) because the pure competitor can sell the added output at a constant price.

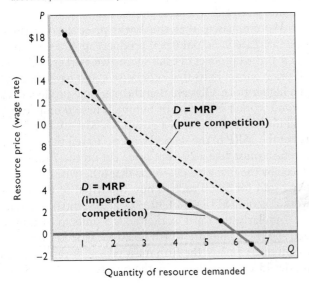

- To maximize profit, a firm will purchase or hire a resource in an amount at which the resource's marginal revenue product equals its marginal resource cost (MRP = MRC).

- Application of the MRP = MRC rule to a firm's MRP curve demonstrates that the MRP curve is the firm's resource demand curve. In a purely competitive resource market, resource price (the wage rate) equals MRC.

- The resource demand curve of a purely competitive seller is downsloping solely because the marginal product of the resource diminishes; the resource demand curve of an imperfectly competitive seller is downsloping because marginal product diminishes *and* product price falls as output is increased.

CONSIDER THIS . . .

Superstars

In what economist Robert Frank calls "winner-take-all markets," a few highly talented performers have huge earnings relative to the average performers in the market. Because consumers and firms seek out "top" performers, small differences in talent or popularity get magnified into huge differences in pay.

In these markets, consumer spending gets channeled toward a few performers. The media then "hypes" these individuals, which further increases the public's awareness of their talents. Many more consumers then buy the stars' products. Although it is not easy to stay on top, several superstars emerge.

The high earnings of superstars result from the high revenues they generate from their work. Consider Beyoncé Knowles. If she sold only a few thousand songs and attracted only a few hundred fans to each concert, the revenue she would produce—her marginal revenue product—would be quite modest. So, too, would be her earnings.

But consumers have anointed Beyoncé as queen of the R&B and hip-hop portion of pop culture. The demand for her music and concerts is extraordinarily high. She sells *millions* of songs, not thousands, and draws *thousands* to her concerts, not hundreds. Her extraordinarily high net earnings derive from her extraordinarily high MRP.

So it is for the other superstars in the "winner-take-all markets." Influenced by the media, but coerced by no one, consumers direct their spending toward a select few. The resulting strong demand for these stars' services reflects their high MRP. And because top talent (by definition) is very limited, superstars receive amazingly high earnings.

Determinants of Resource Demand

What will alter the demand for a resource—that is, shift the resource demand curve? The fact that resource demand is derived from *product demand* and depends on *resource productivity* suggests two "resource demand shifters." Also, our analysis of how changes in the prices of other products can shift a product's demand curve (Chapter 3) suggests another factor: changes in the *prices of other resources*.

Changes in Product Demand

Other things equal, an increase in the demand for a product will increase the demand for a resource used in its production, whereas a decrease in product demand will decrease the demand for that resource.

Let's see how this works. The first thing to recall is that a change in the demand for a product will change its price. In Table 12.1, let's assume that an increase in product demand boosts product price from $2 to $3. You should calculate the new resource demand schedule (columns 1 and 6) that would result and plot it in Figure 12.1 to verify that the new resource demand curve lies to the right of the old demand curve. Similarly, a decline in the product demand (and price) will shift the resource demand curve to the left. This effect—resource demand changing along with product demand—demonstrates that resource demand is derived from product demand.

Example: Assuming no offsetting change in supply, a decrease in the demand for new houses will drive down house prices. Those lower prices will decrease the MRP of construction workers, and therefore the demand for construction workers will fall. The resource demand curve such as in Figure 12.1 or Figure 12.2 will shift to the left.

Changes in Productivity

Other things equal, an increase in the productivity of a resource will increase the demand for the resource and a decrease in productivity will reduce the demand for the resource. If we doubled the MP data of column 3 in Table 12.1, the MRP data of column 6 would also double, indicating a rightward shift of the resource demand curve.

The productivity of any resource may be altered over the long run in several ways:

- ***Quantities of other resources*** The marginal productivity of any resource will vary with the quantities of the other resources used with it. The greater the amount of capital and land resources used with, say, labor, the greater will be labor's marginal productivity and, thus, labor demand.

- *Technological advance* Technological improvements that increase the quality of other resources, such as capital, have the same effect. The better the *quality* of capital, the greater the productivity of labor used with it. Dockworkers employed with a specific amount of real capital in the form of unloading cranes are more productive than dockworkers with the same amount of real capital embodied in older conveyor-belt systems.
- *Quality of the variable resource* Improvements in the quality of the variable resource, such as labor, will increase its marginal productivity and therefore its demand. In effect, there will be a new demand curve for a different, more skilled, kind of labor.

All these considerations help explain why the average level of (real) wages is higher in industrially advanced nations (for example, the United States, Germany, Japan, and France) than in developing nations (for example, Nicaragua, Ethiopia, Angola, and Cambodia). Workers in industrially advanced nations are generally healthier, better educated, and better trained than are workers in developing countries. Also, in most industries they work with a larger and more efficient stock of capital goods and more abundant natural resources. This increases productivity and creates a strong demand for labor. On the supply side of the market, labor is scarcer relative to capital in industrially advanced than in most developing nations. A strong demand and a relatively scarce supply of labor result in high wage rates in the industrially advanced nations.

Changes in the Prices of Other Resources

Changes in the prices of other resources may change the demand for a specific resource. For example, a change in the price of capital may change the demand for labor. The direction of the change in labor demand will depend on whether labor and capital are substitutes or complements in production.

Substitute Resources

Suppose the technology in a certain production process is such that labor and capital are substitutable. A firm can produce some specific amount of output using a relatively small amount of labor and a relatively large amount of capital, or vice versa. Now assume that the price of machinery (capital) falls. The effect on the demand for labor will be the net result of two opposed effects: the substitution effect and the output effect.

- *Substitution effect* The decline in the price of machinery prompts the firm to substitute machinery for labor. This allows the firm to produce its output at lower cost. So at the fixed wage rate, smaller quantities of labor are now employed. This **substitution effect** decreases the demand for labor. More generally, the

substitution effect indicates that a firm will purchase more of an input whose relative price has declined and, conversely, use less of an input whose relative price has increased.
- *Output effect* Because the price of machinery has fallen, the costs of producing various outputs must also decline. With lower costs, the firm finds it profitable to produce and sell a greater output. The greater output increases the demand for all resources, including labor. So this **output effect** increases the demand for labor. More generally, the output effect means that the firm will purchase more of one particular input when the price of the other input falls and less of that particular input when the price of the other input rises.
- *Net effect* The substitution and output effects are both present when the price of an input changes, but they work in opposite directions. For a decline in the price of capital, the substitution effect decreases the demand for labor and the output effect increases it. The net change in labor demand depends on the relative sizes of the two effects: If the substitution effect outweighs the output effect, a decrease in the price of capital decreases the demand for labor. If the output effect exceeds the substitution effect, a decrease in the price of capital increases the demand for labor.

Complementary Resources

Recall from Chapter 3 that certain products, such as computers and software, are complementary goods; they "go together" and are jointly demanded. Resources may also be complementary; an increase in the quantity of one of them used in the production process requires an increase in the amount used of the other as well, and vice versa. Suppose a small design firm does computer-assisted design (CAD) with relatively expensive personal computers as its basic piece of capital equipment. Each computer requires exactly one design engineer to operate it; the machine is not automated—it will not run itself—and a second engineer would have nothing to do.

Now assume that a technological advance in the production of these computers substantially reduces their price. There can be no substitution effect because labor and capital must be used in *fixed proportions*, one person for one machine. Capital cannot be substituted for labor. But there *is* an output effect. Other things equal, the reduction in the price of capital goods means lower production costs. Producing a larger output will therefore be profitable. In doing so, the firm will use both more capital and more labor. When labor and capital are complementary, a decline in the price of capital increases the demand for labor through the output effect.

We have cast our analysis of substitute resources and complementary resources mainly in terms of a decline in

TABLE 12.3 **The Effect of an Increase in the Price of Capital on the Demand for Labor, D_L**

(1) Relationship of Inputs	(2) Increase in the Price of Capital		
	(a) Substitution Effect	(b) Output Effect	(c) Combined Effect
Substitutes in production	Labor substituted for capital	Production costs up, output down, and less of both capital and labor used	D_L increases if the substitution effect exceeds the output effect; D_L decreases if the output effect exceeds the substitution effect
Complements in production	No substitution of labor for capital	Production costs up, output down, and less of both capital and labor used	D_L decreases (because only the output effect applies)

the price of capital. Table 12.3 summarizes the effects of an *increase* in the price of capital on the demand for labor. Please study it carefully.

Now that we have discussed the full list of the determinants of labor demand, let's again review their effects. Stated in terms of the labor resource, the demand for labor will increase (the labor demand curve will shift rightward) when:

- The demand for (and therefore the price of) the product produced by that labor *increases*.
- The productivity (MP) of labor *increases*.
- The price of a substitute input *decreases*, provided the output effect exceeds the substitution effect.
- The price of a substitute input *increases*, provided the substitution effect exceeds the output effect.
- The price of a complementary input *decreases*.

Be sure that you can "reverse" these effects to explain a *decrease* in labor demand.

Table 12.4 provides several illustrations of the determinants of labor demand, listed by the categories of determinants we have discussed. You will benefit by giving them a close look.

Occupational Employment Trends

Changes in labor demand have considerable significance since they affect wage rates and employment in specific occupations. Increases in labor demand for certain occupational groups result in increases in their employment; decreases in labor demand result in decreases in their employment. For illustration, let's first look at occupations for which labor demand is growing and then examine occupations for which it is declining. (Wage rates are the subject of the next chapter.)

The Fastest-Growing Occupations Table 12.5 lists the 10 fastest-growing U.S. occupations for 2008 to 2018, as measured by percentage changes and projected by the Bureau of Labor Statistics. It is no coincidence that the service occupations dominate the list. In general, the demand for service workers in the United States is rapidly outpacing the demand for manufacturing, construction, and mining workers.

Of the 10 fastest-growing occupations in percentage terms, three—personal and home care aides (people who

TABLE 12.4 **Determinants of Labor Demand: Factors That Shift the Labor Demand Curve**

Determinant	Examples
Change in product demand	Gambling increases in popularity, increasing the demand for workers at casinos. Consumers decrease their demand for leather coats, decreasing the demand for tanners. The Federal government increases spending on homeland security, increasing the demand for security personnel.
Change in productivity	An increase in the skill levels of physicians increases the demand for their services. Computer-assisted graphic design increases the productivity of, and demand for, graphic artists.
Change in the price of another resource	An increase in the price of electricity increases the cost of producing aluminum and reduces the demand for aluminum workers. The price of security equipment used by businesses to protect against illegal entry falls, decreasing the demand for night guards. The price of cell phone equipment decreases, reducing the cost of cell phone service; this in turn increases the demand for cell phone assemblers. Health-insurance premiums rise, and firms substitute part-time workers who are not covered by insurance for full-time workers who are.

TABLE 12.5 The 10 Fastest-Growing U.S. Occupations in Percentage Terms, 2008–2018

Occupation	Employment, Thousands of Jobs		Percentage Increase*
	2008	2018	
Biomedical engineers	16	28	72.0
Network systems and data communications analysts	292	448	53.4
Home health aides	922	1383	50.0
Personal and home care aides	817	1193	46.0
Financial examiners	27	38	41.2
Medical scientists, except epidemiologists	109	154	40.4
Physician assistants	75	104	39.0
Skin care specialists	39	54	37.9
Biochemists and biophysicists	23	32	37.4
Athletic trainers	16	22	37.0

*Percentages and employment numbers may not reconcile due to rounding.

Source: Bureau of Labor Statistics, "Employment Projections," **www.bls.gov**.

TABLE 12.6 The 10 Most Rapidly Declining U.S. Occupations in Percentage Terms, 2008–2018

Occupation	Employment, Thousands of Jobs		Percentage Increase*
	2008	2018	
Textile machine operators	35	21	−40.7
Sewing machine operators	212	141	−33.7
Postal service workers	180	125	−30.3
Lathe operators	56	41	−26.7
Order clerks	246	182	−26.1
Photographic processing machine operators	51	39	−24.3
File clerks	212	163	−23.4
Machine feeders and offbearers	141	110	−22.2
Paper goods machine setters operators, tenders	103	81	−21.5
Computer operators	110	90	−18.6

*Percentages and employment numbers may not reconcile due to rounding.

Source: Bureau of Labor Statistics, "Employment Projections," **www.bls.gov**.

provide home care for the elderly and disabled), home health care aides (people who provide short-term medical care after discharge from hospitals), and medical assistants—are related to health care. The rising demands for these types of labor are derived from the growing demand for health services, caused by several factors. The aging of the U.S. population has brought with it more medical problems, the rising standard of income has led to greater expenditures on health care, and the continued presence of private and public insurance has allowed people to buy more health care than most could afford individually.

Two of the fastest-growing occupations are directly related to computers. The increase in the demand for network systems and data communication analysts and computer software engineers arises from the rapid rise in the demand for computers, computer services, and Internet use. It also results from the rising marginal revenue productivity of these particular workers, given the vastly improved quality of the computer and communications equipment they work with. Moreover, price declines on such equipment have had stronger output effects than substitution effects, increasing the demand for these kinds of labor.

The Most Rapidly Declining Occupations In contrast, Table 12.6 lists the 10 U.S. occupations with the greatest projected job loss (in percentage terms) between 2008 and 2018. Several of the occupations owe their declines mainly to "labor-saving" technological change. For example, automated or computerized equipment has greatly

reduced the need for file clerks, model and pattern makers, and telephone operators. The advent of digital photography explains the projected decline in the employment of people operating photographic processing equipment.

Three of the occupations in the declining employment list are related to textiles and apparel. The U.S. demand for these goods is increasingly being filled through imports. Those jobs are therefore rapidly disappearing in the United States.

As we indicated, the "top-10" lists shown in Tables 12.5 and 12.6 are based on percentage changes. In terms of absolute job growth and loss, the greatest projected employment growth between 2008 and 2018 is for home health aids (416,000 jobs) and personal and home care aids (376,000 jobs). The greatest projected absolute decline in employment is for sewing machine operators (−71,000 jobs).

Elasticity of Resource Demand

The employment changes we have just discussed have resulted from shifts in the locations of resource demand curves. Such changes in demand must be distinguished from changes in the quantity of a resource demanded caused by a change in the price of the specific resource under consideration. Such a change is caused not by a shift of the demand curve but, rather, by a movement from one point to another on a fixed resource demand curve. Example: In Figure 12.1 we note that an increase in the wage rate from $5 to $7 will reduce the quantity of labor demanded from 5 to 4 units.

This is a change in the *quantity of labor demanded* as distinct from a *change in the demand for labor.*

The sensitivity of resource quantity to changes in resource prices along a fixed resource demand curve is measured by the **elasticity of resource demand.** In coefficient form,

$$E_{rd} = \frac{\text{percentage change in resource quantity demanded}}{\text{percentage change in resource price}}$$

ORIGIN OF THE IDEA
O 12.1
Elasticity of resource demand

When E_{rd} is greater than 1, resource demand is elastic; when E_{rd} is less than 1, resource demand is inelastic; and when E_{rd} equals 1, resource demand is unit-elastic. What determines the elasticity of resource demand? Several factors are at work.

Ease of Resource Substitutability The degree to which resources are substitutable is a fundamental determinant of elasticity. More specifically, the greater the substitutability of other resources, the more elastic is the demand for a particular resource. As an example, the high degree to which computerized voice recognition systems are substitutable for human beings implies that the demand for human beings answering phone calls at call centers is quite elastic. In contrast, good substitutes for physicians are rare, so demand for them is less elastic or even inelastic. If a furniture manufacturer finds that several types of wood are equally satisfactory in making coffee tables, a rise in the price of any one type of wood may cause a sharp drop in the amount demanded as the producer substitutes some other type of wood for the type of wood whose price has gone up. At the other extreme, there may be no reasonable substitutes; bauxite is absolutely essential in the production of aluminum ingots. Thus, the demand for bauxite by aluminum producers is inelastic.

Time can play a role in the ease of input substitution. For example, a firm's truck drivers may obtain a substantial wage increase with little or no immediate decline in employment. But over time, as the firm's trucks wear out and are replaced, that wage increase may motivate the company to purchase larger trucks and in that way deliver the same total output with fewer drivers.

Elasticity of Product Demand Because the demand for labor is a derived demand, the elasticity of the demand for the output that the labor is producing will influence the elasticity of the demand for labor. Other things equal, the greater the price elasticity of product demand, the greater the elasticity of resource demand. For example, suppose

that the wage rate falls. This means a decline in the cost of producing the product and a drop in the product's price. If the elasticity of product demand is great, the resulting increase in the quantity of the product demanded will be large and thus necessitate a large increase in the quantity of labor to produce the additional output. This implies an elastic demand for labor. But if the demand for the product is inelastic, the increase in the amount of the product demanded will be small, as will be the increases in the quantity of labor demanded. This suggests an inelastic demand for labor.

Remember that the resource demand curve in Figure 12.1 is more elastic than the resource demand curve shown in Figure 12.2. The difference arises because in Figure 12.1 we assume a perfectly elastic product demand curve, whereas Figure 12.2 is based on a downsloping or less than perfectly elastic product demand curve.

Ratio of Resource Cost to Total Cost The larger the proportion of total production costs accounted for by a resource, the greater the elasticity of demand for that resource. In the extreme, if labor cost is the only production cost, then a 20 percent increase in wage rates will shift all the firm's cost curves upward by 20 percent. If product demand is elastic, this substantial increase in costs will cause a relatively large decline in sales and a sharp decline in the amount of labor demanded. So labor demand is highly elastic. But if labor cost is only 50 percent of production cost, then a 20 percent increase in wage rates will increase costs by only 10 percent. With the same elasticity of product demand, this will cause a relatively small decline in sales and therefore in the amount of labor demanded. In this case the demand for labor is much less elastic.

QUICK REVIEW 12.2

- A resource demand curve will shift because of changes in product demand, changes in the productivity of the resource, and changes in the prices of other inputs.

- If resources A and B are substitutable, a decline in the price of A will decrease the demand for B provided the substitution effect exceeds the output effect. But if the output effect exceeds the substitution effect, the demand for B will increase.

- If resources C and D are complements, a decline in the price of C will increase the demand for D.

- Elasticity of resource demand measures the extent to which producers change the quantity of a resource they hire when its price changes.

- The elasticity of resource demand will be less the greater the difficulty of substituting other resources for the resource, the smaller the elasticity of product demand, and the smaller the proportion of total cost accounted for by the resource.

Optimal Combination of Resources*

So far, our main focus has been on one variable input, labor. But in the long run firms can vary the amounts of all the resources they use. That's why we need to consider what combination of resources a firm will choose when *all* its inputs are variable. While our analysis is based on two resources, it can be extended to any number of inputs.

We will consider two interrelated questions:

- What combination of resources will minimize costs at a specific level of output?
- What combination of resources will maximize profit?

The Least-Cost Rule

A firm is producing a specific output with the **least-cost combination of resources** when the last dollar spent on each resource yields the same marginal product. That is, the cost of any output is minimized when the ratios of marginal product to price of the last units of resources used are the same for each resource. To see how this rule maximizes profits in a more concrete setting, consider firms that are competitive buyers in resource markets. Because each firm is too small to affect resource prices, each firm's marginal resource costs will equal market resource prices and each firm will be able to hire as many or as few units as it would like of any and all resources at their respective market prices. Thus, if there are just two resources, labor and capital, a competitive firm will minimize its total cost of a specific output when

$$\frac{\text{Marginal product of labor (MP}_L)}{\text{Price of labor } (P_L)} = \frac{\text{Marginal product of capital (MP}_C)}{\text{Price of capital } (P_C)} \quad (1)$$

Throughout, we will refer to the marginal products of labor and capital as MP_L and MP_C, respectively, and symbolize the price of labor by P_L and the price of capital by P_C.

A concrete example will show why fulfilling the condition in equation 1 leads to least-cost production. Assume that the price of both capital and labor is $1 per unit but that Siam Soups currently employs them in such amounts that the marginal product of labor is 10 and the marginal product of capital is 5. Our equation immediately tells us that this is not the least costly combination of resources:

$$\frac{MP_L = 10}{P_L = \$1} > \frac{MP_C = 5}{P_C = \$1}$$

Suppose Siam spends $1 less on capital and shifts that dollar to labor. It loses 5 units of output produced by the last dollar's worth of capital, but it gains 10 units of output from the extra dollar's worth of labor. Net output increases by 5 ($= 10 - 5$) units for the same total cost. More such shifting of dollars from capital to labor will push the firm *down* along its MP curve for labor and *up* along its MP curve for capital, increasing output and moving the firm toward a position of equilibrium where equation 1 is fulfilled. At that equilibrium position, the MP per dollar for the last unit of both labor and capital might be, for example, 7. And Siam will be producing a greater output for the same (original) cost.

Whenever the same total-resource cost can result in a greater total output, the cost per unit—and therefore the total cost of any specific level of output—can be reduced. Being able to produce a *larger* output with a *specific* total cost is the same as being able to produce a *specific* output with a *smaller* total cost. If Siam buys $1 less of capital, its output will fall by 5 units. If it spends only $.50 of that dollar on labor, the firm will increase its output by a compensating 5 units ($= \frac{1}{2}$ of the MP per dollar). Then the firm will realize the same total output at a $.50 lower total cost.

The cost of producing any specific output can be reduced as long as equation 1 does not hold. But when dollars have been shifted between capital and labor to the point where equation 1 holds, no additional changes in the use of capital and labor will reduce costs further. Siam will be producing that output using the least-cost combination of capital and labor.

All the long-run cost curves developed in Chapter 7 and used thereafter assume that the least-cost combination of inputs has been realized at each level of output. Any firm that combines resources in violation of the least-cost rule would have a higher-than-necessary average total cost at each level of output. That is, it would incur *X-inefficiency*, as discussed in Figure 10.7.

The producer's least-cost rule is analogous to the consumer's utility-maximizing rule described in Chapter 6. In achieving the utility-maximizing combination of goods, the consumer considers both his or her preferences as reflected in diminishing-marginal-utility data and the prices of the various products. Similarly, in achieving the cost-minimizing combination of resources, the producer considers both the marginal-product data and the prices (costs) of the various resources.

The Profit-Maximizing Rule

Minimizing cost is not sufficient for maximizing profit. A firm can produce any level of output in the least costly way by applying equation 1. But only one unique level of output

---

*Note to Instructors: We consider this section to be optional. If desired, it can be skipped without loss of continuity. It can also be deferred until after the discussion of wage determination in the next chapter.

maximizes profit. Our earlier analysis of product markets showed that this profit-maximizing output occurs where marginal revenue equals marginal cost (MR = MC). Near the beginning of this chapter we determined that we could write this profit-maximizing condition as MRP = MRC as it relates to resource inputs.

In a purely competitive resource market the marginal resource cost (MRC) is equal to the resource price P. Thus, for any competitive resource market, we have as our profit-maximizing equation

$$\text{MRP (resource)} = P \text{ (resource)}$$

This condition must hold for every variable resource, and in the long run all resources are variable. In competitive markets, a firm will therefore achieve its **profit-maximizing combination of resources** when each resource is employed to the point at which its marginal revenue product equals its resource price. For two resources, labor and capital, we need both

$$P_L = \text{MRP}_L \quad \text{and} \quad P_C = \text{MRP}_C$$

We can combine these conditions by dividing both sides of each equation by their respective prices and equating the results to get

$$\frac{\text{MRP}_L}{P_L} = \frac{\text{MRP}_C}{P_C} = 1 \qquad (2)$$

Note in equation 2 that it is not sufficient that the MRPs of the two resources be *proportionate* to their prices; the MRPs must be *equal* to their prices and the ratios therefore equal to 1. For example, if $\text{MRP}_L = \$15$, $P_L = \$5$, $\text{MRP}_C = \$9$, and $P_C = \$3$, Siam is underemploying both capital and labor even though the ratios of MRP to resource price are identical for both resources. The firm can expand its profit by hiring additional amounts of both capital and labor until it moves down their downsloping MRP curves to the points at which $\text{MRP}_L = \$5$ and $\text{MRP}_C = \$3$. The ratios will then be 5/5 and 3/3 and equal to 1.

The profit-maximizing position in equation 2 includes the cost-minimizing condition of equation 1. That is, if a firm is maximizing profit according to equation 2, then it must be using the least-cost combination of inputs to do so. However, the converse is not true: A firm operating at least cost according to equation 1 may not be operating at the output that maximizes its profit.

> **WORKED PROBLEMS**
> **W 12.2**
> Optimal combination of resources

Numerical Illustration

A numerical illustration will help you understand the least-cost and profit-maximizing rules. In columns 2, 3, 2′, and 3′ in Table 12.7 we show the total products and marginal products for various amounts of labor and capital that are assumed to be the only inputs Siam needs in producing its soup. Both inputs are subject to diminishing returns.

We also assume that labor and capital are supplied in competitive resource markets at $8 and $12, respectively, and that Siam's soup sells competitively at $2 per unit. For both labor and capital we can determine the total revenue associated with each input level by multiplying total product by the $2 product price. These data are shown in columns 4 and 4′. They enable us to calculate the marginal revenue product of each successive input of labor and capital as shown in columns 5 and 5′, respectively.

TABLE 12.7 Data for Finding the Least-Cost and Profit-Maximizing Combination of Labor and Capital, Siam's Soups*

Labor (Price = $8)					Capital (Price = $12)				
(1) Quantity	(2) Total Product (Output)	(3) Marginal Product	(4) Total Revenue	(5) Marginal Revenue Product	(1′) Quantity	(2′) Total Product (Output)	(3′) Marginal Product	(4′) Total Revenue	(5′) Marginal Revenue Product
0	0		$ 0		0	0		$ 0	
		12		$24			13		$26
1	12		24		1	13		26	
		10		20			9		18
2	22		44		2	22		44	
		6		12			6		12
3	28		56		3	28		56	
		5		10			4		8
4	33		66		4	32		64	
		4		8			3		6
5	37		74		5	35		70	
		3		6			2		4
6	40		80		6	37		74	
		2		4			1		2
7	42		84		7	38		76	

*To simplify, it is assumed in this table that the productivity of each resource is independent of the quantity of the other. For example, the total and marginal products of labor are assumed not to vary with the quantity of capital employed.

Producing at Least Cost What is the least-cost combination of labor and capital for Siam to use in producing, say, 50 units of output? The answer, which we can obtain by trial and error, is 3 units of labor and 2 units of capital. Columns 2 and 2′ indicate that this combination of labor and capital does, indeed, result in the required 50 (= 28 + 22) units of output. Now, note from columns 3 and 3′ that hiring 3 units of labor gives us $MP_L/P_L = \frac{6}{8} = \frac{3}{4}$ and hiring 2 units of capital gives us $MP_C/P_C = \frac{9}{12} = \frac{3}{4}$. So equation (1) is fulfilled. How can we verify that costs are actually minimized? First, we see that the total cost of employing 3 units of labor and 2 of capital is $48 [= (3 × $8) + (2 × $12)].

Other combinations of labor and capital will also yield 50 units of output, but at a higher cost than $48. For example, 5 units of labor and 1 unit of capital will produce 50 (= 37 + 13) units, but total cost is higher, at $52 [= (5 × $8) + (1 × $12)]. This comes as no surprise because 5 units of labor and 1 unit of capital violate the least-cost rule—$MP_L/P_L = \frac{4}{8}$, $MP_C/P_C = \frac{13}{12}$. Only the combination (3 units of labor and 2 units of capital) that minimizes total cost will satisfy equation 1. All other combinations capable of producing 50 units of output violate the cost-minimizing rule, and therefore cost more than $48.

Maximizing Profit Will 50 units of output maximize Siam's profit? No, because the profit-maximizing terms of equation 2 are not satisfied when the firm employs 3 units of labor and 2 of capital. To maximize profit, each input should be employed until its price equals its marginal revenue product. But for 3 units of labor, labor's MRP in column 5 is $12 while its price is only $8. This means the firm could increase its profit by hiring more labor. Similarly, for 2 units of capital, we see in column 5′ that capital's MRP is $18 and its price is only $12. This indicates that more capital should also be employed. By producing only 50 units of output (even though they are produced at least cost), labor and capital are being used in less-than-profit-maximizing amounts. The firm needs to expand its employment of labor and capital, thereby increasing its output.

Table 12.7 shows that the MRPs of labor and capital are equal to their prices, so equation 2 is fulfilled when Siam is employing 5 units of labor and 3 units of capital. So this is the profit-maximizing combination of inputs.[2] The firm's total cost will be $76, made up of $40 (= 5 × $8) of labor and $36 (= 3 × $12) of capital. Total revenue

will be $130, found either by multiplying the total output of 65 (= 37 + 28) by the $2 product price or by summing the total revenues attributable to labor ($74) and to capital ($56). The difference between total revenue and total cost in this instance is $54 (= $130 − $76). Experiment with other combinations of labor and capital to demonstrate that they yield an economic profit of less than $54.

Note that the profit-maximizing combination of 5 units of labor and 3 units of capital is also a least-cost combination for this particular level of output. Using these resource amounts satisfies the least-cost requirement of equation 1 in that $MP_L/P_L = \frac{4}{8} = \frac{1}{2}$ and $MP_C/P_C = \frac{6}{12} = \frac{1}{2}$.

Marginal Productivity Theory of Income Distribution

Our discussion of resource pricing is the cornerstone of the controversial view that fairness and economic justice are one of the outcomes of a competitive capitalist economy. Table 12.7 demonstrates, in effect, that workers receive income payments (wages) equal to the marginal contributions they make to their employers' outputs and revenues. In other words, workers are paid according to the value of the labor services that they contribute to production. Similarly, owners of the other resources receive income based on the value of the resources they supply in the production process.

In this **marginal productivity theory of income distribution,** income is distributed according to contribution to society's output. So, if you are willing to accept the proposition "To each according to the value of what he or she creates," income payments based on marginal revenue product provide a fair and equitable distribution of society's income.

ORIGIN OF THE IDEA

O 12.2

Marginal productivity theory
of distribution

This sounds reasonable, but you need to be aware of serious criticisms of this theory of income distribution:

- *Inequality* Critics argue that the distribution of income resulting from payment according to marginal productivity may be highly unequal because productive resources are very unequally distributed in the first place. Aside from their differences in mental and physical attributes, individuals encounter substantially different opportunities to enhance their productivity through education and training and the use of more and better equipment. Some people may not be able to participate in production at all because of mental or physical disabilities, and they would obtain no income under a system of distribution based solely on marginal productivity. Ownership of property

---

[2]Because we are dealing with discrete (nonfractional) units of the two outputs here, the use of 4 units of labor and 2 units of capital is equally profitable. The fifth unit of labor's MRP and its price (cost) are equal at $8, so that the fifth labor unit neither adds to nor subtracts from the firm's profit; similarly, the third unit of capital has no effect on profit.

Banks Are Using More Automatic Teller Machines (ATMs) and Employing Fewer Human Tellers.

As you have learned from this chapter, a firm achieves its least-cost combination of inputs when the last dollar it spends on each input makes the same contribution to total output. This raises an interesting real-world question: What happens when technological advance makes available a new, highly productive capital good for which *MP/P* is greater than it is for other inputs, say, a particular type of labor? The answer is that the least-cost mix of resources abruptly changes, and the firm responds accordingly. If the new capital is a substitute for labor (rather than a complement), the firm replaces the particular type of labor with the new capital. That is exactly what is happening in the banking industry, in which ATMs are replacing human bank tellers.

ATMs made their debut at a bank in London in 1967. Shortly thereafter, U.S. firms Docutel and Diebold each introduced their own models. Today, Diebold and NCR (also a U.S. firm) dominate global sales, with the Japanese firm Fujitsu being a distant third. The number of ATMs and their usage have exploded, and currently there are nearly 400,000 ATMs in the United States. In 1975, about 10 *million* ATM transactions occurred in the United States. Today there are about 11 *billion* U.S. ATM transactions each year.

ATMs are highly productive: A single machine can handle hundreds of transactions daily, thousands weekly, and millions over the course of several years. ATMs can not only handle cash

withdrawals but also accept deposits and facilitate switches of funds between various accounts. Although ATMs are expensive for banks to buy and install, they are available 24 hours a day, and their cost per transaction is one-fourth the cost for human tellers. They rarely get "held up," and they do not quit their jobs (turnover among human tellers is nearly 50 percent per year). Moreover, ATMs are highly convenient; unlike human tellers, they are located not only at banks but also at busy street corners, workplaces, universities, and shopping malls. The same bank card that enables you to withdraw cash from your local ATM also enables you to withdraw pounds from an ATM in London, yen from an ATM in Tokyo, and rubles from an ATM in Moscow. (All this, of course, assumes that you have money in your checking account!)

In the terminology of this chapter, the more productive, lower-priced ATMs have reduced the demand for a substitute in production—human tellers. Between 1990 and 2000, an estimated 80,000 human teller positions were eliminated, and more positions may disappear in coming years. Where will the people holding these jobs go? Most will eventually move to other occupations. Although the lives of individual tellers are disrupted, society clearly wins. Society obtains more convenient banking services as well as the other goods that these "freed-up" labor resources help produce.

Source: Based partly on Ben Craig, "Where Have All the Tellers Gone?" Federal Reserve Bank of Cleveland, *Economic Commentary*, Apr. 15, 1997; and statistics provided by the American Bankers Association.

resources is also highly unequal. Many owners of land and capital resources obtain their property by inheritance rather than through their own productive effort. Hence, income from inherited property resources conflicts with the "To each according to the value of what he or she creates" idea. Critics say that these inequalities call for progressive taxation and government spending programs aimed at creating an income distribution that will be more equitable than that

which would occur if the income distribution were made strictly according to marginal productivity.

- *Market imperfections* The marginal productivity theory of income distribution rests on the assumptions of competitive markets. But, as we will see in Chapter 13, not all labor markets are highly competitive. In some labor markets employers exert their wage-setting power to pay less-than-competitive wages. And some workers, through labor unions,

261

professional associations, and occupational licensing laws, wield wage-setting power in selling their services. Even the process of collective bargaining over wages suggests a power struggle over the division of income. In wage setting through negotiations, market forces—and income shares based on

marginal productivity—may get partially pushed into the background. In addition, discrimination in the labor market can distort earnings patterns. In short, because of real-world market imperfections, wage rates and other resource prices are not always based solely on contributions to output.

Summary

1. Resource prices help determine money incomes, and they simultaneously ration resources to various industries and firms.

2. The demand for any resource is derived from the product it helps produce. That means the demand for a resource will depend on its productivity and on the market value (price) of the good it is producing.

3. Marginal revenue product is the extra revenue a firm obtains when it employs 1 more unit of a resource. The marginal revenue product curve for any resource is the demand curve for that resource because the firm equates resource price and MRP in determining its profit-maximizing level of resource employment. Thus each point on the MRP curve indicates how many resource units the firm will hire at a specific resource price.

4. The firm's demand curve for a resource slopes downward because the marginal product of additional units declines in accordance with the law of diminishing returns. When a firm is selling in an imperfectly competitive market, the resource demand curve falls for a second reason: Product price must be reduced for the firm to sell a larger output. The market demand curve for a resource is derived by summing horizontally the demand curves of all the firms hiring that resource.

5. The demand curve for a resource will shift as the result of (a) a change in the demand for, and therefore the price of, the product the resource is producing; (b) changes in the productivity of the resource; and (c) changes in the prices of other resources.

6. If resources A and B are substitutable for each other, a decline in the price of A will decrease the demand for B provided the substitution effect is greater than the output effect. But if the output effect *exceeds* the substitution effect, a decline in the price of A will increase the demand for B.

7. If resources C and D are complementary or jointly demanded, there is only an output effect; a change in the price of C will change the demand for D in the opposite direction.

8. The majority of the 10 fastest-growing occupations in the United States—by percentage increase—relate to health

care and computers (review Table 12.5); the 10 most rapidly declining occupations by percentage decrease, however, are more mixed (review Table 12.6).

9. The elasticity of demand for a resource measures the responsiveness of producers to a change in the resource's price. The coefficient of the elasticity of resource demand is

$$E_{rd} = \frac{\text{percentage change in resource quantity demanded}}{\text{percentage change in resource price}}$$

When E_{rd} is greater than 1, resource demand is elastic; when E_{rd} is less than 1, resource demand is inelastic; and when E_{rd} equals 1, resource demand is unit-elastic.

10. The elasticity of demand for a resource will be greater (a) the greater the ease of substituting other resources for labor, (b) the greater the elasticity of demand for the product, and (c) the larger the proportion of total production costs attributable to the resource.

11. Any specific level of output will be produced with the least costly combination of variable resources when the marginal product per dollar's worth of each input is the same—that is, when

$$\frac{\text{MP of labor}}{\text{Price of labor}} = \frac{\text{MP of capital}}{\text{Price of capital}}$$

12. A firm is employing the profit-maximizing combination of resources when each resource is used to the point where its marginal revenue product equals its price. In terms of labor and capital, that occurs when the MRP of labor equals the price of labor and the MRP of capital equals the price of capital—that is, when

$$\frac{\text{MRP of labor}}{\text{Price of labor}} = \frac{\text{MRP of capital}}{\text{Price of capital}} = 1$$

13. The marginal productivity theory of income distribution holds that all resources are paid according to their marginal contribution to output. Critics say that such an income distribution is too unequal and that real-world market imperfections result in pay above and below marginal contributions to output.

Terms and Concepts

derived demand

marginal product (MP)

marginal revenue product (MRP)

marginal resource cost (MRC)

MRP = MRC rule

substitution effect

output effect

elasticity of resource demand

least-cost combination of resources

profit-maximizing combination of resources

marginal productivity theory of income distribution

Questions

1. What is the significance of resource pricing? Explain how the factors determining resource demand differ from those determining product demand. Explain the meaning and significance of the fact that the demand for a resource is a derived demand. Why do resource demand curves slope downward? LO1

2. At the bottom of the page, complete the labor demand table for a firm that is hiring labor competitively and selling its product in a competitive market. LO2
   a. How many workers will the firm hire if the market wage rate is $27.95? $19.95? Explain why the firm will not hire a larger or smaller number of units of labor at each of these wage rates.
   b. Show in schedule form and graphically the labor demand curve of this firm.
   c. Now again determine the firm's demand curve for labor, assuming that it is selling in an imperfectly competitive market and that, although it can sell 17 units at $2.20 per unit, it must lower product price by 5 cents in order to sell the marginal product of each successive labor unit. Compare this demand curve with that derived in question 2b. Which curve is more elastic? Explain.

3. In 2009 General Motors (GM) announced that it would reduce employment by 21,000 workers. What does this decision reveal about how GM viewed its marginal revenue product (MRP) and marginal resource cost (MRC)? Why didn't GM reduce employment by more than 21,000 workers? By fewer than 21,000 workers? LO3

4. What factors determine the elasticity of resource demand? What effect will each of the following have on the elasticity or the location of the demand for resource C, which is being used to produce commodity X? Where there is any uncertainty as to the outcome, specify the causes of that uncertainty. LO4
   a. An increase in the demand for product X.
   b. An increase in the price of substitute resource D.
   c. An increase in the number of resources substitutable for C in producing X.
   d. A technological improvement in the capital equipment with which resource C is combined.
   e. A fall in the price of complementary resource E.
   f. A decline in the elasticity of demand for product X due to a decline in the competitiveness of product market X.

5. Suppose the productivity of capital and labor are as shown in the table on the next page. The output of these resources sells in a purely competitive market for $1 per unit. Both capital and labor are hired under purely competitive conditions at $3 and $1, respectively. LO5
   a. What is the least-cost combination of labor and capital the firm should employ in producing 80 units of output? Explain.
   b. What is the profit-maximizing combination of labor and capital the firm should use? Explain. What is the resulting level of output? What is the economic profit? Is this the least costly way of producing the profit-maximizing output?

Units of Labor	Total Product	Marginal Product	Product Price	Total Revenue	Marginal Revenue Product
0	0	_____	$2	$_____	$_____
1	17	_____	2	_____	_____
2	31	_____	2	_____	_____
3	43	_____	2	_____	_____
4	53	_____	2	_____	_____
5	60	_____	2	_____	_____
6	65	_____	2	_____	_____

Units of Capital	MP of Capital	Units of Labor	MP of Labor
0		0	
1	24	1	11
2	21	2	9
3	18	3	8
4	15	4	7
5	9	5	6
6	6	6	4
7	3	7	1
8	1	8	$\frac{1}{2}$

6. In each of the following four cases, MRP_L and MRP_C refer to the marginal revenue products of labor and capital, respectively, and P_L and P_C refer to their prices. Indicate in each case whether the conditions are consistent with maximum profits for the firm. If not, state which resource(s) should be used in larger amounts and which resource(s) should be used in smaller amounts. LO5
   a. $MRP_L = \$8$; $P_L = \$4$; $MRP_C = \$8$; $P_C = \$4$
   b. $MRP_L = \$10$; $P_L = \$12$; $MRP_C = \$14$; $P_C = \$9$
   c. $MRP_L = \$6$; $P_L = \$6$; $MRP_C = \$12$; $P_C = \$12$
   d. $MRP_L = \$22$; $P_L = \$26$; $MRP_C = \$16$; $P_C = \$19$

7. Florida citrus growers say that the recent crackdown on illegal immigration is increasing the market wage rates necessary to get their oranges picked. Some are turning to $100,000 to $300,000 mechanical harvesters known as "trunk, shake, and catch" pickers, which vigorously shake oranges from the trees. If widely adopted, what will be the effect on the demand for human orange pickers? What does that imply about the relative strengths of the substitution and output effects? LO5

8. **LAST WORD** Explain the economics of the substitution of ATMs for human tellers. Some banks are beginning to assess transaction fees when customers use human tellers rather than ATMs. What are these banks trying to accomplish?

Problems

1. A delivery company is considering adding another vehicle to its delivery fleet, all the vehicles of which are rented for $100 per day. Assume that the additional vehicle would be capable of delivering 1500 packages per day and that each package that is delivered brings in ten cents ($.10) in revenue. Also assume that adding the delivery vehicle would not affect any other costs. LO2
   a. What is the MRP? What is the MRC? Should the firm add this delivery vehicle?
   b. Now suppose that the cost of renting a vehicle doubles to $200 per day. What are the MRP and MRC? Should the firm add a delivery vehicle under these circumstances?
   c. Next suppose that the cost of renting a vehicle falls back down to $100 per day but, due to extremely congested freeways, an additional vehicle would only be able to deliver 750 packages per day. What are the MRP and MRC in this situation? Would adding a vehicle under these circumstances increase the firm's profits?

2. Suppose that marginal product tripled while product price fell by one-half in Table 12.1. What would be the new MRP values in Table 12.1? What would be the net impact on the location of the resource demand curve in Figure 12.1? LO2

3. Suppose that a monopoly firm finds that its MR is $50 for the first unit sold each day, $49 for the second unit sold each day, $48 for the third unit sold each day, and so on. Further suppose that the first worker hired produces 5 units per day, the second 4 units per day, the third 3 units per day, and so on. LO3
   a. What is the firm's MRP for each of the first five workers?
   b. Suppose that the monopolist is subjected to rate regulation and the regulator stipulates that it must charge

exactly $40 per unit for all units sold. At that price, what is the firm's MRP for each of the first five workers?
   c. If the daily wage paid to workers is $170 per day, how many workers will the unregulated monopoly demand? How many will the regulated monopoly demand? Looking at those figures, will the regulated or the unregulated monopoly demand more workers at that wage?
   d. If the daily wage paid to workers falls to $77 per day, how many workers will the unregulated monopoly demand? How many will the regulated monopoly demand? Looking at those figures, will the regulated or the unregulated monopoly demand more workers at that wage?
   e. Comparing your answers to parts c and d, does regulating a monopoly's output price *always* increase its demand for resources?

4. Consider a small landscaping company run by Mr. Viemeister. He is considering increasing his firm's capacity. If he adds one more worker, the firm's total monthly revenue will increase from $50,000 to $58,000. If he adds one more tractor, monthly revenue will increase from $50,000 to $62,000. Additional workers each cost $4000 per month, while an additional tractor would also cost $4000 per month. LO5
   a. What is the marginal product of labor? The marginal product of capital?
   b. What is the ratio of the marginal product of labor to the price of labor (MP_L/P_L)? What is the ratio of the marginal product of capital to the price of capital (MP_K/P_K)?
   c. Is the firm using the least-costly combination of inputs?
   d. Does adding an additional worker or adding an additional tractor yield a larger increase in total revenue for each dollar spent?

FURTHER TEST YOUR KNOWLEDGE AT
www.mcconnell19e.com

At the text's Online Learning Center (OLC), **www.mcconnell19e.com**, you will find one or more Web-based questions that require information from the Internet to answer. We urge you to check them out; they will familiarize you with Web sites that may be helpful in other courses and perhaps even in your career. The OLC also features multiple-choice questions that give instant feedback and provides other helpful ways to further test your knowledge of the chapter.

CHAPTER 12

The Demand for Resources

This chapter is the first of three that examine the market for economic resources such as labor, capital, land, and natural resources. In resource markets the demanders are the employers of the resources and the suppliers are the owners of the resources. As you already know, the demand for and the supply of a resource will determine the resource price and the quantities in a competitive market.

Chapter 12 focuses on the demand or employer side of the resource market. It offers a general explanation of what determines demand for any resource. Chapters 13 and 14 discuss the characteristics of the market for particular resources—labor, capital, land, or entrepreneurial ability—and present the supply side of the resource market.

The **resource market is important** for several reasons, as you will learn in the first section of the chapter. Resource prices determine what resource owners (or households) receive in exchange for supplying their resources, and thus they determine the incomes of households. Prices allocate resources to their most efficient uses and encourage the least costly methods of production in our economy. Many public policy issues also involve resource pricing, such as setting a minimum wage.

The next section of the chapter focuses on the **marginal productivity theory of resource demand.** When a firm wishes to maximize its profits, it produces that output at which marginal revenue and marginal cost are equal. But how much of each resource does the firm hire if it wishes to maximize its profits? You will learn that the firm hires that amount of each resource up to the point that the marginal revenue product and the marginal resource cost of that resource are equal (MRP = MRC).

There is another similarity between the output and the resource markets for the firm. Recall that the competitive firm's supply curve is a portion of its marginal-cost curve. The purely competitive firm's demand curve for a resource is a portion of its marginal-revenue-product curve. Just as cost is the important determinant of supply, the revenue derived from the use of a resource is the important factor determining the demand for that resource in a competitive market for resources.

The next major section of the chapter presents the **determinants of resource demand.** Three major ones are discussed—changes in product demand, productivity, and the prices of other resources. The last one is the most complicated because you must consider whether the other resources are substitutes or complements and also the underlying factors affecting them.

This chapter has a section on the **elasticity of resource demand,** which is no different from the elasticity

concept you learned about in Chapter 6. In this case, it is the relation of the percentage change in quantity demanded of the resource to a percentage change in the price of the resource. As you will discover, three factors that affect elasticity are the availability of other substitute resources, the elasticity of product demand, and the ratio of resource cost to total cost.

Most of the chapter examines the situation in which there is only one variable resource. The next-to-last section of the chapter, however, offers a general perspective on the **combination of resources** the firm will choose to use when multiple inputs are used and all inputs are variable. Two rules are presented. The least-cost rule states that the firm will minimize costs when the last dollar spent on each resource results in the same marginal product. The profit-maximizing rule means that in a competitive market the firm will maximize its profits when each resource is used so that its marginal product is equal to its price. The second rule is equally important because a firm that employs the quantity of resources that maximizes its profits also produces the output that maximizes its profits and is thus producing at the least cost.

The marginal productivity theory of resource demand is not without criticism, as you will learn in the last section of the chapter. If resource prices reflect marginal productivity, then this relationship can produce income inequality in society. In addition, market imperfection may skew the distribution of income.

■ CHECKLIST

When you have studied this chapter you should be able to

☐ Present four reasons for studying resource pricing.
☐ Explain why the demand for an economic resource is a derived demand.
☐ Define the marginal revenue product and relate it to the productivity and price of a resource.
☐ Determine the marginal-revenue-product schedule of a resource for a product sold in a purely competitive market, when given the data.
☐ Define the marginal resource cost.
☐ State the rule used by a profit-maximizing firm to determine how much of a resource it will employ.
☐ Apply the MRP = MRC rule to determine the quantity of a resource a firm will hire, when you are given the necessary data.
☐ Explain why the marginal-revenue-product schedule of a resource is the firm's demand for the resource.

☐ Find the marginal-revenue-product schedule of a resource for a product sold in an imperfectly competitive market, when given the data.

☐ Derive the market demand for a resource.

☐ List the three factors which would change a firm's demand for a resource.

☐ Predict the effect on resource demand of an increase or decrease in one of its three determinants.

☐ Give trends on the occupations with the fastest growth in jobs both in percentage terms and in absolute numbers.

☐ State three determinants of the price elasticity of resource demand.

☐ Describe how a change in each determinant would change the price elasticity of demand for a resource.

☐ State the rule used by a firm for determining the least-cost combination of resources.

☐ Use the least-cost rule to find the least-cost combination of resources for production, when given data.

☐ State the rule used by a profit-maximizing firm to determine the quantity of each of several resources to employ.

☐ Apply the profit-maximizing rule to determine the quantity of each resource a firm will hire, when given the data.

☐ Explain the marginal productivity theory of income distribution.

☐ Give two criticisms of the marginal productivity theory of income distribution.

☐ Explain using the least-cost rule why ATMs have replaced tellers (*Last Word*).

■ **CHAPTER OUTLINE**

1. The study of what determines the prices of resources *is important* because resource prices influence the size of individual incomes and the resulting distribution of income. They allocate scarce resources and affect the way in which firms combine resources in production. Resource pricing also raises policy and ethical issues about income distribution.

2. The marginal productivity theory of resource demand assumes that the firm is a "price taker" or "wage taker" in the resource market.

   a. The demand for a single resource is a **derived demand** that depends on the demand for the goods and services it can produce.

   b. Because resource demand is a derived demand, it depends on two factors: the marginal productivity of the resource and the market price of the good or service it is used to produce.

   (1) **Marginal revenue product (MRP)** is the change in total revenue divided by a one-unit change in resource quantity.

   (2) It combines two factors—the **marginal product** (the additional output from each additional unit of resource) of a resource and the market price of the product it produces—into a single useful tool.

   c. **Marginal resource cost (MRC)** is the change in total resource cost divided by a one-unit change in resource quantity. A firm will hire resources until the marginal revenue product of the resource is equal to its marginal resource cost (**MRP = MRC**).

   d. The firm's marginal-revenue-product schedule for a resource is that firm's demand schedule for the resource.

   e. If a firm sells its output in an **imperfectly competitive product market,** the more the firm sells, the lower the price of the product becomes. This causes the firm's marginal-revenue-product (resource demand) schedule to be less elastic than it would be if the firm sold its output in a purely competitive market.

   f. The market (or total) demand for a resource is the horizontal summation of the demand schedules of all firms using the resource.

3. The **determinants of resource demand** are changes in the demand for the product produced, changes in the productivity of the resource, and changes in the prices of other resources.

   a. A change in the demand for a product produced by a resource will change the demand of a firm for labor in the same direction.

   b. A change in the productivity of a resource will change the demand of a firm for the resource in the same direction.

   c. A change in the price of a

   (1) *substitute resource* will change the demand for a resource in the same direction if the **substitution effect** outweighs the **output effect** and in the opposite direction if the output effect outweighs the substitution effect

   (2) *complementary resource* will change the demand for a resource in the opposite direction

   d. Changes in the demand for labor have significant effects on employment growth in occupations, both in percentage and absolute terms. Projections (2008–2018) are reported for the fastest growing occupations (e.g., biomedical engineers; network systems and data communication analysts; home health aides) and the most rapidly declining occupations (e.g., textile machine operators; sewing machine operators; postal service workers; lathe operators).

4. The price **elasticity of resource demand** measures the sensitivity of resource quantity to changes in resource prices.

   a. Three factors affect the price elasticity of resource demand:

   (1) the ease of substitution of other resources: the greater the substitutability of other resources, the more elastic the resource demand

   (2) the elasticity of the demand for the product that the resource produces: the more elastic the product demand, the more elastic the resource demand

   (3) the ratio of labor cost to total cost: the greater the ratio of labor cost to total cost, the greater the price elasticity of demand for labor.

5. Firms often employ more than one resource in producing a product.

   a. The firm employing resources in purely competitive markets is hiring resources in the **least-cost combination of resources** when the ratio of the marginal product of a resource to its price is the same for all the resources the firm hires.

b. The firm is hiring resources in the *profit-maximizing combination of resources* if it hires resources in a purely competitive market when the marginal revenue product of each resource is equal to the price of that resource.

c. A numerical example illustrates the least-cost and profit-maximizing rules for a firm that employs resources in purely competitive markets.

6. The *marginal productivity theory of income distribution* seems to result in an equitable distribution of income because each unit of a resource receives a payment equal to its marginal contribution to the firm's revenue. The theory has at least two serious faults.

a. The distribution of income will be unequal because resources are unequally distributed among individuals in the economy.

b. The income of those who supply resources will not be based on their marginal productivities if there is monopsony or monopoly in the resource markets of the economy.

7. (*Last Word*). ATMs have eliminated many human teller positions over the past few decades as explained by the resource theory presented in this chapter. The least-cost combination of resources rule implies that firms will change inputs in response to technological change or changes in input prices. If the marginal product of an ATM divided by its price is greater than the marginal product of a human teller divided by its price, then more ATMs will be used in the banking sector.

■ **HINTS AND TIPS**

1. The list of important terms for Chapter 12 is relatively short, but included in the list are two very important concepts—**marginal revenue product** and **marginal resource cost**—which you must grasp if you are to understand how much of a resource a firm will hire. These two concepts are similar to, but not identical with, the marginal-revenue and marginal-cost concepts used in the study of product markets and in the explanation of the quantity of output a firm will produce.

2. Marginal revenue and marginal cost are, respectively, the change in the firm's total revenue and the change in the firm's total cost when it produces and sells an additional unit of *output*. Marginal revenue product and marginal resource cost are, respectively, the change in the firm's total revenue and the change in the firm's total cost when it hires an additional unit of *input*. Note that the two new concepts deal with changes in revenue and costs as a consequence of hiring more of a *resource*.

3. The marginal revenue product (MRP) of a resource is simply the marginal product of the resource (MP) times the price of the product that the resource produces (*P*), or MRP = MP × *P*. Under pure competition, MP changes, but *P* is constant as more resources are added to production. Under imperfect competition, both MP and *P* change as more resources are added, and thus each variable (MP and *P*) affects MRP. Compare the data in Tables 12.1 and 12.2 in the textbook to see this difference.

4. Make sure you understand the rule **MRP = MRC.** A firm will hire one more unit of a resource only so long as the resource adds more to the firm's revenues than it does to its costs. If MRP > MRC, the firm will hire more resources. If MRP < MRC, the firm will cut back on resource use.

5. It can be difficult to figure out what effect a change in the price of a substitute resource (capital) will have on the demand for another resource (labor). It is easy to understand why the demand for labor might decrease if the price of capital decreases because cheaper capital would be substituted for labor. It is harder to explain why the opposite might be true. That insight requires an understanding of both the **substitution effect** and the **output effect.** Find out how one effect may offset the other.

6. The **profit-maximizing rule** for a combination of resources may seem difficult, but it is relatively simple. Just remember that the price of any resource must be equal to its marginal revenue product, and thus *the ratio must always equal 1.*

■ **IIMPORTANT TERMS**

derived demand

marginal product

marginal revenue product (MRP)

marginal resource cost (MRC)

MRP = MRC rule

substitution effect

output effect

elasticity of resource demand

least-cost combination of resources

profit-maximizing combination of resources

marginal productivity theory of income distribution

SELF-TEST

■ **FILL-IN QUESTIONS**

1. Resource prices allocate (revenues, resources) _____ and are one factor that determines household (incomes, costs) _____ and business _____.

2. The demand for a resource is a (constant, derived) _____ demand that depends on the (productivity, cost) of the resource and the (cost, price) _____ of the product made from the resource.

3. A firm will find it profitable to hire units of a resource up to the quantity at which the marginal revenue (cost, product) _____ equals the marginal resource _____.

4. If the firm hires the resource in a purely competitive market, the marginal resource (cost, product) _____ will be (greater than, less than, equal to) _____ the price of the resource.

5. A firm's demand schedule for a resource is the firm's marginal revenue (cost, product) _____ schedule for that resource because both indicate the quantities of the resource the firm will employ at various resource (costs, prices) _____.

6. A producer in an imperfectly competitive market finds that the more of a resource it employs, the (higher, lower) _____ becomes the price at which it can sell its product. As a consequence, the (supply, demand) _____ schedule for the resource is (more, less) _____ elastic than it would be if the output were sold in a purely competitive market.

7. Adding the quantity demanded for the resource at each and every price for each firm using the resource gives the market (supply, demand) _____ curve for the resource.

8. The demand for a resource will change if the (demand, supply) _____ of the product the resource produces changes, if the (productivity, price) _____ of the resource changes, or if the (price, elasticity) _____ of other resources change.

9. If the demand for a product increases, then the demand for the resource that produces that product will (increase, decrease) _____. Conversely, if the demand for a product decreases, then the demand for the resource that produces that product will _____.

10. When the productivity of a resource falls, the demand for the resource (rises, falls) _____, but when the productivity of a resource rises, the demand for the resource _____.

11. The output of the firm being constant, a decrease in the price of resource A will induce the firm to hire (more, less) _____ of resource A and _____ of other resources; this is called the (substitution, output) _____ effect. But if the decrease in the price of A results in lower total costs and an increase in output, the firm may hire (more, less) _____ of both resources; this is called the (substitution, output) _____ effect.

12. A decrease in the price of a complementary resource will cause the demand for labor to (increase, decrease) _____, but an increase in the price of a complementary resource will cause the demand for labor to _____.

13. The three determinants of the price elasticity of demand for a resource are the ease with which other resources can be (substitutes, complements) _____ for it, the price elasticity of (supply, demand) _____ for the product the resource produces, and the ratio of resource (demand, cost) _____ to total (demand, cost) _____.

14. If the marginal product of labor declines slowly when added to a fixed stock of capital, the demand curve for labor (MRP) will decline (rapidly, slowly) _____ and will tend to be highly (elastic, inelastic) _____.

15. The greater the substitutability of other resources for a resource, the (greater, less) _____ will be the elasticity of demand for a resource.

16. Suppose a firm employs resources in purely competitive markets. If the firm wishes to produce any given amount of its output in the least costly way, the ratio of the marginal (cost, product) _____ of each resource to its (demand, price) _____ must be the same for all resources.

17. A firm that hires resources in purely competitive markets is employing the combination of resources that will result in maximum profits for the firm when the marginal (revenue product, resource cost) _____ of every resource is equal to its (demand, price) _____.

18. If the marginal revenue product of a resource is equal to the price of that resource, the marginal revenue product divided by its price is equal to (1, infinity) _____.

19. In the marginal productivity theory, the distribution of income is an equitable one because each unit of each resource is paid an amount equal to its (total, marginal) _____ contribution to the firm's (revenues, costs) _____.

20. The marginal productivity theory rests on the assumption of (competitive, imperfect) _____ markets. In the real world, there are many labor markets with imperfections because of employer pricing or monopoly power, so wage rates and other resource prices (do, do not) _____ perfectly measure contributions to domestic output.

■ **TRUE–FALSE QUESTIONS**

Circle T if the statement is true, F if it is false.

1. In the resource markets of the economy, resources are demanded by business firms and supplied by households.　　　　T　F

2. The prices of resources are an important factor in the determination of resource allocation.　　T　F

3. The demand for a resource is a derived demand based on the demand for the product it produces.　T　F

4. A resource that is highly productive will always be in great demand. **T F**

5. A firm's demand schedule for a resource is the firm's marginal-revenue-product schedule for the resource. **T F**

6. It will be profitable for a firm to hire additional units of labor resources up to the point where the marginal revenue product of labor is equal to its marginal resource cost. **T F**

7. A firm with one worker can produce 30 units of a product that sells for $4 a unit, but the same firm with two workers can produce 70 units of that product. The marginal revenue product of the second worker is $400. **T F**

8. The competitive firm's marginal revenue product of labor will fall as output expands because marginal product diminishes and product price falls. **T F**

9. A producer's demand schedule for a resource will be more elastic if the firm sells its product in a purely competitive market than it would be if it sold the product in an imperfectly competitive market. **T F**

10. The market demand for a particular resource is the sum of the individual demands of all firms that employ that resource. **T F**

11. An increase in the price of a resource will cause the demand for the resource to decrease. **T F**

12. The demand curve for labor will increase when the demand for (and price of) the product produced by that labor increases. **T F**

13. There is an inverse relationship between the productivity of labor and the demand for labor. **T F**

14. The demand for a resource will be increased with improvements in its quality. **T F**

15. When two resources are substitutes for each other, both the substitution effect and the output effect of a decrease in the price of one of these resources operate to increase the quantity of the other resource employed by the firm. **T F**

16. The output effect of an increase in the price of a resource increases the quantity demanded of that resource. **T F**

17. If two resources are complementary, an increase in the price of one will reduce the demand for the other. **T F**

18. Price declines for computer equipment have had stronger output effects than substitution effects, increasing the demand for computer software engineers and specialists. **T F**

19. The greater the substitutability of other resources, the less will be the elasticity of demand for a particular resource. **T F**

20. The greater the elasticity of product demand, the greater the elasticity of resource demand. **T F**

21. The demand for labor will be less elastic when labor is a smaller proportion of the total cost of producing a product. **T F**

Use the following information as the basis for answering Questions 22 and 23. The marginal revenue product and price of resource A are $12 and a constant $2, respectively, and the marginal revenue product and price of resource B are $25 and a constant $5, respectively. The firm sells its product at a constant price of $1.

22. The firm should decrease the amount of A and increase the amount of B it employs if it wishes to decrease its total cost without affecting its total output. **T F**

23. If the firm wishes to maximize its profits, it should increase its employment of both A and B until their marginal revenue products fall to $2 and $5, respectively. **T F**

24. The marginal productivity theory of income distribution results in an equitable distribution if resource markets are competitive. **T F**

25. The marginal productivity theory rests on the assumption of imperfectly competitive markets. **T F**

■ **MULTIPLE-CHOICE QUESTIONS**

Circle the letter that corresponds to the best answer.

1. The prices paid for resources affect
 (a) the money incomes of households in the economy
 (b) the allocation of resources among different firms and industries in the economy
 (c) the quantities of different resources employed to produce a particular product
 (d) all of the above

2. In a competitive resource market, the firm employing a resource such as labor is a
 (a) price maker
 (b) cost maker
 (c) wage taker
 (d) revenue taker

3. The demand for a resource is *derived* from the
 (a) demand for the products it helps produce
 (b) price of the resource
 (c) supply of the resource
 (d) income of the firm selling the resource

4. The law of diminishing returns explains why
 (a) the MRP of an input in a purely competitive market decreases as a firm increases the quantity of an employed resource
 (b) the MRC of an input in a purely competitive market decreases as a firm increases the quantity of an employed resource
 (c) resource demand is a derived demand
 (d) there are substitution and output effects for resources

Answer Questions 5, 6, and 7 on the basis of the information in the following table for a purely competitive market.

Number of workers	Total product	Product price ($)
0	0	4
1	16	4
2	26	4
3	34	4
4	40	4
5	44	4

5. At a wage rate of $15, the firm will choose to employ
(a) 2 workers
(b) 3 workers
(c) 4 workers
(d) 5 workers

6. At a wage rate of $30, the firm will choose to employ
(a) 2 workers
(b) 3 workers
(c) 4 workers
(d) 5 workers

7. If the product price increases to a constant $8, then at a wage rate of $30, the firm will choose to employ
(a) 2 workers
(b) 3 workers
(c) 4 workers
(d) 5 workers

Use the following total-product and marginal-product schedules for a resource to answer Questions 8, 9, 10, and 11. Assume that the quantities of other resources the firm employs remain constant.

Units of resource	Total product	Marginal product
0	0	—
1	8	8
2	14	6
3	18	4
4	21	3
5	23	2

8. If the product the firm produces sells for a constant $3 per unit, the marginal revenue product of the fourth unit of the resource is
(a) $3
(b) $6
(c) $9
(d) $12

9. If the firm's product sells for a constant $3 per unit and the price of the resource is a constant $15, the firm will employ how many units of the resource?
(a) 2
(b) 3
(c) 4
(d) 5

10. If the firm can sell 14 units of output at a price of $1 per unit and 18 units of output at a price of $0.90 per unit,

the marginal revenue product of the third unit of the resource would be
(a) $4
(b) $3.60
(c) $2.20
(d) $0.40

11. If the firm can sell 8 units at a price of $1.50, 14 units at a price of $1.00, 18 units at a price of $0.90, 21 units at a price of $0.70, and 23 units at a price of $0.50, then the firm is
(a) maximizing profits at a product price of $0.50
(b) minimizing its costs at a product price of $1.00
(c) selling in an imperfectly competitive market
(d) selling in a purely competitive market

12. As a firm that sells its product in an imperfectly competitive market increases the quantity of a resource it employs, the marginal revenue product of that resource falls because
(a) the price paid by the firm for the resource falls
(b) the marginal product of the resource falls
(c) the price at which the firm sells its product falls
(d) both the marginal product and the price at which the firm sells its product fall

13. Which would increase a firm's demand for a particular resource?
(a) an increase in the prices of complementary resources used by the firm
(b) a decrease in the demand for the firm's product
(c) an increase in the productivity of the resource
(d) an increase in the price of the particular resource

14. The substitution effect indicates that a firm will use
(a) more of an input whose relative price has decreased
(b) more of an input whose relative price has increased
(c) less of an input whose relative price has decreased
(d) less of an input whose relative price has remained constant

15. Suppose resource A and resource B are substitutes and the price of A increases. If the output effect is greater than the substitution effect,
(a) the quantity of A employed by the firm will increase and the quantity of B employed will decrease
(b) the quantities of both A and B employed by the firm will decrease
(c) the quantities of both A and B employed by the firm will increase
(d) the quantity of A employed will decrease and the quantity of B employed will increase

16. Two resource inputs, capital and labor, are complementary and used in fixed proportions. A decrease in the price of capital will
(a) increase the demand for labor
(b) decrease the demand for labor
(c) decrease the quantity demanded for labor
(d) have no effect because the relationship is fixed

17. Which would result in an increase in the elasticity of demand for a particular resource?
(a) an increase in the demand for the resource
(b) a decrease in the elasticity of demand for the product that the resource helps to produce
(c) an increase in the percentage of the firm's total costs accounted for by the resource
(d) a decrease in the ease of resource substitutability for the particular resource

18. The demand for labor would most likely become more inelastic as a result of
(a) an increase in the elasticity of the demand for the product that the labor produces
(b) an increase in the time for employers to make technological changes or purchase new equipment
(c) a decrease in the proportion of labor costs to total costs
(d) a decrease in the demand for the product

19. A firm is allocating its expenditures for resources in a way that will result in the least total cost of producing any given output when the
(a) amount the firm spends on each resource is the same
(b) marginal revenue product of each resource is the same
(c) marginal product of each resource is the same
(d) marginal product per dollar spent on the last unit of each resource is the same

20. A business is employing inputs such that the marginal product of labor is 20 and the marginal product of capital is 45. The price of labor is $10 and the price of capital is $15. If the business wants to minimize costs while keeping output constant, then it should
(a) use more labor and less capital
(b) use less labor and less capital
(c) use less labor and more capital
(d) make no change in resource use

21. Assume that a computer disk manufacturer is employing resources so that the MRP of the last unit hired for resource X is $240 and the MRP of the last unit hired for resource Y is $150. The price of resource X is $80 and the price of resource Y is $50. To maximize profit the firm should
(a) hire more of resource X and less of resource Y
(b) hire less of resource X and more of resource Y
(c) hire less of both resource X and resource Y
(d) hire more of both resource X and resource Y

22. Which does not suggest that a firm that hires resources in a purely competitive market is maximizing its profits?
(a) The marginal revenue product of every resource is equal to 1.
(b) The marginal revenue product of every resource is equal to its price.
(c) The ratio of the marginal revenue product of every resource to its price is equal to 1.
(d) The ratio of the price of every resource to its marginal revenue product is equal to 1.

23. Assume that a purely competitive firm uses two resources—labor (L) and capital (C)—to produce a product. In which situation would the firm be maximizing profit?

	MRP_L	MRP_C	P_L	P_C
(a)	10	20	30	40
(b)	10	20	10	20
(c)	15	15	10	10
(d)	30	40	10	5

24. In the marginal productivity theory of income distribution, when all markets are purely competitive, each unit of each resource receives a money payment equal to
(a) its marginal product
(b) its marginal revenue product
(c) the needs of the resource owner
(d) the payments received by each of the units of the other resources in the economy

25. A major criticism of the marginal productivity theory of income distribution is that
(a) the demand for labor resources is price elastic
(b) labor markets are often subject to imperfect competition
(c) the theory suggests that there will be equality in incomes
(d) purely competitive firms are only interested in profit maximization

■ **PROBLEMS**

1. The table below shows the total production a firm will be able to obtain if it employs varying amounts of resource **A** while the amounts of the other resources the firm employs remain constant.

Quantity of resource A employed	Total product	Marginal product of A	Total revenue	Marginal revenue product of A
0	0		$____	
1	12	____	____	$____
2	22	____	____	____
3	30	____	____	____
4	36	____	____	____
5	40	____	____	____
6	42	____	____	____
7	43	____	____	____

a. Compute the marginal product of each of the seven units of resource **A** and enter these figures in the table.

b. Assume the product the firm produces sells in the market for $1.50 per unit. Compute the total revenue of the firm at each of the eight levels of output and the marginal revenue product of each of the seven units of resource **A**. Enter these figures in the table below.

c. On the basis of your computations, complete the firm's demand schedule for resource **A** by indicating in the following table how many units of resource **A** the firm would employ at the given prices.

Price of A	Quantity of A demanded
$21.00	_____
18.00	_____
15.00	_____
12.00	_____
9.00	_____
6.00	_____
3.00	_____
1.50	_____

2. In the table below are the marginal product data for resource **B**. Assume that the quantities of other resources employed by the firm remain constant.

a. Compute the total product (output) of the firm for each of the seven quantities of resource **B** employed and enter these figures in the table.

b. Assume that the firm sells its output in an imperfectly competitive market and that the prices at which it can sell its product are those given in the table. Compute and enter in the table:

(1) the total revenue for each of the seven quantities of **B** employed.

(2) the marginal revenue product of each of the seven units of resource **B**.

c. How many units of **B** would the firm employ if the market price of **B** were

(1) $25? _____

(2) $20? _____

(3) $15? _____

(4) $9? _____

(5) $5? _____

(6) $1? _____

3. Use the following total-product schedule as a resource to answer questions **a**, **b**, and **c**. Assume that the quantities of other resources the firm employs remain constant.

Units of resource	Total product
0	0
1	15
2	28
3	38
4	43
5	46

a. If the firm's product sells for a constant $2 per unit, what is the marginal revenue product of the second unit of the resource? _____

b. If the firm's product sells for a constant $2 and the price of the resource is $10, how many units of the resource will the firm employ? _____

c. If the firm can sell 15 units of output at a price of $2.00 and 28 units of output at a price of $1.50, what is the marginal revenue product of the second unit of the resource? _____

4. In the space to the right of each of the following changes, indicate whether the change would tend to increase (+) or decrease (−) a firm's demand for a particular resource.

a. An increase in the demand for the firm's product _____

b. A decrease in the price of the firm's output _____

c. An increase in the productivity of the resource _____

d. An increase in the price of a substitute resource when the output effect is greater than the substitution effect _____

e. A decrease in the price of a complementary resource _____

f. A decrease in the price of a substitute resource when the substitution effect is greater than the output effect _____

Quantity of resource B employed	Marginal product of B	Total product	Product price	Total revenue	Marginal revenue product of B
0	—	0		$0.00	—
1	22	_____	$1.00	_____	_____
2	21	_____	.90	_____	_____
3	19	_____	.80	_____	_____
4	16	_____	.70	_____	_____
5	12	_____	.60	_____	_____
6	7	_____	.50	_____	_____
7	1	_____	.40	_____	_____

Quantity of resource C employed	Marginal product of C	Marginal revenue product of C	Quantity of resource D employed	Marginal product of D	Marginal revenue product of D
1	10	$5.00	1	21	$10.50
2	8	4.00	2	18	9.00
3	6	3.00	3	15	7.50
4	5	2.50	4	12	6.00
5	4	2.00	5	9	4.50
6	3	1.50	6	6	3.00
7	2	1.00	7	3	1.50

5. The table above shows the marginal-product and marginal-revenue-product schedules for resource **C** and resource **D**. Both resources are variable and are employed in purely competitive markets. The price of **C** is $2 and the price of **D** is $3. (Assume that the productivity of each resource is independent of the quantity of the other.)

    a. The least-cost combination of **C** and **D** that would enable the firm to produce

    (1) units of its product is _____ **C** and _____ **D**.

    (2) 99 units of its product is _____ **C** and _____ **D**.

    b. The profit-maximizing combination of **C** and **D** is

    _____ **C** and _____ **D**.

    c. When the firm employs the profit-maximizing combination of **C** and **D**, it is also employing **C** and **D** in

    the least-cost combination because _____

    equals _____.

    d. Examination of the figures in the table reveals that

    the firm sells its product in a _____ com-

    petitive market at a price of $_____.

    e. Employing the profit-maximizing combination of **C** and **D**, the firm's

    (1) total output is _____.

    (2) total revenue is $_____.

    (3) total cost is $_____.

    (4) total profit is $_____.

■ **SHORT ANSWER AND ESSAY QUESTIONS**

1. Give four reasons why it is important to study resource pricing.

2. How does the demand for a product differ from the demand for a resource? Explain why the demand for a resource is a derived demand.

3. What two factors determine the strength of the demand for a resource?

4. Explain why firms that wish to maximize their profits follow the MRP = MRC rule.

5. What effects do marginal product and marginal price have on a firm's resource demand curve under pure competition and under imperfect competition?

6. Why is the demand schedule for a resource less elastic when the firm sells its product in an imperfectly competitive market than when it sells it in a purely competitive market?

7. How do you derive the market demand for a resource?

8. Identify and describe three factors that will cause the demand for a resource to increase or decrease. Give examples of how each factor influences changes in demand.

9. What is the difference between the substitution effect and the output effect?

10. If the price of capital falls, what will happen to the demand for labor if capital and labor are substitutes in production? Describe what happens when the substitution effect outweighs the output effect and when the output effect outweighs the substitution effect. What can you conclude?

11. Why does a change in the price of a complementary resource cause the demand for labor to change in the opposite direction?

12. Describe trends in occupational employment data. Give examples of jobs with the greatest projected growth and decline.

13. What are the three factors that determine the elasticity of demand for a resource?

14. Use an example to explain what happens to elasticity when substitutability for a resource is greater rather than lesser.

15. How can the ratio of labor cost to the total cost influence how producers react to changes in the price of labor?

16. Assume that a firm employs resources in purely competitive markets. How does the firm know that it is spending money on resources in such a way that it can produce a given output for the least total cost?

17. Why is minimizing cost not sufficient for maximizing profit for a firm?

18. When is a firm that employs resources in purely competitive markets using these resources in amounts that will maximize the profits of the firm?

19. What is the marginal productivity theory of income distribution? What ethical proposition must be accepted if this distribution is to be fair and equitable?

20. What are the two major shortcomings of the marginal productivity theory of income distribution?

ANSWERS

Chapter 12 The Demand for Resources

FILL-IN QUESTIONS

1. resources, incomes, costs
2. derived, productivity, price
3. product, cost
4. cost, equal to
5. product, prices
6. lower, demand, less
7. demand
8. demand, productivity, price
9. increase, decrease
10. falls, rises
11. more, less, substitution, more, output
12. increase, decrease
13. substitutes, demand, cost, cost
14. slowly, elastic
15. greater
16. product, price
17. revenue product, price
18. 1
19. marginal, revenues
20. competitive, do not

TRUE–FALSE QUESTIONS

1. T, p. 248	**10.** T, pp. 252–253	**19.** F, pp. 256–257
2. T, p. 249	**11.** F, p. 253	**20.** T, pp. 256–257
3. T, p. 249	**12.** T, p. 253	**21.** T, pp. 256–257
4. F, pp. 249–250	**13.** F, pp. 253–254	**22.** F, pp. 259–260
5. T, p. 250	**14.** T, pp. 253–254	**23.** T, pp. 258–259
6. T, p. 250	**15.** F, p. 254	**24.** F, pp. 260–261
7. F, p. 250	**16.** F, p. 254	**25.** F, pp. 260–262
8. F, p. 250	**17.** T, pp. 254–255	
9. T, pp. 250–252	**18.** T, pp. 254–255	

MULTIPLE-CHOICE QUESTIONS

1. d, p. 249	**10.** c, pp. 250–251	**19.** d, p. 258
2. c, p. 249	**11.** c, pp. 250–251	**20.** c, pp. 259–260
3. a, p. 249	**12.** d, pp. 251–252	**21.** d, p. 260
4. a, pp. 249–250	**13.** c, pp. 253–254	**22.** a, p. 260
5. d, pp. 250–251	**14.** a, p. 254	**23.** b, pp. 259–260
6. b, pp. 250–251	**15.** b, p. 254	**24.** b, pp. 260–261
7. d, pp. 250–251	**16.** a, pp. 254–255	**25.** b, pp. 260–261
8. c, pp. 250–251	**17.** c, pp. 256–257	
9. a, pp. 250–251	**18.** c, pp. 256–257	

PROBLEMS

1. *a.* Marginal product of A: 12, 10, 8, 6, 4, 2, 1; *b.* Total revenue: 0, 18.00, 33.00, 45.00, 54.00, 60.00, 63.00, 64.50; Marginal revenue product of A: 18.00, 15.00, 12.00, 9.00, 6.00, 3.00, 1.50; *c.* 0, 1, 2, 3, 4, 5, 6, 7
2. *a.* Total product: 22, 43, 62, 78, 90, 97, 98; *b.* (1) Total revenue: 22.00, 38.70, 49.60, 54.60, 54.00, 48.50, 39.20, (2) Marginal revenue product of B: 22.00, 16.70, 10.90, 5.00, −0.60, −5.50, −9.30; *c.* (1) 0, (2) 1, (3) 2, (4) 3, (5) 4, (6) 4
3. *a.* $26. The second worker increases TP by 13 units (13 × $2 = $26); *b.* 4 units. The marginal product of the fourth resource is 5 units of output (5 × $2 = $10). Thus MRP = $10 and MRC = $10 when the fourth resource is employed; *c.* $12. The total revenue from 1 unit is $30.00 (15 × $2.00). The total revenue with 2 units is $42 (28 × $1.50). The difference is the MR of the second unit.
4. *a.* +; *b.* −; *c.* +; *d.* −; *e.* +; *f.* −
5. *a.* (1) 1, 3, (2) 3, 5; *b.* 5, 6; *c.* the marginal product of **C** divided by its price, the marginal product of **D** divided by its price; *d.* purely, $.50; *e.* (1) 114, (2) $57, (3) $28, (4) $29

SHORT ANSWER AND ESSAY QUESTIONS

1. p. 249	**8.** pp. 253–255	**15.** p. 257
2. p. 249	**9.** p. 254	**16.** p. 258
3. pp. 249–250	**10.** p. 254	**17.** p. 258
4. p. 250	**11.** pp. 254–255	**18.** pp. 258–260
5. pp. 250–252	**12.** pp. 255–256	**19.** pp. 260–262
6. pp. 251–252	**13.** pp. 256–257	**20.** pp. 260–262
7. pp. 252–253	**14.** p. 257	

13

1 Explain why labor productivity and real hourly compensation track so closely over time.

2 Show how wage rates and employment levels are determined in competitive labor markets.

3 Demonstrate how monopsony (a market with a single employer) can reduce wages below competitive levels.

4 Discuss how unions increase wage rates and how minimum wage laws affect labor markets.

5 List the major causes of wage differentials.

6 Identify the types, benefits, and costs of "pay-for-performance" plans.

7 (Appendix) Relate who belongs to U.S. unions, the basics of collective bargaining, and the economic effects of unions.

Wage Determination

Nearly 140 million Americans go to work each day. We work at an amazing variety of jobs for thousands of different firms and receive considerable differences in pay. What determines our hourly wage or annual salary? Why is the salary for, say, a topflight major-league baseball player $15 million or more a year, whereas the pay for a first-rate schoolteacher is $50,000? Why are starting salaries for college graduates who major in engineering and accounting so much higher than those for graduates majoring in journalism and sociology?

Having explored the major factors that underlie labor demand, we now bring *labor supply* into our analysis to help answer these questions. Generally speaking, labor supply and labor demand interact to determine the level of hourly wage rates or annual salaries in each occupation. Collectively, those wages and salaries make up about 70 percent of all income paid to American resource suppliers.

266

Labor, Wages, and Earnings

Economists use the term "labor" broadly to apply to (1) blue- and white-collar workers of all varieties; (2) professional people such as lawyers, physicians, dentists, and teachers; and (3) owners of small businesses, including barbers, plumbers, and a host of retailers who provide labor as they operate their own businesses.

Wages are the price that employers pay for labor. Wages not only take the form of direct money payments such as hourly pay, annual salaries, bonuses, commissions, and royalties but also fringe benefits such as paid vacations, health insurance, and pensions. Unless stated otherwise, we will use the term "wages" to mean all such payments and benefits converted to an hourly basis. That will remind us that the **wage rate** is the price paid per unit of labor services, in this case an hour of work. It will also let us distinguish between the wage rate and labor earnings, the latter determined by multiplying the number of hours worked by the hourly wage rate.

We must also distinguish between nominal wages and real wages. A **nominal wage** is the amount of money received per hour, day, or year. A **real wage** is the quantity of goods and services a worker can obtain with nominal wages; real wages reveal the "purchasing power" of nominal wages.

Your real wage depends on your nominal wage and the prices of the goods and services you purchase. Suppose you receive a 5 percent increase in your nominal wage during a certain year but in that same year the price level increases by 3 percent. Then your real wage has increased by 2 percent (= 5 percent − 3 percent). Unless otherwise indicated, we will assume that the overall level of prices remains constant. In other words, we will discuss only *real* wages.

General Level of Wages

Wages differ among nations, regions, occupations, and individuals. Wage rates are much higher in the United States than in China or India. They are slightly higher in the north and east of the United States than in the south. Plumbers are paid less than NFL punters. And one physician may earn twice as much as another physician for the same number of hours of work. The average wages earned by workers also differ by gender, race, and ethnic background.

The general, or average, level of wages, like the general level of prices, includes a wide range of different wage rates. It includes the wages of bakers, barbers, brick masons, and brain surgeons. By averaging such wages, we can more easily compare wages among regions and among nations.

As Global Perspective 13.1 suggests, the general level of real wages in the United States is relatively high—although clearly not the highest in the world.

GLOBAL PERSPECTIVE 13.1

Hourly Wages of Production Workers, Selected Nations

Wage differences are pronounced worldwide. The data shown here indicate that hourly compensation in the United States is not as high as in some European nations. It is important to note, however, that the prices of goods and services vary greatly among nations and the process of converting foreign wages into dollars may not accurately reflect such variations.

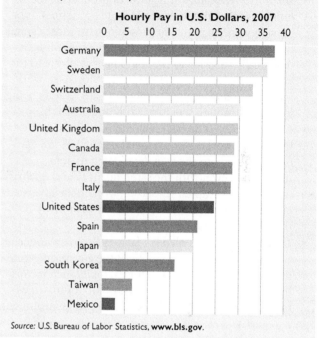

Hourly Pay in U.S. Dollars, 2007

Source: U.S. Bureau of Labor Statistics, **www.bls.gov**.

The simplest explanation for the high real wages in the United States and other industrially advanced economies (referred to hereafter as advanced economies) is that the demand for labor in those nations is relatively large compared to the supply of labor.

Role of Productivity

We know from the previous chapter that the demand for labor, or for any other resource, depends on its productivity. In general, the greater the productivity of labor, the greater is the demand for it. And if the total supply of labor is fixed, then the stronger the demand for labor, the higher is the average level of real wages. The demand for labor in the United States and the other major advanced economies is large because labor in those countries is highly productive. There are several reasons for that high productivity:

- *Plentiful capital* Workers in the advanced economies have access to large amounts of physical capital equipment (machinery and buildings). In the United States in 2008, $118,200 of physical capital was available, on average, for each worker.

- *Access to abundant natural resources* In advanced economies, natural resources tend to be abundant in relation to the size of the labor force. Some of those resources are available domestically and others are imported from abroad. The United States, for example, is richly endowed with arable land, mineral resources, and sources of energy for industry.

- *Advanced technology* The level of production technology is generally high in advanced economies. Not only do workers in these economies have more capital equipment to work with, but that equipment is technologically superior to the equipment available to the vast majority of workers worldwide. Moreover, work methods in the advanced economies are steadily being improved through scientific study and research.

- *Labor quality* The health, vigor, education, and training of workers in advanced economies are generally superior to those in developing nations. This means that, even with the same quantity and quality of natural and capital resources, workers in advanced economies tend to be more efficient than many of their foreign counterparts.

- *Other factors* Less obvious factors also may underlie the high productivity in some of the advanced economies. In the United States, for example, such factors include (a) the efficiency and flexibility of management; (b) a business, social, and political environment that emphasizes production and productivity; (c) the vast size of the domestic market, which enables firms to engage in mass production; and (d) the increased specialization of production enabled by free-trade agreements with other nations.

Real Wages and Productivity

Figure 13.1 shows the close long-run relationship in the United States between output per hour of work and real hourly compensation (= wages and salaries + employers' contributions to social insurance and private benefit plans). Because real income and real output are two ways of viewing the same thing, real income (compensation) per worker can increase only at about the same rate as output per worker. When workers produce more real output per hour, more real income is available to distribute to them for each hour worked.

In the actual economy, however, suppliers of land, capital, and entrepreneurial talent also share in the income from production. Real wages therefore do not always rise in lockstep with gains in productivity over short spans of time. But over long periods, productivity and real wages tend to rise together.

Long-Run Trend of Real Wages

Basic supply and demand analysis helps explain the long-term trend of real-wage growth in the United States. The nation's labor force has grown significantly over the decades. But, as a result of the productivity-increasing

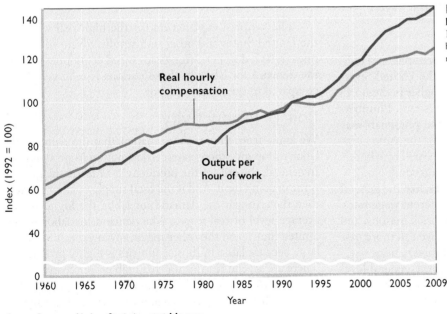

FIGURE 13.1 **Output per hour and real hourly compensation in the United States, 1960–2009.** Over long time periods, output per hour of work and real hourly compensation are closely related.

Source: Bureau of Labor Statistics, **stat.bls.gov**.

FIGURE 13.2 **The long-run trend of real wages in the United States.** The productivity of U.S. labor has increased substantially over the long run, causing the demand for labor *D* to shift rightward (that is, to increase) more rapidly than increases in the supply of labor *S*. The result has been increases in real wages.

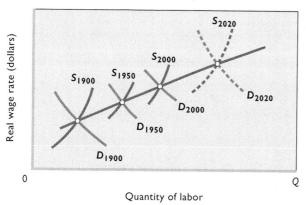

factors we have mentioned, increases in labor demand have outstripped increases in labor supply. Figure 13.2 shows several such increases in labor supply and labor demand. The result has been a long-run, or secular, increase in wage rates and employment. For example, real hourly compensation in the United States has roughly doubled since 1960. Over that same period, employment has increased by about 80 million workers.

A Purely Competitive Labor Market

Average levels of wages, however, disguise the great variation of wage rates among occupations and within occupations. What determines the wage rate paid for a specific type of labor? Demand and supply analysis again is revealing. Let's begin by examining labor demand and labor supply in a **purely competitive labor market.** In this type of market:

- Numerous firms compete with one another in hiring a specific type of labor.
- Each of many qualified workers with identical skills supplies that type of labor.
- Individual firms and individual workers are "wage takers" since neither can exert any control over the market wage rate.

Market Demand for Labor

Suppose 200 firms demand a particular type of labor, say, carpenters. These firms need not be in the same industry; industries are defined according to the products they produce and not the resources they employ. Thus, firms producing wood-framed furniture, wood windows and doors, houses and apartment buildings, and wood cabinets will demand carpenters. To find the total, or market, labor demand curve for a particular labor service, we sum horizontally the labor demand curves (the marginal revenue product curves) of the individual firms, as indicated in **Figure 13.3 (Key Graph).** The horizontal summing of the 200 labor demand curves like *d* in Figure 13.3b yields the market labor demand curve *D* in Figure 13.3a.

Market Supply of Labor

On the supply side of a purely competitive labor market, we assume that no union is present and that workers individually compete for available jobs. The supply curve for each type of labor slopes upward, indicating that employers as a group must pay higher wage rates to obtain more workers. They must do this to bid workers away from other industries, occupations, and localities. Within limits, workers have alternative job opportunities. For example, they may work in other industries in the same locality, or they may work in their present occupations in different cities or states, or they may work in other occupations.

Firms that want to hire these workers (here, carpenters) must pay higher wage rates to attract them away from the alternative job opportunities available to them. They must also pay higher wages to induce people who are not currently in the labor force—who are perhaps doing household activities or enjoying leisure—to seek employment. In short, assuming that wages are constant in other labor markets, higher wages in a particular labor market entice more workers to offer their labor services in that market—a fact expressed graphically by the upsloping market supply-of-labor curve *S* in Figure 13.3a.

Labor Market Equilibrium

The intersection of the market labor demand curve and the market labor supply curve determines the equilibrium wage rate and level of employment in a purely competitive labor market. In Figure 13.3a the equilibrium wage rate is W_c ($10) and the number of workers hired is Q_c (1000). To the individual firm the market wage rate W_c is given. Each of the many firms employs such a small fraction of the total available supply of this type of labor that no single firm can influence the wage rate. As shown by the horizontal line *s* in Figure 13.3b, the supply of labor faced by an individual firm is perfectly elastic. It can hire as many or as few workers as it wants to at the market wage rate.

Each individual firm will maximize its profits (or minimize its losses) by hiring this type of labor up to the point at which marginal revenue product is equal to marginal resource cost. This is merely an application of the MRP = MRC rule we developed in Chapter 12.

FIGURE 13.3 Labor supply and labor demand in (a) a purely competitive labor market and (b) a single competitive firm. In a purely competitive labor market (a), market labor supply S and market labor demand D determine the equilibrium wage rate W_c and the equilibrium number of workers Q_c. Each individual competitive firm (b) takes this competitive wage W_c as given. Thus, the individual firm's labor supply curve $s = \text{MRC}$ is perfectly elastic at the going wage W_c. Its labor demand curve, d, is its MRP curve (here labeled mrp). The firm maximizes its profit by hiring workers up to where MRP = MRC. Area $0abc$ represents both the firm's total revenue and its total cost. The green area is its total wage cost; the blue area is its nonlabor costs, including a normal profit—that is, the firm's payments to the suppliers of land, capital, and entrepreneurship.

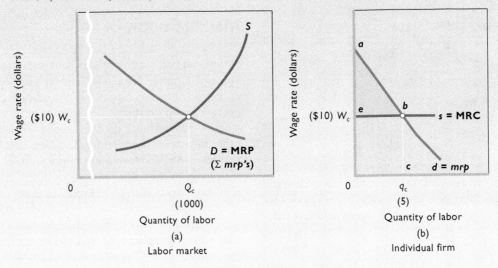

QUICK QUIZ FOR FIGURE 13.3

1. The supply-of-labor curve S slopes upward in graph (a) because:
   a. the law of diminishing marginal utility applies.
   b. the law of diminishing returns applies.
   c. workers can afford to "buy" more leisure when their wage rates rise.
   d. higher wages are needed to attract workers away from other labor markets, household activities, and leisure.

2. This firm's labor demand curve d in graph (b) slopes downward because:
   a. the law of diminishing marginal utility applies.
   b. the law of diminishing returns applies.
   c. the firm must lower its price to sell additional units of its product.
   d. the firm is a competitive employer, not a monopsonist.

3. In employing five workers, the firm represented in graph (b):
   a. has a total wage cost of $6000.
   b. is adhering to the general principle of undertaking all actions for which the marginal benefit exceeds the marginal cost.
   c. uses less labor than would be ideal from society's perspective.
   d. experiences increasing marginal returns.

4. A rightward shift of the labor supply curve in graph (a) would shift curve:
   a. $d = mrp$ leftward in graph (b).
   b. $d = mrp$ rightward in graph (b).
   c. $s = \text{MRC}$ upward in graph (b).
   d. $s = \text{MRC}$ downward in graph (b).

Answers: 1. d; 2. b; 3. b; 4. d

As Table 13.1 indicates, when an individual competitive firm faces the market price for a resource, the marginal cost of that resource (MRC) is constant and is equal to the market price for each and every unit that the competitive firm may choose to purchase. Note that MRC is constant at $10 and matches the $10 wage rate. Each additional worker hired adds precisely his or her own wage rate ($10 in this case) to the firm's total resource cost. So the firm in a purely competitive labor market maximizes its profit by hiring workers to the point at which its wage rate equals MRP. In Figure 13.3b this firm will hire q_c (5) workers, paying each worker the market wage rate W_c ($10). The other 199 firms (not shown) that are hiring workers in this labor market will also each employ 5 workers and pay $10 per hour.

To determine a firm's total revenue from employing a particular number of labor units, we sum the MRPs of those units. For example, if a firm employs 3 labor units with marginal revenue products of $14, $13, and $12, respectively, then the firm's total revenue is

TABLE 13.1 The Supply of Labor: Pure Competition in the Hire of Labor

(1) Units of Labor	(2) Wage Rate	(3) Total Labor Cost	(4) Marginal Resource (Labor) Cost
0	$10	$ 0	
1	10	10	$10
2	10	20	10
3	10	30	10
4	10	40	10
5	10	50	10
6	10	60	10

$39 (= $14 + $13 + $12). In Figure 13.3b, where we are not restricted to whole units of labor, total revenue is represented by area $0abc$ under the MRP curve to the left of q_c. And what area represents the firm's total cost, including a normal profit? Answer: For q_c units, the same area—$0abc$. The green rectangle represents the firm's total wage cost ($0q_c \times 0W_c$). The blue triangle (total revenue minus total wage cost) represents the firm's nonlabor costs—its explicit and implicit payments to land, capital, and entrepreneurship. Thus, in this case, total cost (wages plus other income payments) equals total revenue. This firm and others like it are earning only a normal profit. So Figure 13.3b represents a long-run equilibrium for a firm that is selling its product in a purely competitive product market and hiring its labor in a purely competitive labor market.

INTERACTIVE GRAPHS
G 13.1
Competitive labor market

Monopsony Model

In the purely competitive labor market described in the preceding section, each employer hires too small an amount of labor to influence the wage rate. Each firm can hire as little or as much labor as it needs, but only at the market wage rate, as reflected in its horizontal labor supply curve. The situation is quite different when the labor market is a **monopsony**, a market structure in which there is only a single buyer. A labor market monopsony has the following characteristics:

- There is only a single buyer of a particular type of labor.
- The workers providing this type of labor have few employment options other than working for the monopsony, because they are either geographically immobile or because finding alternative employment would mean having to acquire new skills.

- The firm is a "wage maker," because the wage rate it must pay varies directly with the number of workers it employs.

As is true of monopoly power, there are various degrees of monopsony power. In *pure* monopsony such power is at its maximum because only a single employer hires labor in the labor market. The best real-world examples are probably the labor markets in some towns that depend almost entirely on one major firm. For example, a silver-mining company may be almost the only source of employment in a remote Idaho town. A Colorado ski resort, a Wisconsin paper mill, or an Alaskan fish processor may provide most of the employment in its geographically isolated locale.

ORIGIN OF THE IDEA
O 13.1
Monopsony

In other cases three or four firms may each hire a large portion of the supply of labor in a certain market and therefore have some monopsony power. Moreover, if they tacitly or openly act in concert in hiring labor, they greatly enhance their monopsony power.

Upsloping Labor Supply to Firm

When a firm hires most of the available supply of a certain type of labor, its decision to employ more or fewer workers affects the wage rate it pays to those workers. Specifically, if a firm is large in relation to the size of the labor market, it will have to pay a higher wage rate to attract labor away from other employment or from leisure. Suppose that there is only one employer of a particular type of labor in a certain geographic area. In this pure monopsony situation, the labor supply curve for the *firm* and the total labor supply curve for the *labor market* are identical. The monopsonist's supply curve—represented by curve S in Figure 13.4—is upsloping because the firm must pay higher wage rates if it wants to attract and hire additional workers. This same curve is also the monopsonist's average-cost-of-labor curve. Each point on curve S indicates the wage rate (cost) per worker that must be paid to attract the corresponding number of workers.

MRC Higher Than the Wage Rate

When a monopsonist pays a higher wage to attract an additional worker, it must pay that higher wage not only to the additional worker, but to all the workers it is currently employing at a lower wage. If not, labor morale will deteriorate, and the employer will be plagued with labor unrest because of wage-rate differences existing for the same job. Paying a uniform wage to all workers means that the cost of an extra worker—the marginal resource (labor)

FIGURE 13.4 The wage rate and level of employment in a monopsonistic labor market. In a monopsonistic labor market the employer's marginal resource (labor) cost curve (MRC) lies above the labor supply curve S. Equating MRC with MRP at point b, the monopsonist hires Q_m workers (compared with Q_c under competition). As indicated by point c on S, it pays only wage rate W_m (compared with the competitive wage W_c).

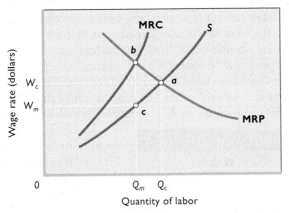

cost (MRC)—is the sum of that worker's wage rate and the amount necessary to bring the wage rate of all current workers up to the new wage level.

Table 13.2 illustrates this point. One worker can be hired at a wage rate of $6. But hiring a second worker forces the firm to pay a higher wage rate of $7. The marginal resource (labor) cost of the second worker is $8—the $7 paid to the second worker plus a $1 raise for the first worker. From another viewpoint, total labor cost is now $14 (= 2 × $7), up from $6 (= 1 × $6). So the MRC of the second worker is $8 (= $14 − $6), not just the $7 wage rate paid to that worker. Similarly, the marginal labor cost of the third worker is $10—the $8 that must be paid to attract this worker from alternative employment plus $1 raises, from $7 to $8, for the first two workers.

Here is the key point: Because the monopsonist is the only employer in the labor market, its marginal resource (labor) cost exceeds the wage rate. Graphically, the monopsonist's MRC curve lies above the average-cost-of-

TABLE 13.2 The Supply of Labor: Monopsony in the Hiring of Labor

(1) Units of Labor	(2) Wage Rate	(3) Total Labor Cost	(4) Marginal Resource (Labor) Cost
0	$ 5	$ 0	
1	6	6	$ 6
2	7	14	8
3	8	24	10
4	9	36	12
5	10	50	14
6	11	66	16

labor curve, or labor supply curve S, as is clearly shown in Figure 13.4.

Equilibrium Wage and Employment

How many units of labor will the monopsonist hire, and what wage rate will it pay? To maximize profit, the monopsonist will employ the quantity of labor Q_m in Figure 13.4, because at that quantity MRC and MRP are equal (point b).[1] The monopsonist next determines how much it must pay to attract these Q_m workers. From the supply curve S, specifically point c, it sees that it must pay wage rate W_m. Clearly, it need not pay a wage equal to MRP; it can attract and hire exactly the number of workers it wants (Q_m) with wage rate W_m. And that is the wage that it will pay.

Contrast these results with those that would prevail in a competitive labor market. With competition in the hiring of labor, the level of employment would be greater (at Q_c) and the wage rate would be higher (at W_c). Other things equal, the monopsonist maximizes its profit by hiring a smaller number of workers and thereby paying a less-than-competitive wage rate. Society obtains a smaller output, and workers receive a wage rate that is less by bc than their marginal revenue product. Just as a monopolistic seller finds it profitable to restrict product output to realize an above-competitive price for its goods, the monopsonistic employer of resources finds it profitable to restrict employment in order to reduce wage rates below those that would occur under competitive conditions.

INTERACTIVE GRAPHS

G 13.2

Monopsony

WORKED PROBLEMS

W 13.1

Labor markets: competition and monopsony

---

[1]The fact that MRC exceeds resource price when resources are hired or purchased under imperfectly competitive (monopsonistic) conditions calls for adjustments in Chapter 12's least-cost and profit-maximizing rules for hiring resources. (See equations 1 and 2 in the "Optimal Combination of Resources" section of Chapter 12.) Specifically, we must substitute MRC for resource price in the denominators of our two equations. That is, with imperfect competition in the hiring of both labor and capital, equation 1 becomes

$$\frac{MP_L}{MRC_L} = \frac{MP_C}{MRC_C} \tag{1'}$$

and equation 2 is restated as

$$\frac{MRP_L}{MRC_L} = \frac{MRP_C}{MRC_C} = 1 \tag{2'}$$

In fact, equations 1 and 2 can be regarded as special cases of 1' and 2' in which firms happen to be hiring under purely competitive conditions and resource price is therefore equal to, and can be substituted for, marginal resource cost.

Examples of Monopsony Power

Fortunately, monopsonistic labor markets are uncommon in the United States. In most labor markets, several potential employers compete for most workers, particularly for workers who are occupationally and geographically mobile. Also, where monopsony labor market outcomes might have otherwise occurred, unions have often sprung up to counteract that power by forcing firms to negotiate wages. Nevertheless, economists have found some evidence of monopsony power in such diverse labor markets as the markets for nurses, professional athletes, public school teachers, newspaper employees, and some building-trade workers.

In the case of nurses, the major employers in most locales are a relatively small number of hospitals. Further, the highly specialized skills of nurses are not readily transferable to other occupations. It has been found, in accordance with the monopsony model, that, other things equal, the smaller the number of hospitals in a town or city (that is, the greater the degree of monopsony), the lower the beginning salaries of nurses.

Professional sports leagues also provide a good example of monopsony, particularly as it relates to the pay of first-year players. The National Football League, the National Basketball Association, and Major League Baseball assign first-year players to teams through "player drafts." That device prohibits other teams from competing for a player's services, at least for several years, until the player becomes a "free agent." In this way each league exercises monopsony power, which results in lower salaries than would occur under competitive conditions.

QUICK REVIEW 13.1

- Real wages have increased over time in the United States because labor demand has increased relative to labor supply.
- Over the long term, real wages per worker have increased at approximately the same rate as worker productivity.
- The competitive employer is a wage taker and employs workers at the point where the wage rate (= MRC) equals MRP.
- The labor supply curve to a monopsonist is upsloping, causing MRC to exceed the wage rate for each worker. Other things equal, the monopsonist, hiring where MRC = MRP, will employ fewer workers and pay a lower wage rate than would a purely competitive employer.

Three Union Models

Our assumption thus far has been that workers compete with one another in selling their labor services. But in some labor markets workers unionize and sell their labor services collectively. (We examine union membership, collective bargaining, and union impacts in detail in an appendix to this chapter. Here our focus is on three union wage models.)

When a union is formed in an otherwise competitive labor market, it usually bargains with a relatively large number of employers. It has many goals, the most important of which is to raise wage rates. It can pursue that objective in several ways.

Demand-Enhancement Model

Unions recognize that their ability to influence the demand for labor is limited. But, from the union's viewpoint, increasing the demand for union labor is highly desirable. As Figure 13.5 shows, an increase in the demand for union labor will create a higher union wage along with more jobs.

Unions can increase the demand for their labor by increasing the demand for the goods or services they help produce. Political lobbying is the main tool for increasing the demand for union-produced goods or services. For example, construction unions have lobbied for new highways, mass-transit systems, and stadium projects. Teachers' unions and associations have pushed for increased public spending on education. Unions in the aerospace industry have lobbied to increase spending on the military and on space exploration. U.S. steel unions and forest-product workers have lobbied for tariffs and quotas on foreign imports of steel and lumber, respectively. Such trade restrictions shift the demand for labor away from foreign countries and toward unionized U.S. labor.

Unions can also increase the demand for union labor by altering the price of other inputs. For example, although union members are generally paid significantly more than the minimum wage, unions have strongly supported increases in the minimum wage. The purpose may be to raise the price of low-wage, nonunion labor, which

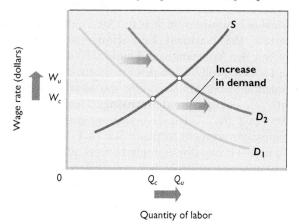

FIGURE 13.5 Unions and demand enhancement. When unions can increase the demand for union labor (say, from D_1 to D_2), they can realize higher wage rates (W_c to W_u) and more jobs (Q_c to Q_u).

in some cases is substitutable for union labor. A higher minimum wage for nonunion workers will discourage employers from substituting such workers for union workers and will thereby bolster the demand for union members.

Similarly, unions have sometimes sought to increase the demand for their labor by supporting policies that will reduce or hold down the price of a complementary resource. For example, unions in industries that represent workers who transport fruits and vegetables may support legislation that allows low-wage foreign agricultural workers to temporarily work in the United States. Where union labor and another resource are complementary, a price decrease for the other resource will increase the demand for union labor through Chapter 12's output effect.

Exclusive or Craft Union Model

Unions can also boost wage rates by reducing the supply of labor, and over the years organized labor has favored policies to do just that. For example, labor unions have supported legislation that has (1) restricted permanent immigration, (2) reduced child labor, (3) encouraged compulsory retirement, and (4) enforced a shorter workweek.

Moreover, certain types of workers have adopted techniques designed to restrict the number of workers who can join their union. This is especially true of *craft unions*, whose members possess a particular skill, such as carpenters, brick masons, or plumbers. Craft unions have frequently forced employers to agree to hire only union members, thereby gaining virtually complete control of the labor supply. Then, by following restrictive membership policies—for example, long apprenticeships, very high initiation fees, and limits on the number of new members admitted—they have artificially restricted labor supply. As indicated in Figure 13.6, such practices result in higher wage rates and constitute what is called **exclusive unionism.** By excluding workers from unions and therefore from the labor supply, craft unions succeed in elevating wage rates.

This craft union model is also applicable to many professional organizations, such as the American Medical Association, the National Education Association, the American Bar Association, and hundreds of others. Such groups seek to prohibit competition for their services from less qualified labor suppliers. One way to accomplish that is through **occupational licensing.** Here a group of workers in a given occupation pressure Federal, state, or municipal government to pass a law that says that some occupational group (for example, barbers, physicians, lawyers, plumbers, cosmetologists, egg graders, pest controllers) can practice their trade only if they meet certain requirements. Those requirements might include level of

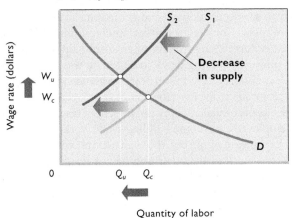

FIGURE 13.6 Exclusive or craft unionism. By reducing the supply of labor (say, from S_1 to S_2) through the use of restrictive membership policies, exclusive unions achieve higher wage rates (W_c to W_u). However, restriction of the labor supply also reduces the number of workers employed (Q_c to Q_u).

education, amount of work experience, the passing of an examination, and personal characteristics ("the practitioner must be of good moral character"). Members of the licensed occupation typically dominate the licensing board that administers such laws. The result is self-regulation, which often leads to policies that serve only to restrict entry to the occupation and reduce labor supply.

The expressed purpose of licensing is to protect consumers from incompetent practitioners—surely a worthy goal. But such licensing, if abused, results in above-competitive wages and earnings for those in the licensed occupation (Figure 13.6). Moreover, licensing requirements often include a residency requirement, which inhibits the interstate movement of qualified workers. Some 600 occupations are now licensed in the United States.

Inclusive or Industrial Union Model

Instead of trying to limit their membership, however, most unions seek to organize all available workers. This is especially true of *industrial unions*, such as those of the automobile workers and steelworkers. Such unions seek as members all available unskilled, semiskilled, and skilled workers in an industry. It makes sense for a union to be exclusive when its members are skilled craft workers for whom the employer has few substitutes. But it does not make sense for a union to be exclusive when trying to organize unskilled and semiskilled workers. To break a strike, employers could then easily substitute unskilled or semiskilled nonunion workers for the unskilled or semiskilled union workers.

By contrast, an industrial union that includes virtually all available workers in its membership can put firms

FIGURE 13.7 Inclusive or industrial unionism.

By organizing virtually all available workers in order to control the supply of labor, inclusive industrial unions may impose a wage rate, such as W_u, which is above the competitive wage rate W_c. In effect, this changes the labor supply curve from S to aeS. At wage rate W_u, employers will cut employment from Q_c to Q_u.

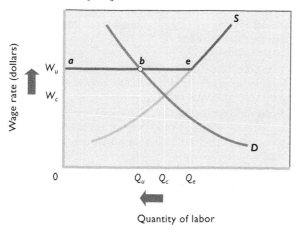

under great pressure to agree to its wage demands. Because of its legal right to strike, such a union can threaten to deprive firms of their entire labor supply. And an actual strike can do just that. Further, with virtually all available workers in the union, it will be difficult in the short run for new nonunion firms to emerge and thereby undermine what the union is demanding from existing firms.

We illustrate such **inclusive unionism** in Figure 13.7. Initially, the competitive equilibrium wage rate is W_c and the level of employment is Q_c. Now suppose an industrial union is formed that demands a higher, above-equilibrium wage rate of, say, W_u. That wage rate W_u would create a perfectly elastic labor supply over the range ae in Figure 13.7. If firms wanted to hire any workers in this range, they would have to pay the union-imposed wage rate. If they decide against meeting this wage demand, the union will supply no labor at all, and the firms will be faced with a strike. If firms decide it is better to pay the higher wage rate than to suffer a strike, they will cut back on employment from Q_c to Q_u.

By agreeing to the union's wage demand, individual employers become wage takers at the union wage rate W_u. Because labor supply is perfectly elastic over range ae, the marginal resource (labor) cost is equal to the wage rate W_u over this range. The Q_u level of employment is the result of employers' equating this MRC (now equal to the union wage rate) with MRP, according to our profit-maximizing rule.

Note from point e on labor supply curve S that Q_e workers desire employment at wage W_u. But as indicated by point b on labor demand curve D, only Q_u workers are employed. The result is a surplus of labor of $Q_e - Q_u$ (also

shown by distance eb). In a purely competitive labor market without the union, the effect of a surplus of unemployed workers would be lower wages. Specifically, the wage rate would fall to the equilibrium level W_c where the quantity of labor supplied equals the quantity of labor demanded (each Q_c). But this drop in wages does not happen, because workers are acting collectively through their union. Individual workers cannot offer to work for less than W_u nor can employers pay less than that.

Wage Increases and Job Loss

Have U.S. unions been successful in raising the wages of their members? Evidence suggests that union members on average achieve a 15 percent wage advantage over nonunion workers. But when unions are successful in raising wages, their efforts also have another major effect.

As Figures 13.6 and 13.7 suggest, the wage-raising actions achieved by both exclusive and inclusive unionism reduce employment in unionized firms. Simply put, a union's success in achieving above-equilibrium wage rates tends to be accompanied by a decline in the number of workers employed. That result acts as a restraining influence on union wage demands. A union cannot expect to maintain solidarity within its ranks if it seeks a wage rate so high that 20-30 percent of its members lose their jobs.

Bilateral Monopoly Model

Suppose a strong industrial union is formed in a monopsonist labor market rather that a competitive labor market, thereby creating a combination of the monopsony model and the inclusive unionism model. Economists call the result **bilateral monopoly** because in its pure form there is a single seller and a single buyer. The union is a monopolistic "seller" of labor that controls labor supply and can influence wage rates, but it faces a monopsonistic "buyer" of labor that can also affect wages by altering the amount of labor that it employs. This is not an uncommon case, particularly in less pure forms in which a single union confronts two, three, or four large employers. Examples: steel, automobiles, construction equipment, professional sports, and commercial aircraft.

Indeterminate Outcome of Bilateral Monopoly

We show this situation in Figure 13.8, where Figure 13.7 is superimposed onto Figure 13.4. The monopsonistic employer will seek the below-competitive-equilibrium wage rate W_m, and the union will press for some above-competitive-equilibrium wage rate such as W_u. Which will

FIGURE 13.8 **Bilateral monopoly in the labor market.**
A monopsonist seeks to hire Q_m workers (where MRC = MRP) and pay wage rate W_m corresponding to quantity Q_m on labor supply curve S. The inclusive union it faces seeks the above-equilibrium wage rate W_u. The actual outcome cannot be predicted by economic theory. It will result from bargaining between the two parties.

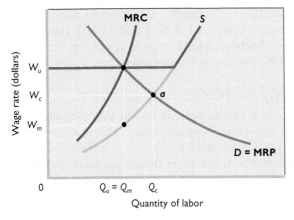

to competitive levels than would be the case if monopoly existed on only one side of the market.

be the outcome? We cannot say with certainty. The outcome is "logically indeterminate" because the bilateral monopoly model does not explain what will happen at the bargaining table. We can expect the wage outcome to lie somewhere between W_m and W_u. Beyond that, about all we can say is that the party with the greater bargaining power and the more effective bargaining strategy will probably get a wage closer to the one it seeks.

Desirability of Bilateral Monopoly

The wage and employment outcomes in this situation might be more economically desirable than the term "bilateral monopoly" implies. The monopoly on one side of the market might in effect cancel out the monopoly on the other side, yielding competitive or near-competitive results. If either the union or management prevailed in this market—that is, if the actual wage rate were either W_u or W_m—employment would be restricted to Q_m (where MRP = MRC), which is below the competitive level.

But now suppose the monopoly power of the union roughly offsets the monopsony power of management, and the union and management agree on wage rate W_c, which is the competitive wage. Once management accepts this wage rate, its incentive to restrict employment disappears; no longer can it depress wage rates by restricting employment. Instead, management hires at the most profitable resource quantity, where the bargained wage rate W_c (which is now the firm's MRC) is equal to the MRP. It hires Q_c workers. Thus, with monopoly on both sides of the labor market, the resulting wage rate and level of employment may be closer

The Minimum-Wage Controversy

Since the passage of the Fair Labor Standards Act in 1938, the United States has had a Federal **minimum wage.** That wage has ranged between 30 and 50 percent of the average wage paid to manufacturing workers and was most recently raised to $7.25 in July 2009. Numerous states, however, have minimum wages that are higher than the Federal minimum wage. Some of these state minimum wages are considerably higher. For example, in 2010 the minimum wage in the state of Washington was $8.55 an hour. The purpose of the minimum wage is to provide a "wage floor" that will help less-skilled workers earn enough income to escape poverty.

Case against the Minimum Wage

Critics, reasoning in terms of Figure 13.7, contend that an above-equilibrium minimum wage (say, W_u) will simply cause employers to hire fewer workers. Downsloping labor demand curves are a reality. The higher labor costs may even force some firms out of business. Then some of the poor, low-wage workers whom the minimum wage was designed to help will find themselves out of work. Critics point out that a worker who is *unemployed* and desperate to find a job at a minimum wage of $7.25 per hour is clearly worse off than he or she would be if *employed* at a market wage rate of, say, $6.50 per hour.

A second criticism of the minimum wage is that it is "poorly targeted" to reduce household poverty. Critics point out that much of the benefit of the minimum wage accrues to workers, including many teenagers, who do not live in impoverished households.

Case for the Minimum Wage

Advocates of the minimum wage say that critics analyze its impact in an unrealistic context. Figure 13.7, advocates claim, assumes a competitive labor market. But in a less competitive, low-pay labor market where employers possess some monopsony power (Figure 13.8), the minimum wage can increase wage rates without causing significant unemployment. Indeed, a higher minimum wage may even produce more jobs by eliminating the motive that monopsonistic firms have for restricting employment. For example, a minimum-wage floor of W_c in Figure 13.8 would change the firm's labor supply curve to W_caS and prompt the firm to increase its employment from Q_m workers to Q_c workers.

Moreover, even if the labor market is competitive, the higher wage rate might prompt firms to find more productive tasks for low-paid workers, thereby raising their productivity. Alternatively, the minimum wage may reduce *labor turnover* (the rate at which workers voluntarily quit). With fewer low-productive trainees, the *average* productivity of the firm's workers would rise. In either case, the alleged negative employment effects of the minimum wage might not occur.

Evidence and Conclusions

Which view is correct? Unfortunately, there is no clear answer. All economists agree that firms will not hire workers who cost more per hour than the value of their hourly output. So there is some minimum wage sufficiently high that it would severely reduce employment. Consider $30 an hour, as an absurd example. Because the majority of U.S. workers earned less than $20 per hour in 2009, a minimum wage of $30 per hour would render the majority of American workers unemployable because the minimum wage that they would have to be paid by potential employers would far exceed their marginal revenue products.

It has to be remembered, though, that a minimum wage will only cause unemployment in labor markets where the minimum wage is higher than the equilibrium wage. Because the current minimum wage of $7.25 per hour is much lower than the average hourly wage of about $18.80 that was earned by American workers in 2009, any unemployment caused by the $7.25 per hour minimum wage is most likely to fall on low-skilled workers who earn low wages due to their low productivity. These workers are mostly teenagers, adults who did not complete high school, and immigrants with low levels of education and poor English proficiency. For members of such groups, recent research suggests that a 10 percent increase in the minimum wage will cause a 1 to 3

percent decline in employment. However, estimates of the employment effect of minimum wage laws vary from study to study so that significant controversy remains.

The overall effect of the minimum wage is thus uncertain. On the one hand, the employment and unemployment effects of the minimum wage do not appear to be as great as many critics fear. On the other hand, because a large part of its effect is dissipated on nonpoverty families, the minimum wage is not as strong an antipoverty tool as many supporters contend.

Voting patterns and surveys make it clear, however, that the minimum wage has strong political support. Perhaps this stems from two realities: (1) More workers are believed to be helped than hurt by the minimum wage and (2) the minimum wage gives society some assurance that employers are not "taking undue advantage" of vulnerable, low-skilled workers.

Wage Differentials

Hourly wage rates and annual salaries differ greatly among occupations. In Table 13.3 we list average annual salaries for a number of occupations to illustrate such occupational **wage differentials.** For example, observe that surgeons on average earn eight times as much as retail salespersons. Not shown, there are also large wage differentials within some of the occupations listed. For example, some highly experienced surgeons earn several times as much income as

TABLE 13.3 Average Annual Wages in Selected Occupations, 2009

Occupation	Average Annual Wages
1. Surgeons	$206,770
2. Aircraft pilots	119,750
3. Petroleum engineers	119,140
4. Financial managers	110,640
5. Law professors	101,170
6. Chemical engineers	88,760
7. Dental hygienists	66,950
8. Registered nurses	65,130
9. Police officers	52,810
10. Electricians	49,890
11. Carpenters	42,940
12. Travel agents	32,470
13. Barbers	26,610
14. Retail sales persons	25,050
15. Janitors	23,500
16. Childcare workers	20,350
17. Fast food cooks	17,620

Source: Bureau of Labor Statistics, **www.bls.gov.**

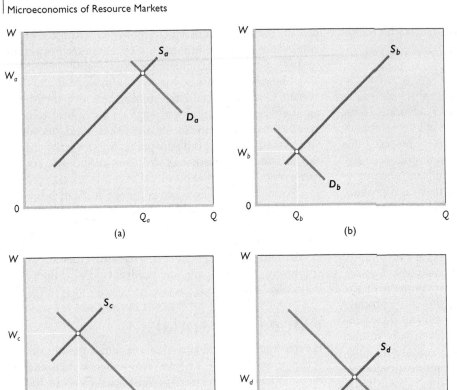

FIGURE 13.9 **Labor demand, labor supply, and wage differentials.** The wage differential between labor markets (a) and (b) results solely from differences in labor demand. In labor markets (c) and (d), differences in labor supply are the sole cause of the wage differential.

surgeons just starting their careers. And, although average wages for retail salespersons are relatively low, some top salespersons selling on commission make several times the average wages listed for their occupation.

What explains wage differentials such as these? Once again, the forces of demand and supply are revealing. As we demonstrate in Figure 13.9, wage differentials can arise on either the supply or the demand side of labor markets. Figure 13.9a and 13.9b represent labor markets for two occupational groups that have identical *labor supply curves*. Labor market (a) has a relatively high equilibrium wage (W_a) because labor demand is very strong. In labor market (b) the equilibrium wage is relatively low (W_b) because labor demand is weak. Clearly, the wage differential between occupations (a) and (b) results solely from differences in the magnitude of labor demand.

Contrast that situation with Figure 13.9c and 13.9d, where the *labor demand curves* are identical. In labor market (c) the equilibrium wage is relatively high (W_c) because labor supply is low. In labor market (d) labor supply is highly abundant, so the equilibrium wage (W_d) is relatively low. The wage differential between (c) and (d) results solely from the differences in the magnitude of labor supply.

Although Figure 13.9 provides a good starting point for understanding wage differentials, we need to know *why* demand and supply conditions differ in various labor markets. There are several reasons.

Marginal Revenue Productivity

The strength of labor demand—how far rightward the labor demand curve is located—differs greatly among occupations due to differences in how much various occupational groups contribute to the revenue of their respective employers. This revenue contribution, in turn, depends on the workers' productivity and the strength of the demand for the products they are helping to produce. Where labor is highly productive and product demand is strong, labor demand also is strong and, other things equal, pay is high. Top professional athletes, for example, are highly productive at producing sports entertainment, for which millions of people are willing to pay billions of dollars over the course of a season. Because the **marginal revenue productivity** of these players is so high, they are in very high demand by sports teams. This high demand leads to their extremely high salaries (as in Figure 13.9a). In contrast, most workers generate much more modest revenue for their employers.

This results in much lower demand for their labor and, consequently, much lower wages (as in Figure 13.9b).

Noncompeting Groups

On the supply side of the labor market, workers are not homogeneous; they differ in their mental and physical capacities and in their education and training. At any given time the labor force is made up of many **noncompeting groups** of workers, each representing several occupations for which the members of a particular group qualify. In some groups qualified workers are relatively few, whereas in others they are plentiful. And workers in one group do not qualify for the occupations of other groups.

Ability Only a few workers have the ability or physical attributes to be brain surgeons, concert violinists, top fashion models, research chemists, or professional athletes. Because the supply of these particular types of labor is very small in relation to labor demand, their wages are high (as in Figure 13.9c). The members of these and similar groups do not compete with one another or with other skilled or semiskilled workers. The violinist does not compete with the surgeon, nor does the surgeon compete with the violinist or the fashion model.

The concept of noncompeting groups can be applied to various subgroups and even to specific individuals in a particular group. Some especially skilled violinists can command higher salaries than colleagues who play the same instrument. A handful of top corporate executives earn 10 to 20 times as much as the average chief executive officer. In each of these cases, the supply of top talent is highly limited since less-talented colleagues are only imperfect substitutes.

Education and Training Another source of wage differentials is differing amounts of **human capital,** which is the personal stock of knowledge, know-how, and skills that enables a person to be productive and thus to earn income.

ORIGIN OF THE IDEA
O 13.2
Human capital

Such stocks result from investments in human capital. Like expenditures on machinery and equipment, productivity-enhancing expenditures on education or training are investments. In both cases, people incur *present costs* with the intention that those expenditures will lead to a greater flow of *future earnings*.

Figure 13.10 indicates that workers who have made greater investments in education achieve higher incomes during their careers. The reason is twofold: (1) There are fewer such workers, so their supply is limited relative to less-educated workers, and (2) more-educated workers tend to be more productive and thus in greater demand.

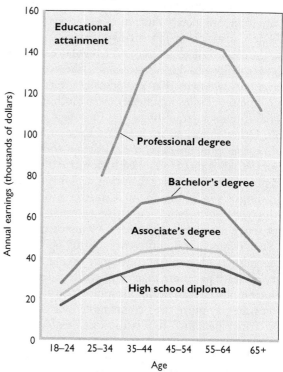

FIGURE 13.10 Education levels and individual annual earnings. Annual income by age is higher for workers with more education than less. Investment in education yields a return in the form of earnings differences enjoyed over one's work life.

Source: U.S. Bureau of the Census. Data are for both sexes in 2008.

Figure 13.10 also indicates that the earnings of better-educated workers rise more rapidly than those of poorly educated workers. The primary reason is that employers provide more on-the-job training to the better-educated workers, boosting their marginal revenue productivity and therefore their earnings.

Although education yields higher incomes, it carries substantial costs. A college education involves not only direct costs (tuition, fees, books) but indirect or opportunity costs (forgone earnings) as well. Does the higher pay received by better-educated workers compensate for these costs? The answer is yes. Rates of return are estimated to be 10 to 13 percent for investments in secondary education and 8 to 12 percent for investments in college education. One generally accepted estimate is that each year of schooling raises a worker's wage by about 8 percent.

Compensating Differences

If the workers in a particular noncompeting group are equally capable of performing several different jobs, you might expect the wage rates to be identical for all these jobs. Not so. A group of high school graduates may be equally capable of becoming salesclerks or general construction workers. But these jobs pay different wages. In virtually all locales, construction laborers receive much higher wages than salesclerks. These wage differentials are called **compensating differences** because they must be paid to compensate for nonmonetary differences in various jobs.

The construction job involves dirty hands, a sore back, the hazard of accidents, and irregular employment, both seasonally and during recessions (the economywide economic slowdowns that periodically affect the economy). The retail sales job means clean clothing, pleasant air-conditioned surroundings, and little fear of injury or layoff. Other things equal, it is easy to see why workers would rather pick up a credit card than a shovel. So the amount of labor that is supplied to construction firms (as in Figure 13.9c) is smaller than that which is supplied to retail shops (as in Figure 13.9d). Construction firms must pay higher wages than retailers to compensate for the unattractive nonmonetary aspects of construction jobs.

Such compensating differences spring up throughout the economy. Other things equal, jobs having high risk of injury or death pay more than comparable, safer jobs. Jobs lacking employer-paid health insurance, pensions, and vacation time pay more than comparable jobs that provide these "fringe benefits." Jobs with more flexible hours pay less than jobs with rigid work-hour requirements. Jobs with greater risk of unemployment pay more than comparable jobs with little unemployment risk. Entry-level jobs in occupations that provide very poor prospects for pay advancement pay more than entry-level jobs that have clearly defined "job ladders."

These and other compensating differences play an important role in allocating society's scarce labor resources. If very few workers want to be garbage collectors, then society must pay high wages to garbage collectors to get the garbage collected. If many more people want to be salesclerks, then society need not pay them as much as it pays garbage collectors to get those services performed.

Market Imperfections

Differences in marginal revenue productivity, amounts of human capital, and nonmonetary aspects of jobs explain most of the wage differentials in the economy. But some persistent differentials result from various market imperfections that impede workers from moving from lower-paying jobs to higher-paying jobs.

Lack of Job Information Workers may simply be unaware of job opportunities and wage rates in other geographic areas and in other jobs for which they qualify. Consequently, the flow of qualified labor from lower-paying to higher-paying jobs—and thus the adjustments in labor supply—may not be sufficient to equalize wages within occupations.

Geographic Immobility Workers take root geographically. Many are reluctant to move to new places. Doing so would involve leaving friends, relatives, and associates. It would mean forcing their children to change schools, having to sell their homes, and incurring the costs and inconveniences of adjusting to a new job and a new community. As Adam Smith noted over two centuries ago, "A [person] is of all sorts of luggage the most difficult to be transported." The reluctance or inability of workers to move enables geographic wage differentials within the same occupation to persist.

Unions and Government Restraints Wage differentials may be reinforced by artificial restrictions on mobility imposed by unions and government. We have noted that craft unions find it to their advantage to restrict membership. After all, if carpenters and bricklayers become too plentiful, the wages they can command will decline. Thus the low-paid nonunion carpenter of Brush, Colorado, may be willing to move to Chicago in the pursuit of higher wages. But her chances for succeeding are slim. She may be unable to get a union card, and no card

My Entire Life

Human capital is the accumulation of outcomes of prior investments in education, training, and other factors that increase productivity and earnings. It is the stock of knowledge, know-how, and skills that enables individuals to be productive and thus earn income. A valuable stock of human capital, together with a strong demand for one's services, can add up to a large capacity to earn income. For some people, high earnings have little to do with actual hours of work and much to do with their tremendous skill, which reflects their accumulated stock of human capital.

The point is demonstrated in the following story: It is said that a tourist once spotted the famous Spanish artist Pablo Picasso (1881–1973) in a Paris café. The tourist asked Picasso if he would do a sketch of his wife for pay. Picasso sketched the wife in a matter of minutes and said, "That will be 10,000 francs [roughly $2000]." Hearing the high price, the tourist became irritated, saying, "But that took you only a few minutes."

"No," replied Picasso, "it took me my entire life!"

means no job. Similarly, an optometrist or lawyer qualified to practice in one state may not meet the licensing requirements of other states, so his or her ability to move is limited. Other artificial barriers involve pension plans, health insurance benefits, and seniority rights that might be jeopardized by moving from one job to another.

Discrimination Despite legislation to the contrary, discrimination sometimes results in lower wages being paid to women and minority workers than to white males doing very similar or even identical work. Also, women and minorities may be crowded into certain low-paying occupations, driving down wages there and raising them elsewhere. If this *occupational segregation* keeps qualified women and minorities from taking higher-paying jobs, then differences in pay will persist. (We discuss discrimination in Chapter 20.)

All four considerations—differences in marginal revenue productivity, noncompeting groups, nonmonetary differences, and market imperfections—come into play in explaining actual wage differentials. For example, the differential between the wages of a physician and those of a construction worker can be explained on the basis of marginal revenue productivity and noncompeting groups. Physicians generate considerable revenue because of their high productivity and the strong willingness of consumers (via insurance) to pay for health care. Physicians also fall into a noncompeting group where, because of stringent training requirements, only relatively few persons qualify. So the supply of labor is small in relation to demand.

In construction work, where training requirements are much less significant, the supply of labor is great relative to demand. So wages are much lower for construction workers than for physicians. However, if not for the unpleasantness of the construction worker's job and the fact that his or her craft union observes restrictive membership policies, the differential would be even greater than it is.

Pay for Performance

The models of wage determination we have described in this chapter assume that worker pay is always a standard amount for each hour's work, for example, $15 per hour. But pay schemes are often more complex than that both in composition and in purpose. For instance, many workers receive annual salaries rather than hourly pay. And workers receive differing proportions of fringe benefits (health insurance, life insurance, paid vacations, paid sick-leave days, pension contributions, and so on) as part of their pay. Finally, some pay plans are designed to elicit a desired level of performance from workers. This last aspect of pay plans requires further elaboration.

The Principal-Agent Problem

The **principal-agent problem** is usually associated with the possible differences in the interests of corporate stockholders (principals) and the executives (agents) they hire. But this problem extends to all paid employees. Firms hire workers because they are needed to help produce the goods and services the firms sell in their attempts to turn a profit. Workers are the firms' agents; they are hired to advance the interest (profit) of the firms. The principals are the firms; they hire agents to advance their goals. Firms and workers have one interest in common: They both want the firm to survive and thrive. That will ensure profit for the firm and continued employment and wages for the workers.

ORIGIN OF THE IDEA
O 13.3
Principal-agent problem

But the interests of firms and workers are not identical. As a result, a principal-agent problem arises. Workers may seek to increase their utility by shirking on the job, that is, by providing less than the agreed-upon effort or by taking unauthorized breaks. They may improve their well-being by increasing their leisure during paid work hours, without forfeiting income. The night security guard in a warehouse may leave work early or spend time reading a novel rather than making the assigned rounds. A salaried manager may spend time away from the office visiting with friends rather than attending to company business.

Firms (principals) have a profit incentive to reduce or eliminate shirking. One option is to monitor workers, but monitoring is difficult and costly. Hiring another worker to supervise or monitor the security guard might double the cost of maintaining a secure warehouse. Another way of resolving a principal-agent problem is through some sort of **incentive pay plan** that ties worker compensation more closely to worker output or performance. Such incentive pay schemes include piece rates; commissions and royalties; bonuses, stock options, and profit sharing; and efficiency wages.

Piece Rates Piece rates consist of compensation paid according to the number of units of output a worker produces. If a principal pays fruit pickers by the bushel or typists by the page, it need not be concerned with shirking or with monitoring costs.

Commissions or Royalties Unlike piece rates, commissions and royalties tie compensation to the value of sales. Employees who sell products or services—including real estate agents, insurance agents, stockbrokers, and retail salespersons—commonly receive *commissions* that are computed as a percentage of the monetary value of their sales. Recording artists and authors are paid *royalties*, computed as a certain percentage of sales revenues from their works. Such types of compensation link the financial interests of the salespeople, artists, and authors to the profit interest of the firms.

Bonuses, Stock Options, and Profit Sharing

Bonuses are payments in addition to one's annual salary that are based on some factor such as the performance of the individual worker, or of a group of workers, or of the firm itself. A professional baseball player may receive a bonus based on a high batting average, the number of home runs hit, or the number of runs batted in. A business manager may receive a bonus based on the profitability of her or his unit. *Stock options* allow workers to buy shares of their employer's stock at a fixed, lower price when the stock price rises. Such options are part of the compensation packages of top corporate officials, as well as many workers in relatively high-technology firms. *Profit-sharing plans* allocate a percentage of a firm's profit to its employees.

Efficiency Wages

The rationale behind *efficiency wages* is that employers will enjoy greater effort from their workers by paying them above-equilibrium wage rates. Glance back at Figure 13.3, which shows a competitive labor market in which the equilibrium wage rate is $10. What if an employer decides to pay an above-equilibrium wage of $12 per hour? Rather than putting the firm at a cost disadvantage compared with rival firms paying only $10, the higher wage might improve worker effort and productivity so that unit labor costs actually fall. For example, if each worker produces 10 units of output per hour at the $12 wage rate compared with only 6 units at the $10 wage rate, unit labor costs for the high-wage firm will be only $1.20 (= $12/10) compared to $1.67 (= $10/6) for firms paying the equilibrium wage.

An above-equilibrium wage may enhance worker efficiency in several ways. It enables the firm to attract higher-quality workers. It lifts worker morale. And it lowers turnover, resulting in a more experienced workforce, greater worker productivity, and lower recruitment and training costs. Because the opportunity cost of losing a higher-wage job is greater, workers are more likely to put forth their best efforts with less supervision and monitoring. In fact, efficiency wage payments have proved effective for many employers.

> **ORIGIN OF THE IDEA**
>
> O 13.4
>
> Efficiency wages

Addenda: Negative Side Effects of Pay for Performance

Although pay for performance may help overcome the principal-agent problem and enhance worker productivity,

such plans may have negative side effects and require careful design. Here are a few examples:

- The rapid production pace that piece rates encourage may result in poor product quality and may compromise the safety of workers. Such outcomes can be costly to the firm over the long run.
- Commissions may cause some salespeople to engage in questionable or even fraudulent sales practices, such as making exaggerated claims about products or recommending unneeded repairs. Such practices may lead to private lawsuits or government legal action.
- Bonuses based on personal performance may disrupt the close cooperation needed for maximum team production. A professional basketball player who receives a bonus for points scored may be reluctant to pass the ball to teammates.
- Since profit sharing is usually tied to the performance of the entire firm, less energetic workers can "free ride" by obtaining their profit share on the basis of the hard work by others.
- Stock options may prompt some unscrupulous executives to manipulate the cost and revenue streams of their firms to create a false appearance of rapidly rising profit. When the firm's stock value rises, the executives exercise their stock options at inflated share prices and reap a personal fortune.
- There may be a downside to the reduced turnover resulting from above-market wages: Firms that pay efficiency wages have fewer opportunities to hire new workers and suffer the loss of the creative energy that they often bring to the workplace.

QUICK REVIEW 13.3

- Proponents of the minimum wage argue that it is needed to assist the working poor and to counter monopsony where it might exist; critics say that it is poorly targeted to reduce poverty and that it reduces employment.
- Wage differentials are attributable in general to the forces of supply and demand, influenced by differences in workers' marginal revenue productivity, education, and skills and by nonmonetary differences in jobs. But several labor market imperfections also play a role.
- As it applies to labor, the principal-agent problem is one of workers pursuing their own interests to the detriment of the employer's profit objective.
- Pay-for-performance plans (piece rates, commissions, royalties, bonuses, stock options, profit sharing, and efficiency wages) are designed to improve worker productivity by overcoming the principal-agent problem.

Word Are Chief Executive Officers (CEOs) Overpaid?

The Multimillion-Dollar Pay of Major Corporate CEOs Has Drawn Considerable Criticism.

Top executives of U.S. corporations typically receive total annual pay (salary, bonuses, and stock options) in the millions of dollars. As shown in Table 1, each of the top five paid U.S. executives earned $90 million or more in 2008.

CEO pay in the United States is not only exceptionally high relative to the average pay of U.S. managers and workers but also high compared to the CEO pay in other industrial countries. For example, in 2005 the CEO pay at firms with about $500 million in annual sales averaged $2.2 million in the United States, compared to $1.2 million in France and Germany and less than $600,000 in South Korea and Japan.*

Is high CEO pay simply the outcome of labor supply and labor demand, as is the pay for star athletes and entertainers? Does it reflect marginal revenue productivity—that is, the contributions by CEOs to their company's output and revenue?

Observers who answer affirmatively point out that decisions made by the CEOs of large corporations affect the productivity of every employee in the organization. Good decisions enhance productivity throughout the organization and increase revenue; bad decisions reduce productivity and revenue. Only executives who have consistently made good business decisions attain the top positions in large corporations.

Because the supply of these people is highly limited and their marginal revenue productivity is enormous, they command huge salaries and performance bonuses.

Also, some economists note that CEO pay in the United States may be like the prizes professional golfers and tennis players receive for winning tournaments. These high prizes are designed to promote the productivity of all those who aspire to achieve them. In corporations the top prizes go to the winners of the "contests" among managers to attain, at least eventually, the CEO positions. Thus high CEO pay does not derive solely from the CEO's direct productivity. Instead, it may exist because the high pay creates incentives that raise the productivity of scores of other corporate executives who seek to achieve the top position. In this view, high CEO pay remains grounded on high productivity.

Critics of existing CEO pay acknowledge that CEOs deserve substantially higher salaries than ordinary workers or typical managers, but they question pay packages that run into the millions of dollars. They reject the "tournament pay" idea on the grounds that corporations require cooperative team effort by managers and executives, not the type of high-stakes competition promoted by "winner-take-most" pay. They believe that corporations, although owned by their shareholders, are controlled by corporate boards and professional executives. Because many board members are present or past CEOs of other corporations, they often exaggerate CEO importance and, consequently, overpay their own CEOs. These overpayments are at the expense of the firm's stockholders.

In summary, defenders of CEO pay say that high pay is justified by the direct or indirect marginal-revenue contribution of CEOs. Like it or not, CEO pay is market-determined pay. In contrast, critics say that multimillion-dollar CEO pay bears little relationship to marginal revenue productivity and is unfair to ordinary stockholders. It is clear from our discussion that this issue remains unsettled.

TABLE 1 The Five Highest-Paid U.S. CEOs, 2008

Name	Company	Total Pay, Millions
Lawrence Ellison	Oracle	$557
Ray Irani	Occidental Petroleum	223
John Hess	Hess Petroleum	155
Michael Watford	Ultra Petroleum	117
Mark Papa	EOG Resources	90

Source: Forbes, www.forbes.com. Reprinted by permission of Forbes Media LLC © 2010.

*Worldwide Total Remuneration, 2005–2006 (New York: Towers Perrin, Jan. 11, 2006, p. 20).

283

Summary

1. The term "labor" encompasses all people who work for pay. The wage rate is the price paid per unit of time for labor. Labor earnings comprise total pay and are found by multiplying the number of hours worked by the hourly wage rate. The nominal wage rate is the amount of money received per unit of time; the real wage rate is the purchasing power of the nominal wage.

2. The long-run growth of real hourly compensation—the average real wage—roughly matches that of productivity, with both increasing over the long run.

3. Global comparisons suggest that real wages in the United States are relatively high, but not the highest, internationally. High real wages in the advanced industrial countries stem largely from high labor productivity.

4. Specific wage rates depend on the structure of the particular labor market. In a competitive labor market the equilibrium wage rate and level of employment are determined at the intersection of the labor supply curve and labor demand curve. For the individual firm, the market wage rate establishes a horizontal labor supply curve, meaning that the wage rate equals the firm's constant marginal resource cost. The firm hires workers to the point where its MRP equals its MRC.

5. Under monopsony the marginal resource cost curve lies above the resource supply curve because the monopsonist must bid up the wage rate to hire extra workers and must pay that higher wage rate to all workers. The monopsonist hires fewer workers than are hired under competitive conditions, pays less-than-competitive wage rates (has lower labor costs), and thus obtains greater profit.

6. A union may raise competitive wage rates by (a) increasing the derived demand for labor, (b) restricting the supply of labor through exclusive unionism, or (c) directly enforcing an above-equilibrium wage rate through inclusive unionism.

7. In many industries the labor market takes the form of bilateral monopoly, in which a strong union "sells" labor to a monopsonistic employer. The wage-rate outcome of this labor market model depends on union and employer bargaining power.

8. On average, unionized workers realize wage rates 15 percent higher than those of comparable nonunion workers.

9. Economists disagree about the desirability of the minimum wage as an antipoverty mechanism. While it causes unemployment for some low-income workers, it raises the incomes of those who retain their jobs.

10. Wage differentials are largely explainable in terms of (a) marginal revenue productivity of various groups of workers; (b) noncompeting groups arising from differences in the capacities and education of different groups of workers; (c) compensating wage differences, that is, wage differences that must be paid to offset nonmonetary differences in jobs; and (d) market imperfections in the form of lack of job information, geographic immobility, union and government restraints, and discrimination.

11. As it applies to labor, the principal-agent problem arises when workers provide less-than-expected effort. Firms may combat this by monitoring workers or by creating incentive pay schemes that link worker compensation to performance.

Terms and Concepts

wage rate

nominal wage

real wage

purely competitive labor market

monopsony

exclusive unionism

occupational licensing

inclusive unionism

bilateral monopoly

minimum wage

wage differentials

marginal revenue productivity

noncompeting groups

human capital

compensating differences

principal-agent problem

incentive pay plan

Questions

1. Explain why the general level of wages is high in the United States and other industrially advanced countries. What is the single most important factor underlying the long-run increase in average real-wage rates in the United States? LO1

2. Why is a firm in a purely competitive labor market a wage taker? What would happen if it decided to pay less than the going market wage rate? LO2

3. Describe wage determination in a labor market in which workers are unorganized and many firms actively compete for the services of labor. Show this situation graphically, using W_1 to indicate the equilibrium wage rate and Q_1 to show the number of workers hired by the firms as a group. Show the labor supply curve of the individual firm, and compare it with that of the total market. Why the differences? In the

diagram representing the firm, identify total revenue, total wage cost, and revenue available for the payment of non-labor resources. LO2

4. Suppose the formerly competing firms in question 3 form an employers' association that hires labor as a monopsonist would. Describe verbally the effect on wage rates and employment. Adjust the graph you drew for question 3, showing the monopsonistic wage rate and employment level as W_2 and Q_2, respectively. Using this monopsony model, explain why hospital administrators sometimes complain about a "shortage" of nurses. How might such a shortage be corrected? LO3

5. Assume a monopsonistic employer is paying a wage rate of W_m and hiring Q_m workers, as indicated in Figure 13.8. Now suppose an industrial union is formed that forces the employer to accept a wage rate of W_c. Explain verbally and graphically why in this instance the higher wage rate will be accompanied by an increase in the number of workers hired. LO4

6. Have you ever worked for the minimum wage? If so, for how long? Would you favor increasing the minimum wage by a dollar? By two dollars? By five dollars? Explain your reasoning. LO5

7. "Many of the lowest-paid people in society—for example, short-order cooks—also have relatively poor working conditions. Hence, the notion of compensating wage differentials is disproved." Do you agree? Explain. LO5

8. What is meant by investment in human capital? Use this concept to explain (a) wage differentials and (b) the long-run rise of real-wage rates in the United States. LO5

9. What is the principal-agent problem? Have you ever worked in a setting where this problem has arisen? If so, do you think increased monitoring would have eliminated the problem? Why don't firms simply hire more supervisors to eliminate shirking? LO6

10. **LAST WORD** Do you think exceptionally high pay to CEOs is economically justified? Why or why not?

Problems

1. Workers are compensated by firms with "benefits" in addition to wages and salaries. The most prominent benefit offered by many firms is health insurance. Suppose that in 2000, workers at one steel plant were paid $20 per hour and in addition received health benefits at the rate of $4 per hour. Also suppose that by 2010 workers at that plant were paid $21 per hour but received $9 in health insurance benefits. LO1
   a. By what percentage did total compensation (wages plus benefits) change at this plant from 2000 to 2010? What was the approximate average annual percentage change in total compensation?
   b. By what percentage did wages change at this plant from 2000 to 2010? What was the approximate average annual percentage change in wages?
   c. If workers value a dollar of health benefits as much as they value a dollar of wages, by what total percentage will they feel that their incomes have risen over this time period? What if they only consider wages when calculating their incomes?
   d. Is it possible for workers to feel as though their wages are stagnating even if total compensation is rising?

2. Complete the following labor supply table for a firm hiring labor competitively: LO2

Units of Labor	Wage Rate	Total Labor Cost	Marginal Resource (Labor) Cost
0	$14	$ _____	
1	14	_____	$ _____
2	14	_____	_____
3	14	_____	_____
4	14	_____	_____
5	14	_____	_____
6	14	_____	_____

   a. Show graphically the labor supply and marginal resource (labor) cost curves for this firm. Are the curves the same or different? If they are different, which one is higher?
   b. Plot the labor demand data of question 2 in Chapter 12 on the graph used in part a above. What are the equilibrium wage rate and level of employment?

3. Assume a firm is a monopsonist that can hire its first worker for $6 but must increase the wage rate by $3 to attract each successive worker (so that the second worker must be paid $9, the third $12, and so on). LO3
   a. Draw the firm's labor supply and marginal resource cost curves. Are the curves the same or different? If they are different, which one is higher?
   b. On the same graph, plot the labor demand data of question 2 in Chapter 12. What are the equilibrium wage rate and level of employment?
   c. Compare these answers with those you found in problem 2. By how much does the monopsonist reduce wages below the competitive wage? By how much does the monopsonist reduce employment below the competitive level?

4. Suppose that low-skilled workers employed in clearing woodland can each clear one acre per month if they are each equipped with a shovel, a machete, and a chainsaw. Clearing one acre brings in $1000 in revenue. Each worker's equipment costs the worker's employer $150 per month to rent and each worker toils 40 hours per week for four weeks each month. LO4
   a. What is the marginal revenue product of hiring one low-skilled worker to clear woodland for one month?
   b. How much revenue per hour does each worker bring in?
   c. If the minimum wage were $6.20, would the revenue per hour in part b exceed the minimum wage? If so, by how much per hour?

d. Now consider the employer's total costs. These include the equipment costs as well as a normal profit of $50 per acre. If the firm pays workers the minimum wage of $6.20 per hour, what will the firm's economic profit or loss be per acre?

e. At what value would the minimum wage have to be set so that the firm would make zero economic profit from employing an additional low-skilled worker to clear woodland?

5. Suppose that a car dealership wishes to see if efficiency wages will help improve its salespeople's productivity. Currently, each salesperson sells an average of one car per day while being paid $20 per hour for an eight-hour day. LO6

   a. What is the current labor cost per car sold?

   b. Suppose that when the dealer raises the price of labor to $30 per hour the average number of cars sold by a salesperson increases to two per day. What is now the labor cost per car sold? By how much is it higher or lower than it was before? Has the efficiency of labor expenditures by the firm (cars sold per dollar of wages paid to salespeople) increased or decreased?

   c. Suppose that if the wage is raised a second time to $40 per hour the number of cars sold rises to an average of 2.5 per day. What is now the labor cost per car sold?

   d. If the firm's goal is to maximize the efficiency of its labor expenditures, which of the three hourly salary rates should it use: $20 per hour, $30 per hour, or $40 per hour?

   e. By contrast, which salary maximizes the productivity of the car dealer's workers (cars sold per worker per day)?

FURTHER TEST YOUR KNOWLEDGE AT
www.mcconnell19e.com

At the text's Online Learning Center (OLC), **www.mcconnell19e.com**, you will find one or more Web-based questions that require information from the Internet to answer. We urge you to check them out; they will familiarize you with Web sites that may be helpful in other courses and perhaps even in your career. The OLC also features multiple-choice questions that give instant feedback and provides other helpful ways to further test your knowledge of the chapter.

Labor Unions and Their Impacts

We have noted that unions can increase wage rates by augmenting the demand for labor (Figure 13.5) or by restricting or controlling the supply of labor (Figures 13.6 and 13.7). The purpose of this appendix is to provide some additional information about American unions, collective bargaining, and union impacts.

Union Membership

In 2009, about 15.3 million U.S. workers—12.3 percent of employed wage and salary workers—belonged to unions. Some 8 million of these U.S. union members belonged to one of many unions that are loosely and voluntarily affiliated with the **American Federation of Labor and the Congress of Industrial Organizations (AFL-CIO).** Examples of AFL-CIO unions are the United Autoworkers, Communications Workers, and United Steelworkers. Another 6 million union members belonged to one of the seven unions, including the Service Workers and Teamsters, loosely federated as **Change to Win.** The remaining union members belonged to other **independent unions** that were not affiliated with either federation.

The likelihood that any particular worker will be a union member depends mainly on the industry in which the worker is employed and his or her occupation. As shown in Figure 1a, the **unionization rate**—the percentage of workers unionized—is high in government,

transportation, telecommunications, construction, and manufacturing. The unionization rate is very low in finance, agriculture, and retail trade. Figure 1b shows that unionism also varies greatly by occupation. Teachers, protective service workers, transportation workers, production workers, and social workers have high unionization rates; sales workers, food workers, and managers have very low rates.

Because disproportionately more men than women work in the industries and occupations with high unionization rates, men are more likely to be union members than women. Specifically, 13 percent of male wage and salary workers belong to unions compared with 11 percent of women. For the same reason, African-Americans have higher unionization rates than whites: 14 percent compared with 12 percent. The unionization rate for Asians is 11 percent; Hispanics, 10 percent. Unionism in the United States is largely an urban phenomenon. Six heavily urbanized, heavily industrialized states (New York, California, Pennsylvania, Illinois, Ohio, and Michigan) account for approximately half of all union members.

The Decline of Unionism

Since the mid-1950s, union membership has not kept pace with the growth of the labor force. While 25 percent of employed wage and salary workers belonged to unions in the

FIGURE 1 **Union membership as a percentage of employed wage and salary workers, selected industries and occupations, 2009.** In percentage terms, union membership varies greatly by (a) industry and (b) occupation.

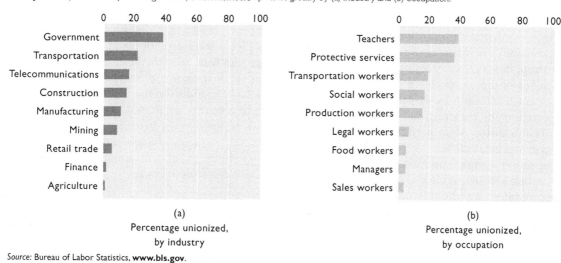

(a)
Percentage unionized,
by industry

(b)
Percentage unionized,
by occupation

Source: Bureau of Labor Statistics, **www.bls.gov.**

mid-1950s, today only 12.3 percent are union members. Over recent years, even the absolute number of union members has declined significantly. More than 22 million workers were unionized in 1980 but only 15.3 million in 2009.

Some of the major reasons for the decline of U.S. unionism involve structural changes in the economy. Employment has shifted away from manufactured goods (where unions have been stronger) and toward services (where unions have been weaker). Consumer demand has shifted toward foreign manufactured goods and away from goods produced by union labor in the United States. Industry has shifted from the northeast and midwest, where unionism is "a way of life," to "hard-to-organize" areas of the south and southwest. These and other factors have reduced the growth of union membership.

Also, management has greatly intensified its opposition to unions and has increasingly engaged in aggressive collective bargaining, including the use of strikebreakers. Within unionized firms, employers have substituted machinery for workers, subcontracted work to nonunion suppliers, and shifted the production of components to low-wage nations. Nonunion firms have greatly improved their wage, fringe benefits, and working conditions. That has reduced the demand for unionism.

Collective Bargaining

Despite the overall decline of unionism, **collective bargaining** (the negotiation of labor contracts) remains an important feature of labor-management relations in several U.S. industries. The goal of collective bargaining is to establish a "work agreement" between the firm and the union.

Collective bargaining agreements (contracts) assume many forms, but typically cover several topics.

Union Status

Union status is the degree of security afforded a union by the work agreement. The strongest form of union security is a **closed shop,** in which a worker must be (or must become) a member of the union before being hired. Under Federal labor law, such shops are illegal in industries other than transportation and construction.

In contrast, a **union shop** permits the employer to hire nonunion workers but provides that these workers must join the union within a specified period, say 30 days, or relinquish their jobs. An **agency shop** allows nonunion workers but requires nonunion workers to either pay union dues or donate an equivalent amount to charity. Union and agency shops are legal, except in the 22 states that expressly prohibit them through so-called **right-to-work laws.**

In an **open shop,** an employer may hire either union or nonunion workers. Those who are nonunion are not obligated to join the union or to pay union dues; they may continue on their jobs indefinitely as nonunion workers. Nevertheless, the wages, hours, and working conditions set forth in the work agreement apply to the nonunion workers as well as to the union workers.

Managerial Prerogatives

Most work agreements contain clauses outlining certain decisions that are reserved solely for management. These managerial prerogatives usually cover such matters as the size and location of plants, the products to be manufactured, and the types of equipment and materials to be used in production and in production scheduling.

Wages and Hours

The focal point of almost all bargaining agreements is wages (including fringe benefits) and hours. Both labor and management press for the advantage in wage bargaining. The arguments that unions use most frequently in demanding wage boosts are (1) "what others are getting"; (2) the employer's ability to pay, based on its profitability; (3) increases in the cost of living; and (4) increases in labor productivity.

Hours of work, voluntary versus mandatory overtime, holiday and vacation provisions, profit sharing, health plans, and pension benefits are other contract issues that must be addressed in the bargaining process.

Seniority and Job Protection

The uncertainty of employment in a market economy, along with the fear of antiunion discrimination on the part of employers, has made workers and their unions "job-conscious." The explicit and detailed provisions covering job opportunities that most agreements contain reflect this concern. Unions stress length of service, or *seniority*, as the basis for worker promotion and for layoff and recall. They want the worker with the longest continuous service to have the first chance at relevant promotions, to be the last one laid off, and to be the first one recalled from layoff.

In recent years, unions have become increasingly sensitive to losing jobs to nonunion subcontractors and to overseas workers. Unions sometimes seek limits on the firm's ability to subcontract out work or to relocate production facilities overseas.

Grievance Procedures

Even the most detailed and comprehensive work agreement cannot spell out all the specific issues and problems that might occur during its life. For example, suppose a particular worker gets reassigned to a less pleasant job. Was this reassignment for legitimate business reasons or, as the person suspects, because of a personality conflict with a particular manager? Labor contracts contain grievance procedures to resolve such matters.

The Bargaining Process

The date for the beginning of collective bargaining on a new contract is usually specified in the existing contract and is typically 60 days before the current one expires.

The union normally takes the initiative, presenting its demands in the form of specific wage, fringe-benefit, and other adjustments to the present union-management contract. The firm counters with an offer relating to these and other contract provisions. It is not unusual for the original union demand and the first offer by the firm to be far apart, not only because of the parties' conflicting goals but also because starting far apart leaves plenty of room for compromise and counter offers during negotiations.

Hanging over the negotiations is the contract deadline, which occurs the moment the present contract expires. At that time there is a possibility of a **strike**—a work stoppage by the union—if it thinks its demands are not being satisfactorily met. But there is also the possibility that at the deadline the firm may engage in a **lockout,** in which it forbids the workers to return to work until a new contract is signed. In this setting of uncertainty prior to the deadline, both parties feel pressure to find mutually acceptable terms.

Although bluster and bickering often occur in collective bargaining, labor and management display a remarkable capacity for compromise and agreement. Typically they reach a compromise that is written into a new contract. Nevertheless, strikes and lockouts occasionally do occur. When they happen, workers lose income and firms lose profit. To stem their losses, both parties usually look for and eventually find ways to settle the labor dispute and get the workers back to work.

Bargaining, strikes, and lockouts occur within a framework of Federal labor law, specifically the **National Labor Relations Act (NLRA).** This act was first passed as the Wagner Act of 1935 and later amended by the Taft-Hartley Act of 1947 and the Landrum-Griffin Act of 1959. The act sets forth the *dos and don'ts* of union and management labor practices. For example, while union members can picket in front of a firm's business, they cannot block access to the business by customers, coworkers, or strikebreakers hired by the firm. Another example: Firms cannot refuse to meet and talk with the union's designated representatives.

Either unions or management can file charges of unfair labor practices under the labor law. The **National** **Labor Relations Board (NLRB)** has the authority to investigate such charges and to issue cease-and-desist orders in the event of a violation. The board also conducts worker elections to decide which specific union, if any, a group of workers might want to have represent them in collective bargaining.

Economic Effects of Unions

The most straightforward effect of unions is an increase in the wage rates for their members. The consensus estimate is that the overall union wage premium (wage advantage) averages about 15 percent. The effects of unions on output and efficiency, however, are slightly more complicated.

Featherbedding and Work Rules

Some unions diminish output and efficiency by engaging in "make-work" or "featherbedding" practices and resisting the introduction of output-increasing machinery and equipment. These productivity-reducing practices often arise in periods of technological change. For example, in 2002 the ILWU (dockworkers' union) obtained a contract provision guaranteeing 40-hour-per week jobs for all current ILWU clerical personnel for as long as they wish to continue working at their current jobs at West Coast ports. However, many of those workers will not be needed because the ports are rapidly moving toward labor-saving computerized systems for tracking cargo. Thus, many of the current clerical personnel will be paid for doing little or nothing. This will be very inefficient.

More generally, unions may reduce efficiency by establishing work rules and practices that impede putting the most productive workers in particular jobs. Under seniority rules, for example, workers may be promoted for their employment tenure rather than for their ability to perform the available job with the greatest efficiency. Also, unions might restrict the kinds of tasks workers may perform. Contract provisions may prohibit sheet-metal workers or bricklayers from doing the simple carpentry work often associated with their jobs. Observance of such rules means, in this instance, that firms must hire unneeded and under-used carpenters.

Finally, critics of unions contend that union contracts often chip away at managerial prerogatives to establish work schedules, determine production targets, introduce new technology, and make other decisions contributing to productive efficiency.

Output Losses from Strikes

A second way unions can impair efficiency and output is through strikes. If union and management reach an impasse during their contract negotiations, a strike may result and the firm's production may cease for the strike's duration. If so, the firm will forgo sales and profit; workers will sacrifice income; and the economy might lose output. U.S. strike activity, however, has dwindled in the past few decades. In 2009 there were only 5 major work stoppages—strikes or lockouts involving 1000 or more employees. This was the lowest number of major work stoppages in a single year since the U.S. government began collecting data on work stoppages in 1947. The prior low was 14 in 2003.

About 13,000 workers were idled by the 5 work stoppages in 2009, with the average length of stoppages being 13 days. It is estimated that the amount of work time lost to the stoppages was less than .005 percent of the total work time provided by employees that year.

But the amount of work time lost is an imprecise indicator of the potential economic costs of strikes. These costs may be greater than indicated if strikes disrupt production in nonstruck firms that either supply inputs to struck firms or buy products from them. Example: An extended strike in the auto industry might reduce output and cause layoffs in firms producing, say, glass, tires, paints, and fabrics used in producing cars. It also may reduce sales and cause layoffs in auto dealerships.

On the other hand, the costs of strikes may be less than is implied by the work time lost by strikers if nonstruck firms increase their output to offset the loss of production by struck firms. While the output of General

Motors declines when its workers strike, auto buyers may shift their demand to Ford, Toyota, or Honda, which will respond by increasing their employment and output. Therefore, although GM and its employees are hurt by a strike, society as a whole may experience little or no decline in employment, real output, and income.

Efficiency Losses from Labor Misallocation

A third and more subtle way that unions might reduce efficiency and output is through the union wage advantage itself. Figure 2 splits the economy into two sectors, showing identical labor demand curves for the unionized sector and the nonunionized sector. If all markets are competitive and no union is initially present in either sector, the wage rate in both parts of the economy will be W_n and N_1 workers will be employed in each sector.

Now suppose workers form a union in sector 1 and succeed in increasing the wage rate from W_n to W_u. As a consequence, $N_1 - N_2$ workers lose their jobs in the union sector. Assume that they all move to nonunion sector 2, where they are employed. This increase in labor supply (not shown) in the nonunion sector increases the quantity of labor supplied there from N_1 to N_3, reducing the wage rate from W_n to W_s.

Recall that the labor demand curves reflect the marginal revenue products (MRPs) of workers or, in other words, the contribution that each additional worker makes

FIGURE 2 The effects of the union wage advantage on the allocation of labor. The higher wage W_u that the union receives in sector 1 causes the displacement of $N_1 - N_2$ workers. The reemployment of these workers in sector 2 increases employment from N_1 to N_3 and reduces the wage rate there from W_n to W_s. The associated loss of output in the union sector is area A + B + C, while the gain in the nonunion sector is only D + E. The net loss of output is area B. This loss of output suggests that the union wage advantage has resulted in a misallocation of labor and a decline in economic efficiency.

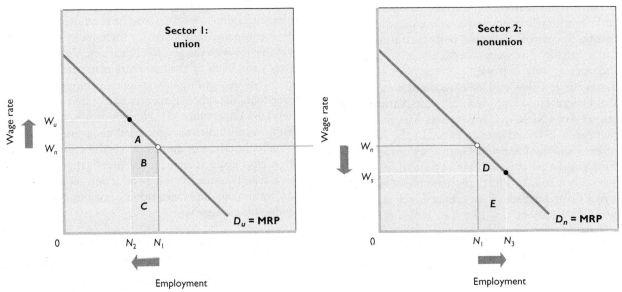

to domestic output. This means that area A + B + C in the union sector represents the sum of the MRPs—the total contribution to domestic output—of the workers displaced by the wage increase achieved by the union. The reemployment of these workers in nonunion sector 2 produces an increase in domestic output shown by area D + E. Because area A + B + C exceeds area D + E, a net loss of domestic output is the result.

More precisely, because A = D and C = E, the efficiency loss attributable to the union wage advantage is represented by area B. Because the same amount of employed labor is now producing a smaller output, labor is being misallocated and used inefficiently. After the shift of N_1N_2 workers to the nonunion sector has occurred, workers in both sectors will be paid wage rates according to their MRPs. But the workers who shifted sectors will be working at a lower MRP than before. An economy always obtains a larger domestic output when labor is reallocated from a low MRP use to a high-MRP use. But here the opposite has occurred. And assuming the union can maintain the W_u wage rate in its sector, a reallocation of labor from sector 2 to sector 1 will never occur.

Attempts to estimate the efficiency loss associated with union wage gains, however, suggest that it is very small: perhaps 0.2 to 0.4 percent (or one-fifth of 1 percent to two-fifths of 1 percent) of U.S. GDP. In 2009 this cost would be about $29 billion to $58 billion.

Offsetting Factors

Some long-run consequences of unionization may enhance productivity and reduce the efficiency loss from unions. One such impact is lower worker turnover within unionized firms. Compared with the rates at nonunion firms, the quit rates (resignation rates) for union workers are 31 to 65 percent lower, depending on the industry.

The union wage premium may reduce worker turnover by increasing the desirability of the union job relative to alternative employment. In economic terms, the higher opportunity cost of quitting reduces the frequency of quitting. Unions also may reduce turnover by using collective communication—the **voice mechanism**—to correct job dissatisfactions that otherwise would be "resolved" by workers quitting and taking other jobs—the **exit mechanism.** It might be risky for individual workers to express their dissatisfaction to employers because employers might retaliate by firing them as "troublemakers." But a union can provide workers with a collective voice to communicate problems and grievances to management and to press for satisfactory resolutions.

A lower quit rate may give a firm a more experienced, more productive workforce. Over time, that might offset a part of the higher costs and reduced profitability associated with the union premium. Also, having fewer resignations might reduce the firm's recruitment, screening, and hiring costs. Additionally, reduced turnover may encourage employers to invest more in the training (and therefore the productivity) of their workers. If a worker quits or "exits" at the end of, say, a year's training, the employer will get no return from providing that training. Lower turnover increases the likelihood that the employer will receive a return on the training it provides, thereby increasing its willingness to upgrade the skills of its workforce. All these factors may increase the long-run productivity of the unionized labor force and therefore reduce the efficiency loss caused by the union wage premium.

Appendix Summary

1. About 8 million of the 15.3 million union members in 2009 belonged to unions affiliated with the AFL-CIO; another 6 million belonged to 7 unions loosely federated under the name Change to Win. The rest were members of other independent unions. About 12.3 percent of U.S. wage and salary workers in 2009 were union members, with government employees having the highest unionization rates. As an occupation, public school teachers have the highest rate of unionization—38 percent.

2. Union membership has declined as a percentage of the labor force and in absolute numbers in recent decades. Some of the key causes are structural changes such as the shift from manufacturing employment to service employment. Other causes include improved wages and working conditions in nonunion firms and increased managerial opposition to unions.

3. Collective bargaining determines the terms of union work agreements, which typically cover (a) union status and managerial prerogatives; (b) wages, hours, and working conditions; (c) control over job opportunities; and (d) grievance procedures. The bargaining process is governed by the National Labor Relations Act.

4. Union wages are on average about 15 percent higher than nonunion wages in comparable jobs. Restrictive union work rules, output losses from strikes, and labor misallocation from the union wage advantage are ways that unions may reduce efficiency, output, and productivity. The efficiency losses from unions may be partially offset in the long run by union productivity advances deriving from reduced labor turnover.

Appendix Terms and Concepts

American Federation of Labor and the Congress of Industrial Organizations (AFL-CIO)

Change to Win

independent unions

unionization rate

collective bargaining

closed shop

union shop

agency shop

right-to-work laws

open shop

strike

lockout

National Labor Relations Act (NLRA)

National Labor Relations Board (NLRB)

voice mechanism

exit mechanism

Appendix Questions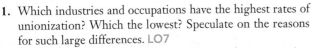

1. Which industries and occupations have the highest rates of unionization? Which the lowest? Speculate on the reasons for such large differences. LO7

2. What percentage of wage and salary workers are union members? Is this percentage higher, or is it lower, than in previous decades? Which of the factors explaining the trend do you think is most dominant? LO7

3. Suppose that you are president of a newly established local union about to bargain with an employer for the first time. List the basic areas you want covered in the work agreement. Why might you begin with a larger wage demand than you actually are willing to accept? What is the logic of a union threatening an employer with a strike during the collective bargaining process? Of an employer threatening the union with a lockout? What is the role of the deadline in encouraging agreement in collective bargaining? LO7

4. Explain how featherbedding and other restrictive work practices can reduce labor productivity. Why might strikes reduce the economy's output less than the loss of production by the struck firms? LO7

5. What is the estimated size of the union wage advantage? How might this advantage diminish the efficiency with which labor resources are allocated in the economy? Normally, labor resources of equal potential productivity flow from low-wage employment to high-wage employment. Why does that not happen to close the union wage advantage? LO7

6. Contrast the voice mechanism and the exit mechanism for communicating dissatisfaction. In what two ways do labor unions reduce labor turnover? How might such reductions increase productivity? LO7

Appendix Problems

1. Suppose that a delivery company currently uses one employee per vehicle to deliver packages. Each driver delivers 50 packages per day, and the firm charges $20 per package for delivery. LO7
   a. What is the MRP per driver per day?
   b. Now suppose that a union forces the company to place a supervisor in each vehicle at a cost of $300 per supervisor per day. The presence of the supervisor causes the number of packages delivered per vehicle per day to rise to 60 packages per day. What is the MRP per supervisor per day? By how much per vehicle per day do firm profits fall after supervisors are introduced?
   c. How many packages per day would each vehicle have to deliver in order to maintain the firm's profit per vehicle after supervisors are introduced?
   d. Suppose that the number of packages delivered per day cannot be increased but that the price per delivery might potentially be raised. What price would the firm have to charge for each delivery in order to maintain the firm's profit per vehicle after supervisors are introduced?

2. Suppose that a car factory initially hires 1500 workers at $30 per hour and that each worker works 40 hours per week.

Then the factory unionizes, and the new union demands that wages be raised by 10 percent. The firm accedes to that request in collective bargaining negotiations but then decides to cut the factory's labor force by 20 percent due to the higher labor costs. LO7
   a. What is the new union wage? How many workers does the factory employ after the agreement goes into effect?
   b. How much in total did the factory's workers receive in wage payments each week before the agreement? How much do the factory's remaining workers receive in wage payments each week after the agreement?
   c. Suppose that the workers who lose their jobs as a result of the agreement end up unemployed. By how much do the total wages received each week by the initial 1500 workers (both those who continue to be employed at the factory and those who lose their jobs) change from before the agreement to after the agreement?
   d. If the workers who lose their jobs as a result of the agreement end up making $15 per hour at jobs where they work 40 hours per week, by how much do the total wages received each week by the initial 1500 workers change from before the agreement to after the agreement?

CHAPTER 13

Wage Determination

The preceding chapter explained the demand for any resource in a competitive resource market. Chapter 13 uses demand and supply analysis to describe what determines the quantity of a particular resource—**labor**—and the price paid for it—**wages**—in different markets.

The chapter begins by defining terms and briefly discussing the general level of wages in the United States and other advanced economies. You will learn about the role that productivity plays in explaining the long-run growth of real wages and the increased demand for labor over time.

In a product market, the degree of competition significantly influences how prices are determined and what output is produced. In a labor resource market, the degree of competition directly affects the determination of **wage rates** and the level of employment. The main purpose of the chapter is to explain how wage rates and the quantity of labor are determined in labor markets varying in competitiveness.

Six labor markets are discussed in the chapter: (1) the **purely competitive** market, in which the number of employers is large and labor is nonunionized; (2) the **monopsony** market, in which a single employer hires labor under competitive (nonunion) conditions; (3) a market in which a union controls the supply of labor, the number of employers is large, and the union attempts to increase the total demand for labor; (4) a similar market in which the union attempts to reduce the total supply of labor; (5) another similar market in which the union attempts to obtain a wage rate that is above the competitive-equilibrium level by threatening to strike; and (6) the **bilateral monopoly** market, in which a single employer faces a labor supply controlled by a single union.

What is important for you to learn is how the characteristics of each labor market affect wage rates and employment. In the purely competitive or monopsony labor market, there is no union. The determination of the wage rate and employment will be quite definite, although different for each market. In the next four types of labor markets, **unions** control the supply of labor, and thus the outcomes for wage rates and employment will be less definite. If the demand for labor is competitive, the wage rate and the amount of employment will depend on how successful the union is in increasing the demand for labor, restricting the supply of labor, or setting a wage rate that employers will accept. If there is both a union and one employer (a bilateral monopoly), wages and employment will fall within certain limits, but exactly where will depend on the bargaining power of the union or the employer.

Three other issues are discussed in the last three sections of the chapter. First, for many years the Federal government has set a legal **minimum wage** for labor. The chapter uses supply and demand analysis to make the case for and against the minimum wage and then discusses its real-world effects. Second, wage rates are not homogeneous and differ across workers and occupations. The chapter presents important reasons why these **wage differentials** exist. Third, there is a **principal–agent problem** in most types of employment that may lead to shirking on the job. Different pay schemes have been devised to tie workers' pay to performance in an effort to overcome this problem. Each of these issues should be of direct interest to you and deepen your understanding about how labor markets work.

■ CHECKLIST

When you have studied this chapter you should be able to

☐ Define wages (or the wage rate).

☐ Distinguish between nominal and real wages.

☐ List five reasons for high productivity in the United States and other advanced economies.

☐ Describe the long-run relationship between real wages and productivity in the United States.

☐ Evaluate the importance of the two factors contributing to the long-run trend of growth in U.S. real wages.

☐ Define the three characteristics of a purely competitive labor market.

☐ Use demand and supply graphs to explain wage rates and the equilibrium level of employment in a purely competitive labor market.

☐ Define the three characteristics of a labor market monopsony and compare it with a purely competitive labor market.

☐ Explain why the marginal resource cost exceeds the wage rate in monopsony.

☐ Use demand and supply graphs to explain wage rates and the equilibrium level of employment in the monopsony model.

☐ Give examples of monopsony power.

☐ List three types of union models.

☐ Identify two strategies of labor unions to increase the demand for labor and their effects on wage rates and employment.

☐ Explain and illustrate graphically the effects of actions taken by craft unions to decrease the supply of labor on wages and the employment of workers.

☐ Explain and illustrate graphically how the organization of workers by an industrial union in a previously competitive labor market would affect the wage rate and the employment level.

☐ Describe the effect of unions on wage increases and union employment.

☐ Use a graph to explain why the equilibrium wage rate and employment level are indeterminate when a labor market is a bilateral monopoly and to predict the range for the wage rate.

☐ Present the case for and the case against a legally established minimum wage.

☐ Use supply and demand analysis to explain wage differentials.

☐ Connect wage differentials to marginal revenue productivity.

☐ Give two reasons why noncompeting groups of workers earn different wages.

☐ Explain why some wage differentials are due to compensatory differences in the nonmonetary aspects of jobs.

☐ Cite four types of labor market imperfections that contribute to wage differentials.

☐ Describe the principal–agent problem in worker pay and performance.

☐ Describe four pay schemes employers use to prevent shirking or to tie worker pay to performance.

☐ Explain the negative side effects of pay-for-performance schemes.

☐ Evaluate from an economic perspective the issue of whether chief executive officers (CEOs) of corporations are overpaid (*Last Word*).

■ **CHAPTER OUTLINE**

1. A *wage* (or the *wage rate*) is the price paid per unit of time for any type of labor. Earnings are equal to the wage multiplied by the amount of time worked. Wages can be measured either in nominal or real terms. A *real wage* is adjusted for the effects of inflation. It reflects the quantity of goods and services a worker can purchase with a *nominal wage.*

2. The *general level of real wages* in the United States and other advanced economies is high because the demand for labor has been large relative to the supply of labor.
   a. The demand for labor in the United States and advanced economies has been strong because labor is highly productive for several reasons: substantial quantities of capital goods and natural resources; technological advancement; improvements in labor quality; and other intangible factors (management techniques, business environment, and size of the domestic market).
   b. The real hourly wage rate and output per hour of labor are closely and directly related to each other, and real income per worker can increase only at the same rate as output per worker (productivity).
   c. The long-run trend shows that real wages have increased because increases in the demand for labor

over time have been greater than increases in the supply of labor in the United States.

3. In a *purely competitive labor market* many firms compete in hiring a specific type of labor and there are many qualified workers with identical skills who independently supply this labor. Both firms and workers are "wage takers" who do not influence the price of labor.
   a. The market *demand curve* for labor is a horizontal summation of the demand curves for individual firms.
   b. The market *supply curve* slopes upward, indicating that a higher wage will entice more workers to supply their labor.
   c. The *wage rate* for labor in this market is determined by the interaction of the market demand for and the supply of that labor. For the individual firm, the supply of labor is perfectly elastic at this wage rate (so the marginal labor cost is equal to the wage rate). The firm will hire the amount of labor at which its marginal revenue product of labor is equal to its marginal labor cost.

4. In a *monopsony* market for labor, there is only one buyer of a particular kind of labor, the labor is relatively immobile, and the hiring firm is a "wage maker" (the wage rate a firm pays varies with the number of workers it employs).
   a. The supply curve is up-sloping and indicates that the firm (the single buyer of labor) must pay higher wages to attract more workers.
   b. A monopsonistic firm's marginal labor costs are greater than the wage rates it must pay to obtain various amounts of labor because once it offers a higher wage to one worker, it must offer the same wage to all workers.
   c. The firm hires the amount of labor at which marginal labor cost and the marginal revenue product of labor are equal. Both the wage rate and the level of employment are less than they would be under purely competitive conditions in labor markets.
   (1) Note that if the firm employs resources in imperfectly competitive markets, it is hiring resources in the least-cost combination when the ratio of the marginal product of a resource to its marginal resource cost is the same for all resources.
   (2) It is hiring resources in the most profitable combination when the marginal revenue product of each resource is equal to its marginal resource cost.
   d. Monopsony power can be found in such situations as small cities where there are one or two firms that hire most of the workers of a particular type in a region or in professional sports franchises that have exclusive rights to obtain the service of professional athletes.

5. In labor markets in which *labor unions* represent workers, the unions attempt to raise wages in three ways.
   a. The union can increase *the demand for labor* by increasing the demand for the products the union workers produce through political lobbying. They also can increase demand by increasing the prices of resources that are substitutes for the labor provided by the mem-

bers of the union or by reducing the price of a complementary resource.

b. With *exclusive unionism,* a *craft union* will seek to increase wages by reducing the supply of labor. *Occupational licensing* is another means of restricting the supply of a particular type of labor.

c. With *inclusive unionism* an industrial union will try to increase wages by forcing employers to pay wages in excess of the equilibrium rate that would prevail in a purely competitive labor market.

d. Labor unions are aware that their actions to increase wage rates may also increase the unemployment of their members, which tends to limit the demands for higher wages.

6. A *bilateral monopoly* is a labor market with a monopsony (single buyer of labor) and an inclusive union (single seller of labor).

a. In this situation, the wage rate depends, within certain limits, on the relative bargaining power of the union and of the employer.

b. This model may be desirable because the monopoly power on the buy side is offset by the monopoly power on the sell side. The resulting wage rate may be close to levels found in purely competitive markets.

7. The *minimum wage* is a price floor that has been used to set a minimum price for unskilled labor.

a. Critics argue that it increases wage rates and reduces the employment of workers. It is a poor policy for reducing household poverty because the benefits largely go to teenagers who do not need the assistance.

b. Defenders think that in a monopsonistic market, it can increase the wage rate and employment. A minimum wage also may increase productivity, thus increasing the demand for labor and reducing labor turnover.

c. The evidence is mixed. In theory, a higher wage should reduce employment, but in practice the negative effects on employment may be minor or nil. The minimum wage, however, is not a strong antipoverty policy, despite its popular appeal in this respect.

8. *Wage differentials* are found across many occupations. They are often explained by the forces of demand and supply.

a. The strength of the demand for workers in an occupation, given the supply of workers, is due largely to the productivity of workers and the revenues they generate for the firm (or *marginal revenue productivity*).

b. One major reason for wage differentials is that workers are not homogeneous and can be thought of as falling into many *noncompeting groups.* The wages for each group differ because of

(1) differences in the abilities or skills possessed by workers, the number of workers in each group, and the demand for those abilities or skills in the labor market

(2) the stock of knowledge and skills people have, called *human capital.* Investment in human capital by workers through education and training can lead to higher future wages.

c. A second reason for wage differentials is that jobs vary in difficulty and attractiveness, so there are *compensating differences.* Higher wages may be necessary to compensate for less desirable nonmonetary aspects of some jobs.

d. A third reason for wage differentials is market imperfections. These arise from a lack of job information, geographic immobilities, union or government restraints, and discrimination.

9. Wage payments in labor markets are often more complex in practice and are often designed to make a connection between *worker pay and performance.*

a. A principal–agent problem arises when the interests of agents (workers) diverge from the interests of the principals (firms). For example, shirking on the job can occur if workers give less than the desired level of performance for pay received.

b. Firms can try to reduce shirking by monitoring worker activity, but this monitoring is costly; therefore, *incentive pay plans* are adopted by firms to tie worker compensation more closely to performance. Among the various incentive schemes are

(1) piece rate payments, commissions, royalties, bonuses, and profit sharing plans

(2) efficiency wages that pay workers above-market wages to get greater effort.

c. Sometimes the "solutions" to principal–agent problems lead to negative results. Commissions may cause employees to pad bills; changes in work rules may demoralize workers.

10. (*Last Word*). The basic argument for why CEOs are highly paid is related to market conditions. On the supply side, there is a restrictive supply of corporate talent to provide leadership and direction. On the demand side, there is a high demand for individuals who have the qualities necessary to make the major managerial decisions and lead corporations. These market conditions of limited supply and high demand explain the high salaries. In addition, becoming a CEO has the elements of a game or tournament. The fact that there is a prize for winning will encourage intense competition and increase productivity. Critics of CEO payment think corporate boards that set CEO pay are too controlled by the CEO and these board members overvalue CEO work.

■ **HINTS AND TIPS**

1. The reason why the market supply curve for labor rises in competitive markets is based on an economic concept from Chapter 2 that you may want to review. To obtain more workers, firms must increase wages to cover the **opportunity cost** of workers' time spent on other alternatives (other employment, household work, or leisure).

2. In monopsony, the marginal resource cost exceeds the wage rate (and the marginal-resource-cost curve lies above the supply curve of labor). The relationship is difficult to understand, so you should pay careful attention to the discussion of Table 13.2 and Figure 13.4.

3. To illustrate the differences in the three union models presented in this chapter, draw supply and demand graphs of each model.

4. The chapter presents the positive economic explanations for the differences in wages between occupations. Remember that whether these wage differentials are "fair" is a normative question. (See Chapter 1 for the positive and normative distinction.)

■ **IMPORTANT TERMS**

wage rate	bilateral monopoly
real wage	minimum wage
nominal wage	wage differentials
purely competitive labor market	marginal revenue productivity
monopsony	noncompeting groups
exclusive unionism	human capital
occupational licensing	compensating differences
inclusive unionism	incentive pay plan

SELF-TEST

■ **FILL-IN QUESTIONS**

1. The price paid for labor per unit of time is the (piece, wage) _____ rate. The earnings of labor are equal to the _____ rate (divided, multiplied) _____ by the amount of time worked. The amount of money received per hour or day by a worker is the (nominal, real) _____ wage, while the purchasing power of that money is the _____ wage.

2. The general level of wages is high in the United States and other advanced economies because the demand for labor in these economies is (weak, strong) _____ relative to the supply of labor. United States labor tends to be highly productive, among other reasons, because it has access to relatively large amounts of (consumer, capital) _____ goods, plentiful (financial, natural) _____ resources, a high-quality (service sector, labor force) _____, and superior (wages, technology) _____. There is a close (short-run, long-run) _____ relationship between output per labor hour and real hourly wages in the United States.

3. In a purely competitive labor market,
a. the supply curve slopes upward from left to right because it is necessary for employers to pay (higher, lower) _____ wages to attract workers from alternative employment. The market supply curve rises because it is an (average cost, opportunity cost) _____ curve.

b. the demand is the sum of the marginal (revenue product, resource cost) _____ schedules of all firms hiring this type of labor.
c. the wage rate will equal the rate at which the total quantity of labor demanded is (less than, equal to, greater than) _____ the total quantity of labor supplied.

4. Insofar as an individual firm hiring labor in a purely competitive market is concerned, the supply of labor is perfectly (elastic, inelastic) _____ because the individual firm is unable to affect the wage rate it must pay. The firm will hire that quantity of labor at which the wage rate, or marginal labor cost, is (less than, equal to, greater than) _____ the marginal revenue product.

5. A monopsonist employing labor in a market that is competitive on the supply side will hire that amount of labor at which the marginal revenue product is (less than, equal to, greater than) _____ marginal labor cost. In such a market, the marginal labor cost is (less, greater) _____ than the wage rate, so the employer will pay a wage rate that is _____ than both the marginal revenue product of labor and the marginal labor cost.

6. A monopsonist facing a competitive supply of labor
a. is employing the combination of resources that enables it to produce any given output in the least costly way when the marginal product of every resource (divided, multiplied) _____ by its marginal resource cost is the same for all resources.
b. is employing the combination of resources that maximizes its profits when the marginal revenue product of every resource is (equal to, greater than) _____ its marginal resource cost or when the marginal revenue product of each resource (divided, multiplied) _____ by its marginal resource cost is equal to (infinity, 1) _____.

7. When compared with a competitive labor market, a market dominated by a monopsonist results in (higher, lower) _____ wage rates and in (more, less) _____ employment.

8. The basic objective of labor unions is to increase wages, and they attempt to accomplish this goal either by increasing the (demand for, supply of) _____ labor, restricting the _____ labor, or imposing (a below, an above) _____-equilibrium wage rate on employers.

9. Labor unions can increase the demand for the services of their members by increasing the (demand for, supply of) _____ the products they produce, by (increasing, decreasing) _____ the prices of resources that are substitutes for the services supplied by their members, and by (increasing, decreasing)

_____ the price of a complementary resource used to produce a product.

10. Restricting the supply of labor to increase wages is the general policy of (exclusive, inclusive) _____ unionism, and imposing above-equilibrium wage rates is the strategy used in _____ unionism. An example of exclusive unionism is (an industrial, a craft) _____ union, while an example of inclusive unionism would be _____ union.

11. If unions are successful in increasing wages, employment in the industry will (increase, decrease) _____, but this effect on members may lead unions to _____ their wage demands. Unions, however, will not worry too much about the effect on employment from the higher wage rates if the economy is growing or if the demand for labor is relatively (elastic, inelastic) _____.

12. In a labor market that is a bilateral monopoly, the monopsonist will try to pay a wage (less, greater) _____ than the marginal revenue product of labor; the union will ask for some wage _____ than the competitive and monopsonist equilibrium wage. Within these limits, the (wage rate, elasticity) _____ of labor will depend on the relative bargaining strength of the union and the monopsonist.

13. Critics of the minimum wage contend that in purely competitive labor markets, the effect of imposing such a wage is to (increase, decrease) _____ the wage rate and to _____ employment. Defenders of the minimum wage argue that such labor markets are monopsonistic, so the effect is to (increase, decrease) _____ the wage rate and to _____ employment. The evidence suggests that the employment and antipoverty effects from increasing the minimum wage are (positive, uncertain) _____.

14. Actual wage rates received by different workers tend to differ because workers (are, are not) _____ homogeneous, jobs (vary, do not vary) _____ in attractiveness, and labor markets may be (perfect, imperfect) _____.

15. The total labor force is composed of a number of (competing, noncompeting) _____ groups of workers. Wages differ among these groups as a consequence of differences in (ability, wealth) _____ and because of different investments in (the stock market, human capital) _____.

16. Within each of these noncompeting groups, some workers receive higher wages than others to compensate these workers for the less desirable (monetary, nonmonetary) _____ aspects of a job. These wage differentials are called (monopsony, compensating) _____ differences.

17. Workers performing identical jobs often receive different wages due to market imperfections such as lack of information about (investment, job) _____ opportunities, geographic (mobility, immobility) _____, union or government (subsidies, restraints) _____, and (taxes, discrimination) _____.

18. Firms, or parties, who hire others to achieve their objectives may be regarded as (agents, principals) _____, while workers, or parties, who are hired to advance firms' interests can be regarded as the firms' _____. The objective of a firm is to maximize (wages, profits) _____ and workers are hired to help a firm achieve that objective in return for _____, but when the interests of a firm and the workers diverge, a principal–agent problem is created.

19. An example of this type of problem is a situation in which workers provide less than the agreed amount of work effort on the job, which is called (licensure, shirking) _____. To prevent this situation, firms can closely monitor job (pay, performance) _____, but this is costly; therefore, many firms offer different incentive _____ plans.

20. Examples of such pay-for-performance schemes include (efficiency, piece) _____ rate payments, commissions and royalties, bonuses and profit sharing, and _____ wages, which means that workers are paid above-equilibrium wages to encourage greater work effort. Such plans must be designed with care because of possible (positive, negative) _____ side effects.

■ **TRUE–FALSE QUESTIONS**

Circle T if the statement is true, F if it is false.

1. If you received a 5% increase in your nominal wage and the price level increased by 3%, then your real wage has increased by 8%. **T F**

2. The general level of wages is high in the United States and other advanced economies because the supply of labor is large relative to the demand for it. **T F**

3. One reason for the high productivity of labor in the United States and other advanced economies is access to large amounts of capital equipment. **T F**

4. Real hourly compensation per worker can increase only at about the same rate as output per worker. **T F**

5. In a purely competitive labor market, there are few qualified workers who supply labor and few firms who employ labor. **T F**

6. If an individual firm employs labor in a purely competitive market, it finds that its marginal labor cost is equal to the wage rate in that market. **T F**

7. Given a purely competitive employer's demand for labor, a lower wage will result in more workers being hired. **T F**

8. Both monopsonists and firms hiring labor in purely competitive markets hire labor up to the quantity at which the marginal revenue product of labor and marginal labor cost are equal. **T F**

9. Political lobbying for special projects or legislation is used by unions to increase the demand for labor. **T F**

10. One strategy unions use to bolster the demand for union workers is to lobby against a higher minimum wage for nonunion workers. **T F**

11. Restricting the supply of labor is a means of increasing wage rates more commonly used by craft unions than by industrial unions. **T F**

12. Occupational licensing is a means of increasing the supply of specific kinds of labor. **T F**

13. Unions that seek to organize all available or potential workers in an industry are called craft unions. **T F**

14. The imposition of an above-equilibrium wage rate will cause employment to fall off more when the demand for labor is inelastic than it will when the demand is elastic. **T F**

15. Union members are paid wage rates that on the average are greater by about 15% than the wage rates paid to nonunion members. **T F**

16. The actions of both exclusive and inclusive unions that raise the wage rates paid to them by competitive employers of labor also cause, other things remaining constant, an increase in the employment of their members. **T F**

17. In a bilateral monopoly, the negotiated wage will be below the competitive equilibrium wage in that labor market. **T F**

18. If a labor market is purely competitive, the imposition of an effective minimum wage will increase the wage rate paid and decrease employment in that market. **T F**

19. If an effective minimum wage is imposed on a monopsonist, the wage rate paid by the firm will increase and the number of workers employed by it may also increase. **T F**

20. The strength of labor demand differs greatly among occupations due to differences in how much each occupation contributes to its employer's revenue. **T F**

21. Actual wage rates received in different labor markets tend to differ because the demands for particular types of labor relative to their supplies differ. **T F**

22. Wage differentials that are used to compensate workers for unpleasant aspects of a job are called efficiency wages. **T F**

23. Market imperfections that impede workers from moving from lower- to higher-paying jobs help explain wage differentials. **T F**

24. Shirking is an example of a principal–agent problem. **T F**

25. There are examples of solutions that have been implemented to solve principal–agent problems that produce negative results. **T F**

■ **MULTIPLE-CHOICE QUESTIONS**

Circle the letter that corresponds to the best answer.

1. Real wages would decline if the
(a) prices of goods and services rose more rapidly than nominal-wage rates
(b) prices of goods and services rose less rapidly than nominal-wage rates
(c) prices of goods and services and wage rates both rose
(d) prices of goods and services and wage rates both fell

2. The basic explanation for high real wages in the United States and other industrially advanced economies is that the
(a) price levels in these nations have increased at a faster rate than nominal wages
(b) governments in these nations have imposed effective minimum wage laws to improve the conditions of labor
(c) demand for labor in these nations is quite large relative to the supply of labor
(d) supply of labor in these nations is quite large relative to the demand for labor

3. A characteristic of a purely competitive labor market would be
(a) firms hiring different types of labor
(b) workers supplying labor under a union contract
(c) wage taker behavior by the firms
(d) price maker behavior by the firms

4. The supply curve for labor in a purely competitive market is up-sloping because the
(a) opportunity costs for workers rise
(b) marginal resource cost is constant
(c) wage rate paid to workers falls
(d) marginal revenue product rises

5. The individual firm that hires labor under purely competitive conditions faces a supply curve for labor that
(a) is perfectly inelastic
(b) is of unitary elasticity
(c) is perfectly elastic
(d) slopes upward from left to right

6. Which is a characteristic of a monopsonist?
(a) The type of labor is relatively mobile.
(b) The supply curve is the marginal resource cost curve.

(c) There are many buyers of a particular kind of labor.
(d) The wage rate it must pay workers varies directly with the number of workers it employs.

7. A monopsonist pays a wage rate that is
(a) greater than the marginal revenue product of labor
(b) equal to the marginal revenue product of labor
(c) equal to the firm's marginal labor cost
(d) less than the marginal revenue product of labor

8. If a firm employs resources in imperfectly competitive markets, to maximize its profits the marginal revenue product of each resource must equal
(a) its marginal product
(b) its marginal resource cost
(c) its price
(d) 1

9. Compared with a purely competitive labor market, a monopsonistic market will result in
(a) higher wage rates and a higher level of employment
(b) higher wage rates and a lower level of employment
(c) lower wage rates and a higher level of employment
(d) lower wage rates and a lower level of employment

10. The monopsonistic labor market for nurses that would be found in a smaller city with two hospitals would lead to
(a) lower starting salaries
(b) higher starting salaries
(c) more employment opportunities
(d) greater demand for nursing services

11. One way that unions can increase the demand for their labor is to
(a) Increase the supply of their labor
(b) decrease in the productivity of their labor
(c) demand an above-equilibrium wage rate
(d) increase the demand for products they help produce

12. Occupational licensing laws have the economic effect of
(a) increasing the demand for labor
(b) decreasing the supply of labor
(c) strengthening the bargaining position of an industrial union
(d) weakening the bargaining position of a craft union

13. Industrial unions typically attempt to increase wage rates by
(a) imposing an above-equilibrium wage rate on employers
(b) decreasing the demand for labor
(c) increasing the supply of labor
(d) forming a bilateral monopoly

14. Which of the following is a significant trade-off that unions face?
(a) Actions by inclusive unions on wages undermine actions by exclusive unions.
(b) When unions obtain higher wage rates it reduces the number of union workers employed.
(c) An increase in the price of a substitute labor resource will decrease the employment of union workers.
(d) A decrease in the price of a complementary resource will decrease the employment of union workers.

Answer Questions 15, 16, and 17 using the data in the following table.

Wage rate	Quantity of labor supplied	Marginal labor cost	Marginal revenue product of labor
$10	0	—	—
11	100	$11	$17
12	200	13	16
13	300	15	15
14	400	17	14
15	500	19	13
16	600	21	12

15. If the firm employing labor were a monopsonist, the wage rate and the quantity of labor employed would be, respectively,
(a) $14 and 300
(b) $13 and 400
(c) $14 and 400
(d) $13 and 300

16. But if the market for this labor were purely competitive, the wage rate and the quantity of labor employed would be, respectively,
(a) $14 and 300
(b) $13 and 400
(c) $14 and 400
(d) $13 and 300

17. If the firm employing labor were a monopsonist and the workers were represented by an industrial union, the wage rate would be
(a) between $13 and $14
(b) between $13 and $15
(c) between $14 and $15
(d) below $13 or above $15

*Answer Questions 18, 19, 20, and 21 on the basis of the following labor market diagram, where **D** is the demand curve for labor, **S** is the supply curve for labor, and **MRC** is the marginal resource (labor) cost.*

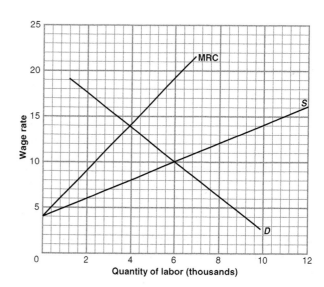

18. If this were a purely competitive labor market, the number of workers hired and the wage rate in equilibrium would be
  (a) 4000 and $14
  (b) 4000 and $8
  (c) 6000 and $10
  (d) 8000 and $12

19. If this were a monopsonistic labor market, the number of workers hired and the wage rate in equilibrium would be
  (a) 4000 and $14
  (b) 4000 and $8
  (c) 6000 and $10
  (d) 8000 and $12

20. Suppose an inclusive union seeks to maximize the employment of workers with the monopsonist. If successful, the number of workers employed and the wage rate would be
  (a) 4000 and $14
  (b) 6000 and $12
  (c) 6000 and $10
  (d) 8000 and $12

21. If the market were characterized as a bilateral monopoly, the number of workers hired and the wage rate in equilibrium would be
  (a) 6000 and $10
  (b) 4000 and $14
  (c) 4000 and $8
  (d) indeterminate

22. The major reason that major league baseball players receive an average salary of over $1 million a year and teachers receive an average salary of about $40,000 a year can best be explained in terms of
  (a) noncompeting labor groups
  (b) compensating differences
  (c) lack of job information
  (d) discrimination

23. The fact that unskilled construction workers typically receive higher wages than bank clerks is best explained in terms of
  (a) noncompeting labor groups
  (b) compensating differences
  (c) geographic immobilities
  (d) union restraints

24. Shirking can be considered to be a principal–agent problem because
  (a) work objectives of the principals (the workers) diverge from the profit objectives of the agent (the firm)
  (b) profit objectives of the principal (the firm) diverge from the work objectives of the agents (the workers)
  (c) the firm is operating in a monopsonistic labor market
  (d) the firm pays efficiency wages to workers in a labor market

25. A firm pays an equilibrium wage of $10 per hour and the workers produce 10 units of output an hour. If the firm

adopts an efficiency wage and it is successful, then the wage rate for these workers will
  (a) rise and output will fall
  (b) fall and output will rise
  (c) rise and output will rise
  (d) fall and output will fall

■ **PROBLEMS**

1. Suppose a single firm has for a particular type of labor the marginal-revenue-product schedule given in the following table.

Number of units of labor	MRP of labor
1	$15
2	14
3	13
4	12
5	11
6	10
7	9
8	8

  a. Assume there are 100 firms with the same marginal-revenue-product schedules for this particular type of labor. Compute the total or market demand for this labor by completing column 1 in the following table.

(1) Quantity of labor demanded	(2) Wage rate	(3) Quantity of labor supplied
_____	$15	850
_____	14	800
_____	13	750
_____	12	700
_____	11	650
_____	10	600
_____	9	550
_____	8	500

  b. Using the supply schedule for labor given in columns 2 and 3,

  (1) what will be the equilibrium wage rate? $_____
  (2) what will be the total amount of labor hired in the market? _____

  c. The individual firm will

  (1) have a marginal labor cost of $_____.
  (2) employ _____ units of labor.
  (3) pay a wage of $_____.

  d. On the following graph, plot the market demand and supply curves for labor and indicate the equilibrium wage rate and the total quantity of labor employed.

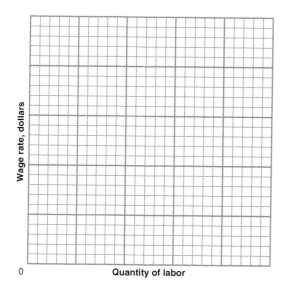

(1) Number of labor units	(2) MRP of labor	(3) Wage rate	(4) Total labor cost	(5) Marginal labor cost
0		$ 2	$_____	
1	$36	4	_____	$_____
2	32	6	_____	_____
3	28	8	_____	_____
4	24	10	_____	_____
5	20	12	_____	_____
6	16	14	_____	_____
7	12	16	_____	_____
8	8	18	_____	_____

a. Compute the firm's total labor costs at each level of employment and the marginal labor cost of each unit of labor, and enter these figures in columns 4 and 5.

b. The firm will

(1) hire _____ units of labor.

(2) pay a wage of $_____.

(3) have a marginal revenue product for labor of

$_____ for the last unit of labor employed.

c. Plot the marginal revenue product of labor, the supply curve for labor, and the marginal-labor-cost curve on the following graph and indicate the quantity of labor the firm will employ and the wage it will pay.

e. On the following graph, plot the individual firm's demand curve for labor, the supply curve for labor, and the marginal-labor-cost curve which confronts the individual firm, and indicate the quantity of labor the firm will hire and the wage it will pay.

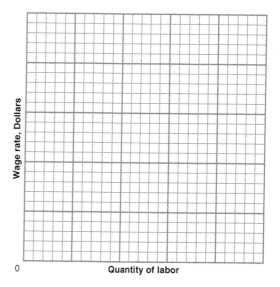

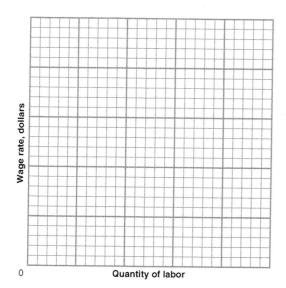

f. The imposition of a $12 minimum wage rate would change the total amount of labor hired in this market

to _____.

2. In the following table, assume a monopsonist has the marginal-revenue-product schedule for a particular type of labor given in columns 1 and 2 and that the supply schedule for labor is that given in columns 1 and 3.

d. If this firm's labor market were competitive, there would

be at least _____ units hired at a wage of at least

$_____.

3. Assume that the employees of the monopsonist in problem 2 organize a strong industrial union. The union demands a wage rate of $16 for its members, and the

447

monopsonist decides to pay this wage because a strike would be too costly.

a. In the following table, compute the supply schedule for labor that now confronts the monopsonist by completing column 2.

(1) Number of labor units	(2) Wage rate	(3) Total labor cost	(4) Marginal labor cost
0	$ _____	$ _____	
1	_____	_____	$ _____
2	_____	_____	_____
3	_____	_____	_____
4	_____	_____	_____
5	_____	_____	_____
6	_____	_____	_____
7	_____	_____	_____
8	_____	_____	_____

b. Compute the total labor cost and the marginal labor cost at each level of employment and enter these figures in columns 3 and 4.

c. The firm will hire_____ units of labor, pay a wage of $_____, and pay total wages of $_____.

d. As a result of unionization, the wage rate has _____, the level of employment has_____, and the earnings of labor have_____.

e. On the graph below plot the firm's marginal revenue product of labor schedule, the labor supply schedule, and the marginal-labor-cost schedule. Indicate also the wage rate the firm will pay and the number of workers it will hire.

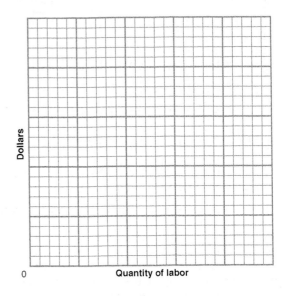

4. Match the following descriptions to one of the six graphs below.

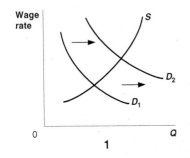

1

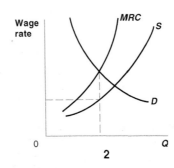

2

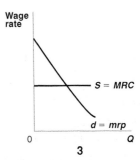

3

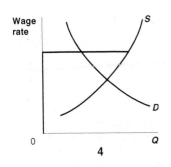

4

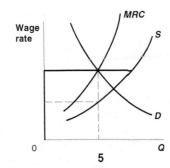

5

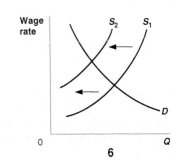

6

a. A bilateral monopoly   Graph _____

b. The supply and demand for labor for a purely competitive firm   Graph _____

c. The labor strategy used by a craft union to raise wages   Graph _____

d. A monopsonistic labor market   Graph _____

e. The strategy used by an industrial union to raise wages above a competitive level   Graph _____

f. A strategy used by a union to get people to buy union-made products   Graph _____

■ **SHORT ANSWER AND ESSAY QUESTIONS**

1. What is meant by the term *wages?* What is the difference between real wages and nominal wages?

2. How does the level of wages in the United States compare with that in other nations?

3. Explain why the productivity of the U.S. labor force has increased to its present high level.

4. Why has the level of real wages continued to increase even though the supply of labor has continually increased?

5. In the competitive model, what determines the market demand for labor and the wage rate? What kind of supply situation do all firms as a group confront? What kind of supply situation does the individual firm confront? Why?

6. In the monopsony model, what determines employment and the wage rate? What kind of supply situation does the monopsonist face? Why? How do the wage rate paid and the level of employment compare with what would result if the market were competitive?

7. In what sense is a worker who is hired by a monopsonist "exploited" and one who is employed in a competitive labor market "justly" rewarded? Why do monopsonists wish to restrict employment?

8. When supply is less than perfectly elastic, marginal labor cost is greater than the wage rate. Why?

9. What political methods do labor unions use to try to increase the wages their members receive? Give examples.

10. When labor unions attempt to restrict the supply of labor to increase wage rates, what devices do they use to do this for the economy as a whole, and what means do they use to restrict the supply of a given type of worker?

11. How do industrial unions attempt to increase wage rates, and what effect does this method of increasing wages have on employment in the industry affected?

12. Both exclusive and inclusive unions are able to raise the wage rates their members receive. Why might unions limit or temper their demands for higher wages? What two factors determine the extent to which they will or will not reduce their demands for higher wages?

13. Have U.S. unions been successful in raising the wages of their members? Evaluate the evidence on wages and employment effects.

14. What is bilateral monopoly? What determines wage rates in a labor market of this type?

15. Using supply and demand graphs, describe the effect of minimum wage laws on wage rates and employment in (a) purely competitive labor markets and (b) monopsony labor markets.

16. Offer an evaluation of the employment and antipoverty effects of the minimum wage based on past and current evidence.

17. What is meant by the term "noncompeting" groups in a labor market? What two factors tend to explain wage differentials in noncompeting groups?

18. How are wages used to equalize differences in the characteristics of jobs? Give examples.

19. Describe four types of imperfections in labor markets. Discuss how these imperfections contribute to wage differentials.

20. Explain what is meant by the principal–agent problem, and relate it to shirking. What are the different pay incentive plans that correct for shirking on the job? How does profit sharing reduce shirking? What is the reason for efficiency wages?

ANSWERS

Chapter 13 Wage Determination

FILL-IN QUESTIONS

1. wage, wage, multiplied, nominal, real
2. strong, capital, natural, labor force, technology, long-run
3. a. higher, opportunity cost; b. revenue product; c. equal to
4. elastic, equal to
5. equal to, greater, less
6. a. divided; b. equal to, divided, 1
7. lower, less
8. demand for, supply of, an above
9. demand for, increasing, decreasing
10. exclusive, inclusive, a craft, an industrial
11. decrease, decrease, inelastic
12. less, greater, wage rate
13. increase, decrease, increase, increase, uncertain
14. are not, vary, imperfect
15. noncompeting, ability, human capital
16. nonmonetary, compensating
17. job, immobility, restraints, discrimination
18. principals, agents, profits, wages
19. shirking, performance, pay
20. piece, efficiency, negative

TRUE–FALSE QUESTIONS

1. F, p. 267
2. F, p. 267
3. T, pp. 267–268
4. T, pp. 268–269
5. F, p. 269
6. T, pp. 269–271
7. T, pp. 269–271
8. T, pp. 271–273
9. T, pp. 273–274
10. F, pp. 273–274

11. T, p. 274
12. F, p. 274
13. F, pp. 274–275
14. F, pp. 274–275
15. T, p. 275
16. F, pp. 274–275
17. F, pp. 275–276
18. T, pp. 276–277

19. T, pp. 276–277
20. T, pp. 278–279
21. T, p. 280
22. F, p. 282
23. T, pp. 280–281
24. T, p. 281
25. T, pp. 281–282

3. *a.* Wage rate: 16.00, 16.00, 16.00, 16.00, 16.00, 16.00, 16.00, 16.00; *b.* Total labor cost: 0, 16.00, 32.00, 48.00, 64.00, 80.00, 96.00, 112.00, 128.00; Marginal labor cost: 16.00, 16.00, 16.00, 16.00, 16.00, 16.00, 16.00, 16.00; *c.* (1) 6, (2) 16.00, (3) 96.00; *d.* increased, increased, increased; *e.* graph (similar to Figure 13.8)
4. *a.* 5; *b.* 3; *c.* 6; *d.* 2; *e.* 4; *f.* 1

MULTIPLE-CHOICE QUESTIONS

1. a, p. 267
2. c, p. 267
3. c, p. 269
4. a, p. 269
5. c, pp. 269–271
6. d, p. 271
7. d, pp. 272–273
8. b, pp. 272–273
9. d, pp. 271–273
10. a, p. 273
11. d, pp. 273–274
12. b, p. 274
13. a, p. 274–275

14. b, p. 275
15. d, pp. 271–273
16. c, pp. 269–271
17. b, pp. 275–276
18. c, pp. 269–271
19. b, pp. 271–273
20. c, pp. 275–276
21. d, pp. 274–275
22. a, p. 279
23. b, pp. 279–280
24. b, pp. 281–282
25. c, p. 282

SHORT ANSWER AND ESSAY QUESTIONS

1. p. 267
2. p. 267
3. pp. 267–268
4. pp. 268–269
5. pp. 269–271
6. pp. 271–273
7. pp. 271–273
8. pp. 271–272
9. pp. 273–274
10. p. 274

11. pp. 274–275
12. pp. 274–275
13. p. 275
14. pp. 275–276
15. pp. 276–277
16. pp. 276–277
17. p. 279
18. pp. 279–280
19. pp. 280–281
20. pp. 281–282

PROBLEMS

1. *a.* Quantity of labor demanded: 100, 200, 300, 400, 500, 600, 700, 800; *b.* (1) 10.00, (2) 600; *c.* (1) 10.00, (2) 6, (3) 10.00; *d.* graph; *e.* graph; *f.* 400
2. *a.* Total labor cost: 0, 4.00, 12.00, 24.00, 40.00, 60.00, 84.00, 112.00, 144.00, Marginal labor cost: 4.00, 8.00, 12.00, 16.00, 20.00, 24.00, 28.00, 32.00; *b.* (1) 5, (2) 12.00, (3) 20.00; *c.* graph; *d.* 6, 14.00

Labor Unions and Their Impacts

This appendix provides some additional information about American **labor unions,** collective bargaining, and union impacts. The labor union is an important economic institution in the U.S. economy. About 15.3 million workers covering about 12.3 percent of the labor force belong to unions. Unions typically focus on specific economic objectives such as improving pay, hours, and working conditions. Union members are more likely to work in government or to be employed in transportation, construction, manufacturing, and mining industries. In spite of its importance, unionism has been on the decline since the mid-1950s.

In Chapter 13 you learned how unions directly and indirectly seek to influence wage rates. The impact of the union on its own membership, on employers, and on the economy is more than just a matter of wages; it involves a contract between a union and an employer. This appendix discusses **collective bargaining** to give you some insights about the union goals and other issues over which employers and employees bargain. Another important idea discussed is that labor-management relations involve more than the periodic signing of a contract; they also involve the day-to-day relations between the union and the employer and the new issues not settled in the contract but which must be resolved under the general provisions of the contract.

The appendix elaborates on the **economic effects of unions** on the economy. Unions improve their members' wage rates relative to the wage rates for nonunionized workers. The effects of unions on output and efficiency, however, are more negative for three reasons that you will learn about in the chapter, although there is one factor that in the long run may offset some of these negative effects.

■ **APPENDIX CHECKLIST**

When you have studied this appendix you should be able to

☐ Identify the number and percentage of union members and the major union organizations.
☐ Describe the characteristics of workers belonging to unions.
☐ State how unions have declined since the mid-1950s.
☐ Present two reasons to explain unionism's decline.
☐ Explain the four basic areas covered by work agreements in collective bargaining.

☐ Describe the bargaining process and major labor relations law.
☐ Draw conclusions about the effects of unions on the wages of workers.
☐ Identify three negative effects unions might have on output and efficiency.
☐ Use a supply and demand model to show how a union might lead to a misallocation of labor resources and reduced output.
☐ Explain the potentially positive effect that unions might have on output and efficiency in the long run because of lower rate of worker turnover.

■ **APPENDIX OUTLINE**

1. About 15.3 million workers in the United States belong to *unions,* and they account for only about 12.3 percent of wage and salary workers. Over half (8 million) of these workers are members of unions affiliated with the *American Federation of Labor and Congress of Industrial Organizations* (AFL-CIO). About 6 million workers are members of a loose federation of seven unions called *Change to Win* that include Service Workers and Teamsters. The rest of the union members belong to *independent unions* that are not affiliated with the other major organizations.

Occupation and industry are important factors that explain who belongs to unions. The **unionization rate** is high in government and in the transportation, construction, manufacturing, and mining industries. Men, African-Americans, and those living in urban areas are more likely to be union members.

2. Union membership has declined since the mid-1950s, when about 25 percent of the workforce was unionized. Two complementary hypotheses explain the decline. One reason for the decline is that changes in the structure of the economy and the labor force have limited the expansion of union membership. A second reason for the decline is that the opposition of management to unions increased because union firms were thought to be less profitable than nonunion firms. The policies management used against unions decreased union membership.

3. *Collective bargaining* between labor and management results in work agreements that take many different forms, but usually cover four basic areas: union status and managerial prerogatives; wages and hours; seniority and job protection; and grievance procedures.

183

a. Union status can be of several types. In a **closed shop,** a worker must be a member of the union before being hired or must become one. In a **union shop,** employers can hire nonunion members but they must become one within a certain period. An **agency shop** requires that nonunion members pay union dues or make a donation to charity similar to the amount of the dues. Twenty-two states prohibit union or agency shops through **right-to-work laws.** In an **open shop,** an employer can hire either union or nonunion members and nonunion members do not have to pay dues. Contracts also typically contain clauses that give management prerogatives over certain work and business practices.

b. Wages (and fringe benefits) and hours of work are the main focus of collective bargaining agreements. Such wage and hour negotiations are influenced by what other workers are being paid, the profitability of the firm, cost of living concerns, and increase in labor productivity.

c. Unions typically are concerned about giving preference for promotion based on the seniority of workers. Unions also may seek job protection for their workers by limiting businesses' discretion to shift work abroad, change production locations, or use nonunion labor,

d. Grievance procedures are specified in labor contracts to help resolve disputes with management over changes in work assignment and other matters affecting workers.

4. The bargaining process on a new contract typically occurs in the 60-day period before the end of the existing contract. After the deadline, a union can **strike,** or there can be a **lockout** by the firm. Most contract agreements are compromises; strikes, lockouts, and violence are rare. The **National Labor Relations Act** specifies legal and illegal practices in collective bargaining, and the **National Labor Relations Board** is authorized to investigate unfair labor practices.

5. Labor unions have economic effects. The most direct effect is that unions typically increase the wages of their members relative to the wages of nonunion members (the wage advantage averages 15 percent). Whether unions increase output and efficiency is more complicated, but the overall effect appears negative.

a. Decreased output and efficiency result from featherbedding and establishing work rules that increase the cost of production.

b. Unions reduce output when they conduct strikes and work stoppages.

c. There are efficiency losses from the misallocation of labor to union and nonunion jobs because of the union wage advantage.

d. One long-run factor that may offset some of these negative effects of unions on output and efficiency is that unions may reduce the turnover or quit rate of workers. Unions offer a collective **voice mechanism** to help correct work problems before workers think they have to express their **exit mechanism** by quitting a job. Reducing the turnover rate may help businesses benefit from their investment in worker training and the experience of workers.

■ **HINTS AND TIPS**

1. This appendix deals with unionism, which can provoke emotional reactions. Make sure you remember the distinction between *positive* and *normative* economics made in Chapter 1. The purpose of the appendix is to analyze and explain the economics of unions (*what is*), and not the ideal world (*what ought to be*).

2. In Figure 2 of the textbook's appendix, the wage rate is plotted on the vertical axis and the quantity of labor is on the horizontal axis. The graph shows how unionization of a labor market affects the wage rate, employment, and domestic output. Make sure you do problem 2 in this Study Guide appendix to help you master this material.

■ **IMPORTANT TERMS**

American Federation of Labor and Congress of Industrial Organizations (AFL-CIO)	right-to-work laws
	open shop
	strike
Change to Win	lockout
independent unions	National Labor Relations Act (NLRA)
unionization rate	
collective bargaining	National Labor Relations Board (NLRB)
closed shop	voice mechanism
union shop	exit mechanism
agency shop	

SELF-TEST

■ **FILL-IN QUESTIONS**

1. About (15.3, 32.4) _____ million workers belong to labor unions in the United States. This number represents about (12.3, 28.9) _____% of wage and salary workers.

2. The unionization rate is relatively (low, high) _____ among workers in government, transportation, construction, and manufacturing, and it is _____ among protective service workers, machine operators, and craft workers. Men are (more, less) _____ likely to be union members than women; African-Americans are _____ likely to be union members than whites; and those in urban areas are _____ likely to be union members than those workers in other locations.

3. Since the mid-1950s, union membership as a percentage of the labor force has (increased, decreased) _____ since 1980, the number of unionized workers has _____.

4. Two reasons can be used to explain the changes in the size of union membership. The (structural-change, managerial-opposition) _____ reason suggests that conditions unfavorable to the expansion of unions have occurred in the economy and labor; the _____ reason suggests that union growth has been deterred by the policies of firms to limit or dissuade workers from joining unions.

5. A typical work agreement between a union and an employer covers the following four basic areas:

a. _____

b. _____

c. _____

d. _____

6. Collective bargaining typically begins about (20, 60) _____ days before a labor contract is set to expire. If the contract demands from workers are not met satisfactorily by the employer, a labor union may authorize a (lockout, strike) _____ that results in a work stoppage, but employers can put pressure on workers to settle the contract by engaging in a _____ that prevents workers from returning to work.

7. Federal labor laws set the framework for bargaining, strikes, and lockout through the National Labor Relations (Act, Board) _____ and the organization that is responsible for investigating charges of unfair labor practices is the National Labor Relations _____.

8. Unionization of workers in the U.S. economy has (increased, decreased) _____ the wage rates of union members relative to the wage rates of nonunion workers, with the wage premium being about (15, 25) _____ percent.

9. Unions have a negative effect on output and efficiency in the economy to the extent that they engage in (collective bargaining, featherbedding) _____ and impose burdensome (exit mechanisms, work rules) _____ on their employers, or impose (above, below) _____-equilibrium wage rates on employers that lead to misallocation of labor resources.

10. In the long run, unions can have a positive effect on output and efficiency in the economy because unions can (increase, decrease) _____ labor turnover.

■ TRUE–FALSE QUESTIONS

Circle T if the statement is true, F if it is false.

1. Most union members in the U.S. belong to independent unions not affiliated with the AFL-CIO.   **T   F**

2. The rate of unionization is relatively high in transportation, construction, and manufacturing industries.   **T   F**

3. Union membership as a percentage of the labor force has been rising since the 1950s.   **T   F**

4. The structural changes in the economy that shift workers from manufacturing employment to service employment is one main reason for the decline in union membership.   **T   F**

5. Collective bargaining between labor and management means no more than deciding on the wage rates employees will receive during the life of the contract.   **T   F**

6. Bargaining, strikes, and lockouts occur within a framework of federal labor laws such as the National Labor Relations Act.   **T   F**

7. The wages of union members exceed the wages of nonunion members on the average by more than 40%.   **T   F**

8. Strikes in the U.S. economy result in little lost work time and reductions in total output.   **T   F**

9. The loss of output in the U.S. economy resulting from increases in wage rates imposed by unions on employers is relatively large.   **T   F**

10. Over time, labor unions reduce worker turnover, which offsets some of the negative effects of union on output and efficiency.   **T   F**

■ MULTIPLE-CHOICE QUESTIONS

Circle the letter that corresponds to the best answer.

1. About what percent of employed wage and salary workers in the United States belong to unions?
(a) 7.5%
(b) 12.3%
(c) 21.3%
(d) 35.4%

2. The rate of unionization is highest in
(a) services
(b) retail trade
(c) government
(d) manufacturing

3. If workers at the time they are hired have a choice of joining the union and paying dues or of not joining the union and paying no dues, there exists
(a) a union shop
(b) an open shop
(c) a nonunion shop
(d) a closed shop

4. A major responsibility of the National Labor Relations Board is to
(a) enforce right-to-work laws
(b) keep unions from becoming politically active
(c) investigate unfair labor practices under labor law
(d) maintain labor peace between the AFL and CIO

5. Unionization has tended to
(a) increase the wages of union workers and decrease the wages of some nonunion workers
(b) increase the wages of some nonunion workers and decrease wages of union workers
(c) increase the wages of both union and nonunion workers
(d) increase the average level of real wages in the economy

6. The higher wages imposed on employers in a unionized labor market tend to result in
(a) lower wage rates in nonunionized labor markets and a decline in domestic output
(b) lower wage rates in nonunionized labor markets and an expansion in domestic output
(c) higher wage rates in nonunionized labor markets and a decline in domestic output
(d) higher wage rates in nonunionized labor markets and an expansion in domestic output

7. Which tends to decrease or have a negative effect on output and efficiency in the economy?
(a) the seniority system
(b) reduced labor turnover
(c) featherbedding and union-imposed work rules
(d) the shock effect of higher union-imposed wage rates

8. The reallocation of a unit of labor from employment where its MRP is $50,000 to employment where its MRP is $40,000 will
(a) increase the output of the economy by $10,000
(b) increase the output of the economy by $90,000
(c) decrease the output of the economy by $10,000
(d) decrease the output of the economy by $90,000

9. Which tends to increase or have a positive effect on output and efficiency in the economy?
(a) strikes
(b) reduced labor turnover
(c) featherbedding and union-imposed work rules
(d) a decrease in the training programs for workers

10. Unions tend to reduce labor turnover by providing workers with all but one of the following. Which one?
(a) an exit mechanism
(b) a voice mechanism
(c) a collective voice
(d) a wage advantage

■ PROBLEMS

1. Match the union term with the phrase using the appropriate number.

1. lockout
2. union shop
3. closed shop
4. right-to-work laws
5. open shop
6. agency shop
7. National Labor Relations Act
8. collective bargaining

a. Employer can hire union or nonunion workers. _____
b. Acts by states to make compulsory union membership, or the union shop, illegal. _____

c. A worker must be a member of the union before he or she is eligible for employment in the firm. _____
d. First passed as the Wagner Act of 1935 and sets forth the dos and don'ts of union and management-labor practices. _____
e. Requires a worker to pay union dues or donate an equivalent amount to charity. _____
f. A firm forbids its workers from returning to work until a new contract is signed. _____
g. Permits the employer to hire nonunion workers, but provides that these workers must join the union within a specified period or relinquish their jobs. _____
h. The negotiations of labor contracts. _____

2. Suppose there are two identical labor markets in the economy. The supply of workers and the demand for workers in each of these markets are shown in the following table.

Quantity of labor demanded	Wage rate (MRP of labor)	Quantity of labor supplied
1	$100	7
2	90	6
3	80	5
4	70	4
5	60	3
6	50	2
7	40	1

a. In each of the two labor markets the equilibrium wage rate in a competitive labor market would be $_____ and employment would be _____ workers.
b. Now suppose that in the first of these labor markets workers form a union and the union imposes an above-equilibrium wage rate of $90 on employers.
(1) Employment in the unionized labor market will (rise, fall) _____ to _____ workers; and
(2) the output produced by workers employed by the firms in the unionized labor market will (expand, contract) _____ by $_____.
c. If the workers displaced by the unionization of the first labor market all enter and find employment in the second labor market which remains nonunionized and competitive,
(1) the wage rate in the second labor market will (rise, fall) _____ to $_____.
(2) the output produced by the workers employed by firms in the second labor market will (expand, contract) _____ by $_____.
d. While the total employment of labor in the two labor markets has remained constant, the total output produced by the employers in the two labor markets has (expanded, contracted) _____ by $_____.

■ SHORT ANSWER AND ESSAY QUESTIONS

1. Describe the current status of unions in the United States and the major union organization.

2. Who belongs to unions? Answer in terms of the types of industries and occupations and the personal characteristics of workers.

3. What evidence is there that the labor movement in the United States has declined? What are two possible causes of this decline?

4. What are the four basic areas usually covered in collective-bargaining agreements between management and labor?

5. What four arguments does labor (management) use in demanding (resisting) higher wages?

6. Describe the bargaining process in labor negotiations. What are the two aspects of federal labor laws that set the framework for this negotiation?

7. How large is the union wage advantage in the United States? How has the unionization of many labor markets affected the average level of real wages in the U.S. economy?

8. Explain how featherbedding and work rules by unions imposes a negative effect on output and efficiency in the economy.

9. What effect does the unionization of a particular labor market have on the wage rate in that market, wage rates in other labor markets, and the total output of the economy?

10. Explain how unions reduce labor turnover and improve the skills of younger workers.

ANSWERS

Appendix to Chapter 13 Labor Unions and Their Impacts

FILL-IN QUESTIONS

1. 15.3, 12.3
2. high, high, more, more, more
3. decreased, decreased
4. structural-change, managerial-opposition
5. *a.* the degree of recognition and status accorded the union and the prerogatives of management; *b.* wages and hours; *c.* seniority and job opportunities; *d.* a procedure for settling grievances (any order for *a–d*)
6. 60, strike, lockout
7. Act, Board
8. increased, 15
9. featherbedding, work rules, above
10. decrease

TRUE–FALSE QUESTIONS

1. F, p. 287
2. T, p. 287
3. F, pp. 287–288
4. T, pp. 287–288
5. F, pp. 288–289
6. T, p. 289
7. F, p. 289
8. T, pp. 289–290
9. F, pp. 290–291
10. T, p. 291

MULTIPLE-CHOICE QUESTIONS

1. b, p. 287
2. c, p. 287
3. b, p. 288
4. c, p. 289
5. a, p. 289
6. a, p. 289
7. c, p. 289
8. c, pp. 290–291
9. b, p. 291
10. a, p. 291

PROBLEMS

1. *a.* 5; *b.* 4; *c.* 3; *d.* 7; *e.* 6; *f.* 1; *g.* 2; *h.* 8
2. *a.* 70, 4; *b.* (1) fall, 2, (2) contract, 150; *c.* (1) fall, 50, (2) expand, 110; *d.* contracted, 40

SHORT ANSWER AND ESSAY QUESTIONS

1. p. 287
2. p. 287
3. pp. 287–288
4. pp. 288–289
5. pp. 288–289
6. p. 289
7. pp. 289–290
8. p. 289
9. pp. 289–291
10. p. 291

37

AFTER READING THIS CHAPTER, YOU SHOULD BE ABLE TO:

1 List and discuss several key facts about international trade.

2 Define comparative advantage, and demonstrate how specialization and trade add to a nation's output.

3 Describe how differences between world prices and domestic prices prompt exports and imports.

4 Analyze the economic effects of tariffs and quotas.

5 Analyze the validity of the most frequently presented arguments for protectionism.

6 Identify and explain the objectives of GATT, WTO, EU, Euro Zone, and NAFTA, and discuss offshoring and trade adjustment assistance.

International Trade*

Backpackers in the wilderness like to think they are "leaving the world behind," but, like Atlas, they carry the world on their shoulders. Much of their equipment is imported—knives from Switzerland, rain gear from South Korea, cameras from Japan, aluminum pots from England, sleeping bags from China, and compasses from Finland. Moreover, they may have driven to the trailheads in Japanese-made Toyotas or German-made BMWs, sipping coffee from Brazil or snacking on bananas from Honduras.

International trade and the global economy affect all of us daily, whether we are hiking in the wilderness, driving our cars, buying groceries, or working at our jobs. We cannot "leave the world behind." We are enmeshed in a global web of economic relationships, such as trading of goods and

---

*Note to Instructors: This chapter is a consolidation of Chapters 5 and 37 of *Economics* 18e. If you prefer to cover international trade early in your course, you can assign this chapter at the end of either Part 1 or Part 2. This chapter builds on the introductory ideas of opportunity costs, supply and demand analysis, and economic efficiency but does not require an understanding of either elasticity or market failures.

services, multinational corporations, cooperative ventures among the world's firms, and ties among the world's financial markets.

The focus of this chapter is the trading of goods and services. Then in Chapter 38, we examine the U.S. balance of payments, exchange rates, and U.S. trade deficits. In Chapter 39W on our Web site, we look at the economics of developing nations.

Some Key Trade Facts

The following are several important facts relating to international trade.

- U.S. exports and imports have more than doubled as percentages of GDP since 1980.
- A *trade deficit* occurs when imports exceed exports. The United States has a trade deficit in goods. In 2009 U.S. imports of goods exceeded U.S. exports of goods by $517 billion.
- A *trade surplus* occurs when exports exceed imports. The United States has a trade surplus in services (such as air transportation services and financial services). In 2009 U.S. exports of services exceeded U.S. imports of services by $138 billion.
- Principal U.S. exports include chemicals, agricultural products, consumer durables, semiconductors, and aircraft; principal imports include petroleum, automobiles, metals, household appliances, and computers.
- As with other advanced industrial nations, the United States imports many goods that are in some of the same categories as the goods that it exports. Examples: automobiles, computers, chemicals, semiconductors, and telecommunications equipment.
- Canada is the United States' most important trading partner quantitatively. In 2009 about 20 percent of U.S. exported goods were sold to Canadians, who in turn provided 15 percent of imported U.S. goods.
- The United States has a sizable trade deficit with China. In 2009 it was $220 billion.
- The U.S. dependence on foreign oil is reflected in its trade with members of OPEC. In 2009 the United States imported $112 billion of goods (mainly oil) from OPEC members, while exporting $48 billion of goods to those countries.
- The United States leads the world in the combined volume of exports and imports, as measured in dollars. China, Germany, the United States, Japan, and the Netherlands were the top five exporters by dollar in 2009.
- Currently, the United States provides about 8.5 percent of the world's exports. (See Global Perspective 37.1.)
- Exports of goods and services (on a national income account basis) make up about 13 percent of total U.S.

GLOBAL PERSPECTIVE 37.1

Shares of World Exports, Selected Nations

China has the largest share of world exports, followed by Germany and the United States. The eight largest export nations account for about 46 percent of world exports.

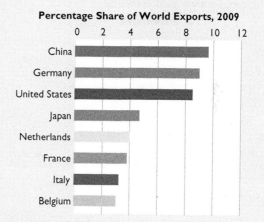

Percentage Share of World Exports, 2009

Source: International Trade Statistics, WTO Publications. Used with permission of the World Trade Organization, www.wto.org.

output. That percentage is much lower than the percentage in many other nations, including Canada, France, Germany, the Netherlands, and South Korea. (See Global Perspective 37.2.)

- China has become a major international trader, with an estimated $1.2 trillion of exports in 2009. Other Asian economies—including South Korea, Taiwan, and Singapore—are also active in international trade. Their combined exports exceed those of France, Britain, or Italy.
- International trade links world economies. Through trade, changes in economic conditions in one place on the globe can quickly affect other places.
- International trade is often at the center of debates over economic policy, both within the United States and internationally.

With this information in mind, let's turn to the economics of international trade.

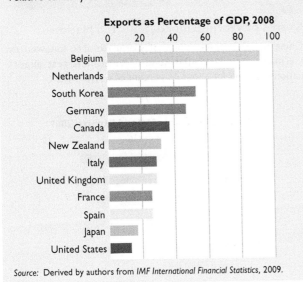

GLOBAL PERSPECTIVE 37.2

Exports of Goods and Services as a Percentage of GDP, Selected Countries

Although the United States is one of the world's largest exporters, as a percentage of GDP, its exports are quite low relative to many other countries.

Exports as Percentage of GDP, 2008

0   20   40   60   80   100

- Belgium
- Netherlands
- South Korea
- Germany
- Canada
- New Zealand
- Italy
- United Kingdom
- France
- Spain
- Japan
- United States

Source: Derived by authors from *IMF International Financial Statistics,* 2009.

The Economic Basis for Trade

Sovereign nations, like individuals and the regions of a nation, can gain by specializing in the products they can produce with the greatest relative efficiency and by trading for the goods they cannot produce as efficiently. The simple answer to the question "Why do nations trade?" is "They trade because it is beneficial." The benefits that emerge relate to three underlying facts:

- The distribution of natural, human, and capital resources among nations is uneven; nations differ in their endowments of economic resources.

- Efficient production of various goods requires different technologies, and not all nations have the same level of technological expertise.

- Products are differentiated as to quality and other attributes, and some people may prefer certain goods imported from abroad rather than similar goods produced domestically.

To recognize the character and interaction of these three facts, think of China, which has abundant and inexpensive labor. As a result, China can produce efficiently (at low cost of other goods forgone) a variety of **labor-intensive goods,** such as textiles, electronics, apparel, toys, and sporting goods.

In contrast, Australia has vast amounts of land and can inexpensively produce such **land-intensive goods** as beef, wool, and meat. Mexico has the soil, tropical climate, rainfall, and ready supply of unskilled labor that allow for the efficient, low-cost production of vegetables. Industrially advanced economies such as the United States and Germany that have relatively large amounts of capital can inexpensively produce goods whose production requires much capital, including such **capital-intensive goods** as airplanes, automobiles, agricultural equipment, machinery, and chemicals.

Also, regardless of their resource intensities, nations can develop individual products that are in demand worldwide because of their special qualities. Examples: fashions from Italy, chocolates from Belgium, software from the United States, and watches from Switzerland.

The distribution of resources, technology, and product distinctiveness among nations is relatively stable in short time periods but certainly can change over time. When that distribution changes, the relative efficiency and success that nations have in producing and selling goods also changes. For example, in the past several decades, South Korea has greatly expanded its stock of capital. Although South Korea was primarily an exporter of agricultural products and raw materials a half-century ago, it now exports large quantities of manufactured goods. Similarly, the new technologies that gave us synthetic fibers and synthetic rubber drastically altered the resource mix needed to produce fibers and rubber and changed the relative efficiency of nations in manufacturing them.

As national economies evolve, the size and quality of their labor forces may change, the volume and composition of their capital stocks may shift, new technologies may develop, and even the quality of land and the quantity of natural resources may be altered. As such changes take place, the relative efficiency with which a nation can produce specific goods will also change. As economists would say, comparative advantage can and does sometimes change.

Comparative Advantage

In an open economy (one with an international sector), a country produces more of certain goods (exports) and fewer of other goods (imports) than it would otherwise. Thus, the country shifts the use of labor and other productive resources toward export industries and away from import industries. For example, in the presence of international trade, the United States uses more resources to make commercial aircraft and to grow wheat and fewer resources to make television sets and sew clothes. So we ask: Do such shifts of resources make economic sense? Do they enhance U.S. total output and thus the U.S. standard of living?

The answers are affirmative. Specialization and international trade increase the productivity of U.S. resources and allow the United States to obtain greater total output than otherwise would be possible. These benefits are the result of exploiting both *absolute advantages* and *comparative advantages*. A country is said to have an *absolute advantage* over other producers of a product if it is the most efficient producer of that product (by which we mean that it can produce more output of that product from any given amount of resource inputs than can any other producer). A country is said to have a *comparative advantage* over other producers of a product if it can produce the product at a lower opportunity cost (by which we mean that it must forgo less output of alternative products when allocating productive resources to producing the product in question).

In 1776 Adam Smith used the concept of absolute advantage to argue for international specialization and trade. His point was that nations would be better off if they each specialized in the production of those products in which they had an absolute advantage and were therefore the most efficient producers:

> It is the maxim of every prudent master of a family, never to attempt to make at home what it will cost him more to make than to buy. The taylor does not attempt to make his own shoes, but buys them of the shoemaker. The shoemaker does not attempt to make his own clothes, but employs a taylor. The farmer attempts to make neither the one nor the other, but employs those different artificers. . . .
>
> What is prudence in the conduct of every private family, can scarce be folly in that of a great kingdom. If a foreign country can supply us with a commodity cheaper than we can make it, better buy it of them with some part of the produce of our own industry, employed in a way in which we have some advantage.[1]

In the early 1800s, David Ricardo extended Smith's idea by demonstrating that it is advantageous for a country to specialize and trade with another country even if it is more productive in all economic activities than that other country. Stated more formally, a nation does not need Smith's absolute advantage—total superiority in the efficiency with which it produces products—to benefit from specialization and trade. It needs only a comparative advantage.

The nearby Consider This box provides a simple, two-person illustration of Ricardo's principle of comparative

---

[1]Adam Smith, *The Wealth of Nations* (originally published, 1776; New York: Modern Library, 1937), p. 424.

CONSIDER THIS . . .

A CPA and a House Painter

Suppose that Madison, a certified public accountant (CPA), is a swifter painter than Mason, the professional painter she is thinking of hiring. Also assume that Madison can earn $50 per hour as an accountant but would have to pay Mason $15 per hour. And suppose that Madison would need 30 hours to paint her house but Mason would need 40 hours.

Should Madison take time from her accounting to paint her own house, or should she hire the painter? Madison's opportunity cost of painting her house is $1500 (= 30 hours of sacrificed CPA time × $50 per CPA hour). The cost of hiring Mason is only $600 (= 40 hours of painting × $15 per hour of painting). Although Madison is better at both accounting and painting, she will get her house painted at lower cost by specializing in accounting and using some of her earnings from accounting to hire a house painter.

Similarly, Mason can reduce his cost of obtaining accounting services by specializing in painting and using some of his income to hire Madison to prepare his income tax forms. Suppose Mason would need 10 hours to prepare his tax return, while Madison could handle the task in 2 hours. Mason would sacrifice $150 of income (= 10 hours of painting time × $15 per hour) to do something he could hire Madison to do for $100 (= 2 hours of CPA time × $50 per CPA hour). By specializing in painting and hiring Madison to prepare his tax return, Mason lowers the cost of getting his tax return prepared.

We will see that what is true for our CPA and house painter is also true for nations. Specializing on the basis of comparative advantage enables nations to reduce the cost of obtaining the goods and services they desire.

---

advantage. Be sure to read it now, because it will greatly help you understand the graphical analysis that follows.

Two Isolated Nations

Our goal is to place the idea of comparative advantage into the context of trading nations. Our method is to build a simple model that relies on the familiar concepts of production possibilities curves. Suppose the world consists of just two nations, the United States and Mexico. Also for simplicity, suppose that the labor forces in the United States and Mexico are of equal size. Each nation can

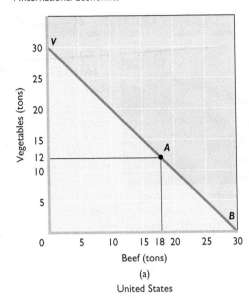

(a)
United States

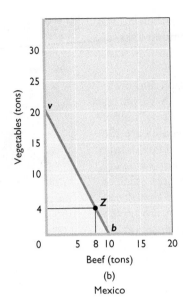

FIGURE 37.1 **Production possibilities for the United States and Mexico.** The two production possibilities curves show the combinations of vegetables and beef that (a) the United States and (b) Mexico can produce domestically. The curves for both countries are straight lines because we are assuming constant opportunity costs. The different cost ratios, 1 vegetables ≡ 1 beef for the United States, and 2 vegetables ≡ 1 beef for Mexico, are reflected in the different slopes of the two lines.

(b)
Mexico

produce both beef and raw (unprocessed) vegetables but at different levels of economic efficiency. Suppose the U.S. and Mexican domestic production possibilities curves for beef and vegetables are those shown in Figure 37.1a and Figure 37.1b. Note three realities relating to the production possibilities curves in the two graphs:

- *Constant costs* The curves derive from the tables and are drawn as straight lines, in contrast to the bowed-outward production possibilities frontiers we examined in Chapter 1. This means that we have replaced the law of increasing opportunity costs with the assumption of constant costs. This substitution simplifies our discussion but does not impair the validity of our analysis and conclusions. Later we will consider the effects of increasing opportunity costs.
- *Different costs* The production possibilities curves of the United States and Mexico reflect different resource mixes and differing levels of technology. Specifically, the differing slopes of the two curves reflect the numbers in the figures and reveal that the opportunity costs of producing beef and vegetables differ between the two nations.
- *U.S. absolute advantage in both* A producer (an individual, firm, or country) has an *absolute advantage* over another producer if it can produce more of a product than the other producer using the same amount of resources. Because of our convenient assumption that the U.S. and Mexican labor forces are the same size, the two production possibilities curves show that the United States has an absolute advantage in producing both products. If the United States and Mexico use

their entire (equal-size) labor forces to produce either vegetables or beef, the United States can produce more of either than Mexico. The United States, using the same number of workers as Mexico, has greater production possibilities. So output per worker—labor productivity—in the United States exceeds that in Mexico in producing both products.

Opportunity-Cost Ratio in the United States In Figure 37.1a, with full employment, the United States will operate at some point on its production possibilities curve. On that curve, it can increase its output of beef from 0 tons to 30 tons by forgoing 30 tons of vegetables output. So the slope of the production possibilities curve is 1 (= 30 vegetables/30 beef), meaning that 1 ton of vegetables must be sacrificed for each extra ton of beef. In the United States the **opportunity-cost ratio** (domestic exchange ratio) for the two products is 1 ton of vegetables (V) for 1 ton of beef (B), or

United States: $1V \equiv 1B$ (The "≡" sign simply means "equivalent to.")

Within its borders, the United States can "exchange" a ton of vegetables from itself for a ton of beef from itself. Our constant-cost assumption means that this exchange or opportunity-cost relationship prevails for all possible moves from one point to another along the U.S. production possibilities curve.

Opportunity-Cost Ratio in Mexico Mexico's production possibilities curve in Figure 37.1b represents a

TABLE 37.1 International Specialization According to Comparative Advantage and the Gains from Trade

Country	(1) Outputs before Specialization	(2) Outputs after Specialization	(3) Amounts Exported (−) and Imported (+)	(4) Outputs Available after Trade	(5) Gains from Specialization and Trade (4) − (1)
United States	18 beef 12 vegetables	30 beef 0 vegetables	−10 beef +15 vegetables	20 beef 15 vegetables	2 beef 3 vegetables
Mexico	8 beef 4 vegetables	0 beef 20 vegetables	+10 beef −15 vegetables	10 beef 5 vegetables	2 beef 1 vegetables

different full-employment opportunity-cost ratio. In Mexico, 20 tons of vegetables must be given up to obtain 10 tons of beef. The slope of the production possibilities curve is 2 (= 20 vegetables/10 beef). This means that in Mexico the opportunity-cost ratio for the two goods is 2 tons of vegetables for 1 ton of beef, or

$$\text{Mexico: } 2V \equiv 1B$$

Self-Sufficiency Output Mix If the United States and Mexico are isolated and self-sufficient, then each country must choose some output mix on its production possibilities curve. It will select the mix that provides the greatest total utility or satisfaction. Let's assume that combination point *A* in Figure 37.1a is the optimal mix in the United States. That is, society deems the combination of 18 tons of beef and 12 tons of vegetables preferable to any other combination of the goods available along the production possibilities curve. Suppose Mexico's optimal product mix is 8 tons of beef and 4 tons of vegetables, indicated by point *Z* in Figure 37.1b. These choices by the two countries are reflected in column 1 of Table 37.1.

Specializing Based on Comparative Advantage

A producer (an individual, firm, or nation) has a **comparative advantage** in producing a particular product if it can produce that product at a lower opportunity cost than other producers. Comparative advantage is the key determinant in whether or not nations can gain from specialization and trade. In fact, absolute advantage turns out to be irrelevant.

In our example, for instance, the United States has an absolute advantage over Mexico in producing both vegetables and beef. But it is still the case that the United States can gain from specialization and trade with Mexico. That is because what actually matters is whether the opportunity costs of producing the two products (beef and vegetables) differ in the two countries. If they do, then each nation will enjoy a comparative advantage in one of the products,

meaning that it can produce that product at a lower opportunity cost than the other country. As a result, total output can increase if each country specializes in the production of the good in which it has the lower opportunity cost.

This idea is summarized in the **principle of comparative advantage**, which says that total output will be greatest when each good is produced by the nation that has the lowest domestic opportunity cost for producing that good. In our two-nation illustration, the United States has the lower domestic opportunity cost for beef; the United States must forgo only 1 ton of vegetables to produce 1 ton of beef, whereas Mexico must forgo 2 tons of vegetables for 1 ton of beef. The United States has a comparative (cost) advantage in beef and should specialize in beef production. The "world" (that is, the United States and Mexico) in our example would clearly not be economizing in the use of its resources if a high-cost producer (Mexico) produced a specific product (beef) when a low-cost producer (the United States) could have produced it. Having Mexico produce beef would mean that the world economy would have to give up more vegetables than is necessary to obtain a ton of beef.

Mexico has the lower domestic opportunity cost for vegetables. It must sacrifice only $\frac{1}{2}$ ton of beef to produce 1 ton of vegetables, while the United States must forgo 1 ton of beef to produce 1 ton of vegetables. Mexico has a comparative advantage in vegetables and should specialize in vegetable production. Again, the world would not be employing its resources economically if vegetables were produced by a high-cost producer (the United States) rather than by a low-cost producer (Mexico). If the United States produced vegetables, the world would be giving up more beef than necessary to obtain each ton of vegetables. Economizing requires that any particular good be produced by the nation having the lowest domestic opportunity cost or the nation having the comparative advantage for that good. The United States should produce beef, and Mexico should produce vegetables. The situation is summarized in Table 37.2.

TABLE 37.2 Comparative-Advantage Example: A Summary

Beef	Vegetables
Mexico: Must give up 2 tons of vegetables to get 1 ton of beef.	*Mexico:* Must give up $\frac{1}{2}$ ton of beef to get 1 ton of vegetables.
United States: Must give up 1 ton of vegetables to get 1 ton of beef.	*United States:* Must give up 1 ton of beef to get 1 ton of vegetables.
Comparative advantage: United States	Comparative advantage: Mexico

A comparison of columns 1 and 2 in Table 37.1 verifies that specialized production enables the world to obtain more output from its fixed amount of resources. By

ORIGIN OF THE IDEA

O 37.1

Absolute and comparative advantage

specializing completely in beef, the United States can produce 30 tons of beef and no vegetables. Mexico, by specializing completely in vegetables, can produce 20 tons of vegetables and no beef. These figures exceed the yields generated without specialization: 26 tons of beef (= 18 in the United States + 8 in Mexico) and 16 tons of vegetables (= 12 in the United States + 4 in Mexico). As a result, the world ends up with 4 more tons of beef (= 30 tons − 26 tons) and 4 more tons of vegetables (= 20 tons − 16 tons) than it would if there were self-sufficiency and unspecialized production.

Terms of Trade

We have just seen that specialization in production will allow for the largest possible amounts of both beef and vegetables to be produced. But with each country specializing in the production of only one item, how will the vegetables that are all produced by Mexico and the beef that is all produced by the United States be divided between consumers in the two countries? The key turns out to be the **terms of trade,** the exchange ratio at which the United States and Mexico trade beef and vegetables.

Crucially, the terms of trade also establish whether each country will find it in its own better interest to bother specializing at all. This is because the terms of trade determine whether each country can "get a better deal" by specializing and trading than it could if it opted instead for self sufficiency. To see how this works, note that because $1B \equiv 1V$ (= $1V \equiv 1B$) in the United States, it must get more than 1 ton of vegetables for each 1 ton of beef exported, otherwise, it will not benefit from exporting beef in exchange for Mexican vegetables. The United States must get a better

"price" (more vegetables) for its beef through international trade than it can get domestically; otherwise, no gain from trade exists and such trade will not occur.

Similarly, because $1B \equiv 2V$ (= $2V \equiv 1B$) in Mexico, Mexico must obtain 1 ton of beef by exporting less than 2 tons of vegetables to get it. Mexico must be able to pay a lower "price" for beef in the world market than it must pay domestically, or else it will not want to trade. The international exchange ratio or terms of trade must therefore lie somewhere between

$$1B \equiv 1V \text{ (United States' cost conditions)}$$

and

$$1B \equiv 2V \text{ (Mexico's cost conditions)}$$

Where between these limits will the world exchange ratio fall? The United States will prefer a rate close to $1B \equiv 2V$, say, $1B \equiv 1\frac{3}{4} V$. The United States wants to obtain as many vegetables as possible for each 1 ton of beef it exports. By contrast, Mexico wants a rate near $1B \equiv 1V$, say, $1B \equiv 1\frac{1}{4} V$. This is true because Mexico wants to export as few vegetables as possible for each 1 ton of beef it receives in exchange.

The actual exchange ratio depends on world supply and demand for the two products. If overall world demand for vegetables is weak relative to its supply and if the demand for beef is strong relative to its supply, the price of vegetables will be lower and the price of beef will be higher. The exchange ratio will settle nearer the $1B \equiv 2V$ figure the United States prefers. If overall world demand for vegetables is great relative to its supply and if the demand for beef is weak relative to its supply, the ratio will settle nearer the $1B \equiv 1V$ level favorable to Mexico. In this manner, the actual exchange ratio that is set by world supply and demand determines how the gains from international specialization and trade are divided between the two nations and, consequently, how the beef that is all produced in the United States and the vegetables that are all produced in Mexico get divided among consumers in the two countries. (We discuss equilibrium world prices later in this chapter.)

Gains from Trade

Suppose the international terms of trade are $1B \equiv 1\frac{1}{2} V$. The possibility of trading on these terms permits each nation to supplant its domestic production possibilities curve with a trading possibilities line (or curve), as shown in **Figure 37.2 (Key Graph).** Just as a production possibilities curve shows the amounts of these products that a full-employment economy can obtain by shifting resources from one to the other, a **trading possibilities line** shows

key graph

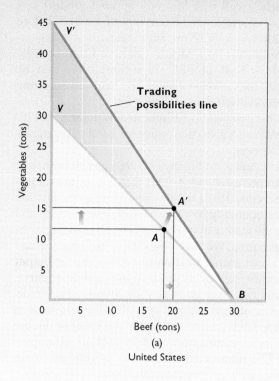

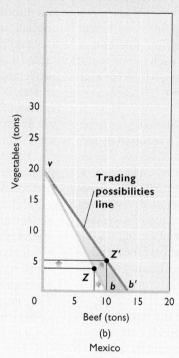

FIGURE 37.2 **Trading possibilities lines and the gains from trade.** As a result of specialization and trade, both the United States and Mexico can have higher levels of output than the levels attainable on their domestic production possibilities curves. (a) The United States can move from point *A* on its domestic production possibilities curve to, say, *A'* on its trading possibilities line. (b) Mexico can move from *Z* to *Z'*.

QUICK QUIZ FOR FIGURE 37.2

1. The production possibilities curves in graphs (a) and (b) imply:
   a. increasing domestic opportunity costs.
   b. decreasing domestic opportunity costs.
   c. constant domestic opportunity costs.
   d. first decreasing, then increasing, domestic opportunity costs.

2. Before specialization, the domestic opportunity cost of producing 1 unit of beef is:
   a. 1 unit of vegetables in both the United States and Mexico.
   b. 1 unit of vegetables in the United States and 2 units of vegetables in Mexico.
   c. 2 units of vegetables in the United States and 1 unit of vegetables in Mexico.
   d. 1 unit of vegetables in the United States and $\frac{1}{2}$ unit of vegetables in Mexico.

3. After specialization and international trade, the world output of beef and vegetables is:
   a. 20 tons of beef and 20 tons of vegetables.
   b. 45 tons of beef and 15 tons of vegetables.
   c. 30 tons of beef and 20 tons of vegetables.
   d. 10 tons of beef and 30 tons of vegetables.

4. After specialization and international trade:
   a. the United States can obtain units of vegetables at less cost than it could before trade.
   b. Mexico can obtain more than 20 tons of vegetables, if it so chooses.
   c. the United States no longer has a comparative advantage in producing beef.
   d. Mexico can benefit by prohibiting vegetables imports from the United States.

Answers: 1. c; 2. b; 3. c; 4. a

---

the amounts of the two products that a nation can obtain by specializing in one product and trading for the other. The trading possibilities lines in Figure 37.2 reflect the assumption that both nations specialize on the basis of comparative advantage: The United States specializes completely in beef (at point *B* in Figure 37.2a), and Mexico specializes completely in vegetables (at point *v* in Figure 37.2b).

Improved Alternatives With specialization and trade, the United States is no longer constrained by its domestic production possibilities line, which requires it to give up 1 ton of beef for every 1 ton of vegetables it wants as it moves up its domestic production possibilities line from, say, point *B*. Instead, the United States, through trade with Mexico, can get $1\frac{1}{2}$ tons of vegetables for every ton of beef that it exports to Mexico, as long as Mexico has vegetables

761

to export. Trading possibilities line BV' thus represents the $1B \equiv 1\frac{1}{2} V$ trading ratio.

Similarly, Mexico, starting at, say, point v, no longer has to move down its domestic production possibilities curve, giving up 2 tons of vegetables for each ton of beef it wants. It can now export just $1\frac{1}{2}$ tons of vegetables for each 1 ton of beef that it wants by moving down its trading possibilities line vb'.

Specialization and trade create a new exchange ratio between beef and vegetables, and that ratio is reflected in each nation's trading possibilities line. For both nations, this exchange ratio is superior to the unspecialized exchange ratio embodied in their respective production possibilities curves. By specializing in beef and trading for Mexico's vegetables, the United States can obtain more than 1 ton of vegetables for 1 ton of beef. By specializing in vegetables and trading for U.S. beef, Mexico can obtain 1 ton of beef for less than 2 tons of vegetables. In both cases, self-sufficiency is inefficient and therefore undesirable.

Greater Output By specializing on the basis of comparative advantage and by trading for goods that are produced in the nation with greater domestic efficiency, the United States and Mexico can achieve combinations of beef and vegetables beyond their own individual production possibilities curves. Specialization according to comparative advantage results in a more efficient allocation of world resources, and larger outputs of both products are therefore available to both nations.

Suppose that at the $1B \equiv 1\frac{1}{2} V$ terms of trade, the United States exports 10 tons of beef to Mexico and in return Mexico exports 15 tons of vegetables to the United States. How do the new quantities of beef and vegetables available to the two nations compare with the optimal product mixes that existed before specialization and trade? Point A in Figure 37.2a reminds us that the United States chose 18 tons of beef and 12 tons of vegetables originally. But by producing 30 tons of beef and no vegetables and by trading 10 tons of beef for 15 tons of vegetables, the United States can obtain 20 tons of beef and 15 tons of vegetables. This new, superior combination of beef and vegetables is indicated by point A' in Figure 37.2a. Compared with the no-trade amounts of 18 tons of beef and 12 tons of vegetables, the United States' **gains from trade** are 2 tons of beef and 3 tons of vegetables.

INTERACTIVE GRAPHS

G 37.1

Comparative advantage

WORKED PROBLEMS

W 37.1

Gains from trade

Similarly, recall that Mexico's optimal product mix was 4 tons of vegetables and 8 tons of beef (point Z) before specialization and trade. Now, after specializing in vegetables and trading for beef, Mexico can have 5 tons of vegetables and 10 tons of beef. It accomplishes that by producing 20 tons of vegetables and no beef and exporting 15 tons of its vegetables in exchange for 10 tons of American beef. This new position is indicated by point Z' in Figure 37.2b. Mexico's gains from trade are 1 ton of vegetables and 2 tons of beef.

Points A' and Z' in Figure 37.2 are superior economic positions to points A and Z. This fact is enormously important! We know that a nation can expand its production possibilities boundary by (1) expanding the quantity and improving the quality of its resources or (2) realizing technological progress. We have now established that international trade can enable a nation to circumvent the output constraint illustrated by its production possibilities curve. An economy can grow by expanding international trade. The outcome of international specialization and trade is equivalent to having more and better resources or discovering and implementing improved production techniques.

Table 37.1 summarizes the transactions and outcomes in our analysis. Please give it one final careful review.

CONSIDER THIS . . .

Misunderstanding the Gains from Trade

It is a common myth that the greatest benefit to be derived from international trade is greater domestic employment in the export sector. This suggests that exports are "good" because they increase domestic employment, whereas imports are "bad" because they deprive people of jobs at home. As we have demonstrated, the true benefit created by international trade is the overall increase in output available through specialization and exchange.

A nation does not need international trade to operate *on* its production possibilities curve. It can fully employ its resources, including labor, with or without international trade. International trade, however, enables a country to reach a point of consumption beyond its domestic production possibilities curve. The gain from trade to a nation is the extra output obtained from abroad—the imports obtained for less sacrifice of other goods than if they were produced at home.

Trade with Increasing Costs

To explain the basic principles underlying international trade, we simplified our analysis in several ways. For example, we limited discussion to two products and two nations. But multiproduct and multinational analysis yield the same conclusions. We also assumed constant opportunity costs (linear production possibilities curves), which is a more substantive simplification. Let's consider the effect of allowing increasing opportunity costs (concave-to-the-origin production possibilities curves) to enter the picture.

Suppose that the United States and Mexico initially are at positions on their concave production possibilities curves where their domestic cost ratios are $1B \equiv 1V$ and $1B \equiv 2V$, as they were in our constant-cost analysis. As before, comparative advantage indicates that the United States should specialize in beef and Mexico in vegetables. But now, as the United States begins to expand beef production, its cost of beef will rise; it will have to sacrifice more than 1 ton of vegetables to get 1 additional ton of beef. Resources are no longer perfectly substitutable between alternative uses, as the constant-cost assumption implied. Resources less and less suitable to beef production must be allocated to the U.S. beef industry in expanding beef output, and that means increasing costs—the sacrifice of larger and larger amounts of vegetables for each additional ton of beef.

Similarly, suppose that Mexico expands vegetable production starting from its $1B \equiv 2V$ cost ratio position. As production increases, it will find that its $1B \equiv 2V$ cost ratio begins to rise. Sacrificing 1 ton of beef will free resources that are capable of producing only something less than 2 tons of vegetables, because those transferred resources are less suitable to vegetable production.

As the U.S. cost ratio falls from $1B \equiv 1V$ and the Mexican ratio rises from $1B \equiv 2V$, a point will be reached where the cost ratios are equal in the two nations, perhaps at $1B \equiv 1\frac{3}{4}V$. At this point the underlying basis for further specialization and trade—differing cost ratios—has disappeared, and further specialization is therefore uneconomical. And, most important, this point of equal cost ratios may be reached while the United States is still producing some vegetables along with its beef and Mexico is producing some beef along with its vegetables. The primary effect of increasing opportunity costs is less-than-complete specialization. For this reason, we often find domestically produced products competing directly against identical or similar imported products within a particular economy.

The Case for Free Trade

The case for free trade reduces to one compelling argument: Through free trade based on the principle of comparative advantage, the world economy can achieve a more efficient allocation of resources and a higher level of material well-being than it can without free trade.

Since the resource mixes and technological knowledge of the world's nations are all somewhat different, each nation can produce particular commodities at different real costs. Each nation should produce goods for which its domestic opportunity costs are lower than the domestic opportunity costs of other nations and exchange those goods for products for which its domestic opportunity costs are high relative to those of other nations. If each nation does this, the world will realize the advantages of geographic and human specialization. The world and each free-trading nation can obtain a larger real income from the fixed supplies of resources available to it.

Government trade barriers lessen or eliminate gains from specialization. If nations cannot trade freely, they must shift resources from efficient (low-cost) to inefficient (high-cost) uses to satisfy their diverse wants. A recent study suggests that the elimination of trade barriers since the Second World War has increased the income of the average U.S. household by at least $7000 and perhaps by as much as $13,000. These income gains are recurring; they happen year after year.[2]

One side benefit of free trade is that it promotes competition and deters monopoly. The increased competition from foreign firms forces domestic firms to find and use the lowest-cost production techniques. It also compels them to be innovative with respect to both product quality and production methods, thereby contributing to economic growth. And free trade gives consumers a wider range of product choices. The reasons to favor free trade are the same as the reasons to endorse competition.

A second side benefit of free trade is that it links national interests and breaks down national animosities. Confronted with political disagreements, trading partners tend to negotiate rather than make war.

QUICK REVIEW 37.1

- International trade enables nations to specialize, increase productivity, and increase output available for consumption.
- Comparative advantage means total world output will be greatest when each good is produced by the nation that has the lowest domestic opportunity cost.
- Specialization is less than complete among nations because opportunity costs normally rise as any specific nation produces more of a particular good.

[2]Scott C. Bradford, Paul L. E. Grieco, and Gary C. Hufbauer, "The Payoff to America from Globalization," *The World Economy*, July 2006, pp. 893–916.

Supply and Demand Analysis of Exports and Imports

Supply and demand analysis reveals how equilibrium prices and quantities of exports and imports are determined. The amount of a good or a service a nation will export or import depends on differences between the equilibrium world price and the equilibrium domestic price. The interaction of *world* supply and demand determines the equilibrium **world price**—the price that equates the quantities supplied and demanded globally. *Domestic* supply and demand determine the equilibrium **domestic price**—the price that would prevail in a closed economy that does not engage in international trade. The domestic price equates quantity supplied and quantity demanded domestically.

In the absence of trade, the domestic prices in a closed economy may or may not equal the world equilibrium prices. When economies are opened for international trade, differences between world and domestic prices encourage exports or imports. To see how, consider the international effects of such price differences in a simple two-nation world, consisting of the United States and

Canada, that are both producing aluminum. We assume there are no trade barriers, such as tariffs and quotas, and no international transportation costs.

Supply and Demand in the United States

Figure 37.3a shows the domestic supply curve S_d and the domestic demand curve D_d for aluminum in the United States, which for now is a closed economy. The intersection of S_d and D_d determines the equilibrium domestic price of $1 per pound and the equilibrium domestic quantity of 100 million pounds. Domestic suppliers produce 100 million pounds and sell them all at $1 a pound. So there are no domestic surpluses or shortages of aluminum.

But what if the U.S. economy were opened to trade and the world price of aluminum were above or below this $1 domestic price?

U.S. Export Supply If the aluminum price in the rest of the world (that is, Canada) exceeds $1, U.S. firms will produce more than 100 million pounds and will export the excess domestic output. First, consider a world price of

FIGURE 37.3 U.S. export supply and import demand. (a) Domestic supply S_d and demand D_d set the domestic equilibrium price of aluminum at $1 per pound. At world prices above $1 there are domestic surpluses of aluminum. At prices below $1 there are domestic shortages. (b) Surpluses are exported (top curve), and shortages are met by importing aluminum (lower curve). The export supply curve shows the direct relationship between world prices and U.S. exports; the import demand curve portrays the inverse relationship between world prices and U.S. imports.

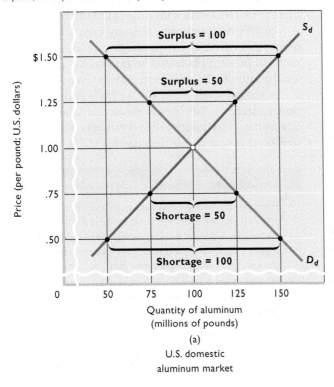

(a)
U.S. domestic
aluminum market

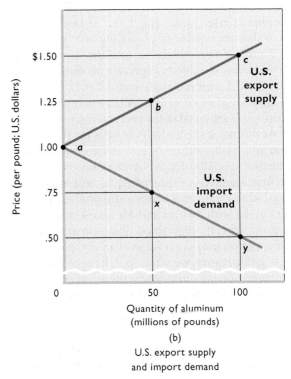

(b)
U.S. export supply
and import demand

$1.25. We see from the supply curve S_d that U.S. aluminum firms will produce 125 million pounds of aluminum at that price. The demand curve D_d tells us that the United States will purchase only 75 million pounds at $1.25. The outcome is a domestic surplus of 50 million pounds of aluminum. U.S. producers will export those 50 million pounds at the $1.25 world price.

What if the world price were $1.50? The supply curve shows that U.S. firms will produce 150 million pounds of aluminum, while the demand curve tells us that U.S. consumers will buy only 50 million pounds. So U.S. producers will export the domestic surplus of 100 million pounds.

Toward the top of Figure 37.3b we plot the domestic surpluses—the U.S. exports—that occur at world prices above the $1 domestic equilibrium price. When the world and domestic prices are equal (= $1), the quantity of exports supplied is zero (point *a*). There is no surplus of domestic output to export. But when the world price is $1.25, U.S. firms export 50 million pounds of surplus aluminum (point *b*). At a $1.50 world price, the domestic surplus of 100 million pounds is exported (point *c*).

The U.S. **export supply curve,** found by connecting points *a*, *b*, and *c*, shows the amount of aluminum U.S. producers will export at each world price above $1. This curve *slopes upward*, indicating a direct or positive relationship between the world price and the amount of U.S. exports. As world prices increase relative to domestic prices, U.S. exports rise.

U.S. Import Demand If the world price is below the domestic $1 price, the United States will import aluminum. Consider a $.75 world price. The supply curve in Figure 37.3a reveals that at that price U.S. firms produce only 75 million pounds of aluminum. But the demand curve shows that the United States wants to buy 125 million pounds at that price. The result is a domestic shortage of 50 million pounds. To satisfy that shortage, the United States will import 50 million pounds of aluminum.

At an even lower world price, $.50, U.S. producers will supply only 50 million pounds. Because U.S. consumers want to buy 150 million pounds at that price, there is a domestic shortage of 100 million pounds. Imports will flow to the United States to make up the difference. That is, at a $.50 world price U.S. firms will supply 50 million pounds and 100 million pounds will be imported.

In Figure 37.3b we plot the U.S. **import demand curve** from these data. This *downsloping curve* shows the amounts of aluminum that will be imported at world prices below the $1 U.S. domestic price. The relationship between world prices and imported amounts is inverse or negative. At a world price of $1, domestic output will satisfy U.S. demand; imports will be zero (point *a*). But at $.75 the United States will import 50 million pounds of aluminum (point *x*); at $.50, the United States will import 100 million pounds (point *y*). Connecting points *a*, *x*, and *y* yields the *downsloping* U.S. import demand curve. It reveals that as world prices fall relative to U.S. domestic prices, U.S. imports increase.

Supply and Demand in Canada

We repeat our analysis in Figure 37.4, this time from the viewpoint of Canada. (We have converted Canadian dollar prices to U.S. dollar prices via the exchange rate.) Note that the domestic supply curve S_d and the domestic demand curve D_d for aluminum in Canada yield a domestic price of $.75, which is $.25 lower than the $1 U.S. domestic price.

The analysis proceeds exactly as above except that the domestic price is now the Canadian price. If the world price is $.75, Canadians will neither export nor import aluminum (giving us point *q* in Figure 37.4b). At world prices above $.75, Canadian firms will produce more aluminum than Canadian consumers will buy. Canadian firms will export the surplus. At a $1 world price, Figure 37.4b tells us that Canada will have and export a domestic surplus of 50 million pounds (yielding point *r*). At $1.25, it will have and will export a domestic surplus of 100 million pounds (point *s*). Connecting these points yields the upsloping Canadian export supply curve, which reflects the domestic surpluses (and hence the exports) that occur when the world price exceeds the $.75 Canadian domestic price.

At world prices below $.75, domestic shortages occur in Canada. At a $.50 world price, Figure 37.4a shows that Canadian consumers want to buy 125 million pounds of aluminum but Canadian firms will produce only 75 million pounds. The shortage will bring 50 million pounds of imports to Canada (point *t* in Figure 37.4b). The Canadian import demand curve in that figure shows the Canadian imports that will occur at all world aluminum prices below the $.75 Canadian domestic price.

Equilibrium World Price, Exports, and Imports

We now have the tools for determining the **equilibrium world price** of aluminum and the equilibrium world levels of exports and imports when the world is opened to trade. Figure 37.5 combines the U.S. export supply curve and import demand curve in Figure 37.3b and the Canadian export supply curve and import demand curve in Figure 37.4b. The two U.S. curves proceed rightward from the $1 U.S. domestic price; the two Canadian curves proceed rightward from the $.75 Canadian domestic price.

FIGURE 37.4 Canadian export supply and import demand. (a) At world prices above the $.75 domestic price, production in Canada exceeds domestic consumption. At world prices below $.75, domestic shortages occur. (b) Surpluses result in exports, and shortages result in imports. The Canadian export supply curve and import demand curve depict the relationships between world prices and exports or imports.

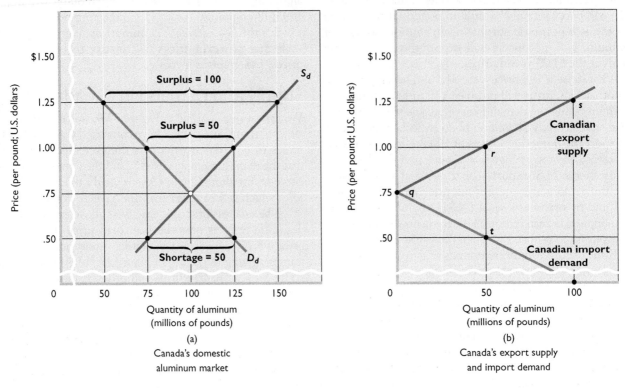

(a)
Canada's domestic
aluminum market

(b)
Canada's export supply
and import demand

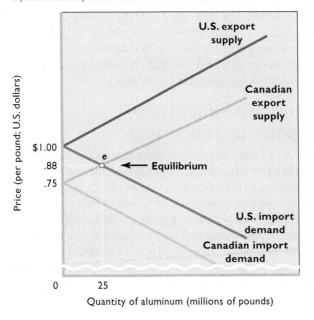

FIGURE 37.5 Equilibrium world price and quantity of exports and imports. In a two-nation world, the equilibrium world price (= $.88) is determined by the intersection of one nation's export supply curve and the other nation's import demand curve. This intersection also decides the equilibrium volume of exports and imports. Here, Canada exports 25 million pounds of aluminum to the United States.

International equilibrium occurs in this two-nation model where one nation's import demand curve intersects another nation's export supply curve. In this case the U.S. import demand curve intersects Canada's export supply curve at *e*. There, the world price of aluminum is $.88. The Canadian export supply curve indicates that Canada will export 25 million pounds of aluminum at this price. Also at this price the United States will import 25 million pounds from Canada, indicated by the U.S. import demand curve. The $.88 world price equates the quantity of imports demanded and the quantity of exports supplied (25 million pounds). Thus, there will be world trade of 25 million pounds of aluminum at $.88 per pound.

Note that after trade, the single $.88 world price will prevail in both Canada and the United States. Only one price for a standardized commodity can persist in a highly competitive world market. With trade, all consumers can buy a pound of aluminum for $.88, and all producers can sell it for that price. This world price means that Canadians will pay more for aluminum with trade ($.88) than without it ($.75). The increased Canadian output caused

WORKED PROBLEMS

W 37.2

Equilibrium world price, exports, and imports

by trade raises Canadian per-unit production costs and therefore raises the price of aluminum in Canada. The United States, however, pays less for aluminum with trade ($.88) than without it ($1). The U.S. gain comes from Canada's comparative cost advantage in producing aluminum.

Why would Canada willingly send 25 million pounds of its aluminum output to the United States for U.S. consumption? After all, producing this output uses up scarce Canadian resources and drives up the price of aluminum for Canadians. Canadians are willing to export aluminum to the United States because Canadians gain the means—the U.S. dollars—to import other goods, say, computer software, from the United States. Canadian exports enable Canadians to acquire imports that have greater value to Canadians than the exported aluminum. Canadian exports to the United States finance Canadian imports from the United States.

QUICK REVIEW 37.2

- A nation will export a particular product if the world price exceeds the domestic price; it will import the product if the world price is less than the domestic price.
- In a two-country world model, equilibrium world prices and equilibrium quantities of exports and imports occur where one nation's export supply curve intersects the other nation's import demand curve.

Trade Barriers and Export Subsidies

While a nation as a whole gains from trade, trade may harm particular domestic industries and their workers. Those industries might seek to preserve their economic positions by persuading their respective governments to protect them from imports—perhaps through tariffs, import quotas, or other trade barriers.

Indeed, the public may be won over by the apparent plausibility ("Cut imports and prevent domestic unemployment") and the patriotic ring ("Buy American!") of the arguments. The alleged benefits of tariffs are immediate and clear-cut to the public, but the adverse effects cited by economists are obscure and dispersed over the entire economy. When political deal-making is added in—"You back tariffs for the apparel industry in my state, and I'll back tariffs for the auto industry in your state"—the outcome can be a politically robust network of trade barriers. These impediments to free international trade can take several forms.

CONSIDER THIS . . .

Buy American?

Will "buying American" make Americans better off? No, says Dallas Federal Reserve economist W. Michael Cox:

A common myth is that it is better for Americans to spend their money at home than abroad. The best way to expose the fallacy of this argument is to take it to its logical extreme. If it is better for me to spend my money here than abroad, then it is even better yet to buy in Texas than in New York, better yet to buy in Dallas than in Houston . . . in my own neighborhood . . . within my own family . . . to consume only what I can produce. Alone and poor.*

*"The Fruits of Free Trade," 2002 Annual Report, by W. Michael Cox and Richard Alm, p. 16, Federal Reserve Bank of Dallas. Used with permission.

Tariffs are excise taxes or "duties" on the dollar values or physical quantities of imported goods. They may be imposed to obtain revenue or to protect domestic firms. A **revenue tariff** is usually applied to a product that is not being produced domestically, for example, tin, coffee, or bananas in the case of the United States. Rates on revenue tariffs tend to be modest and are designed to provide the Federal government with revenue. A **protective tariff** is implemented to shield domestic producers from foreign competition. These tariffs impede free trade by increasing the prices of imported goods and therefore shifting sales toward domestic producers. Although protective tariffs are usually not high enough to stop the importation of foreign goods, they put foreign producers at a competitive disadvantage. A tariff on imported auto tires, for example, would make domestically produced tires more attractive to consumers.

An **import quota** is a limit on the quantities or total values of specific items that are imported in some period. Once a quota is filled, further imports of that product are choked off. Import quotas are more effective than tariffs in impeding international trade. With a tariff, a product can go on being imported in large quantities. But with an import quota, all imports are prohibited once the quota is filled.

A **nontariff barrier (NTB)** includes onerous licensing requirements, unreasonable standards pertaining to product quality, or simply bureaucratic hurdles and delays in customs procedures. Some nations require that importers of foreign goods obtain licenses and then restrict the number of licenses issued. Although many nations carefully inspect imported agricultural products to prevent the introduction of potentially harmful insects, some countries use lengthy inspections to impede imports. Japan and the European countries frequently require that their domestic importers of foreign goods obtain licenses. By restricting the issuance of licenses, governments can limit imports.

A **voluntary export restriction (VER)** is a trade barrier by which foreign firms "voluntarily" limit the amount of their exports to a particular country. VERs have the same effect as import quotas and are agreed to by exporters to avoid more stringent tariffs or quotas. In the late 1990s, for example, Canadian producers of softwood lumber (fir, spruce, cedar, pine) agreed to a VER on exports to the United States under the threat of a permanently higher U.S. tariff.

ORIGIN OF THE IDEA

O 37.2

Trade protectionism

An **export subsidy** consists of a government payment to a domestic producer of export goods and is designed to aid that producer. By reducing production costs, the subsidies enable the domestic firm to charge a lower price and thus to sell more exports in world markets. Two examples: Some European governments have heavily subsidized Airbus Industries, a European firm that produces commercial aircraft. The subsidies help Airbus compete against the American firm Boeing. The United States and other nations have subsidized domestic farmers to boost the domestic food supply. Such subsidies have artificially lowered export prices on agricultural produce.

Later in this chapter we will discuss some of the specific arguments and appeals that are made to justify protection.

Economic Impact of Tariffs

We will confine our in-depth analysis of the effects of trade barriers to the two most common forms: tariffs and quotas. Once again, we turn to supply and demand analysis for help. Curves D_d and S_d in Figure 37.6 show domestic demand and supply for a product in which a nation, say, the United States, does *not* have a comparative advantage—for example, DVD players. (Disregard curve $S_d + Q$ for now.) Without world trade, the domestic price and output would be P_d and q, respectively.

Assume now that the domestic economy is opened to world trade and that Japan, which *does* have a comparative advantage in DVD players, begins to sell its players in the United States. We assume that with free trade the domestic price cannot differ from the world price, which here is P_w. At P_w domestic consumption is d and domestic production is a.

FIGURE 37.6 The economic effects of a protective tariff or an import quota. A tariff that increases the price of a good from P_w to P_t will reduce domestic consumption from d to c. Domestic producers will be able to sell more output (b rather than a) at a higher price (P_t rather than P_w). Foreign exporters are injured because they sell less output (bc rather than ad). The yellow area indicates the amount of tariff paid by domestic consumers. An import quota of bc units has the same effect as the tariff, with one exception: The amount represented by the yellow area will go to foreign producers rather than to the domestic government.

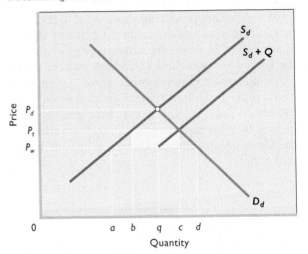

The horizontal distance between the domestic supply and demand curves at P_w represents imports of ad. Thus far, our analysis is similar to the analysis of world prices in Figure 37.3.

Direct Effects Suppose now that the United States imposes a tariff on each imported DVD player. The tariff, which raises the price of imported players from P_w to P_t, has four effects:

- **Decline in consumption** Consumption of DVD players in the United States declines from d to c as the higher price moves buyers up and to the left along their demand curve. The tariff prompts consumers to buy fewer players, and reallocate a portion of their expenditures to less desired substitute products. U.S. consumers are clearly injured by the tariff, since they pay $P_t - P_w$ more for each of the c units they buy at price P_t.
- **Increased domestic production** U.S. producers—who are not subject to the tariff—receive the higher price P_t per unit. Because this new price is higher than the pretariff world price P_w, the domestic DVD-player industry moves up and to the right along its supply curve S_d, increasing domestic output from a to b. Domestic producers thus enjoy both a higher price and expanded sales; this explains why domestic producers lobby for protective tariffs. But from a social point of

view, the increase in domestic production from *a* to *b* means that the tariff permits domestic producers of players to bid resources away from other, more efficient, U.S. industries.

- **Decline in imports** Japanese producers are hurt. Although the sales price of each player is higher by $P_t - P_w$, that amount accrues to the U.S. government, not to Japanese producers. The after-tariff world price, or the per-unit revenue to Japanese producers, remains at P_w, but the volume of U.S. imports (Japanese exports) falls from *ad* to *bc*.

- **Tariff revenue** The yellow rectangle represents the amount of revenue the tariff yields. Total revenue from the tariff is determined by multiplying the tariff, $P_t - P_w$ per unit, by the number of players imported, *bc*. This tariff revenue is a transfer of income from consumers to government and does not represent any net change in the nation's economic well-being. The result is that government gains this portion of what consumers lose by paying more for DVD players.

Indirect Effect Tariffs have a subtle effect beyond what our supply and demand diagram can show. Because Japan sells fewer DVD players in the United States, it earns fewer dollars and so must buy fewer U.S. exports. U.S. export industries must then cut production and release resources. These are highly efficient industries, as we know from their comparative advantage and their ability to sell goods in world markets.

Tariffs directly promote the expansion of inefficient industries that do not have a comparative advantage; they also indirectly cause the contraction of relatively efficient industries that do have a comparative advantage. Put bluntly, tariffs cause resources to be shifted in the wrong direction—and that is not surprising. We know that specialization and world trade lead to more efficient use of world resources and greater world output. But protective tariffs reduce world trade. Therefore, tariffs also reduce efficiency and the world's real output.

Economic Impact of Quotas

We noted earlier that an import quota is a legal limit placed on the amount of some product that can be imported in a given year. Quotas have the same economic impact as a tariff, with one big difference: While tariffs generate revenue for the domestic government, a quota transfers that revenue to foreign producers.

Suppose in Figure 37.6 that, instead of imposing a tariff, the United States prohibits any imports of Japanese DVD players in excess of *bc* units. In other words, an import quota

of *bc* players is imposed on Japan. We deliberately chose the size of this quota to be the same amount as imports would be under a $P_t - P_w$ tariff so that we can compare "equivalent" situations. As a consequence of the quota, the supply of players is $S_d + Q$ in the United States. This supply consists of the domestic supply plus the fixed amount *bc* (= *Q*) that importers will provide at each domestic price. The supply curve $S_w + Q$ does not extend below price P_w because Japanese producers would not export players to the United States at any price below P_w; instead, they would sell them to other countries at the world market price of P_w.

Most of the economic results are the same as those with a tariff. Prices of DVD players are higher (P_t instead of P_w) because imports have been reduced from *ad* to *bc*. Domestic consumption of DVD players is down from *d* to *c*. U.S. producers enjoy both a higher price (P_t rather than P_w) and increased sales (*b* rather than *a*).

The difference is that the price increase of $P_t - P_w$ paid by U.S. consumers on imports of *bc*—the yellow area—no longer goes to the U.S. Treasury as tariff (tax) revenue but flows to the Japanese firms that have acquired the quota rights to sell DVD players in the United States. For consumers in the United States, a tariff produces a better economic outcome than a quota, other things being the same. A tariff generates government revenue that can be used to cut other taxes or to finance public goods and services that benefit the United States. In contrast, the higher price created by quotas results in additional revenue for foreign producers.

Net Costs of Tariffs and Quotas

Figure 37.6 shows that tariffs and quotas impose costs on domestic consumers but provide gains to domestic producers and, in the case of tariffs, revenue to the Federal government. The consumer costs of trade restrictions are calculated by determining the effect the restrictions have on consumer prices. Protection raises the price of a product in three ways: (1) The price of the imported product goes up; (2) the higher price of imports causes some consumers to shift their purchases to higher-priced domestically produced goods; and (3) the prices of domestically produced goods rise because import competition has declined.

Study after study finds that the costs to consumers substantially exceed the gains to producers and government. A sizable net cost or efficiency loss to society arises from trade protection. Furthermore, industries employ large amounts of economic resources to influence Congress to pass and retain protectionist laws. Because these rent-seeking efforts divert resources away from more socially desirable purposes, trade restrictions impose these additional costs on society as well.

Conclusion: The gains that U.S. trade barriers create for protected industries and their workers come at the expense of much greater losses for the entire economy. The result is economic inefficiency, reduced consumption, and lower standards of living.

The Case for Protection: A Critical Review

Despite the logic of specialization and trade, there are still protectionists in some union halls, corporate boardrooms, and congressional conference rooms. What arguments do protectionists make to justify trade barriers? How valid are those arguments?

Military Self-Sufficiency Argument

The argument here is not economic but political-military: Protective tariffs are needed to preserve or strengthen industries that produce the materials essential for national defense. In an uncertain world, the political-military objectives (self-sufficiency) sometimes must take precedence over economic goals (efficiency in the use of world resources).

Unfortunately, it is difficult to measure and compare the benefit of increased national security against the cost of economic inefficiency when protective tariffs are imposed. The economist can only point out that when a nation levies tariffs to increase military self-sufficiency it incurs economic costs.

All people in the United States would agree that relying on hostile nations for necessary military equipment is not a good idea, yet the self-sufficiency argument is open to serious abuse. Nearly every industry can claim that it makes direct or indirect contributions to national security and hence deserves protection from imports.

Diversification-for-Stability Argument

Highly specialized economies such as Saudi Arabia (based on oil) and Cuba (based on sugar) are dependent on international markets for their income. In these economies, wars, international political developments, recessions abroad, and random fluctuations in world supply and demand for one or two particular goods can cause deep declines in export revenues and therefore in domestic income. Tariff and quota protection are allegedly needed in such nations to enable greater industrial diversification. That way, these economies will not be so dependent on exporting one or two products to obtain the other goods they need. Such goods will be available domestically, thereby providing greater domestic stability.

There is some truth in this diversification-for-stability argument. But the argument has little or no relevance to the United States and other advanced economies. Also, the economic costs of diversification may be great; for example, one-crop economies may be highly inefficient at manufacturing.

Infant Industry Argument

The infant industry argument contends that protective tariffs are needed to allow new domestic industries to establish themselves. Temporarily shielding young domestic firms from the severe competition of more mature and more efficient foreign firms will give infant industries a chance to develop and become efficient producers.

This argument for protection rests on an alleged exception to the case for free trade. The exception is that young industries have not had, and if they face mature foreign competition will never have, the chance to make the long-run adjustments needed for larger scale and greater efficiency in production. In this view, tariff protection for such infant industries will correct a misallocation of world resources perpetuated by historically different levels of economic development between domestic and foreign industries.

There are some logical problems with the infant industry argument. In the developing nations it is difficult to determine which industries are the infants that are capable of achieving economic maturity and therefore deserving protection. Also, protective tariffs may persist even after industrial maturity has been realized.

Most economists feel that if infant industries are to be subsidized, there are better means than tariffs for doing so. Direct subsidies, for example, have the advantage of making explicit which industries are being aided and to what degree.

Protection-against-Dumping Argument

The protection-against-dumping argument contends that tariffs are needed to protect domestic firms from "dumping" by foreign producers. **Dumping** is the sale of a product in a foreign country at prices either below cost or below the prices commonly charged at home.

Economists cite two plausible reasons for this behavior. First, with regard to below-cost dumping, firms in country A may dump goods at below cost into country B in an attempt to drive their competitors in country B out of business. If the firms in country A succeed in driving their competitors in country B out of business, they will enjoy monopoly power and monopoly prices and profits on the goods they subsequently sell in country B. Their hope is that the longer-term monopoly profits will more than offset the losses from below-cost sales that must take place while they are attempting to drive their competitors in country B out of business.

Second, dumping that involves selling abroad at a price that is below the price commonly charged in the home country (but that is still at or above production costs) may be a form of price discrimination, which is charging different prices to different customers. As an example, a foreign seller that has a monopoly in its home market may find that it can maximize its overall profit by charging a high price in its monopolized domestic market while charging a lower price in the United States, where it must compete with U.S. producers. Curiously, it may pursue this strategy even if it makes no profit at all from its sales in the United States, where it must charge the competitive price. So why bother selling in the United States? Because the increase in overall production that comes about by exporting to the United States may allow the firm to obtain the per-unit cost savings often associated with large-scale production. These cost savings imply even higher profits in the monopolized domestic market.

Because dumping is an "unfair trade practice," most nations prohibit it. For example, where dumping is shown to injure U.S. firms, the Federal government imposes tariffs called *antidumping duties* on the goods in question. But relatively few documented cases of dumping occur each year, and specific instances of unfair trade do not justify widespread, permanent tariffs. Moreover, antidumping duties can be abused. Often, what appears to be dumping is simply comparative advantage at work.

Increased Domestic Employment Argument

Arguing for a tariff to "save U.S. jobs" becomes fashionable when the economy encounters a recession (such as the severe recession of 2007–2009 in the United States). In an economy that engages in international trade, exports involve spending on domestic output and imports reflect spending to obtain part of another nation's output. So, in this argument, reducing imports will divert spending on another nation's output to spending on domestic output. Thus, domestic output and employment will rise. But this argument has several shortcomings.

While imports may eliminate some U.S. jobs, they create others. Imports may have eliminated the jobs of some U.S. steel and textile workers in recent years, but other workers have gained jobs unloading ships, flying imported aircraft, and selling imported electronic equipment. Import restrictions alter the composition of employment, but they may have little or no effect on the volume of employment.

The *fallacy of composition*—the false idea that what is true for the part is necessarily true for the whole—is also present in this rationale for tariffs. All nations cannot simultaneously succeed in restricting imports while maintaining their exports; what is true for one nation is not true for all nations. The exports of one nation must be the imports of another nation. To the extent that one country is able to expand its economy through an excess of exports over imports, the resulting excess of imports over exports worsens another economy's unemployment problem. It is no wonder that tariffs and import quotas meant to achieve domestic full employment are called "beggar my neighbor" policies: They achieve short-run domestic goals by making trading partners poorer.

Moreover, nations adversely affected by tariffs and quotas are likely to retaliate, causing a "trade war" (more precisely, a *trade barrier war*) that will choke off trade and make all nations worse off. The **Smoot-Hawley Tariff Act** of 1930 is a classic example. Although that act was meant to reduce imports and stimulate U.S. production, the high tariffs it authorized prompted adversely affected nations to retaliate with tariffs equally high. International trade fell, lowering the output and income of all nations. Economic historians generally agree that the Smoot-Hawley Tariff Act was a contributing cause of the Great Depression.

Finally, forcing an excess of exports over imports cannot succeed in raising domestic employment over the long run. It is through U.S. imports that foreign nations earn dollars for buying U.S. exports. In the long run, a nation must import in order to export. The long-run impact of tariffs is not an increase in domestic employment but, at best, a reallocation of workers away from export industries and to protected domestic industries. This shift implies a less efficient allocation of resources.

Cheap Foreign Labor Argument

The cheap foreign labor argument says that domestic firms and workers must be shielded from the ruinous competition of countries where wages are low. If protection is not provided, cheap imports will flood U.S. markets and the prices of U.S. goods—along with the wages of U.S. workers—will be pulled down. That is, domestic living standards in the United States will be reduced.

This argument can be rebutted at several levels. The logic of the argument suggests that it is not mutually beneficial for rich and poor persons to trade with one another. However, that is not the case. A low-income farmworker may pick lettuce or tomatoes for a rich landowner, and both may benefit from the transaction. And both U.S. consumers and Chinese workers gain when they "trade" a pair of athletic shoes priced at $30 as opposed to U.S. consumers being restricted to buying a similar shoe made in the United States for $60.

Also, recall that gains from trade are based on comparative advantage, not on absolute advantage. Look back at Figure 37.1, where we supposed that the United States and Mexico had labor forces of exactly the same size. Noting the positions of the production possibilities curves, observe that U.S. labor can produce more of either good. Thus, it is more productive. Because of this greater productivity, we can expect wages and living standards to be higher for U.S. labor. Mexico's less productive labor will receive lower wages.

The cheap foreign labor argument suggests that, to maintain its standard of living, the United States should not trade with low-wage Mexico. What if it does not trade with Mexico? Will wages and living standards rise in the United States as a result? No. To obtain vegetables, the United States will have to reallocate a portion of its labor from its relatively more-efficient beef industry to its relatively less-efficient vegetables industry. As a result, the average productivity of U.S. labor will fall, as will real wages and living standards. The labor forces of both countries will have diminished standards of living because without specialization and trade they will have less output available to them. Compare column 4 with column 1 in Table 37.1 or points A' and Z' with A and Z in Figure 37.2 to confirm this point.

Another problem with the cheap foreign labor argument is that its proponents incorrectly focus on labor costs per hour when what really matters is labor costs per unit of output. As an example, suppose that a U.S. factory pays its workers $20 per hour while a factory in a developing country pays its workers $4 per hour. The proponents of the cheap foreign labor argument look at these numbers and conclude—incorrectly—that it is impossible for the U.S. factory to compete with the factory in the developing country. But this conclusion fails to take into account two crucial facts:

- What actually matters is labor costs per *unit of output*, not labor costs per *hour of work*.
- Differences in productivity typically mean that labor costs per unit of output are often nearly identical despite huge differences in hourly labor costs.

To see why these points matter so much, let's take into account how productive the two factories are. Because the U.S. factory uses much more sophisticated technology, better trained workers, and a lot more capital per worker, one worker in one hour can produce 20 units of output. Since the U.S. workers get paid $20 per hour, this means the U.S. factory's labor cost *per unit of output* is $1. The factory in the developing country is much less productive

since it uses less efficient technology and its relatively untrained workers have a lot less machinery and equipment to work with. A worker there produces only 4 units per hour. Given the foreign wage of $4 per hour, this means that the labor cost per unit of output at the factory in the developing country is also $1.

As you can see, the lower wage rate per hour at the factory in the developing country does not translate into lower labor costs per unit—meaning that it won't be able to undersell its U.S. competitor just because its workers get paid lower wages per hour.

Proponents of the cheap foreign labor argument tend to focus exclusively on the large international differences that exist in labor costs per hour. They typically fail to mention that these differences in labor costs per hour are mostly the result of tremendously large differences in productivity and that these large differences in productivity serve to equalize labor costs per unit of output. As a result, firms in developing countries only *sometimes* have an advantage in terms of labor costs per unit of output. Whether they do in any specific situation will vary by industry and firm and will depend on differences in productivity as well as differences in labor costs per hour. For many goods, labor productivity in high-wage countries like the United States is so much higher than labor productivity in low-wage countries that it is actually cheaper *per unit of output* to manufacture those goods in high-wage countries. That is why, for instance, Intel still makes microchips in the United States and why most automobiles are still produced in the United States, Japan, and Europe rather than in low-wage countries.

> ### QUICK REVIEW 37.3
>
> - A tariff on a product increases its price, reduces its consumption, increases its domestic production, reduces its imports, and generates tariff revenue for government; an import quota does the same, except a quota generates revenue for foreign producers rather than for the government imposing the quota.
> - Most rationales for trade protections are special-interest requests that, if followed, would create gains for protected industries and their workers at the expense of greater losses for the economy.

Multilateral Trade Agreements and Free-Trade Zones

Aware of the detrimental effects of trade wars and the general weaknesses of arguments for trade protections, nations have worked to lower tariffs worldwide. Their pursuit of freer trade has been aided by recently emerged special-interest groups that have offset the more-established special-interest groups that have traditionally supported tariffs and quotas. Specifically, lower tariffs are now supported by exporters of goods and services, importers of foreign components used in "domestic" products, and domestic sellers of imported products.

General Agreement on Tariffs and Trade

In 1947, 23 nations, including the United States, signed the **General Agreement on Tariffs and Trade (GATT)**. GATT was based on three principles: (1) equal, nondiscriminatory trade treatment for all member nations; (2) the reduction of tariffs by multilateral negotiation; and (3) the elimination of import quotas. Basically, GATT provided a forum for the multilateral negotiation of reduced trade barriers.

Since the Second World War, member nations have completed eight "rounds" of GATT negotiations to reduce trade barriers. The eighth round of negotiations began in Uruguay in 1986. After seven years of complex discussions, in 1993 a new agreement was reached by the 128 nations that were by that time members of GATT. The Uruguay Round agreement took effect on January 1, 1995, and its provisions were phased in through 2005.

Under this agreement, tariffs on thousands of products were eliminated or reduced, with overall tariffs dropping by 33 percent. The agreement also liberalized government rules that in the past impeded the global market for such services as advertising, legal services, tourist services, and financial services. Quotas on imported textiles and apparel were phased out and replaced with tariffs. Other provisions reduced agricultural subsidies paid to farmers and protected intellectual property (patents, trademarks, and copyrights) against piracy.

World Trade Organization

The Uruguay Round agreement established the **World Trade Organization (WTO)** as GATT's successor. Some 153 nations belonged to the WTO in 2010. The WTO oversees trade agreements reached by the member nations, and rules on trade disputes among them. It also provides forums for further rounds of trade negotiations. The ninth and latest round of negotiations—the **Doha Development Agenda**—was launched in Doha, Qatar, in late 2001. (The trade rounds occur over several years in several venues but are named after the city or country of origination.) The negotiations are aimed at further reducing tariffs and quotas, as well as agricultural subsidies that distort trade. You can get an update on the status of the complex negotiations at **www.wto.org**.

GATT and the WTO have been positive forces in the trend toward liberalized world trade. The trade rules agreed upon by the member nations provide a strong and necessary bulwark against the protectionism called for by the special-interest groups in the various nations.

For that reason and others, the WTO is quite controversial. Critics are concerned that rules crafted to expand international trade and investment enable firms to circumvent national laws that protect workers and the environment. Critics ask: What good are minimum-wage laws, worker-safety laws, collective-bargaining rights, and environmental laws if firms can easily shift their production to nations that have weaker laws or if consumers can buy goods produced in those countries?

Proponents of the WTO respond that labor and environmental protections should be pursued directly in nations that have low standards and via international organizations other than the WTO. These issues should not be linked to the process of trade liberalization, which confers widespread economic benefits across nations. Moreover, say proponents of the WTO, many environmental and labor concerns are greatly overblown. Most world trade is among advanced industrial countries, not between them and countries that have lower environmental and labor standards. Moreover, the free flow of goods and resources raises output and income in the developing nations. Historically, such increases in living standards have eventually resulted in stronger, not weaker, protections for the environment and for workers.

The European Union

Countries have also sought to reduce tariffs by creating regional free-trade zones. The most dramatic example is the **European Union (EU)**. Initiated in 1958 as the Common Market, in 2003 the EU comprised 15 European nations—Austria, Belgium, Denmark, Finland, France, Germany, Greece, Ireland, Italy, Luxembourg, the Netherlands, Portugal, Spain, Sweden, and the United Kingdom. In 2004, the EU expanded by 10 additional European countries—Cyprus, the Czech Republic, Estonia, Hungary, Latvia, Lithuania, Malta, Poland, Slovakia, and Slovenia. In 2007, the addition of Bulgaria and Romania expanded the EU to its present size of 27 nations.

The EU has abolished tariffs and import quotas on nearly all products traded among the participating nations and established a common system of tariffs applicable to all goods received from nations outside the EU. It has also liberalized the movement of capital and labor within the EU and has created common policies in other economic matters of joint concern, such as agriculture, transportation, and business practices.

EU integration has achieved for Europe what the U.S. constitutional prohibition on tariffs by individual states has achieved for the United States: increased regional specialization, greater productivity, greater output, and faster economic growth. The free flow of goods and services has created large markets for EU industries. The resulting economies of large-scale production have enabled these industries to achieve much lower costs than they could have achieved in their small, single-nation markets.

One of the most significant accomplishments of the EU was the establishment of the so-called **Euro Zone** in the early 2000s. As of 2010, 16 members of the EU (Austria, Belgium, Cyprus, Germany, Greece, Ireland, Finland, France, Italy, Luxembourg, Malta, the Netherlands, Portugal, Slovenia, Slovakia, and Spain) use the euro as a common currency. Notably, the United Kingdom, Denmark, and Sweden have opted not to use the common currency, at least for now. But gone are French francs, German marks, Italian liras, and other national currencies that were once used by Euro Zone countries.

Economists expect the adoption of the euro to raise the standard of living in the Euro Zone nations over time. By ending the inconvenience and expense of exchanging currencies, the euro has enhanced the free flow of goods, services, and resources among the Euro Zone members. Companies that previously sold products in only one or two European nations have found it easier to price and sell their products in all 16 Euro Zone countries. The euro has also allowed consumers and businesses to comparison shop for outputs and inputs, and this capability has increased competition, reduced prices, and lowered costs.

North American Free Trade Agreement

In 1993 Canada, Mexico, and the United States created a major free-trade zone. The **North American Free Trade Agreement (NAFTA)** established a free-trade area that has about the same combined output as the EU but encompasses a much larger geographic area. NAFTA has eliminated tariffs and other trade barriers between Canada, Mexico, and the United States for most goods and services.

Critics of NAFTA feared that it would cause a massive loss of U.S. jobs as firms moved to Mexico to take advantage of lower wages and weaker regulations on pollution and workplace safety. Also, they were concerned that Japan and South Korea would build plants in Mexico and transport goods tariff-free to the United States, further hurting U.S. firms and workers.

In retrospect, critics were much too pessimistic. Since the passage of NAFTA in 1993, employment in the United States has increased by more than 20 million workers.

NAFTA has increased trade among Canada, Mexico, and the United States and has enhanced the standard of living in all three countries.

Trade Adjustment Assistance

Shifts in patterns of comparative advantage and removal of long-standing trade protection can hurt specific groups of workers. For example, the erosion of the United States' once strong comparative advantage in steel has caused production plant shutdowns and layoffs in the U.S. steel industry. The textile and apparel industries in the United States face similar difficulties. Clearly, not everyone wins from free trade (or freer trade). Some workers lose.

The **Trade Adjustment Assistance Act** of 2002 introduced some innovative policies to help those hurt by shifts in international trade patterns. The law provides cash assistance (beyond unemployment insurance) for up to 78 weeks for workers displaced by imports or plant relocations abroad. To obtain the assistance, workers must participate in job searches, training programs, or remedial education. Also provided are relocation allowances to help displaced workers move geographically to new jobs within the United States. Refundable tax credits for health insurance serve as payments to help workers maintain their insurance coverage during the retraining and job-search period. Workers who are 50 years of age or older are eligible for "wage insurance," which replaces some of the difference in pay (if any) between their old and new jobs. Many economists support trade adjustment assistance because it not only helps workers hurt by international trade but also helps create the political support necessary to reduce trade barriers and export subsidies.

But not all economists favor trade adjustment assistance. Loss of jobs from imports, sending some work abroad, and plant relocations to other countries are only a small fraction (about 4 percent in recent years) of total job losses in the economy each year. Many workers also lose their jobs because of changing patterns of demand, changing technology, bad management, and other dynamic aspects of a market economy. Some critics ask, "What makes losing one's job to international trade worthy of such special treatment, compared to losing one's job to, say, technological change or domestic competition?" Economists can find no totally satisfying answer.

Offshoring of Jobs

Not only are some U.S. jobs lost because of international trade, but some are lost because of globalization of resource markets. In recent years U.S. firms have found the

Word Petition of the Candlemakers, 1845

French Economist Frédéric Bastiat (1801–1850) Devastated the Proponents of Protectionism by Satirically Extending Their Reasoning to Its Logical and Absurd Conclusions.

Petition of the Manufacturers of Candles, Waxlights, Lamps, Candlesticks, Street Lamps, Snuffers, Extinguishers, and of the Producers of Oil Tallow, Rosin, Alcohol, and, Generally, of Everything Connected with Lighting.

TO MESSIEURS THE MEMBERS OF THE CHAMBER OF DEPUTIES.

Gentlemen—You are on the right road. You reject abstract theories, and have little consideration for cheapness and plenty. Your chief care is the interest of the producer. You desire to emancipate him from external competition, and reserve the national market for national industry.

We are about to offer you an admirable opportunity of applying your—what shall we call it? your theory? No; nothing is more deceptive than theory; your doctrine? your system? your principle? but you dislike doctrines, you abhor systems, and as for principles, you deny that there are any in social economy: we shall say, then, your practice, your practice without theory and without principle.

We are suffering from the intolerable competition of a foreign rival, placed, it would seem, in a condition so far superior to ours for the production of light, that he absolutely inundates our national market with it at a price fabulously reduced. The moment he shows himself, our trade leaves us—all consumers apply to him; and a branch of native industry, having countless ramifications, is all at once rendered completely stagnant. This rival . . . is no other than the Sun.

What we pray for is, that it may please you to pass a law ordering the shutting up of all windows, skylights, dormer windows, outside and inside shutters, curtains, blinds, bull's-eyes; in a word, of all openings, holes, chinks, clefts, and fissures, by or through which the light of the sun has been in use to enter houses, to the prejudice of the meritorious manufacturers with which we flatter ourselves we have accommodated our country,— a country which, in gratitude, ought not to abandon us now to a strife so unequal.

If you shut up as much as possible all access to natural light, and create a demand for artificial light, which of our French manufacturers will not be encouraged by it? If more tallow is consumed, then there must be more oxen and sheep; and, consequently, we shall behold the multiplication of artificial meadows, meat, wool, hides, and, above all, manure, which is the basis and foundation of all agricultural wealth.

The same remark applies to navigation. Thousands of vessels will proceed to the whale fishery; and, in a short time, we shall possess a navy capable of maintaining the honor of France, and gratifying the patriotic aspirations of your petitioners, the undersigned candlemakers and others.

Only have the goodness to reflect, Gentlemen, and you will be convinced that there is, perhaps, no Frenchman, from the wealthy coalmaster to the humblest vender of lucifer matches, whose lot will not be ameliorated by the success of this our petition.

Source: Frédéric Bastiat, *Economic Sophisms* (Irvington-on-Hudson, NY: The Foundation for Economic Education, Inc., 1996), abridged. Used with permission of Foundation for Economic Education, **www.FEE.org**.

outsourcing of work abroad to be increasingly profitable. Economists call this business activity **offshoring**—shifting work previously done by American workers to workers located in other nations. Offshoring is not a new practice but traditionally has involved components for U.S. manufacturing goods. For example, Boeing has long offshored the production of major airplane parts for its "American" aircraft.

Recent advances in computer and communications technology have enabled U.S. firms to offshore service jobs such as data entry, book composition, software coding, call-center operations, medical transcription, and

775

477

claims processing to countries such as India. Where off-shoring occurs, some of the value added in the production process accrues to foreign countries rather than the United States. So part of the income generated from the production of U.S. goods is paid to foreigners, not to American workers.

Offshoring is a wrenching experience for many Americans who lose their jobs, but it is not necessarily bad for the overall economy. Offshoring simply reflects growing specialization and international trade in services, or, more descriptively, "tasks." That growth has been made possible by recent trade agreements and new information and communication technologies. As with trade in goods, trade in services reflects comparative advantage and is beneficial to both trading parties. Moreover, the United States has a sizable trade surplus with other nations in services. The United States gains by specializing in high-valued services such as transportation services, accounting services, legal services, and advertising services, where it still has a comparative advantage. It then "trades" to obtain lower-valued services such as call-center and data-entry work, for which comparative advantage has gone abroad.

Offshoring also increases the demand for complementary jobs in the United States. Jobs that are close substitutes for existing U.S. jobs are lost, but complementary jobs in the United States are expanded. For example, the lower price of writing software code in India may mean a lower cost of software sold in the United States and abroad. That, in turn, may create more jobs for U.S.-based workers such as software designers, marketers, and distributors. Moreover, offshoring may encourage domestic investment and the expansion of firms in the United States by reducing their production costs and keeping them competitive worldwide. In some instances, "offshoring jobs" may equate to "importing competitiveness." Entire firms that might otherwise disappear abroad may remain profitable in the United States only because they can offshore some of their work.

QUICK REVIEW 37.4

- The General Agreement on Tariffs and Trade (GATT) of 1947 reduced tariffs and quotas and established a process for numerous subsequent rounds of multinational trade negotiations that have liberalized international trade.
- The World Trade Organization (WTO)—GATT's successor—rules on trade disputes and provides forums for negotiations on further rounds of trade liberalization. The current round of negotiations is called the Doha Development Agenda.
- The European Union (EU) and the North American Free Trade Agreement (NAFTA) have reduced internal trade barriers among their member nations by establishing multination free-trade zones.
- Increased international trade and offshoring of jobs have harmed some specific U.S. workers and have led to policies such as trade adjustment assistance to try to help them with their transitions to new lines of work.

Summary

1. The United States leads the world in the combined volume of exports and imports. Other major trading nations are Germany, Japan, the western European nations, and the Asian economies of China, South Korea, Taiwan, and Singapore. The United States' principal exports include chemicals, agricultural products, consumer durables, semiconductors, and aircraft; principal imports include petroleum, automobiles, metals, household appliances, and computers.

2. World trade is based on three considerations: the uneven distribution of economic resources among nations, the fact that efficient production of various goods requires particular techniques or combinations of resources, and the differentiated products produced among nations.

3. Mutually advantageous specialization and trade are possible between any two nations if they have different domestic opportunity-cost ratios for any two products. By specializing on the basis of comparative advantage, nations can obtain larger real incomes with fixed amounts of resources. The terms of trade determine how this increase in world output is shared by the trading nations. Increasing (rather than constant) opportunity costs limit specialization and trade.

4. A nation's export supply curve shows the quantities of a product the nation will export at world prices that exceed the domestic price (the price in a closed, no-international-trade economy). A nation's import demand curve reveals the quantities of a product it will import at world prices below the domestic price.

5. In a two-nation model, the equilibrium world price and the equilibrium quantities of exports and imports occur where one nation's export supply curve intersects the other nation's import demand curve. A nation will export a particular product if the world price exceeds the domestic price; it will import the product if the world price is less than the domestic price. The country with the lower costs of production will be the exporter and the country with the higher costs of production will be the importer.

6. Trade barriers take the form of protective tariffs, quotas, nontariff barriers, and "voluntary" export restrictions. Export subsidies also distort international trade. Supply and demand analysis demonstrates that protective tariffs and quotas increase the prices and reduce the quantities demanded of the affected goods. Sales by foreign exporters diminish; domestic producers, however, gain higher prices and enlarged sales. Consumer losses from trade restrictions greatly exceed producer and government gains, creating an efficiency loss to society.

7. The strongest arguments for protection are the infant industry and military self-sufficiency arguments. Most other arguments for protection are interest-group appeals or reasoning fallacies that emphasize producer interests over consumer interests or stress the immediate effects of trade barriers while ignoring long-run consequences.

8. The cheap foreign labor argument for protection fails because it focuses on labor costs per hour rather than on what really matters, labor costs per unit of output. Due to higher productivity, firms in high-wage countries like the United States can have lower wage costs per unit of output than competitors in low-wage countries. Whether they do will depend on how their particular wage and productivity levels compare with those of their competitors in low-wage countries.

9. In 1947 the General Agreement on Tariffs and Trade (GATT) was formed to encourage nondiscriminatory treatment for all member nations, to reduce tariffs, and to eliminate import quotas. The Uruguay Round of GATT negotiations (1993) reduced tariffs and quotas, liberalized trade in services, reduced agricultural subsidies, reduced pirating of intellectual property, and phased out quotas on textiles.

10. GATT's successor, the World Trade Organization (WTO), had 153 member nations in 2010. It implements WTO agreements, rules on trade disputes between members, and provides forums for continued discussions on trade liberalization. The latest round of trade negotiations—the Doha Development Agenda—began in late 2001 and as of 2010 was still in progress.

11. Free-trade zones liberalize trade within regions. Two examples of free-trade arrangements are the 27-member European Union (EU) and the North American Free Trade Agreement (NAFTA), comprising Canada, Mexico, and the United States. Sixteen EU nations have abandoned their national currencies for a common currency called the euro.

12. The Trade Adjustment Assistance Act of 2002 recognizes that trade liberalization and increased international trade can create job loss for many workers. The Act therefore provides cash assistance, education and training benefits, health care subsidies, and wage subsidies (for persons aged 50 or older) to qualified workers displaced by imports or relocations of plants from the United States to abroad.

13. Offshoring is the practice of shifting work previously done by Americans in the United States to workers located in other nations. Although offshoring reduces some U.S. jobs, it lowers production costs, expands sales, and therefore may create other U.S. jobs. Less than 4 percent of all job losses in the United States each year are caused by imports, offshoring, and plant relocation abroad.

Terms and Concepts

labor-intensive goods

land-intensive goods

capital-intensive goods

opportunity-cost ratio

comparative advantage

principle of comparative advantage

terms of trade

trading possibilities line

gains from trade

world price

domestic price

export supply curve

import demand curve

equilibrium world price

tariffs

revenue tariff

protective tariff

import quota

nontariff barrier (NTB)

voluntary export restriction (VER)

export subsidy

dumping

Smoot-Hawley Tariff Act

General Agreement on Tariffs and Trade (GATT)

World Trade Organization (WTO)

Doha Development Agenda

European Union (EU)

Euro Zone

North American Free Trade Agreement (NAFTA)

Trade Adjustment Assistance Act

offshoring

Questions

1. Quantitatively, how important is international trade to the United States relative to the importance of trade to other nations? What country is the United States' most important trading partner, quantitatively? With what country does the United States have the largest trade deficit? LO1

2. Distinguish among land-, labor-, and capital-intensive goods, citing an example of each without resorting to book examples. How do these distinctions relate to international trade? How do distinctive products, unrelated to resource intensity, relate to international trade? LO1, LO2

3. Explain: "The United States can make certain toys with greater productive efficiency than can China. Yet we import those toys from China." Relate your answer to the ideas of Adam Smith and David Ricardo. LO2

4. Suppose Big Country can produce 80 units of X by using all its resources to produce X or 60 units of Y by devoting all its resources to Y. Comparable figures for Small Nation are 60 units of X and 60 units of Y. Assuming constant costs, in which product should each nation specialize? Explain why. What are the limits of the terms of trade between these two countries? How would rising costs (rather than constant costs) affect the extent of specialization and trade between these two countries? LO2

5. What is an export demand curve? What is an import supply curve? How do such curves relate to the determination of the equilibrium world price of a tradable good? LO3

6. Why is a quota more detrimental to an economy than a tariff that results in the same level of imports as the quota? What is the net outcome of either tariffs or quotas for the world economy? LO4

7. Draw a domestic supply-and-demand diagram for a product in which the United States does not have a comparative advantage. What impact do foreign imports have on domestic price and quantity? On your diagram show a protective tariff that eliminates approximately one-half of the assumed imports. What are the price-quantity effects of this tariff on (a) domestic consumers, (b) domestic producers, and (c) foreign exporters? How would the effects of a quota that creates the same amount of imports differ? LO4

8. "The potentially valid arguments for tariff protection—military self-sufficiency, infant industry protection, and diversification for stability—are also the most easily abused." Why are these arguments susceptible to abuse? LO4

9. Evaluate the effectiveness of artificial trade barriers, such as tariffs and import quotas, as a way to achieve and maintain full employment throughout the U.S. economy. How might such policies reduce unemployment in one U.S. industry but increase it in another U.S. industry? LO4

10. In 2007, manufacturing workers in the United States earned average compensation of $30.56 per hour. That same year, manufacturing workers in Mexico earned average compensation of $3.91 per hour. How can U.S. manufacturers possibly compete? Why isn't all manufacturing done in Mexico and other low-wage countries? LO4

11. How might protective tariffs reduce both the imports and the exports of the nation that levies tariffs? In what way do foreign firms that "dump" their products onto the U.S. market in effect provide bargains to American consumers? How might the import competition lead to quality improvements and cost reductions by American firms? LO4

12. Identify and state the significance of each of the following trade-related entities: (a) the WTO; (b) the EU; (c) the Euro Zone; and (d) NAFTA. LO5

13. What form does trade adjustment assistance take in the United States? How does such assistance promote political support for free-trade agreements? Do you think workers who lose their jobs because of changes in trade laws deserve special treatment relative to workers who lose their jobs because of other changes in the economy, say, changes in patterns of government spending? LO6

14. What is offshoring of white-collar service jobs and how does that practice relate to international trade? Why has offshoring increased over the past few decades? Give an example (other than that in the textbook) of how offshoring can eliminate some American jobs while creating other American jobs. LO6

15. **LAST WORD** What was the central point that Bastiat was trying to make in his imaginary petition of the candlemakers?

Problems

1. Assume that the comparative-cost ratios of two products—baby formula and tuna fish—are as follows in the nations of Canswicki and Tunata:

   Canswicki: 1 can baby formula ≡ 2 cans tuna fish
   Tunata: 1 can baby formula ≡ 4 cans tuna fish

   In what product should each nation specialize? Which of the following terms of trade would be acceptable to both nations: (a) 1 can baby formula ≡ $2\frac{1}{2}$ cans tuna fish; (b) 1 can baby formula ≡ 1 can tuna fish; (c) 1 can baby formula ≡ 5 cans tuna fish? LO2

2. The accompanying hypothetical production possibilities tables are for New Zealand and Spain. Each country can produce apples and plums. Plot the production possibilities data for each of the two countries separately. Referring to your graphs, answer the following: LO2

New Zealand's Production Possibilities Table (Millions of Bushels)

Product	Production Alternatives			
	A	B	C	D
Apples	0	20	40	60
Plums	15	10	5	0

Spain's Production Possibilities Table (Millions of Bushels)

Product	Production Alternatives			
	R	S	T	U
Apples	0	20	40	60
Plums	60	40	20	0

a. What is each country's cost ratio of producing plums and apples?

b. Which nation should specialize in which product?

c. Show the trading possibilities lines for each nation if the actual terms of trade are 1 plum for 2 apples. (Plot these lines on your graph.)

d. Suppose the optimum product mixes before specialization and trade were alternative B in New Zealand and alternative S in Spain. What would be the gains from specialization and trade?

3. The following hypothetical production possibilities tables are for China and the United States. Assume that before specialization and trade the optimal product mix for China is alternative B and for the United States is alternative U. LO2

a. Are comparative-cost conditions such that the two areas should specialize? If so, what product should each produce?

b. What is the total gain in apparel and chemical output that would result from such specialization?

c. What are the limits of the terms of trade? Suppose that the actual terms of trade are 1 unit of apparel for $1\frac{1}{2}$ units of chemicals and that 4 units of apparel are exchanged for 6 units of chemicals. What are the gains from specialization and trade for each nation?

Product	China Production Possibilities					
	A	B	C	D	E	F
Apparel (in thousands)	30	24	18	12	6	0
Chemicals (in tons)	0	6	12	18	24	30

Product	U.S. Production Possibilities					
	R	S	T	U	V	W
Apparel (in thousands)	10	8	6	4	2	0
Chemicals (in tons)	0	4	8	12	16	20

4. Refer to Figure 3.6, page 57. Assume that the graph depicts the U.S. domestic market for corn. How many bushels of corn, if any, will the United States export or import at a world price of $1, $2, $3, $4, and $5? Use this information to construct the U.S. export supply curve and import demand curve for corn. Suppose that the only other corn-producing nation is France, where the domestic price is $4. Which country will export corn; which county will import it? LO3

FURTHER TEST YOUR KNOWLEDGE AT
www.mcconnell19e.com

CHAPTER 37

International Trade

After a brief review of the facts of international trade, the text uses the concept of production possibilities that you learned in Chapter 1 to explain why nations trade. Nations specialize in and export those goods and services in the production of which they have a **comparative advantage,** which means the domestic opportunity cost of producing a particular good or service is lower in one nation than in another nation. When nations specialize in those products in which they have a comparative advantage, the world can obtain more goods and services from its resources and each nation enjoys a higher standard of living than it would without trade.

Another question the chapter answers is what determines the equilibrium prices and quantities of the imports and exports resulting from trade. The text uses the **supply and demand analysis,** originally presented in Chapter 3, to explain equilibrium in the world market for a product. A simplified two-nation and one-product model of trade is constructed with export supply curves and import demand curves for each nation. Equilibrium occurs where one nation's export supply curve intersects another nation's import demand curve.

Regardless of the advantages of specialization and trade among nations, people in the United States and throughout the world for well over 200 years have debated the question of whether **free trade or protection** was the better policy for their nation. Economists took part in this debate and, with few exceptions, made a strong case for free trade. They also argued that protectionism in the form of tariffs, import quotas, and other trade barriers prevents or reduces specialization and decreases both a nation's and the world's production and standards of living. Despite these arguments, nations have erected and continue to erect trade barriers using an assortment of protection arguments that have questionable validity.

The latter sections of the chapter address questions related to how to make trade among nations work better and resolve trade disputes. **Multilateral agreements** have been made among nations and **free-trade zones** have been established to reduce trade barriers and increase worldwide trade. The World Trade Organization (WTO) is responsible for multilateral trade negotiations among member nations. The European Union (EU) is a free-trade zone among 27 European nations. The North American Free Trade Agreement (NAFTA) established a free-trade zone for the United States, Canada, and Mexico. The U.S. Congress developed policies to assist U.S. workers hurt by the expansion of trade.

Whether the direction of the trade policy in the United States will be toward freer trade or more protectionism is a question that gets debated as each new trade issue is presented to the U.S. public. The decision on each issue may well depend on your economic understanding of trade and the problems with trade protection.

■ CHECKLIST

When you have studied this chapter you should be able to

☐ Cite some key facts about international trade.

☐ State the three economic circumstances that make it desirable for nations to specialize and trade.

☐ Give examples of labor-intensive, capital-intensive, and land-intensive goods.

☐ Explain the difference between absolute advantage and comparative advantage.

☐ State the three assumptions made about the production possibilities graphs for two products in a two-nation example of trade.

☐ Compute the opportunity-cost ratio of producing the two products in the two-nation example.

☐ Determine which nation has a comparative advantage in the two-nation example.

☐ Calculate the range in which the terms of trade will occur in the two-nation example.

☐ Explain how nations gain from trade and specialization based on the two-nation example.

☐ Discuss how increasing costs affect specialization in the two-nation example.

☐ Restate the general case for free trade.

☐ Construct domestic supply and demand curves for two nations that trade a product.

☐ Construct export supply and import demand curves for two nations that trade a product.

☐ Explain how the equilibrium world prices and quantities of exports and imports are determined for two nations that trade a product.

☐ Define and explain the purpose of tariffs, import quotas, nontariff barriers, voluntary export restraints, and export subsidies.

☐ Explain the economic effects of a protective tariff for a product on consumption, production, imports, revenue, and efficiency.

☐ Analyze the economic effects of an import quota and compare them with a tariff.

☐ Discuss the problems with six major arguments for trade protectionism (self-sufficiency, diversification, infant industry, dumping, employment, and cheap labor).

☐ Describe the purpose and outcomes from the General Agreement on Tariffs and Trade (GATT).

☐ Discuss the purpose and controversies surrounding the World Trade Organization (WTO).

☐ Explain how the European Union (EU) operates as a free-trade zone.

☐ Describe the North American Free Trade Agreement (NAFTA).

☐ Discuss the reasons for the Trade Adjustment Assistance Act of 2002.

☐ Evaluate reasons for and outcomes from offshoring.

☐ Explain how Frédéric Bastiat satirized the proponents of protectionism (*Last Word*).

■ **CHAPTER OUTLINE**

1. Some key facts on international trade are worth noting.

   a. About 13 percent of the total output (GDP) of the United States is accounted for by exports of goods and services. The United States provides about 8.5 percent of the world's exports. The United States also leads the world in the combined volume of exports and imports.

   b. The United States has a trade deficit in goods and a trade surplus in services, and overall has a trade deficit in goods and services. The United States has a sizable trade deficit in goods and services with China. Canada is the most important trading partner for the United States in terms of the volume of trade.

   c. The major exports of the United States are chemicals, agricultural products, consumer durables, semiconductors, and aircraft. The major imports are petroleum, automobiles, metals, household appliances, and computers. Most of the U.S. trade occurs with other industrially advanced nations and members of OPEC. Canada is the largest trading partner for the United States.

   d. The major participants in international trade are the United States, Japan, China, and the nations of Western Europe. Other key participants include the Asian economies of South Korea, Taiwan, and Singapore.

   e. International trade links nations and is the focus of economic policy and debate in the United States and other nations.

2. The **economic basis for trade** comprises several circumstances. Specialization and trade among nations is advantageous because the world's resources are not evenly distributed and efficient production of different products requires different technologies and combinations of resources. Also, products differ in quality and other attributes, so people might prefer imported to domestic goods in some cases. Some nations have a cost advantage in making **labor-intensive goods** such as textiles or toys. Other nations have a cost advantage in producing **land-intensive goods** such as beef or vegetables. Industrially advanced economies have a cost advantage in making **capital-intensive goods** such as airplanes or chemicals.

3. Specialization and international trade increase the productivity of a nation's resources and allow a nation to obtain greater output than would be the case without trade. A nation has an absolute advantage in the production of a product over another nation if it can produce more of the product with the same amount of resources as the other nation. To specialize and benefit from trade,

however, a nation only needs to have a comparative advantage, which means that it produces a product at a lower opportunity cost than another nation.

   a. The concept of comparative advantage is presented with an example using two nations (the United States and Mexico) and two products (beef and vegetables). The production possibilities curves are different straight lines because of the assumption of constant opportunity costs, but the curve for each nation is different because of different costs. The United States has an absolute advantage in the production of both beef and vegetables, which means that if all resources were devoted to one product or the other, the United States would produce more of both products (beef: United States 30 tons and Mexico 10 tons; vegetables: United States 30 tons and Mexico 20 tons).

   (1) The **opportunity-cost ratio** is what one nation has to forgo in the output of one domestic product to produce another domestic product. Using tons as units for beef (B) and vegetables (V), the opportunity-cost ratio for the United States is $1V = 1B$.

   (2) The opportunity-cost ratio for Mexico is $2V = 1B$.

   (3) If each nation is self-sufficient, they will pick some combination of the two products to produce. Assume this output mix for the United State is $18B$ and $12V$ and for Mexico it is $8B$ and $4V$.

   b. **Comparative advantage** explains the gains from trade and is directly related to opportunity cost. In essence, a nation has a comparative advantage in the production of a product when it can produce the product at a lower domestic opportunity cost than can a trading partner. A nation will specialize in the production of a product for which it is the low opportunity cost producer and trade for the other products it wants. Although the United States has an absolute advantage in producing both products, it does not have a comparative advantage because of the differences in the domestic opportunity cost of producing the products in both nations. The **principle of comparative advantage** says that total output will be greatest when each nation specializes in the production of a product for which it has the lowest domestic opportunity cost.

   (1) Returning to the two-nation example, for the United States, $1V = 1B$, but for Mexico, $2V = 1B$. The United States has a lower domestic opportunity cost for beef because for the United States to get $1B$ it gives up only $1V$ whereas for Mexico to get $1B$ it gives up $2V$.

   (2) Note that for Mexico, after dividing each side of $2V = 1B$ by 2 it becomes $1V = 0.5B$, Mexico has a lower domestic opportunity cost for vegetables because for Mexico to get $1V$, it gives up only $0.5B$ whereas for the United States to get $1V$ it gives up $1B$.

   c. The **terms of trade** or ratio at which one product is traded for another is between the opportunity-cost ratios of the two nations, or between $1V = 1B$ (U.S. costs) and $1V = 2B$ (Mexico's costs).

   d. Supposing that the terms of trade are $1V = 1.5B$, it is then possible to show a **trading possibilities line** that shifts outward from the original production possibilities line for each nation.

   (1) Each nation will be able to achieve a set of beef and vegetable alternatives by specializing in the production of the product for which it has a low opportunity cost

and trading its output of that product for the product for which has a high opportunity cost.

(2) Each nation gains from this trade because specialization permits a greater total output from the same resources and a better allocation of the world's resources. Given the terms of trade (1V = 1.5B), if the United States uses all its resources to produce beef (30B) and exports 10B to Mexico and in return gets 15V, it is better off with trade (20B and 15V) than without trade (18B and 12V). If Mexico uses all its resources to produce vegetables (20V) and exports 15V to the United States and in return gets 10B, it is better off with trade (10B and 5V) than without trade (8B and 4V).

e. If opportunity cost ratios in the two nations are not constant and there are increasing opportunity costs associated with more production of a product, then specialization may not be complete.

f. The basic argument for free trade among nations is that it leads to a better allocation of resources and a higher standard of living in the world because total output will increase from specialization and trade. Several side benefits from trade are that it increases competition and deters monopoly, and offers consumers a wider array of choices. It also links the interests of nations and can reduce the threat of hostilities or war.

4. *Supply and demand analysis of exports and imports* can be used to explain how the equilibrium price and quantity for a product (e.g., aluminum) are determined when there is trade between two nations (e.g., the United States and Canada).

a. For the United States, there will be *domestic* supply and demand as well as *export* supply and import demand for aluminum.

(1) The price and quantity of aluminum are determined by the intersection of the domestic demand and supply curves in a world without trade.

(2) In a world with trade, the export supply curve for the United States shows the amount of aluminum that U.S. producers will export at each world price above the domestic equilibrium price. U.S. exports will increase when the world price rises relative to the domestic price.

(3) The import demand curve for the United States shows the amount of aluminum that U.S. citizens will import at each world price below the domestic equilibrium price. U.S. imports will increase when world prices fall relative to the domestic price.

b. For Canada, there will be domestic supply and demand as well as export supply and import demand for aluminum. The description of these supply and demand curves is similar to the account of those of the United States previously described in point **a.**

c. The equilibrium world price and equilibrium world levels of exports and imports can be determined with further supply and demand analysis. The export supply curves of the two nations can be plotted on one graph. The import demand curves of both nations can be plotted on the same graph. In this two-nation model, equilibrium will be achieved when one nation's import demand curve intersects another nation's export supply curve.

5. Nations limit international trade by erecting *trade barriers,* which are of several types. *Tariffs* are excise taxes or "duties" on value or quantity of imported goods. They can be revenue tariffs, which typically are placed on products that are not domestically produced and whose basic purpose is to raise money for government. There also can be *protective tariffs,* which are designed to shield domestic producers from foreign competition by raising the price of imports. *Import quotas* are restrictions on the quantity or total value of a product that can be imported from another nation. *Nontariff barriers* are burdensome rules, regulations, licensing procedures, standards, or other practices that make it difficult and costly to import a product. A *voluntary export restraint (VER)* is an agreement among exporters to voluntarily limit the amount of a product exported to another nation; it has the same effect as an import quota. Governments also interfere with trade by giving a domestic producer an *export subsidy,* which is a government payment to a producer that helps the producer sell the product in an export market for a lower price than otherwise would be the case.

a. The imposition of a *tariff* on a product has both direct and indirect economic effects.

(1) The direct effects are an increase in the domestic price of the good, less domestic consumption, more domestic production, less foreign production, and a transfer of income from domestic consumers to the government.

(2) The indirect effects are a reduction in the incomes of foreign producers and thus the incomes of foreign nations to purchase products from the nation imposing the tariff, a shift of resources from efficient industries to inefficient industries, and thus less trade and worldwide output.

b. The imposition of a *quota* on an imported product has the same direct and indirect effects as that of a tariff on that product, with the exception that a tariff generates revenue for government use whereas an import quota transfers that revenue to foreign producers.

c. Special-interest groups benefit from protection and persuade their nations to erect trade barriers, but the costs of tariffs and quotas to consumers and nations exceed any benefits.

6. The arguments for *protectionism* are many, but each one can be challenged for its validity.

a. The military self-sufficiency argument can be challenged because it is difficult to determine which industry is "vital" to national defense and therefore must be protected; it would be more efficient economically to provide a direct subsidy to military producers rather than impose a tariff.

b. Using tariff barriers to permit diversification for stability in the economy is not necessary for advanced economies such as the United States, and there may be great economic costs to diversification in developing nations.

c. It is alleged that infant industries need protection until they are sufficiently large to compete, but the argument may not apply in developed economies: It is difficult to select which industries will prosper; protectionism tends to persist long after it is needed; and direct subsidies may be more economically efficient.

d. Sometimes protection is sought against *dumping,* which is the sale of foreign goods on U.S. markets at prices either below the cost of production or below the prices commonly charged in the home nation. Dumping is a legitimate concern and is restricted under U.S. trade law, but to use dumping as an excuse for widespread tariff protection is unjustified, and the number of documented cases is few. If foreign companies are more efficient (low cost) producers, what may appear to be dumping may actually be comparative advantage at work and domestic consumers can benefit from lower prices.

e. Trade barriers do not necessarily increase domestic employment because imports may eliminate some jobs, but create others, so imports may change only the composition of employment, not the overall level of employment. Also, the exports of one nation become the imports of another, so tariff barriers can be viewed as "beggar thy neighbor" policies. In addition, other nations are likely to retaliate against the imposition of trade barriers that will reduce domestic output and employment. The **Smoot-Hawley Tariff Act** is an example of legislation passed during the Great Depression that caused a trade war with other nations, thus hurting rather than helping the United States. In the long run, barriers create a less efficient allocation of resources by shielding protected domestic industries from the rigors of competition.

f. Protection is sometimes sought because of the cheap foreign labor argument that low-cost labor in other nations will undercut the wages of workers in the United States, but there are several counterpoints. First, there are mutual gains from trade between rich and poor nations and they lower the cost of production for products. Second, it should be realized that nations gain from trade based on comparative advantage, and by specializing at what each nation does best, the productivity of workers and thus their wages and living standards rise. Third, there is an incorrect focus on labor costs per hour rather than labor cost per unit of production. Labor costs or wages per hour can be higher in one nation than in another because of the higher productivity of workers (and it results in lower labor cost per unit of production).

7. International trade policies have changed over the years with the development of *multilateral agreements* and *free-trade zones.* They are used to counter the destructive aspects of trade wars that arise when nations impose high tariffs.

    a. The **General Agreement on Tariffs and Trade (GATT)** that began in 1947 provided equal treatment of all member nations and sought to reduce tariffs and eliminate import quotas by multilateral negotiations. The Uruguay Round of GATT agreements that took effect in 1995 eliminated or reduced tariffs on many products, cut restrictive government rules applying to services, phased out quotas on textiles and apparel, and decreased subsidies for agriculture.

    b. The **World Trade Organization (WTO)** is an international agency that is the successor to GATT. In 2010, 153 nations were members of the WTO. It is responsible for overseeing trade agreements among nations and rules on trade disputes. The WTO also provides a forum for more trade liberalization negotiations under the **Doha Development Agenda** that was begun in Doha, Qatar, in 2001. These negotiations focus on

additional reductions in tariffs and quotas and cutbacks in domestic subsidies for agricultural products.

    c. The **European Union (EU)** is an example of a regional free-trade zone or trade bloc among 27 European nations. The EU abolished tariffs among member nations and developed common policies on various economic issues, such as the tariffs on goods to and from non-member nations. In 2010, 16 EU nations shared a common currency—the **euro.** The chief advantages of such a currency is that it reduces transactions costs for exchanging goods and services in Euro Zone nations and allows consumers and businesses to comparison shop.

    d. In 1993, the **North American Free Trade Agreement (NAFTA)** created a free-trade zone or trade bloc covering the United States, Mexico, and Canada. Critics of this agreement feared job losses and the potential for abuse by other nations using Mexico as a base for production, but the dire outcomes have not occurred. There has been increased trade among Canada, Mexico, and the United States because of the agreement.

8. Although increased trade and trade liberalization raise total output and income, they also create controversies and calls for assistance. The **Trade Adjustment Assistance Act** of 2002 provides support to qualified workers displaced by imports or plant relocations from international trade. It gives cash assistance, education and training benefits, subsides for health care, and wage subsidies (for those aged 50 or older). Critics contend that such dislocations are part of a market economy and workers in the international sector should not get special subsidies for their job losses.

9. The **offshoring** of jobs occurs when jobs done by U.S. workers are shifted to foreign workers and locations. While offshoring has long been used in manufacturing, improvements in communication and technology make it possible to do it in services. Although offshoring causes some domestic workers to lose their jobs, it can be beneficial for an economy. It allows an economy to specialize and use its labor resources in high-valued work for which it has a comparative advantage and obtain services for low-valued work that can be done more efficiently by foreign workers. It can increase the demand for complementary jobs in high-valued industries. It allows domestic businesses to reduce production costs, and thus be more competitive in both domestic and international markets.

10. (*Last Word*). Frédéric Bastiat (1801–1850) was a French economist who wrote a satirical letter to counter the proponents of protectionism. His "petition" to the French government called for blocking out the sun because it provided too much competition for domestic candlestick makers, thus illustrating the logical absurdity of protectionist arguments.

■ **HINTS AND TIPS**

1. In the discussion of **comparative advantage,** the assumption of a constant opportunity-cost ratio means the production possibilities "curves" for each nation can be drawn as straight lines. The slope of the line in each nation is the opportunity cost of one product (beef) in terms of the other product (vegetables). The reciprocal of the slope of each line is the opportunity cost of the other product (vegetables) in terms of the first product (beef).

2. The **export supply and import demand curves** in Figures 37.3 and 37.4 in the text look different from the typical supply and demand curves that you have seen so far, so you should understand how they are constructed. The export supply and import demand curves for a nation do not intersect. Each curve meets at the price point on the Y axis showing the equilibrium price for domestic supply and demand. At this point there are no exports or imports.

    a. The export supply curve is up-sloping from that point because as world prices rise above the domestic equilibrium price, there will be increasing domestic surpluses produced by a nation that can be exported. The export supply curve reflects the positive relationship between rising world prices (above the domestic equilibrium price) and the increasing quantity of exports.

    b. The import demand curve is down-sloping from the domestic equilibrium price because as world prices fall below the domestic equilibrium price, there will be increasing domestic shortages that need to be covered by increasing imports. The import demand curve reflects the inverse relationship between falling world prices (below the domestic price) and the increasing quantity of imports.

3. One of the most interesting sections of the chapter discusses the arguments for and against trade protection. You have probably heard people give one or more of the arguments for trade protection, but now you have a chance to use your economic reasoning to expose the weaknesses in these arguments. Most are half-truths and special pleadings.

■ IMPORTANT TERMS

labor-intensive goods
land-intensive goods
capital-intensive goods
opportunity-cost ratio
comparative advantage
principle of comparative
  advantage
terms of trade
trading possibilities line
gains from trade
world price
domestic price
export supply curve
import demand curve
equilibrium world price
tariffs
revenue tariff
protective tariff

import quota
nontariff barrier (NTB)
voluntary export
  restriction (VER)
export subsidy
dumping
Smoot-Hawley Tariff Act
General Agreement on
  Tariffs and Trade (GATT)
World Trade Organization
  (WTO)
Doha Development Agenda
European Union (EU)
Euro Zone
North American Free Trade
  Agreement (NAFTA)
Trade Adjustment
  Assistance Act
offshoring

SELF-TEST

■ FILL-IN QUESTIONS

1. In the United States, exports of goods and services make up about (13, 26) _____ percent of total U.S. output. The volume of exports and imports in dollar terms makes the United States the world's (largest, smallest) _____ trading nation.

2. A trade deficit occurs when exports are (greater than, less than) _____ imports and a trade surplus occurs when exports are _____ imports. The United States has a trade deficit in (goods, services) _____ and a trade surplus in _____.

3. Nations tend to trade among themselves because the distribution of economic resources among them is (even, uneven) _____, the efficient production of various goods and services necessitates (the same, different) _____ technologies or combinations of resources, and people prefer (more, less) _____ choices in products.

4. The principle of comparative advantage means total world output will be greatest when each good is produced by that nation having the (highest, lowest) _____ opportunity cost. The nations of the world tend to specialize in the production of those goods in which they (have, do not have) _____ a comparative advantage and then export them, and they import those goods in which they _____ a comparative advantage in production.

5. If the cost ratio in country X is 4 Panama hats equal 1 pound of bananas, while in country Y 3 Panama hats equal 1 pound of bananas, then

    a. in country X hats are relatively (expensive, inexpensive) _____ and bananas relatively _____,

    b. in country Y hats are relatively (expensive, inexpensive) _____ and bananas relatively _____,

    c. X has a comparative advantage and should specialize in the production of (bananas, hats) _____, and Y has a comparative advantage and should specialize in the production of _____.

    d. When X and Y specialize and trade, the terms of trade will be somewhere between (1, 2, 3, 4) _____ and _____ hats for each pound of bananas and will depend on world demand and supply for hats and bananas.

e. When the actual terms of trade turn out to be 3 1/2 hats for 1 pound of bananas, the cost of obtaining
(1) 1 Panama hat has been decreased from (2/7, 1/3)

_____ to _____ pounds of bananas in Y.
(2) 1 pound of bananas has been decreased from

(3 1/2, 4) _____ to _____ Panama hats in X.

f. International specialization will not be complete if the opportunity cost of producing either good

(rises, falls) _____ as a nation produces more of it.

6. The basic argument for free trade based on the principle of (bilateral negotiations, comparative advantage) _____ is that it results in a (more, less)

_____ efficient allocation of resources and a

(lower, higher) _____ standard of living.

7. The world equilibrium price is determined by the interaction of (domestic, world) _____ supply and demand, while the domestic equilibrium price is

determined by _____ supply and demand. When the world price of a good falls relative to the domestic price in a nation, the nation will (increase, decrease) _____ its imports, and when the world price rises relative to the domestic price, the nation will

_____ its exports.

8. In a two-nation model for a product, the equilibrium price and quantity of imports and exports occur where one nation's import demand curve intersects another nation's export (supply, demand) _____ curve. In a highly competitive world market, there can be (multiple,

only one) _____ price(s) for a standardized product.

9. Excise taxes on imported products are (quotas, tariffs)

_____, whereas limits on the maximum amount

of a product that can be imported are import _____.
Tariffs applied to a product not produced domestically

are (protective, revenue) _____ tariffs, but tariffs designed to shield domestic producers from foreign

competition are _____ tariffs.

10. There are other types of trade barriers. Imports that are restricted through the use of a licensing requirement or

bureaucratic red tape are (tariff, nontariff) _____
barriers. When foreign firms voluntarily limit their exports to another country, it would represent a voluntary (import,

export) _____ restraint.

11. Nations erect barriers to international trade to benefit the economic positions of (consumers, domestic producers)

_____ even though these barriers (increase,

decrease) _____ economic efficiency and trade among nations and the benefits to that nation are (greater,

less) _____ than the costs to it.

12. When the United States imposes a tariff on a good that is imported from abroad, the price of that good in the

United States will (increase, decrease) _____ and the total purchases of the good in the United States

will _____. The output of U.S. producers of the

good will (increase, decrease) _____ and the

output of foreign producers will _____.

13. When comparing the effects of a tariff with the effects of a quota to restrict the U.S. imports of a product, the basic difference is that with a (tariff, quota)

_____ the U.S. government will receive revenue, but with a _____ foreign producers will receive the revenue.

14. There are counterarguments to the six arguments for trade protectionism.
  a. The military self-sufficiency argument can be challenged because it is difficult to determine which in-

dustry is (essential, unessential) _____ for national defense and must be protected. A direct sub-

sidy to producers would be (more, less) _____ efficient than a tariff.
  b. Using trade barriers to permit diversification for stability in an economy is not necessary for (advanced,

developing) _____ economies such as in the United States, and there may be great economic costs

to forcing diversification in _____ nations.
  c. The problem with the infant industry argument is that it is difficult to determine when (a mature, an infant)

_____ industry becomes _____ industry.
  d. The protection-against-dumping argument does not hold because the lower prices from alleged dumping may be a case of (absolute, comparative)

_____ advantage at work and documented cases of dumping are relatively (common, rare)

_____.
  e. Trade barriers do not necessarily increase domestic employment because imports may change only the

(level, composition) _____ of employment,

such barriers (increase, decrease) _____ the incomes of trading partners thus hurting an exporting nation and other nations can (dump, retaliate)

_____ by imposing their own trade barriers.
  f. Proponents of the cheap foreign labor argument tend to focus exclusively on large international differences that

exist in labor costs (per unit, per hour) _____ and fail to mention that these differences are mostly the result of large national differences in productivity that serve to equalize labor costs _____.

15. The three principles established in the General Agreement on Tariffs and Trade (GATT) of 1947 were

a. _____

b. _____

c. _____

16. The World Trade Organization (WTO) is the successor to GATT and it is responsible for overseeing multilateral trade (barriers, agreements) _____ and rules on trade (licenses, disputes) _____. The current round of multilateral trade negotiations is the (Abba, Doha) _____ Development Agenda that focuses on (increasing, decreasing) _____ tariffs, import quotas, and agricultural subsidies.

17. An example of a regional free-trade zone is the (Western, European) _____ Union. It abolished (imports and exports, tariffs and quotas) _____ among the participating members and established (common, different) _____ tariffs on goods imported from outside this free-trade zone. The common currency of many of the member nations of the regional free-trade zone is the (peso, euro) _____.

18. The North American Free Trade Agreement (NAFTA) formed a free-trade (barrier, zone) _____ among the United States, Canada, and Mexico. This agreement will eliminate (terms of trade, tariffs) _____ among the nations. Critics in the United States said that it would (increase, decrease) _____ jobs, but the evidence shows a(n) _____ in jobs and total output since its passage.

19. The Trade Adjustment Assistance Act of 2002 is designed to help some of the (workers, businesses) _____ hurt by shifts in international trade patterns. Critics contend that such job losses are a (small, large) _____ fraction of the total each year and that such a program is another type of special (tariff, subsidy) _____ that benefits one type of worker over another.

20. The shifting of work previously done by U.S. workers to workers located in other nations is (dumping, offshoring) _____. It reflects a (growth, decline) _____ in the specialization and international trade of services. It may (decrease, increase) _____ some jobs moved to other nations, but also _____ jobs and productivity in the United States.

■ TRUE–FALSE QUESTIONS

Circle T if the statement is true, F if it is false.

1. The combined volume of exports and imports in the United States as measured in dollars is greater than in any other nation.　**T F**

2. A factor that serves as the economic basis for world trade is the even distribution of resources among nations.　**T F**

3. People trade because they seek products of different quality and other nonprice attributes.　**T F**

4. Examples of capital-intensive goods would be automobiles, machinery, and chemicals.　**T F**

5. The relative efficiency with which a nation can produce specific goods is fixed over time.　**T F**

6. Mutually advantageous specialization and trade are possible between any two nations if they have the same domestic opportunity-cost ratios for any two products.　**T F**

7. The principle of comparative advantage is that total output will be greatest when each good is produced by that nation which has the higher domestic opportunity cost.　**T F**

8. By specializing based on comparative advantage, nations can obtain larger outputs with fixed amounts of resources.　**T F**

9. The terms of trade determine how the increase in world output resulting from comparative advantage is shared by trading nations.　**T F**

10. Increasing opportunity costs tend to prevent specialization among trading nations from being complete.　**T F**

11. Trade among nations tends to bring about a more efficient use of the world's resources and a higher level of material well-being.　**T F**

12. Free trade among nations tends to increase monopoly and lessen competition in these nations.　**T F**

13. A nation will export a particular product if the world price is less than the domestic price.　**T F**

14. In a two-country model, equilibrium in world prices and quantities of exports and imports will occur where one nation's export supply curve intersects the other nation's import demand curve.　**T F**

15. A tariff on coffee in the United States is an example of a protective tariff.　**T F**

16. The imposition of a tariff on a good imported from abroad will reduce the amount of the imported good that is bought.　**T F**

17. A cost of tariffs and quotas imposed by the United States is higher prices that U.S. consumers must pay for the protected product.　**T F**

18. The major difference between a tariff and a quota on an imported product is that a quota produces revenue for the government.　**T F**

19. To advocate tariffs that would protect domestic producers of goods and materials essential to national defense is to substitute a political-military objective for the economic objectives of efficiently allocating resources.   **T   F**

20. One-crop economies may be able to make themselves more stable and diversified by imposing tariffs on goods imported from abroad, but these tariffs are also apt to lower the standard of living in these economies. **T   F**

21. Protection against the "dumping" of foreign goods at low prices on the U.S. market is one good justification for widespread, permanent tariffs.   **T   F**

22. Tariffs and import quotas meant to increase domestic full employment achieve short-run domestic goals by making trading partners poorer.   **T   F**

23. The cheap foreign labor argument for protection fails because it focuses on labor costs per hour rather than what really matters, which is labor cost per unit of output. **T   F**

24. Most arguments for protection are special interest appeals that, if followed, would provide gains for consumers at the expense of protected industries and their workers.   **T   F**

25. The General Agreement on Tariffs and Trade sought to reduce tariffs through multilateral negotiations. **T   F**

26. The World Trade Organization (WTO) is the world's major advocate for trade protectionism.   **T   F**

27. The members of the European Union (EU) have experienced freer trade since it was formed.   **T   F**

28. The 1993 North American Free Trade Agreement (NAFTA) includes all Central American nations.   **T   F**

29. The Trade Adjustment Assistance Act of 2002 provided compensation to U.S. workers who were displaced by shifts in international trade patterns.   **T   F**

30. Although offshoring decreases some U.S. jobs, it also lowers production costs, expands sales, and may create other U.S. jobs.   **T   F**

■ **MULTIPLE-CHOICE QUESTIONS**

Circle the letter that corresponds to the best answer.

1. Which nation leads the world in the combined volume of exports and imports?
 (a) Japan
 (b) Germany
 (c) United States
 (d) United Kingdom

2. Which nation is the most important trading partner for the United States in terms of the percentage of imports and exports?
 (a) India
 (b) Russia
 (c) Canada
 (d) Germany

3. Nations engage in trade because
 (a) world resources are evenly distributed among nations

 (b) world resources are unevenly distributed among nations
 (c) all products are produced from the same technology
 (d) all products are produced from the same combinations of resources

Use the following tables to answer Questions 4, 5, 6, and 7.

NEPAL PRODUCTION POSSIBILITIES TABLE

| | Production alternatives | | | | | |
Product	A	B	C	D	E	F
Yak fat	0	4	8	12	16	20
Camel hides	40	32	24	16	8	0

KASHMIR PRODUCTION POSSIBILITIES TABLE

| | Production alternatives | | | | | |
Product	A	B	C	D	E	F
Yak fat	0	3	6	9	12	15
Camel hides	60	48	36	24	12	0

4. The data in the tables show that production in
 (a) both Nepal and Kashmir is subject to increasing opportunity costs
 (b) both Nepal and Kashmir is subject to constant opportunity costs
 (c) Nepal is subject to increasing opportunity costs and Kashmir to constant opportunity costs
 (d) Kashmir is subject to increasing opportunity costs and Nepal to constant opportunity costs

5. If Nepal and Kashmir engage in trade, the terms of trade will be
 (a) between 2 and 4 camel hides for 1 unit of yak fat
 (b) between 1/3 and 1/2 units of yak fat for 1 camel hide
 (c) between 3 and 4 units of yak fat for 1 camel hide
 (d) between 2 and 4 units of yak fat for 1 camel hide

6. Assume that prior to specialization and trade Nepal and Kashmir both choose production possibility C. Now if each specializes according to its comparative advantage, the resulting gains from specialization and trade will be
 (a) 6 units of yak fat
 (b) 8 units of yak fat
 (c) 6 units of yak fat and 8 camel hides
 (d) 8 units of yak fat and 6 camel hides

7. Each nation produced only one product in accordance with its comparative advantage, and the terms of trade were set at 3 camel hides for 1 unit of yak fat. In this case, Nepal could obtain a maximum combination of 8 units of yak fat and
 (a) 12 camel hides
 (b) 24 camel hides
 (c) 36 camel hides
 (d) 48 camel hides

8. What happens to a nation's imports or exports of a product when the world price of the product rises above the domestic price?

(a) Imports of the product increase.

(b) Imports of the product stay the same.

(c) Exports of the product increase.

(d) Exports of the product decrease.

9. What happens to a nation's imports or exports of a product when the world price of the product falls below the domestic price?

(a) Imports of the product increase.

(b) Imports of the product decrease.

(c) Exports of the product increase.

(d) Exports of the product stay the same.

10. Which one of the following is characteristic of tariffs?

(a) They prevent the importation of goods from abroad.

(b) They specify the maximum amounts of specific commodities that may be imported during a given period of time.

(c) They often protect domestic producers from foreign competition.

(d) They enable nations to reduce their exports and increase their imports during periods of recession.

11. The motive for barriers to the importation of goods and services from abroad is to

(a) improve economic efficiency in that nation

(b) protect and benefit domestic producers of those goods and services

(c) reduce the prices of the goods and services produced in that nation

(d) expand the export of goods and services to foreign nations

12. When a tariff is imposed on a good imported from abroad,

(a) the demand for the good increases

(b) the demand for the good decreases

(c) the supply of the good increases

(d) the supply of the good decreases

Answer Questions 13, 14, 15, 16, and 17 on the basis of the following diagram, where S_d and D_d are the domestic supply and demand for a product and P_w is the world price of that product.

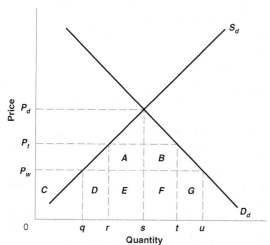

13. In a closed economy (without international trade), the equilibrium price would be

(a) P_d, but in an open economy, the equilibrium price would be P_t

(b) P_d, but in an open economy, the equilibrium price would be P_w

(c) P_w, but in an open economy, the equilibrium price would be P_d

(d) P_w, but in an open economy, the equilibrium price would be P_t

14. If there is free trade in this economy and no tariffs, the total revenue going to the foreign producers is represented by

(a) area **C**

(b) areas **A** and **B** combined

(c) areas **A**, **B**, **E**, and **F** combined

(d) areas **D**, **E**, **F**, and **G** combined

15. If a per-unit tariff was imposed in the amount of P_wP_t then domestic producers would supply

(a) **q** units and foreign producers would supply **qu** units

(b) **s** units and foreign producers would supply **su** units

(c) **r** units and foreign producers would supply **rt** units

(d) **t** units and foreign producers would supply **tu** units

16. Given a per-unit tariff in the amount of P_wP_t, the amount of the tariff revenue paid by consumers of this product is represented by

(a) area **A**

(b) area **B**

(c) areas **A** and **B** combined

(d) areas **D**, **E**, **F**, and **G** combined

17. Assume that an import quota of **rt** units is imposed on the foreign nation producing this product. The amount of *total* revenue going to foreign producers is represented by areas

(a) **A + B**

(b) **E + F**

(c) **A + B + E + F**

(d) **D + E + F + G**

18. Tariffs lead to

(a) the contraction of relatively efficient industries

(b) an overallocation of resources to relatively efficient industries

(c) an increase in the foreign demand for domestically produced goods

(d) an underallocation of resources to relatively inefficient industries

19. Tariffs and quotas are costly to consumers because

(a) the price of the imported good rises

(b) the supply of the imported good increases

(c) import competition increases for domestically produced goods

(d) consumers shift purchases away from domestically produced goods

20. The infant industry argument for tariffs

(a) is especially pertinent for the European Union

(b) generally results in tariffs that are removed after the infant industry has matured

(c) makes it rather easy to determine which infant industries will become mature industries with comparative advantages in producing their goods

(d) might better be replaced by an argument for outright subsidies for infant industries

21. Smoot-Hawley Tariff Act resulted in
(a) a significant decline in tariffs
(b) a trade war with other nations
(c) the elimination of import quotas
(d) the imposition of antidumping duties

22. "The nation needs to protect itself from foreign countries that sell their products in our domestic markets at less than the cost of production." This quotation would be most closely associated with which protectionist argument?
(a) diversification for stability
(b) increased domestic employment
(c) protection against dumping
(d) cheap foreign labor

23. Which is a likely result of imposing tariffs to increase domestic employment?
(a) a short-run increase in domestic employment in import industries
(b) a decrease in the tariff rates of foreign nations
(c) a long-run reallocation of workers from export industries to protected domestic industries
(d) a decrease in consumer prices

24. Which is the likely result of the United States using tariffs to protect its high wages and standard of living from cheap foreign labor?
(a) an increase in U.S. exports
(b) a rise in the U.S. real GDP
(c) a decrease in the average productivity of U.S. workers
(d) a decrease in the quantity of labor employed by industries producing the goods on which tariffs have been levied

25. Which of the following is characteristic of the General Agreement on Tariffs and Trade? Nations signing the agreement were committed to
(a) the expansion of import quotas
(b) the establishment of a world customs union
(c) the reciprocal increase in tariffs by negotiation
(d) the nondiscriminatory treatment of all member nations

26. One important outcome from the Uruguay Round of GATT was
(a) an increase in tariff barriers on services
(b) the elimination or reduction of many tariffs
(c) removal of voluntary export restraints in manufacturing
(d) abolishment of patent, copyright, and trademark protection

27. What international agency is currently charged with overseeing multilateral trade negotiations and with resolving trade disputes among nations?
(a) World Bank
(b) United Nations
(c) World Trade Organization
(d) International Monetary Fund

28. One of the major accomplishments of the European Union was
(a) passing the Trade Assistance Act
(b) enacting minimum wage laws
(c) increasing tariffs on U.S. products
(d) establishing the Euro Zone

29. An example of the formation of a regional free-trade zone would be the
(a) Smoot-Hawley Tariff Act
(b) Doha Development Agenda
(c) North American Free Trade Agreement
(d) General Agreement on Tariffs and Trade

30. The Trade Adjustment Assistance Act
(a) increased funding for the World Trade Organization
(b) provided more foreign aid to nations that trade with the United States
(c) extended normal-trade-relations status to more less-developed countries
(d) gave cash assistance to U.S. workers displaced by imports or plant relocations abroad

■ PROBLEMS

1. Shown below and on the next page are the production possibilities curves for two nations: the United States and Chile. Suppose these two nations do not currently engage in international trade or specialization, and suppose that points **A** and **a** show the combinations of wheat and copper they now produce and consume.

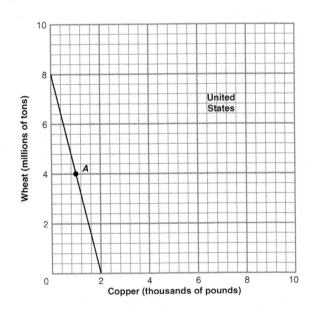

a. The straightness of the two curves indicates that the cost ratios in the two nations are (changing, constant) _____.

b. Examination of the two curves reveals that the cost ratio in

(1) the United States is _____ million tons of wheat

for _____ thousand pounds of copper.

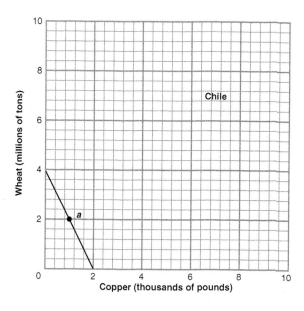

Wheat (millions of tons) vs Copper (thousands of pounds)

Chile

a

a. For nation **A**, the first column of the table is the price of a product. The second column is the quantity demanded domestically (Q_{dd}). The third column is the quantity supplied domestically (Q_{sd}). The fourth column is the quantity demanded for imports (Q_{di}). The fifth column is the quantity of exports supplied (Q_{se}).

(1) At a price of $2.00, there (will, will not) _____ be a surplus or shortage and there _____ be exports or imports.

(2) At a price of $3.00, there will be a domestic (shortage, surplus) _____ of _____ units. This domestic _____ will be eliminated by (exports, imports) _____ of _____ units.

(3) At a price of $1.00, there will be a domestic (shortage, surplus) _____ of _____ units. This domestic _____ will be eliminated by (exports, imports) _____ of _____ units.

NATION B

Price	Q_{dd}	Q_{sd}	Q_{di}	Q_{se}
$2.50	100	300	0	200
2.00	150	250	0	100
1.50	200	200	0	0
1.00	250	150	100	0

b. For nation **B**, the first column is the price of a product. The second column is the quantity demanded domestically (Q_{dd}). The third column is the quantity supplied domestically (Q_{sd}). The fourth column is the quantity demanded for imports (Q_{di}). The fifth column is the quantity of exports supplied (Q_{se}).

(1) At a price of $1.50, there (will, will not) _____ be a surplus or shortage and there _____ be exports or imports.

(2) At a price of $2.50, there will be a domestic (shortage, surplus) _____ of _____ units. This domestic _____ will be eliminated by (exports, imports) _____ of _____ units.

(3) At a price of $1.00, there will be a domestic (shortage, surplus) _____ of _____ units. This domestic _____ will be eliminated by (exports, imports) _____ of _____ units.

c. The following table shows a schedule of the import demand in nation **A** and the export supply in nation **B** at various prices. The first column is the price of the product. The second column is the quantity demanded for imports (Q_{diA}) in nation **A**. The third column is the quantity of exports supplied (Q_{seB}) in nation **B**.

Price	Q_{diA}	Q_{seB}
$2.00	0	100
1.75	50	50
1.50	100	0

(2) Chile is _____ million tons of wheat for _____ thousand pounds of copper.

c. If these two nations were to specialize and trade wheat for copper,

(1) The United States would specialize in the production of wheat because _____.

(2) Chile would specialize in the production of copper because _____.

d. The terms of trade, if specialization and trade occur, will be greater than 2 and less than 4 million tons of wheat for 1000 pounds of copper because _____

_____.

e. Assume the terms of trade turn out to be 3 million tons of wheat for 1000 pounds of copper. Draw in the trading possibilities curves for the United States and Chile.

f. With these trading possibilities curves, suppose the United States decides to consume 5 million tons of wheat and 1000 pounds of copper while Chile decides to consume 3 million tons of wheat and 1000 pounds of copper. The gains from trade to

(1) the United States are _____ million tons of wheat and _____ thousand pounds of copper.

(2) Chile are _____ million tons of wheat and _____ thousand pounds of copper.

2. Following are tables showing the domestic supply and demand schedules and the export supply and import demand schedules for two nations (**A** and **B**).

NATION A

Price	Q_{dd}	Q_{sd}	Q_{di}	Q_{se}
$3.00	100	300	0	200
2.50	150	250	0	100
2.00	200	200	0	0
1.50	250	150	100	0
1.00	300	100	200	0

(1) If the world price is $2.00, then nation (**A**, **B**)

_____ will want to import _____ units and na-

tion _____ will want to export _____ units of the

product.

(2) If the world price is $1.75, then nation (**A**, **B**)

_____ will want to import _____ units and na-

tion _____ will want to export _____ units of the

product.

(3) If the world price is $1.50, then nation (**A**, **B**)

_____ will want to import _____ units and na-

tion _____ will want to export _____ units of the

product.

3. The following table shows the quantities of woolen gloves demanded (**D**) in the United States at several different prices (**P**). Also shown in the table are the quantities of woolen gloves that would be supplied by U.S. producers (**S_a**) and the quantities that would be supplied by foreign producers (**S_f**) at the nine different prices.

P	D	S_a	S_f	S_t	S'_f	S'_t
$2.60	450	275	475	_____	_____	_____
2.40	500	250	450	_____	_____	_____
2.20	550	225	425	_____	_____	_____
2.00	600	200	400	_____	_____	_____
1.80	650	175	375	_____	_____	_____
1.60	700	150	350	_____	_____	_____
1.40	750	125	325	_____	_____	_____
1.20	800	0	300	_____	_____	_____
1.00	850	0	0	_____	_____	_____

a. Compute and enter in the table the total quantities that would be supplied (**S_t**) by U.S. and foreign producers at each of the prices.

b. If the market for woolen gloves in the United States is a competitive one, the equilibrium price for woolen

gloves is $_____ and the equilibrium quantity is

_____.

c. Suppose now that the United States government imposes an 80 cent ($.80) tariff per pair of gloves on all gloves imported into the United States from abroad. Compute and enter into the table the quantities that would be supplied (**S'_f**) by foreign producers at the nine different prices. [*Hint:* If foreign producers were willing to supply 300 pairs at a price of $1.20 when there was no tariff, they are now willing to supply 300 pairs at $2.00 (the $.80 per pair tariff plus the $1.20 they will receive for themselves). The quantities supplied at each of the other prices may be found in a similar fashion.]

d. Compute and enter into the table the total quantities that would be supplied (**S'_t**) by U.S. and foreign producers at each of the nine prices.

e. As a result of the imposition of the tariff the equilib-

rium price has risen to $_____ and the equilibrium

quantity has fallen to _____.

f. The number of pairs sold by

(1) U.S. producers has (increased, decreased) _____

by _____.

(2) foreign producers has (increased, decreased)

_____ by _____.

g. The total revenues (after the payment of the tariff) of

(1) U.S. producers—who do not pay the tariff—have

(increased, decreased) _____ by $_____.

(2) foreign producers—who do pay the tariff—have

(increased, decreased) _____ by $_____.

h. The total amount spent by U.S. buyers of woolen

gloves has _____ by $_____.

i. The total number of dollars earned by foreigners

has _____ by $_____, and, as a result, the total foreign demand for goods and services produced in

the United States has _____ by $_____.

j. The tariff revenue of the United States government

has _____ by $_____.

k. If an import quota were imposed that had the same effect as the tariff on price and output, the amount of

the tariff revenue, $_____, would now be received

as revenue by _____ producers.

■ **SHORT ANSWER AND ESSAY QUESTIONS**

1. What is the economic basis for trade? Explain the underlying facts that support free trade and supply examples of three types of goods produced based on resource differences.

2. Explain the difference between absolute advantage and comparative advantage.

3. Provide a two-nation and two-product example that shows the gains from specialization and trade.

4. What is the case for free trade?

5. Explain how the equilibrium prices and quantities of exports and imports are determined. Why will exports in a nation increase when world prices rise relative to domestic prices?

6. What motivates nations to erect barriers to the importation of goods from abroad, and what types of barriers do they erect?

7. Suppose the United States increases the tariff on automobiles imported from Germany (and other foreign countries). What is the effect of this tariff-rate increase on
  (a) the price of automobiles in the United States;
  (b) the total number of cars sold in the United States during a year;
  (c) the number of cars produced by and employment in the German automobile industry;
  (d) production by and employment in the U.S. automobile industry;
  (e) German income obtained by selling cars in the United States;

(f) the German demand for goods produced in the United States;

(g) the production of and employment in those U.S. industries that now export goods to Germany;

(h) the standards of living in the United States and in Germany;

(i) the allocation of resources in the U.S. economy; and

(j) the allocation of the world's resources?

8. Compare and contrast the economic effects of a tariff with an import quota on a product.

9. Critically evaluate the military self-sufficiency argument for protectionism. What industries should be protected?

10. What is the basis for the diversification-for-stability argument for protectionism? How can it be countered?

11. Explain the arguments and counterarguments for protecting infant industries.

12. Can a strong case for protectionism be made on the basis of defending against the "dumping" of products? How do you determine if a nation is dumping a product? What are the economic effects of dumping on consumers?

13. What are the problems with using trade barriers as a means of increasing domestic employment?

14. Does the economy need to shield domestic workers from competition from "cheap" foreign labor? Explain using comparative advantage, standards of living, productivity, and labor cost per unit of output.

15. What was the purpose of the General Agreement on Tariffs and Trade (GATT), and what did it achieve?

16. Describe the purpose of the World Trade Organization (WTO). Why is it controversial?

17. What is the European Union? What has it achieved?

18. What is the North American Free Trade Agreement (NAFTA)? What do critics and defenders say about the agreement?

19. Discuss the purpose of the Trade Adjustment Assistance Act of 2002 and its advantages and disadvantages.

20. Explain the reasons U.S. businesses have turned to offshoring and evaluate the costs and benefits of such actions.

ANSWERS

Chapter 37 International Trade

FILL-IN QUESTIONS

1. 13, largest
2. less than, greater than, goods, services
3. uneven, different, more
4. lowest, have, do not have
5. *a.* inexpensive, expensive; *b.* expensive, inexpensive; *c.* hats, bananas; *d.* 3, 4; *e.* (1) 1/3, 2/7, (2) 4, 3 1/2; *f.* rises

6. comparative advantage, more, higher
7. world, domestic, increase, increase
8. supply, only one
9. tariffs, quotas, revenue, protective
10. nontariff, export
11. domestic producers, decrease, less
12. increase, decrease, increase, decrease
13. tariff, quota
14. *a.* essential, more; *b.* advanced, developing; *c.* infant, mature; *d.* comparative, rare; *e.* composition, decrease, retaliate; *f.* per hour, per unit
15. *a.* equal, nondiscriminatory treatment of all member nations; *b.* reduction of tariffs by multilateral negotiations; *c.* elimination of import quotas
16. agreements, disputes, Doha, decreasing
17. European, tariffs and quotas, common, euro
18. zone, tariffs, decrease, increase
19. workers, small, subsidy
20. offshoring, growth, decrease, increase

TRUE–FALSE QUESTIONS

1. T, p. 755
2. F, p. 756
3. F, p. 756
4. T, p. 756
5. F, p. 756
6. F, p. 758
7. F, p. 759
8. T, p. 759
9. T, p. 760
10. T, p. 762
11. T, p. 763
12. F, p. 763
13. F, pp. 764–767
14. T, pp. 764–767
15. F, p. 767
16. T, p. 768
17. T, p. 769
18. F, p. 769
19. T, p. 770
20. T, p. 770
21. F, pp. 770–771
22. T, p. 771
23. T, p. 771–772
24. F, p. 772
25. T, p. 773
26. F, p. 773
27. T, p. 773
28. F, p. 774
29. T, p. 774
30. T, p. 774–775

MULTIPLE-CHOICE QUESTIONS

1. c, p. 755
2. c, p. 755
3. b, p. 756
4. b, p. 758
5. a, p. 760
6. a, pp. 760–762
7. c, pp. 760–762
8. c, pp. 764–767
9. a, pp. 764–767
10. c, p. 767
11. b, p. 767
12. d, p. 768
13. b, pp. 768–769
14. d, pp. 768–769
15. c, pp. 768–769
16. c, pp. 768–769
17. c, p. 769
18. a, p. 769
19. a, p. 769
20. d, p. 770
21. b, p. 771
22. c, pp. 770–771
23. c, p. 771
24. c, pp. 771–772
25. d, p. 773
26. b, p. 773
27. c, p. 773
28. d, p. 774
29. c, p. 774
30. d, p. 774

PROBLEMS

1. *a.* constant; *b.* (1) 8, 2, (2) 4, 2; *c.* (1) it has a comparative advantage in producing wheat (its cost of producing wheat is less than Chile's), (2) it has a comparative advantage in producing copper (its cost of producing copper is less than the United States'); *d.* one of the two nations would be unwilling to trade if the terms of trade are outside this range; *f.* (1) 1, 0, (2) 1, 0

2. *a.* (1) will not, will not, (2) surplus, 200, surplus, exports, 200, (3) shortage, 200, shortage, imports, 200; *b.* (1) will not, will not, (2) surplus, 200, surplus, exports, 200, (3) shortage, 100, shortage, imports, 100; *c.* (1) A, 0, B, 100, (2) A, 50, B, 50, (3) A, 100, B, 0

3. *a.* 750, 700, 650, 600, 550, 500, 450, 300, 0; *b.* $2.00, 600; *c.* 375, 350, 325, 300, 0, 0, 0, 0, 0; *d.* 650, 600, 550, 500, 175, 150, 125, 0, 0; *e.* $2.20, 550; *f.* (1) increased, 25, (2) decreased, 75; *g.* (1) increased, $95, (2) decreased, $345; *h.* increased, $10; *i.* decreased, $345, decreased, $345; *j.* increased, $260; *k.* $260, foreign

SHORT ANSWER AND ESSAY QUESTIONS

1. p. 756	**8.** pp. 769–770	**15.** p. 773
2. p. 757	**9.** p. 770	**16.** p. 773
3. pp. 757–763	**10.** p. 770	**17.** p. 773–774
4. p. 763	**11.** p. 770	**18.** p. 774
5. pp. 764–767	**12.** pp. 770–771	**19.** p. 774
6. p. 767	**13.** p. 771	**20.** pp. 774–775
7. pp. 768–769	**14.** pp. 771–772	

38

AFTER READING THIS CHAPTER, YOU SHOULD BE ABLE TO:

1 Explain how currencies of different nations are exchanged when international transactions take place.

2 Analyze the balance sheet the United States uses to account for the international payments it makes and receives.

3 Discuss how exchange rates are determined in currency markets.

4 Describe the difference between flexible exchange rates and fixed exchange rates.

5 Identify the causes and consequences of recent U.S. trade deficits.

The Balance of Payments, Exchange Rates, and Trade Deficits

If you take a U.S. dollar to the bank and ask to exchange it for U.S. currency, you will get a puzzled look. If you persist, you may get a dollar's worth of change: One U.S. dollar can buy exactly one U.S. dollar. But on April 4, 2010, for example, 1 U.S. dollar could buy 1922 Colombian pesos, 1.09 Australian dollars, .66 British pound, 1.01 Canadian dollars, .74 European euro, 94.61 Japanese yen, or 12.30 Mexican pesos. What explains this seemingly haphazard array of exchange rates?

In Chapter 37 we examined comparative advantage as the underlying economic basis of world trade and discussed the effects of barriers to free trade. Now we introduce the highly important monetary and financial aspects of international trade.

International Financial Transactions

This chapter focuses on international financial transactions, the vast majority of which fall into two broad categories: international trade and international asset transactions. International trade involves either purchasing or selling currently produced goods or services across an international border. Examples include an Egyptian firm exporting cotton to the United States and an American company hiring an Indian call center to answer its phones. International asset transactions involve the transfer of the property rights to either real or financial assets between the citizens of one country and the citizens of another country. It includes activities like buying foreign stocks or selling your house to a foreigner.

These two categories of international financial transactions reflect the fact that whether they are from different countries or the same country, individuals and firms can only exchange two things with each other: currently produced goods and services or preexisting assets. With regard to assets, however, money is by far the most commonly exchanged asset. Only rarely would you ever find a barter situation in which people directly exchanged other assets—such as trading a car for 500 shares of Microsoft stock or a cow for 30 chickens and a tank of diesel fuel.

As a result, there are two basic types of transactions:

- People trading either goods or services for money.
- People trading assets for money.

In either case, money flows from the buyers of the goods, services, or assets to the sellers of the goods, services, or assets.

When the people engaged in any such transactions are both from places that use the same currency, what type of money to use is not an issue. Americans from California and Wisconsin will use their common currency, the dollar. People from France and Germany will use their common currency, the euro. However, when the people involved in an exchange are from places that use different currencies, intermediate asset transactions have to take place: the buyers must convert their own currencies into the currencies that the sellers use and accept.

As an example, consider the case of an English software design company that wants to buy a supercomputer made by an American company. The American company sells these high-powered machines for $300,000. To pay for the machine, the English company has to convert some of the money it has (British pounds sterling) into the money that the American company will accept (U.S. dollars). This process is not difficult. As we will soon explain in detail, there are many easy-to-use foreign exchange markets in which those who wish to sell pounds and buy dollars can interact with others who wish to sell dollars and buy pounds. The demand and supply created by these two groups determine the equilibrium exchange rate, which, in turn, determines how many pounds our English company will have to convert to pay for the supercomputer. If, for instance, the exchange rate is $2 = £1, then the English company will have to convert £150,000 to obtain the $300,000 necessary to purchase the computer.

The Balance of Payments

A nation's **balance of payments** is the sum of all the financial transactions that take place between its residents and the residents of foreign nations. Most of these transactions fall into the two main categories that we have just discussed: international trade and international asset transactions. As a result, nearly all the items included in the balance of payments are things such as exports and imports of goods, exports and imports of services, and international purchases and sales of financial and real assets. But the balance of payments also includes international transactions that fall outside of these main categories—things such as tourist expenditures, interest and dividends received or paid abroad, debt forgiveness, and remittances made by immigrants to their relatives back home.

The U.S. Commerce Department's Bureau of Economic Analysis compiles a balance-of-payments statement each year. This statement summarizes all of the millions of payments that individuals and firms in the United States receive from foreigners as well as all of the millions of payments that individuals and firms in the United States make to foreigners. It shows "flows" of inpayments of money *to* the United States and outpayments of money *from* the United States. For convenience, all of these money payments are given in terms of dollars. This is true despite the fact that some of them actually may have been made using foreign currencies—as when, for instance, an American company converts dollars into euros to buy something from an Italian company. When including this outpayment of money from the United States, the accountants who compile the balance-of-payments statement use the number of dollars the American company converted—rather than the number of euros that were actually used to make the purchase.

Table 38.1 is a simplified balance-of-payments statement for the United States in 2009. Because most international financial transactions fall into only two categories—international trade and international asset exchanges—the balance-of-payments statement is organized into two broad

TABLE 38.1 The U.S. Balance of Payments, 2009 (in Billions)

CURRENT ACCOUNT		
(1) U.S. goods exports	$+1046	
(2) U.S. goods imports	−1563	
(3) *Balance on goods*		$−517
(4) U.S. exports of services	+509	
(5) U.S. imports of services	−371	
(6) *Balance on services*		+138
(7) *Balance on goods and services*		−379
(8) Net investment income	+89*	
(9) Net transfers	−130	
(10) **Balance on current account**		**−420**
CAPITAL AND FINANCIAL ACCOUNT		
Capital account		
(11) *Balance on capital account*		−3
Financial account		
(12) Foreign purchases of assets in the United States	+548†	
(13) U.S. purchases of assets abroad	−125†	
(14) *Balance on financial account*		+423
(15) **Balance on capital and financial account**		**+420**
		$ 0

*Includes other, less significant, categories of income.
†Includes one-half of a $225 billion statistical discrepancy that is listed in the capital account.
Source: U.S. Department of Commerce, Bureau of Economic Analysis, **www.bea.gov**. Preliminary 2009 data. The export and import data are on a "balance-of-payment basis," and usually vary from the data on exports and imports reported in the National Income and Product Accounts.

categories. *The current account* located at the top of the table primarily treats international trade. *The capital and financial account* at the bottom of the table primarily treats international asset exchanges.

Current Account

The top portion of Table 38.1 that mainly summarizes U.S. trade in currently produced goods and services is called the **current account.** Items 1 and 2 show U.S. exports and imports of goods (merchandise) in 2009. U.S. exports have a *plus* (+) sign because they are a *credit*; they generate flows of money toward the United States. U.S. imports have a *minus* (−) sign because they are a *debit*; they cause flows of money out of the United States.

Balance on Goods Items 1 and 2 in Table 38.1 reveal that in 2009 U.S. goods exports of $1046 billion were less than U.S. goods imports of $1563 billion. A country's *balance of trade on goods* is the difference between its exports and its imports of goods. If exports exceed imports, the result is a surplus on the balance of goods. If imports exceed exports, there is a trade deficit on the balance of goods.

We note in item 3 that in 2009 the United States incurred a trade deficit on goods of $517 billion.

Balance on Services The United States exports not only goods, such as airplanes and computer software, but also services, such as insurance, consulting, travel, and investment advice, to residents of foreign nations. Item 4 in Table 38.1 shows that these service "exports" totaled $509 billion in 2009. Since they generate flows of money toward the United States, they are a credit (thus the + sign). Item 5 indicates that the United States "imports" similar services from foreigners. Those service imports were $371 billion in 2009, and since they generate flows of money out of the United States, they are a debit (thus the − sign). Summed together, items 4 and 5 indicate that the balance on services (item 6) in 2009 was $138 billion. The **balance on goods and services** shown as item 7 is the difference between U.S. exports of goods and services (items 1 and 4) and U.S. imports of goods and services (items 2 and 5). In 2009, U.S. imports of goods and services exceeded U.S. exports of goods and services by $379 billion. So a **trade deficit** of that amount occurred. In contrast, a **trade surplus** occurs

GLOBAL PERSPECTIVE 38.1

U.S. Trade Balances in Goods and Services, Selected Nations, 2009

The United States has large trade deficits in goods and services with several nations, in particular, China, Mexico, and Germany.

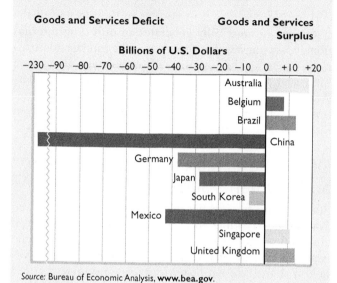

Source: Bureau of Economic Analysis, **www.bea.gov.**

when exports of goods and services exceed imports of goods and services. (Global Perspective 38.1 shows U.S. trade deficits and surpluses with selected nations.)

Balance on Current Account Items 8 and 9 are not items relating directly to international trade in goods and services. But they are listed as part of the current account (which is mostly about international trade in goods and services) because they are international financial flows that in some sense compensate for things that can be conceptualized as being *like* international trade in either goods or services. For instance, item 8, *net investment income*, represents the difference between (1) the interest and dividend payments foreigners paid U.S. citizens and companies for the services provided by U.S. capital invested abroad ("exported" capital) and (2) the interest and dividends the U.S. citizens and companies paid for the services provided by foreign capital invested here ("imported" capital). Observe that in 2009 U.S. net investment income was a positive $89 billion.

Item 9 shows net transfers, both public and private, between the United States and the rest of the world. Included here is foreign aid, pensions paid to U.S. citizens

living abroad, and remittances by immigrants to relatives abroad. These $130 billion of transfers are net U.S. outpayments (and therefore listed as a negative number in Table 38.1). They are listed as part of the current account because they can be thought of as the financial flows that accompany the exporting of goodwill and the importing of "thank you notes."

By adding all transactions in the current account, we obtain the **balance on current account** shown in item 10. In 2009 the United States had a current account deficit of $420 billion. This means that the U.S. current account transactions created outpayments from the United States greater than inpayments to the United States.

Capital and Financial Account

The bottom portion of the current account statement summarizes U.S. international asset transactions. It is called the **capital and financial account** and consists of two separate accounts: the *capital account* and the *financial account*.

Capital Account The capital account mainly measures debt forgiveness—which is an asset transaction because the person forgiving a debt essentially hands the IOU back to the borrower. It is a "net" account (one that can be either + or −). The $3 billion listed in line 11 tells us that in 2009 Americans forgave $3 billion more of debt owed to them by foreigners than foreigners forgave debt owed to them by Americans. The − sign indicates a debit; it is an "on-paper" outpayment (asset transfer) by the net amount of debt forgiven.

Financial Account The financial account summarizes international asset transactions having to do with international purchases and sales of real or financial assets. Line 12 lists the amount of foreign purchases of assets in the United States. It has a + sign because any purchase of an American-owned asset by a foreigner generates a flow of money toward the American who sells the asset. Line 13 lists U.S. purchases of assets abroad. These have a − sign because such purchases generate a flow of money from the Americans who buy foreign assets toward the foreigners who sell them those assets.

Items 11 and 12 combined yielded a $423 billion balance on the financial account for 2009 (line 14). In 2009 the United States "exported" $548 billion of ownership of its real and financial assets and "imported" $125 billion. Thought of differently, this surplus in the financial account brought in income of $423 billion to the United States. The **balance on the capital and financial account** (line 15) is $420 billion. It is the sum of the $3 billion deficit on the capital account and the $423 billion surplus on the financial account. Observe that this $420 billion surplus in the capital and financial account equals the $420 billion deficit in the current account. This is not an accident. The two numbers always equal—or "balance." That's why the statement is called the *balance* of payments. It has to balance. Let's see why.

Why the Balance?

The balance on the current account and the balance on the capital and financial account must always sum to zero because any deficit or surplus in the current account automatically creates an offsetting entry in the capital and financial account. People can only trade one of two things with each other: currently produced goods and services or preexisting assets. Therefore, if trading partners have an imbalance in their trade of currently produced goods and services, the only way to make up for that imbalance is with a net transfer of assets from one party to the other.

To see why this is true, suppose that John (an American) makes shoes and Henri (a Swiss citizen) makes watches and that the pair only trade with each other. Assume that their financial assets consist entirely of money, with each beginning the year with $1000 in his bank account. Suppose that this year John exports $300 of shoes to Henri and imports $500 of watches from Henri. John therefore ends the year with a $200 goods deficit with Henri.

John and Henri's goods transactions, however, also result in asset exchanges that cause a net transfer of assets from John to Henri equal in size to John's $200 goods deficit with Henri. This is true because Henri pays John $300 for his shoes while John pays Henri $500 for his watches. The *net* result of these opposite-direction asset movements is that $200 of John's initial assets of $1000 are transferred to Henri. This is unavoidable, because the $300 John receives from his exports pays for only the first $300 of his $500 of imports. The only way for John to pay for the remaining $200 of imports is for him to transfer $200 of his initial asset holdings to Henri. Consequently, John's assets decline by $200 from $1000 to $800, and Henri's assets rise from $1000 to $1200.

Consider how the transaction between John and Henri affects the U.S. balance-of-payments statement (Table 38.1), other things equal. John's $200 goods deficit with Henri shows up in the U.S. current account as a −$200 entry in the balance on goods account (line 3) and carries down to a −$200 entry in the balance on current account (line 10).

In the capital and financial account, this $200 is recorded as +$200 in the account labeled foreign purchases of assets in the United States (line 12). This +$200 then carries down to the balance on capital and financial account (line 15). Think of it this way: Henri has in essence used $200 worth of watches to purchase $200 of John's initial $1000 holding of assets. The +$200 entry in line 12 (foreign purchases of assets in the United States) simply recognizes this fact. This +$200 exactly offsets the −$200 in the current account.

Thus, the balance of payments always balances. Any current account deficit or surplus in the top half of the statement automatically generates an offsetting international asset transfer that shows up in the capital and financial account in the bottom half of the statement. More specifically, current account deficits simultaneously generate transfers of assets to foreigners, while current account surpluses automatically generate transfers of assets from foreigners.

Official Reserves, Payments Deficits, and Payments Surpluses

Some of the foreign purchases of assets in the United States (line 12, Table 38.1) and the U.S. assets purchased abroad (line 13) are of so-called official reserves. **Official reserves** consist of foreign currencies, certain reserves held with the International Monetary Fund, and stocks of gold. These reserves are owned by governments or their central banks. For simplicity, we will assume for now that the entire stock of U.S. official reserves consists of foreign currency so we can speak of official reserves and foreign currency reserves interchangeably.

Although the balance of payments must always sum to zero, as in Table 38.1, in some years a net sale of official reserves by a nation's treasury or central bank occurs in the process of bringing the capital and financial account into balance with the current account. In such years, a **balance-of-payments deficit** is said to occur. This deficit is in a subset of the overall balance statement and *is not a deficit in the overall account.* Remember, the overall balance of payments is always in balance. But in this case the balancing of the overall account includes sales of official reserves to create an inflow of dollars to the United States. In selling foreign currency in the foreign exchange market, the treasury or central bank must draw down its stock of reserves. This drawdown is an indicator of a balance-of-payments deficit.

These net sales of official reserves in the foreign exchange market show up as a *plus* (+) item on the U.S. balance-of-payments statement, specifically as are foreign purchases of U.S. assets (line 12). They are a credit or an inflow of dollars to the United States, just as are John's proceeds from the sale of $200 of his assets to Henri in our previous example.

In other years, the capital and financial account balances the current account because of government purchases of official reserves from foreigners. The treasury or central bank engineers this balance by selling dollars to obtain foreign currency, and then adding the newly acquired foreign currency to its stock of official reserves. In these years, a **balance-of-payments surplus** is said to exist. This payments surplus therefore can be thought of as either net purchases of official reserves in the balance of payments or, alternatively, as the resulting increase in the stock of official reserves held by the government.

Net purchases of official reserves by the treasury or central bank appear on the U.S. balance sheet as U.S. purchases of foreign assets (line 13)—a *negative* (−) item. These purchases are a debit because they represent an outflow of dollars.

A balance-of-payments deficit is not necessarily bad, just as a balance-of-payments surplus is not necessarily good. Both simply happen. However, any nation's official reserves are limited. Persistent payments deficits must be financed by drawing down those reserves, which would ultimately deplete the reserves. That nation would have to adopt policies to correct its balance of payments. Such policies might require painful macroeconomic adjustments, trade barriers and similar restrictions, or a major depreciation of its currency. For this reason, nations strive for payments balance, at least over several-year periods.

WORKED PROBLEMS

W 38.1

Balance of payments

QUICK REVIEW 38.1

- A nation's balance-of-payments statement summarizes all of the international financial transactions that take place between its residents and the residents of all foreign nations. It includes the current account balance and the capital and financial account balance.

- The current account balance is a nation's exports of goods and services less its imports of goods and services plus its net investment income and net transfers.

- The capital and financial account balance includes the net amount of the nation's debt forgiveness as well as the nation's sale of real and financial assets to people living abroad less its purchases of real and financial assets from foreigners.

- The current account balance and the capital and financial account balance always sum to zero because any current account imbalance automatically generates an offsetting international asset transfer.

- A balance-of-payments deficit exists when net sales of official reserves (mainly foreign currency) occur in the balance-of-payments statement; in contrast, a balance-of-payments surplus exists when net purchases of official reserves occur.

Flexible Exchange Rates

Both the size and the persistence of a nation's balance-of-payments deficits and surpluses and the adjustments it must make to correct those imbalances depend on the system of exchange rates being used. There are two pure types of exchange-rate systems:

- A **flexible- or floating-exchange-rate system** through which demand and supply determine exchange rates and in which no government intervention occurs.

- A **fixed-exchange-rate system** through which governments determine exchange rates and make necessary adjustments in their economies to maintain those rates.

We begin by looking at flexible exchange rates. Let's examine the rate, or price, at which U.S. dollars might be exchanged

INTERACTIVE GRAPHS

G 38.1

Flexible exchange rates

for British pounds. In **Figure 38.1 (Key Graph)** we show demand D_1 and supply S_1 of pounds in the currency market.

The *demand-for-pounds curve* is downsloping because all British goods and services will be cheaper to the United States if pounds become less expensive to the United States. That is, at lower dollar prices for pounds, the United States can obtain more pounds and therefore more British goods and services per dollar. To buy those cheaper British goods, U.S. consumers will increase the quantity of pounds they demand.

The *supply-of-pounds curve* is upsloping because the British will purchase more U.S. goods when the dollar price of pounds rises (that is, as the pound price of dollars falls). When the British buy more U.S. goods, they supply a greater quantity of pounds to the foreign exchange market. In other words, they must exchange pounds for dollars to purchase U.S. goods. So, when the dollar price of pounds rises, the quantity of pounds supplied goes up.

The intersection of the supply curve and the demand curve will determine the dollar price of pounds. Here, that price (exchange rate) is $2 for £1. At this exchange rate, the quantities of pounds supplied and demanded are equal; neither a shortage nor a surplus of pounds occurs.

Depreciation and Appreciation

An exchange rate determined by market forces can, and often does, change daily like stock and bond prices. When the dollar price of pounds *rises*, for example, from $2 = £1 to $3 = £1, the dollar has *depreciated* relative to the pound (and the pound has appreciated relative to the dollar). When a currency depreciates, more units of it (dollars)

key graph

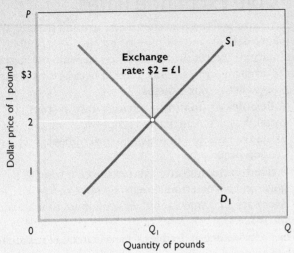

P

Exchange
rate: $2 = £1

S_1

$3

Dollar price of 1 pound

2

1

D_1

0   Q_1 Q

Quantity of pounds

FIGURE 38.1 The market for foreign currency (pounds). The intersection of the demand-for-pounds curve D_1 and the supply-of-pounds curve S_1 determines the equilibrium dollar price of pounds, here, $2. That means that the exchange rate is $2 = £1. Not shown, an increase in demand for pounds or a decrease in supply of pounds will increase the dollar price of pounds and thus cause the pound to appreciate. Also not shown, a decrease in demand for pounds or an increase in the supply of pounds will reduce the dollar price of pounds, meaning that the pound has depreciated.

QUICK QUIZ FOR FIGURE 38.1

1. Which of the following statements is true?
   a. The quantity of pounds demanded falls when the dollar appreciates.
   b. The quantity of pounds supplied declines as the dollar price of the pound rises.
   c. At the equilibrium exchange rate, the pound price of $1 is $£\frac{1}{2}$.
   d. The dollar appreciates if the demand for pounds increases.

2. At the price of $2 for £1 in this figure:
   a. the dollar-pound exchange rate is unstable.
   b. the quantity of pounds supplied equals the quantity demanded.
   c. the dollar price of £1 equals the pound price of $1.
   d. U.S. goods exports to Britain must equal U.S. goods imports from Britain.

3. Other things equal, a leftward shift of the demand curve in this figure:
   a. would depreciate the dollar.

b. would create a shortage of pounds at the previous price of $2 for £1.
   c. might be caused by a major recession in the United States.
   d. might be caused by a significant rise of real interest rates in Britain.

4. Other things equal, a rightward shift of the supply curve in this figure would:
   a. depreciate the dollar and might be caused by a significant rise of real interest rates in Britain.
   b. depreciate the dollar and might be caused by a significant fall of real interest rates in Britain.
   c. appreciate the dollar and might be caused by a significant rise of real interest rates in the United States.
   d. appreciate the dollar and might be caused by a significant fall of interest rates in the United States.

Answers: 1. c; 2. b; 3. c; 4. c

---

are needed to buy a single unit of some other currency (a pound).

When the dollar price of pounds *falls*, for example, from $2 = £1 to $1 = £1, the dollar has *appreciated* relative to the pound. When a currency appreciates, fewer units of it (dollars) are needed to buy a single unit of some other currency (pounds).

In our U.S.-Britain illustrations, depreciation of the dollar means an appreciation of the pound, and vice versa. When the dollar price of a pound jumps from $2 = £1 to $3 = £1, the pound has appreciated relative to the dollar because it takes fewer pounds to buy $1. At $2 = £1, it took $£\frac{1}{2}$ to buy $1; at $3 = £1, it takes only $£\frac{1}{3}$ to buy $1.

Conversely, when the dollar appreciated relative to the pound, the pound depreciated relative to the dollar. More pounds were needed to buy a dollar.

In general, the relevant terminology and relationships between the U.S. dollar and another currency are as follows.

- Dollar price of foreign currency increases ≡ dollar depreciates relative to the foreign currency ≡ foreign currency price of dollar decreases ≡ foreign currency appreciates relative to the dollar.

- Dollar price of foreign currency decreases ≡ dollar appreciates relative to the foreign currency ≡ foreign currency price of dollar increases ≡ foreign currency depreciates relative to the dollar.

786

Determinants of Exchange Rates

What factors would cause a nation's currency to appreciate or depreciate in the market for foreign exchange? Here are three generalizations:

- If the demand for a nation's currency increases (other things equal), that currency will appreciate; if the demand declines, that currency will depreciate.
- If the supply of a nation's currency increases, that currency will depreciate; if the supply decreases, that currency will appreciate.
- If a nation's currency appreciates, some foreign currency depreciates relative to it.

With these generalizations in mind, let's examine the determinants of exchange rates—the factors that shift the demand or supply curve for a certain currency. As we do so, keep in mind that the other-things-equal assumption is always in force. Also note that we are discussing factors *that change the exchange rate*, not things that change *as a result of* a change in the exchange rate.

Changes in Tastes
Any change in consumer tastes or preferences for the products of a foreign country may alter the demand for that nation's currency and change its exchange rate. If technological advances in U.S. wireless phones make them more attractive to British consumers and businesses, then the British will supply more pounds in the exchange market to purchase more U.S. wireless phones. The supply-of-pounds curve will shift to the right, causing the pound to depreciate and the dollar to appreciate.

In contrast, the U.S. demand-for-pounds curve will shift to the right if British woolen apparel becomes more fashionable in the United States. So the pound will appreciate and the dollar will depreciate.

Relative Income Changes
A nation's currency is likely to depreciate if its growth of national income is more rapid than that of other countries. Here's why: A country's imports vary directly with its income level. As total income rises in the United States, people there buy both more domestic goods and more foreign goods. If the U.S. economy is expanding rapidly and the British economy is stagnant, U.S. imports of British goods, and therefore U.S. demands for pounds, will increase. The dollar price of pounds will rise, so the dollar will depreciate.

Relative Inflation Rate Changes
Other things equal, changes in the relative rates of inflation of two nations change their relative price levels and alter the exchange rate between their currencies. The currency of the nation with the higher inflation rate—the more rapidly rising price level—tends to depreciate. Suppose,

for example, that inflation is zero percent in Great Britain and 5 percent in the United States so that prices, on average, are rising by 5 percent per year in the United States while, on average, remaining unchanged in Great Britain. U.S. consumers will seek out more of the now relatively lower-priced British goods, increasing the demand for pounds. British consumers will purchase less of the now relatively higher-priced U.S. goods, reducing the supply of pounds. This combination of increased demand for pounds and reduced supply of pounds will cause the pound to appreciate and the dollar to depreciate.

According to the **purchasing-power-parity theory**, exchange rates should eventually adjust such that they equate the purchasing power of various currencies. If a certain market basket of identical products costs $10,000 in the United States and £5000 in Great Britain, the exchange rate should move to $2 = £1. That way, a dollar spent in the United States will buy exactly as much output as it would if it were first converted to pounds (at the $2 = £1 exchange rate) and used to buy output in Great Britain.

In terms of our example, 5 percent inflation in the United States will increase the price of the market basket from $10,000 to $10,500, while the zero percent inflation in Great Britain will leave the market basket priced at £5000. For purchasing power parity to hold, the exchange rate would have to move from $2 = £1 to $2.10 = £1. That means the dollar therefore would depreciate and the pound would appreciate. In practice, however, not all exchange rates move precisely to equate the purchasing power of various currencies and thereby achieve "purchasing power parity," even over long periods.

Relative Interest Rates
Changes in relative interest rates between two countries may alter their exchange rate. Suppose that real interest rates rise in the United States but stay constant in Great Britain. British citizens will then find the United States a more attractive place in which to loan money directly or loan money indirectly by buying bonds. To make these loans, they will have to supply pounds in the foreign exchange market to obtain dollars. The increase in the supply of pounds results in depreciation of the pound and appreciation of the dollar.

Changes in Relative Expected Returns on Stocks, Real Estate, and Production Facilities
International investing extends beyond buying foreign bonds. It includes international investments in stocks and real estate as well as foreign purchases of factories and production facilities. Other things equal, the extent of this foreign investment depends on relative expected returns. To make the investments, investors in one country must sell their

currencies to purchase the foreign currencies needed for the foreign investments.

For instance, suppose that investing in England suddenly becomes more popular due to a more positive outlook regarding expected returns on stocks, real estate, and production facilities there. U.S. investors therefore will sell U.S. assets to buy more assets in England. The U.S. assets will be sold for dollars, which will then be brought to the foreign exchange market and exchanged for pounds, which will in turn be used to purchase British assets. The increased demand for pounds in the foreign exchange market will cause the pound to appreciate and therefore the dollar to depreciate relative to the pound.

Speculation Currency speculators are people who buy and sell currencies with an eye toward reselling or repurchasing them at a profit. Suppose speculators expect the U.S. economy to (1) grow more rapidly than the British economy and (2) experience more rapid inflation than Britain. These expectations translate into an anticipation that the pound will appreciate and the dollar will depreciate. Speculators who are holding dollars will therefore try to convert them into pounds. This effort will increase the demand for pounds and cause the dollar price of pounds to rise (that is, cause the dollar to depreciate). A self-fulfilling prophecy occurs: The pound appreciates and the dollar depreciates because speculators act on the belief that these changes will in fact take place. In this way, speculation can cause changes in exchange rates. (We discuss currency speculation in more detail in this chapter's Last Word.)

Table 38.2 has more illustrations of the determinants of exchange rates; the table is worth careful study.

Flexible Rates and the Balance of Payments

Flexible exchange rates have an important feature: They automatically adjust and eventually eliminate balance-of-payments deficits or surpluses. We can explain this idea through Figure 38.2, in which S_1 and D_1 are the supply and demand curves for pounds from Figure 38.1. The equilibrium exchange rate of $2 = £1 means that there is no balance-of-payments deficit or surplus between the United States and Britain. At that exchange rate, the quantity of pounds demanded by U.S. consumers to import British goods, buy British transportation and insurance services, and pay interest and dividends on British investments in the United States equals the amount of pounds supplied by the British in buying U.S. exports, purchasing services from the United States, and making interest and dividend payments on U.S. investments in Britain. The United States would have no need to either draw down or build up its official reserves to balance its payments.

Suppose tastes change and U.S. consumers buy more British automobiles; the U.S. inflation rate increases relative to Britain's; or interest rates fall in the United States compared to those in Britain. Any or all of these changes will increase the U.S. demand for British pounds, for example, from D_1 to D_2 in Figure 38.2.

If the exchange rate remains at the initial $2 = £1, a U.S. balance-of-payments deficit will occur in the amount of *ab*. At the $2 = £1 rate, U.S. consumers will demand the quantity of pounds shown by point *b*, but Britain will supply only the amount shown by *a*. There will be a shortage of pounds. But this shortage will not last because this is a

---

TABLE 38.2 Determinants of Exchange Rates: Factors That Change the Demand for or the Supply of a Particular Currency and Thus Alter the Exchange Rate

Determinant	Examples
Change in tastes	Japanese electronic equipment declines in popularity in the United States (Japanese yen depreciates; U.S. dollar appreciates).
	European tourists reduce visits to the United States (U.S. dollar depreciates; European euro appreciates).
Change in relative incomes	England encounters a recession, reducing its imports, while U.S. real output and real income surge, increasing U.S. imports (British pound appreciates; U.S. dollar depreciates).
Change in relative inflation rates	Switzerland experiences a 3% inflation rate compared to Canada's 10% rate (Swiss franc appreciates; Canadian dollar depreciates).
Change in relative real interest rates	The Federal Reserve drives up interest rates in the United States, while the Bank of England takes no such action (U.S. dollar appreciates; British pound depreciates).
Changes in relative expected returns on stocks, real estate, or production facilities	Corporate tax cuts in the United States raise expected after-tax investment returns in the United States relative to those in Europe (U.S. dollar appreciates; the euro depreciates).
Speculation	Currency traders believe South Korea will have much greater inflation than Taiwan (South Korean won depreciates; Taiwanese dollar appreciates).
	Currency traders think Norway's interest rates will plummet relative to Denmark's rates (Norway's krone depreciates; Denmark's krone appreciates).

FIGURE 38.2 **Adjustments under flexible exchange rates and fixed exchange rates.** Under flexible exchange rates, a shift in the demand for pounds from D_1 to D_2, other things equal, would cause a U.S. balance-of-payments deficit ab. That deficit would be corrected by a change in the exchange rate from $2 = £1 to $3 = £1. Under fixed exchange rates, the United States would cover the shortage of pounds ab by selling official reserves (here pounds), restricting trade, implementing exchange controls, or enacting a contractionary stabilization policy.

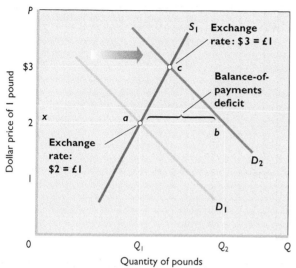

From Britain's standpoint, the exchange rate (the pound price of dollars) has fallen (from £$\frac{1}{2}$ to £$\frac{1}{3}$ for $1). The international value of the pound has appreciated. The British previously got only $2 for £1; now they get $3 for £1. U.S. goods are therefore cheaper to the British, and U.S. exports to Britain will rise.

The two adjustments—a decrease in U.S. imports from Britain and an increase in U.S. exports to Britain—are just what are needed in terms of Figure 38.2 to decrease the quantity of pounds demanded from b to c, increase the quantity of pounds supplied from a to c, and thus correct the U.S. balance-of-payments deficit. These changes end when, at point c, the quantities of British pounds demanded and supplied are equal.

Disadvantages of Flexible Exchange Rates

Even though flexible exchange rates automatically work to eliminate payment imbalances, they may cause several significant problems. These are all related to the fact that flexible exchange rates are often volatile and can change by a large amount in just a few weeks or months. In addition, they often take substantial swings that can last several years or more. This can be seen in Figure 38.3, which plots the dollar-pound exchange rate from 1970 through 2009. (You can track other exchange rates, for example, the dollar-euro or dollar-yen rate, by going to the Federal Reserve Web site, **www.federalreserve.gov**, selecting Economic Research & Data, Statistical Releases and Historical Data, and finally, Exchange Rates and International Data.)

Uncertainty and Diminished Trade The risks and uncertainties associated with flexible exchange rates may discourage the flow of trade. Suppose a U.S. automobile dealer contracts to purchase 10 British cars for £150,000. At the current exchange rate of, say, $2 for £1, the U.S. importer expects to pay $300,000 for these automobiles. But if during the 3-month delivery period the rate of exchange shifts to $3 for £1, the £150,000 payment contracted by the U.S. importer will be $450,000.

That increase in the dollar price of pounds may thus turn the U.S. importer's anticipated profit into a substantial loss. Aware of the possibility of an adverse change in the exchange rate, the U.S. importer may not be willing to assume the risks involved. The U.S. firm may confine its operations to domestic automobiles, so international trade in this product will not occur.

The same thing can happen with investments. Assume that when the exchange rate is $3 to £1, a U.S. firm invests $30,000 (or £10,000) in a British enterprise. It

competitive foreign exchange market. Instead, the dollar price of pounds will rise (the dollar will depreciate) until the balance-of-payments deficit is eliminated. That occurs at the new equilibrium exchange rate of $3 = £1, where the quantities of pounds demanded and supplied are again equal.

To explain why the increase in the dollar price of pounds—the dollar depreciation—eliminates the balance-of-payments deficit ab in Figure 38.2, we need to reemphasize that the exchange rate links all domestic (U.S.) prices with all foreign (British) prices. The dollar price of a foreign good is found by multiplying the foreign price by the exchange rate (in dollars per unit of the foreign currency). At an exchange rate of $2 = £1, a British automobile priced at £15,000 will cost a U.S. consumer $30,000 (= 15,000 × $2).

A change in the exchange rate alters the prices of all British goods to U.S. consumers and all U.S. goods to British buyers. The shift in the exchange rate (here from $2 = £1 to $3 = £1) changes the relative attractiveness of U.S. imports and exports and restores equilibrium in the U.S. (and British) balance of payments. From the U.S. view, as the dollar price of pounds changes from $2 to $3, the British auto priced at £15,000, which formerly cost a U.S. consumer $30,000, now costs $45,000 (= 15,000 × $3). Other British goods will also cost U.S. consumers more, so that U.S. imports of British goods will decline.

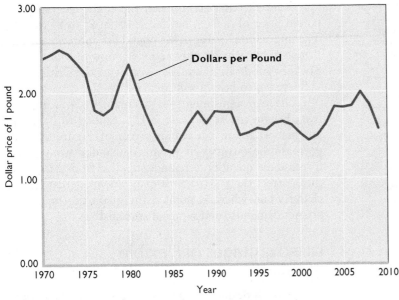

FIGURE 38.3 The dollar-pound exchange rate, 1970–2009. Before January 1971, the dollar-pound exchange rate was fixed at $2.40 = £1. Since that time, its value has been determined almost entirely by market forces, with only occasional government interventions. Under these mostly flexible conditions, the dollar-pound exchange rate has varied considerably. For instance, in 1981 it took $2.02 to buy a pound but by 1985 only $1.50 was needed to buy a pound. In contrast, between 2001 and 2007 the dollar price of a pound rose from $1.44 to $2.00, indicating that the dollar had depreciated relative to the pound. The dollar then sank back to $1.57 per British pound in 2009.

Source: Economic Report of the President, 2010, Table B-110. Earlier years from prior Economic Reports.

estimates a return of 10 percent; that is, it anticipates annual earnings of $3000 or £1000. Suppose these expectations prove correct in that the British firm earns £1000 in the first year on the £10,000 investment. But suppose that during the year, the value of the dollar appreciates to $2 = £1. The absolute return is now only $2000 (rather than $3000), and the rate of return falls from the anticipated 10 percent to only $6\frac{2}{3}$ percent (= $2000/$30,000). Investment is risky in any case. The added risk of changing exchange rates may persuade the U.S. investor not to venture overseas.[1]

Terms-of-Trade Changes A decline in the international value of its currency will worsen a nation's terms of trade. For example, an increase in the dollar price of a pound will mean that the United States must export more goods and services to finance a specific level of imports from Britain.

Instability Flexible exchange rates may destabilize the domestic economy because wide fluctuations stimulate and then depress industries producing exported goods. If the U.S. economy is operating at full employment and its currency depreciates, as in our illustration, the results will

be inflationary, for two reasons. (1) Foreign demand for U.S. goods may rise, increasing total spending and pulling up U.S. prices. Also, the prices of all U.S. imports will increase. (2) Conversely, appreciation of the dollar will lower U.S. exports and increase imports, possibly causing unemployment.

Flexible or floating exchange rates also may complicate the use of domestic stabilization policies in seeking full employment and price stability. This is especially true for nations whose exports and imports are large relative to their total domestic output.

Fixed Exchange Rates

To circumvent the disadvantages of flexible exchange rates, at times nations have fixed or "pegged" their exchange rates. For our analysis of fixed exchange rates, we assume that the United States and Britain agree to maintain a $2 = £1 exchange rate.

The problem is that such a government agreement cannot keep from changing the demand for and the supply of pounds. With the rate fixed, a shift in demand or supply will threaten the fixed-exchange-rate system, and government must intervene to ensure that the exchange rate is maintained.

In Figure 38.2, suppose the U.S. demand for pounds increases from D_1 to D_2 and a U.S. payment deficit *ab* arises. Now, the new equilibrium exchange rate ($3 = £1) is above the fixed exchange rate ($2 = £1). How can the

---

[1]You will see in this chapter's Last Word, however, that a trader can circumvent part of the risk of unfavorable exchange-rate fluctuations by "hedging" in the "futures market" or "forward market" for foreign exchange.

United States prevent the shortage of pounds from driving the exchange rate up to the new equilibrium level? How can it maintain the fixed exchange rate? The answer is by altering market demand or market supply or both so that they will intersect at the $2 = £1 rate. There are several ways to do this.

Use of Official Reserves

One way to maintain a fixed exchange rate is to engage in **currency interventions**. These are situations in which governments or their central banks manipulate an exchange rate through the use of official reserves. For instance, by selling some of its reserves of pounds, the U.S. government could increase the supply of pounds, shifting supply curve S_1 to the right so that it intersects D_2 at b in Figure 38.2, thereby maintaining the exchange rate at $2 = £1.

Notice that when the U.S. government sells some of its reserves of pounds, it is transferring assets to foreigners (since they gain ownership of the pounds). In terms of the balance-of-payments statement shown in Table 38.1, this transfer of assets enters positively on line (12), "Foreign purchases of assets in the United States." This positive entry is what offsets the balance-of-payments deficit caused by the fixed exchange rate and ensures that the U.S. balance of payments does in fact balance.

How do official reserves originate? Perhaps a balance-of-payments surplus occurred in the past. The U.S. government would have purchased that surplus. That is, at some earlier time, the U.S. government may have spent tax dollars to buy the surplus pounds that were threatening to reduce the exchange rate to below the $2 = £1 fixed rate. Those purchases would have bolstered the stock of U.S. official reserves of pounds.

Nations also have used gold as "international money" to obtain official reserves. In our example, the U.S. government could sell some of its gold to Britain to obtain pounds. It could then sell pounds for dollars. That would shift the supply-of-pounds curve to the right, and the $2 = £1 exchange rate could be maintained.

It is critical that the amount of reserves and gold be enough to accomplish the required increase in the supply of pounds. There is no problem if deficits and surpluses occur more or less randomly and are of similar size. Then, last year's balance-of-payments surplus with Britain will increase the U.S. reserve of pounds, and that reserve can be used to "finance" this year's deficit. But if the United States encounters persistent and sizable deficits for an extended period, it may exhaust its reserves, and thus be forced to abandon fixed exchange rates. Or, at the least, a nation whose reserves are inadequate must use less-appealing options to maintain exchange rates. Let's consider some of those options.

Trade Policies

To maintain fixed exchange rates, a nation can try to control the flow of trade and finance directly. The United States could try to maintain the $2 = £1 exchange rate in the face of a shortage of pounds by discouraging imports (thereby reducing the demand for pounds) and encouraging exports (thus increasing the supply of pounds). Imports could be reduced by means of new tariffs or import quotas; special taxes could be levied on the interest and dividends U.S. financial investors receive from foreign investments. Also, the U.S. government could subsidize certain U.S. exports to increase the supply of pounds.

The fundamental problem is that these policies reduce the volume of world trade and change its makeup from what is economically desirable. When nations impose tariffs, quotas, and the like, they lose some of the economic benefits of a free flow of world trade. That loss should not be underestimated: Trade barriers by one nation lead to retaliatory responses from other nations, multiplying the loss.

Exchange Controls and Rationing

Another option is to adopt exchange controls and rationing. Under **exchange controls** the U.S. government could handle the problem of a pound shortage by requiring that all pounds obtained by U.S. exporters be sold to the Federal government. Then the government would allocate or ration this short supply of pounds (represented by xa in Figure 38.2) among various U.S. importers, who demand the quantity xb. This policy would restrict the value of U.S. imports to the amount of foreign exchange earned by U.S. exports. Assuming balance in the capital and financial account, there would then be no balance-of-payments deficit. U.S. demand for British imports with the value ab would simply not be fulfilled.

There are major objections to exchange controls:

- **Distorted trade** Like *trade controls* (tariffs, quotas, and export subsidies), exchange controls would distort the pattern of international trade away from the pattern suggested by comparative advantage.

- **Favoritism** The process of rationing scarce foreign exchange might lead to government favoritism toward selected importers (big contributors to reelection campaigns, for example).

- *Restricted choice* Controls would limit freedom of consumer choice. The U.S. consumers who prefer Volkswagens might have to buy Chevrolets. The business opportunities for some U.S. importers might be impaired if the government were to limit imports.
- *Black markets* Enforcement problems are likely under exchange controls. U.S. importers might want foreign exchange badly enough to pay more than the $2 = £1 official rate, setting the stage for black-market dealings between importers and illegal sellers of foreign exchange.

Domestic Macroeconomic Adjustments

A final way to maintain a fixed exchange rate would be to use domestic stabilization policies (monetary policy and fiscal policy) to eliminate the shortage of foreign currency. Tax hikes, reductions in government spending, and a high-interest-rate policy would reduce total spending in the U.S. economy and, consequently, domestic income. Because the volume of imports varies directly with domestic income, demand for British goods, and therefore for pounds, would be restrained.

If these "contractionary" policies served to reduce the domestic price level relative to Britain's, U.S. buyers of consumer and capital goods would divert their demands from British goods to U.S. goods, reducing the demand for pounds. Moreover, the high-interest-rate policy would lift U.S. interest rates relative to those in Britain.

Lower prices on U.S. goods and higher U.S. interest rates would increase British imports of U.S. goods and would increase British financial investment in the United States. Both developments would increase the supply of pounds. The combination of a decrease in the demand for and an increase in the supply of pounds would reduce or eliminate the original U.S. balance-of-payments deficit. In Figure 38.2 the new supply and demand curves would intersect at some new equilibrium point on line *ab*, where the exchange rate remains at $2 = £1.

Maintaining fixed exchange rates by such means is hardly appealing. The "price" of exchange-rate stability for the United States would be a decline in output, employment, and price levels—in other words, a recession. Eliminating a balance-of-payments deficit and achieving domestic stability are both important national economic goals, but to sacrifice macroeconomic stability simply to balance international payments would be to let the tail wag the dog.

- In a system in which exchange rates are flexible (meaning that they are free to float), the rates are determined by the demand for and supply of individual national currencies in the foreign exchange market.
- Determinants of flexible exchange rates (factors that shift currency supply and demand curves) include changes in (a) tastes; (b) relative national incomes; (c) relative inflation rates; (d) real interest rates; (e) relative expected returns on stocks, real estate, and production facilities; and (f) speculation.
- Under a system of fixed exchange rates, nations set their exchange rates and then maintain them by buying or selling official reserves of currencies, establishing trade barriers, employing exchange controls, or incurring inflation or recession.

The Current Exchange Rate System: The Managed Float

Over the past 130 years, the world's nations have used three different exchange-rate systems. From 1879 to 1934, most nations used a gold standard, which implicitly created fixed exchange rates. From 1944 to 1971, most countries participated in the Bretton Woods system, which was a fixed-exchange-rate system indirectly tied to gold. And since 1971, most have used managed floating exchange rates, which mix mostly flexible exchange rates with occasional currency interventions. Naturally, our focus here is on the current exchange rate system. However, the history of the previous systems and why they broke down is highly fascinating. For that reason, we have included a discussion of these systems at the book's Web site (see Content Option for Instructors 2 [COI 2]).

The current international exchange-rate system (1971–present) is an "almost" flexible system called **managed floating exchange rates.** Exchange rates among major currencies are free to float to their equilibrium market levels, but nations occasionally use currency interventions in the foreign exchange market to stabilize or alter market exchange rates.

Normally, the major trading nations allow their exchange rates to float up or down to equilibrium levels based on supply and demand in the foreign exchange market. They recognize that changing economic conditions among nations require continuing changes in equilibrium exchange rates to avoid persistent payments deficits or surpluses. They rely on freely operating foreign exchange markets to accomplish the necessary adjustments. The result has been considerably more volatile exchange rates than those during the Bretton Woods era.

But nations also recognize that certain trends in the movement of equilibrium exchange rates may be at odds with national or international objectives. On occasion, nations therefore intervene in the foreign exchange market by buying or selling large amounts of specific currencies. This way, they can "manage" or stabilize exchange rates by influencing currency demand and supply.

The leaders of the *G8 nations* (Canada, France, Germany, Italy, Japan, Russia, United Kingdom, and United States) meet regularly to discuss economic issues and try to coordinate economic policies. At times they have collectively intervened to try to stabilize currencies. For example, in 2000 they sold dollars and bought euros in an effort to stabilize the falling value of the euro relative to the dollar. In the previous year the euro (€) had depreciated from €1 = \$1.17 to €1 = \$.87.

The current exchange-rate system is thus an "almost" flexible exchange-rate system. The "almost" refers mainly to the occasional currency interventions by governments; it also refers to the fact that the actual system is more complicated than described. While the major currencies such as dollars, euros, pounds, and yen fluctuate in response to changing supply and demand, some developing nations peg their currencies to the dollar and allow their currencies to fluctuate with it against other currencies. Also, some nations peg the value of their currencies to a "basket" or group of other currencies.

How well has the managed float worked? It has both proponents and critics.

In Support of the Managed Float Proponents of the managed-float system argue that it has functioned far better than many experts anticipated. Skeptics had predicted that fluctuating exchange rates would reduce world trade and finance. But in real terms world trade under the managed float has grown tremendously over the past several decades. Moreover, as supporters are quick to point out, currency crises such as those in Mexico and southeast Asia in the last half of the 1990s were not the result of the floating-exchange-rate system itself. Rather, the abrupt currency devaluations and depreciations resulted from internal problems in those nations, in conjunction with the nations' tendency to peg their currencies to the dollar or to a basket of currencies. In some cases, flexible exchange rates would have made these adjustments far more gradual.

Proponents also point out that the managed float has weathered severe economic turbulence that might have caused a fixed-rate system to break down. Such events as extraordinary oil price increases in 1973–1974 and again in 1981–1983, inflationary recessions in several nations in the mid-1970s, major national recessions in the early 1980s, and large U.S. budget deficits in the 1980s and the first half of the 1990s all caused substantial imbalances in international trade and finance, as did the large U.S. budget deficits and soaring world oil prices that occurred in the middle of the first decade of the 2000s. The U.S. financial crisis and the severe recession of 2007–2009 greatly disrupted world trade. Flexible rates enabled the system to adjust to all these events, whereas the same events would have put unbearable pressures on a fixed-rate system.

Concerns with the Managed Float There is still much sentiment in favor of greater exchange-rate stability. Those favoring more stable exchange rates see problems with the current system. They argue that the excessive volatility of exchange rates under the managed float threatens the prosperity of economies that rely heavily on exports. Several financial crises in individual nations (for example, Mexico, South Korea, Indonesia, Thailand, Russia, and Brazil) have resulted from abrupt changes in exchange rates. These crises have led to massive "bailouts" of those economies via loans from the International Monetary Fund (IMF). The IMF bailouts, in turn, may encourage nations to undertake risky and inappropriate economic policies since they know that, if need be, the IMF will come to the rescue. Moreover, some exchange-rate volatility has occurred even when underlying economic and financial conditions were relatively stable, suggesting that speculation plays too large a role in determining exchange rates.

Skeptics say the managed float is basically a "nonsystem" because the guidelines as to what each nation may or may not do with its exchange rates are not specific enough to keep the system working in the long run. Nations inevitably will be tempted to intervene in the foreign exchange market, not merely to smooth out short-term fluctuations in exchange rates but to prop up their currency if it is chronically weak or to manipulate the exchange rate to achieve domestic stabilization goals.

So what are we to conclude? Flexible exchange rates have not worked perfectly, but they have not failed miserably. Thus far they have survived, and no doubt have eased, several major shocks to the international trading system. Meanwhile, the "managed" part of the float has given nations some sense of control over their collective economic destinies. On balance, most economists favor continuation of the present system of "almost" flexible exchange rates.

Recent U.S. Trade Deficits

As shown in Figure 38.4a, the United States has experienced large and persistent trade deficits in recent years. These deficits rose rapidly between 2001 and 2006 before declining when consumers and businesses greatly curtailed their purchase of imports during the recession of 2007–2009. Even in 2009, however, the trade deficit on goods was still at $517 billion and the trade deficit on goods and services was $379 billion. The current account deficit (Figure 38.4b) reached a record high of $806 billion in 2006, and that amount was 6.0 percent of GDP. The current account deficit declined to $420 billion—2.9 percent of GDP—in the recession year 2009. Economists expect the trade deficits to expand, absolutely and relatively, toward prerecession levels when the economy recovers and U.S. income and imports again rise.

Causes of the Trade Deficits

The large U.S. trade deficits have several causes. First, the U.S. economy expanded more rapidly between 2001 and 2007 than the economies of several U.S. trading partners. The strong U.S. income growth that accompanied that economic growth enabled Americans to greatly increase their purchases of imported products. In contrast, Japan and some European nations suffered recession or experienced relatively slow income growth over that same period. So consumers in those countries increased their purchases of U.S. exports much less rapidly than Americans increased their purchases of foreign imports.

Another factor explaining the large trade deficits is the enormous U.S. trade imbalance with China. In 2007 the United States imported $257 billion more of goods and services than it exported to China. Even in the recession year 2009, the trade deficit with China was $220 billion.

FIGURE 38.4 U.S. trade deficits, 2001–2009. (a) The United States experienced large deficits in *goods* and in *goods and services* between 2001 and 2009. (b) The U.S. current account, generally reflecting the goods and services deficit, was also in substantial deficit. Although reduced significantly by the recession of 2007–2009, large trade deficits are expected to continue for many years to come.

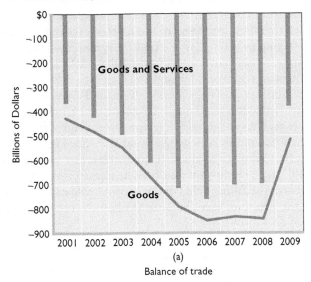

(a)
Balance of trade

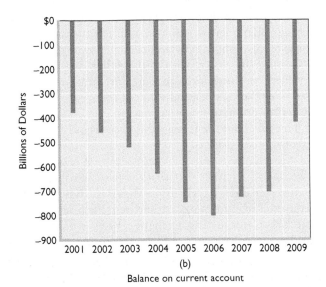

(b)
Balance on current account

Source: Bureau of Economic Analysis, **www.bea.gov**.

That deficit was double the combined deficits with Mexico ($43 billion), Germany ($37 billion), and Japan ($28 billion). The United States is China's largest export market, and although China has greatly increased its imports from the United States, its standard of living has not yet risen sufficiently for its households to afford large quantities of U.S. products. Adding to the problem, China's government has fixed the exchange rate of it currency, the yuan, to a basket of currencies that includes the U.S. dollar.

Therefore, China's large trade surpluses with the United States have not caused the yuan to appreciate much against the U.S. dollar. Greater appreciation of the yuan would have made Chinese goods more expensive in the United States and reduced U.S. imports from China. In China a stronger yuan would have reduced the dollar price of U.S. goods and increased Chinese purchases of U.S. exports. That combination—reduced U.S. imports from China and increased U.S. exports to China—would have reduced the large U.S. trade imbalance.

Another factor underlying the large U.S. trade deficits is a continuing trade deficit with oil-exporting nations. For example, in 2009 the United States had a $54 billion trade deficit with the OPEC countries.

A declining U.S. saving rate (= saving/total income) also contributed to the large U.S. trade deficits. Up until the recession of 2007–2009, the U.S. saving rate declined substantially, while its investment rate (= investment/total income) increased. The gap between U.S. investment and U.S. saving was filled by foreign purchases of U.S. real and financial assets, which created a large surplus on the U.S. capital and financial account. Because foreign savers were willing to finance a large part of U.S. investment, Americans were able to save less and consume more. Part of that added consumption spending was on imported goods.

Finally, many foreigners simply view U.S. assets favorably because of the relatively high risk-adjusted rates of return they provide. The purchase of those assets provides foreign currency to Americans that enables them to finance their strong appetite for imported goods. The capital account surpluses therefore may partially cause the high U.S. trade deficits, not just result from those high deficits. The point is that the causes of the high U.S. trade deficits are numerous and not so easy to disentangle.

Implications of U.S. Trade Deficits

The prerecession U.S. trade deficits were the largest ever run by a major industrial nation. Whether the large trade deficits should be of significant concern to the United States and the rest of the world is debatable. Most economists see both benefits and costs to trade deficits.

Increased Current Consumption At the time a trade deficit or a current account deficit is occurring, American consumers benefit. A trade deficit means that the United States is receiving more goods and services as imports from abroad than it is sending out as exports. Taken alone, a trade deficit allows the United States to consume outside its production possibilities curve. It augments the domestic standard of living. But here is a catch: The gain in present consumption may come at the expense of reduced future consumption. When and if the current account deficit declines, Americans may have to consume less than before and perhaps even less than they produce.

Increased U.S. Indebtedness A trade deficit is considered unfavorable because it must be financed by borrowing from the rest of the world, selling off assets, or dipping into official reserves. Recall that current account deficits are financed by surpluses in the capital and financial accounts. Such surpluses require net inpayments of dollars to buy U.S. assets, including debt issued by Americans. Therefore, when U.S. exports are insufficient to finance U.S. imports, the United States increases both its debt to people abroad and the value of foreign claims against assets in the United States. Financing of the U.S. trade deficit has resulted in a larger foreign accumulation of claims against U.S. financial and real assets than the U.S. claim against foreign assets. In 2008, foreigners owned about $3.5 trillion more of U.S. assets (corporations, land, stocks, bonds, loan notes) than U.S. citizens and institutions owned in foreign assets.

If the United States wants to regain ownership of these domestic assets, at some future time it will have to export more than it imports. At that time, domestic consumption will be lower because the United States will need to send more of its output abroad than it receives as imports. Therefore, the current consumption gains delivered by U.S. current account deficits may mean permanent debt, permanent foreign ownership, or large sacrifices of future consumption.

We say "may mean" above because the foreign lending to U.S. firms and foreign investment in the United States increases the U.S. capital stock. U.S. production capacity therefore might increase more rapidly than otherwise because of a large surplus on the capital and financial account. Faster increases in production capacity and real GDP enhance the economy's ability to service foreign debt and buy back real capital, if that is desired.

Trade deficits therefore are a mixed blessing. The long-term impacts of the record-high U.S. trade deficits are largely unknown. That "unknown" worries some economists, who are concerned that foreigners will lose financial confidence in the United States. If that happens, they would restrict their lending to American households and businesses and also reduce their purchases of U.S. assets. Both actions would decrease the demand for U.S. dollars in the foreign exchange market and cause the U.S. dollar to depreciate. A sudden, large depreciation of the U.S. dollar might disrupt world trade and negatively affect economic growth worldwide. Other economists, however, downplay this scenario. Because any decline in the U.S. capital and financial account surplus is automatically met with a decline in the current account deficit, U.S. net exports would rise and the overall impact on the American economy would be slight.

Are Speculators a Negative or a Positive Influence in Currency Markets and International Trade?

Most people buy foreign currency to facilitate the purchase of goods, services, or assets from another country. A U.S. importer buys Japanese yen to purchase Japanese autos. A Hong Kong financial investor purchases Australian dollars to invest in the Australian stock market. But there is another group of participants in the currency market—speculators—that buys and sells foreign currencies in the hope of reselling or rebuying them later at a profit.

Contributing to Exchange-Rate Fluctuations Speculators were much in the news in late 1997 and 1998 when they were widely accused of driving down the values of the South Korean won, Thai baht, Malaysian ringgit, and Indonesian rupiah. The value of these currencies fell by as much as 50 percent within one month, and speculators undoubtedly contributed to the swiftness of those declines. The expectation of currency depreciation (or appreciation) can be self-fulfilling. If speculators, for example, expect the Indonesian rupiah to be devalued or to depreciate, they quickly sell rupiah and buy currencies that they think will increase in relative value. The sharp increase in the supply of rupiah indeed reduces its value; this reduction then may trigger further selling of rupiah in expectation of further declines in its value.

But changed economic realities, not speculation, are normally the underlying causes of changes in currency values. That was largely the case with the southeast Asian countries in which actual and threatened bankruptcies in the financial and manufacturing sectors undermined confidence in the strength of the currencies. Anticipating the eventual declines in currency values, speculators simply hastened those declines. That is, the declines in value probably would have occurred with or without speculators.

Moreover, on a daily basis, speculation clearly has positive effects in foreign exchange markets.

Smoothing Out Short-Term Fluctuations in Currency Prices When temporarily weak demand or strong supply reduces a currency's value, speculators quickly buy the currency, adding to its demand and strengthening its value. When temporarily strong demand or weak supply increases a currency's value, speculators sell the currency. That selling increases the supply of the currency and reduces its value. In this way speculators smooth out supply and demand, and thus exchange rates, over short time periods. This day-to-day exchange-rate stabilization aids international trade.

Absorbing Risk Speculators also absorb risk that others do not want to bear. Because of potential adverse changes in exchange rates, international transactions are riskier than

Summary

1. International financial transactions involve trade either in currently produced goods and services or in preexisting assets. Exports of goods, services, and assets create inflows of money, while imports cause outflows of money. If buyers and sellers use different currencies, then foreign exchange transactions take place so that the exporter can be paid in his or her own currency.

2. The balance of payments records all international trade and financial transactions taking place between a given nation and the rest of the world. The balance on goods and services (the trade balance) compares exports and imports of both goods and services. The current account balance includes not only goods and services transactions but also net investment income and net transfers.

3. The capital and financial account includes (a) the net amount of the nation's debt forgiveness and (b) the nation's sale of real and financial assets to people living abroad less its purchases of real and financial assets from foreigners.

4. The current account and the capital and financial account always sum to zero. A deficit in the current account is always offset by a surplus in the capital and financial account. Conversely, a surplus in the current account is always offset by a deficit in the capital and financial account.

5. Official reserves are owned by national governments and their central banks and consist of stocks of foreign currencies, certain reserves held with the International Monetary Fund, and stocks of gold.

796

domestic transactions. Suppose AnyTime, a hypothetical retailer, signs a contract with a Swiss manufacturer to buy 10,000 Swatch watches to be delivered in three months. The stipulated price is 75 Swiss francs per watch, which in dollars is $50 per watch at the present exchange rate of, say, $1 = 1.5 francs. AnyTime's total bill for the 10,000 watches will be $500,000 (= 750,000 francs).

But if the Swiss franc were to appreciate, say, to $1 = 1 franc, the dollar price per watch would rise from $50 to $75 and Any-Time would owe $750,000 for the watches (= 750,000 francs). AnyTime may reduce the risk of such an unfavorable exchange-rate fluctuation by hedging in the futures market. Hedging is an action by a buyer or a seller to protect against a change in future prices. The futures market is a market in which currencies are bought and sold at prices fixed now, for delivery at a specified date in the future.

AnyTime can purchase the needed 750,000 francs at the current $1 = 1.5 francs exchange rate, but with delivery in three months when the Swiss watches are delivered. And here is where speculators come in. For a price determined in the futures market, they agree to deliver the 750,000 francs to AnyTime in three months at the $1 = 1.5 francs exchange rate, regardless of the exchange rate then. The speculators need not own francs when the agreement is made. If the Swiss franc depreciates to, say, $1 = 2 francs in this period, the speculators profit. They can buy the 750,000 francs stipulated in the contract for $375,000, pocketing the difference between that amount and the $500,000 Any Time has agreed to pay for the 750,000 francs. If the Swiss franc appreciates, the speculators, but not AnyTime, suffer a loss.

The amount AnyTime must pay for this "exchange-rate insurance" will depend on how the market views the likelihood of the franc depreciating, appreciating, or staying constant over the three-month period. As in all competitive markets, supply and demand determine the price of the futures contract.

The futures market thus eliminates much of the exchange-rate risk associated with buying foreign goods for future delivery. Without it, AnyTime might have decided against importing Swiss watches. But the futures market and currency speculators greatly increase the likelihood that the transaction will occur. Operating through the futures market, speculation promotes international trade.

In short, although speculators in currency markets occasionally contribute to swings in exchange rates, on a day-to-day basis they play a positive role in currency markets.

6. A balance-of-payments deficit is said to occur when a nation draws down its stock of official reserves to purchase dollars from abroad to balance the capital and financial account with the current account. A balance-of-payments surplus occurs when a nation adds to its stock of official reserves by selling dollars to foreigners to obtain foreign currencies to balance the two accounts. The desirability of a balance-of-payments deficit or surplus depends on its size and its persistence.

7. Flexible or floating exchange rates between international currencies are determined by the demand for and supply of those currencies. Under flexible rates, a currency will depreciate or appreciate as a result of changes in tastes, relative income changes, relative changes in inflation rates, relative changes in real interest rates, and speculation.

8. The maintenance of fixed exchange rates requires adequate official reserves to accommodate periodic payments deficits. If reserves are inadequate, nations must invoke protectionist trade policies, engage in exchange controls, or endure undesirable domestic macroeconomic adjustments.

9. Since 1971 the world's major nations have used a system of managed floating exchange rates. Market forces generally set rates, although governments intervene with varying frequency to alter their exchange rates.

10. Between 1997 and 2007, the United States had large and rising trade deficits, which are projected to last well into the future. Causes of the trade deficits include (a) more rapid income growth in the United States than in Japan and some European nations, resulting in expanding U.S. imports

relative to exports, (b) the emergence of a large trade deficit with China, (c) continuing large trade deficits with oil-exporting nations, and (d) a large surplus in the capital and financial account, which enabled Americans to reduce their saving and buy more imports. The severe recession of 2007–2009 in the United States substantially lowered the U.S. trade deficit by reducing American spending on imports.

11. U.S. trade deficits have produced current increases in the living standards of U.S. consumers. The accompanying surpluses on the capital and financial account have increased U.S. debt to the rest of the world and increased foreign ownership of assets in the United States. This greater foreign investment in the United States, however, has undoubtedly increased U.S. production possibilities.

Terms and Concepts

balance of payments

current account

balance on goods and services

trade deficit

trade surplus

balance on current account

capital and financial account

balance on capital and financial account

official reserves

balance-of-payments deficits and surpluses

flexible- or floating-exchange-rate system

fixed-exchange-rate system

purchasing-power-parity theory

currency interventions

exchange controls

managed floating exchange rates

Questions

1. Do all international financial transactions necessarily involve exchanging one nation's distinct currency for another? Explain. Could a nation that neither imports goods and services nor exports goods and services still engage in international financial transactions? LO1

2. Explain: "U.S. exports earn supplies of foreign currencies that Americans can use to finance imports." Indicate whether each of the following creates a demand for or a supply of European euros in foreign exchange markets: LO1
   a. A U.S. airline firm purchases several Airbus planes assembled in France.
   b. A German automobile firm decides to build an assembly plant in South Carolina.
   c. A U.S. college student decides to spend a year studying at the Sorbonne in Paris.
   d. An Italian manufacturer ships machinery from one Italian port to another on a Liberian freighter.
   e. The U.S. economy grows faster than the French economy.
   f. A U.S. government bond held by a Spanish citizen matures, and the loan amount is paid back to that person.
   g. It is widely expected that the euro will depreciate in the near future.

3. What do the plus signs and negative signs signify in the U.S. balance-of-payments statement? Which of the following items appear in the current account and which appear in the capital and financial account? U.S. purchases of assets abroad; U.S. services imports; foreign purchases of assets in the United States; U.S. good exports, U.S. net investment income. Why must the current account and the capital and financial account sum to zero? LO2

4. What are official reserves? How do net sales of official reserves to foreigners and net purchases of official reserves from foreigners relate to U.S. balance-of-payment deficits and surpluses? Explain why these deficits and surpluses are not actual deficits and surpluses in the *overall* balance-of-payments statement. LO2

5. Generally speaking, how is the dollar price of euros determined? Cite a factor that might increase the dollar price of euros. Cite a different factor that might decrease the dollar price of euros. Explain: "A rise in the dollar price of euros necessarily means a fall in the euro price of dollars." Illustrate and elaborate: "The dollar-euro exchange rate provides a direct link between the prices of goods and services produced in the Euro Zone and in the United States." Explain the purchasing-power-parity theory of exchange rates, using the euro-dollar exchange rate as an illustration. LO3

6. Suppose that a Swiss watchmaker imports watch components from Sweden and exports watches to the United States. Also suppose the dollar depreciates, and the Swedish krona appreciates, relative to the Swiss franc. Speculate as to how each would hurt the Swiss watchmaker. LO3

7. Explain why the U.S. demand for Mexican pesos is downsloping and the supply of pesos to Americans is upsloping. Assuming a system of flexible exchange rates between Mexico and the United States, indicate whether each of the following would cause the Mexican peso to appreciate or depreciate, other things equal: LO3
   a. The United States unilaterally reduces tariffs on Mexican products.
   b. Mexico encounters severe inflation.

c. Deteriorating political relations reduce American tourism in Mexico.

d. The U.S. economy moves into a severe recession.

e. The United States engages in a high-interest-rate monetary policy.

f. Mexican products become more fashionable to U.S. consumers.

g. The Mexican government encourages U.S. firms to invest in Mexican oil fields.

h. The rate of productivity growth in the United States diminishes sharply.

8. Explain why you agree or disagree with the following statements. Assume other things equal. LO3

   a. A country that grows faster than its major trading partners can expect the international value of its currency to depreciate.

   b. A nation whose interest rate is rising more rapidly than interest rates in other nations can expect the international value of its currency to appreciate.

   c. A country's currency will appreciate if its inflation rate is less than that of the rest of the world.

9. "Exports pay for imports. Yet in 2009 the nations of the world exported about $379 billion more of goods and services to the United States than they imported from the United States." Resolve the apparent inconsistency of these two statements. LO2

10. Diagram a market in which the equilibrium dollar price of 1 unit of fictitious currency zee (Z) is $5 (the exchange rate is $5 = Z1). Then show on your diagram a decline in the demand for zee. LO4

a. Referring to your diagram, discuss the adjustment options the United States would have in maintaining the exchange rate at $5 = Z1 under a fixed-exchange-rate system.

b. How would the U.S. balance-of-payments surplus that is caused by the decline in demand be resolved under a system of flexible exchange rates?

11. Suppose that a country follows a managed-float policy but that its exchange rate is currently floating freely. In addition, suppose that it has a massive current account deficit. Does it also necessarily have a balance-of-payments deficit? If it decides to engage in a currency intervention to reduce the size of its current account deficit, will it buy or sell its own currency? As it does so, will its official reserves of foreign currencies get larger or smaller? Would that outcome indicate a balance-of-payments deficit or a balance-of-payments surplus? LO4

12. What have been the major causes of the large U.S. trade deficits in recent years? What are the major benefits and costs associated with trade deficits? Explain: "A trade deficit means that a nation is receiving more goods and services from abroad than it is sending abroad." How can that be considered to be "unfavorable"? LO5

13. **LAST WORD** Suppose Super D'Hiver—a hypothetical French snowboard retailer—wants to order 5000 snowboards made in the United States. The price per board is $200, the present exchange rate is 1 euro = $1, and payment is due in dollars when the boards are delivered in 3 months. Use a numerical example to explain why exchange-rate risk might make the French retailer hesitant to place the order. How might speculators absorb some of Super D'Hiver's risk?

Problems

1. Alpha's balance-of-payments data for 2010 are shown below. All figures are in billions of dollars. What are the (a) balance on goods, (b) balance on goods and services, (c) balance on current account, and (d) balance on capital and financial account? Suppose Alpha sold $10 billion of official reserves abroad to balance the capital and financial account with the current account. Does Alpha have a balance-of-payments deficit or does it have a surplus? LO2

Goods exports	$+40
Goods imports	−30
Service exports	+15
Service imports	−10
Net investment income	−5
Net transfers	+10
Balance on capital account	0
Foreign purchases of Alpha assets	+20
Alpha purchases of assets abroad	−40

2. China had a $372 billion overall current account surplus in 2007. Assuming that China's net debt forgiveness was zero in 2007 (its capital account balance was zero), by how much did Chinese purchases of financial and real assets abroad exceed foreign purchases of Chinese financial and real assets? LO2

3. Refer to the following table, in which Q_d is the quantity of yen demanded, P is the dollar price of yen, Q_s is the quantity of yen supplied in year 1, and Q_s' is the quantity of yen supplied in year 2. All quantities are in billions and the dollar-yen exchange rate is fully flexible. LO3

Q_d	P	Q_s	Q_s'
10	125	30	20
15	120	25	15
20	115	20	10
25	110	15	5

a. What is the equilibrium dollar price of yen in year 1?
b. What is the equilibrium dollar price of yen in year 2?
c. Did the yen appreciate or did it depreciate relative to the dollar between years 1 and 2?
d. Did the dollar appreciate or did it depreciate relative to the yen between years 1 and 2?
e. Which one of the following could have caused the change in relative values of the dollar and yen between years 1 and 2: (1) More rapid inflation in the United States than in Japan, (2) an increase in the real interest rate in the United States but not in Japan, or (3) faster income growth in the United States than in Japan.

4. Suppose that the current Canadian dollar (CAD) to U.S. dollar exchange rate is $.85 CAD = $1 US and that the U.S. dollar price of an Apple iPhone is $300. What is the Canadian dollar price of an iPhone? Next, suppose that the CAD to U.S. dollar exchange rate moves to $.96 CAD = $1 US. What is the new Canadian dollar price of an iPhone? Other things equal, would you expect Canada to import more or fewer iPhones at the new exchange rate? LO3

5. Return to problem 3 and assume the exchange rate is fixed against the dollar at the equilibrium exchange rate that occurs in year 1. Also suppose that Japan and the United States are the only two countries in the world. In year 2, what quantity of yen would the Japanese government have to buy or sell to balance its capital and financial account with its current account? In what specific account would this purchase or sale show up in Japan's balance-of-payments statement: Foreign purchases of assets in Japan or Japanese purchase of assets abroad? Would this transaction increase Japan's stock of official reserves or decrease its stock? LO5

FURTHER TEST YOUR KNOWLEDGE AT
www.mcconnell19e.com

At the text's Online Learning Center (OLC), **www.mcconnell19e.com**, you will find one or more Web-based questions that require information from the Internet to answer. We urge you to check them out; they will familiarize you with Web sites that may be helpful in other courses and perhaps even in your career. The OLC also features multiple-choice questions that give instant feedback and provides other helpful ways to further test your knowledge of the chapter.

The Balance of Payments, Exchange Rates, and Trade Deficits

As you know from Chapter 37, nations buy and sell large quantities of goods and services across national boundaries. The residents of these nations also buy and sell such financial assets as stocks and bonds and such real assets as land and capital goods in other nations, and the governments and individuals in one nation make gifts (or give remittances) to other nations. In Chapter 38 you will learn *how* nations using different currencies are able to make these international financial transactions, the accounting system used to measure them, and what the accounts mean for a nation.

The market in which one currency is sold and is paid for with another currency is the **foreign exchange market.** When the residents of a nation (its consumers, business firms, or governments) buy products or real or financial assets from, make loans or give gifts to, or pay interest and dividends to the residents of other nations, they must *buy* some of the currency used in that nation and pay for it with some of their own currency. And when the residents of a nation sell products or real or financial assets to, receive loans or gifts from, or are paid dividends or interest by the residents of other nations, they *sell* this foreign currency in return for some of their own currency. The price paid (in one currency) for a unit of another currency is called the foreign exchange rate, and like most prices, it is determined by the demand for and the supply of that foreign currency.

At the end of a year, nations summarize their international financial transactions. This summary is called the nation's **balance of payments:** a record of how it obtained foreign currency during the year and what it did with this foreign currency. Of course, all foreign currency obtained was used for some purpose—it did not evaporate—consequently, the balance of payments *always* balances. The balance of payments is an extremely important and useful device for understanding the amounts and kinds of international transactions in which the residents of a nation engage. A balance-of-payments deficit occurs when the foreign currency receipts are less than foreign currency payments and the nation must reduce the **official reserves** of its central bank to balance its payments. Conversely, a balance-of-payments surplus occurs when foreign currency receipts are greater than foreign currency payments, and the nation must expand its official reserves to balance its payments.

How nations correct balance-of-payments deficits or surpluses or adjust trade imbalances often depends on the **exchange-rate systems** used. There are two basic types of such systems—flexible and fixed. In a flexible or floating system, exchange rates are set by the forces of the demand for and supply of a nation's currency relative to the currency of other nations. If the demand for a nation's currency increases, there will be an *appreciation* in its value relative to another currency, and if the demand of a nation's currency declines, there will be a *depreciation* in its value relative to another currency. Fixed-exchange-rate systems have been used by nations to peg or fix a specific amount of one nation's currency that must be exchanged for another nation's currency. Both types of systems have their advantages and disadvantages. Currently, the major trading nations of the world use a **managed float exchange-rate system** that corrects balance-of-payments deficits and surpluses.

The final section of the chapter examines the U.S. **trade deficits** that arise when the value of exports is less than the value of imports. As you will learn, these deficits are the result of several factors such as differences in national growth rates and a declining saving rate that have contributed to imports rising faster than exports. They also have several implications such as increased current consumption at the expense of future consumption and increased U.S. indebtedness to foreigners.

■ CHECKLIST

When you have studied this chapter you should be able to

☐ Describe examples of transactions in international trade and the role that money plays in them.
☐ Explain how money is used for the international buying and selling of real and financial assets.
☐ Give a definition of a nation's balance of payments.
☐ Use the items in the current account to calculate the balance on goods, balance on goods and services, and balance on the current account when given the data.
☐ Describe how balance is achieved in the capital and financial account.
☐ Explain the relationship between the current account and the capital and financial account.
☐ Use a supply and demand graph to illustrate how a flexible-exchange-rate system works to establish the price and quantity of a currency.
☐ Discuss the role of official reserves when there is a balance-of-payments deficit or balance-of-payments surplus.
☐ Describe the depreciation and appreciation of a nation's currency under a flexible-exchange-rate system.
☐ Identify the six principal determinants of the demand for and supply of a particular foreign currency and explain how they alter exchange rates.

461

☐ Explain how flexible exchange rates eventually eliminate balance-of-payments deficits or surpluses.

☐ Describe three disadvantages of flexible exchange rates.

☐ Use a supply and demand graph to illustrate how a fixed exchange-rate system functions.

☐ Explain how nations use official reserves to maintain a fixed exchange rate.

☐ Describe how trade policies can be used to maintain a fixed exchange rate.

☐ Discuss advantages and disadvantages of using exchange controls to maintain a fixed exchange rate.

☐ Explain what domestic macroeconomic adjustments are needed to maintain a fixed exchange rate.

☐ Identify three different exchange-rate systems used by the world's nations in recent years.

☐ Discuss the pros and cons of the system of managed floating exchange rates.

☐ Describe the causes of recent trade deficits in the United States.

☐ Explain the economic implications of recent trade deficits in the United States.

☐ Assess the role that speculators play in currency markets (*Last Word*).

■ **CHAPTER OUTLINE**

1. International financial transactions are used for two purposes. First, there is the international trade of goods and services, such as food or insurance, that people buy or sell for money. Second, there is the international exchange of financial assets, such as real estate, stocks, or bonds, that people also buy or sell with money. International trade between nations or the international exchange of assets differs from domestic trade or asset exchanges because the nations use different currencies. This problem is resolved by the existence of foreign exchange markets, in which the currency of one nation can be purchased and paid for with the currency of the other nation.

2. The **balance of payments** for a nation is a summary of all the financial transactions with foreign nations; it records all the money payments received from and made to foreign nations. Most of the payments in the balance of payments accounts are for exports or imports of goods and services or for the purchase or sale of real and financial assets. The accounts show the inflows of money to the United States and the outflows of money from the United States. For convenience, both the inflows and outflows are stated in terms of U.S. dollars so they can be easily and consistently measured.

  a. The **current account** section of a nation's balance of payments records the imports and exports of goods and services. Within this section
  (1) the *balance on goods* of the nation is equal to its exports of goods minus its imports of goods;
  (2) the *balance on services* of the nation is equal to its exports of services minus its imports of services;
  (3) the **balance on goods and services** is equal to its exports of goods and services minus its imports of goods and services; and

(4) the **balance on the current account** is equal to its balance on goods and services and two other "net" items (which can be positive or negative). First there is net investment income (such as dividends and interest), which is the difference in investment income received from other nations minus any investment income paid to foreigners. Second, there are net private and public transfers, which is the difference between such transfers to other nations minus any transfers from other nations. This balance on the current account may be positive, zero, or negative. In 2009, it was a negative $420 billion.

  b. International asset transactions are shown in the **capital and financial account** of a nation's balance of payments.
  (1) The *capital account* primarily measures debt forgiveness and is a "net" account. If Americans forgave more debt owed to them by foreigners than foreigners forgave debt owed to them by Americans, then the capital account would be entered as a negative (−).
  (2) The financial account shows foreign purchases of real and financial assets in the United States. This item brings a flow of money into the United States, so it is entered as a plus (+) in the capital account. U.S. purchases of real and financial assets abroad result in a flow of money from the United States to other nations, so this item is entered as a minus (−) in the capital account. The nation has a surplus in its financial account if foreign purchases of U.S. assets (and its inflow of money) are greater than U.S. purchases of assets abroad (and its outflow of money). The nation has a deficit in its financial account if foreign purchases of U.S. assets are less than U.S. purchases of assets abroad. The **balance on the capital and financial account** is the difference between the value of the capital account and the value of the financial account.

  c. The balance of payments must always sum to zero. For example, any deficit in the current account would be offset by a surplus in the capital and financial account. The reason that the account balances is that people trade current produced goods and services or preexisting assets. If a nation imports more goods and services than it exports, then the deficit in the current account (and outflow of money) must be offset by sales of real and financial assets to foreigners (and inflow of money).

  d. Sometimes economists and government officials refer to **balance-of-payments deficits or surpluses**. Whether a nation has a balance-of-payments deficit or surplus depends on what happens to its **official reserves**. These reserves are central bank holdings of foreign currencies, reserves at the International Monetary Fund, and stocks of gold.
  (1) A nation has a *balance-of-payments deficit* when an imbalance in the combined current account and capital and financial account leads to a decrease in official reserves. These official reserves are an inpayment to the capital and financial account.
  (2) A *balance-of-payments surplus* arises when an imbalance in the combined current account and capital and financial account results in an increase in official

reserves. These official reserves become an outpayment from the capital and financial account.

(3) Deficits in the balance-of-payments will happen over time and they are not necessarily bad. What is of concern, however, for any nation is whether the deficits are persistent over time because in that case they require that a nation continually draw down its official reserves. Such official reserves are limited and if they are depleted, a nation will have to adopt tough macroeconomic policies (discussed later in the chapter). In the case of the United States, there are ample official reserves and their depletion is not a major concern.

3. There are two basic types of exchange-rate systems that nations use to correct imbalances in the balance of payments. The first is a *flexible- or floating-exchange-rate system* that will be described in this section of the chapter outline. The second is a *fixed-exchange-rate system* that will be described in the next section of the chapter outline. If nations use a flexible- or floating-exchange-rate system, the demand for and the supply of foreign currencies determine foreign exchange rates. The exchange rate for any foreign currency is the rate at which the quantity of that currency demanded is equal to the quantity of it supplied.

   a. A change in the demand for or the supply of a foreign currency will cause a change in the exchange rate for that currency. When there is an increase in the price paid in dollars for a foreign currency, the dollar has *depreciated* and the foreign currency has *appreciated* in value. Conversely, when there is a decrease in the price paid in dollars for a foreign currency, the dollar has *appreciated* and the foreign currency has *depreciated* in value.

   b. Changes in the demand for or supply of a foreign currency are largely the result of changes in the *determinants of exchange rates* such as tastes, relative incomes, relative inflation rates, relative interest rates, expected returns, and speculation.

   (1) A change in tastes for foreign goods that leads to an increase in demand for those goods will increase the value of the foreign currency and decrease the value of the U.S. currency.

   (2) If the growth of U.S. national income is more rapid than other nations', then the value of U.S. currency will depreciate because it will expand its imports over its exports.

   (3) *Purchasing-power-parity theory* is the idea that exchange rates equate the purchasing power of various currencies. Exchange rates, however, often deviate from this parity. If the inflation rate rises sharply in the United States and it remains constant in another nation, then foreign currency of the other nation will appreciate in value and the U.S. currency will depreciate in value.

   (4) Changes in the relative interest rate in two nations may change their exchange rate. If real interest rates rise in the United States relative to another major trading partner, the U.S. dollar will appreciate in value because people will want to invest more money in the United States and the value of the other nation's currency will depreciate.

(5) Changes in the expected returns on stocks, real estate, and production facilities may change the exchange rate. If corporate tax rates are cut in the United States, then such a change would make investing in U.S. stock or production facilities more attractive relative to other nations, so foreigners may demand more U.S. dollars. The U.S. dollar will appreciate in value and the value of the foreigner's currency may depreciate.

(6) If speculators think the U.S. currency will depreciate, they can sell that currency and that act will help depreciate its value.

   c. Flexible exchange rates can be used to eliminate a balance-of-payments deficit or surplus.

   (1) When a nation has a payment deficit, foreign exchange rates will increase, thus making foreign goods and services more expensive and decreasing imports. These events will make a nation's goods and services less expensive for foreigners to buy, thus increasing exports.

   (2) With a payment surplus, the exchange rates will increase, thus making foreign goods and services less expensive and increasing imports. This situation makes a nation's goods and services more expensive for foreigners to buy, thus decreasing exports.

   d. Flexible exchange rates have three disadvantages.

   (1) Flexible rates can change often so they increase the uncertainties exporters, importers, and investors face when exchanging one nation's currency for another, thus reducing international trade and international purchase and sale of real and financial assets.

   (2) This system also changes the terms of trade. A depreciation of the U.S. dollar means that the United States must supply more dollars to the foreign exchange market to obtain the same amount of goods and services it previously obtained. Other nations will be able to purchase more U.S. goods or services because their currencies have appreciated relative to the dollar.

   (3) The changes in the value of imports and exports can change the demand for goods and services in export and import industries, thus creating more instability in industrial production and in implementing macroeconomic policy.

4. If nations use a *fixed-exchange-rate system,* the nations fix (or peg) a specific exchange rate (for example, $2 will buy one British pound). To maintain this fixed exchange rate, the governments of these nations must intervene in the foreign exchange markets to prevent shortages and surpluses of currencies caused by shifts in demand and supply.

   a. One way a nation can stabilize foreign exchange rates is through *currency interventions.* In this case, its government sells its reserves of a foreign currency in exchange for its own currency (or gold) when there is a shortage of the foreign currency. Conversely, a government would buy a foreign currency in exchange for its own currency (or gold) when there is a surplus of the foreign currency. The problem with this policy is that it only works when the currency needs are relatively minor and the intervention is of short duration. If there are persistent deficits, currency reserves may be inadequate for sustaining an intervention, so nations may need to use other means to maintain fixed exchange rates.

b. A nation might adopt trade policies that discourage imports and encourage exports. The problem with such policies is that they decrease the volume of international trade and make it less efficient, so that the economic benefits of free trade are diminished.

c. A nation might impose **exchange controls** so that all foreign currency is controlled by the government, and then rationed to individuals or businesses in the domestic economy who say they need it for international trade purposes. This policy too has several problems because it distorts trade, leads to government favoritism of specific individuals or businesses, restricts consumer choice of goods and services they can buy, and creates a black market in foreign currencies.

d. Another way a nation can stabilize foreign exchange rates is to use monetary and fiscal policy to reduce its national output and price level and raise its interest rates relative to those in other nations. These events would lead to a decrease in demand for and increase in the supply of different foreign currencies. But such macroeconomic policies would be harsh because they could lead to recession and deflation, and cause civil unrest.

5. In the past, some type of fixed-exchange-rate system was used such as the gold standard or the Bretton Woods system. The exchange-rate system used today is a more flexible one. Under the system of **managed floating exchange rates,** exchange rates are allowed to float in the long term to correct balance-of-payments deficits and surpluses, but if necessary there can be short-term interventions by governments to stabilize and manage currencies so they do not cause severe disruptions in international trade and finance. For example, the G8 nations (United States, United Kingdom, Canada, Germany, France, Japan, Russia, and Italy) regularly discuss economic issues and evaluate exchange rates, and at times have coordinated currency interventions to strengthen a nation's currency. This "almost" flexible system is favored by some and criticized by others.

a. Its proponents contend that this system has *not* led to any decrease in world trade, and has enabled the world to adjust to severe economic shocks throughout its history.

b. Its critics argue that it has resulted in volatile exchange rates that can hurt those developing nations that are dependent on exports, has *not* reduced balance-of-payments deficits and surpluses, and is a "nonsystem" that a nation may use to achieve its own domestic economic goals.

6. The United States had large and persistent **trade deficits** in the past decade and they are likely to continue.

a. Those trade deficits are the result of several factors:
(1) more rapid growth in the domestic economy than in the economies of several major trading partners, which caused imports to rise more than exports;
(2) the emergence of large trade deficits with China and the use of a relatively fixed exchange rate by the Chinese;

(3) a rapid rise in the price of oil that must be imported from oil-producing nations; and
(4) a decline in the rate of saving and a capital account surplus, which allowed U.S. citizens to consume more imported goods.

b. The trade deficits of the United States have had two principal effects.
(1) They increased current domestic consumption beyond what is being produced domestically, which allows the nation to operate outside its production possibilities frontier. This increased current consumption, however, may come at the expense of future consumption.
(2) They increased the indebtedness of U.S. citizens to foreigners. A negative implication of these persistent trade deficits is that they will lead to permanent debt and more foreign ownership of domestic assets, or lead to large sacrifices of future domestic consumption. But if the foreign lending increases the U.S. capital stock, then it can contribute to long-term U.S. economic growth. Thus, trade deficits may be a mixed blessing.

7. (*Last Word*). Speculators buy foreign currency in hopes of reselling it later at a profit. They also sell foreign currency in hopes of rebuying it later when it is cheaper. Although speculators are often accused of creating severe fluctuations in currency markets, that criticism is overstated because economic conditions rather than speculation are typically the chief source of the problem. One positive function of speculators is that they smooth out temporary fluctuations in the value of foreign currencies. Another positive role speculators play in currency markets is that they bear risks that others do not want by delivering the specified amount of foreign exchange at the contract price on the date of delivery.

■ **HINTS AND TIPS**

1. The chapter is filled with many new terms, some of which are just special words used in international economics to mean things with which you are already familiar. Other terms are entirely new to you, so you must spend time learning them if you are to understand the chapter.

2. The terms **depreciation** and **appreciation** can be confusing when applied to foreign exchange markets. First, know the related terms. "Depreciate" means decrease or fall, whereas "appreciate" means increase or rise. Second, think of depreciation or appreciation in terms of *quantities*: what decreases when the currency of Country A *depreciates* is the quantity of Country B's currency that can be purchased for 1 unit of Country A's currency; what increases when the currency of Country A *appreciates* is the quantity of Country B's currency that can be purchased for 1 unit of Country A's currency. Third, consider the effect of changes in *exchange rates:* when the exchange rate for Country B's currency increases, this means that Country A's currency has *depreciated* in value because 1 unit of Country A's currency will now purchase a smaller quantity of Country B's currency; when the exchange rate for Country B's currency decreases, this means that Country A's currency has *appreciated* in value because 1 unit of

Country A's currency will now purchase a larger quantity of Country B's currency.

3. The meaning of the balance of payments can also be confusing because of the number of accounts in the balance sheet. Remember that the balance of payments must always balance and sum to zero because the current account in the balance of payments can be in deficit, but it will be exactly offset by a surplus in the capital and financial account. When economists speak of a balance-of-payments deficit or surplus, however, they are referring to adding *official reserves* or subtracting *official reserves* from the capital and financial account so that it just equals the current account.

■ **IMPORTANT TERMS**

balance of payments

current account

balance on goods and services

balance on current account

capital and financial account

balance on the capital and financial account

balance-of-payments deficit

balance-of-payments surplus

official reserves

flexible- or floating- exchange-rate system

fixed-exchange-rate system

purchasing-power-parity theory

currency interventions

exchange controls

managed floating exchange rate

trade deficit

trade surplus

SELF-TEST

■ **FILL-IN QUESTIONS**

1. The rate of exchange for the European euro is the amount in (euros, dollars) _____ that a U.S. citizen must pay to obtain 1 (euro, dollar) _____. The rate of exchange for the U.S. dollar is the amount in (euros, dollars) _____ that a citizen in the euro zone must pay to obtain 1 (euro, dollar) _____. If the rate of exchange for the euro is (1.05 euros, $0.95) _____, the rate of exchange for the U.S. dollar is _____.

2. The balance of payments of a nation records all payments (domestic, foreign) _____ residents make to and receive from _____ residents. Any transaction that *earns* foreign exchange for that nation is a (debit, credit) _____, and any transaction that *uses up* foreign exchange is a _____. A debit is shown with a $(+, -)$ _____ sign, and a credit is shown with a _____ sign.

3. If a nation has a deficit in its balance of goods, its exports of goods are (greater, less) _____ than its imports of goods. If a nation has a surplus in its balance of services, its exports of services are (greater, less) _____ than its imports of services. If a nation has a deficit in its balance on goods and services, its exports of these items are (greater, less) _____ than its imports of them.

4. The current account is equal to the balance on goods and services (plus, minus) _____ net investment income and net transfers. When investment income received by U.S. individuals and businesses from foreigners is greater than investment income Americans pay to foreigners, then net investment income is a (negative, positive) _____ number; when transfer payments from the United States to other nations are greater than transfer payments from other nations to the United States, then net transfers are a _____ number.

5. The capital account is a net measure of (investment, debt forgiveness) _____. When Americans forgive more debt owed to them by foreigners than foreigners forgive debt owed to them by Americans, the capital account has a (debit, credit) _____ that reflects an outpayment of funds.

6. The financial account measures the flow of monetary payments from the sale or purchase of real or financial assets. Foreign purchases of real and financial assets in the United States earn foreign currencies, so they are entered as a (plus, minus) _____ in the financial account, but U.S. purchases of real and financial assets abroad draw down U.S. holding of foreign currencies, so this item is entered as a _____.

7. If foreign purchases of U.S. assets are greater than U.S. purchases of assets abroad, the nation has a (surplus, deficit) _____ in its financial account, but if foreign purchases of U.S. assets are less than U.S. purchases of assets abroad, it has a _____.

8. A nation may finance a current account deficit by (buying, selling) _____ real or financial assets and may use a current account surplus to (buy, sell) _____ real or financial assets.

9. The sum of the current account and the capital and financial accounts must equal (0, 1) _____ so the balance of payments always balances. When economists or government officials speak of a balance-of-payments deficit or surplus, however, they are referring to the use of official reserves, which are the quantities of (foreign currencies, its own money) _____ owned by a nation's central bank.

10. If a nation has a balance-of-payments deficit, then its official reserves (increase, decrease) _____ in the capital and financial account, but with a balance-of-payments surplus its official reserves _____ in the capital and financial account.

11. If foreign exchange rates float freely and a nation has a balance-of-payments *deficit,* that nation's currency in the foreign exchange markets will (appreciate, depreciate) _____ and foreign currencies will _____ compared to it. As a result of these changes in foreign exchange rates, the nation's imports will (increase, decrease) _____, its exports will _____, and the size of its deficit will (increase, decrease) _____.

12. What effect would each of the following have—the appreciation (**A**) or depreciation (**D**) of the euro compared to the U.S. dollar in the foreign exchange market, *ceteris paribus*?

  a. The increased preference in the United States for domestic wines over wines produced in Europe: ____

  b. A rise in the U.S. national income: ____

  c. An increase in the inflation rate in Europe: ____
  d. A rise in real interest rates in the United States:

                                  ____

  e. A large cut in corporate tax rates in Europe: ____
  f. The belief of speculators in Europe that the dollar will appreciate in the foreign exchange market: ____

13. There are three disadvantages of freely floating foreign exchange rates: the risks and uncertainties associated with flexible rates tend to (expand, diminish) _____ trade between nations; when a nation's currency depreciates, its terms of trade with other nations are (worsened, improved) _____; and fluctuating exports and imports can (stabilize, destabilize) _____ an economy.

14. To fix or peg the rate of exchange for the Mexican peso when the exchange rate for the peso is rising, the United States would (buy, sell) _____ pesos in exchange for dollars, and when the exchange rate for the peso is falling, the United States would _____ pesos in exchange for dollars.

15. Under a fixed-exchange-rate system, a nation with a balance-of-payments deficit might attempt to eliminate the deficit by (taxing, subsidizing) _____ imports or by _____ exports. The nation might use exchange controls and ration foreign exchange among those who wish to (export, import) _____ goods and services and require all those who _____

goods and services to sell the foreign exchange they earn to the (businesses, government) _____.

16. If the United States has a payments deficit with Japan and the exchange rate for the Japanese yen is rising, under a fixed-exchange-rate system the United States might adopt (expansionary, contractionary) _____ fiscal and monetary policies to reduce the demand for the yen, but this would bring about (inflation, recession) _____ in the United States.

17. The international monetary system has moved to a system of managed (fixed, floating) _____ exchange rates. This means that exchange rates of nations are (restricted from, free to) _____ find their equilibrium market levels, but nations may occasionally (leave, intervene in) _____ the foreign exchange markets to stabilize or alter market exchange rates.

18. The advantages of the current system are that the growth of trade (was, was not) _____ accommodated and that it has survived much economic (stability, turbulence) _____. Its disadvantages are its (equilibrium, volatility) _____ and the lack of guidelines for nations that make it a (bureaucracy, non-system) _____.

19. In recent years, the United States had large trade and current account (surpluses, deficits) _____. One cause of these deficits was (stronger, weaker) _____ economic growth in the United States relative to Europe and Japan. Other contributing factors were a (rise, fall) _____ in trade deficits with China, a _____ in the price of oil, and a _____ in the saving rate.

20. One effect of the recent trade deficits of the United States has been a(n) (decrease, increase) _____ in current domestic consumption that allows the nation to operate outside its production possibility frontier, but may lead to a(n) _____ in future consumption. Another effect was a (rise, fall) _____ in the indebtedness of U.S. citizens to foreigners.

■ **TRUE–FALSE QUESTIONS**

Circle T if the statement is true, F If it is false.

1. The two basic categories of international financial transactions are international trade and international assets.   **T F**

2. The balance of payments of the United States records all the payments its residents receive from and make to the residents of foreign nations.   **T F**

3. Exports are a debit item and are shown with a minus sign (−), and imports are a credit item and are shown with a plus sign (+) in the balance of payments of a nation. **T F**

4. The current account balance is a nation's export of goods and services minus its imports of goods and services. **T F**

5. The capital account will be a negative number when Americans forgive more debt owed to them by foreigners than the debt foreigners forgive that was owed to them by Americans. **T F**

6. The nation's current account balance and the capital and financial account in any year are always equal to zero. **T F**

7. When a nation must make an inpayment of official reserves to its capital and financial account to balance it with the current account, a balance-of-payments deficit has occurred. **T F**

8. The two "pure" types of exchange-rate systems are flexible (or floating) and fixed. **T F**

9. When the U.S. dollar price of a British pound rises, the dollar has depreciated relative to the pound. **T F**

10. If the supply of a nation's currency increases, that currency will appreciate in value. **T F**

11. The purchasing-power-parity theory basically explains why there is an inverse relationship between the price of dollars and the quantity demanded. **T F**

12. If income growth is robust in Europe, but sluggish in the United States, then the U.S. dollar will appreciate. **T F**

13. If the expected returns on stocks, real estate, or production facilities increased in the United States relative to Japan, the U.S. dollar would depreciate in value relative to the Japanese yen. **T F**

14. The expectations of speculators in the United States that the exchange rate for Japanese yen will fall in the future will increase the supply of yen in the foreign exchange market and decrease the exchange rate for the yen. **T F**

15. If a nation has a balance-of-payments deficit and exchange rates are flexible, the price of that nation's currency in the foreign exchange markets will fall; this will reduce its imports and increase its exports. **T F**

16. Were the United States' terms of trade with Nigeria to worsen, Nigeria would obtain a greater quantity of U.S. goods and services for every barrel of oil it exported to the United States. **T F**

17. If a nation wishes to fix (or peg) the foreign exchange rate for the Swiss franc, it must buy Swiss francs with its own currency when the rate of exchange for the Swiss franc rises. **T F**

18. If exchange rates are stable or fixed and a nation has a balance-of- payments surplus, prices and currency incomes in that nation will tend to rise. **T F**

19. A nation using exchange controls to eliminate a balance-of-payments surplus might depreciate its currency. **T F**

20. Using the managed floating system of exchange rates, a nation with a persistent balance-of-payments surplus should allow the value of its currency in foreign exchange markets to decrease. **T F**

21. Two criticisms of the current managed floating-exchange-rate system are its potential for volatility and its lack of clear policy rules or guidelines for nations to manage exchange rates. **T F**

22. The trade deficits of the United States in recent years were caused by sharp increases in U.S. exports and slight increases in U.S. imports. **T F**

23. Improved economic growth in the economies of the major trading partners of the United States would tend to worsen the trade deficit. **T F**

24. The decline in the saving rate in the United States contributed to the persistent trade deficit of the past decade. **T F**

25. The negative net exports of the United States have increased the indebtedness of U.S. citizens to foreigners. **T F**

■ **MULTIPLE-CHOICE QUESTIONS**

Circle the letter that corresponds to the best answer.

1. If a U.S. citizen could buy £25,000 for $100,000, the rate of exchange for the pound would be
  (a) $40
  (b) $25
  (c) $4
  (d) $.25

2. U.S. residents demand foreign currencies to
  (a) produce goods and services exported to foreign countries
  (b) pay for goods and services imported from foreign countries
  (c) receive interest payments on investments in the United States
  (d) have foreigners make real and financial investments in the United States

3. Which of the following would be a credit in the current account?
  (a) U.S. imports of goods
  (b) U.S. exports of services
  (c) U.S. purchases of assets abroad
  (d) U.S. interest payments for foreign capital invested in the United States

4. A nation's balance on the current account is equal to its exports less its imports of
  (a) goods and services
  (b) goods and services, plus U.S. purchases of assets abroad
  (c) goods and services, plus net investment income and net transfers
  (d) goods and services, minus foreign purchases of assets in the United States

5. The net investment income of the United States in its international balance of payments is the
(a) interest income it receives from foreign residents
(b) value of dividends it receives from foreign residents
(c) excess of interest and dividends it receives from foreign residents over what it paid to them
(d) excess of public and private transfer payments it receives from foreign residents over what it paid to them

Answer Questions 6, 7, and 8 using the following table that contains data for the United States' balance of payments in a prior year. All figures are in billions of dollars.

(1)	U.S. goods exports	$+1149
(2)	U.S. goods imports	−1965
(3)	U.S. service exports	+479
(4)	U.S. service imports	−372
(5)	Net investment income	+74
(6)	Net transfers	−104
(7)	Balance on capital account	−2
(8)	Foreign purchases of U.S. assets	+1905
(9)	U.S. purchases of foreign assets	−1164

6. The balance on goods and services was a deficit of
(a) $107 billion
(b) $709 billion
(c) $816 billion
(d) $935 billion

7. The balance on the current account was a
(a) surplus of $739 billion
(b) deficit of $739 billion
(c) surplus of $816 billion
(d) deficit of $816 billion

8. The balance on the financial account was a
(a) deficit of $372 billion
(b) surplus of $479 billion
(c) deficit of $739 billion
(d) surplus of $741 billion

9. In a flexible- or floating-exchange-rate system, when the U.S. dollar price of a British pound rises, this means that the dollar has
(a) appreciated relative to the pound and the pound has appreciated relative to the dollar
(b) appreciated relative to the pound and the pound has depreciated relative to the dollar
(c) depreciated relative to the pound and the pound has appreciated relative to the dollar
(d) depreciated relative to the pound and the pound has depreciated relative to the dollar

10. Which statement is correct about a factor that causes a nation's currency to appreciate or depreciate in value?
(a) If the supply of a nation's currency decreases, all else equal, that currency will depreciate.
(b) If the supply of a nation's currency increases, all else equal, that currency will depreciate.
(c) If the demand for a nation's currency increases, all else equal, that currency will depreciate.
(d) If the demand for a nation's currency decreases, all else equal, that currency will appreciate.

11. Assuming exchange rates are flexible, which of the following should increase the dollar price of the Swedish krona?
(a) a rate of inflation greater in Sweden than in the United States
(b) real interest rate increases greater in Sweden than in the United States
(c) national income increases greater in Sweden than in the United States
(d) the increased preference of Swedish citizens for U.S. automobiles over Swedish automobiles

12. Under a flexible-exchange-rate system, a nation may be able to correct or eliminate a persistent (long-term) balance-of-payments deficit by
(a) lowering the barriers on imported goods
(b) reducing the international value of its currency
(c) expanding its national income
(d) reducing its official reserves

13. If a nation had a balance-of-payments surplus and exchange rates floated freely, the foreign exchange rate for its currency would
(a) rise, its exports would increase, and its imports would decrease
(b) rise, its exports would decrease, and its imports would increase
(c) fall, its exports would increase, and its imports would decrease
(d) fall, its exports would decrease, and its imports would increase

Answer Questions 14, 15, and 16 using the graph below.

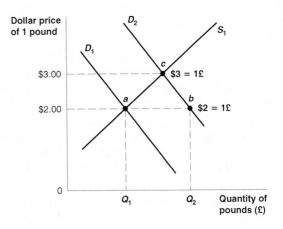

14. If D_1 moves to D_2, the U.S. dollar has
(a) appreciated, and the British pound has depreciated
(b) appreciated, and the British pound has appreciated
(c) depreciated, and the British pound has depreciated
(d) depreciated, and the British pound has appreciated

15. If D_1 moves to D_2, there will be a balance-of-payments
(a) deficit of Q_1
(b) surplus of Q_2
(c) deficit of Q_2 minus Q_1
(d) surplus of Q_2 minus Q_1

16. If **D₁** moves to **D₂**, but the British government seeks to keep the exchange rate at $2 = 1£, then it can do so through policies that

(a) increase the supply of pounds and decrease the demand for pounds

(b) decrease the supply of pounds and increase the demand for pounds

(c) increase the supply of pounds and increase the demand for pounds

(d) decrease the supply of pounds and decrease the demand for pounds

17. Which would be a result associated with the use of freely floating foreign exchange rates to correct a nation's balance-of-payments surplus?

(a) The nation's terms of trade with other nations would be worsened.

(b) Importers in the nation who had made contracts for the future delivery of goods would find that they had to pay a higher price than expected for the goods.

(c) If the nation were at full employment, the decrease in exports and the increase in imports would be inflationary.

(d) Exporters in the nation would find their sales abroad had decreased.

18. The use of exchange controls to eliminate a nation's balance-of-payments deficit results in decreasing the nation's

(a) imports

(b) exports

(c) price level

(d) income

19. Assume a nation has a balance-of-payments deficit and it seeks to maintain a fixed exchange rate. To eliminate the shortage of foreign currency, it may have to adopt monetary policies that

(a) lower the interest rate

(b) raise the interest rate

(c) reduce the tax rate

(d) increase the tax rate

20. A system of managed floating exchange rates

(a) allows nations to stabilize exchange rates in the short term

(b) requires nations to stabilize exchange rates in the long term

(c) entails stable exchange rates in both the short and long term

(d) fixes exchange rates at market levels

21. Floating exchange rates

(a) tend to correct balance-of-payments imbalances

(b) reduce the uncertainties and risks associated with international trade

(c) increase the world's need for international monetary reserves

(d) tend to have no effect on the volume of trade

22. The trade problem that faced the United States in recent years was a

(a) deficit in its capital account

(b) surplus in its balance on goods

(c) deficit in its current account

(d) surplus in its current account

23. Which was a cause of the growth of U.S. trade deficits in recent years?

(a) protective tariffs imposed by the United States

(b) slower economic growth in the United States

(c) direct foreign investment in the United States

(d) a declining saving rate in the United States

24. What would be the effect on U.S. imports and exports when the United States experiences strong economic growth but its major trading partners experience sluggish economic growth?

(a) U.S. imports will increase more than U.S. exports

(b) U.S. exports will increase more than U.S. imports

(c) U.S. imports will decrease but U.S. exports will increase

(d) there will be no effect on U.S. imports and exports

25. Two major outcomes from the trade deficits of recent years were

(a) decreased domestic consumption and U.S. indebtedness

(b) increased domestic consumption and U.S. indebtedness

(c) increased domestic consumption but decreased U.S. indebtedness

(d) decreased domestic consumption but increased U.S. indebtedness

■ PROBLEMS

1. Assume a U.S. exporter sells $3 million worth of wheat to an importer in Colombia. If the rate of exchange for the Colombian peso is $.02 (2 cents), the wheat has a total value of 150 million pesos. There are two ways the importer in Colombia may pay for the wheat.

a. It might write a check for 150 million pesos drawn on its bank in Bogotá and send it to the U.S. exporter. The U.S. exporter would then send the check to its bank in New Orleans and its checking account there would increase by $_____ million. The New Orleans bank would then arrange to have the check converted to U.S. dollars through a correspondent bank (a U.S. commercial bank that keeps an account in the Bogotá bank).

b. The second way for the importer to pay for the wheat is to buy from its bank in Bogotá a draft on a U.S. bank for $3 million, pay for this draft by writing a check for 150 million pesos drawn on the Bogotá bank, and send the draft to the U.S. exporter. The U.S. exporter would then deposit the draft in its account in the New Orleans bank and its checking account there would increase by $_____ million. The New Orleans bank would then collect the amount of the draft from the U.S. bank on which it is drawn through the Federal Reserve Banks.

2. The following table contains hypothetical balance-of-payments data for the United States. All figures are in billions. Compute with the appropriate sign (+ or −) and enter in the table the six missing items.

Current account		
(1)	U.S. goods exports	$+150
(2)	U.S. goods imports	−200
(3)	*Balance on goods*	___
(4)	U.S. exports of services	+75
(5)	U.S. imports of services	−60
(6)	*Balance on services*	___
(7)	*Balance on goods and services*	___
(8)	Net investment income	+12
(9)	Net transfers	−7
(10)	**Balance on current account**	___

Capital Account and Financial Account		
(11)	Capital Account	−5

Financial Account:		
(12)	Foreign purchases of assets in the U.S.	+90
(13)	U.S. purchases of assets abroad	−55
(14)	*Balance on financial account*	___
(15)	**Balance on capital and financial account**	___
		$ 0

3. The following table shows supply and demand schedules for the British pound.

Quantity of pounds supplied	Price	Quantity of pounds demanded
400	$5.00	100
360	4.50	200
300	4.00	300
286	3.50	400
267	3.00	500
240	2.50	620
200	2.00	788

a. If the exchange rates are flexible
(1) what will be the rate of exchange for the pound?

$_____
(2) what will be the rate of exchange for the dollar?

£_____
(3) how many pounds will be purchased in the market?

_____
(4) how many dollars will be purchased in the market?

_____
b. If the U.S. government wished to fix or peg the price of the pound at $5.00, it would have to (buy, sell)

_____ (how many) _____ pounds for $_____.
c. And if the British government wished to fix the price of the dollar at £ 2/5, it would have to (buy, sell)

_____ (how many) _____ pounds for $_____.

■ SHORT ANSWER AND ESSAY QUESTIONS

1. Explain the two basic types of international transactions and give an example of each one.

2. What is meant when it is said that "A nation's exports pay for its imports"? Do nations pay for all their imports with exports? Explain.

3. What is a balance of payments? What are the principal sections in a nation's balance-of-payments, and what are the principal "balances" to be found in it?

4. How can a nation finance a current account deficit? Explain the relationship between the current account and the capital and financial account.

5. Why do the balance-of-payments balance? Explain.

6. What is a balance-of-payments deficit, and what is a balance-of-payments surplus? What role do official reserves play in the matter?

7. Is a balance-of-payments deficit bad or a balance-of-payments surplus good? Explain.

8. Use a supply and demand graph to help describe how exchange rates for a currency appreciate and depreciate.

9. What types of events cause the exchange rate for a foreign currency to appreciate or to depreciate? How will each event affect the exchange rate for a foreign currency and for a nation's own currency?

10. How can flexible foreign exchange rates eliminate balance-of-payments deficits and surpluses?

11. What are the problems associated with flexible-exchange-rate systems for correcting payments imbalances?

12. How may a nation use its international monetary reserves to fix or peg foreign exchange rates? Be precise. How does a nation obtain or acquire these monetary reserves?

13. What kinds of trade policies may nations with payments deficits use to eliminate their deficits?

14. How can foreign exchange controls be used to restore international equilibrium? Why do such exchange controls necessarily involve the rationing of foreign exchange? What effect do these controls have on prices, output, and employment in nations that use them?

15. If foreign exchange rates are fixed, what kind of domestic macroeconomic adjustments are required to eliminate a payments deficit? To eliminate a payments surplus?

16. Explain what is meant by a managed floating system of foreign exchange rates.

17. When are exchange rates managed and when are they allowed to float? What organization is often responsible for currency interventions?

18. Explain the arguments of the proponents and the critics of the managed floating system.

19. What were the causes of the trade deficits of the United States in recent years?

20. What were the effects of the trade deficits of recent years on the U.S. economy?

ANSWERS

Chapter 38 The Balance of Payments, Exchange Rates, and Trade Deficits

FILL-IN QUESTIONS

1. dollars, euro, euros, dollar, $0.95, 1.05 euros
2. domestic, foreign, credit, debit, −, +
3. less, greater, less
4. plus, positive, negative
5. debt forgiveness, debit
6. plus, minus
7. surplus, deficit
8. selling, buy
9. 0, foreign currencies
10. decrease, increase
11. depreciate, appreciate, decrease, increase, decrease
12. *a.* D; *b.* A; *c.* D; *d.* D; *e.* A; *f.* D
13. diminish, worsened, destabilize
14. sell, buy
15. taxing, subsidizing, import, export, government
16. contractionary, recession
17. floating, free to, intervene in
18. was, turbulence, volatility, nonsystem
19. deficits, stronger, rise, rise, fall
20. increase, decrease, rise

TRUE–FALSE QUESTIONS

1. T, p. 781
2. T, p. 782
3. F, p. 782
4. F, pp. 782–783
5. T, p. 783
6. T, p. 784
7. T, pp. 784–785
8. T, p. 785
9. T, pp. 785–786
10. F, pp. 785–786
11. F, p. 787
12. T, p. 787
13. F, p. 787–788
14. T, p. 788
15. T, pp. 788–789
16. T, p. 790
17. F, p. 790–791
18. T, p. 791
19. F, pp. 791–792
20. F, pp. 792–793
21. T, p. 793
22. F, pp. 794–795
23. F, pp. 794–795
24. T, p. 795
25. T, p. 795

MULTIPLE-CHOICE QUESTIONS

1. c, p. 781
2. b, p. 781
3. b, p. 782
4. c, pp. 782–783
5. c, p. 783
6. b, pp. 782–783
7. b, pp. 782–783
8. d, pp. 783–784
9. c, pp. 785–786
10. b, pp. 785–786
11. b, p. 787
12. b, pp. 788–789
13. b, pp. 788–789
14. d, pp. 788–789
15. c, pp. 788–789
16. a, pp. 790–791
17. d, pp. 789–790
18. a, pp. 791–792
19. b, pp. 792
20. a, pp. 792–793
21. a, pp. 792–793
22. c, p. 794
23. d, pp. 794–795
24. a, pp. 794–795
25. b, p. 795

PROBLEMS

1. *a.* 3; *b.* 3
2. −50, +15, −35, −30, +35, +30
3. *a.* (1) 4.00, (2) 1/4, (3) 300, (4) 1200; *b.* buy, 300, 1500; *c.* sell, 380, 950

SHORT ANSWER AND ESSAY QUESTIONS

1. p. 781
2. p. 781
3. pp. 781–784
4. pp. 782–784
5. p. 784
6. pp. 784–785
7. pp. 784–785
8. pp. 785–786
9. pp. 787–788
10. pp. 788–789
11. pp. 789–790
12. pp. 790–791
13. p. 791
14. pp. 791–792
15. p. 792
16. p. 792
17. pp. 792–793
18. p. 793
19. p. 794–795
20. p. 795

AFTER READING THIS CHAPTER, YOU SHOULD BE ABLE TO:

1 Describe how the World Bank distinguishes between industrially advanced countries (high-income nations) and developing countries (middle-income and low-income nations).

2 List some of the obstacles to economic development.

3 Explain the vicious circle of poverty that afflicts low-income nations.

4 Discuss the role of government in promoting economic development within low-income nations.

5 Describe how industrial nations attempt to aid low-income countries.

The Economics of Developing Countries

It is difficult for those of us in the United States, where per capita GDP in 2009 was about $48,000, to grasp the fact that about 2.5 billion people, or nearly half the world's population, live on $2 or less a day. And about 1.4 billion live on less than $1.25 a day. Hunger, squalor, and disease are the norm in many nations of the world.

In this bonus Web chapter we identify the developing countries, discuss their characteristics, and explore the obstacles that have impeded their growth. We also examine the appropriate roles of the private sector and government in economic development. Finally, we look at policies that might help developing countries increase their growth rates.

The Rich and the Poor

Just as there is considerable income inequality among families within a nation, so too is there great income inequality among the family of nations. According to the United Nations, the richest 20 percent of the world's population receive more than 80 percent of the world's income; the poorest 20 percent receive less than 2 percent. The poorest 60 percent receive less than 6 percent of the world's income.

Classifications

The World Bank classifies countries into high-income, medium-income, and low-income countries on the basis of national income per capita, as shown in Figure 39W.1. The *high-income nations*, shown in gold, are known as the **industrially advanced countries (IACs);** they include the United States, Japan, Canada, Australia, New Zealand, and most of the nations of western Europe. In general, these nations have well-developed market economies based on large stocks of capital goods, advanced production technologies, and well-educated workers. In 2008 this group of economies had a per capita income of $37,665.

The remaining nations of the world are called **developing countries (DVCs).** They have wide variations of income per capita and are mainly located in Africa, Asia, and Latin America. The DVCs are a highly diverse group that can be subdivided into two groups:

- The *middle-income nations*, shown in green in Figure 39W.1, include such countries as Brazil, Iran, Poland, Russia, South Africa, and Thailand. Per capita output of these middle-income nations ranged all the way from $925 to $11,906 in 2008 and averaged $3251.
- The *low-income nations*, shown in purple, had a per capita income of $925 or less in 2008 and averaged only $523 of income per person. The sub-Saharan nations of Africa dominate this group. Low-income DVCs have relatively low levels of industrialization. In general, literacy rates are low, unemployment is high, population growth is rapid, and exports consist largely of agricultural produce (such as cocoa, bananas, sugar, raw cotton) and raw materials (such as copper, iron ore, natural rubber). Capital equipment is minimal, production technologies are simple, and labor productivity is very low. About 15 percent of the world's population live in these low-income DVCs, all of which suffer widespread poverty.

Comparisons

Several comparisons will bring the differences in world income into sharper focus:

- In 2008 U.S. GDP was $14.6 trillion; the combined GDPs of the 144 DVCs in that year added up to $15.6 trillion.
- The United States, with only 4.5 percent of the world's population in 2008, produces 25.1 percent of the world's output.
- Per capita GDP of the United States in 2008 was 150 times greater than per capita GDP in Sierra Leone, one of the world's poorest nations.
- The annual sales of the world's largest corporations exceed the national incomes of many of the DVCs. Walmart's annual world revenues of $379 billion in 2008 were greater than the national incomes of all but 23 nations.

Growth, Decline, and Income Gaps

Two other points relating to the nations shown in Figure 39W.1 should be noted. First, the various nations have demonstrated considerable differences in their ability to improve circumstances over time. On the one hand, DVCs such as Chile, China, India, Malaysia, and Thailand achieved high annual growth rates in their GDPs in recent decades. Consequently, their real output per capita increased severalfold. Several former DVCs, such as Singapore, Greece, and Hong Kong (now part of China), have achieved IAC status. In contrast, a number of DVCs in sub-Saharan Africa have recently been experiencing stagnant or even declining per capita GDPs.

Second, the absolute income gap between rich and poor nations has been widening. Suppose the per capita incomes of the advanced and developing countries were growing at about 2 percent per year. Because the income base in the advanced countries is initially much higher, the absolute income gap grows. If per capita income is $400 a year in a DVC, a 2 percent growth rate means an $8 increase in income. Where per capita income is $20,000 per year in an IAC, the same 2 percent growth rate translates into a $400 increase in income. Thus the absolute income gap will have increased from $19,600 (= $20,000 − $400) to $19,992 (= $20,400 − $408). The DVCs must grow faster than the IACs for the gap to be narrowed.

A quick glance back at Figure 25.1 in our chapter on economic growth will confirm the "great divergence" in standards of living that has emerged between the United States, Western Europe, and Japan relative to Africa, Latin America, and Asia (excluding Japan).

FIGURE 39W.1 **Groups of economies.** The world's nations are grouped into industrially advanced countries (IACs) and developing countries (DVCs). The IACs (shown in gold) are high-income countries. The DVCs are middle-income and low-income countries (shown respectively in green and in purple).

☐ Low-income economies ☐ Middle-income economies ☐ High-income economies

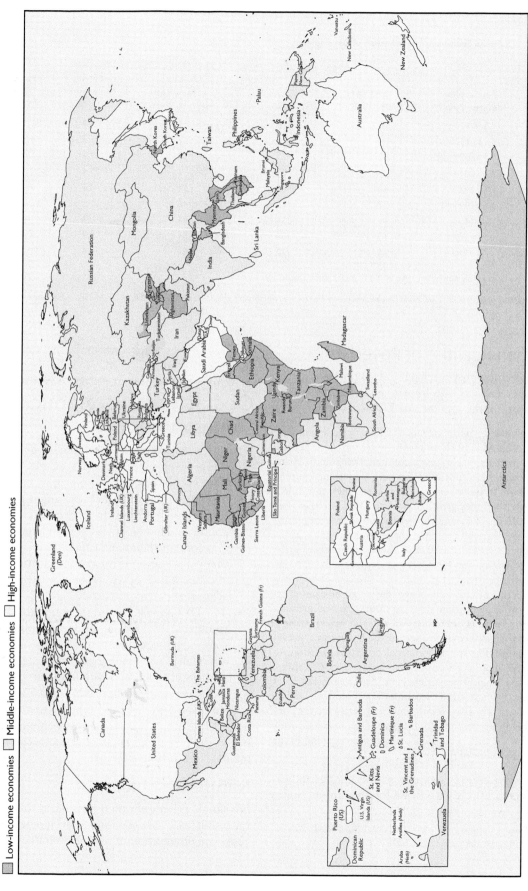

Source: World Bank data, **www.worldbank.org.** National income per capita is converted to U.S. dollars using the World Bank's Atlas Method, which adjusts national amounts to U.S. dollars using 3-year exchange rate averages. See the World Bank's Web site for more details.

TABLE 39W.1 Selected Socioeconomic Indicators of Development

Country	(1) Per Capita Income, 2008*	(2) Life Expectancy at Birth, 2008	(3) Under-5 Mortality Rate per 1000, 2008	(4) Adult Illiteracy Rate, Percent, 2007	(5) Internet Users per 100, 2008	(6) Per Capita Energy Consumption, 2007**
United States	$48,430	78	8	1	75.9	7766
Japan	35,190	83	4	1	75.2	4019
Brazil	10,070	72	22	10	37.5	1239
China	6010	73	21	7	22.5	1484
India	2930	64	69	44	4.5	529
Mauritania	1990	57	118	46	1.9	111
Bangladesh	1450	66	54	47	0.3	163
Ethiopia	870	55	109	54	0.4	4198
Mozambique	770	48	130	56	1.6	418

*Purchasing power parity basis (see World Bank Web site for definition and methodology).
**Kilograms of oil equivalent.
Source: World Development Indicators 2010 and World Development Report 2010, **www.worldbank.org**. Used with permission of World Bank Publications, via Copyright Clearance Center, Inc.

The Human Realities of Poverty

Development economist Michael Todaro points out that mere statistics conceal the human implications of the extreme poverty in the low-income DVCs:

> Let us examine a typical "extended" family in rural Asia. The Asian household is likely to comprise ten or more people, including parents, five to seven children, two grandparents, and some aunts and uncles. They have a combined annual income, both in money and in "kind" (i.e., they consume a share of the food they grow), of $250 to $300. Together they live in a poorly constructed one-room house as tenant farmers on a large agricultural estate owned by an absentee landlord who lives in the nearby city. The father, mother, uncle, and the older children must work all day on the land. None of the adults can read or write; of the five school-age children, only one attends school regularly; and he cannot expect to proceed beyond three or four years of primary education. There is only one meal a day; it rarely changes and it is rarely sufficient to alleviate the children's constant hunger pains. The house has no electricity, sanitation, or fresh water supply. There is much sickness, but qualified doctors and medical practitioners are far away in the cities attending to the needs of wealthier families. The work is hard, the sun is hot and aspirations for a better life are constantly being snuffed out. In this part of the world the only relief from the daily struggle for physical survival lies in the spiritual traditions of the people.[1]

Table 39W.1 contrasts various socioeconomic indicators for selected DVCs with those for the United States

and Japan. These data confirm the major points stressed in the quotation from Todaro.

Obstacles to Economic Development

The paths to economic development are essentially the same for developing countries as for the industrially advanced economies:

- The DVCs must use their existing supplies of resources more efficiently. This means that they must eliminate unemployment and underemployment and also combine labor and capital resources in a way that will achieve lowest-cost production. They must also direct their scarce resources so that they will achieve allocative efficiency.
- The DVCs must expand their available supplies of resources. By achieving greater supplies of raw materials, capital equipment, and productive labor, and by advancing its technological knowledge, a DVC can push its production possibilities curve outward.

All DVCs are aware of these two paths to economic development. Why, then, have some of them traveled those paths while others have lagged far behind? The difference lies in the physical, human, and socioeconomic environments of the various nations.

Natural Resources

No simple generalization is possible as to the role of natural resources in the economic development of DVCs because the distribution of natural resources among them is

---

[1]Michael P. Todaro, *Economic Development in the Third World*, 7th ed. (New York: Addison Wesley Longman, 2000), p. 4.

so uneven. Some DVCs have valuable deposits of bauxite, tin, copper, tungsten, nitrates, and petroleum and have been able to use their natural resource endowments to achieve rapid growth. This is true, for instance, of Kuwait and several other members of the Organization of Petroleum Exporting Countries (OPEC). In other instances, natural resources are owned or controlled by the multinational corporations of industrially advanced countries, with the economic benefits from these resources largely diverted abroad. Furthermore, world markets for many of the farm products and raw materials that the DVCs export are subject to large price fluctuations that contribute to instability in their economies.

Other DVCs lack mineral deposits, have little arable land, and have few sources of power. Moreover, most of the poor countries are situated in Central and South America, Africa, the Indian subcontinent, and southeast Asia, where tropical climates prevail. The heat and humidity hinder productive labor; human, crop, and livestock diseases are widespread; and weed and insect infestations plague agriculture.

A weak resource base can be a serious obstacle to growth. Real capital can be accumulated and the quality of the labor force improved through education and training. But it is not as easy to augment the natural resource base. It may be unrealistic for many of the DVCs to envision an economic destiny comparable with that of, say, the United States or Canada. But we must be careful in generalizing: Japan, for example, has achieved a high standard of living despite limited natural resources. It simply imports the large quantities of natural resources that it needs to produce goods for consumption at home and export abroad.

Human Resources

Three statements describe many of the poorest DVCs with respect to human resources:

- Populations are large.
- Unemployment and underemployment are widespread.
- Educational levels and labor productivity are low.

Large Populations As demonstrated by equation (1), a nation's standard of living or real income per capita depends on the size of its total output (or income) relative to its total population:

$$\text{Standard of living} = \frac{\text{Total output (or income)}}{\text{Population}} \quad (1)$$

Some of the DVCs with the most meager natural and capital resources not only have low total incomes but also large populations. These large populations often produce high population densities (population per square mile). In

TABLE 39W.2 Population Statistics, Selected Countries

(1) Country	(2) Population per Square Km, 2008*	(3) Annual Rate of Population Increase, 1990–2008
United States	33	1.1%
Pakistan	215	2.4
Bangladesh	1229	1.8
Venezuela	32	1.9
India	383	1.6
China	142	0.9
Kenya	68	2.8
Philippines	303	2.1
Yemen	43	3.5
World	**52**	**1.3**

*1 square kilometer (km) = 0.386 square miles.
Source: World Development Indicators 2010, **www.worldbank.org**.

column 1 of Table 39W.2, note the high population densities of the selected DVCs relative to the lower densities of the United States and the world.

The high population densities of many DVCs have resulted from decades of higher rates of population growth than most IACs. Column 3 of Table 39W.2 shows the varying rates of population growth in selected countries over a recent period: 1990–2008. Although *fertility rates*—the number of children per woman's lifetime—are dramatically declining in many DVCs, the population growth rates of the DVCs remain considerably higher than for the IACs. Between 1990 and 2008, the annual population growth rate was 2.2 percent for the low-income DVCs and 1.3 percent for the middle-income DVCs. Those numbers compare to only a 0.7 percent rate of population growth for the IACs. Because a large percentage of the world's current population already lives in DVCs, their population growth remains significant. Over the next 15 years, 9 out of every 10 people added to the world population are projected to be born in developing nations. Figure 39W.2 dramatically illustrates the effect of population growth in the DVCs on past, present, and projected world population numbers. Population growth in the DVCs will continue to increase the world's population through midcentury, at which time world population is expected to begin to level off.

In some of the poorest DVCs, rapid population growth actually strains the levels of income growth so severely that per capita income remains stagnant or even falls toward subsistence levels. In the worst instances, death rates rise sharply as war, drought, and natural disasters cause severe malnutrition and disease.

FIGURE 39W.2 Population growth in developing countries and advanced industrial countries, 1950–2050.
The majority of the world's population lives in the developing nations, and those nations will account for most of the rapid increase in population over the next 40 years.

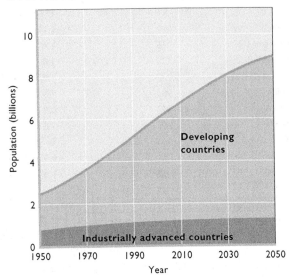

Source: Population Reference Bureau, **www.prb.org**. The underlying data are from the United Nations Population Division, *World Population Prospects: The 2008 Revision.*

Boosting the standard of living in countries that have subsistence- or near-subsistence levels of income is a daunting task. When a DVC is just starting to modernize its economy, initial increases in real income can for a time increase population and short-circuit the process. If population increases are sufficiently large, they simply spread the higher level of total income among more people such that the original gain in per capita income disappears.

Why might income gains in the poorest DVC increase population growth, at least for a while? First, such income growth often reduces the nation's death rate. The increase in income means better nutrition and that improves health and increases life expectancy. Also, the death rate falls as a result of the basic medical and sanitation programs that accompany greater economic development. Second, the birthrate initially rises, particularly if medical and sanitation programs reduce infant mortality. For these reasons, the rapid population growth that results from income increases can convert an expanding standard of living into a stagnant or very slow-growing standard of living.

Population expansion can also impede economic development in four additional ways:

- *Reduced saving and investment* The expenses associated with raising large families often reduce the capacity of households to save, thereby restricting the economy's ability to accumulate capital.

- *Lower productivity* As population increases, added investment is required to maintain the amount of real capital per person. If investment fails to keep pace, then on average each worker will have fewer tools and less equipment, and that will reduce worker productivity (output per worker). Declining productivity implies stagnating or declining per capita incomes.

- *Overuse of land resources* Because most developing countries are heavily dependent on agriculture, rapid population growth may cause an overuse of land resources. The much-publicized African famines are partly the result of overgrazing and overplanting of land caused by the pressing need to feed a growing population. Population pressures also can encourage excessive cutting down of trees for use as fuel. This denuding of the landscape contributes to severe soil erosion from wind and water. Finally, in some cases population pressure leads to the use of crop waste and animal dung as needed fuel rather than as fertilizer to replenish the productivity of the soil. (We say more about the African famines in this chapter's Last Word.)

- *Contribution to urban problems* Rapid population growth in the cities of the DVCs, accompanied by unprecedented inflows of rural migrants, generates massive urban problems. Rapid population growth aggravates problems such as substandard housing, poor public services, congestion, pollution, and crime. Resolving or reducing these difficulties necessitates diverting resources from growth-oriented uses.

Most authorities see birth control as the most effective means for breaking out of the population dilemma. And breakthroughs in contraceptive technology in recent decades have made this solution increasingly relevant. As we have indicated, fertility rates have dropped significantly in the DVCs. But obstacles to population control are still present. Low literacy rates make it difficult to disseminate information about contraceptive devices. In peasant agriculture, large families are a major source of labor. Adults may regard having many children as a kind of informal social security system: the more children, the greater the probability of the parents' having a relative to care for them in old age.

Finally, many nations that stand to gain the most through birth control are often the least willing, for religious reasons, to embrace contraception programs. For example, population growth in Latin America (which has a high proportion of Catholics) is among the most rapid in the world.

China, which has about one-fifth of the world's population, began its harsh "one-child" program in 1980. The government advocates late marriages and one child per family. Couples having more than one child are fined or lose various social benefits. Even though the rate of population growth has diminished under this program, China's population continues to expand. Between 1990 and 2008 it increased by 190 million people. India, the world's second most populous nation, had a 291 million person increase in population—a 34 percent rise—during the 1990–2008 period. With a total population of about 1.1 billion, India has 17 percent of the world's population but less than 2.5 percent of the world's landmass.

Qualifications We need to qualify our focus on population growth as a major cause of low per-capita incomes, however. As with the relationship between natural resources and living standards, the relationship between population sizes and living standards is less clear than one might expect. High population density certainly does not confine a nation to poverty. China and India have immense populations and are poor, but Japan, Singapore, and Hong Kong are densely populated and are wealthy. Moreover, the standard of living in many parts of China and India has rapidly increased in recent years.

Also, the population growth rate for the DVCs as a group has declined significantly in recent decades. Between 1990 and 2008, their annual population growth rate was about 1.4 percent; for 2008 through 2015, it is projected to fall to 1.2 percent (compared to 0.4 percent in the IACs). The world's population actually is projected to decline in the last part of this century.

Finally, not everyone agrees that reducing population growth is the best way to increase per capita GDP in the developing countries. Economists point to a **demographic transition** that occurs as economic growth takes off. In this transition, rising income transforms the population dynamics of a nation by reducing birthrates. In this view, high fertility rates and large populations are a consequence of low income, not the underlying cause. The task of a nation is to increase output and income. With success, declining birthrates will automatically follow.

This view recognizes both marginal benefits and marginal costs of having another child. In DVCs the marginal benefits are relatively large, because the extra child becomes an extra worker who can help support the family. Extra children can provide financial support and security for parents in their old age, so people in poor countries have high birthrates. But in wealthy IACs, the marginal cost of having another child is relatively high. Care of children may require that one of the parents incur the opportunity cost of sacrificing high earnings or that the parents purchase expensive child care. Also, children require extended and expensive education for the highly skilled jobs characteristic of the IAC economies. At the same time, the marginal benefits of having a child may also be lower in a wealthy IAC.

In particular, most IACs are wealthy enough to afford extensive "social safety nets" (such as retirement and disability benefits) that protect adults from the insecurity associated with old age and the inability to work. People in the IACs therefore recognize that high birthrates are not in the family's short-term or long-term interest. Thus, many of them choose to have fewer children.

Note the differences in causation between the traditional view and the demographic transition view of population. The traditional view is that reduced birthrates must first be achieved and then higher per capita income can follow. Lower birthrates enable per capita income to rise. The demographic transition view is that higher output and income should first be achieved and then lower rates of population growth eventually will follow. Higher incomes reduce population growth.

Development economists typically suggest a dual approach to development that combines both views. The surest way for the poorest DVCs to break out of their poverty is to implement policies that expand output and income while establishing independent policies that give families greater access to birth control information and methods. In terms of equation (1) on page 39W-5, a set of policies that raises the numerator (total income) and holds constant or lowers the denominator (population) will provide the biggest lift to a developing nation's standard of living.

Unemployment and Underemployment A second human resource dimension of developing countries relates to employment. For many DVCs, employment-related data are either nonexistent or highly unreliable. But observation suggests that unemployment is high. There is also significant **underemployment,** which means that a large number of people are employed fewer hours per week than they want, work at jobs unrelated to their training, or spend much of the time on their jobs unproductively.

Many economists contend that unemployment may be as high as 15 to 20 percent in the rapidly growing urban areas of the DVCs. There has been substantial migration in most developing countries from rural to urban areas, motivated by the expectation of finding jobs with higher wage rates than are available in agricultural and other rural employment. But this huge migration to the cities reduces a migrant's chance of obtaining a job. In many cases, migration to the cities has greatly exceeded the growth of urban job opportunities, resulting in very high urban unemployment rates. Thus, rapid rural-urban migration has given rise to urban unemployment rates that are two or three times as great as rural rates.

Underemployment is widespread and characteristic of most DVCs. In many of the poorer DVCs, rural agricultural labor is so abundant relative to capital and natural resources that a significant percentage of the labor contributes little or nothing to agricultural output. Similarly, many DVC workers are self-employed as proprietors of small shops, in handicrafts, or as street vendors. Unfortunately, however, many of them must endure long stretches of idle time at work due to a lack of demand. While they are not unemployed, they are clearly underemployed.

Low Labor Productivity The final human resource reality in developing nations is that labor productivity is low. As we will see, DVCs have found it difficult to invest in physical capital. As a result, their workers are poorly equipped with machinery and tools and therefore are relatively unproductive. Remember that rapid population growth tends to reduce the amount of physical capital available per worker, and that reduction erodes labor productivity and decreases real per capita incomes.

Moreover, most poor countries have not been able to invest adequately in their human capital (see Table 39W.1, columns 3 and 4); consequently, expenditures on health and education have been meager. Low levels of literacy, malnutrition, lack of proper medical care, and insufficient educational facilities all contribute to populations that are ill equipped for industrialization and economic expansion. Attitudes may also play a role: In countries where hard work is associated with slavery and inferiority, many people try to avoid it. Also, by denying educational and work opportunities to women, many of the poorest DVCs forgo vast amounts of productive human capital.

Particularly vital is the absence of a vigorous entrepreneurial class willing to bear risks, accumulate capital, and provide the organizational requisites essential to economic growth. Closely related is the lack of labor trained to handle the routine supervisory functions basic to any program of development. Ironically, the higher-education systems of some DVCs emphasize the humanities and offer relatively few courses in business, engineering, and the sciences. Some DVCs are characterized by an authoritarian view of human relations, sometimes fostered by repressive governments, that creates an environment hostile to thinking independently, taking initiatives, and assuming economic risks. Authoritarianism discourages experimentation and change, which are the essence of entrepreneurship.

While migration from the DVCs has modestly offset rapid population growth, it has also deprived some DVCs of highly productive workers. Often the best-trained and most highly motivated workers, such as physicians, engineers, teachers, and nurses, leave the DVCs to better their circumstances in the IACs. This so-called **brain drain** contributes to the deterioration in the overall skill level and productivity of the labor force.

Capital Accumulation

The accumulation of capital goods is an important focal point of economic development. All DVCs have a relative dearth of capital goods such as factories, machinery and equipment, and public utilities. Better-equipped labor forces would greatly enhance productivity and would help boost per capita output. There is a close relationship between output per worker (labor productivity) and real income per worker. A nation must produce more goods and services per worker as output to enjoy more goods and services per worker as income. One way of increasing labor productivity is to provide each worker with more tools and equipment.

Increasing the stock of capital goods is crucial, because the possibility of augmenting the supply of arable land is slight. An alternative is to supply the available agricultural workforce with more and better capital equipment. And, once initiated, the process of capital accumulation may be cumulative. If capital accumulation increases output faster than the growth in population, a margin of saving may arise that permits further capital formation. In a sense, capital accumulation feeds on itself.

Let's first consider the possibility that developing nations will manage to accumulate capital domestically. Then we will consider the possibility that foreign funds will flow into developing nations to support capital expansion.

Domestic Capital Formation A developing nation, like any other nation, accumulates capital through saving and investing. A nation must save (refrain from consumption) to free some of its resources from the production of consumer goods. Investment spending must then absorb those released resources in the production of capital goods. But impediments to saving and investing are much greater in a low-income nation than they are in an advanced economy.

Savings Potential Consider first the savings side of the picture. The situation here is mixed and varies greatly between countries. Some of the very poor countries, such as Burundi, Chad, Ghana, Guinea, Liberia, Madagascar, Mozambique, and Sierra Leone, have negative saving or save only 0 to 7 percent of their GDPs. The people are simply too poor to save a significant portion of their incomes. Interestingly, however, some middle-income countries save a larger percentage of their domestic outputs than do advanced industrial countries. In 2008 India and China saved 38 and 54 percent of their domestic outputs, respectively, compared to 29 percent for Japan, 26 percent for Germany, and 14 percent for the United States. The problem is that the domestic outputs of the DVCs are so low that even when saving rates are larger than those of advanced nations, the total volume of saving is not large.

Capital Flight Some of the developing countries have suffered **capital flight,** the transfer of private DVC savings to accounts held in the IACs. (In this usage, "capital" is simply "money," "money capital," or "financial capital.") Many wealthy citizens of DVCs have used their savings to invest in the more economically advanced nations, enabling them to avoid the high investment risks at home, such as loss of savings or real capital from government expropriation, abrupt changes in taxation, potential hyperinflation, or high volatility of exchange rates. If a DVC's political climate is unsettled, savers may shift their funds overseas to a "safe haven" in fear that a new government might confiscate their wealth. Rapid or skyrocketing inflation in a DVC would have similar detrimental effects. The transfer of savings overseas may also be a means of evading high domestic taxes on interest income or capital gains. Finally, money capital may flow to the IACs to achieve higher interest rates or a greater variety of investment opportunities.

Whatever the motivation, the amount of capital flight from some DVCs is significant and offsets much of the IACs' lending and granting of other financial aid to the developing nations.

Investment Obstacles There are as many obstacles on the investment side of capital formation in DVCs as on the saving side. Those obstacles include a lack of investors and a lack of incentives to invest.

In some developing nations, the major obstacle to investment is the lack of entrepreneurs who are willing to assume the risks associated with investment. This is a special case of the human capital limitations of the labor force mentioned above.

But the incentive to invest may be weak even in the presence of substantial savings and a large number of willing entrepreneurs. Several factors may combine in a DVC to reduce investment incentives, including political instability, high rates of inflation, and lack of economies of scale. Similarly, very low incomes in a DVC result in a lack of buying power and thus weak demand for all but agricultural goods. This factor is crucial because the chances of competing successfully with mature industries in the international market are slim. Then, too, lack of trained administrative personnel may be a factor in retarding investment.

Finally, the **infrastructure** (stock of public capital goods) in many DVCs is insufficient to enable private

firms to achieve adequate returns on their investments. Poor roads and bridges, inadequate railways, little gas and electricity production, poor communications, unsatisfactory housing, and inadequate educational and public health facilities create an inhospitable environment for private investment. A substantial portion of any new private investment would have to be used to create the infrastructure needed by all firms. Rarely can firms provide an investment in infrastructure themselves and still earn a positive return on their overall investment.

For all these reasons, investment incentives in many DVCs are lacking. It is significant that four-fifths of the overseas investments of multinational firms go to the IACs and only one-fifth to the DVCs. If the multinationals are reluctant to invest in the DVCs, we can hardly blame local entrepreneurs for being reluctant too.

How then can developing nations build up the infrastructure needed to attract investment? The higher-income DVCs may be able to accomplish this through taxation and public spending. But in the poorest DVCs there is little income to tax. Nevertheless, with leadership and a willingness to cooperate, a poor DVC can accumulate capital by transferring surplus agricultural labor to the improvement of the infrastructure. If each agricultural village allocated its surplus labor to the construction of irrigation canals, wells, schools, sanitary facilities, and roads, significant amounts of capital might be accumulated at no significant sacrifice of consumer goods production. Such investment bypasses the problems inherent in the financial aspects of the capital accumulation process. It does not require that consumers save portions of their money income, nor does it presume the presence of an entrepreneurial class eager to invest. When leadership and cooperative spirit are present, this "in-kind" investment is a promising avenue for accumulation of basic capital goods.

Technological Advance

Technological advance and capital formation are frequently part of the same process. Yet there are advantages in discussing technological advance separately.

Given the rudimentary state of technology in the DVCs, they are far from the frontiers of technological advance. But the IACs have accumulated an enormous body of technological knowledge that the developing countries might adopt and apply without expensive research. Crop rotation and contour plowing require no additional capital equipment and would contribute significantly to productivity. By raising grain storage bins a few inches aboveground, a large amount of grain spoilage could be avoided. Although such changes may sound trivial to people of advanced nations, the resulting gains in productivity might mean the difference between subsistence and starvation in some poverty-ridden nations.

The application of either existing or new technological knowledge often requires the use of new and different capital goods. But, within limits, a nation can obtain at least part of that capital without an increase in the rate of capital formation. If a DVC channels the annual flow of replacement investment from technologically inferior to technologically superior capital equipment, it can increase productivity even with a constant level of investment spending. Actually, it can achieve some advances through **capital-saving technology** rather than **capital-using technology**. A new fertilizer, better adapted to a nation's topography and climate, might be cheaper than the fertilizer currently being used. A seemingly high-priced metal plow that will last 10 years may be cheaper in the long run than an inexpensive but technologically inferior wooden plow that has to be replaced every year.

To what extent have DVCs adopted and effectively used available IAC technological knowledge? The picture is mixed. There is no doubt that such technological borrowing has been instrumental in the rapid growth of such Pacific Rim countries as Japan, South Korea, Taiwan, and Singapore. Similarly, the OPEC nations have benefited significantly from IAC knowledge of oil exploration, production, and refining. Recently Russia, the nations of eastern Europe, and China have adopted Western technology to hasten their conversion to market-based economies.

Still, the transfer of advanced technologies to the poorest DVCs is not an easy matter. In IACs technological advances usually depend on the availability of highly skilled labor and abundant capital. Such advances tend to be capital-using or, to put it another way, labor-saving. Developing economies require technologies appropriate to quite different resource endowments: abundant unskilled labor and very limited quantities of capital goods. Although labor-using and capital-saving technologies are appropriate to DVCs, much of the highly advanced technology of advanced nations is inappropriate to them. They must develop their own appropriate technologies. Moreover, many DVCs have "traditional economies" and are not highly receptive to change. That is particularly true of peasant agriculture, which dominates the economies of most of the poorer DVCs. Since technological change that fails may well mean hunger and malnutrition, there is a strong tendency to retain traditional production techniques.

Sociocultural and Institutional Factors

Economic considerations alone do not explain why an economy does or does not grow. Substantial sociocultural and institutional readjustments are usually an integral part of the growth process. Economic development means not only changes in a nation's physical environment (new transportation and communications facilities, new schools, new housing, new plants and equipment) but also changes in the way people think, behave, and associate with one another. Emancipation from custom and tradition is frequently a prerequisite of economic development. A critical but intangible ingredient in that development is the **will to develop.** Economic growth may hinge on what individuals within DVCs want for themselves and their children. Do they want more material abundance? If so, are they willing to make the necessary changes in their institutions and old ways of doing things?

Sociocultural Obstacles Sociocultural impediments to growth are numerous and varied. Some of the very-low-income countries have failed to achieve the preconditions for a national economic entity. Tribal and ethnic allegiances take precedence over national allegiance. Each tribe confines its economic activity to the tribal unit, eliminating any possibility for production-increasing specialization and trade. The desperate economic circumstances in Somalia, Sudan, Liberia, Zaire, Rwanda, and Afghanistan are due in no small measure to military and political conflicts among rival groups.

In countries with a formal or informal caste system, labor is allocated to occupations on the basis of status or tradition rather than on the basis of skill or merit. The result is a misallocation of human resources.

Religious beliefs and observances may seriously restrict the length of the workday and divert to ceremonial uses resources that might have been used for investment. Some religious and philosophical beliefs are dominated by the fatalistic view that the universe is capricious, the idea that there is little or no correlation between an individual's activities and endeavors and the outcomes or experiences that person encounters. The **capricious universe view** leads to a fatalistic attitude. If "providence" rather than hard work, saving, and investing is the cause of one's lot in life, why save, work hard, and invest? Why engage in family planning? Why innovate?

Other attitudes and cultural factors may impede economic activity and growth: emphasis on the performance of duties rather than on individual initiative; focus on the group rather than on individual achievement; and the belief in reincarnation, which reduces the importance of one's current life.

Institutional Obstacles Political corruption and bribery are common in many DVCs. School systems and public service agencies are often ineptly administered, and their functioning is frequently impaired by petty politics. Tax systems are frequently arbitrary, unjust, cumbersome, and detrimental to incentives to work and invest. Political decisions are often motivated by a desire to enhance the nation's international prestige rather than to foster development.

Because of the predominance of farming in DVCs, the problem of achieving an optimal institutional environment in agriculture is a vital consideration in any growth program. Specifically, the institutional problem of **land reform** demands attention in many DVCs. But the reform that is needed may vary tremendously from nation to nation. In some DVCs the problem is excessive concentration of land ownership in the hands of a few wealthy families. This situation is demoralizing for tenants, weakens their incentive to produce, and typically does not promote capital improvements. At the other extreme is the situation in which each family owns and farms a piece of land far too small for the use of modern agricultural technology. An important complication to the problem of land reform is that political considerations sometimes push reform in the direction of farms that are too small to achieve economies of scale. For many nations, land reform is the most acute institutional problem to be resolved in initiating economic development.

Examples: Land reform in South Korea weakened the political control of the landed aristocracy and opened the way for the emergence of strong commercial and industrial middle classes, all to the benefit of the country's economic development. In contrast, the prolonged dominance of the landed aristocracy in the Philippines may have stifled economic development in that nation.

QUICK REVIEW 39W.1

- About 15 percent of the world's population lives in the low-income DVCs, which typically are characterized by scarce natural resources, inhospitable climates, large populations, high unemployment and underemployment, low education levels, and low labor productivity.

- For DVCs just beginning to modernize, high birthrates caused by improved medical care and sanitation can increase population faster than income growth, leading to lower living standards; but as development continues, the opportunity costs of having children rise and population growth typically slows.

- Low saving rates, capital flight, weak infrastructures, and lack of investors impair capital accumulation in many DVCs.

- Sociocultural and institutional factors are often serious impediments to economic growth in DVCs.

The Vicious Circle

Many of the characteristics of the poorest of the DVCs just described are both causes and consequences of their poverty. These countries are caught in a **vicious circle of poverty.** They stay poor because they are poor! Consider Figure 39W.3. Common to most DVCs is low per capita income. A family that is poor has little ability or incentive to save. Furthermore, low incomes mean low levels of product demand. Thus, there are few available resources, on the one hand, and no strong incentives, on the other hand, for investment in physical or human capital. Consequently, labor productivity is low. And since output per

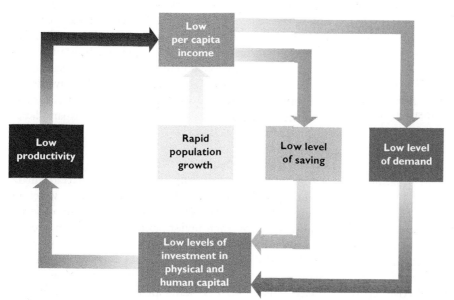

FIGURE 39W.3 The vicious circle of poverty. Low per capita incomes make it difficult for poor nations to save and invest, a condition that perpetuates low productivity and low incomes. Furthermore, rapid population growth may quickly absorb increases in per capita real income and thereby destroy the possibility of breaking out of the poverty circle.

person is real income per person, it follows that per capita income is low.

Many economists think that the key to breaking out of this vicious circle is to increase the rate of capital accumulation, to achieve a level of investment of, say, 10 percent of the national income. But Figure 39W.3 reminds us that rapid population growth may partially or entirely undo the potentially beneficial effects of a higher rate of capital accumulation. Suppose that initially a DVC is realizing no growth in its real GDP but somehow manages to increase saving and investment to 10 percent of its GDP. As a result, real GDP begins to grow at, say, 2.5 percent per year. With a stable population, real GDP per capita will also grow at 2.5 percent per year. If that growth persists, the standard of living will double in about 28 years. But what if population also grows at the rate of 2.5 percent per year, as it does in parts of the Middle East, northern Africa, and sub-Saharan Africa? Then real income per person will remain unchanged and the vicious circle will persist.

But if population can be kept constant or limited to some growth rate significantly below 2.5 percent, real income per person will rise. Then the possibility arises of further enlargement of the flows of saving and investment, continuing advances in productivity, and the continued growth of per capita real income. If a process of self-sustaining expansion of income, saving, investment, and productivity can be achieved, the self-perpetuating vicious circle of poverty can be transformed into a self-regenerating, beneficent circle of economic progress. The challenge is to make effective policies and strategies that will accomplish that transition.

ORIGIN OF THE IDEA
O 39W.1
Economic development

The Role of Government

Economists see a positive role for government in fostering DVC growth, but they generally agree that government efforts must be support private efforts, not substitute for them. That is not always the case in practice.

A Positive Role

Economists suggest that developing nations have several avenues for fostering economic growth and improving their standards of living.

Establishing the Rule of Law Some of the poorest countries of the world are plagued by banditry and inter-tribal warfare that divert attention and resources from the task of development. A strong, stable national government is needed to establish domestic law and order and to achieve peace and unity. Research demonstrates that political instability (as measured by the number of revolutions and coups per decade) and slow economic growth go hand in hand.

Clearly defined and strictly enforced property rights bolster economic growth by ensuring that individuals receive and retain the fruits of their labor. Because legal protections reduce investment risk, the rule of law encourages direct investments by firms in the IACs. Government itself must live by the law. The presence of corruption in the government sanctions criminality throughout the economic system. Such criminality discourages the growth of output because it lowers the returns available to honest workers and honest businesspeople.

Building Infrastructure Many obstacles to economic growth are related to an inadequate infrastructure. Sanitation and basic medical programs, education, irrigation and soil conservation projects, and construction of transportation links and communication facilities are all essentially nonmarketable goods and services that yield widespread spillover benefits. Government is the only institution that is in a position to provide public infrastructure. But it need not do all the work through government entities. It can contract out much of the work to private enterprises.

With respect to both private and public infrastructure, DVCs have an unexpected advantage over more developed countries, because they can act as *follower countries* when it comes to technology. As explained in Chapter 25 on economic growth, DVCs can simply adopt technologies that were developed at high cost in the more technologically advanced *leader countries* without having to pay any of the development costs of those technologies. DVCs can often jump directly to the most modern and highly productive infrastructure without going through the long process of development and replacement that was required in the IACs. As a good example, many DVCs have developed Internet-capable wireless phone networks instead of using their scarce resources to build and expand landline systems.

Embracing Globalization Other things equal, open economies that participate in international trade grow faster than closed economies. Also, DVCs that welcome foreign direct investment enjoy greater growth rates than DVCs that view such investment suspiciously or even as exploitation and therefore put severe obstacles in its way.

Realistic exchange-rate policies by government also help. Exchange rates that are fixed at unrealistic levels invite balance-of-payments problems and speculative trading in currencies. Often, such trading forces a nation into an abrupt devaluation of its currency, sending shock waves throughout its economy. More flexible exchange rates enable more gradual adjustments and thus less susceptibility to major currency shocks and the domestic disruption they cause.

Building Human Capital Government programs that encourage literacy, education, and labor market skills enhance economic growth by building human capital. In particular, policies that close the education gap between women and men spur economic growth in developing countries. Promoting the education of women pays off in terms of reduced fertility, greater productivity, and greater emphasis on educating children.

And government is in a position to nurture the will to develop, to change a philosophy of "Heaven and faith will determine the course of events" to one of "God helps those who help themselves." That change encourages personal educational attainment and enhanced human capital.

Promoting Entrepreneurship The lack of a sizable and vigorous entrepreneurial class, ready and willing to accumulate capital and initiate production, indicates that in some DVCs private enterprise is not capable of spearheading the growth process. Government may have to take the lead, at least at first. But many DVCs would benefit by converting some of their state enterprises into private firms. State enterprises often are inefficient, more concerned with providing maximum employment than with introducing modern technology and delivering goods and services at minimum per-unit cost. Moreover, state enterprises are poor "incubators" for developing profit-focused, entrepreneurial persons who leave the firm to set up their own businesses.

Developing Credit Systems The banking systems in some of the poorest DVCs are nearly nonexistent and that makes it difficult for domestic savers and international lenders to lend money to DVC borrowers, who in turn wish to create capital goods. An effective first step in developing credit systems is through **microfinance,** in which groups of people pool their money and make small loans to budding entrepreneurs and owners of small businesses. People from the IACs can do the same, helping nurture the spirit of enterprise and foster the benefits that it brings. The benefits of microlending accrue not only to the entrepreneurs in the DVCs but to the country as a whole, because the lending creates jobs, expands output, and raises the standard of living.

At the national level, DVC governments must guard against excessive money creation and the high inflation that it brings. High rates of inflation simply are not conducive to economic investment and growth, because inflation lowers the real returns generated by investments. DVCs can help keep inflation in check by establishing independent central banks to maintain proper control over their money supplies. Studies indicate that DVCs that control inflation enjoy higher growth rates than those that do not.

Controlling Population Growth Government can provide information about birth control options. We have seen that slower population growth can convert increases in real output and income to increases in real *per capita* output and income. Families with fewer children consume less and save more; they also free up time for women for education and participation in the labor market. As women participate in the labor market, they tend to reduce their fertility rate, which further helps to control population growth.

Making Peace with Neighbors Countries at war or in fear of war with neighboring nations divert scarce resources to armaments, rather than to private capital or public infrastructure. Sustained peace among neighboring nations eventually leads to economic cooperation and integration, broadened markets, and stronger economic growth.

Public Sector Problems

Although the public sector can positively influence economic development, serious problems can and do arise with government-directed initiatives. If entrepreneurial talent is lacking in the private sector, are quality leaders likely to surface in the ranks of government? Is there not a real danger that government bureaucracy will impede, not stimulate, social and economic change? And what of the tendency of some political leaders to favor spectacular "showpiece" projects at the expense of less showy but more productive programs? Might not political objectives take precedence over the economic goals of a governmentally directed development program?

Development experts are less enthusiastic about the role of government in the growth process than they were 30 years ago. Unfortunately, government misadministration and **corruption** are common in many DVCs, and government officials sometimes line their own pockets with foreign-aid funds. Moreover, political leaders often confer monopoly privileges on relatives, friends, and political supporters and grant exclusive rights to relatives or friends to produce, import, or export certain products. Such monopoly privileges lead to higher domestic prices and diminish the DVC's ability to compete in world markets.

GLOBAL PERSPECTIVE 39W.1

The Corruption Perceptions Index, Selected Nations, 2009*

The corruption perceptions index measures the degree of corruption existing among public officials and politicians as seen by businesspeople, risk analysts, and the general public. An index value of 10 is highly clean and 0 is highly corrupt.

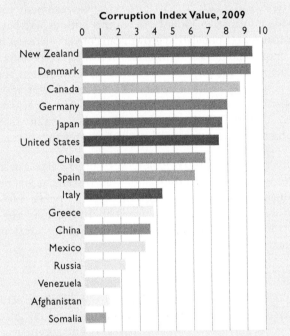

Corruption Index Value, 2009

*Index values are subject to change on the basis of election outcomes, military coups, and so on.
Source: Adapted from The Corruption Perceptions Index. Copyright 2009 Transparency International: the global coalition against corruption. Used with permission. For more information, visit **www.transparency.org**.

Similarly, managers of state-owned enterprises are often appointed on the basis of cronyism rather than competence. Many DVC governments, particularly in Africa, have created "marketing boards" as the sole purchaser of agricultural products from local farmers. The boards buy farm products at artificially low prices and sell them at higher world prices; the "profit" ends up in the pockets of government officials. In recent years the perception of government has shifted from that of catalyst and promoter of growth to that of a potential impediment to development. According to a recent ranking of 179 nations based on perceived corruption, the 40 nations at the bottom of the list (most corrupt) were DVCs. Global Perspective 39W.1 shows the corruption scores for 16 selected nations, including the two least corrupt (New Zealand and Denmark) and the two most corrupt (Afghanistan and Somalia).

The Role of Advanced Nations

How can the IACs help developing countries in their pursuit of economic growth? To what degree have IACs provided assistance?

Expanding Trade

Some authorities maintain that the simplest and most effective way for the United States and other industrially advanced nations to aid developing nations is to lower international trade barriers. Such action would enable DVCs to elevate their national incomes through increased trade. Trade barriers instituted by the IACs are often highest for labor-intensive manufactured goods, such as textiles, clothing, footwear, and processed agricultural products. These are precisely the sorts of products for which the DVCs have a comparative advantage. Also, many IACs' tariffs rise as the degree of product processing increases; for example, tariffs on chocolates are higher than those on cocoa. This practice discourages the DVCs from developing processing industries of their own.

Additionally, large agricultural subsidies in the IACs encourage excessive production of food and fiber in the IACs. The overproduction flows into world markets, where it depresses agricultural prices. DVCs, which typically do not subsidize farmers, therefore face artificially low prices for their farm exports. The IACs could greatly help DVCs by reducing farm subsidies along with tariffs.

But lowering trade barriers is certainly not a panacea. Some poor nations need only large foreign markets for their raw materials to achieve growth. But the problem for many poor nations is not to obtain markets in which to sell existing products or relatively abundant raw materials but to get the capital and technical assistance they need to produce products for domestic consumption.

Also, close trade ties with advanced nations entail certain disadvantages. Dependence by the DVCs on exports to the IACs leaves the DVCs highly vulnerable to recessions in the IACs. As firms cut back production in the IACs, the demand for DVC resources declines; and as income in the IACs declines, the demand for DVC-produced goods declines. By reducing the demand for DVC exports, recessions in the IACs can severely reduce the prices of raw materials exported by the DVCs. For example, during the recession of 2007–2009, the world price of zinc fell from $2.02 per pound to $.49 per pound, and the world price of copper fell from $4.05 per pound to $1.40 per pound. These declines in prices severely reduce the export earnings of the DVCs. Because mineral exports are a significant source of DVC income, stability and growth in IACs are important to improved standards of living in the developing nations.

Admitting Temporary Workers

Some economists recommend that the IACs help the DVCs by accepting more seasonal or other temporary workers from the DVCs. Temporary migration provides an outlet for surplus DVC labor. Moreover, migrant remittances to families in the home country serve as a sorely needed source of income. The problem, of course, is that some temporary workers illegally blend into the fabric of the IACs and do not leave when their visas or work permits expire. That may not be in the long-run best interest of the IACs.

Discouraging Arms Sales

Finally, the IACs can help the DVCs as a group by discouraging the sale of military equipment to the DVCs. Such purchases by the DVCs divert public expenditures from infrastructure and education and heighten tensions in DVCs that have long-standing disputes with neighbors.

Foreign Aid: Public Loans and Grants

Official development assistance (ODA), or simply "foreign aid," is another route through which IACs can help DVCs. This aid can play a crucial role in breaking an emerging country's circle of poverty by supplementing its saving and investment. As previously noted, many DVCs lack the infrastructure needed to attract either domestic or foreign private capital. The infusion of foreign aid that strengthens infrastructure could enhance the flow of private capital to the DVCs.

Direct Aid The United States and other IACs have assisted DVCs directly through a variety of programs designed to stimulate economic development. Over the past 10 years, U.S. loans and grants to the DVCs totaled $15 billion to $28 billion per year. The U.S. Agency for International Development (USAID) administers most of this aid. Some of it, however, consists of grants of surplus food under the Food for Peace program. Other advanced nations also have substantial foreign aid programs. In 2008 foreign aid from the IACs to the developing nations totaled $129 billion. This amounted to about one-fourth of 1 percent of the collective GDP of the IACs that year (see Global Perspective 39W.2 for percentages for selected nations).

A large portion of foreign aid is distributed on the basis of political and military rather than strictly economic considerations. Afghanistan, Egypt, Israel, Pakistan, and Turkey, for example, are major recipients of U.S. aid. Asian, Latin American, and African nations with lower standards of living receive less.

Only one-fourth of foreign aid goes to the 10 countries in which 70 percent of the world's poorest people

GLOBAL PERSPECTIVE 39W.2

Development Assistance as a Percentage of GDP, Selected Nations

In terms of absolute amounts, the United States was the leading provider of development assistance in 2008. It provided $26.8 billion to developing nations. But many other industrialized nations contribute a larger percentage of their GDPs to foreign aid than does the United States.

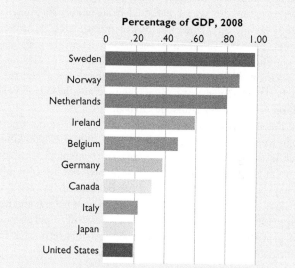

Percentage of GDP, 2008

Sweden, Norway, Netherlands, Ireland, Belgium, Germany, Canada, Italy, Japan, United States

Source: Based on data from OECD (2009); Development aid at its highest level ever in 2008 [Press release]. Table 1: Net Official Development Assistance in 2008: Preliminary data for 2008 (March 30, 2009), **www.oecd.org/dac**.

live. The most affluent 40 percent of the DVC population receives over twice as much aid as the poorest 40 percent. Many economists argue that the IACs should shift foreign aid away from the middle-income DVCs and toward the poorest DVCs.

Some of the world's poorest nations *do* receive large amounts of foreign aid relative to their meager GDPs. For example, in 2008 foreign aid relative to GDP was 44 percent in Burundi, 32 percent in Guinea-Bissau, 22 percent in Mozambique, 21 percent in Malawi, 19 percent in Rwanda, and 19 percent in Sierra Leone.

Also, these and many other low-income developing nations receive large amounts of support from private donors in the IACs. In fact, in recent years the private giving to the DVCs by private U.S. universities, foundations (such as the Gates Foundation), voluntary organizations, and religious organizations has exceeded the foreign aid provided by the U.S. government.

The large accumulated debts of some of the poorest DVCs have become a severe roadblock to their growth.

LAST Word Famine in Africa

The Roots of Africa's Persistent Famines Lie in Both Natural and Human Causes.

A number of sub-Saharan African nations are periodically threatened by famine. For example, in the early 1990s about 300,000 children under the age of five died from famine in Somalia. In 2003 famine threatened the lives of an estimated 10 million people in several southern Africa nations (Lesotho, Malawi, Mozambique, Swaziland, Zambia, and Zimbabwe). Although most African countries were self-sufficient in food at the time they became independent nations, they are now heavily dependent on imported foodstuffs for survival.

The immediate cause of famine often is drought. For example, in Kenya drought and crop failures in 1999 and 2000 killed much of the nation's livestock, leaving an estimated 3.5 million people at risk of starvation. But as first pointed out by economist Amartya Sen, the ultimate causes of sub-Saharan Africa's inability to feed itself are rooted in a complex interplay of natural and human conditions. Lack of rainfall, chronic civil strife, rapid population growth, widespread soil erosion, and counterproductive public policies all contribute to Africa's famines.

Civil Strife Regional rebellions, prolonged civil wars, and wars between nations have devastated several African nations. Ethiopia, Sudan, and Rwanda, for example, have been plagued by decades of civil strife. As another example, Ethiopia has recently been at war with its neighbor Eritrea. Not only do these conflicts divert precious resources from civilian uses, but they seriously complicate the ability of wealthy nations to provide famine and developmental aid. Governments frequently divert donated food to the army and deny it to starving civilians. In Somalia, factional feuding destroyed most of the existing schools, factories, and government ministries and reduced the country to anarchy. Armed gangs stole water pumps, tractors, and livestock from farms and looted ports of donated foodstuffs.

Population Growth Although substantially slowing from previous growth rates, the population of sub-Saharan Africa is still growing very rapidly. Population is projected to grow by 2.4 percent annually from 2008 to 2015, compared to 0.5 percent in the industrially advanced economies. When crops are abundant, the sub-Saharan nations are able to feed their growing population. But when war or drought hits, hunger and malnutrition quickly follow.

Ecological Degradation Population growth has also contributed to the ecological degradation of Africa. With population pressures and the increasing need for food, marginal land has been deforested and put into crop production. In many cases trees that have served as a barrier to the encroachment of the desert have been cut down for fuel, allowing the fragile topsoil to be blown away by desert winds. The scarcity of wood that has accompanied deforestation in some cases has resulted in the use of animal dung for fuel, thereby denying its traditional use as fertilizer.

Therefore, some of the recent direct assistance by the IACs to the DVCs has taken the form of forgiving parts of the past IAC-government loans to low-income DVCs. In 2005 the G8 nations canceled $55 billion of debt owed by developing countries to the World Bank, the International Monetary Fund, and the African Development Bank. Of course, debt forgiveness creates a *moral hazard problem*. If current debt forgiveness creates an expectation of later debt forgiveness, a country has little incentive against running up a new debt. Therefore, future loans by the IACs must be extended cautiously to the low-income developing nations that receive current debt forgiveness.

The World Bank Group The United States and other IACs also support the DVCs by participating in the **World Bank**, whose major objective is helping DVCs achieve economic growth. [The World Bank was established in 1945, along with the International Monetary Fund (IMF).] Supported by about 185 member nations, the World Bank not only lends out of its capital funds but also sells bonds and lends the proceeds and guarantees and insures private loans:

- The World Bank is a "last-resort" lending agency; its loans are limited to economic projects for which private funds are not readily available.
- Many World Bank loans have been for basic development projects—dams, irrigation projects, health and sanitation programs, communications, and transportation facilities. Consequently, the Bank has helped finance the infrastructure needed to encourage the flow of private capital.

39W-16

Furthermore, traditional fallow periods have been shortened, resulting in overplanting and overgrazing and a wearing out of the soil. Deforestation and land overuse have reduced the capacity of the land to absorb moisture, diminishing its productivity and its ability to resist drought. All this is complicated by the fact that there are few facilities for crop storage, making it difficult, even when crops are good, to accumulate a surplus for future lean years. A large percentage of domestic farm output in some parts of Africa is lost to rats, insects, and spoilage.

Public Policies Ill-advised public policies have contributed to Africa's famines.

First, many African governments generally have neglected investment in agriculture in favor of industrial development and military strength. It is estimated that African governments on the average spend four times as much on armaments as they do on agriculture.

Second, many African governments have adopted a policy of setting the prices of agricultural commodities at low levels to provide cheap food for growing urban populations. That policy has diminished the incentives of farmers to increase production. While foreign aid has helped ease the effects of Africa's food-population problems, most experts reject aid as a long-term solution. Experience suggests that aid in the form of food can provide only temporary relief and may undermine the achievement of long-run local self-sufficiency in food production. Foreign food aid, it is contended, treats symptoms, not causes.

Most dramatically, Zimbabwe's seizure of thousands of white-owned commercial farms for redistribution to black settlers collapsed the food supply. Along with severe drought, the policy threatened half the Zimbabwe population with severe malnutrition in 2003.

External Debt All this is made more complex by the fact that the sub-Saharan nations are burdened with large external debts. The World Bank reports that the aggregate external debt of these nations was $84 billion in 1980 and grew to $231 billion in 2009. As a condition of further aid, these nations have had to invoke austerity programs that have contributed to declines in their per capita incomes. One tragic consequence is that many of these nations have cut back on social service programs such as health care for children. For that reason, in 2000 the major industrial nations and the World Bank initiated a program to forgive $50 billion of total debt owed by some of these nations, on the condition that they end warfare and use the savings in interest and principal to ease the plight of their populations.

- The Bank has provided technical assistance to the DVCs by helping them determine what avenues of growth seem appropriate for their economic development.

Affiliates of the World Bank function in areas where the World Bank has proved weak. The *International Finance Corporation (IFC)*, for example, invests in private enterprises in the DVCs. The *International Development Association (IDA)* makes "soft loans" (which may not be self-liquidating) to the poorest DVCs on more liberal terms than does the World Bank.

Foreign Harm? Although official development assistance directly from the IACs and indirectly through the World Bank has generally helped the DVCs expand their economies, the foreign-aid approach to helping DVCs has met with several criticisms.

Dependency and Incentives A basic criticism is that foreign aid may promote dependency rather than self-sustaining growth. Critics argue that injections of funds from the IACs encourage the DVCs to ignore the painful economic decisions, the institutional and cultural reforms, and the changes in attitudes toward thrift, industry, hard work, and self-reliance that are needed for economic growth. They say that, after some five decades of foreign aid, the DVCs' demand for foreign aid has increased rather than decreased. These aid programs should have withered away if they had been successful in promoting sustainable growth.

Bureaucracy and Centralized Government

IAC aid is given to the governments of the DVCs, not to their residents or businesses. The consequence is that the aid typically generates massive, ineffective government bureaucracies and centralizes government power over the economy. The stagnation and collapse of the Soviet Union and communist countries of eastern Europe is evidence that highly bureaucratized economies are not very conducive to economic growth and development. Furthermore, not only does the bureaucratization of the DVCs divert valuable human resources from the private to the public sector, but it often shifts the nation's focus from producing more output to bickering over how unearned "income" should be distributed.

Corruption and Misuse

Critics also allege that foreign aid is being used ineffectively. As we noted previously, corruption is a major problem in many DVCs, and some estimates suggest that from 10 to 20 percent of the aid is diverted to government officials. Also, IAC-based aid consultants and multinational corporations are major beneficiaries of aid programs. Some economists contend that as much as one-fourth of each year's aid is spent on expert consultants. Furthermore, because IAC corporations manage many of the aid projects, they are major beneficiaries of, and lobbyists for, foreign aid.

Current Level of Foreign Aid After declining in the late 1990s, foreign aid increased between 2000 and 2008. This increase resulted from a renewed international emphasis on reducing global poverty and also from expanded efforts by the IACs to enlist the cooperation of DVCs in fighting terrorism. In 2008 foreign direct aid by IAC governments to developing countries was $129 billion.

Flows of Private Capital

The IACs also send substantial amounts of private capital to the DVCs. Among the private investors are corporations, commercial banks, and, more recently, financial investment companies. General Motors or Ford might finance the construction of plants in Mexico or Brazil to assemble autos or produce auto parts. JPMorgan Chase or Bank of America might make loans to private firms operating in Argentina or China or to the governments of Thailand and Malaysia. And individuals living in IACs might purchase shares in "emerging markets" mutual funds run by investment companies like Fidelity. Those funds make financial investments in the stock of promising firm in DVCs such as Hungary and Chile.

The total flow of private capital to DVCs was $770 billion in 2008, but the makeup of this flow differed from the flow in earlier decades. The main private investors and lenders are now private IAC firms and individuals, not commercial banks. Also, more of the flow is in the form of **foreign direct investment** in DVCs, rather than loans to DVC governments. Such direct investment includes the building of new factories in DVCs by multinational firms and the purchase of DVC firms (or parts of them). Whereas DVCs once viewed foreign direct investment as "exploitation," many of them now seek out foreign direct investment as a way to expand their capital stock and improve their citizens' job opportunities and wages. Those wages are often very low by IAC standards but high by DVC standards. Another benefit of direct investment in DVCs is that management skills and technological knowledge often accompany the capital.

Unfortunately for the low-income DVCs, the strong flow of private capital to the DVCs has been very selective. The vast majority of IAC investment and lending has been directed toward China, India, Mexico, and other middle-income DVCs, with only small amounts flowing toward such extremely impoverished DVCs as those in Africa.

In fact, as we have indicated, many of the lowest-income countries face staggering debt burdens from previous government and private loans. Payment of interest and principal on this external debt is diverting expenditures away from maintenance of infrastructure, new infrastructure, education, and private investment.

Further, the flows of private capital to both the middle-income and low-income DVCs plummeted during the worldwide recession of 2007–2009. It may be several years before foreign direct investment regains its momentum.

QUICK REVIEW 39W.2

- DVC governments may encourage economic growth by (a) providing law and order, (b) taking the lead in establishing enterprises, (c) improving infrastructure, (d) forcing higher levels of saving and investing, and (e) resolving social-institutional problems.

- The IACs can assist the DVCs through expanded trade, foreign aid, and flows of private capital.

- Many of the poorest DVCs have large external debts that pose an additional obstacle to economic growth.

- The worldwide recession of 2007–2009 greatly reduced direct investment by the IACs in the DVC economies.

Summary

1. The majority of the world's nations are developing countries (low- and middle-income nations). While some DVCs have been realizing rapid growth rates in recent years, others have experienced little or no growth.

2. Scarcities of natural resources make it more challenging—but certainly not impossible—for a nation to develop.

3. The large and rapidly growing populations in many DVCs contribute to low per capita incomes. Increases in per capita incomes frequently induce greater population growth, often reducing per capita incomes to near-subsistence levels. The demographic transition view, however, suggests that rising living standards must precede declining birthrates.

4. Most DVCs suffer from unemployment and underemployment. Labor productivity is low because of insufficient investment in physical and human capital.

5. In many DVCs, formidable obstacles impede both saving and investment. In some of the poorest DVCs, the savings potential is very low, and many savers transfer their funds to the IACs rather than invest them domestically. The lack of a vigorous entrepreneurial class and the weakness of investment incentives also impede capital accumulation.

6. Appropriate social and institutional changes and, in particular, the presence of the will to develop, are essential ingredients in economic development.

7. The vicious circle of poverty brings together many of the obstacles to growth, supporting the view that poor countries stay poor because of their poverty. Low incomes inhibit saving and the accumulation of physical and human capital, making it difficult to increase productivity and incomes. Overly rapid population growth, however, may offset promising attempts to break the vicious circle.

8. The nature of the obstacles to growth—the absence of an entrepreneurial class, the dearth of infrastructure, the saving-investment dilemma, and the presence of social-institutional obstacles to growth—suggests that government should play a major role in initiating growth. Economists suggest that DVCs could make further development progress through such policies as establishing the rule of law, building infrastructure, opening their economies to international trade, setting realistic exchange rates, encouraging foreign direct investment, building human capital, encouraging entrepreneurship, controlling population growth, and making peace with neighbors. However, the corruption and maladministration that are common to the public sectors of many DVCs suggest that government may not be very effective in instigating growth.

9. Advanced nations can encourage development in the DVCs by reducing IAC trade barriers and by directing foreign aid (official development assistance) to the neediest nations, providing debt forgiveness to the poorest DVCs, allowing temporary low-skilled immigration from the DVCs, and discouraging arms sales to the DVCs. Critics of foreign aid, however, say that it (a) creates DVC dependency, (b) contributes to the growth of bureaucracies and centralized economic control, and (c) is rendered ineffective by corruption and mismanagement.

10. In recent years the IACs have reduced foreign aid to the DVCs but have increased direct investment and other private capital flows to the DVCs. Little of the foreign direct investment, however, has gone to the poorest DVCs. Also, foreign direct investment plummeted during the worldwide recession of 2007–2009.

Terms and Concepts

industrially advanced countries (IACs)	infrastructure	vicious circle of poverty
developing countries (DVCs)	capital-saving technology	microfinance
demographic transition	capital-using technology	corruption
underemployment	will to develop	World Bank
brain drain	capricious universe view	foreign direct investment
capital flight	land reform	

Questions

1. What are the three categories used by the World Bank to classify nations on the basis of national income per capita? Identify any two nations of your choice for each of the three categories. LO1

2. Explain how the absolute per capita income gap between rich and poor nations might increase, even though per capita income (or output) is growing faster in DVCs than in IACs. LO1

3. Explain how each of the following can be obstacles to the growth of income per capita in the DVCs: lack of natural resources, large populations, low labor productivity, poor infrastructure, and capital flight. LO2

4. What is the demographic transition? Contrast the demographic transition view of population growth with the traditional view that slower population growth is a prerequisite for rising living standards in the DVCs. LO2

5. As it relates to the vicious circle of poverty, what is meant by the saying "Some DVCs stay poor because they are poor"? Change the box labels as necessary in Figure 39W.3 to explain rapid economic growth in countries such as South Korea and Chile. What factors other than those contained in the figure might contribute to that growth? LO3

6. Because real capital is supposed to earn a higher return where it is scarce, how do you explain the fact that most international investment flows to the IACs (where capital is relatively abundant) rather than to the DVCs (where capital is very scarce)? LO3

7. List and discuss five policies that DVC governments might undertake to promote economic development and expansion of income per capita in their countries? LO4

8. Do you think that the nature of the problems the DVCs face requires a government-directed or a private-sector directed development process? Explain your reasoning. LO4

9. Why do you think there is so much government corruption in some developing countries? LO4

10. What types of products do the DVCs typically export? How do those exports relate to the law of comparative advantage? How do tariffs by IACs reduce the standard of living of DVCs? LO5

11. Do you favor debt forgiveness to all DVCs, just the poorest ones, or none at all? What incentive problem might debt relief create? Would you be willing to pay $20 a year more in personal income taxes for debt forgiveness? How about $200? How about $2000? LO5

12. Do you think that IACs such as the United States should open their doors wider to the immigration of low-skilled DVC workers as a way to help DVCs develop? Do you think that it is appropriate for students from DVC nations to stay in IAC nations to work and build careers? LO5

13. **LAST WORD** Explain how civil wars, population growth, and public policy decisions have contributed to periodic famines in Africa.

Problems

1. Assume a DVC and an IAC currently have real per capita outputs of $500 and $5000, respectively. If both nations have a 3 percent increase in their real per capita outputs, by how much will the per capita output gap change? LO1

2. Assume that a very tiny and very poor DVC has income per capita of $300 and total national income of $3 million. How large is its population? If its population grows by 2 percent in some year while its total income grows by 3 percent, what will be its new income per capita rounded to full dollars? If population had not grown during the year, what would have been its income per capita? LO2

FURTHER TEST YOUR KNOWLEDGE AT
www.mcconnell19e.com

At the text's Online Learning Center (OLC), **www.mcconnell19e.com**, you will find one or more Web-based questions that require information from the Internet to answer. We urge you to check them out; they will familiarize you with Web sites that may be helpful in other courses and perhaps even in your career. The OLC also features multiple-choice questions that give instant feedback and provides other helpful ways to further test your knowledge of the chapter.

Agriculture: Economics and Policy

If you eat, you are part of agriculture! In the United States, agriculture is important for a number of reasons. It is one of the nation's largest industries and major segments of it provide real-world examples of the pure-competition model developed in Chapters 8 and 9. Also, agriculture clearly shows the effects of government policies that interfere with supply and demand. Further, the industry provides excellent illustrations of Chapter 17's special-interest effect and rent-seeking behavior. Finally, it demonstrates the globalization of markets for farm commodities.

This chapter examines the circumstances in agriculture that have resulted in government intervention, the types and outcomes of government intervention, and recent major changes in farm policy.

Economics of Agriculture

Although economists refer to *the* agriculture industry, this segment of the economy is extremely diverse. Agriculture encompasses cattle ranches, fruit orchards, dairies, poultry plants, pig farms, grain farms, feed lots, vegetable plots, sugar-cane plantations, and much more. Some farm commodities (for example, soybeans and corn) are produced by thousands of individual farmers. Other farm commodities (such as poultry) are produced by just a handful of large firms. Some farm products (for example, wheat, milk, and sugar) are heavily subsidized through Federal government programs; other farm products (such as fruits, nuts, and potatoes) have much less government support.

Moreover, agriculture includes both farm products, or **farm commodities** (for example, wheat, soybeans, cattle, and rice), and also **food products** (items sold through restaurants or grocery stores). Generally, the number of competing firms in the market diminishes as farm products are refined into commercial food products. Although thousands of ranches and farms raise cattle, only four firms (Tyson, Cargill, JBS, and National) account for about 80 percent of red meat produced at cattle slaughtering/meat packing plants. And thousands of farms grow tomatoes, but only three companies (Heinz, Del-Monte, and Hunt) make the bulk of the ketchup sold in the United States.

Our focus in this chapter will be on farm commodities (or farm products) and the farms and ranches that produce them. Farm commodities usually are sold in highly competitive markets, whereas food products tend to be sold in markets characterized by monopolistic competition or oligopoly.

Partly because of large government subsidies, farming remains a generally profitable industry. U.S. consumers allocate 12 percent of their spending to food, and farmers and ranchers receive about $291 billion of revenue annually from sales of crops and livestock. Over the years, however, American farmers have experienced severely fluctuating prices and periodically low incomes. Further, they have had to adjust to the reality that agriculture is a declining industry. The farm share of GDP has declined from about 7 percent in 1950 to 1 percent today.

Let's take a close look at both the short-run and long-run economics of U.S. agriculture.

The Short Run: Price and Income Instability

Price and income instability in agriculture results from (1) an inelastic demand for agricultural products, combined with (2) fluctuations in farm output and (3) shifts of the demand curve for farm products.

Inelastic Demand for Agricultural Products In industrially advanced economies, the price elasticity of demand for agricultural products is low. For agricultural products in the aggregate, the elasticity coefficient is between .20 and .25. These figures suggest that the prices of farm products would have to fall by 40 to 50 percent for consumers to increase their purchases by a mere 10 percent. Consumers apparently put a low value on additional farm output compared with the value they put on additional units of alternative goods.

Why is this so? Recall that the basic determinant of elasticity of demand is substitutability. When the price of one product falls, the consumer tends to substitute that product for other products whose prices have not fallen. But in relatively wealthy societies this "substitution effect" is very modest for food. Although people may eat more, they do not switch from three meals a day to, say, five or six meals a day in response to a decline in the relative prices of farm products. Real biological factors constrain an individual's capacity to substitute food for other products.

The inelasticity of agricultural demand is also related to diminishing marginal utility. In a high-income economy, the population is generally well fed and well clothed; it is relatively saturated with the food and fiber of agriculture. Additional farm products therefore are subject to rapidly diminishing marginal utility. So very large price cuts are needed to induce small increases in food and fiber consumption.

Fluctuations in Output Farm output tends to fluctuate from year to year, mainly because farmers have limited control over their output. Floods, droughts, unexpected frost, insect damage, and similar disasters can mean poor crops, while an excellent growing season means bumper crops (unusually large outputs). Such natural occurrences are beyond the control of farmers, yet they exert an important influence on output.

In addition to natural phenomena, the highly competitive nature of many parts of farming and ranching makes it difficult for those producers to form huge combinations to control production. If the thousands of widely scattered and independent producers happened to plant an unusually large or abnormally small portion of their land one year, an extra-large or a very small farm output would result even if the growing season were normal.

Curve *D* in Figure 19.1 illustrates the inelastic demand for agricultural products. Combining that inelastic demand with the instability of farm production, we can see why agricultural prices and incomes are unstable. Even if the market demand for farm products remains fixed at *D*, its price inelasticity will magnify small changes in output

FIGURE 19.1 **The effects of changes in farm output on agricultural prices and income.** Because of the inelasticity of demand for farm products, a relatively small change in farm output (from Q_n to Q_p or Q_b) will cause a relatively large change in agricultural prices (from P_n to P_p or P_b). Farm income will change from the yellow area to the larger $0P_ppQ_p$ area or to the smaller $0P_bbQ_b$ area.

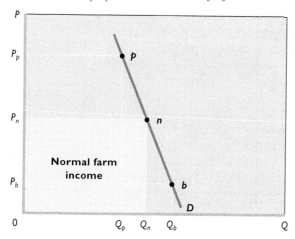

FIGURE 19.2 **The effect of a demand shift on agricultural prices and income.** Because of the highly inelastic demand for farm products, a small shift in demand (from D_1 to D_2) for farm products can drastically alter agricultural prices (P_1 to P_2) and farm income (area $0P_1aQ_n$ to area $0P_2bQ_n$), given a fixed level of production Q_n.

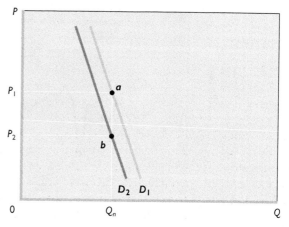

into relatively large changes in agricultural prices and income. For example, suppose that a "normal" crop of Q_n results in a "normal" price of P_n and a "normal" farm income represented by the yellow rectangle. A bumper crop or a poor crop will cause large deviations from these normal prices and incomes because of the inelasticity of demand.

If a good growing season occurs, the resulting large crop of Q_b will reduce farm income to that of area $0P_bbQ_b$. When demand is inelastic, an increase in the quantity sold will be accompanied by a more-than-proportionate decline in price. The net result is that total revenue, that is, total farm income, will decline disproportionately.

Similarly, a small crop caused by, say, drought will boost total farm income to that represented by area $0P_ppQ_p$. A decline in output will cause more-than-proportionate increases in price and income when demand is inelastic. Ironically, for farmers as a group, a poor crop may be a blessing and a bumper crop a hardship.

Conclusion: With a stable market demand for farm products, the inelasticity of that demand will turn relatively small changes in output into relatively larger changes in agricultural prices and income.

Fluctuations in Demand The third factor in the short-run instability of farm income results from shifts in the demand curve for agricultural products. Suppose that somehow farm output is stabilized at the "normal" level of Q_n in Figure 19.2. Now, because of the inelasticity of the demand for farm products, short-run changes in the

demand for those products will cause markedly different prices and incomes to be associated with this fixed level of output.

A slight decline in demand from D_1 to D_2 will reduce farm income from area $0P_1aQ_n$ to $0P_2bQ_n$. So a relatively small decline in demand gives farmers significantly less income for the same amount of farm output. Conversely, a slight increase in demand—as from D_2 to D_1—provides a sizable increase in farm income for the same volume of output. Again, large price and income changes occur because demand is inelastic.

It is tempting to argue that the sharp declines in agricultural prices that accompany a decrease in demand will cause many farmers to close down in the short run, reducing total output and alleviating the price and income declines. But farm production is relatively insensitive to price changes in the short run because farmers' fixed costs are high compared with their variable costs.

Interest, rent, tax, and mortgage payments on land, buildings, and equipment are the major costs faced by the farmer. These are all fixed charges. Furthermore, the labor supply of farmers and their families can also be regarded as a fixed cost. As long as they stay on their farms, farmers cannot reduce their costs by firing themselves. Their variable costs are the costs of the small amounts of extra help they may employ, as well as expenditures for seed, fertilizer, and fuel. As a result of their high proportion of fixed costs, farmers are usually better off working their land even when they are losing money since they would lose much more by shutting down their operations for the year.

FIGURE 19.3 **U.S. farm exports as a percentage of farm output, 1950–2008.** Exports of farm output have increased as a percentage of total farm output (the value of agricultural-sector production) in the United States. But this percentage has been quite variable, contributing to the instability of the demand for U.S. farm output.

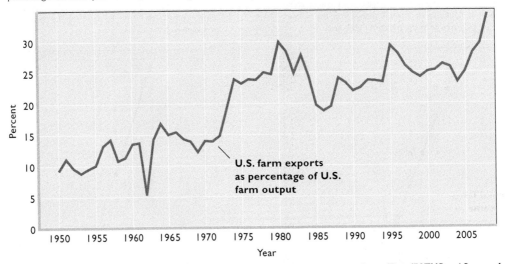

Source: Derived by the authors from *Foreign Agricultural Trade of the United States,* **www.ers.usda.gov/Data/FATUS**; and Bureau of Economic Analysis, **www.bea.gov**.

Only in the long run will exiting the industry make sense for them.

But why is agricultural demand unstable? The major source of demand volatility in U.S. agriculture springs from its dependence on world markets. As we show in Figure 19.3, that dependency has increased since 1950. The yearly ups and downs of the line in the figure also reveal that, as a percentage of total U.S. farm output, farm exports are highly unstable.

The incomes of U.S. farmers are sensitive to changes in weather and crop production in other countries: Better crops abroad mean less foreign demand for U.S. farm products. Similarly, cyclical fluctuations in incomes in Europe or Southeast Asia, for example, may shift the demand for U.S. farm products. Changes in foreign economic policies may also change demand. For instance, if the nations of western Europe decide to provide their farmers with greater protection from foreign competition, U.S. farmers will have less access to those markets and demand for U.S. farm exports will fall.

International politics also add to demand instability. Changing political relations between the United States and China and the United States and Russia have boosted exports to those countries in some periods and reduced them in others. Changes in the international value of the dollar may also be critical. Depreciation of the dollar increases the demand for U.S. farm products (which become cheaper to foreigners), whereas appreciation of the dollar diminishes foreign demand for U.S. farm products.

Figure 19.4 shows inflation-adjusted U.S. prices for cattle, hogs, corn, and wheat from 1950 through 2009. The short-run economics of price volatility is evident. So, too, is the general decline of real (inflation-adjusted) agricultural prices from 1950 through the late 1990s.

Since the late 1990s, however, the prices of these four commodities have not continued the overall downward trend that they had previously followed. Prices continued to be volatile but remained in 2009 about where they had been in the late 1990s. In addition, there were significant spikes in corn and wheat prices in 2006 and 2007. For example, the inflation-adjusted price of corn increased from $1.91 per bushel in 2005 to $4.15 per bushel in 2007 before declining to $3.14 in early 2010.

The lack of a downward trend in commodity prices starting in the late 1990s coupled with the doubling of wheat and corn prices in 2006 and 2007 led some economists to wonder whether the era of inflation-adjusted price decreases in agriculture had come to an end. They speculated that the rising demand for food in emerging economies such as China together with the growing demand for farm products to produce ethanol might reverse the long-run downward trend. But, as Figure 19.4 reveals, several previous price spikes as well as flat periods in agricultural prices have occurred. Each of these events eventually yielded to the general historical downward trend in agricultural prices. Whether this pattern will occur again remains to be seen.

FIGURE 19.4 Inflation-adjusted U.S. agricultural prices, selected commodities, 1950–2009. Inflation-adjusted U.S. prices (in 2005 dollars) for cattle, hogs, corn, and wheat during the second half of the twentieth century reflected both volatility and general decline.

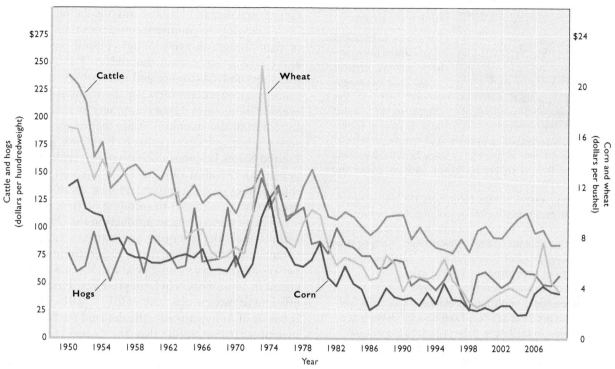

Source: Author calculations using nominal values from Global Financial Data, **globalfinancialdata.com**, adjusted for inflation with the GDP deflator published by the Bureau of Economic Analysis, **bea.gov**.

The Long Run: A Declining Industry

Two dynamic characteristics of agricultural markets explain why agriculture has been a declining industry:

- Over time, the supply of farm products has increased rapidly because of technological progress.
- The demand for farm products has increased slowly because it is inelastic with respect to income and because it is largely limited by population growth, which has not been rapid in the United States.

Let's examine each of these supply and demand forces.

Technology and Supply Increases A rapid rate of technological advance has significantly increased the supply of agricultural products. This technological progress has many roots: the mechanization of farms, improved techniques of land management, soil conservation, irrigation, development of hybrid crops, availability of improved fertilizers and insecticides, polymer-coated seeds, and improvements in the breeding and care of livestock. The amount of capital used per farmworker increased 15 times between 1930 and 1980, permitting a fivefold increase in the amount of land cultivated per farmer. The simplest

measure of these advances is the U.S. Agriculture Department's index of farm output per unit of farm labor. In 1950 a single unit of farm labor could produce 14 units of farm output. This amount increased to 43 in 1970, 60 in 1980, 91 in 1990, 128 in 2000, and 154 in 2008. Over the last half-century, productivity in agriculture has advanced twice as fast as productivity in the nonfarm economy.

Most of the technological advances in agriculture were not initiated by farmers. Rather, they are the result of government-sponsored programs of research and education and the initiative of the suppliers of farm inputs. Land-grant colleges, experiment stations, county agents of the Agricultural Extension Service, educational pamphlets issued by the United States Department of Agriculture (USDA), and the research departments of farm machinery, pesticide, and fertilizer producers have been the primary sources of technological advance in U.S. agriculture.

More recently, technological advance has been fueled by the incorporation of advanced information technologies into farming. Computers and the Internet give farmers instant access to information about soil conditions, estimated crop yields, farm-product prices, available land for purchase or lease, and much more. They also provide

CONSIDER THIS . . .

Risky Business

The short-run instability of agricultural prices and farm income creates considerable risk in agriculture. Later in this chapter we will find that farm programs (direct payments, countercyclical payments, and "repay-or-default" loans) reduce the risk of farming for many farmers. But these programs are limited to certain crops, such as grains and oilseeds.

Fortunately, several private techniques for managing risk have become commonplace in agriculture. The purpose of these measures is to "smooth" income over time, "hedging" against short-run output and price fluctuations. Hedging is an action by a buyer or seller to protect against a change in future prices prior to an anticipated purchase or sale.

Farm risk-management techniques include:

- *Futures markets.* In the futures market, farmers can buy or sell farm products at prices fixed now, for delivery at a specified date in the future. If the price falls, farmers will still obtain revenue based on the higher price fixed in the futures market. If the price rises, the buyer will benefit by getting the farm commodity at the lower price fixed in the futures market.
- *Contracting with processors.* In advance of planting, farmers can directly contract with food processors (firms such as sugar beet refiners, ethanol plants, and feed lots) to assure themselves of a fixed price per unit of their farm or ranch output.
- *Crop revenue insurance.* Farmers can buy crop revenue insurance, which insures them against gross revenue losses resulting from storm damage and other natural occurrences.
- *Leasing land.* Farm operators can reduce their risk by leasing some of their land to other operators who pay them cash rent. The rent payment is stable, regardless of the quality of the crop and crop prices.
- *Nonfarm income.* Many farm households derive substantial parts of their total income from off-farm income, such as spousal work and agricultural investments. These more-stable elements of income cushion the instability of farm income.

Although farming remains a risky business, farm operators have found creative ways to manage the inherent risks of price and income instability.

farmers with sophisticated business software to help track and manage their operations.

Lagging Demand

Increases in the demand for agricultural products have failed to keep pace with these technologically created increases in the supply of the products. The reason lies in the two major determinants of agricultural demand: income and population.

In developing countries, consumers must devote most of their meager incomes to agricultural products—food and clothing—to sustain themselves. But as income expands beyond subsistence and the problem of hunger diminishes, consumers increase their outlays on food at ever-declining rates. Once consumers' stomachs are filled, they turn to the amenities of life that manufacturing and services, not agriculture, provide. Economic growth in the United States has boosted average per capita income far beyond the level of subsistence. As a result, increases in the incomes of U.S. consumers now produce less-than-proportionate increases in spending on farm products.

The demand for farm products in the United States is income-inelastic; it is quite insensitive to increases in income. Estimates indicate that a 10 percent increase in real per capita after-tax income produces about a 1 percent increase in consumption of farm products. That means a coefficient of income elasticity of 0.1 ($= 0.01/.10$). So as the incomes of Americans rise, the demand for farm products increases far less rapidly than the demand for goods and services in general.

The second reason for lagging demand relates to population growth. Once a certain income level has been reached, each consumer's intake of food and fiber becomes relatively fixed. Thus subsequent increases in demand depend directly on growth in the number of consumers. In most advanced nations, including the United States, the demand for farm products increases at a rate roughly equal to the rate of population growth. Because U.S. population growth has not been rapid, the increase in U.S. demand for farm products has not kept pace with the rapid growth of farm output.

Graphical Portrayal

The combination of an inelastic and slowly increasing demand for agricultural products with a rapidly increasing supply puts strong downward pressure on agricultural prices and income. Figure 19.5 shows a large increase in agricultural supply accompanied by a very modest increase in demand. Because of the inelasticity of demand, those shifts result in a sharp decline in agricultural prices, accompanied by a relatively small increase in output. So farm income declines. On the graph, we see that farm income before the increases in demand and supply (measured by rectangle $0P_1aQ_1$) exceeds farm income after those increases ($0P_2bQ_2$). Because farm products have inelastic demand, an increase in supply relative to demand creates persistent downward pressure on farm income.

Consequences

The actual consequences of the demand and supply changes over time have been those

FIGURE 19.5 **The long-run decline of agricultural prices and farm income.** In the long run, increases in the demand for U.S. farm products (from D_1 to D_2) have not kept pace with the increases in supply (from S_1 to S_2) resulting from technological advances. Because agricultural demand is inelastic, these shifts have tended to depress agricultural prices (from P_1 to P_2) and reduce farm income (from $0P_1aQ_1$ to $0P_2bQ_2$) while increasing output only modestly (from Q_1 to Q_2).

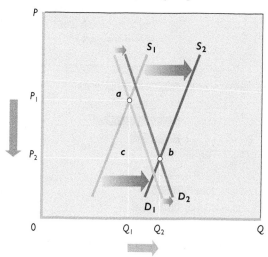

GLOBAL PERSPECTIVE 19.1

Average Percentage of Labor Force in Agriculture, Selected Nations, 2002–2008 Data

High-income nations devote a much smaller percentage of their labor forces to agriculture than do low-income nations. Because their workforces are so heavily committed to producing the food and fiber needed for their populations, low-income nations have relatively less labor available to produce housing, schools, autos, and the other goods and services that contribute to a high standard of living.

Source: World Development Indicators 2010, World Bank, **databank.worldbank.org**.

predicted by the pure-competition model. The supply and demand conditions just outlined have increased the minimum efficient scale (MES) in agriculture and reduced crop prices. Farms that are too small to realize productivity gains and take advantage of economies of scale have discovered that their average total costs exceed the (declining) prices for their crops. So they can no longer operate profitably. In the long run, financial losses in agriculture have triggered a massive exit of workers to other sectors of the economy, as shown by Table 19.1.

TABLE 19.1 U.S. Farm Employment and Number of Farms, 1950–2008

Year	Farm Employment* In Millions of People	As Percentage of Total Employment	Number of Farms, Thousands
1950	9.3	15.8	5388
1960	6.2	9.4	3962
1970	4.0	5.0	2954
1980	3.5	3.5	2440
1990	2.5	2.1	2146
2000	2.2	1.6	2172
2008	1.8	1.2	2200

*Includes self-employed farmers, unpaid farmworkers, and hired farmworkers.

Sources: Derived by the authors from *Economic Report of the President, 2010,* Table B-100; U.S. Bureau of Labor Statistics, **www.bls.gov**, and Department of Agriculture, Economic Research Service, **www.ers.usda.gov**.

They have also caused a major consolidation of smaller farms into larger ones. A person farming, say, 240 acres of corn three decades ago is today likely to be farming two or three times that number of acres. Large corporate firms, collectively called **agribusiness,** have emerged in some areas of farming such as potatoes, beef, fruits, vegetables, and poultry. Today, there are 2.2 million farms compared to about 4 million in 1960, and farm labor constitutes about 1.2 percent of the U.S. labor force compared to 9.4 percent in 1960. (Global Perspective 19.1 compares the most recent labor-force percentages for several nations.)

Farm-Household Income

Traditionally, the income of farm households was well below that of nonfarm households. But even with the lower real crop prices, that imbalance has reversed. In 2008—a particularly good year for agriculture—the average income of farm households was $78,803, compared to $68,424 for all U.S. households. Outmigration, consolidation, rising farm productivity, and significant government subsidies have boosted farm income *per farm household* (of which there are fewer than before).

Also, members of farm households operating smaller farms have increasingly taken jobs in nearby towns and cities. On average, only about 11 percent of the income of farm households derives from farming activities. This average, however, is pulled downward by the many households living in rural areas and operating small "residential farms." For households operating "commercial farms"—farms with annual sales of $250,000 or more—about 73 percent of the average income of $182,842 in 2008 derived from farming. Although agriculture is a declining industry, the 8 percent of farm households operating commercial farms in the United States are doing remarkably well, at least as a group.

QUICK REVIEW 19.1

- Agricultural prices and incomes are volatile in the short run because an inelastic demand converts small changes in farm output and demand into relatively larger changes in prices and income.
- Technological progress has generated large increases in the supply of farm products over time.
- Increases in demand for farm products have been modest in the United States because demand is inelastic with respect to income and because population growth has been modest.
- The combination of large increases in supply and small increases in demand has made U.S. agriculture a declining industry (as measured by the value of agricultural output as a percentage of GDP).

Economics of Farm Policy

The U.S. government has subsidized agriculture since the 1930s with a "farm program" that includes (1) support for agricultural prices, income, and output; (2) soil and water conservation; (3) agricultural research; (4) farm credit; (5) crop insurance; and (6) subsidized sale of farm products in world markets.

We will focus on the main element of farm policy: the programs designed to prop up prices and income. This topic is particularly timely because in recent years (specifically, 1996, 2002, and 2008) Congress passed new farm laws replacing traditional forms of farm subsidies with new forms. To understand these new policies, we need to understand the policies they replaced and the purposes and outcomes of farm subsidies. Between 2000 and 2009, American farmers received an average of $16.4 billion of direct government subsidies each year. (As indicated in

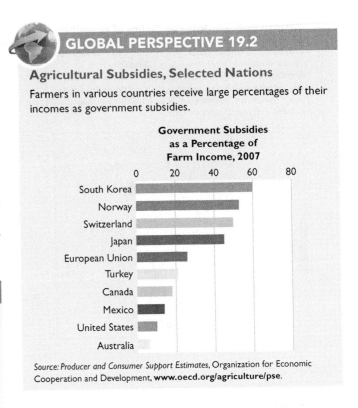

GLOBAL PERSPECTIVE 19.2

Agricultural Subsidies, Selected Nations

Farmers in various countries receive large percentages of their incomes as government subsidies.

Government Subsidies as a Percentage of Farm Income, 2007

South Korea, Norway, Switzerland, Japan, European Union, Turkey, Canada, Mexico, United States, Australia

Source: Producer and Consumer Support Estimates, Organization for Economic Cooperation and Development, www.oecd.org/agriculture/pse.

Global Perspective 19.2, farm subsidies are common in many nations.)

Rationale for Farm Subsidies

A variety of arguments have been made to justify farm subsidies over the decades:

- Although farm products are necessities of life, many farmers have relatively low incomes, so they should receive higher prices and incomes through public help.
- The "family farm" is a fundamental U.S. institution and should be nurtured as a way of life.
- Farmers are subject to extraordinary hazards—floods, droughts, and insects—that most other industries do not face. Without government help, farmers cannot fully insure themselves against these disasters.
- While many farmers face purely competitive markets for their outputs, they buy inputs of fertilizer, farm machinery, and gasoline from industries that have considerable market power. Whereas those resource-supplying industries are able to control their prices, farmers are at the "mercy of the market" in selling their output. The supporters of subsidies argue that agriculture warrants public aid to offset the disadvantageous market-power imbalances faced by farmers.

Background: The Parity Concept

The Agricultural Adjustment Act of 1933 established the **parity concept** as a cornerstone of agricultural policy. The rationale of the parity concept can be stated in both real and nominal terms. In real terms, parity says that year after year for a fixed output of farm products, a farmer should be able to acquire a specific total amount of other goods and services. A particular real output should always result in the same real income: "If a farmer could take a bushel of corn to town in 1912 and sell it for enough money to buy a shirt, he should be able to sell a bushel of corn today and buy a shirt." In nominal terms, the parity concept suggests that the relationship between the prices received by farmers for their output and the prices they must pay for goods and services should remain constant. The parity concept implies that if the price of shirts tripled over some time period, then the price of corn should have tripled too. Such a situation is said to represent 100 percent of parity.

The **parity ratio** is the ratio of prices received to prices paid, expressed as a percentage. That is:

$$\text{Parity ratio} = \frac{\text{prices received by farmers}}{\text{prices paid by farmers}}$$

Why farmers would benefit from having the prices of their products based on 100 percent of parity is obvious. By 2010 nominal prices paid by farmers had increased 24-fold since 1900–1914, whereas nominal prices received by farmers had increased only about 9-fold. In 2010 the parity ratio stood at .36 (or 36 percent), indicating that prices received in 2010 could buy 36 percent as much as prices received in the 1910–1914 period. So a farm policy that enforced 100 percent of parity would generate substantially higher prices for farmers.

Economics of Price Supports

The concept of parity provides the rationale for government price floors on farm products. In agriculture those minimum prices are called **price supports.** We have shown that, in the long run, the market prices received by farmers have not kept up with the prices paid by them. One way to achieve parity, or some percentage thereof, is to have the government establish above-equilibrium price supports for farm products.

Many different price-support programs have been tried, but they all tend to have similar effects, some of which are subtle and negative. Suppose in Figure 19.6 that the equilibrium price is P_e and the price support is P_s. Then the major effects would be as follows.

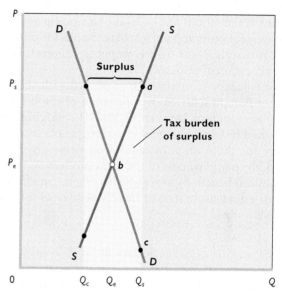

FIGURE 19.6 Price supports, agricultural surpluses, and transfers to farmers. The market demand D and supply S of a farm product yield equilibrium price P_e and quantity Q_e. An above-equilibrium price support P_s results in consumption of quantity Q_c, production of quantity Q_s and a surplus of quantity $Q_s - Q_c$. The yellow rectangle represents a transfer of money from taxpayers to farmers. Triangle *bac* within the yellow rectangle shows the efficiency loss (or a deadweight loss) to society.

Surplus Output The most obvious result is a product surplus. Consumers are willing to purchase only Q_c units at the supported price, while farmers supply Q_s units. What about the $Q_s - Q_c$ surplus that results? The government must buy it to make the above-equilibrium price support effective. As you will see, this surplus farm output means that agriculture receives an overallocation of resources.

Gain to Farmers Farmers benefit from price supports. In Figure 19.6, gross farm revenue rises from the free-market level represented by area $0P_e b Q_e$ to the larger, supported level shown by area $0P_s a Q_s$.

Loss to Consumers Consumers lose; they pay a higher price (P_s rather than P_e) and consume less (Q_c rather than Q_e) of the product. In some instances differences between the market price and the supported price are substantial. For example, the U.S.-supported price of a pound of sugar is about 32 percent higher than the world market price, and a quart of fluid milk is estimated to cost consumers twice as much as it would without government programs. Moreover, the burden of higher food prices falls disproportionately on the poor because they spend a larger part of their incomes on food.

Efficiency Losses Society loses because price supports create allocative inefficiency by encouraging an overallocation of resources to agriculture. A price floor (P_s) attracts more resources to the agricultural sector than would the free-market price (P_e). Viewed through the pure-competition model, the market supply curve in Figure 19.6 represents the marginal costs of all farmers producing this product at the various output levels. An efficient allocation of resources occurs at point *b*, where the market price P_e is equal to marginal cost. So the output Q_e reflects that efficient allocation of resources.

In contrast, the output Q_s associated with the price support P_s represents an overallocation of resources; for all units of output between Q_e and Q_s, marginal costs (measured on curve *S*) exceed the prices people are willing to pay for those units (measured on curve *D*). Simply stated, the marginal cost of the extra production exceeds its marginal benefit to society. Society incurs an efficiency loss (or a deadweight loss) of area *bac* because of the price-support system.

Other Social Losses Society at large loses in other ways.

Taxpayers pay higher taxes to finance the government's purchase of the surplus. This added tax burden is equal to the surplus output $Q_s - Q_c$ multiplied by its price P_s, as shown by the yellow area in Figure 19.6. Recall, too, that the mere collection of taxes imposes an efficiency loss (Figure 16.10). Also, the cost of storing surplus farm output adds to this tax burden.

Government's intervention in agriculture also entails administrative costs. Thousands of government workers are needed to administer U.S. price supports and other farm programs.

Finally, the rent-seeking activity involved—the pursuit of political support to maintain price supports—is costly and socially wasteful. Farm groups spend considerable sums to sustain political support for price floors and other programs that enhance farm incomes.

Environmental Costs We know from Figure 19.6 that price supports encourage additional production. Although some of that extra output may come from the use of additional land, much of it comes from heavier use of fertilizer and pesticides. Those pesticides and fertilizers may pollute the environment (for example, groundwater) and create residues in food that pose health risks to farmworkers and consumers. Research shows a positive relationship between the level of price-support subsidies and the use of agrochemicals.

Farm policy also may cause environmental problems in less obvious ways. Farmers benefit from price supports only when they use their land consistently for a specific crop such as corn or wheat. That creates a disincentive to practice crop rotation, which is a nonchemical technique for controlling pests. Farm policy thus encourages the substitution of chemicals for other forms of pest control.

Also, we know from the concept of derived demand that an increase in the price of a product will increase the demand for relevant inputs. In particular, price supports for farm products increase the demand for land. And the land that farmers bring into farm production is often environmentally sensitive "marginal" land, such as steeply sloped, erosion-prone land, or wetlands that provide wildlife habitat. Similarly, price supports result in the use of more water for irrigation, and the resulting runoff may contribute to soil erosion.

International Costs Actually, the costs of farm price supports go beyond those indicated by Figure 19.6. Price supports generate economic distortions that cross national boundaries. For example, the high prices caused by price supports make the U.S. agricultural market attractive to foreign producers. But inflows of foreign agricultural products would serve to increase supplies in the United States, aggravating the problem of U.S. surpluses. To prevent that from happening, the United States is likely to impose import barriers in the form of tariffs or quotas. Those barriers tend to restrict the output of more-efficient foreign producers while encouraging more output from less-efficient U.S. producers. The result is a less-efficient use of world agricultural resources. This chapter's Last Word suggests that this is indeed the case for sugar.

Similarly, as the United States and other industrially advanced countries with similar agricultural programs dump surplus farm products on world markets, the prices of such products are depressed. Developing countries are often heavily dependent on world commodity markets for their incomes. So they are particularly hurt because their export earnings are reduced. Thus, U.S. subsidies for rice production have imposed significant costs on Thailand, a major rice exporter. Similarly, U.S. cotton programs have adversely affected Egypt, Mexico, and other cotton-exporting nations.

Reduction of Surpluses

Figure 19.6 suggests that programs designed to reduce market supply (shift *S* leftward) or increase market demand (shift *D* rightward) would help boost the market price toward the supported price P_s. Further, such programs would reduce or eliminate farm surpluses. The U.S. government has tried both supply and demand approaches to reduce or eliminate surpluses.

Restricting Supply Until recently, public policy focused mainly on restricting farm output. In particular, **acreage allotments** accompanied price supports. In return for guaranteed prices for their crops, farmers had to agree to limit the number of acres they planted in that crop. The U.S. Department of Agriculture first set the price support and then estimated the amount of the product consumers would buy at the supported price. It then translated that amount into the total number of planted acres necessary to provide it. The total acreage was apportioned among states, counties, and ultimately individual farmers.

These supply-restricting programs were only partially successful. They did not eliminate surpluses, mainly because acreage reduction did not result in a proportionate decline in production. Some farmers retired their worst land and kept their best land in production. They also cultivated their tilled acres more intensively. Superior seed, more and better fertilizer and insecticides, and improved farm equipment were used to enhance output per acre. And nonparticipating farmers expanded their planted acreage in anticipation of overall higher prices. Nevertheless, the net effect of acreage allotment undoubtedly was a reduction of farm surpluses and their associated costs to taxpayers.

Bolstering Demand Government has tried several ways to increase demand for U.S. agricultural products. For example, both government and private industry have spent large sums on research to create new uses for agricultural goods. The production of "gasohol," which is a blend of gasoline and alcohol (ethanol) made mainly from corn, is one such successful attempt to increase the demand for farm output. (See the nearby Consider This box for a fuller discussion of ethanol.) Recent attempts to promote "biodiesel," a fuel made from soybean oil and other natural vegetable oils, also fit the demand-enhancement approach.

The government has also created a variety of programs to stimulate consumption of farm products. For example, the objective of the food-stamp program is not only to reduce hunger but also to bolster the demand for food. Similarly, the Food for Peace program has enabled developing countries to buy U.S. surplus farm products with their own currencies, rather than having to use dollars. The Federal government spends millions of dollars each year to advertise and promote global sales of U.S. farm products. Furthermore, U.S. negotiators have pressed hard in international trade negotiations to

CONSIDER THIS . . .

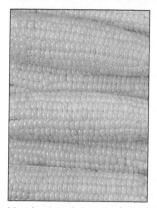

Putting Corn in Your Gas Tank

Government's promotion of greater production and use of corn-based ethanol serves both as a good example of an attempt by government to bolster the demand for U.S. farm products and as an example of how price changes can ripple through markets and produce myriad secondary effects. Gasoline producers blend ethanol (an alcohol-like substance) with conventional gasoline refined from oil. The government's rationale for promoting ethanol is to reduce U.S. dependency on foreign oil, but the strongest proponents are from states in the Corn Belt.

The ethanol program has several facets, including tariffs on imported ethanol, subsidies to oil refineries that buy ethanol, and mandates to industry to increase their use of alternative fuels. The rising demand for ethanol that resulted contributed to a 50 percent rise in the inflation-adjusted price of a bushel of corn between 2005 and 2007.

But numerous secondary effects from the increased price of corn also occurred. Farmers shifted production toward corn and away from soybeans, sorghum, and other crops. The decreases in the supply of these other crops raised their prices, too. Also, because corn is used as a major feedstock, the price of beef, pork, and chicken rose.

The ethanol subsidies had other secondary effects. The prices of seed, fertilizer, and farmland all increased. Because corn is a water-intensive crop, its expanded production resulted in faster withdrawals of irrigation water from underground aquifers. The refining of ethanol also depleted ground water or removed it from rivers. Moreover, the increased use of fertilizer in corn production increased the runoff of nitrogen from fertilizer into streams and rivers, causing environmental damage.

The price effects of ethanol subsidies, however, may moderate as farmers shift additional land to corn, increasing its supply and reducing its price. Nevertheless, the multiple impacts of public policy illustrate an important economic maxim: In the economy, it is difficult to do just *one* thing.

persuade foreign nations to reduce trade barriers to the importing of farm products.

During the era of price supports, the government's supply-restricting and demand-increasing efforts boosted agricultural prices and reduced surplus production, but they did not succeed in eliminating the sizable surpluses.

Criticisms and Politics

After decades of experience with government price-support programs, it became apparent in the 1990s that farm policy was not working well. Major criticisms of farm subsidies emerged, as did a more skeptical analysis of the politics of those subsidies.

Criticisms of the Parity Concept

Economists uniformly rejected the rationale of the parity concept. They found no economic logic in the proposition that if a bushel of wheat could buy a shirt in 1900, it should still be able to buy a shirt several decades later. The relative values of goods and services are established by supply and demand, and those relative values change over time as technology changes, resource prices change, tastes change, and substitute resources and new products emerge. A fully equipped personal computer, monitor, and printer cost as much as a cheap new automobile in 1985. That was not true just a decade later because the price of computer equipment had dropped so dramatically. Based on the parity concept, one could argue that price supports and subsidies were justified for computer manufacturers!

Criticisms of the Price-Support System

Criticisms of the price-support system were equally severe.

Symptoms, Not Causes The price-support strategy in agriculture was designed to treat the symptoms, not the causes of the farm problem. The root cause of the long-run farm problem was misallocation of resources between agriculture and the rest of the economy. Historically, the problem had been one of too many farmers. The effect of

that misallocation was relatively low agricultural prices and low farm income. But the price and income supports encouraged people to stay in farming rather than move to nonfarm occupations. That is, the price and income orientation of the farm program slowed the reallocation of resources necessary to resolve the long-run farm problem.

Misguided Subsidies Because price supports were on a per-bushel basis, the subsidy system benefited those farmers who needed subsidies the least. If the goal of farm policy was to raise low farm incomes, it followed that any program of Federal aid should have been aimed at farmers with the lowest incomes. But the poor, low-output farmer did not produce and sell enough in the market to get much aid from price supports. Instead, the large, prosperous farmer reaped the benefits because of sizable output. On equity grounds, direct income payments to struggling farmers are highly preferable to indirect price-support subsidies that go primarily to large-scale, prosperous farmers. Better yet, say many economists, would be transition and retraining support for farmers willing to move out of farming and into other occupations and businesses in greater demand.

A related point concerns land values. The price and income benefits that the price-support system provided increased the value of farmland. By making crops more valuable, price supports made the land itself more valuable. That was helpful to farmers who owned the land they farmed but not to farmers who rented land. Farmers rented about 40 percent of their farmland, mostly from well-to-do nonfarm landlords. So, price supports became a subsidy to people who were not actively engaged in farming.

Policy Contradictions Because farm policy had many objectives, it often led to contradictions. Whereas most subsidized research was aimed at increasing farm productivity and the supply of farm products, acreage-allotment programs required that farmers take land out of production in order to reduce supply. Price supports for crops meant increased feed costs for ranchers and farmers and high consumer prices for animal products. Tobacco farmers were subsidized even though tobacco consumption was causing serious health problems. The U.S. sugar program raised prices for domestic producers by imposing import quotas that conflicted with free-trade policies. Conservation programs called for setting aside land for wildlife habitat, while price supports provided incentives to bring such acreage into production.

All these criticisms helped spawn policy reform. Nevertheless, as we will see, those reforms turned out to be less substantive than originally conceived. Nearly all these criticisms are as valid for current farm policy as they were for the price-support program.

The Politics of Farm Policy

In view of these criticisms, why did the United States continue its price-support program for 60 years and why does it still continue that program for sugar, milk, and tobacco? Why do farm subsidies in the billions of dollars still occur?

Public Choice Theory Revisited Public choice theory (Chapter 17) helps answer these questions. Recall that rent-seeking behavior occurs when a group (a labor union, firms in a specific industry, or farmers producing a particular crop) uses political means to transfer income or wealth to itself at the expense of another group or of society as a whole. And recall that the special-interest effect involves a program or policy from which a small group receives large benefits at the expense of a much larger group whose members individually suffer small losses. Both rent-seeking behavior and the special-interest effect help explain the politics of farm subsidies.

Suppose a certain group of farmers, say, peanut or sugar producers, organize and establish a well-financed political action committee (PAC). The PAC's job is to promote government programs that will transfer income to the group (this is rent-seeking behavior). The PAC vigorously lobbies U.S. senators and representatives to enact or to continue price supports, production quotas, or import quotas for peanuts or sugar. The PAC does this in part by making political contributions to sympathetic legislators. Although peanut production is heavily concentrated in a few states such as Georgia, Alabama, and Texas, the peanut PAC will also make contributions to legislators from other states in order to gain support.

But how can a small interest group like peanut or sugar growers successfully lobby to increase its own income at the expense of society as a whole? Because even though the total cost of the group's programs might be considerable, the cost imposed on each individual taxpayer is small (this is the special-interest effect). Taxpayers are likely to be uninformed about and indifferent to such programs since they have little at stake. Unless you grow sugar beets or peanuts, you probably have no idea how much these programs cost you as an individual taxpayer and consumer and therefore do not object when your legislator votes for, say, a sugar-support program. Thus, the PAC encounters little or no lobbying against its efforts.

Political logrolling—the trading of votes on policies and programs—also works to perpetuate certain programs: Senator Foghorn agrees to vote for a program that benefits Senator Moribund's constituents, and Moribund returns the favor. Example: Many members of Congress who represent low-income urban areas vote in favor of farm subsidies. In return, representatives of agricultural areas support such programs as food stamps, which subsidize food for the poor. The result is a rural-urban coalition through which representatives from both areas provide benefits for their constituents and enhance their reelection chances. Such coalitions help explain why farm subsidies persist and why the food-stamp program has been expanded over the years.

Large agribusinesses that supply inputs to agriculture also lend political support to farm subsidies because subsidies increase the amounts of agrochemicals and farm machinery that farmers are able to buy. And most of the thousands of government employees whose jobs depend on farm programs are highly supportive. So, too, are owners of farmland.

Public choice theory also tells us that politicians are likely to favor programs that have hidden costs. As we have seen, that is often true of farm programs. Our discussion of Figure 19.6 indicated that price supports involve not simply a transfer of money from taxpayer to farmer but costs that are hidden as higher food prices, storage costs for surplus output, costs of administering farm programs, and costs associated with both domestic and international misallocations of resources. Because those costs are largely indirect and hidden, farm programs are much more acceptable to politicians and the public than they would be if all costs were explicit.

Changing Politics In spite of rent seeking, special interests, and logrolling, a combination of factors has somewhat altered the politics of farm subsidies in recent decades.

Declining Political Support As the farm population declines, agriculture's political power weakens. The farm population was about 25 percent of the general population in the 1930s, when many U.S. farm programs were established; now it is less than 2 percent. Urban congressional representatives now constitute a 10-to-1 majority over their rural colleagues. An increasing number of legislators are critically examining farm programs for their effects on consumers' grocery bills as well as on farm incomes. Also, more farmers themselves are coming to resent the intrusion of the Federal government into their farming decisions. A few rural-state congressional members now support free-market agriculture.

World Trade Considerations The United States has taken the lead to reduce barriers to world trade in

Word The Sugar Program: A Sweet Deal

The Sugar Program Is a Sweet Deal for Domestic Sugar Producers, but It Imposes Heavy Costs on Domestic Consumers, Domestic Candy Manufacturers, Foreign Producers, and the American Economy.

The continuing U.S. sugar program uses price supports and import quotas to guarantee a minimum price of sugar for domestic sugar producers. The program has significant effects, both domestically and internationally.

Domestic Costs Price supports and import quotas have boosted the domestic price of sugar to approximately 32 percent above the world price (for 2009, $.25 per pound compared to the international price of $.19 per pound). The aggregate cost to domestic consumers has been estimated at between $1.5 billion and $1.9 billion per year. In contrast, each sugar producer receives from subsidies alone an amount estimated to be twice the nation's average family income. In one particular year, a single producer received an estimated $30 million in benefits. Many sugar producers obtain more than $1 million each year in benefits.

Import Quotas As a consequence of high U.S. domestic price supports, foreign sugar producers have a strong incentive to sell

their output in the United States. But an influx of lower-priced foreign sugar into the U.S. domestic market would undermine U.S. price supports. The government therefore has imposed import quotas on foreign sugar. It decides how much sugar can be imported at a zero or very low tariff rate, and then it charges a prohibitively high tariff for any quantities above that amount. As the gap between U.S.-supported prices and world prices has widened, imports have declined as a percentage of sugar consumed in the United States. In 1975, about 30 percent of the sugar consumed in the United States was imported; currently about 20 percent comes from abroad. Domestic policy regarding the U.S. sugar industry largely dictates the nation's international trade policy with respect to sugar.

Developing Countries The loss of the U.S. market has had several harmful effects on sugar-exporting developing countries such as the Philippines, Brazil, and several Central American countries.

First, exclusion from the U.S. market has significantly reduced their export revenues—by an amount estimated to be many billions of dollars per year. That decline in export revenues is important because many of the sugar-producing countries depend on such revenues to pay interest and principal on large debts owed to the United States and other industrially advanced nations.

agricultural products. This has also contributed to the more critical attitude toward farm subsidies, particularly price supports. The nations of the European Union (EU) and many other nations support agricultural prices. And, to maintain their high domestic prices, they restrict imports of foreign farm products by imposing tariffs and quotas. They then try to rid themselves of their domestic surpluses by subsidizing exports into world markets. The effects on the United States are that (1) trade barriers hinder U.S. farmers from selling to EU nations and (2) subsidized exports from those nations depress world prices for agricultural products, making world markets less attractive to U.S. farmers.

Perhaps most important, farm programs such as those maintained by the EU and the United States distort both world agricultural trade and the international allocation of agricultural resources. Encouraged by artificially high prices, farmers in industrially advanced

nations produce more food and fiber than they would otherwise. The resulting surpluses flow into world markets, where they depress prices. This means that farmers in countries with no farm programs—many of them developing countries—face artificially low prices for their exports, which signals them to produce less. Overall, the result is a shift in production away from what would occur on the basis of comparative advantage. As an example, price supports cause U.S. agricultural resources to be used for sugar production, even though sugar can be produced at perhaps half the cost in the Caribbean countries and Australia.

Recognizing these distortions, in 1994 the 128 nations then belonging to the World Trade Organization (WTO) agreed to reduce farm price-support programs by 20 percent by the year 2000 and to reduce tariffs and quotas on imported farm products by 15 percent. Larger, more significant, reductions of farm subsidies and

404

Second, barred by quotas from sale in the U.S. market, the sugar produced by the developing countries has been added to world markets, where the increased supply has depressed the world price of sugar.

Third, domestic price supports have caused U.S. sugar production to expand to the extent that the United States may soon change from a sugar-importing to a sugar-exporting nation. That is, the U.S. sugar program may soon be a source of new competition for the sugar producers of the developing countries. Sugar price supports in the European Union have already turned that group of nations into sugar exporters.

U.S. Efficiency Loss The sugar program benefits sugar producers by about $1 billion annually but costs U.S. consumers about $1.5 billion to $1.9 billion each year. The excess of losses over gains is therefore $500 million to $900 million annually. This efficiency loss (or deadweight loss) results from the overallocation of U.S. resources to growing and processing sugar beets and sugar cane.

As a secondary effect, the higher domestic sugar prices have encouraged several U.S. confectionery firms (candy manufacturers) to relocate their operations to Canada or Mexico.

According to the U.S. Commerce Department, for every American job that has been added by the price supports in the cane sugar and sugar beet industries, three American jobs have been lost in the industries buying sugar. Government economists estimate that the confectionery industry has lost a total of about 17,000 jobs since 2003.

Global Resource Misallocation Both domestically and globally, the sugar price-support programs of the United States and other industrially advanced economies have distorted the worldwide allocation of agricultural resources. Price supports have caused a shift of resources to sugar production by less efficient U.S. producers, and U.S. import quotas and consequent low world sugar prices have caused more efficient foreign producers to restrict their production. Thus high-cost producers are producing more sugar and low-cost producers are producing less, resulting in the inefficient use of the world's agricultural resources.

Adding to the inefficient use of world resources, the relocation of candy manufacturers—to avoid artificially sweetened U.S. sugar prices—is moving capital and labor resources away from their place of comparative advantage.

agricultural tariffs are part of the agenda of the most recent round of trade negotiations (the Doha Development Agenda). But reaching agreement on those reductions has proved difficult. As of mid-2010, negotiations over these issues were completely stalled.

Recent Farm Policies

In the mid-1990s there was a common feeling among economists and political leaders that the goals and techniques of farm policy needed to be reexamined and revised. Moreover, crop prices were relatively high at the time and Congress wanted to reduce large Federal budget deficits.

Freedom to Farm Act of 1996

In 1996 Congress radically revamped 60 years of U.S. farm policy by passing the **Freedom to Farm Act.** The

law ended price supports and acreage allotments for wheat, corn, barley, oats, sorghum, rye, cotton, and rice. Farmers were allowed to respond to changing crop prices by planting as much or as little of these crops as they chose. Also, they were free to plant crops of their choice. If the price of, say, oats increased, farmers could plant more oats and less barley. Markets, not government programs, were to determine the kinds and amounts of crops grown.

To ease the transition away from price supports, the Freedom to Farm Act granted declining annual transition payments through 2002. The $37 billion of total scheduled payments through 2002 was based on the production levels of the crops each farmer previously had grown under the price-support system. So a previous wheat farmer, for example, would receive cash payments for 7 years regardless of the current price of wheat or amount of wheat presently grown.

But this ambitious plan to wean American agriculture from subsidies unraveled in 1998 and 1999, when sharply reduced export demand and strong crop production in the United States depressed the prices of many farm products. Congress responded by supplementing the previously scheduled transition payments with large "emergency aid" payments to farmers. Agricultural subsidies for 1999–2002 averaged $20 billion annually—even more than they were before passage of the Freedom to Farm Act.

The Food, Conservation, and Energy Act of 2008

Since 2002, agricultural policy in the United States has substantially retreated from the free-market intent of the 1996 law. Current subsidy programs continue the "freedom to plant" approach and provide revenue guarantees for farmers by ironically transforming the "transition payments" policy into a permanent program known as "direct payments." These revenue guarantees kick in automatically when crop prices (or total revenues) fall below targeted levels.

The **Food, Conservation, and Energy Act of 2008** is the present law under which subsidies are provided. The law extends through 2012 and provides three main forms of cash commodity subsidies, with an option on one of them.

Direct Payments The **direct payments** under the 2008 law are similar to the transition payments paid under the Freedom to Farm Act. The cash payments are fixed for each crop based on a farmer's historical pattern of production and are unaffected by current crop prices or current production. Farmers are free to plant as much or as little of any particular crop as they want and still receive these payments. These direct payments do not decline from year to year. They are a permanent transfer payment from the Federal government (general taxpayers) to farmers.

Countercyclical Payments This component of farm policy ties a separate set of subsidies to the difference between market prices of specified farm products and a target price set for each crop. Like direct payments, these **countercyclical payments (CCPs)** are based on previous crops grown and are received regardless of the current crop planted. For example, the target price for corn in the years 2008–2012 is $2.63 per bushel. If corn is at or exceeds $2.63 in one of those years, the farmer who qualifies will receive no CCP. But if the price is below $2.63, the farmer will receive CCP payments geared to the size of the price gap. The CCP system has returned a form of price supports to a prominent role in farm policy, but it bases those supports on past crops grown, not current crops planted.

Beginning in 2009, farmers obtained the option of withdrawing from the CCP program and instead participating in the Average Crop Revenue Election (ACRE). This program bases farmers' counter cyclical payments on average crop yields per acre in their states over the past five years along with the average national price for the crop in the past two years.

Marketing Loans Finally, current law contains a **marketing loan program** under which farmers can receive a loan (on a per-unit-of-output basis) from a government lender. If the crop price at harvest is higher than the price specified in the loan (the loan price), farmers can repay their loans, with interest. If the crop price is lower than the loan price, farmers can forfeit their harvested crops to the lender and be free of their loans. In this second case, farmers receive what amounts to a subsidy because the proceeds from the loan exceed the revenues from the sale of the crop in the market.

The 2008 farm law reduces the risk of price and revenue variability for farmers and increases farm income. But the law fails to address the problem of subsidies. However structured, subsidies slow the exodus of resources from agriculture and maintain high production levels. This means lower crop prices and less market income for farmers. These lower prices and reduced market incomes, in turn, provide the rationale for continued government subsidies!

QUICK REVIEW 19.3

- Farm policy in the United States has been heavily criticized for delaying the shift of resources away from farming, directing most subsidies to wealthier farmers, and being fraught with policy contradictions.

- The persistence of farm subsidies can largely be explained in terms of rent-seeking behavior, the special-interest effect, political logrolling, and other aspects of public choice theory.

- The Freedom to Farm Act of 1996 eliminated price supports and acreage allotments for many of the nation's crops, while continuing direct subsidies to farmers.

- The Food, Conservation, and Energy Act of 2008 provides three major kinds of farm subsidies: direct payments, countercyclical payments, and marketing loans.

Summary

1. In the short run, the highly inelastic demand for farm products transforms small changes in output and small shifts in demand into large changes in prices and income.

2. Over the long run, rapid technological advance, together with a highly inelastic and relatively slow-growing demand for agricultural output, has made agriculture a declining industry in the United States and dictated that resources exit the industry.

3. Historically, farm policy has been centered on price and based on the parity concept, which suggests that the relationship between prices received and paid by farmers should be constant over time.

4. The use of price floors or price supports has a number of economic effects: It (a) causes surplus production; (b) increases the incomes of farmers; (c) causes higher consumer prices for farm products; (d) creates an overallocation of resources to agriculture; (e) obliges society to pay higher taxes to finance the purchase and storage of surplus output; (f) increases pollution because of the greater use of agrochemicals and vulnerable land; and (g) forces other nations to bear the costs associated with import barriers and depressed world agricultural prices.

5. With only limited success, the Federal government has pursued programs to reduce agricultural supply and increase agricultural demand as a way to reduce the surpluses associated with price supports.

6. Economists have criticized U.S. farm policy for (a) confusing symptoms (low farm incomes) with causes (excess capacity), (b) providing the largest subsidies to high-income farmers, and (c) creating contradictions among specific farm programs.

7. The persistence of agricultural subsidies can be explained by public choice theory and, in particular, as

rent-seeking behavior; the special-interest effect; and political logrolling.

8. Political backing for price supports and acreage allotments has eroded for several reasons: (a) The number of U.S. farmers, and thus their political clout, has declined relative to the number of urban consumers of farm products; and (b) successful efforts by the United States to get other nations to reduce their farm subsidies have altered the domestic debate on the desirability of U.S. subsidies.

9. The Freedom to Farm Act of 1996 ended price supports and acreage allotments for wheat, corn, barley, oats, sorghum, rye, cotton, and rice. The law established declining annual transition payments through the year 2002, but those payments were no longer tied to crop prices or the current crop produced.

10. When crop prices plummeted in 1998 and 1999, Congress supplemented the transition payments of the Freedom to Farm Act with large amounts of emergency aid. Total subsidies to agriculture averaged $20 billion annually in the years 1999–2002.

11. Beginning in 2002, the Federal government retreated from the free-market principles of the Freedom to Farm Act, setting up a system of permanent direct payments to farmers along with countercyclical farm-revenue guarantees.

12. The Food, Conservation, and Energy Act of 2008 provides farmers with direct payments (based on previous crops planted), countercyclical payments (based on the differences between market prices and targeted prices), and marketing loans (based on a specified crop price and an option to either pay back the loan or forfeit the crop to the government lender).

Terms and Concepts

farm commodities	price supports	direct payments
food products	acreage allotments	countercyclical payments (CCPs)
agribusiness	Freedom to Farm Act	marketing loan program
parity concept	Food, Conservation, and Energy	
parity ratio	Act of 2008	

Questions

1. Carefully evaluate: "The supply and demand for agricultural products are such that small changes in agricultural supply result in drastic changes in prices. However, large changes in agricultural prices have modest effects on agricultural output." (Hint: A brief review of the distinction between *supply* and *quantity supplied* may be helpful.) Do exports

increase or reduce the instability of demand for farm products? Explain. LO1

2. What relationship, if any, can you detect between the facts that farmers' fixed costs of production are large and the supply of most agricultural products is generally inelastic? Be specific in your answer. LO1

3. Explain how each of the following contributes to the farm problem: LO1, LO2
   a. The inelasticity of demand for farm products.
   b. The rapid technological progress in farming.
   c. The modest long-run growth in demand for farm commodities.
   d. The volatility of export demand.
4. The key to efficient resource allocation is shifting resources from low-productivity to high-productivity uses. In view of the high and expanding physical productivity of agricultural resources, explain why many economists want to divert additional resources away from farming in order to achieve allocative efficiency. LO2
5. Explain and evaluate: "Industry complains of the higher taxes it must pay to finance subsidies to agriculture. Yet the trend of agricultural prices has been downward, while industrial prices have been moving upward, suggesting that on balance agriculture is actually subsidizing industry." LO3
6. "Because consumers as a group must ultimately pay the total income received by farmers, it makes no real difference whether the income is paid through free farm markets or through price supports supplemented by subsidies financed out of tax revenue." Do you agree? LO3
7. If in a given year the indexes of prices received and paid by farmers were 120 and 165, respectively, what would the parity ratio be? Explain the meaning of that ratio. LO3
8. Explain the economic effects of price supports. Explicitly include environmental and global impacts in your answer. On what grounds do economists contend that price supports cause a misallocation of resources? LO3
9. Use supply and demand curves to depict equilibrium price and output in a competitive market for some farm product. Then show how an above-equilibrium price floor (price support) would cause a surplus in this market. Demonstrate in your graph how government could reduce the surplus through a policy that (a) changes supply or (b) changes demand. Identify each of the following

actual government policies as primarily affecting the supply of or the demand for a particular farm product: acreage allotments, the food-stamp program, the Food for Peace program, a government buyout of dairy herds, and export promotion. LO3
10. Do you agree with each of the following statements? Explain why or why not. LO3, LO4
    a. The problem with U.S. agriculture is that there are too many farmers. That is not the fault of farmers but the fault of government programs.
    b. The Federal government ought to buy up all U.S. farm surpluses and give them away to developing nations.
    c. All industries would like government price supports if they could get them; agriculture has obtained price supports only because of its strong political clout.
11. What are the effects of farm subsidies such as those of the United States and the European Union on (a) domestic agricultural prices, (b) world agricultural prices, and (c) the international allocation of agricultural resources? LO3
12. Use public choice theory to explain the persistence of farm subsidies in the face of major criticisms of those subsidies. If the special-interest effect is so strong, what factors made it possible in 1996 for the government to end price supports and acreage allotments for several crops? LO4
13. What was the major intent of the Freedom to Farm Act of 1996? Do you agree with the intent? Why or why not? Did the law succeed in reducing overall farm subsidies? Why or why not? LO5
14. Distinguish the major features of direct subsidies, countercyclical payments, and marketing loan subsidies under the Food, Conservation, and Energy Act of 2008. In what way do countercyclical payments and marketing loans help reduce the volatility of farm income? In what way do direct subsidies perpetuate the long-run farm problem of too many resources in agriculture? LO5
15. **LAST WORD** What groups benefit and what groups lose from the U.S. sugar subsidy program?

Problems

1. Suppose that corn currently costs $4 per bushel and that wheat currently costs $3 per bushel. Also assume that the price elasticity of corn is .10, while the price elasticity of wheat is .15. For the following questions about elasticities, simply use the percentage changes that are provided rather than attempting to calculate those percentage changes yourself using the midpoint formula given in Chapter 4. LO1
   a. If the price of corn fell by 25 percent to $3 per bushel, by what percentage would the quantity demanded of corn increase? What if the price of corn fell by 50 percent to $2 per bushel?
   b. To what value would the price of wheat have to fall to induce consumers to increase their purchases of wheat by 5 percent?

c. If the government imposes a $.40 per bushel tax on corn so that the price of corn rises by 10 percent to $4.40 per bushel, by what percentage would the quantity demanded of corn decrease? If the initial quantity demanded is 10 billion bushels per year, by how many bushels would the quantity demanded decrease in response to this tax?
2. Suppose that both wheat and corn have an income elasticity of .1. LO1
   a. If the average income in the economy increases by 2 percent each year, by what percentage does the quantity demanded of wheat increase each year, holding all other factors constant? Holding all other factors constant, if 10 billion bushels are demanded this year, by how many

bushels will the quantity demanded increase next year if incomes rise by 2 percent?

b. Given that average personal income doubles in the United States about every 30 years, by about what percentage does the quantity demanded of corn increase every 30 years, holding all other factors constant?

3. Suppose that 10 workers were required in 2010 to produce 40,000 bushels of wheat on a 1000-acre farm. LO2

    a. What is the average output per acre? Per worker?

    b. If in 2020 only 8 workers produce 44,000 bushels of wheat on that same 1000-acre farm, what will be the average output per acre? Per worker?

    c. By how what percentage does productivity (output per worker) increase over those 10 years? Over those 10 years, what is the average annual percentage increase in productivity?

4. In 2009, it was estimated that the total value of all corn-production subsidies in the United States totaled about $4 billion. The population of the United States was approximately 300 million people that year. LO3

    a. On average, how much did corn subsidies cost per person in the United States in 2009? (Hint: A billion is a 1 followed by nine zeros. A million is a 1 followed by six zeros.)

    b. If each person in the United States is only willing to spend $.50 to support efforts to overturn the corn subsidy, and if antisubsidy advocates can only raise funds from 10 percent of the population, how much money will they be able to raise for their lobbying efforts?

    c. If the recipients of corn subsidies donate just one percent of the total amount that they receive in subsidies, how much could they raise to support lobbying efforts to continue the corn subsidy?

    d. By how many dollars does the amount raised by the recipients of the corn subsidy exceed the amount raised by the opponents of the corn subsidy?

FURTHER TEST YOUR KNOWLEDGE AT
www.mcconnell19e.com

At the text's Online Learning Center (OLC), **www.mcconnell19e.com**, you will find one or more Web-based questions that require information from the Internet to answer. We urge you to check them out; they will familiarize you with Web sites that may be helpful in other courses and perhaps even in your career. The OLC also features multiple-choice questions that give instant feedback and provides other helpful ways to further test your knowledge of the chapter.

Health Care

On March 23, 2010, President Barack Obama signed into law the **Patient Protection and Affordable Care Act (PPACA)**, a wide-ranging law that proponents claimed would lower health care costs while increasing access to quality health care for millions of poorer Americans.

At over 2400 pages, the legislation was designed to address a wide set of concerns relating to the provision, delivery, and cost of health care. These included the high and rapidly rising cost of health insurance for those who did have health insurance, the fact that tens of millions of Americans at any given moment were without health insurance, and the inability of many people with preexisting conditions to obtain health insurance.

The controversial law gave the Federal government sweeping new powers to promote universal insurance coverage and to regulate the details of insurance policies. Because health care spending was 17.3 percent of GDP in 2009, the law effectively put the Federal government in control of one-sixth

433

of the U.S. economy. This chapter applies microeconomic analysis to help explain the origin of the problems that the law was designed to address as well as the heated debate over whether the policies prescribed by the law are likely to achieve their goals.

The Health Care Industry

Because the boundaries of the health care industry are not precise, defining the industry is difficult. In general, it includes services provided in hospitals, nursing homes, laboratories, and physicians' and dentists' offices. It also includes prescription and nonprescription drugs, artificial limbs, and eyeglasses. Note, however, that many goods and services that may affect health are not included, for example, low-fat foods, vitamins, and health club services.

Health care is one of the largest U.S. industries, employing about 16 million people, including about 817,000 practicing physicians, or 271 doctors per 100,000 of population. There are about 5800 hospitals containing 951,000 beds. Americans make more than 1 billion visits to office-based physicians each year.

The U.S. Emphasis on Private Health Insurance

Many of the provisions of the Patient Protection and Affordable Care Act are focused on health insurance. This is because a high proportion of health care spending in the United States is provided through private health insurance policies paid for by employers. By contrast, many countries such as Canada have systems of **national health insurance** in which the government uses tax revenues to provide a basic package of health care to every resident at either no charge or at low cost-sharing levels. In such countries only a relatively few people bother to buy private health insurance—and then only to cover services that are not paid for by the national health insurance system.

The uniquely American emphasis on private health insurance paid for by employers is a relatively recent phenomenon. It began during the Second World War in response to price and wage controls that the Federal government imposed to prevent inflation. The wage controls were problematic for the private companies charged with building the tanks, planes, and boats needed to win the war. These firms needed to expand output rapidly and knew that doing so would be possible only if they could attract workers away from other industries. Several manufacturers stumbled on the strategy of offering free health insurance as a way of attracting workers. Unable to raise wages, the companies recruited the workers they needed by offering health insurance as a fringe benefit paid for by the employer.

After the war, price and wage controls were lifted. Nevertheless, more and more companies began to offer "free" health insurance to their employees. They did so because of a provision in the Federal tax law that makes it cheaper for companies to purchase insurance for their employees than it would be for employees to purchase insurance on their own behalf. By 2007, this incentive structure led to a situation in which nearly 88 percent of people with private health insurance received it as a benefit provided by their employer rather than by purchasing it themselves directly from an insurance company.

The prominence of employer-provided health insurance in the United States has had several important consequences. Perhaps the most important is that health care paid for via insurance can create perverse incentives for overuse that, in turn, lead to higher prices.

Another consequence of employer-provided health care is that health care reform efforts have focused on regulating the health insurance system with which most people are familiar rather than attempting alternatives that most people have never experienced. Later, we will explore how this tendency to regulate—rather than replace—the current insurance system has affected recent reform efforts including the Patient Protection and Affordable Care Act.

Twin Problems: Costs and Access

In recent decades, the U.S. health care system has suffered from two highly publicized problems:

- The cost of health care has risen rapidly in response to higher prices and an increase in the quantity of services provided. (Spending on health care involves both "prices" and "quantities" and is often loosely referred to as "health care costs.") The price of medical care has increased faster than the overall price level. For example, the December-to-December index of medical care prices rose by 3.6 percent in 2006, 5.2 percent in 2007, 2.6 percent in 2008, and 3.4 percent in 2009. (The overall price index increased by an annual average of 2.4 percent for those four years.) Health care spending (price × quantity) grew by 6.9 percent in 2005, 6.6 percent in 2006, 6.0 percent in 2007, and 4.4 percent in 2008. It is projected to grow at an annual rate of 6.1 percent over the next 10 years.

- Some 46 million Americans do not have health insurance coverage and, as a result, have significantly reduced access to quality health care.

434

Efforts to reform health care have focused on controlling costs and making it accessible to everyone. Those two goals are related, since high and rising prices make health care services unaffordable to a significant portion of the U.S. population. In fact, a dual system of health care may be evolving in the United States. Those with insurance or other financial means receive the world's highest-quality medical treatment, but many people, because of their inability to pay, often fail to seek out even the most basic treatment. When they do seek treatment, they may receive poorer care than those who have insurance. Free county hospitals and private charity hospitals do provide services to those without insurance, but the quality of care can be considerably lower than that which is available to people who have insurance.

High and Rising Health Care Costs

We need to examine several aspects of health care costs, or, alternatively, health care spending.

Health Care Spending

Health care spending in the United States is high and rising in both absolute terms and as a percentage of domestic output.

Total Spending on Health Care Figure 21.1a gives an overview of the major types of U.S. health care spending ($2.3 trillion in 2008). It shows that 31 cents of each

health care dollar goes to hospitals, while 21 cents goes to physicians, and 22 cents is spent on dental, vision, and other miscellaneous health care services.

Figure 21.1b shows the sources of funds for health care spending. It reveals that four-fifths of health care spending is financed by insurance. Public insurance (Medicaid, Medicare, and insurance for veterans, current military personnel, and government employees) is the source of 48 cents of each dollar spent. Private insurance accounts for 33 cents. So public and private insurance combined provide 81 cents of each dollar spent. The remaining 19 cents comes directly out of the health care consumer's pocket. It is paid mainly as insurance **deductibles** (that is, the insured pays the first $250 or $500 of each year's health care costs before the insurer begins paying) or **copayments** (that is, the insured pays, say, 20 percent of all health care costs and the insurance company pays 80 percent).

As we discuss in Chapter 20, Medicare is a nationwide Federal health care program available to Social Security beneficiaries and persons with disabilities. One part of Medicare is a hospital insurance program that, after a deductible of $1100 in 2010, covers all reasonable costs for the first 60 days of inpatient care per "benefit period" and lesser amounts (on a cost-sharing basis) for additional days. Coverage is also provided for posthospital nursing services, home health care, and hospice care for the terminally ill. Other parts of Medicare (including insurance programs for physicians' services, laboratory and other diagnostic tests, outpatient hospital services, and prescription drugs) are

FIGURE 21.1 Health care expenditures and finance. Total U.S. health care expenditures are extremely large ($2.3 trillion in 2008). (a) Most health care expenditures are for hospitals and the services of physicians and other skilled professionals. (b) Public and private insurance pay for four-fifths of health care.

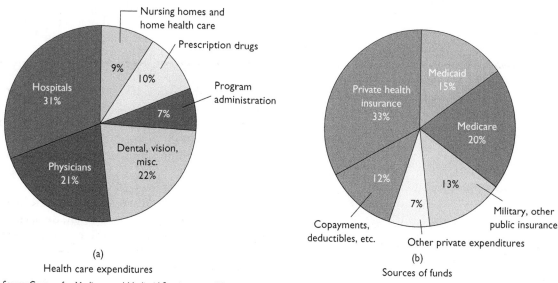

(a)
Health care expenditures

(b)
Sources of funds

Source: Centers for Medicare and Medicaid Services, **cms.hhs.gov**. Data are for 2008 and are compiled by the authors.

voluntary but heavily subsidized by government. The monthly premiums that most participants pay cover about one-fourth of the cost of the benefits provided.

Medicaid provides payment for medical benefits to certain low-income people, including the elderly, the blind, persons with disabilities, children, and adults with dependent children. Those who qualify for Temporary Aid for Needy Families (TANF) and the Supplemental Security Income (SSI) program are automatically eligible for Medicaid. Nevertheless, Medicaid covers less than half of those living in poverty. The Federal government and the states share the cost of Medicaid. On average, the states fund 42 percent and the Federal government 58 percent of each Medicaid dollar spent.

Overall, about 19 percent of each dollar spent on health care is financed by direct out-of-pocket payments by individuals. The fact that most U.S. health care is paid for by private insurance companies or the government is an important contributor to rising health care costs.

Percentage of GDP Figure 21.2 shows how U.S. health care spending has been increasing as a percentage of GDP. Health care spending absorbed 5.2 percent of GDP in 1960 but rose to 17.3 percent in 2009.

International Comparisons Global Perspective 21.1 reveals that among the industrialized nations, health care

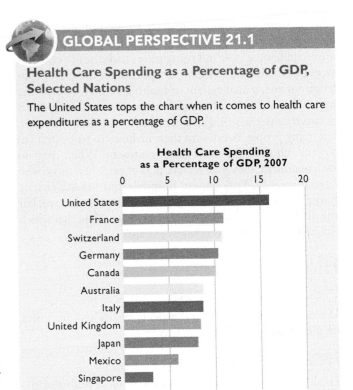

GLOBAL PERSPECTIVE 21.1

Health Care Spending as a Percentage of GDP, Selected Nations

The United States tops the chart when it comes to health care expenditures as a percentage of GDP.

Sources: Organization for Economic Cooperation and Development, **www.oecd.org.**

FIGURE 21.2 **U.S. health care expenditures as a percentage of GDP.** U.S. health care spending as a percentage of GDP has greatly increased since 1960.

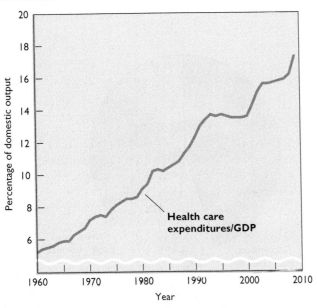

Source: Centers for Medicare and Medicaid Services, **cms.hhs.gov.**

spending as a percentage of GDP is highest in the United States. It is reasonable to assume that health care spending varies positively with output and incomes, but that doesn't account for the higher U.S. health expenditures as a percentage of GDP. Later in the chapter we discuss various explanations for why the United States is "in a league of its own" as to its proportion of output devoted to health care.

Quality of Care: Are We Healthier?

To compare the quality of health care from country to country is difficult. Yet there is general agreement that medical care (although not health and not "preventive treatment") in the United States is probably the best in the world. Average life expectancy in the United States has increased by about 7 years since 1970, and U.S. physicians and hospitals employ the most advanced medical equipment and technologies. Also, more than half the world's medical research funding is done in the United States. As a result, the incidence of disease has been declining and the quality of treatment has been improving. Polio has been virtually eliminated, ulcers are successfully treated without surgery, angioplasty and coronary bypass surgery greatly benefit those with heart disease, sophisticated body scanners are increasingly available diagnostic tools, and organ transplants and prosthetic joint replacements are more and more common.

That is the good news. But there is other news as well. Despite new screening and treatment technologies, the breast cancer mortality rate has shown only modest improvement. Tuberculosis, a virtually forgotten disease, has reappeared. The AIDS epidemic has claimed more than 583,000 American lives. More generally, some experts say that high levels of health care spending have not produced significantly better health and well-being. U.S. health care expenditures are the highest in the world absolutely, as a proportion of GDP, and on a per capita basis. Yet many nations have lower rates of maternal and infant mortality and longer life expectancies.

Economic Implications of Rising Costs

The most visible economic effects of rising health care costs are higher health insurance premiums to employers and higher out-of-pocket costs to workers. But rising health care costs have other economic effects as well.

Reduced Access to Care Higher health care costs and insurance premiums reduce access to health care. Some employers reduce or eliminate health insurance as part of their pay packages and some uninsured workers go without private health insurance. Consequently, the number of uninsured grows. We will consider this issue in detail momentarily.

Labor Market Effects Surging health care costs have three main effects on labor markets:

- ***Slower wage growth*** First, gains in workers' total compensation (wages plus fringe benefits, including health insurance paid for by employers) generally match gains in productivity. When health care costs (and thus insurance prices) rise more rapidly than productivity, firms wanting to maintain the existing level of health care benefits for their workers must reduce the growth of the wage portion of the total compensation package. Thus, in the long run, workers bear the burden of rising health care costs in the form of slower-growing wages.
- ***Use of part-time and temporary workers*** The high cost of employer-provided health insurance has led some employers to restructure their workforces: Full-time workers with health insurance benefits are employed in smaller numbers, and uninsured part-time or temporary workers are employed in greater numbers. Similarly, an employer with a generous but expensive health care plan might reduce its health

insurance expense by discharging its insured lower-wage workers—janitors, gardeners, and cafeteria staff—and replacing them with workers employed by outside independent contractors that provide little or no health insurance for their employees.

- ***Outsourcing (and Offshoring)*** Burdened by rising insurance costs, some firms may find it profitable to shift part of their production to outside suppliers that may be either domestic or international. This outsourcing may lower labor costs in situations where the outside suppliers provide fewer medical benefits to their workers. Offshoring (international outsourcing) has shifted jobs to developing economies such as Mexico, India, and China. Although labor productivity in these countries is considerably lower than that in the United States, lower wages and employer-provided medical benefits may be sufficient to make offshoring profitable. Rising domestic medical expenses therefore may join a host of other factors, including shifts in comparative advantage, in encouraging this practice.

Personal Bankruptcies Large, uninsured medical bills are one of the major causes of personal bankruptcy. Health care experts point out that medical bills are often the last to be paid because unlike other bills there is nothing to repossess, shut off, or foreclose. So medical bills sometimes build up beyond the point of a realistic means for full repayment. Even individuals who pay all bills in a timely fashion can find themselves in tremendous financial difficulty when they face large, uninsured medical bills for major operations (such as open-heart surgery) and expensive medical procedures (such as cancer treatment).

Impact on Government Budgets The budgets of Federal, state, and local governments are negatively affected by spiraling and sometimes unpredictable health care expenditures. In the past two decades, spending for health care through Medicare and Medicaid has been by far the fastest-growing segment of the Federal budget. To cover those rising expenditures, the government must either raise taxes or reduce the portion of the budget used for national defense, education, environmental programs, scientific research, and other spending categories.

The states are also finding it difficult to cover their share of the Medicaid bill. Most of them have been forced to raise their tax rates and search for new sources of revenue, and many of them have had to reduce spending on nonhealth programs such as infrastructure maintenance, welfare, and education. Local governments face similar budget strains in trying to finance public health services, hospitals, and clinics.

Too Much Spending?

Increased spending on computers or houses would be a sign of prosperity, not a cause for alarm, because society is obtaining more of each. What is different about increased spending on health care? Maybe nothing, say some economists. William Nordhaus of Yale, for example, estimated that the economic value of increases in longevity over the last 100 years nearly equals the total value of the additional GDP produced during that period. According to Kevin Murphy and Robert Topel, economists at the University of Chicago, reduced mortality from heart disease alone contributes $1.5 trillion of benefits a year in the United States. That amount exceeds the entire annual GDP of Canada.

While all economists agree that improved health care has greatly contributed to society's GDP and well-being, many economists think that health care expenditures in the United States are inefficiently large. The production of health care requires scarce resources such as capital in the form of hospitals and diagnostic equipment and the highly skilled labor of physicians, technicians, and nurses. The total output of health care in the United States may be so large that health care, at the margin, is worth less than the alternative goods and services these resources could otherwise have produced. The United States therefore may be consuming health care beyond the MB = MC point that defines efficiency.

If resources are overallocated to health care, society incurs an efficiency loss. Resources used excessively in health care could be used more productively to build new factories, support research and development, construct new bridges and roads, support education, improve the environment, or provide more consumer goods.

The suggested "too much of a good thing" results from peculiarities in the market for health care. We will see that the possibility of overspending arises from the way health care is financed, the asymmetry of information between consumers and providers, and the interaction of health insurance with technological progress in the industry.

Limited Access

The other health care problem is limited access. Even though there may be an overallocation of resources to health care, not all Americans can obtain the health care they need. Extrapolations from government surveys indicate that in 2008 about 46 million Americans, or roughly 15 percent of the population, had no health insurance for the entire year. As health care costs (and therefore health care insurance premiums) continue to rise, the number of uninsured could grow.

Who are the medically uninsured? As incomes rise, so does the probability of being insured. So it is no surprise that the uninsured are concentrated among the poor. Medicaid is designed to provide health care for the poor who are on welfare. But many poor people work at low or minimum-wage jobs without health care benefits, earning "too much" to qualify for Medicaid yet not enough to afford private health insurance. About half of the uninsured have a family head who works full-time. Many single-parent families, African Americans, and Hispanics are uninsured simply because they are more likely to be poor.

Curiously, those with excellent health and those with the poorest health also tend to be uninsured. Many young people with excellent health simply choose not to buy health insurance. The chronically ill find it very difficult and too costly to obtain insurance because of the likelihood that they will incur substantial health care costs in the future. Because private health insurance is most frequently obtained through an employer, the unemployed are also likely to lack insurance.

Workers for smaller firms are also less likely to have health insurance. The main reason is that administrative expenses for a small firm may be 30 to 40 percent of insurance premiums, as opposed to only 10 percent for a large firm. Also, corporations can deduct health insurance premiums from income to obtain substantial tax savings. Small unincorporated businesses can deduct only part of their health insurance expenses.

Low-wage workers are also less likely to be insured. Earlier we noted that in the long run employers pass on the increasing expense of health care insurance to workers as lower wages. This option is not available to employers who are paying the minimum wage. Thus as health care insurance premiums rise, employers cut or eliminate this benefit from the compensation package for their minimum- and low-wage workers. As a result, these workers are typically uninsured.

Although many of the uninsured forgo health care, some do not. A few are able to pay for it out of pocket. Others may wait until their illness reaches a critical stage and then go to a hospital for admittance or to be treated in the emergency room. This form of treatment is more costly than if the patient had insurance and therefore had been treated earlier by a physician. It is estimated that hospitals provide about $36 billion of uncompensated ("free") health care per year. The hospitals then try to shift these costs to those who have insurance or who can pay out of pocket.

- Private, employer-funded health insurance plays a much larger role in the delivery of health care in the United States than it does in other countries.
- Health care spending in the United States has been increasing absolutely and as a percentage of gross domestic output.
- Rising health care costs have caused (a) more people to find health insurance unaffordable; (b) adverse labor market effects, including slower real-wage growth and increased use of part-time and temporary workers; and (c) restriction of nonhealth spending by governments.
- Rising health care spending may reflect an overallocation of resources to the health care industry.
- Approximately 15 percent of all Americans have no health insurance and, hence, inferior access to quality health care.

Why the Rapid Rise in Costs?

The rising prices, quantities, and costs of health care services are the result of the demand for health care increasing much more rapidly than supply. We will examine the reasons for this in some detail. But first it will be helpful to understand certain characteristics of the health care market.

Peculiarities of the Health Care Market

We know that purely competitive markets achieve both allocative and productive efficiency: The most desired products are produced in the least costly way. We also have found that many imperfectly competitive markets, perhaps aided by regulation or the threat of antitrust action, provide outcomes generally accepted as efficient. What, then, are the special features of the health care market that have contributed to rising prices and thus escalating costs to buyers?

- **Ethical and equity considerations** Ethical questions inevitably intervene in markets when decisions involve the quality of life, or literally life or death. Although we might not consider it immoral or unfair if a person cannot buy a Mercedes or a personal computer, society regards it as unjust for people to be denied access to basic health care or even to the best available health care. In general, society regards health care as an "entitlement" or a "right" and is reluctant to ration it solely by price and income.
- **Asymmetric information** Health care buyers typically have little or no understanding of complex diagnostic and treatment procedures, while the physicians who are the health care sellers of those procedures

possess detailed information. This creates the unusual situation in which the doctor (supplier) as the agent of the patient (consumer) tells the patient what health care services he or she should consume. We will say more about this shortly.

- **Positive externalities** The medical care market often generates positive externalities (spillover benefits). For example, an immunization against polio, smallpox, or measles benefits the immediate purchaser, but it also benefits society because it reduces the risk that other members of society will be infected with a highly contagious disease. Similarly, a healthy labor force is more productive, contributing to the general prosperity and well-being of society.
- **Third-party payments: insurance** Because four-fifths of all health care expenses are paid through public or private insurance, health care consumers pay much lower out-of-pocket "prices" than they would otherwise. Those lower prices are a distortion that results in "excess" consumption of health care services.

The Increasing Demand for Health Care

With these four features in mind, let's consider some factors that have increased the demand for health care over time.

Rising Incomes: The Role of Elasticities Because health care is a normal good, increases in domestic income have caused increases in the demand for health care. While there is some disagreement as to the exact income elasticity of demand for health care, several studies for industrially advanced countries suggest that the income elasticity coefficient is about 1. This means that per capita health care spending rises approximately in proportion to increases in per capita income. For example, a 3 percent increase in income will generate a 3 percent increase in health care expenditures. Some evidence suggests that income elasticity may be higher in the United States, perhaps as high as 1.5.

Estimates of the price elasticity of demand for health care imply that it is quite inelastic, with this coefficient being as low as .2. This means that the quantity of health care consumed declines relatively little as price increases. For example, a 10 percent increase in price would reduce quantity demanded by only 2 percent. An important consequence is that total health care spending will increase as the price of health care rises.

The relative insensitivity of health care spending to price changes results from four factors. First, people consider health care a necessity, not a luxury. Few, if any, good substitutes exist for medical care in treating injuries and infections and alleviating various ailments. Second, medical treatment is often provided in an emergency situation in which price considerations are secondary or irrelevant. Third, most consumers prefer a long-term relationship with their doctors and therefore do not "shop around" when health care prices rise. Fourth, most patients have insurance and are therefore not directly affected by the price of health care. If insured patients pay, for example, only 20 percent of their health care expenses, they are less concerned with price increases or price differences between hospitals and between doctors than they would be if they paid 100 percent themselves.

An Aging Population The U.S. population is aging. People 65 years of age and older constituted approximately 9 percent of the population in 1960 but 12.4 percent in 2000. Projections for the year 2030 indicate 20 percent of the population will be 65 or over by that year.

This aging of the population affects the demand for health care because older people encounter more frequent and more prolonged spells of illness. Specifically, those 65 and older consume about three and one-half times as much health care as those between 19 and 64. In turn, people over 84 consume almost two and one-half times as much health care as those in the 65 to 69 age group. Health care expenditures are often extraordinarily high in the last year of one's life.

In 2011 the oldest of the 76 million members of the baby boom generation born between 1946 and 1964 began turning 65. We can expect that fact to create a substantial surge in the demand for health care.

Unhealthy Lifestyles Substance abuse helps drive up health care costs. The abuse of alcohol, tobacco, and illicit drugs damages health and is therefore an important component of the demand for health care services. Alcohol is a major cause of injury-producing traffic accidents and liver disease. Tobacco use markedly increases the probability of cancer, heart disease, bronchitis, and emphysema. Illicit drugs are a major contributor to violent crime, health problems in infants, and the spread of AIDS. In addition, illicit-drug users make hundreds of thousands of costly visits to hospital emergency rooms each year. And overeating and lack of exercise contribute to heart disease, diabetes, and many other ailments. Obesity-related medical costs are estimated to be about $147 billion per year, with taxpayers picking up more than half the tab through Medicare and Medicaid.

The Role of Doctors Physicians may increase the demand for health care in several ways.

Supplier-Induced Demand As we mentioned before, doctors, the suppliers of medical services, have much more information about those services than consumers, who are the demanders. While a patient might be well informed about food products or more complex products such as cameras, he or she is not likely to be well informed about diagnostic tests such as magnetic resonance imaging or medical procedures such as joint replacements. Because of this asymmetric information (informational imbalance), a principal-agent problem emerges: The supplier, not the demander, decides what types and amounts of health care are to be consumed. This situation creates a possibility of "supplier-induced demand."

This possibility becomes especially relevant when doctors are paid on a **fee-for-service** basis, that is, paid separately for each service they perform. In light of the asymmetric information and fee-for-service arrangement, doctors have an opportunity and an incentive to suggest more health care services than are absolutely necessary (just as an auto repair shop has an opportunity and an incentive to recommend replacement of parts that are worn but still working).

More surgery is performed in the United States, where many doctors are paid a fee for each operation, than in foreign countries, where doctors are often paid annual salaries unrelated to the number of operations they perform. Furthermore, doctors who own X-ray or ultrasound machines do four times as many tests as doctors who refer their patients to radiologists. More generally, studies suggest that up to one-third of common medical tests and procedures are either inappropriate or of questionable value.

The seller's control over consumption decisions has another result: It eliminates much of the power buyers might have in controlling the growth of health care prices and spending.

Defensive Medicine "Become a doctor and support a lawyer," says a bumper sticker. The number of medical malpractice lawsuits admittedly is high. To a medical doctor, each patient represents not only a person in need but also a possible malpractice suit. As a result, physicians tend to practice **defensive medicine.** They recommend more tests and procedures than are warranted medically or economically to protect themselves against malpractice suits.

Medical Ethics Medical ethics may drive up the demand for health care in two ways. First, doctors are legally and ethically committed to use "best-practice" techniques in serving their patients. This often means the use of costly medical procedures that may be of only slight benefit to patients.

Second, public values seem to support the medical ethic that human life should be sustained as long as possible. This makes it difficult to confront the notion that health care is provided with scarce resources and therefore must be rationed like any other good. Can society afford to provide $5000-per-day intensive care to a comatose patient unlikely to be restored to reasonable health? Public priorities seem to indicate that such care should be provided, and those values again increase the demand for health care.

Role of Health Insurance

As we noted in Figure 21.1, 81 percent of health care spending is done not by health care consumers through direct out-of-pocket payments but by private health insurance companies or by the government through Medicare and Medicaid.

Individuals and families face potentially devastating monetary losses from a variety of hazards. Your house may burn down; you may be in an auto accident; or you may suffer a serious illness. An insurance program is a means of protection against the huge monetary losses that can result from such hazards. A number of people agree to pay certain amounts (premiums) periodically in return for the guarantee that they will be compensated if they should incur a particular misfortune. Insurance is a means of paying a relatively small known cost in exchange for obtaining protection against an uncertain but potentially much larger cost.

This financial arrangement can be highly advantageous to those purchasing insurance, but it also alters incentives in ways that can contribute to rising costs and the overconsumption of health care.

The Moral Hazard Problem
The moral hazard problem is the tendency of one party to an agreement to alter her or his behavior in a way that is costly to the other party. Health care insurance can change behavior in two ways. First, some insured people may be less careful about their health, taking fewer steps to prevent accident or illness. Second, insured individuals have greater incentives to use health care more intensively than they would if they did not have insurance. Let's consider both aspects of moral hazard.

Less Prevention Health insurance may increase the demand for health care by encouraging behaviors that require more health care. Although most people with health care insurance are probably as careful about their health as are those without insurance, some may be more inclined to smoke, avoid exercise, and eat unhealthful foods, knowing they have insurance. Similarly, some individuals may take

up ski jumping or rodeo bull riding if they have insurance covering the costs of orthopedic surgeons. And if their insurance covers rehabilitation programs, some people may be more inclined to experiment with alcohol or drugs.

Overconsumption Insured people go to doctors more often and request more diagnostic tests and more complex treatments than they would if they were uninsured because, with health insurance, the price or opportunity cost of consuming health care is minimal. For example, many individuals with private insurance pay a fixed premium for coverage, and beyond that, aside from a modest deductible, their health care is "free." This situation differs from most markets, in which the price to the consumer reflects the full opportunity cost of each unit of the good or service. In all markets, price provides a direct economic incentive to restrict use of the product. The minimal direct price to the insured consumer of health care, in contrast, creates an incentive to overuse the health care system. Of course, the penalty for overuse will ultimately show up in higher insurance premiums, but all policyholders will share those premiums. The cost increase for the individual health consumer will be relatively small.

Also, the availability of insurance removes the consumer's budget constraint (spending limitation) when he or she decides to consume health care. Recall from Chapter 6 that budget constraints limit the purchases of most products. But insured patients face minimal or no out-of-pocket expenditures at the time they purchase health care. Because affordability is not the issue, health care may be overconsumed.

Government Tax Subsidy
Federal tax policy toward employer-financed health insurance works as a **tax subsidy** that strengthens the demand for health care services. Specifically, employees do not pay Federal income or payroll tax (Social Security) on the value of the health insurance they receive as an employee benefit. Employees thus request and receive more of their total compensation as nontaxed health care benefits and less in taxed wages and salaries.

The government rationale for this tax treatment is that positive spillover benefits are associated with having a healthy, productive workforce. So it is appropriate to encourage health insurance for workers. The tax break does enable more of the population to have health insurance, but it also contributes to greater consumption of health care. Combined with other factors, the tax break may result in an overconsumption of health care.

To illustrate: If the marginal tax rate is, say, 28 percent, $1 worth of health insurance is equivalent to 72 cents in after-tax pay. Because the worker can get more insurance

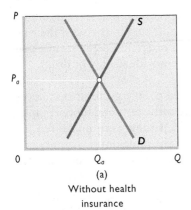

(a)
Without health
insurance

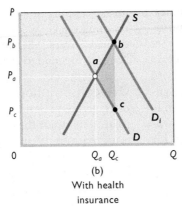

(b)
With health
insurance

FIGURE 21.3 Insurance and the overallocation of resources to health care. (a) Without health insurance, the optimal amount of health care consumed is Q_a, where the marginal benefit and marginal cost of health care are equal. (b) The availability of private and public insurance increases the demand for health care, as from D to D_i, and reduces the price to the consumer from P_a to P_c (here, equal to one-third of the full price P_b). This lower after-insurance price results in overconsumption (Q_c rather than Q_a). Area abc represents the efficiency loss (or deadweight loss) from the overallocation of resources to health care.

for $1 than for 72 cents, the exclusion of health insurance from taxation increases purchases of health insurance, thus increasing the demand for health care. In essence, the 28-cent difference acts as a government subsidy to health care. One estimate suggests that this subsidy costs the Federal government $120 billion per year in forgone tax revenue and boosts private health insurance spending by about one-third. Actual health care spending may be 10 to 20 percent higher than otherwise because of the subsidy.

Graphical Portrayal A simple demand and supply model illustrates the effect of health insurance on the health care market. Figure 21.3a depicts a competitive market for health care services; curve D shows the demand for health care services if all consumers are uninsured, and S represents the supply of health care. At market price P_a the equilibrium quantity of health care is Q_a.

Recall from our discussion of competitive markets that output Q_a results in allocative efficiency, which means there is no better alternative use for the resources allocated to producing that level of health care. To see what we mean by "no better use," recall that:

- As we move down along demand curve D, each succeeding point indicates, via the price it represents, the marginal benefit that consumers receive from that unit.
- The supply curve is the producers' marginal-cost curve. As we move up along supply curve S, each succeeding point indicates the marginal cost of each successive unit of health care.
- For each unit produced up to the equilibrium quantity Q_a, marginal benefit exceeds marginal cost (because points on D are above those on S). At Q_a marginal benefit equals marginal cost, designating allocative efficiency. No matter what else those resources could have produced, the greatest net

benefit to society is obtained by using those resources to produce Q_a units of health care.

But allocative efficiency occurs only when consumers pay the full market price for a product, as is assumed in Figure 21.3a. What happens when we introduce health insurance that covers, say, two-thirds of all health care costs? In Figure 21.3b, with private or public health insurance in place, consumers increase their demand for health care, as from D to D_i. At each possible price they desire more health care than before because insurance will pick up a large part of the bill. Given the supply curve of health care S, this increase in demand raises the price of health care to P_b. But with the insurance, consumers pay only one-third of the new higher price. This is less than without the insurance because the new price is only P_c (= $\frac{1}{3}P_b$)—rather than the previous price P_a. So they increase their consumption of health care from Q_a to Q_c.

The added consumption (and production) of health care is inefficient. Between Q_a and Q_c each unit's marginal cost to society (measured on curve S) exceeds its marginal benefit (measured on before-insurance demand curve D). Each unit of health care between Q_a and Q_c is an overallocation of resources to health care. Area abc shows the efficiency loss (or deadweight loss) that results.

Figure 21.3b implies that a trade-off exists between efficiency and equity. Standards of fairness or equity in the United States lead people to believe that all citizens should have access to basic health care, which is why government created social insurance in the form of Medicare and Medicaid. Also, it helps explain the Federal tax subsidy to private health insurance, which again makes health care more accessible. The problem, as Figure 21.3b shows, is that the greater the availability of insurance (and thus the more equitable society makes access to health care), the greater the overallocation of resources to the health care industry. This overallocation would be even greater if health care were provided completely "free" under a program of national health insurance. Consumers would purchase health care as long as the marginal benefit to themselves as individuals was positive, regardless of the true cost to society.

Rationing to Control Costs We have just seen that by reducing the marginal costs facing patients, both private health insurance and government health insurance drive up prices. But then why is it that the United States, with its emphasis on private health insurance, spends so much more on health care than countries like the United Kingdom and Canada that provide national health insurance? If both types of insurance promote higher prices, why do we see higher health care spending in the United States than in those other countries?

One contributing factor is that the countries with national health insurance use various nonprice mechanisms to ration care. These mechanisms restrict the quantity of health care services supplied and, consequently, the amount of money spent providing health care.

Some nonprice rationing is done by committees of medical and budgetary experts. In the United Kingdom, for instance, the National Committee for Health and Clinical Excellence has set a general limit of £30,000 (approximately $44,000) on the cost of extending life for a year. Applying this rule to a specific situation, if an anti-cancer treatment would cost more than £30,000 to extend a cancer patient's life for a year, the United Kingdom's national health service would not pay for it. This cost rule keeps a lid on expenditures.

Waiting is another nonprice mechanism that rations care in countries with national health insurance. In the Canadian system, patients often have waits of weeks, months, or even years for certain diagnostic procedures and surgeries. This is the result of the Canadian government's effort to control expenditures by restricting hospitals' capital spending. To illustrate, there are only one-fifth as many magnetic resonance imaging (MRI) machines per million people in Canada as in the United States. This results in a substantial waiting list for MRI scans in Canada.

By contrast, private health insurers in the United States have not had to obey national committees that set spending limits. Nor have they had to answer to government budget officials attempting to control expenditures by restricting capital spending. Instead, private health insurers have faced a very different regulatory system that has tended to increase rather than decrease spending.

To see why this is true, note that until the Patient Protection and Affordable Care Act of 2010, private health insurers were regulated almost entirely at the state level. In addition, each state insurance regulator had very different incentives compared to the national health insurance regulators found in other countries.

In a country with national health insurance, regulators are confronted by their government's budget constraint and the fact that the government has a limited supply of tax dollars to spend on health care. As a result, they have a strong incentive to deny care and limit spending. By contrast, state insurance regulators in the United States did not have to worry about exhausting government budgets because private health insurance is paid for with private money rather than government money. This led to a tendency for state insurance regulators to focus on benefits more than costs.

To see why this happened, note that requiring insurance companies to cover more people or treat more conditions is politically popular, while requiring them to cut coverage to save money is politically unpopular. With many states having popularly elected state insurance commissioners and the rest having insurance commissioners appointed either by the governor or the legislature, there was constant political pressure for state insurance regulators to pass new regulations requiring insurance companies to spend more rather than less. States incrementally imposed various rules expanding the number of conditions that had to be covered by insurers as well as the amounts that insurers had to spend on patient care.

Because these requirements involved the costly provision of additional care, insurance companies responded by raising insurance premiums. Thus, America's state-based system of government insurance regulation tended to increase rather than decrease the amount spent on health care.

Many economists view this regulatory system as one of the factors that has contributed to the United States spending more of its GDP on health care than any other nation on earth. While regulators in other countries have sought out ways to deny care and reduce costs, state regulators in America have tended to mandate that insurance companies expand treatment and incur additional costs.

As we will discuss later, the Patient Protection and Affordable Care Act creates a new set of Federal insurance regulators that will largely supersede state insurance regulators. Part of the controversy related to the bill is whether the new Federal regulators might eventually be tasked with denying care in the way that European regulators have.

Supply Factors in Rising Health Care Prices

Supply factors have also played a role in rising health care prices. Specifically, the supply of health care services has increased, but more slowly than demand. A combination of factors has produced this relatively slow growth of supply.

Supply of Physicians

The supply of physicians in the United States has increased over the years; in 1975 there were 169 physicians per 100,000 people; by 2008 there were 271. But this increase in supply has not kept up with the increase in the demand for physicians' services. As a result, physicians' fees and incomes have increased more rapidly than average prices and incomes for the economy as a whole.

Conventional wisdom has been that physician groups, for example, the American Medical Association, have purposely kept admissions to medical schools, and therefore the supply of doctors, artificially low. But that is too simplistic. A rapidly rising cost of medical education seems to be the main cause of the relatively slow growth of doctor supply. Medical training requires 4 years of college, 4 years of medical school, an internship, and perhaps 3 or 4 years of training in a medical specialty. The opportunity cost of this education has increased because the salaries of similarly capable people have soared in other professions. The direct expenses have also increased, largely due to the increasingly sophisticated levels of medical care and therefore of medical training.

High and rising education and training costs have necessitated high and rising doctors' fees to ensure an adequate return on this sort of investment in human capital. Physicians' incomes are indeed high, averaging in 2009 from about $169,000 for family care physicians up to $530,000 for neurosurgeons. But the costs of obtaining the skills necessary to become a physician are also very high. Data show that while doctors have high rates of return on their educational expenses, those returns are below the returns for lawyers and holders of masters of business administration degrees.

Slow Productivity Growth

Productivity growth in an industry tends to reduce costs and increase supply. In the health care industry, such productivity growth has been modest. One reason is that health care is a service, and it is generally more difficult to increase productivity for services than for goods. It is relatively easy to increase productivity in manufacturing by mechanizing the production process. With more and better machinery, the same number of workers can produce greater output. But services often are a different matter. It is not easy, for example, to mechanize haircuts, child care, and pizza delivery. How do you significantly increase the productivity of physicians, nurses, and home care providers?

Also, competition for patients among many providers of health care has not been sufficiently brisk to force them to look for ways to reduce costs by increasing productivity. When buying most goods, customers typically shop around for the lowest price. This shopping requires that sellers keep their prices low and look to productivity increases to maintain or expand their profits. But patients rarely shop for the lowest prices when seeking medical care. In fact, a patient may feel uncomfortable about being operated on by a physician who charges the lowest price. Moreover, if insurance pays for the surgery, there is no reason to consider price at all. The point is that unusual features of the market for health care limit competitive pricing and thus reduce incentives to achieve cost saving via advances in productivity.

Changes in Medical Technology

Some technological advances in medicine have lowered costs. For example, the development of vaccines for polio, smallpox, and measles has greatly reduced health care expenditures for the treatment of those diseases. And reduced lengths of stays in hospitals have lowered the costs of medical care.

But many medical technologies developed since the Second World War have significantly increased the cost of medical care either by increasing prices or by extending procedures to a greater number of people. For example, because they give more accurate information, advanced body scanners costing up to $1000 per scan are often used in place of X-rays that cost less than $100 for each scan. Desiring to offer the highest quality of service, hospitals want to use the very latest equipment and procedures. These newer, more expensive treatments are believed to be more effective than older ones. But doctors and hospital administrators both realize that the high fixed cost of such equipment means it must be used extensively to reduce the average cost per patient and recoup the investment at "fair return" charges per procedure.

As another example, organ transplants are extremely costly. Before the development of this technology, a person with a serious liver malfunction died. Now a liver transplant can cost $200,000 or more, with subsequent medical attention costing $10,000 to $20,000 per year for the rest of the patient's life.

Finally, consider new prescription medications. Pharmaceutical companies have developed very expensive drugs that often replace less expensive ones and are prescribed for a much wider range of physical and mental illnesses. Although these remarkable new medications greatly improve health care, they also contribute to rising health care costs.

The historical willingness of private and public insurance to pay for new treatments without regard to price and number of patients has contributed to the incentive to

CONSIDER THIS . . .

Cancer Fight Goes Nuclear

Medical technology often improves health care but adds to health-care costs. *The New York Times* reports that several major medical centers are turning nuclear particle accelerators into medical devices to treat cancer. The machines, previously used only for physics research, accelerate protons to near the speed of light and direct them into cancerous tumors. Because the proton beams are more precise than are conventional radiation X-ray beams, the side effects are reduced and the treatment outcomes may be improved.

Each accelerator costs $100 million! The building housing the machine is the size of a football field and requires walls up to 18 feet thick. A concern has arisen that competition among medical centers will result in too many machines, each being underutilized. Also, once medical centers have invested in the machines, they will want to recoup their investment as soon as possible at the "fair-return" prices allowed by insurance companies. So physicians may feel pressure from the centers to use the devices on cancer patients even though less-costly alternatives might be equally effective. Patients, desiring the latest and best technology, will pressure physicians to use the proton therapies.

Welcome to the world of modern medicine—advanced technology, new and improved procedures, and rising medical costs!

Source: Based on Andrew Pollack, "Cancer Fight Goes Nuclear, with Heavy Price Tag," *New York Times*, December 26, 2007, **www.nytimes.com**.

develop and use new technologies. Insurers, in effect, have encouraged research into and development of health care technologies, regardless of their cost. Recently, when insurance companies resisted paying for new expensive treatments such as bone marrow transplants, public outcries led them to change their minds. So expanding insurance coverage leads to new, often more expensive medical technologies, which in turn lead to a demand for a wider definition of what should be covered by insurance.

Relative Importance

According to most analysts, the demand and supply factors we have discussed vary in their impact on escalating health care costs. As we noted, the income elasticity of demand for health care is estimated to be upward of 1.5 in the United States, meaning that increased income brings with

it more-than-proportionate increases in health care spending. But rising income does not alone explain the rocketing increase in health care spending as a percentage of total domestic output (income). Furthermore, government studies estimate that the aging population accounts for less than 10 percent of the current increase in per capita health care spending.

Most experts attribute the relative rise in health care spending to (1) advances in medical technology, combined with (2) the medical ethic of providing the best treatment available, (3) private and public health insurance, and (4) fee-for-service physicians' payments by health insurance firms. Through technological progress, great strides have been made in the diagnosis, treatment, and prevention of illness. But the third-party (insurance) payment system provides little incentive to limit the development or use of such technologies because it has no mechanism to force an equating of marginal costs and marginal benefits. And the "best treatment available" ethic, together with the fee-for-service payment system, ensures that any new technology with a positive marginal benefit will get used and be billed for, regardless of the marginal cost to society.

QUICK REVIEW 21.2

- Characteristics of the health care market are (a) the widespread view of health care as a "right," (b) asymmetric information between consumers and suppliers, (c) the presence of positive externalities, and (d) payment mostly by insurance.

- The demand for health care has increased for many reasons, including rising incomes, an aging population, unhealthy lifestyles, the role of doctors as advisers to patients, the practice of defensive medicine, and a fee-for-service payment system via health insurance.

- Countries with national health insurance systems contain costs by denying care for certain procedures and by limiting capital expenditures.

- The supply of health care has grown slowly, primarily because of (a) relatively slow productivity growth in the health care industry, (b) rising costs of medical education and training, and (c) greater use of very-high-cost health care technologies.

Cost Containment: Altering Incentives

The Patient Protection and Affordable Care Act is the latest in a long series of attempts to control the growth of health care costs, prices, and spending. Many of these efforts have been focused on reducing the incentives to overconsume health care.

Deductibles and Copayments

Insurance companies have reacted to rising health care costs by imposing sizable deductibles and copayments on those they insure. Instead of covering all of an insured's medical costs, a policy might now specify that the insured pay the first $250 or $500 of each year's health care costs (the deductible) and 15 or 20 percent of all additional costs (the copayment). The deductible and copayment are intended to alleviate the overuse problem by creating a direct payment and therefore an opportunity cost to the health care consumer. The deductible has the added advantage of reducing the administrative costs of insurance companies in processing many small claims.

Health Savings Accounts

A Federal law enacted in 2003 established **health savings accounts (HSAs).** These accounts are available to all workers who are covered by health insurance plans with annual deductibles of $1000 or more and do not have other first-dollar insurance coverage. Individuals can make tax-deductible contributions into their HSAs, even if they do not itemize deductions on their tax forms. Employers can also make tax-free contributions to workers' accounts if they choose. Earnings on the funds in HSAs are not taxable, and the owners of these accounts can use them to pay for approved medical expenses. Unused funds in HSAs accumulate and remain available for later out-of-pocket medical expenses. Account holders can place additional money into their accounts each year between age 55 and the year they become eligible for Medicare.

HSAs are designed to promote personal saving out of which workers can pay routine health care expenses while working and Medicare copayments and deductibles later, during retirement. HSAs are also designed to reduce escalating medical expenses by injecting an element of competition into health care delivery. Because individuals are using some of their own HSA money to pay for health care, they presumably will assess their personal marginal costs and marginal benefits in choosing how much and what type of health care to obtain. They will also have a strong incentive to inquire about and compare prices charged by various qualified medical providers. Holders of HSAs never lose their accumulated funds. They can remove money for nonmedical purchases but must pay income taxes and a 10 percent penalty on such withdrawals.

Managed Care

Managed-care organizations (or systems) are those in which medical services are controlled or coordinated by insurance companies or health care organizations to reduce health care expenditures. In 2009 nearly 90 percent of all U.S. workers received health care through such "managed care." These organizations are of two main types.

Some insurance companies have set up **preferred provider organizations (PPOs),** which require that hospitals and physicians accept discounted prices for their services as a condition for being included in the insurance plan. The policyholder receives a list of participating hospitals and doctors and is given, say, 80 to 100 percent reimbursement of health care costs when treated by PPO physicians and hospitals. If a patient chooses a doctor or hospital outside the PPO, the insurance company reimburses only 60 to 70 percent. In return for being included as a PPO provider, doctors and hospitals agree to rates set by the insurance company for each service. Because these fees are less than those usually charged, PPOs reduce health insurance premiums and health care expenditures.

Many Americans now receive their medical care from **health maintenance organizations (HMOs),** which provide health care services to a specific group of enrollees in exchange for a set annual fee per enrollee. HMOs employ their own physicians and contract for specialized services with outside providers and hospitals. They then contract with firms or government units to provide medical care for their workers, who thereby become HMO members. Because HMOs have fixed annual revenue, they may lose money if they provide "too much" care. So they have an incentive to hold down costs. They also have an incentive to provide preventive care in order to reduce the potentially far larger expense of corrective care.

Both PPOs and HMOs are managed-care organizations, because medical use and spending are "managed" by closely monitoring physicians' and hospitals' behavior. The purpose of close monitoring is to eliminate unnecessary tests and treatments. Doctors in managed-care organizations might not order an MRI scan or an ultrasound test or suggest surgery, because their work is monitored and because they may have a fixed budget. In contrast, an independent fee-for-service physician facing little or no oversight may have a financial incentive to order the test or do the surgery. Doctors and hospitals in a managed-care organization often share in an "incentive pool" of funds when they meet their cost-control goals.

The advantages of managed-care plans are that they provide health care at lower prices than traditional insurance and emphasize preventive medicine. The disadvantages are that the patient usually is restricted to physicians employed by or under contract with the managed-care plan. Also, some say that the focus on reducing costs has gone too far, resulting in denial of highly expensive, but effective, treatment. This "too far" criticism was mainly leveled at HMOs, where incentives to reduce costs were the greatest. Perhaps because of a backlash against HMOs, firms have increasingly shifted managed care toward PPOs.

Medicare and DRG

In 1983 the Federal government altered the way it makes payments for hospital services received by Medicare patients. Rather than automatically paying all costs related to a patient's treatment and length of hospital stay, Medicare authorized payments based on a **diagnosis-related-group (DRG) system.** Under DRG, a hospital receives a fixed payment for treating each patient; that payment is an amount associated with the diagnosis—one of several hundred carefully detailed diagnostic categories—that best characterizes the patient's condition and needs.

DRG payments obviously give hospitals the incentive to restrict the amount of resources used in treating patients. It is no surprise that under DRG the length of hospital stays has fallen sharply and more patients are treated on an outpatient basis. Critics, however, argue that this is evidence of diminished health-care quality.

Limits on Malpractice Awards

Congress has, for many years, debated whether to cap (at, say, $250,000 or $500,000) the "pain and suffering" awards on medical malpractice lawsuits against physicians. Those who support malpractice caps say that patients should receive full compensation for economic losses but not be made wealthy through huge jury awards. They contend that capping the awards will reduce medical malpractice premiums and therefore lower health care costs. Opponents of caps counter that large "pain and suffering" awards deter medical malpractice. If so, such awards improve the overall quality of the health care system. Opponents also point out that malpractice awards are a negligible percentage of total health care costs. Thirty-three states have placed caps on the "pain and suffering" portion of malpractice awards.

The Patient Protection and Affordable Care Act

The primary goal of the Patient Protection and Affordable Care Act (PPACA) passed in 2010 was not cost containment but rather the extension of health care coverage to all Americans. In truth, covering every single citizen would have been possible only if America had moved to a national health insurance system similar to that used in Canada. Such a move would have been impossible politically, how-

ever, because opinion polls indicated that 75 percent of Americans with employer-provided health insurance rated their coverage as good or very good.

Thus, President Obama and like-minded members of Congress did not pursue the creation of a national health insurance system. Rather, they moved to extend and expand the existing system in which nearly all Americans receive their health care through either employer-provided health insurance or government-provided health insurance (Medicaid and Medicare). In promoting the PPACA, the president reassured audiences by telling them, "If you like your health care plan, you can keep it."

Major Provisions

The authors of the PPACA understood that extending insurance coverage to millions of previously uninsured people would be costly. As with any group of people enrolled in a health insurance program, many would eventually become sick and need costly treatments. This problem was exacerbated by the fact that many of those without insurance were known to suffer from extremely costly medical conditions. Indeed, these individuals were without insurance precisely because private insurance companies (which have to either break even or go bankrupt) considered them too expensive to insure. Thus, if those with costly medical conditions were to be covered, significant new revenue sources had to be found.

The PPACA aims to obtain the needed revenue from two main sources: a personal mandate to buy insurance and an assortment of new taxes. We will discuss each as we go over the PPACA's major provisions.

Preexisting Conditions, Caps, and Drops The PPACA makes it illegal for insurance companies to deny coverage to anyone on the basis of a preexisting medical condition. As just discussed, this ban will lead to the enrollment of millions of individuals with costly health conditions, as these individuals will be almost certain to enroll as soon as the ban goes into effect.

The PPACA also increases the amount of money that insurance companies will be spending in the future by prohibiting them from imposing annual or lifetime expenditure caps.

To prevent insurance companies from dropping policyholders just because they develop a costly illness, the PPACA also makes fraud the only legal reason that an insurance company can drop a policyholder. Because this provision will force insurance companies to keep very sick people enrolled, it too is expected to entail significant cost increases for insurance companies.

LAST Word Singapore's Efficient and Effective Health Care System

How Does Singapore Deliver Some of the Best Health Care in the World While Spending Nearly 80 Percent Less per Person than the United States?

In every health-quality category monitored by the World Health Organization, the small island nation of Singapore is either number one in the world or near the top of the list. Among other achievements, Singapore has the world's lowest rate of infant mortality and the world's fourth highest life expectancy.

One might expect that achieving these exceptional outcomes would be extremely expensive. But Singapore is also number one in another category. It spends less per person on health care than any other developed nation. In 2009 the United States spent 17.3 percent of its GDP on health care. Singapore spent just 3.8 percent.

How does Singapore deliver world-class health care while spending less than any other developed nation? The answer is a unique combination of government mandates to encourage competition, high out-of-pocket costs for consumers, and laws requiring people to save for future health expenditures.

Competition is encouraged by forcing hospitals to post prices for each of their services. Armed with this information,

patients can shop around for the best deal. The government also publishes the track record of each hospital on each service so that consumers can make informed decisions about quality as well as price. With consumers choosing on the basis of cost and quality, local hospitals compete to reduce costs and improve quality.

Singapore also insists upon high out-of-pocket costs to avoid the overconsumption and high prices that result when insurance policies pick up most of the price for medical procedures. Indeed, out-of-pocket spending represents about 92 percent of all nongovernment health-care spending in Singapore, compared to just 12 percent in the United States.

Having to pay for most medical spending out of pocket, however, means that Singapore's citizens are faced with having to pay for most of their health care themselves. How can this be done without bankrupting the average citizen? The answer is mandatory health savings accounts.

Singapore's citizens are required to save about 6 percent of their incomes into "MediSave" accounts. MediSave deposits are private property, so people have an incentive to spend the money in their accounts wisely. In addition, the citizens of Singapore also know that they won't be left helpless if the money in their MediSave accounts runs out. The government subsidizes the health care of those who have exhausted their MediSave

Employer Mandate The PPACA has an **employer mandate** (requirement) that every firm with 50 or more employees must either purchase health insurance for their employees or pay a fine of $2000 per employee. This provision of the law is intended to extend employer-paid health insurance to as many workers as possible so that private employers, rather than the government, will bear as much of the cost of extending insurance coverage to the uninsured as possible.

Firms with fewer than 50 employees are exempt from the employer mandate because the high cost of health insurance might bankrupt many smaller firms.

Personal Mandate The PPACA contains a **personal mandate** (requirement) that individuals must purchase health insurance for themselves and their dependents unless they are already covered by either government insurance or employer-provided insurance.

Anyone refusing will be fined. The fine is the larger of either $695 per uninsured family member or 2.5 percent of family income.

As we will explain next, the PPACA contains extensive subsidies to ensure that poorer people will not be financially devastated by the personal mandate's requirement to buy health insurance. However, it must be understood that the point of the personal mandate is to force higher-income healthy people (especially healthy young workers) to buy health insurance so that their insurance premiums can help pay for the high health care bills of those with costly medical conditions as well as the subsidies needed to make health insurance affordable for those with lower incomes.

Covering the Poor Millions of poorer Americans lacked private health insurance either (*a*) because they were unemployed and thus not receiving employer-

448

accounts as well as the health care of the poor and others who have not been able to accumulate much money in their Medi-Save accounts.

Could elements of Singapore's system help to hold down medical costs in the United States? Two cases suggest that the answer is yes.

First, consider the health care plan offered by Whole Foods Markets to its employees. The company deposits $1800 per year into a "personal wellness account" for each of its full-time employees. It simultaneously pays for a high-deductible health insurance plan that will pick up 100 percent of all medical expenses exceeding $2500 in a given year. This combination implies that employees are *at most* on the hook for $700 a year—that is, for the difference between the $1800 in their personal wellness accounts and the $2500 deductible on their health insurance policy (above which, all medical expenses are covered).

Because both the money in the personal wellness account as well as the $700 that employees might have to spend before reaching the $2500 deductible are personal property, Whole Foods Markets has effectively created a system in which all medical spending up to $2500 is an out-of-pocket expense. This forces employees to examine the opportunity cost of any potential medical expenditure. The result is less spending.

A similar plan offered to employees of the State of Indiana puts $2750 per year into a health savings account and then provides an insurance policy that covers 80 percent of any medical expenses between $2750 and $8000 and 100 percent of any expenses above $8000. The Indiana plan's design means that any state employee volunteering for the plan must pay 100 percent of all spending up to $2750 from their health savings accounts. As with Singapore's system and Whole Foods' system, this encourages prudence. The result has been a 35 percent decline in total health care spending for those who volunteered for the plan versus state employees who opted to stick with the state's traditional PPO option. In addition, an independent audit showed that participants in the new plan were not cutting corners by skimping on preventive care like annual mammogram screenings for cancer. Thus, the savings appear to be permanent and sustainable.

The program is also popular, with positive personal recommendations causing voluntary participation to rise from 2 percent of state employees in the program's first year to 70 percent of state employees in the program's second year.

provided health insurance or (*b*) because their employers did not provide health insurance. Some of these poorer Americans could obtain government health insurance through either Medicaid or Medicare, but those who did not found themselves without any health insurance, either private or public.

The PPACA attempts to cover those with lower incomes in three ways. First, the employer mandate will induce many larger employers to provide insurance for all of their employees, including the poorer ones. Second, the law expands the Medicaid system to cover anyone whose income is less than 133 percent of the poverty level. Third, the PPACA subsidizes the purchase price of health insurance for those who must buy their own health insurance to comply with the individual mandate.

The subsidies actually extend well into the middle class, because they extend upward along the income scale even to persons making up to four times the Federal poverty level. Taking into account the fact that individuals and households have different Federal poverty levels, the subsidies would extend to individuals making up to about $44,000 per year and families of four making up to about $88,000 per year. By comparison, full-time workers had median annual earnings of about $41,000 in 2008, while the median family income in 2008 was about $50,300. The subsidies extend into the upper half of the income distribution because health insurance is so expensive that the personal mandate would have been financially ruinous for even middle-income workers if it had not been accompanied by subsidies.

A complicated formula adjusts the size of the subsidies by income level. The formula kicks in at 133 percent of the Federal poverty level because anyone earning less will receive free government health insurance through Medicaid. For those earning slightly more than 133 percent of the poverty level (about $14,000 for an individual and

449

about $29,000 for a family for four), the subsidies would be large enough so that they would not have to spend more than about 4 percent of their incomes purchasing health insurance. The subsidies get progressively less generous as incomes rise, so that those earning three to four times the poverty level would be subsidized such that they would have to pay about 10 percent of their incomes to buy health insurance.

Insurance Exchanges Individuals shopping for their own insurance will do so in government-regulated markets called **insurance exchanges.** There will be one exchange for each state, and Federal regulators will only allow policies meeting certain standards to be offered. The regulators cannot set prices directly but will have the authority to withdraw approval from any insurer that requests a price increase that regulators deem to be unjustified on the basis of higher costs. It is hoped that the exchanges will reduce the growth of health care spending by fostering competition among insurance companies.

Other Provisions The 2400-page PPACA contains hundreds of additional provisions. Some of the more publicized include:

- Mandating that the adult children of parents with employer-provided health insurance can remain covered by their parents' insurance through age 26.
- Making it illegal for insurance companies to charge copayments or apply deductibles to annual check ups or preventive care.
- Requiring insurers to spend at least 80 percent of the money they receive in premiums on either health care or improving health care.

Taxes To help pay for the extension of health insurance to millions of previously uninsured people, the PPACA imposes several new taxes. The more prominent are:

- A 0.9 percentage point increase in the Medicare payroll tax for individuals earning more than $200,000 per year and for married couples earning more than $250,000 per year.
- A 3.8 percentage point increase in the capital gains tax for individuals earning more than $200,000 per year and for married couples earning more than $250,000 per year.
- A 40 percent tax payable by employers on any employer-provided insurance policy whose premium exceeds $10,200 per year for individual coverage or $27,500 per year for family coverage.

- A 2.9 percent excise tax applied to everything sold by medical device manufacturers.
- A 10 percent tax levied on indoor tanning.

Objections and Alternatives

The PPACA was strongly opposed and passed Congress without a single approving vote in either chamber of Congress from members of the minority (Republican) party. The legislation also failed to achieve majority support in public opinion polls conducted on the eve of the legislation's passage. Leading into the midterm congressional elections of 2010, many opponents called for repeal.

Some of those voicing objections worried that Federal control over the pricing and content of insurance policies would lead to greater inefficiencies in health care by adding additional layers of bureaucracy. Others objected because they felt that the PPACA might be the first step toward the creation of a national health insurance system in which nonprice rationing might become necessary to hold down expenditures. Yet others pointed to financial projections indicating that the revenue sources legislated by the PPACA would not be nearly sufficient to cover future health care expenses, especially over the longer run.

An additional concern was whether the PPACA would reduce the growth rate of health care expenditures and thereby fulfill the president's promise that the law would "bend the cost curve down." Many economists worried that the large subsidies provided by the law would raise prices and increase consumption (as in Figure 21.3 and the nearby discussion). With even middle-class individuals and families eligible for significant government subsidies, inefficient health care spending might increase significantly.

As an alternative, some opponents of the PPACA pointed to the health care system in Singapore and recent experiments with the health insurance offered to employees of the State of Indiana. Both systems reduce wasteful expenditures by increasing the percentage of health care spending that comes directly out of consumer's pockets, thereby forcing them to consider opportunity costs and weigh marginal benefits against marginal costs. (See this chapter's Last Word for more.)

In evaluating the pros and cons of the PPACA, one thing seems clear. It will not be the last word on health care reform in America. Indeed, the economic challenges related to health care will only get stronger. The combination of an aging population and advances in medical technology seem to be on a collision course with the reality of economic scarcity such that individuals and society will face increasingly difficult choices about how much health care to consume and how to pay for it.

Summary

1. The U.S. health care industry comprises 16 million workers (including about 817,000 practicing physicians) and 5800 hospitals.

2. Unlike nations with publicly funded systems of national health insurance, the United States delivers a large fraction of its health care through private, employer-provided health insurance.

3. U.S. health care spending has increased both absolutely and as a percentage of GDP.

4. Rising health care costs and prices have (*a*) reduced access to the health care system, (*b*) contributed to slower real wage growth and expanded the employment of part-time and temporary workers, and (*c*) caused governments to restrict spending on nonhealth programs and to raise taxes.

5. The core of the health care problem is an alleged overallocation of resources to the health care industry.

6. About 46 million Americans, or 15 percent of the population, did not have health insurance in 2008. The uninsured were concentrated among the poor, the chronically ill, the unemployed, the young, those employed by small firms, and low-wage workers.

7. Special characteristics of the health care market include (*a*) the belief that health care is a "right," (*b*) an imbalance of information between consumers and suppliers, (*c*) the presence of positive externalities, and (*d*) the payment of most health care expenses by private or public insurance.

8. While rising incomes, an aging population, and substance abuse have all contributed to an increasing demand for health care, the role of doctors is also significant. Because of asymmetric information, physicians influence the demand for their own services. The fee-for- service payment system, combined with defensive medicine to protect against malpractice suits, also increases the demand for health care.

9. The moral hazard problem arising from health insurance takes two forms: (*a*) People may be less careful of their health, and (*b*) there is an incentive to overconsume health care.

10. The exemption of employer-paid health insurance from the Federal income tax subsidizes health care. The subsidy increases demand, leading to higher prices and a likely overallocation of resources to health care.

11. Countries with systems of national health insurance also increase demand by subsidizing health care. Facing limited budgets, those countries engage in nonprice rationing to restrict health-care expenditures. Rationing mechanisms include waiting lists, committees that set standards for denial of service, and restrictions on capital spending.

12. Because private insurance does not involve government expenditures, the state regulators charged with regulating private insurance companies in the United States focus more on expanding politically popular benefits than on restricting costs.

13. Slow productivity growth in the health care industry and, more important, cost-increasing advances in health-care technology have restricted the expansion of the supply of medical care and have boosted prices.

14. Strategies that have attempted to contain health care prices and spending include (*a*) insurance deductibles and copayments to confront consumers with opportunity costs, (*b*) managed-care organizations—preferred provider organizations (PPOs) and health maintenance organizations (HMOs)—that attempt to restrict their members' use of health services, (*c*) the diagnosis-related-group (DRG) system that caps the amount Medicare will spend on any procedure, and (*d*) health savings accounts (HSAs) that also confront individuals with opportunity costs when they spend out of their tax-free HSA accounts.

15. The Patient Protection and Affordable Care Act (PPACA) of 2010 is an attempt to extend either private or public (Medicare and Medicaid) insurance coverage to all U.S. citizens and legal residents.

16. Enrolling millions of previously uninsured people (including the chronically ill) into health insurance will be costly, so the PPACA includes a personal mandate that requires all citizens and legal residents to purchase insurance coverage for themselves and their dependents if they are not already provided with insurance by their employer or by the government. The goal is to compel healthy people to purchase insurance so that their premiums can help to pay for the health care costs of the previously uninsured (many of whom are likely to be chronically ill.)

17. The PPACA also (*a*) bans insurance companies from denying coverage on the basis of preexisting conditions, (*b*) includes various subsidies so that the personal mandate will not bankrupt the poor and middle class, (*c*) provides for the creation of state insurance exchanges where individuals can comparison shop for government-approved health insurance policies, and (*d*) imposes various taxes to help pay for the increased expenditures that will be required to extend insurance coverage to the previously uninsured.

Terms and Concepts

Patient Protection and Affordable Care Act (PPACA)

national health insurance

deductibles

copayments

fee for service

defensive medicine

tax subsidy

health savings accounts (HSAs)

preferred provider organizations (PPOs)

health maintenance organizations (HMOs)

diagnosis-related-group (DRG) system

employer mandate

personal mandate

insurance exchanges

Questions

1. Why would increased spending as a percentage of GDP on, say, household appliances or education in a particular economy be regarded as economically desirable? Why, then, is there so much concern about rising expenditures as a percentage of GDP on health care? LO1

2. What are the "twin problems" of the health care industry as viewed by society? How are they related? LO1

3. Briefly describe the main features of Medicare and Medicaid, indicating how each is financed. LO1

4. What are the implications of rapidly rising health care prices and spending for (a) the growth of real wage rates, (b) government budgets, and (c) offshoring of U.S. jobs? Explain. LO2

5. What are the main groups without health insurance? LO3

6. List the special characteristics of the U.S. health care market and specify how each affects health care problems. LO3

7. What are the estimated income and price elasticities of demand for health care? How does each relate to rising health care costs? LO4

8. Briefly discuss the demand and supply factors that contribute to rising health costs. Specify how (a) asymmetric information, (b) fee-for-service payments, (c) defensive medicine, and (d) medical ethics might cause health care costs to rise. LO4

9. How do advances in medical technology and health insurance interact to drive up the cost of medical care? LO4

10. Using the concepts in Chapter 6's discussion of consumer behavior, explain how health care insurance results in an overallocation of resources to the health care industry. Use a demand and supply diagram to specify the resulting efficiency loss. LO4

11. How is the moral hazard problem relevant to the health care market? LO4

12. What is the rationale for exempting a firm's contribution to its workers' health insurance from taxation as worker income? What is the impact of this exemption on allocative efficiency in the health care industry? LO4

13. What are (a) preferred provider organizations and (b) health maintenance organizations? In your answer, explain how each is designed to alleviate the overconsumption of health care. LO4

14. What are health savings accounts (HSAs)? How might they reduce the overconsumption of health care resulting from traditional insurance? How might they introduce an element of price competition into the health care system? LO4

15. Why is the PPACA's attempt to extend insurance coverage to all Americans so costly? How does the PPACA attempt to obtain the funds needed to extend insurance coverage to all Americans? LO5

16. How does the PPACA attempt to ensure affordable insurance for the poor? LO5

17. What were the objections made by opponents of the PPACA? LO5

18. **LAST WORD** What are the three major cost-reducing features of the Singapore health care system? Which one do you think has the largest effect on holding down the price of medical care in Singapore? What element of the Singapore system is shared by the Whole Foods and State of Indiana systems? What elements are missing? How difficult do you think it would be to implement those missing elements in the United States? Explain.

Problems

1. Suppose that the price elasticity for hip replacement surgeries is 0.2. Further suppose that hip replacement surgeries are originally not covered by health insurance and that at a price of $50,000 each, 10,000 such surgeries are demanded each year. LO2
   a. Suppose that health insurance begins to cover hip replacement surgeries and that everyone interested in getting a hip replacement has health insurance. If insurance covers 50 percent of the cost of the surgery, by what percentage would you expect the quantity demanded of hip replacements to increase? What if insurance covered 90 percent of the price? (Hint: Do not bother to calculate the percentage changes using the midpoint formula given in

Chapter 4. If insurance covers 50 percent of the bill, just assume that the price paid by consumers falls 50 percent.)
   b. Suppose that with insurance companies covering 90 percent of the price, the increase in demand leads to a jump in the price per hip surgery from $50,000 to $100,000. How much will each insured patient now pay for a hip replacement surgery? Compared to the original situation, where hip replacements cost $50,000 each but people had no insurance to help subsidize the cost, will the quantity demanded increase or decrease? By how much?

2. The Federal tax code allows businesses but not individuals to deduct the cost of health insurance premiums from their taxable income. Consider a company named HeadBook that

could either spend $5000 on an insurance policy for an employee named Vanessa or could increase her annual salary by $5000 instead. LO4

a. As far as the tax code is concerned, HeadBook will increase its expenses by $5000 in either case. If it pays for the policy, it incurs a $5000 health care expense. If it raises Vanessa's salary by $5000, it incurs $5000 of salary expense. If HeadBook is profitable and pays corporate profit taxes at a marginal 35 percent rate, by how much will HeadBook's tax liability be reduced in either case?

b. Suppose that Vanessa pays personal income tax at a marginal 20 percent rate. If HeadBook increases her salary by $5000, how much of that increase will she have after paying taxes on that raise? If Vanessa can only devote what remains after paying taxes on the $5000 to purchasing health insurance, how much will she be able to spend on health insurance for herself?

c. If HeadBook spends the $5000 on a health insurance policy for Vanessa instead of giving it to her as a raise, how many more dollars will HeadBook be able to spend on Vanessa's health insurance than if she had to purchase it herself after being given a $5000 raise and paying taxes on that raise?

d. Would Vanessa prefer to have the raise or to have HeadBook purchase insurance for her? Would HeadBook have any profit motive for denying Vanessa her preference?

e. Suppose the government changes the tax law so that individuals can now deduct the cost of health insurance from their personal incomes. If Vanessa gets the $5000 raise and then spends all of it on health insurance, how much will her tax liability change? How much will she be able to spend on health insurance? Will she now have a preference for HeadBook to buy insurance on her behalf?

3. Preventive care is not always cost effective. Suppose that it costs $100 per person to administer a screening exam for a particular disease. Also suppose that if the screening exam finds the disease, the early detection given by the exam will avert $1000 of costly future treatment. LO4

a. Imagine giving the screening test to 100 people. How much will it cost to give those 100 tests? Imagine a case in which 15 percent of those receiving the screening exam test positive. How much in future costly treatments will be averted? How much is saved by setting up a screening system?

b. Imagine that everything is the same as in part a except that now only 5 percent of those receiving the screening exam test positive. In this case, how much in future costly treatments will be averted? How much is lost by setting up a screening system?

AFTER READING THIS CHAPTER, YOU SHOULD BE ABLE TO:

1 Differentiate between invention, innovation, and technological diffusion.

2 Explain how entrepreneurs and other innovators further technological advance.

3 Summarize how a firm determines its optimal amount of research and development (R&D).

4 Relate why firms can benefit from their innovation even though rivals have an incentive to imitate it.

5 Discuss the role of market structure in promoting technological advance.

6 Show how technological advance enhances productive efficiency and allocative efficiency.

Technology, R&D, and Efficiency

- "Just do it!" In 1968 two entrepreneurs from Oregon developed a lightweight sport shoe and formed a new company called Nike, incorporating a "swoosh" logo (designed by a graduate student for $35). Today, Nike sells $18 billion worth of goods annually.
- "Leap Ahead." In 1967 neither Intel nor its product existed. Today it is the world's largest producer of microprocessors for personal computers, with about $35 billion of annual sales.
- "Save money, live better." Expanding from a single store in 1962 to about 7000 stores worldwide today, Walmart's annual revenue ($400 billion) exceeds that of General Motors or IBM.

Nike, Intel, and Walmart owe much of their success to **technological advance,** broadly defined as new and better goods and services or new and better ways of producing or distributing them. Nike and Intel pioneered innovative new products, and Walmart developed creative ways to manage inventories and distribute goods.

Multiply these examples—perhaps on a smaller scale—by thousands in the economy! The pursuit of technological advance is a major competitive activity among firms. In this chapter, we examine some of the microeconomics of that activity.

Invention, Innovation, and Diffusion

For economists, technological advance occurs over a theoretical time period called the *very long run*, which can be as short as a few months or as long as many years. Compare the concept of the very long run with the two shorter-duration time concepts that we developed while discussing our four market models (pure competition, monopolistic competition, oligopoly, and pure monopoly). In the short run, technology and plant and equipment are fixed. In the long run, technology is constant but firms can change their plant sizes and are free to enter or exit industries. In contrast, the **very long run** is a period in which technology can change and in which firms can develop and offer entirely new products.

In Chapter 1 we saw that technological advance shifts an economy's production possibilities curve outward, enabling the economy to obtain more goods and services. Technological advance is a three-step process of invention, innovation, and diffusion.

Invention

The basis of technological advance is **invention:** the discovery of a product or process combined with the first proof that it will work. Invention is a process of imagination, ingenious thinking, and experimentation. The result of the process is called *an* invention. The prototypes (basic working models) of the telephone, the automobile, and the microchip were inventions.

Invention usually is based on scientific knowledge and is the product of individuals, working either on their own or as members of corporate research and development (R&D) teams. Later on you will see how governments encourage invention by providing the inventor with a **patent,** an exclusive right to sell any new and useful process, machine, or product for a set period of time. In 2009, the top 10 firms in terms of securing the most U.S. patents were IBM (4914), Samsung (3611), Microsoft (2906), Canon (2206), Panasonic (1829), Toshiba (1696), Sony (1680), Intel (1537), Seiko Epson (1330), and Hewlett-Packard (1273). Numbers like these, of course, do not reveal the quality of the patents received; some patents are much more significant than other patents. Patents have a worldwide duration of 20 years from the time of application for the patent.

Innovation

Innovation draws directly on invention. While invention is the discovery and first proof of workability, **innovation** is the first successful commercial introduction of a new product, the first use of a new method, or the creation of a new form of business enterprise. Innovation is of two types: **product innovation,** which refers to new and improved products or services; and **process innovation,** which refers to new and improved methods of production or distribution.

Unlike inventions, innovations cannot be patented. Nevertheless, innovation is a major factor in competition, since it sometimes enables a firm to leapfrog competitors by rendering their products or processes obsolete. For example, personal computers coupled with software for word processing pushed some major typewriter manufacturers into obscurity. More recently, innovations in hardware retailing (by large warehouse stores such as Home Depot and Lowe's) have threatened the existence of smaller, more traditional hardware stores.

But innovation need not weaken or destroy existing firms. Aware that new products and processes may threaten their survival, existing firms have a powerful incentive to engage continuously in R&D of their own. Innovative products and processes often enable such firms to maintain or increase their profits. The introduction of disposable contact lenses by Johnson & Johnson, scientific calculators by Hewlett-Packard, and iPhones by Apple are good examples. Thus, innovation can either diminish or strengthen market power.

Diffusion

Diffusion is the spread of an innovation to other products or processes through imitation or copying. To take advantage of new profit opportunities or to slow the erosion of profit, both new and existing firms emulate the successful innovations of others. Alamo greatly increased its auto rentals by offering customers unlimited mileage, and Hertz, Avis, Budget, and others eventually followed. Chrysler profitably introduced a luxury version of its Jeep Grand Cherokee; other manufacturers, including Acura, Mercedes, and Lexus, countered with luxury sport-utility vehicles of their own. In 2007 Apple introduced the iPhone, a palm-sized telephone that was also a music player, camera, Internet browser, and mini personal computer. Blackberry, Nokia, Samsung, and Palm soon brought out similar products.

Other recent examples: Early successful cholesterol-reducing drugs (statins) such as Bristol-Myers Squibb's Pravachol were soon followed by chemically distinct but similar statins such as Merck's Zocor and Pfizer's Lipitor. Early video game consoles such as those by Atari eventually gave rise to more popular consoles by Nintendo (Wii), Sony (PlayStation), and Microsoft (Xbox). MySpace, Facebook, and LinkedIn mimicked the social networking innovation pioneered by Classmates.com.

In each of these cases, other firms incorporated the new innovation into their own businesses and products through imitation, modification, and extension. The original innovation thus became commonplace and mainly of historical interest.

Although not as dramatic as invention and innovation, diffusion is a critical element of technological change.

R&D Expenditures

As related to *businesses*, the term "research and development" is used loosely to include direct efforts toward invention, innovation, and diffusion. However, *government* also engages in R&D, particularly R&D having to do with national defense. In 2008 *total* U.S. R&D expenditures (business *plus* government) were $398 billion. Relative to GDP that amount was about 2.8 percent, which is a reasonable measure of the emphasis the U.S. economy puts on technological advance. As shown in Global Perspective 11W.1, this is a high percentage of GDP compared to several other nations.

American businesses spent $263 billion on R&D in 2008. Figure 11W.1 shows how these R&D expenditures were allocated. Observe that U.S. firms collectively channeled 75 percent of their R&D expenditures to "development" (innovation and imitation, the route to diffusion). They spent another 20 percent on applied research, or on pursuing invention. For reasons we will mention later, only 5 percent of business R&D expenditures went for basic research, the search for general scientific principles. Of course, industries, and firms within industries, vary greatly in the amount of emphasis they place on these three processes.

Modern View of Technological Advance

For decades most economists regarded technological advance as being a random *external* force to which the economy adjusted. In their opinion, advances in scientific and technological knowledge were unforeseeable lucky events unrelated to anything going on in the economy. But when

GLOBAL PERSPECTIVE 11W.1

Total R&D Expenditures as a Percentage of GDP, Selected Nations

Relative R&D spending varies among leading industrial nations. From a microeconomic perspective, R&D helps promote economic efficiency; from a macroeconomic perspective, R&D helps promote economic growth.

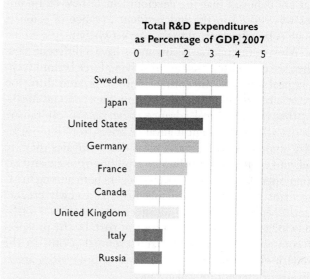

Source: National Science Foundation, **www.nsf.gov**, and *OECD Factbook 2009: Economic, Environmental and Social Statistics*, **www.oecd.org**. Latest available data.

FIGURE 11W.1 The composition of business R&D outlays in the United States, 2008. Firms channel the bulk of their R&D spending to innovation and imitation because both have direct commercial value; less to applied research, that is, invention; and a relatively small amount to basic scientific research.

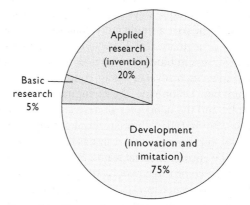

Source: Science Resource Statistics, National Science Foundation, **www.nsf.gov**.

they occurred from time to time, they paved the way for major new products (automobiles, airplanes) and major new production processes (assembly lines). Firms and industries incorporated a new technology into their products or processes to enhance or maintain their profits. After integrating the new technology, they settled back into new long-run equilibrium positions. Although they agreed with modern economists that technological advance was vitally important to the economy, economists of that era believed that the development of new technologies was rooted in the independent advance of science, which is largely external to the market system.

Most contemporary economists have a different view. They see capitalism itself as the driving force behind technological advance. Invention, innovation, and diffusion occur in response to incentives within the economy, meaning that technological advance is *internal* to capitalism. Specifically, technological advance arises from intense rivalry among individuals and firms that motivates them to seek and exploit new profit opportunities or to expand existing opportunities. That rivalry occurs both among existing firms and between existing firms and newly created firms. Moreover, many advances in "pure" scientific knowledge are motivated, at least in part, by the prospect of commercial applicability and eventual profit. In the modern view, entrepreneurs and other innovators are at the heart of technological advance.

Role of Entrepreneurs and Other Innovators

It will be helpful to distinguish between "entrepreneurs" and "other innovators":

- *Entrepreneurs* Recall that the entrepreneur is an initiator, innovator, and risk bearer. His or her entrepreneurial ability is the productive resource that combines the other productive resources of land, labor, and capital in new and unique ways to produce new goods and services. In the past a single individual, for example, Andrew Carnegie in steel, Henry Ford in automobiles, or Levi Strauss in blue jeans, carried out the entrepreneurial role. Such advances as air conditioning, the ballpoint pen, cellophane, the jet engine, insulin, xerography, and the helicopter all have an individualistic heritage. But in today's more technologically complex economy, entrepreneurship is just as likely to be carried out by entrepreneurial teams. Such teams may include only two or three people working "as their own bosses" on some new product idea or it may consist of larger groups of entrepreneurs who have pooled their financial resources to pursue a business idea.

- *Other innovators* This designation includes other key people involved in the pursuit of innovation who do not bear personal financial risk. Among them are key executives, scientists, and other salaried employees engaged in commercial R&D activities. (They are sometimes referred to as *intrapreneurs* since they provide the spirit of entrepreneurship within existing firms.)

Forming Start-Ups

Entrepreneurs often form small new companies called **start-ups** that focus on creating and introducing a new product or employing a new production or distribution technique. Two twenty-somethings named Steve Jobs and Steve Wozniak formed such a start-up in the mid-1970s after months of tinkering on a prototype personal computer that they had built in a garage during their free time. When neither of their employers—Hewlett-Packard and Atari, the developer of Pong (the first video game)—was interested in funding the development of their new computer, they founded their own computer company: Apple. Other examples of successful start-ups are Amgen, a biotechnology firm specializing in new medical treatments; Starbucks, a seller of gourmet coffee; Amazon, an Internet retailer; and Google, an Internet search provider.

Innovating within Existing Firms

Innovators are also at work within existing corporations, large and small. Such innovators are salaried workers, although many firms have pay systems that provide them with substantial bonuses or profit shares. Examples of firms known for their skillful internal innovators are 3M Corporation, the U.S. developer of Scotch tape, Post-it notes, and Thinsulate insulation; and General Electric, the developer of innovative major kitchen appliances, medical imaging machines, and jet aircraft engines. R&D work in major corporations has produced significant technological improvements in such products as television sets, telephones, home appliances, automobiles, automobile tires, and sporting equipment.

Some large firms, aware that excessive bureaucracy can stifle creative thinking and technological advance, have separated part of their R&D and manufacturing divisions to form new, more flexible, innovative firms. Three significant examples of such "spin-off firms" are Lucent Technologies (now Alcatel-Lucent), a telephone equipment and R&D firm created by AT&T; Imation, a high-technology firm spun off by the 3M Corporation; and Yum! Brands, which operates restaurant chains Taco Bell, KFC, and Pizza Hut. It was spun off by Pepsi.

Anticipating the Future

In 1949 a writer for *Popular Mechanics* magazine boldly predicted, "Computers in the future may weigh no more than 1.5 tons." Today's notebook computers weigh less than 3 pounds, while an iPhone weighs just 4.8 ounces.

Anticipating the future is difficult, but that is what innovators try to do. Those with strong anticipatory ability and determination have a knack for introducing new and improved products or services at just the right time.

The rewards for success are both monetary and nonmonetary. Product innovation and development are creative endeavors, with such intangible rewards as personal satisfaction. Also, many people simply enjoy participating in the competitive "contest." Of course, the "winners" can reap huge monetary rewards in the form of economic profits, stock appreciation, or large bonuses. Extreme examples are Bill Gates and Paul Allen, who founded Microsoft in 1975, and had a net worth in 2009 of $50 billion and $11 billion, respectively, mainly in the form of Microsoft stock.

Past successes often give entrepreneurs and innovative firms access to resources for further innovations that anticipate consumer wants. Although they may not succeed a second time, the market tends to entrust the production of goods and services to businesses that have consistently succeeded in filling consumer wants. And the market does not care whether these "winning" entrepreneurs and innovative firms are American, Brazilian, Japanese, German, or Swiss. Entrepreneurship and innovation are global in scope.

Exploiting University and Government Scientific Research

In Figure 11W.1 we saw that only 5 percent of business R&D spending in the United States goes to basic scientific research. The reason the percentage is so small is that scientific principles, as such, cannot be patented, nor do they usually have immediate commercial uses. Yet new scientific knowledge is highly important to technological advance. For that reason, entrepreneurs study the scientific output of university and government laboratories to identify discoveries with commercial applicability.

Government and university labs have been the scene of many technological breakthroughs, including hybrid seeds, nuclear energy, satellite communications, the computer mouse, genetic engineering, and the Internet. Entire high-tech industries such as computers and biotechnology have their roots in major research universities and government laboratories. And nations with strong scientific communities tend to have the most technologically progressive firms and industries.

Also, firms increasingly help fund university research that relates to their products. Business funding of R&D at universities has grown rapidly, rising to more than $2.9 billion in 2008. Today, the separation between university scientists and innovators is narrowing; scientists and universities increasingly realize that their work may have commercial value and are teaming up with innovators to share in the potential profit.

A few firms, of course, find it profitable to conduct basic scientific research on their own. New scientific knowledge can give them a head start in creating an invention or a new product. This is particularly true in the pharmaceutical industry, where it is not uncommon for firms to parlay new scientific knowledge generated in their corporate labs into new, patentable drugs.

> ### QUICK REVIEW 11W.1
>
> - Broadly defined, technological advance means new or improved products and services as well as new or improved production and distribution processes.
> - Invention is the *discovery* of a new product or method; innovation is the *successful commercial application* of some invention; and diffusion is the *widespread adoption* of the innovation.
> - Many economists view technological advance as mainly a response to profit opportunities arising within a capitalist economy.
> - Technological advance is fostered by entrepreneurs and other innovators and is supported by the scientific research of universities and government-sponsored laboratories.

A Firm's Optimal Amount of R&D

How does a firm decide on its optimal amount of research and development? That amount depends on the firm's perception of the marginal benefit and marginal cost of R&D activity. The decision rule here flows from basic economics: To earn the greatest profit, expand a particular activity until its marginal benefit (MB) equals its marginal cost (MC). A firm that sees the marginal benefit of a particular R&D activity, say, innovation, as exceeding the marginal cost should expand that activity. In contrast, an activity whose marginal benefit promises to be less than its marginal cost should be cut back. But the R&D spending decision is complex since it involves a present sacrifice for a future expected gain. While the cost of R&D is immediate, the expected benefits occur at some future time and are highly uncertain. So estimating those benefits is often more art than science. Nevertheless, the MB = MC way of thinking remains relevant for analyzing R&D decisions.

Interest-Rate Cost of Funds

Firms have several ways of obtaining the funds they need to finance R&D activities:

- **Bank loans** Some firms are able to obtain a loan from a bank or other financial institution. The cost of using the funds is the interest paid to the lender. The marginal cost is the cost per extra dollar borrowed, which is simply the market interest rate for borrowed funds.

- **Bonds** Bonds are financial contracts through which a borrower (typically a firm or a government) is obligated to pay the owner of a bond both the principal and interest due on a loan on dates specified in the bond contract. Established, profitable firms may be able to borrow funds for R&D by issuing bonds and selling them in the bond market. In this case, the cost is the interest paid to the lenders—the bondholders. Again the marginal cost of using the funds is the interest rate.

- **Retained earnings** A large, well-established firm may be able to draw on its own corporate savings to finance R&D. Typically, such a firm retains part of its profit rather than paying it all out as dividends to corporate owners. Some of the undistributed profit, called *retained earnings*, can be used to finance R&D activity. The marginal cost of using retained earnings for R&D is an opportunity cost—the rate of interest that those funds could have earned as deposits in a financial institution.

- **Venture capital** A small start-up firm may be able to attract venture capital to finance its R&D projects. Venture capital is financial capital, or simply money, not real capital. **Venture capital** consists of that part of household saving used to finance high-risk business ventures in exchange for shares of the profit if the ventures succeed. The marginal cost of venture capital is the share of expected profit that the firm will have to pay to those who provided the money. This can be stated as a percentage of the venture capital, so it is essentially an interest rate.

- **Personal savings** Finally, individual entrepreneurs might draw on their own savings to finance the R&D for a new venture. The marginal cost of the financing is again the forgone interest rate.

Thus, whatever the source of the R&D funds, we can state the marginal cost of these funds as an interest rate *i*. For simplicity, let's assume that this interest rate is the same no matter how much financing is required. Further, we assume that a certain firm called MedTech must pay an interest rate of 8 percent for the least expensive funding available to it. Then a graph of the marginal cost of each funding amount for this firm is a horizontal line at the 8 percent interest

FIGURE 11W.2 The interest-rate cost-of-funds schedule and curve. As it relates to R&D, a firm's interest-rate cost-of-funds schedule (the table) and curve (the graph) show the interest rate the firm must pay to obtain any particular amount of funds to finance R&D. Curve *i* indicates the firm can finance as little or as much R&D as it wants at a constant 8 percent rate of interest.

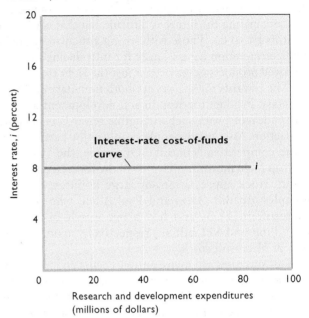

R&D, Millions	Interest-Rate Cost of Funds, %
$10	8
20	8
30	8
40	8
50	8
60	8
70	8
80	8

rate, as shown in Figure 11W.2. Such a graph is called an **interest-rate cost-of-funds curve.** This one tells us that MedTech can borrow any amount of money at the 8 percent interest rate. The table accompanying the graph contains the data used to construct the graph and tells us much the same thing.

With these data in hand, MedTech wants to determine how much R&D it should finance in the coming year.

Expected Rate of Return

A firm's marginal benefit from R&D is its expected profit (or return) from the last (marginal) dollar spent on R&D. That is, the R&D is expected to result in a new product or production method that will increase revenue, reduce production costs, or both (in ways we will soon explain). This return

FIGURE 11W.3 **The expected-rate-of-return schedule and curve.** As they relate to R&D, a firm's expected-rate-of-return schedule (the table) and curve (the graph) show the firm's expected gain in profit, as a percentage of R&D spending, for each level of R&D spending. Curve r slopes downward because the firm assesses its potential R&D projects in descending order of expected rates of return.

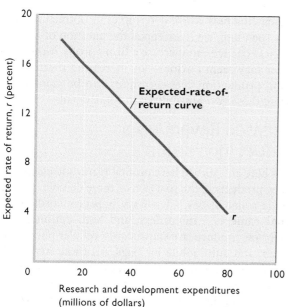

R&D, Millions	Expected Rate of Return, %
$10	18
20	16
30	14
40	12
50	10
60	8
70	6
80	4

FIGURE 11W.4 **A firm's optimal level of R&D expenditures.** The firm's optimal level of R&D expenditures ($60 million) occurs where its expected rate of return equals the interest-rate cost of funds, as shown in both the table and the graph. At $60 million of R&D spending, the firm has taken advantage of all R&D opportunities for which the expected rate of return, r, exceeds or equals the 8 percent interest cost of borrowing, i.

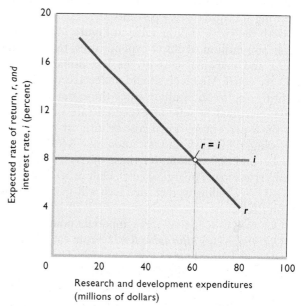

Expected Rate of Return, %	R&D, Millions	Interest-Rate Cost of Funds, %
18	$10	8
16	20	8
14	30	8
12	40	8
10	50	8
8	**60**	**8**
6	70	8
4	80	8

is expected, not certain—there is risk in R&D decisions. Let's suppose that after considering such risks, MedTech anticipates that an R&D expenditure of $1 million will result in a new product that will yield a one-time added profit of $1.2 million a year later. As a result, the expected rate of return r on the $1 million R&D expenditure (after the $1 million has been repaid) is 20 percent (= $200,000/$1,000,000). This is the marginal benefit of the first $1 million of R&D. (Stretching the return over several years complicates the computation of r, but it does not alter the basic analysis. We discuss this "present-value complication" in Chapter 15.)

MedTech can use this same method to estimate the expected rates of return for R&D expenditures of $2 million, $3 million, $4 million, and so on. Suppose those marginal rates of return are the ones indicated in the table in

Figure 11W.3, where they are also graphed as the **expected-rate-of-return curve.** This curve shows the expected rate of return, which is the marginal benefit of each dollar of expenditure on R&D. The curve slopes downward because of diminishing returns to R&D expenditures. A firm will direct its initial R&D expenditures to the highest expected-rate-of-return activities and then use additional funding for activities with successively lower expected rates of return. That is, the firm will experience lower and lower expected rates of return as it expands its R&D spending.

Optimal R&D Expenditures

Figure 11W.4 combines the interest-rate cost-of-funds curve (Figure 11W.2) and the expected-rate-of-return curve (Figure 11W.3). The curves intersect at MedTech's **optimal**

amount of R&D, which is $60 million. This amount can also be determined from the table as the amount of funding for which the expected rate of return and the interest cost of borrowing are equal (here, 8 percent).

Both the curve and the table in Figure 11W.4 tell us that at $60 million of R&D expenditures, the marginal benefit and marginal cost of the last dollar spent on R&D are equal. MedTech should undertake all R&D expenditures up to $60 million since those outlays yield a higher marginal benefit or expected rate of return, r, than the 8 percent marginal cost or interest-rate cost of borrowing, i. But it should not undertake R&D expenditures beyond $60 million; for these outlays, r (marginal benefit) is less than i (marginal cost). Only at $60 million do we have $r = i$, telling us that MedTech will spend $60 million on R&D.

Our analysis reinforces three important points:

- *Optimal versus affordable R&D* From earlier discussions we know there can be too much, as well as too little, of a "good thing." So it is with R&D and technological advance. Figure 11W.4 shows that R&D expenditures make sense to a firm only as long as the expected return from the outlay equals or exceeds the cost of obtaining the funds needed to finance it. Many R&D expenditures may be affordable but not worthwhile because their marginal benefit is likely to be less than their marginal cost.

- *Expected, not guaranteed, returns* The outcomes from R&D are expected, not guaranteed. With 20-20 hindsight, a firm can always look back and decide whether a particular expenditure for R&D was worthwhile. But that assessment is irrelevant to the original decision. At the time of the decision, the expenditure was thought to be worthwhile on the basis of existing information and expectations. Some R&D decisions may be more like an informed gamble than the typical business decision. Invention and innovation, in particular, carry with them a great deal of risk. For every successful outcome, there are scores of costly disappointments.

- *Adjustments* Firms adjust their R&D expenditures when expected rates of return on various projects change (when curves such as r in Figure 11W.4 shift). The U.S. war on terrorism, for example, increased the expected rate of return on R&D for improved security devices used at airports, train stations, harbors, and other public places. It also increased the expected return on new methods of detecting and responding

to potential bioterrorism. The revised realities prompted many firms to increase their R&D expenditures for these purposes.

Increased Profit via Innovation

In discussing how a firm determines its optimal amount of R&D spending, we sidestepped the question of how technological change can increase a firm's profit. Although the answer may seem obvious—by increasing revenue or reducing production costs—insights can be gained by exploring these two possibilities in some detail.

Increased Revenue via Product Innovation

Firms here and abroad have profitably introduced hundreds of new products in the past two or three decades. Examples include roller blades, microwave popcorn, cordless drills, digital cameras, camcorders, and high-definition TVs. Other new products are snowboards, cellular phones, MP3 players, and automobile air bags. All these items reflect technological advance in the form of product innovation.

How do such new products gain consumer acceptance? As you know from Chapter 6, to maximize their satisfaction, consumers purchase products that have the highest marginal utility per dollar. They determine which products to buy in view of their limited money incomes by comparing the ratios of MU/price for the various goods. They first select the unit of the good with the highest MU/price ratio, then the one with the next highest, and so on, until their incomes are used up.

The first five columns of Table 11W.1 repeat some of the information in Table 6.1. Before the introduction of new product C, the consumer maximized the total utility she could get from $10 of income by buying 2 units of A at $1 per unit and 4 units of B at $2 per unit. Her total budget of $10 was thus fully expended, with $2 spent on A and $8 on B. As shown in columns 2b and 3b, the marginal utility per dollar spent on the last unit of each product was 8 (= 8/$1 = 16/$2). The total utility, derived from columns 2a and 3a, was 96 utils (= 10 + 8 from the first 2 units of A plus 24 + 20 + 18 + 16 from the first 4 units of B). (If you are uncertain about this outcome, please review the discussion of Table 6.1.)

Now suppose an innovative firm offers new product C (columns 4a and 4b in Table 11W.1), priced at $4 per unit. Note that the first unit of C has a higher marginal utility per dollar (13) than any unit of A and B and that the second unit of C and the first unit of B have equal MU/price ratios of 12. To maximize satisfaction, the consumer now buys 2 units of C at $4 per unit, 1 unit of B at $2 per unit,

TABLE 11W.1 Utility Maximization with the Introduction of a New Product (Income = $10)*

(1) Unit of Product	(2) Product A: Price = $1		(3) Product B: Price = $2		(4) New Product C: Price = $4	
	(a) Marginal Utility, Utils	(b) Marginal Utility per Dollar (MU/Price)	(a) Marginal Utility, Utils	(b) Marginal Utility per Dollar (MU/Price)	(a) Marginal Utility, Utils	(b) Marginal Utility per Dollar (MU/Price)
First	10	10	24	12	52	13
Second	8	8	20	10	48	12
Third	7	7	18	9	44	11
Fourth	6	6	16	8	36	9
Fifth	5	5	12	6	32	8

*It is assumed in this table that the amount of marginal utility received from additional units of each of the three products is independent of the quantity purchased of the other products. For example, the marginal-utility schedule for product C is independent of the amount of A and B purchased by the consumer.

and zero units of A. Our consumer has spent all of her $10 income ($8 on C and $2 on B), and the MU/price ratios of the last units of B and C are equal at 12. But as determined via columns 3a and 4a, the consumer's total utility is now 124 utils (= 24 from the first unit of B plus 52 + 48 from the first 2 units of C).

Total utility has increased by 28 utils (= 124 utils − 96 utils), and that is why product C was purchased. Consumers will buy a new product only if it increases the total utility they obtain from their limited incomes.

From the innovating firm's perspective, these "dollar votes" represent new product demand that yields increased revenue. When per-unit revenue exceeds per-unit cost, the product innovation creates per-unit profit. Total profit rises by the per-unit profit multiplied by the number of units sold. As a percentage of the original R&D expenditure, the rise in total profit is the return on that R&D expenditure. It was the basis for the expected-rate-of-return curve r in Figure 11W.4.

Other related points:

- **Importance of price** Consumer acceptance of a new product depends on both its marginal utility and its price. (Confirm that the consumer represented in Table 11W.1 would buy zero units of new product C if its price were $8 rather than $4.) To be successful, a new product must not only deliver utility to consumers but do so at an acceptable price.

- **Unsuccessful new products** For every successful new product, hundreds do not succeed; the expected return that motivates product innovation is not always realized. Examples of colossal product flops are Ford's Edsel automobile, quadraphonic stereo, New Coke by Coca-Cola, Kodak disc cameras, and XFL football. Less dramatic failures include the hundreds of dot-com firms that have gone out of business

since the late 1990s. In each case, millions of dollars of R&D and promotion expense ultimately resulted in loss, not profit.

- **Product improvements** Most product innovation consists of incremental improvements to existing products rather than radical inventions. Examples: more fuel-efficient automobile engines, new varieties of pizza, lighter-weight shafts for golf clubs, more flavorful bubble gum, "rock shocks" for mountain bikes, and clothing made of wrinkle-free fabrics.

Reduced Cost via Process Innovation

The introduction of better methods of producing products—process innovation—is also a path toward enhanced profit and a positive return on R&D expenditures. Suppose a firm introduces a new and better production process, say, assembling its product by teams rather than by a standard assembly line. Alternatively, suppose this firm replaces old equipment with more productive equipment embodying a technological advance. In either case, the innovation yields an upward shift in the firm's total-product curve from TP_1 to TP_2 in Figure 11W.5a. As a result, more units of output can now be produced at each level of resource usage. Note from the figure, for example, that this firm can now produce 2500 units of output, rather than 2000, when using 1000 units of labor. So its average product has increased from 2 (= 2000 units of output/1000 units of labor) to 2.5 (= 2500 units of output/1000 units of labor).

The result is a downward shift in the firm's average-total-cost curve, from ATC_1 to ATC_2 in Figure 11W.5b. To understand why, let's assume this firm pays $1000 for the use of its capital and $9 for each unit of labor. Since it uses 1000 units of labor, its labor cost is $9000 (= $9 × 1000); its capital cost is $1000; and thus its total cost is $10,000. When its output increases from 2000 to 2500

FIGURE 11W.5 **Process innovation, total product, and average total cost.** (a) Process innovation shifts a firm's total-product curve upward from TP_1 to TP_2, meaning that with a given amount of capital the firm can produce more output at each level of labor input. As shown, with 1000 units of labor it can produce 2500 rather than 2000 units of output. (b) The upward shift in the total-product curve results in a downward shift in the firm's average-total-cost curve, from ATC_1 to ATC_2. This means the firm can produce any particular unit of output at a lower average total cost than it could previously. For example, the original 2000 units can be produced at less than $4 per unit, versus $5 per unit originally. Or 2500 units can now be produced at $4 per unit.

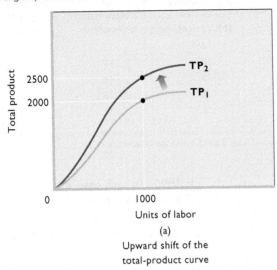

(a)
Upward shift of the
total-product curve

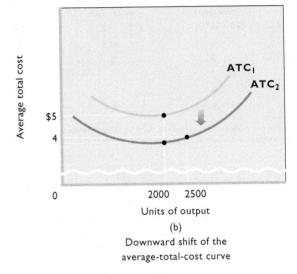

(b)
Downward shift of the
average-total-cost curve

units as a result of the process innovation, its total cost remains $10,000. So its average total cost declines from $5 (= $10,000/2000) to $4 (= $10,000/2500). Alternatively, the firm could produce the original 2000 units of output with fewer units of labor at an even lower average total cost.

This reduction in average total cost enhances the firm's profit. As a percentage of the R&D expenditure that fostered it, this extra profit is the expected return r that was the basis for the rate-of-return curve in Figure 11W.3. In this case, the expected increase in profit arose from the prospect of lower production costs through process innovation.

Example: Computer-based inventory control systems, such as those pioneered by Walmart, enabled innovators to reduce the number of people needed to keep track of inventories. The new systems also enabled firms to keep goods arriving "just in time," reducing the cost of storing inventories. The consequence? Significant increases in sales per worker, declines in average total cost, and increased profit.

Imitation and R&D Incentives

Our analysis of product and process innovation explains how technological advance enhances a firm's profit. But it also hints at a potential **imitation problem:** A firm's rivals may be able to imitate its new product or process, greatly reducing the originator's profit from its R&D effort. As just one example, in the 1980s U.S. auto firms took apart Japanese Honda Accords, piece by piece, to discover the secrets of their high quality. This reverse engineering—which ironically was perfected earlier by the Japanese—helped the U.S. firms incorporate innovative features into their own cars. This type of imitation is perfectly legitimate and fully anticipated; it is often the main path to widespread diffusion of an innovation.

In fact, a dominant firm that is making large profits from its existing products may let smaller firms in the industry incur the high costs of product innovation while it closely monitors their successes and failures. The dominant firm then moves quickly to imitate any successful new product; its goal is to become the second firm to embrace the innovation. In using this so-called **fast-second strategy,** the dominant firm counts on its own product-improvement abilities, marketing prowess, or economies of scale to prevail.

Examples abound: Royal Crown introduced the first diet cola, but Diet Coke and Diet Pepsi dominate diet-cola sales today. Meister Brau introduced the first low-calorie beer, but Miller popularized the product with its Miller Lite. Gillette moved quickly with its own stainless-steel razor blade only after a smaller firm, Wilkinson, introduced this product innovation. Creative Technology (the maker of Sound Blaster audio cards for personal computers) introduced the first miniature MP3 player, but Apple popularized the product with its iPod.

Benefits of Being First

Imitation and the fast-second strategy raise an important question: What incentive is there for any firm to bear the expenses and risks of innovation if competitors can imitate its new or improved product? Why not let others bear the costs and risks of product development and then just imitate the successful innovations? Although we have seen that this may be a plausible strategy in some situations, there are several protections for, and potential advantages to, taking the lead.

Patents   Some technological breakthroughs, specifically inventions, can be patented. Once patented, they cannot be legally imitated for two decades from time of patent application. The purpose of patents is, in fact, to reduce imitation and its negative effect on the incentive for engaging in R&D. Example: Polaroid's patent of its instant camera enabled it to earn high economic profits for many years. When Kodak "cloned" the camera, Polaroid won a patent-infringement lawsuit against its rival. Kodak not only had to stop producing its version of the camera but had to buy back the Kodak instant cameras it had sold and pay millions of dollars in damages to Polaroid.

There are hundreds of other examples of long-run profits based on U.S. patents; they involve products from prescription drugs to pop-top cans to weed trimmers. As shown in Global Perspective 11W.2, foreign citizens and firms hold U.S. patents along with American citizens and firms.

Copyrights and Trademarks   *Copyrights* protect publishers of books, computer software, movies, videos, and musical compositions from having their works copied. *Trademarks* give the original innovators of products the exclusive right to use a particular product name ("M&Ms," "Barbie" dolls, "Wheaties"). By reducing the problem of direct copying, these legal protections increase the incentive for product innovation. They have been strengthened worldwide through recent international trade agreements.

Brand-Name Recognition   Along with trademark protection, brand-name recognition may give the original innovator a major marketing advantage for years or even decades. Consumers often identify a new product with the firm that first introduced and popularized it in the mass market. Examples: Levi's blue jeans, Kleenex soft tissues, Johnson & Johnson's Band-Aids, Gatorade sports drink, and Kellogg's Corn Flakes.

Trade Secrets and Learning by Doing   Some innovations involve trade secrets, without which competitors cannot imitate the product or process. Example: Coca-Cola has

GLOBAL PERSPECTIVE 11W.2

Distribution of U.S. Patents, by Foreign Nation

Foreign citizens, corporations, and governments hold 42 percent of U.S. patents. The top 10 foreign countries in terms of U.S. patent holdings since 1963 are listed below, with the number of U.S. patents (through 2008) in parentheses.

Top 10 Foreign Countries

Japan (725,866)
Germany (313,078)
U.K. (129,762)
France (117,133)
Canada (84,321)
Taiwan (70,643)
South Korea (57,968)
Switzerland (54,349)
Italy (46,346)
Sweden (40,577)

Source: U.S. Patent and Trademark Office, **www.uspto.gov.**

successfully kept its formula for Coke a secret from potential rivals. Many other firms have perfected special production techniques known only to them. In a related advantage, a firm's head start with a new product often allows it to achieve substantial cost reductions through learning by doing. The innovator's lower cost may enable it to continue to profit even after imitators have entered the market.

Time Lags   Time lags between innovation and diffusion often enable innovating firms to realize a substantial economic profit. It takes time for an imitator to gain knowledge of the properties of a new innovation. And once it has that knowledge, the imitator must design a substitute product, gear up a factory for its production, and conduct a marketing campaign. Various entry barriers, such as large financial requirements, economies of scale, and price-cutting, may extend the time lag between innovation and imitation. In practice, it may take years or even decades before rival firms can successfully imitate a profitable new product and cut into the market share of the innovator. In the meantime, the innovator continues to profit.

Profitable Buyouts

A final advantage of being first arises from the possibility of a buyout (outright purchase) of the innovating firm by a larger firm. Here, the innovative entrepreneurs take their

CONSIDER THIS . . .

Trade Secrets

Trade secrets have long played an important role in maintaining returns from research and development (R&D). Long before Coca-Cola's secret formula or Colonel Sanders' secret herbs and spices, legend has it that the Roman citizen Erasmo (c. A.D. 130) had a secret ingredient for violin strings.* As the demand for his new product grew, he falsely identified his strings as *catgut,* when they were actually made of sheep intestines. Why the deception? At the time, it was considered to be extremely bad luck to kill a cat. By identifying his strings as catgut, he hoped that nobody would imitate his product and reduce his monopoly profit. Moreover, his product name would help him preserve his valuable trade secret.

---

*We found this anecdote in Dennis W. Carleton and Jeffrey Perloff, *Modern Industrial Organization,* 2d ed. (New York: HarperCollins, 1994), p. 139. Their source, in turn, was L. Boyd, *San Francisco Chronicle,* October 27, 1984, p. 35.

year. As shown in Figure 11W.6, business R&D spending in the United States not only remains substantial but has grown over the past quarter-century. The high levels of spending simply would not continue if imitation consistently and severely depressed rates of return on R&D expenditures.

QUICK REVIEW 11W.2

- A firm's optimal R&D expenditure is the amount at which the expected rate of return (marginal benefit) from the R&D expenditure just equals the interest-rate cost of borrowing (marginal cost) required to finance it.
- Product innovation can entice consumers to substitute a new product for existing products to increase their total utility, thereby increasing the innovating firm's revenue and profit.
- Process innovation can lower a firm's production costs and increase its profit by increasing total product and decreasing average total cost.
- A firm faces reduced profitability from R&D if competitors can successfully imitate its new product or process. Nevertheless, there are significant potential protections and benefits to being first, including patents, copyrights, and trademarks; brand-name recognition; trade secrets; cost reductions from learning by doing; and major time lags between innovation and imitation.

rewards immediately, as cash or as shares in the purchasing firm, rather than waiting for perhaps uncertain long-run profits from their own production and marketing efforts.

Examples: Once the popularity of cellular communications became evident, AT&T bought out McCaw Communications, an early leader in this new technology. When Minnetonka's Softsoap became a huge success, it sold its product to Colgate-Palmolive. More recently, Swiss conglomerate Nestlé bought out Chef America, the highly successful maker of Hot Pockets frozen meat-and-cheese sandwiches. Such buyouts are legal under current antitrust laws as long as they do not substantially lessen competition in the affected industry. For this to be the case, there must be other strong competitors in the market. That was not true, for example, when Microsoft tried to buy out Intuit (maker of Quicken, the best-selling financial software). That buyout was disallowed because Intuit and Microsoft were the two main suppliers of financial software for personal computers.

In short, despite the imitation problem, significant protections and advantages enable most innovating firms to profit from their R&D efforts, as implied by the continuing high levels of R&D spending by firms year after

FIGURE 11W.6 The growth of business R&D expenditures in the United States, 1980–2008. Inflation-adjusted R&D expenditures by firms are substantial and growing, suggesting that R&D continues to be profitable for firms, even in the face of possible imitation.

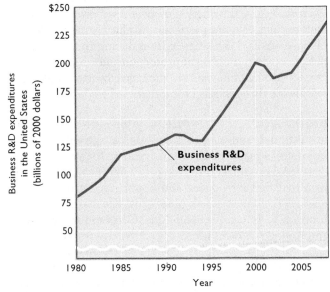

Source: *Science Resource Statistics,* National Science Foundation, **www.nsf.gov.**

Role of Market Structure

In view of our discussion of market structures in the previous four chapters, asking whether some particular market structure or firm size is best suited to technological progress is logical. Is a highly competitive industry consisting of thousands of relatively small firms likely to produce faster technological progress than a monopoly? Or is perhaps an intermediate market structure like oligopoly the most likely to produce rapid technological progress?

Market Structure and Technological Advance

As a first step toward answering these questions, we survey the strengths and shortcomings of our four market models as related to technological advance.

Pure Competition Does a pure competitor have a strong incentive and strong ability to undertake R&D? On the positive side, strong competition provides a reason for such firms to innovate; competitive firms tend to be less complacent than monopolists. If a pure competitor does not seize the initiative, one or more rivals may introduce a new product or cost-reducing production technique that could drive it from the market. As a matter of short-term profit and long-term survival, the pure competitor is under continual pressure to improve products and lower costs through innovation. Also, where there are many competing firms, there is less chance that an idea for improving a product or process will be overlooked by a single firm.

On the negative side, the expected rate of return on R&D may be low or even negative for a pure competitor. Because of easy entry, its profit rewards from innovation may quickly be competed away by existing or entering firms that also produce the new product or adopt the new technology. Also, the small size of competitive firms and the fact that they earn only a normal profit in the long run lead to serious questions as to whether they can finance substantial R&D programs. Observers have noted that the high rate of technological advance in the purely competitive agricultural industry, for example, has come not from the R&D of individual farmers but from government-sponsored research and from the development of fertilizers, hybrid seed, and farm implements by oligopolistic firms.

Monopolistic Competition Like pure competitors, monopolistic competitors cannot afford to be complacent. But unlike pure competitors, which sell standardized products, monopolistic competitors have a strong profit incentive to engage in product innovation. This incentive to differentiate products from those of competitors stems from the fact that sufficiently novel products may create monopoly power and thus economic profit. There are many examples of innovative firms (McDonald's, Starbucks, Redbox video rentals) that started out as monopolistic competitors in localized markets but soon gained considerable national market power, with the attendant economic profit.

For the typical firm, however, the shortcomings of monopolistic competition in relation to technological advance are the same as those of pure competition. Most monopolistic competitors remain small, which limits their ability to secure inexpensive financing for R&D. In addition, monopolistic competitors find it difficult to extract large profits from technological advances. Any economic profits from innovation are usually temporary because entry to monopolistically competitive industries is relatively easy. In the long run, new entrants with similar goods reduce the demand for the innovator's product, leaving the innovator with only a normal profit. Monopolistic competitors therefore usually have relatively low expected rates of return on R&D expenditures.

Oligopoly Many of the characteristics of oligopoly are conducive to technological advance. First, the large size of oligopolists enables them to finance the often large R&D costs associated with major product or process innovation. In particular, the typical oligopolist realizes an ongoing economic profit, a part of which is retained. This undistributed profit serves as a major source of readily available, relatively low-cost funding for R&D. Moreover, the existence of barriers to entry gives the oligopolist some assurance that it can maintain any economic profit it gains from innovation. Then, too, the large sales volume of the oligopolist enables it to spread the cost of specialized R&D equipment and teams of specialized researchers over a great many units of output. Finally, the broad scope of R&D activity within oligopolistic firms helps them offset the inevitable R&D "misses" with more-than-compensating R&D "hits." Thus, oligopolists clearly have the means and incentive to innovate.

But there is also a negative side to R&D in oligopoly. In many instances, the oligopolist's incentive to innovate may be far less than we have just implied because oligopoly tends to breed complacency. An oligopolist may reason that introducing costly new technology and producing new products makes little sense when it currently is earning a sizable economic profit without them. The oligopolist wants to maximize its profit by exploiting fully all its capital assets. Why rush to develop a new product (say, batteries for electric automobiles) when that product's success will render obsolete much of the firm's current equipment designed to produce its existing product (say, gasoline engines)? It is not difficult to cite oligopolistic industries in which the largest firms' interest in R&D has been quite modest. Examples: the steel, cigarette, and aluminum industries.

Pure Monopoly In general, the pure monopolist has little incentive to engage in R&D; it maintains its high profit through entry barriers that, in theory, are complete. The only incentive for the pure monopolist to engage in R&D is defensive: to reduce the risk of being blindsided by some new product or production process that destroys its monopoly. If such a product is out there to be discovered, the monopolist may have an incentive to find it. By so doing, it can either exploit the new product or process for continued monopoly profit or suppress the product until the monopolist has extracted the maximum profit from its current capital assets. But, in general, economists agree that pure monopoly is the market structure least conducive to innovation.

Inverted-U Theory of R&D

Analysis like this has led some experts on technological progress to postulate a so-called **inverted-U theory of R&D**, which deals with the relationship between market structure and technological advance. This theory is illustrated in Figure 11W.7, which relates R&D spending as a percentage of a firm's sales (vertical axis) to the industry's four-firm concentration ratio (horizontal axis). The "inverted-U" shape of the curve suggests that R&D effort is at best weak in both very-low-concentration industries (pure competition) and very-high-concentration industries (pure monopoly). Starting from the lowest concentrations, R&D spending as a percentage of sales rises with

concentration until a concentration ratio of 50 percent or so is reached, meaning that the four largest firms account for about one-half the total industry output. Beyond that, relative R&D spending decreases as concentration rises.

The logic of the inverted-U theory follows from our discussion. Firms in industries with very low concentration ratios are mainly competitive firms. They are small, and this makes it difficult for them to finance R&D. Moreover, entry to these industries is easy, making it difficult to sustain economic profit from innovations that are not supported by patents. As a result, firms in these industries spend little on R&D relative to their sales. At the other end (far right) of the curve, where concentration is exceptionally high, monopoly profit is already high and innovation will not add much more profit. Furthermore, innovation typically requires costly retooling of very large factories, which will cut into whatever additional profit is realized. As a result, the expected rate of return from R&D is quite low, as are expenditures for R&D relative to sales. Finally, the lack of rivals makes the monopolist quite complacent about R&D.

The optimal industry structure for R&D is one in which expected returns on R&D spending are high and funds to finance it are readily available and inexpensive. From our discussion, those factors seem to occur in industries where a few firms are absolutely and relatively large but where the concentration ratio is not so high as to prohibit vigorous competition by smaller rivals. Rivalry among the larger oligopolistic firms and competition between the larger and the smaller firms then provide a strong incentive for R&D. The inverted-U theory of R&D, as represented by Figure 11W.7, also points toward this "loose" oligopoly as the optimal structure for R&D spending.

Market Structure and Technological Advance: The Evidence

Various industry studies and cross-industry studies collectively support the inverted-U theory of R&D.[1] Other things equal, the optimal market structure for technological advance seems to be an industry in which there is a mix of large oligopolistic firms (a 40 to 60 percent concentration ratio), with several highly innovative smaller firms.

But our "other-things-equal" qualification is quite important here. Whether or not a particular industry is highly technical may well be a more important determinant of R&D than its structure. While some concentrated industries (electronics, aircraft, and petroleum) devote

FIGURE 11W.7 The inverted-U theory of R&D expenditures. The inverted-U theory suggests that R&D expenditures as a percentage of sales rise with industry concentration until the four-firm concentration ratio reaches about 50 percent. Further increases in industry concentration are associated with lower relative R&D expenditures.

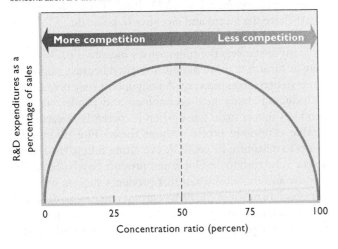

[1]One such study is that by Philippe Aghion et al., "Competition and Innovation: An Inverted-U Relationship," *Quarterly Journal of Economics,* May 2005, pp. 701–728.

large quantities of resources to R&D and are very innovative, others (cigarettes, aluminum, gypsum products) are not. The level of R&D spending within an industry seems to depend as much on its technical character and "technological opportunities" as on its market structure. There simply may be more opportunities to innovate in the computer and pharmaceutical industries, for example, than in the brick-making and coal-mining industries.

Conclusion: The inverted-U curve shown in Figure 11W.7 is a useful depiction of the general relationship between R&D spending and market structure, other things equal.

Technological Advance and Efficiency

Technological advance contributes significantly to economic efficiency. New and better processes and products enable society to produce more output, as well as a higher-valued mix of output.

Productive Efficiency

Technological advance as embodied in process innovation improves *productive efficiency* by increasing the productivity of inputs (as indicated in Figure 11W.5a) and by reducing average total costs (as in Figure 11W.5b). In other words, it enables society to produce the same amount of a particular good or service while using fewer scarce resources, thereby freeing the unused resources to produce other goods and services. Or if society desires more of the now less expensive good, process innovation enables it to have that greater quantity without sacrificing other goods. Viewed either way, process innovation enhances productive efficiency: It reduces society's per-unit cost of whatever mix of goods and services it chooses. It is thus an important means of shifting an economy's production possibilities curve rightward.

Allocative Efficiency

Technological advance as embodied in *product* (or service) innovation enhances allocative efficiency by giving society a more preferred mix of goods and services. Recall from our earlier discussion that consumers buy a new product rather than an old product only when buying the new one increases the total utility obtained from their limited incomes. Obviously, then, a popular new product—and the new mix of products it implies—creates a higher level of total utility for society.

In terms of markets, the demand for the new product rises and the demand for the old product declines. The high economic profit engendered by the new product attracts resources away from less valued uses and to the production of the new product. In theory, such shifting of resources continues until the price of the new product equals its marginal cost.

There is a caveat here, however. Innovation (either product or process) can create monopoly power through patents or through the many advantages of being first. When new monopoly power results from an innovation, society may lose part of the improved efficiency it otherwise would have gained from that innovation. The reason is that the profit-maximizing monopolist restricts output to keep its product price above marginal cost. For example, Microsoft's innovative Windows product has resulted in dominance in the market for Intel-compatible operating systems for personal computers. Microsoft's substantial monopoly power permits it to charge prices that are well above marginal cost and minimum average total cost.

Creative Destruction

Although innovation can create monopoly power, it also can reduce or eliminate it. By increasing competition where it previously was weak, innovation can push prices down toward marginal cost. For example, Intel's microprocessor enabled personal computers, and their ease of production eventually diminished IBM's monopoly power in the sale of computer hardware. More recently, Linux's new computer operating system has provided some promising competition for Microsoft Windows.

At the extreme, innovation may cause *creative destruction*, the phenomenon discussed in Chapter 9 whereby the market positions of firms committed to existing products and old ways of doing business are destroyed by the creation and spread of new products and new production methods.

According to early proponents like MIT economist Joseph Schumpeter, creative destruction is such a powerful force that it will automatically displace any monopolist that no longer delivers superior performance. But many contemporary economists think this notion reflects more wishful thinking than fact. In this view, the idea that creative destruction is automatic

> . . . neglects the ability of powerful established firms to erect private storm shelters—or lobby government to build public storm shelters for them—in order to shield themselves from the Schumpeterian gales of creative destruction. It ignores the difference between the legal freedom of entry and the economic reality deterring the entry of potential newcomers into concentrated industries.[2]

---

[2]Walter Adams and James Brock, *The Structure of American Industry*, 10th ed. (Upper Saddle River, N.J.: Prentice Hall, 2001), pp. 363–364.

LAST Word On the Path to the Personal Computer and Internet

Technological Advance Is Clearly Evident in the Development of the Modern Personal Computer and the Emergence of the Internet. Here Is a Brief History of Those Events.

1945 Grace Murray Hopper finds a dead moth between relay contacts in the experimental Mark II computer at Harvard University. Whenever the computer subsequently malfunctions, workers set out to "debug" the device.

1946 ENIAC is revealed. A precursor to the modern-day computer, it relies on 18,000 vacuum tubes and fills 3000 cubic feet of space.

1947 AT&T scientists invent the "transfer resistance device," later known as the transistor. It replaces the less reliable vacuum tubes in computers.

1961 Bob Noyce (who later founded Intel Corporation) and Jack Kilby invent the first integrated circuit, which miniaturizes electronic circuitry onto a single silicon chip.

1964 IBM introduces the System/360 computer. Configured as a system, it takes up nearly the same space as two tennis courts.

1965 Digital Equipment Corporation unveils its PDP-8, the first relatively small-size computer (a "minicomputer").

1969 A networking system called ARPANET is born; it is the beginning of the Internet.

1971 Intel introduces its 4004 processor (a "microprocessor"). The $200 chip is the size of a thumbnail and has as much computing capability as the earlier ENIAC.

1975 Xerox markets Alto, the first personal computer (a "microcomputer"). Bill Gates and Paul Allen found Microsoft. MITS Corporation's Altair 8800 arrives on the scene. It contains Intel's 8080 microprocessor that Intel developed a year earlier to control traffic lights.

1977 The Apple II, Commodore PET, and Radio Shack TRS-80 go on sale, setting the stage for the personal computer revolution.

1981 IBM enters the personal computer market with a computer powered by the Intel 8800 chip and operated by the Microsoft Disc Operating System (MS-DOS). Logitech commercializes the "X-Y Position Indicator for a Display System," invented earlier by Douglas Engelbart in a government-funded research lab. Someone dubs it a "computer mouse" because it appears to have a tail.

1982 Compaq Computer "clones" the IBM machines; others do the same. Eventually Compaq becomes one of the leading sellers of personal computers.

1984 Apple introduces its Macintosh computer. It features user-friendly icons, a mouse, and preloaded software. College student Michael Dell founds Dell Computers, which builds customized personal computers and sells them through mail order. IBM, Sears Roebuck, and CBS team up to launch Prodigy Services, the first online computer business.

1985 Microsoft releases its Windows graphical interface operating system that improves upon MS-DOS. Ted Waitt starts a mail-order personal computer business (Gateway 2000) out of his South Dakota barn.

That is, some dominant firms may be able to use strategies such as selective price cutting, buyouts, and massive advertising to block entry and competition from even the most innovative new firms and existing rivals. Moreover, politically active dominant firms have been known to persuade government to give them tax breaks, subsidies, and tariff protection that strengthen their market power.

In short, while innovation in general enhances economic efficiency, in some cases it may lead to entrenched monopoly power. Further innovation may eventually destroy that monopoly power, but the process of creative destruction is neither automatic nor inevitable. On the other hand, the possession of monopoly power does not necessarily preclude rapid technological advance, innovation, or efficiency.

11W-16

1990 Microsoft introduces Windows 3.0, which, like Macintosh, features windows, icons, and pull-down menus.

1991 The World Wide Web (an Internet system) is invented.

1993 Intel introduces its first of several Pentium chips, which greatly speed up computing.

1994 Marc Andreessen starts up Netscape Communications and markets Netscape Navigator, which quickly becomes the leading software for browsing the emerging Internet. David Filo and Jerry Yang develop Yahoo, a system for locating material stored on the Internet.

1995 Microsoft releases the Windows 95 operating system, which becomes the dominant operating system of personal computers (90 percent market share). Microsoft is now well established as the world's leading software producer. Sun Microsystems introduces Java, an Internet programming language.

1996 Playing catch-up with Netscape, Microsoft develops Microsoft Internet Explorer and gives it away free.

1999 Netscape's market share plunges and it merges with America Online. More than 100 million personal computers are manufactured worldwide this year alone.

2000 Sixty percent of American households have access to the Internet either at home or at work, and the Internet spreads worldwide. Internet commerce in the United States reaches $300 billion, and an estimated 1.2 million U.S. jobs are Internet-related.

2002 A Federal court of appeals finds that Microsoft has a monopoly in operating system software for Intel-compatible personal computers and has maintained its monopoly through illegal actions aimed at thwarting threats from rivals. The court imposes a set of specific restrictions on Microsoft's anticompetitive business practices.

2005 Google, the innovative Internet search company, becomes the "darling" of Wall Street as its share price rises from $85 at its initial public offering (IPO) in August 2004 to $700 at the end of 2007.

2007 Apple's iPhone combines a cellular telephone, camera, media player, Web browser, and computer into a single hand-held device. The iPhone is also the first popular consumer electronic product to utilize a touch screen for input and control.

Source: Based partly on Diedtra Henderson, "Moore's Law Still Reigns," *Seattle Times*, Nov. 24, 1996, augmented and updated.

Summary

1. Technological advance is evidenced by new and improved goods and services and new and improved production or distribution processes. In economists' models, technological advance occurs only in the *very long run*.

2. Invention is the discovery of a product or process through the use of imagination, ingenuity, and experimentation. Innovation is the first successful commercial introduction of a new product, the first use of a new method, or the creation of a

new form of business enterprise. Diffusion is the spread of an earlier innovation among competing firms. Firms channel a majority of their R&D expenditures to innovation and imitation, rather than to basic scientific research and invention.

3. Historically, most economists viewed technological advance as a random, external force to which the economy adjusted. Many contemporary economists see technological advance as occurring in response to profit incentives within the economy and thus as an integral part of capitalism.

4. Entrepreneurs and other innovators try to anticipate the future. They play a central role in technological advance by initiating changes in products and processes. Entrepreneurs often form start-up firms that focus on creating and introducing new products. Sometimes, innovators work in the R&D labs of major corporations. Entrepreneurs and innovative firms often rely heavily on the basic research done by university and government scientists.

5. A firm's optimal amount of R&D spending occurs where its expected return (marginal benefit) from R&D equals its interest-rate cost of funds (marginal cost) to finance R&D. Entrepreneurs and firms use several sources to finance R&D, including (a) bank loans, (b) bonds, (c) venture capital (funds given in return for a share of the profits if the business succeeds), (d) undistributed corporate profits (retained earnings), and (e) personal savings.

6. Product innovation, the introduction of new products, succeeds when it provides consumers with a higher marginal utility per dollar spent than do existing products. The new product enables consumers to obtain greater total utility from a given income. From the firm's perspective, product innovation increases net revenue sufficiently to yield a positive rate of return on the R&D spending that produced the innovation.

7. Process innovation can lower a firm's production costs by improving its internal production techniques. Such improvement increases the firm's total product, thereby lowering its average total cost and increasing its profit. The added profit provides a positive rate of return on the R&D spending that produced the process innovation.

8. Imitation poses a potential problem for innovators since it threatens their returns on R&D expenditures. Some dominant firms use a fast-second strategy, letting smaller firms initiate new products and then quickly imitating the successes. Nevertheless, there are significant protections and potential benefits for firms that take the lead with R&D and innovation, including (a) patent protection, (b) copyrights and trademarks, (c) lasting brand-name recognition, (d) benefits from trade secrets and learning by doing, (e) high economic profits during the time lag between a product's introduction and its imitation, and (f) the possibility of lucrative buyout offers from larger firms.

9. Each of the four basic market structures has potential strengths and weaknesses regarding the likelihood of R&D and innovation. The inverted-U theory of R&D holds that a firm's R&D spending as a percentage of its sales rises with its industry four-firm concentration ratio, reaches a peak at a 50 percent concentration ratio, and then declines as concentration increases further. Empirical evidence is not clear-cut but lends general support to this theory. For any specific industry, however, the technological opportunities that are available may count more than market structure in determining R&D spending and innovation.

10. In general, technological advance enhances both productive and allocative efficiency. But in some situations patents and the advantages of being first with an innovation can increase monopoly power. While in some cases creative destruction eventually destroys monopolies, most economists doubt that this process is either automatic or inevitable.

Terms and Concepts

technological advance	process innovation	optimal amount of R&D
very long run	diffusion	imitation problem
invention	start-ups	fast-second strategy
patent	venture capital	inverted-U theory of R&D
innovation	interest-rate cost-of-funds curve	
product innovation	expected-rate-of-return curve	

Questions

1. What is meant by technological advance, as broadly defined? How does technological advance enter into the definition of the very long run? Which of the following are examples of technological advance, and which are not: an improved production process; entry of a firm into a profitable purely competitive industry; the imitation of a new production process by another firm; an increase in a firm's advertising expenditures? LO1

2. Listed below are several possible actions by firms. Write "INV" beside those that reflect invention, "INN" beside those that reflect innovation, and "DIF" beside those that reflect diffusion. LO1

   a. An auto manufacturer adds "heated seats" as a standard feature in its luxury cars to keep pace with a rival firm whose luxury cars already have this feature.

   b. A television production company pioneers the first music video channel.

   c. A firm develops and patents a working model of a self-erasing whiteboard for classrooms.

   d. A light bulb firm is the first to produce and market lighting fixtures with LEDs (light-emitting diodes).

   e. A rival toy maker introduces a new Jezebel doll to compete with Mattel's Barbie doll.

3. Contrast the older and the modern views of technological advance as they relate to the economy. What is the role of entrepreneurs and other innovators in technological advance? How does research by universities and government affect innovators and technological advance? Why do you think some university researchers are becoming more like entrepreneurs and less like "pure scientists"? LO2

4. Consider the effect that corporate profit taxes have on investing. Look back at Figure 11W.4. Suppose that the r line is the rate of return a firm earns before taxes. If corporate profit taxes are imposed, the firm's after-tax returns will be lower (and the higher the tax rate, the lower the after-tax returns). If the firm's decisions about R&D spending are based on comparing after-tax returns with the interest-rate cost of funds, how will increased corporate profit taxes affect R&D spending? Does this effect modify your views on corporate profit taxes? Discuss. LO3

5. Answer the following lettered questions on the basis of the information in this table: LO3

Amount of R&D, Millions	Expected Rate of Return on R&D, %
$10	16
20	14
30	12
40	10
50	8
60	6

   a. If the interest-rate cost of funds is 8 percent, what will be the optimal amount of R&D spending for this firm?

   b. Explain why $20 million of R&D spending will not be optimal.

   c. Why won't $60 million be optimal either?

6. Explain: "The success of a new product depends not only on its marginal utility but also on its price." LO3

7. Learning how to use software takes time. So once customers have learned to use a particular software package, it is easier to sell them software upgrades than to convince them to switch to new software. What implications does this have for expected rates of return on R&D spending for software firms developing upgrades versus firms developing imitative products? LO4

8. Why might a firm making a large economic profit from its existing product employ a fast-second strategy in relationship to new or improved products? What risks does it run in pursuing this strategy? What incentive does a firm have to engage in R&D when rivals can imitate its new product? LO4

9. Do you think the overall level of R&D would increase or decrease over the next 20 to 30 years if the lengths of new patents were extended from 20 years to, say, "forever"? What if the duration were reduced from 20 years to, say, 3 years? LO4

10. Make a case that neither pure competition nor pure monopoly is conducive to a great deal of R&D spending and innovation. Why might oligopoly be more favorable to R&D spending and innovation than either pure competition or pure monopoly? What is the inverted-U theory of R&D, and how does it relate to your answers to these questions? LO5

11. Evaluate: "Society does not need laws outlawing monopolization and monopoly. Inevitably, monopoly causes its own self-destruction, since its high profit is the lure for other firms or entrepreneurs to develop substitute products." LO6

12. **LAST WORD** Identify a specific example of each of the following in this chapter's Last Word: (*a*) entrepreneurship, (*b*) invention, (*c*) innovation, and (*d*) diffusion.

Problems

1. Suppose a firm expects that a $20 million expenditure on R&D in the current year will result in a new product that can be sold next year. Selling that product next year would increase the firm's revenue next year by $30 million and its costs next year by $29 million. LO3

   a. What is the expected rate of return on this R&D expenditure?

   b. Suppose the firm can get a bank loan at 6 percent interest to finance its $20 million R&D project. Will the firm undertake the project?

   c. Now suppose the interest-rate cost of borrowing, in effect, falls to 4 percent because the firm decides to use its own retained earnings to finance the R&D. Will this lower interest rate change the firm's R&D decision?

d. Now suppose that the firm has savings of $20 million—enough money to fund the R&D expenditure without borrowing. If the firm has the chance to invest this money either in the R&D project or in government bonds that pay 3.5 percent per year, which should it do?

e. What if the government bonds were paying 6.5 percent per year?

2. A firm faces the following costs: total cost of capital = $1000; price paid for labor = $12 per labor unit; and price paid for raw materials = $4 per raw-material unit. LO3

    a. Suppose the firm can produce 5000 units of output this year by combining its fixed capital with 100 units of labor and 450 units of raw materials. What are the total cost and average total cost of producing the 5000 units of output?

b. Now assume the firm improves its production process so that it can produce 6000 units of output this year by combining its fixed capital with 100 units of labor and 450 units of raw materials. What are the total cost and average total cost of producing the 6000 units of output?

c. If units of output can always be sold for $1 each, then by how much does the firm's profit increase after it improves its production process?

d. Suppose that implementing the improved production process would require a one-time-only cost of $1100. If the firm only considers this year's profit, would the firm implement the improved production process? What if the firm considers its profit not just this year but in future years as well?

FURTHER TEST YOUR KNOWLEDGE AT
www.mcconnell19e.com

At the text's Online Learning Center (OLC), **www.mcconnell19e.com**, you will find one or more Web-based questions that require information from the Internet to answer. We urge you to check them out; they will familiarize you with Web sites that may be helpful in other courses and perhaps even in your career. The OLC also features multiple-choice questions that give instant feedback and provides other helpful ways to further test your knowledge of the chapter.

Note: Terms set in *italic* type are defined separately in this glossary.

ability-to-pay principle The idea that those who have greater *income* (or *wealth*) should pay a greater proportion of it as taxes than those who have less income (or wealth).

absolute advantage A situation in which a person or country can produce more of a particular product from a specific quantity of resources than some other person or country.

accounting profit The *total revenue* of a *firm* less its *explicit costs;* the profit (or net income) that appears on accounting statements and that is reported to the government for tax purposes.

acreage allotments A pre-1996 government program that determined the total number of acres to be used in producing (reduced amounts of) various food and fiber products and allocated these acres among individual farmers. These farmers had to limit their plantings to the allotted number of acres to obtain *price supports* for their crops.

actively managed funds *Mutual funds* that have portfolio managers who constantly buy and sell *assets* in an attempt to generate higher returns than some benchmark rate of return for similar *portfolios*.

actual investment The amount that *firms* invest; equal to *planned investment* plus *unplanned investment*.

actual reserves The funds that a bank has on deposit at the *Federal Reserve Bank* of its district (plus its *vault cash*).

adverse selection problem A problem arising when information known to one party to a contract or agreement is not known to the other party, causing the latter to incur major costs. Example: Individuals who have the poorest health are most likely to buy health insurance.

advertising A seller's activities in communicating its message about its product to potential buyers.

AFL-CIO An acronym for the American Federation of Labor–Congress of Industrial Organizations; the largest federation of *labor unions* in the United States.

agency shop A place of employment where the employer may hire either *labor union* members or nonmembers but where those who do not join the union must either pay union dues or donate an equivalent amount of money to a charity.

aggregate A collection of specific economic units treated as if they were one. For example, all prices of individual goods and services are combined into a *price level*, or all units of output are aggregated into *gross domestic product*.

aggregate demand A schedule or curve that shows the total quantity of goods and services demanded (purchased) at different *price levels*.

aggregate demand–aggregate supply (AD-AS) model The macroeconomic model that uses *aggregate demand* and *aggregate supply* to determine and explain the *price level* and the real *domestic output*.

aggregate expenditures The total amount spent for final goods and services in an economy.

aggregate expenditures–domestic output approach Determination of the equilibrium *gross domestic product* by finding the real GDP at which *aggregate expenditures* equal *domestic output*.

aggregate expenditures schedule A schedule or curve showing the total amount spent for final goods and services at different levels of *real GDP*.

aggregate supply A schedule or curve showing the total quantity of goods and services supplied (produced) at different *price levels*.

aggregate supply shocks Sudden, large changes in resource costs that shift an economy's aggregate supply curve.

agribusiness The portion of the agricultural and food product industries that is dominated by large corporations.

Alcoa case A 1945 case in which the courts ruled that the possession of monopoly power, no matter how reasonably that power had been used, was a violation of the antitrust laws; temporarily overturned the *rule of reason* applied in the *U.S. Steel case*.

allocative efficiency The apportionment of resources among firms and industries to obtain the production of the products most wanted by society (consumers); the output of each product at which its *marginal cost* and *price* or *marginal benefit* are equal, and at which the sum of *consumer surplus* and *producer surplus* is maximized.

anchoring The tendency people have to unconsciously base, or "anchor," the valuation of an item they are currently thinking about on previously considered but logically irrelevant information.

anticipated inflation Increases in the price level (*inflation*) that occur at the expected rate.

antitrust laws Legislation (including the *Sherman Act* and *Clayton Act*) that prohibits anticompetitive business activities such as *price fixing*, bid rigging, monopolization, and *tying contracts*.

antitrust policy The use of the *antitrust laws* to promote *competition* and economic efficiency.

appreciation (of the dollar) An increase in the value of the dollar relative to the currency of another nation, so a dollar buys a larger amount of the foreign currency and thus of foreign goods.

arbitrage The activity of selling one *asset* and buying an identical or nearly identical asset to benefit from temporary differences in prices or rates of return; the practice that equalizes prices or returns on similar financial instruments and thus eliminates further opportunities for riskless financial gains.

asset Anything of monetary value owned by a firm or individual.

asset demand for money The amount of *money* people want to hold as a *store of value;* this amount varies inversely with the *interest rate.*

asymmetric information A situation where one party to a market transaction has much more information about a product or service than the other. The result may be an under- or overallocation of resources.

average expected rate of return The *probability-weighted average* of an investment's possible future returns.

average fixed cost (AFC) A firm's total *fixed cost* divided by output (the quantity of product produced).

average product (AP) The total output produced per unit of a *resource* employed (*total product* divided by the quantity of that employed resource).

average propensity to consume (APC) Fraction (or percentage) of *disposable income* that households plan to spend for consumer goods and services; consumption divided by *disposable income.*

average propensity to save (APS) Fraction (or percentage) of *disposable income* that households save; *saving* divided by *disposable income.*

average revenue Total revenue from the sale of a product divided by the quantity of the product sold (demanded); equal to the price at which the product is sold when all units of the product are sold at the same price.

average tax rate Total tax paid divided by total *taxable income* or some other base (such as total income) against which to compare the amount of tax paid. Expressed as a percentage.

average total cost (ATC) A firm's *total cost* divided by output (the quantity of product produced); equal to *average fixed cost* plus *average variable cost.*

average variable cost (AVC) A firm's total *variable cost* divided by output (the quantity of product produced).

backflows The return of workers to the countries from which they originally emigrated.

balance of payments (See *international balance of payments.*)

balance-of-payments deficit The net amount of *official reserves* (mainly foreign currencies) that a nation's treasury or central bank must sell to achieve balance between that nation's *capital and financial account* and its *current account* (in its *balance of payments*).

balance-of-payments surplus The net amount of *official reserves* (mainly foreign currencies) that a nation's treasury or central bank must buy to achieve balance between that nation's *capital and financial account* and its *current accounts* (in its *balance of payments*).

balance on capital and financial account The sum of the *capital account balance* and the *financial account balance.*

balance on current account The exports of goods and services of a nation less its imports of goods and services plus its *net investment income* and *net transfers* in a year.

balance on goods and services The exports of goods and services of a nation less its imports of goods and services in a year.

balance sheet A statement of the *assets, liabilities,* and *net worth* of a firm or individual at some given time.

bank deposits The deposits that individuals or firms have at banks (or thrifts) or that banks have at the *Federal Reserve Banks.*

bankers' bank A bank that accepts the deposits of and makes loans to *depository institutions;* in the United States, a *Federal Reserve Bank.*

bank reserves The deposits of commercial banks and thrifts at *Federal Reserve Banks* plus bank and thrift *vault cash.*

bankrupt A legal situation in which an individual or *firm* finds that it cannot make timely interest payments on money it has borrowed. In such cases, a bankruptcy judge can order the individual or firm to liquidate (turn into cash) its assets in order to pay lenders at least some portion of the amount they are owed.

barrier to entry Anything that artificially prevents the entry of firms into an industry.

barter The exchange of one good or service for another good or service.

base year The year with which other years are compared when an index is constructed; for example, the base year for a *price index.*

beaten paths Migration routes taken previously by family, relatives, friends, and other migrants.

behavioral economics The branch of economics that combines insights from economics, psychology, and neuroscience to give a better explanation of choice behavior than previous theories that incorrectly concluded that consumers were always rational, deliberate, and unemotional. Behavioral economics explains: *framing effects, anchoring, mental accounting,* the *endowment effect,* and how people are *loss averse.*

benefits-received principle The idea that those who receive the benefits of goods and services provided by government should pay the taxes required to finance them.

beta A relative measure of *nondiversifiable risk* that measures how the nondiversifiable risk of a given *asset* or *portfolio* compares with that of the *market portfolio* (the portfolio that contains every asset available in the financial markets).

bilateral monopoly A market in which there is a single seller *(monopoly)* and a single buyer *(monopsony).*

Board of Governors The seven-member group that supervises and controls the money and banking system of the United States; the Board of Governors of the *Federal Reserve System;* the Federal Reserve Board.

bond A financial device through which a borrower (a firm or government) is obligated to pay the principal and interest on a loan at a specific date in the future.

brain drains The exit or *emigration* of highly educated, highly skilled workers from a country.

break-even income The level of *disposable income* at which *households* plan to consume (spend) all their income and to save none of it.

break-even output Any output at which a (competitive) firm's *total cost* and *total revenue* are equal; an output at which a firm has neither an *economic profit* nor an economic loss, at which it earns only a *normal profit*.

break-even point An output at which a firm makes a *normal profit* (*total revenue = total cost*) but not an *economic profit*.

British thermal unit (BTU) The amount of energy required to raise the temperature of 1 pound of water by 1 degree Fahrenheit.

budget constraint The limit that the size of a consumer's income (and the prices that must be paid for goods and services) imposes on the ability of that consumer to obtain goods and services.

budget deficit The amount by which the expenditures of the Federal government exceed its revenues in any year.

budget line A line that shows the different combinations of two products a consumer can purchase with a specific money income, given the products' prices.

budget surplus The amount by which the revenues of the Federal government exceed its expenditures in any year.

built-in stabilizer A mechanism that increases government's budget deficit (or reduces its surplus) during a recession and increases government's budget surplus (or reduces its deficit) during an expansion without any action by policymakers. The tax system is one such mechanism.

Bureau of Economic Analysis (BEA) An agency of the U.S. Department of Commerce that compiles the national income and product accounts.

business cycle Recurring increases and decreases in the level of economic activity over periods of years; consists of peak, recession, trough, and expansion phases.

businesses Economic entities (*firms*) that purchase resources and provide goods and services to the economy.

business firm (See *firm*.)

cap-and-trade program A government strategy for reducing harmful emissions or discharges by placing a limit on their total amounts and then allowing firms to buy and sell the rights to emit or discharge specific amounts within the total limits.

capital Human-made resources (buildings, machinery, and equipment) used to produce goods and services; goods that do not directly satisfy human wants; also called capital goods.

capital and financial account The section of a nation's *international balance of payments* that records (1) debt forgiveness by and to foreigners and (2) foreign purchases of assets in the United States and U.S. purchases of assets abroad.

capital and financial account deficit A negative balance on its *capital and financial account* in a country's *international balance of payments*.

capital and financial account surplus A positive balance on its *capital and financial account* in a country's *international balance of payments*.

capital flight (Web chapter) The transfer of savings from *developing countries* to *industrially advanced countries* to avoid government expropriation, taxation, higher rates of inflation, or simply to realize greater returns on *financial investments*.

capital gain The gain realized when securities or properties are sold for a price greater than the price paid for them.

capital goods (See *capital*.)

capital-intensive goods Products that require relatively large amounts of *capital* to produce.

capitalism An economic system in which property resources are privately owned and markets and prices are used to direct and coordinate economic activities.

capital-saving technology (Web chapter) An improvement in *technology* that permits a greater quantity of a product to be produced with a specific amount of *capital* (or permits the same amount of the product to be produced with a smaller amount of capital).

capital stock The total available *capital* in a nation.

capital-using technology (Web chapter) An improvement in *technology* that requires the use of a greater amount of *capital* to produce a specific quantity of a product.

capricious-universe view (Web chapter) The view held by some people that fate and outside events, rather than hard work and enterprise, will determine their economic destinies.

cardinal utility Satisfaction (*utility*) that can be measured via cardinal numbers (1, 2, 3...), with all the mathematical properties of those numbers such as addition, subtraction, multiplication, and division being applicable.

cartel A formal agreement among firms (or countries) in an industry to set the price of a product and establish the outputs of the individual firms (or countries) or to divide the market for the product geographically.

causation A relationship in which the occurrence of one or more events brings about another event.

CEA (See *Council of Economic Advisers*.)

cease-and-desist order An order from a court or government agency to a corporation or individual to stop engaging in a specified practice.

ceiling price (See *price ceiling*.)

Celler-Kefauver Act The Federal law of 1950 that amended the *Clayton Act* by prohibiting the acquisition of the assets of one firm by another firm when the effect would be less competition.

central bank A bank whose chief function is the control of the nation's *money supply*; in the United States, the Federal Reserve System.

central economic planning Government determination of the objectives of the economy and how resources will be directed to attain those goals.

ceteris paribus assumption (See *other-things-equal assumption*.)

change in demand A movement of an entire *demand curve* or schedule such that the *quantity demanded* changes at every particular price; caused by a change in one or more of the *determinants of demand*.

change in quantity demanded A change in the *quantity demanded* along a fixed *demand curve* (or within a fixed demand schedule) as a result of a change in the price of the product.

change in quantity supplied A change in the *quantity supplied* along a fixed *supply curve* (or within a fixed supply schedule) as a result of a change in the product's price.

change in supply A movement of an entire *supply curve* or schedule such that the *quantity supplied* changes at every particular price; caused by a change in one or more of the *determinants of supply*.

Change to Win A loose federation of American unions that includes the Service Workers and Teamsters and has a total membership of 6 million workers.

checkable deposit Any deposit in a *commercial bank* or *thrift institution* against which a check may be written.

checkable-deposit multiplier (See *monetary multiplier*.)

check clearing The process by which funds are transferred from the checking accounts of the writers of checks to the checking accounts of the recipients of the checks.

checking account A *checkable deposit* in a *commercial bank* or *thrift institution*.

circular flow diagram An illustration showing the flow of resources from *households* to *firms* and of products from firms to households. These flows are accompanied by reverse flows of money from firms to households and from households to firms.

Clayton Act The Federal antitrust law of 1914 that strengthened the *Sherman Act* by making it illegal for firms to engage in certain specified practices.

closed economy An economy that neither exports nor imports goods and services.

closed shop A place of employment where only workers who are already members of a labor union may be hired.

Coase theorem The idea, first stated by economist Ronald Coase, that some *externalities* can be resolved through private negotiations of the affected parties.

coincidence of wants A situation in which the good or service that one trader desires to obtain is the same as that which another trader desires to give up and an item that the second trader wishes to acquire is the same as that which the first trader desires to surrender.

COLA (See *cost-of-living adjustment*.)

collective action problem The idea that getting a group to pursue a common, collective goal gets harder the larger the group's size. Larger groups are more costly to organize and their members more difficult to motivate because the larger the group, the smaller each member's share of the benefits if the group succeeds.

collective bargaining The negotiation of labor contracts between *labor unions* and *firms* or government entities.

collective voice The function a *labor union* performs for its members as a group when it communicates their problems and grievances to management and presses management for a satisfactory resolution.

collusion A situation in which firms act together and in agreement (collude) to fix prices, divide a market, or otherwise restrict competition.

command system A method of organizing an economy in which property resources are publicly owned and government uses *central economic planning* to direct and coordinate economic activities; command economy; communism.

commercial bank A firm that engages in the business of banking (accepts deposits, offers checking accounts, and makes loans).

commercial banking system All *commercial banks* and *thrift institutions* as a group.

communism (See *command system*.)

comparative advantage A situation in which a person or country can produce a specific product at a lower opportunity cost than some other person or country; the basis for specialization and trade.

compensating differences Differences in the *wages* received by workers in different jobs to compensate for the nonmonetary differences between the jobs.

compensating wage differential (See *compensating differences*.)

compensation to employees *Wages* and salaries plus wage and salary supplements paid by employers to workers.

competition The presence in a market of independent buyers and sellers competing with one another along with the freedom of buyers and sellers to enter and leave the market.

competitive industry's short-run supply curve The horizontal summation of the short-run supply curves of the *firms* in a purely competitive industry (see *pure competition*); a curve that shows the total quantities offered for sale at various prices by the firms in an industry in the short run.

competitive labor market A resource market in which a large number of (noncolluding) employers demand a particular type of labor supplied by a large number of nonunion workers.

complementary goods Products and services that are used together. When the price of one falls, the demand for the other increases (and conversely).

complementary resources Productive inputs that are used jointly with other inputs in the production process; resources for which a decrease in the price of one leads to an increase in the demand for the other.

compound interest The accumulation of money that builds over time in an investment or interest-bearing account as new interest is earned on previous interest that is not withdrawn.

concentration ratio The percentage of the total sales of an industry made by the four (or some other number) largest sellers in the industry.

conflict diamonds Diamonds that are mined and sold by combatants in war zones in Africa as a way to provide the currency needed to finance their military activities.

conglomerate merger The merger of a *firm* in one *industry* with a firm in another industry (with a firm that is not a supplier, customer, or competitor).

conglomerates Firms that produce goods and services in two or more separate industries.

constant-cost industry An industry in which expansion by the entry of new firms has no effect on the prices firms in the industry must pay for resources and thus no effect on production costs.

constant opportunity cost An *opportunity cost* that remains the same for each additional unit as a consumer (or society) shifts purchases (production) from one product to another along a straight-line *budget line (production possibilities curve)*.

constant returns to scale Unchanging *average total cost* of producing a product as the firm expands the size of its plant (its output) in the *long run*.

consumer equilibrium In marginal utility theory, the combination of goods purchased based on *marginal utility* (MU) and *price* (P) that maximizes *total utility*; the combination for goods X and Y at which $MU_x/P_x = MU_y/P_y$. In indifference curve analysis, the combination of goods purchased that maximize *total utility* by enabling the consumer to reach the highest *indifference curve*, given the consumer's *budget line* (or *budget constraint*).

consumer goods Products and services that satisfy human wants directly.

Consumer Price Index (CPI) An index that measures the prices of a fixed "market basket" of some 300 goods and services bought by a "typical" consumer.

consumer sovereignty Determination by consumers of the types and quantities of goods and services that will be produced with the scarce resources of the economy; consumers' direction of production through their *dollar votes*.

consumer surplus The difference between the maximum price a consumer is (or consumers are) willing to pay for an additional unit of a product and its market price; the triangular area below the demand curve and above the market price.

consumption of fixed capital An estimate of the amount of *capital* worn out or used up (consumed) in producing the *gross domestic product*; also called depreciation.

consumption schedule A schedule showing the amounts *households* plan to spend for *consumer goods* at different levels of *disposable income*.

contractionary fiscal policy A decrease in *government purchases* of goods and services, an increase in *net taxes*, or some combination of the two, for the purpose of decreasing *aggregate demand* and thus controlling inflation.

coordination failure A situation in which people do not reach a mutually beneficial outcome because they lack some way to jointly coordinate their actions; a possible cause of macroeconomic instability.

copayment The percentage of (say, health care) costs that an insured individual pays while the insurer pays the remainder.

copyright A legal protection provided to developers and publishers of books, computer software, videos, and musical compositions against the copying of their works by others.

core inflation The underlying increases in the *price level* after volatile food and energy prices and removed.

corporate income tax A tax levied on the net income (accounting profit) of corporations.

corporation A legal entity ("person") chartered by a state or the Federal government that is distinct and separate from the individuals who own it.

correlation A systematic and dependable association between two sets of data (two kinds of events); does not necessarily indicate causation.

corruption The misuse of government power, with which one has been entrusted or assigned, to obtain private gain; includes payments from individuals or companies to secure advantages in obtaining government contracts, avoiding government regulations, or obtaining inside knowledge about forthcoming policy changes.

cost-benefit analysis A comparison of the *marginal costs* of a government project or program with the *marginal benefits* to decide whether or not to employ resources in that project or program and to what extent.

cost-of-living adjustment (COLA) An automatic increase in the incomes (wages) of workers when inflation occurs; guaranteed by a collective bargaining contract between firms and workers.

cost-push inflation Increases in the price level (inflation) resulting from an increase in resource costs (for example, raw-material prices) and hence in *per-unit production costs*; inflation caused by reductions in *aggregate supply*.

Council of Economic Advisers (CEA) A group of three persons that advises and assists the president of the United States on economic matters (including the preparation of the annual *Economic Report of the President*).

countercyclical payments (CCPs) Cash *subsidies* paid to farmers when market prices for certain crops drop below targeted prices. Payments are based on previous production and are received regardless of the current crop grown.

craft union A labor union that limits its membership to workers with a particular skill (craft).

creative destruction The hypothesis that the creation of new products and production methods simultaneously destroys the market power of existing monopolies.

credible threat In *game theory*, a statement of harmful intent by one party that the other party views as believable; often issued in conditional terms of "if you do this; we will do that."

credit An accounting item that increases the value of an asset (such as the foreign money owned by the residents of a nation).

credit union An association of persons who have a common tie (such as being employees of the same firm or members of the same labor union) that sells shares to (accepts deposits from) its members and makes loans to them.

cross elasticity of demand The ratio of the percentage change in *quantity demanded* of one good to the percentage change in the price of some other good. A positive coefficient indicates the two products are *substitute goods;* a negative coefficient indicates they are *complementary goods.*

crowding model of occupational discrimination A model of labor markets suggesting that *occupational discrimination* has kept many women and minorities out of high-paying occupations and forced them into a limited number of low-paying occupations.

crowding-out effect A rise in interest rates and a resulting decrease in *planned investment* caused by the Federal government's increased borrowing to finance budget deficits and refinance debt.

currency Coins and paper money.

currency appreciation (See *exchange-rate appreciation.*)

currency depreciation (See *exchange-rate depreciation.*)

currency intervention A government's buying and selling of its own currency or foreign currencies to alter international exchange rates.

current account The section in a nation's *international balance of payments* that records its exports and imports of goods and services, its net *investment income*, and its *net transfers.*

cyclical asymmetry The idea that *monetary policy* may be more successful in slowing expansions and controlling *inflation* than in extracting the economy from severe recession.

cyclical deficit A Federal *budget deficit* that is caused by a recession and the consequent decline in tax revenues.

cyclically adjusted budget A comparison of the government expenditures and tax collections that would occur if the economy operated at *full employment* throughout the year; the full-employment budget.

cyclical unemployment A type of *unemployment* caused by insufficient total spending (or by insufficient *aggregate demand*).

deadweight loss (See *efficiency loss.*)

debit An accounting item that decreases the value of an asset (such as the foreign money owned by the residents of a nation).

declining industry An industry in which *economic profits* are negative (losses are incurred) and that will, therefore, decrease its output as firms leave it.

decreasing-cost industry An industry in which expansion through the entry of firms lowers the prices that firms in the industry must pay for resources and therefore decreases their production costs.

deductible The dollar sum of (for example, health care) costs that an insured individual must pay before the insurer begins to pay.

defaults Situations in which borrowers stop making loan payments or do not pay back loans that they took out and are now due.

defensive medicine The recommendation by physicians of more tests and procedures than are warranted medically or economically as a way of protecting themselves against later malpractice suits.

deflating Finding the *real gross domestic product* by decreasing the dollar value of the GDP for a year in which prices were higher than in the *base year.*

deflation A decline in the economy's *price level.*

demand A schedule showing the amounts of a good or service that buyers (or a buyer) wish to purchase at various prices during some time period.

demand curve A curve illustrating *demand.*

demand factor (in growth) The increase in the level of *aggregate demand* that brings about the *economic growth* made possible by an increase in the production potential of the economy.

demand management The use of *fiscal policy* and *monetary policy* to increase or decrease *aggregate demand.*

demand-pull inflation Increases in the price level (inflation) resulting from an excess of demand over output at the existing price level, caused by an increase in *aggregate demand.*

demand schedule (See *demand.*)

demand shocks Sudden, unexpected changes in demand.

demand-side market failures Underallocations of resources that occur when private demand curves understate consumers' full willingness to pay for a good or service.

demographers Scientists who study the characteristics of human populations.

demographic transition (Web chapter) The idea that population growth slows once a developing country achieves higher standards of living because the perceived marginal cost of additional children begins to exceed the perceived marginal benefit.

dependent variable A variable that changes as a consequence of a change in some other (independent) variable; the "effect" or outcome.

depository institutions Firms that accept deposits of *money* from the public (businesses and persons); *commercial banks, savings and loan associations, mutual savings banks,* and *credit unions.*

depreciation (See *consumption of fixed capital.*)

depreciation (of the dollar) A decrease in the value of the dollar relative to another currency, so a dollar buys a smaller amount of the foreign currency and therefore of foreign goods.

derived demand The demand for a resource that depends on the demand for the products it helps to produce.

determinants of aggregate demand Factors such as consumption spending, *investment*, government spending, and *net exports* that, if they change, shift the aggregate demand curve.

determinants of aggregate supply Factors such as input prices, *productivity*, and the legal-institutional environment that, if they change, shift the aggregate supply curve.

determinants of demand Factors other than price that determine the quantities demanded of a good or service.

determinants of supply Factors other than price that determine the quantities supplied of a good or service.

developing countries Many countries of Africa, Asia, and Latin America that are characterized by lack of capital goods, use of nonadvanced technologies, low literacy rates, high unemployment, rapid population growth, and labor forces heavily committed to agriculture.

diagnosis-related group (DRG) system Payments to doctors and hospitals under *Medicare* based on which of hundreds of carefully detailed diagnostic categories best characterize the patient's condition and needs.

differentiated oligopoly An *oligopoly* in which firms produce a *differentiated product*.

differentiated product A product that differs physically or in some other way from the similar products produced by other firms; a product such that buyers are not indifferent to the seller when the price charged by all sellers is the same.

diffusion (Web chapter) The spread of an *innovation* through its widespread imitation.

dilemma of regulation The tradeoff faced by a *regulatory agency* in setting the maximum legal price a monopolist may charge: The *socially optimal price* is below *average total cost* (and either bankrupts the *firm* or requires that it be subsidized), while the higher, *fair-return price* does not produce *allocative efficiency*.

diminishing marginal returns (See *law of diminishing returns*.)

diminishing marginal utility (See *law of diminishing marginal utility*.)

direct foreign investment (See *foreign direct investment*.)

direct payments Cash subsidies paid to farmers based on past production levels; unaffected by current crop prices and current production.

direct relationship The relationship between two variables that change in the same direction, for example, product price and quantity supplied; positive relationship.

discount rate The interest rate that the *Federal Reserve Banks* charge on the loans they make to *commercial banks* and *thrift institutions*.

discouraged workers Employees who have left the *labor force* because they have not been able to find employment.

discretionary fiscal policy Deliberate changes in taxes (tax rates) and government spending by Congress to promote full employment, price stability, and economic growth.

discrimination The practice of according individuals or groups inferior treatment in hiring, occupational access, education and training, promotion, wage rates, or working conditions even though they have the same abilities, education, skills, and work experience as other workers.

discrimination coefficient A measure of the cost or disutility of prejudice; the monetary amount an employer is willing to pay to hire a preferred worker rather than a nonpreferred worker.

diseconomies of scale Increases in the *average total cost* of producing a product as the *firm* expands the size of its *plant* (its output) in the *long run*.

disinflation A reduction in the rate of *inflation*.

disposable income (DI) *Personal income* less personal taxes; income available for *personal consumption expenditures* and *personal saving*.

dissaving Spending for consumer goods and services in excess of *disposable income*; the amount by which *personal consumption expenditures* exceed disposable income.

diversifiable risk Investment *risk* that investors can reduce via *diversification*; also called idiosyncratic risk.

diversification The strategy of investing in a large number of investments in order to reduce the overall risk to an entire investment *portfolio*.

dividends Payments by a corporation of all or part of its profit to its stockholders (the corporate owners).

division of labor The separation of the work required to produce a product into a number of different tasks that are performed by different workers; *specialization* of workers.

Doha Development Agenda The latest, uncompleted (as of mid-2010) sequence of trade negotiations by members of the *World Trade Organization*; named after Doha, Qatar, where the set of negotiations began. Also called the Doha Round.

dollar votes The "votes" that consumers and entrepreneurs cast for the production of consumer and capital goods, respectively, when they purchase those goods in product and resource markets.

domestic capital formation The process of adding to a nation's stock of *capital* by saving and investing part of its own domestic output.

domestic output *Gross* (or net) *domestic product*; the total output of final goods and services produced in the economy.

domestic price The price of a good or service within a country, determined by domestic demand and supply.

dominant strategy In *game theory*, an option that is better than any other alternative option regardless of what the other firm does.

dumping The sale of a product in a foreign country at prices either below cost or below the prices commonly charged at home.

DuPont cellophane case The antitrust case brought against DuPont in which the U.S. Supreme Court ruled (in 1956) that while DuPont had a monopoly in the narrowly defined market for cellophane, it did not monopolize the more broadly defined market for flexible packaging materials. It was thus not guilty of violating the *Sherman Act*.

durable good A consumer good with an expected life (use) of three or more years.

earmarks Narrow, specially designated spending authorizations placed in broad legislation by Senators and representatives for the purpose of providing benefits to firms and organizations within their constituencies without undergoing the usual evaluation process or competitive bidding.

earned-income tax credit (EITC) A refundable Federal tax credit for low-income working people designed to reduce poverty and encourage labor-force participation.

earnings The money income received by a worker; equal to the *wage* (rate) multiplied by the amount of time worked.

economic concentration A description or measure of the degree to which an industry is dominated by one or a handful of firms or is characterized by many firms. (See *concentration ratio*.)

economic cost A payment that must be made to obtain and retain the services of a *resource*; the income a firm must provide to a resource supplier to attract the resource away from an alternative use; equal to the quantity of other products that cannot be produced when resources are instead used to make a particular product.

economic efficiency The use of the minimum necessary resources to obtain the socially optimal amounts of goods and services; entails both *productive efficiency* and *allocative efficiency*.

economic growth (1) An outward shift in the *production possibilities curve* that results from an increase in resource supplies or quality or an improvement in *technology*; (2) an increase of real output (*gross domestic product*) or real output per capita.

economic immigrants International migrants who have moved to a country from another to obtain economic gains such as better employment opportunities.

economic investment (See *investment*.)

economic law An *economic principle* that has been tested and retested and has stood the test of time.

economic model A simplified picture of economic reality; an abstract generalization.

economic perspective A viewpoint that envisions individuals and institutions making rational decisions by comparing the marginal benefits and marginal costs associated with their actions.

economic policy A course of action intended to correct or avoid a problem.

economic principle A widely accepted generalization about the economic behavior of individuals or institutions.

economic profit The *total revenue* of a firm less its *economic costs* (which include both *explicit costs* and *implicit costs*); also called "pure profit" and "above-normal profit."

economic regulation (See *industrial regulation* and *social regulation*.)

economic rent The price paid for the use of land and other natural resources, the supply of which is fixed (*perfectly inelastic*).

economic resources The *land*, *labor*, *capital*, and *entrepreneurial ability* that are used in the production of goods and services; productive agents; factors of production.

economics The social science concerned with how individuals, institutions, and society make optimal (best) choices under conditions of scarcity.

economic system A particular set of institutional arrangements and a coordinating mechanism for solving the economizing problem; a method of organizing an economy, of which the *market system* and the *command system* are the two general types.

economic theory A statement of a cause-effect relationship; when accepted by all or nearly all economists, an *economic principle*.

economies of scale Reductions in the *average total cost* of producing a product as the firm expands the size of plant (its output) in the *long run*; the economies of mass production.

economizing problem The choices necessitated because society's economic wants for goods and services are unlimited but the resources available to satisfy these wants are limited (scarce).

efficiency factors (in growth) The capacity of an economy to combine resources effectively to achieve growth of real output that the *supply factors* (of growth) make possible.

efficiency gains from migration Additions to output from *immigration* in the destination nation that exceed the loss of output from *emigration* from the origin nation.

efficiency loss Reductions in combined consumer and producer surplus caused by an underallocation or overallocation of resources to the production of a good or service. Also called *deadweight loss*.

efficiency loss of a tax The loss of net benefits to society because a tax reduces the production and consumption of a taxed good below the level of *allocative efficiency*. Also called the deadweight loss of the tax.

efficiency wage A wage that minimizes wage costs per unit of output by encouraging greater effort or reducing turnover.

efficient allocation of resources That allocation of an economy's resources among the production of different products that leads to the maximum satisfaction of consumers' wants, thus producing the socially optimal mix of output with society's scarce resources.

elastic demand Product or resource demand whose *price elasticity* is greater than 1. This means the resulting change in *quantity demanded* is greater than the percentage change in *price*.

elasticity coefficient The number obtained when the percentage change in *quantity demanded* (or supplied) is divided by the percentage change in the *price* of the commodity.

elasticity formula (See *price elasticity of demand*.)

elasticity of resource demand A measure of the responsiveness of firms to a change in the price of a particular *resource* they employ or use; the percentage change in the quantity of the resource demanded divided by the percentage change in its price.

elastic supply Product or resource supply whose price elasticity is greater than 1. This means the resulting change in quantity supplied is greater than the percentage change in price.

electronic payments Purchases made by transferring funds electronically. Examples: Fedwire transfers, automated clearinghouse transactions (ACHs), payments via the PayPal system, and payments made through stored-value cards.

emigration The exit (outflow) of residents from a country to reside in foreign countries.

employer mandate The requirement under the *Patient Protection and Affordable Care Act (PPACA)* of 2010 that firms with 50 or more employees pay for insurance policies for their employees or face a fine of $2000 per employee per year. Firms with fewer than 50 employees are exempt.

employment rate The percentage of the *labor force* employed at any time.

empty threat In *game theory*, a statement of harmful intent that is easily dismissed by the recipient because the threat is not viewed as being believable; compare to *credible threat*.

endowment effect The tendency people have to place higher valuations on items they own than on identical items that they do not own. Perhaps caused by people being *loss averse*.

entitlement programs Government programs such as *social insurance*, *Medicare*, and *Medicaid* that guarantee particular levels of transfer payments or noncash benefits to all who fit the programs' criteria.

entrepreneurial ability The human resource that combines the other resources to produce a product, makes nonroutine decisions, innovates, and bears risks.

equality-efficiency trade-off The decrease in *economic efficiency* that may accompany a decrease in *income inequality*; the presumption that some income inequality is required to achieve economic efficiency.

equation of exchange $MV = PQ$, in which M is the supply of money, V is the *velocity* of money, P is the *price level*, and Q is the physical volume of *final goods and services* produced.

equilibrium GDP (See *equilibrium real domestic output*.)

equilibrium position In the indifference curve model, the combination of two goods at which a consumer maximizes his or her *utility* (reaches the highest attainable *indifference curve*), given a limited amount to spend (a *budget constraint*).

equilibrium price The *price* in a competitive market at which the *quantity demanded* and the *quantity supplied* are equal, there is neither a shortage nor a surplus, and there is no tendency for price to rise or fall.

equilibrium price level The price level at which the aggregate demand curve intersects the aggregate supply curve.

equilibrium quantity (1) The quantity at which the intentions of buyers and sellers in a particular market match at a particular price such that the *quantity demanded* and the *quantity supplied* are equal; (2) the profit-maximizing output of a firm.

equilibrium real domestic output The *gross domestic product* at which the total quantity of final goods and services purchased *(aggregate expenditures)* is equal to the total quantity of final goods and services produced (the real domestic output); the real domestic output at which the aggregate demand curve intersects the aggregate supply curve.

equilibrium real output (See *equilibrium real domestic output*.)

equilibrium world price The price of an internationally traded product that equates the quantity of the product demanded by importers with the quantity of the product supplied by exporters; the price determined at the intersection of the export supply curve and the import demand curve.

euro The common currency unit used by 16 European nations (as of mid-2010) in the *Euro Zone*, which consists of Austria, Belgium, Cyprus, Finland, France, Germany, Greece, Ireland, Italy, Luxembourg, Malta, the Netherlands, Portugal, Slovakia, Slovenia, and Spain.

European Union (EU) An association of 27 European nations (as of mid-2010) that has eliminated tariffs and quotas among them, established common tariffs for imported goods from outside the member nations, eliminated barriers to the free movement of capital, and created other common economic policies.

Euro Zone The 16 nations (as of 2010) of the 25-member (as of 2010) *European Union* that use the *euro* as their common currency. The Euro Zone countries are Austria, Belgium, Cyprus, Finland, France, Germany, Greece, Ireland, Italy, Luxembourg, Malta, the Netherlands, Portugal, Slovakia, Slovenia, and Spain.

excess capacity Plant resources that are underused when imperfectly competitive firms produce less output than that associated with achieving minimum average total cost.

excess reserves The amount by which a bank's or thrift's *actual reserves* exceed its *required reserves*; actual reserves minus required reserves.

exchange controls (See *foreign exchange controls*.)

exchange rate The *rate of exchange* of one nation's currency for another nation's currency.

exchange-rate appreciation An increase in the value of a nation's currency in foreign exchange markets; an increase in the *rate of exchange* with foreign currencies.

exchange-rate depreciation A decrease in the value of a nation's currency in foreign exchange markets; a decrease in the *rate of exchange* with foreign currencies.

exchange-rate determinant Any factor other than the *rate of exchange* that determines a currency's demand and supply in the *foreign exchange market*.

excise tax A tax levied on the production of a specific product or on the quantity of the product purchased.

excludability The characteristic of a *private good*, for which the seller can keep nonbuyers from obtaining the good.

exclusive unionism The practice of a *labor union* of restricting the supply of skilled union labor to increase the wages received by union members; the policies typically employed by a *craft union*.

exhaustive expenditure An expenditure by government resulting directly in the employment of *economic resources* and in the absorption by government of the goods and services those resources produce; a *government purchase*.

exit mechanism The process of leaving a job and searching for another one as a means of improving one's working conditions.

expanding industry An industry whose firms earn *economic profits* and for which an increase in output occurs as new firms enter the industry.

expansion A phase of the *business cycle* in which *real GDP*, *income*, and employment rise.

expansionary fiscal policy An increase in *government purchases* of goods and services, a decrease in *net taxes*, or some combination of the two for the purpose of increasing *aggregate demand* and expanding real output.

expansionary monetary policy *Federal Reserve System* actions to increase the *money supply*, lower *interest rates*, and expand *real GDP*; an easy money policy.

expectations The anticipations of consumers, firms, and others about future economic conditions.

expected rate of return The increase in profit a firm anticipates it will obtain by purchasing capital (or engaging in research and development); expressed as a percentage of the total cost of the investment (or R&D) activity.

expected-rate-of-return curve (Web chapter) As it relates to research and development (*R&D*), a curve showing the anticipated gain in *profit*, as a percentage of R&D expenditure, from an additional dollar spent on R&D.

expenditures approach The method that adds all expenditures made for *final goods and services* to measure the *gross domestic product*.

expenditures-output approach (See *aggregate expenditures–domestic output approach*.)

explicit cost The monetary payment a *firm* must make to an outsider to obtain a *resource*.

exports Goods and services produced in a nation and sold to buyers in other nations.

export subsidy A government payment to a domestic producer to enable the firm to reduce the price of a good or service to foreign buyers.

export supply curve An upward-sloping curve that shows the amount of a product that domestic firms will export at each *world price* that is above the *domestic price*.

export transaction A sale of a good or service that increases the amount of foreign currency flowing to a nation's citizens, firms, and government.

external benefit (See *positive externality*.)

external cost (See *negative externality*.)

external debt Private or public debt owed to foreign citizens, firms, and institutions.

externality A cost or benefit from production or consumption, accruing without compensation to someone other than the buyers and sellers of the product (see *negative externality* and *positive externality*).

external public debt The portion of the public debt owed to foreign citizens, firms, and institutions.

extraction cost All costs associated with extracting a natural resource and readying it for sale.

face value The dollar or cents value placed on a U.S. coin or piece of paper money.

factors of production *Economic resources: land, capital, labor,* and *entrepreneurial ability*.

fair-return price The price of a product that enables its producer to obtain a *normal profit* and that is equal to the *average total cost* of producing it.

fallacy of composition The false notion that what is true for the individual (or part) is necessarily true for the group (or whole).

farm commodities Agricultural products such as grains, milk, cattle, fruits, and vegetables that are usually sold to processors, who use the products as inputs in creating *food products*.

fast-second strategy (Web chapter) An approach by a dominant firm in which it allows other firms in its industry to bear the risk of innovation and then quickly becomes the second firm to offer any successful new product or adopt any improved production process.

FDIC (See *Federal Deposit Insurance Corporation*.)

Federal Deposit Insurance Corporation (FDIC) The federally chartered corporation that insures deposit liabilities (up to $250,000 per account) of *commercial banks* and *thrift institutions* (excluding *credit unions*, whose deposits are insured by the *National Credit Union Administration*).

Federal funds rate The interest rate banks and other depository institutions charge one another on overnight loans made out of their *excess reserves*.

Federal government The government of the United States, as distinct from the state and local governments.

Federal Open Market Committee (FOMC) The 12-member group that determines the purchase and sale policies of the *Federal Reserve Banks* in the market for U.S. government securities.

Federal Reserve Banks The 12 banks chartered by the U.S. government to control the *money supply* and perform other functions. (See *central bank, quasi-public bank,* and *bankers' bank*.)

Federal Reserve Note Paper money issued by the *Federal Reserve Banks*.

Federal Reserve System The U.S. central bank, consisting of the *Board of Governors* of the Federal Reserve and the 12 *Federal Reserve Banks*, which controls the lending activity of the nation's banks and thrifts and thus the *money supply;* commonly referred to as the "Fed."

Federal Trade Commission (FTC) The commission of five members established by the *Federal Trade Commission Act* of 1914 to investigate unfair competitive practices of firms, to hold hearings on the complaints of such practices, and to issue *cease-and-desist orders* when firms are found to engage in such practices.

Federal Trade Commission Act The Federal law of 1914 that established the *Federal Trade Commission.*

fee for service In the health care industry, payment to physicians for each visit made or procedure performed rather than payment as an annual salary.

fiat money Anything that is *money* because government has decreed it to be money.

final goods Goods that have been purchased for final use and not for resale or further processing or manufacturing.

financial capital (See *money capital.*)

financial investment The purchase of a financial asset (such as a *stock, bond,* or *mutual fund*) or real asset (such as a house, land, or factories) or the building of such assets in the expectation of financial gain.

financial services industry The broad category of firms that provide financial products and services to help households and businesses earn *interest,* receive *dividends,* obtain *capital gains,* insure against losses, and plan for retirement. Includes *commercial banks, thrifts,* insurance companies, mutual fund companies, pension funds, investment banks, and securities firms.

firm An organization that employs resources to produce a good or service for profit and owns and operates one or more *plants.*

first-mover advantage In *game theory,* the benefit obtained by the party that moves first in a *sequential game.*

fiscal policy Changes in government spending and tax collections designed to achieve a full-employment and noninflationary domestic output; also called *discretionary fiscal policy.*

fishery A stock of fish or other marine animal that is composed of a distinct group, for example New England cod, Pacific tuna, or Alaskan crab.

fishery collapse A rapid decline in a fishery's population because its fish are being harvested faster than they can reproduce.

fixed cost Any cost that in total does not change when the *firm* changes its output; the cost of *fixed resources.*

fixed exchange rate A *rate of exchange* that is set in some way and therefore prevented from rising or falling with changes in currency supply and demand.

fixed resource Any resource whose quantity cannot be changed by a firm in the *short run.*

flexible exchange rate A *rate of exchange* determined by the international demand for and supply of a nation's money; a rate free to rise or fall (to float).

flexible prices Product prices that freely move upward or downward when product demand or supply changes.

floating exchange rate (See *flexible exchange rate.*)

follower countries As it relates to *economic growth,* countries that adopt advanced technologies that previously were developed and used by *leader countries.*

Food, Conservation, and Energy Act of 2008 Farm legislation that continued and extended previous agricultural subsides of three basic kinds: *direct payments, countercyclical payments,* and *marketing loans.*

food products Processed agricultural commodities sold through grocery stores and restaurants. Examples: bread, meat, fish, chicken, pork, lettuce, peanut butter, and breakfast cereal.

foreign competition (See *import competition.*)

foreign direct investment (Web chapter) Financial investments made to obtain a lasting ownership interest in firms operating outside the economy of the investor; may involve purchasing existing assets or building new production facilities.

foreign exchange controls Controls that a government may exercise over the quantity of foreign currency demanded by its citizens and firms and over the *rates of exchange* as a way to limit the nation's quantity of *outpayments* relative to its quantity of *inpayments* (to eliminate a *payments deficit*).

foreign exchange market A market in which the money (currency) of one nation can be used to purchase (can be exchanged for) the money of another nation; currency market.

foreign exchange rate (See *rate of exchange.*)

foreign purchase effect The inverse relationship between the *net exports* of an economy and its price level relative to foreign price levels.

45° (degree) line A line along which the value of *GDP* (measured horizontally) is equal to the value of *aggregate expenditures* (measured vertically).

four-firm concentration ratio The percentage of total industry sales accounted for by the top four firms in the industry.

fractional reserve banking system A system in which *commercial banks* and *thrift institutions* hold less than 100 percent of their checkable-deposit liabilities as *required reserves.*

framing effects In *prospect theory,* changes in people's decision-making caused by new information that alters the context, or "frame of reference," that they use to judge whether options are viewed as gains or losses.

freedom of choice The freedom of owners of property resources to employ or dispose of them as they see fit, of workers to enter any line of work for which they are qualified, and of consumers to spend their incomes in a manner that they think is appropriate.

freedom of enterprise The freedom of *firms* to obtain economic resources, to use those resources to produce products of the firm's own choosing, and to sell their products in markets of their choice.

Freedom to Farm Act A law passed in 1996 that revamped 60 years of U.S. farm policy by ending *price supports* and *acreage allotments* for wheat, corn, barley, oats, sorghum, rye, cotton, and rice.

free-rider problem The inability of potential providers of an economically desirable good or service to obtain payment from those who benefit, because of *nonexcludability*.

free trade The absence of artificial (government-imposed) barriers to trade among individuals and firms in different nations.

frictional unemployment A type of unemployment caused by workers voluntarily changing jobs and by temporary layoffs; unemployed workers between jobs.

fringe benefits The rewards other than *wages* that employees receive from their employers and that include pensions, medical and dental insurance, paid vacations, and sick leaves.

full employment (1) The use of all available resources to produce want-satisfying goods and services; (2) the situation in which the *unemployment rate* is equal to the *full-employment rate of unemployment* and where *frictional* and *structural* unemployment occur but not *cyclical unemployment* (and the *real GDP* of the economy equals *potential output*).

full-employment rate of unemployment The *unemployment rate* at which there is no *cyclical unemployment* of the *labor force*; equal to between 4 and 5 percent in the United States because some *frictional* and *structural unemployment* is unavoidable.

functional distribution of income The manner in which *national income* is divided among the functions performed to earn it (or the kinds of resources provided to earn it); the division of national income into wages and salaries, proprietors' income, corporate profits, interest, and rent.

future value The amount to which some current amount of money will grow if the interest earned on the amount is left to compound over time. (See *compound interest.*)

gains from trade The extra output that trading partners obtain through specialization of production and exchange of goods and services.

game theory A means of analyzing the business behavior of oligopolists that uses the theory of strategy associated with games such as chess and bridge.

GDP (See *gross domestic product.*)

GDP gap Actual *gross domestic product* minus potential output; may be either a positive amount (a *positive GDP gap*) or a negative amount (a *negative GDP gap*).

GDP price index A *price index* for all the goods and services that make up the *gross domestic product;* the price index used to adjust *nominal gross domestic product* to *real gross domestic product.*

G8 nations A group of eight major nations (Canada, France, Germany, Italy, Japan, Russia, United Kingdom, and United States) whose leaders meet regularly to discuss common economic problems and try to coordinate economic policies.

General Agreement on Tariffs and Trade (GATT) The international agreement reached in 1947 in which 23 nations agreed to give equal and nondiscriminatory treatment to one another, to reduce tariff rates by multinational negotiations, and to eliminate *import quotas.* It now includes most nations and has become the *World Trade Organization.*

generalization Statement of the nature of the relationship between two or more sets of facts.

Gini ratio A numerical measure of the overall dispersion of income among households, families, or individuals; found graphically by dividing the area between the diagonal line and the *Lorenz curve* by the entire area below the diagonal line.

gold standard A historical system of fixed exchange rates in which nations defined their currencies in terms of gold, maintained a fixed relationship between their stocks of gold and their money supplies, and allowed gold to be freely exported and imported.

government failure Inefficiencies in resource allocation caused by problems in the operation of the public sector (government), specifically, rent-seeking pressure by special-interest groups, shortsighted political behavior, limited and bundled choices, and bureaucratic inefficiencies.

government purchases (G) Expenditures by government for goods and services that government consumes in providing public goods and for public capital that has a long lifetime; the expenditures of all governments in the economy for those *final goods and services.*

government transfer payment The disbursement of money (or goods and services) by government for which government receives no currently produced good or service in return.

grievance procedure The method used by a *labor union* and a *firm* to settle disputes that arise during the life of the collective bargaining agreement between them.

gross domestic product (GDP) The total market value of all *final goods and services* produced annually within the boundaries of the United States, whether by U.S.- or foreign-supplied resources.

gross private domestic investment (I_g) Expenditures for newly produced *capital goods* (such as machinery, equipment, tools, and buildings) and for additions to inventories.

growth accounting The bookkeeping of the supply-side elements such as productivity and labor inputs that contribute to changes in *real GDP* over some specific time period.

guiding function of prices The ability of price changes to bring about changes in the quantities of products and resources demanded and supplied.

H1-B provision A provision of the U.S. immigration law that allows the annual entry of 65,000 high-skilled workers in "specialty occupations" such as science, *R&D*, and computer programming to work legally and continuously in the United States for six years.

health maintenance organizations (HMOs) Health care providers that contract with employers, insurance companies, labor unions, or government units to provide health care for their workers or others who are insured.

health savings accounts (HSAs) Accounts into which people with high-deductible health insurance plans can place tax-free funds each year and then draw on these funds to pay out-of-pocket medical expenses such as *deductibles* and *copayments.*

Unused funds accumulate from year to year and later can be used to supplement *Medicare*.

Herfindahl index A measure of the concentration and competitiveness of an industry; calculated as the sum of the squared percentage market shares of the individual firms in the industry.

homogeneous oligopoly An *oligopoly* in which the firms produce a *standardized product*.

horizontal axis The "left-right" or "west-east" measurement line on graph or grid.

horizontal merger The merger into a single *firm* of two firms producing the same product and selling it in the same geographic market.

households Economic entities (of one or more persons occupying a housing unit) that provide *resources* to the economy and use the *income* received to purchase goods and services that satisfy economic wants.

human capital The knowledge and skills that make a person productive.

human capital investment Any expenditure undertaken to improve the education, skills, health, or mobility of workers, with an expectation of greater productivity and thus a positive return on the investment.

hyperinflation A very rapid rise in the price level; an extremely high rate of inflation.

hypothesis A tentative explanation of cause and effect that requires testing.

illegal immigrants People who have entered a country unlawfully to reside there; also called unauthorized immigrants.

IMF (See *International Monetary Fund.*)

imitation problem (Web chapter) The potential for a firm's rivals to produce a close variation of (imitate) a firm's new product or process, greatly reducing the originator's profit from *R&D* and *innovation*.

immediate short-run aggregate supply curve An aggregate supply curve for which real output, but not the price level, changes when the aggregate demand curves shifts; a horizontal aggregate supply curve that implies an inflexible price level.

immigration The inflow of people into a country from another country. The immigrants may be either *legal immigrants or illegal immigrants.*

immobility The inability or unwillingness of a worker to move from one geographic area or occupation to another or from a lower-paying job to a higher-paying job.

imperfect competition All market structures except *pure competition*; includes *monopoly, monopolistic competition,* and *oligopoly.*

implicit cost The monetary income a *firm* sacrifices when it uses a resource it owns rather than supplying the resource in the market; equal to what the resource could have earned in the best-paying alternative employment; includes a *normal profit.*

import competition The competition that domestic firms encounter from the products and services of foreign producers.

import demand curve A downsloping curve showing the amount of a product that an economy will import at each *world price* below the *domestic price.*

import quota A limit imposed by a nation on the quantity (or total value) of a good that may be imported during some period of time.

imports Spending by individuals, *firms,* and governments for goods and services produced in foreign nations.

import transaction The purchase of a good or service that decreases the amount of foreign money held by citizens, firms, and governments of a nation.

incentive function The inducement that an increase in the price of a commodity gives to sellers to make more of it available (and conversely for a decrease in price), and the inducement that an increase in price offers to buyers to purchase smaller quantities (and conversely for a decrease in price).

incentive pay plan A compensation structure that ties worker pay directly to performance. Such plans include piece rates, bonuses, *stock options,* commissions, and *profit sharing.*

inclusive unionism The practice of a labor union of including as members all workers employed in an industry.

income A flow of dollars (or purchasing power) per unit of time derived from the use of human or property resources.

income approach The method that adds all the income generated by the production of *final goods and services* to measure the *gross domestic product.*

income effect A change in the quantity demanded of a product that results from the change in *real income (purchasing power)* caused by a change in the product's price.

income elasticity of demand The ratio of the percentage change in the *quantity demanded* of a good to a percentage change in consumer income; measures the responsiveness of consumer purchases to income changes.

income inequality The unequal distribution of an economy's total income among households or families.

income-maintenance system A group of government programs designed to eliminate poverty and reduce inequality in the distribution of income.

income mobility The extent to which income receivers move from one part of the income distribution to another over some period of time.

increase in demand An increase in the *quantity demanded* of a good or service at every price; a shift of the *demand curve* to the right.

increase in supply An increase in the *quantity supplied* of a good or service at every price; a shift of the *supply curve* to the right.

increasing-cost industry An *industry* in which expansion through the entry of new firms raises the prices *firms* in the industry must pay for resources and therefore increases their production costs.

increasing marginal returns An increase in the *marginal product* of a resource as successive units of the resource are employed.

increasing returns An increase in a firm's output by a larger percentage than the percentage increase in its inputs.

independent goods Products or services for which there is little or no relationship between the price of one and the demand for the other. When the price of one rises or falls, the demand for the other tends to remain constant.

independent unions U.S. unions that are not affiliated with the *AFL-CIO*.

independent variable The variable causing a change in some other (dependent) variable.

index funds *Mutual funds* that select stock or bond *portfolios* to exactly match a stock or bond index (a collection of stocks or bonds meant to capture the overall behavior of a particular category of investments) such as the Standard & Poor's 500 Index or the Russell 3000 Index.

indifference curve A curve showing the different combinations of two products that yield the same satisfaction or *utility* to a consumer.

indifference map A set of *indifference curves*, each representing a different level of *utility*, that together show the preferences of a consumer.

individual demand The demand schedule or *demand curve* of a single buyer.

individual supply The supply schedule or *supply curve* of a single seller.

individual transferable quotas (ITQs) Limits set by government or a fisheries commission on the total number or total weight of a species that an individual fisher can harvest during some particular time period; fishers holding the quotas can sell all or part of the rights to other fishers.

industrially advanced countries High-income countries such as the United States, Canada, Japan, and the nations of western Europe that have highly developed *market economies* based on large stocks of technologically advanced capital goods and skilled labor forces.

industrial regulation The older and more traditional type of regulation in which government is concerned with the prices charged and the services provided to the public in specific industries, in contrast to *social regulation*.

industrial union A *labor union* that accepts as members all workers employed in a particular industry (or by a particular firm).

industry A group of (one or more) *firms* that produce identical or similar products.

inelastic demand Product or resource demand for which the *elasticity coefficient* for price is less than 1. This means the resulting percentage change in *quantity demanded* is less than the percentage change in *price*.

inelastic supply Product or resource supply for which the price elasticity coefficient is less than 1. The percentage change in *quantity supplied* is less than the percentage change in *price*.

inferior good A good or service whose consumption declines as income rises, prices held constant.

inflating Determining *real gross domestic product* by increasing the dollar value of the *nominal gross domestic product* produced in a year in which prices are lower than those in a *base year*.

inflation A rise in the general level of prices in an economy.

inflationary expectations The belief of workers, firms, and consumers about future rates of inflation.

inflationary expenditure gap The amount by which the *aggregate expenditures schedule* must shift downward to decrease the *nominal GDP* to its full-employment noninflationary level.

inflation premium The component of the *nominal interest rate* that reflects anticipated inflation.

inflation targeting The annual statement by a *central bank* of a goal for a specific range of inflation in a future year, coupled with monetary policy designed to achieve the goal.

inflexible prices Product prices that remain in place (at least for a while) even though supply or demand has changed; stuck prices or sticky prices.

information technology New and more efficient methods of delivering and receiving information through the use of computers, fax machines, wireless phones, and the Internet.

infrastructure The capital goods usually provided by the *public sector* for use by citizens and firms (for example, highways, bridges, transit systems, wastewater treatment facilities, municipal water systems, and airports).

injection An addition of spending to the income-expenditure stream: *investment, government purchases*, and *net exports*.

injunction A court order directing a person or organization not to perform a certain act because the act would do irreparable damage to some other person or persons; a restraining order.

in-kind transfer The distribution by government of goods and services to individuals for which the government receives no currently produced good or service in return; a *government transfer payment* made in goods or services rather than in money; also called a noncash transfer.

innovation The first commercially successful introduction of a new product, the use of a new method of production, or the creation of a new form of business organization.

inpayments The receipts of domestic or foreign money that individuals, firms, and governments of one nation obtain from the sale of goods and services abroad, as investment income and remittances, and from foreign purchases of domestic assets.

insider-outsider theory The hypothesis that nominal wages are inflexible downward because firms are aware that workers ("insiders") who retain employment during recession may refuse to work cooperatively with previously unemployed workers ("outsiders") who offer to work for less than the current wage.

insurable risk An event that would result in a loss but whose frequency of occurrence can be estimated with considerable accuracy. Insurance companies are willing to sell insurance against such losses.

insurance exchanges Government-regulated markets for health insurance in which individuals seeking to purchase health insurance to comply with the *personal mandate* of the *Patient Protection and Affordable Care Act (PPACA)* of 2010 will be able to comparison shop among insurance policies approved by regulators. Each state will have its own exchange.

interest The payment made for the use of money (of borrowed funds).

interest income Payments of income to those who supply the economy with *capital*.

interest rate The annual rate at which *interest* is paid; a percentage of the borrowed amount.

interest-rate-cost-of-funds curve (Web chapter) As it relates to research and development (*R&D*), a curve showing the *interest rate* the firm must pay to obtain any particular amount of funds to finance R&D.

interest-rate effect The tendency for increases in the *price level* to increase the demand for money, raise interest rates, and, as a result, reduce total spending and real output in the economy (and the reverse for price-level decreases).

interindustry competition The competition for sales between the products of one industry and the products of another industry.

interlocking directorate A situation where one or more members of the board of directors of a *corporation* are also on the board of directors of a competing corporation; illegal under the *Clayton Act.*

intermediate goods Products that are purchased for resale or further processing or manufacturing.

internally held public debt *Public debt* owed to citizens, firms, and institutions of the same nation that issued the debt.

international balance of payments A summary of all the transactions that took place between the individuals, firms, and government units of one nation and those of all other nations during a year.

international balance-of-payments deficit (See *balance-of-payments deficit.*)

international balance-of-payments surplus (See *balance-of-payments surplus.*)

international gold standard (See *gold standard.*)

International Monetary Fund (IMF) The international association of nations that was formed after the Second World War to make loans of foreign monies to nations with temporary *payments deficits* and, until the early 1970s, to administer the *adjustable pegs*. It now mainly makes loans to nations facing possible defaults on private and government loans.

international monetary reserves The foreign currencies and other assets such as gold that a nation can use to settle a *balance-of-payments deficit.*

international value of the dollar The price that must be paid in foreign currency (money) to obtain one U.S. dollar.

intertemporal choice Choices between benefits obtainable in one time period and benefits achievable in a later time period; comparisons that individuals and society must make between the reductions in current consumption that are necessary to fund current investments and the higher levels of future consumption that those current investments can produce.

intrinsic value The market value of the metal within a coin.

invention (Web chapter) The first discovery of a product or process through the use of imagination, ingenious thinking, and experimentation and the first proof that it will work.

inventories Goods that have been produced but remain unsold.

inverse relationship The relationship between two variables that change in opposite directions, for example, product price and quantity demanded; a negative relationship.

inverted-U theory (Web chapter) The idea that, other things equal, *R&D* expenditures as a percentage of sales rise with industry concentration, reach a peak at a four-firm *concentration ratio* of about 50 percent, and then fall as the ratio further increases.

investment In economics, spending for the production and accumulation of *capital* and additions to inventories. (For contrast, see *financial investment.*)

investment banks Firms that help corporations and government raise money by selling stocks and bonds; they also offer advisory services for corporate mergers and acquisitions in addition to providing brokerage services and advice.

investment demand curve A curve that shows the amounts of *investment* demanded by an economy at a series of *real interest rates.*

investment goods Same as *capital* or capital goods.

investment in human capital (See *human capital investment.*)

investment schedule A curve or schedule that shows the amounts firms plan to invest at various possible values of *real gross domestic product.*

"invisible hand" The tendency of firms and resource suppliers that seek to further their own self-interests in competitive markets to also promote the interests of society.

Joint Economic Committee (JEC) Committee of senators and representatives that investigates economic problems of national interest.

kinked-demand curve The demand curve for a noncollusive oligopolist, which is based on the assumption that rivals will match a price decrease and will ignore a price increase.

labor People's physical and mental talents and efforts that are used to help produce goods and services.

labor force Persons 16 years of age and older who are not in institutions and who are employed or are unemployed and seeking work.

labor-force participation rate   The percentage of the working-age population that is actually in the *labor force*.

labor-intensive goods   Products requiring relatively large amounts of *labor* to produce.

labor productivity   Total output divided by the quantity of labor employed to produce it; the *average product* of labor or output per hour of work.

labor union   A group of workers organized to advance the interests of the group (to increase wages, shorten the hours worked, improve working conditions, and so on).

Laffer Curve   A curve relating government tax rates and tax revenues and on which a particular tax rate (between zero and 100 percent) maximizes tax revenues.

laissez-faire capitalism   (See *capitalism*.)

land   Natural resources ("free gifts of nature") used to produce goods and services.

land-intensive goods   Products requiring relatively large amounts of *land* to produce.

land reform   (Web chapter) A set of policies designed to create more efficient distribution of land ownership in developing countries; policies vary country to country and can involve everything from government purchasing large land estates and dividing the land into smaller farms to consolidating tiny plots of land into larger, more efficient private farms.

law of demand   The principle that, other things equal, an increase in a product's price will reduce the quantity of it demanded, and conversely for a decrease in price.

law of diminishing marginal utility   The principle that as a consumer increases the consumption of a good or service, the *marginal utility* obtained from each additional unit of the good or service decreases.

law of diminishing returns   The principle that as successive increments of a variable resource are added to a fixed resource, the *marginal product* of the variable resource will eventually decrease.

law of increasing opportunity costs   The principle that as the production of a good increases, the *opportunity cost* of producing an additional unit rises.

law of supply   The principle that, other things equal, an increase in the price of a product will increase the quantity of it supplied, and conversely for a price decrease.

leader countries   As it relates to *economic growth*, countries that develop and use advanced technologies, which then become available to *follower countries*.

leakage   (1) A withdrawal of potential spending from the income-expenditures stream via *saving*, tax payments, or *imports*; (2) a withdrawal that reduces the lending potential of the banking system.

learning by doing   Achieving greater *productivity* and lower *average total cost* through gains in knowledge and skill that accompany repetition of a task; a source of *economies of scale*.

least-cost combination of resources   The quantity of each resource a firm must employ in order to produce a particular output at the lowest total cost; the combination at which the ratio of the *marginal product* of a resource to its *marginal resource cost* (to its *price* if the resource is employed in a competitive market) is the same for the last dollar spent on each of the resources employed.

legal cartel theory of regulation   The hypothesis that some industries seek regulation or want to maintain regulation so that they may form or maintain a legal *cartel*.

legal immigrant   A person who lawfully enters a country for the purpose of residing there.

legal tender   A nation's official currency (bills and coins). Payment of debts must be accepted in this monetary unit, but creditors can specify the form of payment, for example, "cash only" or "check or credit card only."

lending potential of an individual commercial bank   The amount by which a single bank can increase the *money supply* by making new loans to (or buying securities from) the public; equal to the bank's excess reserves.

lending potential of the banking system   The amount by which the banking system can increase the *money supply* by making new loans to (or buying securities from) the public; equal to the *excess reserves* of the banking system multiplied by the *monetary multiplier*.

liability   A debt with a monetary value; an amount owed by a firm or an individual.

limited liability rule   Rule limiting the risks involved in investing in corporations and encouraging investors to invest in stocks by capping their potential losses at the amount that they paid for their shares.

liquidity   The ease with which an asset can be converted quickly into cash with little or no loss of purchasing power. Money is said to be perfectly liquid, whereas other assets have a lesser degree of liquidity.

liquidity trap   A situation in a severe *recession* in which the Fed's injection of additional reserves into the banking system has little or no additional positive impact on lending, borrowing, *investment*, or *aggregate demand*.

loanable funds   *Money* available for lending and borrowing.

loanable funds theory of interest   The concept that the supply of and demand for *loanable funds* determine the equilibrium rate of interest.

lockout   An action by a firm that forbids workers to return to work until a new collective bargaining contract is signed; a means of imposing costs (lost wages) on union workers in a collective bargaining dispute.

logrolling   The trading of votes by legislators to secure favorable outcomes on decisions concerning the provision of *public goods* and *quasi-public goods*.

long run   (1) In *microeconomics*, a period of time long enough to enable producers of a product to change the quantities of all the resources they employ; period in which all resources and costs are variable and no resources or costs are fixed. (2) In *macroeconomics*, a period sufficiently long for *nominal wages* and other input prices to change in response to a change in a nation's *price level*.

long-run aggregate supply curve The aggregate supply curve associated with a time period in which input prices (especially *nominal wages*) are fully responsive to changes in the *price level*.

long-run competitive equilibrium The price at which firms in *pure competition* neither obtain *economic profit* nor suffer economic losses in the *long run* and in which the total quantity demanded and supplied are equal; a price equal to the *marginal cost* and the minimum long-run *average total cost* of producing the product.

long-run supply In *microeconomics*, a schedule or curve showing the prices at which a purely competitive industry will make various quantities of the product available in the *long run*.

long-run supply curve As it applies to macroeconomics, a supply curve for which price, but not real output, changes when the demand curves shifts; a vertical supply curve that implies fully flexible prices.

long-run vertical Phillips Curve The *Phillips Curve* after all nominal wages have adjusted to changes in the rate of inflation; a line emanating straight upward at the economy's *natural rate of unemployment*.

Lorenz curve A curve showing the distribution of income in an economy. The cumulated percentage of families (income receivers) is measured along the horizontal axis and the cumulated percentage of income is measured along the vertical axis.

loss averse In *prospect theory*, the property of people's preferences that the pain generated by losses feels substantially more intense than the pleasure generated by gains.

lump-sum tax A tax that collects a constant amount (the tax revenue of government is the same) at all levels of GDP.

M1 The most narrowly defined *money supply*, equal to *currency* in the hands of the public and the *checkable deposits* of commercial banks and thrift institutions.

M2 A more broadly defined *money supply*, equal to *M1* plus *noncheckable savings accounts* (including *money market deposit accounts*), small *time deposits* (deposits of less than $100,000), and individual *money market mutual fund* balances.

macroeconomics The part of economics concerned with the economy as a whole; with such major aggregates as the household, business, and government sectors; and with measures of the total economy.

managed floating exchange rate An *exchange rate* that is allowed to change (float) as a result of changes in currency supply and demand but at times is altered (managed) by governments via their buying and selling of particular currencies.

managerial prerogatives The decisions that a firm's management has the sole right to make; often enumerated in the labor contract (work agreement) between a *labor union* and a *firm*.

marginal analysis The comparison of marginal ("extra" or "additional") benefits and marginal costs, usually for decision making.

marginal benefit The extra (additional) benefit of consuming 1 more unit of some good or service; the change in total benefit when 1 more unit is consumed.

marginal cost (MC) The extra (additional) cost of producing 1 more unit of output; equal to the change in *total cost* divided by the change in output (and, in the short run, to the change in total *variable cost* divided by the change in output).

marginal cost–marginal benefit rule As it applies to *cost-benefit analysis*, the tenet that a government project or program should be expanded to the point where the *marginal cost* and *marginal benefit* of additional expenditures are equal.

marginal product (MP) The additional output produced when 1 additional unit of a resource is employed (the quantity of all other resources employed remaining constant); equal to the change in *total product* divided by the change in the quantity of a resource employed.

marginal productivity theory of income distribution The contention that the distribution of income is equitable when each unit of each resource receives a money payment equal to its marginal contribution to the firm's revenue (its *marginal revenue product*).

marginal propensity to consume (MPC) The fraction of any change in *disposable income* spent for *consumer goods*; equal to the change in consumption divided by the change in disposable income.

marginal propensity to save (MPS) The fraction of any change in *disposable income* that households save; equal to the change in *saving* divided by the change in disposable income.

marginal rate of substitution (MRS) The rate at which a consumer is willing to substitute one good for another (from a given combination of goods) and remain equally satisfied (have the same *total utility*); equal to the slope of a consumer's *indifference curve* at each point on the curve.

marginal resource cost (MRC) The amount the total cost of employing a *resource* increases when a firm employs 1 additional unit of the resource (the quantity of all other resources employed remaining constant); equal to the change in the *total cost* of the resource divided by the change in the quantity of the resource employed.

marginal revenue The change in *total revenue* that results from the sale of 1 additional unit of a firm's product; equal to the change in total revenue divided by the change in the quantity of the product sold.

marginal-revenue–marginal-cost approach A method of determining the total output where *economic profit* is a maximum (or losses are a minimum) by comparing the *marginal revenue* and the *marginal cost* of each additional unit of output.

marginal revenue product (MRP) The change in a firm's *total revenue* when it employs 1 additional unit of a resource (the quantity of all other resources employed remaining constant); equal to the change in total revenue divided by the change in the quantity of the resource employed.

marginal revenue productivity (See *marginal revenue product*.)

marginal tax rate The tax rate paid on an additional dollar of income.

marginal utility The extra *utility* a consumer obtains from the consumption of 1 additional unit of a good or service; equal to the change in total utility divided by the change in the quantity consumed.

market Any institution or mechanism that brings together buyers (demanders) and sellers (suppliers) of a particular good or service.

market demand (See *total demand*.)

market economy An economy in which the private decisions of consumers, resource suppliers, and firms determine how resources are allocated; the *market system*.

market failure The inability of a market to bring about the allocation of resources that best satisfies the wants of society; in particular, the overallocation or underallocation of resources to the production of a particular good or service because of *externalities* or informational problems or because markets do not provide desired *public goods*.

market for externality rights A market in which firms can buy rights to discharge pollutants. The price of such rights is determined by the demand for the right to discharge pollutants and a *perfectly inelastic supply* of such rights (the latter determined by the quantity of discharge that the environment can assimilate).

market period A period in which producers of a product are unable to change the quantity produced in response to a change in its price and in which there is a *perfectly inelastic supply*.

market portfolio The portfolio consisting of every financial asset (including every *stock* and *bond*) traded in the financial markets. The market portfolio is used to calculate *beta* (a measure of the degree of riskiness) for specific stocks, bonds, and mutual funds.

market system All the product and resource markets of a *market economy* and the relationships among them; a method that allows the prices determined in those markets to allocate the economy's scarce resources and to communicate and coordinate the decisions made by consumers, firms, and resource suppliers.

marketing loan program A Federal farm subsidy under which certain farmers can receive a loan (on a per-unit-of-output basis) from a government lender and then, depending on the price of the crop, either pay back the loan with interest or keep the loan proceeds while forfeiting their harvested crop to the lender.

median-voter model The theory that under majority rule the median (middle) voter will be in the dominant position to determine the outcome of an election.

Medicaid A Federal program that helps finance the medical expenses of individuals covered by the *Supplemental Security Income (SSI)* and *Temporary Assistance for Needy Families (TANF)* programs.

Medicare A Federal program that is financed by *payroll taxes* and provides for (1) compulsory hospital insurance for senior citizens, (2) low-cost voluntary insurance to help older Americans pay physicians' fees, and (3) subsidized insurance to buy prescription drugs.

Medicare Part D The portion of Medicare that enables enrollees to shop among private health insurance companies to buy highly subsidized insurance to help reduce the out-of-pocket expense of prescription drugs.

medium of exchange Any item sellers generally accept and buyers generally use to pay for a good or service; *money*; a convenient means of exchanging goods and services without engaging in *barter*.

mental accounting The tendency people have to create separate "mental boxes" (or "accounts") in which they deal with particular financial transactions in isolation rather than dealing with them as part of their overall decision-making process that considers how to best allocate their limited budgets using the *utility-maximizing rule*.

menu costs The reluctance of firms to cut prices during recessions (that they think will be short-lived) because of the costs of altering and communicating their price reductions; named after the cost associated with printing new menus at restaurants.

merger The combination of two (or more) firms into a single firm.

microeconomics The part of economics concerned with decision making by individual units such as a *household*, a *firm*, or an *industry* and with individual markets, specific goods and services, and product and resource prices.

microfinance (Web chapter) A credit system through which groups of people pool their money and make small loans to budding *entrepreneurs* and owners of small businesses in *developing countries*.

Microsoft case A 2002 antitrust case in which Microsoft was found guilty of violating the *Sherman Act* by engaging in a series of unlawful activities designed to maintain its monopoly in operating systems for personal computers; as a remedy the company was prohibited from engaging in a set of specific anticompetitive business practices.

midpoint formula A method for calculating *price elasticity of demand* or *price elasticity of supply* that averages the two prices and two quantities as the reference points for computing percentages.

minimum efficient scale (MES) The lowest level of output at which a firm can minimize long-run *average total cost*.

minimum wage The lowest *wage* that employers may legally pay for an hour of work.

modern economic growth The historically recent phenomenon in which nations for the first time have experienced sustained increases in *real GDP per capita*.

monetarism The macroeconomic view that the main cause of changes in aggregate output and *price level* is fluctuations in the *money supply*; espoused by advocates of a *monetary rule*.

monetary multiplier The multiple of its *excess reserves* by which the banking system can expand *checkable deposits* and thus the *money supply* by making new loans (or buying securities); equal to 1 divided by the *reserve requirement*.

monetary policy A central bank's changing of the *money supply* to influence interest rates and assist the economy in achieving price stability, full employment, and economic growth.

monetary rule The rule suggested by *monetarism*. As traditionally formulated, the rule says that the *money supply* should be expanded each year at the same annual rate as the potential rate of growth of the *real gross domestic product;* the supply of money should be increased steadily between 3 and 5 percent per year. (Also see *Taylor rule*.)

money Any item that is generally acceptable to sellers in exchange for goods and services.

money capital Money available to purchase *capital;* simply *money,* as defined by economists.

money income (See *nominal income*.)

money market The market in which the demand for and the supply of money determine the *interest rate* (or the level of interest rates) in the economy.

money market deposit accounts (MMDAs) Bank- and thrift-provided interest-bearing accounts that contain a variety of short-term securities; such accounts have minimum balance requirements and limits on the frequency of withdrawals.

money market mutual funds (MMMFs) Interest-bearing accounts offered by investment companies, which pool depositors' funds for the purchase of short-term securities. Depositors can write checks in minimum amounts or more against their accounts.

money supply Narrowly defined, $M1$; more broadly defined, $M2$. (See $M1$ and $M2$)

monopolistic competition A market structure in which many firms sell a *differentiated product,* into which entry is relatively easy, in which the firm has some control over its product price, and in which there is considerable *nonprice competition.*

monopoly A market structure in which there is only a single seller of a good, service, or resource. In antitrust law, a dominant firm that accounts for a very high percentage of total sales within a particular market.

monopsony A market structure in which there is only a single buyer of a good, service, or resource.

moral hazard problem The possibility that individuals or institutions will change their behavior as the result of a contract or agreement. Example: A bank whose deposits are insured against losses may make riskier loans and investments.

mortgage-backed securities *Bonds* that represent claims to all or part of the monthly mortgage payments from the pools of mortgage loans made by leaders to borrowers to help them purchase residential property.

mortgage debt crisis The period beginning in late 2007 when thousands of homeowners defaulted on mortgage loans when they experienced a combination of higher mortgage interest rates and falling home prices.

MR = MC rule The principle that a firm will maximize its profit (or minimize its losses) by producing the output at which *marginal revenue* and *marginal cost* are equal, provided product price is equal to or greater than *average variable cost.*

MRP = MRC rule The principle that to maximize profit (or minimize losses), a firm should employ the quantity of a resource at which its *marginal revenue product* (MRP) is equal to its *marginal resource cost* (MRC), the latter being the wage rate in a purely competitive labor market.

multinational corporations Firms that own production facilities in two or more countries and produce and sell their products globally.

multiple counting Wrongly including the value of *intermediate goods* in the *gross domestic product;* counting the same good or service more than once.

multiplier The ratio of a change in equilibrium GDP to the change in *investment* or in any other component of *aggregate expenditures* or *aggregate demand;* the number by which a change in any such component must be multiplied to find the resulting change in equilibrium GDP.

multiplier effect The effect on equilibrium GDP of a change in *aggregate expenditures* or *aggregate demand* (caused by a change in the *consumption schedule, investment,* government expenditures, or *net exports*).

mutual funds *Portfolios* of *stocks* and *bonds* selected and purchased by mutual fund companies, which finance the purchases by pooling money from thousands of individual fund investors; includes both *index funds* as well as *actively managed funds.* Fund returns (profits or losses) pass through to the individual fund investors who invest in the funds.

mutual interdependence A situation in which a change in price strategy (or in some other strategy) by one firm will affect the sales and profits of another firm (or other firms). Any firm that makes such a change can expect the other rivals to react to the change.

Nash equilibrium In *game theory,* an outcome from which neither firm wants to deviate; the outcome that once achieved is stable and therefore lasting.

national bank A *commercial bank* authorized to operate by the U.S. government.

National Credit Union Administration (NCUA) The federally chartered agency that insures deposit liabilities (up to $250,000 per account) in *credit unions.*

national health insurance A program in which a nation's government provides a basic package of health care to all citizens at no direct charge or at a low cost-sharing level. Financing is out of general tax revenues.

national income Total income earned by resource suppliers for their contributions to *gross domestic product* plus *taxes on production and imports;* the sum of wages and salaries, *rent, interest, profit, proprietors' income,* and such taxes.

national income accounting The techniques used to measure the overall production of the economy and other related variables for the nation as a whole.

National Labor Relations Act (NLRA) Act first passed as the Wagner Act of 1935; as amended, the basic labor-relations law in the United States; defines the legal rights of unions and management and identifies unfair union and management labor practices; established the *National Labor Relations Board.*

National Labor Relations Board (NLRB) The board established by the *National Labor Relations Act* of 1935 to investigate unfair labor practices, issue *cease-and-desist orders*, and conduct elections among employees to determine if they wish to be represented by a *labor union*.

natural monopoly An industry in which *economies of scale* are so great that a single firm can produce the product at a lower average total cost than would be possible if more than one firm produced the product.

natural rate of unemployment (NRU) The *full-employment rate of unemployment*; the unemployment rate occurring when there is no cyclical unemployment and the economy is achieving its potential output; the unemployment rate at which actual inflation equals expected inflation.

near-money Financial assets, the most important of which are *noncheckable savings accounts*, *time deposits*, and U.S. short-term securities and savings bonds, which are not a medium of exchange but can be readily converted into money.

negative externality A cost imposed without compensation on third parties by the production or consumption of sellers or buyers. Example: A manufacturer dumps toxic chemicals into a river, killing fish prized by sports fishers; an external cost or a spillover cost.

negative GDP gap A situation in which actual *gross domestic product* is less than *potential output*. Also known as a recessionary output gap.

negative relationship (See *inverse relationship*.)

negative self-selection As it relates to international *migration*, the idea that those who choose to move to another country have poorer wage opportunities in the origin country than those with similar skills who choose not to *emigrate*.

negative-sum game In *game theory*, a game in which the gains (+) and losses (−) add up to some amount less than zero; one party's losses exceed the other party's gains.

net benefits The total benefits of some activity or policy less the total costs of that activity or policy.

net domestic product (NDP) *Gross domestic product* less the part of the year's output that is needed to replace the *capital goods* worn out in producing the output; the nation's total output available for consumption or additions to the *capital stock*.

net exports (X_n) *Exports* minus *imports*.

net foreign factor income Receipts of resource income from the rest of the world minus payments of resource income to the rest of the world.

net investment income The interest and dividend income received by the residents of a nation from residents of other nations less the interest and dividend payments made by the residents of that nation to the residents of other nations.

net private domestic investment *Gross private domestic investment* less *consumption of fixed capital*; the addition to the nation's stock of *capital* during a year.

net taxes The taxes collected by government less *government transfer payments*.

net transfers The personal and government transfer payments made by one nation to residents of foreign nations less the personal and government transfer payments received from residents of foreign nations.

network effects Increases in the value of a product to each user, including existing users, as the total number of users rises.

net worth The total *assets* less the total *liabilities* of a firm or an individual; for a firm, the claims of the owners against the firm's total assets; for an individual, his or her wealth.

new classical economics The theory that, although unanticipated price-level changes may create macroeconomic instability in the short run, the economy is stable at the full-employment level of domestic output in the long run because prices and wages adjust automatically to correct movements away from the full-employment, noninflationary output.

NLRB (See *National Labor Relations Board*.)

nominal gross domestic product (GDP) *GDP* measured in terms of the price level at the time of measurement; *GDP* not adjusted for inflation.

nominal income The number of dollars received by an individual or group for its resources during some period of time.

nominal interest rate The interest rate expressed in terms of annual amounts currently charged for interest and not adjusted for inflation.

nominal wage The amount of money received by a worker per unit of time (hour, day, etc.); money wage.

noncash transfer A *government transfer payment* in the form of goods and services rather than money, for example, food stamps, housing assistance, and job training; also called in-kind transfers.

noncollusive oligopoly An *oligopoly* in which the firms do not act together and in agreement to determine the price of the product and the output that each firm will produce.

noncompeting groups Collections of workers who do not compete with each other for employment because the skill and training of the workers in one group are substantially different from those of the workers in other groups.

nondiscretionary fiscal policy (See *built-in stabilizer*.)

nondiversifiable risk Investment *risk* that investors are unable to reduce via *diversification*; also called systemic risk.

nondurable good A *consumer good* with an expected life (use) of less than three years.

nonexcludability The inability to keep nonpayers (free riders) from obtaining benefits from a certain good; a characteristic of a *public good*.

nonexhaustive expenditure An expenditure by government that does not result directly in the use of economic resources or the production of goods and services; see *government transfer payment*.

nonincome determinants of consumption and saving All influences on consumption and saving other than the level of *GDP*.

noninterest determinants of investment All influences on the level of investment spending other than the *interest rate*.

noninvestment transaction An expenditure for stocks, bonds, or secondhand *capital goods*.

nonmarket transactions The value of the goods and services that are not included in the *gross domestic product* because they are not bought and sold.

nonprice competition Competition based on distinguishing one's product by means of *product differentiation* and then *advertising* the distinguished product to consumers.

nonproduction transaction The purchase and sale of any item that is not a currently produced good or service.

nonrenewable natural resource Things such as oil, natural gas, and metals, which are either in actual fixed supply or which renew so slowly as to be in virtual fixed supply when viewed from a human time perspective.

nonrivalry The idea that one person's benefit from a certain good does not reduce the benefit available to others; a characteristic of a *public good*.

nontariff barriers (NTBs) All barriers other than *protective tariffs* that nations erect to impede international trade, including *import quotas*, licensing requirements, unreasonable product-quality standards, unnecessary bureaucratic detail in customs procedures, and so on.

normal good A good or service whose consumption increases when income increases and falls when income decreases, price remaining constant.

normal profit The payment made by a firm to obtain and retain *entrepreneurial ability;* the minimum income entrepreneurial ability must receive to induce it to perform entrepreneurial functions for a firm.

normative economics The part of economics involving value judgments about what the economy should be like; focused on which economic goals and policies should be implemented; policy economics.

North American Free Trade Agreement (NAFTA) A 1993 agreement establishing, over a 15-year period, a free-trade zone composed of Canada, Mexico, and the United States.

occupation A category of activities or tasks performed by a set of workers for pay, independent of employer or industry. Examples are managers, nurses, farmers, and cooks.

occupational licensing The laws of state or local governments that require that a worker satisfy certain specified requirements and obtain a license from a licensing board before engaging in a particular occupation.

occupational segregation The crowding of women or minorities into less desirable, lower-paying occupations.

official reserves Foreign currencies owned by the central bank of a nation.

offshoring The practice of shifting work previously done by American workers to workers located abroad.

Okun's law The generalization that any 1-percentage-point rise in the *unemployment rate* above the *full-employment rate of unemployment* is associated with a rise in the negative *GDP gap* by 2 percent of *potential output* (potential GDP).

oligopoly A market structure in which a few firms sell either a *standardized* or *differentiated product*, into which entry is difficult, in which the firm has limited control over product price because of *mutual interdependence* (except when there is collusion among firms), and in which there is typically *nonprice competition*.

one-time game In *game theory*, a game in which the parties select their optimal strategies in a single time period without regard to possible interaction in subsequent time periods.

OPEC (See *Organization of Petroleum Exporting Countries*.)

open economy An economy that exports and imports goods and services.

open-market operations The buying and selling of U.S. government securities by the *Federal Reserve Banks* for purposes of carrying out *monetary policy*.

open shop A place of employment in which the employer may hire nonunion workers and in which the workers need not become members of a *labor union*.

opportunity cost The amount of other products that must be forgone or sacrificed to produce a unit of a product.

opportunity-cost ratio An equivalency showing the number of units of two products that can be produced with the same resources; the cost 1 corn ≡ 3 olives shows that the resources required to produce 3 units of olives must be shifted to corn production to produce 1 unit of corn.

optimal amount of R&D (Web chapter) The level of *R&D* at which the *marginal benefit* and *marginal cost* of R&D expenditures are equal.

optimal reduction of an externality The reduction of a *negative externality* such as pollution to the level at which the *marginal benefit* and *marginal cost* of reduction are equal.

ordinal utility Satisfaction that is measured by having consumers compare and rank products (or combinations of products) as to preference, without asking them to specify the absolute amounts of satisfaction provided by the products.

Organization of Petroleum Exporting Countries (OPEC) A cartel of 12 oil-producing countries (Algeria, Angola, Ecuador, Iran, Iraq, Kuwait, Libya, Nigeria, Qatar, Saudi Arabia, Venezuela, and the United Arab Emirates) that attempts to control the quantity and price of crude oil exported by its members and that accounts for a large percentage of the world's export of oil.

other-things-equal assumption The assumption that factors other than those being considered are held constant; *ceteris paribus* assumption.

outpayments The expenditures of domestic or foreign currency that the individuals, firms, and governments of one nation make to purchase goods and services, for remittances, to pay investment income, and for purchases of foreign assets.

output effect The situation in which an increase in the price of one input will increase a firm's production costs and reduce its level of output, thus reducing the demand for other inputs; conversely for a decrease in the price of the input.

paper money Pieces of paper used as a *medium of exchange;* in the United States, *Federal Reserve Notes.*

paradox of thrift The seemingly self-contradictory but nevertheless true statement that increased *saving* can be both good and bad for the economy. It is good in the long run when matched with increased *investment* spending, but bad during a *recession* because it reduces spending, which further reduces output and employment. In fact, attempts by *households* to save more during a recession may simply worsen the recession and result in less saving.

paradox of voting A situation where paired-choice voting by majority rule fails to provide a consistent ranking of society's preferences for *public goods* or services.

parity concept The idea that year after year the sale of a specific output of a farm product should enable a farmer to purchase a constant amount of nonagricultural goods and services.

parity ratio The ratio of the price received by farmers from the sale of an agricultural commodity to the prices of other goods paid by them; usually expressed as a percentage; used as a rationale for *price supports.*

partnership An unincorporated firm owned and operated by two or more persons.

passively managed funds *Mutual funds* whose *portfolios* are not regularly updated by a fund manager attempting to generate high returns. Rather, once an initial portfolio is selected, it is left unchanged so that investors receive whatever return that unchanging portfolio subsequently generates. *Index funds* are a type of passively managed fund.

patent An exclusive right given to inventors to produce and sell a new product or machine for 20 years from the time of patent application.

Patient Protection and Affordable Care Act (PPACA) A major health care law passed by the Federal government in 2010. Major provisions include an individual health insurance mandate, a ban on insurers refusing to accept patients with preexisting conditions, and Federal (rather than state) regulation of health insurance policies.

payments deficit (See *balance-of-payments deficit.*)

payments surplus (See *balance-of-payments surplus.*)

payroll tax A tax levied on employers of labor equal to a percentage of all or part of the wages and salaries paid by them and on employees equal to a percentage of all or part of the wages and salaries received by them.

P = MC rule The principle that a purely competitive firm will maximize its profit or minimize its loss by producing that output at which the *price* of the product is equal to *marginal cost,* provided that price is equal to or greater than *average variable cost* in the short run and equal to or greater than *average total cost* in the long run.

peak The point in a business cycle at which business activity has reached a temporary maximum; the economy is near or at full employment and the level of real output is at or very close to the economy's capacity.

per capita GDP *Gross domestic product* (GDP) per person; the average GDP of a population.

per capita income A nation's total income per person; the average income of a population.

percentage rate of return The percentage gain or loss, relative to the buying price, of an *economic investment* or *financial investment* over some period of time.

perfectly elastic demand Product or resource demand in which *quantity demanded* can be of any amount at a particular product *price;* graphs as a horizontal *demand curve.*

perfectly elastic supply Product or resource supply in which *quantity supplied* can be of any amount at a particular product or resource *price;* graphs as a horizontal *supply curve.*

perfectly inelastic demand Product or resource demand in which *price* can be of any amount at a particular quantity of the product or resource demanded; *quantity demanded* does not respond to a change in price; graphs as a vertical *demand curve.*

perfectly inelastic supply Product or resource supply in which *price* can be of any amount at a particular quantity of the product or resource demanded; *quantity supplied* does not respond to a change in price; graphs as a vertical *supply curve.*

per se violations Collusive actions, such as attempts by firms to fix prices or divide a market, that are violations of the *antitrust laws,* even if the actions themselves are unsuccessful.

personal consumption expenditures (C) The expenditures of *households* for *durable* and *nondurable consumer goods* and *services.*

personal distribution of income The manner in which the economy's *personal* or *disposable income* is divided among different income classes or different households or families.

personal income (PI) The earned and unearned income available to resource suppliers and others before the payment of personal taxes.

personal income tax A tax levied on the taxable income of individuals, households, and unincorporated firms.

personal mandate The requirement under the *Patient Protection and Affordable Care Act (PPACA)* of 2010 that all U.S. citizens and legal residents purchase health insurance unless they are already covered by employer-sponsored health insurance or government-sponsored health insurance (*Medicaid* or *Medicare*).

personal saving The *personal income* of households less personal taxes and *personal consumption expenditures; disposable income* not spent for *consumer goods.*

per-unit production cost The average production cost of a particular level of output; total input cost divided by units of output.

Phillips Curve A curve showing the relationship between the *unemployment rate* (on the horizontal axis) and the annual rate of increase in the *price level* (on the vertical axis).

planned investment The amount that *firms* plan or intend to invest.

plant A physical establishment that performs one or more functions in the production, fabrication, and distribution of goods and services.

policy economics The formulation of courses of action to bring about desired economic outcomes or to prevent undesired occurrences.

political business cycle Fluctuations in the economy caused by the alleged tendency of Congress to destabilize the economy by reducing taxes and increasing government expenditures before elections and to raise taxes and lower expenditures after elections.

political corruption The unlawful misdirection of governmental resources or actions that occurs when government officials abuse their entrusted powers for personal gain. (Also see *corruption*.)

Ponzi scheme A financial fraud in which the returns paid to earlier investors come from contributions made by later investors (rather than from the financial investment that the perpetrator of the fraud claims to be making). Named after notorious fraudster Charles Ponzi.

portfolio A specific collection of *stocks*, *bonds*, or other *financial investments* held by an individual or a *mutual fund*.

positive economics The analysis of facts or data to establish scientific generalizations about economic behavior.

positive externality A benefit obtained without compensation by third parties from the production or consumption of sellers or buyers. Example: A beekeeper benefits when a neighboring farmer plants clover. An *external benefit* or a spillover benefit.

positive GDP gap A situation in which actual *gross domestic product* exceeds *potential output*. Also known as an inflationary output gap.

positive relationship (See *direct relationship*.)

positive sum game In *game theory*, a game in which the gains (+) and losses (−) add up to more than zero; one party's gains exceeds the other party's losses.

post hoc, ergo propter hoc **fallacy** The false belief that when one event precedes another, the first event must have caused the second event.

potential competition The new competitors that may be induced to enter an industry if firms now in that industry are receiving large *economic profits*.

potential output The real output *(GDP)* an economy can produce when it fully employs its available resources.

poverty A situation in which the basic needs of an individual or family exceed the means to satisfy them.

poverty rate The percentage of the population with incomes below the official poverty income levels that are established by the Federal government.

preferred provider organization (PPO) An arrangement in which doctors and hospitals agree to provide health care to insured individuals at rates negotiated with an insurer.

present value Today's value of some amount of money that is to be received sometime in the future.

price The amount of money needed to buy a particular good, service, or resource.

price ceiling A legally established maximum price for a good or service.

price discrimination The selling of a product to different buyers at different prices when the price differences are not justified by differences in cost.

price elasticity of demand The ratio of the percentage change in *quantity demanded* of a product or resource to the percentage change in its *price*; a measure of the responsiveness of buyers to a change in the price of a product or resource.

price elasticity of supply The ratio of the percentage change in *quantity supplied* of a product or resource to the percentage change in its *price*; a measure of the responsiveness of producers to a change in the price of a product or resource.

price fixing The conspiring by two or more firms to set the price of their products; an illegal practice under the *Sherman Act*.

price floor A legally determined minimum price above the *equilibrium price*.

price index An index number that shows how the weighted-average price of a "market basket" of goods changes over time.

price leadership An informal method that firms in an *oligopoly* may employ to set the price of their product: One firm (the leader) is the first to announce a change in price, and the other firms (the followers) soon announce identical or similar changes.

price level The weighted average of the prices of all the final goods and services produced in an economy.

price-level stability A steadiness of the price level from one period to the next; zero or low annual inflation; also called "price stability."

price-level surprises Unanticipated changes in the price level.

price maker A seller (or buyer) that is able to affect the product or resource price by changing the amount it sells (or buys).

price support A minimum price that government allows sellers to receive for a good or service; a legally established or maintained minimum price.

price taker A seller (or buyer) that is unable to affect the price at which a product or resource sells by changing the amount it sells (or buys).

price war Successive and continued decreases in the prices charged by firms in an oligopolistic industry. Each firm lowers its price below rivals' prices, hoping to increase its sales and revenues at its rivals' expense.

prime interest rate The benchmark *interest rate* that banks use as a reference point for a wide range of loans to businesses and individuals.

principal-agent problem A conflict of interest that occurs when agents (workers or managers) pursue their own objectives to the detriment of the principals' (stockholders') goals.

principle of comparative advantage The proposition that an individual, region, or nation will benefit if it specializes in producing goods for which its own *opportunity costs* are lower than the opportunity costs of a trading partner, and then exchanging some of the products in which it specializes for other desired products produced by others.

private good A good or service that is individually consumed and that can be profitably provided by privately owned firms because they can exclude nonpayers from receiving the benefits.

private property The right of private persons and firms to obtain, own, control, employ, dispose of, and bequeath *land, capital,* and other property.

private sector The *households* and business *firms* of the economy.

probability-weighted average Each of the possible future rates of return from an investment multiplied by its respective probability (expressed as a decimal) of happening.

process innovation (Web chapter) The development and use of new or improved production or distribution methods.

producer surplus The difference between the actual price a producer receives (or producers receive) and the minimum acceptable price; the triangular area above the supply curve and below the market price.

product differentiation A strategy in which one firm's product is distinguished from competing products by means of its design, related services, quality, location, or other attributes (except price).

product innovation (Web chapter) The development and sale of a new or improved product (or service).

production possibilities curve A curve showing the different combinations of two goods or services that can be produced in a *full-employment, full-production* economy where the available supplies of resources and technology are fixed.

productive efficiency The production of a good in the least costly way; occurs when production takes place at the output at which *average total cost* is a minimum and *marginal product* per dollar's worth of input is the same for all inputs.

productivity A measure of average output or real output per unit of input. For example, the productivity of labor is determined by dividing real output by hours of work.

productivity growth The increase in *productivity* from one period to another.

product market A market in which products are sold by *firms* and bought by *households.*

profit The return to the resource *entrepreneurial ability* (see *normal profit*); *total revenue* minus *total cost* (see *economic profit*).

profit-maximizing combination of resources The quantity of each resource a firm must employ to maximize its profit or minimize its loss; the combination in which the *marginal revenue product* of each resource is equal to its *marginal resource cost* (to its *price* if the resource is employed in a competitive market).

profit-sharing plan A compensation device through which workers receive part of their pay in the form of a share of their employer's profit (if any).

progressive tax A tax whose *average tax rate* increases as the taxpayer's income increases and decreases as the taxpayer's income decreases.

property tax A tax on the value of property (*capital, land, stocks* and *bonds,* and other *assets*) owned by *firms* and *households.*

proportional tax A tax whose *average tax rate* remains constant as the taxpayer's income increases or decreases.

proprietor's income The net income of the owners of unincorporated firms (proprietorships and partnerships).

prospect theory A *behavioral economics* theory of preferences having three main features: (1) people evaluate options on the basis of whether they generate gains or losses relative to the *status quo;* (2) gains are subject to diminishing marginal utility, while losses are subject to diminishing marginal disutility; and (3) people are *loss averse.*

protective tariff A *tariff* designed to shield domestic producers of a good or service from the competition of foreign producers.

public assistance programs Government programs that pay benefits to those who are unable to earn income (because of permanent disabilities or because they have very low income and dependent children); financed by general tax revenues and viewed as public charity (rather than earned rights).

public choice theory The economic analysis of government decision making, politics, and elections.

public debt The total amount owed by the Federal government to the owners of government securities; equal to the sum of past government *budget deficits* less government *budget surpluses.*

public good A good or service that is characterized by *nonrivalry* and *nonexcludability*; a good or service with these characteristics provided by government.

public interest theory of regulation The presumption that the purpose of the regulation of an *industry* is to protect the public (consumers) from abuse of the power possessed by *natural monopolies.*

public investments Government expenditures on public capital (such as roads, highways, bridges, mass-transit systems, and electric power facilities) and on *human capital* (such as education, training, and health).

public sector The part of the economy that contains all government entities; government.

public utility A firm that produces an essential good or service, has obtained from a government the right to be the sole supplier of the good or service in the area, and is regulated by that government to prevent the abuse of its monopoly power.

purchasing power The amount of goods and services that a monetary unit of income can buy.

purchasing power parity The idea that exchange rates between nations equate the purchasing power of various currencies. Exchange rates between any two nations adjust to reflect the price-level differences between the countries.

pure competition A market structure in which a very large number of firms sells a *standardized product,* into which entry is very easy, in which the individual seller has no control over the product price, and in which there is no nonprice competition; a market characterized by a very large number of buyers and sellers.

purely competitive labor market A *resource market* in which many firms compete with one another in hiring a specific kind of labor, numerous equally qualified workers supply that labor, and no one controls the market wage rate.

pure monopoly A market structure in which one firm sells a unique product, into which entry is blocked, in which the single firm has considerable control over product price, and in which *nonprice competition* may or may not be found.

pure profit (See *economic profit*.)

pure rate of interest An essentially risk-free, long-term interest rate that is free of the influence of market imperfections.

quantity demanded The amount of a good or service that buyers (or a buyer) are willing and able to purchase at a specific price during a specified period of time.

quantity supplied The amount of a good or service that producers (or a producer) are willing and able to make available for sale at a specific price during a specified period of time.

quasi-public bank A bank that is privately owned but governmentally (publicly) controlled; each of the U.S. *Federal Reserve Banks*.

quasi-public good A good or service to which excludability could apply but that has such a large *positive externality* that government sponsors its production to prevent an underallocation of resources.

R&D Research and development activities undertaken to bring about *technological advance*.

rate of exchange The price paid in one's own money to acquire 1 unit of a foreign currency; the rate at which the money of one nation is exchanged for the money of another nation.

rate of return The gain in net revenue divided by the cost of an investment or an *R&D* expenditure; expressed as a percentage.

rational behavior Human behavior based on comparison of marginal costs and marginal benefits; behavior designed to maximize total utility.

rational expectations theory The hypothesis that firms and households expect monetary and fiscal policies to have certain effects on the economy and (in pursuit of their own self-interests) take actions that make these policies ineffective.

rationing function of prices The ability of market forces in competitive markets to equalize *quantity demanded* and *quantity supplied* and to eliminate shortages and surpluses via changes in prices.

real-balances effect The tendency for increases in the *price level* to lower the real value (or purchasing power) of financial assets with fixed money value and, as a result, to reduce total spending and real output, and conversely for decreases in the price level.

real-business-cycle theory A theory that *business cycles* result from changes in technology and resource availability, which affect *productivity* and thus increase or decrease long-run aggregate supply.

real capital (See *capital*.)

real GDP (See *real gross domestic product*.)

real GDP per capita *Inflation*-adjusted output per person; *real GDP*/population.

real gross domestic product (GDP) *Gross domestic product* adjusted for inflation; gross domestic product in a year divided by the GDP *price index* for that year, the index expressed as a decimal.

real income The amount of goods and services that can be purchased with *nominal income* during some period of time; nominal income adjusted for inflation.

real interest rate The interest rate expressed in dollars of constant value (adjusted for *inflation*) and equal to the *nominal interest rate* less the expected rate of inflation.

real wage The amount of goods and services a worker can purchase with his or her *nominal wage*; the purchasing power of the nominal wage.

recession A period of declining real GDP, accompanied by lower real income and higher unemployment.

recessionary expenditure gap The amount by which the *aggregate expenditures schedule* must shift upward to increase the real GDP to its full-employment, noninflationary level.

refinancing the public debt Selling new government securities to owners of expiring securities or paying them money gained from the sale of new securities to others.

regressive tax A tax whose *average tax rate* decreases as the taxpayer's income increases and increases as the taxpayer's income decreases.

regulatory agency An agency, commission, or board established by the Federal government or a state government to control the prices charged and the services offered by a *natural monopoly*.

remittances Payments by *immigrants* to family members and others located in the origin countries of the immigrants.

rental income The payments (income) received by those who supply *land* to the economy.

renewable natural resources Things such as forests, water in reservoirs, and wildlife that are capable of growing back or building back up (renewing themselves) if they are harvested at moderate rates.

rent-seeking behavior The actions by persons, firms, or unions to gain special benefits from government at the taxpayers' or someone else's expense.

repeated game In *game theory*, a game that is played again sometime after the previous game ends.

replacement rate The birthrate necessary to offset deaths in a country and therefore to keep the size of its population constant (without relying on immigration). For most countries, the replacement rate is about 2.1 births per woman per lifetime.

required reserves The funds that banks and thrifts must deposit with the *Federal Reserve Bank* (or hold as *vault cash*) to meet the legal *reserve requirement;* a fixed percentage of the bank's or thrift's checkable deposits.

reserve ratio The fraction of *checkable deposits* that a bank must hold as reserves in a *Federal Reserve Bank* or in its own bank vault; also called the *reserve requirement.*

reserve requirement The specified minimum percentage of its checkable deposits that a bank or thrift must keep on deposit at the Federal Reserve Bank in its district or hold as *vault cash.*

resource A natural, human, or manufactured item that helps produce goods and services; a productive agent or factor of production.

resource market A market in which *households* sell and *firms* buy resources or the services of resources.

restrictive monetary policy *Federal Reserve System* actions to reduce the *money supply,* increase *interest rates,* and reduce *inflation;* a tight money policy.

revenue tariff A *tariff* designed to produce income for the Federal government.

right-to-work law A state law (in 22 states) that makes it illegal to require that a worker join a *labor union* in order to retain his or her job; laws that make *union shops* and *agency shops* illegal.

risk The uncertainty as to the actual future returns of a particular *financial investment* or *economic investment.*

risk-free interest rate The *interest rate* earned on short-term U.S. government bonds.

risk premium The *interest rate* above the *risk-free* interest rate that must be paid and received to compensate a lender or investor for *risk.*

rivalry (1) The characteristic of a *private good,* the consumption of which by one party excludes other parties from obtaining the benefit; (2) the attempt by one firm to gain strategic advantage over another firm to enhance market share or profit.

rule of reason The rule stated and applied in the *U.S. Steel case* that only combinations and contracts unreasonably restraining trade are subject to actions under the antitrust laws and that size and possession of monopoly power are not illegal.

rule of 70 A method for determining the number of years it will take for some measure to double, given its annual percentage increase. Example: To determine the number of years it will take for the *price level* to double, divide 70 by the annual rate of *inflation.*

sales and excise taxes (See *sales tax; see excise tax.*)

sales tax A tax levied on the cost (at retail) of a broad group of products.

saving Disposable income not spent for consumer goods; equal to *disposable income* minus *personal consumption expenditures;* saving is a flow.

savings The accumulation of funds that results when people in an economy spend less (consume less) than their incomes during a given time period; savings are a stock.

savings account A deposit in a *commercial bank* or *thrift institution* on which interest payments are received; generally used for saving rather than daily transactions; a component of the *M2* money supply.

savings and loan association (S&L) A firm that accepts deposits primarily from small individual savers and lends primarily to individuals to finance purchases such as autos and homes; now nearly indistinguishable from a *commercial bank.*

saving schedule A schedule that shows the amounts *households* plan to save (plan not to spend for *consumer goods*), at different levels of *disposable income.*

savings deposit A deposit that is interest-bearing and that the depositor can normally withdraw at any time.

savings institution (See *thrift institution.*)

Say's law The largely discredited macroeconomic generalization that the production of goods and services (supply) creates an equal *demand* for those goods and services.

scarce resources The limited quantities of *land, capital, labor,* and *entrepreneurial ability* that are never sufficient to satisfy people's virtually unlimited economic wants.

scientific method The procedure for the systematic pursuit of knowledge involving the observation of facts and the formulation and testing of hypotheses to obtain theories, principles, and laws.

secular trend A long-term tendency; a change in some variable over a very long period of years.

securitization The process of aggregating many individual financial debts, such as mortgages or student loans, into a pool and then issuing new securities (financial instruments) backed by the pool. The holders of the new securities are entitled to receive the debt payments made on the individual financial debts in the pool.

Security Market Line (SML) A line that shows the average expected rate of return of all financial investments at each level of *nondiversifiable risk,* the latter measured by *beta.*

self-interest That which each firm, property owner, worker, and consumer believes is best for itself and seeks to obtain.

self-selection As it relates to international migration, the idea that those who choose to move tend to have greater motivation for economic gain or greater willingness to sacrifice current consumption for future consumption than those with similar skills who choose to remain at home.

seniority The length of time a worker has been employed absolutely or relative to other workers; may be used to determine which workers will be laid off when there is insufficient work for them all and who will be rehired when more work becomes available.

separation of ownership and control The fact that different groups of people own a *corporation* (the stockholders) and manage it (the directors and officers).

sequential game In *game theory,* a game in which the parties make their moves in turn, with one party making the first move, followed by the other party making the next move, and so on.

service An (intangible) act or use for which a consumer, firm, or government is willing to pay.

Sherman Act The Federal antitrust law of 1890 that makes monopoly and conspiracies to restrain trade criminal offenses.

shirking Workers' neglecting or evading work to increase their *utility* or well-being.

shocks Sudden, unexpected changes in *demand* (or *aggregate demand*) or supply (or *aggregate supply*).

shortage The amount by which the *quantity demanded* of a product exceeds the *quantity supplied* at a particular (below-equilibrium) price.

short run (1) In microeconomics, a period of time in which producers are able to change the quantities of some but not all of the resources they employ; a period in which some resources (usually plant) are fixed and some are variable. (2) In macroeconomics, a period in which nominal wages and other input prices do not change in response to a change in the price level.

short-run aggregate supply curve An *aggregate supply* curve relevant to a time period in which input prices (particularly *nominal wages*) do not change in response to changes in the *price level*.

short-run competitive equilibrium The price at which the total quantity of a product supplied in the *short run* in a purely competitive industry equals the total quantity of the product demanded and that is equal to or greater than *average variable cost*.

short-run supply curve A supply curve that shows the quantity of a product a firm in a purely competitive industry will offer to sell at various prices in the *short run*; the portion of the firm's short-run marginal cost curve that lies above its *average-variable-cost* curve.

shutdown case The circumstance in which a firm would experience a loss greater than its total *fixed cost* if it were to produce any output greater than zero; alternatively, a situation in which a firm would cease to operate when the *price* at which it can sell its product is less than its *average variable cost*.

simple multiplier The *multiplier* in any economy in which government collects no *net taxes*, there are no *imports*, and *investment* is independent of the level of income; equal to 1 divided by the *marginal propensity to save*.

simultaneous consumption The same-time derivation of *utility* from some product by a large number of consumers.

simultaneous game In *game theory*, a game in which both parties choose their strategies and execute them at the same time.

single-tax movement The political efforts by followers of Henry George (1839-1897) to impose a single tax on the value of land and eliminate all other taxes.

skill transferability The ease with which people can shift their work talents from one job, region, or country to another job, region, or country.

slope of a straight line The ratio of the vertical change (the rise or fall) to the horizontal change (the run) between any two points on a line. The slope of an upward-sloping line is positive, reflecting a direct relationship between two variables; the slope of a downward-sloping line is negative, reflecting an inverse relationship between two variables.

Smoot-Hawley Tariff Act Legislation passed in 1930 that established very high tariffs. Its objective was to reduce imports and stimulate the domestic economy, but it resulted only in retaliatory tariffs by other nations.

social insurance programs Programs that replace the earnings lost when people retire or are temporarily unemployed, that are financed by payroll taxes, and that are viewed as earned rights (rather than charity).

socially optimal price The price of a product that results in the most efficient allocation of an economy's resources and that is equal to the *marginal cost* of the product.

social regulation Regulation in which government is concerned with the conditions under which goods and services are produced, their physical characteristics, and the impact of their production on society; in contrast to *industrial regulation*.

Social Security The social insurance program in the United States financed by Federal payroll taxes on employers and employees and designed to replace a portion of the earnings lost when workers become disabled, retire, or die.

Social Security trust fund A Federal fund that saves excessive Social Security tax revenues received in one year to meet Social Security benefit obligations that exceed Social Security tax revenues in some subsequent year.

sole proprietorship An unincorporated *firm* owned and operated by one person.

special-interest effect Any result of government promotion of the interests (goals) of a small group at the expense of a much larger group.

specialization The use of the resources of an individual, a firm, a region, or a nation to concentrate production on one or a small number of goods and services.

speculation The activity of buying or selling with the motive of later reselling or rebuying for profit.

SSI (See *Supplemental Security Income*.)

stagflation Inflation accompanied by stagnation in the rate of growth of output and an increase in unemployment in the economy; simultaneous increases in the *inflation rate* and the *unemployment rate*.

standardized product A product whose buyers are indifferent to the seller from whom they purchase it as long as the price charged by all sellers is the same; a product all units of which are identical and thus are perfect substitutes for each other.

Standard Oil case A 1911 antitrust case in which Standard Oil was found guilty of violating the *Sherman Act* by illegally monopolizing the petroleum industry. As a remedy the company was divided into several competing firms.

start-up firm A new firm focused on creating and introducing a particular new product or employing a specific new production or distribution method.

state bank A *commercial bank* authorized by a state government to engage in the business of banking.

statistical discrimination The practice of judging an individual on the basis of the average characteristics of the group to which he or she belongs rather than on his or her own personal characteristics.

status quo The existing state of affairs; in *prospect theory*, the current situation from which gains and losses are calculated.

sticky prices (See *inflexible prices*.)

stock (corporate) An ownership share in a corporation.

stock options Contracts that enable executives or other key employees to buy shares of their employers' stock at fixed, lower prices even when the market price subsequently rises.

store of value An *asset* set aside for future use; one of the three functions of *money*.

strategic behavior Self-interested economic actions that take into account the expected reactions of others.

strike The withholding of labor services by an organized group of workers (a *labor union*).

structural unemployment Unemployment of workers whose skills are not demanded by employers, who lack sufficient skill to obtain employment, or who cannot easily move to locations where jobs are available.

subprime mortgage loans High-interest rate loans to home buyers with above-average credit risk.

subsidy A payment of funds (or goods and services) by a government, firm, or household for which it receives no good or service in return. When made by a government, it is a *government transfer payment*.

substitute goods Products or services that can be used in place of each other. When the price of one falls, the demand for the other product falls; conversely, when the price of one product rises, the demand for the other product rises.

substitute resources Productive inputs that can be used instead of other inputs in the production process; resources for which an increase in the price of one leads to an increase in the demand for the other.

substitution effect (1) A change in the quantity demanded of a *consumer good* that results from a change in its relative expensiveness caused by a change in the product's price; (2) the effect of a change in the price of a *resource* on the quantity of the resource employed by a firm, assuming no change in its output.

sunk cost A cost that has been incurred and cannot be recovered.

Supplemental Nutrition Assistance Program (SNAP) A government program that provides food money to low-income recipients by depositing electronic money onto special debit cards. Formerly known as the food-stamp program.

Supplemental Security Income (SSI) A federally financed and administered program that provides a uniform nationwide minimum income for the aged, blind, and disabled who do not qualify for benefits under *Social Security* in the United States.

supply A schedule showing the amounts of a good or service that sellers (or a seller) will offer at various prices during some period.

supply curve A curve illustrating *supply*.

supply factor (in growth) An increase in the availability of a resource, an improvement in its quality, or an expansion of technological knowledge that makes it possible for an economy to produce a greater output of goods and services.

supply schedule (See *supply*.)

supply shocks Sudden, unexpected changes in *aggregate supply*.

supply-side economics A view of macroeconomics that emphasizes the role of costs and *aggregate supply* in explaining *inflation*, *unemployment*, and *economic growth*.

supply-side market failures Overallocations of resources that occur when private supply curves understate the full cost of producing a good or service.

surplus The amount by which the *quantity supplied* of a product exceeds the *quantity demanded* at a specific (above-equilibrium) price.

surplus payment A payment exceeding the minimum payment necessary to ensure the availability of a resource in a production process; for example, land rent.

tacit understanding An unspoken, unwritten agreement by an oligopolist to set prices and outputs that does not involve outright (or overt) *collusion*. *Price leadership* is a frequent example.

TANF (See *Temporary Assistance for Needy Families*.)

tariff A tax imposed by a nation on an imported good.

taste-for-discrimination model A theory that views discrimination as a preference for which an employer is willing to pay.

tax An involuntary payment of money (or goods and services) to a government by a *household* or *firm* for which the household or firm receives no good or service directly in return.

taxes on production and imports A *national income accounting* category that includes such taxes as *sales*, *excise*, business property taxes, and *tariffs* which firms treat as costs of producing a product and pass on (in whole or in part) to buyers by charging a higher price.

tax incidence The degree to which a *tax* falls on a particular person or group.

tax subsidy A grant in the form of reduced taxes through favorable tax treatment. For example, employer-paid health insurance is exempt from Federal income and payroll taxes.

tax-transfer disincentives Decreases in the incentives to work, save, invest, innovate, and take risks that result from high *marginal tax rates* and *transfer payments*.

Taylor rule A modern monetary rule proposed by economist John Taylor that would stipulate exactly how much the Federal Reserve should change real interest rates in response to divergences of real GDP from potential GDP and divergences of actual rates of inflation from a target rate of inflation.

technological advance New and better goods and services and new and better ways of producing or distributing them.

technology The body of knowledge and techniques that can be used to combine *economic resources* to produce goods and services.

Temporary Assistance for Needy Families (TANF) A state-administered and partly federally funded program in the United States that provides financial aid to poor families; the basic welfare program for low-income families in the United States; contains time limits and work requirements.

term auction facility The *monetary policy* procedure used by the Federal Reserve, in which commercial banks anonymously bid to obtain loans being made available by the Fed as a way to expand reserves in the banking system.

terms of trade The rate at which units of one product can be exchanged for units of another product; the price of a good or service; the amount of one good or service that must be given up to obtain 1 unit of another good or service.

theoretical economics The process of deriving and applying economic theories and principles.

theory of human capital The generalization that *wage differentials* are the result of differences in the amount of *human capital investment* and that the incomes of lower-paid workers are raised by increasing the amount of such investment.

thrift institution A *savings and loan association, mutual savings bank,* or *credit union.*

till money (See *vault cash.*)

time deposit An interest-earning deposit in a *commercial bank* or *thrift institution* that the depositor can withdraw without penalty after the end of a specified period.

time preference The human tendency for people, because of impatience, to prefer to spend and consume in the present rather than save and wait to spend and consume in the future; this inclination varies in strength among individuals.

time-value of money The idea that a specific amount of money is more valuable to a person the sooner it is received because the money can be placed in a financial account or investment and earn *compound interest* over time; the *opportunity cost* of receiving a sum of money later rather than earlier.

token money Bills or coins for which the amount printed on the *currency* bears no relationship to the value of the paper or metal embodied within it; for currency still circulating, money for which the face value exceeds the commodity value.

total allowable catch (TAC) A limit set by government or a fisheries commission on the total number of fish or tonnage of fish that fishers collectively can harvest during some particular time period.

total cost The sum of *fixed cost* and *variable cost.*

total demand The demand schedule or the *demand curve* of all buyers of a good or service; also called market demand.

total demand for money The sum of the *transactions demand for money* and the *asset demand for money.*

total fertility rate The average total number of children that a woman is expected to have during her lifetime.

total product (TP) The total output of a particular good or service produced by a firm (or a group of firms or the entire economy).

total revenue (TR) The total number of dollars received by a firm (or firms) from the sale of a product; equal to the total expenditures for the product produced by the firm (or firms); equal to the quantity sold (demanded) multiplied by the price at which it is sold.

total-revenue test A test to determine elasticity of *demand* between any two prices: Demand is elastic if *total revenue* moves in the opposite direction from price; it is inelastic when it moves in the same direction as price; and it is of unitary elasticity when it does not change when price changes.

total spending The total amount that buyers of goods and services spend or plan to spend; also called *aggregate expenditures.*

total supply The supply schedule or the *supply curve* of all sellers of a good or service; also called market supply.

total utility The total amount of satisfaction derived from the consumption of a single product or a combination of products.

Trade Adjustment Assistance Act A U.S. law passed in 2002 that provides cash assistance, education and training benefits, health care subsidies, and wage subsidies (for persons age 50 or older) to workers displaced by imports or relocations of U.S. plants to other countries.

trade balance The export of goods (or goods and services) of a nation less its imports of goods (or goods and services).

trade controls *Tariffs, export subsidies, import quotas,* and other means a nation may employ to reduce *imports* and expand *exports.*

trade deficit The amount by which a nation's *imports* of goods (or goods and services) exceed its *exports* of goods (or goods and services).

trademark A legal protection that gives the originators of a product an exclusive right to use the brand name.

trade-off The sacrifice of some or all of one economic goal, good, or service to achieve some other goal, good, or service.

trade surplus The amount by which a nation's *exports* of goods (or goods and services) exceed its *imports* of goods (or goods and services).

trading possibilities line A line that shows the different combinations of two products that an economy is able to obtain (consume) when it specializes in the production of one product and trades (exports) it to obtain the other product.

tragedy of the commons The tendency for commonly owned *natural resources* to be overused, neglected, or degraded because their common ownership gives nobody an incentive to maintain or improve them.

transactions demand for money The amount of money people want to hold for use as a *medium of exchange* (to make payments); varies directly with *nominal GDP.*

transfer payment A payment of *money* (or goods and services) by a government to a *household* or *firm* for which the payer receives no good or service directly in return.

Troubled Asset Relief Program (TARP) A 2008 Federal government program that authorized the U.S. Treasury to loan up to $700 billion to critical financial institutions and other U.S. firms that were in extreme financial trouble and therefore at high risk of failure.

trough The point in a *business cycle* at which business activity has reached a temporary minimum; the point at which a *recession* has ended and an expansion (recovery) begins.

tying contract A requirement imposed by a seller that a buyer purchase another (or other) of its products as a condition for buying a desired product; a practice forbidden by the *Clayton Act*.

unanticipated inflation Increases in the price level (*inflation*) at a rate greater than expected.

underemployment (Web chapter) A situation in which workers are employed in positions requiring less education and skill than they have.

undistributed corporate profits After-tax corporate profits not distributed as dividends to stockholders; corporate or business saving; also called retained earnings.

unemployment The failure to use all available *economic resources* to produce desired goods and services; the failure of the economy to fully employ its *labor force*.

unemployment compensation (See *unemployment insurance*).

unemployment insurance The social insurance program that in the United States is financed by state *payroll taxes* on employers and makes income available to workers who become unemployed and are unable to find jobs.

unemployment rate The percentage of the *labor force* unemployed at any time.

unfulfilled expectations Situations in which households and businesses were expecting one thing to happen but instead find that something else has happened; unrealized anticipations or plans relating to future economic conditions and outcomes.

uninsurable risk An event that would result in a loss and whose occurrence is uncontrollable and unpredictable. Insurance companies are not willing to sell insurance against such a loss.

union (See *labor union*.)

unionization rate The percentage of a particular population of workers that belongs to *labor unions*; alternatively, the percentage of the population of workers whom unions represent in *collective bargaining*.

union shop A place of employment where the employer may hire either *labor union* members or nonmembers but where nonmembers must become members within a specified period of time or lose their jobs.

unit elasticity Demand or supply for which the *elasticity coefficient* is equal to 1; means that the percentage change in the quantity demanded or supplied is equal to the percentage change in price.

unit labor cost Labor cost per unit of output; total labor cost divided by total output; also equal to the *nominal wage* rate divided by the *average product* of labor.

unit of account A standard unit in which prices can be stated and the value of goods and services can be compared; one of the three functions of *money*.

unlimited wants The insatiable desire of consumers for goods and services that will give them satisfaction or *utility*.

unplanned changes in inventories Changes in inventories that firms did not anticipate; changes in inventories that occur because of unexpected increases or decreases of aggregate spending (or of *aggregate expenditures*).

unplanned investment Actual investment less *planned investment*; increases or decreases in the *inventories* of firms resulting from production greater than sales.

Uruguay Round A 1995 trade agreement (fully implemented in 2005) that established the *World Trade Organization (WTO)*, liberalized trade in goods and services, provided added protection to intellectual property (for example, *patents* and *copyrights*), and reduced farm subsidies.

user cost The *opportunity* cost of extracting and selling a nonrenewable resource today rather than waiting to extract and sell the resource in the future; the *present value* of the decline in future revenue that will occur because a nonrenewable resource is extracted and sold today rather than being extracted and sold in the future.

U.S. securities U.S. Treasury bills, notes, and bonds used to finance *budget deficits*; the components of the *public debt*.

U.S. Steel case The antitrust action brought by the Federal government against the U.S. Steel Corporation in which the courts ruled (in 1920) that only unreasonable restraints of trade were illegal and that size and the possession of monopoly power were not by themselves violations of the antitrust laws.

usury laws State laws that specify the maximum legal interest rate at which loans can be made.

utility The want-satisfying power of a good or service; the satisfaction or pleasure a consumer obtains from the consumption of a good or service (or from the consumption of a collection of goods and services).

utility-maximizing rule The principle that to obtain the greatest *utility*, a consumer should allocate *money income* so that the last dollar spent on each good or service yields the same marginal utility.

value added The value of a product sold by a *firm* less the value of the products (materials) purchased and used by the firm to produce that product.

value-added tax A tax imposed on the difference between the value of a product sold by a firm and the value of the goods purchased from other firms to produce that product; used in several European countries.

value judgment Opinion of what is desirable or undesirable; belief regarding what ought or ought not to be in terms of what is right (or just) or wrong (or unjust).

value of money The quantity of goods and services for which a unit of money (a dollar) can be exchanged; the purchasing power of a unit of money; the reciprocal of the *price index*.

variable cost A cost that in total increases when the firm increases its output and decreases when the firm reduces its output.

VAT (See *value-added tax*.)

vault cash The *currency* a bank has in its vault and cash drawers.

velocity The number of times per year that the average dollar in the *money supply* is spent for *final goods and services*; nominal GDP divided by the money supply.

venture capital (Web chapter) That part of household saving used to finance high-risk business enterprises in exchange for shares of the profit if the enterprise succeeds.

vertical axis The "up-down" or "north-south" measurement line on a graph or grid.

vertical integration A group of *plants* engaged in different stages of the production of a final product and owned by a single *firm*.

vertical intercept The point at which a line meets the vertical axis of a graph.

vertical merger The merger of one or more *firms* engaged in different stages of the production of a final product.

very long run (Web chapter) A period long enough that *technology* can change and *firms* can introduce new products.

vicious circle of poverty (Web chapter) A problem common in some *developing countries* in which their low *per capita incomes* are an obstacle to realizing the levels of saving and investment needed to achieve rates of growth of output that exceed their rates of population growth.

voice mechanism Communication by workers through their union to resolve grievances with an employer.

voluntary export restrictions (VER) Voluntary limitations by countries or firms of their exports to a particular foreign nation to avoid enactment of formal trade barriers by that nation.

wage The price paid for the use or services of *labor* per unit of time (per hour, per day, and so on).

wage differential The difference between the *wage* received by one worker or group of workers and that received by another worker or group of workers.

wage rate (See *wage*.)

wages The income of those who supply the economy with *labor*.

Wall Street Reform and Consumer Protection Act of 2010 A law that gave authority to the Federal Reserve to regulate all large financial institutions, created an oversight council to look for growing risk to the financial system, established a process for the Federal government to sell off the assets of large failing financial institutions, provided Federal regulatory oversight of asset-backed securities, and created a financial consumer protection bureau within the Fed.

wealth Anything that has value because it produces income or could produce income. Wealth is a stock; *income* is a flow. Assets less liabilities; net worth.

wealth effect The tendency for people to increase their consumption spending when the value of their financial and real assets rises and to decrease their consumption spending when the value of those assets falls.

welfare programs (See *public assistance programs*.)

Wheeler-Lea Act The Federal law of 1938 that amended the *Federal Trade Commission Act* by prohibiting and giving the commission power to investigate unfair and deceptive acts or practices of commerce (such as false and misleading advertising and the misrepresentation of products).

will to develop (Web chapter) The state of wanting *economic growth* strongly enough to change from old to new ways of doing things.

World Bank (Web chapter) A bank that lends (and guarantees loans) to developing nations to assist them in increasing their *capital stock* and thus in achieving *economic growth*.

world price The international market price of a good or service, determined by world demand and supply.

World Trade Organization (WTO) An organization of 153 nations (as of mid-2010) that oversees the provisions of the current world trade agreement, resolves trade disputes stemming from it, and holds forums for further rounds of trade negotiations.

WTO (See *World Trade Organization*.)

X-inefficiency The production of output, whatever its level, at a higher average (and total) cost than is necessary for producing that level of output.

zero-sum game In *game theory*, a game in which the gains (+) and losses (−) add up to zero; one party's gain equals the other party's loss.

Credits

Part Openers © Peter Gridley/Getty Images
Chapter Openers © Peter Gridley/Getty Images
Page 4 Courtesy of Robbins Recreation, www.4americanrecreation.com, and artist Katherine Robbins.
Page 5 © Syracuse Newspapers/The Image Works
Page 9 © Mike Theiler/Reuters/Corbis
Page 14 © Royalty-Free/Corbis
Page 16 © James Leynse/Corbis
Page 35 © The McGraw-Hill Companies, Inc./John Flournoy, photographer
Page 39 © Stocktrek Images/Getty Images
Page 42 © Royalty-Free/Corbis
Page 58 © Robert W. Ginn/PhotoEdit
Page 61 © Nancy R. Cohen/Getty Images
Page 63 © Olivier Matthys/epa/Corbis
Page 78 © Nancy R. Cohen/Getty Images
Page 87 © Tom Prettyman/PhotoEdit
Page 101 © David Frazier/PhotoEdit
Page 100 © Colin Young-Wolff/PhotoEdit
Page 106 © Digital Vision/Getty Images
Page 111 © Royalty-Free/Corbis
Page 117 © Kim Kulish/Corbis
Page 126 © Stewart Cohen/Index Stock/Photolibrary
Page 129 © Manoj Shah/Getty Images
Page 137 © Ryan McVay/Getty Images
Page 144 © BananaStock/JupiterImages
Page 159 © Jonnie Miles/Getty Images
Page 173 © Getty Images
Page 177 © iStockphoto
Page 190 © Katrin Thomas/Getty Images
Page 191 © Tannen Maury/epa/Corbis
Page 208 © Getty Images
Page 212 © PhotoLink/Getty Images
Page 224 © Richard Cummins/Corbis
Page 227 © Brand X Pictures
Page 237 © Burke/Triolo Productions/Getty Images
Page 253 © PRNewsFoto/Diamond Information Center
Page 261 © age fotostock/SuperStock
Page 280 Reunion des Musees Nationaux/Art Resource, NY. © 2007 Estate of Pablo Picasso / Artists Rights Society (ARS), New York
Page 283 © Peter Weber/Getty Images
Page 301 © Matthew Borkoski/Index Stock Imagery, Inc.
Page 305 © AFP/Getty Images
Page 307 © Royalty-Free/Corbis
Page 314 © Digital Vision/Getty Images
Page 320 © T. O'Keefe/PhotoLink/Getty Images
Page 331 © PhotoLink/Getty Images
Page 342 © Mark Steinmetz/Amanita Pictures
Page 346 © Steve Cole/Getty Images
Page 352 © PhotoDisc/Getty Images
Page 360 © Bruce Ayres/Getty Images
Page 366 © Hein von Horsten/Getty Images
Page 370 © Royalty-Free/Corbis
Page 381 © AP Photo/Stephen Lance Dennee
Page 387 © AP Photo/Paul Sakuma

Page 396 © Digital Vision/PunchStock
Page 401 © Burke/Triolo Productions/Getty Images
Page 405 © Envision/Corbis
Page 417 © PrNewsFoto/Dream Works Home Entertainment
Page 419 © Royalty-Free/Corbis
Page 428 © Kelly Ryerson/Getty Images
Page 445 © Don Farrall/Getty Images
Page 449 © Comstock Images/PictureQuest
Page 459 © Royalty-Free/Corbis
Page 466 © Getty Images
Page 476 © Getty Images
Page 479 © Getty Images
Page 481 © Macduff Everton/Corbis
Page 490 Courtesy USDA/NRCS, photo by Lynn Betts
Page 501 © Getty Images
Page 510 © Getty Images
Page 512 © Photodisc Collection/Getty Images
Page 516 © Dynamic Graphics/JupiterImages
Page 522 © Travelpix Ltd/Getty Images
Page 537 © Royalty-Free/Corbis
Page 542 © Ryan McVay/Getty Images
Page 554 © Digital Vision/Getty Images
Page 560 © Getty Images
Page 563 © Getty Images
Page 584 Cover image from *The General Theory of Employment, Interest, and Money*, by John Maynard Keynes. (Amherst, NY: Prometheus Books, 1997). Copyright © 1997 by Prometheus Books. Reprinted with permission of the publisher.
Page 603 © Royalty-Free/Corbis
Page 605 © Getty Images
Page 631 © Royalty-Free/Corbis
Page 640 © Getty Images
Page 651 © Canadian Press via AP Images
Page 666 © Thomas Kitchin & Victoria Hurst/Getty Images
Page 683 © Royalty-Free/Corbis
Page 689 © Steve Allen/Getty Images
Page 710 © AP Photo/Mary Altaffer
Page 712 © Creasource/Corbis
Page 732 © Bettmann/Corbis
Page 733 © Thinkstock/Corbis
Page 741 © Baron Wolman/Getty Images
Page 746 © Getty Images
Page 749 © Matthias Kulka/zefa/Corbis
Page 757 © David Frazier/PhotoEdit
Page 762 © Bloomberg via Getty Images
Page 767 © Robert W. Ginn/PhotoEdit
Page 775 © Steve Allen/Getty Images
Page 797 © PhotoLink/Getty Images

Photos on the Web

Page 11W–12 © Don Farrall/Getty Images
Page 11W–17 © AP Photo/George Nikitin
Page 39W–17 © Jon Jones/Sygma/Corbis
Page COI1–7 © David Frazier/PhotoEdit
Page COI1–12 © Robert W. Ginn/PhotoEdit
Page COI1–17 © Getty Images

Selected Economics Statistics for Various Years, 1929–1982

Statistics in rows 1–5 are in billions of dollars in the year specified. Numbers may not add to totals because of rounding.

GDP AND INCOME DATA	1929	1933	1939	1940	1942	1944	1946	1948	1950	1952	1954
1 Gross domestic product	103.6	56.4	92.2	101.4	161.9	219.8	222.2	269.1	293.7	358.3	380.4
1A Personal consumption expenditures	77.4	45.9	67.2	71.3	89.0	108.7	144.3	175.0	192.2	219.5	240.0
1B Gross private domestic investment	16.5	1.7	9.3	13.6	10.4	7.8	31.1	48.1	54.1	54.0	53.8
1C Government purchases	9.4	8.7	14.8	15.0	62.7	105.3	39.6	40.5	46.7	83.6	86.1
1D Net exports of goods and services	0.4	0.1	0.8	1.5	−0.3	−2.0	7.2	5.5	0.7	1.2	0.4
2 Net domestic product	93.9	49.0	82.9	91.8	148.2	200.2	199.1	240.7	263.8	322.0	339.8
3 National income	93.9	48.1	82.0	90.9	149.5	198.0	198.6	242.6	263.9	321.3	338.7
3A Wages and salaries	51.1	29.6	48.1	52.2	85.3	121.3	119.6	142.0	155.3	196.2	209.2
3B Rent	6.2	2.9	3.8	3.9	5.5	6.4	7.1	7.8	9.1	11.2	13.4
3C Interest	4.6	4.0	3.6	3.3	3.2	2.4	1.9	2.6	3.2	4.1	5.6
3D Profits	10.7	−0.3	6.4	9.6	20.4	24.8	17.9	30.9	35.6	38.8	38.3
3E Proprietor's income	14.1	5.3	11.1	12.3	23.4	29.4	35.7	39.2	37.5	43.1	42.3
3F Taxes on production and imports*	7.2	6.6	9.0	9.6	11.7	13.7	16.4	20.1	23.2	27.9	29.9
4 Personal income	84.9	65.2	72.9	78.4	123.4	166.0	178.6	209.7	228.9	275.2	294.3
5 Disposable income	83.2	46.0	71.4	76.8	118.5	148.3	161.4	190.5	209.9	243.2	264.1
6 Disposable income per capita	683	366	545	581	879	1072	1142	1299	1384	1550	1627
7 Personal saving as percent of DI	4.3	3.7	4.4	5.7	24.1	26.0	9.6	6.9	7.1	8.4	7.5

OTHER STATISTICS	1929	1933	1939	1940	1942	1944	1946	1948	1950	1952	1954
8 Real GDP (billions of 2005 dollars)	977.0	716.4	1072.8	1166.9	1618.2	2035.2	1792.2	1854.2	2006.0	2243.9	2332.4
9 Economic growth rate (change in real GDP)	—	−1.3	8.1	8.8	18.5	8.1	−10.9	4.4	8.7	3.8	−0.6
10 Consumer Price Index (1982–1984 = 100)	17.1	13.0	13.9	14.0	16.3	17.6	19.5	24.1	24.1	26.5	26.9
11 Rate of inflation (percent change in CPI)	0.0	−5.1	−1.4	0.7	10.9	1.7	8.3	8.1	1.3	1.9	0.7
12 Money supply, M1 (billions of $)	26.6	19.9	34.2	39.7	55.4	85.3	106.5	112.5	114.1	125.2	130.3
13 Federal funds interest rate (%)	—	—	—	—	—	—	—	1.75	2.07	3.00	3.05
14 Prime interest rate (%)	5.50	1.50	1.50	1.50	1.50	1.50	1.50	1.75	2.70	3.00	3.05
15 Population (millions)	121.8	125.6	131.0	132.1	134.9	138.4	141.4	146.6	152.3	157.6	163.0
16 Civilian labor force (millions)	49.2	51.6	55.2	55.6	56.4	54.6	57.5	60.6	62.2	62.1	63.6
16A Employment (millions)	47.6	38.8	45.7	47.5	53.8	54.0	55.3	58.3	58.9	60.3	60.1
16B Unemployment (millions)	1.6	12.8	9.5	8.1	2.7	0.7	2.3	2.3	3.3	1.9	3.5
17 Unemployment rate (%)	3.2	24.9	17.2	14.6	4.7	1.2	3.9	3.8	5.3	3.0	5.5
18 Productivity growth, business sector (%)	—	—	—	—	—	—	—	4.6	8.2	2.8	2.1
19 After-tax manufacturing profit per dollar of sales (cents)	—	—	—	—	—	—	—	7.0	7.1	4.3	4.5
20 Price of crude oil (U.S. average, dollars per barrel)	1.27	0.67	1.02	1.02	1.19	1.21	1.41	2.60	2.51	2.53	2.78
21 Federal budget surplus (+) or deficit (−) (billions of dollars)	—	—	—	−2.9	−20.5	−47.6	−15.2	11.8	−3.1	−1.5	−1.2
22 Public debt (billions of dollars)	16.9	22.5	48.2	50.7	79.2	204.1	271.0	252.0	256.9	259.1	270.8
23 Trade balance on current account (billions of dollars)	—	—	—	—	—	—	4.9	2.4	−1.8	0.6	0.2

*Combines items from other smaller accounts.

1956	1958	1960	1962	1964	1966	1968	1970	1972	1974	1976	1978	1980	1982
437.4	467.2	526.4	585.7	663.6	787.7	909.8	1038.3	1237.9	1499.5	1824.6	2293.8	2788.1	3253.2
271.7	296.2	331.8	363.3	411.5	480.9	558.0	648.3	770.2	932.9	1151.3	1427.6	1755.8	2075.5
72.0	64.5	78.9	88.1	102.1	131.3	141.2	152.4	207.6	249.4	292.0	438.0	479.3	517.2
91.4	106.0	111.5	130.1	143.2	171.6	209.3	233.7	263.4	317.9	383.0	453.6	566.1	680.4
2.4	0.5	4.2	4.1	6.9	3.9	1.4	4.0	-3.4	-0.8	-1.6	-25.4	-13.1	-20.0
390.3	413.9	469.9	525.1	597.3	711.2	819.4	930.0	1110.7	1335.8	1616.4	2032.3	2444.1	2819.7
394.9	415.6	473.9	528.9	601.4	710.1	821.2	929.5	1110.3	1341.5	1609.8	2027.9	2433.0	2851.4
244.5	259.5	296.4	327.1	370.7	442.7	524.3	617.2	725.1	890.2	1059.3	1335.5	1647.6	1919.6
14.1	15.2	17.0	18.6	19.4	20.5	20.6	21.1	23.1	24.0	22.1	20.9	28.5	38.1
6.9	9.5	10.6	14.2	17.4	22.4	27.1	39.1	47.9	70.8	85.5	115.0	181.8	271.1
48.0	42.5	53.1	62.3	75.5	92.5	97.3	82.5	111.4	115.1	161.6	218.4	201.4	205.7
45.9	50.2	50.7	55.3	59.4	68.2	74.2	78.5	96.0	113.5	132.2	167.5	173.5	174.8
35.5	38.7	46.1	51.4	59.0	63.8	77.7	91.1	106.8	127.9	169.1	244.1	200.2	242.1
339.5	368.9	411.3	456.4	514.3	603.8	711.7	838.6	992.6	1222.7	1474.7	1836.7	2301.5	2766.8
302.9	330.4	365.2	404.9	462.3	537.4	624.7	735.5	869.0	1071.7	1302.3	1607.3	2002.7	2412.7
1800	1897	2020	2170	2408	2733	3112	3586	4140	5010	5972	7220	8794	10,390
8.5	8.5	7.2	8.3	8.8	8.2	8.4	9.4	8.9	10.7	9.4	8.9	9.8	10.9

1956	1958	1960	1962	1964	1966	1968	1970	1972	1974	1976	1978	1980	1982
2549.7	2577.6	2830.9	3072.4	3392.3	3845.3	4133.4	4269.9	4647.7	4889.9	5141.3	5677.6	5839.0	5870.9
2.0	-0.9	2.5	6.1	5.8	6.5	4.8	0.2	5.3	-0.6	5.4	5.6	-0.3	-1.9
27.2	28.9	29.6	30.2	31.0	32.4	34.8	38.8	41.8	49.3	56.9	65.2	82.4	96.5
1.5	2.8	1.7	1.0	1.3	2.9	4.2	5.7	3.2	11.0	5.8	7.6	13.5	6.2
136.0	138.4	140.7	145.2	160.3	172.0	197.4	214.4	249.2	274.2	306.2	357.3	408.5	474.8
2.73	1.57	3.21	2.71	3.50	5.11	5.66	7.17	4.44	10.51	5.05	7.94	13.35	12.24
3.77	3.83	4.82	4.50	4.50	5.63	6.31	5.25	5.73	10.81	6.84	9.06	15.26	14.85
168.9	174.9	180.7	186.5	191.9	196.6	200.7	205.1	209.9	213.9	218.0	222.6	227.7	232.2
66.6	67.6	69.6	70.6	73.1	75.8	78.7	82.8	87.0	91.9	96.2	102.3	106.9	110.2
63.8	63.0	65.8	66.7	69.3	72.9	75.9	78.7	82.2	86.8	88.8	96.0	99.3	99.5
2.8	4.6	3.9	3.9	3.8	2.9	2.8	4.1	4.9	5.2	7.4	6.2	7.6	10.7
4.1	6.8	5.5	5.5	5.2	3.8	3.6	4.9	5.6	5.6	7.7	6.1	7.1	9.7
0.1	2.8	1.7	4.6	3.4	4.1	3.4	2.0	3.2	-1.7	3.2	1.1	-0.3	-0.8
5.3	4.2	4.4	4.5	5.2	5.6	5.1	4.0	4.3	5.5	5.4	5.4	4.8	3.5
2.79	3.01	2.88	2.90	2.88	2.88	2.94	3.18	3.39	6.87	8.19	9.00	21.59	28.52
3.9	-2.8	0.3	-7.1	-5.9	-3.7	-25.2	-2.8	-23.4	-6.1	-73.7	-59.2	-73.8	-128.0
72.7	279.7	290.5	302.9	316.1	328.5	368.7	380.9	435.9	483.9	629.0	776.6	909.1	1137.3
2.7	0.8	2.8	3.4	6.8	3.0	0.6	2.3	-5.8	2.0	4.3	-15.1	2.3	-5.5

(Continued in back of book)

Selected Economics Statistics for Various Years, 1984–2009

Statistics in rows 1–5 are in billions of dollars in the year specified. Numbers may not add to totals because of rounding.

GDP AND INCOME DATA	1984	1986	1987	1988	1989	1990	1991	1992	1993	1994	1995
1 Gross domestic product	3930.9	4460.1	4736.4	5100.4	5482.1	5800.5	5992.1	6342.3	6667.4	7085.2	7414.7
1A Personal consumption expenditures	2501.1	2896.7	3097.0	3350.1	3594.5	3835.5	3980.1	4236.9	4483.6	4750.8	4987.3
1B Gross private domestic investment	735.6	746.5	785.0	821.6	874.9	861.0	802.9	864.8	953.3	1097.3	1144.0
1C Government purchases	796.9	949.3	999.4	1038.9	1100.6	1181.7	1236.1	1273.5	1294.8	1329.8	1374.0
1D Net exports of goods and services	−102.7	−132.5	−145.0	−110.1	−87.9	−77.6	−27.0	−32.8	−64.4	−92.7	−90.7
2 Net domestic product	3456.5	3921.6	4165.3	4489.4	4830.7	5109.3	5267.7	5598.0	5889.3	6266.0	6545.2
3 National income	3461.3	3871.5	4150.0	4522.3	4800.5	5059.5	5217.9	5517.1	5784.7	6181.3	6522.3
3A Wages and salaries	2245.4	2557.7	2735.6	2954.2	3131.3	3326.3	3438.3	3631.4	3797.1	3998.5	4195.2
3B Rent	40.0	33.8	34.2	40.2	42.4	49.8	61.6	84.6	114.1	142.9	154.6
3C Interest	327.1	367.1	366.7	385.3	434.1	444.2	418.2	387.7	364.6	362.2	358.3
3D Profits	318.6	314.1	367.8	426.6	425.6	434.4	457.3	496.2	543.7	628.2	716.2
3E Proprietor's income	233.1	262.6	294.2	334.8	351.6	365.1	367.3	414.9	449.6	485.1	516.0
3F Taxes on production and imports*	297.1	336.2	351.5	381.2	415.5	439.7	475.2	502.5	515.6	564.4	582.0
4 Personal income	3268.9	3696.0	3924.4	4231.2	4557.5	4846.7	5031.5	5347.3	5568.1	5874.8	6200.9
5 Disposable income	2891.5	3258.8	3435.3	3726.3	3991.4	4254.0	4444.9	4736.7	4921.6	5184.3	5457.0
6 Disposable income per capita	12,232	13,540	14,146	15,206	16,134	17,004	17,532	18,436	18,909	19,678	20,470
7 Personal saving as percent of DI	10.2	7.6	6.5	6.9	6.6	6.5	7.0	7.3	5.8	5.2	5.2

OTHER STATISTICS	1984	1986	1987	1988	1989	1990	1991	1992	1993	1994	1995
8 Real GDP (billions of 2005 dollars)	6577.1	7086.5	7313.3	7613.9	7885.9	8033.9	8015.1	8287.1	8523.4	8870.7	9093.7
9 Economic growth rate (change in real GDP)	7.2	3.5	3.2	4.1	3.6	1.9	−0.2	3.4	2.9	4.1	2.5
10 Consumer Price Index (1982–1984 =100)	103.9	109.6	113.6	118.3	124.0	130.7	136.2	140.3	144.5	148.2	152.4
11 Rate of inflation (percent change in CPI)	4.3	1.9	3.6	4.1	4.8	5.4	4.2	3.0	3.0	2.6	2.8
12 Money supply, M1 (billions of $)	551.6	724.7	750.2	786.7	792.9	824.7	897.0	1024.9	1129.6	1150.6	1127.5
13 Federal funds interest rate (%)	10.23	6.80	6.66	7.57	9.21	8.10	5.69	3.52	3.02	4.21	5.8
14 Prime interest rate (%)	12.04	8.33	8.21	9.32	10.87	10.01	8.46	6.25	6.00	7.15	8.1
15 Population (millions)	236.3	240.7	242.8	245.0	247.3	250.1	253.5	256.9	260.3	263.4	266.7
16 Civilian labor force (millions)	113.5	117.8	119.9	121.7	123.9	125.8	126.3	128.1	129.2	131.1	132.7
16A Employment (millions)	105.0	109.6	112.4	115.0	117.3	118.8	117.7	118.5	120.3	123.1	124.9
16B Unemployment (millions)	8.5	8.2	7.4	6.7	6.5	7.0	8.6	9.6	8.9	8.0	7.4
17 Unemployment rate (%)	7.5	7.0	6.2	5.5	5.3	5.6	6.8	7.5	6.9	6.1	5.
18 Productivity growth, business sector (%)	2.7	2.9	0.3	1.5	1.0	2.1	1.5	4.2	0.5	0.9	0
19 After-tax manufacturing profit per dollar of sales (cents)	4.6	3.7	4.9	5.9	4.9	3.9	2.4	0.8	2.8	5.4	5
20 Price of crude oil (U.S. average, dollars per barrel)	25.88	12.51	15.40	12.58	15.86	20.03	16.54	15.99	14.25	13.19	14
21 Federal budget surplus (+) or deficit (−) (billions of dollars)	−185.4	−221.2	−149.7	−155.2	−152.6	−221.0	−269.2	−290.3	−255.1	−203.2	−164
22 Public debt (billions of dollars)	1564.7	2120.6	2346.1	2601.3	2868.0	3206.6	3598.5	4002.1	4351.4	4643.7	4921
23 Trade balance on current account (billions of dollars)	−94.3	−147.2	−160.7	−121.1	−99.5	−79.0	2.9	−50.1	−84.8	−121.6	−113

*Combines items from other smaller accounts.

1996	1997	1998	1999	2000	2001	2002	2003	2004	2005	2006	2007	2008	2009**
7838.5	8332.4	8793.5	9353.5	9951.5	10,286.2	10,642.3	11,142.1	11,867.8	12,638.4	13,398.9	14,077.6	14,441.4	14,256.3
5273.6	5570.6	5918.5	6342.8	6830.4	7148.8	7439.2	7804.0	8285.1	8819.0	9322.7	9826.4	10,129.9	10,089.1
1240.2	1388.7	1510.8	1641.5	1772.2	1661.9	1647.0	1729.7	1968.6	2172.2	2327.2	2288.5	2136.1	1628.8
1421.0	1474.4	1526.1	1631.3	1731.0	1846.4	1983.3	2112.6	2232.8	2369.9	2518.4	2676.5	2883.2	2930.7
−96.3	−101.4	−161.8	−262.1	−382.1	−371.0	−427.2	−504.1	−618.7	−722.7	−769.3	−713.8	−707.8	−392.4
6925.9	7368.6	7772.9	8259.1	8767.2	9029.9	9337.3	9788.1	10,435.0	11,097.0	11,738.2	12,317.6	12,594.3	12,392.3
6931.7	7406.0	7875.6	8358.0	8938.9	9185.2	9408.5	9840.2	10,534.0	11,273.8	12,031.2	12,448.2	12,635.2	12,288.1
4391.4	4665.6	5023.2	5353.9	5788.8	5979.3	6110.8	6382.6	6693.4	7065.0	7477.0	7856.5	8037.4	7791.6
170.4	176.5	191.5	208.2	215.3	232.4	218.7	204.2	198.4	178.2	146.5	144.9	210.4	268.1
371.1	407.6	479.3	481.4	539.3	544.4	506.4	504.1	461.6	543.0	652.2	739.2	815.1	788.2
801.5	884.8	812.4	856.3	819.2	784.2	872.2	977.8	1246.9	1456.1	1608.3	1541.7	1360.4	1308.9
583.7	628.2	687.5	746.8	817.5	870.7	890.3	930.6	1033.8	1069.8	1133.0	1096.4	1106.3	1041.0
613.3	643.3	681.7	711.6	758.8	774.2	810.1	840.9	889.9	961.7	1014.2	1069.5	1105.6	1090.3
6591.6	7000.7	7525.4	7910.8	8559.4	8883.3	9060.1	9378.1	9937.2	10,485.9	11,268.1	11,894.1	12,238.8	12,026.1
5759.6	6074.6	6498.9	6803.3	7327.2	7648.5	8009.7	8377.8	8889.4	9277.3	9915.7	10,403.1	10,806.4	10,923.6
21,355	22,255	23,534	24,356	25,944	26,805	27,799	28,805	30,287	31,318	33,157	34,445	35,450	35,526
4.9	4.6	5.3	3.1	2.9	2.7	3.5	3.5	3.4	1.4	2.4	1.7	2.7	4.3

1996	1997	1998	1999	2000	2001	2002	2003	2004	2005	2006	2007	2008	2009**
9433.9	9854.3	10,283.5	10,779.8	11,226.0	11,347.2	11,553.0	11,840.7	12,263.8	12,638.4	12,976.2	13,254.1	13,312.2	12,987.4
3.7	4.5	4.4	4.8	4.1	1.1	1.8	2.5	3.6	3.1	2.7	2.1	0.4	−2.4
156.9	160.5	163.0	166.6	172.2	177.1	179.9	184.0	188.9	195.3	201.6	207.3	215.3	214.5
3.0	2.3	1.6	2.2	3.4	2.8	1.6	2.3	2.7	3.4	3.2	2.8	3.8	−0.4
1081.6	1072.8	1095.8	1122.7	1087.7	1182.2	1220.4	1306.9	1377.1	1375.3	1367.9	1375.8	1594.7	1693.3
5.30	5.46	5.35	4.97	6.24	3.88	1.67	1.13	1.35	3.22	4.97	5.02	1.92	0.16
8.27	8.44	8.35	8.00	9.23	6.91	4.67	4.12	4.34	6.19	7.96	8.05	5.09	3.25
269.7	272.9	276.1	279.3	282.4	285.3	288.0	290.7	293.3	296.0	298.8	301.7	304.5	307.2
133.9	136.3	137.7	139.4	142.6	143.7	144.9	146.5	147.4	149.3	151.4	153.1	154.3	154.1
126.7	129.6	131.5	133.5	136.9	136.9	136.5	137.8	139.3	141.7	144.4	146.0	145.4	139.9
7.2	6.7	6.2	5.9	5.7	6.8	8.4	8.8	8.1	7.6	7.0	7.1	8.9	14.3
5.4	4.9	4.5	4.2	4.0	4.7	5.8	6.0	5.5	5.1	4.6	4.6	5.8	9.3
2.9	1.8	3.0	3.5	3.5	3.0	4.5	3.8	2.9	1.7	1.0	1.8	2.1	3.8
6.0	6.2	5.9	6.2	6.1	0.8	3.2	5.4	7.1	7.4	8.1	7.3	4.2	5.4
18.46	17.23	10.87	15.56	26.72	21.84	22.51	27.56	36.77	50.28	59.63	66.52	94.04	56.39
−107.4	−21.9	69.3	125.6	236.2	128.2	−157.8	−377.6	−412.7	−318.3	−248.2	−160.7	−458.6	−1412.7
5181.9	5369.7	5478.7	5605.5	5628.7	5769.9	6198.4	6760.0	7354.7	7905.3	8451.4	8950.7	9986.1	11,875.9
−124.8	−140.7	−215.1	−301.6	−417.4	−398.3	−459.2	−521.5	−631.1	−748.7	−803.5	−726.6	−706.1	−419.9

**Data for 2009 and the years immediately prior are subject to change because of subsequent government data revisions.

Sources: Bureau of Economic Analysis; Bureau of Labor Statistics; Federal Reserve System; *Economic Report of the President, 2010;* and U.S. Energy Information Administration.